D0077658

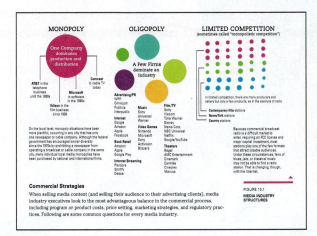

MONOPOLY

One Company dominates production and distribution

AT&T in the telephone business until the 1980s
Microsoft in software in the 1990s
Comcast in cable TV today
Edison in the film business circa 1908

On the local level, monopoly situations have been more plentiful, occurring in any city that has only one newspaper or cable company. Although the federal government has encouraged owner diversity since the 1970s by prohibiting a newspaper from operating a broadcast or cable company in the same city, many individual local media monopolies have been purchased by national and international firms.

OLIGOPOLY

A Few Firms dominate an industry

Advertising/PR
WPP
Omnicom
Publicis
Interpublic
Internet
Google
Amazon
Apple
Facebook
Book Retail
Amazon
Apple
Google Play
Internet Streaming
Pandora
Spotify
Deezer

Music
Sony
Universal
Warner
Video Games
Nintendo
Microsoft
Sony
Activision
Blizzard

Film/TV
Sony
Viacom
Time Warner
Disney
NBC Universal
Netflix
Google/YouTube
Theaters
Regal
AMC Entertainment
Cinemark
Carmike
Cineplex
Marcus

LIMITED COMPETITION
(sometimes called "monopolistic competition")

In limited competition, there are many producers and sellers but only a few products, as in the example of radio

Contemporary Hits stations
News/Talk stations
Country stations

Because commercial broadcast radio is a difficult market to enter, requiring an FCC license and major capital investment, most stations play one of the few formats that attract sizable audiences. Under these circumstances, fans of blues, jazz, or classical music may not be able to find a radio station. That is changing, though, with the Internet.

Commercial Strategies
When selling media content (and selling their audience to their advertising clients), media industry executives look to the most advantageous balance in the commercial process, including program or product costs, price setting, marketing strategies, and regulatory practices. Following are some common questions for every media industry.

FIGURE 13.1
MEDIA INDUSTRY
STRUCTURES

◀ **A heavily revised chapter on Economics and the Global Marketplace** conveys key concepts with new, easy-to-read visuals and a fresh perspective on media conglomerates, ownership, and globalization.

An all-new Extended Case Study examines the possible effects of social media on happiness through the book's trademark five-step critical process, asking students to examine their own relationships with the media through critical-thinking questions. ▶

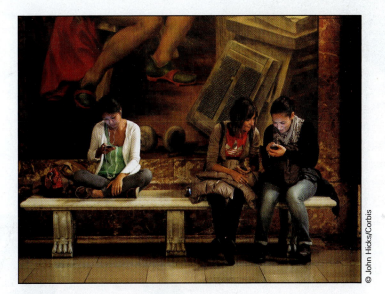

© John Hicks/Corbis

New coverage of important developments in mass media includes cord-cutting, socially conscious digital gaming, shifting revenues in the music industry, new distribution channels for film, the rise of Vine and Snapchat, safety issues in the NFL, and more.

The critical and cultural perspective illustrates how the mass media and our shared culture fit together, addressing digital age-convergence and media literacy.

For more information about *Media & Culture*, please visit macmillanhighered.com/mediaculture/catalog.

Praise for *Media & Culture*

The updated material in each edition makes the thought-provoking text relevant and offers plenty of resources for students considering a communications-related career.

ARNOLD MACKOWIAK,
EASTERN MICHIGAN UNIVERSITY

Excellent and well-researched materials, excellent writing, and strong ideas for stimulating critical thinking for students.

DAVID BRADFORD,
EASTERN FLORIDA STATE COLLEGE

The text consistently reminds us of the strands that weave their way through the material—regularly pointing out how all of the information is intimately connected.

MARCIA LADENDORFF,
UNIVERSITY OF NORTH FLORIDA

It is simply the best intro to mass communication book available.

MATTHEW CECIL,
SOUTH DAKOTA STATE UNIVERSITY

I think the Campbell text is outstanding. It is a long-overdue media text that is grounded in pressing questions about American culture and its connection to the techniques and institutions of commercial communication. It is, indeed, an important book. At the undergraduate level, that's saying something.

STEVE M. BARKIN,
UNIVERSITY OF MARYLAND

Media & Culture respects students' opinions, while challenging them to take more responsibility and to be accountable for their media choices. This text is essential for professors who are truly committed to teaching students how to understand the media.

DREW JACOBS,
CAMDEN COUNTY COLLEGE

The critical perspective has enlightened the perspective of all of us who study media, and Campbell has the power to infect students with his love of the subject.

ROGER DESMOND,
UNIVERSITY OF HARTFORD

I will switch to Campbell because it is a tour de force of coverage and interpretation, it is the best survey text in the field hands down, and it challenges students. Campbell's text is the most thorough and complete in the field. . . . No other text is even close.

RUSSELL BARCLAY,
QUINNIPIAC UNIVERSITY

The feature boxes are excellent and are indispensable to any classroom.

MARVIN WILLIAMS,
*KINGSBOROUGH
COMMUNITY COLLEGE*

I love *Media & Culture*! I have used it since the first edition. *Media & Culture* integrates the history of a particular medium or media concept with the culture, economics, and the technological advances of the time. But more than that, the authors are explicit in their philosophy that media and culture cannot be separated.

DEBORAH LARSON,
MISSOURI STATE UNIVERSITY

Media & Culture

Mass Communication in a Digital Age

Tenth Edition

Richard Campbell
Miami University

Christopher R. Martin
University of Northern Iowa

Bettina Fabos
University of Northern Iowa

BEDFORD/ST. MARTIN'S
Boston • New York

"WE ARE NOT ALONE."
For my family—Chris, Caitlin, and Dianna

"YOU MAY SAY I'M A DREAMER, BUT I'M NOT THE ONLY ONE."
For our daughers—Olivia and Sabine

For Bedford/St. Martin's

Vice President, Editorial, Macmillan Higher Education Humanities: Edwin Hill
Publisher for Communication: Erika Gutierrez
Developmental Editor: Jesse Hassenger
Senior Production Editor: Jessica Gould
Senior Production Supervisor: Dennis J. Conroy
Marketing Manager: Tom Digiano
Copy Editor: Jennifer Greenstein

Photo Researcher: Sue McDermott Barlow
Director of Rights and Permissions: Hilary Newman
Senior Art Director: Anna Palchik
Text Design: TODA (The Office of Design and Architecture)
Cover Design: Billy Boardman
Cover Art: The High Line public park, NYC, Section 2 © Claire Takacs/Getty Images; Blue Cubes © mareandmare/Getty Images; 3D Architecture Abstract © nadla/Getty Images
Composition: Cenveo Publisher Services
Printing and Binding: RR Donnelley and Sons

Manufactured in the United States of America

0 9 8 7 6 5
f   e   d   c   b   a

For information, write: Bedford/St. Martin's, 75 Arlington Street, Boston, MA 02116
(617-399-4000)

ISBN 978-1-4576-6873-9 (Paperback)
ISBN 978-1-319-01055-3 (Loose-leaf Edition)

About the Authors

Richard Campbell, Chair of the Department of Media, Journalism and Film at Miami University, is the author of *"60 Minutes" and the News: A Mythology for Middle America* (1991) and coauthor of *Cracked Coverage: Television News, the Anti-Cocaine Crusade, and the Reagan Legacy* (1994). Campbell has written for numerous publications, including *Columbia Journalism Review*, *Journal of Communication*, and *Media Studies Journal*, and he is on the editorial boards of *Critical Studies in Mass Communication* and *Television Quarterly*. He also serves on the board of directors for Cincinnati Public Radio. He holds a Ph.D. from Northwestern University and has also taught at the University of Wisconsin—Milwaukee, Mount Mary College, the University of Michigan, and Middle Tennessee State University.

Christopher R. Martin is Professor and Head of the Department of Communication Studies at the University of Northern Iowa and author of *Framed! Labor and the Corporate Media* (2003). He has written articles and reviews on journalism, televised sports, the Internet, and labor for several publications, including *Communication Research*, *Journal of Communication*, *Journal of Communication Inquiry*, *Labor Studies Journal*, *Culture, Sport, and Society,* and *Perspectives on Politics*. He is also on the editorial board of the *Journal of Communication Inquiry*. Martin holds a Ph.D. from the University of Michigan and has also taught at Miami University.

Bettina Fabos, an award-winning video maker and former print reporter, is an associate professor of visual communication and interactive digital studies at the University of Northern Iowa. She is the author of *Wrong Turn on the Information Superhighway: Education and the Commercialized Internet* (2004). Her areas of expertise include critical media literacy, Internet commercialization, the role of the Internet in education, and media representations of popular culture. Her work has been published in *Library Trends*, *Review of Educational Research*, and *Harvard Educational Review*. She is also a recipient of Fulbright and Spencer Fellowships. Fabos has taught at Miami University and has a Ph.D. from the University of Iowa.

Brief Contents

1 Mass Communication: A Critical Approach 3

DIGITAL MEDIA AND CONVERGENCE
2 The Internet, Digital Media, and Media Convergence 39
3 Digital Gaming and the Media Playground 73

SOUNDS AND IMAGES
4 Sound Recording and Popular Music 113
5 Popular Radio and the Origins of Broadcasting 149
6 Television and Cable: The Power of Visual Culture 187
7 Movies and the Impact of Images 231

WORDS AND PICTURES
8 Newspapers: The Rise and Decline of Modern Journalism 269
9 Magazines in the Age of Specialization 309
10 Books and the Power of Print 341

THE BUSINESS OF MASS MEDIA
11 Advertising and Commercial Culture 375
12 Public Relations and Framing the Message 413
13 Media Economics and the Global Marketplace 443

DEMOCRATIC EXPRESSION AND THE MASS MEDIA
14 The Culture of Journalism: Values, Ethics, and Democracy 477
15 Media Effects and Cultural Approaches to Research 511
16 Legal Controls and Freedom of Expression 537
Extended Case Study: Social Media and Finding Real Happiness 569

Preface

The digital future of mass media is here—we're living it right now. E-books are outselling print books on Amazon, digital album sales and streaming songs dominate the music industry, and social networking sites like Facebook and Twitter reach hundreds of millions of users world-wide. As mass media converge, the newest devices multitask as e-readers, music players, Web browsers, TV and movie screens, gaming systems, and phones.

But while many of today's students have integrated digital media into their daily lives, they may not understand how the media evolved to this point; how technology converges text, audio, and visual media; and what all these developments mean. This is why we believe the critical and cultural perspectives at the core of *Media & Culture*'s approach are more important than ever. *Media & Culture* pulls back the curtain to show students how the media really work—from the roots and economics of each media industry to the implications of today's consolidated media ownership to how these industries have changed in our digital world. By looking at the full history of media through a critical lens, students will leave this course with a better understanding of the complex relationship between the mass media and our shared culture.

The tenth edition of *Media & Culture* confronts the digital realities of how we consume media—and how students learn in today's classroom. Throughout the book, new "Elsewhere" pages cross-reference media stories and statistics, showing the Web-like connections between media industries and key issues. New part-opening infographics convey complex media relationships with eye-catching statistics and factoids about shifts in media consumption, ownership, and the most important and vital digital companies. New "Digital Job Outlook" boxes offer perspectives from industry insiders on how media jobs actually work. And a heavily revised Chapter 13, "Media Economics and the Global Marketplace," addresses the new economic realities of the media world with more visuals and greater digital savvy.

Media & Culture shares stories about the history of media, the digital revolution, and ongoing convergence—and the book itself practices convergence, too. The tenth edition is available packaged with LaunchPad, combining print and digital media together in an interactive e-book featuring video clips of media texts, links to streaming media, and an insider's look at the media industries—along with quizzes, activities, and instructor resources—free to the student with purchase of the book.

Of course, *Media & Culture* retains its well-loved and teachable organization that supports instructors in their quest to provide students with a clear understanding of the historical and cultural contexts for each media industry. Our signature five-step approach to studying the media has struck a chord with hundreds of instructors and thousands of students across the United States and North America. We continue to be enthusiastic about—and humbled by—the chance to work with the amazing community of teachers that has developed around *Media & Culture*. We hope the text enables students to become more knowledgable media consumers and engaged, media-literate citizens who are ready to take a critical stake in shaping our dynamic world.

The Tenth Edition

Media & Culture has taken the digital turn, and the new tenth edition continues to keep pace with the technological, economic, and social effects of today's rapidly changing media landscape.

- **All-new part-opening infographics show how convergence shapes our media experience.** Each of the book's five parts opens with a new overview, offering broad, cross-medium context for the chapters that follow and drawing connections to other sections of the book. These openers also include all-new infographics, connecting facts and figures about how we consume media with visually engaging and readable style.

- **New "Elsewhere" pages cross-reference and converge related topics.** As the mass media continue to converge, overlap, and influence one another, *Media & Culture* highlights those connections with new "Elsewhere" pages. Each of the book's five parts includes a page telling students where to find related information in other sections of the book, connecting the inner workings of media industries like video games, music, and movies with concepts like media effects studies, monopolies, and government regulation.

- **All-new Digital Job Outlook boxes give students the inside scoop.** *Media & Culture* takes students behind the scenes of the media with the brand-new Digital Job Outlook feature. Each of the chapters on media industries includes a box highlighting real advice and observations from media professionals, explaining what they look for, how they find those qualities in employees, or how they got where they are today.

- **Print and media converge with LaunchPad.** LaunchPad for *Media & Culture* merges and converges the book with the Web. A variety of video clips for each chapter gets students to think critically about media texts. Clips of movies and TV shows, streaming links, and videos provide an insider's look at the media industries through the eyes of leading professionals, including Noam Chomsky, Amy Goodman, and Junot Díaz. These clips are showcased throughout the book and are easily accessible through LaunchPad, where accompanying questions make them perfect for media response papers and class discussions. For more ideas on how using LaunchPad can enhance your course, see the Instructor's Resource Manual. For a complete list of available clips and access information, see the inside back cover of the book or visit **macmillanhighered.com/mediaculture10e**.

- **Revised Chapter 13 brings media economics up to date.** Over the past decade, the economics of the mass media have changed drastically, with changes in ownership and the domination of five major digital companies: Google, Amazon, Apple, Microsoft, and Facebook. We've revised Chapter 13, "Media Economics and the Global Marketplace," to reflect these changes—and to offer more accessible, visually literate coverage of this important topic. Chapter 13 explores deregulation, wage gaps, mergers, and acquisitions—all as they relate to media companies that students need to know about.

The Best and Broadest Introduction to the Mass Media

- **A critical approach to media literacy.** *Media & Culture* introduces students to five stages of the critical thinking and writing process—description, analysis, interpretation, evaluation, and engagement. The text uses these stages as a lens for examining the historical context and current processes that shape mass media as part of our culture. This framework informs the writing throughout, including the "Media Literacy and the Critical Process" boxed features in each chapter.

- **A cultural perspective.** The text focuses on the vital relationship between mass media and our shared culture—how cultural trends influence the mass media and how specific historical developments, technical innovations, and key decision makers in the history of the media have affected the ways our democracy and society have evolved.

- **Comprehensive coverage.** The text supports the instructor in providing students with the nuts-and-bolts content they need to understand each media industry's history, organizational structure, economic models, and market statistics.

- **An exploration of media economics and democracy.** *Media & Culture* spotlights the significance and impact of multinational media systems throughout the text. It also invites students to explore the implications of the Telecommunications Act of 1996 and other deregulation resolutions. Additionally, each chapter ends with a discussion of the effects of various mass media on the nature of democratic life.

- **Compelling storytelling.** Most mass media make use of storytelling to tap into our shared beliefs and values, and so does *Media & Culture*. Each chapter presents the events and issues surrounding media culture as intriguing and informative narratives, rather than as a series of unconnected facts and feats, and maps the uneasy and parallel changes in consumer culture and democratic society.

- **The most accessible book available.** Learning tools in every chapter help students find and remember the information they need to know. Bulleted lists at the beginning of every chapter give students a road map to key concepts, annotated timelines offer powerful visual guides that highlight key events and refer to more coverage in the chapter, Media Literacy and the Critical Process boxes model the five-step process, and the Chapter Reviews help students study and review for quizzes and exams and set them up for success.

Student Resources

For more information on student resources or to learn about package options, please visit the online catalog at **macmillanhighered.com/mediaculture/catalog**.

Your e-book. Your way.

A variety of e-book formats are available for use on computers, tablets, and e-readers, featuring portability, customization options, and affordable prices. For more information, see **macmillanhighered.com/ebooks**.

Discover What LaunchPad Can Do for Your Course

LaunchPad offers our acclaimed content curated and organized for easy assignability in an interface that can be used as is or adapted to your needs. Bedford provides multimedia content and assessments—including the e-book—which you can assign in units along with your own materials. An entire unit's worth of work can be assigned in seconds, significantly decreasing the amount of time it takes for you to get your course up and running. In addition, you can customize as much or as little as you like. LaunchPad also provides access to analytics that provide a clear window on performance for your whole class, for individual students, and for individual assignments. And all of this is done with an intuitive interface and design, ensuring that everyone in the class is on the same page. Free study aids on the book's Web site help students gauge their understanding of the text material through concise chapter summaries with study questions, visual activities that combine images and critical-thinking analysis, and pre- and post-chapter quizzes to help students assess their strengths and weaknesses and focus their studying.

Media Career Guide: Preparing for Jobs in the 21st Century, Tenth Edition

Sherri Hope Culver, *Temple University;* ISBN: 978-1-319-01953-2

Practical, student-friendly, and revised with recent trends in the job market (like the role of social media in a job search), this guide includes a comprehensive directory of media jobs, practical tips, and career guidance for students who are considering a major in the media industries. *Media Career Guide* can also be packaged for free with the print book.

Instructor Resources

For more information or to order or download the instructor resources, please visit the online catalog at **macmillanhighered.com/mediaculture/catalog**.

Instructor's Resource Manual

Bettina Fabos, *University of Northern Iowa*; Christopher R. Martin, *University of Northern Iowa*; and Marilda Oviedo, *University of Iowa*

This downloadable manual improves on what has always been the best and most comprehensive instructor teaching tool available for introduction to mass communication courses. This extensive resource provides a range of teaching approaches, tips for facilitating in-class discussions, writing assignments, outlines, lecture topics, lecture spin-offs, critical-process exercises, classroom media resources, and an annotated list of more than two hundred video resources.

Test Bank

Christopher R. Martin, *University of Northern Iowa*; Bettina Fabos, *University of Northern Iowa;* and Marilda Oviedo, *University of Iowa*

Available as software formatted for Windows and Macintosh, the Test Bank includes multiple choice, true/false, matching, fill-in-the-blank, and short and long essay questions for every chapter in *Media & Culture*.

PowerPoint Slides

PowerPoint presentations to help guide your lecture are available for downloading for each chapter in *Media & Culture*.

The Online Image Library for *Media & Culture*

This free instructor resource provides access to hundreds of dynamic images from the pages of *Media & Culture*. These images can be easily incorporated into lectures or used to spark in-class discussion.

Questions for Classroom Response Systems

Questions for every chapter in *Media & Culture* help integrate the latest classroom response systems (such as i>clicker) into your lecture to get instant feedback on students' understanding of course concepts as well as their opinions and perspectives.

Acknowledgments

We are very grateful to everyone at Bedford/St. Martin's who supported this project through its many stages. We wish that every textbook author could have the kind of experience we had with these people: Chuck Christensen, Joan Feinberg, Denise Wydra, Erika Gutierrez, Erica Appel, Stacey Propps, Simon Glick, and Noel Hohnstine. Over the years, we have also collaborated with superb and supportive developmental editors: on the tenth edition, Jesse Hassenger. We particularly appreciate the tireless work of Jessica Gould, senior project editor, who kept the book on schedule while making sure we got the details right, and Dennis J. Conroy, senior production supervisor. Thanks also to Billy Boardman for a fantastic cover design. We are especially grateful to our research assistant, Susan Coffin, who functioned as a one-person clipping service throughout the process. We are also grateful to Jimmie Reeves, our digital gaming expert, who contributed his great knowledge of this medium to the development of Chapter 3.

We also want to thank the many fine and thoughtful reviewers who contributed ideas to the tenth edition of *Media & Culture*: Mariam Alkazemi, *University of Florida*; Ronald Becker, *Miami University*; Tanya Biami, *Cochise College*; Dave Bostwick, *Baker University*; David Bradford, *Eastern Florida State College*; Alexis Carreiro, *Queens University of Charlotte*; David Cassady, *Pacific University*; John Chalfa, *Mercer University*; Jon Conlogue, *Westfield State University*; Don Diefenbach, *UNC Asheville*; Larry Hartsfield, *Fort Lewis College*; Phelps Hawkins, *Savannah State University*; Deborah Lev, *Centenary College*; Thomas Lindlof, *University of Kentucky*; Steve Liu, *University of Incarnate Word*; Maureen Louis, *Cazenovia College*;

Mary Lowney, *American International College*; Arnold Mackowiak, *Eastern Michigan University*; Bob Manis, *College of Southern Nevada*; Michael McCluskey, *Ohio State University*; Andrea McDonnell, *Emmanuel College*; Ryan Medders, *California Lutheran University*; Alicia Morris, *Virginia State University*; Lanie Steinwart, *Valparaiso University*; Stephen Swanson, *McLennan Community College*; Shauntae White, *North Carolina Central University*.

For the ninth edition: Glenda Alvarado, *University of South Carolina*; Lisa Burns, *Quinnipiac University*; Matthew Cecil, *South Dakota University*; John Dougan, *Middle Tennessee State University*; Lewis Freeman, *Fordham University*; Cindy Hing-Yuk Wong, *College of Staten Island*; K. Megan Hopper, *Illinois State University*; John Kerezy, *Cuyahoga Community College*; Marcia Ladendorff, *University of North Florida*; Julie Lellis, *Elon University*; Joy McDonald, *Hampton University*; Heather McIntosh, *Boston College*; Kenneth Nagelberg, *Delaware State University*; Eric Pierson, *University of San Diego*; Jennifer Tiernan, *South Dakota State University*; Erin Wilgenbusch, *Iowa State University*.

For the eighth edition: Frank A. Aycock, *Appalachian State University*; Carrie Buchanan, *John Carroll University*; Lisa M. Burns, *Quinnipiac University*; Rich Cameron, *Cerritos College*; Katherine Foss, *Middle Tennessee State University*; Myleea D. Hill, *Arkansas State University*; Sarah Alford Hock, *Santa Barbara City College*; Sharon R. Hollenback, *Syracuse University*; Drew Jacobs, *Camden County College*; Susan Katz, *University of Bridgeport*; John Kerezy, *Cuyahoga Community College*; Les Kozaczek, *Franklin Pierce University*; Deborah L. Larson, *Missouri State University*; Susan Charles Lewis, *Minnesota State University–Mankato*; Rick B. Marks, *College of Southern Nevada*; Donna R. Munde, *Mercer County Community College*; Wendy Nelson, *Palomar College*; Charles B. Scholz, *New Mexico State University*; Don W. Stacks, *University of Miami*; Carl Sessions Stepp, *University of Maryland*; David Strukel, *University of Toledo*; Lisa Turowski, *Towson University*; Lisa M. Weidman, *Linfield College*.

For the seventh edition: Robert Blade, *Florida Community College*; Lisa Boragine, *Cape Cod Community College*; Joseph Clark, *University of Toledo*; Richard Craig, *San Jose State University*; Samuel Ebersole, *Colorado State University–Pueblo*; Brenda Edgerton-Webster, *Mississippi State University*; Tim Edwards, *University of Arkansas at Little Rock*; Mara Einstein, *Queens College*; Lillie M. Fears, *Arkansas State University*; Connie Fletcher, *Loyola University*; Monica Flippin-Wynn, *University of Oklahoma*; Gil Fowler, *Arkansas State University*; Donald G. Godfrey, *Arizona State University*; Patricia Homes, *University of Southwestern Louisiana*; Daniel McDonald, *Ohio State University*; Connie McMahon, *Barry University*; Steve Miller, *Rutgers University*; Siho Nam, *University of North Florida*; David Nelson, *University of Colorado–Colorado Springs*; Zengjun Peng, *St. Cloud State University*; Deidre Pike, *University of Nevada–Reno*; Neil Ralston, *Western Kentucky University*; Mike Reed, *Saddleback College*; David Roberts, *Missouri Valley College*; Donna Simmons, *California State University–Bakersfield*; Marc Skinner, *University of Idaho*; Michael Stamm, *University of Minnesota*; Bob Trumpbour, *Penn State University*; Kristin Watson, *Metro State University*; Jim Weaver, *Virginia Polytechnic and State University*; David Whitt, *Nebraska Wesleyan University*.

For the sixth edition: Boyd Dallos, *Lake Superior College*; Roger George, *Bellevue Community College*; Osvaldo Hirschmann, *Houston Community College*; Ed Kanis, *Butler University*; Dean A. Kruckeberg, *University of Northern Iowa*; Larry Leslie, *University of South Florida*; Lori Liggett, *Bowling Green State University*; Steve Miller, *Rutgers University*; Robert Pondillo, *Middle Tennessee State University*; David Silver, *University of San Francisco*; Chris White, *Sam Houston State University*; Marvin Williams, *Kingsborough Community College*.

For the fifth edition: Russell Barclay, *Quinnipiac University*; Kathy Battles, *University of Michigan*; Kenton Bird, *University of Idaho*; Ed Bonza, *Kennesaw State University*; Larry L. Burris, *Middle Tennessee State University*; Ceilidh Charleson-Jennings, *Collin County Community College*; Raymond Eugene Costain, *University of Central Florida*; Richard Craig, *San Jose State University*; Dave Deeley, *Truman State University*; Janine Gerzanics, *West Valley College*;

Beth Haller, *Towson University*; Donna Hemmila, *Diablo Valley College*; Sharon Hollenback, *Syracuse University*; Marshall D. Katzman, *Bergen Community College*; Kimberly Lauffer, *Towson University*; Steve Miller, *Rutgers University*; Stu Minnis, *Virginia Wesleyan College*; Frank G. Perez, *University of Texas at El Paso*; Dave Perlmutter, *Louisiana State University–Baton Rouge*; Karen Pitcher, *University of Iowa*; Ronald C. Roat, *University of Southern Indiana*; Marshel Rossow, *Minnesota State University*; Roger Saathoff, *Texas Tech University*; Matthew Smith, *Wittenberg University*; Marlane C. Steinwart, *Valparaiso University*.

For the fourth edition: Fay Y. Akindes, *University of Wisconsin–Parkside*; Robert Arnett, *Mississippi State University*; Charles Aust, *Kennesaw State University*; Russell Barclay, *Quinnipiac University*; Bryan Brown, *Southwest Missouri State University*; Peter W. Croisant, *Geneva College*; Mark Goodman, *Mississippi State University*; Donna Halper, *Emerson College*; Rebecca Self Hill, *University of Colorado*; John G. Hodgson, *Oklahoma State University*; Cynthia P. King, *American University*; Deborah L. Larson, *Southwest Missouri State University*; Charles Lewis, *Minnesota State University–Mankato*; Lila Lieberman, *Rutgers University*; Abbus Malek, *Howard University*; Anthony A. Olorunnisola, *Pennsylvania State University*; Norma Pecora, *Ohio University–Athens*; Elizabeth M. Perse, *University of Delaware*; Hoyt Purvis, *University of Arkansas*; Alison Rostankowski, *University of Wisconsin–Milwaukee*; Roger A. Soenksen, *James Madison University*; Hazel Warlaumont, *California State University–Fullerton*.

For the third edition: Gerald J. Baldasty, *University of Washington*; Steve M. Barkin, *University of Maryland*; Ernest L. Bereman, *Truman State University*; Daniel Bernadi, *University of Arizona*; Kimberly L. Bissell, *Southern Illinois University*; Audrey Boxmann, *Merrimack College*; Todd Chatman, *University of Illinois*; Ray Chavez, *University of Colorado*; Vic Costello, *Gardner-Webb University*; Paul D'Angelo, *Villanova University*; James Shanahan, *Cornell University*; Scott A. Webber, *University of Colorado*.

For the second edition: Susan B. Barnes, *Fordham University*; Margaret Bates, *City College of New York*; Steven Alan Carr, *Indiana University/Purdue University–Fort Wayne*; William G. Covington Jr., *Bridgewater State College*; Roger Desmond, *University of Hartford*; Jules d'Hemecourt, *Louisiana State University*; Cheryl Evans, *Northwestern Oklahoma State University*; Douglas Gomery, *University of Maryland*; Colin Gromatzky, *New Mexico State University*; John L. Hochheimer, *Ithaca College*; Sheena Malhotra, *University of New Mexico*; Sharon R. Mazzarella, *Ithaca College*; David Marc McCoy, *Kent State University*; Beverly Merrick, *New Mexico State University*; John Pantalone, *University of Rhode Island*; John Durham Peters, *University of Iowa*; Lisa Pieraccini, *Oswego State College*; Susana Powell, *Borough of Manhattan Community College*; Felicia Jones Ross, *Ohio State University*; Enid Sefcovic, *Florida Atlantic University*; Keith Semmel, *Cumberland College*; Augusta Simon, *Embry-Riddle Aeronautical University*; Clifford E. Wexler, *Columbia-Greene Community College*.

For the first edition: Paul Ashdown, *University of Tennessee*; Terry Bales, *Rancho Santiago College*; Russell Barclay, *Quinnipiac University*; Thomas Beell, *Iowa State University*; Fred Blevens, *Southwest Texas State University*; Stuart Bullion, *University of Maine*; William G. Covington Jr., *Bridgewater State College*; Robert Daves, *Minneapolis Star Tribune*; Charles Davis, *Georgia Southern University*; Thomas Donahue, *Virginia Commonwealth University*; Ralph R. Donald, *University of Tennessee–Martin*; John P. Ferre, *University of Louisville*; Donald Fishman, *Boston College*; Elizabeth Atwood Gailey, *University of Tennessee*; Bob Gassaway, *University of New Mexico*; Anthony Giffard, *University of Washington*; Zhou He, *San Jose State University*; Barry Hollander, *University of Georgia*; Sharon Hollenbeck, *Syracuse University*; Anita Howard, *Austin Community College*; James Hoyt, *University of Wisconsin–Madison*; Joli Jensen, *University of Tulsa*; Frank Kaplan, *University of Colorado*; William Knowles, *University of Montana*; Michael Leslie, *University of Florida*; Janice Long, *University of Cincinnati*; Kathleen Maticheck, *Normandale Community College*; Maclyn McClary, *Humboldt State University*; Robert McGaughey, *Murray State University*; Joseph McKerns, *Ohio State University*; Debra

Merskin, *University of Oregon*; David Morrissey, *Colorado State University*; Michael Murray, *University of Missouri at St. Louis*; Susan Dawson O'Brien, *Rose State College*; Patricia Bowie Orman, *University of Southern Colorado*; Jim Patton, *University of Arizona*; John Pauly, *St. Louis University*; Ted Pease, *Utah State University*; Janice Peck, *University of Colorado*; Tina Pieraccini, *University of New Mexico*; Peter Pringle, *University of Tennessee*; Sondra Rubenstein, *Hofstra University*; Jim St. Clair, *Indiana University Southeast*; Jim Seguin, *Robert Morris College*; Donald Shaw, *University of North Carolina*; Martin D. Sommernes, *Northern Arizona State University*; Linda Steiner, *Rutgers University*; Jill Diane Swensen, *Ithaca College*; Sharon Taylor, *Delaware State University*; Hazel Warlaumont, *California State University–Fullerton*; Richard Whitaker, *Buffalo State College*; Lynn Zoch, *University of South Carolina*.

Special thanks from Richard Campbell: I would also like to acknowledge the number of fine teachers at both the *University of Wisconsin–Milwaukee and Northwestern University* who helped shape the way I think about many of the issues raised in this book, and I am especially grateful to my former students at the *University of Wisconsin–Milwaukee, Mount Mary College,* the *University of Michigan, Middle Tennessee State University*, and my current students at *Miami University*. Some of my students have contributed directly to this text, and thousands have endured my courses over the years—and made them better. My all-time favorite former students, Chris Martin and Bettina Fabos, are now essential coauthors, as well as the creators of our book's Instructor's Resource Manual and Test Bank. I am grateful for Chris and Bettina's fine writing, research savvy, good stories, and tireless work amid their own teaching schedules and writing careers, all while raising two spirited daughters. I remain most grateful, though, to the people I most love: my son, Chris; my daughter, Caitlin; and, most of all, my wife, Dianna, whose line editing, content ideas, daily conversations, shared interests, and ongoing support are the resources that make this project go better with each edition.

Special thanks from Christopher Martin and Bettina Fabos: We would also like to thank Richard Campbell, with whom it is always a delight working on this project. We also appreciate the great energy, creativity, and talent that everyone at Bedford/St. Martin's brings to the book. From edition to edition, we also receive plenty of suggestions from *Media & Culture* users and reviewers and from our own journalism and media students. We would like to thank them for their input and for creating a community of sorts around the theme of critical perspectives on the media. Most of all, we'd like to thank our daughters, Olivia and Sabine, who bring us joy and laughter every day, and a sense of mission to better understand the world of media and culture in which they live.

Please feel free to e-mail us at **mediaandculture@bedfordstmartins.com** with any comments, concerns, or suggestions!

Photo by Rick Kern/Getty Image for Comedy Central

Contents

ABOUT THE AUTHORS iii
BRIEF CONTENTS iv
PREFACE v

1 Mass Communication: A Critical Approach 3

Culture and the Evolution of Mass Communication 5
    Oral and Written Eras in Communication 6
    The Print Revolution 7
    The Electronic Era 8
    The Digital Era 8
    The Linear Model of Mass Communication 9
    A Cultural Model for Understanding Mass Communication 9

The Development of Media and Their Role in Our Society 10
    The Evolution of Media: From Emergence to Convergence 10
    Media Convergence 11
    Stories: The Foundation of Media 13
    The Power of Media Stories in Everyday Life 14
    © Agenda Setting and Gatekeeping 15

Surveying the Cultural Landscape 16
    Culture as a Skyscraper 17
    ◢ EXAMINING ETHICS Covering War 18
    Culture as a Map 21
    ◢ CASE STUDY Is *Anchorman* a Comedy or a Documentary? 22
    Cultural Values of the Modern Period 26
    Shifting Values in Postmodern Culture 27

Critiquing Media and Culture 29
    Media Literacy and the Critical Process 30
    Benefits of a Critical Perspective 30
    ◢ GLOBAL VILLAGE Bedouins, Camels, Transistors, and Coke 31
    ◢ MEDIA LITERACY AND THE CRITICAL PROCESS 32

CHAPTER REVIEW 34
    © LaunchPad 35

© For videos, review quizzing, and more, visit **LaunchPad for** *Media & Culture*
at **macmillanhighered.com/mediaculture10e.**

PhotoInc/Getty Images

PART 1: DIGITAL MEDIA AND CONVERGENCE   36

2   The Internet, Digital Media, and Media Convergence   39

The Development of the Internet and the Web   41
The Birth of the Internet   41
The Net Widens   43
The Commercialization of the Internet   44

The Web Goes Social   47
Types of Social Media   47
◉ *The Net* (1995)   47
Social Media and Democracy   49
◣ EXAMINING ETHICS The "Anonymous" Hackers of the Internet   50

Convergence and Mobile Media   53
Media Converges on Our PCs and TVs   53
Mobile Devices Propel Convergence   53
The Impact of Media Convergence and Mobile Media   54
The Next Era: The Semantic Web   56

The Economics and Issues of the Internet   57
Ownership: Controlling the Internet   57
Targeted Advertising and Data Mining   60
◣ GLOBAL VILLAGE Designed in California, Assembled in China   61
◣ MEDIA LITERACY AND THE CRITICAL PROCESS Tracking and Recording Your Every Move   63
Security: The Challenge to Keep Personal Information Private   64
Appropriateness: What Should Be Online?   64
Access: The Fight to Prevent a Digital Divide   65
◉ Net Neutrality   66
Net Neutrality: Maintaining an Open Internet   66
Alternative Voices   67

The Internet and Democracy   68
◣ DIGITAL JOB OUTLOOK   69

CHAPTER REVIEW   70
◉ LaunchPad   71

Getty Images

3 Digital Gaming and the Media Playground   73

The Development of Digital Gaming   75
  Mechanical Gaming   76
  The First Video Games   78
  Arcades and Classic Games   78
  Consoles and Advancing Graphics   79
  Gaming on Home Computers   80

The Internet Transforms Gaming   81
  MMORPGs, Virtual Worlds, and Social Gaming   81
  Convergence: From Consoles to Mobile Gaming   83

The Media Playground   84
  Video Game Genres   84
  ◢ CASE STUDY *Watch Dogs* **Hacks Our Surveillance Society   85**
  Communities of Play: Inside the Game   90
  Communities of Play: Outside the Game   90

Trends and Issues in Digital Gaming   92
  Electronic Gaming and Media Culture   92
  ⊙ **Video Games at the Movies**   92
  Electronic Gaming and Advertising   93
  Addiction and Other Concerns   94
  ◢ **GLOBAL VILLAGE South Korea's Gaming Obsession   96**
  ◢ **MEDIA LITERACY AND THE CRITICAL PROCESS**
     First-Person Shooter Games: Misogyny as Entertainment?   98
  Regulating Gaming   98
  The Future of Gaming and Interactive Environments   99

The Business of Digital Gaming   99
  The Ownership and Organization of Digital Gaming   100
  The Structure of Digital Game Publishing   103
  Selling Digital Games   104
  Alternative Voices   105

Digital Gaming, Free Speech, and Democracy   106
  ◢ **DIGITAL JOB OUTLOOK   107**

  CHAPTER REVIEW   108
  ⊙ **LaunchPad**   109

Tim Mosenfelder/Getty Images

PART 2: SOUNDS AND IMAGES   110

4   Sound Recording and Popular Music   113

The Development of Sound Recording   115

From Cylinders to Disks: Sound Recording Becomes a Mass Medium   116

From Phonographs to CDs: Analog Goes Digital   118

Convergence: Sound Recording in the Internet Age   119

▶ Recording Music Today   120

The Rocky Relationship between Records and Radio   121

U.S. Popular Music and the Formation of Rock   122

The Rise of Pop Music   122

Rock and Roll Is Here to Stay   123

Rock Muddies the Waters   124

Battles in Rock and Roll   126

A Changing Industry: Reformations in Popular Music   129

The British Are Coming!   129

Motor City Music: Detroit Gives America Soul   130

Folk and Psychedelic Music Reflect the Times   130

◢ MEDIA LITERACY AND THE CRITICAL PROCESS
Music Preferences across Generations   132

Punk, Grunge, and Alternative Respond to Mainstream Rock   133

Hip-Hop Redraws Musical Lines   134

The Reemergence of Pop   135

The Business of Sound Recording   136

Music Labels Influence the Industry   137

◢ TRACKING TECHNOLOGY The Song Machine: The Hitmakers
behind Rihanna   138

Making, Selling, and Profiting from Music   139

▶ Alternative Strategies for Music Marketing   141

◢ CASE STUDY Psy and the Meaning of "Gangnam Style"   142

Alternative Voices   143

▶ Streaming Music Videos   144

Sound Recording, Free Expression, and Democracy   144

◢ DIGITAL JOB OUTLOOK   145

Tim Pannell/Corbis

CHAPTER REVIEW   146
   ⊙ **LaunchPad**   147

5   Popular Radio and the Origins of Broadcasting   149

Early Technology and the Development of Radio   **151**
   Maxwell and Hertz Discover Radio Waves   152
   Marconi and the Inventors of Wireless Telegraphy   152
   Wireless Telephony: De Forest and Fessenden   154
   Regulating a New Medium   156

The Evolution of Radio   **157**
   Building the First Networks   158
   Sarnoff and NBC: Building the "Blue" and "Red" Networks   159
   Government Scrutiny Ends RCA-NBC Monopoly   160
   CBS and Paley: Challenging NBC   161
   Bringing Order to Chaos with the Radio Act of 1927   161
   The Golden Age of Radio   163

Radio Reinvents Itself   **165**
   Transistors Make Radio Portable   166
   The FM Revolution and Edwin Armstrong   166
   The Rise of Format and Top 40 Radio   167
   Resisting the Top 40   168

The Sounds of Commercial Radio   **169**
   Format Specialization   169
   ◢ **CASE STUDY Host: The Origins of Talk Radio**   **171**
   Nonprofit Radio and NPR   173
   ◢ **MEDIA LITERACY AND THE CRITICAL PROCESS**
      Comparing Commercial and Noncommercial Radio   **174**
   New Radio Technologies Offer More Stations   175
   Radio and Convergence   175
   ⊙ **Going Visual: Video, Radio, and the Web**   175
   ◢ **GLOBAL VILLAGE Radio Mogadishu**   **176**
   ⊙ **Radio: Yesterday, Today, and Tomorrow**   178

The Economics of Broadcast Radio   **178**
   Local and National Advertising   178
   Manipulating Playlists with Payola   179

Eric Leibowitz/© Netflix/courtesy Everett Collection

Radio Ownership: From Diversity to Consolidation   179
Alternative Voices   181

Radio and the Democracy of the Airwaves   182
   ◢ **DIGITAL JOB OUTLOOK   183**

CHAPTER REVIEW   184
   ◉ **LaunchPad**   185

6   Television and Cable: The Power of Visual Culture   187

The Origins and Development of Television   189
   Early Innovations in TV Technology   190
   Electronic Technology: Zworykin and Farnsworth   190
   Controlling Content—TV Grows Up   193

The Development of Cable   195
   CATV—Community Antenna Television   195
   The Wires and Satellites behind Cable Television   195
   Cable Threatens Broadcasting   196
   Cable Services   197
   ◢ **CASE STUDY ESPN: Sports and Stories   198**
   DBS: Cable without Wires   199

Technology and Convergence Change Viewing Habits   199
   ◉ **Television Networks Evolve**   199
   Home Video   200
   The Third Screen: TV Converges with the Internet   200
   Fourth Screens: Smartphones and Mobile Video   202

Major Programming Trends   203
   TV Entertainment: Our Comic Culture   203
   TV Entertainment: Our Dramatic Culture   205
   ◉ **Television Drama: Then and Now**   206
   TV Information: Our Daily News Culture   207
   Reality TV and Other Enduring Trends   208
   Public Television Struggles to Find Its Place   209
   ◢ **MEDIA LITERACY AND THE CRITICAL PROCESS**
   TV and the State of Storytelling   210

Regulatory Challenges to Television and Cable 211

  Government Regulations Temporarily Restrict Network Control 211

  ▶ **What Makes Public Television Public?** 211

  Balancing Cable's Growth against Broadcasters' Interests 212

  Franchising Frenzy 214

  The Telecommunications Act of 1996 215

The Economics and Ownership of Television and Cable 216

  Production 217

  Distribution 218

  Syndication Keeps Shows Going and Going . . . 218

  Measuring Television Viewing 220

  ▲ **TRACKING TECHNOLOGY Changing Channels: Big Studios Diversify on YouTube 222**

  The Major Programming Corporations 223

  Alternative Voices 225

Television, Cable, and Democracy 225

  ▲ **DIGITAL JOB OUTLOOK 227**

CHAPTER REVIEW 228

  ▶ **LaunchPad** 229

7 Movies and the Impact of Images 231

Early Technology and the Evolution of Movies 233

  The Development of Film 234

  The Introduction of Narrative 237

  The Arrival of Nickelodeons 237

The Rise of the Hollywood Studio System 238

  Production 239

  Distribution 239

  Exhibition 240

The Studio System's Golden Age 241

  Hollywood Narrative and the Silent Era 242

  The Introduction of Sound 242

  The Development of the Hollywood Style 243

  Outside the Hollywood System 246

  ▶ **Breaking Barriers with *12 Years a Slave* 246**

AP Photo/John Minchillo

▲ CASE STUDY **Breaking through Hollywood's Race Barrier** 247

▲ GLOBAL VILLAGE **Beyond Hollywood: Asian Cinema** 250

The Transformation of the Studio System 251

    The Hollywood Ten 251

    The Paramount Decision 252

    Moving to the Suburbs 252

    Television Changes Hollywood 253

    Hollywood Adapts to Home Entertainment 254

The Economics of the Movie Business 255

    Production, Distribution, and Exhibition Today 255

    The Major Studio Players 258

    ▲ **MEDIA LITERACY AND THE CRITICAL PROCESS**
    The Blockbuster Mentality 259

    Convergence: Movies Adjust to the Digital Turn 260

    Alternative Voices 261

Popular Movies and Democracy 262

    ⓒ **More Than a Movie: Social Issues and Film** 262

    ▲ **DIGITAL JOB OUTLOOK** 263

CHAPTER REVIEW 264

    ⓒ **LaunchPad** 265

PART 3: WORDS AND PICTURES 266

8   Newspapers: The Rise and Decline of Modern Journalism 269

The Evolution of American Newspapers 271

    Colonial Newspapers and the Partisan Press 272

    The Penny Press Era: Newspapers Become Mass Media 274

    The Age of Yellow Journalism: Sensationalism and Investigation 276

Competing Models of Modern Print Journalism 278

    "Objectivity" in Modern Journalism 278

    Interpretive Journalism 280

    Literary Forms of Journalism 281

    Contemporary Journalism in the TV and Internet Age 282

    ⓒ **Newspapers and the Internet: Convergence** 284

Robert Caplin/The New York Times/Redux

The Business and Ownership of Newspapers 284

Consensus versus Conflict: Newspapers Play Different Roles 285

Newspapers Target Specific Readers 285

◢ **MEDIA LITERACY AND THE CRITICAL PROCESS**
Covering Business and Economic News 286

Newspaper Operations 291

◢ **CASE STUDY Alternative Journalism: Dorothy Day and I. F. Stone 292**

Newspaper Ownership: Chains Lose Their Grip 294

Joint Operating Agreements Combat Declining Competition 295

Challenges Facing Newspapers Today 296

Readership Declines in the United States 296

Going Local: How Small and Campus Papers Retain Readers 297

Blogs Challenge Newspapers' Authority Online 297

ⓒ **Community Voices: Weekly Newspapers 298**

Convergence: Newspapers Struggle in the Move to Digital 298

New Models for Journalism 301

Alternative Voices 302

Newspapers and Democracy 303

◢ **DIGITAL JOB OUTLOOK 305**

CHAPTER REVIEW 306

ⓒ **LaunchPad** 307

9 Magazines in the Age of Specialization 309

The Early History of Magazines 311

The First Magazines 311

Magazines in Colonial America 312

U.S. Magazines in the Nineteenth Century 313

National, Women's, and Illustrated Magazines 314

The Development of Modern American Magazines 315

Social Reform and the Muckrakers 316

The Rise of General-Interest Magazines 317

The Fall of General-Interest Magazines 319

◢ **CASE STUDY The Evolution of Photojournalism 320**

Convergence: Magazines Confront the Digital Age 324

The Domination of Specialization 325

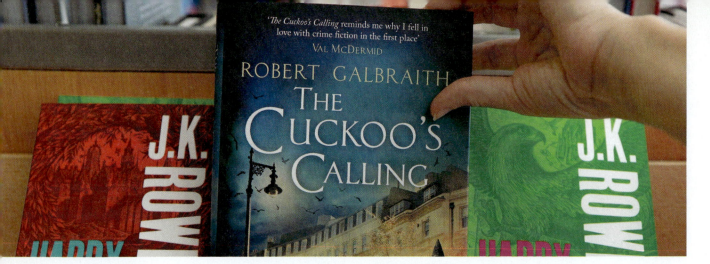

Andy Rain/EPA/Newscom

◢ **TRACKING TECHNOLOGY The New "Touch" of Magazines 326**

Men's and Women's Magazines 327

Sports, Entertainment, and Leisure Magazines 327

ⓒ **Magazine Specialization Today** 327

Magazines for the Ages 328

Elite Magazines 329

Minority-Targeted Magazines 329

◢ **MEDIA LITERACY AND THE CRITICAL PROCESS
Uncovering American Beauty 330**

Supermarket Tabloids 331

ⓒ **Narrowcasting in Magazines** 332

The Organization and Economics of Magazines 332

Magazine Departments and Duties 332

Major Magazine Chains 334

Alternative Voices 335

Magazines in a Democratic Society 336

◢ **DIGITAL JOB OUTLOOK 337**

CHAPTER REVIEW 338

ⓒ **LaunchPad** 339

10 Books and the Power of Print 341

The History of Books from Papyrus to Paperbacks 344

The Development of Manuscript Culture 345

The Innovations of Block Printing and Movable Type 346

The Gutenberg Revolution: The Invention of the Printing Press 346

The Birth of Publishing in the United States 347

Modern Publishing and the Book Industry 348

The Formation of Publishing Houses 348

Types of Books 348

◢ **CASE STUDY Comic Books: Alternative Themes, but Superheroes Prevail 352**

Trends and Issues in Book Publishing 355

ⓒ **Based On: Making Books into Movies** 356

Influences of Television and Film 356

Audio Books 357

Convergence: Books in the Digital Age 357

Kevin Mazur/BET/Getty Images for BET

◎ **Books in the New Millennium** 357

Preserving and Digitizing Books 358

◢ **GLOBAL VILLAGE France and the Anti-Amazon Law 359**

◢ **MEDIA LITERACY AND THE CRITICAL PROCESS
Banned Books and "Family Values" 360**

Censorship and Banned Books 360

The Organization and Ownership of the Book Industry 361

Ownership Patterns 361

The Structure of Book Publishing 362

Selling Books: Brick-and-Mortar Stores, Clubs, and Mail Order 364

Selling Books Online 365

Alternative Voices 366

Books and the Future of Democracy 367

◢ **DIGITAL JOB OUTLOOK 369**

CHAPTER REVIEW 370

◎ **LaunchPad** 371

PART 4: THE BUSINESS OF MASS MEDIA 372

11 Advertising and Commercial Culture 375

Early Developments in American Advertising 378

The First Advertising Agencies 379

Advertising in the 1800s 379

Promoting Social Change and Dictating Values 381

Early Ad Regulation 382

The Shape of U.S. Advertising Today 383

The Influence of Visual Design 383

Types of Advertising Agencies 384

The Structure of Ad Agencies 386

Trends in Online Advertising 390

◎ **Advertising in the Digital Age** 391

Persuasive Techniques in Contemporary Advertising 393

Conventional Persuasive Strategies 393

The Association Principle 394

Kevin Mazur/WireImage for Parkwood Entertainment/Getty Images

▲ **CASE STUDY Hey, Super Bowl Sponsors: Your Ads Are Already Forgotten 395**

Advertising as Myth and Story 396

Product Placement 397

▲ **EXAMINING ETHICS Brand Integration, Everywhere 398**

▲ **MEDIA LITERACY AND THE CRITICAL PROCESS The Branded You 399**

Commercial Speech and Regulating Advertising 399

Critical Issues in Advertising 400

⊙ Advertising and Effects on Children 401

▲ **GLOBAL VILLAGE Smoking Up the Global Market 404**

Watching Over Advertising 405

Alternative Voices 407

Advertising, Politics, and Democracy 408

Advertising's Role in Politics 408

▲ **DIGITAL JOB OUTLOOK 409**

The Future of Advertising 409

CHAPTER REVIEW 410

⊙ LaunchPad 411

---

12 Public Relations and Framing the Message 413

Early Developments in Public Relations 416

P. T. Barnum and Buffalo Bill 416

Big Business and Press Agents 418

The Birth of Modern Public Relations 418

The Practice of Public Relations 421

Approaches to Organized Public Relations 422

Performing Public Relations 423

▲ **CASE STUDY The NFL's Concussion Crisis 426**

▲ **EXAMINING ETHICS What Does It Mean to Be Green? 428**

Public Relations Adapts to the Internet Age 431

Public Relations during a Crisis 431

Tensions between Public Relations and the Press 433

Elements of Professional Friction 433

⊙ Give and Take: Public Relations and Journalism 434

Shaping the Image of Public Relations   435

Alternative Voices   436

Public Relations and Democracy   436

◢ **MEDIA LITERACY AND THE CRITICAL PROCESS**
The Invisible Hand of PR   437

◢ **DIGITAL JOB OUTLOOK   439**

CHAPTER REVIEW   440

ⓒ **LaunchPad**   441

13   Media Economics and the Global Marketplace   443

Analyzing the Media Economy   445

The Structure of the Media Industry   446

The Performance of Media Organizations   446

The Transition to an Information Economy   448

Deregulation Trumps Regulation   449

Media Powerhouses: Consolidation, Partnerships, and Mergers   450

Business Tendencies in Media Industries   451

Economics, Hegemony, and Storytelling   453

Specialization, Global Markets, and Convergence   455

The Rise of Specialization and Synergy   455

Disney: A Postmodern Media Conglomerate   456

ⓒ **Disney's Global Brand**   456

◢ **CASE STUDY   Minority and Female Media Ownership: Why It Matters   458**

Global Audiences Expand Media Markets   460

The Internet and Convergence Change the Game   460

◢ **MEDIA LITERACY AND THE CRITICAL PROCESS**
Cultural Imperialism and Movies   461

Social Issues in Media Economics   463

The Limits of Antitrust Laws   465

ⓒ **The Impact of Media Ownership**   465

◢ **CASE STUDY   From Fifty to a Few: The Most Dominant Media Corporations   466**

The Fallout from a Free Market   467

Cultural Imperialism   468

The Media Marketplace and Democracy   469

The Effects of Media Consolidation on Democracy   470

The Media Reform Movement   471

The Granger Collection

CHAPTER REVIEW 472

◎ LaunchPad 473

PART 5: DEMOCRATIC EXPRESSION AND THE MASS MEDIA 474

14 The Culture of Journalism: Values, Ethics, and Democracy 477

Modern Journalism in the Information Age 479

What Is News? 479

Values in American Journalism 481

⏷ CASE STUDY Bias in the News 484

Ethics and the News Media 485

Ethical Predicaments 485

Resolving Ethical Problems 488

Reporting Rituals and the Legacy of Print Journalism 490

Focusing on the Present 490

◢ MEDIA LITERACY AND THE CRITICAL PROCESS
Telling Stories and Covering Disaster 491

Relying on Experts 492

Balancing Story Conflict 494

Acting as Adversaries 494

Journalism in the Age of TV and the Internet 495

Differences between Print, TV, and Internet News 495

Pundits, "Talking Heads," and Politics 497

◎ The Contemporary Journalist: Pundit or Reporter? 498

Convergence Enhances and Changes Journalism 498

The Power of Visual Language 499

◎ Fake News/Real News: A Fine Line 499

Alternative Models: Public Journalism and "Fake" News 500

The Public Journalism Movement 500

⏷ CASE STUDY A Lost Generation of Journalists? 501

"Fake" News and Satiric Journalism 503

Democracy and Reimagining Journalism's Role 505

Social Responsibility 505

Scott Garfield/© Columbia Pictures/courtesy Everett Collection

Deliberative Democracy   505

▲ EXAMINING ETHICS WikiLeaks, Secret Documents, and Good Journalism   506

CHAPTER REVIEW   508
© LaunchPad   509

15 Media Effects and Cultural Approaches to Research   511

Early Media Research Methods   513
Propaganda Analysis   514
Public Opinion Research   514
Social Psychology Studies   515
Marketing Research   516
▲ CASE STUDY The Effects of TV in a Post-TV World   517

Research on Media Effects   518
© Media Effects Research   518
Early Theories of Media Effects   518
Conducting Media Effects Research   520
▲ MEDIA LITERACY AND THE CRITICAL PROCESS
Wedding Media and the Meaning of the Perfect Wedding Day   523
Contemporary Media Effects Theories   523
Evaluating Research on Media Effects   526

Cultural Approaches to Media Research   526
Early Developments in Cultural Studies Research   527
Conducting Cultural Studies Research   527
▲ CASE STUDY Our Masculinity Problem   529
Cultural Studies' Theoretical Perspectives   530
Evaluating Cultural Studies Research   531

Media Research and Democracy   532

CHAPTER REVIEW   534
© LaunchPad   535

16 Legal Controls and Freedom of Expression   537

The Origins of Free Expression and a Free Press   539
Models of Expression   540
The First Amendment of the U.S. Constitution   541

© Shawn Thew/epa/Corbis

Censorship as Prior Restraint 542

Unprotected Forms of Expression 543

▲ **MEDIA LITERACY AND THE CRITICAL PROCESS**
Who Knows the First Amendment? 544

▲ **CASE STUDY Is "Sexting" Pornography? 550**

First Amendment versus Sixth Amendment 551

Film and the First Amendment 553

Social and Political Pressures on the Movies 554

Self-Regulation in the Movie Industry 554

The MPAA Ratings System 556

Expression in the Media: Print, Broadcast, and Online 557

The FCC Regulates Broadcasting 559

Dirty Words, Indecent Speech, and Hefty Fines 559

Political Broadcasts and Equal Opportunity 561

◉ **Bloggers and Legal Rights** 562

The Demise of the Fairness Doctrine 562

Communication Policy and the Internet 562

▲ **EXAMINING ETHICS A Generation of Copyright Criminals? 564**

The First Amendment and Democracy 565

CHAPTER REVIEW 566

◉ **LaunchPad** 567

Extended Case Study: Social Media and Finding Real Happiness 569

Step 1: Description 571
Step 2: Analysis 572
Step 3: Interpretation 573
Step 4: Evaluation 574
Step 5: Engagement 574

Notes N-1
Glossary G-1
Credits C-1
Index I-1

While the media used to be owned by numerous different companies, today six large conglomerates—**Sony, Disney, Comcast/NBC Universal, News Corp., Time Warner, and CBS**—dominate. However, in the wake of the digital turn, several more companies have emerged as leaders in digital media. These five digital companies—**Apple, Amazon, Google, Microsoft,** and **Facebook**—began in software or as Web sites, but their reach has expanded to compete with traditional media companies in many areas as they have begun producing, distributing, and consuming content. This visualization breaks down the media holdings of these digital companies to help you understand their growing influence.

As you examine this information, think about how much of your daily media consumption is owned by these top digital companies (as well as more traditional conglomerates like Sony or Disney). Which companies have the most influence on your entertainment and news consumption? What about on the technology you use every day? What does it mean that so few companies own so much of the media? Are there areas where the newer digital companies have a weaker hold?

Top Digital Companies and Their 2013 Revenue

Apple
$171 billion

The company Steve Jobs built sells computers, iPods, iPads, iPhones—and the music, movies, and e-books you consume on them.

Microsoft
$77.8 billion

Thanks to their widely used Windows operating system and their Xbox gaming console, Microsoft is still a major force in the digital world.

Amazon
$74.5 billion

What began as an online bookstore now commands a high share of printed and recorded media in traditional and digital forms—and dominates the e-reader market.

Google
$55.5 billion

Still the most-used search engine, Google has branched out into other media with its Google Play service and the Android phone.

Facebook
$7.9 billion

Facebook doesn't yet have as broad a multimedia reach as Amazon or Apple, but it is easily the biggest and most powerful social networking site, which provides a platform for games, music, news feeds, and plenty of crowd-sourced content.

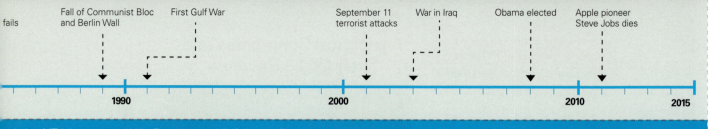

fails

Fall of Communist Bloc and Berlin Wall

First Gulf War

September 11 terrorist attacks

War in Iraq

Obama elected

Apple pioneer Steve Jobs dies

1990   **2000**   **2010**   **2015**

explodes. MTV changes
ok and sound of televi-
music, advertising, and
verall attention spans.
offers 24/7 news to view-
while *USA Today* brings
and bite-sized reports to
rs. The Reagan adminis-
n deregulates the mass
entation emerges—
che media through cable
magazines.

1990s: The digital era is in full swing. The Internet becomes a mass medium, computers become home appliances, and e-mail—born in the 1970s—revolutionizes the way people and businesses communicate around the world. CDs and DVDs deliver music, movies, and video games. Corporate media dominate through consolidation and the Telecommunications Act of 1996, which discards most ownership limits.

2000s: Media fragmentation deepens and political polarization divides the U.S. Cable and the Internet become important news sources but no longer require that we share common cultural ground, as did older forms of radio, TV, and the movies. E-commerce booms. Movies, TV shows, music, books, magazines, and newspapers converge on the Internet. The rise of smartphones and touchscreen devices makes it easier than ever to consume a variety of media at any time and in any place.

2010s: Devices like smartphones and touchscreen tablets become more prevalent, making it simpler to consume a wide variety of media at any time and in any place. In this emerging era of media convergence, it will be fascinating to see what the future of media holds.

1987
Beloved published

1995
Amazon.com launched

1997
First Harry Potter book published

2003
The Da Vinci Code published

2007
Amazon introduces the Kindle e-book reader

2011
Borders declares bankruptcy and closes stores

2011
Amazon.com sells more e-books than print books

1989
First newspaper sold by homeless

1995
Demise of many big-city dailies

2001
Dominance of newspaper chains

2006
Knight Ridder sold

2007
News Corp. buys the *Wall Street Journal*

2007
Tribune Co. sold

2008
Newspapers start rapid decline

2011
New York Times puts up paywall

2013
Jeff Bezos buys *Washington Post*

1995
Salon.com founded

2003
AARP Bulletin and *Magazine* top circulation

2008
U.S. News becomes a monthly magazine

2010
Wired sells 24,000 downloads of its iPad app on the first day

2009
Magazine ad pages drop 26%

1990s
Talk radio becomes most popular format

1996
Telecommunications Act of 1996 consolidates ownership

2002
Satellite radio begins

2004
Podcasting debuts

2007
HD radio introduced

2008
Sirius and XM satellite radio companies merge

2010
Pandora brings back portable radio listening with an iPad app

---

roduced as new

1997
DVDs introduced

2000
MP3 format compresses digital files

2001
File sharing

2003
iTunes online music store

2013
iTunes celebrates its 25 billionth download

2011
Spotify debuts in the U.S.

1990s
The rise of independent films as a source of new talent

1995
Megaplex cinemas emerge

1997
DVDs largely replace VHS cassettes

2000
Digital production and distribution gain strength

2006
Movie theaters continue to add IMAX screens to their megaplexes

2009
James Cameron uses specially created 3-D cameras (developed with Sony) to present a whole new world in *Avatar*

---

*S*H* finale
es highest-
rogram in
n TV

1987
Fox network launches *The Simpsons*

1994
DBS, direct broadcast satellite, offers service

1996
Telecommunications Act of 1996 consolidates ownership

2002
TV standard changed to digital

2008
TV shows widely available online and on demand

2006
TV programs are available on iTunes

2009
Switch to DTV

2010
Hulu Plus debuts

2013
Netflix receives Emmy nomination for its original programming

---

1985
Super Mario Bros. released

1992
Web browsers make the Internet navigable

1995
Amazon.com launches online shopping

1999
Blogger software released

2001
Instant messenger services flourish

2002
Xbox LIVE debuts

2004
World of Warcraft debuts

2006
Google buys YouTube.com

2008
Broadband in 60% of American homes

2010
Apple launches the iPad

2011
Wireless devices popularize cloud computing

2013
Grand Theft Auto V generates more than $1 billion in three days

2014
Facebook buys Oculus Rift for $2 billion

Top Music Retailers by Market Share

1. **iTunes (Apple):** 29%
2. **Amazon/Amazon MP3:** 19%
3. **Walmart:** 11%

Source: "iTunes Continues to Dominate Music Retailing," NPD Group, September 19, 2012, https://www.npd.com/wps/portal /npd/us/news/press-releases/itunes-continues-to-dominate-music -retailing-but-nearly-60-percent-of-itunes-music-buyers-also-use -pandora/.

Search Engine Market Share

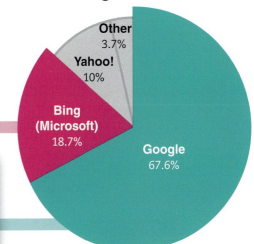

- Other 3.7%
- Yahoo! 10%
- Bing (Microsoft) 18.7%
- Google 67.6%

Top Book Retailers by Market Share

1. **Amazon:** 29%
2. **Barnes & Noble:** 20%
3. **Other online stores:** 10%
4. **Independent brick-and-mortar store:** 6%

Source: "Amazon Picks Up Market Share," *Publishers Weekly*, July 27, 2012, http://www.publishersweekly.com/pw/by-topic /industry-news/financial-reporting/article/53336-amazon-picks -up-market-share.html.

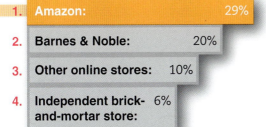

Top Online Movie Distribu[tion] Market Share

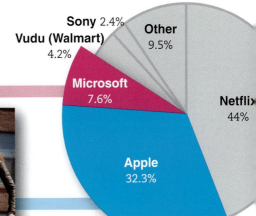

- Sony 2.4%
- Vudu (Walmart) 4.2%
- Other 9.5%
- Microsoft 7.6%
- Netflix 44%
- Apple 32.3%

Source: "Report: Netflix Beats Apple as No. 1 Online M[ovie...]" paidcontent, June 1, 2012, http://paidcontent.org/2012[...] -netflix-Beats-apple-as-no-1-online-movie-supplier/.

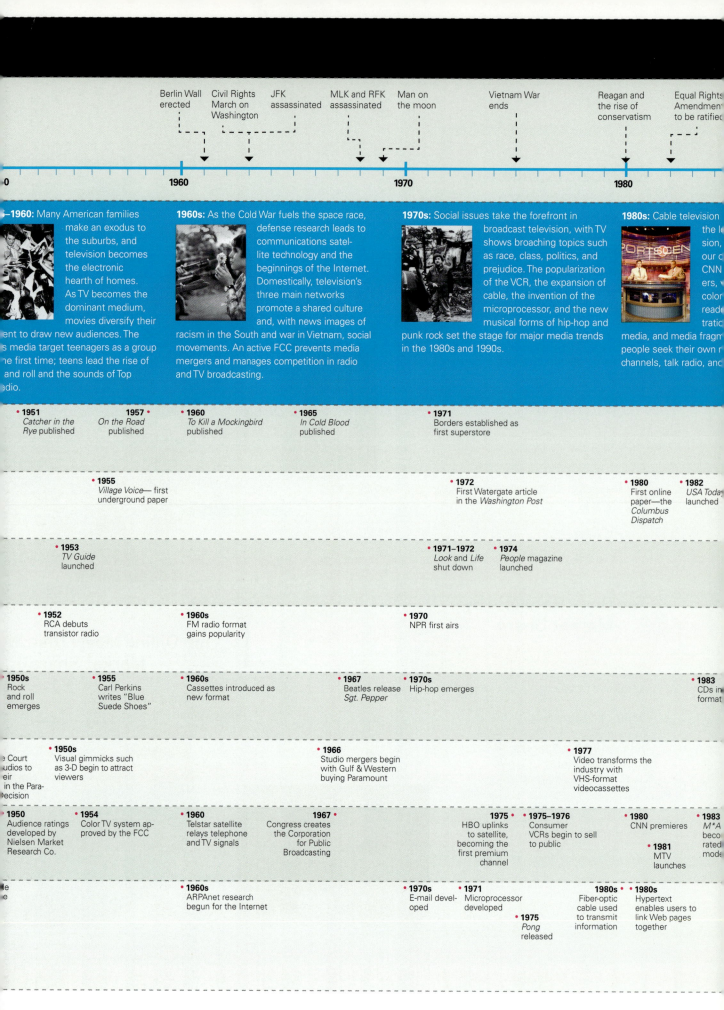

Timeline markers (top):

Berlin Wall erected | Civil Rights March on Washington | JFK assassinated | MLK and RFK assassinated | Man on the moon | Vietnam War ends | Reagan and the rise of conservatism | Equal Rights Amendment to be ratified

Timeline axis: 0 — 1960 — 1970 — 1980

…–1960: Many American families make an exodus to the suburbs, and television becomes the electronic hearth of homes. As TV becomes the dominant medium, movies diversify their [content] to draw new audiences. The [mass] media target teenagers as a group [for the] first time; teens lead the rise of [rock] and roll and the sounds of Top [40 r]adio.

1960s: As the Cold War fuels the space race, defense research leads to communications satellite technology and the beginnings of the Internet. Domestically, television's three main networks promote a shared culture and, with news images of racism in the South and war in Vietnam, social movements. An active FCC prevents media mergers and manages competition in radio and TV broadcasting.

1970s: Social issues take the forefront in broadcast television, with TV shows broaching topics such as race, class, politics, and prejudice. The popularization of the VCR, the expansion of cable, the invention of the microprocessor, and the new musical forms of hip-hop and punk rock set the stage for major media trends in the 1980s and 1990s.

1980s: Cable television [enters] the le[vision], [and] our c[…] CNN [and oth]ers, [and] color [television] read[er]... [frag]men[tation] media, and media fragm[entation as] people seek their own [news] channels, talk radio, and […]

• 1951 *Catcher in the Rye* published

1957 • *On the Road* published

• 1960 *To Kill a Mockingbird* published

• 1965 *In Cold Blood* published

• 1971 Borders established as first superstore

• 1955 *Village Voice*— first underground paper

• 1972 First Watergate article in the *Washington Post*

• 1980 First online paper—the *Columbus Dispatch*

• 1982 *USA Today* launched

• 1953 *TV Guide* launched

• 1971–1972 *Look* and *Life* shut down

• 1974 *People* magazine launched

• 1952 RCA debuts transistor radio

• 1960s FM radio format gains popularity

• 1970 NPR first airs

• 1950s Rock and roll emerges

• 1955 Carl Perkins writes "Blue Suede Shoes"

• 1960s Cassettes introduced as new format

• 1967 Beatles release *Sgt. Pepper*

• 1970s Hip-hop emerges

• 1983 CDs in[troduced as] format

[Supreme] Court [order s]tudios to [sell th]eir [theaters] in the Para[mount D]ecision

• 1950s Visual gimmicks such as 3-D begin to attract viewers

• 1966 Studio mergers begin with Gulf & Western buying Paramount

• 1977 Video transforms the industry with VHS-format videocassettes

• 1950 Audience ratings developed by Nielsen Market Research Co.

• 1954 Color TV system approved by the FCC

• 1960 Telstar satellite relays telephone and TV signals

• 1967 Congress creates the Corporation for Public Broadcasting

• 1975 HBO uplinks to satellite, becoming the first premium channel

• 1975–1976 Consumer VCRs begin to sell to public

• 1980 CNN premieres

• 1981 MTV launches

• 1983 *M*A*[S*H]* beco[mes] rated [...] mode[l]

• 1960s ARPAnet research begun for the Internet

• 1970s E-mail developed

• 1971 Microprocessor developed

• 1975 *Pong* released

• 1980s Fiber-optic cable used to transmit information

• 1980s Hypertext enables users to link Web pages together

Projected Revenue Share of Digital Ad Revenue in the U.S.

1.	Google:	40.8%
2.	Facebook:	8.2%
3.	Microsoft:	5.7%
4.	Yahoo!:	5.4%

Source: "Mobile Growth Pushes Facebook to Become No. 2 Digital Ad Seller," eMarketer, December 19, 2013.

Percentage of Online Adults Using . . .

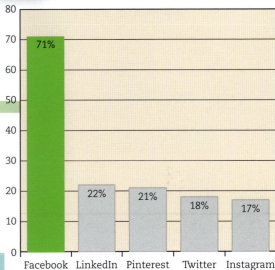

Facebook: 71%
LinkedIn: 22%
Pinterest: 21%
Twitter: 18%
Instagram: 17%

Source: "Social Media Update 2013,"
http://pewinternet.org/2013/12/30/social-media-update-2013

ators

Most Popular News Sites

1. Yahoo! News
2. Google News
3. Huffington Post
4. CNN
5. *New York Times*
6. Fox News
7. NBC News
8. *Mail* Online
9. *Washington Post*
10. *The Guardian*

Source: eBizMBA, "Top 15 Most Popular News Websites,"
www.ebizmba.com/articles/news-websites

Top-Selling Video Game Consoles in 2014

1.	PlayStation 4 (Sony):	4.7 million
2.	XboxOne (Microsoft):	4.2 million
3.	3DS (Nintendo):	2.7 million
4.	Wii U (Nintendo):	1.6 million

Source: "USA Yearly Chart," VGChartz, http://vgchartz.com/yearly/2014/USA

ovie Supplier,"
06/01/report

1880   1900   1920   1930   1940   19

1880–1920: The Industrial Revolution gains full steam, and the majority of the U.S. population shifts from rural to urban areas. As urban centers grow, muckraking journalists focus on social issues and big business. Media formats explode: Nickelodeons bring film to cities, recorded music is popularized, and radio becomes a full-fledged mass medium. The U.S. becomes an international power, advertising fuels the booming consumer economy, and public relations spurs the U.S. into World War I.

1920–1936: Networks take hold of radio broadcasting, uniting the U.S. with nationwide programming and advocating an ad-based system. But as the Roaring Twenties turn into the Great Depression of the 1930s, many Americans grow distrustful of big business. Citizens' groups push to reserve part of the airwaves as nonprofit, but commercial broadcasters convince Congress that their interests best represent the public interest.

1937–1945: Public relations shapes world events through print, radio, and movies. In Europe, fascism rises with overwhelming propaganda campaigns, while in the U.S., Edward Bernays and others use the "engineering of consent" to sell consumer products and a positive image of big business. Movies offer both newsreels and escape from harsh realities.

194

con
mas
for t
rock
40 r

1870 Mass market paperbacks

1880 Linotype and offset lithography

1884 *The Adventures of Huckleberry Finn* published

1906 *The Jungle* published

1925 *The Great Gatsby* published

1926 Book clubs

1940 *Native Son* published

---

ng
on

1880s–1890s The age of yellow journalism

1914 First U.S.-based Spanish paper, *El Diario-La Prensa*

1930 Syndicated columns flourish

1879 Postal Act increases magazine circulation

1903 *Ladies' Home Journal* circulation hits 1 million

1922 *Reader's Digest* launched

1923 *Time* magazine launched

1936 *Life* magazine launched

1894 Marconi experiments on wireless telegraph

1912 *Titanic* lives saved by onboard wireless operators

1922 First commercial radio advertisements

1927 Congress issues radio licenses

1930s Golden age of radio

1933–1944 FDR's Fireside Chats

1877 Edison's wax cylinder phonograph

1889 First flat disk and gramophone by Berliner

1910 Phonographs enter homes

1920s Electricity and microphones introduced

1940s Audiotape developed in Germany

1889 Celluloid, a transparent film, developed by Hannibal Goodwin

1895 Film screenings in Paris by Lumière brothers

1907 Nickelodeons—storefront theaters

1910s Movie studio system develops

1927 Sound comes to movies

1947 HUAC convicts 10 men from film industry of alleged communist sympathies

1948 Suprem forces s divest t theaters mount I

Late 1880s Cathode ray tube invented

1927 First TV transmission by Farnsworth

1935 First public demonstration of television

1940s Community antenna television systems

1941 FCC sets TV standards

1880s Penny arcades

1940s Digital technology developed

1945 Modern pinball machines

Catho
ray tu

How much do media companies make, really?

$575,000,000,000
$575 billion Department of Defense proposed budget for 2013

$200,000,000,000
$200 billion Facebook's estimated value in 2014

$85,000,000,000
$85 billion Amount of 2008 U.S. government loan to insurance giant AIG

$82,000,000,000
$82 billion Estimated worth of Bill Gates in 2013

$75,410,000,000
$75.4 billion Sony's 2013 revenue

$73,610,000,000
$73.6 billion Libya's Gross Domestic Product (GDP) in 2013 (projected)

$59,800,000,000
$59.8 billion Google's 2013 revenue

$45,000,000,000
$45 billion Disney's 2013 revenue

$34,000,000,000
$34 billion 21st Century Fox's 2013 revenue

$29,400,000,000
$29.4 billion Time Warner's 2013 revenue

$27,100,000,000
$27.1 billion President's fiscal year budget for the U.S. Department of Justice in 2013

$21,530,000,000
$21.5 billion Total U.S. retail sales in the video game industry in 2013

$18,010,000,000
$18.01 billion NASA proposed budget for 2015

$16,100,000,000
$16.1 billion Net worth of Mark Zuckerberg (CEO of Facebook) in 2013

$13,800,000,000
$13.8 billion Viacom's 2013 revenue

$10,300,000,000
$10.3 billion Total U.S. movie box-office receipts in 2013

$8,340,000,000
$8.34 billion Environmental Protection Agency proposed budget for 2013

$1,274,000,000
$1.27 billion Worldwide gross for *Frozen*

$315,000,000
$315 million Amount AOL paid for the *Huffington Post* in 2011

$40,000,000
$40 million Estimated cost of the 2012 London Olympics opening ceremony

$35,000,000
$35 million Amount News Corp. sold MySpace for in 2011

$1,500,000
$1.5 million Amount *People* magazine paid for the exclusive photos from Kim Kardashian's wedding

$142,544
$142,544 Average four-year tuition and room and board at a private university

$53,891
$53,891 Median U.S. household income in 2014

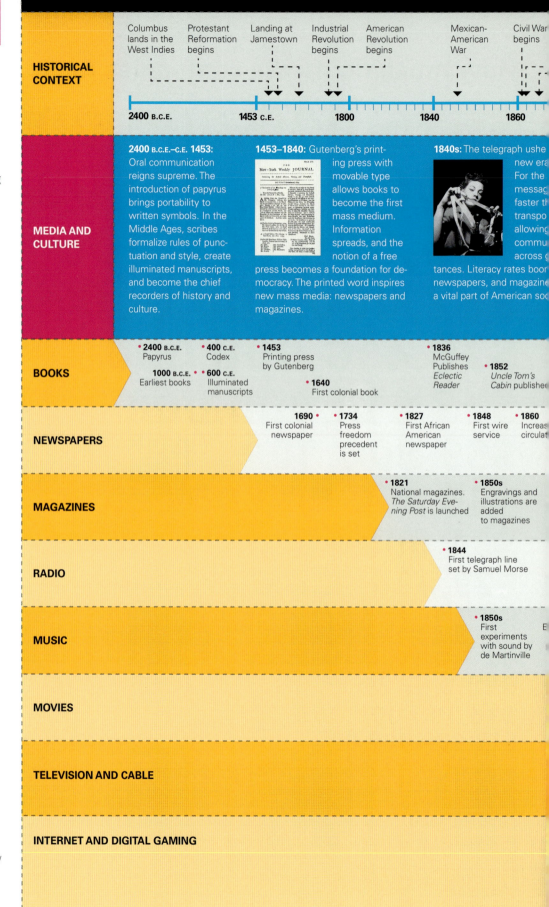

Timeline: Media and Culture through History

HISTORICAL CONTEXT

Columbus lands in the West Indies | Protestant Reformation begins | Landing at Jamestown | Industrial Revolution begins | American Revolution begins | Mexican-American War | Civil War begins

2400 B.C.E. — 1453 C.E. — 1800 — 1840 — 1860

MEDIA AND CULTURE

2400 B.C.E.–C.E. 1453: Oral communication reigns supreme. The introduction of papyrus brings portability to written symbols. In the Middle Ages, scribes formalize rules of punctuation and style, create illuminated manuscripts, and become the chief recorders of history and culture.

1453–1840: Gutenberg's printing press with movable type allows books to become the first mass medium. Information spreads, and the notion of a free press becomes a foundation for democracy. The printed word inspires new mass media: newspapers and magazines.

1840s: The telegraph ushe new era. For the first messag faster th transpo allowing commu across tances. Literacy rates boor newspapers, and magazine a vital part of American soc

BOOKS

- **2400 B.C.E.** Papyrus
- **1000 B.C.E.** Earliest books
- **400 C.E.** Codex
- **600 C.E.** Illuminated manuscripts
- **1453** Printing press by Gutenberg
- **1640** First colonial book
- **1836** McGuffey Publishes *Eclectic Reader*
- **1852** *Uncle Tom's Cabin* published

NEWSPAPERS

- **1690** First colonial newspaper
- **1734** Press freedom precedent is set
- **1827** First African American newspaper
- **1848** First wire service
- **1860** Increas circulat

MAGAZINES

- **1821** National magazines. *The Saturday Evening Post* is launched
- **1850s** Engravings and illustrations are added to magazines

RADIO

- **1844** First telegraph line set by Samuel Morse

MUSIC

- **1850s** First experiments with sound by de Martinville

MOVIES

TELEVISION AND CABLE

INTERNET AND DIGITAL GAMING

Media & Culture

1

Mass Communication

A Critical Approach

5
Culture and the
Evolution of Mass
Communication

10
The Development of
Media and Their Role in
Our Society

16
Surveying the Cultural
Landscape

29
Critiquing Media and
Culture

The 2014 midterm election had the lowest percentage of voter turnout since 1942 (the middle of World War II).[1] One effect: the Republican Party took control of Congress during President Obama's last term, just as the Democrats won both houses during George W. Bush's last term in 2006. Turnout among eighteen- to twenty-nine-year-olds was particularly small, representing only 13 percent of voters, compared to 19 percent in the 2012 presidential election.[2]

The local and national media played key roles 2014, as they do in every election cycle. The main narrative threads that dominated the news and TV-Internet punditry pointed to an unpopular president advised by his own party not to campaign for a number of Democratic candidates who eventually lost. Despite economic improvements, intense partisanship by the parties and enormous amounts of media advertising turned off many moderate voters and helped win the day for the GOP.

These changes in political power are common, and enabled in part by ubiquitous political ads that run on radio, TV, and the Internet during election cycles.

Photo by Rick Kern/Getty Images
for Comedy Central

These ads, which usually offer stories designed to build up one candidate while tearing down the other, are expensive, and candidates now depend on both their parties and outside partisan groups for additional money—the 2014 election, for example, cost parties and donors about $3.7 billion.[3] Following the *Citizens United v. Federal Election Commission* ruling by the Supreme Court in 2010 (see Chapter 16), election campaigns now benefit from unlimited funds raised by corporations, rich individuals, and unknown groups, prompting concern about rich donors dictating election outcomes.

Much of this money is spent, of course, on TV ads. In 2014 marketing firm Kantar Media estimated that local TV stations raked in $2.4 billion from political ads, with another $600–$800 million going for local ad purchases on national cable channels like AMC and USA. Media business reporter Brian Stelter sees a conflict of interest that may prevent local TV news from covering this story: "Station owners are the ones benefiting . . . so might their newsrooms be a little less likely to cover proposals to reduce the amount of money in politics?"[4]

Notably, local and large media firms do not invest this money in more reporters, whose numbers have declined precipitously over the past decade. Faced with a need for complex narratives, documented information, and sharp analysis about the world, large chunks of our media instead fill twenty-four-hour news cycles with sensational crime and corruption stories and partisan sniping.

Following the digital turn, most media today communicate not to the mass audiences of the past but to niche markets and interest groups, to sports fans and history buffs—and to conservatives and liberals. It's in the economic interest, then, of many media outlets to stoke the flames of partisanship. But Harvard law professor Cass Sunstein describes a phenomenon he calls *partyism*: "In 1960, 5 percent of Republicans and 4 percent of Democrats said they would feel 'displeased' if their son or daughter married outside their political party. By 2010, those numbers had reached 49 percent and 33 percent." Citing current research, Sunstein says that "when people are exposed to messages that attack members of the opposing party, their biases increase [and] the destructive power of partyism is extending well beyond politics into people's behavior in daily life."[5]

So in the end, do the media help us understand the complex issues of our time or merely reinforce our biases? Do they discourage young people from voting? In election cycles, news media often reduce the story of an election to two-dimensional "right versus left" narratives, obscuring complex policy issues like affordable health care, technological innovation, climate change, economic recovery, and stateless terrorism. In a democracy, we depend on the media to provide information to help make decisions about our leaders, and should expect that media outlets who earn so much money from political ads will use that money to further investigate the issues of the day. Despite their limitations, the media's job of presenting the world to us and documenting what's going on is enormously important. But we also have a job to do that is equally important. As media watchers, we can point a critical lens back at the media and describe, analyze, and interpret their stories, arriving at informed judgments about the media's performance. This textbook offers a map to help us become more *media literate*, critiquing the media not as detached cynics or rabid partisans, but as informed citizens with a stake in the outcome.

◢ SO WHAT EXACTLY ARE THE RESPONSIBILITIES OF NEWSPAPERS AND MEDIA IN GENERAL? In an age of highly partisan politics, economic and unemployment crises, and upheaval in several Arab nations, how do we demand the highest standards from our media to describe and analyze such complex events and issues—especially at a time when the business models for newspapers and most other media are in such flux? At their best, in all their various forms, from mainstream newspapers and radio talk shows to blogs, the media try to help us understand the events that affect us. But at their worst, the media's appetite for telling and selling stories leads them not only to document tragedy but also to misrepresent or exploit it. Many viewers and critics disapprove of how media, particularly TV and cable, hurtle from one event to another, often dwelling on trivial, celebrity-driven content.

Visit **LaunchPad** for *Media & Culture* and use **LearningCurve** to review concepts from this chapter.

In this book, we examine the history and business of mass media and discuss the media as a central force in shaping our culture and our democracy. We start by examining key concepts and introducing the critical process for investigating media industries and issues. In later chapters, we probe the history and structure of media's major institutions. In the process, we will develop an informed and critical view of the influence these institutions have had on national and global life. The goal is to become media literate—to become critical consumers of mass media institutions and engaged participants who accept part of the responsibility for the shape and direction of media culture. In this chapter, we will:

- Address key ideas, including communication, culture, mass media, and mass communication
- Investigate important periods in communication history: the oral, written, print, electronic, and digital eras
- Examine the development of a mass medium from emergence to convergence
- Learn about how convergence has changed our relationship to media
- Look at the central role of storytelling in media and culture
- Discuss two models for organizing and categorizing culture: a skyscraper and a map
- Trace important cultural values in both modern and postmodern societies
- Study media literacy and the five stages of the critical process: description, analysis, interpretation, evaluation, and engagement

As you read through this chapter, think about your early experiences with the media. Identify a favorite media product from your childhood—a song, book, TV show, or movie. Why was it so important to you? How much of an impact did your early taste in media have on your identity? How has your taste shifted over time? What do your current preferences indicate about your identity now? Do your current media preferences reveal anything about you? For more questions to help you think about the role of media in your life, see "Questioning the Media" in the Chapter Review.

Culture and the Evolution of Mass Communication

One way to understand the impact of the media on our lives is to explore the cultural context in which the media operate. Often, culture is narrowly associated with art, the unique forms of creative expression that give pleasure and set standards about what is true, good, and beautiful. Culture, however, can be viewed more broadly as the ways in which people live and represent themselves at particular historical times. This idea of culture encompasses fashion, sports, literature, architecture, education, religion, and science, as well as mass media.

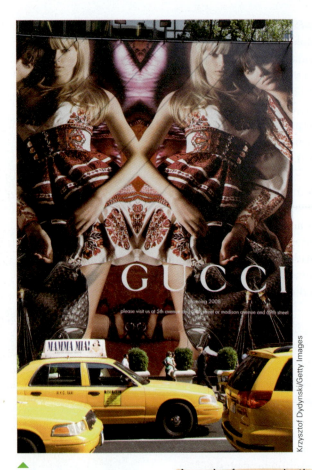

CULTURAL VALUES AND IDEALS are transmitted through the media. Many fashion advertisements show beautiful people using a company's products; such images imply that anyone who buys the products can obtain such ideal beauty. What other societal ideas are portrayed through the media?

Krzysztof Dydynski/Getty Images

Although we can study discrete cultural products, such as novels or songs from various historical periods, culture itself is always changing. It includes a society's art, beliefs, customs, games, technologies, traditions, and institutions. It also encompasses a society's modes of **communication**: the creation and use of symbol systems that convey information and meaning (e.g., languages, Morse code, motion pictures, and one-zero binary computer codes).

Culture is made up of both the products that a society fashions and, perhaps more important, the processes that forge those products and reflect a culture's diverse values. Thus **culture** may be defined as the symbols of expression that individuals, groups, and societies use to make sense of daily life and to articulate their values. According to this definition, when we listen to music, read a book, watch television, or scan the Internet, we are usually not asking "Is this art?" but are instead trying to identify or connect with something or someone. In other words, we are assigning meaning to the song, book, TV program, or Web site. Culture, therefore, is a process that delivers the values of a society through products or other meaning-making forms. The American ideal of "rugged individualism"—depicting heroic characters overcoming villains or corruption, for instance—has been portrayed on television for decades through a tradition of detective stories like HBO's *True Detective* and crime procedurals like CBS's *NCIS*. This ideal has also been a staple in movies and books, and even in political ads.

Culture links individuals to their society by providing both shared and contested values, and the mass media help circulate those values. The **mass media** are the cultural industries—the channels of communication—that produce and distribute songs, novels, TV shows, newspapers, movies, video games, Internet services, and other cultural products to large numbers of people. The historical development of media and communication can be traced through several overlapping phases or eras in which newer forms of technology disrupted and modified older forms—a process that many academics, critics, and media professionals began calling *convergence* with the arrival of the Internet.

These eras, which all still operate to some degree, are oral, written, print, electronic, and digital. The first two eras refer to the communication of tribal or feudal communities and agricultural economies. The last three phases feature the development of **mass communication**: the process of designing cultural messages and stories and delivering them to large and diverse audiences through media channels as old and distinctive as the printed book and as new and converged as the Internet. Hastened by the growth of industry and modern technology, mass communication accompanied the shift of rural populations to urban settings and the rise of a consumer culture.

Oral and Written Eras in Communication

In most early societies, information and knowledge first circulated slowly through oral traditions passed on by poets, teachers, and tribal storytellers. As alphabets and the written word emerged, however, a manuscript, or written, culture began to develop and eventually overshadowed oral communication. Documented and transcribed by philosophers, monks, and stenographers, the manuscript culture served the ruling classes. Working people were generally illiterate, and the economic and educational gap between rulers and the ruled was vast. These eras of oral and written communication developed slowly over many centuries. Although exact time frames are disputed, historians generally consider these eras as part of Western civilization's premodern period, spanning the epoch from roughly 1000 B.C.E. to the beginnings of the Industrial Revolution.

Early tensions between oral and written communication played out among ancient Greek philosophers and writers. Socrates (470–399 B.C.E.), for instance, made his arguments through public conversations and debates. Known as the Socratic method, this dialogue style of communication and inquiry is still used in college classrooms and university law schools. Many philosophers who believed in the superiority of the oral tradition feared that the written word would threaten public discussion. In fact, Socrates' most famous student, Plato (427–347 B.C.E.), sought to banish poets, whom he saw as purveyors of ideas less rigorous than those generated in oral, face-to-face, question-and-answer discussions. These debates foreshadowed similar discussions in our time in which we ask whether TV news, Twitter, or online comment sections cheapen public discussion and discourage face-to-face communication.

The Print Revolution

While paper and block printing developed in China around 100 C.E. and 1045, respectively, what we recognize as modern printing did not emerge until the middle of the fifteenth century. At that time in Germany, Johannes Gutenberg's invention of movable metallic type and the printing press ushered in the modern print era. Printing presses and publications spread rapidly across Europe in the late fifteenth century and early sixteenth century. Early on, the size and expense of books limited them to an audience of wealthy aristocrats, royal families, church leaders, prominent merchants, and powerful politicians. Gradually, printers reduced the size and cost of books, making them available and affordable to more people. Books eventually became the first mass-marketed products in history because of the way the printing press combined three necessary elements.

First, machine duplication replaced the tedious system in which scribes hand-copied texts. Second, duplication could occur rapidly, so large quantities of the same book could be reproduced easily. Third, the faster production of multiple copies brought down the cost of each unit, which made books more affordable to less-affluent people.

Since mass-produced printed materials could spread information and ideas faster and farther than ever before, writers could use print to disseminate views counter to traditional civic doctrine and religious authority—views that paved the way for major social and cultural changes, such as the Protestant Reformation and the rise of modern nationalism. People started to resist traditional clerical authority and also began to think of themselves not merely as members of families, isolated communities, or tribes but as part of a country whose interests were broader than local or regional concerns. While oral and written societies had favored decentralized local governments, the print era supported the ascent of more centralized nation-states.

Eventually, the machine production of mass quantities that had resulted in a lower cost per unit for books became an essential factor in the mass production of other goods, which led to the Industrial Revolution, modern capitalism, and the consumer culture of the twentieth century. With the revolution in industry came the rise of the middle class and an elite business class of owners and managers who acquired the kind of influence formerly held only by the nobility or the clergy. Print media became key tools that commercial and political leaders used to distribute information and maintain social order.

As with the Internet today, however, it was difficult for a single business or political leader, certainly in a democratic society, to gain exclusive control over printing technology (although

Biblioteque Nationale, Paris/Scala–Art Resource, NY

EARLY BOOKS
Before the invention of the printing press, books were copied by hand in a labor-intensive process. This beautifully illuminated page is from an Italian Bible made in the early fourteenth century.

the king or queen did control printing press licenses in England until the early nineteenth century, and even today, governments in many countries control presses, access to paper, advertising, and distribution channels). Instead, the mass publication of pamphlets, magazines, and books in the United States helped democratize knowledge, and literacy rates rose among the working and middle classes. Industrialization required a more educated workforce, but printed literature and textbooks also encouraged compulsory education, thus promoting literacy and extending learning beyond the world of wealthy upper-class citizens.

Just as the printing press fostered nationalism, it also nourished the ideal of individualism. People came to rely less on their local community and their commercial, religious, and political leaders for guidance. By challenging tribal life, the printing press "fostered the modern idea of individuality," disrupting "the medieval sense of community and integration."[6] In urban and industrial environments, many individuals became cut off from the traditions of rural and small-town life, which had encouraged community cooperation in premodern times. By the mid-nineteenth century, the ideal of individualism affirmed the rise of commerce and increased resistance to government interference in the affairs of self-reliant entrepreneurs. The democratic impulse of individualism became a fundamental value in American society in the nineteenth and twentieth centuries.

The Electronic Era

In Europe and the United States, the impact of industry's rise was enormous: Factories replaced farms as the main centers of work and production. During the 1880s, roughly 80 percent of Americans lived on farms and in small towns; by the 1920s and 1930s, most had moved to urban areas, where new industries and economic opportunities beckoned. The city had overtaken the country as the focal point of national life.

The gradual transformation from an industrial, print-based society to one grounded in the Information Age began with the development of the telegraph in the 1840s. Featuring dot-dash electronic signals, the telegraph made four key contributions to communication. First, it separated communication from transportation, making media messages instantaneous—unencumbered by stagecoaches, ships, or the pony express.[7] Second, the telegraph, in combination with the rise of mass-marketed newspapers, transformed "information into a commodity, a 'thing' that could be bought or sold irrespective of its uses or meaning."[8] By the time of the Civil War, news had become a valuable product. Third, the telegraph made it easier for military, business, and political leaders to coordinate commercial and military operations, especially after the installation of the transatlantic cable in the late 1860s. Fourth, the telegraph led to future technological developments, such as wireless telegraphy (later named radio), the fax machine, and the cell phone, which ironically resulted in the telegraph's demise: In 2006, Western Union telegraph offices sent their final messages.

The rise of film at the turn of the twentieth century and the development of radio in the 1920s were early signals, but the electronic phase of the Information Age really boomed in the 1950s and 1960s with the arrival of television and its dramatic impact on daily life. Then, with the coming of ever more communication gadgetry—personal computers, cable TV, DVDs, DVRs, direct broadcast satellites, cell phones, smartphones, PDAs, and e-mail—the Information Age passed into its digital phase, where old and new media began to converge, thus dramatically changing our relationship to media and culture.

The Digital Era

In **digital communication**, images, texts, and sounds are converted (encoded) into electronic signals (represented as varied combinations of binary numbers—ones and zeros) that are then reassembled (decoded) as a precise reproduction of, say, a TV picture, a magazine article, a song, or a telephone voice. On the Internet, various images, texts, and sounds are all digitally reproduced and transmitted globally.

New technologies, particularly cable television and the Internet, developed so quickly that traditional leaders in communication lost some of their control over information. For example, starting with the 1992 presidential campaign, the network news shows (ABC, CBS, and NBC) began to lose their audiences, first to MTV and CNN, and later to MSNBC, Fox News, Comedy Central, and partisan radio talk shows. By the 2012 national elections, Facebook, Twitter, and other social media sites had become key players in news and politics, especially as information resources for younger generations who had grown up in an online and digital world.

Moreover, e-mail—a digital reinvention of oral culture—has assumed some of the functions of the postal service and is outpacing attempts to control communications beyond national borders. A professor sitting at her desk in Cedar Falls, Iowa, sends e-mail or Skype messages routinely to research scientists in Budapest. Moreover, many repressive and totalitarian regimes have had trouble controlling messages sent out over the borderless Internet, as opposed to hard copy "snail mail."

Oral culture has been further reinvented by the emergence of *social media*, such as Twitter and in particular Facebook, which now has nearly one billion users worldwide. Social media allow people from all over the world to have ongoing online conversations, share stories and interests, and generate their own media content. This turn to digital media forms has fundamentally overturned traditional media business models, the ways we engage with and consume media products, and the ways we organize our daily lives around various media choices.

The Linear Model of Mass Communication

The digital era also brought about a shift in the models that media researchers have used over the years to explain how media messages and meanings are constructed and communicated in everyday life. In one of the older and more enduring explanations of how media operate, mass communication has been conceptualized as a linear process of producing and delivering messages to large audiences. **Senders** (authors, producers, and organizations) transmit **messages** (programs, texts, images, sounds, and ads) through a **mass media channel** (newspapers, books, magazines, radio, television, or the Internet) to large groups of **receivers** (readers, viewers, and consumers). In the process, **gatekeepers** (news editors, executive producers, and other media managers) function as message filters. Media gatekeepers make decisions about what messages actually get produced for particular receivers. The process also allows for **feedback**, in which citizens and consumers, if they choose, return messages to senders or gatekeepers through phone calls, e-mail, Web postings, talk shows, or letters to the editor.

But the problem with the linear model is that in reality, media messages—especially in the digital era—do not usually move smoothly from a sender at point A to a receiver at point Z. Words and images are more likely to spill into one another, crisscrossing in the daily media deluge of ads, TV shows, news reports, social media, smartphone apps, and—of course—everyday conversation. Media messages and stories are encoded and sent in written and visual forms, but senders often have very little control over how their intended messages are decoded or whether the messages are ignored or misread by readers and viewers.

A Cultural Model for Understanding Mass Communication

A more contemporary approach to understanding media is through a cultural model. This concept recognizes that individuals bring diverse meanings to messages, given factors and differences such as gender, age, educational level, ethnicity, and occupation. In this model of mass communication, audiences actively affirm, interpret, refashion, or reject the messages and stories that flow through various media channels. For example, when controversial singer Lady Gaga released her nine-minute music video for the song "Telephone" in 2010, fans and critics had very different interpretations of the video. Some saw Lady Gaga as a cutting-edge artist pushing boundaries and celebrating alternative lifestyles—and the rightful heir to Madonna. Others, however, saw the video as tasteless and cruel, making fun of transsexuals and exploiting women—not to mention celebrating the poisoning of an old boyfriend.

While the linear model may demonstrate how a message gets from a sender to a receiver, the cultural model suggests the complexity of this process and the lack of control that "senders" (such as media executives, moviemakers, writers, news editors, and ad agencies) often have over how audiences receive messages and interpret their intended meanings. Sometimes, producers of media messages seem to be the active creators of communication while audiences are merely passive receptacles. But as the Lady Gaga example illustrates, consumers also shape media messages to fit or support their own values and viewpoints. This phenomenon is known as **selective exposure**: People typically seek messages and produce meanings that correspond to their own cultural beliefs, values, and interests. For example, studies have shown that people with political leanings toward the left or the right tend to seek out blogs or news outlets that reinforce their preexisting views.

The rise of the Internet and social media has also complicated the traditional roles in both the linear and the cultural models of communication. While there are still senders and receivers, the borderless, decentralized, and democratic nature of the Internet means that anyone can become a sender of media messages—whether it's by uploading a video mash-up to YouTube or by writing a blog post. The Internet has also largely eliminated the gatekeeper role. Although some governments try to control Internet servers, and some Web sites have restrictions on what can and cannot be posted, for the most part, the Internet allows senders to transmit content without first needing approval from, or editing by, a gatekeeper. For example, some authors who are unable to find a traditional book publisher for their work turn to self-publishing on the Internet. And musicians who don't have deals with major record labels can promote, circulate, and sell their music online.

The Development of Media and Their Role in Our Society

The mass media constitute a wide variety of industries and merchandise, from moving documentary news programs about famines in Africa to shady infomercials about how to retrieve millions of dollars in unclaimed money online. The word *media* is, after all, a Latin plural form of the singular noun *medium*, meaning an intervening substance through which something is conveyed or transmitted. Television, newspapers, music, movies, magazines, books, billboards, radio, broadcast satellites, and the Internet are all part of the media, and they are all quite capable of either producing worthy products or pandering to society's worst desires, prejudices, and stereotypes. Let's begin by looking at how mass media develop, and then at how they work and are interpreted in our society.

The Evolution of Media: From Emergence to Convergence

The development of most mass media is initiated not only by the diligence of inventors, such as Thomas Edison (see Chapters 4 and 7), but also by social, cultural, political, and economic circumstances. For instance, both telegraph and radio evolved as newly industrialized nations sought to expand their military and economic control and to transmit information more rapidly. The Internet is a contemporary response to new concerns: transporting messages and sharing information more rapidly for an increasingly mobile and interconnected global population.

Media innovations typically go through four stages. First is the *emergence*, or *novelty*, *stage*, in which inventors and technicians try to solve a particular problem, such as making pictures move, transmitting messages from ship to shore, or sending mail electronically. Second is the *entrepreneurial stage*, in which inventors and investors determine a practical and marketable use for the new device. For example, early radio relayed messages to and from places where telegraph wires could not go, such as military ships at sea. Part of the Internet also had its roots in the ideas of military leaders, who wanted a communication system that was decentralized and distributed widely enough to survive nuclear war or natural disasters.

The third phase in a medium's development involves a breakthrough to the *mass medium stage*. At this point, businesses figure out how to market the new device or medium as a consumer product. Although the government and the U.S. Navy played a central role in radio's early years, it was commercial entrepreneurs who pioneered radio broadcasting and figured out how to reach millions of people. In the same way, Pentagon and government researchers helped develop early prototypes for the Internet, but commercial interests extended the Internet's global reach and business potential.

Finally, the fourth and newest phase in a medium's evolution is the *convergence stage*. This is the stage in which older media are reconfigured in various forms on newer media. However, this does not mean that these older forms cease to exist. For example, you can still get the *New York Times* in print, but it's also now accessible on laptops and smartphones via the Internet. During this stage, we see the merging of many different media forms onto online platforms, but we also see the fragmenting of large audiences into smaller niche markets. With new technologies allowing access to more media options than ever, mass audiences are morphing into audience subsets that chase particular lifestyles, politics, hobbies, and forms of entertainment.

Media Convergence

Developments in the electronic and digital eras enabled and ushered in this latest stage in the development of media—**convergence**—a term that media critics and analysts use when describing all the changes that have occurred over the past decade, and are still occurring, in media content and within media companies. The term actually has two different meanings—one referring to technology and one to business—and it describes changes that have a great impact on how media companies are charting a course for the future.

The Dual Roles of Media Convergence

The first definition of media convergence involves the technological merging of content across different media channels—the magazine articles, radio programs, songs, TV shows, video games, and movies now available on the Internet through laptops, tablets, and smartphones.

Culver Pictures/The Art Archive at Art Resource, NY

© The Toronto Star/ZUMApress.com

MEDIA CONVERGENCE
In the 1950s, television sets—like radios in the 1930s and 1940s—were often encased in decorative wood and sold as stylish furniture that occupied a central place in many American homes. Today, using our computers, we can listen to a radio talk show, watch a movie, or download a favorite song—usually on the go—as older media forms now converge online.

Such technical convergence is not entirely new. For example, in the late 1920s, the Radio Corporation of America (RCA) purchased the Victor Talking Machine Company and introduced machines that could play both radio and recorded music. In the 1950s, this collaboration helped radio survive the emergence of television. Radio lost much of its content to TV and could not afford to hire live bands, so it became more dependent on deejays to play records produced by the music industry. However, contemporary media convergence is much broader than the simple merging of older and newer forms. In fact, the eras of communication are themselves reinvented in this "age of convergence." Oral communication, for example, finds itself reconfigured, in part, in e-mail and social media. And print communication is re-formed in the thousands of newspapers now available online. Also, keep in mind the wonderful ironies of media convergence: The first major digital retailer, Amazon, made its name by selling the world's oldest mass medium—the book—on the world's newest mass medium—the Internet.

A second definition of media convergence—sometimes called **cross platform** by media marketers—describes a business model that involves consolidating various media holdings, such as cable connections, phone services, television transmissions, and Internet access, under one corporate umbrella. The goal is not necessarily to offer consumers more choice in their media options but to better manage resources and maximize profits. For example, a company that owns TV stations, radio outlets, and newspapers in multiple markets—as well as in the same cities—can deploy a reporter or producer to create three or four versions of the same story for various media outlets. So rather than having each radio station, TV station, newspaper, and online news site generate diverse and independent stories about an issue, a media corporation employing the convergence model can use fewer employees to generate multiple versions of the same story.

Media Businesses in a Converged World

The ramifications of media convergence are best revealed in the business strategies of digital age companies like Amazon, Facebook, Apple, and especially Google—the most profitable company of the digital era so far (see Chapter 2). Google is the Internet's main organizer and aggregator because it finds both "new" and "old" media content—like blogs and newspapers—and delivers that content to vast numbers of online consumers. Google does not produce any of the content, and most consumers who find a news story or magazine article through a Google search pay nothing to the original media content provider or to Google. Instead, as the "middleman" or distributor, Google makes most of its money by selling ads that accompany search results. But not all ads are created equal; as writer and journalism critic James Fallows points out, Google does not necessarily sell ads on the news sites it aggregates: Almost all of the company's money comes from shopping-related searches, rather than from the information searches it is best known for. In fact, Fallows writes that Google, which has certainly done its part in contributing to the decline of newspapers, still has a large stake in seeing newspapers succeed online.[9] Over the last few years, Google has undertaken a number of experiments to help older news media make the transition into the converged world. Google executives believe that since they aren't in the content creation business, they are dependent on news organizations to produce the quality information and journalism that healthy democracies need—and that Google can deliver.

Today's converged media world has broken down the old definitions of distinct media forms like newspapers and television—both now available online and across multiple platforms. And it favors players like Google, whose business model works in a world where customers expect to get their media in multiple places—and often for free. But the next challenge ahead in the new, converged world is to resolve who will pay for quality content and how that system will emerge. In the upcoming industry chapters, we take a closer look at how media convergence is affecting each industry in terms of both content production and business strategies.

Media Convergence and Cultural Change

The Internet and social media have led to significant changes in the ways we consume and engage with media culture. In the pre-Internet days (say, back in the late 1980s), most people would watch popular TV shows like the *Cosby Show*, *Cheers*, or *Roseanne* at the time they originally aired. Such scheduling provided common media experiences at specific times within our culture. While we still watch TV shows, we are increasingly likely to do so at our own convenience through Web sites like Hulu and Netflix or DVR/On-Demand options. We are also increasingly making our media choices on the basis of Facebook, YouTube, or Twitter recommendations from friends. Or we upload our own media—from photos of last night's party to homemade videos of our lives, pets, and hobbies—to share with friends instead of watching "mainstream" programming. While these options allow us to connect with friends or family and give us more choices, they also break down shared media experiences in favor of our individual interests and pursuits.

The ability to access many different forms of media in one place is also changing the ways we engage with and consume media. In the past, we read newspapers in print, watched TV on our televisions, and played video games on a console. Today, we are able to do all these things on a computer, tablet, or smartphone, making it easy—and very tempting—to multitask. Media multitasking has led to growing media consumption, particularly for young people. A recent Kaiser Family Foundation study found that today's youth—now doing two or more things at once—packed ten hours and forty-five minutes worth of media content into the seven and a half hours they spent daily consuming media.[10] But while we might be consuming more media, are we really engaging with it? And are we really engaging with our friends when we communicate with them by texting or posting on Facebook? Some critics and educators feel that media multitasking means that we are more distracted, that we engage less with each type of media we consume, and that we often pay closer attention to the media we are using than to people immediately in our presence.

However, media multitasking could have other effects. In the past, we would wait until the end of a TV program, if not until the next day, to discuss it with our friends. Now, with the proliferation of social media, and in particular Twitter, we can discuss that program with our friends—and with strangers—as we watch the show. Many TV shows now gauge their popularity with audiences by how many people are "live-tweeting" it and by how many related trending topics they have on Twitter. In fact, commenting on a TV show on social media grew by 194 percent between April 2011 and April 2012.[11] This type of participation could indicate that audiences are in fact engaging more with the media they consume, even though they are multitasking. Some media critics even posit that having more choice actually makes us more engaged media consumers, because we have to actively choose the media we want to consume from the growing list of options.

Stories: The Foundation of Media

The stories that circulate in the media can shape a society's perceptions and attitudes. Throughout the twentieth century and during the recent wars in Afghanistan and Iraq, for instance, courageous professional journalists covered armed conflicts, telling stories that helped the public comprehend the magnitude and tragedy of such events. In the 1950s and 1960s, network television news stories on the Civil Rights movement led to crucial legislation that transformed the way many white people viewed the grievances and aspirations of African Americans. In the late 1960s to early 1970s, the persistent media coverage of the Vietnam War ultimately led to a loss of public support for the war. In the late 1990s, news and tabloid magazine stories about the President Clinton–Monica Lewinsky affair sparked heated debates over private codes of behavior and public abuses of authority. In each of these instances, the stories told through a variety of media outlets played a key role in changing individual awareness, cultural attitudes, and public perception.

While we continue to look to the media for narratives today, the kinds of stories we seek and tell are changing in the digital era. During Hollywood's Golden Age in the 1930s and 1940s, as many as ninety million people each week went to the movies on Saturday to take in a professionally produced double feature and a newsreel about the week's main events. In the 1980s, during TV's Network Era, most of us sat down at night to watch the polished evening news or the scripted sitcoms and dramas written by paid writers and performed by seasoned actors. But in the digital age, where reality TV and social media now seem to dominate storytelling, many of the performances are enacted by "ordinary" people. Audiences are fascinated by the stories of couples finding love, relationships gone bad, and backstabbing friends on shows like the *Real Housewives* series and its predecessors, like *Jersey Shore*. Other reality shows—like *Pawn Stars*, *Deadliest Catch*, and *Duck Dynasty*—give us glimpses into the lives and careers of everyday people, while amateurs entertain us in singing, dancing, and cooking shows like *The Voice*, *So You Think You Can Dance*, and *Top Chef*. While these shows are all professionally produced, the performers are almost all ordinary people (or celebrities and professionals performing alongside amateurs), which is part of the appeal of reality TV—we are better able to relate to the characters, or compare our lives against theirs, because they seem just like us.

Online, many of us are entertaining each other with videos of our pets, Facebook posts about our achievements or relationship issues, photos of a good meal, or tweets about a funny thing that happened at work. This cultural blending of old and new ways of telling stories—told by both professionals and amateurs—is just another form of convergence that has disrupted and altered the media landscape in the digital era. More than ever, ordinary citizens are able to participate in, and have an effect on, the stories being told in the media. For example, when the Russian government took control of Crimea and threatened the borders of other parts of the Ukraine in 2014, many ordinary people caught between allegiances to different nations got their stories out via videos, tweets, social media, and blog posts. They were able to communicate in an online world that was much harder for autocratic leaders to control, and their messages allowed the more traditional media to find and report stories that in another age would not have been told. Our varied media institutions and outlets are basically in the **narrative**—or story-telling—business. Media stories put events in context, helping us to better understand both our daily lives and the larger world. As psychologist Jerome Bruner argues, we are storytelling creatures, and as children we acquire language to tell the stories we have inside us. In his book *Making Stories*, he says, "Stories, finally, provide models of the world."[12] The common denominator, in fact, between our entertainment and information cultures is the narrative. It is the media's main cultural currency—whether it's Michael Jackson's "Thriller" video, a post on a gossip blog, a Fox News "exclusive," a *New York Times* article, a tweet about a bad breakfast, or a funny TV commercial. The point is that the popular narratives of our culture are complex and varied. Roger Rosenblatt, writing in *Time* magazine during the 2000 presidential election, made this observation about the importance of stories: "We are a narrative species. We exist by storytelling—by relating our situations—and the test of our evolution may lie in getting the story right."[13]

The Power of Media Stories in Everyday Life

The earliest debates, at least in Western society, about the impact of cultural narratives on daily life date back to the ancient Greeks. Socrates, himself accused of corrupting young minds, worried that children exposed to popular art forms and stories "without distinction" would "take into their souls teachings that are wholly opposite to those we wish them to be possessed of when they are grown up."[14] He believed art should uplift us from the ordinary routines of our lives. The playwright Euripides, however, believed that art should imitate life, that characters should be "real," and that artistic works should reflect the actual world—even when that reality is sordid.

Marc Riboud/Magnum Photos

In *The Republic*, Plato developed the classical view of art: It should aim to instruct and uplift. He worried that some staged performances glorified evil and that common folk watching might not be able to distinguish between art and reality. Aristotle, Plato's student, occupied a middle ground in these debates, arguing that art and stories should provide insight into the human condition but should entertain as well.

The cultural concerns of classical philosophers are still with us. In the early 1900s, for example, newly arrived immigrants to the United States who spoke little English gravitated toward cultural events (such as boxing, vaudeville, and the emerging medium of silent film) whose enjoyment did not depend solely on understanding English. Consequently, these popular events occasionally became a flash point for some groups, including the Daughters of the American Revolution, local politicians, religious leaders, and police vice squads, who not only resented the commercial success of immigrant culture but also feared that these "low" cultural forms would undermine what they saw as traditional American values and interests.

In the United States in the 1950s, the emergence of television and rock and roll generated several points of contention. For instance, the phenomenal popularity of Elvis Presley set the stage for many of today's debates over hip-hop lyrics and television's influence, especially on young people. In 1956 and 1957, Presley made three appearances on the *Ed Sullivan Show*. The public outcry against Presley's "lascivious" hip movements was so great that by the third show the camera operators were instructed to shoot the singer only from the waist up. In some communities, objections to Presley were motivated by class bias and racism. Many white adults believed that this "poor white trash" singer from Mississippi was spreading rhythm and blues, a "dangerous" form of black popular culture.

Today, with the reach of print, electronic, and digital communications and the amount of time people spend consuming them (see Figure 1.1 on page 16), mass media play an even more controversial role in society. Many people are critical of the quality of much contemporary culture and are concerned about the overwhelming amount of information now available. Many see popular media culture as unacceptably commercial and sensationalistic. Too many talk

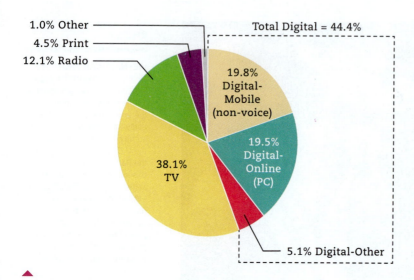

FIGURE 1.1

DAILY MEDIA CONSUMPTION BY PLATFORM, 2013

Data from: "Media Consumption Estimates: Mobile > PC; Digital > TV," Marketing Charts, www.marketingcharts.com/wp/wp-content/uploads/2013/08/eMarketer-Share-Media-Consumption-by-Medium-2010-2013-Aug2013.png.

shows exploit personal problems for commercial gain, reality shows often glamorize outlandish behavior and dangerous stunts, and television research continues to document a connection between aggression in children and violent entertainment programs or video games. Children, who watch nearly forty thousand TV commercials each year, are particularly vulnerable to marketers selling junk food, toys, and "cool" clothing. Even the computer, once heralded as an educational salvation, has created confusion. Today, when kids announce that they are "on the computer," many parents wonder whether they are writing a term paper, playing a video game, chatting on Facebook, or peering at pornography.

Yet how much the media shape society—and how much they simply respond to existing cultural issues—is still unknown. Although some media depictions may worsen social problems, research has seldom demonstrated that the media directly cause our society's major afflictions. For instance, when a middle-school student shoots a fellow student over designer clothing, should society blame the ad that glamorized clothes and the network that carried the ad? Or are parents, teachers, and religious leaders failing to instill strong moral values? Are economic and social issues involving gun legislation, consumerism, and income disparity at work as well? Even if the clothing manufacturer bears responsibility as a corporate citizen, did the ad alone bring about the tragedy, or is the ad symptomatic of a larger problem?

With American mass media industries earning more than $200 billion annually, the economic and societal stakes are high. Large portions of media resources now go toward studying audiences, capturing their attention through stories, and taking their consumer dollars. To increase their revenues, media outlets try to influence everything from how people shop to how they vote. Like the air we breathe, the commercially based culture that mass media help create surrounds us. Its impact, like the air, is often taken for granted. But to monitor that culture's "air quality"—to become media literate—we must attend more thoughtfully to diverse media stories that are too often taken for granted. (For further discussion, see "Examining Ethics: Covering War" on pages 18–19.)

Surveying the Cultural Landscape

Some cultural phenomena gain wide popular appeal, and others do not. Some appeal to certain age groups or social classes. Some, such as rock and roll, jazz, and classical music, are popular worldwide; other cultural forms, such as Tejano, salsa, and Cajun music, are popular primarily in certain regions or ethnic communities. Certain aspects of culture are considered elite in one place (e.g., opera in the United States) and popular in another (e.g., opera in Italy). Though categories may change over time and from one society to another, two metaphors offer contrasting views about the way culture operates in our daily lives: culture as a hierarchy, represented by a *skyscraper* model, and culture as a process, represented by a *map* model.

Culture as a Skyscraper

Throughout twentieth-century America, critics and audiences perceived culture as a hierarchy with supposedly superior products at the top and inferior ones at the bottom. This can be imagined, in some respects, as a modern skyscraper. In this model, the top floors of the building house high culture, such as ballet, the symphony, art museums, and classic literature. The bottom floors—and even the basement—house popular or low culture, including such icons as soap operas, rock music, radio shock jocks, and video games (see Figure 1.2 on page 20). High culture, identified with "good taste" and higher education, and supported by wealthy patrons and corporate donors, is associated with "fine art," which is available primarily in libraries, theaters, and museums. In contrast, low or popular culture is aligned with the "questionable" tastes of the masses, who enjoy the commercial "junk" circulated by the mass media, such as reality TV, celebrity-gossip Web sites, and violent action films. Whether or not we agree with this cultural skyscraper model, the high–low hierarchy often determines or limits the ways we view and discuss culture today.[15] Using this model, critics have developed at least five areas of concern about so-called low culture: the depreciation of fine art, the exploitation of high culture, the disposability of popular culture, the driving out of high culture, and the deadening of our cultural taste buds.

An Inability to Appreciate Fine Art

Some critics claim that popular culture, in the form of contemporary movies, television, and music, distracts students from serious literature and philosophy, thus stunting their imagination and undermining their ability to recognize great art.[16] This critical view pits popular culture against high art, discounting a person's ability to value Bach and the Beatles or Shakespeare and *The Simpsons* concurrently. The assumption is that because popular forms of culture are made for profit, they cannot be experienced as valuable artistic experiences in the same way as more elite art forms, such as classical ballet, Italian opera, modern sculpture, or Renaissance painting—even though many of what we regard as elite art forms today were once supported and even commissioned by wealthy patrons.

A Tendency to Exploit High Culture

Another concern is that popular culture exploits classic works of literature and art. A good example may be Mary Wollstonecraft Shelley's dark Gothic novel *Frankenstein*, written in 1818 and ultimately transformed into multiple popular forms. Today, the tale is best remembered by virtue of two movies: a 1931 film version starring Boris Karloff as the towering and tragic monster, and the 1974 Mel Brooks comedy *Young Frankenstein*. In addition to the many cinematic versions, television turned the tale into *The Munsters*, a mid-1960s situation comedy. The monster was even resurrected as sugarcoated Franken Berry cereal. In the recycled forms of the original story, Shelley's powerful themes about abusing science and judging people on the basis of appearances are often lost or trivialized in favor of a simplistic horror story, a comedy spoof, or a form of junk food.

A Throwaway Ethic

Unlike an Italian opera or a Shakespearean tragedy, many elements of popular culture have a short life span. The average newspaper circulates for about twelve hours, then lands in a recycling bin; a hit song might top the charts for a few weeks at a time; and most new Web sites or blogs are rarely visited and doomed to oblivion. Although endurance does not necessarily denote quality, many critics think that so-called better or higher forms of culture have more staying power. In this argument, lower or popular forms of culture are unstable and fleeting; they follow rather than lead public taste. In the TV industry in the 1960s and 1970s, for example, network executives employed the "least objectionable programming" (or LOP) strategy that

Covering War

By 2014, as the United States withdrew most of its military forces from Afghanistan—from a war that was in its thirteenth year (making it the longest war in U.S. history)—journalistic coverage of Middle East war efforts had declined dramatically. This was partly due to the tendency of news organizations to lose interest in an event when it drags on for a long time and becomes "old news." The news media are often biased in favor of timeliness and "current events." But war reporting also declined because of the financial crisis—more than twenty thousand reporters lost their jobs or took buyouts between 2009 and 2013 as papers cut staff to save money. In fact, most news organizations stopped sending

reporters to cover the wars in Iraq and Afghanistan, depending instead on wire service reporters, foreign correspondents from other countries, or major news organizations like the *New York Times* or CNN for their coverage. Despite the decreasing coverage, the news media continue to confront ethical challenges about the best way to cover the wars, including reporting on the deaths of soldiers; documenting drug abuse or the high suicide rate among Iraq and Afghanistan war veterans; dealing with First Amendment issues; and knowing what is appropriate for their audiences to view, read, or hear.

When President Obama took office in 2009, he suspended the previous Bush administration ban on media coverage of soldiers' coffins returning to U.S. soil from the Iraq and Afghanistan wars. First Amendment advocates praised Obama's decision, although after a flurry of news coverage of these arrivals in April 2009, media outlets grew less interested as the wars dragged on. Later, though, the Obama

administration upset some of the same First Amendment supporters when it withheld more prisoner and detainee abuse photos from earlier in the wars, citing concerns for the safety of current U.S. troops and fears of further inflaming anti-American opinion. Both issues—one opening up news access and one closing it down—suggest the difficult and often tense relationship between presidential administrations and the news media.

In May 2011, these issues surfaced again when U.S. Navy SEALs killed Osama bin Laden, long credited with perpetrating the 9/11 tragedy. As details of the SEAL operation began to emerge, the Obama administration weighed the appropriateness of releasing photos of bin Laden's body and video of his burial at sea. While some news organizations and First Amendment advocates demanded the release of the photos, the Obama administration ultimately decided against it, saying that the government did not want to spur any further terrorist actions against the United States and its allies.

IMAGES OF WAR
The photos and images that news outlets choose to show greatly influence their audience members' opinions. In each of the photos below, what message about war is being portrayed? How much freedom do you think news outlets should have in showing potentially controversial scenes from war?

Wissam al-Okaili/AFP/Getty Images   ZUMApress.com

How much freedom should the news media have to cover a war?

Back in 2006, President George W. Bush criticized the news media for not showing enough "good news" about U.S. efforts to bring democracy to Iraq. Bush's remarks raised ethical questions about the complex relationship between the government and the news media during times of war: How much freedom should the news media have to cover a war? How much control, if any, should the military have over reporting a war? Are there topics that should not be covered?

These kinds of questions have also created ethical quagmires for local TV stations that cover war and its effects on communities where soldiers have been called to duty and then injured or killed. In one extreme case, the nation's largest TV station owner—Sinclair Broadcast Group—would not air the ABC News program *Nightline* in 2004 because it devoted an episode to reading the names of all U.S. soldiers killed in the Iraq War up to that time. Here is an excerpt from a *New York Times* account of that event:

Sinclair Broadcast Group, one of the largest owners of local television stations, will preempt tonight's edition of the ABC News program "Nightline," saying the program's plan to have Ted Koppel [who then anchored the program] read aloud the names of every member of the armed forces killed in action in Iraq was motivated by an antiwar agenda and threatened to undermine American efforts there.

The decision means viewers in eight cities, including St. Louis and Columbus, Ohio, will not see "Nightline." ABC News disputed

that the program carried a political message, calling it "an expression of respect which simply seeks to honor those who have laid down their lives for their country."

But Mark Hyman, the vice president of corporate relations for Sinclair, who is also a conservative commentator on the company's newscasts, said tonight's edition of "Nightline" is biased journalism. "Mr. Koppel's reading of the fallen will have no proportionality," he said in a telephone interview, pointing out that the program will ignore other aspects of the war effort.

Mr. Koppel and the producers of "Nightline" said earlier this week that they had no political motivation behind the decision to devote an entire show, expanded to 40 minutes, to reading the names and displaying the photos of those killed. They said they only intended to honor the dead and document what Mr. Koppel called "the human cost" of the war.[1]

Given such a case, how might a local TV news director today—under pressure from the station's manager or owner—formulate guidelines to help negotiate such ethical territory? While most TV news divisions have ethical codes to guide journalists' behavior in certain situations, could ordinary citizens help shape ethical discussions and decisions? Following is a general plan for dealing with an array of ethical dilemmas that media practitioners face and for finding ways in which nonjournalists might participate in this decision-making process.

Arriving at ethical decisions is a particular kind of criticism involving several steps. These include (1) laying out the case; (2) pinpointing the key issues; (3) identifying the parties involved, their intents, and their potentially competing values; (4) studying ethical models and theories; (5) presenting strategies and options; and (6) formulating a decision or policy.[2]

As a test case, let's look at how local TV news directors might establish ethical guidelines for war-related events. By following the six steps above, our goal is to make some ethical decisions and to lay the groundwork for policies that address TV images or photographs—for example, those of protesters, supporters, memorials, or funerals—used in war coverage. (See Chapter 14 for details on confronting ethical problems.)

Examining Ethics Activity

As a class or in smaller groups, design policies that address one or more of the issues raised here. Start by researching the topic; find as much information as possible. For example, you can research guidelines that local stations already use by contacting local news directors and TV journalists.

Do the local stations have guidelines? If so, are they adequate? Are there certain types of images they will not show? If the Obama administration had released photographic evidence of bin Laden's death, would a local station have shown it? Finally, if time allows, send the policies you designed to various TV news directors and/or station managers; ask for their evaluations, and ask whether they would consider implementing the policies. ▲

FIGURE 1.2

CULTURE AS A SKYSCRAPER

Culture is diverse and difficult to categorize. Yet throughout the twentieth century, we tended to think of culture not as a social process but as a set of products sorted into high, low, or middle positions on a cultural skyscraper. Look at this highly arbitrary arrangement and see if you agree or disagree. Write in some of your own examples.

Why do we categorize or classify culture in this way? Who controls this process? Is control of making cultural categories important? Why or why not?

▶

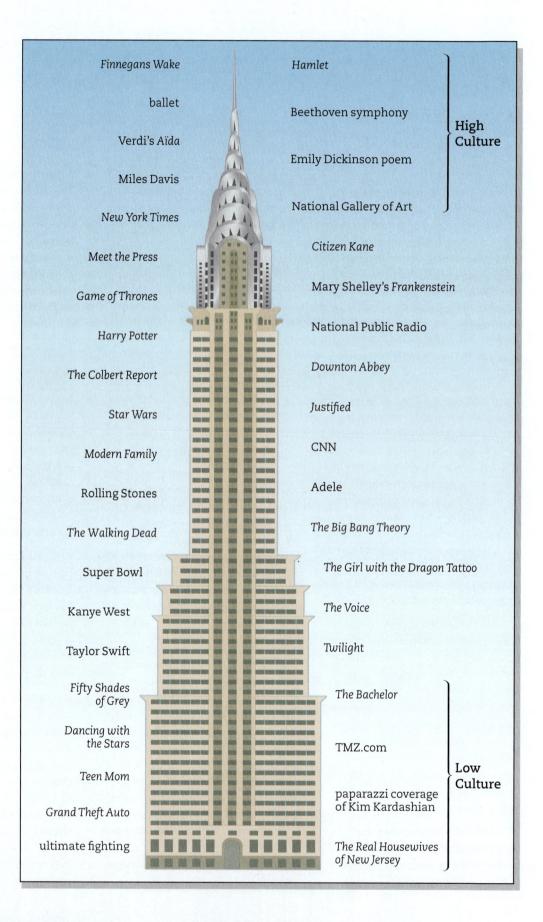

Finnegans Wake

ballet

Verdi's Aïda

Miles Davis

New York Times

Meet the Press

Game of Thrones

Harry Potter

The Colbert Report

Star Wars

Modern Family

Rolling Stones

The Walking Dead

Super Bowl

Kanye West

Taylor Swift

Fifty Shades of Grey

Dancing with the Stars

Teen Mom

Grand Theft Auto

ultimate fighting

Hamlet

Beethoven symphony

Emily Dickinson poem

National Gallery of Art

High Culture

Citizen Kane

Mary Shelley's Frankenstein

National Public Radio

Downton Abbey

Justified

CNN

Adele

The Big Bang Theory

The Girl with the Dragon Tattoo

The Voice

Twilight

The Bachelor

TMZ.com

paparazzi coverage of Kim Kardashian

The Real Housewives of New Jersey

Low Culture

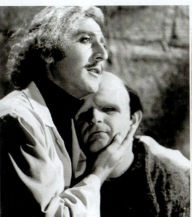

Photofest   20th Century Fox/Photofest   © Lionsgate/Everett Collection

critics said pandered to mediocrity with bland, disposable programs that a "regular" viewer would not find objectionable, challenging, or disturbing.

A Diminished Audience for High Culture

Some observers also warn that popular culture has inundated the cultural environment, driving out higher forms of culture and cheapening public life.[17] This concern is supported by data showing that TV sets are in use in the average American home for nearly eight hours a day, exposing adults and children each year to thousands of hours of trivial TV commercials, violent crime dramas, and superficial reality programs. According to one story critics tell, the prevalence of so many popular media products prevents the public from experiencing genuine art—though this view fails to note the number of choices and options now available to media consumers.

Dulling Our Cultural Taste Buds

One cautionary story, frequently recounted by academics, politicians, and pundits, tells how popular culture, especially its more visual forms (such as TV advertising and YouTube videos), undermines democratic ideals and reasoned argument. According to this view, popular media may inhibit not only rational thought but also social progress by transforming audiences into cultural dupes lured by the promise of products. A few multinational conglomerates that make large profits from media products may be distracting citizens from examining economic disparity and implementing change. Seductive advertising images showcasing the buffed and airbrushed bodies of professional models, for example, frequently contradict the actual lives of people who cannot hope to achieve a particular "look" or may not have the money to obtain the high-end cosmetic or clothing products offered. In this environment, art and commerce have become blurred, restricting the audience's ability to make cultural and economic distinctions. Sometimes called the "Big Mac" theory, this view suggests that people are so addicted to mass-produced media menus that they lose their discriminating taste for finer fare and, much worse, their ability to see and challenge social inequities.

Culture as a Map

While the skyscraper model is one way to view culture, another way to view it is as a map. Here, culture is an ongoing and complicated process—rather than a high–low vertical hierarchy—that allows us to better account for our diverse and individual tastes. In the map model, we judge forms of culture as good or bad based on a combination of personal taste and the aesthetic judgments a society makes at particular historical times. Because such tastes and evaluations are "all over the map," a cultural map suggests that we can pursue many

Is *Anchorman* a Comedy or a Documentary?

One fascinating media phenomenon of the first few decades of the twenty-first century is that fictional storytelling has changed dramatically over this time while TV news stories, especially local TV news, have hardly changed at all.

Why is this?

They are both media products that depend on storytelling to draw audiences and make money. But while complex and controversial TV narratives like HBO's *Game of Thrones*, Showtime's *Penny Dreadful*, FX's *Fargo*, AMC's *Breaking Bad* and *The Walking Dead*, Netflix's *House of Cards*, and NBC's *The Blacklist* were not possible in the 1960s, when just three networks—careful not to offend or challenge viewers—dominated, the lead crime story on most local TV newscasts around the country looks pretty much like it did decades earlier. In the film *Anchorman 2*, Will Ferrell and Adam McKay follow up their satire of small-minded local news anchors in the 1970s with a story about the birth of pandering twenty-four-hour news coverage

in the 1980s. The film points out that nonfictional storytelling on television remains locked in narrative patterns from the 1960s and 1970s—making Ferrell's newscaster comedies, at times, seem more like documentaries.

The reason for the lack of advances in news narratives is itself a story—one that's about money, and which stories sell and why.

American filmmakers from D. W. Griffith and Orson Welles to Steven Spielberg and Wes Anderson have understood the allure of narrative. But narrative is such a large category—encompassing everything from poetry and novels to movies and TV shows to TV newscasts and political ads—that it demands subdivisions. So over time we developed the idea of genre as a way to differentiate the vast array of stories. In *Poetics*, Aristotle first talked about generic categories in his analysis of poetry, which he divided into three basic types: "Epic poetry and Tragedy, Comedy also and Dithyrambic poetry, and the music of the flute and of the lyre." Fast-forwarding to more contemporary takes

on popular genres, literary scholar John Cawelti, in his book *Adventure, Mystery, and Romance*, identified five popular literary formulas: adventure, romance, mystery, melodrama, and "alien beings or states."[1]

In fact, most local and national TV news stories function as a kind of melodrama as defined by Cawelti and others. In the melodrama, "the city" is often the setting—as it is in most TV newscasts—and has degenerated into a corrupt and mysterious place, full of crime and mayhem. Historically, heroes of fictional melodramas are small-town sheriffs and big-city cops who must rise above the corruption to impose their individual moral values to defeat various forms of evil. In today's popular culture, cities like Los Angeles and New York are portrayed as places that conceal evil terrorist cells, corrupt cops, maniacal corporate bosses, and other assorted "bad guys," until the strong cops or triumphant lawyers conquer evil and restore order through the convictions of their strong individual character. Variations on these melodramatic themes can be found as the major organizing structure in everything from cop shows like *NCIS*, *The Good Wife*, and *Justified* to newsmagazines like *60 Minutes* or cable TV shows like Fox News' *The O'Reilly Factor* and *Hannity*. This is not surprising given that individualism is probably our most persistent American value and that the melodrama generally celebrates the rugged tenacity of tough-minded heroes—whether they are gunfighters, cops, reporters, or even news anchors.

The appropriation of these narratives by news shows has been satirized by the likes of *Anchorman*, *Saturday Night*

Gemma LaMana/© Paramount Pictures/Everett Collection

Live, and, more pointedly, Comedy Central's *The Daily Show* and *The Colbert Report*. These satires often critique the way news producers repeat stale formulas rather than invent dynamic new story forms for new generations of viewers. As much as the world has changed since the 1970s (when *SNL*'s "Weekend Update" debuted), local TV news story formulas have gone virtually unaltered. Modern newscasts still limit reporters' stories to two minutes or less and promote stylish male/female anchor teams, a sports "guy," and a certified meteorologist as familiar personalities, usually leading with a dramatic local crime story and teasing viewers to stay tuned for a possible weather disaster.

Dana Edelson/NBC/NBCU Photo Bank via Getty Images

By indulging these formulas, TV news continues to address viewers not primarily as citizens and members of communities but as news consumers who build the TV ratings that determine the ad rates for local stations and the national networks. In the book *The Elements of Journalism*, Bill Kovach and Tom Rosenstiel argue that "journalists must make the significant interesting and relevant."[2] Too often, however, on cable, the Internet, and local news, we are awash in news stories that try to make something significant out of the obviously trivial, mildly interesting, or narrowly relevant—like stories about troubled celebrities, attention-seeking politicians, or decontextualized stock-market numbers.

In fictional TV, however, storytelling has evolved over time, becoming increasingly dynamic and complex with shows like *Mad Men, Breaking Bad, Game of Thrones, The Good Wife, Fargo, Homeland*, and *Girls*. In *Everything Bad Is Good for You*, Steven Johnson argues that in contrast to older popular 1970s programs like *Dallas* or *Dynasty*, the

best TV stories today layer "each scene with a thick network of affiliations. You have to focus to follow the plot, and in focusing you're exercising the parts of your brain that map social networks, that fill in missing information, that connect multiple narrative threads."[3] Johnson says that younger audiences today—brought up in an era of the Internet and complicated interactive visual games—bring high expectations to other kinds of popular culture as well, including television. "The mind," he writes, "likes to be challenged; there's real pleasure to be found in solving puzzles, detecting patterns or unpacking a complex narrative system."[4]

This evolution of fictional storytelling has not yet happened with its nonfictional counterparts; TV news remains entrenched in old formulas and time constraints. The reasons for this, of course, are money and competition. Whereas national networks today have begun to adjust their programming decisions to better compete against cable services like AMC and HBO and

new story "content" providers like Netflix and Amazon, local TV news still competes against just three or four other news stations and just one (if any) local newspaper. Even with diminished viewership (most local TV stations have lost half their audience over the past ten to fifteen years), local TV news still draws enough viewers in a fragmented media landscape to attract top ad dollars.

But those viewership levels continue to decline as older audiences give way to new generations more likely to comb social media networks for news and information. Perhaps younger audiences crave news stories that match the more complicated storytelling that surrounds them in everything from TV dramas to interactive video games to their own conversations. Viewers raised on the irony of *Saturday Night Live, The Simpsons, Family Guy, South Park*, and *The Daily Show* are not buying—and not watching—news stories that seem as if they still belong to their grandparents' generation. ◢

THE POPULAR *HUNGER GAMES* book series, which has also become a blockbuster film franchise, mixes elements that have, in the past, been considered "low" culture (young-adult stories, science fiction) with the "high" culture of literature and satire. It also doubles as a cautionary story about media used to transform and suppress its audience: In the books and films, the media, controlled by a totalitarian government, broadcast a brutal fight to the death between child "tributes," fascinating the population while attempting to quash any hope of revolution.

Lionsgate/Photofest

connections from one cultural place to another and can appreciate a range of cultural experiences without simply ranking them from high to low.

Our attraction to and choice of cultural phenomena—such as the stories we read in books or watch at the movies—represent how we make our lives meaningful. Culture offers plenty of places to go that are conventional, familiar, and comforting. Yet at the same time, our culture's narrative storehouse contains other stories that tend toward the innovative, unfamiliar, and challenging. Most forms of culture, however, demonstrate multiple tendencies. We may use online social networks because they are both comforting (an easy way to keep up with friends) and innovative (new tools or apps that engage us). We watch televised sporting events for their familiarity and conventional organization, and because the unknown outcome can be unpredictable or challenging. The map offered here (see Figure 1.3) is based on a familiar subway grid. Each station represents tendencies or elements related to why a person may be attracted to different cultural products. Also, more popular culture forms congregate in more congested areas of the map, while less popular cultural forms are outliers. Such a large, multidirectional map may be a more flexible, multidimensional, and inclusive way of imagining how culture works.

The Comfort of Familiar Stories

The appeal of culture is often its familiar stories, pulling audiences toward the security of repetition and common landmarks on the cultural map. Consider, for instance, early television's *Lassie* series, about the adventures of a collie named Lassie and her owner, young Timmy. Of the more than five hundred episodes, many have a familiar and repetitive plotline: Timmy, who arguably possessed the poorest sense of direction and suffered more concussions than any TV character in history, gets lost or knocked unconscious. After finding Timmy and licking his face, Lassie goes for help and saves the day. Adult critics might mock this melodramatic formula, but many children found comfort in the predictability of the story. This quality is also evident when night after night children ask their parents to read them the same book, such as Margaret Wise Brown's *Goodnight Moon* or Maurice Sendak's *Where the Wild Things Are*, or watch the same DVD, such as *Snow White* or *The Princess Bride*.

Innovation and the Attraction of "What's New"

Like children, adults also seek comfort, often returning to an old Beatles or Guns N' Roses song, a William Butler Yeats or Emily Dickinson poem, or a TV rerun of *Seinfeld* or *Andy Griffith*. But we

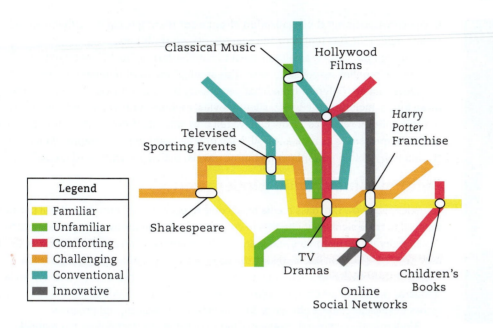

Classical Music Hollywood Films

Televised Sporting Events

Harry Potter Franchise

Legend

- Familiar
- Unfamiliar
- Comforting
- Challenging
- Conventional
- Innovative

Shakespeare

TV Dramas

Children's Books

Online Social Networks

FIGURE 1.3
CULTURE AS A MAP

In this map model, culture is not ranked as high or low. Instead, the model shows culture as spreading out in several directions across a variety of dimensions. For example, some cultural forms can be familiar, innovative, and challenging, like the *Harry Potter* books and movies. This model accounts for the complexity of individual tastes and experiences. The map model also suggests that culture is a process by which we produce meaning—that is, make our lives meaningful—as well as a complex collection of media products and texts. The map shown is just one interpretation of culture. What cultural products would you include in your own model? What dimensions would you link to and why?

also like cultural adventure. We may turn from a familiar film on cable's AMC to discover a new movie from Iran or India on the Sundance Channel. We seek new stories and new places to go—those aspects of culture that demonstrate originality and complexity. For instance, James Joyce's *Finnegans Wake* (1939) created language anew and challenged readers, as the novel's poetic first sentence illustrates: "riverrun, past Eve and Adam's, from swerve of shore to bend of bay, brings us by a commodius vicus of recirculation back to Howth Castle and Environs." A revolutionary work, crammed with historical names and topical references to events, myths, songs, jokes, and daily conversation, Joyce's novel remains a challenge to understand and decode. His work demonstrated that part of what culture provides is the impulse to explore new places, to strike out in new directions, searching for something different that may contribute to growth and change.

A Wide Range of Messages

We know that people have complex cultural tastes, needs, and interests based on different backgrounds and dispositions. It is not surprising, then, that our cultural treasures, from blues music and opera to comic books and classical literature, contain a variety of messages. Just as Shakespeare's plays—popular entertainments in his day—were packed with both obscure and popular references, TV episodes of *The Simpsons* have included allusions to the Beatles, Kafka, *Teletubbies*, Tennessee Williams, Apple, *Star Trek*, *The X-Files*, Freud, *Psycho*, and *Citizen Kane*. In other words, as part of an ongoing process, cultural products and their meanings are "all over the map," spreading out in diverse directions.

Challenging the Nostalgia for a Better Past

Some critics of popular culture assert—often without presenting supportive evidence—that society was better off before the latest developments in mass media. These critics resist the idea of reimagining an established cultural hierarchy as a multidirectional map. The nostalgia for some imagined "better past" has often operated as a device for condemning new cultural phenomena. This impulse to criticize something that is new is often driven by fear of change or of cultural differences. Back in the nineteenth century, in fact, a number of intellectuals and politicians worried that rising literacy rates among the working class might create havoc: How would the aristocracy and intellectuals maintain their authority and status if everyone could read? A recent example includes the fear that some politicians, religious leaders, and citizens

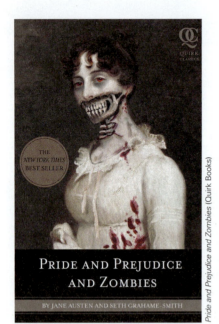

Pride and Prejudice and Zombies (Quirk Books)

PRIDE AND PREJUDICE AND ZOMBIES is a famous "mash-up"—a new creative work made by mixing together disparate cultural pieces. In this case, the classic novel by Jane Austen is reimagined as taking place among zombies and ninjas, mixing elements of English literature and horror and action films. Usually intended as satire, such mash-ups allow us to enjoy an array of cultural elements in a single work and are a direct contradiction to the cultural hierarchy model.

have expressed about the legalization of same-sex marriage, claiming that it would violate older religious tenets or the sanctity of past traditions.

Throughout history, a call to return to familiar terrain, to "the good old days," has been a frequent response to new, "threatening" forms of popular culture or to any ideas that are different from what we already believe. Yet over the years many of these forms, including the waltz, silent movies, ragtime, and jazz, have themselves become cultural "classics." How can we tell now what the future has in store for such cultural expressions as rock and roll, soap operas, fashion photography, dance music, hip-hop, tabloid newspapers, graphic novels, reality TV, and social media?

Cultural Values of the Modern Period

To understand how the mass media have come to occupy their current cultural position, we need to trace significant changes in cultural values from the modern period until today. In general, U.S. historians and literary scholars think of the **modern period** as beginning with the Industrial Revolution of the nineteenth century and extending until about the mid-twentieth century. Although there are many ways to define what it means to be "modern," we will focus on four major features or values that resonate best with changes across media and culture: efficiency, individualism, rationalism, and progress.

Modernization involved captains of industry using new technology to create efficient manufacturing centers, produce inexpensive products to make everyday life better, and make commerce more profitable. Printing presses and assembly lines made major contributions in this transformation, and then modern advertising spread the word about new gadgets to American consumers. In terms of culture, the modern mantra has been "form follows function." For example, the growing populations of big cities placed a premium on space, creating a new form of building that fulfilled that functional demand by building upwards. Modern skyscrapers made of glass, steel, and concrete replaced the supposedly wasteful decorative and ornate styles of premodern Gothic cathedrals. This new value was echoed in journalism, where a front-page style rejected decorative and ornate adjectives and adverbs for "just the facts." To be lean and efficient, modern news de-emphasized complex analysis and historical context and elevated the new and the now.

Cultural responses to and critiques of modern efficiency often manifested themselves in the mass media. For example, in *Brave New World* (1932), Aldous Huxley created a fictional world in which he cautioned readers that the efficiencies of modern science and technology posed a threat to individual dignity. Charlie Chaplin's film *Modern Times* (1936), set in a futuristic manufacturing plant, also told the story of the dehumanizing impact of modernization and machinery. Writers and artists, in their criticisms of the modern world, have often pointed to technology's ability to alienate people from one another, capitalism's tendency to foster greed, and government's inclination to create bureaucracies whose inefficiency oppresses rather than helps people.

While the values of the premodern period (before the Industrial Revolution) were guided by a strong belief in a natural or divine order, modernization elevated individual self-expression to a more central position. Modern print media allowed ordinary readers to engage with new ideas beyond what their religious leaders and local politicians communicated to them. Modern individualism and the Industrial Revolution also triggered new forms of hierarchy in which certain individuals and groups achieved higher standing in the social order. For example, those who managed commercial enterprises gained more control over the economic ladder, while an intellectual class of modern experts acquired increasing power over the nation's economic, political, and cultural agendas.

To be modern also meant valuing the ability of logical and scientific minds to solve problems by working in organized groups and expert teams. Progressive thinkers maintained that the printing press, the telegraph, and the railroad, in combination with a scientific attitude, would foster a new type of informed society. At the core of this society, the printed mass media—particularly newspapers—would educate the citizenry, helping to build and maintain an organized social framework.[18]

A leading champion for an informed rational society was Walter Lippmann, who wrote the influential book *Public Opinion* in 1922. He distrusted both the media and the public's ability to navigate a world that was "altogether too big, too complex, and too fleeting for direct acquaintance," and to reach the rational decisions needed in a democracy. Instead, he advocated a "machinery of knowledge" that might be established through "intelligence bureaus" staffed by experts. While such a concept might look like the modern think tank, Lippmann saw these as independent of politics, unlike think tanks today, such as the Brookings Institution or the Heritage Foundation, which have strong partisan ties.[19]

Walter Lippmann's ideas were influential throughout the twentieth century and were a product of the **Progressive Era**—a period of political and social reform that lasted roughly from the 1890s to the 1920s. On both local and national levels, Progressive Era reformers championed social movements that led to constitutional amendments for both Prohibition and women's suffrage, political reforms that led to the secret ballot during elections, and economic reforms that ushered in the federal income tax to try to foster a more equitable society. Muckrakers—journalists who exposed corruption, waste, and scandal in business and politics—represented media's significant contribution to this era (see Chapter 9).

Influenced by the Progressive movement, the notion of being modern in the twentieth century meant throwing off the chains of the past, breaking with tradition, and embracing progress. For example, twentieth-century journalists, in their quest for modern efficiency, focused on "the now" and the reporting of timely events. Newly standardized forms of front-page journalism that championed "just the facts" and events that "just happened yesterday" did help reporters efficiently meet tight deadlines. But realizing one of Walter Lippmann's fears, modern newspapers often failed to take a historical perspective or to analyze sufficiently the ideas and interests underlying these events.

Shifting Values in Postmodern Culture

For many people, the changes occurring in the **postmodern period**—from roughly the mid-twentieth century to today—are identified by a confusing array of examples: music videos, remote controls, Nike ads, shopping malls, fax machines, e-mail, video games, blogs, *USA Today*, YouTube, iPads, hip-hop, and reality TV (see Table 1.1). Some critics argue that postmodern culture represents a way of seeing—a new condition, or even a malady, of the human spirit. Although there are many ways to define the postmodern, this textbook focuses on four major features or values that resonate best with changes across media and culture: populism, diversity, nostalgia, and paradox.

TABLE 1.1

TRENDS ACROSS HISTORICAL PERIODS

▼

Trend	Premodern (pre-1800s)	Modern Industrial Revolution (1800s-1950s)	Postmodern (1950s-present)
Work hierarchies	peasants/merchants/rulers	factory workers/managers/national CEOs	temp workers/global CEOs
Major work sites	field/farm	factory/office	office/home/"virtual" or mobile office
Communication reach	local	national	global
Communication transmission	oral/manuscript	print/electronic	electronic/digital
Communication channels	storytellers/elders/town criers	books/newspapers/magazines/radio	television/cable/Internet/multimedia
Communication at home	quill pen	typewriter/office computer	personal computer/laptop/smartphone/social networks
Key social values	belief in natural or divine order	individualism/rationalism/efficiency/antitradition	antihierarchy/skepticism (about science, business, government, etc.)/diversity/multiculturalism/irony & paradox
Journalism	oral & print-based/partisan/controlled by political parties	print-based/"objective"/efficient/timely/controlled by publishing families	TV- & Internet-based/opinionated/conversational/controlled by global entertainment conglomerates

As a political idea, *populism* tries to appeal to ordinary people by highlighting or even creating an argument or conflict between "the people" and "the elite." In virtually every campaign, populist politicians often tell stories and run ads that criticize big corporations and political favoritism. Meant to resonate with middle-class values and regional ties, such narratives generally pit southern or midwestern small-town "family values" against the supposedly coarser, even corrupt, urban lifestyles associated with big cities like Washington or Los Angeles.

In postmodern culture, populism has manifested itself in many ways. For example, artists and performers, like Chuck Berry in "Roll Over Beethoven" (1956) or Queen in "Bohemian Rhapsody" (1975), intentionally blurred the border between high and low culture. In the visual arts, following Andy Warhol's 1960s pop art style, advertisers have borrowed from both fine art and street art, while artists appropriated styles from commerce and popular art. Film stars, like Angelina Jolie and Ben Affleck, often champion oppressed groups while appearing in movies that make the actors wealthy global icons of consumer culture.

Other forms of postmodern style blur modern distinctions not only between art and commerce but also between fact and fiction. For example, television vocabulary now includes infotainment (such as *Entertainment Tonight* and *Access Hollywood*) and infomercials (such as fading celebrities selling antiwrinkle cream). On cable, MTV's reality programs—such as *The Real World* and *16 and Pregnant*—blur boundaries between the staged and the real, mixing serious themes and personal challenges with comedic interludes and romantic entanglements; Comedy Central's fake news programs, *The Daily Show with Jon Stewart* and *The Colbert Report*, have combined real, insightful news stories with biting satires of traditional broadcast and cable news programs.

Closely associated with populism, another value (or vice) of the postmodern period is the emphasis on *diversity* and fragmentation, including the wild juxtaposition of old and new cultural styles. In a suburban shopping mall, for instance, Gap stores border a food court with Vietnamese, Italian, and Mexican options, while techno-digitized instrumental versions of 1960s protest music play in the background to accompany shoppers. Part of this stylistic diversity involves borrowing and transforming earlier ideas from the modern period. In music, hip-hop deejays and performers sample old R&B, soul, and rock classics, both reinventing old songs and creating something new. Critics of postmodern style contend that such borrowing devalues originality, emphasizing surface over depth and recycled ideas over new ones. Throughout the twentieth century, for example, films were adapted from books and short stories. More recently, films often derive from old popular TV series: *Mission Impossible*, *Charlie's Angels*, and *The A-Team*, to name just a few. Video games like the *Resident Evil* franchise and *Tomb Raider* have been made into Hollywood blockbusters. In fact, by 2013, more than twenty-five video games, including *BioShock* and the *Warcraft* series, were in various stages of script or film development.

Another tendency of postmodern culture involves rejecting rational thought as "the answer" to every social problem, reveling instead in *nostalgia* for the premodern values of small communities, traditional religion, and even mystical experience. Rather than seeing science purely as enlightened thinking or rational deduction that relies on evidence, some artists, critics, and politicians criticize modern values for laying the groundwork for dehumanizing technological advances and bureaucratic problems. For example, in the renewed debates over evolution, one cultural narrative that plays out often pits scientific evidence against religious belief and literal interpretations of the Bible. And in popular culture, many TV programs—such as *The X-Files*, *Buffy the Vampire Slayer*, *Charmed*, *Angel*, *Lost*, and *Fringe*—emerged to offer mystical and supernatural responses to the "evils" of our daily world and the limits of science and the purely rational.

Lastly, the fourth aspect of our postmodern time is the willingness to accept *paradox*. While modern culture emphasized breaking with the past in the name of progress, postmodern culture stresses integrating—or converging—retro beliefs and contemporary culture. So at the same time that we seem nostalgic for the past, we embrace new technologies with a vengeance. For example, fundamentalist religious movements that promote seemingly

Chaplin/Zuma Press   © Warner Bros./Photofest

outdated traditions (e.g., rejecting women's rights to own property or seek higher education) still embrace the Internet and modern technology as recruiting tools or as channels for spreading messages. Culturally conservative politicians, who seem most comfortable with the values of the 1950s nuclear family, welcome talk shows, Twitter, Facebook, and Internet and social media ad campaigns as venues to advance their messages and causes.

Although, as modernists warned, new technologies can isolate people or encourage them to chase their personal agendas (e.g., a student perusing his individual interests online), new technologies can also draw people together to advance causes; to solve community problems; or to discuss politics on radio talk shows, Facebook, or smartphones. For example, in 2011 and 2012, Twitter made the world aware of protesters in many Arab nations, including Egypt and Libya, when governments there tried to suppress media access. Our lives today are full of such incongruities.

Critiquing Media and Culture

In contemporary life, cultural boundaries are being tested; the arbitrary lines between information and entertainment have become blurred. Consumers now read newspapers on their computers. Media corporations do business across vast geographic boundaries. We are witnessing media convergence, in which televisions, computers, and smartphones easily access new and old forms of mass communication. For a fee, everything from magazines to movies is channeled into homes through the Internet and cable or satellite TV.

Considering the diversity of mass media, to paint them all with the same broad brush would be inaccurate and unfair. Yet that is often what we seem to do, which may in fact reflect the distrust many of us have of prominent social institutions, from local governments to daily newspapers. Of course, when one recent president leads us into a long war based on faulty intelligence that mainstream news failed to uncover, or one of the world's leading media companies—with former editors in top government jobs—engages in phone hacking and privacy invasion, our distrust of both government and media may be understandable. It's ultimately more useful, however, to replace a cynical perception of the media with an attitude of genuine criticism. To deal with these shifts

FILMS OFTEN REFLECT THE KEY SOCIAL VALUES of an era—as represented by the modern and postmodern movies pictured. Charlie Chaplin's *Modern Times* (1936, above left) satirized modern industry and the dehumanizing impact of a futuristic factory on its overwhelmed workers. Similarly, Ridley Scott's *Blade Runner* (1982, above right), set in futuristic Los Angeles in 2019, questioned the impact on humanity when technology overwhelms the natural world. Author William Romanowski suggested of *Blade Runner* in *Pop Culture Wars* that the movie managed to "capture some postmodern themes" that were not fully recognized then by "trying to balance the promise of technology with the threats of technology."[20]

in how we experience media and culture and their impact, we need to develop a profound understanding of the media focused on what they offer or produce and what they downplay or ignore.

Media Literacy and the Critical Process

Developing **media literacy**—that is, attaining an understanding of mass media and how they construct meaning—requires following a **critical process** that takes us through the steps of description, analysis, interpretation, evaluation, and engagement (see "Media Literacy and the Critical Process" on pages 32–33). We will be aided in our critical process by keeping an open mind, trying to understand the specific cultural forms we are critiquing, and acknowledging the complexity of contemporary culture.

Just as communication cannot always be reduced to the linear sender-message-receiver model, many forms of media and culture are not easily represented by the high–low model. We should, perhaps, strip culture of such adjectives as *high, low, popular,* and *mass.* These modifiers may artificially force media forms and products into predetermined categories. Rather than focusing on these worn-out labels, we might instead look at a wide range of issues generated by culture, from the role of storytelling in the mass media to the global influences of media industries on the consumer marketplace. We should also be moving toward a critical perspective that takes into account the intricacies of the cultural landscape. A fair critique of any cultural form, regardless of its social or artistic reputation, requires a working knowledge of the particular book, program, or music under scrutiny. For example, to understand W. E. B. Du Bois's essays, critics immerse themselves in his work and in the historical context in which he wrote. Similarly, if we want to develop a meaningful critique of TV's *Dexter* (in which the protagonist is a serial killer) or Rush Limbaugh's radio program or a gossip magazine's obsession with Justin Bieber, it is essential to understand the contemporary context in which these cultural phenomena are produced.

To begin this process of critical assessment, we must imagine culture as richer and more complicated than the high–low model allows. We must also assume a critical stance that enables us to get outside our own preferences. We may like or dislike hip-hop, R&B, pop, or country, but if we want to criticize these musical genres intelligently, we should understand what the various types of music have to say and why their messages appeal to particular audiences that may be different from us. The same approach applies to other cultural forms. If we critique a newspaper article, we must account for the language that is chosen and what it means; if we analyze a film or TV program, we need to slow down the images in order to understand how they make sense and create meaning.

Benefits of a Critical Perspective

Developing an informed critical perspective and becoming media literate allow us to participate in a debate about media culture as a force for both democracy and consumerism. On the one hand, the media can be a catalyst for democracy and social progress. Consider the role of television in spotlighting racism and injustice in the 1960s; the use of video technology to reveal oppressive conditions in China and Eastern Europe or to document crimes by urban police departments; the impact of TV coverage of both business and government's slow response to the 2010 Gulf oil spill on people's understanding of the event; and the role of blogs and Twitter in debunking bogus claims or protesting fraudulent elections. The media have also helped to renew interest in diverse cultures around the world and other emerging democracies (see "Global Village: Bedouins, Camels, Transistors, and Coke" on page 31).

On the other hand, competing against these democratic tendencies is a powerful commercial culture that reinforces a world economic order controlled by relatively few multinational corporations. For instance, when Poland threw off the shackles of the Soviet Union in the late 1980s, one of the first things its new leadership did was buy and dub the American soap operas

Bedouins, Camels, Transistors, and Coke

Upon receiving the Philadelphia Liberty Medal in 1994, President Václav Havel of the Czech Republic described postmodernism as the fundamental condition of global culture, "when it seems that something is on the way out and something else is painfully being born." He described this "new world order" as a "multicultural era" or state in which consistent value systems break into mixed and blended cultures:

For me, a symbol of that state is a Bedouin mounted on a camel and clad in traditional robes under which he is wearing jeans, with a transistor radio in his hands and an ad for Coca-Cola on the camel's back. . . . New meaning is gradually born from the . . . intersection of many different elements.[1]

Many critics, including Havel, think that there is a crucial tie between global politics and postmodern culture. They contend that the people who overthrew governments in the former Yugoslavia and the Soviet Union were the same people who valued American popular culture—especially movies, pop music, and television—for its free expression and democratic possibilities.

Back in the 1990s, as modern communist states were undermined by the growth and influence of transnational corporations, citizens in these nations capitalized on the developing global market, using portable video cameras, digital cameras and phones, and audio technology to smuggle out recordings of repression perpetrated by totalitarian regimes. Thus it was difficult for political leaders to hide repressive acts from the rest of the world. In *Newsweek*, former CBS news anchor Dan Rather wrote about the role of television in the 1989 student uprising in China:

Television brought Beijing's battle for democracy to Main Street. It made students who live on the other side of the planet just as human, just as vulnerable as the boy on the next block. The miracle of television is that the triumph and tragedy of Tiananmen Square would not have been any more vivid had it been Times Square.[2]

This trend continues today through the newer manifestations of our digital world, like Facebook, Twitter, and YouTube. As protesters sent out messages and images on smartphones and laptops during the Arab Spring uprisings in 2011 and 2012, they spread stories that could not be contained by totalitarian governments.

At the same time, we need to examine the impact on other nations of the influx of U.S. popular culture (movies, TV shows, music, etc.), our second-biggest export (after military and airplane equipment). Has access to an American consumer lifestyle fundamentally altered Havel's Bedouin on the camel? What happens when Westernized popular culture encroaches on the mores of Islamic countries, where the spread of American music, movies, and television is viewed as a danger to tradition? These questions still need answers. A global village, which through technology shares culture and communication, can also alter traditional customs forever.

To try to grasp this phenomenon, we might imagine how we would feel if the culture from a country far away gradually eroded our own established habits. This, in fact, is happening all over the world, as U.S. culture has become the world's global currency. Although newer forms of communication such as tweeting and texting have in some ways increased citizen participation in global life, in what ways have they threatened the values of older cultures?

Our current postmodern period is double-coded: It is an agent both for the renewed possibilities of democracy and, even in tough economic times, for the worldwide spread of consumerism and American popular culture. ◢

Media Literacy and the Critical Process

1 DESCRIPTION. If we decide to focus on how well the news media serve democracy, we might critique the fairness of several programs or individual stories from, say, *60 Minutes* or the *New York Times*. We start by describing the programs or articles, accounting for their reporting strategies, and noting those featured as interview subjects. We might further identify central characters, conflicts, topics, and themes. From the notes taken at this stage, we can begin comparing what we have found to other stories on similar topics. We can also document what we think is missing from these news narratives—the questions, viewpoints, and persons that were not included—and other ways to tell the story.

2 ANALYSIS. In the second stage of the critical process, we isolate patterns that call for closer attention. At this point, we decide how to focus the critique. Because *60 Minutes* has produced thousands of hours of programs in its nearly fifty-year history, our critique might spotlight just a few key patterns. For example, many of the program's reports are organized like detective stories, reporters are almost always visually represented at a medium distance, and interview subjects are generally shot in tight close-ups. In studying the *New York Times*, in contrast, we might limit our

It is easy to form a cynical view about the stream of TV advertising, reality programs, video games, celebrities, gossip blogs, tweets, and news tabloids that floods the cultural landscape. But cynicism is no substitute for criticism. To become literate about media involves striking a balance between taking a critical position (developing knowledgeable interpretations and judgments) and becoming tolerant of diverse forms of expression (appreciating the distinctive variety of cultural products and processes).

A cynical view usually involves some form of intolerance and either too little or too much information. For example, after enduring the glut of news coverage and political advertising devoted to the 2008 and 2012 presidential elections, we might easily become cynical about our political system. However, information in the form of "factual" news bits and knowledge about a complex social process such as a national election are not the same thing. The critical process stresses the subtle distinctions between amassing information and becoming media literate.

analysis to social or political events in certain countries that get covered more often than events in other areas of the world. Or we could focus on recurring topics chosen for front-page treatment, or the number of quotes from male and female experts.

3 INTERPRETATION. In the interpretation stage, we try to determine the meanings of the patterns we have analyzed. The most difficult stage in criticism, interpretation demands an answer to the "So what?" question. For instance, the greater visual space granted to *60 Minutes*

reporters—compared with the close-up shots used for interview subjects—might mean that the reporters appear to be in control. They are given more visual space in which to operate, whereas interview subjects have little room to maneuver within the visual frame. As a result, the subjects often look guilty and the reporters look heroic—or, at least, in charge. Likewise, if we look again at the *New York Times*, its attention to particular countries could mean that the paper tends to cover nations in which the United States has more vital political or economic interests,

Santa Barbara and *Dynasty*. For some, these shows were a relief from sober Soviet political propaganda, but others worried that Poles might inherit another kind of indoctrination—one starring American consumer culture and dominated by large international media companies.

This example illustrates that contemporary culture cannot easily be characterized as one thing or another. Binary terms such as *liberal* and *conservative* or *high* and *low* have less meaning in an environment where so many boundaries have been blurred, so many media forms have converged, and so many diverse cultures coexist. Modern distinctions between print and electronic culture have begun to break down largely because of the increasing number of individuals who have come of age in what is both a print and an electronic culture.[21] Either/or models of culture, such as the high–low approach, are giving way to more inclusive ideas, like the map model for culture discussed earlier.

Developing a media-literate critical perspective involves mastering five overlapping stages that build on one another:

- **_Description:_** paying close attention, taking notes, and researching the subject under study
- **_Analysis:_** discovering and focusing on significant patterns that emerge from the description stage
- **_Interpretation:_** asking and answering "What does that mean?" and "So what?" questions about one's findings
- **_Evaluation:_** arriving at a judgment about whether something is good, bad, or mediocre, which involves subordinating one's personal taste to the critical "bigger picture" resulting from the first three stages
- **_Engagement:_** taking some action that connects our critical perspective with our role as citizens to question our media institutions, adding our own voice to the process of shaping the cultural environment

Let's look at each of these stages in greater detail.

even though the *Times* might claim to be neutral and evenhanded in its reporting of news from around the world.

4 EVALUATION. The fourth stage of the critical process focuses on making an informed judgment. Building on description, analysis, and interpretation, we are better able to evaluate the fairness of a group of *60 Minutes* or *New York Times* reports. At this stage, we can grasp the strengths and weaknesses of the news media under study and make critical judgments measured against our own frames of reference—what we like and dislike, as well as what seems good or bad or missing, in the stories and coverage we analyzed.

This fourth stage differentiates the reviewer (or previewer) from the critic. Most newspaper reviews, for example, are limited by daily time or space constraints. Although these reviews may give us key information about particular programs, they often begin and end with personal judgments—"This is a quality show" or "That was a piece of trash"—that should be saved for the final stage in the critical process. Regrettably, many reviews do not reflect such a process; they do not move much beyond the writer's own frame of reference or personal taste.

5 ENGAGEMENT. To be fully media literate, we must actively work to create a media world that helps serve democracy. So we propose a fifth stage in the critical process—engagement. In our *60 Minutes* and *New York Times* examples, engagement might involve something as simple as writing a formal letter or an e-mail to these media outlets to offer a critical take on the news narratives we are studying.

But engagement can also mean participating in Web discussions, contacting various media producers or governmental bodies like the Federal Communications Commission (FCC) with critiques and ideas, organizing or participating in public media literacy forums, or learning to construct different types of media narratives ourselves—whether print, audio, video, or online—to participate directly in the creation of mainstream or alternative media. Producing actual work for media outlets might involve writing news stories for a local newspaper (and its Web site), producing a radio program on a controversial or significant community issue, or constructing a Web site that critiques various news media. The key to this stage is to challenge our civic imaginations, to refuse to sit back and cynically complain about the media without taking some action that lends our own voices and critiques to the process.

What are the social implications of the new, blended, and merging cultural phenomena? How do we deal with the fact that public debate and news about everyday life now seem as likely to come from *Facebook, Twitter,* Jon Stewart, Stephen Colbert, or bloggers as from the *Wall Street Journal*, the *NBC Nightly News*, or *Time* magazine?[22] Clearly, such changes challenge us to reassess and rebuild the standards by which we judge our culture. The search for answers lies in recognizing the links between cultural expression and daily life. The search also involves monitoring how well the mass media serve democracy, not just by providing us with consumer culture but by encouraging us to help improve political, social, and economic practices. A healthy democracy requires the active involvement of everyone. Part of this involvement means watching over the role and impact of the mass media, a job that belongs to every one of us—not just the paid media critics and watchdog organizations. ▶

CHAPTER REVIEW

COMMON THREADS

In telling the story of mass media, several plotlines and major themes recur and help provide the "big picture"—the larger context for understanding the links between forms of mass media and popular culture. Under each thread that follows, we pose a set of questions that we will investigate together to help you explore media and culture:

- **Developmental stages of mass media.** How did the media evolve, from their origins in ancient oral traditions to their incarnation on the Internet today? What discoveries, inventions, and social circumstances drove the development of different media? What roles do new technologies play in changing contemporary media and culture?

- **The commercial nature of mass media.** What role do media ownership and government regulation play in the presentation of commercial media products and serious journalism? How do the desire for profit and other business demands affect and change the media landscape? What role should government oversight play? What role do we play as ordinary viewers, readers, students, critics, and citizens?

- **The converged nature of media.** How has convergence changed the experience of media from the print to the digital era? What are the significant differences between reading a printed newspaper and reading the news online? What changes have to be made in the media business to help older forms of media, like newspapers, transition to an online world?

- **The role that media play in a democracy.** How are policy decisions and government actions affected by the news media and other mass media? How do individuals find room in the media terrain to express alternative (nonmainstream) points of view? How do grassroots movements create media to influence and express political ideas?

- **Mass media, cultural expression, and storytelling.** What are the advantages and pitfalls of the media's appetite for telling and selling stories? As we reach the point where almost all media exist on the Internet in some form, how have our culture and our daily lives been affected?

- **Critical analysis of the mass media.** How can we use the critical process to understand, critique, and influence the media? How important is it to be media literate in today's world? At the end of each chapter, we will examine the historical contexts and current processes that shape media products. By becoming more critical consumers and more engaged citizens, we will be in a better position to influence the relationships among mass media, democratic participation, and the complex cultural landscape that we all inhabit.

KEY TERMS

The definitions for the terms listed below can be found in the glossary at the end of the book. The page numbers listed with the terms indicate where the term is highlighted in the chapter.

communication, 6
culture, 6
mass media, 6
mass communication, 6
digital communication, 8
senders, 9
messages, 9
mass media channel, 9
receivers, 9

gatekeepers, 9
feedback, 9
selective exposure, 10
convergence, 11
cross platform, 12
narrative, 14
high culture, 17
low culture, 17
modern period, 26

Progressive Era, 27
postmodern period, 27
media literacy, 30
critical process, 30
description, 32
analysis, 32
interpretation, 32
evaluation, 33
engagement, 33

For review quizzes, chapter summaries, links to media-related Web sites, and more, go to macmillanhighered.com/mediaculture10e.

REVIEW QUESTIONS

Culture and the Evolution of Mass Communication

1. Define *culture, mass communication,* and *mass media,* and explain their interrelationships.

2. What key technological breakthroughs accompanied the transition to the print and electronic eras? Why were these changes significant?

3. Explain the linear model of mass communication and its limitations.

The Development of Media and Their Role in Our Society

4. Describe the development of a mass medium from emergence to convergence.

5. In looking at the history of popular culture, explain why newer and emerging forms of media seem to threaten status quo values.

Surveying the Cultural Landscape

6. Describe the skyscraper model of culture. What are its strengths and limitations?

7. Describe the map model of culture. What are its strengths and limitations?

8. What are the chief differences between modern and postmodern values?

Critiquing Media and Culture

9. What are the five steps in the critical process? Which of these is the most difficult, and why?

10. What is the difference between cynicism and criticism?

11. Why is the critical process important?

QUESTIONING THE MEDIA

1. Drawing on your experience, list the kinds of media stories you like and dislike. You might think mostly of movies and TV shows, but remember that news, sports, political ads, and product ads are also usually structured as stories. Conversations on Facebook can also be considered narratives. What kinds of stories do you like and dislike on Facebook, and why?

2. Cite some examples in which the media have been accused of unfairness. Draw on comments from parents, teachers, religious leaders, friends, news media, and so on. Discuss whether these criticisms have been justified.

3. Pick an example of a popular media product that you think is harmful to children. How would you make your concerns known? Should the product be removed from circulation? Why or why not? If you think the product should be banned, how would you do so?

4. Make a critical case either defending or condemning Comedy Central's *South Park,* a TV or radio talk show, a hip-hop group, a soap opera, or TV news coverage of the ongoing wars in the Middle East. Use the five-step critical process to develop your position.

5. Although in some ways postmodern forms of communication, such as e-mail, MTV, smartphones, and Twitter, have helped citizens participate in global life, in what ways might these forms harm more traditional or native cultures?

LAUNCHPAD FOR *MEDIA & CULTURE*

Visit LaunchPad for *Media & Culture at* macmillanhighered.com/mediaculture10e *for additional learning tools:*

- REVIEW WITH LEARNINGCURVE
  LearningCurve, available on LaunchPad for *Media & Culture,* uses gamelike quizzing to help you master the concepts you need to learn from this chapter.

- VIDEO: *THE MEDIA AND DEMOCRACY*
  This video traces the history of the media's role in democracy, from newspapers and television to the Internet.

PART 1
Digital Media and Convergence

Think about the main media technologies in your life when you were growing up. How did you watch TV shows, listen to music, or read books? How did you communicate with friends?

Now consider this: Apple began selling music through iTunes in 2003; Facebook was born in 2004, but was only opened to the full public in 2006; smartphones debuted in 2007; Hulu and Netflix launched their streaming video services in 2008; the iPad was introduced in 2010; and Apple's Siri first spoke in 2011. In less than fifteen years, we have moved from a world in which each type of media was consumed separately and in its own distinct format to a world in which we can experience every form of mass media content—books, music, newspapers, television, video games—on almost any Internet-connected device.

As you can see on the infographic on the opposite page, media didn't always develop this quickly; an early medium like radio could take decades to fully emerge, while today a Web site or an app can reach similar audience thresholds in a matter of years or even days. With these changes, the history of mass media has moved from *emergence* to *convergence*. While electronic media have been around for a long time, it was the development of the Web and the emergence of the Internet as a mass medium in the early 1990s that allowed an array of media—text, photos, audio, video, and interactive games—to converge in one space and be easily shared. This convergence has been happening since the early 1990s, but more recently we have experienced the **digital turn**. Ever-growing download speeds and the development of more portable devices have fundamentally changed the ways in which we access and consume media.

The digital turn has made us more fragmented—but also more connected. We might not be able to count on our friends all watching the same television show, but Facebook and Twitter have made it easier for us to connect with friends—and strangers—and tell them what we watched, read, and listened to. Mass media are more integrated into our lives than ever before.

FROM MEDIUM TO MASS MEDIA

TIME IT TOOK TO REACH 50 MILLION USERS

RADIO

TV

INTERNET

FACEBOOK

DRAW SOMETHING APP

38 YEARS

13 YEARS

4 YEARS

3.5 YEARS

50 DAYS

HOW TIME IS SPENT ON SMARTPHONES

6% SOCIAL NETWORKING

8% ENTERTAINMENT

18% WEB BROWSER

2% PRODUCTIVITY

32% GAMES

2% NEWS

18% FACEBOOK

8% UTILITY

6% OTHER

MEDIA CONSUMPTION: 7 HOURS OF 24 HOURS TOTAL

7 HOURS A DAY

MOBILE **1.8**

TV **1.5**

COMPUTER **1.6**

OTHER **2.1**

2

The Internet, Digital Media, and Media Convergence

41
The Development of the Internet and the Web

47
The Web Goes Social

53
Convergence and Mobile Media

57
The Economics and Issues of the Internet

68
The Internet and Democracy

The cassette tape. The VHS video. The mass market paperback book. The digital turn in mass media has consigned all these objects to the dustbin (or thrift shop) of media history. Our digital culture and economy are in the process of outmoding yet another familiar object: the wallet. Traditionally, a wallet would hold a person's money, credit cards, and perhaps photos of loved ones. Now, all these things can be accomplished with what has become the one essential device to take with you out of the home: a smartphone.

Photos have already shifted to smartphones (why carry a few photos of family, friends, and pets when you can have several hundred with you?), and soon credit cards and money will be right there on the same device. Several companies even make smartphone cases with a compartment for carrying ID cards, credit cards, and a few bills of old-fashioned cash—essentially an interim stop on the way to full digitalization.

This shift of mobile phones into money exchange devices is already underway, with a number of digital start-ups offering innovative devices and apps. Retailers can turn a mobile phone or tablet into a point of sale (that is, a digital cash register) with Square, a small, square credit card reader that plugs into a mobile device's headphone jack. Square was released in 2010 by digital entrepreneur Jack Dorsey, cofounder of Twitter. Square also has the Square Wallet, an app that turns a smartphone into a credit card for payments at places like Starbucks.

Of course, there is a cost to digital transactions. Credit cards typically charge merchants about 2 to 4 percent in various fees on each traditional credit card sale. (Visa and MasterCard control over 77 percent of the global market share of credit card purchases.)[1] Square charges merchants 2.75 percent per swipe for transactions with major credit cards, although the retailers get the Square device and software for free. PayPal (owned by eBay since 2002), AT&T, Verizon Wireless, Google, Amazon, Apple, and start-ups like Braintree and Stripe either have already launched their mobile payment systems or plan to, but these payment systems all charge the same kinds of transaction fees.[2]

The biggest goal in digital transactions is enabling people to use their mobile phones to exchange money without involving the credit card companies and their high fees. One start-up doing this is Dwolla, which provides an app that allows users to exchange money for just $.25 per transaction, or for free for transactions less than $10. "Money is basically data. We should be able to exchange it without paying huge fees. When I saw the opportunity to replace this infrastructure with something newer, safer, better, faster, I thought, Why not?" says Ben Milne, the founder and CEO of the Iowa-based Dwolla.[3] Milne's motivation for creating Dwolla was that his e-commerce business in Iowa was paying $55,000 a year in credit card fees. Dwolla claims that its system of payment is more secure than credit and debit card payment, as it requires only a user name and ID. Because no other information is exchanged, there is less information at risk. Other digital companies are following with similar apps and networks, including Square Cash (released by Square in 2013), Venmo (now owned by PayPal), and Popmoney. With recent security breaches of credit card or account information at retail chains like Target, Staples, and Home Depot, the need for more secure digital transactions may also give mobile-device payments a boost.

Of course, cash is still the most secure medium for information security—it contains no personal information at all. But wallets can only hold so much, and with a smartphone already in your pocket, it is becoming easier to just leave the cash and credit cards at home—just another way that mobile devices bring Internet tech into your pockets.

▲ **THE INTERNET,** the vast network of telephone and cable lines, wireless connections, and satellite systems designed to link and carry digital information worldwide, was initially described as an *information superhighway*. This description implied that the goal of the Internet was to build a new media network, a new superhighway, to replace traditional media (e.g., books, newspapers, television, and radio), the old highway system. In many ways, the original description of the Internet has turned out to be true. The Internet has expanded dramatically from its initial establishment in the 1960s to an enormous media powerhouse that encompasses—but has not replaced—all other media today.

In this chapter, we examine the many dimensions of the Internet, digital media, and convergence. We will:

- Review the birth of the Internet and the development of the Web
- Provide an overview of the key features of the Internet, including instant messaging, search engines, and social media
- Discuss the convergence of the Internet with mobile media, such as smartphones and tablets, and how the Internet has changed our relationship with media
- Examine the economics of the Internet, including the control of Internet content, ownership issues, and the five leading Internet companies
- Investigate the critical issues of the Internet, such as targeted advertising, free speech, security, net neutrality, and access

As you read through this chapter, think back to your first experiences with the Internet. What was your first encounter like? What were some of the things you remember using the Internet for then? How did it compare with your first encounters with other mass media? How has the Internet changed since your first experiences with it? For more questions to help you think through the role of the Internet in our lives, see "Questioning the Media" in the Chapter Review.

Courtesy Google, Inc.

YOUTUBE is the most popular Web site for watching videos online. Full of amateur and home videos, the site now partners with mainstream television and movie companies to provide professional content as well (a change that occurred after Google bought the site in 2006).

The Development of the Internet and the Web

From its humble origins as a military communications network in the 1960s, the **Internet** became increasingly interactive by the 1990s, allowing immediate two-way communication and one-to-many communication. By 2000, the Internet was a multimedia source for both information and entertainment as it quickly became an integral part of our daily lives. For example, in 2000, about 50 percent of American adults were connected to the Internet; by 2014, about 87 percent of American adults used the Internet.[4]

The Birth of the Internet

The Internet originated as a military-government project, with computer time-sharing as one of its goals. In the 1960s, computers were relatively new, and there were only a few of the expensive, room-sized mainframe computers across the country for researchers to use. The

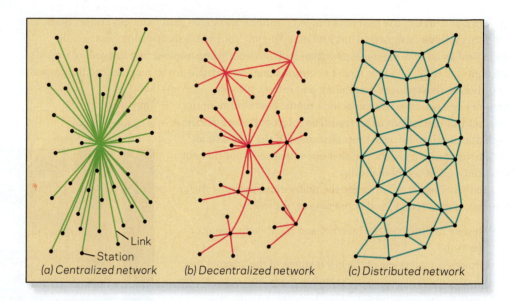

FIGURE 2.1

DISTRIBUTED NETWORKS

In a centralized network (*a*), all the paths lead to a single nerve center. Decentralized networks (*b*) contain several main nerve centers. In a distributed network (*c*), which resembles a net, there are no nerve centers; if any connection is severed, information can be immediately rerouted and delivered to its destination. But is there a downside to distributed networks when it comes to the circulation of network viruses?

Data from: Katie Hafner and Matthew Lyon, Where Wizards Stay Up Late (New York: Simon & Schuster, 1996).

(a) Centralized network   (b) Decentralized network   (c) Distributed network

Link
Station

Defense Department's Advanced Research Projects Agency (ARPA) developed a solution to enable researchers to share computer processing time starting in the late 1960s. This original Internet—called ARPAnet and nicknamed the Net—enabled military and academic researchers to communicate on a distributed network system (see Figure 2.1). First, ARPA created a wired network system in which users from multiple locations could log into a computer whenever they needed it. Second, to prevent logjams in data communication, the network used a system called *packet switching*, which broke down messages into smaller pieces to more easily route them through the multiple paths on the network before reassembling them on the other end.

▼ **The Internet, Digital Media, and Media Convergence**

Digital Technology
In the late 1940s, images, texts, and sounds are first converted into "binary code"—ones and zeros—vastly improving the rate at which information is stored and reproduced (pp. 45–46).

Microprocessors
These miniature computer circuits, developed in 1971, enable personal computers to be born. PCs become increasingly smaller, cheaper, and more powerful (p. 43).

NSF Network
In 1982, the National Science Foundation bankrolls a high-speed communications network, connecting computers across the country (p. 44).

| 1940 | 1950 | 1960 | 1970 | 1980 |

ARPAnet
The U.S. Defense Department begins research in the late 1960s on a distributed communication network—the groundwork for the Internet (p. 42).

E-mail
The process by which electronic messages are sent from computer to computer on a network is first developed in the early 1970s, revolutionizing modes of communication (p. 43).

Ironically, one of the most hierarchically structured and centrally organized institutions in our culture—the national defense industry—created the Internet, possibly the least hierarchical and most decentralized social network ever conceived. Each computer hub in the Internet has similar status and power, so nobody can own the system outright, and nobody has the power to kick others off the network. There isn't even a master power switch, so authority figures cannot shut off the Internet—although as we will discuss later, some nations and corporations have attempted to restrict access for political or commercial benefit.

To enable military personnel and researchers involved in the development of ARPAnet to better communicate with one another from separate locations, an essential innovation during the development stage of the Internet was **e-mail**. It was invented in 1971 by computer engineer Ray Tomlinson, who developed software to send electronic mail messages to any computer on ARPAnet. He decided to use the @ symbol to signify the location of the computer user, thus establishing the "login name@host computer" convention for e-mail addresses.

At this point in the development stage, the Internet was primarily a tool for universities, government research labs, and corporations involved in computer software and other high-tech products to exchange e-mail and to post information. As the use of the Internet continued to proliferate, the entrepreneurial stage quickly came about.

The Net Widens

From the early 1970s until the late 1980s, a number of factors (both technological and historical) brought the Net to the entrepreneurial stage, in which it became a marketable medium. The first signal of the Net's marketability came in 1971 with the introduction of **microprocessors**, miniature circuits that process and store electronic signals. This innovation facilitated the integration of thousands of transistors and related circuitry into thin strands of silicon along which binary codes traveled. Using microprocessors, manufacturers were eventually able to introduce the first *personal computers (PCs)*, which were smaller, cheaper, and

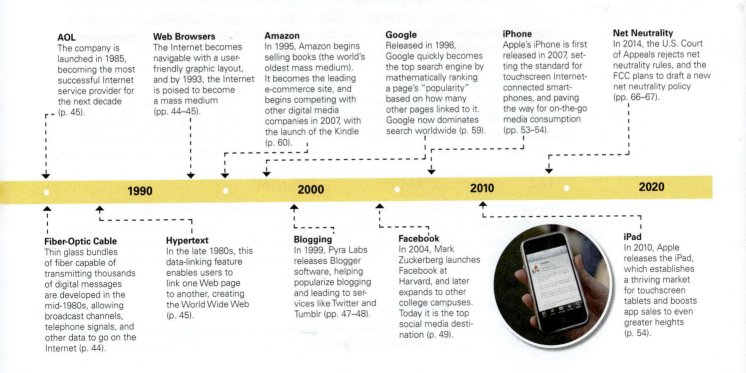

AOL
The company is launched in 1985, becoming the most successful Internet service provider for the next decade (p. 45).

Web Browsers
The Internet becomes navigable with a user-friendly graphic layout, and by 1993, the Internet is poised to become a mass medium (pp. 44–45).

Amazon
In 1995, Amazon begins selling books (the world's oldest mass medium). It becomes the leading e-commerce site, and begins competing with other digital media companies in 2007, with the launch of the Kindle (p. 60).

Google
Released in 1998, Google quickly becomes the top search engine by mathematically ranking a page's "popularity" based on how many other pages linked to it. Google now dominates search worldwide (p. 59).

iPhone
Apple's iPhone is first released in 2007, setting the standard for touchscreen Internet-connected smart-phones, and paving the way for on-the-go media consumption (pp. 53–54).

Net Neutrality
In 2014, the U.S. Court of Appeals rejects net neutrality rules, and the FCC plans to draft a new net neutrality policy (pp. 66–67).

1990   **2000**   **2010**   **2020**

Fiber-Optic Cable
Thin glass bundles of fiber capable of transmitting thousands of digital messages are developed in the mid-1980s, allowing broadcast channels, telephone signals, and other data to go on the Internet (p. 44).

Hypertext
In the late 1980s, this data-linking feature enables users to link one Web page to another, creating the World Wide Web (p. 45).

Blogging
In 1999, Pyra Labs releases Blogger software, helping popularize blogging and leading to services like Twitter and Tumblr (pp. 47–48).

Facebook
In 2004, Mark Zuckerberg launches Facebook at Harvard, and later expands to other college campuses. Today it is the top social media destination (p. 49).

iPad
In 2010, Apple releases the iPad, which establishes a thriving market for touchscreen tablets and boosts app sales to even greater heights (p. 54).

▶

COMMODORE 64
This advertisement for the
Commodore 64, one of the
first home PCs, touts the
features of the computer.
Although it was heralded in its
time, today's PCs far exceed
its abilities.

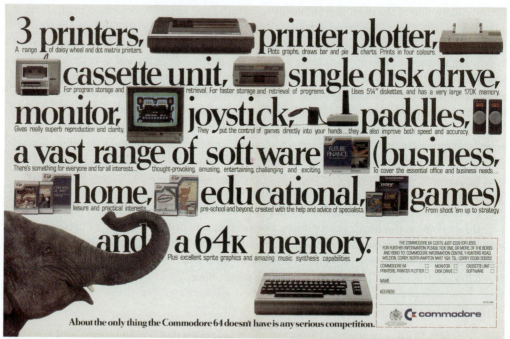

Image courtesy of the Advertising Archives

more powerful than the bulky computer systems of the 1960s. With personal computers now readily available, a second opportunity for marketing the Net came in 1986, when the National Science Foundation developed a high-speed communications network (NSFNET) designed to link university research computer centers around the country and also encourage private investment in the Net. This innovation led to a dramatic increase in Internet use and further opened the door to the widespread commercial possibilities of the Internet.

In the mid-1980s, **fiber-optic cable** became the standard for transmitting communication data speedily. Featuring thin glass bundles of fiber capable of transmitting thousands of messages simultaneously (via laser light), fiber-optic cables began replacing the older, bulkier copper wire used to transmit computer information. This development made the commercial use of computers even more viable than before. With this increased speed, few limits exist with regard to the amount of information that digital technology can transport.

With the dissolution of the Soviet Union in the late 1980s, the ARPAnet military venture officially ended. By that time, a growing community of researchers, computer programmers, amateur hackers, and commercial interests had already tapped into the Net, creating tens of thousands of points on the network and the initial audience for its emergence as a mass medium.

The Commercialization of the Internet

The introduction of the World Wide Web and the first Web browsers, Mosaic and Netscape, in the 1990s helped transform the Internet into a mass medium. Soon after these developments, the Internet quickly became commercialized, leading to battles between corporations vying to attract the most users, and others who wished to preserve the original public, nonprofit nature of the Net.

The World Begins to Browse

Prior to the 1990s, most of the Internet's traffic was for e-mail, file transfers, and remote access of computer databases. The **World Wide Web** (or the Web) changed all that. Developed in the late

1980s by software engineer Tim Berners-Lee at the CERN particle physics lab in Switzerland to help scientists better collaborate, the Web was initially a text data-linking system that allowed computer-accessed information to associate with, or link to, other information no matter where it was on the Internet. Known as *hypertext*, this data-linking feature of the Web was a breakthrough for those attempting to use the Internet. **HTML (hypertext markup language),** the written code that creates Web pages and links, is a language that all computers can read, so computers with different operating systems, such as Windows or Macintosh, can communicate easily. The Web and HTML allow information to be organized in an easy-to-use nonlinear manner, making way for the next step in using the Internet.

The release of Web **browsers**—the software packages that help users navigate the Web—brought the Web to mass audiences. In 1993, computer programmers led by Marc Andreessen at the National Center for Supercomputing Applications (NCSA) at the University of Illinois in Urbana-Champaign released Mosaic, the first window-based browser to load text and graphics together in a magazine-like layout, with attractive fonts and easy-to-use back, forward, home, and bookmark buttons at the top. In 1994, Andreessen joined investors in California's Silicon Valley to introduce a commercial browser, Netscape. As *USA Today* wrote that year, this "new way to travel the Internet, the World Wide Web," was "the latest rage among Net aficionados."[5] The Web soon became everyone else's rage, too, as universities and businesses, and later home users, got connected.

As the Web became the most popular part of the Internet, many thought that the key to commercial success on the Net would be through a Web browser. In 1995, Microsoft released its own Web browser, Internet Explorer, and within a few years, Internet Explorer—strategically bundled with Microsoft operating system software—overtook Netscape as the most popular Web browser. Today, Chrome and Firefox are the top browsers, with Internet Explorer, Safari, and Opera as the leading alternatives.

Users Link in through Telephone and Cable Wires

In the first decades of the Internet, most people connected to "cyberspace" through telephone wires. AOL (formerly America Online) began connecting millions of home users in 1985 to its proprietary Web system through dial-up access, and quickly became the United States' top **Internet service provider (ISP)**. AOL's success was so great that by 2001, the Internet start-up bought the world's largest media company, Time Warner—a deal that shocked the industry and signaled the Internet's economic significance as a vehicle for media content. As **broadband** connections, which can quickly download multimedia content, became more available (about 70 percent of all American households had such connections by 2014), users moved away from the slower telephone dial-up ISP service (AOL's main service) to high-speed service from cable, telephone, or satellite companies.[6] By 2007, both AT&T (offering DSL and cable broadband) and Comcast (cable broadband) surpassed AOL in numbers of customers. Today, other major ISPs include Verizon, Time Warner Cable, Cox, and Charter. These are accompanied by hundreds of local services, many offered by regional telephone and cable companies that compete to provide consumers with access to the Internet. Yet in the United States, there is little competition in the broadband Internet market. Only 9 percent of Americans have access to three or more ISPs. As a result, according to a 2013 study, American consumers "pay more money for lower speeds" compared to Internet customers in countries like Korea, Japan, Canada, Mexico, and most of Europe.[7]

People Embrace Digital Communication

In **digital communication**, an image, a text, or a sound is converted into electronic signals represented as a series of binary numbers—ones and zeros—which are then reassembled as

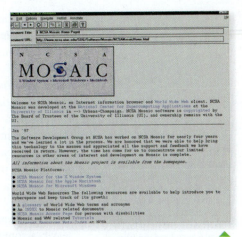

WEB BROWSERS
The GUI (graphical user interface) of the World Wide Web changed overnight with the release of Mosaic in 1993. As the first popular Web browser, Mosaic unleashed the multimedia potential of the Internet. Mosaic was the inspiration for the commercial browser Netscape, which was released in 1994.

Courtesy of the National Center for Supercomputing Applications and the Board of Trustees of the University of Illinois.

a precise reproduction of an image, a text, or a sound. Digital signals operate as pieces, or bits (from *BI*nary digi*TS*), of information representing two values, such as yes/no, on/off, or 0/1. For example, a typical compact disc track uses a binary code system in which zeros are microscopic pits in the surface of the disc and ones are represented on the unpitted surface. Used in various combinations, these digital codes can duplicate, store, and play back the most complex kinds of media content.

In the early days of e-mail, the news media constantly marveled at the immediacy of this new form of communication. Describing a man from Long Island e-mailing a colleague on the Galapagos Islands, the *New York Times* wrote in 1994 that his "magical new mailbox is inside his personal computer at his home, and his correspondence with the Galapagos now travels at the speed of electricity over the global computer network known as the Internet."[8]

E-mail was one of the earliest services of the Internet, and people typically used the e-mail services connected to their ISPs before major Web corporations such as Google, Yahoo!, and Microsoft (Hotmail) began to offer free Web-based e-mail accounts to draw users to their sites; each now has millions of users. Today, all the top e-mail services also include advertisements in their users' e-mail messages, one of the costs of the "free" e-mail accounts. Google's Gmail goes one step further by scanning messages to dynamically match a relevant ad to the text each time an e-mail message is opened. Such targeted advertising has become a hallmark feature of the Internet.

Instant messaging, or IM, remains the easiest way to communicate over the Internet in real time and has become increasingly popular as a smartphone and tablet app, with free IM services supplanting costly text messages. Major IM services—many with voice and video chat capabilities—include Google Chat (through its e-mail service), Facebook Chat, Microsoft's Skype, AOL Instant Messenger (AIM), Yahoo!'s Messenger, and Apple's iChat. IM users fill out detailed profiles when signing up for the service, providing advertisers with multiple ways to target them as they chat with their friends. IM has evolved and expanded with the Internet, embracing multimedia capabilities with apps like Snapchat, a photo messaging service that thrives on the cultural popularity of sending "selfies" and captions to friends. The images erase themselves in one to ten seconds, depending on the user's settings. In 2014 (after reportedly offering $3 billion to buy Snapchat in a failed deal the year before), Facebook paid $19 billion for WhatsApp, a cross-platform IM service with more than 480 million users worldwide.

Search Engines Organize the Web

As the number of Web sites on the Internet quickly expanded, companies seized the opportunity to provide ways to navigate this vast amount of information by providing directories and search engines. One of the more popular search engines, Yahoo!, began as a directory. In 1994, Stanford University graduate students Jerry Yang and David Filo created a Web page—"Jerry and David's Guide to the World Wide Web"—to organize their favorite Web sites, first into categories, then into more and more subcategories as the Web grew. At that point, the entire World Wide Web was almost manageable, with only about twenty-two thousand Web sites. (By 2014,

SNAPCHAT allows users to send one another photos, videos, and/or text that will disappear after a certain amount of time. Like a lot of popular apps, the program gained a large following from a young audience and expanded out from there. Hundreds of millions of photos are sent through the application every day.

Courtesy of Snapchat

Google announced it had indexed more than sixty trillion Web pages, up from one billion in 2000.) The guide made a lot of sense to other people, and soon enough Yang and Filo renamed it the more memorable Yahoo!

Eventually, though, having employees catalog individual Web sites became impractical. **Search engines** offer a more automated route to finding content by allowing users to enter key words or queries to locate related Web pages. Search engines are built on mathematic algorithms. Google, released in 1998, became a major success because it introduced a new algorithm that mathematically ranked a page's "popularity" on the basis of how many other pages linked to it. Google later moved to maintain its search dominance with its Google Voice Search and Google Goggles apps, which allow smartphone users to conduct searches by voicing search terms or by taking a photo. By 2014, Google's global market share accounted for nearly 70 percent of searches, while China's Baidu claimed 16.8 percent, Yahoo! reached 6.5 percent, and Microsoft's Bing claimed about 6 percent.[9]

The Web Goes Social

Aided by faster microprocessors, high-speed broadband networks, and a proliferation of digital content, the Internet has become more than just an information source in its third decade as a mass medium. The third generation of the Internet is a much more robust and social environment, having moved toward being a fully interactive medium with user-created content like blogs, Tumblrs, YouTube videos, Flickr photostreams, Photobucket albums, social networking, and other collaborative sites. In the words of law professor and media scholar Lawrence Lessig, we have moved from a "Read/Only" culture on the Internet, in which users can only read content, to a "Read/Write" culture, in which users have the power not only to read content but also to develop their own.[10] It's the users who ultimately rule here, sharing the words, sounds, images, and creatively edited music remixes and mash-up videos that make these Web communities worth visiting.

Social media are new digital media platforms that engage users to create content, add comments, and interact with others. Social media have become a new distribution system for media as well, challenging the one-to-many model of traditional mass media with the many-to-many model of social media.

Types of Social Media

In less than a decade, a number of different types of social media have evolved, with multiple platforms for the creation of user-generated content. European researchers Andreas M. Kaplan and Michael Haenlein identify six categories of social media on the Internet: blogs, collaborative projects, content communities, social networking sites, virtual game worlds, and virtual social worlds.[11]

Blogs

Years before there were status updates or Facebook, **blogs** enabled people to easily post their ideas to a Web site. Popularized with the release of Blogger (now owned by Google) in 1999, blogs contain articles or posts in chronological, journal-like form, often with reader

LaunchPad ⓒ

macmillanhighered.com /mediaculture10e

The Net (1995)
Sandra Bullock communicates using her computer in this clip from the 1995 thriller.
Discussion: How does this 1995 movie portray online communication? What does it get right, and what seems silly now?

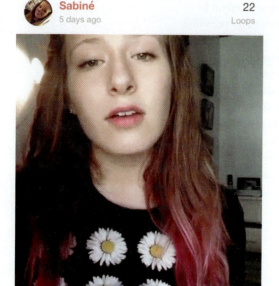

Sabiné
5 days ago

22
Loops

|Everybody~ Ingrid Michelson|

Liv likes this

😊   💬   ⬆   •••

Courtesy of Vine

VINE, a short video-sharing service, launched in 2012 and was acquired by Twitter later that year. The most popular Vine stars have millions of followers, and some of them can make a living through product placements in their six-second videos.

comments and links to other sites. Blogs can be personal or corporate multimedia sites, sometimes with photos, graphics, podcasts, and video. Some blogs have developed into popular news and culture sites, such as the *Huffington Post*, *TechCrunch*, *Mashable*, *Gawker*, *HotAir*, *ThinkProgress*, and *TPM Muckraker*.

Blogs have become part of the information and opinion culture of the Web, giving regular people and citizen reporters a forum for their ideas and views, and providing a place for even professional journalists to informally share ideas before a more formal news story gets published. Some of the leading platforms for blogging include Blogger, WordPress, Tumblr, Weebly, and Wix. But by 2013, the most popular form of blogging was microblogging, with about 241 million active users on Twitter, sending out 500 million tweets (a short message with a 140-character limit) per day.[12] In 2013, Twitter introduced an app called Vine that enabled users to post short video clips. A few months later, Facebook's Instagram responded with its own video-sharing service.

Collaborative Projects

Another Internet development involves collaborative projects in which users build something together, often using *wiki* (which means "quick" in Hawaiian) technology. **Wiki Web sites** enable anyone to edit and contribute to them. There are several large wikis, such as Wikitravel (a global travel guide), Wikimapia (combining Google Maps with wiki comments), and WikiLeaks (an organization publishing sensitive documents leaked by anonymous whistleblowers). WikiLeaks gained notoriety for its release of thousands of United States diplomatic cables and other sensitive documents beginning in 2010 (see page 506 in Chapter 14). But the most notable wiki is Wikipedia, an online encyclopedia launched in 2001 that is constantly updated and revised by interested volunteers. All previous page versions of Wikipedia are stored, allowing users to see how each individual topic develops. The English version of Wikipedia is the largest, containing over four million articles, but Wikipedias are also being developed in 287 other languages.

Businesses and other organizations have developed social media platforms for specific collaborative projects. Tools like Basecamp and Podio provide social media interfaces for organizing project and event-planning schedules, messages, to-do lists, and workflows. Kickstarter is a popular fund-raising tool for creative projects like books, recordings, and films. InnoCentive is a crowd-sourcing community that offers award payments for people who can solve business and scientific problems. And Change.org has become an effective petition project to push for social change. For example, in 2013 Lucien Tessier of Maryland began a campaign to petition the Boy Scouts of America (BSA) to drop its ban against openly gay scouts. After nearly 130,000 people signed the Change.org petition, and after additional lobbying by others, the BSA dropped its ban on gay scouts under the age of eighteen.[13]

Content Communities

Content communities are the best examples of the many-to-many ethic of social media. **Content communities** exist for the sharing of all types of content, from text (FanFiction.net) to photos (Flickr, Photobucket) and videos (YouTube, Vimeo). YouTube, created in 2005 and bought by Google in 2006, is the most well-known content community, with hundreds of millions of users around the world uploading and watching amateur and professional videos. YouTube gave rise to the viral video—a video that becomes immediately popular by millions sharing it through social media platforms. The most popular video of all time—Psy's 2012 music video "Gangnam Style"—has more than 2.2 billion views. In 2014, YouTube reported that one hundred hours of video are uploaded to the site every minute, and it has more than one billion unique users each month.

Social Networking Sites

Perhaps the most visible examples of social media are **social networking sites** like Facebook, LiveJournal, Pinterest, Orkut, LinkedIn, and Google+. On these sites, users can create content, share ideas, and interact with friends and colleagues.

Courtesy of kickstarter.com

KICKSTARTER has funded 59,000 creative projects since its launch in 2009. According to Kickstarter's data, 5.9 million people have pledged a total of $1 billion for the projects. Some notable successes from 2013 include the Oculus Rift (9,522 backers pledging $2.4 million), a virtual reality gaming headset bought in 2014 by Facebook for $2 billion; a human-powered helicopter (479 backers pledging $34,424); student-built classrooms made from shipping containers (242 backers pledging $16,567); and the movie *Blue Ruin* (438 backers pledging $37,828), which won an award at the Cannes Film Festival.

Facebook is the most popular social media site on the Internet. Started at Harvard in 2004 as an online substitute to the printed facebooks the school created for incoming first-year students, Facebook was instantly a hit and soon eclipsed MySpace as the leading social media destination. The site enables users to construct personal profiles, upload photos, share music lists, play games, and post messages to connect with old friends and meet new ones. Originally, access was restricted to college students, but in 2006 the site expanded to include anyone. Soon after, Facebook grew at an astonishing rate, and by 2014 it had 1.3 billion active users and was available in more than seventy languages.

In 2011, Google introduced Google+, a social networking interface designed to compete with Facebook. Google+ enables users to develop distinct "circles," by dragging and dropping friends into separate groups, rather than having one long list of friends. In response, Facebook created new settings to enable users to control who sees their posts.

Virtual Game Worlds and Virtual Social Worlds

Virtual game worlds and virtual social worlds invite users to role-play in rich 3-D environments, in real time, with players throughout the world. In virtual game worlds (also known as massively multiplayer online role-playing games, or MMORPGs) such as *World of Warcraft* and *Elder Scrolls Online*, players can customize their online identity, or avatar, and work with others through the game's challenges. Community forums for members extend discussion and shared play outside of the game. Virtual social worlds, like *Second Life*, enable players to take their avatars through simulated environments and even make transactions with virtual money. (See Chapter 3 for a closer look at virtual game worlds and virtual social worlds.)

Social Media and Democracy

In just a decade, social media have changed the way we consume and relate to media and the way we communicate with others. Social media tools have put unprecedented power in our hands to produce and distribute our own media. We can share our thoughts and opinions, write or update an encyclopedic entry, start a petition or fund-raising campaign, post a video, and create and explore virtual worlds. But social media have also proven to be an effective tool for democracy and for undermining repressive regimes that thrive on serving up propaganda and hiding their atrocities from view.

The wave of protests in more than a dozen Arab nations in North Africa and the Middle East that began in late 2010 resulted in four rulers being forced from power by mid-2012. The Arab Spring began in Tunisia, with a twenty-six-year-old street vendor named Mohamed

The "Anonymous" Hackers of the Internet

Anonymous, the loosely organized hacktivist collective that would become known for its politically and socially motivated Internet vigilantism, first attracted major public attention in 2008.

If you haven't seen Anonymous, you have probably seen the chosen "face" of Anonymous—a Guy Fawkes mask, portraying the most renowned member of the 1605 anarchist plot to assassinate King James I of England. The mask has been a part of Guy Fawkes Day commemorations in England for centuries but was made even more popular by the 2006 film *V for Vendetta*, based on the graphic novel series of the same name. Today, the mask has become a widespread international symbol for groups protesting financial institutions and politicians, from the Occupy Wall Street movement to Arab Spring to Anonymous.

The issue was a video featuring a fervent Tom Cruise—meant for internal promotional use within the Church of Scientology—that had been leaked to the Web site *Gawker*. When the church tried to suppress the video footage on grounds of copyright, Anonymous went to work. They launched a DDoS, or Distributed Denial of Service, attack (flooding a server or network with external requests so that it becomes overloaded and slows down or crashes) on the church's Web sites, bombarded the church headquarters with prank phone calls and faxes, and "doxed" the church by publishing sensitive internal documents.

United by their libertarian distrust of government, their commitment to a free and open Internet, their opposition to child pornography, and their distaste for corporate conglomerates, Anonymous has targeted organizations as diverse as

the Indian government (to protest the country's plan to block Web sites like The Pirate Bay and Vimeo) and the agricultural conglomerate Monsanto (to protest the company's malicious patent lawsuits and the company's dominant control of the food industry). As Anonymous wrote in a message to Monsanto:

> You have continually introduced harmful, even deadly products into our food supply without warning, without care, all for your own profit. . . . Rest assured, we will continue to dox your employees and executives, continue to knock down your Web sites, continue to fry your mail servers, continue to be in your systems.[1]

While Anonymous agrees on an agenda and coordinates the campaign, the individual hackers all act independently of the group, without expecting recognition. A reporter from the *Baltimore Sun* aptly characterized Anonymous as "a group, in the sense that a flock of birds is a group. How do you know they're a group? Because they're traveling in the same direction. At any given moment, more birds could join, leave, peel off in another direction entirely."[2]

In some cases, it's easy to find moral high ground in the activities of hacktivists. For example, Anonymous reportedly hacked the computer network of Tunisian tyrant Zine el-Abidine Ben Ali; his downfall in 2011 was the first victory of the Arab Spring movement. And in *The Girl with the Dragon Tattoo* book and film series, it is hard not to cheer on the master hacker character Lisbeth Salander as she exacts justice

Vivek Prakash/Reuters/Landov

on rapists and other criminals. In a world of large, impersonal governments and organizations, hackers level the playing field for the ordinary people, responding quickly in ways much more powerful than traditional forms of protest, like writing a letter or publicly demonstrating in front of headquarters or embassies. In fact, hacktivism could be seen as an update on the long tradition of peaceful protest.

Yet hackers can run afoul of ethics. Because the members of Anonymous are indeed anonymous, there aren't any checks or balances on those who dox a corporate site, revealing thousands of credit card or Social Security numbers and making regular citizens vulnerable to identity theft and fraud, as some hackers have done.

The work of Anonymous also raises questions about how we as a society weigh the ethics of the hacktivists when their illegal work may expose the truth and bring people to justice. One of the most controversial cases is of Anonymous hacker Deric Lostutter, a twenty-six-year-old programmer from Lexington, Kentucky. Lostutter (not unlike the fictional Lisbeth Salander) helped expose the cover-up of a rape of a sixteen-year-old girl in Steubenville, Ohio, by two high school football players in 2012. Lostutter posted a video taken by the rapists and their friends that showed that the girl was

Thomas Ondrey/The Plain Dealer/Landov

unconscious during the sexual violence. For some, Lostutter was a hero, shedding light on a cover-up that ultimately led to indictments against the school superintendent, coaches, and others. But for others, Lostutter was a criminal. His house was raided by the FBI, and by 2013, he was facing more than ten years in jail for his hacking work. *Rolling Stone* magazine pointed out the cruel irony: "Now he's facing more jail time than the convicted rapists." (One rapist received a minimum sentence of one year; the other got two years.)[3]

The very existence of Anonymous is a sign that many of our battles are now in the digital domain. We fight for equal access and free speech on the Internet. We are in a perpetual struggle with corporations and other institutions over the privacy of our digital information. And, although our government prosecutes hackers for computer crimes, governments themselves are increasingly using hacking to fight each other. Yet this new kind of warfare carries risks for the United States as well. As the *New York Times* noted, "No country's infrastructure is more dependent on computer systems, and thus more vulnerable to attack, than that of the United States."[4]

Bouazizi, who had his vegetable cart confiscated by police. Humiliated when he tried to get it back, he set himself on fire. While there had been protests before in Tunisia, the stories were never communicated widely. This time, protesters posted videos on Facebook, and satellite news networks spread the story with reports based on those videos. The protests spread across Tunisia, and in January 2011, Tunisia's dictator of nearly twenty-four years fled the country.

In Egypt, a similar circumstance occurred when twenty-eight-year-old Khaled Said was pulled from a café and beaten to death by police. Said's fate might have made no impact but for the fact that his brother used his mobile phone to snap a photo of Said's disfigured face and released it to the Internet. The success of protesters in Tunisia spurred Egyptians to organize their own protests, using the beating of Said as a rallying point. During the pro-democracy gatherings at Tahrir Square in Cairo, protesters used social media like Facebook, Twitter, and YouTube to stay in touch. Global news organizations tracked the protesters' feeds to stay abreast of what was happening, especially because the state news media ignored the protests and carried pro-Mubarak propaganda. Even though Egyptian leader Hosni Mubarak tried to shut down the Internet in Egypt, word of the protests spread quickly, and he was out eighteen days after the demonstrations started. In 2013, more protests aided by social media led to the ouster of Mohamed Morsi, Mubarak's democratically elected successor. In Yemen and Libya, other dictators were ousted. And although Syria's repressive government was still in power in 2014 after years of protests and fighting, citizens continued to use social media to provide evidence of the government's killing thousands of civilians.

Even in the United States, social media have helped call attention to issues that might not have received any media attention otherwise. In 2011 and 2012, protesters in the Occupy Wall Street movement in New York and at hundreds of sites across the country took to Twitter, Tumblr, YouTube, and Facebook to point out the inequalities of the economy and the income disparity between the wealthiest 1 percent and the rest of the population—the 99 percent. The physical occupations didn't last, but the movement changed the discourse in the United States about economic inequality.[14]

NEW PROTEST LANGUAGE
It has become more and more commonplace to see protest signs with information about Facebook groups, Twitter hashtags, URLs, and other social media references.

The flexible and decentralized nature of the Internet and social media is in large part what makes them such powerful tools for subverting control. In China, the Communist Party has tightly controlled mass communication for decades. As more and more Chinese citizens take to the Internet, an estimated thirty thousand government censors monitor or even block Web pages, blogs, chat rooms, and e-mails. Social media sites like Twitter, YouTube, Flickr, WordPress, and Blogger have frequently been blocked, and Google moved its Chinese search engine (Google.cn) to Hong Kong after the Chinese government repeatedly censored it. And for those who persist in practicing "subversive" free speech, there can be severe penalties: Paris-based Reporters without Borders reports that thirty Chinese journalists and seventy-four netizens were in prison in 2014 for writing articles and blogs that criticized the government.[15] Still, Chinese dissenters bravely play cat-and-mouse with Chinese censors, using free services like Hushmail, Freegate, and Ultrasurf (the latter two produced by Chinese immigrants in the United States) to break through the Chinese government's blockade. (For more on using the Internet for political and social statements, see "Examining Ethics: The 'Anonymous' Hackers of the Internet" on pages 50–51.)

Khaled Desouki/AFP/Getty Images

Convergence and Mobile Media

The innovation of digital communication—central to the development of the first computers in the 1940s—enables all media content to be created in the same basic way, which makes *media convergence*, the technological merging of content in different mass media, possible.

In recent years, the Internet has really become the hub for convergence, a place where music, television shows, radio stations, newspapers, magazines, books, games, and movies are created, distributed, and presented. Although convergence initially happened on desktop computers, the popularity of notebook computers and then the introduction of smartphones and tablets have hastened the pace of media convergence and made the idea of accessing any media content, anywhere, a reality.

Media Converges on Our PCs and TVs

First there was the telephone, invented in the 1870s. Then came radio in the 1920s, TV in the 1950s, and eventually the personal computer in the 1970s. Each device had its own unique and distinct function. Aside from a few exceptions, like the clock radio (a hybrid device popular since the 1950s), that was how electronic devices worked.

The rise of the personal computer industry in the mid-1970s first opened the possibility for unprecedented technological convergence. A *New York Times* article on the new "home computers" in 1978 noted that "the long-predicted convergence of such consumer electronic products as television sets, videotape recorders, video games, stereo sound systems and the coming video-disk machines into a computer-based home information-entertainment center is getting closer."[16] However, PC-based convergence didn't really materialize until a few decades later, when broadband Internet connections improved the multimedia capabilities of computers.

By the early 2000s, computers connected to the Internet allowed an array of digital media to converge in one space and be easily shared. A user can now access television shows, movies, music, books, games, newspapers, magazines, and lots of other Web content on a computer. And with Skype, iChat, and other live voice and video software, PCs can replace landline telephones. Other devices, like iPods, quickly capitalized on the Internet's ability to distribute such content and were adapted to play and exhibit multiple media content forms.

Media are also converging on our television sets, as the electronics industry manufactures Internet-ready TVs. Video game consoles like the Xbox, Wii, and PS4, and set-top devices like Apple TV, Google Chromecast, Roku, and Amazon Fire TV, offer additional entertainment content access via their Internet connections. In the early years of the Web, people would choose only one gateway to the Internet and media content, usually a computer or a television. Today however, wireless networks and the recent technological developments in various media devices mean that consumers regularly use more than one avenue to access all types of media content.

Mobile Devices Propel Convergence

Mobile telephones have been around for decades (like the giant "brick" mobile phones of the 1970s and 1980s), but the smartphones of the twenty-first century are substantially different creatures. Introduced in 2002, the BlackBerry was the first popular Internet-capable smartphone in the United States. Users' ability to check their e-mail messages at any time created addictive e-mail behavior and earned the phones their "Crackberry" nickname. Convergence on mobile phones took another big leap in 2007 with Apple's introduction of the iPhone, which combined qualities of its iPod digital music player and telephone and Internet service, all accessed through a sleek touchscreen. The next year, Apple opened its App Store, featuring free and low-cost software applications for the iPhone (and the iPod Touch and, later, the iPad) created by third-party developers, vastly increasing the utility of the iPhone. By 2014, there were about 1.2 million apps available to do thousands of things on Apple devices—from playing interactive games to finding locations with a GPS or using the iPhone like a carpenter's level.

In 2008, the first smartphone to run on Google's competing Android platform was released. By 2014, Android phones (sold by companies such as Samsung, HTC, LG, and Motorola, and supported by the Google Play app market and the Amazon Appstore) held 52.1 percent of the smartphone market share in the United States, while Apple's iPhone had a 41.3 percent share; Microsoft and BlackBerry smartphones constituted the remainder of the market.[17] The precipitous drop of the BlackBerry's market standing in just ten years (the company was late to add touchscreens and apps to its phones) illustrates the tumultuous competition in mobile devices. It also illustrates how apps and the ability to consume all types of media content on the go have surpassed voice call quality to become the most important feature to consumers purchasing a phone today.

In 2010, Apple introduced the iPad, a tablet computer suitable for reading magazines, newspapers, and books; watching video; and using visual applications. The tablets became Apple's fastest-growing product line, selling at a rate of twenty-five million a year. Apple added cameras, faster graphics, and a thinner design to subsequent generations of the iPad, as companies like Samsung (Galaxy), Amazon (Kindle Fire), Microsoft (Surface), and Google (Nexus) rolled out competing tablets.

The Impact of Media Convergence and Mobile Media

Convergence of media content and technology has forever changed our relationship with media. Today, media consumption is mobile and flexible; we don't have to miss out on media content just because we weren't home in time to catch a show, didn't find the book at the bookstore, or forgot to buy the newspaper yesterday. Increasingly, we demand access to media when we want it, where we want it, and in multiple formats. In order to satisfy those demands and to stay relevant in such a converged world, traditional media companies have had to dramatically change their approach to media content and their business models.

John MacDougall/AFP/Getty Images

SMARTWATCHES have been a part of pulp- and science-fiction tales since the thirties, and real-life versions were developed in the seventies and eighties before electronics companies shifted their attention to laptops and cell phones. By 2014, many top digital conglomerates had begun developing, and in some cases manufacturing, new smartwatches; Samsung and Sony released their own models; and Apple announced the Apple watch, to debut in early 2015.

Our Changing Relationship with the Media

The merging of all media onto one device, such as a tablet or smartphone, blurs the distinctions of what used to be separate media. For example, *USA Today* (a newspaper) and CBS News (network television news) used to deliver the news in completely different formats, but today their Web forms look quite similar, with listings of headlines, rankings of the most popular stories, local weather forecasts, photo galleries, and video. With the Amazon Kindle, on which one can read books, newspapers, and magazines, new forms like the Kindle Single challenge old categories. Are the fictional Kindle Singles novellas, or are they more like the stories found in literary magazines? And what about the investigative reports released as Kindle Singles? Should they be considered long-form journalism, or are they closer to nonfiction books? Is listening to an hour-long archived episode of public radio's *This American Life* on an iPod more like experiencing a radio program or an audio book? (It turns out you can listen to that show on the radio, as a downloadable podcast, as a Web stream, on mobile apps, or purchased on a USB drive or on a CD.)

Not only are the formats morphing, but we can now also experience the media in more than one manner, simultaneously. Fans of television shows like *The Voice, Glee,* and *Top Chef,* or viewers of live events like NFL football, often multitask, reading live blogs during broadcasts or sharing their own commentary with friends on Facebook and Twitter. For those who miss the initial broadcasts, converged media offer a second life for media content through deep archive access and repurposed content on other platforms. For example, cable shows like *Game of Thrones* and *Mad Men* have found audiences beyond their initial broadcasts through their DVD collections and online video services like Amazon Instant Video and Apple's iTunes. In fact, some fans even prefer to watch these more complex shows this way, enjoying the ability to rewind an episode in order to catch a missed detail, as well as the ability to binge-watch several episodes back-to-back. Similarly, *Arrested Development,* critically acclaimed but canceled by Fox in 2006, garnered new fans through the streaming episodes on Hulu and Netflix. As a result of this renewed interest, it was revived with new episodes produced for Netflix in 2013. Netflix also revived the canceled AMC series *The Killing* in 2014, with six new episodes for its fourth and final season.

AFP/Getty Images

Our Changing Relationship with the Internet

Mobile devices and social media have altered our relationship with the Internet. Two trends are noteworthy: (1) Apple now makes more than five times as much money selling iPhones, iPads, and iPods and accessories as it does selling computers, and (2) the number of Facebook users (1.23 billion in 2014) keeps increasing. The significance of these two trends is that through Apple devices and Facebook, we now inhabit a different kind of Internet—what some call a closed Internet, or a walled garden.[18]

In a world where the small screens of smartphones are becoming the preferred medium for linking to the Internet, we typically don't get the full, open Internet, one represented by the vast searches brought to us by Google. Instead we get a more managed Internet, brought to us by apps or platforms that carry out specific functions via the Internet. Are you looking for a nearby restaurant? Don't search on the Internet—use this app especially designed for that purpose. And the distributors of these apps act as gatekeepers. Apple has more than 1.2 million apps in its App Store, and Apple approves every one of them. The competing Android app stores on Google Play and Amazon have a similar number of apps (with many fewer apps in the Windows Store), but Google and Amazon exercise less control over approval of apps than Apple does.

Facebook offers a similar walled garden experience. Facebook began as a highly managed environment, only allowing those with .edu e-mail addresses. Although all are now invited to join Facebook, the interface and the user experience on the site are still highly managed by Facebook CEO Mark Zuckerberg and his staff. For example, if you click on a link to a news article that your friend has shared using a social reader app on Facebook, you will be prompted to add the same app—giving it permission to post your activity to your Wall—before you can access the article. In addition, Facebook has severely restricted what content can be accessed through the open Internet. Facebook has installed measures to stop search engines from indexing users' photos, Wall posts, videos, and other data. The effect of both Apple's devices and the Facebook interface is a clean, orderly, easy-to-use environment but one in which we are "tethered" to the Apple App Store or to Facebook.[19]

© Danny Moloshok/Reuters/Corbis

The open Internet—best represented by Google (but not its Google+ social networking service, which is more confining, like Facebook) and a Web browser—promised to put the entire World Wide Web at your fingertips. On the one hand, the appeal of the Internet *is* its openness, its free-for-all nature. But of course the trade-off is that the open Internet can be chaotic and unruly, and apps and other walled garden services have streamlined the cacophony of the Internet considerably.

The Changing Economics of Media and the Internet

The digital turn in the mass media has profoundly changed the economics of the Internet. Since the advent of Napster in 1999, which brought (illegal) file sharing to the music industry, each media industry has struggled to rethink how to distribute its content for the digital age. The content itself is still important—people still want quality news, television, movies, music, and games—but they want it in digital formats and for mobile devices.

Apple's response to Napster established the new media economics. The late Apple CEO Steve Jobs struck a deal with the music industry. Apple would provide a new market for music on the iTunes store, selling digital music customers could play on their iPods (and later on their iPhones and iPads). In return, Apple got a 30 percent cut of the revenue for all music sales on iTunes, simply for being the "pipes" that delivered the music. As music stores went out of business all across America, Apple sold billions of songs and hundreds of millions of iPods, all without requiring a large chain of retail stores.

Amazon started as a more traditional online retailer, taking orders online and delivering merchandise from its warehouses. As books took the turn into the digital era, Amazon created its own device, the Kindle, and followed Apple's model. Amazon started selling e-books, taking its cut for delivering the content. Along the way, Amazon and Apple (and Google through its Android apps) have become leading media companies. They don't make the content (although Amazon is now publishing books, too, and Amazon CEO Jeff Bezos purchased the *Washington Post* in 2013), but they are among the top digital distributors of books, newspapers, magazines, music, television, movies, and games.

THE SPIKE JONZE FILM
HER, set in the near future, explores the relationship between a human and an operating system. The voice-based operating system brings to mind Apple's Siri, which moves users toward a deeper, more personally relevant Web. Google Now and Microsoft Cortana are similar voice-activated personal digital assistants for mobile devices.

Warner Bros. Pictures/Everett Collection

The Next Era: The Semantic Web

Many Internet visionaries talk about the next generation of the Internet as the *Semantic Web*, a term that gained prominence after hypertext inventor Tim Berners-Lee and two coauthors published an influential article in a 2001 issue of *Scientific American*.[20] If "semantics" is the study of meanings, then the Semantic Web is about creating a more meaningful—or more organized—Web. To do that, the future promises a layered, connected database of information that software agents will sift through and process automatically for us. Whereas the search engines of today generate relevant Web pages for us to read, the software of the Semantic Web will make our lives even easier as it places the basic information of the Web into meaningful categories—family, friends, calendars, mutual interests, location—and makes significant connections for us. In the words of Tim Berners-Lee and his colleagues, "The Semantic Web is not a separate Web but an extension of the current one, in which information is given well-defined meaning, better enabling computers and people to work in cooperation."[21]

The best example of the Semantic Web is Apple's voice recognition assistant Siri, first shipped with its iPhone 4S in 2011. Siri uses conversational voice recognition to answer questions, find locations, and interact with various iPhone functionalities, such as the calendar, reminders, the weather app, the music player, the Web browser, and the maps function. Some of its searches get directed to Wolfram Alpha, a computational search engine that provides direct answers to questions, rather than the traditional list of links for search results. Other Siri searches draw on the databases of external services, such as Yelp for restaurant locations and reviews, and StubHub for ticket information. Another example of the Semantic Web is the Siemens refrigerator (available in Europe) that takes a photo of the interior every time the door closes. The owner may be away at the supermarket but can call up a photo of the interior to be reminded of what should be on the shopping list.[22]

The Economics and Issues of the Internet

One of the unique things about the Internet is that no one owns it. But that hasn't stopped some corporations from trying to control it. Since the **Telecommunications Act of 1996**, which overhauled the nation's communications regulations, most regional and long-distance phone companies and cable operators have competed against one another to provide connections to the Internet. However, there is more to controlling the Internet than being the service provider for it. Companies have realized the potential of dominating the Internet business through search engines, software, social networking, and providing access to content, all in order to sell the essential devices that display the content, or to amass users who become an audience for advertising.

Ownership and control of the Internet are connected to three Internet issues that command much public attention: the security of personal and private information, the appropriateness of online materials, and the accessibility and openness of the Internet. Important questions have been raised: Should personal or sensitive government information be private, or should the Internet be an enormous public record? Should the Internet be a completely open forum, or should certain types of communications be limited or prohibited? Should all people have equal access to the Internet, or should it be available only to those who can afford it? For each of these issues, there have been heated debates but no easy resolutions.

Ownership: Controlling the Internet

By the end of the 1990s, four companies— AOL, Yahoo!, Microsoft, and Google—had emerged as the leading forces on the Internet, each with a different business angle. AOL attempted to dominate the Internet as the top ISP, connecting millions of home users to its proprietary Web system through dial-up access. Yahoo!'s method has been to make itself an all-purpose entry point—or **portal**—to the Internet. Computer software behemoth Microsoft's approach began by integrating its Windows software with its Internet Explorer Web browser, drawing users to its MSN.com site and other Microsoft applications. Finally, Google made its play to seize the Internet with a more elegant, robust search engine to help users find Web sites.

Since the end of the 1990s, the Internet's digital turn toward convergence has changed the Internet and the fortunes of its original leading companies. While AOL's early success led to the huge AOL–Time Warner corporate merger of 2001, its technological shortcomings in broadband contributed to its devaluation and eventual spin-off from Time Warner in 2009. Yahoo! was eclipsed by Google in the search engine business but tried to regain momentum with its purchase of Tumblr in 2013.

In today's converged world, in which mobile access to digital content prevails, Microsoft and Google still remain powerful. Those two, along with Apple, Amazon, and Facebook, constitute the leading companies of digital media's rapidly changing world. Of the five, all but

ELSEWHERE IN
MEDIA & CULTURE

The **cathode-ray tube** was also instrumental in the invention of television

p. 190

25%

how much of a $60 video game goes to art and design

p. 103

WHO DECIDES WHAT INFORMATION IS LEGAL FOR CORPORATIONS TO USE?

p. 448

7.4 cents

amount of each dollar spent on textbooks that goes to college store operations

p. 351

How has the digital turn changed media distribution?

p. 187

THE TRANSITION FROM WIRED TO WIRELESS HAPPENED FIRST IN RADIO

p. 152

Facebook also operate proprietary cloud services and encourage their customers to store all their files in their "walled garden" for easy access across all devices. This ultimately builds brand loyalty and generates customer fees for file storage.[23]

Microsoft

Microsoft, the oldest of the dominant digital firms (established by Bill Gates and Paul Allen in 1975), is an enormously wealthy software company that struggled for years to develop an Internet strategy. Although its software business is in a gradual decline, its flourishing digital game business (Xbox) helped it to continue to innovate and find a different path to a future in digital media. The company finally found moderate success on the Internet with its search engine Bing. With the 2012 release of the Windows Phone 8 mobile operating system and the Surface tablet, Microsoft was prepared to offer a formidable challenge in the mobile media business. In 2014, Microsoft brought its venerable office software to mobile devices, with Office for iPad and Office Mobile for iPhones and Android phones, all of which work with OneDrive, Microsoft's cloud service.

Google

Google, established in 1998, had instant success with its algorithmic search engine and now controls about 70 percent of the search market, generating billions of dollars of revenue yearly through the pay-per-click advertisements that accompany key-word searches. Google has also branched out into a number of other Internet offerings, including shopping (Google Shopping), mapping (Google Maps), e-mail (Gmail), blogging (Blogger), browsing (Chrome), books (Google Books), video (YouTube), and television (Chromecast). Google has also challenged Microsoft's Office programs with Google Apps, a cloud-based bundle of word processing, spreadsheet, calendar, IM, and e-mail software. Google competes against Apple's iTunes with Google Play, an online media store, and challenges Facebook with the social networking tool Google+.

As the Internet goes wireless, Google has acquired other companies in its quest to replicate its online success in the wireless world. Beginning in 2005, Google bought the Android operating system (now the leading mobile phone platform, and also a tablet computer platform) and mobile phone ad placement company AdMob. Google continues to experiment with new devices, such as Google Glass, which layers virtual information over one's real view of the world through eyeglasses, and Android Wear, its new line of wearable technology (the first product is a smartwatch). Google's biggest challenge is the "closed Web": companies like Facebook and Apple that steer users to online experiences that are walled off from search engines and threaten Google's reign as the Internet's biggest advertising conglomerate.

Apple

Apple, Inc., was founded by Steve Jobs and Steve Wozniak in 1976 as a home computer company and is today the most valuable company in the world (by 2014, Google was the second most valuable company, ExxonMobil was third, and Microsoft was fourth).[24] Apple was only moderately successful until 2001, when Jobs, having been forced out of the company for a decade, returned. Apple introduced the iPod and iTunes in 2003, two innovations that led the company to become the No. 1 music retailer in the United States. Then in 2007, Jobs introduced the iPhone, transforming the mobile phone industry. With Apple's release of the intensely anticipated iPad in 2010, the company further redefined portable computing.

With the iPhone and iPad now at the core of Apple's business, the company expanded to include providing content—music, television shows, movies, games, newspapers, magazines—to sell its media devices. The next wave of Apple's innovations was the iCloud, a new storage and syncing service that enables users to access media content anywhere (with a wireless connection) on its mobile devices. The iCloud also helps ensure that customers purchase their media content through Apple's iTunes store, further tethering users to its media systems. (For more on Apple devices and how they are made, see "Global Village: Designed in California, Assembled in China" on page 61.)

AFTER YEARS IN THE RETAIL BUSINESS, Amazon has been experimenting with content creation, commissioning groups of series, making the pilots available on its Amazon Prime streaming service, and taking both viewer and critical feedback into account when deciding which pilot episodes to expand into series. *Betas*, a comedy about Web developers, was turned into a series in 2013 but was not renewed after its first eleven-episode season. Amazon is continuing to develop more shows, recruiting high-profile filmmakers like Woody Allen (*Blue Jasmine*) and David Gordon Green (*Pineapple Express*).

Amazon

Amazon started its business in 1995 in Seattle, selling the world's oldest mass medium (books) online. Since that time, Amazon has developed into the world's largest e-commerce store, selling not only books but also electronics, garden tools, clothing, appliances, and toys. To keep its lead in e-commerce, Amazon also acquired Zappos, the popular online shoe seller. Yet by 2007, with the introduction of its Kindle e-reader, Amazon was following Apple's model of using content to sell devices. The Kindle became the first widely successful e-reader, and by 2010, e-books were outselling hardcovers and paperbacks at Amazon. In 2011, in response to Apple's iPad, Amazon released its own color touchscreen tablet, the Kindle Fire, giving Amazon a device that can play all the media—including music, TV, movies, and games—it sells online and in its Appstore. Like Apple, Amazon has a Cloud Player for making media content portable and offers an additional 5 gigabytes of free Cloud Drive space to all users, to use however they like. Amazon is now also competing with television, cable networks, and Netflix by producing at least ten Amazon Originals television series for its streaming service.

Facebook

Facebook's immense, socially dynamic audience (about two-thirds of the U.S. population and over 1.28 billion total users across the globe) is its biggest resource, and Facebook, like Google, has become a data processor as much as a social media service, collecting every tidbit of information about its users—what we "like," where we live, what we read, and what we want—and selling this information to advertisers. Because Facebook users reveal so much about themselves in their profiles and the messages they share with others, Facebook can offer advertisers exceptionally tailored ads: A user who recently got engaged gets ads like "Impress Your Valentine," "Vacation in Hawaii," and "Are You Pregnant?" while a teenage girl sees ads for prom dresses, sweet-sixteen party venues, and "Chat with Other Teens" Web sites.

As a young company, Facebook has suffered growing pains while trying to balance its corporate interests (capitalizing on its millions of users) with its users' interest in controlling the privacy of their own information. In 2012, Facebook had the third-largest public offering in U.S. history, behind General Motors and Visa, with the company valued at $104 billion. Facebook's valuation is a reflection of investors' hopes of what the company can do with more than one billion users rather than evidence of the company's financial success so far. In recent years, Facebook has focused on moving its main interface from the computer screen to mobile phones. Its purchase of Instagram, the photo-sharing app, in 2012 for $1 billion was part of that strategy. Facebook's approach appears to be successful: "Americans spend about one-fifth of their time on mobile phones checking Facebook," the *New York Times* reported.[25] Facebook continues to make investments to expand beyond its core service, with purchases in 2014 of WhatsApp, an instant messaging service, and Oculus VR, a virtual reality technology company.

Targeted Advertising and Data Mining

In the early years of the Web, advertising took the form of traditional display ads placed on pages. The display ads were no more effective than newspaper or magazine advertisements, and because they reached small, general audiences, they weren't very profitable. But in the late 1990s, Web advertising began to shift to search engines. Paid links appeared as "sponsored links" at the top, bottom, and side of a search engine result list and even, depending on the search engine, within the "objective" result list itself. Every time a user clicks on a sponsored link, the advertiser pays the search engine for the click-through. For online shopping, having paid placement in searches can be a good thing. But search engines doubling as ad brokers may undermine the utility of search engines as neutral locators of Web sites (see "Media

Designed in California, Assembled in China

There is a now-famous story involving the release of the iPhone in 2007. The late Apple CEO Steve Jobs was carrying the prototype in his pocket about one month prior to its release and discovered that his keys, also in his pocket, were scratching the plastic screen. Known as a stickler for design perfection, Jobs reportedly gathered his fellow executives in a room and told them (angrily), "I want a glass screen, and I want it perfect in six weeks."[1] This demand would have implications for a factory complex in China, called Foxconn, where iPhones are assembled. When the order trickled down to a Foxconn foreman, he woke up eight thousand workers in the middle of the night, gave them a biscuit and a cup of tea, and then started them on twelve-hour shifts fitting glass screens into the iPhone frames. Within four days, Foxconn workers were churning out ten thousand iPhones daily.

On its sleek packaging, Apple proudly proclaims that its products are "Designed by Apple in California," a slogan that evokes beaches, sunshine, and Silicon Valley—where the best and brightest in American engineering ingenuity reside. The products also say, usually in a less visible location, "Assembled in China," which suggests little, except that the components of the iPhone, iPad, iPod, or Apple computer were put together in a factory in the world's most populous country.

It wasn't until 2012 that most Apple customers learned that China's Foxconn was the company where their devices are assembled. Investigative reports by the *New York Times* revealed a company with ongoing problems with labor conditions and worker safety, including fatal explosions and a spate of worker suicides.[2] (Foxconn responded in part by erecting nets around its buildings to prevent fatal jumps.)

Foxconn (also known as Hon Hai Precision Industry Co., Ltd., with headquarters in Taiwan) is China's largest and most prominent private employer, with 1.2 million employees—more than any American company except Walmart. Foxconn assembles an incredible 40 percent of the world's electronics and earns more revenue than ten of its competitors combined.[3] And Foxconn is not just Apple's favorite place to outsource production; nearly every global electronics company is connected to the manufacturing giant: Amazon (Kindle), Microsoft (Xbox), Sony (PlayStation), Dell, Hewlett-Packard, IBM, Motorola, and Toshiba all feed their products to the vast Foxconn factory network.

Behind this manufacturing might is a network of factories now legendary for its enormity. Foxconn's largest factory compound is in Shenzhen. Dubbed "Factory City," it employs roughly 300,000 people—all squeezed into one square mile, many of whom live in the dormitories (dorms sleep seven to a room) on the Foxconn campus.[4] Workers, many of whom come from rural areas in China, often start a shift at 4 A.M. and work until late at night, performing monotonous, routinized work—for example, filing the aluminum shavings from iPad casings six thousand times a day. Thousands of these

full-time workers are under the age of eighteen.

Conditions at Foxconn might, in some ways, be better than the conditions in the poverty-stricken small villages from which most of its workers come. But the low pay, long hours, dangerous work conditions, and suicide nets are likely *not* what the young workers had hoped for when they left their families behind.

In light of the news reports about the problems at Foxconn, Apple joined the Fair Labor Association (FLA), an international nonprofit that monitors labor conditions. The FLA inspected factories and surveyed more than thirty-five thousand Foxconn workers. Its 2012 study verified a range of serious issues. Workers regularly labored more than sixty hours per week, with some employees working more than seven days in a row. Other workers weren't compensated for overtime. More than 43 percent of the workers reported they had witnessed or experienced an accident, and 64 percent of the employees surveyed said that the compensation does not meet their basic needs. In addition, the FLA found the labor union at Foxconn an unsatisfactory channel for addressing worker concerns, as representatives from management dominated the union's membership.[5]

In 2014, Apple reported that its supplier responsibility program had resulted in improved labor conditions at supplier factories. But Apple might not have taken any steps had it not been for the *New York Times* investigative reports and the intense public scrutiny that followed. What is our role as consumers in ensuring that Apple and other companies are ethical and transparent in the treatment of the workers who make our electronic devices?

Victor Idrogo/El Comercio de Peru/Newscom

WHATSAPP

Facebook's acquisition of Instagram in 2012 aided the social networking site's future as a provider of mobile interfaces. Yet Facebook is preparing for the possibility that its social network's popularity may fade. In 2014, Facebook paid $19 billion for WhatsApp, a cross-platform instant messaging service with more than 480 million users worldwide. The price was steep, but Facebook wanted a stake in the global IM business to complement its social media business. Prior to WhatsApp's purchase by Facebook, the service's owners had vowed to keep advertising off its platform. Facebook said it would honor that pledge.

Literacy and the Critical Process: Tracking and Recording Your Every Move" on page 63).

Advertising has since spread to other parts of the Internet, including social networking sites, e-mail, and mobile apps. For advertisers—who for years struggled with how to measure people's attention to ads—these activities make advertising easy to track, effective in reaching the desired niche audience, and relatively inexpensive, because ads get wasted less often on the uninterested. For example, Yahoo! gleans information from search terms; Google scans the contents of Gmail messages; and Facebook uses profile information, status updates, and "likes" to deliver individualized, real-time ads to users' screens. Similarly, a mobile social networking application for smartphones, Foursquare, encourages users to earn points and "badges" by checking in at business locations, such as museums, restaurants, and airports (or other user-added locations), and to share that information via Twitter, Facebook, and text message. Other companies, like Poynt and Yelp, are also part of the location-based ad market. The rise in smartphone use has contributed to extraordinary growth in mobile advertising, which jumped from $3.4 billion in 2012 to $7.1 billion in 2013, accounting for 17 percent of the $42.8 billion in total Internet advertising that year.[26]

Gathering users' location and purchasing habits has been a boon for advertising, but these data-collecting systems also function as consumer surveillance and **data mining** operations. The practice of data mining also raises issues of Internet security and privacy. Millions of people, despite knowing that transmitting personal information online can make them vulnerable to online fraud, have embraced the ease of **e-commerce**: the buying and selling of products and services on the Internet, which took off in 1995 with the launch of Amazon. What many people don't know is that their personal information may be used without their knowledge for commercial purposes, such as targeted advertising. For example, in 2011, the Federal Trade Commission charged Facebook with a list of eight violations in which Facebook told consumers their information would be private but made it public to advertisers and third-party applications. Facebook CEO Mark Zuckerberg admitted the company had made "a bunch of mistakes" and settled with the FTC by fixing the problems and agreeing to submit to privacy audits for twenty years.[27]

One common method that commercial interests use to track the browsing habits of computer users is **cookies**, or information profiles that are automatically collected and transferred between computer servers whenever users access Web sites.[28] The legitimate purpose of a cookie is to verify that a user has been cleared for access to a particular Web site, such as a library database that is open only to university faculty and students. However, cookies can also be used to create marketing profiles of Web users to target them for advertising. Many Web sites require the user to accept cookies in order to gain access to the site.

Even more unethical and intrusive is **spyware**, information-gathering software that is often secretly bundled with free downloaded software. Spyware can be used to send pop-up ads to users' computer screens, to enable unauthorized parties to collect personal or account information of users, or even to plant a malicious click-fraud program on a computer, which generates phony clicks on Web ads that force an advertiser to pay for each click.

In 1998, the FTC developed fair information practice principles for online privacy to address the unauthorized collection of personal data. These principles require Web sites to (1) disclose their data-collection practices, (2) give consumers the option to choose whether their data may be collected and to provide information on how that data is collected, (3) permit individuals access to their records to ensure data accuracy, and (4) secure personal data from unauthorized use. Unfortunately, the FTC has no power to enforce these principles, and most Web sites either do not self-enforce them or deceptively appear to enforce them when they in fact don't.[29] As a

Media Literacy and the Critical Process

Imagine if you went into a department store and someone followed you the whole time, noting every place you stopped to look at something and recording every item you purchased. Then imagine that the same person followed you the same way on every return visit. It's likely that you would be outraged by such surveillance. Now imagine that the same thing happens when you search the Web—except in this case, it really happens.

1 DESCRIPTION. Do an audit of your Web browser's data collection—the cookie files deposited on your computer, and your recorded search histories. (For this critical process, use either Chrome or Firefox, the two most popular browsers.) On Google's Chrome browser, go to Chrome at the left of the top menu, and select Preferences, Settings, Advanced Settings (at the bottom of the Settings page), Privacy, Content Settings, and then All Cookies and Site Data. You can then click on each individual cookie file (some Web sites establish multiple cookies on your computer) to discover when the cookie was set and when it is scheduled to expire. Chrome also saves your search history forever: Go to History in the top menu, then Show Full History. On Firefox, go to Firefox, Preferences, Privacy, and Remove Individual Cookies. Here, you can again click on each cookie and find when the cookie is set to expire. To see your browsing history in Firefox, go to History in the top menu, then Show All History. For either browser, try to count how many cookies are on your computer and determine how far back in time your browser history is recorded. Finally, delete all cookies and search history, and then start fresh with the browser and spend just five minutes browsing five different Web sites.

2 ANALYSIS. From your five minutes of browsing five Web sites, look for patterns in the cookies. How many total were there? Which types of sites had multiple cookies? Sample ten to twenty cookies for a close-up look: What is the planned life span of cookies? (That is, when are they set to expire?) What kinds of companies are the cookies from?

3 INTERPRETATION. Why are our searches tracked with cookies and our search histories recorded? Is this done solely for the convenience of advertisers, marketers, and Google, which mine our search data for commercial purposes, or is there value to you in this? (Firefox is owned by a nonprofit, the Mozilla Foundation.)[1]

4 EVALUATION. Web sites don't tell you they are installing cookies on your computer. Cookies and search histories can be found and deleted, but do the browsers make this easy or difficult for you? Did you know this information was being collected? Should you have more say in the data being collected on your searches? Overall, should Web sites be more transparent and honest about what they do in placing cookies and their purpose? Should Web browsers be more transparent and honest about the cookies and histories they save and whether they are used for data mining?

5 ENGAGEMENT. What can you do to preserve your privacy? On a personal level, start by clearing out your cookies and search history after every session. On Firefox (under Privacy), you can check "Tell sites that I do not want to be tracked." On Chrome, you can select Clear Browsing Data in the main menu. Alternatively, Chrome offers "incognito mode" for browsing, with the following warning: "You've gone incognito. Pages you view in incognito tabs won't stick around in your browser's history, cookie store, or search history after you've closed *all* of your incognito tabs. Any files you download or bookmarks you create will be kept. *Going incognito doesn't hide your browsing from your employer, your internet service provider, or the websites you visit.*" For greater privacy, you can use the search engine DuckDuckGo (launched in 2008), which doesn't track your searches or put them in a "filter bubble" (that is, it doesn't filter search results based on what the search engine knows about your previous searches, which is what Google does). On a social level, you can file a complaint with the Federal Trade Commission. Go to www.ftccomplaintassistant.gov, but be aware that even the FTC may use cookies to process your complaint.

result, consumer and privacy advocates are calling for stronger regulations, such as requiring Web sites to adopt **opt-in** or **opt-out policies**. Opt-in policies, favored by consumer and privacy advocates, require Web sites to obtain explicit permission from consumers before the sites can collect browsing history data. Opt-out policies, favored by data-mining corporations, allow for the automatic collection of browsing history data unless the consumer requests to "opt out" of the practice. In 2012, the Federal Trade Commission approved a report recommending that Congress adopt "Do Not Track" legislation to limit tracking of user information on Web sites and mobile

THE UNGOOGLABLE MAN

Even the most powerful search engines CANNOT DETECT HIM!

No Facebook page... no MySpace page... no NOTHING!

And yet HE WALKS AMONGST US.

© Roz Chast/The New Yorker Collection/www.cartoonbank.com

THIS *NEW YORKER* CARTOON illustrates an increasingly rare phenomenon.

devices and enable users to easily opt out of data collection. Several Web browsers now offer "Do Not Track" options, while other Web tools, like Ghostery, detect Web tags, bugs, and other trackers, generating a list of all the sites following your moves.

Security: The Challenge to Keep Personal Information Private

When you watch television, listen to the radio, read a book, or go to the movies, you do not need to provide personal information to others. However, when you use the Internet, whether you are signing up for an e-mail account, shopping online, or even just surfing the Web, you give away personal information—voluntarily or not. As a result, government surveillance, online fraud, and unethical data-gathering methods have become common, making the Internet a potentially treacherous place.

Government Surveillance

Since the inception of the Internet, government agencies worldwide have obtained communication logs, Web browser histories, and the online records of individual users who thought their online activities were private. In the United States, for example, the USA PATRIOT Act (which became law about a month after the September 11 attacks in 2001 and was renewed in 2006) grants sweeping powers to law-enforcement agencies to intercept individuals' online communications, including e-mail messages and browsing records. The act was intended to allow the government to more easily uncover and track potential terrorists and terrorist organizations, but many now argue that it is too vaguely worded, allowing the government to unconstitutionally probe the personal records of citizens without probable cause and for reasons other than preventing terrorism. Moreover, searches of the Internet permit law-enforcement agencies to gather huge amounts of data, including the communications of people who are not the targets of an investigation. Documents leaked to the news media in 2013 by former CIA employee and former National Security Agency (NSA) contractor Edward Snowden revealed that the NSA has continued its domestic spying program, collecting bulk Internet and mobile phone data on millions of Americans for more than a decade.

Online Fraud

In addition to being an avenue for surveillance, the Internet is increasingly a conduit for online robbery and *identity theft*, the illegal obtaining of personal credit and identity information in order to fraudulently spend other people's money. Computer hackers have the ability to infiltrate Internet databases (from banks to hospitals to even the Pentagon) to obtain personal information and to steal credit card numbers from online retailers. Identity theft victimizes hundreds of thousands of people a year, and clearing one's name can take a very long time and cost a lot of money. According to the U.S. Department of Justice, about 7 percent of Americans were victims of identity theft in 2012, totaling about $24.7 billion in losses.[30] One particularly costly form of Internet identity theft is known as phishing. This scam involves phony e-mail messages that appear to be from official Web sites—such as eBay, PayPal, or the user's university or bank—asking customers to update their credit card numbers, account passwords, and other personal information.

Appropriateness: What Should Be Online?

The question of what constitutes appropriate content has been part of the story of most mass media, from debates over the morality of lurid pulp-fiction books in the nineteenth century to arguments over the appropriateness of racist, sexist, and homophobic content in films and music. Although it is not the only material to come under intense scrutiny, most of the debate about appropriate media content, despite the medium, has centered on sexually explicit imagery.

As has always been the case, eliminating some forms of sexual content from books, films, television, and other media remains a top priority for many politicians and public interest groups. So it should not be surprising that public objection to indecent and obscene Internet content has led to various legislative efforts to tame the Web. Although the Communications Decency Act of 1996 and the Child Online Protection Act of 1998 were both judged unconstitutional, the Children's Internet Protection Act of 2000 was passed and upheld in 2003. This act requires schools and libraries that receive federal funding for Internet access to use software that filters out any visual content deemed obscene, pornographic, or harmful to minors, unless disabled at the request of adult users. Regardless of new laws, pornography continues to flourish on commercial sites, individuals' blogs, and social networking pages. As the American Library Association notes, there is "no filtering technology that will block out all illegal content, but allow access to constitutionally protected materials."[31]

Although the "back alleys of sex" on the Internet have caused considerable public concern, Internet sites that carry potentially dangerous information (bomb-building instructions, hate speech) have also incited calls for Internet censorship, particularly after the terrorist attacks of September 11, 2001, and several tragic school shootings. Nevertheless, many people—fearing that government regulation of speech would inhibit freedom of expression in a democratic society—want the Web to be completely unregulated.

Access: The Fight to Prevent a Digital Divide

A key economic issue related to the Internet is whether the cost of purchasing a personal computer and paying for Internet services will undermine equal access. Coined to echo the term *economic divide* (the disparity of wealth between the rich and the poor), the term **digital divide** refers to the growing contrast between the "information haves," those who can afford to purchase computers and pay for Internet services, and the "information have-nots," those who may not be able to afford a computer or pay for Internet services.

Although about 87 percent of U.S. households are connected to the Internet, there are big gaps in access. For example, a 2014 study found that only 57 percent of Americans age sixty-five and up go online, compared with 88 percent of Americans ages fifty to sixty-four, 93 percent of Americans ages thirty to forty-nine, and 98 percent of Americans ages eighteen to twenty-nine. Education has an even more pronounced effect: Only 76 percent of people with a high school education or less have Internet access, compared with 91 percent of people with some college and 97 percent of college graduates.[32]

The rising use of smartphones is helping to narrow the digital divide, particularly along racial lines. In the United States, African American and Hispanic families have generally lagged behind whites in home access to the Internet, which requires a computer and broadband access. However, the Pew Internet & American Life Project reported that African Americans and Hispanics are active users of mobile Internet devices. The report concluded, "While blacks and Latinos are less likely to have access to home broadband than whites, their use of smartphones nearly eliminates that difference."[33]

Globally, though, the have-nots face an even greater obstacle to crossing the digital divide. Although the Web claims to be worldwide, the most economically powerful countries—the United States, Sweden, Japan, South Korea, Australia, the United Kingdom—account for most of its international flavor. In nations such as Jordan, Saudi Arabia, Syria, and Myanmar (Burma), the governments permit limited or no access to the Web. In other countries, an inadequate telecommunications infrastructure hampers access to the Internet. And in underdeveloped countries, phone lines and computers are almost nonexistent. For example, in

Brad Fleet/Newspix/Getty Images

Sierra Leone—a West African nation of about six million people, with poor public utilities and intermittent electrical service—less than a hundred thousand people, or about 1.7 percent of the population, are Internet users.[34] However, as mobile phones become more popular in the developing world, they can provide one remedy for the global digital divide.

Even as the Internet matures and becomes more accessible, wealthy users are still more able to buy higher levels of privacy and faster speeds of Internet access than are other users. Whereas traditional media made the same information available to everyone who owned a radio or a TV set, the Internet creates economic tiers and classes of service. Policy groups, media critics, and concerned citizens continue to debate the implications of the digital divide, valuing the equal opportunity to acquire knowledge.

Net Neutrality: Maintaining an Open Internet

For more than a decade, the debate over net neutrality has framed the shape of the Internet's future. **Net neutrality** refers to the principle that every Web site and every user—whether a multinational corporation or you—has the right to the same Internet network speed and access. The idea of an open and neutral network has existed since the origins of the Internet, but there had never been a formal policy until 2010, when the Federal Communications Commission approved a limited set of net neutrality rules. Still, the debate forges on.

The dispute over net neutrality and the future of the Internet is dominated by some of the biggest communications corporations. These major telephone and cable companies—including Verizon, Comcast, AT&T, Time Warner Cable, and Cox—control 98 percent of broadband access in the United States through DSL and cable modem service. They want to offer faster connections and priority to clients willing to pay higher rates, and provide preferential service for their own content or for content providers who make special deals with them—effectively eliminating net neutrality. For example, tiered Internet access might mean that these

companies would charge customers more for data-heavy services like Netflix, YouTube, Hulu, or iTunes. These companies argue that the profits they could make with tiered Internet access would allow them to build expensive new networks, benefiting everyone. In 2014, Netflix (which accounts for 30 percent of Internet traffic) decided to go this route and revealed that it paid Comcast (the nation's biggest cable company and cable modem provider) for a faster connection to its service to ensure better video streaming for its customers. Netflix's willingness to pay more to Comcast undercut content providers' collective backing of net neutrality.[35]

Supporters of net neutrality—mostly bloggers, video gamers, educators, religious groups, unions, and small businesses—argue that the cable and telephone giants actually have incentive to rig their services and cause net congestion in order to force customers to pay a premium for higher-speed connections. They claim that an Internet without net neutrality would hurt small businesses, nonprofits, and Internet innovators, who might be stuck in the "slow lane" and not be able to afford the fastest connections that large corporations can afford. Large Internet corporations like Google, Yahoo!, Amazon, eBay, Microsoft, Skype, and Facebook also support net neutrality because their businesses depend on their millions of customers having equal access to the Web.

In late 2010, the FCC adopted rules on net neutrality, noting that "the Internet's openness promotes innovation, investment, competition, free expression, and other national broadband goals."[36] But the FCC's rules were twice rejected by federal courts, most recently in 2014. Afterward, FCC chairman Tom Wheeler proposed that the FCC's new policy on the Internet would allow cable and telephone companies to charge tiered fees for slow and fast service. The *New York Times* argued that if the policy is approved, it would create "a two-speed Internet."[37] The proposal pleased the telecommunication companies, but critics noted that while big companies like Netflix, Amazon, and Google could pay up, smaller start-ups (which Netflix, Amazon, and Google once were) would never be able to pay for the Internet's "fast lane," thus undermining the Internet's spirit of equality and discouraging digital entrepreneurs.

Alternative Voices

Independent programmers continue to invent new ways to use the Internet and communicate over it. While some of their innovations have remained free of corporate control, others have been taken over by commercial interests. Despite commercial buyouts, however, the pioneering spirit of the Internet's independent early days endures; the Internet continues to be a participatory medium in which anyone can be involved. Two of the most prominent areas in which alternative voices continue to flourish relate to open-source software and digital archiving.

Open-Source Software

In the early days of computer code writing, amateur programmers were developing open-source software on the principle that it was a collective effort. Programmers openly shared program source codes and their ideas to upgrade and improve programs. Beginning in the 1970s, Microsoft put an end to much of this activity by transforming software development into a business in which programs were developed privately and users were required to pay for both the software and its periodic upgrades.

However, programmers are still developing noncommercial, open-source software, if on a more limited scale. One open-source operating system, Linux, was established in 1991 by Linus Torvalds, a twenty-one-year-old student at the University of Helsinki in Finland. Since the establishment of Linux, professional computer programmers and hobbyists around the world have participated in improving it, creating a sophisticated software system that even Microsoft has acknowledged is a credible alternative to expensive commercial programs. Linux can operate across disparate platforms, and companies such as IBM, Dell, and Oracle, as well as other corporations and governmental organizations, have developed applications and systems that run on it. Still, the greatest impact of Linux is evident not on the desktop screens of everyday computer users but in the operation of behind-the-scenes computer servers.

Digital Archiving

Librarians have worked tirelessly to build nonprofit digital archives that exist outside of any commercial system in order to preserve libraries' tradition of open access to information. One of the biggest and most impressive digital preservation initiatives is the Internet Archive, established in 1996. The Internet Archive aims to ensure that researchers, historians, scholars, and all citizens have universal access to human knowledge—that is, everything that's digital: text, moving images, audio, software, and more than 150 billion archived Web pages reaching back to the earliest days of the Internet. The archive is growing at staggering rates as the general public and partners such as the Smithsonian and the Library of Congress upload cultural artifacts. For example, the Internet Archive stores more than 134,000 live music concerts, including performances by Jack Johnson, the Grateful Dead, and the Smashing Pumpkins.

Media activist David Bollier has likened open-access initiatives to an information "commons," underscoring the idea that the public collectively owns (or should own) certain public resources, like airwaves, the Internet, and public spaces (such as parks). "Libraries are one of the few, if not the key, public institutions defending popular access and sharing of information as a right of all citizens, not just those who can afford access," Bollier says.[38]

The Internet and Democracy

Throughout the twentieth century, Americans closely examined emerging mass media for their potential contributions to democracy. As radio became more affordable in the 1920s and 1930s, we hailed the medium for its ability to reach and entertain even the poorest Americans caught in the Great Depression. When television developed in the 1950s and 1960s, it also held promise as a medium that could reach everyone, including those who were illiterate or cut off from printed information. Despite continuing concerns over the digital divide, many have praised the Internet for its democratic possibilities. Some advocates even tout the Internet as the most democratic social network ever conceived.

The biggest threat to the Internet's democratic potential may well be its increasing commercialization. As happened with radio and television, the growth of commercial "channels" on the Internet has far outpaced the emergence of viable nonprofit channels, as fewer and fewer corporations have gained more and more control. The passage of the 1996 Telecommunications Act cleared the way for cable TV systems, computer firms, and telephone companies to merge their interests and become even larger commercial powers. Although there was a great deal of buzz about lucrative Internet start-ups in the 1990s and 2000s, it has been large corporations—such as Microsoft, Apple, Amazon, Google, and Facebook—that have weathered the low points of the dot-com economy and maintained a controlling hand.

About three-quarters of households in the United States are now linked to the Internet, thus greatly increasing its democratic possibilities but also tempting commercial interests to gain even greater control over it and intensifying problems for agencies trying to regulate it. If the histories of other media are any predictor, it seems realistic to expect that the Internet's potential for widespread use by all could be partially preempted by narrower commercial interests. As media economist Douglas Gomery warns, "Technology alone does not a communication revolution make. Economics trumps technology every time."[39]

DIGITAL JOB OUTLOOK

Media Professionals Speak about Internet Jobs

Eric Bonzer, Web Designer, Spinutech

You'll want to learn HTML and know how to write it from scratch, not using Dreamweaver. And then the CSS—also learn how to write that from scratch. Certainly the Adobe Creative Suite is great, but for the most part it's really knowing how to write that stuff from scratch.

Gina Bianchini, CEO, Mightybell

If Zuckerberg, the Google guys, and Bill Gates are the pattern creators, Steve Jobs may be the best counterevidence to the creation myth. He didn't study computer science during his brief time at Reed College. He didn't need to be an ace at coding. Instead, he relentlessly and passionately focused on products. He marketed. He sold. He inspired. He challenged. He succeeded. He failed. He kept going. Then, he succeeded again. These are the true characteristics of a successful entrepreneur in the consumer Internet space. And there is nothing stopping women from performing just as well as men.

Visual Designer Ad for Uber, New York Office

You are . . .

- A utility player. You're willing to find resolutions to customer issues early, late, and often.

- Cool and calm under pressure. You have superior organizational skills, integrity, and great follow-through on tasks. You don't get overwhelmed easily . . . tons of design requests from the Community and Operations teams? No prob!

- Graceful. You are self-aware, well-spoken on the phone, and eloquent in e-mails.

- Fun. You're a charismatic people person who can talk to anyone; you're flexible, fearless, and excited to help build something awesome and share it with the world.

- Motivated. You're ready to hit the ground running; you are slightly obsessive-compulsive about grinding away at projects for the team.

Alexa Andrzejewski, Ux Designer and Founding CEO of Foodspotting

Share your idea with anyone who will listen. There is a temptation to keep it to yourself so no one will steal it. The truth is, finding someone with the time and money to do it better and faster than you is so rare, and the value of sharing your idea is so much more. I shared the idea when I first had it, and I felt validated and motivated to pursue it.

However, defenders of the digital age argue that inexpensive digital production and social media distribution allow greater participation than does any traditional medium. In response to these new media forms, older media are using Internet technology to increase their access to and feedback from varied audiences. Skeptics raise doubts about the participatory nature of discussions on the Internet. For instance, they warn that Internet users may be communicating with people whose beliefs and values are similar to their own—in other words, just their Facebook friends and Google+ circles. Although it is important to be able to communicate across vast distances with people who have similar viewpoints, these kinds of discussions may not serve to extend the diversity and tolerance that are central to democratic ideals. There is also the threat that we may not be interacting with anyone at all. In the wide world of the Web, we are in a shared environment of billions of people. In the emerging ecosystem of apps, we live in an efficient but gated community, walled off from the rest of the Internet. However, we are still in the early years of the Internet. The democratic possibilities of the Internet's future are endless. ▶

CHAPTER REVIEW

COMMON THREADS

One of the Common Threads discussed in Chapter 1 is the commercial nature of mass media. The Internet is no exception, as advertisers have capitalized on its ability to be customized. How might this affect other media industries?

People love the simplicity of Pinterest, the visual social media site where users "pin" images and videos to their "board," creating a customized site that reflects their own personal style on topics like home décor, apparel, food, crafts, or travel. To sign up for an account, users provide their name, e-mail address, and gender (male or female). The final choice is already prechecked by Pinterest and says, "Let Pinterest personalize your experience based on other sites you visit."

Pinterest is just one example of the mass customization the Internet offers—something no other mass medium has been able to provide. (When is the last time a television, radio, newspaper, or movie spoke directly to you, or let you be the content producer?) This is one of the Web's greatest strengths—it can connect us to the world in a personally meaningful way. But a casualty of the Internet may be our shared common culture. A generation ago, students and coworkers across the country gathered on Friday mornings to discuss what happened the previous night on NBC's

"must-see" TV shows, like *Cosby, Seinfeld, Friends,* and *Will & Grace.* Today it's more likely that they watched vastly different media the night before. And if they did view the same thing—say, a funny YouTube video—it's likely they all laughed alone, as they watched it individually, although they may have later shared it with their friends on a social media site.

We have become a society divided by the media, often split into our basic entity, the individual. One would think that advertisers dislike this, since it is easier to reach a mass audience by showing commercials during *The Voice.* But mass customization gives advertisers the kind of personal information they once only dreamed about: your e-mail address, hometown, zip code, and birthday, and a record of your interests—what Web pages you visit and what you buy online. If you have a Facebook profile or a Gmail account, they may know even more about you—what you did last night or what you are doing right now. What will advertisers have the best chance of selling to you with all this information? With the mass-customized Internet, you may have already told them.

KEY TERMS

The definitions for the terms listed below can be found in the glossary at the end of the book. The page numbers listed with the terms indicate where the term is highlighted in the chapter.

Internet, 41
ARPAnet, 42
e-mail, 43
microprocessors, 43
fiber-optic cable, 44
World Wide Web, 44
HTML (hypertext markup language), 45
browsers, 45
Internet service provider (ISP), 45
broadband, 45

digital communication, 45
instant messaging, 46
search engines, 47
social media, 47
blogs, 47
wiki Web sites, 48
content communities, 48
social networking sites, 49
Telecommunications
  Act of 1996, 57

portal, 57
data mining, 62
e-commerce, 62
cookies, 62
spyware, 62
opt-in *or* opt-out policies, 63
phishing, 64
digital divide, 65
net neutrality, 66
open-source software, 67

REVIEW QUESTIONS

The Development of the Internet and the Web

1. When did the Internet reach the novelty (development), entrepreneurial, and mass medium stages?

2. How did the Internet originate? What role did the government play?

3. How does the World Wide Web work? What is its significance in the development of the Internet?

4. Why did Google become such a force in Web searching?

The Web Goes Social

5. What is the difference between a "Read/Only" culture and a "Read/Write" culture on the Internet?

6. What are the six main types of social media?

7. What are the democratic possibilities of social media? How can social media aid political repression?

Convergence and Mobile Media

8. What conditions enabled media convergence?

9. What role do mobile devices play in media convergence, and what significant mobile milestones can you think of?

10. How has convergence changed our relationship with media and with the Internet?

11. What elements of today's digital world are part of the Semantic Web?

The Economics and Issues of the Internet

12. Which of the five major digital companies are most aligned with the "open Internet," and which are most aligned with the "closed Internet"?

13. What is the role of data mining in the digital economy? What are the ethical concerns?

14. What is the digital divide, and what is being done to close the gap?

15. Why is net neutrality such an important issue?

16. What are the major alternative voices on the Internet?

The Internet and Democracy

17. How can the Internet make democracy work better?

18. What are the key challenges to making the Internet itself more democratic?

QUESTIONING THE MEDIA

1. What possibilities for the Internet's future are you most excited about? Why? What possibilities are most troubling? Why?

2. What advantages of media convergence enable all types of media content to be accessed on a single device?

3. Google's corporate motto is "Don't be evil." Which of the five major digital corporations (Microsoft, Google, Apple, Amazon, and Facebook) seems to have the greatest tendency for evil? Which seems to do the most good? Why?

4. As we move from a print-oriented Industrial Age to a digitally based Information Age, how do you think individuals, communities, and nations have been affected positively? How have they been affected negatively?

LAUNCHPAD FOR MEDIA & CULTURE

Visit LaunchPad for *Media & Culture* at macmillanhighered.com/mediaculture10e for additional learning tools:

- REVIEW WITH LEARNINGCURVE
  LearningCurve, available on LaunchPad for *Media & Culture*, uses gamelike quizzing to help you master the concepts you need to learn from this chapter.

- VIDEO: USER-GENERATED CONTENT
  Editors, producers, and advertisers discuss the varieties of user-generated content and how they can contribute to the democratization of media.

Dan R. Krauss/Getty Images

3

Digital Gaming and the Media Playground

75
The Development
of Digital Gaming

81
The Internet
Transforms Gaming

84
The Media Playground

92
Trends and Issues
in Digital Gaming

99
The Business of
Digital Gaming

106
Digital Gaming,
Free Speech, and
Democracy

Because they have been inherently digital for much of their history, electronic games have not always felt the full force of the digital turn—at least compared to more traditional media. While the Internet turned much of the media world upside down and gave rise to powerful companies like Amazon, Apple, Facebook, Google, and Microsoft, the digital gaming industry was already well equipped to chart its own path. It's almost as if the Super Mario Bros. (created by Nintendo in 1985) just kept chugging along in their mission on a console monitor or Game Boy screen, oblivious to the changing media world around them.

But eventually digital games became more fully absorbed into the new digital conglomerates. Microsoft, the world's largest software company, entered the video game console business in 2001 with the Xbox. At the time, the *New York Times* called the Xbox "a Trojan horse of sorts, part of the company's ambitious effort to extend its reach from the personal computer to the television."[1] Today, that characterization remains true: Microsoft itself calls the console's latest version, the Xbox

One, an "all-in-one entertainment system" in which games, movies, music, sports, and live television are equal offerings. Apple, Google, Amazon, and Facebook have begun to notice digital games, too, especially those on mobile phone, tablet, and social media platforms, giving rise to tens of thousands of gaming apps. But often gaming has been a way to expand the business or add to the bottom line, rather than a central component of these companies' operations.

Which is why Facebook's purchase of a small virtual reality company in 2014 is—depending on one's viewpoint— either the craziest or the most brilliant move yet to integrate gaming into a digital corporation. Oculus VR invented the Oculus Rift, a virtual reality headset developed with funds from Kickstarter, and had only demonstrated experimental versions of the device. The company was headed by a twenty-one-year-old inventor named Palmer Luckey and had never made any money or sold consumer versions of Oculus Rift when Facebook bought Oculus for $2 billion. Responses to Facebook's purchase varied widely. A columnist for the *Wall Street Journal*'s *MarketWatch* said Facebook's decision was "bold" and "smart," while a *Forbes* magazine columnist wrote, "[Facebook founder and CEO] Mark Zuckerberg is nuts."[2]

Zuckerberg's purchase means that Facebook, like Microsoft, wants gaming to be part of its business. (Up until this point, Facebook's foray into games consisted of hosting social media games like *Words with Friends* and *FarmVille*.) But Zuckerberg's bigger bet is that virtual reality will be the next generation of gaming style and that virtual reality will then be the leading interface for everything else in the media business. On the announcement of the purchase, Zuckerberg described his vision:

> This is just the start. After games, we're going to make Oculus a platform for many other experiences. Imagine enjoying a court side seat at a game, studying in a classroom of students and teachers all over the world or consulting with a doctor face-to-face—just by putting on goggles in your home.

> This is really a new communication platform. By feeling truly present, you can share unbounded spaces and experiences with the people in your life. Imagine sharing not just moments with your friends online, but entire experiences and adventures.[3]

While Microsoft used digital games as a way to enter into our living rooms, Facebook envisions digital games as a way to enter into every part of our lives. After all, why would we want to "share" our experiences via two-dimensional posts on Facebook when we can be there— virtually—on the Facebook of the future?

Visit **LaunchPad** for
Media & Culture and
use **LearningCurve** to review
concepts from this chapter.

◀ **ELECTRONIC GAMES OFFER PLAY, ENTERTAINMENT, AND SOCIAL INTERACTION.**
Like the Internet, they combine text, audio, and moving images. But they go even further than
the Internet by enabling players to interact with aspects of the medium in the context of the
game—from deciding when an onscreen character jumps or punches to controlling the
direction of the "story." This interactive
quality creates an experience so compelling
that vibrant communities of fans have cropped
up around the globe. And the games have
powerfully shaped the everyday lives of
millions of people. Indeed, for players around
the world, digital gaming has become a social
medium as compelling and distracting as other
social media. The U.S. Supreme Court has even
granted digital gaming First Amendment
freedom of speech rights, ensuring its place as
a mass medium.

Getty Images

In this chapter, we will take a look at the
evolving mass medium of digital gaming and:

- Examine the early history of electronic
  gaming, including its roots in penny arcades
- Trace the evolution of electronic gaming,
  from arcades and bars into living rooms
  and our hands
- Discuss gaming as a social medium that
  forms communities of play
- Analyze the economics of gaming, including the industry's major players and various
  revenue streams
- Raise questions about the role of digital gaming in our democratic society

▲

**THE SUPER MARIO
BROTHERS**, Mario and
Luigi, have been video game
mainstays for over thirty
years. In addition to the
various Mario Brothers games
(including the influential
Nintendo original, released
in 1985), the characters have
appeared in cartoons, comic
books, a live-action movie, and
an enormous variety of sequel
and spin-off games, including
games centered on fighting,
racing, and puzzle-solving.

The Development of Digital Gaming

When the Industrial Revolution swept Western civilization two centuries ago, the technological
advances involved weren't simply about mass production. They also promoted mass consumption and the emergence of *leisure time*—both of which created moneymaking opportunities
for media makers. By the late nineteenth century, the availability of leisure time had sparked
the creation of mechanical games like pinball. Technology continued to grow, and by the 1950s,
computer science students in the United States had developed early versions of the video
games we know today.

In their most basic form, digital games involve users in an interactive computerized environment where they strive to achieve a desired outcome. These days, most digital games go
beyond a simple competition like the 1975 tennis-style game of *Pong*: They often entail sweeping narratives and offer imaginative and exciting adventures, sophisticated problem-solving
opportunities, and multiple possible outcomes.

But the boundaries were not always so varied. Digital games evolved from their simplest forms in the arcade into four major formats: television, handheld devices, computers, and the Internet. As these formats evolved and graphics advanced, distinctive types of games emerged and became popular. These included action games, sports games, shooter games, family entertainment games, role-playing games, adventure games, racing games, strategy games, fighting games, simulation games, computerized versions of card games, fantasy sports leagues, and virtual social environments. Together, these varied formats constitute an industry that analysts predict will reach $111 billion in annual revenues worldwide by 2015—and one that has become a socially driven mass medium.[4]

Mechanical Gaming

In the 1880s, the seeds of the modern entertainment industry were planted by a series of coin-operated contraptions devoted to cashing in on idleness. First appearing in train depots, hotel lobbies, bars, and restaurants, these leisure machines (also called "counter machines") would find a permanent home in the first thoroughly modern indoor playground: the **penny arcade**.[5]

Arcades were like nurseries for fledgling forms of amusement that would mature into mass entertainment industries during the twentieth century. For example, automated phonographs used in arcade machines evolved into the jukebox, while the kinetoscope (see Chapter 7) set the stage for the coming wonders of the movies. But the machines most relevant to today's electronic gaming were more interactive and primitive than the phonograph and kinetoscope. Some were strength testers that dared young men to show off their muscles by punching a boxing bag or arm wrestling a robotlike Uncle Sam. Others required more refined skills and sustained play, such as those that simulated bowling, horse racing, and football.[6]

Another arcade game, the bagatelle, spawned the **pinball machine**, the most prominent of the mechanical games. In pinball, players score points by manipulating

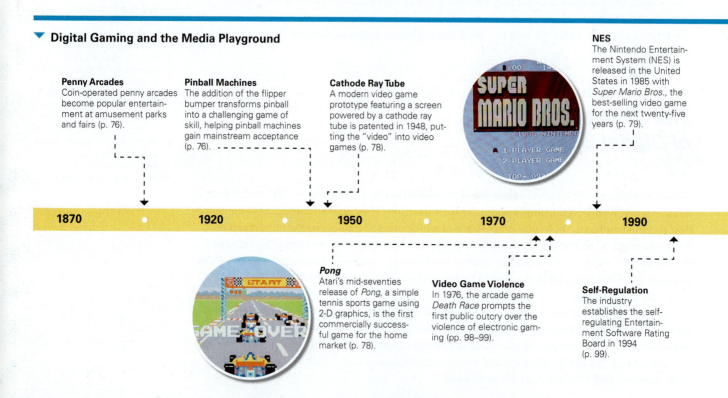

Digital Gaming and the Media Playground

Penny Arcades Coin-operated penny arcades become popular entertainment at amusement parks and fairs (p. 76).

Pinball Machines The addition of the flipper bumper transforms pinball into a challenging game of skill, helping pinball machines gain mainstream acceptance (p. 76).

Cathode Ray Tube A modern video game prototype featuring a screen powered by a cathode ray tube is patented in 1948, putting the "video" into video games (p. 78).

NES The Nintendo Entertainment System (NES) is released in the United States in 1985 with *Super Mario Bros.*, the best-selling video game for the next twenty-five years (p. 79).

1870 1920 1950 1970 1990

Pong Atari's mid-seventies release of *Pong*, a simple tennis sports game using 2-D graphics, is the first commercially successful game for the home market (p. 78).

Video Game Violence In 1976, the arcade game *Death Race* prompts the first public outcry over the violence of electronic gaming (pp. 98–99).

Self-Regulation The industry establishes the self-regulating Entertainment Software Rating Board in 1994 (p. 99).

the path of a metal ball on a playfield in a glass-covered case. In the 1930s and 1940s, players could control only the launch of the ball. For this reason, pinball was considered a sinister game of chance that, like the slot machine, fed the coffers of the gambling underworld. As a result, pinball was banned in most American cities, including New York, Chicago, and Los Angeles.[7] However, pinball gained mainstream acceptance and popularity after World War II with the addition of the flipper bumper, which enables players to careen the ball back up the play table. This innovation transformed pinball into a challenging game of skill, touch, and timing—all of which would become vital abilities for video game players years later.

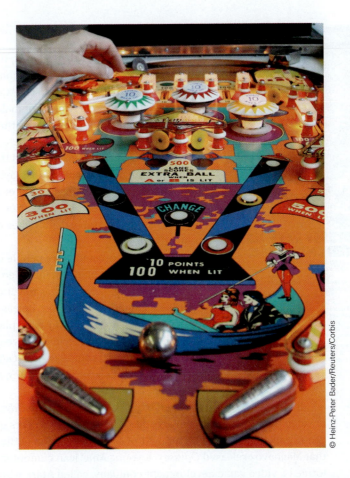

MODERN GAMING EVENTS and obsessions can be traced back to the emergence of penny arcades in the late nineteenth century. Today, pinball machines remain in many bars and arcades, and pinball expos are held all over the country.

Adding Internet Access
Sega introduces the 128-bit Sega Dreamcast, the first console to feature a built-in modem, in 1999 (p. 79).

MMORPG
World of Warcraft, the most successful MMORPG to date, is released in 2004 by Blizzard Entertainment (p. 82).

Full-Body Interactivity
Nintendo's Wii allows the user to mimic full-body motion controls and detect movement in three dimensions (pp. 79–80).

Apple
In 2010, Apple introduces the social gaming platform Game Center, which allows iOS users to connect with each other for multiplayer games (p. 83).

Kinect
In 2010, Microsoft unveils the Kinect, which reads body movement and voice commands for the Xbox (p. 80).

2000   **2003**   **2006**   **2009**   **2012**

PlayStation
In 1994, Sony introduces PlayStation, the first of a series of best-selling console and handheld game devices (p. 80).

Xbox LIVE
Microsoft, the first American company to get into game consoles, debuts the Xbox LIVE online service in 2002 (p. 80).

Oculus
In 2014, Facebook purchases the maker of the Oculus Rift, a virtual reality headset that Facebook plans to deploy for digital games and as a new communication device for everyday virtual experiences (p. 74).

THE WIZARD OF ODYSSEY REVEALS
THE KEY TO GREATER CHALLENGE.

The Keyboard!
It makes the fun go further with Odyssey² than any other video game. The keyboard lets you program mazes and grids. Type numbers and letters on the screen. Increase skill levels. It even lets you change opponents and fields of play! And only Odyssey² offers—The Master Strategy Series²! Each game comes with its own game board. You use it to plan your strategy

input that strategy through the keyboard, and play out the action on your TV screen.
Plus, Odyssey² offers over 50 games including arcade, educational, sports and strategy games.
So take the word of the Wizard of Odyssey. If you're looking for greater challenge in a video game, look to Odyssey²! For your nearest dealer call (800) 447-2882. In Illinois call (800) 322-4400.

ODYSSEY²
The keyboard is the key to greater challenge.

Image courtesy the Advertising Archives

THE *ODYSSEY*², a later model of the *Odyssey* console, was released in 1978 and featured a full keyboard that could be used for educational games.

The First Video Games

Not long after the growth of pinball, the first video game patent was issued on December 14, 1948, to Thomas T. Goldsmith and Estle Ray Mann for what they described as a "Cathode Ray Tube Amusement Device." The invention would not make much of a splash in the history of digital gaming, but it did feature the key component of the first video games: the cathode ray tube (CRT).

CRT-powered screens provided the images for analog television and for early computers' displays, where the first video games appeared a few years later. Computer science students developed these games as novelties in the 1950s and 1960s. But because computers consisted of massive mainframes at the time, the games couldn't be easily distributed.

However, more and more people owned televisions, and this development provided a platform for video games. The first home television game, called *Odyssey*, was developed by German immigrant and television engineer Ralph Baer. Released by Magnavox in 1972 and sold for a whopping $100, *Odyssey* used player controllers that moved dots of light around the screen in a twelve-game inventory of simple aiming and sports games. From 1972 until *Odyssey*'s replacement by a simpler model (the *Odyssey 100*) in 1975, Magnavox sold roughly 330,000 consoles.[8]

In the next decade, a ripped-off version of one of the *Odyssey* games brought the delights of video gaming into modern **arcades**. These establishments gather multiple coin-operated games together and can be thought of as a later version of the penny arcade. The same year that Magnavox released *Odyssey*, a young American computer engineer named Nolan Bushnell formed a video game development company, called Atari, with a friend. The enterprise's first creation was *Pong*, a simple two-dimensional tennis-style game, with two vertical paddles that bounced a white dot back and forth. The game kept score on the screen. Unlike *Odyssey*, *Pong* made blip noises when the ball hit the paddles or bounced off the sides of the court. *Pong* quickly became the first video game to become popular in arcades.

In 1975, Atari began successfully marketing a home version of *Pong* through an exclusive deal with Sears. The arrangement established the home video game market. Just two years later, Bushnell started the Chuck E. Cheese pizza–arcade restaurant chain and sold Atari to Warner Communications for an astounding $28 million. Although Atari folded in 1984, plenty of companies—including Nintendo, Sony, and Microsoft—followed its early lead, transforming the video game business into a full-fledged industry.

Arcades and Classic Games

By the late 1970s and early 1980s, games like *Asteroids*, *Pac-Man*, and *Donkey Kong* filled arcades and bars, competing directly with traditional pinball machines. In a way, arcades signaled electronic gaming's potential as a social medium, because many games allowed players to play with or compete against each other, standing side by side. To be sure, arcade gaming has been superseded by the console and computer. But the industry still attracts fun-seekers to businesses like Dave and Buster's, a gaming–restaurant chain operating in more than fifty locations, as well as to amusement parks, malls, and casinos.

To play the classic arcade games, as well as many of today's popular console games, players use controllers like joysticks and buttons to interact with graphical elements on a video screen. With a few notable exceptions (puzzle games like *Tetris*, for instance), these types of video games require players to identify with a position on the screen. In *Pong*, this position is represented by an electronic paddle; in *Space Invaders*, it's an earthbound shooting position. After *Pac-Man*, the **avatar** (a graphic interactive "character" situated within the world of the game) became the most common figure of player control and position identification. In the United States, the most popular video games today assume a "first-person" perspective, in which the player "sees" the virtual environment through the eyes of an avatar. In South Korea and other Asian countries, many real-time strategy games take an elevated "three-quarters" perspective, which affords a grander and more strategic vantage point on the field of play.

© ArcadeImages/Alamy

Consoles and Advancing Graphics

Today, many electronic games are played on home **consoles**, devices specifically used to play video games. These systems have become increasingly more powerful since the appearance of the early Atari consoles in the 1970s. One way of charting the evolution of consoles is to track the number of bits (binary digits) that they can process at one time. The bit rating of a console is a measure of its power at rendering computer graphics. The higher the bit rating, the more detailed and sophisticated the graphics. The Atari 2600, released in 1977, used an 8-bit processor, as did the wildly popular Nintendo Entertainment System, first released in Japan in 1983. Sega Genesis, the first 16-bit console, appeared in 1989. In 1992, 32-bit computers appeared on the market; the following year, 64 bits became the new standard. The 128-bit era dawned with the marketing of Sega Dreamcast in 1999. With the current generation of consoles, 256-bit processors are the standard.

POPULAR ARCADE GAMES in the 1970s and 1980s were simple two-dimensional games with straightforward goals, like driving a racecar, destroying asteroids, or gobbling up little dots. Today, most video games have more complex story lines based in fully fleshed-out worlds.

Of course, more detailed graphics have not always replaced simpler games. Nintendo, for example, offers many of its older, classic games for download onto its newest consoles even as updated versions are released, for the nostalgic gamers as well as new fans. Perhaps the best example of enduring games is the *Super Mario Bros.* series. Created by Nintendo mainstay Shigeru Miyamoto in 1983, the original *Mario Bros.* game began in arcades. The 1985 sequel *Super Mario Bros.*, developed for the 8-bit Nintendo Entertainment System, became the best-

THE ATARI 2600 was followed by the Atari 400, Atari 800, and Atari 5200, but none matched the earlier success of the 2600 model.

selling video game of all time (holding this title until 2009, when it was unseated by Nintendo's *Wii Sports*). Graphical elements from the *Mario Bros.* games, like the "1UP" mushroom that gives players an extra life, remain instantly recognizable to gamers of all ages. Some even appear on nostalgic T-shirts, as toys and cartoons, and in updated versions of newer games.

Photo by SSPL/Getty Images

Through decades of ups and downs in the electronic gaming industry (Atari folded in 1984, and Sega no longer makes video consoles), three major home console makers now compete for gamers: Nintendo, Sony, and Microsoft. Nintendo has been making consoles since the 1980s; Sony and Microsoft came later, but both companies were already major media conglomerates and thus well positioned to support and promote their interests in the video game market.

Nintendo released a new kind of console, the Wii, in 2006. The device supported traditional video games like

New Super Mario Bros. However, it was the first of the three major consoles to add a wireless motion-sensing controller, which took the often-sedentary nature out of gameplay. Games like *Wii Sports* require the user to mimic the full-body motion of bowling or playing tennis, while *Wii Fit* uses a wireless balance board for interactive yoga, strength, aerobic, and balance games. Although the Wii has lagged behind Xbox and PlayStation in establishing an online community, its controller enabled a host of games that appealed to broader audiences, and upon its release, it became the best-selling of the three major console systems. In 2012, Nintendo introduced the Wii U, which features the GamePad: a controller with an embedded touch-screen, on which games can be played without a television set (making it like a handheld video player).

Veteran electronics manufacturer Sony has the PlayStation series, introduced in 1994. Its current console, the PlayStation 4 (PS4, launched in 2013), boasts more than 110 million users on its free online PlayStation Network. Sony's PlayStation Plus is a paid subscription service that adds additional features, such as game downloads, to the PlayStation Network. Sony introduced PlayStation Move, its handheld remote motion-sensing controller, in 2010.

Microsoft's first foray into video game consoles was the Xbox, released in 2001; it was linked to the Xbox LIVE online service in 2002 and released as Xbox 360 in 2005. Xbox LIVE lets its 48 million subscribers play online and enables users to download new content directly to its console. In 2013, Microsoft released the Xbox One, with an upgraded Kinect (a motion-sensing controller first introduced in 2010), as an advanced gaming device and voice-controlled entertainment system. By 2014, Sony's PlayStation 4 and Microsoft's Xbox One were the most popular of the new generation of consoles, with the Wii U lagging in third place in sales.

Each of the three major digital game consoles has its niche. Sony's PlayStation is mostly about gaming, although like the other two consoles, it offers television entertainment features. Microsoft's Xbox is also about gaming, but Microsoft also wants its console to be the entertainment hub of the house. Wii features more devices and family-oriented games (the *Super Mario Bros.* are still an omnipresent franchise for Nintendo). All three of the consoles have motion-controlled sensors, online networks, and Internet entertainment links to services like Netflix and Hulu.

Although the major consoles share some game content, not every popular game is multi-platform (that is, one that is released on all three platforms)—so game offerings become a major selling point for a particular system. For example, *Destiny* (by Activision Blizzard), *Assassin's Creed IV: Black Flag* (by Ubisoft), and *Child of Light* (by Ubisoft) come in versions for all three consoles (and personal computers running Microsoft Windows, too). But the console makers also create or license games just for their own platform: *Titanfall* and *Halo 5: Guardians* for the Xbox One, *inFAMOUS Second Son* for the PlayStation 4, and *Mario Kart 8* for the Wii.

Gaming on Home Computers

Like the early console games, very early home computer games often mimicked (and sometimes ripped off) popular arcade games, like *Frogger*, *Centipede*, *Pac-Man*, and *Space Invaders*. Computer-based gaming also featured certain genres not often seen on consoles, like digitized card and board games. The early days of the personal computer saw the creation of electronic versions of games like Solitaire, Hearts, Spades, and Chess, all simple games still popular today. But for a time in the late 1980s and much of the 1990s, personal computers held some clear advantages over

THE ORIGINAL *MARIO BROS.* GAME made its arcade debut in 1983, but it was the 1985 home console sequel *Super Mario Bros.* that made the series a household name. *Super Mario* titles have been developed for the original Nintendo, Super Nintendo, Nintendo 64, GameCube, Game Boy, Wii, and 3DS, for which *Super Mario Bros. 3* was released in 2014.

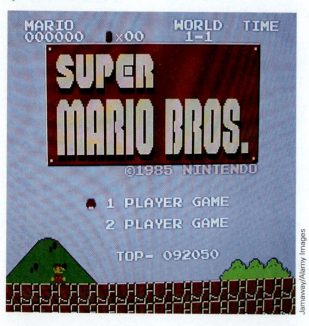

Jamaway/Alamy Images

console gaming. The versatility of keyboards, compared with the relatively simple early console controllers, allowed for ambitious puzzle-solving games like *Myst*. Moreover, faster processing speeds gave some computer games richer, more detailed three-dimensional (3-D) graphics. Many of the most popular early first-person shooter games, like *Doom* and *Quake*, were developed for home computers rather than consoles.

As consoles caught up with greater processing speeds and disc-based games in the late 1990s, elaborate personal computer games attracted less attention. But more recently, PC gaming has experienced a resurgence, due to the advent of free-to-play games (like *Spelunky* and *League of Legends*), subscription games (such as *World of Warcraft* and *Diablo 3*), and social media games (such as *Candy Crush Saga* on Facebook)—all trends aided by the Internet. With powerful processors for handling rich graphics, and more stable Internet connectivity for downloading games or playing games via social media sites and other gaming sites, personal computers can adeptly handle a wide range of activities.

KRT/Newscom

DOOM, an early first-person shooter game that influenced later hits like *Halo,* was first developed for home computers. The first game was released in 1993. It has spawned several sequels and a 2005 feature film.

The Internet Transforms Gaming

With the introduction of the Sega Dreamcast in 1999, the first console to feature a built-in modem, gaming emerged as an online, multiplayer social activity. The Dreamcast didn't last, but online connections are now a normal part of console video games, with Internet-connected players opposing one another in combat, working together against a common enemy, or teaming up to achieve a common goal (like sustaining a medieval community). Some of the biggest titles have been first-person shooter games like *Counter-Strike*, an online spin-off of the popular *Half-Life* console game. Each player views the game from the first-person perspective but also plays in a team as either a terrorist or a counterterrorist.

The ability to play online has added a new dimension to other, less combat-oriented games, too. For example, football and music enthusiasts playing already-popular console games like *Madden NFL* and *Rock Band* can now engage with others in live online multiplayer play. And young and old alike can compete against teams in other locations in Internet-based bowling tournaments using the Wii.

The Internet enabled the spread of video games to converged devices, like tablets and mobile phones, making games more portable and creating whole new segments in the gaming industry. The connectivity of the Internet also opened the door to social gaming, virtual worlds, and massively multiplayer online games.

MMORPGs, Virtual Worlds, and Social Gaming

It is one of the longest acronyms in the world of gaming: **massively multiplayer online role-playing games (MMORPGs)**. These games are set in virtual worlds that require users to play through an avatar of their own design. The "massively multiplayer" aspect of MMORPGs indicates that electronic games—once designed for solo or small-group play—have expanded to reach large groups, like traditional mass media do.

The fantasy adventure game *World of Warcraft* is the most popular MMORPG, peaking at 12 million subscribers in 2010 and leveling off to 7.8 million subscribers in 2014. Users can select from twelve different "races" of avatars, including dwarves, gnomes, night elves, orcs, trolls, goblins, and humans. To succeed in the game, many players join with other players to form guilds or tribes, working together toward in-game goals that can be achieved only by teams. *Second Life*, a 3-D social simulation set in real time, also features social interaction. Players build human avatars, selecting from an array of physical characteristics and clothing. Then they use real money to buy virtual land and to trade in virtual goods and services.

MMORPGs like *World of Warcraft* and simulations like *Second Life* are aimed at teenagers and adults. One of the most overlooked areas (at least by adults) in online gaming is the children's market. *Club Penguin*, a moderated virtual world purchased by Disney, enables kids to play games and chat as colorful penguins. Disney later developed additional *Club Penguin* games for handheld players. Toy maker Ganz developed the online *Webkinz* game to revive its stuffed-animal sales. Each Webkinz stuffed animal comes with a code that lets players access the online game and care for the virtual version of their plush pets. In 2009, as Webkinz sales declined, Ganz started *Webkinz Jr.* to market bigger, more expensive plush animals to preschoolers. *Woozworld* offers a virtual shopping world and chat for the tween market, ages nine to fourteen. All these virtual worlds offer younger players their own age-appropriate environment to experiment with virtual socializing, but they have also attracted criticism for their messages of consumerism. In many of these games, children can buy items with virtual currency or acquire "bling" more quickly through a premium membership. The games also market merchandise to their young players, such as stuffed animals, movies, and clothing.

Online fantasy sports games also reach a mass audience with a major social component. Players—real-life friends, virtual acquaintances, or a mix of both—assemble teams and use actual sports results to determine scores in their online games. But rather than experiencing the visceral thrills of, say, *Madden NFL 15*, fantasy football participants take a more detached, managerial perspective on the game—a departure from the classic video game experience. Fantasy sports' managerial angle makes it even more fun to watch almost any televised game because players focus more on making strategic investments in individual performances scattered across the various professional teams than they do on rooting for local teams. In the process, players become statistically savvy aficionados of the game overall, rather than rabid fans of a particular team. In 2013, about 34 million people played fantasy sports in the United States and Canada; the Fantasy Sports Trade Association currently estimates a market size of more than $3.6 billion.[9]

The increasingly social nature of video games has made them a natural fit for social networking sites. Game apps for Facebook have drawn millions of fans. London-based game developer King is the maker of several of the most popular games on Facebook, including *Candy Crush Saga*, *Farm Heroes Saga*, and *Pet*

THE GAMEMAKER KING has made massive casual-gaming hits out of *Candy Crush Saga* and *Bubble Witch Saga*. The company's sales came close to the $2 billion mark in 2013, with over 400 million active users playing its games.

AFP/Getty Images

Rescue Saga. Facebook reported in 2014 that over 375 million people play games on its social network site each month.[10]

Convergence: From Consoles to Mobile Gaming

Digital games made their initial appearance on computers and consoles and were very much wedded to those platforms. Today, though, games can be consumed the same way so much music and so many books, television shows, and films are consumed: just about anywhere and in a number of different ways. And video game consoles are increasingly part of the same technological convergence that gives devices like smartphones and tablets multiple functions.

Consoles Become Entertainment Centers

Video game consoles, once used exclusively for games, now work as part computer, part cable box. They've become powerful entertainment centers, with multiple forms of media converging in a single device. For example, the Xbox One and PS4 can function as DVD players and digital video recorders (with hard drives of up to 500 gigabytes) and offer access to Twitter, Facebook, blogs, and video chat. The PS4 can also play Blu-ray discs, and all three competing console systems (PS4, Xbox, and Wii) offer connections to stream programming from sources like Netflix and Hulu. Microsoft's Xbox—which has Kinect's voice recognition system, allowing viewers to communicate with the box—has been the most successful in becoming a converged device for home entertainment.

Portable Players and Mobile Gaming

Simple handheld players made games portable long before the advent of Internet-connected touchscreen mobile devices. Nintendo popularized handheld digital games with the release of its Game Boy line of devices and sold nearly 120 million of them from 1989 to 2003 with games like *Tetris*, *Metroid*, and *Pokémon Red/Blue*.[11] The early handhelds gave way to later generations of devices offering more advanced graphics and wireless capabilities. These include the top-selling Nintendo 3DS, released in 2011, and PlayStation Portable (PSP), released in 2005 and succeeded by the PlayStation Vita in 2012. Both brands are Wi-Fi capable, so players can interface with other users to play games or browse the Internet.

While portable players remain immensely popular (the Nintendo 3DS sold more than 154 million units through 2014), they face competition from the widespread use of smartphones and touchscreen tablets like iPads. These devices are not designed principally for gaming, but their capabilities have provided another option for casual gamers who may not have been interested in owning a handheld console. Manufacturers of these converged devices are catching on to their gaming potential: After years of relatively little interest in video games, Apple introduced Game Center in 2010. This social gaming network enables users to invite friends or find others for multiplayer gaming, track their scores, and view high scores on a leader board—which the 3DS and PSP do as well. With more than 500 million iPhones and 210 million iPads sold worldwide by 2014 (and millions more iPod Touch devices in circulation), plus more than 260,000 games (like *Blek* and *Minecraft—Pocket Edition*) available in its App Store, Apple is transforming the portable video game business with its devices, games, and distribution system.[12] Handheld video games have made the medium more accessible and widespread. Even people who wouldn't identify themselves as gamers may kill time between classes or waiting in line by playing *Don't Touch the White Tile 4* on their phones.

Google Play (formerly the Android Market) rivals Apple's App Store in number of apps and provides a substantial platform for gaming on Android mobile phones and tablet devices

© Alex Segre/Alamy

▲
HANDHELD GAMING used to require a specific piece of hardware, like the classic Game Boy. But as technology has grown more sophisticated, handheld games can be played on smaller, more versatile devices, like smartphones and PDAs, and some handheld gaming systems can provide more than just games.

like the Kindle, Galaxy, and Nexus. Microsoft got a later start with its Windows phones and Surface tablet, so its game offerings lag far behind those of the Android and Apple stores.

This portable and mobile gaming convergence is changing the way people look at digital games and their systems. The games themselves are no longer confined to arcades or home television sets, while the mobile media have gained power as entertainment tools, reaching a wider and more diverse audience. Thus gaming has become an everyday form of entertainment, rather than the niche pursuit of hard-core enthusiasts.

With its increased profile and flexibility across platforms, the gaming industry has achieved a mass medium status on a par with film or television. This rise in status has come with stiffer and more complex competition, not just within the gaming industry but across media. Rather than Sony competing with Nintendo, or TV networks competing among themselves for viewers, or new movies facing off at the box office, media must now compete against other media for an audience's attention. Recent statistics mark how far the digital game industry has come: Global box office revenue for the film industry hit a record $35.9 billion in 2013. (The movie industry makes billions more on DVD, streaming, television licensing, and merchandising deals.) In that same year, the worldwide digital game marketplace, including hardware, software, online games, and mobile games, reached $93 billion.[13]

The Media Playground

To fully explore the larger media playground, we need to look beyond electronic gaming's technical aspects and consider the human faces of gaming. The attractions of this interactive playground validate electronic gaming's status as one of today's most powerful social media. Electronic games occupy an enormous range of styles, from casual games like *Tetris*, *Angry Birds*, *Bejeweled*, and *Fruit Ninja*—described by one writer as "stupid games" that are typically "a repetitive, storyless puzzle that could be picked up, with no loss of potency, at any moment, in any situation"—to full-blown, Hollywood-like immersive adventure games like *Final Fantasy*.[14] No matter what the style, digital games are compelling entertainment and mass media because they pose challenges (mental and physical), allow us to engage in situations both realistic and fantastical, and allow us to socialize with others as we play with friends and form communities inside and outside of games. (See "Case Study: *Watch Dogs* Hacks Our Surveillance Society" on page 85 for more on the narrative power of video games.)

Video Game Genres

Electronic games inhabit so many playing platforms and devices, and cover so many genres, that they are not easy to categorize. The game industry, as represented by the Entertainment Software Association, organizes games by **gameplay**—the way in which the rules structure how players interact with the game—rather than by any sort of visual or narrative style. There

Watch Dogs Hacks Our Surveillance Society

by Olivia Mossman

With the revelations of government surveillance brought to light by WikiLeaks and Edward Snowden, many Americans are now aware of the possibility that their phone calls are being overheard, their Internet searches observed, and other surveillance conducted without their permission. But what if individual American citizens had the same kind of almost-omniscient hacking powers? Would they use these powers for good?

A new open-world action-adventure game aims to help players discover their stance on modern-day technologies and hacking. *Watch Dogs*, created by Ubisoft and released in 2014, allows players to take the persona of "Aiden Pearce," a hacker in a vaguely futuristic Chicago. The *New York Times* called the game "impossibly well-timed for the year of Edward Snowden."[1]

The Aiden character uses hacking, government records, and surveillance to track down the killer of his niece. However, the game eerily puts into perspective a "futuristic," technologically connected world that looks even more similar to current society than the game designers planned. Players will see a Chicago that is heavily monitored by technology, and while some of the game still uses fantastical versions of smart systems, *Watch Dogs* also predicts where society is headed. In fact, when game developers began constructing the video game in 2009, smartphones were only just emerging. Now they are Aiden's primary weapon and a keystone of society. In reality, the interconnectivity of Chicago is not far from the vision of *Watch Dogs*. A report by video gaming Web site Polygon explains how Chicago's surveillance systems are

© Fred Prouser/Reuters/Corbis

primarily used for fighting crime but have increased in number, decreased in size, and infiltrated the city, even using facial recognition to assist in catching culprits.[2] As Aiden, players can access people's history, identity, and personal accounts for their own self-gain. To actually control the character with such power will no doubt have an impact on players' views of the National Security Agency, its gathering of information through its PRISM program, and their own habits regarding personal disclosure.

Watch Dogs offers another element that is more fact than fiction: It requires users to use game information to make moral decisions. As the game promo says, when playing as Aiden Pearce, you "use your hacking abilities for good or bad—it's up to you."[3] Unlike other games such as *Grand Theft Auto*, in which a player in a car can mindlessly run down nameless pedestrians, *Watch Dogs* gives the main character a means to reflect on whom he chooses to kill and why. Each player has the ability to hack information about each individual, giving the player access to the name and backstory of each

computerized, nonplayer character, turning the "extras" into "people."[4]

With this context, killing or hacking game characters with names, faces, and stories is not as easy as it is in other games. Would players hack into the Webcam of a rich woman, who had recently lost her daughter, and then steal money from her bank account to line their own character's pockets? To avoid getting arrested in a car chase, would players knowingly run over a civilian who is a tobacco executive but also volunteers his time and money at homeless shelters? The game makes players question what truly matters, which evils are "worse," and whether they would sacrifice themselves for others. Even the multiplayer version of the game allows players to hack into another *real* player's game, giving them the option to "kill" a real player's character. In *Watch Dogs*, players determine their own morality and act on it—and as in real life, there are consequences for these decisions. ◢

Olivia Mossman is a game player, a writer, and a communication studies student at the University of Northern Iowa.

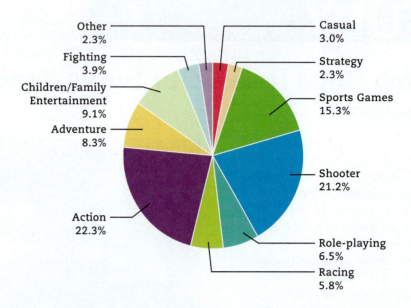

▶

FIGURE 3.1

TOP VIDEO GAME GENRES BY UNITS SOLD, 2012

Data from: Entertainment Software Association, "Essential Facts about the Computer and Video Game Industry," 2013.

Note: Percentages were rounded up to the next decimal point.

(Pie chart labels:)

Other 2.3%
Casual 3.0%
Fighting 3.9%
Strategy 2.3%
Children/Family Entertainment 9.1%
Sports Games 15.3%
Adventure 8.3%
Shooter 21.2%
Action 22.3%
Role-playing 6.5%
Racing 5.8%

are many hybrid forms, but the major gameplay genres are discussed in the following sections. (See Figure 3.1 for a breakdown of top video game genres.)

Action and Shooter Games

Usually emphasizing combat-type situations, **action games** ask players to test their reflexes and to punch, slash, shoot, or throw as strategically and accurately as possible so as to strategically make their way through a series of levels. Some action games feature hand-to-hand combat (*Street Fighter*, *Marvel vs. Capcom*); others feature more sophisticated weaponry and obstacles, such as bladed spears against groups of enemy combatants (*Hidden Blade*, *Bushido Blade*). Shooter games offer a selection of guns and missiles for obliterating opponents.

Most *shooter games* have a **first-person shooter (FPS)** perspective, which allows players to feel as though they are actually holding the weapon and to feel physically immersed in the drama. (See Table 3.1 for more on major video game conventions.) *Doom*, for example, released in 1993, was one of the first major FPS breakthroughs, requiring players to shoot their way through a military base on Mars's moon, killing the demons from Hell first using a pistol, then moving up to a chainsaw, shotgun, chain gun, rocket launcher, plasma rifle, and finally the coveted BFG 9000, all the while negotiating pits of toxic slime and locating the "exit door" that leads to the next level. *Halo*, Microsoft's impressive launch title for the Xbox 360 in 2001, has become the top FPS game of all time. In the *Halo* series (the fourth sequel was released in 2012), players assume the identity of "Master Chief," a super-soldier living in the twenty-sixth century and fighting aliens, with the ultimate goal of uncovering secrets about the ring-shaped world, Halo. The weapons allotted to Master Chief all require the player to think strategically about how and when to launch them. Plasma weapons need time to cool between firings; guns need both ammunition and time to reload; fragmentation grenades bounce and detonate immediately; plasma grenades attach to the target before exploding. Players have to negotiate all these (and many more) variables as they move through various futuristic landscapes in order to unlock the secrets of Halo.

Maze games like *Pac-Man* also fit into the "action" genre, involving maze navigation to avoid or chase adversaries. Finally, *platform games* gained notoriety through the very successful *Super Mario Bros.* series. Using quick reflexes and strategic time management, players move Mario and Luigi between various platform levels of the Mushroom Kingdom in order to rescue

Convention	Description	Examples	Visual Representation
Avatars	Onscreen figures of player identification	Pac-Man, Mario from the *Mario Bros.* series, Sonic the Hedgehog, Link from *Legend of Zelda*	
Bosses	Powerful enemy characters that represent the final challenge in a stage or the entire game	Ganon from the *Zelda* series, Hitler in *Castle Wolfenstein*, Dr. Eggman from *Sonic the Hedgehog*, Mother Brain from *Metroid*	
Vertical and Side Scrolling	As opposed to a fixed screen, scrolling that follows the action as it moves up, down, or sideways in what is called a "tracking shot" in the cinema	Platform games like *Jump Bug*, *Donkey Kong*, and *Super Mario Bros.*; also integrated into the design of *Angry Birds*	
Isometric Perspective *(or Three-Quarters Perspective)*	An elevated and angled perspective that enhances the sense of three-dimensionality by allowing players to see the tops and sides of objects	*Zaxxon*, *StarCraft*, *Civilization*, and *Populous*	
First-Person Perspective	Presents the gameplay through the eyes of your avatar	First-person shooter (FPS) games like *Quake*, *Doom*, *Halo*, and *Call of Duty*	
Third-Person Perspective *(or Over-the-Shoulders Perspective)*	Enables you to view your heroic avatar in action from an external viewpoint	*Tomb Raider*, *Assassin's Creed*, and the default viewpoint in *World of Warcraft*	

(top to bottom) © Jamaway/Alamy; © Jamaway/Alamy; © Jamaway/Alamy; © ArcadeImages/Alamy; KRT/Newscom; KRT/Newscom

TABLE 3.1

MAJOR VIDEO GAME CONVENTIONS

This table breaks down six common elements of video game layout. Many of these elements have been in place since the earliest games and continue to be used today.

Princess Toadstool (later called Princess Peach) from Bowser. Action and shooter games are the best-selling game genres, accounting for more than 43 percent of all game units sold.[15]

Adventure Games

Developed in the 1970s, **adventure games** involve a type of gameplay that is in many ways the opposite of action games. Typically nonconfrontational in nature, adventure games such as *Myst* require players to interact with individual characters and the sometimes-hostile environment in order to solve puzzles. In the case of *Myst* (released in 1991), the player is "the Stranger" who travels to different worlds and finds clues to solve various puzzles that, if solved correctly, lead to the "deserted" island of Myst. The genre peaked in popularity in 1993 and has spawned derivative genres, such as *action-adventure* (*Zelda, Metroid*) and *survival horror* games (*Resident Evil*), which are inspired by horror fiction.

Role-Playing Games

Role-playing games (RPGs) are typically set in a fantasy or sci-fi world in which each player (there can be multiple players in a game) chooses to play as a character that specializes in a particular skill set (such as magic spells or "finesse"). Players embark on a predetermined adventure and interact with the game's other inhabitants and each other, making choices throughout the game that bring about various diverse outcomes. *Neverwinter Nights* (2002), for example, challenges its players to collaboratively collect four Waterdhavian creatures needed to stop the Wailing Death plague, defeat the cult that is spreading the plague, and finally thwart an attack on the city of Neverwinter. The game is derived from *Dungeons & Dragons*, one of the most popular face-to-face, paper-and-pencil role-playing games. More complex role-playing games, like the *Final Fantasy* series, involve branching plots and changing character destinies. MMORPGs are obviously a subgenre of this game category. Sandbox (or open-world) RPGs, such as the *Grand Theft Auto* series and *Minecraft*, tend to offer the greatest leeway in how players may roam through a game's environment and create their own narratives. Other subgenres, such as MOBAs (multiplayer online battle arena games, which can combine RPG elements with real-time strategy; see below), make up some of the most successful digital games on the market. A good example is *League of Legends*, a free-to-play PC game in which players control "champions" who gain levels by winning player-versus-player battles against opposing champions. The game has become immensely popular, with more than 27 million players worldwide each day, and has spawned university leagues and live tournaments in which top players from around the world compete for large cash prizes.[16]

Strategy and Simulation Games

Strategy video games often involve military battles (real or imaginary) and focus on gameplay that requires careful thinking and skillful planning in order to achieve victory. Unlike FPS games, the perspective in **strategy games** is omniscient, with the player surveying the entire "world," or playing field, and making strategic decisions—such as building bases, researching technologies, managing resources, and waging battles—that will make or break this world. No doubt the most popular *real-time strategy game* (*RTS*) is Blizzard's *StarCraft*, which is played competitively throughout South Korea and televised to large audiences. Taking place during the twenty-sixth century in a distant part of the Milky Way galaxy, *StarCraft* involves three races (one human) that are at war with one another. To develop better strategic advantages, players download and memorize maps, study up on minute game details (such as race characteristics), and participate in *StarCraft*-centered advice boards.

Like strategy games, **simulation games** involve managing resources and planning worlds, but these worlds are typically based in reality. A good example is *SimCity*, which asks players to build a city given real-world constraints, such as land-use zoning (commercial, industrial, residential); tax rates (to tax or not to tax); and transportation (buses, cars, trams). A player may also face unanticipated natural disasters, such as floods or tornadoes. Another example is *The Oregon Trail*, an educational simulation game that aims at reproducing the circumstances and drastic choices faced by white settlers traveling the two-thousand-mile journey from Independence, Kansas, to the Willamette Valley in Oregon. Throughout the game, players make choices to help their ox-driven wagon parties survive numerous potential horrors, including measles, dysentery, typhoid, cholera, snakebites, drowning, physical injuries, floods, mountains, heat, and cold, all the while maintaining provisions and predicting weather conditions. First developed by educators in 1971, *The Oregon Trail* has been played by millions of students.

Casual Games

This category of gaming, which encompasses everything from *Minesweeper* to *Angry Birds* to *Words with Friends*, includes games that have very simple rules and are usually quick to play. The historical starting point of **casual games** was 1989, when the game *Tetris* came bundled with every new Game Boy (Nintendo). *Tetris* requires players to continuously (frantically, for some) rotate colored blocks and fit them into snug spaces before the screen fills up with badly stacked blocks. There is no story to *Tetris*, and no real challenge other than mastering the rather numbing pattern of rotating and stacking, a process that keeps getting faster as the player achieves higher levels. For many people, the ceaseless puzzle is like a drug: Millions of people have purchased and played *Tetris* since its release. Today, *Tetris* has given way to *Angry Birds*, *Candy Crush Saga*, and other such games that have exploded in popularity due in large part to the rise in mobile devices.

Sports, Music, and Dance Games

"There is apparently a video game for every sport except for competitive mushroom picking," commented a *Milwaukee Journal* editorial in 1981.[17] Today, there really does seem to be a game for every sport. Gaming consoles first featured 3-D graphics in the early to mid-1990s with the arrival of Sega Saturn and Sony's PlayStation in 1994. Today's game technology, with infrared motion detectors, accelerometers (devices that measure proper acceleration), and tuning fork gyroscopes (devices that determine rotational motion), allows players to control their avatar through physical movements, making the 3-D sports games experience even more realistic. Players in a soccer game, for example, might feel as though they are in the thick of things, kicking, dribbling, shooting, and even getting away with a foul if referees aren't watching. In sports games, players engage in either competitive gameplay (player versus player) or cooperative gameplay (two or more teammates work together against the artificial intelligence, or AI, opponents within the game).

One of the most consistently best-selling sports games is *Madden NFL*, which is based on famed NFL football player and former coach John Madden. Among the game's realistic features are character collisions, with varying speeds and trajectories that differ based on player control; sophisticated playbooks and player statistics; and voice commentary, which allows players to hear the game as if it were a real TV broadcast. With Xbox Kinect functionality, players can even select and alter screen actions with the power of their own voice (*they* are Madden, screaming from the sidelines).

Other experiential games tie into music and dance categories. *Rock Band*, developed by Harmonix Systems and published by Mad Catz, allows up to four players to simulate the popular rock band performances of fifty-eight songs—from the Pixies and OK Go to Black Sabbath and the Rolling Stones—as well as more than fourteen hundred additional downloadable songs for $1.99 apiece. Each instrument part (lead guitar, bass, drums, and vocal) can be played at one of four difficulty levels (Easy, Medium, Hard, and Expert), and if players don't keep up, they "fail" out of the song, and their instruments are muted. The gameplay is

Gautier Stephane/Sagaphoto.com/Alamy

THE *JUST DANCE* SERIES has become a popular experiential game; it has also provided a new revenue stream for the music industry, which can license songs for use with the game.

derivative of *Guitar Hero* (vertical scrolling, colored music notes, and karaoke-like vocals), but the experience of *Rock Band*—with four players; a variety of venues, from clubs to concert halls; and screaming fans (who are also prone to boo)—is far more "real." Dance-oriented video games, such as *Dance Dance Revolution* and *Just Dance*, use motion-detecting technology and challenge players to match their rhythm and dance moves to figures on the screen.

Communities of Play: Inside the Game

Virtual communities often crop up around online video games and fantasy sports leagues. Indeed, players may get to know one another through games without ever meeting in person. They can interact in two basic types of groups. **PUGs** (short for "pick-up groups") are temporary teams usually assembled by matchmaking programs integrated into the game. The members of a PUG may range from elite players to **noobs** (clueless beginners) and may be geographically and generationally diverse. PUGs are notorious for harboring ninjas and trolls—two universally despised player types (not to be confused with ninja or troll avatars). **Ninjas** are players who snatch loot out of turn and then leave the group; **trolls** are players who delight in intentionally spoiling the gaming experience for others.

Because of the frustration of dealing with noobs, ninjas, and trolls, most experienced players join organized groups called **guilds** or **clans**. These groups can be small and easygoing or large and demanding. Guild members can usually avoid PUGs and team up with guildmates to complete difficult challenges requiring coordinated group activity. As the terms *ninja*, *troll*, and *noob* suggest, online communication is often encoded in gamespeak, a language filled with jargon, abbreviations, and acronyms relevant to gameplay. The typical codes of text messaging (OMG, LOL, ROFL, and so forth) form the bedrock of this language system.

Players communicate in two forms of in-game chat—voice and text. Xbox LIVE, for example, uses three types of voice chat that allow players to socialize and strategize, in groups or one-on-one, even as they are playing the game. Other in-game chat systems are text-based, with chat channels for trading in-game goods or coordinating missions within a guild. These methods of communicating with fellow players who may or may not know one another outside the game create a sense of community around gameplay. Some players have formed lasting friendships or romantic relationships through their video game habit. Avid gamers have even held in-game ceremonies, like weddings or funerals—sometimes for game-only characters, sometimes for real-life events.

Communities of Play: Outside the Game

Communities also form outside games, through Web sites and even face-to-face gatherings dedicated to electronic gaming in its many forms. This phenomenon is similar to the formation of online and in-person groups to discuss other mass media, like movies, TV shows, or books. These communities extend beyond gameplay, enhancing the social experience gained through the games.

Collective Intelligence

Mass media productions are almost always collaborative efforts, as is evident in the credits for movies, television shows, and music recordings. The same goes for digital games. But what is unusual about game developers and the game industry is their interest in listening to gamers and their communities in order to gather new ideas and constructive criticism and to gauge popularity. Gamers, too, collaborate with one another to share shortcuts and "cheats" to solving tasks and quests, and to create their own modifications to games. This sharing of knowledge and ideas is an excellent example of **collective intelligence.** French professor Pierre Lévy coined the term *collective intelligence* in 1997 to describe the Internet, "this new dimension of communication," and its ability to "enable us to share our knowledge and acknowledge it to others."[18] In the world of gaming, where users are active participants (more than in any other medium), the collective intelligence of players informs the entire game environment.

For example, collective intelligence (and action) is necessary to work through levels of many games. In *World of Warcraft*, collective intelligence is highly recommended. According to the beginner's guide, "If you want to take on the greatest challenges *World of Warcraft* has to offer, you will need allies to fight by your side against the tides of darkness."[19] Players form guilds and use their play experience and characters' skills to complete quests and move to higher levels. Gamers also share ideas through chats and wikis, and those looking for tips and cheats provided by fellow players need only Google what they want. The largest of the sites devoted to sharing collective intelligence is the *World of Warcraft* wiki (www.wowwiki.com). Similar user-generated sites are dedicated to a range of digital games, including *Age of Conan*, *Assassin's Creed*, *Grand Theft Auto*, *Halo*, *Mario*, *Metal Gear*, *Pokémon*, *Sonic the Hedgehog*, and *Spore*.

The most advanced form of collective intelligence in gaming is **modding,** slang for "modifying game software or hardware." In many mass communication industries, modifying hardware or content would land someone in a copyright lawsuit. In gaming, modding is often encouraged, as it is yet another way players become more deeply invested in a game, and it can improve the game for others. For example, *Counter-Strike*, a popular first-person shooter game, is a mod of the game *Half-Life*. *Half-Life* is a critically acclaimed science-fiction first-person shooter game (a physicist fighting aliens), released by Valve Corporation in 1998 for PCs, and later PlayStation. The developers of *Half-Life* encouraged mods by including software development tools with it. By 1999, *Counter-Strike*, in which counterterrorists fight terrorists, emerged as the most popular of many mods, and Valve formed a partnership with the game's developers. *Counter-Strike* was released to retailers as a PC game in 2000 and an Xbox game in 2004, eventually selling more copies than *Half-Life*. Today, many other games, such as *The Elder Scrolls*, have active modding communities.

Game Sites

Game sites and blogs are among the most popular external communities for gamers. IGN (owned by Ziff Davis), GameSpot (owned by CBS), GameTrailers (MTV Networks/Viacom), and Kotaku (Gawker Media) are four of the leading Web sites for gaming. GameSpot and IGN are apt examples of giant industry sites, each with sixteen to nineteen million unique, mostly male, eighteen- to thirty-four-year-old visitors per month—a desirable demographic to major media corporations. Penny Arcade is perhaps the best known of the independent community-building sites. Founded by Jerry Holkins and Mike Krahulik, the site started out as a Webcomic focused on video game culture. It has since expanded to include forums and a Web series called *PA* that documents behind-the-scenes work at Penny Arcade. Penny Arcade organizes a live festival to celebrate gamers and gamer culture called the Penny Arcade Expo (PAX), as well as a children's charity called Child's Play.

Conventions

In addition to online gaming communities, there are conventions and expos where video game enthusiasts can come together in person to test out new games and other new products, play old games in competition, and meet video game developers. One of the most significant is the

Jason Merritt/Getty Images for Take-Two

▲

RITA ORA performs at the Electronic Entertainment Expo in 2014. Other musicians who have played E3 in recent years include Drake, Usher, David Guetta, deadmau5, and Eminem, reflecting the increased convergence of the video game and music industries.

Electronic Entertainment Expo (E3), which draws more than 45,000 industry professionals, investors, developers, and retailers to its annual meeting. E3 is the place where the biggest new game titles and products are unveiled, and it is covered by hundreds of journalists, televised on Spike TV, and streamed to mobile devices and Xbox consoles.

The Penny Arcade Expo (PAX) is a convention created by gamers for gamers, held each year in Seattle and Boston. One of its main attractions is the Omegathon, a three-day elimination game tournament, in which twenty randomly selected attendees compete in games across several genres, culminating in the championship match at the convention's closing. Other conventions include BlizzCon (operated by Blizzard Entertainment to feature developments to their games, including their top franchises—*World of Warcraft*, *Diablo*, and *StarCraft*) and the Tokyo Game Show, the world's largest gaming convention, with more than 200,000 attendees annually.

Trends and Issues in Digital Gaming

The ever-growing relationship between video games and other media, such as books, movies, and television, leaves no doubt that digital gaming has a permanent place in our culture. Like other media, games are a venue for advertising. A virtual billboard in a video game is usually more than just a digital prop; as in television and the movies, it's a paid placement. And like other media, games are a subject of social concern. Violent and misogynistic content has from time to time spurred calls for more regulation of electronic games. But as games permeate more aspects of culture and become increasingly available in nonstandard formats and genres, they may also become harder to define and, therefore, regulate.

Electronic Gaming and Media Culture

Beyond the immediate industry, electronic games have had a pronounced effect on media culture. For example, fantasy league sports have spawned a number of draft specials on ESPN as well as a regular podcast, *Fantasy Focus*, on ESPN Radio. Fantasy football has even inspired an adult comedy called *The League* on the cable channel FXX. In the case of the Web site Twitch, streaming and archived video of digital games being played *is* the content. In just three years, the site became so popular that Amazon bought it for almost $1 billion to add to its collection of original video programming.

Like television shows, books, and comics before them, electronic games have inspired movies, such as *Lara Croft: Tomb Raider* (2001), the *Resident Evil* series (2001–present, including a sixth installment due in 2015), and *Need for Speed* (2014). *Tron* (1982), a movie inspired by video games, spurred an entire franchise of books, comic books, and arcade and console video games in the 1980s; and it was revived a generation later with an Xbox LIVE game in 2008, a movie sequel (*Tron: Legacy*) in 2010, and a Disney television series. For many Hollywood blockbusters today, a video game spin-off is a must-have item. Box office hits like *Transformers: Dark of the Moon* (2011), *Brave* (2012), *The Amazing Spider-Man 2* (2014), and *Maleficent* (2014) all have companion video games for consoles, portable players, or mobile devices.

LaunchPad ▶

macmillanhighered.com
/mediaculture10e

Video Games at the Movies

Alice, the hero of the *Resident Evil* film series, fights zombies in this clip. **Discussion:** In what ways does this clip replicate the experience of game play? In what ways is a film inherently different from a game?

Books and electronic games have also had a long history of influencing each other. Japanese manga and anime (comic books and animation) have also inspired video games, such as *Akira*, *Astro Boy*, and *Naruto. Batman: Arkham Asylum*, a top video game title introduced in 2009, is based closely on the *Batman* comic-book stories, while *The Witcher*, an action role-playing game for PCs, is based on Polish fantasy writer Andrzej Sapkowski's saga, *The Witcher*. Perhaps the most unusual link between books and electronic games is the *Marvel vs. Capcom* series. In this series, characters from Marvel comic books (Captain America, Hulk, Spider-Man, Wolverine) battle characters from Capcom games like *Street Fighter* and *Resident Evil* (Akuma, Chun-Li, Ryu, Albert Wesker).

© Warner Bros. Pictures/Everett Collection

BIG-BUDGET MOVIES LIKE *GODZILLA* **(2014)** inspire an increasing number of game tie-ins. In the past, these games would often trail their movie counterparts by months; for *Godzilla*, a simpler mobile game was released concurrently with the movie, while a more elaborate console-based game was promised for the PlayStation 3 at a later date.

Electronic Gaming and Advertising

Commercialism is as prevalent in video games as it is in most entertainment media. **Advergames**, like television's infomercials or newspapers and magazines' advertorials, are video games created for purely promotional purposes. The first notable advergame debuted in 1992, when Chester Cheetah, the official mascot for Cheetos snacks, starred in two video games for the Sega Genesis and Super Nintendo systems—*Chester Cheetah: Too Cool to Fool* and *Chester Cheetah: Wild Wild Quest*. In late 2006, Burger King sold three advergame titles for Xbox and Xbox 360 consoles for $3.99 each with value-meal purchases. One title, *Sneak King*, required the player to have the Burger King mascot deliver food to other characters before they faint from hunger. More recent is the innovative interactive Web commercial "Magnum Pleasure Hunt," for gourmet Magnum chocolate ice cream bars. In this platform game, the user manipulates the constantly jogging, barefoot "Magnum Girl" up and over the game's Internet-based environments (such as Bing travel pages, YouTube videos, and luxury hotel Web sites). A player earns points by strategically timing Magnum Girl's jumps so that she connects with—or consumes—the game's many chocolate bonbons, and Magnum's specialty chocolate bar is the final reward for Magnum Girl's (and the player's) hard work. **In-game advertisements** are more subtle; ads are integrated into the game as billboards, logos, or storefronts (e.g., a Farmers Insurance airship floating by in *FarmVille* or Dove soap spas appearing in *The Sims Social*), or advertised products appear as components of the game (e.g., in the game *Splinter Cell: Chaos Theory*, a large glowing billboard for Axe deodorant becomes an obstacle for the player to overcome).[20]

Some in-game advertisements are static, which means the ads are permanently placed in the game. Other in-game ads are dynamic, which means the ads are digitally networked and can be altered remotely, so agencies can tailor them according to release time, geographical location, or user preferences. A movie ad, for example, can have multiple configurations to reflect the movie's release date and screening markets. Advertisers can also record data on users who come in contact with a dynamic ad, such as how long they look at it, from what angle, and how often, and can thus determine how to alter their ad campaigns in the future. The Xbox Kinect has taken dynamic advertising one step further with its newest consoles, enabling players to engage with the in-game ads using motion and voice control to learn more about a product.

Google's game advertising strategy, launched in 2008, is to place increasing numbers of ads in well-known social game titles, like *Frogger* and *Dance Dance Revolution*—an indication of the tremendous potential growth in social gaming. All in-game advertising is estimated to generate $1 billion in global revenue in 2014.[21]

Addiction and Other Concerns

Though many people view gaming as a simple leisure activity, the electronic gaming industry has sparked controversy. Parents, politicians, the medical establishment, and media scholars have expressed concern about the addictive quality of video games, especially MMORPGs, and have raised the alarm about violent and misogynistic game content—standard fare for many of the most heavily played games.

Addiction

No serious—and honest—gamer can deny the addictive qualities of electronic gaming. In fact, an infamous *South Park* episode from 2006 ("Make Love, Not Warcraft") satirized the obsessive, addictive behavior of video game playing. In a 2011 study of more than three thousand third through eighth graders from Singapore, one in ten were considered pathological gamers, meaning that their gaming addiction was jeopardizing multiple areas of their lives, including school, social and family relations, and psychological well-being. Indeed, the more the children were addicted, the more prone they were to depression, social phobias, and increased anxiety, which led to poorer grades in school. Singapore's high percentage of pathological youth gamers is in line with numbers reported in other countries, including the United States, where studies found 8.5 percent of gamers to be addicted. In China, the number is 10.3 percent, and in Germany, 11.9 percent.[22]

Gender is a factor in game addiction: A 2013 study found that males are much more susceptible to game addiction. This makes sense, given that the most popular games—action and shooter games—are heavily geared toward males.[23] These findings are also not entirely surprising, given that many electronic games are addictive not by accident but by design. Just as habit formation is a primary goal of virtually every commercial form of electronic media, from newspapers to television to radio, cultivating compulsiveness is the aim of most game designs. From recognizing high scores to incorporating various difficulty settings (encouraging players to try easy, medium, and hard versions) and levels that gradually increase in difficulty, designers provide constant in-game incentives for obsessive play.

This is especially true of multiplayer online games—like *Halo*, *Call of Duty*, and *World of Warcraft*—that make money from long-term engagement by selling expansion packs or charging monthly subscription fees. These games have elaborate achievement systems with hard-to-resist rewards that include military ranks like "General" or fanciful titles like "King Slayer," as well as special armor, weapons, and mounts (creatures your avatar can ride, including bears, wolves, or even dragons), all aimed at turning casual players into habitual ones.

This strategy of promoting habit formation may not differ from the cultivation of other media obsessions, like watching televised sporting events. Even so, real-life stories, such as that of the South Korean couple whose three-month-old daughter died of malnutrition while the negligent parents spent ten-hour overnight sessions in an Internet café raising a virtual daughter, bring up serious questions about video games and addiction.[24] South Korea, one of the world's most Internet-connected countries, is already sponsoring efforts to battle Internet addiction, along with China, the Netherlands, and Australia (see "Global Village: South Korea's Gaming Obsession" on pages 96–97).

Meanwhile, industry executives and others cite the positive impact of digital games, such as the mental stimulation and educational benefits of games like *SimCity*, the health benefits of *Wii Fit*, and the socially rewarding benefits of playing games together as a family or with friends.

Violence and Misogyny

The Entertainment Software Association (ESA), the main trade association of the gaming industry, likes to point out that nearly half of game players are women, that nearly three-quarters of games sold are rated in the family- and teen-friendly categories, and that the average age of a game player is thirty. While these statements are true, they also mask a troubling aspect of some of game culture's most popular games: their violent and sexist imagery.

Most games involving combat, guns, and other weapons are intentionally violent, with representations of violence becoming all the more graphic as game visuals reach cinematic hyperrealism. The most violent video games, rated M for "Mature," often belong to the first-person shooter, dark fantasy, or survival horror genres (or a combination of all three) and cast players in a variety of sinister roles—serial killers, mortal combat soldiers, chain-gun-wielding assassins, nut jobs going "postal," father-hating sons, mutated guys out for revenge, not-quite-executed death-row inmates, and underworld criminals (to name a few)—in which they earn points by killing and maiming their foes (sometimes monsters but often "ordinary people") through the most horrendous means possible. In this genre of games, violence is a celebration, as is clear from one Top 10 list featuring the most "delightfully violent video games of all time."[25]

That some games can be violent and misogynistic is not a point of dispute. But the possible effects of such games have been debated for years, and video games have been accused of being a factor in violent episodes, such as the Columbine High School shootings in 1999. Earlier research linked playing violent video games to aggressive thoughts or hostility, but those effects don't necessarily transfer to real-world environments. Instead, more recent studies suggest that the personality traits of certain types of players should be of greater concern than the violence of video games. For example, a study in the *Review of General Psychology* noted that individuals with a combination of "high neuroticism (e.g., easily upset, angry, depressed, emotional, etc.), low agreeableness (e.g., little concern for others, indifferent to others' feelings, cold, etc.), and low conscientiousness (e.g., break rules, don't keep promises, act without thinking, etc.)" are more susceptible to the negative outcomes measured in studies of violent video games.[26] For the vast majority of players, the study concluded, violent video games have no adverse effects.

There is less research on misogyny (hatred of women) in video games. One of the most extreme game narratives is from *Grand Theft Auto 3*, in which male characters can pick up female prostitutes, pay money for sex, get an increase in player "health," and then beat up or kill the hooker to get their money back. Although women are close to half of the digital game audience in the United States, it's likely that many aren't engaged by this story. The source of the problem may be the male insularity of the game development industry—for reasons that are unclear, few women are on the career path to be involved in game development. According to the National Center for Women & Information Technology, "Women hold 56% of all professional occupations in the U.S. workforce, but only 25% of IT occupations." And even as the digital game industry gets bigger, the impact of women gets smaller. "In 2009, just 18% of undergraduate Computing and Information Sciences degrees were awarded to women; in 1985, women earned 37% of these degrees."[27] (See "Media Literacy and the Critical Process: First-Person Shooter Games: Misogyny as Entertainment?" on page 98 for more on violence and misogyny in video games.)

GAMES IN THE *GRAND THEFT AUTO* series typically receive a rating of "Mature," indicating they should not be sold to players under seventeen. However, the ratings do not distinguish between overall game violence and misogynistic attitudes.

David J. Green–Lifestyle/Alamy

GLOBAL VILLAGE

South Korea's Gaming Obsession

In 1997–98, a deep economic crisis hit the formerly booming economies of East Asia. Banks and corporations failed, exports fell, and unemployment soared. South Korea's new president responded to the crisis with a unique recovery plan for his country: Make South Korea the world's leader in Internet connectivity. By 2004, South Korea had achieved this goal and then some, with more than 70 percent of the nation connected to the fiber-optic broadband network. Today, that number is 95 percent.[1] Perhaps the most interesting phenomenon arising from this degree of broadband penetration is the advent of Internet cafés known as *PC bangs*—literally "PC rooms"—in South Korea.

By 2004, more than thirty thousand PC bangs dotted the country, and they became the main hangout for teenagers and young adults. "In America they have lots of fields and grass and outdoor space. They have lots of room to play soccer and baseball and other sports," explained one PC bang operator. "We don't have that here. Here, there are very few places for young people to go and very little for them to do, so they found PC games, and it's their way to spend time together and relax."[2] Some PC bangs, like Intercool in Seoul's Shinlim district, cover two floors, one for smoking patrons and the other for nonsmoking. In a country where most young adults live with their parents until they are married, PC

bangs have become a necessary outlet for socializing.

By far the biggest draw of PC bangs, with their rows of late-model computers and ultrafast Internet connections, are online video games like *StarCraft* and *Lineage*. Because of long-standing resentment against Japan for its years as an imperial ruler over Korea, Koreans shunned Japanese-made video game consoles, such as Sony PlayStations and those made by Nintendo and Sega, and instead preferred to play video games on PCs, a pastime that now feeds the popularity of the broadband network. The PC game *StarCraft* is so popular in South Korea that two-hour battles among the nation's best *StarCraft* players are featured on prime-time television, and an entire sports channel (OnGameNet) is devoted to *StarCraft* competitions and interviews with the biggest *StarCraft* celebrities. One player, Lim Yo-hwan (also known by his *StarCraft* identity, "BoxeR"), began playing in PC bangs as a boy because he couldn't afford his own computer.[3] Lim became the first professional Korean gamer to be signed to a salaried corporate sponsorship contract: South Korea's largest cell phone company hired him to captain its now-legendary gaming team, SK Telecom T1, which went on to win four hundred televised matches.

Today, e-gaming is a legitimate career in South Korea, where league champions can earn as much as $500,000 a year.[4] Gamers who reach the competitive circuit are followed like "characters" in any televised drama, can draw millions of members to their fan clubs, and can become such huge celebrities that they need disguises to walk outside their

Kim Jae-Hwan/AFP/Getty Images/Newscom

houses. "When you look at gaming around the world, Korea is the leader in many ways. It just occupies a different place in the culture there than anywhere else," said Rich Wickham, the global head of Microsoft's PC game business.[5]

With more than half of Korea's fifty million people playing video games, and a culture that celebrates gaming as a sport, it's no surprise that some Koreans spend large amounts of time in front of their PCs.[6] Generally, Koreans view gaming as a good stress reliever, especially given the enormous pressure put on Korean youth to succeed academically. A typical Korean student plays about twenty-three hours a week.[7] But studies have also confirmed that 4 percent of adolescent players in Korea are seriously addicted to gaming. Dramatic stories of addicted users playing fifty to eighty-five hours nonstop, getting fired from their jobs, failing school, and even dying in the midst of a gaming binge because they're neglecting grave medical symptoms

point to the dark underbelly of Korean gaming culture.[8]

The Korean government has responded with numerous approaches to combat addiction, including public awareness campaigns, offers of free software to limit the time people spend on the Web, government-sponsored counseling clinics and treatment programs for gaming

addicts, and Internet "rest camps." Most recently, the government has opted for industry regulation: It has banned all teenagers under the age of sixteen from access to highly addictive (MMORPG and first-person shooter) games between midnight and 6 A.M. (a ban that some have found can be bypassed with an alternative ID). ◢

Media Literacy and the Critical Process

First-Person Shooter Games: Misogyny as Entertainment?

Historical first-person shooter games are a significant sub-genre of action games, the biggest-selling genre of the digital game industry. *Call of Duty: Modern Warfare 3* (set in a fictional WWIII) made $775 million in its first five days. And with thirteen million units sold by 2012, Rockstar Games' critically acclaimed *Red Dead Redemption* (*RDR*, set in the Wild West) was applauded for its realism and called a "tour de force" by the *New York Times*.[1] But as these games proliferate through our culture, what are we learning as we are launched back and forth in time and into the worlds of these games?

1 **DESCRIPTION.** *Red Dead Redemption* features John Madsen, a white outlaw turned federal agent, who journeys to the "uncivilized" West to capture or kill his old gang members. Within this game, gamers encounter breathtaking vistas and ghost towns with saloons, prostitutes, and gunslingers; large herds of cattle; and scenes of the Mexican Rebellion. Shootouts are common in towns and on the plains, and gamers earn points for killing animals and people. The *New York Times* review notes that "*Red Dead Redemption* is perhaps most distinguished by the brilliant voice acting and pungent, pitch-perfect writing we have come to expect from Rockstar."[2]

2 **ANALYSIS.** *RDR* may have "pitch-perfect writing," but a certain tune emerges. For example, African Americans and Native Americans are absent from the story line (although they were clearly present in the West of 1911). The roles of women are limited: They are portrayed as untrustworthy and chronically nagging wives, prostitutes, or nuns—and they can be blithely killed in front of sheriffs and husbands without ramifications. One special mission is to hogtie a nun or prostitute and drop her onto tracks in front of an oncoming train. One gamer in his popular how-to demo on YouTube calls this mission "the coolest achievement I've ever seen in a game."[3]

3 **INTERPRETATION.** *RDR* may give us a technologically rich immersion into the Wild West of 1911, but it relies on clichés to do so (macho white gunslinger as leading man, weak or contemptible women, vigilante justice). If the macho/misogynistic narrative possibilities and value system of *RDR* seem familiar, it's because the game is based on Rockstar's other video game hit, *Grand Theft Auto* (*GTA*), which lets players have sex with and then graphically kill hookers. *GTA* was heavily criticized for creating an "X-Rated wonderland" and was dubbed "Grand Theft Misogyny."[4] Indeed, Rockstar simply took the *GTA* engine and interface and overlaid new scenes, narratives, and characters, moving from the urban streets of Liberty City to the American frontier towns.[5]

4 **EVALUATION.** The problem with *Red Dead Redemption* is its limited view of history, lack of imagination, and reliance on misogyny as entertainment. Since its gameplay is so similar to that of *GTA*, the specifics of time and place are beside the point—all that's left is killing and hating women. Video games are fun, but what effect do they have on men's attitudes toward women?

5 **ENGAGEMENT.** Talk to friends about games like *GTA*, *RDR*, and Rockstar's latest, *L.A. Noire* (set in 1940s Los Angeles, it also contains scenes with nudity and graphic violence against women). Comment on blog sites about the ways some games can provide a mask for misogyny, and write to Rockstar itself (www.rockstargames.com), demanding less demeaning narratives regarding women and ethnic minorities.

Regulating Gaming

For decades, concern about violence in video games has led to calls for regulation. Back in 1976, an arcade game called *Death Race* prompted the first public outcry over the violence of electronic gaming. The primitive graphics of the game depicted a blocky car running down stick-figure Gremlins that, if struck, turned into grave markers. Described as "sick and morbid" by the National Safety Council, *Death Race* inspired a *60 Minutes* report on the potential psychological damage of playing video games. Over the next thirty-five years, violent video games would prompt citizen groups and politicians to call for government regulation of electronic games' content.

In 1993, after the violence of *Mortal Kombat* and *Night Trap* attracted the attention of religious and educational organizations, Senator Joe Lieberman conducted a hearing that proposed federal regulation of the gaming industry. Following a pattern established in the movie and music industries, the gaming industry implemented a self-regulation system enforced by an industry panel. The industry founded the **Entertainment Software Rating Board (ESRB)** in 1994 to institute a labeling system designed to inform parents of sexual and violent content that might not be suitable for younger players. Publishers aren't required to submit their games to the ESRB for a rating, but many retailers will only sell rated games, so gamemakers usually consent to the process. To get a rating, the game companies submit scripts that include any dialogue and music lyrics, and also fill out a questionnaire to describe the story and identify possibly offensive content.[28] Currently the ESRB sorts games into six categories: EC (Early Childhood), E (Everyone), E 10+, T (Teens), M (17+), and AO (Adults Only 18+).

In the most recent effort to regulate video games, California passed a law in 2005 to fine stores $1,000 for selling video games rated M or AO to minors. In 2011, the U.S. Supreme Court struck down the law in a 7–2 decision, setting a difficult precedent for the establishment of other laws regulating electronic games.

The Future of Gaming and Interactive Environments

Gaming technology of the future promises a more immersive and portable experience that will touch even more aspects of our lives. The Wii has been successful in harnessing more interactive technology to attract nongamers with its motion-controlled games. Nintendo's latest Wii U system goes a step further—in one game, the controller serves as a shield to block virtual arrows shot by pirates on the TV screen. Microsoft's motion-sensing Xbox Kinect has been a hit since its introduction in late 2010, and with Avatar Kinect, users can control their avatar's motions as the Kinect senses even small physical gestures. In 2012, Sony released its SOEmote facial-tracking and voice-font software with its popular *Everquest II* game, enabling players to give their facial expressions and voices to their avatars. The anticipated release of the Oculus Rift virtual reality headset could further deepen the immersive play of games.

Video games in the future will also continue to move beyond just entertainment. The term *gamification* describes how interactive game experiences are being embedded to bring competition and rewards to everyday activities.[29] Games are already used in workforce training, for social causes, in classrooms, and as part of multimedia journalism. For example, to accompany a news report about texting while driving, the *New York Times* developed an interactive game, *Gauging Your Distraction*, to demonstrate the consequences of distractions (such as cell phones) on driving ability. All these developments continue to make games a larger part of our media experiences.

The Business of Digital Gaming

Today, about 72 percent of households play computer or video games. The entire U.S. video game market, including portable and console hardware and accessories, adds up to about $20.8 billion annually, while global sales are expected to reach $111 billion by 2015. Thanks largely to the introduction of the Wii and mobile games, today's audience for games extends beyond the young-male gamer stereotype. Though the obsessive gamers who frequent GameSpot and IGN are largely youthful and male, the population of casual gamers has grown much more diverse. According to the video and computer game industry's main trade group, the Entertainment Software Association, the average game player is thirty years old and has been playing games for thirteen years. Women constitute 46 percent of game players. Gamers play across a range of platforms: 51 percent of U.S. households have a video console, 43 percent play games on smartphones, and 37 percent play on a dedicated handheld player. Gamers are social, too: 62 percent of them play games with others, either in person or online.[30] These numbers speak to the economic health of the electronic gaming industry, which has proved recession-proof so far. Digital gaming companies can make money selling not just consoles and games but also online subscriptions, companion books, and movie rights.

The Ownership and Organization of Digital Gaming

For years, the two major components of the gaming industry have been console makers and game publishers. The biggest blockbuster games are still produced and distributed by the leading game publishers, and many are designed to be played on the leading game consoles connected to big television sets. At the same time, the emergence of game platforms on mobile devices and on social networks has expanded the game market and brought new game publishers into the field.

Console Makers

The video game console business is dominated by three major players: Nintendo, Sony, and Microsoft. Nintendo got its start manufacturing Japanese playing cards in 1889. After seventy-seven years, the playing card business was becoming less profitable, and Nintendo began venturing into toy production in the 1960s. By 1974, the toy business evolved into the company distributing Magnavox's *Odyssey* home video console by 1974. Nintendo would release its own video game console three years later. In the early 1980s, Nintendo had two major marketing successes. First, the company developed and released the very successful platform game *Donkey Kong* (1981), in which players help Jumpman rescue Lady from the giant ape, Donkey Kong. Developed for multiple consoles, the video game was the Japanese company's breakthrough into the U.S. console market. Second, Nintendo developed the Nintendo Entertainment System (NES) console, which reached U.S. markets in 1985 bundled with the *Super Mario Bros.* platform game. With this package, Nintendo set the standard for video game consoles, Mario and Luigi became household names, and *Super Mario Bros.* became the most successful video series for the next twenty-five years.

Sony, also headquartered in Japan, emerged after World War II as a manufacturer of tape recorders and radios (the name Sony is rooted in the Latin word *sonus*, meaning "sound"). Since then, Sony has been a major player in the consumer electronics industry, producing televisions, VCRs, computers, cameras, and, beginning in the mid-1990s, video game consoles. Its venture into video games came about because of a deal gone bad with Nintendo. Sony had been partnering with Nintendo to create an add-on device to Nintendo's NES that would control music CDs (hence the name they proposed: "play station"). When the partnership fell through, Sony went into direct competition with Nintendo, launching in 1994 the impressive PlayStation console, which doubled the microprocessor size introduced by Sega (from 16 bits to 32 bits) and played both full-motion and 3-D video. Described in the *New York Times* as the "CD-based video game machine," PlayStation was also capable of playing music CDs—a nice retort to Nintendo.[31]

Continuing the console battle, in 1996 Nintendo released Nintendo 64, a doubly powerful 64-bit microprocessor complete with even more realistic images and even clearer 3-D motion graphics. This launch created a buyer's frenzy—for the Nintendo 64 as well as for the *Super Mario 64* game **cartridge** that launched with the console, dubbed by critics "the best video game ever."[32] Meanwhile, other console makers—such as Sega, Atari, and SNK—were trying to compete, sometimes making incredible technological leaps, like Sega's 128-bit Dreamcast, which came equipped with a built-in modem. Ultimately, these advancements were copied, and then overshadowed, by Nintendo and Sony products.

The main rivalry between Nintendo and Sony was more or less resolved by 1997, with Nintendo claiming the market for children up to age fourteen and Sony's PlayStation becoming the console of choice for serious young-adult gamers. By 1997, the newly broadened audience had created an impressive market for the video game industry worth $5.5 billion.[33] PlayStation 2, released in 2000, heightened this trend. As a masterpiece in console engineering, and through Sony's alliance with third-party game publishers who were churning out the world's most innovative titles (*Call of Duty*, *Final Fantasy*), PlayStation 2 would become the most successful console of all time.

And yet into this new world of serious gaming—so securely dominated by Sony PlayStation—came the computer software goliath Microsoft. "The machine, called Xbox," wrote *New York Times* technology writer John Markoff in 2000, "is both a technical tour de force by the world's largest software publisher and a shot fired across the bow of the giant Sony Corporation, which now dominates the $20 billion video game industry."[34] The Xbox, which represented a $500 million commitment from Microsoft, had many firsts: the first console to feature a built-in hard disk drive; the first to be connected to an online service (Xbox LIVE); and the first to have Dolby Digital sound, for a cinematic sound experience. While Xbox could not offer the arsenal of games that PlayStation gamers had access to, the console did launch with one particular game, *Halo*. Game critics and players immediately recognized this sci-fi first-person shooter game—now a multibillion-dollar franchise—as Microsoft's "killer app."[35]

Today, Sony's PlayStation 4 (2013), Microsoft's Xbox One (2013), and Nintendo's Wii U (2012) are the leading consoles, providing the most creative, interactive, hyperrealistic, and stimulating entertainments.

Game Publishers

As the video game industry moves away from consoles and toward streaming services, browsers, smartphones, and tablets, game publishers have had to adapt to new technological innovations and predict future media trends, all while still offering good gameplay and stories. In some cases, the game-console makers are also the game publishers (sometimes making the game *proprietary*, meaning it only plays on that company's system). For example, Microsoft famously published its *Halo* game series to drive sales of the Xbox. Similarly, Sony publishes the *Uncharted* game series just for PlayStation, and Nintendo publishes *The Legend of Zelda* series solely for its gaming platforms.

More often, game publishers are independent companies, distributing games that play across multiple platforms. Sometimes the publishers are also the developers of the game—the people who write the actual code for the game. But publishers may also be just the distributors for the game developers (just as film studios may distribute the work of independent filmmakers). Two leading independent game publishing companies, Activision Blizzard and Electronic Arts, have been particularly good at adaptation and innovation, producing the most imaginative and ambitious titles and selling the most games across multiple platforms. King (*Candy Crush Saga*) and Rovio (*Angry Birds*) are two other major players, respectively dominating in social gaming and mobile gaming.

Activision Blizzard was created through the merging of Activision and Vivendi's Blizzard division in 2008. One half of the company—Activision—got its start in the 1970s as the first independent game developer and distributor, initially providing games for the Atari platform (before Activision, console makers like Atari created only proprietary games for their own systems). Activision was unique in that it rewarded its developers with royalty payments and name credits on game box covers, something that hadn't yet been considered by other game publishing companies, which kept their developers anonymous. As a result, top game designers and programmers migrated to Activision, and Activision began to produce a number of top-selling games, including the *X-Men* series (2000–), the *Call of Duty* series (2003–), and *Guitar Hero* (2006–2011).

Meanwhile, Blizzard Entertainment, established in 1991 as an independent game publisher, has three famous franchises in game publishing: *Diablo* (1996–), *StarCraft* (1998–), and *World of Warcraft* (2001–). Dedicated, as the company says in its mission statement, to "creating the most epic entertainment experiences . . . ever,"[36] and known for its obsession with game quality, artistic achievement, and commitment to its fans, Blizzard has dominated in real-time strategy games and remains one of the most critically acclaimed game publishers in the world. As one company, Activision Blizzard has become a publishing giant in the industry.

Electronic Arts (EA) got its name by recognizing that the video game is an art form and that software developers are indeed artists; the name Electronic Arts is also a tribute to the United Artists film studio, established in 1919 by three actors and one director—Charlie Chaplin, Mary Pickford, Douglas Fairbanks, and D. W. Griffith—who broke away from the studio-dominated film industry (see page 239). Operating under the same principle that Activision pioneered—of recognizing game developers on the package and paying them high royalty fees—EA was able to secure a stable of top talent and begin producing a promising lineup of titles: *Archon*, *Pinball Construction Set*, *M.U.L.E.*, *Seven Cities of Gold*, *The Bard's Tale*, *Starflight*, and *Wasteland*.

The company's big breakthrough, though, was signing a contract with Super Bowl–winning coach and television football commentator John Madden in 1984. The game, *John Madden Football*, was released in 1988, with annual versions coming out every year since 1990. This became the modus operandi for EA: Create a popular game (or, more typically, buy the company that produces the popular game) and then create annual updates until the game stops selling. The *Madden* series has become a billion-dollar enterprise, and EA has since developed a reputation for specializing in sports games, with such series as *FIFA* (soccer) and *NASCAR* (racing). EA also struck gold with *Battlefield*, *Crysis*, *Rock Band*, *Mass Effect*, and *Dragon Age: Origins*.

Unlike Activision Blizzard, EA has quickly moved toward mobile and social gaming platforms. Electronic Arts acquired PopCap Games, the company that produces both *Bejeweled* and *Plants vs. Zombies*, as well as other social media gaming start-ups, and has more than 127 iPhone game apps and 41 Android game apps for direct download. The company has also sought to compete directly with Activision Blizzard's *World of Warcraft* series by developing (through its Canadian subsidiary, BioWare) the lavish new MMORPG game *Star Wars: The Old Republic* (2012), the most expensive game made to date, with a price tag approaching $200 million.[37]

One of the newest major game publishers, Zynga, was established in 2007 and specializes in casual games. *FarmVille*, *Draw Something*, *Zynga Poker*, and *Hidden Chronicles* are among its hit games. But in recent years, Zynga's games on the Facebook platform have lost players to competing developers like King (*Candy Crush Saga*, *Bubble Witch Saga*) and Wooga (*Diamond Dash*, *Bubble Island*). Zynga's next step is developing games for mobile devices to decrease its reliance on Facebook.

The most well-known developer and publisher of games for mobile devices is Rovio, founded in Finland in 2003. In 2010, Rovio's *Angry Birds* became an international phenomenon, as millions of players downloaded the game on touchscreen devices for the chance to slingshot-launch birds at pigs hiding in increasingly complex structures. By 2012 (as Rovio released *Angry Birds Space*), the downloads of all of the company's *Angry Birds* titles reached a billion.[38] Like Zynga, Rovio has moved to diversify, and it brought *Angry Birds* to Facebook in 2012.

Other top game publishers around the world include Square Enix (*Deus Ex*, *Final Fantasy*), Ubisoft (*Assassin's Creed*, *Rayman*), Sega (*Sonic the Hedgehog*, *Super Monkey Ball*), THQ (*Saints Row*, *Red Faction*), and Namco Bandai (*Dark Souls*, *Tekken*).

The Structure of Digital Game Publishing

AAA game titles (games that represent the current standard for technical excellence) can cost as much as a blockbuster film to make and promote. For example, Activision Blizzard's MMORPG *Star Wars: The Old Republic* (2012) took six years of production, with hundreds of programmers, writers, and artists working on the game, as well as an untold number of contract workers. Using recorded voice dialogue rather than text, *Star Wars: The Old Republic* has more voice acting than any previous game, online or off. To get the game ready for its global launch, EA assembled 1.6 million players to test an early version of the game.[39] Development, licensing, manufacturing, and marketing constitute the major expenditures in game publishing (see Figure 3.2).

"Of course I'm angry—look at me."

© Kim Warp/The New Yorker Collection/www.CartoonBank.com.

Development

The largest part of the **development** budget—the money spent designing, coding, scoring, and testing a game—goes to paying talent, digital artists, and game testers. Each new generation of gaming platforms doubles the number of people involved in designing, programming, and mixing digitized images and sounds.

Licensing

Independent gamemakers must also deal with two types of licensing. First, they have to pay royalties to console manufacturers (Microsoft, Sony, or Nintendo) for the right to distribute a game using their system. These royalties vary from $3 to $10 per unit sold. (Of course, if a console manufacturer such as Nintendo makes its own games exclusively for the Wii, then it doesn't have to pay a console royalty to itself.) The other form of licensing involves **intellectual properties**—stories, characters, personalities, and music that require licensing

ANGRY BIRDS, Rovio's popular mobile video game, had over 2 billion downloads across all mobile platforms by 2014. With a mention on NBC's *30 Rock,* a tie-in with Twentieth Century Fox's animated film *Rio,* and a *New Yorker* cartoon, these fearsome birds have permeated our media culture.

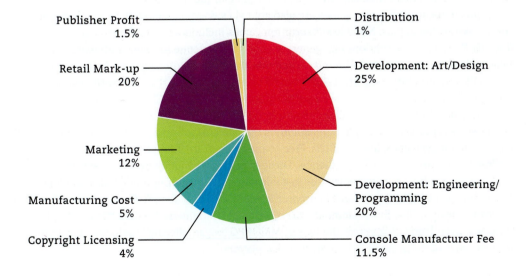

FIGURE 3.2

WHERE THE MONEY GOES ON A $60 VIDEO GAME

Data from: Altered Gamer, March 30, 2012, www.alteredgamer.com /free-pcgaming/21118-why-are-video -games-so-expensive.

Publisher Profit
1.5%

Distribution
1%

Retail Mark-up
20%

Development: Art/Design
25%

Marketing
12%

Development: Engineering/ Programming
20%

Manufacturing Cost
5%

Copyright Licensing
4%

Console Manufacturer Fee
11.5%

agreements. In 2005, for instance, John Madden reportedly signed a $150 million deal with EA Sports that allowed the company to use his name and likeness for the next ten years.[40]

Marketing

The marketing costs of launching an electronic game often equal or exceed the development costs. The successful launch of a game involves online promotions, banner ads, magazine print ads, in-store displays, and the most expensive of all: television advertising. In many ways, the marketing blitz associated with introducing a major new franchise title, including cinematic television trailers, resembles the promotional campaign surrounding the debut of a blockbuster movie. For example, Rockstar Games reportedly spent $150 million for the marketing of its 2013 blockbuster release, *Grand Theft Auto V*. In this case, the marketing budget eclipsed the $115 million development budget.[41] Just as avid fans line up for the midnight release of a new *Spider-Man* or *Hunger Games* movie, devoted gamers mob participating retail outlets during the countdown to the midnight launch of a hotly anticipated new game.

Selling Digital Games

Just as digital distribution has altered the relationship between other mass media and their audiences, it has transformed the selling of electronic games. Although the selling of $60 AAA console games at retail stores is an enduring model, many games are now free (with opportunities for hooked players to pay for additional play features), and digital stores are making access to games almost immediate.

Pay Models

There are three main pay models in the electronic game industry: the boxed game/retail model, the subscription model, and free-to-play.

The *boxed game/retail model* is the most traditional and dates back to the days of cartridges on Atari, Sega, and Nintendo console systems from the 1970s to the 1990s. By the 1990s, games were being released on CD-ROMs, and later DVDs, to better handle the richer game files. Many boxed games are now sold with offers of additional downloadable content, known as DLC in gaming circles. For blockbuster console games, retail sales of boxed games still reign as the venue for a game premiere. As of 2013, the biggest game launch ever—in fact, the biggest launch of *any* media product ever—was the September 17, 2013, release of *Grand Theft Auto V*. The game, published by Rockstar Games, generated more than $1 billion in sales in just three days, more than any other previous game or movie release.[42]

Some of the most popular games are also sold via *subscription models*, in which gamers pay a monthly fee to play. Notable subscription games include *World of Warcraft* and *Star Wars: The Old Republic*. Subscriptions can generate enormous revenue for game publishers. At its height of popularity, *World of Warcraft* earned more than $1 billion a year for Activision Blizzard.[43] Players first buy the game (either boxed or as a download at $19.99, with expansions costing $29.99–$39.99) and then pay a subscription from $12.99 to $14.99 a month. EA's *Star Wars: The Old Republic* has a similar subscription cost.

Free-to-play (sometimes called *freemium*) is the latest pay model and is common with casual and online games, like *100 Balls*. Free-to-play games are offered online or as downloads for free to gain or retain a large audience. These games make money by selling extras, like power boosters (to aid in gameplay), or in-game subscriptions for upgraded play. In addition to free casual games (like *Angry Birds Seasons*, *Clash of Clans*, and *Temple Run*), popular MMORPG games like Sony Online Entertainment's *EverQuest* and *DC Universe Online* offer free-to-play versions. Even *World of Warcraft*, the largest MMORPG, began offering free-to-play for up to twenty levels of the game in 2011 to lure in new players.

Video Game Stores

Apart from buying boxed game titles at stores like Walmart, Best Buy, and Target, or online stores like Amazon, there is really only one major video game store chain devoted entirely to new and used video games: GameStop. The chain, which started in Dallas, Texas, in 1984 as Babbage's, today operates more than sixty-six hundred company stores in the United States and in fourteen other countries, including Canada, Australia, Austria, Denmark, Finland, France, and Germany.[44] GameStop stores usually appear in shopping and strip malls, and beyond video titles, they also specialize in gaming magazines (including their own proprietary title, *Game Informer*), strategy guides, and video game accessories.

Today, the traditional brick-and-mortar chain GameStop is trying to negotiate the shifting ground of the digital turn. Some of GameStop's digital survival strategies include selling customers video game access codes to digital game downloads in the stores, selling Android tablets and refurbished iPads, and investing in other digital gaming companies.

Digital Distribution

With the advent and growing popularity of digital game distribution, game players don't need to go to a department store or retail game shop to buy video games. All three major consoles are Wi-Fi capable, and each has its own digital store—Xbox Games Store, Wii Shop Channel, and PlayStation Store. Customers can purchase and download games, get extra downloadable content, and buy other media—including television shows and movies—as the consoles compete to be the sole entertainment center of people's living rooms. These console-connected digital stores present the biggest threat to brick-and-mortar game stores.

Although the three major console companies control digital downloads to their devices, several companies compete for the download market in PC games. The largest is Steam, with more than seventy-five million subscribers and about 50 percent of the PC game distribution market.[45] Steam is owned by Valve Corporation, which used the digital store to help distribute its *Counter-Strike* game online starting in 2003. Steam also carries more than three thousand games from a wide range of game publishers. Other companies that sell digital game downloads for PCs include Amazon's Appstore, GameStop, Microsoft's Games Marketplace, Origin (owned by EA), and GameFly.

Of course, the most ubiquitous digital game distributors are Apple's App Store and Google Play, where users can purchase games on mobile devices. Although Google's Android system has surpassed the iPhone in market penetration, Apple customers are more likely to purchase apps, including games. This has drawn more independent developers to work in the Apple operating system. As one technology writer summarized, "Quite simply, developers have long known that Apple device owners are closely locked into the Apple ecosystem, with credit cards on file."[46]

Alternative Voices

The advent of mobile gaming has provided a new entry point for independent game developers. As *Canadian Business* magazine noted, the cost of entry has decreased substantially. "The average cost of making a major console game for Xbox 360 and PlayStation3 is about $20 million, but almost anyone can churn out a new game app for the iPhone. And independent

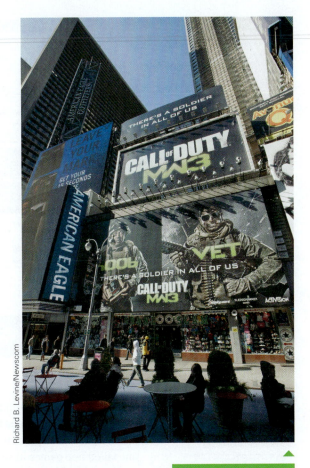

MAJOR GAME FRANCHISES like *Call of Duty* from Activision receive launches that rival the biggest film events (like *The Avengers* or the *Transformers* movies) or book publications (like *Harry Potter* or *The Hunger Games*). In fact, the most popular games can match the grosses of the year's biggest movies in a matter of days, thanks to sky-high demand as well as higher prices.

GOOGLE PLAY, formerly known as the Android Market, allows Android users to browse and download their favorite video games directly to their mobile devices. And while it has been shown that Apple customers are more likely to purchase apps, Google Play kept pace with Apple's App Store, with 1.2 million apps available by 2014. Google, Inc. Reprinted by permission.

developers need only pay Apple's $99 fee for a developer's account to get their creations to the market—no Best Buy or Walmart shelf space required."[47]

But even so, time and money are still required to develop quality games. Many independent game developers and smaller game companies, shunned by big game publishers who are focused on the next big blockbuster games, are finding funding through Kickstarter, the crowdsource fund-raising social media Web site for creative projects. Video game developers make a brief pitch on Kickstarter and then request a modest amount—sometimes just a few thousand dollars—from supporters to get started. "Rather than seeking help from publishers who demand a high rate of return and, thus, a product that appeals to a broad group of gamers, developers can turn directly to their most devoted fans," the *Washington Post* explained. "And if enough of those fans are willing to pony up cash for the promise of a game that suits their tastes, it gets made, regardless of how quirky or niche-oriented it is."[48] (The Oculus Rift virtual reality headset that Facebook bought for $2 billion got its start in a comparatively modest Kickstarter campaign, which raised more than $2.4 million, far exceeding its $250,000 goal.) A number of top games at Apple's App Store—including *Temple Run*, *Tiny Wings*, and *Jetpack Joyride*—are great success stories, started by small independent developers. But the cautionary tale is that it takes incredible persistence against great odds to make a successful game. Rovio made fifty-one failed app games in six years and nearly folded before *Angry Birds* became a worldwide success in 2009.

Digital Gaming, Free Speech, and Democracy

Though 80 percent of retail outlets voluntarily chose to observe the ESRB guidelines and not sell M- and AO-rated games to minors, the ratings did not have force of law. That changed in 2005, when California enacted a law to make renting or selling an M-rated game to a minor an offense enforced by fines. The law was immediately challenged by the industry and struck down by a lower court as unconstitutional. California petitioned the Supreme Court to hear the case. In a landmark decision handed down in 2011, the Supreme Court granted electronic games speech protections afforded by the First Amendment. According to the opinion written by Justice Antonin Scalia, video games communicate ideas worthy of such protection:

Like the protected books, plays, and movies that preceded them, video games communicate ideas—and even social messages—through many familiar literary devices (such as characters, dialogue, plot, and music) and through features distinctive to the medium (such as the player's interaction with the virtual world).[49]

DIGITAL JOB OUTLOOK

Media Professionals Speak about Jobs in the Video Game Industry

Ian Williams, Student and Freelance Writer

I started as a QA (Quality Assurance) engineer, and a QA's job is to break things in-game, record how the things were broken, and then pass the information to the content creation team, who would hopefully fix them. It's a common entry-level gig in the industry, one that gives you a broad enough knowledge of how things work to eventually launch something more specialized.

Lisa Brown, Designer, Insomniac Games

Should people learn to code? I think so! Even if you aren't planning on becoming a programmer, it really helps you get a feel and an appreciation for the medium you're working in—and will help you talk to your programmer teammates in the future.

Sarah Ford, Indie Developer

I'm useless with code, so most of my beginner games were made in conjunction with coders and designers, many of whom found my art online and dug it enough to want to work with me. It helps if you think in assets, if you're wanting to get into games art. It's not just about creating a picture of a cool car in a neon cityscape—it's about thinking about all the little parts that make up that scene, from the car to the buildings that create the skyline down to the surface of the road itself.

Andy Grossman, Video Game Developer

Even if you're lucky enough to land that dream job at Valve or Nintendo or Blizzard, and you get to work on a beloved franchise, you'll hate it when you're done. Try enjoying *Halo* after you get reprimanded for slightly coloring Master Chief's helmet off the style guide. You won't. The magic will be gone: An endless universe filled with infinite stories will be replaced by a group of bug logs reporting that Nathan Drake's eyes are missing in cut scenes.

Allison Salmon, Game Developer and Software Engineer, Learning Games Network

I experienced far more discrimination and harassment during my time in college than I did while working in AAA. So I guess some of my advice would be don't let the unfriendliness of certain gamer cultures scare you away from the video game industry.

Keith Stuart, Games Editor, the *Guardian*

We are entering an era of diverse artistic and emotional expression. It's no longer about dumb muscle-heads saving the princess (not that games were ever about just that)—this is a creative medium bursting with interesting, weird, and challenging ideas. In the seventies, kids turned to guitars and the punk movement to express themselves. Now they're just as likely to write and distribute games that reach thousands.

Scalia even mentions *Mortal Kombat* in footnote 4 of the decision:

Reading Dante is unquestionably more cultured and intellectually edifying than playing Mortal Kombat. *But these cultural and intellectual differences are not constitutional ones. Crudely violent video games, tawdry TV shows, and cheap novels and magazines are no less forms of speech than* The Divine Comedy. . . . *Even if we can see in them "nothing of any possible value to society . . . they are as much entitled to the protection of free speech as the best of literature."*

With the Supreme Court decision, electronic games achieved the same First Amendment protection afforded to other mass media. However, as in the music, television, and film industries, First Amendment protections will not make the rating system for the gaming industry go away. Parents continue to have legitimate concerns about the games their children play. Game publishers and retailers understand it is still in their best interest to respect those concerns even though the ratings cannot be enforced by law. ▶

CHAPTER REVIEW

COMMON THREADS

One of our favorite quotes that we like to use in our teaching is from writer Joan Didion, in her book **The White Album.** *She wrote: "We tell ourselves stories in order to live." Telling stories is one of the constants of cultural expression across the mass media. But with digital games, is it still a story—or, better yet, what is it that is being communicated—if we are crafting our own individual narrative as we play through a game?*

Books, television, movies, newspapers, magazines, and even musical recordings tell us stories about the human experience. Digital games, especially ones in which we play as a character or an avatar, offer perhaps the most immersive storytelling experience of any medium.

Gamers have already shifted away from traditional media stories to those of video games. The Entertainment Software Association reported that gamers who played more video games than they had three years earlier were spending less time going to the movies (47 percent of respondents), watching TV (48 percent), and watching movies at home (47 percent).[50] Clearly, video games are in competition with movies and television for consumers' attention. But as we move from the kind of storytelling we experience as audience members of TV and movies to the storytelling we experience as players of games, what happens to the story? Is it still a mass mediated story, or is it something else?

Jon Spaihts, screenwriter of the science-fiction film *Prometheus* (2012), identified an essential difference between the stories and storytelling in games and in films. "The central character of a game is most often a cipher—an avatar into which the player projects himself or herself. The story has to have a looseness to accommodate the player's choices," Spaihts said. Conversely, "a filmmaker is trying to make you look at something a certain way—almost to force an experience on you," he added.[51] Thus the question of who is doing the storytelling—a producer/director or the game player—is a significant one.

Such was the case in the furor over *Mass Effect 3* in 2012. After players spent from 120 to 150 hours advancing through the trilogy, in which they could make hundreds of choices in the sequence of events, the final act took that power away from them with a tightly scripted finish. The players complained loudly, and the cofounder of BioWare, the game's developer, issued an apology: "*Mass Effect 3* concludes a trilogy with so much player control and ownership of the story that it was hard for us to predict the range of emotions players would feel when they finished playing through it. The journey you undertake in *Mass Effect* provokes an intense range of highly personal emotions in the player; even so, the passionate reaction of some of our most loyal players to the current endings in *Mass Effect 3* is something that has genuinely surprised us." BioWare said that it would create a new ending with "a number of game content initiatives that will help answer the questions, providing more clarity for those seeking further closure to their journey."[52]

Certainly the audience of a movie will have a range of interpretations of the movie's story. But what of the stories we are telling ourselves as players of games like *Mass Effect*? Is such personally immersive storytelling better, worse, or just different? And who is doing the storytelling?

KEY TERMS

The definitions for the terms listed below can be found in the glossary at the end of the book. The page numbers listed with the terms indicate where the term is highlighted in the chapter.

penny arcade, 76
pinball machine, 76
arcades, 78
avatar, 79
consoles, 79
massively multiplayer online role-playing
  games (MMORPGs), 81
online fantasy sports, 82
gameplay, 84
action games, 86

first-person shooter (FPS), 86
adventure games, 88
role-playing games (RPGs), 88
strategy games, 88
simulation games, 88
casual games, 89
PUGs, 90
noobs, 90
ninjas, 90
trolls, 90

guilds *or* clans, 90
collective intelligence, 91
modding, 91
advergames, 93
in-game advertisements, 93
Entertainment Software Rating Board
  (ESRB), 99
cartridge, 100
development, 103
intellectual properties, 103

REVIEW QUESTIONS

The Development of Digital Gaming

1. What sparked the creation of mechanical games in both the nineteenth and the twentieth centuries?

2. What technology enabled the evolution of the first video games?

3. How are classic arcade games and the culture of the arcade similar to today's popular console games and gaming culture?

4. What are the three major consoles, and what distinguishes them from each other?

5. What advantages did personal computers have over video game consoles in the late 1980s and much of the 1990s?

The Internet Transforms Gaming

6. How are MMORPGs, virtual worlds, and online fantasy sports built around online social interaction?

7. How has digital convergence changed the function of gaming consoles?

The Media Playground

8. What are the main genres within digital gaming?

9. What are the two basic kinds of virtual communities?

10. How do collective intelligence, gaming Web sites, and game conventions enhance the social experience of gaming and make games different from other mass media?

Trends and Issues in Digital Gaming

11. How have digital games influenced media culture, and vice versa?

12. In what ways has advertising become incorporated into electronic games?

13. To what extent are video game addiction and violent and misogynistic representations problems for the gaming industry?

14. How are digital games regulated?

15. What might video games be like in the future?

The Business of Digital Gaming

16. What are the roles of two major components of the gaming industry—console makers and game publishers?

17. How do game publishers develop, license, and market new titles?

18. What are the three major pay models for selling video games today?

19. How can small, independent game developers get their start in the industry?

Digital Gaming, Free Speech, and Democracy

20. Why did the U.S. Supreme Court rule that games count as speech?

21. Why does the game industry still rate digital games, even if it isn't required by law to do so?

QUESTIONING THE MEDIA

1. Do you have any strong memories from playing early video games? To what extent did these games define your childhood?

2. What role does digital gaming play in your life today? Are you more inclined to play casual games or more involved games, and why?

3. Do you have a story about game addiction, either your own or from someone you know? Explain.

4. Have you ever been appalled at the level of violence, misogyny, or racism in a video game you played (or watched being played)? Discuss the game narrative and what made it problematic.

5. Most electronic games produced have a white, male, heterosexual point of view. Why is that? If you were a game developer, what kinds of game narratives would you like to see developed?

LAUNCHPAD FOR *MEDIA & CULTURE*

Visit **LaunchPad for *Media & Culture*** *at* **macmillanhighered.com/mediaculture10e** *for additional learning tools:*

- REVIEW WITH LEARNINGCURVE
  LearningCurve, available on LaunchPad for *Media & Culture*, uses gamelike quizzing to help you master the concepts you need to learn from this chapter.

PART 2

Sounds and Images

Richard B. Levine/Newscom

The dominant media of the twentieth century were all about sounds and images: music, radio, television, and film. Each of these media industries was built around a handful of powerful groups—record labels, radio networks, television networks, and film studios—that set the terms for creating and distributing this popular media content. The main story of these media industries was one of ever-improving technology. For example, television moved from black-and-white to color, from analog broadcast transmissions to digital cable.

Music, radio, TV, and movies are still significant media in our lives. But convergence and the digital turn have changed the story of our sound and image media. Starting with the music industry and the introduction of Napster in 1999, one by one these media industries have had to cope with revolutionary changes. More than a decade later, the traditional media corporations have much less power in dictating what we listen to and watch. The narrative of ever-improving technology has been upended and replaced with wholly different technology.

We now live in a world where any and all media can be consumed via the Internet on laptops, tablets, smartphones, and video game consoles. As a result, we have seen the demise of record stores and video stores, local radio deejays, and the big network TV hit. Traditional media corporations are playing catch-up, devising new online services to bring their offerings to us and still make money. (Hulu, NBC.com, and iHeartRadio are good examples.) Meanwhile, start-up technology and content companies and anyone with a video camera and a YouTube account are competing with the major media corporations on the same Internet playing field. Pandora, iTunes, Vevo, YouTube, Amazon, and Netflix have all become significant distributors of sounds and images.

Moreover, as we consume all types of media content on a single device or through a single service, the traditionally separate "identities" of music, radio, television, and film have become blurred. For example, people might download an audio book and the latest pop single onto their iPods, or stream an album on a subscription service like Spotify, or listen to a genre of music on streaming radio. Similarly, more and more people are choosing to watch their video content on Netflix or Hulu—where TV programs and movies exist side by side.

The major media of the twentieth century are mostly still with us, but the twenty-first-century story of what form that content will take, how we will experience it, and even what we might call the activity (we may need new words for incessantly snapchatting our friends, or creating a customized Internet radio channel) is still up for grabs.

HOW WE WATCH AND LISTEN TODAY

iTunes Downloads Totals (Billions of Units, Months after Launch)

Historical Trend. Average Active Sessions (Domestic, Mon–Sun 6a–12m)

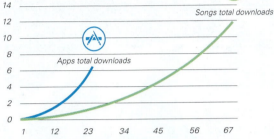

Songs total downloads

Apps total downloads

iTunes Revenues. Shown in Billions (USD)

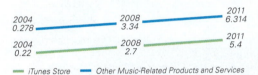

2004	2008	2011
0.278	3.34	6.314
2004	2008	2011
0.22	2.7	5.4

— iTunes Store   — Other Music-Related Products and Services

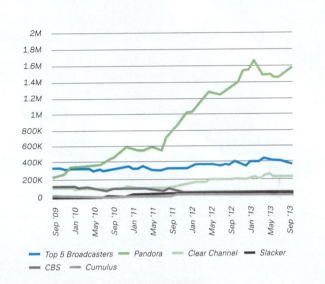

— Top 5 Broadcasters   — Pandora   — Clear Channel   — Slacker
— CBS   — Cumulus

NETFLIX, YOUTUBE, AND APPLE REINVENT HOW WE WATCH MOVIES AND TELEVISION

1. NETFLIX **32%**
2. GOOGLE **22%**
3. APPLE **4.3%**
4. TWITCH **1.8%**
5. HULU **1.7%**
6. FACEBOOK **1.5%**
7. VALVE **1.3%**
8. AMAZON **1.2%**
9. PANDORA **0.5%**
10. TUMBLR **0.4%**

Percentage of U.S. peak Internet traffic produced by companies' networks

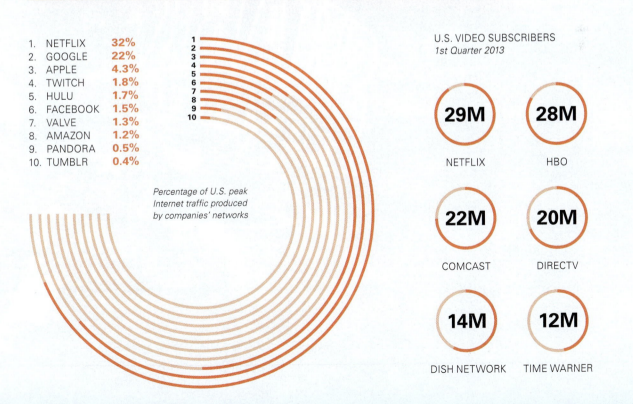

U.S. VIDEO SUBSCRIBERS
1st Quarter 2013

29M
NETFLIX

28M
HBO

22M
COMCAST

20M
DIRECTV

14M
DISH NETWORK

12M
TIME WARNER

4

Sound Recording and Popular Music

115
The Development of Sound Recording

122
U.S. Popular Music and the Formation of Rock

129
A Changing Industry: Reformations in Popular Music

136
The Business of Sound Recording

144
Sound Recording, Free Expression, and Democracy

The story of how Seattle rapper/producer duo Macklemore & Ryan Lewis broke onto the international music scene is also the story of how the music industry has been completely upended in the last fifteen years.

Macklemore began 2013 with the *Billboard* No. 1 hit "Thrift Shop." The video for the song had been posted on YouTube the previous summer and had generated more than 380 million views a year later. Most interesting about this success is that Macklemore & Ryan Lewis can take complete credit for it: They don't have a recording contract with a major label. The quirky repeating saxophone line and irreverent lyrics made "Thrift Shop" the first No. 1 hit from an independent group since 1994.[1] They did it again later in the year, hitting the top spot with "Can't Hold Us."

Their success had already defied the typical when they released the song "Same Love," written and recorded in 2012 as a way to support Macklemore's gay uncle, his uncle's partner, and his gay godfather—and also after he read a report of a bullied teenager who committed suicide.[2]

The song became an anthem for support of Referendum 74, a measure to uphold same-sex marriage in Washington State. It would soon have national resonance.

Although other songs, such as Lady Gaga's "Born This Way," have addressed the battle for gay equality, "Same Love" is one of the most politically direct songs to emerge as a hit in decades. (One would have to go back to rock and roll's protest years in the Vietnam War era to find a major hit as pointed.) Macklemore targets politics in the song ("The right-wing conservatives think it's a decision / And you can be cured with some treatment and religion") and his own form of music ("If I was gay, I would think hip-hop hates me / Have you read the YouTube comments lately?"). The refrain, by openly gay singer Mary Lambert, laments, "I can't change / Even if I tried / Even if I wanted to."

Corporate radio was not hot on the trail of this song. But with 60 million YouTube views by the summer of 2013, some radio programmers understood the song's connection to larger issues in the nation (the U.S. Supreme Court's decisions that summer upholding California's gay marriage law and overturning the Defense of Marriage Act, which had denied federal recognition of same-sex marriage since 1996). Other radio programmers, particularly at reluctant hip-hop stations, eventually responded to listener demand, and the song raced up the music charts. By the summer of 2014, "Same Love" had more than 120 million views on YouTube—a level of exposure that would have been unthinkable for a political song

on an independent label even twenty years earlier.

In today's sound recording business, industry revenues are finally leveling out after Napster's file-sharing network turned the music industry upside down starting in 1999. The industry is now half its former size, and many artists, like Macklemore & Ryan Lewis, are finding that they can leverage the Internet to reach a fan base without the help of a big music label.

Big stars with enormous recording contracts—like Adele, Beyoncé, and Taylor Swift—still remain. But even their paths have changed: Adele became famous through MySpace, while Beyoncé and Swift have become bigger than their recording contracts, gaining millions in endorsements and sponsorships to chart their own career courses.

Given their new fame and fortune, one might expect Macklemore & Ryan Lewis to entertain major-label offers. Yet they've already addressed that scenario in another song, titled "Jimmy Iovine," named after the chairman of Universal Music Group's hip-hop powerhouse label, Interscope Geffen A&M. In the song, the artists finally make it to their dream, a visit to Iovine's office. Then they reconsider: "I replied I appreciate the offer, thought that this is what I wanted / Rather be a starving artist than succeed at getting f—ed."

The digital turn in the music industry has changed the calculus for musical artists. Macklemore proves that it's possible to shun the big contract and not end up a starving artist.

▲ **THE MEDIUM OF SOUND RECORDING** has had an immense impact on our culture. The music that helps shape our identities and comforts us during the transition from childhood to adulthood resonates throughout our lives, and it often stirs debate among parents and teenagers, teachers and students, and politicians and performers, many times leading to social change. Throughout its history, popular music has been banned by parents, school officials, and even governments under the guise of protecting young people from corrupting influences. As far back as the late eighteenth century, authorities in Europe, thinking that it was immoral for young people to dance close together, outlawed waltz music as "savagery." Between the 1920s and the 1940s, jazz music was criticized for its unbridled and sometimes free-form sound and the unrestrained dance crazes (such as the Charleston and the jitterbug) it inspired. Rock and roll from the 1950s onward and hip-hop from the 1980s to today have also added their own chapters to the age-old musical battle between generations.

☑ Visit **LaunchPad** for *Media & Culture* and use **LearningCurve** to review concepts from this chapter.

In this chapter, we will place the impact of popular music in context and:

- Investigate the origins of recording's technological "hardware," from Thomas Edison's early phonograph to Emile Berliner's invention of the flat disk record and the development of audiotape, compact discs, and MP3s
- Study radio's early threat to sound recording and the subsequent alliance between the two media when television arrived in the 1950s
- Explore the impact of the Internet on music, including the effects of online piracy and how the industry is adapting to the new era of convergence with new models for distributing and promoting music, from downloads to streaming
- Examine the content and culture of the music industry, focusing on the predominant role of rock music and its extraordinary impact on mass media forms and a diverse array of cultures, both American and international
- Explore the economic and democratic issues facing the recording industry

As you consider these topics, think about your own relationship with popular music and sound recordings. Who was your first favorite group or singer? How old were you, and what was important to you about this music? How has the way you listen to music changed in the past five years? For more questions to help you think through the role of music in our lives, see "Questioning the Media" in the Chapter Review.

The Development of Sound Recording

New mass media have often been defined in terms of the communication technologies that preceded them. For example, movies were initially called *motion pictures*, a term that derived from photography; radio was known as *wireless telegraphy*, referring back to telegraphs; and television was often called *picture radio*. Likewise, sound recording instruments were initially described as talking machines and later as phonographs, indicating the existing innovations, the tele*phone* and the tele*graph*. This early blending of technology foreshadowed our contemporary era, in which media as diverse as newspapers and movies converge on the Internet. Long before the Internet, however, the first major media convergence involved the relationship between the sound recording and radio industries.

From Cylinders to Disks: Sound Recording Becomes a Mass Medium

In the 1850s, the French printer Édouard-Léon Scott de Martinville conducted the first experiments with sound recording. Using a hog's hair bristle as a needle, he tied one end to a thin membrane stretched over the narrow part of a funnel. When the inventor spoke into the funnel, the membrane vibrated and the free end of the bristle made grooves on a revolving cylinder coated with a thick liquid called *lamp black*. De Martinville noticed that different sounds made different trails in the lamp black, but he could not figure out how to play back the sound. However, his experiments did usher in the *development stage* of sound recording as a mass medium. In 2008, audio researchers using high-resolution scans of the recordings and a digital stylus were finally able to play back some of de Martinville's recordings for the first time.[3]

In 1877, Thomas Edison had success playing back sound. He recorded his own voice by using a needle to press his voice's sound waves onto tinfoil wrapped around a metal cylinder about the size of a cardboard toilet-paper roll. After recording his voice, Edison played it back by repositioning the needle to retrace the grooves in the foil. The machine that played these cylinders became known as the *phonograph*, derived from the Greek terms for "sound" and "writing."

Thomas Edison was more than an inventor—he was also able to envision the practical uses of his inventions and ways to market them. Moving sound recording into its *entrepreneurial stage*, Edison patented his phonograph in 1878 as a kind of answering machine. He thought the phonograph would be used as a "telephone repeater" that would "provide invaluable records, instead of being the recipient of momentary and fleeting communication."[4] Edison's phonograph patent was specifically for a device that recorded and played back foil cylinders. Because of this limitation, in 1886 Chichester Bell (cousin of telephone inventor Alexander Graham Bell) and Charles Sumner Tainter were able to further sound recording by patenting an improvement on the phonograph. Their sound recording device,

THOMAS EDISON
In addition to inventing the phonograph, Edison (1847–1931) ran an industrial research lab that is credited with inventing the motion picture camera, the first commercially successful lightbulb, and a system for distributing electricity.
© Bettmann/Corbis

Sound Recording and Popular Music

de Martinville
The first experiments with sound are conducted in the 1850s using a hog's hair bristle as a needle; de Martinville can record sound, but he can't play it back (p. 116).

Flat Disk
Berliner invents the flat disk in 1887 and develops the gramophone to play it. The disks are easily mass-produced, a labeling system is introduced, and sound recording becomes a mass medium (p. 117).

Radio Threatens the Sound Recording Industry
By 1925, "free" music can be heard over the airwaves (p. 121).

Audiotape
Developed in Germany in the early 1940s, audiotape enables multitrack recording. Taping technology comes to the United States after WWII (p. 118).

1850 — 1880 — 1890 — 1900 — 1910 — 1920 — 1930 — 1940

Phonograph
In 1877, Edison figures out how to play back sound, thinking this invention would make a good answering machine (p. 116).

Victrolas
Around 1910, music players enter living rooms as elaborate furniture centerpieces, replacing pianos as musical entertainment (p. 117).

Photo by Robert Johnson Estate/Hulton Archive /Getty Images (top); Popperfoto/Getty Images (bottom)

known as the *graphophone*, played back more durable wax cylinders.[5] Both Edison's phonograph and Bell and Tainter's graphophone had only marginal success as voice-recording office machines. Eventually, both sets of inventors began to produce cylinders with prerecorded music, which proved to be more popular but difficult to mass-produce and not very durable for repeated plays.

Using ideas from Edison, Bell, and Tainter, Emile Berliner, a German engineer who had immigrated to America, developed a better machine that played round, flat disks, or records. Made of zinc and coated with beeswax, these records played on a turntable, which Berliner called a *gramophone* and patented in 1887. Berliner also developed a technique that enabled him to mass-produce his round records, bringing sound recording into its *mass medium stage*. Previously, using Edison's cylinder, performers had to play or sing into the speaker for each separate recording. Berliner's technique featured a master recording from which copies could be easily duplicated in mass quantities. In addition, Berliner's records could be stamped with labels, allowing the music to be differentiated by title, performer, and songwriter. This led to the development of a "star system," wherein fans could identify and choose their favorite artists across many records.

By the first decade of the twentieth century, record-playing phonographs were widely available for home use. In 1906, the Victor Talking Machine Company placed the hardware, or "guts," of the record player inside a piece of furniture. These early record players, known as Victrolas, were mechanical and had to be primed with a crank handle. As more homes were wired for electricity, electric record players, first available in 1925, gradually replaced Victrolas, and the gramophone soon became an essential appliance in most American homes.

The appeal of recorded music was limited at first because of sound quality. The original wax records were replaced by shellac discs, but these records were also very fragile and didn't improve the sound quality much. By the 1930s, in part because of the advent of radio and in part because of the Great Depression, record and phonograph sales declined dramatically. However, in the early 1940s, shellac was needed for World War II munitions production, so the record industry turned to manufacturing polyvinyl plastic records instead. The vinyl

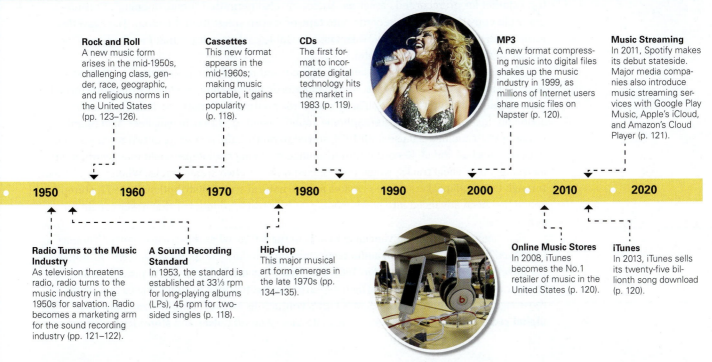

Rock and Roll
A new music form arises in the mid-1950s, challenging class, gender, race, geographic, and religious norms in the United States (pp. 123–126).

Cassettes
This new format appears in the mid-1960s; making music portable, it gains popularity (p. 118).

CDs
The first format to incorporate digital technology hits the market in 1983 (p. 119).

MP3
A new format compressing music into digital files shakes up the music industry in 1999, as millions of Internet users share music files on Napster (p. 120).

Music Streaming
In 2011, Spotify makes its debut stateside. Major media companies also introduce music streaming services with Google Play Music, Apple's iCloud, and Amazon's Cloud Player (p. 121).

1950   1960   1970   1980   1990   2000   2010   2020

Radio Turns to the Music Industry
As television threatens radio, radio turns to the music industry in the 1950s for salvation. Radio becomes a marketing arm for the sound recording industry (pp. 121–122).

A Sound Recording Standard
In 1953, the standard is established at 33⅓ rpm for long-playing albums (LPs), 45 rpm for two-sided singles (p. 118).

Hip-Hop
This major musical art form emerges in the late 1970s (pp. 134–135).

Online Music Stores
In 2008, iTunes becomes the No.1 retailer of music in the United States (p. 120).

iTunes
In 2013, iTunes sells its twenty-five billionth song download (p. 120).

recordings turned out to be more durable than shellac records and less noisy, paving the way for a renewed consumer desire to buy recorded music.

In 1948, CBS Records introduced the 33⅓-rpm (revolutions per minute) *long-playing record* (LP), with about twenty minutes of music on each side, creating a market for multisong albums and classical music. This was an improvement over the three to four minutes of music contained on the existing 78-rpm records. The next year, RCA developed a competing 45-rpm record that featured a quarter-size hole (best for jukeboxes) and invigorated the sales of songs heard on jukeboxes throughout the country. Unfortunately, the two new record standards were not technically compatible, meaning the two types of records could not be played on each other's machines. A five-year marketing battle ensued, similar to the Macintosh-versus-Windows conflict over computer-operating-system standards in the 1980s and 1990s or the battle between Blu-ray and HD DVD in the mid-2000s. In 1953, CBS and RCA compromised. The LP became the standard for long-playing albums, the 45 became the standard for singles, and record players were designed to accommodate 45s, LPs, and, for a while, 78s.

From Phonographs to CDs: Analog Goes Digital

The inventions of the phonograph and the record were the key sound recording advancements until the advent of magnetic **audiotape** and tape players in the 1940s. Magnetic tape sound recording was first developed as early as 1929 and further refined in the 1930s, but it didn't catch on initially because the first machines were bulky reel-to-reel devices, the amount of tape required to make a recording was unwieldy, and the tape itself broke or became damaged easily. However, owing largely to improvements by German engineers who developed plastic magnetic tape during World War II, audiotape eventually found its place.

Audiotape's lightweight magnetized strands finally made possible sound editing and multiple-track mixing, in which instrumentals or vocals could be recorded at one location and later mixed onto a master recording in another studio. This led to a vast improvement in studio recordings and subsequent increases in sales, although the recordings continued to be sold primarily in vinyl format rather than on reel-to-reel tape. By the mid-1960s, engineers had placed miniaturized reel-to-reel audiotape inside small plastic *cassettes* and had developed portable cassette players, permitting listeners to bring recorded music anywhere and creating a market for prerecorded cassettes. Audiotape also permitted "home dubbing": Consumers could copy their favorite records onto tape or record songs from the radio. The cassette format also gave rise to the Sony Walkman, a portable cassette player that foreshadowed the release of the iPod two decades later.

Some thought the portability, superior sound, and recording capabilities of audiotape would mean the demise of records. Although records had retained essentially the same format since the advent of vinyl, the popularity of records continued, in part due to the improved sound fidelity that came with stereophonic sound. Invented in 1931 by engineer Alan Blumlein, but not put to commercial use until 1958, **stereo** permitted the recording of two separate channels, or tracks, of sound. Recording-studio engineers, using audiotape, could now record many instrumental or vocal tracks, which they "mixed down" to two stereo tracks. When played back through two loudspeakers, stereo creates a more natural sound distribution. By 1971, stereo sound had been advanced into *quadraphonic*, or four-track, sound, but that never caught on commercially.

The biggest recording advancement came in the 1970s, when electrical engineer Thomas Stockham made the first digital audio recordings on standard computer equipment. Although the digital recorder was invented in 1967, Stockham was the first to put it to practical use. In contrast to **analog recording**, which captures the fluctuations of sound waves and stores those signals in a record's grooves or a tape's continuous stream of magnetized particles, **digital recording** translates sound waves into binary on-off pulses and stores that information

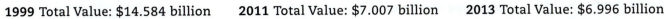

1999 Total Value: $14.584 billion   **2011** Total Value: $7.007 billion   **2013** Total Value: $6.996 billion

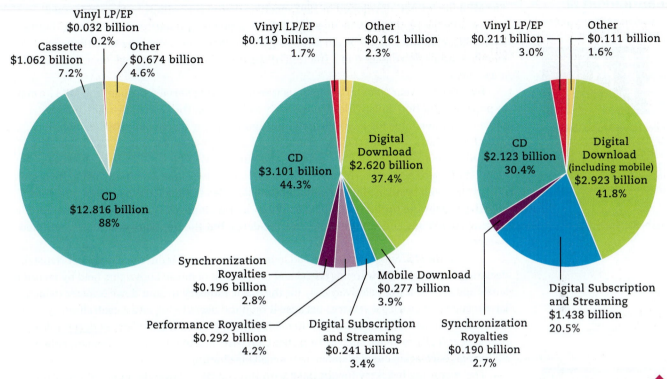

1999

Vinyl LP/EP
$0.032 billion
0.2%

Cassette
$1.062 billion
7.2%

Other
$0.674 billion
4.6%

CD
$12.816 billion
88%

2011

Vinyl LP/EP
$0.119 billion
1.7%

Other
$0.161 billion
2.3%

CD
$3.101 billion
44.3%

Digital
Download
$2.620 billion
37.4%

Synchronization
Royalties
$0.196 billion
2.8%

Performance Royalties
$0.292 billion
4.2%

Digital Subscription
and Streaming
$0.241 billion
3.4%

Mobile Download
$0.277 billion
3.9%

2013

Vinyl LP/EP
$0.211 billion
3.0%

Other
$0.111 billion
1.6%

CD
$2.123 billion
30.4%

Digital
Download
(including mobile)
$2.923 billion
41.8%

Synchronization
Royalties
$0.190 billion
2.7%

Digital Subscription
and Streaming
$1.438 billion
20.5%

as numerical code. When a digital recording is played back, a microprocessor translates those numerical codes back into sounds and sends them to loudspeakers. By the late 1970s, Sony and Philips were jointly working on a way to design a digitally recorded disc and player to take advantage of this new technology, which could be produced at a lower cost than either vinyl records or audiocassettes. As a result of their efforts, digitally recorded **compact discs (CDs)** hit the market in 1983.

By 1987, CD sales were double the amount of LP record album sales. By 2000, CDs rendered records and audiocassettes nearly obsolete, except for DJs and record enthusiasts who continued to play and collect vinyl LPs. In an effort to create new product lines and maintain consumer sales, the music industry promoted two advanced digital disc formats in the late 1990s, which it hoped would eventually replace standard CDs. However, the introduction of these formats was ill-timed for the industry, because the biggest development in music formatting was already on the horizon—the MP3.

Convergence: Sound Recording in the Internet Age

Music, perhaps more so than any other mass medium, is bound up in the social fabric of our lives. Ever since the introduction of the tape recorder and the heyday of homemade mixtapes, music has been something that we have shared eagerly with friends.

It is not surprising, then, that the Internet, a mass medium that links individuals and communities together like no other medium, became a hub for sharing music. In fact, the reason college student Shawn Fanning said he developed the groundbreaking file-sharing site Napster in 1999 was "to build communities around different types of music."[6] But this convergence with the Internet began to unravel the music industry in the 2000s. The changes in the music industry were set in motion about two decades ago with the proliferation of Internet use and the development of a new digital file format.

FIGURE 4.1

THE EVOLUTION OF DIGITAL SOUND RECORDING SALES (REVENUE IN BILLIONS)

Data from: Recording Industry Association of America, Annual Year-End Statistics

Note: The year 1999 is the year Napster arrived, and the peak year of industry revenue. In 2011, digital product revenue surpassed physical product revenue for the first time. In 2013, digital download revenue dropped for the first time as digital subscriptions and streaming gained in popularity. Synchronization royalties are those from music being licensed for use in television, movies, and advertisements.

MP3s and File-Sharing

The **MP3** file format, developed in 1992, enables digital recordings to be compressed into smaller, more manageable files. With the increasing popularity of the Internet in the mid-1990s, computer users began swapping MP3 music files online because they could be uploaded or downloaded in a fraction of the time it took to exchange noncompressed music files.

By 1999, the year Napster's infamous free file-sharing service brought the MP3 format to popular attention, music files were widely available on the Internet—some for sale, some legally available for free downloading, and many for trading in possible violation of copyright laws. Despite the higher quality of industry-manufactured CDs, music fans enjoyed the convenience of downloading and burning MP3 files to CD. Some listeners skipped CDs altogether, storing their music on hard drives and essentially using their computers as stereo systems. Losing countless music sales to illegal downloading, the music industry fought the proliferation of the MP3 format with an array of lawsuits (aimed at file-sharing companies and at individual downloaders), but the popularity of MP3s continued to increase.

In 2001, the U.S. Supreme Court ruled in favor of the music industry and against Napster, declaring free music file-swapping illegal and in violation of music copyrights held by recording labels and artists. It was relatively easy for the music industry to shut down Napster (which later relaunched as a legal service) because it required users to log into a centralized system. However, the music industry's elimination of file-sharing was not complete, as decentralized *peer-to-peer* (P2P) systems, such as Grokster, LimeWire, Morpheus, Kazaa, eDonkey, eMule, and BitTorrent, once again enabled online free music file-sharing.

The recording industry fought back with thousands of lawsuits, many of them successful. In 2005, P2P service Grokster shut down after it was fined $50 million by U.S. federal courts, and in upholding the lower court rulings, the Supreme Court reaffirmed that the music industry could pursue legal action against any P2P service that encouraged its users to illegally share music or other media. By 2010, eDonkey, Morpheus, and LimeWire had been shut down, while Kazaa settled a lawsuit with the music industry and became a legal service.[7] By 2011, several major Internet service providers, including AT&T, Cablevision, Comcast, Time Warner Cable, and Verizon, agreed to help the music industry identify customers who may be illegally downloading music and try to prevent them from doing so by sending them "copyright alert" warning letters, redirecting them to Web pages about digital piracy, and ultimately slowing download speeds or closing their broadband accounts.

As it cracked down on digital theft, the music industry also realized that it would have to somehow adapt its business to the digital format and embraced services like iTunes (launched by Apple in 2003 to accompany the iPod), which has become the model for legal online distribution. In 2008, iTunes became the top music retailer in the United States, surpassing Walmart, and by 2013, iTunes had sold more than twenty-five billion songs. Ironically, iTunes' 2013 sales milestone came in the same year that global digital download sales fell for the first time.[8] What happened? It was the arrival of the next big digital format.

Richard B. Levine/Newscom

The Next Big Thing: Streaming Music

If the history of recorded music tells us anything, it's that over time tastes change and formats change. The digital music era began in 1983 with the debut of the CD. Next was the digital download, made a commercially viable option by iTunes in 2003. Today, streaming music is quickly growing in popularity. In the language of the music industry, we are shifting from *ownership* of music to *access* to music.[9] The access model has been driven by the availability of streaming services such as the Sweden-based Spotify, which made its debut in the United States in 2011 and hit ten million worldwide paying subscribers in 2014. Other services include Rhapsody, Rdio, Deezer (outside of the United States), and Google Play Music; Amazon has also added a streaming music component to its Prime subscription accounts. With these services, listeners can pay a subscription fee (typically $5 to $10 per month), or in some cases sign up for an ad-supported free account, and instantly play millions of songs on demand via the Internet. One of the newest services is Beats Music, a subscription-only streaming service founded by music executive Jimmy Iovine and the renowned artist/producer Dr. Dre, the same team behind the trendy and pricey Beats by Dr. Dre headphones (some of which cost up to $450). Just a few months after the Beats Music streaming service launched in early 2014, Apple purchased the company for $3 billion. Apple gained a premium headphone brand to sell and, more importantly, acquired a streaming service to complement its iTunes download business.[10] The streaming market also includes ad-supported streaming services that initially specialized in video, such as YouTube and Vevo, which have wide international use.

The Rocky Relationship between Records and Radio

Some streaming services, like Pandora, closely resemble commercial radio; the recording industry and radio have always been closely linked. Although they work almost in unison now, in the beginning they had a tumultuous relationship. Radio's very existence sparked the first battle. By 1915, the phonograph had become a popular form of entertainment. The recording industry sold thirty million records that year, and by the end of the decade, sales more than tripled each year. In 1924, though, record sales dropped to only half of what they had been the previous year. Why? Because radio had arrived as a competing mass medium, providing free entertainment over the airwaves, independent of the recording industry.

The battle heated up when, to the alarm of the recording industry, radio stations began broadcasting recorded music without compensating the music industry. The American Society of Composers, Authors, and Publishers (ASCAP), founded in 1914 to collect copyright fees for music publishers and writers, charged that radio was contributing to plummeting sales of records and sheet music. By 1925, ASCAP established music rights fees for radio, charging stations between $250 and $2,500 a week to play recorded music—and causing many stations to leave the air.

But other stations countered by establishing their own live, in-house orchestras, disseminating "free" music to listeners. This time, the recording industry could do nothing, as original radio music did not infringe on any copyrights. Throughout the late 1920s and the 1930s, record and phonograph sales continued to fall, although the recording industry got a small boost when Prohibition ended in 1933 and record-playing jukeboxes became the standard musical entertainment in neighborhood taverns.

The recording and radio industries only began to cooperate with each other after television became popular in the early 1950s. Television pilfered radio's variety shows, crime dramas, and comedy programs, and, along with those formats, much of its advertising revenue and audience. Seeking to reinvent itself, radio turned to the record industry, and this time

SPOTIFY became popular in Europe before the streaming service made its U.S. debut in 2011. Now available in more than fifty-five countries, it has a vast catalog of music, with more than twenty million songs globally.

Courtesy Spotify

both industries greatly benefited from radio's new "hit songs" format. The alliance between the recording industry and radio was aided enormously by rock-and-roll music, which was just emerging in the 1950s. Rock created an enduring consumer youth market for sound recordings and provided much-needed new content for radio precisely when television made it seem like an obsolete medium.

After the digital turn, that mutually beneficial arrangement between the recording and radio industries began to fray. While Internet streaming radio stations were being required to pay royalties to music companies when they played their songs, radio stations still got to play music royalty-free over the air. In 2012, Clear Channel, the largest radio station chain in the United States and one of the largest music streaming companies, with more than 1,500 live stations on iHeartRadio, was the first company to strike a new deal with the recording industry and pay royalties for music played over the air. Clear Channel pledged to pay royalties to Big Machine Label Group—one of the country's largest independent labels—for broadcasting the songs of its artists (including Taylor Swift, Tim McGraw, and the Band Perry) in exchange for a limit on royalties it must pay for streaming those artists' music. With the agreement, Big Machine Label Group gained a new source of royalty income, and Clear Channel (which renamed itself iHeartMedia in 2014) crafted a more stable future for its growing digital streaming operations. Since the first deal, other radio groups have begun to forge agreements with Big Machine and other music labels, paying royalties for on-air play while getting reduced rates for streaming music.

U.S. Popular Music and the Formation of Rock

Popular music, or **pop music**, is music that appeals either to a wide cross section of the public or to sizable subdivisions within the larger public based on age, region, or ethnic background (e.g., teenagers, southerners, and Mexican Americans). U.S. pop music today encompasses styles as diverse as blues, country, Tejano, salsa, jazz, rock, reggae, punk, hip-hop, and dance. The word *pop* has also been used to distinguish popular music from classical music, which is written primarily for ballet, opera, ensemble, or symphony. As various subcultures have intersected, U.S. popular music has developed organically, constantly creating new forms and reinvigorating older musical styles.

The Rise of Pop Music

The Granger Collection

SCOTT JOPLIN (1868–1917) published more than fifty compositions during his life, including "Maple Leaf Rag"—arguably his most famous piece.

Although it is commonly assumed that pop music developed simultaneously with the phonograph and radio, it actually existed prior to these media. In the late nineteenth century, the sale of sheet music for piano and other instruments sprang from a section of Broadway in Manhattan known as Tin Pan Alley, a derisive term used to describe the sound of these quickly produced tunes, which supposedly resembled cheap pans clanging together. Tin Pan Alley's tradition of song publishing began in the late 1880s with such music as the marches of John Philip Sousa and the ragtime piano pieces of Scott Joplin. It continued through the first half of the twentieth century with the show tunes and vocal ballads of Irving Berlin, George Gershwin, and Cole Porter, and into the 1950s and 1960s with such rock-and-roll writing teams as Jerry Leiber–Mike Stoller and Carole King–Gerry Goffin.

At the turn of the twentieth century, with the newfound ability of song publishers to mass-produce sheet music for a growing middle class, popular songs moved from being a novelty to being a major business enterprise. With the emergence of the phonograph, song publishers also discovered that recorded tunes boosted interest in and sales of sheet music. Thus songwriting and Tin Pan Alley played a key role in transforming popular music into a mass medium.

As sheet music grew in popularity, **jazz** developed in New Orleans. An improvisational and mostly instrumental musical form, jazz absorbed and integrated a diverse body of musical styles, including African rhythms, blues, and gospel. Jazz influenced many bandleaders throughout the 1930s and 1940s. Groups led by Louis Armstrong, Count Basie, Tommy Dorsey, Duke Ellington, Benny Goodman, and Glenn Miller were among the most popular of the "swing" jazz bands, whose rhythmic music also dominated radio, recordings, and dance halls in their day.

The first pop vocalists of the twentieth century were products of the vaudeville circuit, which radio, movies, and the Depression would bring to an end in the 1930s. In the 1920s, Eddie Cantor, Belle Baker, Sophie Tucker, and Al Jolson were all extremely popular. By the 1930s, Rudy Vallée and Bing Crosby had established themselves as the first "crooners," or singers of pop standards. Bing Crosby also popularized Irving Berlin's "White Christmas," one of the most covered songs in recording history. (A song recorded or performed by another artist is known as **cover music**.) Meanwhile, the Andrews Sisters' boogie-woogie style helped them sell more than sixty million records in the late 1930s and 1940s. In one of the first mutually beneficial alliances between sound recording and radio, many early pop vocalists had their own network of regional radio programs, which vastly increased their exposure.

Frank Sinatra arrived in the 1940s, and his romantic ballads foreshadowed the teen love songs of rock and roll's early years. Nicknamed "the Voice" early in his career, Sinatra, like Crosby, parlayed his music and radio exposure into movie stardom. Helped by radio, pop vocalists like Sinatra were among the first vocalists to become popular with a large national teen audience. Their record sales helped stabilize the industry, and in the early 1940s, Sinatra's concerts caused the kind of audience riots that would later characterize rock-and-roll performances.

Rock and Roll Is Here to Stay

The cultural storm called **rock and roll** hit in the mid-1950s. As with the term *jazz, rock and roll* was a blues slang term for "sex," lending it instant controversy. Early rock and roll was considered the first "integrationist music," merging the black sounds of rhythm and blues, gospel, and Robert Johnson's screeching blues guitar with the white influences of country, folk, and pop vocals.[11] From a cultural perspective, only a few musical forms have ever sprung from such a diverse set of influences, and no new style of music has ever had such a widespread impact on so many different cultures as rock and roll. From an economic perspective, rock and roll was the first musical form to simultaneously transform the structure of sound recording and radio. Rock's development set the stage for how music is produced, distributed, and performed today. Many social, cultural, economic, and political factors leading up to the 1950s contributed to the growth of rock and roll, including black migration, the growth of youth culture, and the beginnings of racial integration.

The migration of southern blacks to northern cities in search of better jobs during the first half of the twentieth century had helped spread different popular music styles. In particular, **blues** music, the foundation of rock and roll, came to the North. Influenced by African American spirituals, ballads, and work songs

ROBERT JOHNSON (1911–1938), who ranks among the most influential and innovative American guitarists, played the Mississippi delta blues and was a major influence on early rock and rollers, especially the Rolling Stones and Eric Clapton. His intense slide-guitar and finger-style playing also inspired generations of blues artists, including Muddy Waters, Howlin' Wolf, Bonnie Raitt, and Stevie Ray Vaughan. To get a sense of his style, visit the Internet Archive's Robert Johnson collection: www.archive.org/details /RobertJohnsonMp3Audio Songs.

Photo by Robert Johnson Estate/Hulton Archive/Getty Images

BESSIE SMITH (1895–1937) is considered the best female blues singer of the 1920s and 1930s. Mentored by the famous Ma Rainey, Smith had many hits, including "Down Hearted Blues" and "Gulf Coast Blues." She also appeared in the 1929 film *St. Louis Blues.*

Michael Ochs Archives/Getty Images

from the rural South, blues music was exemplified in the work of Robert Johnson, Ma Rainey, Son House, Bessie Smith, Charley Patton, and others. The introduction in the 1930s of the electric guitar—a major contribution to rock music—gave southern blues its urban style, popularized in the work of Muddy Waters, Howlin' Wolf, Sonny Boy Williamson, B.B. King, and Buddy Guy.[12]

During this time, blues-based urban black music began to be marketed under the name **rhythm and blues**, or **R&B**. Featuring "huge rhythm units smashing away behind screaming blues singers," R&B appealed to young listeners fascinated by the explicit (and forbidden) sexual lyrics in songs like "Annie Had a Baby," "Sexy Ways," and "Wild Wild Young Men."[13] Although it was banned on some stations, by 1953 R&B continued to gain airtime. In those days, black and white musical forms were segregated: Trade magazines tracked R&B record sales on "race" charts, which were kept separate from white record sales tracked on "pop" charts.

Another reason for the growth of rock and roll can be found in the repressive and uneasy atmosphere of the 1950s. To cope with the threat of the atomic bomb, the Cold War, and communist witch-hunts, young people sought escape from the menacing world created by adults. Teens have always sought out music that has a beat—music they can dance to—from the waltz in eighteenth-century Europe to the Charleston in 1920s America. More recent musical forms like disco and hip-hop began as dance and party music before their growing popularity eventually energized both record sales and radio formats.

Perhaps the most significant factor in the growth of rock and roll was the beginning of the integration of white and black cultures. In addition to increased exposure of black literature, art, and music, several key historical events in the 1950s broke down the borders between black and white cultures. In 1948, President Truman had signed an executive order integrating the armed forces, bringing young men from very different ethnic and economic backgrounds together at the time of the Korean War. Even more significant was the Supreme Court's *Brown v. Board of Education* decision in 1954. With this ruling, "separate but equal" laws, which had kept white and black schools, hotels, restaurants, rest rooms, and drinking fountains segregated for decades, were declared unconstitutional. A cultural reflection of the times, rock and roll would burst forth from the midst of these social and political tensions.

Rock Muddies the Waters

In the 1950s, legal integration accompanied a cultural shift, and the music industry's race and pop charts blurred. White deejay Alan Freed had been playing black music for his young audiences in Cleveland and New York since the early 1950s, and such white performers as Johnnie Ray and Bill Haley had crossed over to the race charts to score R&B hits. Meanwhile, black artists like Chuck Berry were performing country songs, and for a time Ray Charles even played in an otherwise all-white country band. Although continuing the work of breaking down racial borders was one of rock and roll's most important contributions, the genre also blurred other long-standing distinctions between high and low culture, masculinity and femininity, the country and the city, the North and the South, and the sacred and the secular.

High and Low Culture

In 1956, Chuck Berry's "Roll Over Beethoven" merged rock and roll, considered low culture by many, with high culture, thus forever blurring the traditional boundary between these cultural forms with lyrics like "You know my temperature's risin' / the jukebox is blowin' a fuse . . . / Roll over Beethoven / and tell Tchaikovsky the news." Although such early rock-and-roll lyrics seem tame by today's standards, at the time they sounded like sacrilege. Rock and rollers also challenged music decorum and the rules governing how musicians should behave or misbehave: Berry's "duck walk" across the stage, Elvis Presley's pegged pants and gyrating hips, and Bo Diddley's use of the guitar as a phallic symbol were an affront to the norms of well-behaved, culturally elite audiences.

The blurring of cultures works both ways. Since the advent of rock and roll, some musicians performing in traditionally high-culture genres such as classical have even adopted some of rock and roll's ideas in an effort to boost sales and popularity, for example, performing in casual dress or in untraditional venues, like bars and subway stations.

Masculinity and Femininity

Rock and roll was also the first popular music genre to overtly confuse issues of sexual identity and orientation. Although early rock and roll largely attracted males as performers, the most fascinating feature of Elvis Presley, according to the Rolling Stones' Mick Jagger, was his androgynous appearance.[14] During this early period, though, the most sexually outrageous rock-and-roll performer was Little Richard (Penniman).

Wearing a pompadour hairdo and assaulting his Steinway piano, Little Richard was considered rock and roll's first drag queen, blurring the boundary between masculinity and femininity. Little Richard has said that given the reality of American racism, he blurred gender and sexuality lines because he feared the consequences of becoming a sex symbol for white girls: "I decided that my image should be crazy and way out so that adults would think I was harmless. I'd appear in one show dressed as the Queen of England and in the next as the pope."[15] Little Richard's playful blurring of gender identity and sexual orientation paved the way for performers like David Bowie, Elton John, Boy George, Annie Lennox, Prince, Grace Jones, Marilyn Manson, Lady Gaga, and Adam Lambert.

The Country and the City

Rock and roll also blurred geographic borders between country and city, between the black urban rhythms of Memphis and the white country & western music of Nashville. Early white rockers such as Buddy Holly and Carl Perkins combined country or hillbilly music, southern gospel, and Mississippi delta blues to create a sound called **rockabilly**. At the same time, an urban R&B influence on early rock came from Fats Domino ("Blueberry Hill"), Willie Mae "Big Mama" Thornton ("Hound Dog"), and Big Joe Turner ("Shake, Rattle, and Roll"). Many of these songs, first popular on R&B labels, crossed over to the pop charts during the mid to late 1950s (although many were performed by more widely known white artists). Chuck Berry borrowed from white country & western music (an old country song called "Ida Red") and combined it with R&B to write "Maybellene." His first hit, the song was No. 1 on the R&B chart in July 1955 and crossed over to the pop charts the next month.

Although rock lyrics in the 1950s may not have been especially provocative or overtly political, soaring record sales and the crossover appeal of the music itself represented an enormous threat to long-standing racial and class boundaries. In 1956, the secretary of the North Alabama White Citizens Council bluntly spelled out the racism and white fear concerning the new blending of urban-black and rural-white culture: "Rock and roll is a means of pulling the white man down to the level of the Negro. It is part of a plot to undermine the morals of the youth of our nation."[16] These days, distinctions between traditionally rural music and urban music continue to blur, with older hybrids such as country rock (think of the Eagles) and newer forms like alternative country performed by artists like Ryan Adams, Steve Earle, the Avett Brothers, and Kings of Leon.

© Bettmann/Corbis

ROCK-AND-ROLL PIONEER
A major influence on early rock and roll, Chuck Berry, born in 1926, scored major hits between 1955 and 1958, writing "Maybellene," "Roll Over Beethoven," "School Day," "Sweet Little Sixteen," and "Johnny B. Goode." At the time, he was criticized by some black artists for sounding white, and his popularity among white teenagers was bemoaned by conservative critics. Today, young guitar players routinely imitate his style.

© Paul Martinka/Splash News/Corbis

KATY PERRY
Many of today's biggest pop music stars show off not just catchy radio-ready singles but also eye-grabbing fashion, memorable music videos, and multimillion-dollar live shows. Perry's 2014 Prismatic World Tour featured a spectacular concert production with at least seven different "acts" and costume and set changes.

The North and the South

Not only did rock and roll muddy the urban and rural terrain, but it also combined northern and southern influences. In fact, with so much blues, R&B, and rock and roll rising from the South in the 1950s, this region regained some of its cultural flavor, which (along with a sizable portion of the population) had migrated to the North after the Civil War and during the early twentieth century. Meanwhile, musicians and audiences in the North had absorbed blues music as their own, eliminating the understanding of blues as specifically a southern style. Like the many white teens today who are fascinated by hip-hop, musicians such as Carl Perkins, Elvis Presley, and Buddy Holly—all from the rural South—were fascinated with and influenced by the black urban styles they had heard on the radio or seen in nightclubs. These artists in turn brought southern culture to northern listeners.

But the key to record sales and the spread of rock and roll, according to famed record producer Sam Phillips of Sun Records, was to find a white man who sounded black. Phillips found that man in Elvis Presley. Commenting on Presley's cultural importance, one critic wrote: "White rockabillies like Elvis took poor white southern mannerisms of speech and behavior deeper into mainstream culture than they had ever been taken."[17]

The Sacred and the Secular

Although many mainstream adults in the 1950s complained that rock and roll's sexuality and questioning of moral norms constituted an offense against God, in fact many early rock figures had close ties to religion. Jerry Lee Lewis attended a Bible institute in Texas (although he was eventually thrown out); Ray Charles converted an old gospel tune he had first heard in church as a youth into "I Got a Woman," one of his signature songs; and many other artists transformed gospel songs into rock and roll.

Still, many people did not appreciate the blurring of boundaries between the sacred and the secular. In the late 1950s, public outrage over rock and roll was so great that even Little Richard and Jerry Lee Lewis, both sons of southern preachers, became convinced that they were playing the "devil's music." By 1959, Little Richard had left rock and roll to become a minister. Lewis had to be coerced into recording "Great Balls of Fire," a song by Otis Blackwell that turned an apocalyptic biblical phrase into a sexually charged teen love song that was banned by many radio stations but nevertheless climbed to No. 2 on the pop charts in 1957. The boundaries between sacred and secular music have continued to blur in the years since, with some churches using rock and roll to appeal to youth, and some Christian-themed rock groups recording music as seemingly incongruous as heavy metal.

Battles in Rock and Roll

The blurring of racial lines and the breakdown of other conventional boundaries meant that performers and producers were forced to play a tricky game to get rock and roll accepted by the masses. Two prominent white disc jockeys used different methods. Cleveland deejay Alan Freed, credited with popularizing the term *rock and roll*, played original R&B recordings from the race charts and black versions of early rock and roll on his program. In contrast, Philadelphia deejay Dick Clark believed that making black music acceptable to white audiences required cover versions by white artists. By the mid-1950s, rock and roll was gaining

© Bettmann/Corbis

Kevin Winter/Getty Images

acceptance with the masses, but rock-and-roll artists and promoters still faced further obstacles: Black artists found that their music was often undermined by white cover versions; the payola scandals portrayed rock and roll as a corrupt industry; and fears of rock and roll as a contributing factor in juvenile delinquency resulted in censorship.

White Cover Music Undermines Black Artists

By the mid-1960s, black and white artists routinely recorded and performed one another's original tunes. For example, established black R&B artist Otis Redding covered the Rolling Stones' "Satisfaction" and Jimi Hendrix covered Bob Dylan's "All along the Watchtower," while just about every white rock-and-roll band, including the Beatles and the Rolling Stones, established its career by covering R&B classics.

Although today we take such rerecordings for granted, in the 1950s the covering of black artists' songs by white musicians was almost always an attempt to capitalize on popular songs from the R&B "race" charts by transforming them into hits on the white pop charts. Often, not only would white producers give cowriting credit to white performers for the tunes they merely covered, but the producers would also buy the rights to potential hits from black songwriters who seldom saw a penny in royalties or received songwriting credit.

During this period, black R&B artists, working for small record labels, saw many of their popular songs covered by white artists working for major labels. These cover records, boosted by better marketing and ties to white deejays, usually outsold the original black versions. For instance, the 1954 R&B song "Sh-Boom," by the Chords on Atlantic's Cat label, was immediately covered by a white group, the Crew Cuts, for the major Mercury label. Record sales declined for the Chords, although jukebox and R&B radio play remained strong for their original version. By 1955, R&B hits regularly crossed over to the pop charts, but inevitably the cover music versions were more successful. Pat Boone's cover of Fats Domino's "Ain't That a Shame" went to No. 1 and stayed on the Top 40 pop chart for twenty weeks, whereas Domino's original made it only to No. 10. Boone's record sales at the time were second only to Elvis Presley's, and Boone found this success through releasing dozens of covers. Slowly, however, the cover situation changed. After watching Boone outsell his song "Tutti Frutti" in 1956, Little Richard wrote "Long Tall Sally," which included lyrics written and delivered in such a way that he believed Boone

ELVIS PRESLEY AND HIS LEGACY
Elvis Presley remains the most popular solo artist of all time. From 1956 to 1962, he recorded seventeen No. 1 hits, from "Heartbreak Hotel" to "Good Luck Charm." According to Little Richard, Presley's main legacy was that he opened doors for many young performers and made black music popular in mainstream America. Presley's influence continues to be felt today in the music of artists such as Bruno Mars.

would not be able to adequately replicate them. "Long Tall Sally" went to No. 6 for Little Richard and charted for twelve weeks; Boone's version got to No. 8 and stayed there for nine weeks.

Overt racism lingered in the music business well into the 1960s. A turning point, however, came in 1962, the last year that Pat Boone, then aged twenty-eight, ever had a Top 40 rock-and-roll hit. That year, Ray Charles covered "I Can't Stop Loving You," a 1958 country song by the Grand Ole Opry's Don Gibson. This marked the first time that a black artist, covering a white artist's song, had notched a No. 1 pop hit. With Charles's cover, the rock-and-roll merger between gospel and R&B, on one hand, and white country and pop, on the other, was complete. In fact, the relative acceptance of black crossover music provided a more favorable cultural context for the political activism that spurred important Civil Rights legislation in the mid-1960s.

Payola Scandals Tarnish Rock and Roll

The payola scandals of the 1950s were another cloud over rock-and-roll music and its artists. In the music industry, *payola* is the practice of record promoters paying deejays or radio programmers to play particular songs. As recorded rock and roll became central to commercial radio's success in the 1950s and the demand for airplay grew enormous, independent promoters hired by record labels used payola to pressure deejays into playing songs by the artists they represented.

Although payola was considered a form of bribery, no laws prohibited its practice. However, following closely on the heels of television's quiz-show scandals (see Chapter 6), congressional hearings on radio payola began in December 1959. The hearings were partly a response to generally fraudulent business practices, but they were also an opportunity to blame deejays and radio for rock and roll's supposedly negative impact on teens by portraying rock and roll (and its radio advocates) as a corrupt industry.

The payola scandals threatened, ended, or damaged the careers of a number of rock-and-roll deejays and undermined rock and roll's credibility for a number of years. When Chicago deejay Phil Lind broadcast secretly taped discussions in which a representative of a small independent record label acknowledged that it had paid $22,000 to ensure that a record would get airplay, he received calls threatening his life and received police protection. At the hearings in 1960, Alan Freed admitted to participating in payola, although he said he did not believe there was anything illegal about such deals, and his career soon ended. Dick Clark, then an influential deejay and the host of TV's *American Bandstand*, would not admit to participating in payola. But the hearings committee chastised Clark and alleged that some of his complicated business deals were ethically questionable, a censure that hung over him for years. Congress eventually added a law concerning payola to the Federal Communications Act, prescribing a $10,000 fine and/or a year in jail for each violation (see Chapter 5).

Fears of Corruption Lead to Censorship

Since rock and roll's inception, one of the uphill battles the genre faced was the perception that it was a cause of juvenile delinquency, which was statistically on the rise in the 1950s. Looking for an easy culprit rather than considering contributing factors such as neglect, the rising consumer culture, or the growing youth population, many assigned blame to rock and roll. The view that rock and roll corrupted youth was widely accepted by social authorities, and rock-and-roll music was often censored, eventually even by the industry itself.

By late 1959, many key figures in rock and roll had been tamed. Jerry Lee Lewis was exiled from the industry, labeled southern "white trash" for marrying his thirteen-year-old third cousin; Elvis Presley, having already been censored on television, was drafted into the army; Chuck Berry was run out of Mississippi and eventually jailed for gun possession and transporting a minor across state lines; and Little Richard felt forced to tone down his image and left rock and roll to sing gospel music. A tragic accident led to the final taming of rock and roll's first front line. In February 1959, Buddy Holly ("Peggy Sue"), Ritchie Valens ("La Bamba"), and the Big Bopper ("Chantilly Lace") all died in an Iowa plane crash—a tragedy mourned in Don McLean's 1971 hit "American Pie" as "the day the music died."

Although rock and roll did not die in the late 1950s, the U.S. recording industry decided that it needed a makeover. To protect the enormous profits the new music had been generating, record companies began to discipline some of rock and roll's rebellious impulses. In the early 1960s, the industry introduced a new generation of clean-cut white singers, like Frankie Avalon, Connie Francis, Ricky Nelson, Lesley Gore, and Fabian. Rock and roll's explosive violations of racial, class, and other boundaries were transformed into simpler generation gap problems, and the music developed a milder reputation.

A Changing Industry: Reformations in Popular Music

As the 1960s began, rock and roll was tamer and "safer," as reflected in the surf and road music of the Beach Boys and Jan & Dean, but it was also beginning to branch out. For instance, the success of all-female groups, such as the Shangri-Las ("Leader of the Pack") and the Angels ("My Boyfriend's Back"), challenged the male-dominated world of early rock and roll. In the 1960s and the following decades, rock-and-roll music and other popular styles went through cultural reformations that significantly changed the industry, including the international appeal of the "British invasion"; the development of soul and Motown; the political impact of folk-rock; the experimentalism of psychedelic music; the rejection of music's mainstream by punk, grunge, and alternative rock movements; the reassertion of black urban style in hip-hop; and the transformation of music distribution, which resulted in an unprecedented market growth of music from independent labels.

The British Are Coming!

The global trade of pop music is evident in the exchanges and melding of rhythms, beats, vocal styles, and musical instruments across cultures. The origin of this global impact can be traced to England in the late 1950s, when the young Rolling Stones listened to the blues of Robert Johnson and Muddy Waters, and the young Beatles tried to imitate Chuck Berry and Little Richard.

Until 1964, rock-and-roll recordings had traveled on a one-way ticket to Europe. Even though American artists regularly reached the top of the charts overseas, no British performers had yet appeared on any Top 10 pop lists in the States. This changed almost overnight. In 1964, the Beatles invaded America with their mop haircuts and pop reinterpretations of American blues and rock and roll. Within the next few years, British bands as diverse as the Kinks, the Rolling Stones, the Zombies, the Animals, Herman's Hermits, the Who, the Yardbirds, Them, and the Troggs had hit the American Top 40 charts.

With the British invasion, "rock and roll" unofficially became "rock," sending popular music and the industry in two directions. On the one hand, the Rolling Stones would influence generations of musicians emphasizing gritty, chord-driven, high-volume rock, including bands in the glam rock, hard rock, punk, heavy metal, and grunge genres. On the other hand, the Beatles would influence countless artists interested in a more accessible, melodic, and softer sound, in genres such as pop-rock, power-pop, new wave, and alternative rock. In the end, the British invasion verified what Chuck Berry and Little Richard had already demonstrated—that rock-and-roll performers could write and produce popular songs as well as Tin Pan Alley had. The success of British groups helped change an industry arrangement in which most pop music was produced by songwriting teams hired by major labels and matched with selected performers. Even more

Popperfoto/Getty Images

Michael Putland/Getty Images

BRITISH ROCK GROUPS
Ed Sullivan, who booked the Beatles several times on his TV variety show in 1964, helped promote their early success. Sullivan, though, reacted differently to the Rolling Stones, who were perceived as the "bad boys" of rock and roll in contrast to the "good" Beatles. The Stones performed black-influenced music without "whitening" the sound and exuded a palpable aura of sexuality, particularly frontman Mick Jagger. Although the Stones appeared on his program as early as 1964 and returned on several occasions, Sullivan remained wary and forced them to change the lyrics of "Let's Spend the Night Together" to "Let's Spend Some Time Together" for a 1967 broadcast.

important, the British invasion showed the recording industry how older American musical forms, especially blues and R&B, could be repackaged as rock and exported around the world.

Motor City Music: Detroit Gives America Soul

Ironically, the British invasion, which drew much of its inspiration from black influences, drew many white listeners away from a new generation of black performers. Gradually, however, throughout the 1960s, black singers like James Brown, Aretha Franklin, Otis Redding, Ike and Tina Turner, and Wilson Pickett found large and diverse audiences. Transforming the rhythms and melodies of older R&B, pop, and early rock and roll into what became labeled as **soul**, they countered the British invaders with powerful vocal performances. Mixing gospel and blues with emotion and lyrics drawn from the American black experience, soul contrasted sharply with the emphasis on loud, fast instrumentals and lighter lyrical concerns that characterized much of rock music.[18]

The most prominent independent label that nourished soul and black popular music was Motown, started in 1959 by former Detroit autoworker and songwriter Berry Gordy with a $700 investment and named after Detroit's "Motor City" nickname. Beginning with Smokey Robinson and the Miracles' "Shop Around," Motown enjoyed a long string of hit records that rivaled the pop success of British bands throughout the decade. Motown's many successful artists included the Temptations ("My Girl"), Mary Wells ("My Guy"), the Four Tops ("I Can't Help Myself"), Martha and the Vandellas ("Heat Wave"), Marvin Gaye ("I Heard It through the Grapevine"), and, in the early 1970s, the Jackson 5 ("ABC"). But the label's most successful group was the Supremes, featuring Diana Ross, which scored twelve No. 1 singles between 1964 and 1969 ("Where Did Our Love Go," "Stop! In the Name of Love"). The Motown groups had a more stylized, softer sound than the grittier southern soul (later known as funk) of Brown and Pickett.

Folk and Psychedelic Music Reflect the Times

Popular music has always been a product of its time, so the social upheavals of the Civil Rights movement, the women's movement, the environmental movement, and the Vietnam War naturally brought social concerns into the music of the 1960s and early 1970s. By the late 1960s, the

THE SUPREMES
One of the most successful groups in rock-and-roll history, the Supremes started out as the Primettes in Detroit in 1959. They signed with Motown's Tamla label in 1960 and changed their name in 1961. Between 1964 and 1969, they recorded twelve No. 1 hits, including "Where Did Our Love Go," "Baby Love," "Come See about Me," "Stop! In the Name of Love," "I Hear a Symphony," "You Can't Hurry Love," and "Someday We'll Be Together." Lead singer Diana Ross (*center*) left the group in 1969 for a solo career. The group was inducted into the Rock and Roll Hall of Fame in 1988.

Beatles had transformed themselves from a relatively lightweight pop band to one that spoke for the social and political concerns of their generation, and many other groups followed the same trajectory. (To explore how the times and personal taste influence music choices, see "Media Literacy and the Critical Process: Music Preferences across Generations" on page 132.)

Folk Inspires Protest

The musical genre that most clearly responded to the political happenings of the time was folk music, which had long been the sound of social activism. In its broadest sense, **folk music** in any culture refers to songs performed by untrained musicians and passed down mainly through oral traditions, from the banjo and fiddle tunes of Appalachia to the accordion-led zydeco of Louisiana and the folk-blues of the legendary Lead Belly (Huddie Ledbetter). During the 1930s, folk was defined by the music of Woody Guthrie ("This Land Is Your Land"), who not only brought folk to the city but also was extremely active in social reforms. Groups such as the Weavers, featuring labor activist and songwriter Pete Seeger, carried on Guthrie's legacy and inspired a new generation of singer-songwriters, including Joan Baez; Arlo Guthrie; Peter, Paul, and Mary; Phil Ochs; and—perhaps the most influential—Bob Dylan. Dylan's career as a folk artist began with acoustic performances in New York's Greenwich Village in 1961, and his notoriety was spurred by his measured nonchalance and unique nasal voice. Significantly influenced by the blues, Dylan identified folk as "finger pointin'" music that addressed current social circumstances. At a key moment in popular music's history, Dylan walked onstage at the 1965 Newport Folk Festival fronting a full electric rock band. He was booed and cursed by traditional "folkies," who saw amplified music as a sellout to the commercial recording industry. However, Dylan's change inspired the formation of **folk-rock** artists like the Byrds, who had a No. 1 hit with a cover of Dylan's "Mr. Tambourine Man," and led millions to protest during the turbulent 1960s.

Rock Turns Psychedelic

Alcohol and drugs have long been associated with the private lives of blues, jazz, country, and rock musicians. These links, however, became much more public in the late 1960s and

CHAPTER 4 ● SOUND RECORDING AND POPULAR MUSIC   131

Media Literacy and the Critical Process

Music Preferences across Generations

We make judgments about music all the time. Older generations don't like some of the music younger people prefer, and young people often dismiss some of the music of previous generations. Even among our peers, we have different tastes in music and often reject certain kinds of music that have become too popular or that don't conform to our own preferences. The following exercise aims to understand musical tastes beyond our own individual choices. Be sure to include yourself in this project.

1 DESCRIPTION. Arrange to interview four to eight friends or relatives of different ages about their musical tastes and influences. Devise questions about what music they listen to and have listened to at different stages of their lives. What music do they buy or collect? What's the first album (or single) they acquired? What's the latest album? What stories or vivid memories do they relate to particular songs or artists? Collect demographic and consumer information: age, gender, occupation, educational background, place of birth, and current place of residence.

2 ANALYSIS. Chart and organize your results. Do you recognize any patterns emerging from the data or stories? What kinds of music did your interview subjects listen to when they were younger? What kinds of music do they listen to now? What formed/influenced their musical interests? If their musical interests changed, what happened? (If they stopped listening to music, note that and find out why.) Do they have any associations between music and their everyday lives? Are these music associations and lifetime interactions with songs and artists important to them?

3 INTERPRETATION. Based on what you have discovered and the patterns you have charted, determine what the patterns mean. Does age, gender, geographic location, or education matter in musical tastes? Over time, are the changes in musical tastes and buying habits significant? Why or why not? What kind of music is most important to your subjects? Finally, and most important, why do you think their music preferences developed as they did?

4 EVALUATION. Determine how your interview subjects came to like particular kinds of music. What constitutes "good" and "bad" music for them? Did their ideas change over time? How? Are they open- or closed-minded about music? How do they form judgments about music? What criteria did your interview subjects offer for making judgments about music? Do you think their criteria are a valid way to judge music?

5 ENGAGEMENT. To expand on your findings, consider the connections of music across generations, geography, and genres. Take a musical artist you like and input the name at www.music-map.com. Use the output of related artists to discover new bands. Input favorite artists of the people you interviewed in Step 1, and share the results with them. Expand your musical tastes.

early 1970s, when authorities busted members of the Rolling Stones and the Beatles. With the increasing role of drugs in youth culture and the availability of LSD (not illegal until the mid-1960s), more and more rock musicians experimented with and sang about drugs in what were frequently labeled rock's psychedelic years. Many groups and performers of the *psychedelic* era (named for the mind-altering effects of LSD and other drugs), like Jefferson Airplane, Big Brother and the Holding Company (featuring Janis Joplin), the Jimi Hendrix Experience, the Doors, and the Grateful Dead (as well as established artists like the Beatles and the Stones), believed that artistic expression could be enhanced through mind-altering drugs. The 1960s drug explorations coincided with the free-speech movement, in which many artists and followers saw experimenting with drugs as a form of personal expression and a response to the failure of traditional institutions to deal with social and political problems such as racism and America's involvement in the Vietnam War. But after a surge of optimism that culminated in the historic Woodstock concert in August 1969, the psychedelic movement was quickly overshadowed. In 1969, a similar concert at the Altamont racetrack in California started in chaos and ended in tragedy when one of the Hell's Angels hired as a bodyguard for the show murdered a concertgoer. Around the same time, the shocking multiple murders committed by the Charles Manson "family" cast a negative light on hippies, drug use, and psychedelic culture. Then, in quick succession, a number of the psychedelic movement's greatest stars died from drug overdoses, including Janis Joplin, Jimi Hendrix, and Jim Morrison of the Doors.

Punk, Grunge, and Alternative Respond to Mainstream Rock

By the 1970s, rock music was increasingly viewed as just another part of mainstream consumer culture. With major music acts earning huge profits, rock soon became another product line for manufacturers and retailers to promote, package, and sell—primarily to middle-class white male teens. According to critic Ken Tucker, this situation gave rise to "faceless rock—crisply recorded, eminently catchy"—featuring anonymous hits by bands with "no established individual personalities outside their own large but essentially discrete audiences" of young white males.[19] Some rock musicians like Bruce Springsteen and Elton John; glam artists like David Bowie, Lou Reed, and Iggy Pop; and soul artists like Curtis Mayfield and Marvin Gaye continued to explore the social possibilities of rock or at least keep its legacy of outrageousness alive. But they had, for the most part, been replaced by "faceless" supergroups, like REO Speedwagon, Styx, Boston, and Kansas. By the late 1970s, rock could only seem to define itself by saying what it wasn't; "Disco Sucks" became a standard rock slogan against the popular dance music of the era.

Punk Revives Rock's Rebelliousness

Punk rock rose in the late 1970s to challenge the orthodoxy and commercialism of the record business. By this time, the glory days of rock's competitive independent labels had ended, and rock music was controlled by just a half-dozen major companies. By avoiding rock's consumer popularity, punk attempted to return to the basics of rock and roll: simple chord structures, catchy melodies, and politically or socially challenging lyrics. The premise was "do it yourself": Any teenager with a few weeks of guitar practice could learn the sound and make music that was both more democratic and more provocative than commercial rock.

The punk movement took root in the small dive bar CBGB in New York City around bands such as the Ramones, Blondie, and the Talking Heads. (The roots of punk essentially lay in four pre-punk groups from the late 1960s and early 1970s—the Velvet Underground, the Stooges, the New York Dolls, and the MC5—none of which experienced commercial success in their day.) Punk quickly spread to England, where a soaring unemployment rate and growing class inequality ensured the success of socially critical rock. Groups like the Sex Pistols, the Clash, the Buzzcocks, and Siouxsie and the Banshees sprang up and even scored Top 40 hits on the U.K. charts.

Punk was not a commercial success in the United States, where (not surprisingly) it was shunned by radio. However, punk's contributions continue to be felt. Punk broke down the "boy's club" mentality of rock, launching unapologetic and unadorned frontwomen like Patti Smith, Joan Jett, Debbie Harry, and Chrissie Hynde, and it introduced all-women bands (writing and performing their own music) like the Go-Go's into the mainstream. It also reopened the door to rock experimentation at a time when the industry had turned music into a purely commercial enterprise. The influence of experimental, or post-punk, music is still felt today in alternative and indie bands such as the Yeah Yeah Yeahs, Speedy Ortiz, and Parquet Courts.

Andrew DeLory

BOB DYLAN
Born Robert Allen Zimmerman in Minnesota, Bob Dylan took his stage name from Welsh poet Dylan Thomas. He led a folk music movement in the early 1960s with engaging, socially provocative lyrics. He was also an astute media critic, as is evident in the seminal documentary *Don't Look Back* (1967).

© Gonzales Photo/Malthe Ivarsson/The Hell Gate/Corbis

SAVAGES
All-female bands like Savages continue to take on the boy's-club mentality of rock and roll. The band formed in London in 2011 and gained critical acclaim for what *Pitchfork* calls its "post-punk aesthetics" and "classic rock chops."

Grunge and Alternative Reinterpret Rock

Taking the spirit of punk and updating it, the **grunge** scene represented a significant development in rock in the 1990s. Getting its name from its often-messy guitar sound and the anti-fashion torn jeans and flannel shirt appearance of its musicians and fans, grunge's lineage can be traced back to 1980s bands like Sonic Youth, the Minutemen, and Hüsker Dü. In 1992, after years of limited commercial success, the younger cousin of punk finally broke into the American mainstream with the success of Nirvana's "Smells Like Teen Spirit" on the album *Nevermind*. Led by enigmatic singer Kurt Cobain—who committed suicide in 1994—Nirvana produced songs that one critic described as "stunning, concise bursts of melody and rage that occasionally spilled over into haunting, folk-styled acoustic ballad."[20] Nirvana opened the floodgates to bands such as Green Day, Pearl Jam, Soundgarden, the Breeders, Hole, and Nine Inch Nails.

In some critical circles, both punk and grunge are considered subcategories or fringe movements of **alternative rock**. This vague label describes many types of experimental rock music that offered a departure from the theatrics and staged extravaganzas of 1970s glam rock, which showcased such performers as David Bowie and Kiss. Appealing chiefly to college students and twentysomethings, alternative rock has traditionally opposed the sounds of Top 40 and commercial FM radio. In the 1980s and 1990s, U2 and R.E.M. emerged as successful groups often associated with alternative rock. A key dilemma for successful alternative performers, however, is that their popularity results in commercial success, ironically a situation that their music often criticizes. While alternative rock music has more variety than ever, it is also not producing new mega-groups like Nirvana, Pearl Jam, and Green Day. Still, alternative groups like Arctic Monkeys, Vampire Weekend, and Deafheaven have launched successful recording careers the old-school way, but with a twist: starting out on independent labels, playing small concerts, and growing popular quickly with alternative music audiences through the immediate buzz of the Internet.

Hip-Hop Redraws Musical Lines

With the growing segregation of radio formats and the dominance of mainstream rock by white male performers, the place of black artists in the rock world diminished from the late 1970s onward. By the 1980s, few popular black successors to Chuck Berry or Jimi Hendrix had emerged in rock, though Prince and Lenny Kravitz were exceptions. These trends, combined with the rise of "safe" dance disco by white bands (the Bee Gees), black artists (Donna Summer), and integrated groups (the Village People), created a space for a new sound to emerge: **hip-hop**, a term for the urban culture that includes *rapping*, *cutting* (or *sampling*) by deejays, breakdancing, street clothing, poetry slams, and graffiti art.

In the same way that punk opposed commercial rock, hip-hop music stood in direct opposition to the polished, professional, and often less political world of soul. Its combination of social politics, swagger, and confrontational lyrics carried forward long-standing traditions in blues, R&B, soul, and rock and roll. Like punk and early rock and roll, hip-hop was driven by a democratic, nonprofessional spirit and was cheap to produce, requiring only a few mikes, speakers, amps, turntables, and vinyl records. Deejays, like the pioneering Jamaican émigré

Clive Campbell (a.k.a. DJ Kool Herc), emerged first in New York, scratching and re-cueing old reggae, disco, soul, and rock albums. These deejays, or MCs (masters of ceremony), used humor, boasts, and "trash talking" to entertain and keep the peace at parties.

The music industry initially saw hip-hop as a novelty, despite the enormous success of the Sugarhill Gang's "Rapper's Delight" in 1979 (which sampled the bass beat of a disco hit from the same year, Chic's "Good Times"). Then, in 1982, Grandmaster Flash and the Furious Five released "The Message" and forever infused hip-hop with a political take on ghetto life, a tradition continued by artists like Public Enemy and Ice-T. By 1985, hip-hop had exploded as a popular genre with the commercial successes of groups like Run-DMC, the Fat Boys, and LL Cool J. That year, Run-DMC's album *Raising Hell* became a major crossover hit, the first No. 1 hip-hop album on the popular charts (thanks in part to a collaboration with Aerosmith on a rap version of the group's 1976 hit "Walk This Way"). But because most major labels and many black radio stations rejected the rawness of hip-hop, the music spawned hundreds of new independent labels. Although initially dominated by male performers, hip-hop was open to women, and some—Salt-N-Pepa and Queen Latifah among them—quickly became major players. Soon, white groups like the Beastie Boys, Limp Bizkit, and Kid Rock were combining hip-hop and punk rock in a commercially successful way, while Eminem found enormous success emulating black rap artists.

On the one hand, the conversational style of rap makes it a forum in which performers can debate issues of gender, class, sexuality, violence, and drugs. On the other hand, hip-hop, like punk, has often drawn criticism for lyrics that degrade women, espouse homophobia, and applaud violence. Although hip-hop encompasses many different styles, including various Latin and Asian offshoots, its most controversial subgenre is probably **gangster rap**, which, in seeking to tell the truth about gang violence in American culture, has been accused of creating violence. Gangster rap drew national attention in 1996 with the shooting death of Tupac Shakur, who lived the violent life he rapped about on albums like *Thug Life*. Then, in 1997, Notorious B.I.G. (Christopher Wallace, a.k.a. Biggie Smalls), whose followers were prominent suspects in Shakur's death, was shot to death in Hollywood. The result was a change in the hip-hop industry. Most prominently, Sean "Diddy" Combs led Bad Boy Entertainment (former home of Notorious B.I.G.) away from gangster rap to a more danceable hip-hop that combined singing and rapping with musical elements of rock and soul. Today, hip-hop's stars include artists such as YG, who emulates the gangster genre, and artists like will.i.am, Lupe Fiasco, Talib Kweli, and M.I.A., who bring an old-school social consciousness to their performances.

© Pycha/DAPR/Zuma Press

NIRVANA'S lead singer, Kurt Cobain, is pictured here during his brief career in the early 1990s. The release of Nirvana's *Nevermind* in September 1991 bumped Michael Jackson's *Dangerous* from the top of the charts and signaled a new direction in popular music. Other grunge bands soon followed Nirvana onto the charts, including Pearl Jam, Alice in Chains, Stone Temple Pilots, and Soundgarden.

The Reemergence of Pop

After waves of punk, grunge, alternative, and hip-hop; the decline of Top 40 radio; and the demise of MTV's *Total Request Live* countdown show, it seemed as though pop music and the era of big pop stars was waning. But pop music has endured and even flourished in recent years, especially with the advent of iTunes. The era of digital downloads has again made the single (as opposed to the album) the dominant unit of music, with digital single download sales more than ten times as popular as digital album download sales. The dominance of singles has aided the reemergence of pop, since songs with catchy hooks generate the most digital sales. By 2014, iTunes offered more than twenty-eight million songs, and the top artists were leading

ITUNES shifted the music business toward a singles-based model. While artists still release full albums, it's also possible to produce a massive iTunes hit, like Carly Rae Jepsen's "Call Me Maybe," before an album is even available (Jepsen's full album sold modestly upon its later release). But some artists can still sell full-album packages: Beyoncé's self-titled album (including a series of music videos to accompany the music) was released exclusively to iTunes for its first few weeks and promptly broke sales records for the site.

FilmMagic/Getty Images

CHANCE THE RAPPER gained an enormous following based on the self-release of his mixtapes on DatPiff, the leading mixtape download site. In 2013, the Chicago-based rapper began touring with Kendrick Lamar and Macklemore, and was named "Rookie of the Year" by *The Source* magazine.

pop acts such as Katy Perry, Lana Del Rey, Rihanna, Jason Derulo, and Luke Bryan. Similarly, streaming services such as Spotify, Rdio, and Deezer, each offering more than twenty million tracks, have also greatly expanded accessibility to music. The digital formats in music have resulted in a leap in viability and market share for independent labels and have changed the cultural landscape of the music industry in the twenty-first century.

The Business of Sound Recording

For many in the recording industry, the relationship between music's business and artistic elements is an uneasy one. The lyrics of hip-hop or alternative rock, for example, often question the commercial value of popular music. Both genres are built on the assumption that musical integrity requires a complete separation between business and art. But, in fact, the line between commercial success and artistic expression is hazier than simply arguing that the business side is driven by commercialism and the artistic side is free of commercial concerns. The truth, in most cases, is that the business needs artists who are provocative, original, and appealing to the public, and the artists need the expertise of the industry's marketers, promoters, and producers to hone their sound and reach the public. And both sides stand to make a lot of money from the relationship. But such factors as the enormity of the major labels and the complexities of making, selling, and profiting from music in an industry still adapting to the digital turn affect the economies of sound recording (see "Tracking Technology: The Song Machine: The Hitmakers behind Rihanna," on page 138).

Music Labels Influence the Industry

After several years of steady growth, revenues for the recording industry experienced significant losses beginning in 2000 as file-sharing began to undercut CD sales. In 2013, U.S. music sales were about $7 billion, down from a peak of $14.5 billion in 1999, but relatively stable since 2010 (file-sharing peaked in 2005, having since declined). The U.S. market accounts for about one-third of global sales, followed by Japan, the United Kingdom, France, Germany, and Canada. Despite the losses, the U.S. and global music business still constitutes a powerful **oligopoly**: a business situation in which a few firms control most of an industry's production and distribution resources. This global reach gives these firms enormous influence over what types of music gain worldwide distribution and popular acceptance.

Fewer Major Labels and Falling Market Share

From the 1950s through the 1980s, the music industry, though powerful, consisted of a large number of competing major labels, along with numerous independent labels. Over time, the major labels began swallowing up the independents and then buying one another. By 1998, only six major labels remained—Universal, Warner, Sony, BMG, EMI, and Polygram. That year, Universal acquired Polygram; and in 2003, BMG and Sony merged. (BMG left the partnership in 2008.) By 2012, Universal gained regulatory approval to purchase EMI's recorded music division, and then only three major music corporations remained: Universal Music Group, Sony Music Entertainment, and Warner Music Group. Together, these companies control about 65 percent of the recording industry market in the United States (see Figure 4.2). Although their revenue has eroded over the past decade, the major music corporations still wield great power, with a number of music stars under contract and enormous back catalogs of recordings that continue to sell. Despite the oligopoly in the music industry, the biggest change has been the rise in market share for independent music labels.

The Indies Grow with Digital Music

The rise of rock and roll in the 1950s and early 1960s showcased a rich diversity of independent labels—including Sun, Stax, Chess, and Motown—all vying for a share of the new music. That tradition lives on today. In contrast to the three global players, some five thousand large and small independent production houses—or **indies**—record less commercially viable music, or music they hope will become commercially viable. Often struggling enterprises, indies require only a handful of people to operate them. For years, indies accounted for 10 to 15 percent of all music releases. But with the advent of downloads and streaming, the enormous diversity of independent-label music became much more accessible, and the market share of indies more than doubled in size. Indies often still depend on wholesale distributors to promote and sell their music, or enter into deals with one of the three majors to gain wider distribution for their artists (in the same way that independent filmmakers use major studios for film distribution). Independent labels have produced some of the best-selling artists of recent years; examples include Big Machine Records (Taylor Swift, Rascal Flatts), Dualtone Records (the Lumineers), XL Recordings

FIGURE 4.2

U.S. MARKET SHARE OF THE MAJOR LABELS IN THE RECORDING INDUSTRY, 2013

Data from: Nielsen SoundScan, 2013. Figures are rounded.

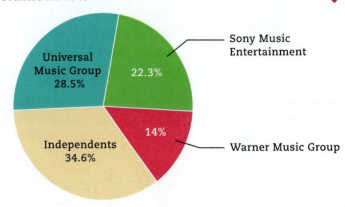

Universal Music Group 28.5%

Sony Music Entertainment 22.3%

Warner Music Group 14%

Independents 34.6%

TRACKING TECHNOLOGY

The Song Machine: The Hitmakers behind Rihanna

by John Seabrook

On a mild Monday afternoon in mid-January, Ester Dean, a songwriter and vocalist, arrived at Roc the Mic Studios in Manhattan for the first of five days of songwriting sessions. Her engineer, Aubry Delaine, whom she calls Big Juice, accompanied her. Tor Hermansen and Mikkel Eriksen, the team of Norwegian writer-producers professionally known as Stargate, were waiting there for Dean.

Most of the songs played on Top Forty radio are collaborations between producers like Stargate and "top line" writers like Ester Dean. The producers compose the chord progressions, program the beats, and arrange the "synths," or computer-made instrumental sounds; the top-liners come up with primary melodies, lyrics, and the all-important hooks, the ear-friendly musical phrases that lock you into the song. "It's not enough to have one hook anymore," Jay Brown, the president of Roc Nation, and Dean's manager, told me recently. "You've got to have a hook in the intro, a hook in the pre-chorus, a hook in the chorus, and a hook in the bridge." The reason, he explained, is that "people on average give a song seven seconds on the radio before they change the channel, and you got to hook them."

Today's Top Forty is almost always machine-made: lush sonic landscapes of beats, loops, and synths in which all the sounds have square edges and shiny surfaces, the voices are Auto-Tuned for pitch, and there are no mistakes. The music sounds sort of like this: *thump thooka whompa whomp pish pish pish thumpaty wompah pah pah pah*. The people who create the songs are

Kevin Winter/Getty Images

often in different places. The artists, who spend much of the year touring, don't have time to come into the studio; they generally record new material in between shows, in mobile recording studios and hotel rooms, working with demos that producers and top-line writers make for them to use as a kind of vocal stencil pattern.

As was the case in the pre-rock era, when Phil Spector–produced girl groups led the hit parade, many of the leading artists of the post-rock era are women. Rarely a month goes by without a new song from Lady Gaga, Katy Perry, Beyoncé, Kelly Clarkson, Ke$ha, Rihanna, Nicki Minaj, or Pink near the top of the charts. But the artist who best embodies the music and the style of the new Top Forty is Rihanna, the Barbados-born pop singer. At twenty-four [in 2012], she is the queen of urban pop, and the

consummate artist of the digital age, in which quantity is more important than quality and personality trumps song craft. She releases an album a year, often recording a new one while she is on an eighty-city world tour promoting the last one. To keep her supplied with material, her label, Def Jam, and her manager, Jay Brown, periodically convene "writer camps"— weeklong conclaves, generally held in Los Angeles, where dozens of top producers and writers from around the world are brought in to brainstorm on songs. After an album comes out, she may release remixes, like her recent ill-advised collaborations with Chris Brown, to give singles a boost. She has sold more digital singles than any other artist—a hundred and twenty million.

Rihanna is often described as a "manufactured" pop star, because she doesn't write her songs, but neither did Sinatra or Elvis. She embodies a song in the way an actor inhabits a role—and no one expects the actor to write the script. In the rock era, when the album was the standard unit of recorded music, listeners had ten or eleven songs to get to know the artist, but in the singles-oriented business of today the artist has only three or four minutes to put her personality across. The song must drip with attitude and swagger, or "swag," and nobody delivers that better than Rihanna, even if a good deal of the swag originates with Ester Dean. ◢

Source: Excerpted from John Seabrook, "The Song Machine: The Hitmakers behind Rihanna," New Yorker, *March 26, 2012, www.newyorker.com/ reporting/2012/03/26/120326fa_fact_seabrook.*

(Adele, Vampire Weekend), and Cash Money Records (Drake, Nicki Minaj). (See "Alternative Voices" on page 143.)

Making, Selling, and Profiting from Music

Like most mass media, the music business is divided into several areas, each working in a different capacity. In the music industry, those areas are making the music (signing, developing, and recording the artist), selling the music (selling, distributing, advertising, and promoting the music), and dividing the profits. All these areas are essential to the industry but have always shared in the conflict between business concerns and artistic concerns.

Making the Music

Labels are driven by **A&R (artist & repertoire) agents**, the talent scouts of the music business, who discover, develop, and sometimes manage artists. A&R executives scan online music sites and listen to demonstration tapes, or *demos*, from new artists and decide whom to sign and which songs to record. A&R executives naturally look for artists they think will sell, and they are often forced to avoid artists with limited commercial possibilities or to tailor artists to make them viable for the recording studio.

A typical recording session is a complex process that involves the artist, the producer, the session engineer, and audio technicians. In charge of the overall recording process, the producer handles most nontechnical elements of the session, including reserving studio space, hiring session musicians (if necessary), and making final decisions about the sound of the recording. The session engineer oversees the technical aspects of the recording session, everything from choosing recording equipment to managing the audio technicians. Most popular records are recorded part by part. Using separate microphones, the vocalists, guitarists, drummers, and other musical sections are digitally recorded onto separate audio tracks, which are edited and remixed during postproduction and ultimately mixed down to a two-track stereo master copy for reproduction to CD or online digital distribution.

Selling the Music

Selling and distributing music is a tricky part of the business. For years, the primary sales outlets for music were direct-retail record stores (independents or chains) and general retail outlets like Walmart, Best Buy, and Target. Such direct retailers could specialize in music, carefully monitoring new releases and keeping large, varied inventories. But as digital sales climbed, CD sales fell, forcing direct-retail record stores out of business and leaving general retail outlets to offer considerably less variety, stocking only top-selling CDs.

As recently as 2011, physical recordings (CDs and some vinyl) accounted for about 50 percent of U.S. music sales. But CD sales continue to decline and now constitute about 35 percent of the market. In some other Top 10 global music markets, such as Japan and Germany, CDs are still the top format, and the cultural shift from physical recordings to digital formats is just beginning.

Conversely, digital sales—which include digital downloads (like iTunes and Amazon), subscription streaming services (like Rhapsody and the paid version of Spotify), free streaming

Tim Mosenfelder/Getty Images

INDIE LABELS are able to take chances on artists like Majical Cloudz, an indie pop duo from Montreal signed to Matador, an independent label based in New York. Majical Cloudz gained exposure by touring in summer 2014 with Lorde, who has a contract with Universal, the largest major label.

services (like the ad-supported Spotify, Rdio, YouTube, and Vevo), streaming radio services (like Pandora and iHeartRadio), ringtones, and synchronization fees (payments for use of music in media like film, TV, and advertising)—have grown to capture almost two-thirds of the U.S. market and 39 percent of the global market.[21] About 40 percent of all music recordings purchased in the United States are downloads, and iTunes is the leading retailer of downloads.

Subscription and streaming services have been a big growth area in the United States and now account for about 21 percent of U.S. music industry revenues. The difference between a streaming music service (e.g., Spotify) and streaming radio (e.g., Pandora) is that streaming services enable listeners to stream specific songs, whereas streaming radio services allow listeners to select only a genre or style of music.

The international recording industry is a major proponent of music streaming services because they are a new revenue source. Although **online piracy**—unauthorized online file-sharing—still exists, the advent of advertising-supported music streaming services has satisfied consumer demand for free music and weakened interest in illegal file swapping. There are now about 450 licensed online music services worldwide.[22] Spotify, one of the leading services, has more than twenty million licensed songs to stream globally, with over twenty thousand songs added every day. Spotify carries so many songs that 20 percent of them have never been played.[23] Another service, Forgotify, creates playlists composed of these neglected songs.

Dividing the Profits

The digital upheaval in the music industry has shaken up the once-predictable sale of music through CDs. Now there are multiple digital venues for selling music and an equally high number of methods for dividing the profits. Although the digital download and streaming market has now surpassed physical sales, for the sake of example, we will first look at the various costs and profits from a typical CD that retails at $17.98.

The wholesale price for that CD is about $12.50, leaving the remainder as retail profit. Discount retailers like Walmart and Best Buy sell closer to the wholesale price to lure customers to buy other things (even if they make less profit on the CD itself). The wholesale price represents the actual cost of producing and promoting the recording, plus the recording label's profits. The record company reaps the highest revenue (close to $9.74 on a typical CD) but, along with the artist, bears the bulk of the expenses: manufacturing costs, packaging and CD design, advertising and promotion, and artists' royalties (see Figure 4.3 on page 141). The physical product of the CD itself costs less than a quarter to manufacture.

New artists usually negotiate a royalty rate of between 8 and 12 percent on the retail price of a CD, while more established performers might negotiate for 15 percent or higher. An artist who has negotiated a typical 11 percent royalty rate would earn about $1.93 per CD whose suggested retail price is $17.98. So a CD that "goes gold"—that is, sells 500,000 units—would net the artist around $965,000. But out of this amount, artists must repay the record company the money they have been advanced (from $100,000 to $500,000). And after band members, managers, and attorneys are paid with the remaining money, it's quite possible that an artist will end up with almost nothing—even after a certified gold CD. The financial risk is much lower for the songwriter/publisher, who makes a standard mechanical royalty rate of about 9.1 cents per song, or $0.91 for a ten-song CD, without having to bear any production or promotional costs.

The profits are divided somewhat differently in digital download sales. A $1.29 iTunes download generates about $0.40 for Apple (it gets 30 percent of every song sale) and a standard $0.09 mechanical royalty for the song publisher and writer, leaving about $0.60 for the record company. Artists at a typical royalty rate of about 15 percent would get $0.20 from the song download. With no CD printing and packaging costs, record companies can retain more of the revenue on download sales. Digital music sales also sometimes involve lucrative side deals: Jay-Z's 2013 album *Magna Carta Holy Grail* was packaged as a freebie with his Samsung

... ON A $17.98 CD
(ten tracks)

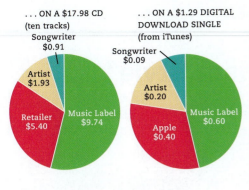

Songwriter
$0.91

Artist
$1.93

Retailer
$5.40

Music Label
$9.74

... ON A $1.29 DIGITAL
DOWNLOAD SINGLE
(from iTunes)

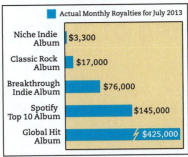

Songwriter
$0.09

Artist
$0.20

Apple
$0.40

Music Label
$0.60

... ON A SONG STREAMED 60 TIMES ON A
MUSIC STREAMING SERVICE, PER MONTH,
FOR AN ALBUM (e.g., Spotify)

■ Actual Monthly Royalties for July 2013

Niche Indie Album — $3,300
Classic Rock Album — $17,000
Breakthrough Indie Album — $76,000
Spotify Top 10 Album — $145,000
Global Hit Album — $425,000

FIGURE 4.3
WHERE THE MONEY GOES
Data from: Steve Knopper, "The New Economics of the Music Industry," Rolling Stone, *October 25, 2011, www.rollingstone.com/music/news /the-new-economics-of-the-music -industry-20111025; and Spotify, "Spotify Explained," accessed June 7, 2014, www.spotifyartists .com/spotify-explained/.*

... ON A SONG PLAYED ON INTERNET RADIO
(Pandora, Slacker)
$0.002 per performance (per play, per listener)
Nonfeatured Artist

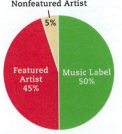

5%

Featured Artist
45%

Music Label
50%

... ON A SONG PLAYED IN AN ONLINE VIDEO
SERVICE

$1 per 1,000 video plays to record label,
e.g., "Forever" by Chris Brown on the
"JK Wedding Entrance Dance" video
earned $87,000 for 87 million plays.

app, which meant Samsung "bought" over a million copies of it in advance, surpassing the album's first-week sales of 528,000 (the Samsung deal was not counted as part of the album's official sales).

Another venue for digital music is streaming services like Spotify, Rdio, and Beats Music. Some leading artists initially held back their new releases from such services due to concerns that streaming would eat into their digital download and CD sales and that the compensation from streaming services wasn't sufficient. One of the leading services, Spotify, reports that on average, each stream is worth about $0.007.[24] Depending on the popularity of the song, that could add up to a little or a lot of money. For example, Spotify reports that similar to Apple's iTunes, it pays out about 70 percent of its revenue to music rights holders (divided between the label, performers, and songwriters) and retains about 30 percent for itself. Spotify provided examples of what typical payouts might be for a range of albums in a single month (see Figure 4.3). For contrast, contemporary cellist Zoë Keating, an independent recording artist, reported that she earned just $808 in the first half of 2013 from 201,412 Spotify streams of two of her older recordings distributed by CD Baby.[25]

Songs played on Internet radio, like Pandora, Slacker, or iHeartRadio, have yet another formula for determining royalties. In 2000, the nonprofit group SoundExchange was established to collect royalties for Internet radio. (The significant difference between Internet radio and subscription streaming services is that on Internet radio, listeners can't select specific songs to play. Instead, Internet stations have "theme" stations.) SoundExchange charges fees of $0.002 per play, per listener. Large Internet radio stations can pay up to 25 percent of their gross revenue (less for smaller Internet radio stations, and a small flat fee for streaming nonprofit stations). About 50 percent of the fees go to the music label, 45 percent go to the featured artists, and 5 percent go to nonfeatured artists.

Finally, video services like YouTube and Vevo have become sites to generate advertising revenue through music videos, which can attract tens of millions of views (see "Case Study: Psy and the Meaning of 'Gangnam Style'" on page 142). For example, Beyoncé's 2014 video for "Drunk in Love" drew more than 166 million views in just five months. Even popular amateur

LaunchPad ©
macmillanhighered.com
/mediaculture10e

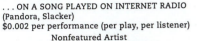

Alternative Strategies for Music Marketing
This video explores the strategies independent artists and marketers now employ to reach audiences.
Discussion: Even with the ability to bypass major record companies, many of the most popular artists still sign with those companies. Why do you think that is?

Psy and the Meaning of "Gangnam Style"

by Michael Park

South Korean musician Psy (aka Park Jae-Sang) became a pop-cultural sensation in the fall of 2012 with his viral Internet meme "Gangnam Style." The video has now generated over two billion views, making it the most popular YouTube video ever. Within a few months of the video's release, Psy was making appearances on national talk shows, such as *The Today Show*, *Ellen*, *Chelsea Lately*, and even an appearance on *Saturday Night Live*. Never before had a Korean pop ("K-pop") artist reached such epic crossover success, despite dozens of music acts from Korea and Asia making the attempt.

Although Psy's crossover appeal is largely unprecedented, his overwhelming popularity has many Koreans both gratified and puzzled.[1] The K-pop music industry is primarily made up of young and attractive singers who often flaunt their sexuality. Psy, however, is a comedic performer who is significantly older (mid-30s), portly, and without the leading-man looks that have come to dominate the K-pop scene. Without question, the "Gangnam Style" music video is visually seductive, with its colorful setups,

its catchy melody, and Psy's signature horse dance. As a seasoned comedic performer, Psy offers wacky juxtapositions, and the video has been the subject of exhaustive parody by mainstream and user-generated media. Unbeknownst to most viewers, the video and the song's lyrics offer a subversive message: Psy's scathing critique of materialism and conspicuous superficiality run amok in Korea's trendiest district—"Gangnam" ("south of the river" in Korean).

On one hand, it is possible to conclude that Psy's crossover success represents greater social acceptance of Asian men who have historically been absent or marginalized in mainstream media representations. However, Psy and his physicality in the video also evoke one of the stereotyped roles that mainstream media has situated Asian men in: the emasculated and clownish Asian male. The celebratory reception of Psy's "Gangnam Style" indicates that in order for Asian males to find popular appeal in the audiovisual realm, they too must negotiate with a "codified visual hierarchy" where consumers will only accept caricatured images of Asian men.

On *The Ellen DeGeneres Show*, it becomes clear that Psy's value as a guest is centered on his comical dance; he is relegated to an object of humor who elicits laughs with his minstrel performance. Psy teaches Britney Spears and Ellen his horse dance before performing the song

PHANTOM   PHANTOM
Ozan Kose/AFP/Getty Images

for the audience. Ellen fails to properly introduce Psy, and the audience and viewers learn nothing about him, nor are the song's lyrics or subversive message inquired about. On *Saturday Night Live*, Psy's comical horse dance and minstrelsy are further exploited in a sketch featuring host Seth MacFarlane. The point is clear: the comical dance moves and wacky visuals are consumed as silly entertainment and comic relief. Psy never speaks a word except for "Oppa Gangnam Style." Like his debut on *Ellen*, Psy stands as a recognizable prop, eager to entertain with his comical physicality. On *Chelsea Lately*, Psy makes an appearance in a bit that has him galloping his signature horse dance while performing menial office tasks, such as stomping on cardboard boxes, dusting office portraits, and stapling papers. Throughout the skit, he never speaks; he never even blurts out "Gangnam Style" while performing his dance.

Psy's "crossover success" into America's mainstream cultural imaginary, coupled with the absence of prototypical male K-pop artists (e.g., Rain, Se7en, or Big Bang), who display high fashion and flaunt hyper-sexuality, bolsters the assertion that a codified visual hierarchy operates in the audiovisual space as well. While Psy's popular appeal and celebrated reception in the American cultural imaginary are unprecedented, his image and physicality are tightly aligned with popular constructions of Asian men that define Asian masculinity as synonymous with emasculation and comic relief. ◢

Source: Adapted from Michael Park, "Psy-zing Up the Mainstreaming of 'Gangnam Style': Embracing Asian Masculinity as Neo-minstrelsy?" an award-winning paper presented at the Association for Education in Journalism and Mass Communication conference, Montreal, Canada, August 2014.

Al Pereira/WireImage/Getty Images

videos that use copyrighted music can create substantial revenue for music labels and artists. The 2009 amateur video "JK Wedding Entrance Dance" (reprised in a wedding scene in TV's *The Office*) has about 87 million views. Instead of asking YouTube to remove the wedding video for its unauthorized use of Chris Brown's song "Forever," Sony licensed the video to stay on YouTube. At the rate of $1 per thousand video plays, it ultimately generated about $87,000 in ad revenue.

There aren't standard formulas for sharing ad revenue from music videos, but there is movement in that direction. In 2012, Universal Music Group and the National Music Publishers' Association agreed that music publishers would be paid 15 percent of advertising revenues generated by music videos licensed for use on YouTube and Vevo.

Alternative Voices

A vast network of independent (indie) labels, distributors, stores, publications, and Internet sites devoted to music outside of the major label system has existed since the early days of rock and roll. The indie industry nonetheless continues to thrive, providing music fans access to all styles of music, including some of the world's most respected artists.

Independent labels have become even more viable by using the Internet as a low-cost distribution and promotional outlet for downloads, streaming, and merchandise sales, as well as for fan discussion groups, regular e-mail updates of tour schedules, and promotion of new releases. Consequently, bands that in previous years would have signed to a major label have found another path to success in the independent music industry, with labels like Merge Records (Arcade Fire, She & Him, the Mountain Goats), Matador (Yo La Tengo, Sonic Youth, Pavement), 4AD (the National, Bon Iver), and Epitaph (Bad Religion, Alkaline Trio, Frank Turner). Unlike artists on major labels who need to sell 500,000 copies

ChinaFotoPress/ChinaFotoPress via Getty Images

or more in order to recoup expenses and make a profit, indie artists "can turn a profit after selling roughly 25,000 copies of an album."[26] Some musical artists also self-publish CDs and sell them at concerts or use popular online services like CD Baby, the largest online distributer of independent music, where artists can earn $6 to $12 per CD. One of the challenges of being an independent, unsigned artist is figuring out how to sell one's music on iTunes, Amazon, Spotify, YouTube, and other digital music services. TuneCore, founded in 2006, is one of many companies (including CD Baby) that have emerged to fulfill that need. For less than $100, the company will distribute recordings to online music services and then collect royalties for the artist (charging an additional 10 percent for recovered royalty fees).

Some established rock acts, like Nine Inch Nails and Amanda Palmer, are taking another approach to their business model, shunning major labels and independents and using the Internet to directly reach their fans. By selling music online at their own Web sites or selling CDs at live concerts, music acts generally do better, cutting out the retailer and keeping more of the revenue themselves. Artists and bands can also build online communities around their Web sites, listing shows, news, tours, photos, and downloadable songs. Social networking sites are another place for fans and music artists to connect. MySpace was one of the first dominant sites, but Facebook eventually eclipsed it as the go-to site for music lovers. In addition, social music media sites like the Hype Machine and SoundCloud; music streaming sites like Blip.fm, Rhapsody, Grooveshark, and DatPiff; Internet radio stations like Pandora, Slacker, and 8tracks; and video sites like YouTube and Vevo are becoming increasingly popular places for fans to sample and discover new music.

LaunchPad ⊚

macmillanhighered.com
/mediaculture10e

Streaming Music Videos
On LaunchPad for *Media & Culture,* watch a clip of recent music videos from Katy Perry.
Discussion: Music videos get less TV exposure than they did in their heyday, but they can still be a crucial part of major artists' careers. How do these videos help sell Perry's music?

Sound Recording, Free Expression, and Democracy

From sound recording's earliest stages as a mass medium, when the music industry began stamping out flat records, to the breakthrough of MP3s and Internet-based music services, fans have been sharing music and pushing culture in unpredictable directions. Sound recordings allowed for the formation of rock and roll, a genre drawing from such a diverse range of musical styles that its impact on culture is unprecedented: Low culture challenged high-brow propriety, black culture spilled into white, southern culture infused the North, masculine and feminine stereotypes broke down, rural and urban styles came together, and artists mixed the sacred and the profane. Attempts to tame music were met by new affronts, including the British invasion, the growth of soul, and the political force of folk and psychedelic music. The gradual mainstreaming of rock led to the establishment of other culture-shaking genres, including punk, grunge, alternative, and hip-hop.

The battle over rock's controversial aspects speaks to the heart of democratic expression. Nevertheless, rock and other popular recordings—like other art forms—also have a history of reproducing old stereotypes: limiting women's access as performers, fostering racist or homophobic attitudes, and celebrating violence and misogyny.

Popular musical forms that test cultural boundaries face a dilemma: how to uphold a legacy of free expression while resisting giant companies bent on consolidating independents and maximizing profits. Since the 1950s, forms of rock music have been breaking boundaries, then becoming commercial, then reemerging as rebellious, and then repeating the pattern. The congressional payola hearings of 1959 and the Senate hearings of the mid-1980s triggered by Tipper Gore's Parents Music Resource Center (which led to music advisory labels) are just two

DIGITAL JOB OUTLOOK

Media Professionals Speak about Jobs in the Music Industry

Ariel Hyatt, Founder, Ariel Publicity and Cyber PR (firms that have worked with over one thousand musicians and bands of all genres)

If you love a specific band or artist, look up whom they work with and put those companies on your list because nothing is more thrilling and satisfying than working for your *favorite* artists and bands (I still get a thrill out of that, and I've been working in the music industry for fourteen years).

Morna Cook, Head of Human Resources, Universal Music UK

Any music-related experience is valuable, whether you've volunteered at a festival, done work experience for a small label, or worked on a blog or Web site on your own time. It's always good to see work experience on candidates' CVs. Volunteering to work not only shows that you are dedicated and proactive, but will also mean you have a better understanding of how things work in a practical sense. This will give you the edge over candidates who have purely theoretical knowledge.

John Kellogg, Assistant Chair of Music Business/ Management Department, Berklee College of Music

I think the growth area is in management. [Managers] can coordinate all the various activities of creative talents and maximize those careers. It used to be [that] record companies were the central place where that happened. . . . That's completely different now.

Lauren Drell, Branded Content Editor, *Mashable*

If you're applying for a tech position, and the Spotify team likes what they see on your résumé, you'll be contacted for a phone or Skype interview with an engineer. Then you'll have a half day of on-site interviews (three hour-long meetings with engineers, and lunch with an engineer). Depending on the position, you may have to complete a coding challenge at home before arriving on-site. If you're applying to work on the business side, you can expect one or two phone interviews and two or three hours of on-site interviews. The ideal candidate [according to Alexandra Cohen, Technical Director at Spotify]: "We are looking for motivated, passionate people who want to accept the mission of helping people find the right music for every moment."

Lady Gaga

Stop taking selfies, because that won't make you a star.

---

of the many attempts to rein in popular music, whereas the infamous antics of performers from Elvis Presley onward, the blunt lyrics of artists from rock and roll and rap, and the independent paths of the many garage bands and cult bands of the early rock-and-roll era through the present are among those actions that pushed popular music's boundaries.

Still, this dynamic between popular music's clever innovations and capitalism's voracious appetite is crucial to sound recording's constant innovation and mass appeal. Ironically, successful commerce requires periodic infusions of the diverse sounds that come from ethnic communities, backyard garages, dance parties, and neighborhood clubs. No matter how it is produced and distributed, popular music endures because it speaks to both individual and universal themes, from a teenager's first romantic adventure to a nation's outrage over social injustice. Music often reflects the personal or political anxieties of a society. It also breaks down artificial or hurtful barriers better than many government programs do. Despite its tribulations, music at its best continues to champion a democratic spirit. Writer and free-speech advocate Nat Hentoff addressed this issue in the 1970s when he wrote, "Popular music always speaks, among other things, of dreams—which change with the times."[27] The recording industry continues to capitalize on and spread those dreams globally, but in each generation, musicians and their fans keep imagining new ones. ▶

CHAPTER REVIEW

COMMON THREADS

One of the Common Threads discussed in Chapter 1 is the developmental stages of mass media. But as new audio and sound recording technologies evolve, do they drive the kind of music we hear?

In the recent history of the music industry, it would seem as if technology has been the driving force behind the kind of music we hear. Case in point: The advent of the MP3 file as a new format in 1999 led to a new emphasis on single songs as the primary unit of music sales. The Recording Industry Association of America reports that there were more than 1.3 billion downloads of digital singles in 2013. In that year, digital singles outsold physical CD albums more than 7 to 1. In the past decade, we have come to live in a music business dominated by digital singles.

What have we gained by this transition? Thankfully, there are fewer CD jewel boxes (which always shattered with the greatest of ease). And there is no requirement to buy the lackluster "filler" songs that often come with the price of an album, when all we want are the two or three hit songs. But what have we lost culturally in the transition away from albums?

First, there is no physical album art for digital singles (although department stores now sell frames to turn vintage 12-inch album covers into art). And second, we have lost the concept of an album as a thematic collection of music, and a medium that provides a much broader canvas to a talented musical artist. Consider this: How would the Beatles' *The White Album* have been created in a business dominated by singles? A look at *Rolling Stone* magazine's 500 Greatest Albums and *Time* magazine's All-Time 100 Albums indicates the apex of album creativity in earlier decades, with selections such as Jimi Hendrix's *Are You Experienced* (1967), the Beatles' *Sgt. Pepper's Lonely Hearts Club Band* (1967), David Bowie's *The Rise and Fall of Ziggy Stardust* (1972), Public Enemy's *It Takes a Nation of Millions to Hold Us Back* (1988), and Radiohead's *OK Computer* (1997). Has the movement away from albums changed possibilities for musical artists? That is, if an artist wants to be commercially successful, is there more pressure just to generate hit singles instead of larger bodies of work that constitute the album? Have the styles of artists like Kesha, Nicki Minaj, OneRepublic, and Lil Wayne been shaped by the predominance of the single?

Still, there is a clear case against technological determinism—the idea that technological innovations determine the direction of the culture. Back in the 1950s, the vinyl album caught on despite its newness—and despite the popularity of the 45-rpm single format, which competed with it at the same time. When the MP3 single format emerged in the late 1990s, the music industry had just rolled out two formats of advanced album discs that were technological improvements on the CD. Neither caught on. Of course, music fans may have been lured by the ease of acquiring music digitally via the Internet, and by the price—usually free (but illegal).

So, if it isn't technological determinism, why doesn't a strong digital album market coexist with the digital singles of today? Can you think of any albums of the past few years that merit being listed among the greatest albums of all time?

KEY TERMS

The definitions for the terms listed below can be found in the glossary at the end of the book. The page numbers listed with the terms indicate where the term is highlighted in the chapter.

audiotape, 118
stereo, 118
analog recording, 118
digital recording, 118
compact discs (CDs), 119
MP3, 120
pop music, 122
jazz, 123
cover music, 123

rock and roll, 123
blues, 123
rhythm and blues (R&B), 124
rockabilly, 125
soul, 130
folk music, 131
folk-rock, 131
punk rock, 133
grunge, 134

alternative rock, 134
hip-hop, 134
gangster rap, 135
oligopoly, 137
indies, 137
A&R (artist & repertoire)
    agents, 139
online piracy, 140

REVIEW QUESTIONS

The Development of Sound Recording

1. The technological configuration of a particular medium sometimes elevates it to mass market status. Why did Emile Berliner's flat disk replace the wax cylinder, and why did this reconfiguration of records matter in the history of the mass media? Can you think of other mass media examples in which the size and shape of the technology have made a difference?

2. How did sound recording survive the advent of radio?

3. How did the music industry attempt to curb illegal downloading and file-sharing?

U.S. Popular Music and the Formation of Rock

4. How did rock and roll significantly influence two mass media industries?

5. Although many rock-and-roll lyrics from the 1950s are tame by today's standards, this new musical development represented a threat to many parents and adults at that time. Why?

6. What moral and cultural boundaries were blurred by rock and roll in the 1950s?

7. Why did cover music figure so prominently in the development of rock and roll and the record industry in the 1950s?

A Changing Industry: Reformations in Popular Music

8. Explain the British invasion. What was its impact on the recording industry?

9. What were the major influences of folk music on the recording industry?

10. Why did hip-hop and punk rock emerge as significant musical forms in the late 1970s and 1980s? What do their developments have in common, and how are they different?

11. Why does pop music continue to remain powerful today?

The Business of Sound Recording

12. What companies control the bulk of worldwide music production and distribution?

13. Why have independent labels grown to have a significantly larger market share in the 2010s?

14. Which major parties receive profits when a digital download, music stream, or physical CD is sold?

15. How is a mechanical royalty different from a performance royalty?

Sound Recording, Free Expression, and Democracy

16. Why is it ironic that so many forms of alternative music become commercially successful?

QUESTIONING THE MEDIA

1. If you ran a noncommercial campus radio station, what kind of music would you play, and why?

2. Think about the role of the 1960s drug culture in rock's history. How are drugs and alcohol treated in contemporary and alternative forms of rock and hip-hop today?

3. Is it healthy for, or detrimental to, the music business that so much of the recording industry is controlled by just a few large international companies? Explain.

4. Do you think the Internet as a technology helps or hurts musical artists? Why do so many contemporary musical performers differ in their opinions about the Internet?

5. How has the Internet changed your musical tastes? Has it exposed you to more global music? Do you listen to a wider range of music because of the Internet?

LAUNCHPAD FOR *MEDIA & CULTURE*

Visit LaunchPad for *Media & Culture* at macmillanhighered.com/mediaculture10e for additional learning tools:

- REVIEW WITH LEARNINGCURVE
  LearningCurve, available on LaunchPad for *Media & Culture*, uses gamelike quizzing to help you master the concepts you need to learn from this chapter.

SOUNDS AND IMAGES

5

Popular Radio and the Origins of Broadcasting

151
Early Technology and the Development of Radio

157
The Evolution of Radio

165
Radio Reinvents Itself

169
The Sounds of Commercial Radio

178
The Economics of Broadcast Radio

182
Radio and the Democracy of the Airwaves

A few years ago, a young woman named Kristin* took an entry-level position running the audio board for the on-air radio personalities at an AM radio station. She loved radio and hoped that this job would jump-start her career in the industry. "When I went to college to get my bachelor's degree, that's what I wanted to do," she said. Kristin got her break when she was asked to fill in at the microphone when one of the radio personalities went on maternity leave. Soon, she won a regular shift while just a college student. And because the station was owned by Atlanta-based Cumulus Media, one of the largest radio groups in the country, there were opportunities for Kristin to grow within the company. She was transferred to host a show on a popular contemporary hits FM station in a larger market, playing the latest songs. "I was so excited to be living my dream," Kristin said, so much so that she didn't mind that she was earning only minimum wage.

* Her name has been changed for confidentiality reasons.

Tim Pannell/Corbis

That dream soon revealed its darker side—the realities of today's homogenized radio industry. Kristin's station was one of three FM stations owned by Cumulus in that market. Kristin was asked to do voice-tracking, a cost-saving measure in which a radio deejay prerecords voice breaks that are then inserted into an automated shift. To listeners, it may have seemed as if they were getting three different deejays on Cumulus's contemporary hits station, rock station, and country station. After all, they were hearing three different names, with three slightly different personalities. In reality, Kristin was the midday deejay on the contemporary hits radio station, the evening deejay on the rock format station, and the weekend voice of the company's country format station. Some days, due to scheduling, Kristin's three on-air personalities could be heard at the exact same time. But she would only be paid for the one hour it took her to lay down a voice track for each four- to five-hour shift.

Kristin and her fellow voice-tracked deejays felt disconnected from their listeners. "You can see that the phones ring all day long," she said, referring to listeners calling in requests. "Even if you voice-track, you say, 'Call in with your request, or leave a message.'" But because the songs are scheduled days in advance in the automated system, if a request happens to be played, it's only by coincidence.

After four years, Kristin finished her BA in communication, left the radio station, and went to grad school. "I wouldn't have been able to pay my college loans with the money I was making," she said.

But even with the low wages, for Kristin, the biggest disappointment was that the kind of commercial radio she had grown up listening to was being phased out by the time she went to work in the business.

The consolidation of stations into massive radio groups like Cumulus and Clear Channel (now iHeartMedia) in the 1990s and 2000s resulted in budget-cutting demands from the corporate offices and, ultimately, stations with less connection to their local audience. And even with growing complaints from listeners and community groups about the decline in minority ownership, the lack of musical diversity on the airwaves, and the near disappearance of local radio news, little has changed. It is simply more profitable for radio conglomerates to use prerecorded or syndicated programming, even if it means losing sight of their duty to serve the public interest and stifling their deejays' individuality and passion for the medium. Kristin's contemporary hits station had five full-time on-air deejays when she started. Today, it has just one.

▲ *EVEN WITH THE ARRIVAL OF TV IN THE 1950s* and the "corporatization" of broadcasting in the 1990s, the historical and contemporary roles played by radio have been immense. From the early days of network radio, which gave us "a national identity" and "a chance to share in a common experience,"[1] to the more customized, demographically segmented medium today, radio's influence continues to reverberate throughout our society. Though television displaced radio as our most common media experience, radio specialized and adapted. The daily music and persistent talk that resonate from radios all over the world continue to play a key role in contemporary culture.

Visit **LaunchPad** for *Media & Culture* and use **LearningCurve** to review concepts from this chapter.

In this chapter, we examine the scientific, cultural, political, and economic factors surrounding radio's development and perseverance. We will:

- Explore the origins of broadcasting, from the early theories about radio waves to the critical formation of RCA as a national radio monopoly
- Probe the evolution of commercial radio, including the rise of NBC as the first network, the development of CBS, and the establishment of the first federal radio legislation
- Review the fascinating ways in which radio reinvented itself in the 1950s
- Examine television's impact on radio programming, the invention of FM radio, radio's convergence with sound recording, and the influence of various formats
- Investigate newer developments, like satellite and HD radio; radio's convergence with the Internet; and radio's hopes for greater convergence with the mobile phone industry
- Survey the economic health, increasing conglomeration, and cultural impact of commercial and noncommercial radio today, including the emergence of noncommercial low-power FM service

As you read through this chapter, think about your own relationship with radio. What are your earliest memories of radio listening? Do you remember a favorite song or station? How old were you when you started listening? Why did you listen? What types of radio stations are in your area today? How has the Internet made radio better? How has it made it worse? For more questions to help you think through the role of radio in our lives, see "Questioning the Media" in the Chapter Review.

Early Technology and the Development of Radio

Radio did not emerge as a full-blown mass medium until the 1920s, though the technology that made radio possible had been evolving for years. The telegraph—the precursor of radio technology—was invented in the 1840s. American inventor Samuel Morse developed the first practical system, sending electrical impulses from a transmitter through a cable to a reception point. Using what became known as Morse code—a series of dots and dashes that stood for letters in the alphabet—telegraph operators transmitted news and messages simply by interrupting the electrical current along a wire cable. By 1844, Morse had set up the first telegraph line between Washington, D.C., and Baltimore. By 1861, telegraph lines ran coast to coast. By 1866, the first transatlantic cable, capable of transmitting about six words a minute, ran between Newfoundland and Ireland along the ocean floor.

Although it was a revolutionary technology, the telegraph had its limitations. For instance, while it dispatched complicated language codes, it was unable to transmit the human voice. Moreover, ships at sea still had no contact with the rest of the world. As a result, navies could not find out that wars had ceased on land and often continued fighting for months. Commercial

A TELEGRAPH OPERATOR
reads the perforated tape.
Sending messages using
Morse code across telegraph
wires was the precursor to
radio, which did not fully
become a mass medium until
the 1920s.

shipping interests also lacked an efficient way to coordinate and relay information from land and between ships. What was needed was a telegraph without the wires.

Maxwell and Hertz Discover Radio Waves

The key development in wireless transmissions came from James Maxwell, a Scottish physicist who in the mid-1860s theorized the existence of electromagnetic waves: invisible electronic impulses similar to visible light. Maxwell's equations showed that electricity, magnetism, light, and heat are part of the same electromagnetic spectrum and that they radiate in space at the speed of light, about 186,000 miles per second (see Figure 5.1). Maxwell further theorized that a portion of these phenomena, later known as radio waves, could be harnessed so that signals could be sent from a transmission point to a reception point.

It was German physicist Heinrich Hertz, however, who in the 1880s proved Maxwell's theories. Hertz created a crude device that permitted an electrical spark to leap across a small gap between two steel balls. As the electricity jumped the gap, it emitted waves; this was the first recorded transmission and reception of an electromagnetic wave. Hertz's experiments significantly advanced the development of wireless communication.

Marconi and the Inventors of Wireless Telegraphy

In 1894, Guglielmo Marconi—a twenty-year-old, self-educated Italian engineer—read Hertz's work and understood that developing a way to send high-speed messages over great distances would transform communication, the military, and commercial shipping. Although revolutionary, the

▼ Popular Radio and the Origins of Broadcasting

Samuel Morse
The first telegraph line is set up between Washington, D.C., and Baltimore, Maryland, in 1844. For the first time in history, communication exceeds the speed of land transportation (p. 151).

Guglielmo Marconi
The Italian inventor begins experiments on wireless telegraphy in 1894. He sees his invention as a means for point-to-point communication (pp. 152–153).

Practical Use for Wireless Technology
Wireless operators save 705 lives during the *Titanic* tragedy in 1912, boosting interest in amateur radio across the United States (p. 156).

Commercial Radio
The first advertisements beginning in 1922 cause an uproar as people question the right to pollute the public airwaves with commercial messages (p. 158).

1830	1850	1870	1890	1910

Nikola Tesla
The Serbian-Croatian inventor creates a wireless device in America in 1892. His transmitter can make a tube thirty feet away light up (p. 154).

Lee De Forest
The American inventor writes the first dissertation on wireless technology in 1899 and goes on to invent wireless telephony and a means for amplifying radio sound (p. 154).

Wireless Ship Act
In 1910, Congress passes this act requiring that all major ships be equipped with wireless radio (p. 156).

Amateur Radio Shutdown
The navy closes down all amateur radio operations in 1917 to ensure military security as the United States enters World War I (p. 156).

telephone and the telegraph were limited by their wires, so Marconi set about trying to make wireless technology practical. First, he attached Hertz's spark-gap transmitter to a Morse telegraph key, which could send out dot-dash signals. The electrical impulses traveled into a Morse inker, the machine that telegraph operators used to record the dots and dashes onto narrow strips of paper. Second, Marconi discovered that grounding—connecting the transmitter and receiver to the earth—greatly increased the distance over which he could send signals.

In 1896, Marconi traveled to England, where he received a patent on **wireless telegraphy**, a form of voiceless point-to-point communication. In London, in 1897, he formed the Marconi Wireless Telegraph Company, later known as British Marconi, and began installing wireless technology on British naval and private commercial ships. In 1899, he opened a branch in the United States, establishing a company nicknamed American Marconi. That same year, he sent the first wireless Morse-code signal across the English Channel to France, and in 1901 he relayed the first wireless signal across the Atlantic Ocean. Although Marconi was a successful innovator and entrepreneur, he saw wireless telegraphy only as point-to-point communication, much like the telegraph and the telephone, not as a one-to-many mass medium. He also confined his applications to Morse-code messages for military and commercial ships, leaving others to explore the wireless transmission of voice and music.

History often cites Marconi as the "father of radio," but another inventor unknown to him was making parallel discoveries about wireless telegraphy in Russia. Alexander Popov, a professor of physics in St. Petersburg, was also experimenting with sending wireless messages over distances. Popov announced to the Russian Physicist Society of St. Petersburg on May 7, 1895, that he had transmitted and received signals over a distance of six hundred yards.[2] Yet Popov was an academic, not an entrepreneur, and after Marconi accomplished a similar feat that same summer, Marconi was the first to apply for and receive a patent. However, May 7 is celebrated as Radio Day in Russia.

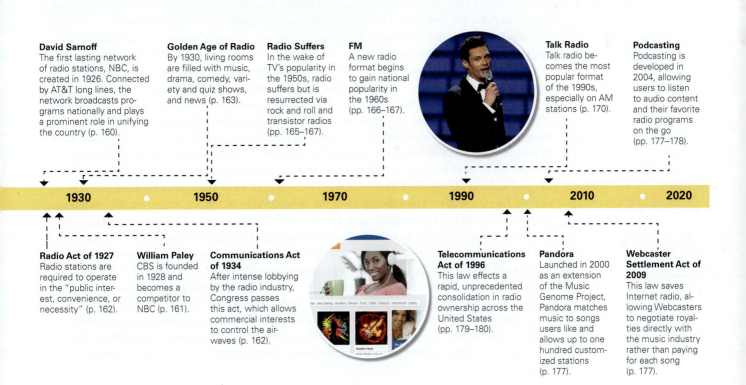

David Sarnoff
The first lasting network of radio stations, NBC, is created in 1926. Connected by AT&T long lines, the network broadcasts programs nationally and plays a prominent role in unifying the country (p. 160).

Golden Age of Radio
By 1930, living rooms are filled with music, drama, comedy, variety and quiz shows, and news (p. 163).

Radio Suffers
In the wake of TV's popularity in the 1950s, radio suffers but is resurrected via rock and roll and transistor radios (pp. 165–167).

FM
A new radio format begins to gain national popularity in the 1960s (pp. 166–167).

Talk Radio
Talk radio becomes the most popular format of the 1990s, especially on AM stations (p. 170).

Podcasting
Podcasting is developed in 2004, allowing users to listen to audio content and their favorite radio programs on the go (pp. 177–178).

| 1930 | 1950 | 1970 | 1990 | 2010 | 2020 |

Radio Act of 1927
Radio stations are required to operate in the "public interest, convenience, or necessity" (p. 162).

William Paley
CBS is founded in 1928 and becomes a competitor to NBC (p. 161).

Communications Act of 1934
After intense lobbying by the radio industry, Congress passes this act, which allows commercial interests to control the airwaves (p. 162).

Telecommunications Act of 1996
This law effects a rapid, unprecedented consolidation in radio ownership across the United States (pp. 179–180).

Pandora
Launched in 2000 as an extension of the Music Genome Project, Pandora matches music to songs users like and allows up to one hundred customized stations (p. 177).

Webcaster Settlement Act of 2009
This law saves Internet radio, allowing Webcasters to negotiate royalties directly with the music industry rather than paying for each song (p. 177).

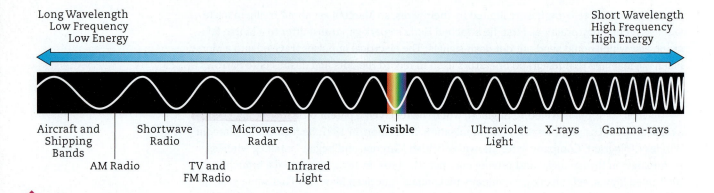

Long Wavelength
Low Frequency
Low Energy

Short Wavelength
High Frequency
High Energy

Aircraft and Shipping Bands

AM Radio

Shortwave Radio

TV and FM Radio

Microwaves Radar

Infrared Light

Visible

Ultraviolet Light

X-rays

Gamma-rays

FIGURE 5.1

THE ELECTROMAGNETIC SPECTRUM

Data from: NASA, http://imagine .gsfc.nasa.gov/docs/science /know_l1/emspectrum.html.

It is important to note that the work of Popov and Marconi was preceded by that of Nikola Tesla, a Serbian-Croatian inventor who immigrated to New York in 1884. Tesla, who also conceived the high-capacity alternating current systems that made worldwide electrification possible, invented a wireless system in 1892. A year later, Tesla successfully demonstrated his device in St. Louis, with his transmitter lighting up a receiver tube thirty feet away.[3] However, Tesla's work was overshadowed by Marconi's; Marconi used much of Tesla's work in his own developments, and for years Tesla was not associated with the invention of radio. Tesla never received great financial benefits from his breakthroughs, but in 1943 (a few months after he died penniless in New York), the U.S. Supreme Court overturned Marconi's wireless patent and deemed Tesla the inventor of radio.[4]

Wireless Telephony: De Forest and Fessenden

In 1899, inventor Lee De Forest (who, in defiance of other inventors, liked to call himself the "father of radio") wrote the first Ph.D. dissertation on wireless technology, building on others' innovations. In 1901, De Forest challenged Marconi, who was covering New York's International Yacht Races for the Associated Press, by signing up to report the races for a rival news service. The competing transmitters jammed each other's signals so badly, however, that officials ended up relaying information on the races in the traditional way—with flags and hand signals. The event exemplified a problem that would persist throughout radio's early development: noise and interference from competition for the finite supply of radio frequencies.

In 1902, De Forest set up the Wireless Telephone Company to compete head-on with American Marconi, by then the leader in wireless communication. A major difference between Marconi and De Forest was the latter's interest in wireless voice and music transmissions, later known as **wireless telephony** and, eventually, radio. Although sometimes an unscrupulous competitor (inventor Reginald Fessenden won a lawsuit against De Forest for using one of his patents without permission), De Forest went on to patent more than three hundred inventions.

De Forest's biggest breakthrough was the development of the Audion, or triode, vacuum tube, which detected radio signals and then amplified them. De Forest's improvements greatly increased listeners' ability to hear dots and dashes and, later, speech and music on a receiver set. His modifications were essential to the development of voice transmission, long-distance radio, and television. In fact, the Audion vacuum tube, which powered radios until the arrival of transistors and solid-state circuits in the 1950s, is considered by many historians to be the beginning of modern electronics. But again, bitter competition taints De Forest's legacy; although De Forest won a twenty-year court battle for the rights to the Audion patent, most engineers at the time agreed that Edwin Armstrong (who later developed FM radio) was the true inventor and disagreed with the U.S. Supreme Court's 1934 decision on the case that favored De Forest.[5]

Bettmann/Corbis

The credit for the first voice broadcast belongs to Canadian engineer Reginald Fessenden, formerly a chief chemist for Thomas Edison. Fessenden went to work for the U.S. Navy and eventually for General Electric (GE), where he played a central role in improving wireless signals. Both the navy and GE were interested in the potential for voice transmissions. On Christmas Eve in 1906, after GE built Fessenden a powerful transmitter, he gave his first public demonstration, sending a voice through the airwaves from his station at Brant Rock, Massachusetts. A radio historian describes what happened:

That night, ship operators and amateurs around Brant Rock heard the results: "someone speaking! . . . a woman's voice rose in song. . . . Next someone was heard reading a poem." Fessenden himself played "O Holy Night" on his violin. Though the fidelity was not all that it might be, listeners were captivated by the voices and notes they heard. No more would sounds be restricted to mere dots and dashes of the Morse code.[6]

Ship operators were astonished to hear voices rather than the familiar Morse code. (Some operators actually thought they were having a supernatural encounter.) This event showed that the wireless medium was moving from a point-to-point communication tool (wireless operator to wireless operator) toward a one-to-many communication tool. **Broadcasting**, once an agricultural term that referred to the process of casting seeds over a large area, would come to mean the transmission of radio waves (and, later, TV signals) to a broad public audience. Prior to radio broadcasting, wireless was considered a form of **narrowcasting**, or person-to-person communication, like the telegraph and the telephone.

In 1910, De Forest transmitted a performance of *Tosca* by the Metropolitan Opera to friends in the New York area with wireless receivers. At this point in time, radio passed from the novelty stage to the entrepreneurial stage, during which various practical uses would be tested before radio would launch as a mass medium.

St. Louis Post-Dispatch headline:

ST. LOUIS POST-DISPATCH HOME EDITION

1302 LIVES LOST WHEN "TITANIC" SANK; 868 SAVED

Carpathia Steaming to New York With Survivors; None on Other Ships

2-THIRDS WOMEN IN PARTIAL LIST OF THOSE RESCUED

7 ST. LOUISANS ARE REPORTED SAFE ON BOARD CARPATHIA

Getty Images

NEWS OF THE *TITANIC*
Despite the headline in the *St. Louis Post-Dispatch*, actually 1,523 people died and only 705 were rescued when the *Titanic* hit an iceberg on April 14, 1912 (the ship technically sank at 2:20 A.M. on April 15). The crew of the *Titanic* used the Marconi wireless equipment on board to send distress signals to other ships. Of the eight ships nearby, the *Carpathia* was the first to respond with lifeboats.

Regulating a New Medium

The two most important international issues affecting radio in the first decade of the twentieth century were ship radio requirements and signal interference. Congress passed the Wireless Ship Act in 1910, which required that all major U.S. seagoing ships carrying more than fifty passengers and traveling more than two hundred miles off the coast be equipped with wireless equipment with a one-hundred-mile range. The importance of this act was underscored by the *Titanic* disaster two years later. A brand-new British luxury steamer, the *Titanic* sank in 1912. Although more than fifteen hundred people died in the tragedy, wireless reports played a critical role in pinpointing the *Titanic*'s location, enabling rescue ships to save over seven hundred lives.

Radio Waves as a Natural Resource

In the wake of the *Titanic* tragedy, Congress passed the **Radio Act of 1912**, which addressed the problem of amateur radio operators increasingly cramming the airwaves. Because radio waves crossed state and national borders, legislators determined that broadcasting constituted a "natural resource"—a kind of interstate commerce. This meant that radio waves could not be owned; they were the collective property of all Americans, just like national parks. Therefore, transmitting on radio waves would require licensing in the same way that driving a car requires a license.

A short policy guide, the first Radio Act required all wireless stations to obtain radio licenses from the Commerce Department. This act, which governed radio until 1927, also formally adopted the SOS Morse-code distress signal that other countries had been using for several years. Further, the "natural resource" mandate led to the idea that radio, and eventually television, should provide a benefit to society—in the form of education and public service. The eventual establishment of public radio stations was one consequence of this idea; the Fairness Doctrine was another.

The Impact of World War I

By 1915, more than twenty American companies sold wireless point-to-point communication systems, primarily for use in ship-to-shore communication. Having established a reputation for efficiency and honesty, American Marconi (a subsidiary of British Marconi) was the biggest and best of these companies. But in 1914, with World War I beginning in Europe and with America warily watching the conflict, the U.S. Navy questioned the wisdom of allowing a foreign-controlled company to wield so much power. American corporations, especially GE and AT&T, capitalized on the navy's xenophobia and succeeded in undercutting Marconi's influence.

As wireless telegraphy played an increasingly large role in military operations, the navy sought tight controls on information. When the United States entered the war in 1917, the navy closed down all amateur radio operations and took control of key radio transmitters to ensure military security. As the war was nearing its end in 1919, British Marconi placed an order with GE for twenty-four potent new alternators, which were strong enough to power a transoceanic system of radio stations that could connect the world. But the U.S. Navy, influenced by Franklin Roosevelt—at that time the navy's assistant secretary—grew concerned and moved to ensure that such powerful new radio technology would not fall under foreign control.

Roosevelt was guided in turn by President Woodrow Wilson's goal of developing the United States as an international power, a position greatly enhanced by American military successes during the war. Wilson and the navy saw an opportunity to slow Britain's influence over communication and to promote a U.S. plan for the control of the emerging wireless operations. Thus corporate heads and government leaders conspired to make sure radio communication would serve American interests.

The Formation of RCA

Some members of Congress and the corporate community opposed federal legislation that would grant the government or the navy a radio monopoly. Consequently, GE developed a compromise plan that would create a *private sector monopoly*—that is, a private company that would have the government's approval to dominate the radio industry. First, GE broke off negotiations to sell key radio technologies to European-owned companies like British Marconi, thereby limiting those companies' global reach. Second, GE took the lead in founding a new company, **Radio Corporation of America (RCA)**, which soon acquired American Marconi and radio patents of other U.S. companies. Upon its founding in 1919, RCA had pooled the necessary technology and patents to monopolize the wireless industry and expand American communication technology throughout the world.[7]

Under RCA's patent pool arrangement, wireless patents from the navy, AT&T, GE, the former American Marconi, and other companies were combined to ensure U.S. control over the manufacture of radio transmitters and receivers. Initially AT&T, then the government-sanctioned monopoly provider of telephone services, manufactured most transmitters, while GE (and later Westinghouse) made radio receivers. RCA administered the pool, collecting patent royalties and distributing them to pool members. To protect these profits, the government did not permit RCA to manufacture equipment or to operate radio stations under its own name for several years. Instead, RCA's initial function was to ensure that radio parts were standardized by manufacturers and to control frequency interference by amateur radio operators, which increasingly became a problem after the war.

A government restriction at the time mandated that no more than 20 percent of RCA could be owned by foreigners. This restriction, later raised to 25 percent, became law in 1927 and applied to all U.S. broadcasting stocks and facilities. Because of this rule, Rupert Murdoch—the head of Australia's News Corp.—became a U.S. citizen in 1985, so he could buy a number of TV stations and form the Fox television network. In 2013, the FCC ruled it would allow exemptions to the 25 percent foreign ownership limit on a case-by-case basis.

RCA's most significant impact was that it gave the United States almost total control over the emerging mass medium of broadcasting. At the time, the United States was the only country that placed broadcasting under the care of commercial, rather than military or government, interests. By pooling more than two thousand patents and sharing research developments, RCA ensured the global dominance of the United States in mass communication, a position it maintained in electronic hardware into the 1960s and maintains in program content today.

The Evolution of Radio

When Westinghouse engineer Frank Conrad set up a crude radio studio above his Pittsburgh garage in 1916, placing a microphone in front of a phonograph to broadcast music and news to his friends (whom Conrad supplied with receivers) two evenings a week on experimental station 8XK, he unofficially became one of the medium's first disc jockeys. In 1920, a Westinghouse executive, intrigued by Conrad's curious hobby, realized the potential of radio as a mass medium. Westinghouse then established station KDKA, which is generally regarded as the first commercial broadcast station. KDKA is most noted for airing national returns from the Cox–Harding presidential election on November 2, 1920, an event most historians consider the first professional broadcast.

Other amateur broadcasters could also lay claim to being first. One of the earliest stations, operated by Charles "Doc" Herrold in San Jose, California, began in 1909 and later became KCBS. Additional experimental stations—in places like New York; Detroit; Medford, Massachusetts; and Pierre, South Dakota—broadcast voice and music prior to the establishment of KDKA. But KDKA's success, with the financial backing of Westinghouse, signaled the start of broadcast radio.

In 1921, the U.S. Commerce Department officially licensed five radio stations for operation; by early 1923, more than six hundred commercial and noncommercial stations were operating. Some stations were owned by AT&T, GE, and Westinghouse, but many were run by amateurs or were independently owned by universities or businesses. By the end of 1923, as many as 550,000 radio receivers, most manufactured by GE and Westinghouse, had been sold for about $55 each (about $701 in today's dollars). Just as the "guts" of the phonograph had been put inside a piece of furniture to create a consumer product, the vacuum tubes, electrical posts, and bulky batteries that made up the radio receiver were placed inside stylish furniture and marketed to households. By 1925, 5.5 million radio sets were in use across America, and radio was officially a mass medium.

Building the First Networks

In a major power grab in 1922, AT&T, which already had a government-sanctioned monopoly in the telephone business, decided to break its RCA agreements in an attempt to monopolize radio as well. Identifying the new medium as the "wireless telephone," AT&T argued that broadcasting was merely an extension of its control over the telephone. Ultimately, the corporate giant complained that RCA had gained too much monopoly power. In violation of its early agreements with RCA, AT&T began making and selling its own radio receivers.

In the same year, AT&T started WEAF (now WNBC) in New York, the first radio station to regularly sell commercial time to advertisers. AT&T claimed that under the RCA agreements it had the exclusive right to sell ads, which AT&T called *toll broadcasting*. Most people in radio at the time recoiled at the idea of using the medium for crass advertising, viewing it instead as a public information service. In fact, stations that had earlier tried to sell ads received "cease and desist" letters from the Department of Commerce. But by August 1922, AT&T had nonetheless sold its first ad to a New York real estate developer for $50. The idea of promoting the new medium as a public service, along the lines of today's noncommercial National Public Radio (NPR), ended when executives realized that radio ads offered another opportunity for profits long after radio-set sales had saturated the consumer market.

The initial strategy behind AT&T's toll broadcasting idea was an effort to conquer radio. By its agreements with RCA, AT&T retained the rights to interconnect the signals between two or more radio stations via telephone wires. In 1923, when AT&T aired a program simultaneously on its flagship WEAF station and on WNAC in Boston, the phone company created the first **network**: a cost-saving operation that links (at that time, through special phone lines; today, through satellite relays) a group of broadcast stations that share programming produced at a central location. By the end of 1924, AT&T had interconnected twenty-two stations to air a talk by President Calvin Coolidge. Some of these

WESTINGHOUSE ENGINEER FRANK CONRAD
Broadcasting from his garage, Conrad turned his hobby into Pittsburgh's KDKA, one of the first radio stations. Although this early station is widely celebrated in history books as the first broadcasting outlet, one can't underestimate the influence Westinghouse had in promoting this "historical first." Westinghouse clearly saw the celebration of Conrad's garage studio as a way to market the company and its radio equipment. The resulting legacy of Conrad's garage studio has thus overshadowed other individuals who also experimented with radio broadcasting.

Bettmann/Corbis

stations were owned by AT&T, but most simply consented to become AT&T "affiliates," agreeing to air the phone company's programs. These network stations informally became known as the *telephone group* and later as the Broadcasting Corporation of America (BCA).

In response, GE, Westinghouse, and RCA interconnected a smaller set of competing stations, known as the *radio group*. Initially, their network linked WGY in Schenectady, New York (then GE's national headquarters), and WJZ in Manhattan. The radio group had to use inferior Western Union telegraph lines when AT&T denied them access to telephone wires. By this time, AT&T had sold its stock in RCA and refused to lease its lines to competing radio networks. The telephone monopoly was now enmeshed in a battle to defeat RCA for control of radio.

This clash, among other problems, eventually led to a government investigation and an arbitration settlement in 1925. In the agreement, the Justice Department, irritated by AT&T's power grab, redefined patent agreements. AT&T received a monopoly on providing the wires, known as *long lines*, to interconnect stations nationwide. In exchange, AT&T sold its BCA network to RCA for $1 million and agreed not to reenter broadcasting for eight years (a banishment that actually extended into the 1990s).

Sarnoff and NBC: Building the "Blue" and "Red" Networks

After Lee De Forest, David Sarnoff was among the first to envision wireless telegraphy as a modern mass medium. From the time he served as Marconi's personal messenger (at age fifteen), Sarnoff rose rapidly at American Marconi. He became a wireless operator, helping relay information about the *Titanic* survivors in 1912. Promoted to a series of management positions, Sarnoff was closely involved in RCA's creation in 1919, when most radio executives saw wireless merely as point-to-point communication. But with Sarnoff as RCA's first commercial manager, radio's potential as a mass medium was quickly realized. In 1921, at age thirty, Sarnoff became RCA's general manager.

DAVID SARNOFF
As a young man, Sarnoff taught himself Morse code and learned as much as possible in Marconi's experimental shop in New York. He was then given a job as wireless operator for the station on Nantucket Island. He went on to create NBC and network radio. Sarnoff's calculated ambition in the radio industry can easily be compared to Bill Gates's drive to control the computer software and Internet industries.

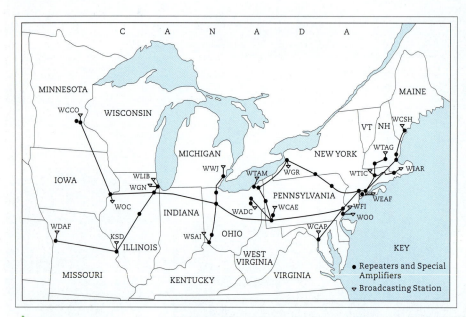

CANADA

MINNESOTA

WCCO

WISCONSIN

MICHIGAN

IOWA

WLIB
WGN

WOC

INDIANA

WDAF

KSD

ILLINOIS

WSAI

OHIO

MISSOURI

KENTUCKY

WWJ

WTAM

WGR

WADC

WCAE

WEST
VIRGINIA

VIRGINIA

MAINE

WCSH

VT NH

WTAG

NEW YORK

WTIC

WIAR

PENNSYLVANIA

WEAF

WFI

WOO

WCAP

KEY

● Repeaters and Special
  Amplifiers

▽ Broadcasting Station

NBC'S RED NETWORK was formed by RCA in 1926. WEAF, the first station in New York, was the Red network's flagship station.

After RCA bought AT&T's telephone group network (BCA), Sarnoff created a new subsidiary in September 1926 called the National Broadcasting Company (NBC). Its ownership was shared by RCA (50 percent), General Electric (30 percent), and Westinghouse (20 percent). This loose network of stations would be hooked together by AT&T long lines. Shortly thereafter, the original telephone group became known as the NBC-Red network, and the radio group (the network previously established by RCA, GE, and Westinghouse) became the NBC-Blue network.

Although NBC owned a number of stations by the late 1920s, many independent stations also began affiliating with the NBC networks to receive programming. NBC affiliates, though independently owned, signed contracts to be part of the network and paid NBC to carry its programs. In exchange, NBC reserved time slots, which it sold to national advertisers. NBC centralized costs and programming by bringing the best musical, dramatic, and comedic talent to one place, where programs could be produced and then distributed all over the country. By 1933, NBC-Red had twenty-eight affiliates, and NBC-Blue had twenty-four.

Network radio may have actually helped modernize America by de-emphasizing the local and the regional in favor of national programs broadcast to nearly everyone. For example, when Charles Lindbergh returned from the first solo transatlantic flight in 1927, an estimated twenty-five to thirty million people listened to his welcome-home party on the six million radio sets then in use. At the time, it was the largest shared audience experience in the history of any mass medium.

David Sarnoff's leadership at RCA was capped by two other negotiations that solidified his stature as the driving force behind radio's development as a modern medium: cutting a deal with General Motors for the manufacture of car radios (under the brand name Motorola) in 1929, and merging RCA with the Victor Talking Machine Company. Afterward, until the mid-1960s, the company was known as RCA Victor, adopting as its corporate symbol the famous terrier sitting alertly next to a Victrola radio-phonograph. The merger gave RCA control over Victor's records and recording equipment, making the radio company a major player in the sound recording industry. In 1930, David Sarnoff became president of RCA, and he ran it for the next forty years.

Government Scrutiny Ends RCA-NBC Monopoly

As early as 1923, the Federal Trade Commission had charged RCA with violations of antitrust laws, but the FTC allowed the monopoly to continue. By the late 1920s, the government, concerned about NBC's growing control over radio content, intensified its scrutiny. Then, in 1930, federal marshals charged RCA-NBC with a number of violations, including exercising too much control over manufacturing and programming. The government had originally sanctioned a closely supervised monopoly for wireless communication, but following the collapse of the stock market in 1929, the public became increasingly distrustful of big business.

RCA acted quickly. To eliminate its monopolizing partnerships, Sarnoff's company proposed buying out GE's and Westinghouse's remaining shares in RCA's manufacturing business.

Now RCA would compete directly against GE, Westinghouse, and other radio manufacturers, encouraging more competition in the radio manufacturing industry. In 1932, days before the antitrust case against RCA was to go to trial, the government accepted RCA's proposal for breaking up its monopoly. Ironically, in the mid-1980s, GE bought RCA, a shell of its former self and no longer competitive with foreign electronics firms.[8] GE was chiefly interested in RCA's brand-name status and its still-lucrative subsidiary, NBC.

CBS and Paley: Challenging NBC

Even with RCA's head start and its favored status, the two NBC networks faced competitors in the late 1920s. The competitors, however, all found it tough going. One group, United Independent Broadcasters (UIB), even lined up twelve prospective affiliates and offered them $500 a week for access to ten hours of station time in exchange for quality programs. UIB was cash-poor, however, and AT&T would not rent the new company its lines to link the affiliates.

Enter the Columbia Phonograph Company, which was looking for a way to preempt RCA's merger with the Victor Company, then the record company's major competitor. With backing from Columbia, UIB launched the new Columbia Phonograph Broadcasting System (CPBS), a wobbly sixteen-affiliate network, in 1927. But after losing $100,000 in the first month, the record company pulled out. Later, CPBS dropped the word *Phonograph* from its title, creating the Columbia Broadcasting System (CBS).

In 1928, William Paley, the twenty-seven-year-old son of Sam Paley, owner of a Philadelphia cigar company, bought a controlling interest in CBS to sponsor their cigar brand, La Palina. One of Paley's first moves was to hire the public relations pioneer Edward Bernays to polish the new network's image. (Bernays played a significant role in the development of the public relations industry; see Chapter 12.) Paley and Bernays modified a concept called **option time**, in which CBS paid affiliate stations $50 per hour for an option on a portion of their time. The network provided programs to the affiliates and sold ad space or sponsorships to various product companies. In theory, CBS could now control up to twenty-four hours a day of its affiliates' radio time. Some affiliates received thousands of dollars per week merely to serve as conduits for CBS programs and ads. Because NBC was still charging some of its affiliates as much as $96 a week to carry its network programs, the CBS offer was extremely appealing.

By 1933, Paley's efforts had netted CBS more than ninety affiliates, many of them defecting from NBC. Paley also concentrated on developing news programs and entertainment shows, particularly soap operas and comedy-variety series. In the process, CBS successfully raided NBC, not just for affiliates but for top talent as well. Throughout the 1930s and 1940s, Paley lured a number of radio stars from NBC, including Jack Benny, Frank Sinatra, George Burns, Gracie Allen, and Groucho Marx. During World War II, Edward R. Murrow's powerful firsthand news reports from bomb-riddled London established CBS as the premier radio news network, a reputation it carried forward to television. In 1949, near the end of big-time network radio, CBS finally surpassed NBC as the highest-rated network. Although William Paley had intended to run CBS only for six months to help get it off the ground, he ultimately ran it for more than fifty years.

Bringing Order to Chaos with the Radio Act of 1927

In the 1920s, as radio moved from narrowcasting to broadcasting, the battle for more frequency space and less channel interference intensified. Manufacturers, engineers, station

© Bettmann/Corbis

CBS HELPED ESTABLISH ITSELF as a premier radio network by attracting top talent from NBC, like comedic duo George Burns and Gracie Allen. They first brought their "Dumb Dora" and straight man act from stage to radio in 1929, and then continued on various radio programs in the 1930s and 1940s, with the most well known being *The Burns and Allen Show*. CBS also reaped the benefits when Burns and Allen moved their eponymous show to television in 1950.

operators, network executives, and the listening public demanded action. Many wanted more sweeping regulation than the simple licensing function granted under the Radio Act of 1912, which gave the Commerce Department little power to deny a license or to unclog the airwaves.

Beginning in 1924, Commerce Secretary Herbert Hoover ordered radio stations to share time by setting aside certain frequencies for entertainment and news, and others for farm and weather reports. To challenge Hoover, a station in Chicago jammed the airwaves, intentionally moving its signal onto an unauthorized frequency. In 1926, the courts decided that based on the existing Radio Act, Hoover had the power only to grant licenses, not to restrict stations from operating. Within the year, two hundred new stations clogged the airwaves, creating a chaotic period in which nearly all radios had poor reception. By early 1927, sales of radio sets had declined sharply.

To restore order to the airwaves, Congress passed the **Radio Act of 1927**, which stated an extremely important principle—licensees did not *own* their channels but could only license them as long as they operated to serve the "public interest, convenience, or necessity." To oversee licenses and negotiate channel problems, the 1927 act created the **Federal Radio Commission (FRC)**, whose members were appointed by the president. Although the FRC was intended as a temporary committee, it grew into a powerful regulatory agency. With passage of the **Communications Act of 1934**, the FRC became the **Federal Communications Commission (FCC)**. Its jurisdiction covered not only radio but also the telephone and the telegraph (and later television, cable, and the Internet). More significantly, by this time Congress and the president had sided with the already-powerful radio networks and acceded to a system of advertising-supported commercial broadcasting as best serving the "public interest, convenience, or necessity," overriding the concerns of educational, labor, and citizen broadcasting advocates.[9] (See Table 5.1.)

In 1941, an activist FCC went after the networks. Declaring that NBC and CBS could no longer force affiliates to carry programs they did not want, the government outlawed the practice of option time that Paley had used to build CBS into a major network. The FCC also demanded that RCA sell one of its two NBC networks. RCA and NBC claimed that the rulings would bankrupt them. The Supreme Court sided with the FCC, however, and RCA eventually sold NBC-Blue to a group of businessmen for $8 million in the mid-1940s. It became the American Broadcasting Company (ABC). These government crackdowns brought long-overdue reform to the radio industry, but they had not come soon enough to prevent considerable damage to noncommercial radio.

TABLE 5.1

MAJOR ACTS IN THE HISTORY OF U.S. RADIO

▼

Act	Provisions	Effects
Wireless Ship Act of 1910	Required U.S. seagoing ships carrying more than fifty passengers and traveling more than two hundred miles off the coast to be equipped with wireless equipment with a one-hundred-mile range.	Saved lives at sea, including more than seven hundred rescued by ships responding to the *Titanic*'s distress signals two years later.
Radio Act of 1912	Required radio operators to obtain a license, gave the Commerce Department the power to deny a license, and began a uniform system of assigning call letters to identify stations.	The federal government began to assert control over radio. Penalties were established for stations that interfere with other stations' signals.
Radio Act of 1927	Established the Federal Radio Commission (FRC) as a temporary agency to oversee licenses and negotiate channel assignments.	First expressed the now-fundamental principle that licensees did not *own* their channels but could only license them as long as they operated to serve the "public interest, convenience, or necessity."
Communications Act of 1934	Established the Federal Communications Commission (FCC) to replace the FRC. The FCC regulated radio, the telephone, the telegraph, and later television, cable, and the Internet.	Congress tacitly agreed to a system of advertising-supported commercial broadcasting despite concerns of the public.
Telecommunications Act of 1996	Eliminated most radio and television station ownership rules, some dating back more than fifty years.	Enormous national and regional station groups formed, dramatically changing the sound and localism of radio in the United States.

The Golden Age of Radio

Many programs on television today were initially formulated for radio. The first weather forecasts and farm reports on radio began in the 1920s. Regularly scheduled radio news analysis started in 1927, with H. V. Kaltenborn, a reporter for the *Brooklyn Eagle*, providing commentary on AT&T's WEAF. The first regular network news analysis began on CBS in 1930, featuring Lowell Thomas, who would remain on radio for forty-four years.

Early Radio Programming

Early on, only a handful of stations operated in most large radio markets, and popular stations were affiliated with CBS, NBC-Red, or NBC-Blue. Many large stations employed their own in-house orchestras and aired live music daily. Listeners had favorite evening programs, usually fifteen minutes long, to which they would tune in each night. Families gathered around the radio to hear such shows as *Amos 'n' Andy*, *The Shadow*, *The Lone Ranger*, *The Green Hornet*, and *Fibber McGee and Molly*, or one of President Franklin Roosevelt's fireside chats.

Among the most popular early programs on radio, the variety show was the forerunner to popular TV shows like the *Ed Sullivan Show*. The variety show, developed from stage acts and vaudeville, began with the *Eveready Hour* in 1923 on WEAF. Considered experimental, the program presented classical music, minstrel shows, comedy sketches, and dramatic readings. Stars from vaudeville, musical comedy, and New York theater and opera would occasionally make guest appearances.

By the 1930s, studio-audience quiz shows—*Professor Quiz* and the *Old Time Spelling Bee*—had emerged. Other quiz formats, used on *Information Please* and *Quiz Kids*, featured guest panelists. The quiz formats were later copied by television, particularly in the 1950s. *Truth or Consequences*, based on a nineteenth-century parlor game, first aired on radio in 1940 and featured guests performing goofy stunts. It ran for seventeen years on radio and another twenty-seven years on television, influencing TV stunt shows like CBS's *Beat the Clock* in the 1950s and NBC's *Fear Factor* in the early 2000s.

Dramatic programs, mostly radio plays that were broadcast live from theaters, developed as early as 1922. Historians mark the appearance of *Clara, Lu, and Em* on WGN in 1931 as the first soap opera. One year later, Colgate-Palmolive bought the program, put it on NBC, and began selling the soap products that gave this dramatic genre its distinctive nickname. Early "soaps" were fifteen minutes in length and ran five or six days a week. By 1940, sixty different soap operas occupied nearly eighty hours of network radio time each week.

Most radio programs had a single sponsor that created and produced each show. The networks distributed these programs live around the country, charging the sponsors advertising fees. Many shows—the *Palmolive Hour*, *General Motors Family Party*, the *Lucky Strike Orchestra*, and the *Eveready Hour* among them—were named after the sole sponsor's product.

Radio Programming as a Cultural Mirror

The situation comedy, a major staple of TV programming today, began on radio in the mid-1920s. By the early 1930s, the most popular comedy was *Amos 'n' Andy*, which started on Chicago radio in 1925 before moving to NBC-Blue in 1929. *Amos 'n' Andy* was based on the conventions of the nineteenth-century minstrel show and featured black characters stereotyped as shiftless and stupid. Created as a blackface stage act by two white comedians, Charles Correll and Freeman Gosden, the program was criticized as racist. But NBC and the program's producers claimed that *Amos 'n' Andy* was as popular among black audiences as among white listeners.[10]

Amos 'n' Andy also launched the idea of the serial show: a program that featured continuing story lines from one day to the next. The format was soon copied by soap operas

© Bettmann/Corbis

and other radio dramas. *Amos 'n' Andy* aired six nights a week from 7:00 to 7:15 P.M. During the show's first year on the network, radio-set sales rose nearly 25 percent nationally. To keep people coming to restaurants and movie theaters, owners broadcast *Amos 'n' Andy* in lobbies, rest rooms, and entryways. Early radio research estimated that the program aired in more than half of all radio homes in the nation during the 1930–31 season, making it the most popular radio series in history. In 1951, it made a brief transition to television (Correll and Gosden sold the rights to CBS for $1 million), becoming the first TV series to have an entirely black cast. But amid a strengthening Civil Rights movement and a formal protest by the NAACP (which argued that "every character is either a clown or a crook"), CBS canceled the program in 1953.[11]

The Authority of Radio

The most famous single radio broadcast of all time was an adaptation of H. G. Wells's *War of the Worlds* on the radio series *Mercury Theater of the Air*. Orson Welles produced, hosted, and acted in this popular series, which adapted science fiction, mystery, and historical adventure dramas for radio. On Halloween eve in 1938, the twenty-three-year-old Welles aired the 1898 Martian invasion novel in the style of a radio news program. For people who missed the opening disclaimer, the program sounded like a real news report, with eyewitness accounts of battles between Martian invaders and the U.S. Army.

Hulton Archive/Getty Images

© Bettmann/Corbis

The program created a panic that lasted several hours. In New Jersey, some people walked through the streets with wet towels around their heads for protection from deadly Martian heat rays. In New York, young men reported to their National Guard headquarters to prepare for battle. Across the nation, calls jammed police switchboards. Afterward, Orson Welles, once the radio voice of *The Shadow*, used the notoriety of this broadcast to launch a film career. Meanwhile, the FCC called for stricter warnings both before and during programs that imitated the style of radio news.

Radio Reinvents Itself

Older media forms do not generally disappear when confronted by newer forms. Instead, they adapt. Although radio threatened sound recording in the 1920s, the recording industry adjusted to the economic and social challenges posed by radio's arrival. Remarkably, the arrival of television in the 1950s marked the only time in media history when a new medium stole virtually every national programming and advertising strategy from an older medium. Television snatched radio's advertisers, program genres, major celebrities, and large evening audiences. The TV set even physically displaced the radio as the living room centerpiece of choice across America. Nevertheless, radio adapted and continued to reach an audience.

The story of radio's evolution and survival is especially important today, as newspapers and magazines appear online and as publishers produce e-books for new generations of readers. In contemporary culture, we have grown accustomed to such media convergence, but to best understand this blurring of the boundaries between media forms, it is useful to look at the 1950s and the ways in which radio responded to the advent of television.

New from Motorola
ALL-TRANSISTOR
Shirt-pocket radio
with powerful built-in speaker

Slips into your pocket...plays with the sound of a set twice its size.
New miniaturized transistor radio lets you enjoy favorite programs wherever you go. Powerful chassis pulls in stations loud and clean . . . plays them clear and mellow through a newly designed built-in speaker. A *single* low-cost battery gives many hours of listening pleasure. Motorola extras include magnifying lens for easy-to-read dial . . . durable case in black, blue, red, or green. *90-day warranty on all parts and labor at no additional cost.*

Perfect gift for you or someone extra special

ONLY
$29 95*
MODEL
X11

Built-In Easel Stand in back for stable "stand-up" position.

Power-Packed Chassis with 6 transistors provides plenty of volume.

Built-In Antenna pulls in stations like a magnet for finest reception.

Perfect Companion for sports events. Earphone jack for private listening.

More Ⓜ *to enjoy* **MOTOROLA**

Image courtesy of the Advertising Archives

▲

ADVERTISEMENTS for pocket transistor radios, which became popular in the 1950s, emphasized their portability.

Transistors Make Radio Portable

A key development in radio's adaptation to television occurred with the invention of the transistor by Bell Laboratories in 1947. **Transistors** were small electrical devices that, like vacuum tubes, could receive and amplify radio signals. However, they used less power and produced less heat than vacuum tubes, and they were more durable and less expensive. Best of all, they were tiny. Transistors, which also revolutionized hearing aids, constituted the first step in replacing bulky and delicate tubes, leading eventually to today's integrated circuits.

Texas Instruments marketed the first transistor radio in 1953 for about $40. Using even smaller transistors, Sony introduced the pocket radio in 1957. But it wasn't until the 1960s that transistor radios became cheaper than conventional tube and battery radios. For a while, the term *transistor* became a synonym for a small, portable radio.

The development of transistors let radio go where television could not—to the beach, to the office, into bedrooms and bathrooms, and into nearly all new cars. (Before the transistor, car radios were a luxury item.) By the 1960s, most radio listening took place outside the home.

The FM Revolution and Edwin Armstrong

By the time the broadcast industry launched commercial television in the 1950s, many people, including David Sarnoff of RCA, were predicting radio's demise. To fund television's development and to protect his radio holdings, Sarnoff had even delayed a dramatic breakthrough in broadcast sound, what he himself called a "revolution"—FM radio.

Edwin Armstrong, who first discovered and developed FM radio in the 1920s and early 1930s, is often considered the most prolific and influential inventor in radio history. He used De Forest's vacuum tube to invent an amplifying system that enabled radio receivers to pick up distant signals, rendering the enormous alternators used for generating power in early radio transmitters obsolete. In 1922, he sold a "super" version of his circuit to RCA for $200,000 and sixty thousand shares of RCA stock, which made him a millionaire as well as RCA's largest private stockholder.

Armstrong also worked on the major problem of radio reception—electrical interference. Between 1930 and 1933, the inventor filed five patents on **FM**, or frequency modulation. Offering static-free radio reception, FM supplied greater fidelity and clarity than AM, making FM ideal for music. **AM**, or amplitude modulation (*modulation* refers to the variation in waveforms), stressed the volume, or height, of radio waves; FM accentuated the pitch, or distance, between radio waves (see Figure 5.2).

Although David Sarnoff, RCA's president, thought that television would replace radio, he helped Armstrong set up the first experimental FM station atop the Empire State Building in New York City. Eventually, though, Sarnoff thwarted FM's development (which he was able to do because RCA had an option on Armstrong's new patents). Instead, in 1935 Sarnoff threw RCA's considerable weight behind the development of television. With the FCC allocating and reassigning scarce frequency spaces, RCA wanted to ensure that channels went to television before they went to FM. But most of all, Sarnoff wanted to protect RCA's existing AM empire. Given the high costs of converting to FM and the revenue needed for TV experiments, Sarnoff decided to close down Armstrong's station.

Armstrong forged ahead without RCA. He founded a new FM station and advised other engineers, who started more than twenty experimental stations between 1935 and the early 1940s. In 1941, the FCC approved limited space allocations for commercial FM licenses. During the next few years, FM grew in fits and starts. Between 1946 and early 1949, the number of commercial FM stations expanded from 48 to 700. But then the FCC moved FM's frequency space to a new band on the electromagnetic spectrum, rendering some 400,000 prewar FM receiver sets useless. FM's future became uncertain, and by 1954, the number of FM stations had fallen to 560.

On January 31, 1954, Edwin Armstrong—weary from years of legal skirmishes over patents with RCA, Lee De Forest, and others—wrote a note apologizing to his wife, removed the air conditioner from his thirteenth-story New York apartment window, and jumped to his death. A month later, David Sarnoff announced record profits of $850 million for RCA, with TV sales accounting for 54 percent of the company's earnings. In the early 1960s, the FCC opened up more spectrum space for the superior sound of FM, infusing new life into radio.

Although AM stations had greater reach, they could not match the crisp fidelity of FM, which made FM preferable for music. In the early 1970s, about 70 percent of listeners tuned almost exclusively to AM radio. By the 1980s, however, FM had surpassed AM in profitability. By the 2010s, more than 75 percent of all listeners preferred FM, and about 6,660 commercial and about 4,000 educational FM stations were in operation. The expansion of FM represented one of the chief ways radio survived television and Sarnoff's gloomy predictions.

The Rise of Format and Top 40 Radio

Live and recorded music had long been radio's single biggest staple, accounting for 48 percent of all programming in 1938. Although live music on radio was generally considered superior to recorded music, early disc jockeys made a significant contribution to the latter, demonstrating that music alone could drive radio. In fact, when television snatched radio's program ideas and national sponsors, radio's dependence on recorded music became a necessity and helped the medium survive the 1950s.

As early as 1949, station owner Todd Storz in Omaha, Nebraska, experimented with formula-driven radio, or **format radio**. Under this system, management rather than deejays controlled programming each hour. When Storz and his program manager noticed that bar patrons and waitresses repeatedly played certain favorite songs from the records available in a jukebox, they began researching record sales to identify the most popular tunes. From observing jukebox culture, Storz hit on the idea of **rotation**: playing the top songs many times during the day. By the mid-1950s,

FIGURE 5.2
AM AND FM WAVES
Data from: Adapted from David Cheshire, The Video Manual, *1982.*

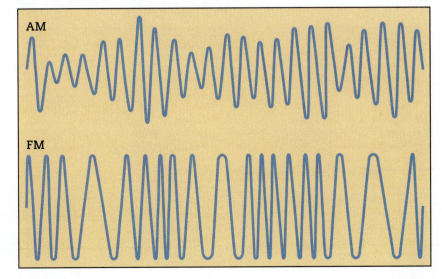

the management-control idea combined with the rock-and-roll explosion, and the **Top 40 format** was born. The term *Top 40* came to refer to the forty most popular hits in a given week as measured by record sales.

As format radio grew, program directors combined rapid deejay chatter with the best-selling songs of the day and occasional oldies—popular songs from a few months earlier. By the early 1960s, to avoid "dead air," managers asked deejays to talk over the beginning and the end of a song so that listeners would feel less compelled to switch stations. Ads, news, weather forecasts, and station identifications were all designed to fit a consistent station environment. Listeners, tuning in at any moment, would recognize the station by its distinctive sound.

In format radio, management carefully coordinates, or programs, each hour, dictating what the deejay will do at various intervals throughout each hour of the day (see Figure 5.3). Management creates a program log—once called a *hot clock* in radio jargon—that deejays must follow. By the mid-1960s, one study had determined that in a typical hour on Top 40 radio, listeners could expect to hear about twenty ads; numerous weather, time, and contest announcements; multiple recitations of the station's call letters; about three minutes of news; and approximately twelve songs.

Radio managers further sectioned off programming into *day parts*, which typically consisted of time blocks covering 6 to 10 A.M., 10 A.M. to 3 P.M., 3 to 7 P.M., and 7 P.M. to midnight. Each day part, or block, was programmed through ratings research according to who was listening. For instance, a Top 40 station would feature its top deejays in the morning and afternoon periods when audiences, many riding in cars, were largest. From 10 A.M. to 3 P.M., research determined that women at home and secretaries at work usually controlled the dial, so program managers, capitalizing on the gender stereotypes of the day, played more romantic ballads and less hard rock. Teenagers tended to be heavy evening listeners, so program managers often discarded news breaks at this time, since research showed that teens turned the dial when news came on.

Critics of format radio argued that only the top songs received play and that lesser-known songs deserving airtime received meager attention. Although a few popular star deejays continued to play a role in programming, many others quit when managers introduced formats. Program directors approached programming as a science, but deejays considered it an art form. Program directors argued that deejays had different tastes from those of the average listener and therefore could not be fully trusted to know popular audience tastes. The program directors' position, which generated more revenue, triumphed.

FIGURE 5.3

RADIO PROGRAM LOG FOR AN ADULT CONTEMPORARY (AC) STATION

Data from: KCVM, Cedar Falls, IA, 2014.

Time	Title	Artist	Length
9:00:00 AM ===== New Hour =====			
9:02:00 AM	Pompeii	Bastille	3:31
9:03:00 AM	Shotgun	Sweeper	00:10
9:04:00 AM	Rumor Has It (12)	Adele	0:03:39
9:05:00 AM	80s Liner	Sweeper	
9:06:00 AM	Lover Girl	Teena Marie	0:05:36
9:07:00 AM	Shotgun	Sweeper	00:10
9:08:00 AM	Maps	Maroon 5	3:08
9:08:00 AM ===== :15 Spot Break =====			
9:20:00 AM	Jingle	Sweeper	00:10
9:21:00 AM	Me and My Broken Heart	Rixton	3:10
9:22:00 AM	Sweeper B	Sweeper	00:10
9:23:00 AM	Found Out About You (92)	Gin Blossoms	0:03:45
9:24:00 AM	Shotgun	Sweeper	00:10
9:25:00 AM	Somebody That I Used To Know	Gotye	0:04:02

Resisting the Top 40

The expansion of FM in the mid-1960s created room for experimenting, particularly with classical music, jazz, blues, and non–Top 40 rock songs. **Progressive rock** emerged as an alternative to conventional formats. Many noncommercial stations broadcast from college campuses, where student deejays and managers rejected the commercialism associated with Top 40 tunes and began playing lesser-known alternative music and longer album cuts (such as Bob Dylan's "Desolation Row" and the Doors' "The End"). Until that time, most rock on radio had been consigned almost exclusively to Top 40 AM formats, with song length averaging about three minutes.

Experimental FM stations, both commercial and noncommercial, offered a cultural space for hard-edged political folk music and for rock music that commented on the Civil Rights movement and protested America's involvement in the Vietnam War. By the 1970s, however, progressive rock had been copied, tamed, and absorbed by mainstream radio under the format labeled **album-oriented rock (AOR)**. By 1972, AOR-driven album sales accounted for more than 85 percent of the retail record business. By the 1980s, as first-generation rock and rollers aged and became more affluent, AOR stations became less political and played mostly white, post-Beatles music featuring such groups as Pink Floyd, Genesis, AC/DC, and Queen. Today, AOR has been subsumed under the more general classic rock format.

RYAN SEACREST may be best known for his job hosting TV's *American Idol*, but he began his career in radio when he hosted a local radio show while attending the University of Georgia. In the style of his own idols—Dick Clark and Casey Kasem—Seacrest now hosts two nationally syndicated radio shows, *On Air with Ryan Seacrest* and *American Top 40*, in addition to his television projects.

Mark Davis/Getty Images

The Sounds of Commercial Radio

Contemporary radio sounds very different from its predecessor. In contrast to the few stations per market in the 1930s, most large markets today include more than forty stations that vie for listener loyalty. With the exception of national network–sponsored news segments and nationally syndicated programs, most programming is locally produced and heavily dependent on the music industry for content. Although a few radio personalities, such as Glenn Beck, Ryan Seacrest, Rush Limbaugh, Tom Joyner, Tavis Smiley, and Jim Rome, are nationally prominent, local deejays and their music are the stars at most radio stations.

However, listeners today are unlike radio's first audiences in several ways. First, listeners in the 1930s tuned in to their favorite shows at set times. Listeners today do not say, "Gee, my favorite song is coming on at 8 P.M., so I'd better be home to listen." Instead, radio has become a secondary, or background, medium that follows the rhythms of daily life. Radio programmers today worry about channel cruising—listeners' tendency to search the dial until they find a song they like.

Second, in the 1930s, peak listening time occurred during the evening hours—dubbed *prime time* in the TV era—when people were home from work and school. Now, the heaviest radio listening occurs during **drive time**, between 6 and 9 A.M. and between 4 and 7 P.M., when people are commuting to and from work or school.

Third, stations today are more specialized. Listeners are loyal to favorite stations, music formats, and even radio personalities, rather than to specific shows. People generally listen to only four or five stations that target them. More than fifteen thousand radio stations now operate in the United States, customizing their sounds to reach niche audiences through format specialization and alternative programming.

Format Specialization

Stations today use a variety of formats based on managed program logs and day parts. All told, more than forty different radio formats, plus variations, serve diverse groups of listeners

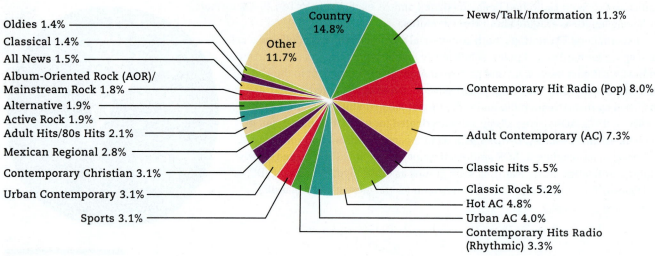

Oldies 1.4%
Classical 1.4%
All News 1.5%
Album-Oriented Rock (AOR)/ Mainstream Rock 1.8%
Alternative 1.9%
Active Rock 1.9%
Adult Hits/80s Hits 2.1%
Mexican Regional 2.8%
Contemporary Christian 3.1%
Urban Contemporary 3.1%
Sports 3.1%

Other 11.7%
Country 14.8%

News/Talk/Information 11.3%
Contemporary Hit Radio (Pop) 8.0%
Adult Contemporary (AC) 7.3%
Classic Hits 5.5%
Classic Rock 5.2%
Hot AC 4.8%
Urban AC 4.0%
Contemporary Hits Radio (Rhythmic) 3.3%

FIGURE 5.4

THE MOST POPULAR RADIO FORMATS IN THE UNITED STATES AMONG PERSONS AGE TWELVE AND OLDER

Data from: Nielsen report: "State of the Media: Audio Today 2014, How America Listens," February 6, 2014, www.nielsen.com/us/en/reports /2014/state-of-the-media-audio -today-2014.html.

Note: Based on listener shares for primary AM and FM stations, plus HD stations and Internet streams of radio stations.

(see Figure 5.4). To please advertisers, who want to know exactly who is listening, formats usually target audiences according to their age, income, gender, or race/ethnicity. Radio's specialization enables advertisers to reach smaller target audiences at costs that are much lower than those for television.

Targeting listeners has become extremely competitive, however, because forty or fifty stations may be available in a large radio market. About 10 percent of all stations across the country switch formats each year in an effort to find a formula that generates more advertising money. Some stations, particularly those in large cities, even rent blocks of time to various local ethnic or civic groups; this enables the groups to dictate their own formats and sell ads.

News, Talk, and Information Radio

The nation's fastest-growing format throughout much of the 1990s was the **news/talk/ information** format (see "Case Study: Host: The Origins of Talk Radio" on page 171). In 1987, only 170 radio stations operated formats dominated by either news programs or talk shows, which tend to appeal to adults over age thirty-five (except for sports talk programs, which draw mostly male sports fans of all ages). By 2014, more than 2,183 stations carried the format—more stations than any other format. It is the most dominant format on AM radio and the second most popular format (by number of listeners) in the nation (see Figure 5.4 and Table 5.2). A news/talk/information format, though more expensive to produce than a music format, appeals to advertisers looking to target working- and middle-class adult consumers. Nevertheless, most radio stations continue to be driven by a variety of less expensive music formats.

TABLE 5.2

TALK RADIO WEEKLY AUDIENCE (IN MILLIONS)

Data from: Talkers magazine, "The Top Talk Radio Audiences," June 2014.

Note: * = Information unavailable; N/A = Talk host not nationally broadcast.

Talk Show Host	2003	2008	2014
Rush Limbaugh (Conservative)	14.5	14.25	13
Sean Hannity (Conservative)	11.75	13.25	12.25
Dave Ramsey (Financial Advice)	*	4.5	7.5
Glenn Beck (Conservative)	*	6.75	7
Mark Levin (Conservative)	N/A	5.5	7
Michael Savage (Conservative)	7	8.25	5.5
Jim Bohannon (Moderate)	4	3.5	3

Host: The Origins of Talk Radio

by David Foster Wallace

The origins of contemporary political talk radio can be traced to three phenomena of the 1980s. The first of these involved AM music stations getting absolutely murdered by FM, which could broadcast music in stereo and allowed for much better fidelity on high and low notes. The human voice, on the other hand, is midrange and doesn't require high fidelity. The eighties' proliferation of talk formats on the AM band also provided new careers for some music deejays—e.g., Don Imus, Morton Downey Jr.—whose chatty personas didn't fit well with FM's all-about-the-music ethos.

The second big factor was the repeal, late in Ronald Reagan's second term, of what was known as the Fairness Doctrine. This was a 1949 FCC rule designed to minimize any possible restrictions on free speech caused by limited access to broadcasting outlets. The idea was that, as one of the conditions for receiving an FCC broadcast license, a station had to "devote reasonable attention to the coverage of controversial issues of public importance," and consequently had to provide "reasonable, although not necessarily equal," opportunities for opposing sides to express their views. Because of the Fairness Doctrine, talk stations had to hire and program symmetrically: If you had a three-hour program whose host's politics were on one side of the ideological spectrum, you had to have another long-form program whose host more or less spoke for the other side. Weirdly enough, up through the mid-eighties it was usually the U.S. right that benefited most from the Doctrine. Pioneer talk syndicator Ed McLaughlin, who managed San Francisco's KGO in the 1960s, recalls that "I had more liberals on the air than I had conservatives or even moderates for that matter, and I had a hell of a time finding the other voice."

The Fairness Doctrine's repeal was part of the sweeping deregulations of the Reagan era, which aimed to liberate all sorts of industries from government interference and allow them to compete freely in the marketplace. The old, Rooseveltian logic of the Doctrine had been that since the airwaves belonged to everyone, a license to profit from those airwaves conferred on the broadcast industry some special obligation to serve the public interest. Commercial radio broadcasting was not, in other words, originally conceived as just another for-profit industry; it was supposed to meet a higher standard of social responsibility. After 1987, though, just another industry is pretty much what radio became, and its only real responsibility now is to attract and retain listeners in order to generate revenue. In other words, the sort of distinction explicitly drawn by FCC Chairman Newton Minow in the 1960s—namely, that between "the public interest" and "merely what interests the public"—no longer exists.

More or less on the heels of the Fairness Doctrine's repeal came the West Coast and then national syndication of *The Rush Limbaugh Show* through Mr. McLaughlin's EFM Media. Limbaugh is the third great progenitor of today's political talk radio partly because he's a host of extraordinary, once-in-a-generation talent and charisma—bright, loquacious, witty, complexly authoritative—whose show's blend of news, entertainment, and partisan analysis became the model for legions of imitators. But he was also the first great promulgator of the Mainstream Media's Liberal Bias (MMLB) idea. This turned out to be a brilliantly effective rhetorical move, since the MMLB concept functioned simultaneously as a standard around which Rush's audience could rally, as an articulation of the need for right-wing (i.e., unbiased) media, and as a mechanism by which any criticism or refutation of conservative ideas could be dismissed (either as biased or as the product of indoctrination by biased media). Boiled way down, the MMLB thesis is able both to exploit and to perpetuate many conservatives' dissatisfaction with extant media sources—and it's this dissatisfaction that cements political talk radio's large and loyal audience. ◢

Source: Excerpted from David Foster Wallace, "Host: The Origins of Talk Radio," Atlantic, April 2005, pp. 66–68.

GLENN BECK is the conservative host of *The Glenn Beck Program*, a nationally syndicated talk-radio show that also promulgates the MMLB idea.

WireImage/Getty Images

AP Photo/Julie Jacobson

John Parra/Getty Images

WENDY WILLIAMS refers to herself as the "Queen of All Media," but before her daytime TV talk show, she got her start with a nearly two-decade career in radio. She began as a substitute deejay on an urban contemporary station in New York before gaining notoriety with her celebrity interviews and gossip.

EL ZOL 106.7 is a top Spanish-language radio station in the Miami market, visited here by Puerto Rican–American singer Ivy Queen. El Zol is home to Betzy "La Gatita" Vázquez, named the "Best Spanish-Language Radio Personality" by *Miami New Times*.

Music Formats

The **adult contemporary (AC)** format, also known as middle-of-the-road, or MOR, is among radio's oldest and most popular formats, reaching about 7.3 percent of all listeners, most of them over age forty, with an eclectic mix of news, talk, oldies, and soft rock music—what *Broadcasting* magazine describes as "not too soft, not too loud, not too fast, not too slow, not too hard, not too lush, not too old, not too new." Variations on the AC format include urban AC, hot AC, rhythmic AC, modern AC, and smooth AC. Now encompassing everything from rap to pop punk songs, Top 40 radio—also called **contemporary hit radio (CHR)**—still appeals to many teens and young adults. A renewed focus on producing pop singles in the sound recording industry has recently boosted listenership of this format.

Country is the most popular format in the nation (except during morning drive time, when news/talk/information is number one). Many stations are in tiny markets where country is traditionally the default format for communities with only one radio station. Country music has old roots in radio, starting in 1925 with the influential *Grand Ole Opry* program on WSM in Nashville. Although Top 40 drove country music out of many radio markets in the 1950s, the growth of FM in the 1960s brought it back, as station managers looked for market niches not served by rock music.

Many formats appeal to particular ethnic or racial groups. In 1947, WDIA in Memphis was the first station to program exclusively for black listeners. Now called **urban contemporary**, this format targets a wide variety of African American listeners, primarily in large cities. Urban contemporary, which typically plays popular dance, rap, R&B, and hip-hop music (featuring performers like Wiz Khalifa and Tyler the Creator), also subdivides by age, featuring an urban AC category with performers like Maxwell, Alicia Keys, and Robin Thicke.

Spanish-language radio, one of radio's fastest-growing formats, is concentrated mostly in large Hispanic markets such as Miami, New York, Chicago, Las Vegas, California, Arizona, New Mexico, and Texas (where KCOR, the first all-Spanish-language station, originated in San Antonio in 1947). Besides talk shows and news segments in Spanish, this format features a variety of Spanish, Caribbean, and Latin American musical styles, including calypso, flamenco, mariachi, merengue, reggae, samba, salsa, and Tejano.

In addition, today there are other formats that are spin-offs from album-oriented rock. Classic rock serves up rock favorites from the mid-1960s through the 1980s to the baby-boom generation and other listeners who have outgrown Top 40. The oldies format originally served adults who grew up on 1950s and early-1960s rock and roll. As that audience has aged, oldies formats now target younger audiences with the classic-hits format, featuring songs from the 1970s, 1980s, and 1990s. The alternative format recaptures some of the experimental approach of the FM stations of the 1960s, although with much more controlled playlists, and has helped introduce artists such as the Dead Weather and Cage the Elephant.

Research indicates that most people identify closely with the music they listened to as adolescents and young adults. This tendency partially explains why classic hits and classic rock stations combined have surpassed CHR stations today. It also helps explain the recent nostalgia for music from the 1980s and 1990s.

Nonprofit Radio and NPR

Although commercial radio (particularly those stations owned by huge radio conglomerates) dominates the radio spectrum, nonprofit radio maintains a voice. But the road to viability for nonprofit radio in the United States has not been easy. In the 1930s, the Wagner-Hatfield Amendment to the 1934 Communications Act intended to set aside 25 percent of radio for a wide variety of nonprofit stations. When the amendment was defeated in 1935, the future of educational and noncommercial radio looked bleak. Many nonprofits had sold out to for-profit owners during the Great Depression of the 1930s. The stations that remained were often banished from the air during the evening hours or assigned weak signals by federal regulators who favored commercial owners and their lobbying agents. Still, nonprofit public radio survived. Today, more than three thousand nonprofit stations operate, most of them on the FM band.

AP Photo/David Goldman

PUBLIC RADIO STATIONS in rural areas, like WMMT—which services eastern Kentucky, southwestern Virginia, and southern West Virginia—connect people in far-flung and remote areas by broadcasting local programming that speaks to their listeners' needs and tastes. Rural stations like this one rely heavily on federal funding and are thus more likely to go under if budgets are cut.

The Early Years of Nonprofit Radio

Two government rulings, both in 1948, aided nonprofit radio. First, the government began authorizing noncommercial licenses to stations not affiliated with labor, religious, education, or civic groups. The first license went to Lewis Kimball Hill, a radio reporter and pacifist during World War II who started the **Pacifica Foundation** to run experimental public stations. Pacifica stations, like Hill, have often challenged the status quo in radio as well as in government. Most notably, in the 1950s they aired the poetry, prose, and music of performers considered radical, left-wing, or communist who were blacklisted by television and seldom acknowledged by AM stations. Over the years, Pacifica has been fined and reprimanded by the FCC and Congress for airing programs that critics considered inappropriate for public airwaves. Today, Pacifica has more than one hundred affiliate stations.

Second, the FCC approved 10-watt FM stations. Prior to this time, radio stations had to have at least 250 watts to get licensed. A 10-watt station with a broadcast range of only about seven miles took very little capital to operate, allowing more people to participate, and such stations became training sites for students interested in broadcasting. Although the FCC stopped licensing new 10-watt stations in 1978, about one hundred longtime 10-watters are still in operation.

Creation of the First Noncommercial Networks

During the 1960s, nonprofit broadcasting found a Congress sympathetic to an old idea: using radio and television as educational tools. As a result, **National Public Radio (NPR)** and the **Public Broadcasting Service (PBS)** were created as the first noncommercial networks. Under the provisions of the **Public Broadcasting Act of 1967** and the **Corporation for Public Broadcasting (CPB)**, NPR and PBS were mandated to provide alternatives to commercial broadcasting. Now, NPR's popular news and interview programs, such as *Morning Edition* and *All Things Considered*, are thriving, and they contribute to the network's audience of thirty-two million listeners per week.

Media Literacy and the Critical Process

1 DESCRIPTION. Listen to a typical morning or late-afternoon hour of a popular local commercial talk-news radio station and a typical hour of your local NPR station from the same time period over a two- to three-day period. Keep a log of what topics are covered and what news stories are reported. For the commercial station, log what commercials are carried and how much time in an hour is devoted to ads. For the noncommercial station, note how much time is devoted to recognizing the station's sources of funding support and who the supporters are.

2 ANALYSIS. Look for patterns. What kinds of stories are covered? What kinds of topics are discussed? Create a chart to categorize the stories. To cover events and issues, do the stations use actual reporters at the scene? How much time is given to reporting compared to time devoted to opinion? How many sources are cited in each story? What kinds of interview sources are used? Are they expert sources or regular person-on-the-street interviews? How many sources are men, and how many are women?

Comparing Commercial and Noncommercial Radio

After the arrival and growth of commercial TV, the Corporation for Public Broadcasting (CPB) was created in 1967 as the funding agent for public broadcasting—an alternative to commercial TV and radio featuring educational and cultural programming that could not be easily sustained by commercial broadcasters in search of large general audiences. As a result, National Public Radio (NPR) developed to provide national programming to public stations to supplement local programming efforts. Today, NPR affiliates get just 2 percent of their funding from the federal government. Most money for public radio comes instead from corporate sponsorships, individual grants, and private donations.

3 INTERPRETATION. What do these patterns mean? Is there a balance between reporting and opinion? Do you detect any bias, and if so, how did you determine this? Are the stations serving as watchdogs to ensure that democracy's best interests are being served? What effect, if any, do you think the advertisers/supporters have on the programming? What arguments might you make about commercial and noncommercial radio based on your findings?

4 EVALUATION. Which station seems to be doing a better job serving its local audience? Why? Do you buy the 1930s argument that noncommercial stations serve narrow, special interests while commercial stations serve capitalism and the public interest? Why or why not? From which station did you learn the most, and which station did you find most entertaining? Explain. What did you like and dislike about each station?

5 ENGAGEMENT. Join your college radio station. Talk to the station manager about the goals for a typical hour of programming and what audience the station is trying to reach. Finally, pitch program or topic ideas that would improve your college station's programming.

Over the years, however, public radio has faced waning government support and the threat of losing its federal funding. In 1994, a conservative majority in Congress cut financial support and threatened to scrap the CPB, the funding authority for public broadcasting. In 2011, the House voted to end financing for the CPB, but the Senate voted against the measure. Consequently, stations have become more reliant on private donations and corporate sponsorship, which could cause some public broadcasters to steer clear of controversial subjects, especially those that critically examine corporations. (See "Media Literacy and the Critical Process: Comparing Commercial and Noncommercial Radio" above.)

Like commercial stations, nonprofit radio has adopted the format style. However, the dominant style in public radio is a loose variety format whereby a station may actually switch from jazz, classical music, and alternative rock to news and talk during different parts of the day. Noncommercial radio remains the place for both tradition and experimentation, as well as for programs that do not draw enough listeners for commercial success. (See "Global Village: Radio Mogadishu" on page 176 for more on public radio internationally.)

New Radio Technologies Offer More Stations

Over the past decade or so, two alternative radio technologies have helped expand radio beyond its traditional AM and FM bands and bring more diverse sounds to listeners: satellite and HD (digital) radio.

Satellite Radio

A series of satellites launched to cover the continental United States created a subscription-based national **satellite radio** service. Two companies, XM and Sirius, completed their national introduction by 2002 and merged into a single provider in 2008. The merger was precipitated by their struggles to make a profit after building competing satellite systems and battling for listeners. SiriusXM offers about 165 digital music, news, and talk channels to the continental United States, with monthly prices starting at $14.49 and satellite radio receivers costing from $50 to $110. SiriusXM access is also available to mobile devices via an app.

Programming includes a range of music channels, from rock and reggae to Spanish Top 40 and opera, as well as channels dedicated to NASCAR, NPR, cooking, and comedy. Another feature of satellite radio's programming is popular personalities who host their own shows or have their own channels, including Howard Stern, Martha Stewart, Oprah Winfrey, and Bruce Springsteen. U.S. automakers (investors in the satellite radio companies) now equip most new cars with a satellite band, in addition to AM and FM, in order to promote further adoption of satellite radio. SiriusXM had more than twenty-five million subscribers by 2014.

HD Radio

Available to the public since 2004, **HD radio** is a digital technology that enables AM and FM radio broadcasters to multicast up to three additional compressed digital signals within their traditional analog frequency. For example, KNOW, a public radio station at 91.1 FM in Minneapolis–St. Paul, runs its National Public Radio news/talk/information format on 91.1 HD1, runs Radio Heartland (acoustic and Americana music) on 91.1 HD2, and runs the BBC News service on 91.1 HD3. About 2,200 radio stations now broadcast in HD. To tune in, listeners need a radio with the HD band, which brings in CD-quality digital signals. Digital HD radio also provides program data, such as artist name and song title, and enables listeners to tag songs for playlists that can later be downloaded to an iPod and purchased on iTunes. The rollout of HD has been slow, but by 2014, a new car was being sold with HD radio technology every 4.5 seconds.

Radio and Convergence

Like every other mass medium, radio is moving into the future by converging with the Internet. Interestingly, this convergence is taking radio back to its roots in some aspects. Internet radio allows for much more variety in radio, which is reminiscent of radio's earliest years, when nearly any individual or group with some technical skill could start a radio station. Moreover, *podcasts* bring back such content as storytelling, instructional programs, and local topics of interest, which have largely been missing in corporate radio. And portable listening devices like the iPod and radio apps for the iPad and smartphones hark back to the compact portability that first came with the popularization of transistor radios in the 1950s.

Internet Radio

Internet radio emerged in the 1990s with the popularity of the Web. Internet radio stations come in two types. The first involves an existing AM, FM, satellite, or HD station "streaming" a simulcast version of its on-air signal over the Web. More than 10,500 radio stations

LaunchPad ▶

macmillanhighered.com
/mediaculture10e

Going Visual: Video, Radio, and the Web
This video looks at how radio stations adapted to the Internet by providing multimedia on their Web sites to attract online listeners.
Discussion: If video is now important to radio, what might that mean for journalism and broadcasting students who are considering a job in radio?

Radio Mogadishu

For more than two decades, Somalia has been without a properly functioning government. The nation of about nine million people on the eastern coast of Africa has been embroiled in a civil war since 1991 in which competing clans and militias have fought in seesaw battles for control of the country. During this time, more than a half-million Somalis have died from famine and war. Although Somalia was once a great economic and cultural center, its biggest contribution to global culture in recent years has been modern-day seagoing pirates.

A more moderate transitional government has tried to take leadership of the war-weary nation, but radical Islamist militias, including one called Al-Shabaab with ties to Al-Qaeda, have been its biggest adversaries. Al-Shabaab has terrorized African Union peacekeepers and humanitarian aid workers with assassinations and suicide bombings, and it has used amputations, stonings, and beatings to enforce its harsh rules against civilians.

Journalists in Somalia (the National Union of Somali Journalists estimates there are seven hundred of them) have not been immune from the terror. More than fifty-two journalists have been killed there since 1992, earning Somalia the world's No. 2 ranking (behind only Iraq) as a nation "where journalist murders go unpunished."[1] The media workers under attack include radio workers, who were threatened by militias in April 2010 to stop playing foreign programs from the BBC and Voice of America, and then to stop playing all music (which was deemed un-Islamic), or face "serious consequences."[2] Although most radio stations in Somalia's capital, Mogadishu, have succumbed to the threats, they have found creative (and ironic) ways to jab back at the militants, like playing sound effects instead of music to introduce programs. A newscast, for example, might be introduced by recorded gunshots, animal noises, or car sounds.

One station, Radio Mogadishu, is still bravely broadcasting music and independent newscasts. The station is supported by the transitional government as a critical tool in bringing democracy back to the country, but radio work in the name of democracy has never been more dangerous than it is in Somalia today. "Radio Mogadishu's 100 or so employees are marked men and women, because the insurgents associate them with the government," the New York Times reported.[3] Many of the journalists, sound engineers, and deejays eat and sleep at the station for fear of being killed; some have not left the radio station compound to visit their families for months, even though they live in the same city. Their fears are well founded: Another veteran reporter was gunned down by assassins as he returned to his house in April 2013.[4]

Radio Mogadishu (in English, Somali, and Arabic on the Web at http://radiomuqdisho.net/) speaks to the enduring power of independent radio around the globe and its particular connection to Somali citizens, for whom it is a cultural lifeline. The BBC reports that Somali citizens love pop music (like that of popular Somali artists Abdi Shire Jama [Jooqle] and K'naan, who record abroad), and they resent being told that they cannot listen to it on the radio. Somali bus drivers reportedly sneak music radio for their passengers, turning the music on and off depending on whether they are in a safe, government-controlled district or a dangerous, militia-controlled area. The news portion of radio broadcasts is also important, especially in a country where only about 1 percent of the population has Internet access. "In a fractured state like Somalia, radio remains the most influential medium," the BBC noted.[5]

For radio stations in the United States, the most momentous decision is what kind of music to play—maybe CHR, country, or hot AC. For Radio Mogadishu, simply deciding to play music and broadcast independent news is a far more serious, and life-threatening, matter.

Jehad Nga/The New York Times/Redux

stream their programming over the Web today.[12] IHeartRadio is one of the major streaming sites for broadcast and custom digital stations. The second kind of online radio station is one that has been created exclusively for the Internet. Pandora, 8tracks, Slacker, and Last.fm are some of the leading Internet radio services. In fact, services like Pandora allow users to have more control over their listening experience and the selections that are played. Listeners can create individualized stations based on a specific artist or song that they request. Pandora also enables users to share their musical choices on Facebook. AM/FM radio is used by nearly eight out of ten people who like to learn about new music, but YouTube, Facebook, Pandora, iTunes, iHeartRadio, Spotify, and blogs are among the competing sources for new music fans.[13]

Beginning in 2002, a Copyright Royalty Board established by the Library of Congress began to assess royalty fees for streaming copyrighted songs over the Internet based on a percentage of each station's revenue. Webcasters complained that royalty rates set by the board were too high and threatened their financial viability, particularly compared to satellite radio, which pays a lower royalty rate, and broadcasters, who pay no royalty rates at all. For decades, radio broadcasters have paid mechanical royalties to songwriters and music publishers but no royalties to the performing artists or record companies. Broadcasters have argued that the promotional value of getting songs played is sufficient compensation.

In 2009, Congress passed the Webcaster Settlement Act, which was considered a lifeline for Internet radio. The act enabled Internet stations to negotiate royalty fees directly with the music industry, at rates presumably more reasonable than what the Copyright Royalty Board had proposed. In 2012, Clear Channel became the first company to strike a deal directly with the recording industry. Clear Channel (now iHeartMedia) pledged to pay royalties to Big Machine Label Group—one of the country's largest independent labels—for broadcasting the songs of Taylor Swift and its other artists in exchange for a limit on royalties it must pay for streaming those artists' music on its iHeartRadio.com site.

Clear Channel's deal with the music industry opened up new dialogue about equalizing the royalty rates paid by broadcast radio, satellite radio, and Internet radio. Tim Westergren, founder of Pandora, argued before Congress in 2012 that the rates were most unfair to companies like his. In the previous year, Westergren said, Pandora paid 50 percent of its revenue for performance royalties, whereas satellite radio service SiriusXM paid 7.5 percent of its revenue for performance royalties, and broadcast radio paid nothing. He noted that a car equipped with an AM/FM radio, satellite radio, and streaming Internet radio could deliver the same song to a listener through all three technologies, but the various radio services would pay markedly different levels of performance royalties to the artist and recording company.[14]

Podcasting and Portable Listening

Developed in 2004, **podcasting** (the term marries *iPod* and *broadcasting*) refers to the practice of making audio files available on the Internet so listeners can download them onto their computers and either transfer them to portable MP3 players or listen to the files on the computer. This distribution method quickly became mainstream, as mass media companies created commercial podcasts to promote and extend existing content, such as news and reality TV, while independent producers developed new programs, such as public radio's *Serial*, a popular weekly audio nonfiction narrative.

INTERNET RADIO SITES like RadioTunes typically offer a variety of ways to listen: free streaming supported by ads, or a pay model that charges more for higher-quality audio or an ad-free stream.

Courtesy RadioTunes.com

LaunchPad ▶

macmillanhighered.com
/mediaculture10e

Radio: Yesterday, Today, and Tomorrow
Scholars and radio producers explain how radio adapts to and influences other media.
Discussion: Do you expect that the Internet will be the end of radio, or will radio stations still be around decades from now?

Podcasts have led the way for people to listen to radio on mobile devices like smartphones. Satellite radio, Internet-only stations like Pandora and Slacker, sites that stream traditional broadcast radio like iHeartRadio, and public radio like NPR all offer apps for smartphones and touchscreen devices like the iPad, which has also led to a resurgence in portable listening. Traditional broadcast radio stations are becoming increasingly mindful that they need to reach younger listeners on the Internet, and that Internet radio is no longer tethered to a computer.

For the broadcast radio industry, portability used to mean listening on a transistor or car radio. But with the digital turn to iPods and mobile phones, broadcasters haven't been as easily available on today's primary portable audio devices. Hoping to change that, the National Association of Broadcasters (NAB) has been lobbying the FCC and the mobile phone industry to include FM radio capability in all mobile phones. New mobile phones in the United States now have FM radio chips, but Sprint is the only major cell phone company to enable the chips with the NextRadio app.[15] Although the NAB argues that the enabled radio chip would be most important for enabling listeners to access local broadcast radio in times of emergencies and disasters, the chip would also be commercially beneficial for radio broadcasters, putting them on the same digital devices as their nonbroadcast radio competitors, like Pandora.

The Economics of Broadcast Radio

Radio continues to be one of the most used mass media, reaching about 92 percent of American teenagers and adults every week.[16] Because of radio's broad reach, the airwaves are very desirable real estate for advertisers, who want to reach people in and out of their homes; for record labels, who want their songs played; and for radio station owners, who want to create large radio groups to dominate multiple markets.

Local and National Advertising

About 10 percent of all U.S. spending on media advertising goes to radio stations. Like newspapers, radio generates its largest profits by selling local and regional ads. Thirty-second radio spot ads range from $1,500 in large markets to just a few dollars in the smallest markets. Today, gross advertising receipts for radio are more than $17.6 billion (about 80 percent of the revenues from local ad sales, with the remainder in national spot, network, and digital radio sales), up from about $16 billion in 2009.[17] Although industry revenue has dropped from a peak of $21.7 billion in 2006, the number of stations keeps growing, now totaling 15,406 stations (4,725 AM stations, 6,624 FM commercial stations, and 4,057 FM educational stations).[18] Unlike television, in which nearly 40 percent of a station's expenses goes toward buying syndicated programs, local radio stations get much of their content free from the recording industry. Therefore, only about 20 percent of a typical radio station's budget goes toward covering programming costs. But, as noted earlier, that free music content is in doubt as the music industry—which already charges performance royalties for Internet radio stations—moves toward charging radio broadcasters performance royalties for playing music on the air.

When radio stations want to purchase programming, they often turn to national network radio, which generates more than $1 billion in ad sales annually by offering dozens of specialized services. For example, Westwood One, the nation's largest radio network service, managed by Cumulus Media, reaches more than 225 million consumers a week with a range of programming, including regular network radio news (e.g., ABC, CBS, and NBC), entertainment programs (e.g., *The Bob & Tom Show*), talk shows (e.g., *The Mark Levin Show*), and complete twenty-four-hour formats (e.g., *Hot Country*, *Hits Now!*, and *Jack FM*). Dozens of companies offer national program and format services, typically providing local stations with programming in exchange for time slots for national ads. The most successful radio network programs are the shows broadcast by affiliates in the Top 20 markets, which offer advertisers half of the country's radio audience.

Manipulating Playlists with Payola

Radio's impact on music industry profits—radio airplay serves to popularize recordings—has required ongoing government oversight to expose illegal playlist manipulation. **Payola**, the practice by which record promoters pay deejays to play particular records, was rampant during the 1950s as record companies sought to guarantee record sales (see Chapter 4). In response, management took control of programming, arguing that if individual deejays had less impact on which records would be played, the deejays would be less susceptible to bribery.

Despite congressional hearings and new regulations, payola persisted. Record promoters showered their favors on a few influential, high-profile deejays, whose backing could make or break a record nationally, or on key program managers in charge of Top 40 formats in large urban markets. Although a 1984 congressional hearing determined that there was "no credible evidence" of payola, NBC News broke a story in 1986 about independent promoters who had alleged ties to organized crime. A subsequent investigation led major recording companies to break most of their ties with independent promoters. Prominent record labels had been paying such promoters up to $80 million per year to help records become hits.

More recently, in 2007 four of the largest broadcasting companies—CBS Radio, Clear Channel, Citadel, and Entercom—agreed to pay $12.5 million to settle an FCC payola investigation. The companies also agreed to an unprecedented "independent music content commitment," which required them to provide 8,400 half-hour blocks of airtime to play music from independent record labels over three years. In 2010, Univision Radio paid $1 million to settle allegations of payola and end an FCC investigation.

CLEAR CHANNEL COMMUNICATIONS has been a target for protesters who object to the company's media dominance, allowed by FCC deregulation. Clear Channel has shed some stations in recent years, but as a result of an economic downturn rather than increased regulation. The company changed its name to iHeartMedia in 2014 to reflect its future in streaming digital radio.

Radio Ownership: From Diversity to Consolidation

The **Telecommunications Act of 1996** substantially changed the rules concerning ownership of the public airwaves because the FCC eliminated most ownership restrictions on radio. As a result, 2,100 stations and $15 billion changed hands that year alone. From 1995 to 2005, the number of radio station owners declined by one-third, from 6,600 to about 4,400.[19]

Once upon a time, the FCC tried to encourage diversity in broadcast ownership. From the 1950s through the 1980s, a media company could not own more than seven AM, seven FM, and seven TV stations nationally, and could own only one radio station per

Richard B. Levine/Newscom

WAVES BELONG TO THE PEOPLE, NOT CLEAR CHANNEL

market. Just prior to the 1996 act, the ownership rules were relaxed to allow any single person or company to own up to twenty AM, twenty FM, and twelve TV stations nationwide, but only two in the same market.

The 1996 act allows individuals and companies to acquire as many radio stations as they want, with relaxed restrictions on the number of stations a single broadcaster may own in the same city: The larger the market or area, the more stations a company may own within that market. For example, in areas where forty-five or more stations are available to listeners, a broadcaster may own up to eight stations, but not more than five of one type (AM or FM). In areas with fourteen or fewer stations, a broadcaster may own up to five stations (three of any one type). In very small markets with a handful of stations, a broadcast company may not own more than half the stations.

With few exceptions, for the past two decades the FCC has embraced the consolidation schemes pushed by the powerful National Association of Broadcasters lobbyists in Washington, D.C., under which fewer and fewer owners control more and more of the airwaves.

The consequences of the 1996 Telecommunications Act and other deregulation have been significant. Consider the cases of Clear Channel Communications (now iHeartMedia) and Cumulus, the two largest radio chain owners in terms of number of stations owned (see Table 5.3). Clear Channel Communications was formed in 1972 with one San Antonio station. In 1998, it swallowed up Jacor Communications, the fifth-largest radio chain, and became the nation's second-largest group, with 454 stations in 101 cities. In 1999, Clear Channel gobbled up another growing conglomerate, AMFM (formerly Chancellor Media Corporation). Due to the recession of 2007–2009, Clear Channel shed some of the 1,205 stations it owned at its peak in 2005. Today, as iHeartMedia, it owns 840 radio stations and about 600,000 billboard and outdoor displays in over thirty countries across five continents, including 914 digital displays across thirty-seven U.S. markets. IHeartMedia also distributes many of the leading syndicated programs, including *The Rush Limbaugh Show*, *The Glenn Beck Program*, *On Air with Ryan Seacrest*, and *Delilah*. IHeartMedia is also an Internet radio source, with iheartradio, which has more than 30 million registered users. Cumulus became the second-largest radio conglomerate when it merged with Citadel in 2011 in a $2.5 billion deal and bought radio network service Dial Global (now Westwood One) in 2013. Cumulus also owns a stake in Rdio, a subscription music streaming service.

TABLE 5.3

TOP TWELVE RADIO COMPANIES (BY NUMBER OF STATIONS), 2014

Data from: The 10-K annual reports and business profiles for each radio company; Radio Lineup, "Large Radio Station Owners," 2014, www.radiolineup.com /owners/.

▶

Rank	Company	Number of Stations
1	iHeartMedia (Top property: WLTW-FM, New York)	840
2	Cumulus (KNBR-AM, San Francisco)	525
3	Townsquare Media (KSAS-FM, Boise)	312
4	Educational Media Foundation (KLVB, Citrus Heights, Calif.)	289
5	American Family Association (WAFR, Tupelo, Miss.)	193
6	CBS Radio (KROQ-FM, Los Angeles)	126
7	Entercom (WEEI-AM, Boston)	103
8	Salem Communications (KLTY, Dallas–Ft. Worth)	95
9	Saga Communications (WSNY, Columbus, Ohio)	92
10	Univision (KLVE-FM, Los Angeles)	68
11	Midwest Communications (WTAQ-FM, Green Bay)	62
12	Cox (WSB-AM, Atlanta)	57

Townsquare Media, launched in 2010 with the buyout of a 62-station group, grew to 312 stations by 2014 by focusing on acquiring stations in midsize markets. Two other major radio groups, the Educational Media Foundation and the American Family Association, are nonprofit religious broadcasters. The Educational Media Foundation also syndicates the K-Love and Air1 contemporary Christian music formats to hundreds of stations. The American Family Association is a conservative Christian activist organization that was originally established by Rev. Donald Wildmon in 1977 as the National Federation for Decency.

Combined, the top three commercial groups—iHeartMedia, Cumulus, and Townsquare Media—own almost 1,700 radio stations (about 11 percent of all U.S. stations), dominate the fifty largest markets in the United States, and control at least one-third of the entire radio industry's $17.6 billion revenue. As a result of the consolidations permitted by deregulation, in most American cities just a few corporations dominate the radio market.

A smaller radio conglomerate, but one that is perhaps the most dominant in a single format area, is Univision. With a $3 billion takeover of Hispanic Broadcasting in 2003, Univision is the top Spanish-language radio broadcaster in the United States. The company is also the largest Spanish-language television broadcaster in the United States (see Chapter 6), as well as the owner of the top two Spanish-language cable networks (Galavisión and UniMás) and Univision Online, the most popular Spanish-language Web site in the United States.

Alternative Voices

As large corporations gained control of America's radio airwaves, activists in hundreds of communities across the United States protested in the 1990s by starting up their own noncommercial "pirate" radio stations capable of broadcasting over a few miles with low-power FM signals of 1 to 10 watts. The NAB and other industry groups pressed to have the pirate broadcasters closed down, citing their illegality and their potential to create interference with existing stations. Between 1995 and 2000, more than five hundred illegal micropower radio stations were shut down. Still, an estimated one hundred to one thousand pirate stations are in operation in the United States, in both large urban areas and small rural towns.

The major complaint of pirate radio station operators was that the FCC had long ago ceased licensing low-power community radio stations. In 2000, the FCC, responding to tens of thousands of inquiries about the development of a new local radio broadcasting service, approved a new noncommercial **low-power FM (LPFM)** class of 100-watt stations (with a broadcast coverage reach of about five miles) in order to give voice to local groups lacking access to the public airwaves. LPFM station licensees included mostly religious groups but also high schools, colleges and universities, Native American tribes, labor groups, and museums.

LPFM stations are located in unused frequencies on the FM dial. Still, the NAB and National Public Radio fought to delay and limit the number of LPFM stations, arguing that such stations would cause interference with existing full-power FM stations. Then FCC chairman William E. Kennard, who fostered the LPFM initiative, responded: "This is about the haves—the broadcast industry—trying to prevent many have-nots—small community and educational organizations—from having just a little piece of the pie. Just a little piece of the airwaves which belong to all of the people."[20] By 2014, about 830 LPFM stations were broadcasting.

ALTERNATIVE RADIO VOICES can also be found on college stations, typically started by students and community members. There are around 520 such stations currently active in the United States, broadcasting in an eclectic variety of formats. As rock radio influence has declined, college radio has become a major outlet for new indie bands.

© Thomas Fricke/Corbis

JJ Tiziou Photography

The passage of the Local Community Radio Act in 2011 created opportunities for more LPFM station applications in 2013. A major advocate of LPFM stations is the Prometheus Radio Project, a nonprofit formed by radio activists in 1998. Prometheus has helped educate community organizations about low-power radio and has sponsored at least a dozen "barn raisings" to build community stations in places like Hudson, New York; Opelousas, Louisiana; and Woodburn, Oregon.

Radio and the Democracy of the Airwaves

As radio was the first national electronic mass medium, its influence in the formation of American culture cannot be overestimated. Radio has given us soap operas, situation comedies, and broadcast news; it helped popularize rock and roll, car culture, and the politics of talk radio. Yet for all its national influence, broadcast radio is still a supremely local medium. For decades, listeners have tuned in to hear the familiar voices of their community's deejays and talk-show hosts and hear the regional flavor of popular music over airwaves that the public owns.

The early debates over radio gave us one of the most important and enduring ideas in communication policy: a requirement to operate in the "public interest, convenience, or necessity." But the broadcasting industry has long been at odds with this policy, arguing that radio corporations invest heavily in technology and should be able to have more control over the radio frequencies on which they operate and, moreover, own as many stations as they want. Deregulation in the past few decades has moved closer to that corporate vision, as nearly every radio market in the nation is dominated by a few owners, and those owners are required to renew their broadcasting licenses only every eight years.

This trend in ownership has moved radio away from its localism, as radio groups often manage hundreds of stations from afar. Given broadcasters' reluctance to publicly raise

DIGITAL JOB OUTLOOK

Media Professionals Speak about Jobs in the Radio Industry

Corey Deitz, Radio Personality, KDJE-FM, Little Rock, Arkansas

If you want to be in radio so you can play your favorite music because you're absolutely positive you can put together a great show, leave now. Few stations are going to let you pick the music you play, except maybe a college station or a tiny local station in the middle of Nowhere, Oklahoma.

Melissa Chase, Morning Show Host and Program Director, WURV-FM, Richmond, Virginia

If you want to become a "Radio Personality" versus just being a liner-reading deejay, you have to be an interesting person and have cool things to talk about. So in college, I did wild stuff like taking time to build houses in Miami with Habitat for Humanity, signed [myself] up for the school Broomball Team, took a *Harry Potter* class for my English requirement, interned at MTV, volunteered at our local PBS station. . . . I just tried to go out and meet crazy people and have a good story to tell. I would also say don't get too focused on the job you want, which sounds crazy. But the people who get so eagle-eye focused on "*this* is where I want to work and have *this* job title and *this* salary" . . . they close themselves off to so much!

Erica Farber, President and CEO, Radio Advertising Bureau

We need to be certain that our sellers have the tools to be competitive in today's marketplace. Sellers today must be well versed in the nuances of being a marketing partner—understanding the challenges and business needs of their clients. And as technology changes, education and training in how to understand, use, and market radio with these changes will be essential.

Tim Westergren, Founder and CEO, Pandora

My advice to undergraduates is "learn to pitch," which is a euphemism for public speaking. And if I could go back and do college again, . . . one thing that I would make as a mandatory course for all students all four years would be a public speaking course. Because there is just no substitute for learning how to communicate, and it applies to everything you do for the rest of your life.

questions about their own economic arrangements, public debate regarding radio as a natural resource has remained minuscule. As citizens look to the future, a big question remains to be answered: With a few large broadcast companies now permitted to dominate radio ownership nationwide, how much is consolidation of power restricting the number and kinds of voices permitted to speak over public airwaves? To ensure that mass media industries continue to serve democracy and local communities, the public needs to play a role in developing the answer to this question. ▶

CHAPTER REVIEW

COMMON THREADS

One of the Common Threads discussed in Chapter 1 is the developmental stages of mass media. Like other mass media, radio evolved in three stages, but it also influenced an important dichotomy in mass media technology: wired versus wireless.

In radio's novelty stage, several inventors transcended the wires of the telegraph and telephone to solve the problem of wireless communication. In the entrepreneurial stage, inventors tested ship-to-shore radio, while others developed person-to-person toll radio transmissions and other schemes to make money from wireless communication. Finally, when radio stations began broadcasting to the general public (who bought radio receivers for their homes), radio became a mass medium.

As the first electronic mass medium, radio set the pattern for an ongoing battle between wired and wireless technologies. For example, television brought images to wireless broadcasting. Then, cable television's wires brought television signals to places where receiving antennas didn't work. Satellite television (wireless from outer space) followed as an innovation to bring TV where cable didn't exist. Now, broadcast, cable, and satellite all compete against one another.

Similarly, think of how cell phones have eliminated millions of traditional phone, or land, lines. The Internet, like the telephone, also began with wires, but Wi-Fi and home wireless systems are eliminating those wires, too. And radio? Most listeners get traditional local (wireless) radio broadcast signals, but now listeners may use a wired Internet connection to stream Internet radio or download Webcasts and podcasts. The radio industry's push for the future is to ensure that all mobile phones have enabled FM radio chips so that local radio listening through the Internet can be (again) wireless.

Both wired and wireless technologies have advantages and disadvantages. Do we want the stability and the tethers of a wired connection? Or do we want the freedom and occasional instability ("Can you hear me now?") of wireless media? Can radio's development help us understand wired-versus-wireless battles in other media?

KEY TERMS

The definitions for the terms listed below can be found in the glossary at the end of the book. The page numbers listed with the terms indicate where the term is highlighted in the chapter.

telegraph, 151
Morse code, 151
electromagnetic waves, 152
radio waves, 152
wireless telegraphy, 153
wireless telephony, 154
broadcasting, 155
narrowcasting, 155
Radio Act of 1912, 156
Radio Corporation of America (RCA), 157
network, 158
option time, 161
Radio Act of 1927, 162
Federal Radio Commission (FRC), 162
Communications Act of 1934, 162

Federal Communications Commission (FCC), 162
transistors, 166
FM, 166
AM, 166
format radio, 167
rotation, 167
Top 40 format, 168
progressive rock, 168
album-oriented rock (AOR), 169
drive time, 169
news/talk/information, 170
adult contemporary (AC), 172
contemporary hit radio (CHR), 172
country, 172

urban contemporary, 172
Pacifica Foundation, 173
National Public Radio (NPR), 173
Public Broadcasting Service (PBS), 173
Public Broadcasting Act of 1967, 173
Corporation for Public Broadcasting (CPB), 173
satellite radio, 175
HD radio, 175
Internet radio, 175
podcasting, 177
payola, 179
Telecommunications Act of 1996, 179
low-power FM (LPFM), 181

For review quizzes, chapter summaries, links to media-related Web sites, and more, go to **macmillanhighered.com/mediaculture10e**.

REVIEW QUESTIONS

Early Technology and the Development of Radio

1. Why was the development of the telegraph important in media history? What were some of the disadvantages of telegraph technology?

2. How is the concept of wireless different from that of radio?

3. What was Guglielmo Marconi's role in the development of wireless telegraphy?

4. What were Lee De Forest's contributions to radio?

5. Why were there so many patent disputes in the development of radio?

6. Why was the RCA monopoly formed?

7. How did broadcasting, unlike print media, come to be federally regulated?

The Evolution of Radio

8. What was AT&T's role in the early days of radio?

9. How did the radio networks develop? What were the contributions of David Sarnoff and William Paley to network radio?

10. Why did the government-sanctioned RCA monopoly end?

11. What is the significance of the Radio Act of 1927 and the Communications Act of 1934?

Radio Reinvents Itself

12. How did radio adapt to the arrival of television?

13. What was Edwin Armstrong's role in the advancement of radio technology? Why did RCA hamper Armstrong's work?

14. How did music on radio change in the 1950s?

15. What is format radio, and why was it important to the survival of radio?

The Sounds of Commercial Radio

16. Why are there so many radio formats today?

17. Why did Top 40 radio diminish as a format in the 1980s and 1990s?

18. What is the state of nonprofit radio today?

19. Why are performance royalties a topic of debate between broadcast radio, satellite radio, Internet radio, and the recording industry?

20. Why do radio broadcasters want FM radio chips enabled for use in mobile phones?

The Economics of Broadcast Radio

21. What are the current ownership rules governing American radio?

22. What has been the main effect of the Telecommunications Act of 1996 on radio station ownership?

23. Why did the FCC create a new class of low-power FM stations?

Radio and the Democracy of the Airwaves

24. Throughout the history of radio, why did the government encourage monopoly or oligopoly ownership of radio broadcasting?

25. What is the relevance of localism to debates about ownership in radio?

QUESTIONING THE MEDIA

1. Count the number and types of radio stations in your area today. What formats do they use? Do a little research, and find out who are the owners of the stations in your market. How much diversity is there among the highest-rated stations?

2. If you could own and manage a commercial radio station, what format would you choose, and why?

3. If you ran a noncommercial radio station in your area, what services would you provide to address needs that are not being met by commercial format radio?

4. How might radio be used to improve social and political discussions in the United States?

5. If you were a broadcast radio executive, what arguments would you make in favor of broadcast radio over Internet radio?

LAUNCHPAD FOR *MEDIA & CULTURE*

Visit LaunchPad for *Media & Culture* at macmillanhighered.com/mediaculture10e *for additional learning tools:*

- REVIEW WITH LEARNINGCURVE
  LearningCurve, available on LaunchPad for *Media &*

Culture, uses gamelike quizzing to help you master the concepts you need to learn from this chapter.

6

Television and Cable

The Power of Visual Culture

189
The Origins and
Development of
Television

195
The Development
of Cable

199
Technology and
Convergence Change
Viewing Habits

203
Major Programming
Trends

211
Regulatory Challenges
to Television and Cable

216
The Economics
and Ownership of
Television and Cable

225
Television, Cable,
and Democracy

Television may be our final link to true "mass" communication—a medium that in the 1960s through the 1980s could attract forty million viewers to a single episode of a popular prime-time drama like *Bonanza* (1959–1973) or a "must-see" comedy like *Seinfeld* (1989–1998). Today, the only program that attracts that kind of audience happens once a year—the Super Bowl. Back in its full-blown mass media stage, television was available only on traditional TV sets, and people mostly watched only the original broadcast networks—ABC, CBS, and NBC.

Things are different today, as television has entered the fourth stage in the life cycle of a mass medium—convergence. Today, audiences watch TV on everything from big flat-screen digital sets to tiny smartphones and tablet screens. Back in the day, the networks either made or bought almost all TV shows, usually bankrolled by Hollywood film studios. These days, everyone from broadcast networks to cable channels to Internet services like Netflix and Amazon is producing original shows.

The first major crack in the networks' mass audience dominance came when cable TV developed in the 1970s. At first, cable channels like HBO and TNT survived by redistributing old movies and network TV programs. But when HBO (and its parent company, Time Warner, a major owner of cable companies) began producing popular award-winning original series like *The Sopranos*, the networks' hold on viewers started to erode. Premium cable services like HBO (*True Detective*) and Showtime (*Homeland*) led the way, but now basic cable channels like USA Network (*Royal Pains*), AMC (*The Walking Dead*), and FX (*Justified*) are producing popular original programming. Cable shows routinely win more Emmys each year than do broadcast networks (e.g., for Best Drama, AMC's *Mad Men* won the Emmy from 2008 to 2011 and AMC's *Breaking Bad* won that category in 2014).

What cable really did was introduce a better business model—earning money from monthly subscription fees *and* advertising. The old network model relied solely on advertising revenue. The networks, worried about the loss both of viewers and of ad dollars to its upstart competitor, decided they wanted a piece of that action. Some networks started buying cable channels (NBC, for example, has purchased stakes in Bravo, E!, Syfy, USA Network, and the Weather Channel). The networks and local TV stations also championed something called *retransmission consent*—fees that cable providers like Comcast and Time Warner pay to local TV stations and the major networks each month for the right to carry their channels. Typically, cable companies in large-market cities pay their local broadcasters and the national networks about fifty to seventy-five cents per month for each cable subscriber. Those fees are then passed along to subscribers.

In recent years, retransmission fees have caused some friction between broadcasters and cable companies. For example, in 2013,

when fee negotiations between CBS and Time Warner broke down, the station was dropped from Time Warner's lineup in some markets for almost a month. In the same year, the evolving relationship between broadcasters and cable TV took a dramatic turn when General Electric, which started and owned NBC (and Universal Studios), sold majority control of its flagship network (and the film company) to Comcast, the nation's largest cable provider. Comcast now produces or owns a significant amount of programming for use on its broadcast and cable channels, and exercises better control over retransmission fees.

While the major tensions between cable and broadcasters appear to have quieted down, a new battle is brewing as the Internet and smaller screens are quickly becoming the future of television. On the surface, a mutually beneficial relationship has developed among streaming online services and broadcasters and cable providers—Hulu, after all, is jointly owned by Disney (ABC), 21st Century Fox (Fox), and Comcast (NBC). Internet streaming services help cable and broadcast networks increase their audiences through time shifting, as viewers watch favorite TV shows days, even weeks, after they originally aired. But these services are no longer satisfied to distribute network reruns and old cable shows—Hulu (*Deadbeat*), Netflix (*Orange Is the New Black*), and Amazon (*Mozart in the Jungle*) have begun developing original programming.

As the newest battle shakes up the television landscape, one thing remains unchanged: high-quality stories that resonate with viewers. And in the fragmented marketplace, in which the "mass" audience has shrunk and morphed into niche viewers, there may be plenty of room for small, quirky shows that attract younger fans who grew up on the Internet.

Visit **LaunchPad for** *Media & Culture* and use **LearningCurve** to review concepts from this chapter.

▲ *BROADCAST NETWORKS TODAY* may resent cable networks developing original programming, but in the beginning, network television actually stole most of its programming and business ideas from radio. Old radio scripts began reappearing in TV form, snatching radio's sponsors, its program ideas, and even its prime-time evening audience. In 1949, for instance, *The Lone Ranger* rode over to television from radio, where the program had originated in 1933. *Amos 'n' Andy*, a fixture on network radio since 1928, became the first TV series to have an entirely black cast in 1951. Since replacing radio in the 1950s as our most popular mass medium, television has sparked repeated arguments about its social and cultural impact. Television has been accused of having a negative impact on children and young people and has also faced criticism for enabling and sustaining a sharply partisan political system. But there are other sides to this story. In times of crisis, our fragmented and pluralistic society has embraced television as common ground. It was TV that exposed many to Civil Rights violations in the South and to the shared loss after the Kennedy and King assassinations in the 1960s. On September 11, 2001—in shock and horror—we turned on television sets to learn that nearly three thousand people had been killed in that day's terrorist attacks. And in 2013, we viewed the Boston Marathon bombing attacks on our TVs and online. For better or worse, television remains a central touchstone in our daily lives.

In this chapter, we examine television and cable's cultural, social, and economic impact. We will:

- Review television's early technological development
- Discuss TV's boom in the 1950s and the impact of the quiz-show scandals
- Examine cable's technological development and basic services
- Explore new viewing technologies, such as computers, smartphones, and tablets
- Learn about major programming genres: comedy, drama, news, and reality TV
- Trace the key rules and regulations of television and cable
- Inspect the costs related to the production, distribution, and syndication of programs
- Investigate the impact of television and cable on democracy and culture

As you read through this chapter, think about your own experiences with television programs and the impact they have on you. What was your favorite show as a child? Were there shows you weren't allowed to watch when you were young? If so, why? What attracts you to your favorite programs now? For more questions to help you think through the role of television and cable in our lives, see "Questioning the Media" in the Chapter Review.

The Origins and Development of Television

In 1948, only 1 percent of America's households had a TV set; by 1953, more than 50 percent had one; and since the early 1960s, more than 90 percent of all homes have TV. Television's rise throughout the 1950s created fears that radio—as well as books, magazines, and movies—would become irrelevant and unnecessary, but both radio and print media adapted. In fact, today more radio stations are operating and more books and magazines are being published than ever before; only ticket sales for movies have declined slightly since the 1960s.

Three major historical developments in television's early years helped shape it: (1) technological innovations and patent wars, (2) the wresting of content control from advertisers, and (3) the sociocultural impact of the infamous quiz-show scandals.

CIVIL RIGHTS
In the 1950s and 1960s, television images of Civil Rights struggles visually documented the inequalities faced by black citizens. Seeing these images made the events and struggles more "real" to a nation of viewers and helped garner support for the movement.

Early Innovations in TV Technology

In its novelty stage, television's earliest pioneers were trying to isolate TV waves from the electro-magnetic spectrum (as radio's pioneers had done with radio waves). The big question was, If a person could transmit audio signals from one place to another, why not visual images as well? Inventors from a number of nations toyed with the idea of sending "tele-visual" images for nearly a hundred years before what we know as TV developed.

From roughly 1897 to 1907, the development by several inventors of the *cathode ray tube*, the fore-runner of the TV picture tube, combined principles of the camera and electricity. Because television images could not physically float through the air, technicians and inventors developed a method of encoding them at a transmission point (TV station) and decoding them at a reception point (TV set). In the 1880s, German inventor Paul Nipkow developed the *scanning disk*, a large flat metal disk with a series of small perforations organized in a spiral pattern. As the disk rotated, it separated pictures into pinpoints of light that could be transmitted as a series of electronic lines. As the disk spun, each small hole scanned one line of a scene to be televised. For years, Nipkow's mechanical disk served as the foundation for experiments on the transmission of visual images.

Electronic Technology: Zworykin and Farnsworth

The story of television's invention included a complex patents battle between two independent inventors: Vladimir Zworykin and Philo Farnsworth. It began in Russia in 1907, when physicist

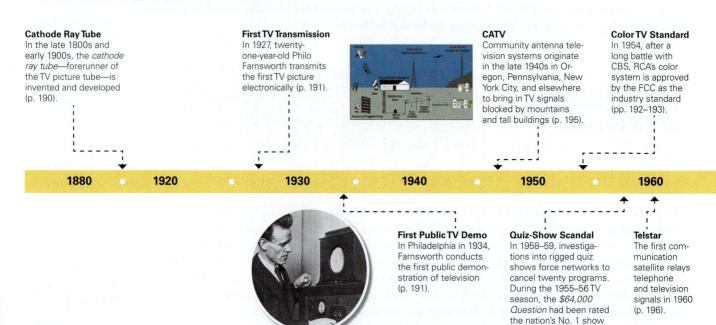

▼ Television and Cable: The Power of Visual Culture

Cathode Ray Tube
In the late 1800s and early 1900s, the *cathode ray tube*—forerunner of the TV picture tube—is invented and developed (p. 190).

First TV Transmission
In 1927, twenty-one-year-old Philo Farnsworth transmits the first TV picture electronically (p. 191).

CATV
Community antenna television systems originate in the late 1940s in Oregon, Pennsylvania, New York City, and elsewhere to bring in TV signals blocked by mountains and tall buildings (p. 195).

Color TV Standard
In 1954, after a long battle with CBS, RCA's color system is approved by the FCC as the industry standard (pp. 192–193).

| 1880 | 1920 | 1930 | 1940 | 1950 | 1960 |

First Public TV Demo
In Philadelphia in 1934, Farnsworth conducts the first public demonstration of television (p. 191).

Quiz-Show Scandal
In 1958–59, investigations into rigged quiz shows force networks to cancel twenty programs. During the 1955–56 TV season, the *$64,000 Question* had been rated the nation's No. 1 show (p. 194).

Telstar
The first communication satellite relays telephone and television signals in 1960 (p. 196).

Boris Rosing improved Nipkow's mechanical scanning device. Rosing's lab assistant, Vladimir Zworykin, left Russia for America in 1919 and went to work for Westinghouse and then RCA. In 1923, Zworykin invented the *iconoscope*, the first TV camera tube to convert light rays into electrical signals, and he received a patent for it in 1928.

Around the same time, Idaho teenager Philo Farnsworth also figured out that a mechanical scanning system would not send pictures through the air over long distances. On September 7, 1927, the twenty-one-year-old Farnsworth transmitted the first electronic TV picture: He rotated a straight line scratched on a square of painted glass by 90 degrees. RCA, then the world leader in broadcasting technology, challenged Farnsworth in a major patents battle, in part over Zworykin's innovations for Westinghouse and RCA. Farnsworth had to rely on his high school science teacher to retrieve his original drawings from 1922. Finally, in 1930, Farnsworth received a patent for the first electronic television.

After the company's court defeat, RCA's president, David Sarnoff, had to negotiate to use Farnsworth's patents. Farnsworth later licensed these patents to RCA and AT&T for use in the commercial development of television. At the end of television's development stage, Farnsworth conducted the first public demonstration of television at the Franklin Institute in Philadelphia in 1934—five years *before* RCA's famous public demonstration at the 1939 World's Fair.

Setting Technical Standards

Figuring out how to push TV as a business and elevate it to a mass medium meant creating a coherent set of technical standards for product manufacturers. In the late 1930s, the National Television Systems Committee (NTSC), a group representing major electronics firms, began outlining industry-wide manufacturing practices and compromising on technical standards. As a result, in 1941 the Federal Communications Commission (FCC) adopted an ==analog== standard (based on radio waves) for all U.S. TV sets. About thirty countries, including Japan, Canada, Mexico, Saudi Arabia, and most Latin American nations, also adopted this system. (Most of Europe and Asia, however, adopted a slightly superior technical system shortly thereafter.)

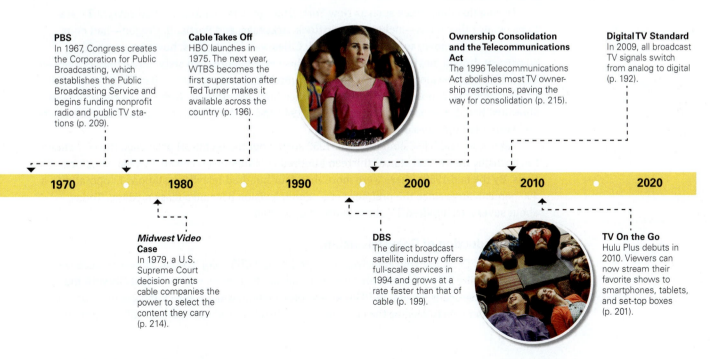

PBS
In 1967, Congress creates the Corporation for Public Broadcasting, which establishes the Public Broadcasting Service and begins funding nonprofit radio and public TV stations (p. 209).

Cable Takes Off
HBO launches in 1975. The next year, WTBS becomes the first superstation after Ted Turner makes it available across the country (p. 196).

Ownership Consolidation and the Telecommunications Act
The 1996 Telecommunications Act abolishes most TV ownership restrictions, paving the way for consolidation (p. 215).

Digital TV Standard
In 2009, all broadcast TV signals switch from analog to digital (p. 192).

1970   1980   1990   2000   2010   2020

Midwest Video **Case**
In 1979, a U.S. Supreme Court decision grants cable companies the power to select the content they carry (p. 214).

DBS
The direct broadcast satellite industry offers full-scale services in 1994 and grows at a rate faster than that of cable (p. 199).

TV On the Go
Hulu Plus debuts in 2010. Viewers can now stream their favorite shows to smartphones, tablets, and set-top boxes (p. 201).

© Bettmann/Corbis

The United States continued to use analog signals until 2009, when they were replaced by **digital** signals. These translate TV images and sounds into binary codes (ones and zeros like computers use) and allow for increased channel capacity and improved image quality and sound. HDTV, or *high-definition television*, digital signals offer the highest resolution and sharpest image. Receiving a "hi-def" picture depends on two factors: The programmer must use a high-definition signal, and consumers must have HDTV equipment to receive and view it. The switch to digital signals has also opened up new avenues for receiving and viewing television on laptops, smartphones, and tablets.

Assigning Frequencies and Freezing TV Licenses

In the early days of television, the number of TV stations a city or market could support was limited because airwave spectrum frequencies interfered with one another. Thus a market could have a channel 2 and a channel 4 but not a channel 3. Cable systems "fixed" this problem by sending channels through cable wires that don't interfere with one another. Today, a frequency that once carried one analog TV signal can carry eight or nine compressed digital channels.

In the 1940s, the FCC began assigning channels in specific geographic areas to make sure there was no interference. As a result, for years New Jersey had no TV stations because those signals would have interfered with the New York stations. But by 1948 the FCC had issued nearly one hundred TV licenses, and there was growing concern about the finite number of channels and the frequency-interference problems. The FCC declared a freeze on new licenses from 1948 to 1952.

During this time, cities such as New York, Chicago, and Los Angeles had several TV stations, while other areas—including Little Rock, Arkansas, and Portland, Oregon—had none. In non-TV cities, movie audiences increased. Cities with TV stations, however, saw a 20 to 40 percent drop in movie attendance during this period; more than sixty movie theaters closed in the Chicago area alone. Taxi receipts and nightclub attendance also fell in TV cities, as did library book circulation. Radio listening also declined; for example, Bob Hope's network radio show lost half its national audience between 1949 and 1951. By 1951, the sales of television sets had surpassed the sales of radio receivers.

After a second NTSC conference in 1952 sorted out the technical problems, the FCC ended the licensing freeze, and almost thirteen hundred communities received TV channel allocations. By the mid-1950s, there were more than four hundred television stations in operation—a 400 percent surge since the prefreeze era—and television became a mass medium. Today, about seventeen hundred TV stations are in operation.

The Introduction of Color Television

In 1952, the FCC tentatively approved an experimental CBS color system. However, because black-and-white TV sets could not receive its signal, the system was incompatible with the sets most Americans owned. In 1954, RCA's color system, which sent TV images in color but allowed older sets to receive the color images as black-and-white, usurped CBS's system to become the color standard. Although NBC began broadcasting a few shows in color in the mid-1950s, it wasn't until 1966, when the consumer market for color sets had taken off, that the Big Three networks (CBS, NBC, and ABC) broadcast their entire evening lineups in color.

Controlling Content—TV Grows Up

By the early 1960s, television had become a dominant mass medium and cultural force, with more than 90 percent of U.S. households owning at least one set. Television's new standing came as its programs moved away from the influence of radio and established a separate identity. Two important contributors to this identity were a major change in the sponsorship structure of television programming and, more significant, a major scandal.

Program Format Changes Inhibit Sponsorship

Like radio in the 1930s and 1940s, early TV programs were often developed, produced, and supported by a single sponsor. Many of the top-rated programs in the 1950s even included the sponsor's name in the title: *Buick Circus Hour*, *Camel News Caravan*, and *Colgate Comedy Hour*. Having a single sponsor for a show meant that the advertiser could easily influence the program's content. In the early 1950s, the broadcast networks became increasingly unhappy with the lack of creative control in this arrangement. Luckily, the growing popularity, and growing cost, of television offered opportunities to alter this financial setup. In 1952, for example, a single one-hour TV show cost a sponsor about $35,000, a figure that rose to $90,000 by the end of the decade.

David Sarnoff, then head of RCA-NBC, and William Paley, head of CBS, saw an opportunity to diminish the sponsors' role. In 1953, Sarnoff appointed Sylvester "Pat" Weaver (father of actress Sigourney Weaver) as the president of NBC. Previously an advertising executive, Weaver undermined his former profession by increasing program length from fifteen minutes (then the standard for radio programs) to thirty minutes or longer, substantially raising program costs for advertisers and discouraging some from sponsoring programs.

In addition, the introduction of two new types of programs—the magazine format and the TV spectacular—greatly helped the networks gain control over content. The *magazine program* featured multiple segments—news, talk, comedy, and music—similar to the varied content found in a general-interest publication or newsmagazine of the day, such as *Life* or *Time*. In January 1952, NBC introduced the *Today* show as a three-hour morning talk-news program. Then, in September 1954, NBC premiered the ninety-minute *Tonight Show*. Because both shows ran daily rather than weekly, studio production costs were prohibitive for a single sponsor. Consequently, NBC offered spot ads within the shows: Advertisers paid the network for thirty- or sixty-second time slots. The network, not the sponsor, now produced and owned the programs or bought them from independent producers.

The television spectacular is today recognized by a more modest term, the *television special*. At NBC, Weaver bought the rights to special programs, like the Broadway production of *Peter Pan*, and sold spot ads to multiple sponsors. The 1955 TV version of *Peter Pan* was a particular success, with sixty-five million viewers. More typical specials featured music-variety shows hosted by famous singers, such as Judy Garland, Frank Sinatra, and Nat King Cole.

THE TODAY SHOW, the first magazine-style show, has been on the air since 1952. A groundbreaking concept that forever changed television, morning news shows are now common. They include *Good Morning America* (ABC), *The Early Show* (CBS), *Fox & Friends* (Fox), and *American Morning* (CNN).

Peter Kramer/NBC/NBCU Photo Bank via Getty Images

The Rise and Fall of Quiz Shows

In 1955, CBS aired the *$64,000 Question*, reviving radio's quiz-show genre (radio's version was the more modest *$64 Question*). Sponsored by Revlon, the program ran in **prime time** (the hours between 8 and 11 P.M., when networks traditionally draw their largest audiences and charge their highest advertising rates) and became the most popular TV show in America during its first year. Revlon followed the show's success with the *$64,000 Challenge* in 1956; by the end of 1958, twenty-two quiz shows aired on network television. Revlon's cosmetic sales skyrocketed from $1.2 million before its sponsorship of the quiz shows to nearly $10 million by 1959.

Compared with dramas and sitcoms, quiz shows were (and are) cheap to produce, with inexpensive sets and mostly nonactors as guests. The problem was that most of these shows were rigged. To heighten the drama, key contestants were rehearsed and given the answers.

The most notorious rigging occurred on *Twenty-One*, a quiz show owned by Geritol (whose profits climbed by $4 million one year after it began to sponsor the program in 1956). A young Columbia University English professor from a famous literary family, Charles Van Doren, won $129,000 in 1957 during his fifteen-week run on the program; his fame even landed him a job on NBC's *Today* show. But in 1958, after a series of contestants accused the quiz show *Dotto* of being fixed, the networks quickly dropped twenty quiz shows. Following further rumors, a *TV Guide* story, a New York grand jury probe, and a 1959 congressional investigation during which Van Doren admitted to cheating, big-money prime-time quiz shows ended.

Quiz-Show Scandal Hurts the Promise of TV

The impact of the quiz-show scandals was enormous. First, the sponsors' pressure on TV executives to rig the programs and the subsequent fraud put an end to any role that major sponsors had in creating TV content. Second, and more important, the fraud undermined Americans' expectation of the democratic promise of television—to bring inexpensive information and entertainment into every household. Many people had trusted their own eyes—what they saw on TV—more than the *words* they heard on radio or read in print.

TWENTY-ONE
In 1957, the most popular contestant on the quiz show *Twenty-One* was college professor Charles Van Doren (*left*). Congressional hearings on rigged quiz shows revealed that Van Doren had been given some answers. Host Jack Barry, pictured here above the sponsor's logo, nearly had his career ruined, but made a comeback in the late 1960s with the syndicated game show *The Joker's Wild*.

Everett Collection

But the scandals provided the first dramatic indication that TV images could be manipulated. In fact, our contemporary love-hate relationship with electronic culture and new gadgets began during this time.

The third, and most important, impact of the quiz-show scandals was that they magnified the division between "high" and "low" culture attitudes toward television. The fact that Charles Van Doren had come from a family of Ivy League intellectuals and cheated for fame and money drove a wedge between intellectuals—who were already skeptical of television—and the popular new medium. This was best expressed in 1961 by FCC commissioner Newton Minow, who labeled game shows, westerns, cartoons, and other popular genres as part of television's "vast wasteland." Critics have used the wasteland metaphor ever since to admonish the TV industry for failing to live up to its potential.

After the scandal, quiz shows were kept out of network prime time for forty years. Finally, in 1999, ABC gambled that the nation was ready once again for a quiz show in prime time. The network had great, if brief, success with *Who Wants to Be a Millionaire*, which hit No. 1 that year.

The Development of Cable

Most historians mark the period from the late 1950s, when the networks gained control over TV's content, to the end of the 1970s as the **network era**. Except for British and American anthology dramas on PBS, this was a time when the Big Three broadcast networks—CBS, NBC, and ABC—dictated virtually every trend in programming and collectively accounted for more than 95 percent of all prime-time TV viewing. In 2012, however, this figure was less than 40 percent. Why the drastic drop? Because cable television systems—along with VCRs and DVD players—had cut into the broadcast networks' audience.

CATV—Community Antenna Television

The first small cable systems—called CATV, or community antenna television—originated in the late 1940s in Oregon, Pennsylvania, and New York City, where mountains or tall buildings blocked TV signals. These systems served roughly 10 percent of the country and, because of early technical and regulatory limits, contained only twelve channels. Even at this early stage, though, TV sales personnel, broadcasters, and electronics firms recognized two big advantages of cable. First, by routing and reamplifying each channel in a separate wire, cable eliminated over-the-air interference. Second, running signals through coaxial cable increased channel capacity.

In the beginning, small communities with CATV often received twice as many channels as were available over the air in much larger cities. That technological advantage, combined with cable's ability to deliver clear reception, would soon propel the new cable industry into competition with conventional broadcast television. But unlike radio, which freed mass communication from unwieldy wires, early cable technology relied on wires.

The Wires and Satellites behind Cable Television

The idea of using space satellites to receive and transmit communication signals is right out of science fiction: In 1945, Arthur C. Clarke (who studied physics and mathematics and would later write dozens of sci-fi books, including *2001: A Space Odyssey*) published the original theories for a global communications system based on three satellites equally spaced from one another, rotating with the earth's orbit. In the mid-1950s, these theories became reality, as the Soviet Union and then the United States successfully sent satellites into orbit around the earth.

In 1960, AT&T launched Telstar, the first communication satellite capable of receiving, amplifying, and returning signals. Telstar was able to process and relay telephone and occasional television signals between the United States and Europe. By the mid-1960s, scientists had figured out how to lock communication satellites into *geosynchronous orbit*. Hovering 22,300 miles above the earth, satellites travel at nearly 7,000 mph and circle the earth at the same speed at which the earth revolves on its axis. For cable television, the breakthrough was the launch of domestic communication satellites: Canada's *Anik* in 1972 and the United States' *Westar* in 1974.

Cable TV signals are processed at a computerized nerve center, or *headend*, which operates various large satellite dishes that receive and distribute long-distance signals from, say, CNN in Atlanta or ESPN in Connecticut. In addition, the headend's receiving equipment can pick up an area's local signals or a nearby city's PBS station. The headend relays each channel, local network affiliate, or public TV signal along its own separate line. Headend computers relay the channels in the same way that telephone calls and electric power reach individual households: through *trunk* and *feeder cables* attached to existing utility poles. Cable companies rent space on these poles from phone and electric companies. Signals are then transmitted to *drop* or *tap lines* that run from the utility poles into subscribers' homes (see Figure 6.1).

Advances in satellite technology in the 1970s dramatically changed the fortunes of cable by creating a reliable system for the distribution of programming to cable companies across the nation. The first cable network to use satellites for regular transmission of TV programming was Home Box Office (HBO), which began delivering programming such as uncut, commercial-free movies and exclusive live coverage of major boxing matches for a monthly fee in 1975. The second cable network began in 1976, when media owner Ted Turner distributed his small Atlanta broadcast TV station, WTBS, to cable systems across the country.

Cable Threatens Broadcasting

While only 14 percent of all U.S. homes received cable in 1977, by 1985 that percentage had climbed to 46. By the summer of 1997, basic cable channels had captured a larger prime-time audience than the broadcast networks had. The cable industry's rapid rise to prominence was partly due to the shortcomings of broadcast television. Beyond improving signal reception in most communities, the cable era introduced **narrowcasting**—the providing of specialized programming for diverse and fragmented groups. Attracting both advertisers and audiences, cable programs provide access to certain target audiences that cannot be guaranteed in broadcasting. For example, a golf-equipment manufacturer can buy ads on the Golf Channel and reach only golf enthusiasts. (See "Case Study: ESPN: Sports and Stories" on page 198 for more on narrowcasting.)

As cable channels have become more and more like specialized magazines or radio formats, they have siphoned off network viewers, and the networks' role as the chief programmer of our shared culture has eroded. For example, back in 1980, the Big Three evening news programs had a combined audience of more than fifty million on a typical weekday evening. By 2012 and 2013, though, that audience had shrunk to twenty million.[1] In addition, through its greater channel capacity, cable has provided more access. In many communities, various public, government, and educational channels have

FIGURE 6.1

A BASIC CABLE TELEVISION SYSTEM

Data from: Clear Creek Telephone & Television, www.ccmtc.com.

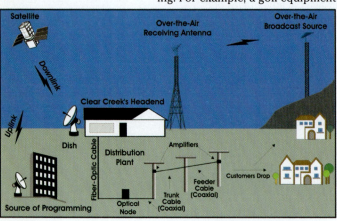

made it possible for anyone to air a point of view or produce a TV program. When it has lived up to its potential, cable has offered the public opportunities to participate more fully in the democratic promise of television.

Cable Services

Cable consumers usually choose programming from a two-tiered structure: basic cable services like CNN and premium cable services like HBO. These services are the production arm of the cable industry, supplying programming to the nation's six-thousand-plus cable operations, which function as program distributors to cable households.

Basic Cable Services

A typical basic cable system today includes a hundred-plus channel lineup composed of local broadcast signals; access channels (for local government, education, and general public use); regional PBS stations; and a variety of cable channels, such as ESPN, CNN, MTV, USA, Bravo, Nickelodeon, Disney, Comedy Central, BET, Telemundo, the Weather Channel, superstations (independent TV stations uplinked to a satellite, such as WGN in Chicago), and others, depending on the cable system's capacity and regional interests. Typically, local cable companies pay each of these satellite-delivered services between a few cents per month per subscriber ($.06 per month per subscriber for low-cost, low-demand channels like C-SPAN) and over $4 per month per subscriber (for high-cost, high-demand channels like ESPN). That fee is passed along to consumers as part of their basic monthly cable rate, which averaged—depending on the study and the location—between $70 and $90 per month by 2014. In addition, cable system capacities continue to increase as a result of high-bandwidth fiber-optic cable and *digital cable*, allowing for expanded offerings such as premium channels, pay-per-view programs, and video-on-demand.

Premium Cable Services

Besides basic programming, cable offers a wide range of special channels, known as premium channels, which lure customers with the promise of no advertising; recent and classic Hollywood movies; and original movies or series, like HBO's *Game of Thrones, True Detective,* or *Girls,* and Showtime's *Homeland, Masters of Sex,* or *Penny Dreadful*. These channels are a major source of revenue for cable companies: The cost to them is $4 to $6 per month per subscriber to carry a premium channel, but the cable company can charge customers $10 or more per month and reap a nice profit. Premium services also include pay-per-view (PPV) programs; video-on-demand (VOD); and interactive services that enable consumers to use their televisions to bank, shop, play games, and access the Internet.

Beginning in 1985, cable companies began introducing new viewing options for their customers. Pay-per-view (PPV) channels came first, offering recently released movies or special one-time sporting events to subscribers who paid a designated charge to their cable company, allowing them to view the program. In the early 2000s, cable companies

Jeff Kravitz/FilmMagic/Getty Images

"FAKE NEWS" SHOWS like *The Daily Show* and *Last Week Tonight* are available on the basic cable channel Comedy Central and the premium channel HBO, respectively. While their audiences are not as large as those of other basic cable news shows like *The O'Reilly Factor*, critics argue that the satiric shows have become a major source of news for the eighteen- to thirty-four-year-old age group because of their satire and sharp-witted lampoon of politics and the news media.

CASE STUDY

ESPN: Sports and Stories

A common way many of us satisfy our cultural and personal need for storytelling is through sports: We form loyalties to local and national teams. We follow the exploits of favorite players. We boo our team's rivals. We suffer with our team when the players have a bad game or an awful season. We celebrate the victories.

The appeal of sports is similar to the appeal of our favorite books, TV shows, and movies—we are interested in characters, in plot development, in conflict and drama. Sporting events have all of this. It's no coincidence, then, that the Super Bowl is annually the most watched single TV show around the world.

One of the best sports stories on television over the past thirty years, though, may be not a single sporting event but the tale of an upstart cable network based in Bristol, Connecticut. ESPN (Entertainment Sports Programming Network) began in 1979 and has now surpassed all the major broadcast networks as the "brand" that frames and presents sports on TV. In fact, cable operators around the country regard ESPN as the top service when it comes to helping them "gain and retain customers."[1] One of ESPN's main attractions is its "live" aspect and its ability to draw large TV and cable audiences—many of them young men—to events in real time. In a third-screen world full of mobile devices, this is a big plus for ESPN and something that advertisers especially like.

Today, the ESPN flagship channel reaches more than 100 million U.S. homes. And ESPN, Inc., now provides a sports smorgasbord—a menu of media offerings that includes ESPN2 (sporting events, news, and original programs), ESPN Classic (historic sporting events), ESPN Deportes (Spanish-language sports network), ESPN HD (high-definition channel), ESPNEWS (twenty-four-hour sports news channel), ESPNU (college games), ESPN Radio, and *ESPN The Magazine*. ESPN also creates original programming for TV and radio and operates ESPN.go.com, which is among the most popular sites on the Internet. Like CNN and MTV, ESPN makes its various channels available in more than two hundred countries.

Each year, ESPN's channels air more than five thousand live and original hours of sports programming, covering more than sixty-five different sports. In 2002, ESPN even outbid NBC for six years of NBA games—offering $2.4 billion, which at the time was just over a year's worth of ESPN revenues. But the major triumph of ESPN over the broadcast networks was probably wrestling the *Monday Night Football* contract away from its sports partner, ABC (both ESPN and ABC are owned by Disney). For eight years, starting in 2006, ESPN agreed to pay the NFL $1.1 billion a year for the broadcasting rights to *MNF*, the most highly rated sports series in prime-time TV history. In 2006, ABC turned over control of its sports programming division, ABC Sports, to ESPN, which now carries games on ABC under the ESPN logo.

The story of ESPN's birth also has its share of drama. The creator of ESPN was Bill Rasmussen, an out-of-work sports announcer who had been fired in 1978 by the New England Whalers (now the Carolina Hurricanes), a professional hockey team. Rasmussen wanted to bring sports programs to cable TV, which was just emerging from the shadow of broadcast television. But few backers thought this would be a good idea. Eventually, Rasmussen managed to land a contract with the NCAA to cover college games. He also lured Anheuser-Busch to become cable's first million-dollar advertiser. Getty Oil then agreed to put up $10 million to finance this sports adventure, and ESPN took off.

Today, ESPN is 80 percent owned by the Disney Company, while the Hearst Corporation holds the other 20 percent interest. The sports giant earned over $10 billion in worldwide revenue in 2012, and ESPN's cable ad sales and higher subscription fees were major reasons why Disney's sales revenue rose 8 percent in 2013, to more than $45 billion. ◢

Richard Freeda/Aurora Photos

introduced **video-on-demand (VOD)**. This service enables customers to choose among hundreds of titles and watch their selection whenever they want in the same way as a video, pausing and fast-forwarding when desired. Along with online downloading and streaming services and digital video recorders (DVRs), VOD services today are ending the era of the local video store.

DBS: Cable without Wires

By 1999, cable penetration had hit 70 percent. But **direct broadcast satellite (DBS)** services presented a big challenge to cable—especially in regions with rugged terrain and isolated homes, where the installation of cable wiring hasn't always been possible or profitable. Instead of using wires, DBS transmits its signal directly to small satellite dishes near or on customers' homes. As a result, cable penetration dropped to 44 percent by 2012. In addition, new over-the-air digital signals and better online options meant that many customers began moving away from either cable or DBS subscriptions.

Jojo Whilden/© HBO/Everett Collection

HBO series don't always attract massive audiences by broadcast standards: *Girls*, for example, a comedy about twentysomething women in New York City, averages about a million views per episode. They do, however, attract positive buzz, Emmy nominations, and pay-channel subscribers.

Satellite service began in the mid-1970s, when satellite dishes were set up to receive cable programming. Small-town and rural residents bypassed FCC restrictions by buying receiving dishes and downlinking, for free, the same channels that cable companies were supplying to wired communities. Not surprisingly, satellite programmers filed a flurry of legal challenges against those who were receiving their signals for free. Rural communities countered that they had the rights to the airspace above their own property; the satellite firms contended that their signals were being stolen. Because the law was unclear, a number of cable channels began scrambling their signals, and most satellite users had to buy or rent descramblers and subscribe to services, just as cable customers did.

Signal scrambling spawned companies that provided both receiving dishes and satellite program services for a monthly fee. In 1978, Japanese companies, which had been experimenting with "wireless cable" alternatives for years, started the first DBS system in Florida. By 1994, full-scale DBS service was available. Today, DBS companies like DirecTV and Dish (formerly the Dish Network) offer consumers most of the channels and tiers of service that cable companies carry (including Internet, television, and phone services) at a comparable and often cheaper monthly cost.

Technology and Convergence Change Viewing Habits

Among the biggest technical innovations in TV are nontelevision delivery systems. We can skip a network broadcast and still watch our favorite shows on DVRs, on laptops, or on mobile devices for free or for a nominal cost. Not only is TV being reinvented, but its audiences—although fragmented—are also growing. A few years ago, televisions glimmered in the average U.S. household just over seven hours a day; but by 2012, when you add in downloading, streaming, DVR playback, and smartphone/tablet viewing, that figure has expanded to more

LaunchPad ⊚
macmillanhighered.com
/mediaculture10e

David Gale
VP of New Media, MTV

Television Networks Evolve
Insiders discuss how cable and satellite have changed the television market.
Discussion: How might definitions of a TV network change in the realm of new digital media?

than eight hours a day. All these options mean that we are still watching TV but at different times, in different places, and on different kinds of screens.

Home Video

In 1975–76, the consumer introduction of videocassettes and *videocassette recorders (VCRs)* enabled viewers to tape-record TV programs and play them back later. Sony introduced the Betamax ("Beta") in 1975, and in 1976 JVC in Japan introduced a slightly larger format, VHS (Video Home System), which was incompatible with Beta. This triggered a marketing war, which helped drive costs down and put VCRs in more homes. Beta ultimately lost the consumer marketplace battle to VHS, whose larger tapes held more programming space.

VCRs also got a boost from a failed suit brought against Sony by Disney and MCA (now NBC Universal) in 1976: The two film studios alleged that home taping violated their movie copyrights. In 1979, a federal court ruled in favor of Sony and permitted home taping for personal use. In response, the movie studios quickly set up videotaping facilities so that they could rent and sell movies in video stores, which became popular in the early 1980s.

Over time, the VHS format gave way to DVDs. But today the standard DVD is threatened by both the Internet and a consumer market move toward *high-definition* DVDs. In fact, in 2007 another format war pitted high-definition Blu-ray DVDs (developed by Sony and used in the PlayStation 3) against the HD DVD format (developed by Toshiba and backed by Microsoft). Blu-ray was declared the victor when, in February 2008, Best Buy and Walmart, the nation's leading sellers of DVDs, decided to stop carrying HD DVD players and discs.

By 2012, more than 50 percent of U.S. homes had *DVRs (digital video recorders)*, which enable users to download specific programs onto the DVR's computer memory and watch at a later time. While offering greater flexibility for viewers, DVRs also provide a means to "watch" the watchers. DVRs give advertisers information about what each household views, allowing them to target viewers with specific ads when they play back their programs. This kind of technology has raised concerns among some lawmakers and consumer groups over the tracking of personal viewing and buying habits by marketers.

The impact of home video has been enormous. More than 95 percent of American homes today are equipped with either DVD or DVR players, resulting in two major developments: video rentals and time shifting. Video rental, formerly the province of walk-in video stores like Blockbuster, has given way to mail services like Netflix or online services like iTunes. **Time shifting,** which began during the VCR era, occurs when viewers record shows and watch them at a later, more convenient time. Time shifting and video rentals, however, have threatened the TV industry's advertising-driven business model; when viewers watch programs on DVDs and DVRs, they often aren't watching the ads that normally accompany network or cable shows.

The Third Screen: TV Converges with the Internet

The Internet has transformed the way many of us, especially younger generations, watch movies, TV, and cable programming. These new online viewing experiences are often labeled **third screens,**

WATCHING TV ONLINE
Hulu is the second most popular site for watching videos online—after Google's YouTube. Launched in 2008, the site offers content from NBC, ABC/Disney, Fox, PBS, Bravo, FX, USA, E!, movie studios, and others. Many viewers use Hulu for catch-up viewing, or watching episodes of current shows after they first air.

Kyodo/Newscom

usually meaning that computer screens are the third major way we view content (movie screens and traditional TV sets are the first and second screens, respectively). By far the most popular site for viewing video online is YouTube. Containing some original shows, classic TV episodes, full-length films, and of course the homemade user-uploaded clips that first made the site famous, YouTube remains at the center of video consumption online. Owned by Google, YouTube by 2014 was drawing more than one billion unique visitors per month and reporting these statistics on its Web site: "Over 6 billion hours of video are watched each month on YouTube . . . [and] 100 hours of video are uploaded [to the site] every minute."[2]

But YouTube has competition from sites that offer full-length episodes of current and recent programming. While viewers might be able to watch snippets of a show on YouTube, it's rare that they will find a full episode of popular, professionally produced TV shows like *Mad Men*, *New Girl*, and *Homeland*. Services like iTunes or Amazon Instant Video offer the ability to download full seasons of these shows, charging just $0.99 to $2.99 per episode. And streaming site Hulu (a partnership among NBC, Fox, and Disney) allows viewers to watch a certain number of episodes of a show for free—but with ads.

In late 2010, Hulu started Hulu Plus, a paid subscription service. For about $8 a month, viewers can stream full seasons of current and older programs and some movies and documentaries on their computer, TV, or mobile device. Hulu Plus had more than 6 million subscribers by 2014, up from 2 million in early 2012. Netflix, which started streaming videos back in 2008, has moved further away from a DVD-through-mail model and has become more focused on a less expensive (no postal costs) online streaming model. According to Nielsen's 2014 "Digital Consumer" report, "38 percent of U.S. consumers say they subscribe to or use Netflix to stream video."[3] With nearly 36 million U.S. subscribers by 2014 (Netflix reported 48 million streaming customers worldwide in June 2014), Netflix has become much bigger than Comcast, the largest cable company, with its 22 million U.S. subscribers.[4] Netflix has also been negotiating with major film and TV studios for the rights to stream current episodes of prime-time television shows—and seemed willing to pay between $70,000 and $100,000 per episode.[5]

In addition, cable TV giants like Comcast, Time Warner, and HBO are making programs available to download or stream through sites like Xfinity TV, TV Everywhere, and HBO GO. These programs are open only to subscribers who can download cable TV shows using a password and username. In 2012, Netflix, looking to increase its subscriber base, started talks with some of the largest U.S. cable operators about adding Netflix as part of their cable packages. However, cable and DBS companies are, thus far, resisting Netflix's proposition and are rolling out their own video-streaming services instead. Comcast introduced Xfinity Streampix in February 2012, expanding the Xfinity offerings to include even more movies from top Hollywood studios and past seasons of TV shows. The goal, according to Comcast executive Marcien Jenckes, is "to be the single stop for video needs for consumers."[6] Other companies have attempted to create streaming services of their own, though some, like Redbox, have failed to catch on.

In most cases, these third-screen sites operate as *catch-up services* rather than as replacements for broadcast or cable TV, allowing viewers and fans to "catch up" on movies and programs that played earlier in theaters or on television (see Figure 6.2 on page 202).

COMMUNITY aired on NBC for five seasons; the network canceled the low-rated cult favorite in 2014. However, Yahoo!, seeking to expand its original programming lineup, commissioned a new sixth season of thirteen episodes—a continuation that would have been unthinkable just five years earlier.

© NBC/Photofest

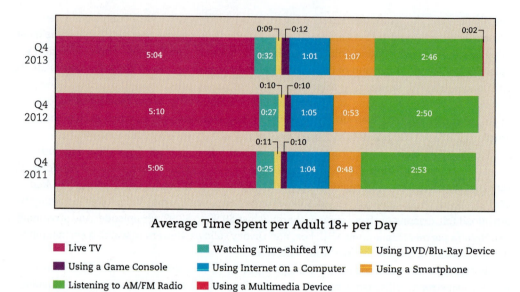

Q4 2013	5:04 · 0:32 · 0:09 · 0:12 · 1:01 · 1:07 · 2:46 · 0:02	
Q4 2012	5:10 · 0:27 · 0:10 · 0:10 · 1:05 · 0:53 · 2:50	
Q4 2011	5:06 · 0:25 · 0:11 · 0:10 · 1:04 · 0:48 · 2:53	

Average Time Spent per Adult 18+ per Day

■ Live TV   ■ Watching Time-shifted TV   ■ Using DVD/Blu-Ray Device
■ Using a Game Console   ■ Using Internet on a Computer   ■ Using a Smartphone
■ Listening to AM/FM Radio   ■ Using a Multimedia Device

Now, with devices like the Roku box and gaming consoles that can stream programming directly to our television sets, and newer television sets that are Internet ready, the TV has become one of the latest converged devices.

Fourth Screens: Smartphones and Mobile Video

According to Nielsen's 2014 "Digital Consumer" report, 84 percent of smartphone and tablet owners said they used those devices as an additional screen while they were watching television "at the same time."[7] Such multitasking has further accelerated with new **fourth-screen** technologies like smartphones, iPods, iPads, and mobile TV devices. For the past few years, these devices have forced major changes in consumer viewing habits and media content creation. Thus cable and DBS operators have begun to capitalize on this trend: Cablevision, Time Warner, and the Dish Network released iPad apps in 2011, allowing their subscribers to watch live TV on their iPads at no additional charge in the hopes of deterring their customers from cutting their subscriptions. However, some cable programmers—like Discovery and Viacom— are pushing back, arguing that their existing contracts with cable and DBS operators don't cover third or fourth screens.

The multifunctionality and portability of third- and fourth-screen devices means that consumers may no longer need television sets—just as landline telephones have fallen out of favor as more people rely solely on their mobile phones. If *where* we watch TV programming changes, does TV programming also need to change to keep up? Reality shows like *The Voice* and dramas like *Game of Thrones*—with many contestants or characters and multiple plotlines—are considered best suited for the digital age, enabling viewers to talk to one another on various social networks about favorite singers, characters, and plot twists at the same time as they watch these programs on traditional—or nontraditional—TV.

MEDIA ON THE GO
Downloading or streaming TV episodes to smartphones and other mobile devices lets us take our favorite shows with us wherever we go. By expanding where and when we consume such programming, these devices encourage the development of new ways to view and engage with the media. How have your own viewing habits changed over the last few years?

J. Emilio Flores/The New York Times/Redux Pictures

Major Programming Trends

Television programming began by borrowing genres from radio, such as variety shows, sitcoms, soap operas, and newscasts. Starting in 1955, the Big Three networks gradually moved their entertainment divisions to Los Angeles because of its proximity to Hollywood production studios. Network news operations, however, remained in New York. Ever since, Los Angeles and New York came to represent the two major branches of TV programming: *entertainment* and *information*. Although there is considerable blurring between these categories today, the two were once more distinct. In the sections that follow, we focus on these long-standing program developments and explore newer trends (see Figure 6.3).

TV Entertainment: Our Comic Culture

The networks began to move their entertainment divisions to Los Angeles partly because of the success of the pioneering comedy series *I Love Lucy* (1951–1957). *Lucy*'s owners and costars, Lucille Ball and Desi Arnaz, began filming the top-rated sitcom in California near their home. In 1951, *Lucy* became the first TV program to be filmed before a live Hollywood audience. Prior to the days of videotape (invented in 1956), the only way to preserve a live broadcast, other than filming it like a movie, was through a technique called **kinescope**. In this process, a film camera recorded a live TV show off a studio monitor. The quality of the kinescope was poor, and most series that were saved in this way have not survived. *I Love Lucy*, *Alfred Hitchcock Presents*, and *Dragnet* are among a handful of series from the 1950s that have endured

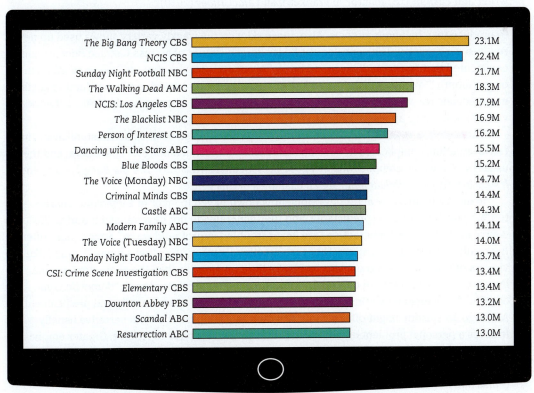

Show	Viewers
The Big Bang Theory CBS	23.1M
NCIS CBS	22.4M
Sunday Night Football NBC	21.7M
The Walking Dead AMC	18.3M
NCIS: Los Angeles CBS	17.9M
The Blacklist NBC	16.9M
Person of Interest CBS	16.2M
Dancing with the Stars ABC	15.5M
Blue Bloods CBS	15.2M
The Voice (Monday) NBC	14.7M
Criminal Minds CBS	14.4M
Castle ABC	14.3M
Modern Family ABC	14.1M
The Voice (Tuesday) NBC	14.0M
Monday Night Football ESPN	13.7M
CSI: Crime Scene Investigation CBS	13.4M
Elementary CBS	13.4M
Downton Abbey PBS	13.2M
Scandal ABC	13.0M
Resurrection ABC	13.0M

FIGURE 6.3

THE TOP 20 SHOWS OF THE 2013–14 SEASON*

*In millions of viewers, including first seven days of DVR data.

Data from: TV Guide, *"America's Most Watched: The Top 50 Shows of the 2013–2014 TV Season,"* June 6, 2014, www.tvguide.com /news/most-watched-shows-2013 -2014-1082628.aspx.

CBS Photo Archive/Getty Images

COMEDIES are often among the most popular shows on television. *I Love Lucy* was the top-ranked show from 1952 to 1955 and was a model for other shows, such as *Dick Van Dyke, Laverne & Shirley, Roseanne,* and *Will & Grace.*

because they were originally shot and preserved on film, like movies. In capturing *I Love Lucy* on film for future generations, the program's producers understood the enduring appeal of comedy, which is a central programming strategy both for broadcast networks and cable. TV comedy is usually delivered in two formats: sketch comedy and situation comedy (usually referred to as sitcoms).

Sketch comedy, or short comedy skits, was a key element in early TV variety shows, which also included singers, dancers, acrobats, animal acts, stand-up comics, and ventriloquists. According to one TV historian, variety shows "resurrected the essentials of stage variety entertainment" and played to noisy studio audiences.[8] Vaudeville and stage performers were TV's first stars of sketch comedy. They included Milton Berle, TV's first major celebrity, in *Texaco Star Theater* (1948–1967), and Sid Caesar, Imogene Coca, and Carl Reiner in *Your Show of Shows* (1950–1954), for which playwright Neil Simon, filmmakers Mel Brooks and Woody Allen, and writer Larry Gelbart (*M*A*S*H*) all served for a time as writers. Today, NBC's *Saturday Night Live* (1975–) carries on the sketch comedy tradition. Sketches on *SNL* have inspired several feature-length movies over the years, including *The Blues Brothers* (1980), *Wayne's World* (1992), *Stuart Saves His Family* (1995, starring former *SNL* writer and current U.S. senator Al Franken), and *MacGruber* (2010).

However, the hour-long variety series in which these skits appeared were more expensive to produce than half-hour sitcoms. Also, these skits on the weekly variety shows used up new routines very quickly. The ventriloquist Edgar Bergen (father of actress Candice Bergen) once commented that "no comedian should be on TV once a week; he shouldn't be on more than once a month."[9] With original skits and new sets being required each week, production costs mounted, and the vaudeville-influenced variety series faded. Since the early 1980s, network variety shows have appeared only as yearly specials.

The **situation comedy**, or *sitcom*, features a recurring cast; each episode establishes a narrative situation, complicates it, develops increasing confusion among its characters, and then usually resolves the complications.[10] *I Love Lucy, Seinfeld, New Girl, The Big Bang Theory,* and *It's Always Sunny in Philadelphia* are all examples of this genre.

In most sitcoms, character development is downplayed in favor of zany plots. Characters are usually static and predictable, and they generally do not develop much during the course of a series. Such characters "are never troubled in profound ways." Stress, more often the result of external confusion rather than emotional anxiety, "is always funny."[11] Much like viewers of soap operas, sitcom fans feel just a little bit smarter than the characters, whose lives seem wacky and out of control. In some sitcoms (once referred to as "domestic comedies"), characters and settings are typically more important than complicated predicaments. Although an episode might offer a goofy situation as a subplot, the main narrative usually features a personal problem or family crisis that characters have to resolve. Greater emphasis is placed on character development than on reestablishing the order that has been disrupted by confusion. Such comedies take place primarily at home (*Modern Family*), at the workplace (*Parks and Recreation*), or at both (*Curb Your Enthusiasm*).

In TV history, some sitcoms of the domestic variety have mixed dramatic and comedic elements. This blurring of serious and comic themes marks a contemporary hybrid, sometimes labeled *dramedy*, which has included such series as *The Wonder Years* (1988–1993), *Ally McBeal* (1997–2002), HBO's *Sex and the City* (1999–2004), Showtime's *The Big C* (2010–2013), and Fox's musical-dramedy *Glee* (2009–).

TV Entertainment: Our Dramatic Culture

Because the production of TV entertainment was centered in New York City in its early days, many of its ideas, sets, technicians, actors, and directors came from New York theater. Young stage actors—including Anne Bancroft, Ossie Davis, James Dean, Grace Kelly, Paul Newman, Sidney Poitier, Robert Redford, and Joanne Woodward—often worked in television if they could not find stage work. The TV dramas that grew from these early influences fit roughly into two categories: the anthology drama and the episodic series.

ABC/Photofest

Anthology Drama and the Miniseries

In the early 1950s, television—like cable in the early 1980s—served a more elite and wealthier audience. **Anthology dramas** brought live dramatic theater to that audience. Influenced by stage plays, anthologies offered new, artistically significant *teleplays* (scripts written for television), casts, directors, writers, and sets from one week to the next. In the 1952–53 season alone, there were eighteen anthology dramas, including *Alfred Hitchcock Presents* (1955–1965), the *Twilight Zone* (1959–1964), and *Kraft Television Theater* (1947–1958), which was created to introduce Kraft's Cheez Whiz.

The anthology's brief run as a dramatic staple on television ended for both economic and political reasons. First, advertisers disliked anthologies because they often presented stories containing complex human problems that were not easily resolved. The commercials that interrupted the drama, however, told upbeat stories in which problems were easily solved by purchasing a product; by contrast, anthologies made the simplicity of the commercial pitch ring false. A second reason for the demise of anthology dramas was a change in audience. The people who could afford TV sets in the early 1950s could also afford tickets to a play. For these viewers, the anthology drama was a welcome addition given their cultural tastes. By 1956, however, working- and middle-class families were increasingly able to afford television, and the prices of sets dropped. Anthology dramas were not as popular in this newly expanded market. Third, anthology dramas were expensive to produce—double the cost of most other TV genres in the 1950s—because each week meant a new story line, along with new writers, casts, and sets. Sponsors and networks came to realize that it would be easier and less expensive to build audience allegiance with an ongoing program featuring the same cast and set.

Finally, anthologies that dealt seriously with the changing social landscape were sometimes labeled "politically controversial." This was especially true during the attempts by Senator Joseph McCarthy and his followers to rid media industries and government agencies of left-leaning political influences. (See Chapter 16 for more on blacklisting.) By the early 1960s, this dramatic form had virtually disappeared from network television, although its legacy continues on public television with the imported British program *Masterpiece Theatre* (1971–)—now known as either *Masterpiece Classic* or *Masterpiece Mystery!*—the longest-running prime-time drama series on U.S. television.

In fact, these British shows resemble U.S. TV *miniseries*—serialized TV shows that run over a two-day to two-week period, usually on consecutive evenings. A cross between an extended anthology drama and a network serial, the most famous U.S. miniseries was probably *Roots* (1977), based on Alex Haley's novelized version of his family's slave history. The final episode of *Roots,* which ran on eight consecutive nights, drew an audience of more than 100 million viewers. Contemporary British series like *Doc Martin* (2005–), *Downton Abbey* (2010–), and *Sherlock* (2011–) last three to eight episodes over a few weeks, making them more like miniseries than traditional network dramas, even though they have multiple seasons. The miniseries has also experienced a recent resurgence in the United States, with high-quality and popular miniseries on cable like *True Detective* (HBO), *American Horror Story* (FX), and *Hatfields and McCoys* (History Channel).

Episodic Series

Abandoning anthologies, producers and writers increasingly developed **episodic series**, first used on radio in 1929. In this format, main characters continue from week to week, sets and locales remain the same, and technical crews stay with the program. The episodic series comes in two general types: chapter shows and serial programs.

Chapter shows are self-contained stories with a recurring set of main characters who confront a problem, face a series of conflicts, and find a resolution. This structure can be used in a wide range of sitcoms like *The Big Bang Theory* (2007–) and dramatic genres, including adult westerns like *Gunsmoke* (1955–1975); police/detective shows like *CSI: Crime Scene Investigation* (2000–); and science fiction like *Star Trek* (1966–1969). Culturally, television dramas often function as a window into the hopes and fears of the American psyche. For example, in the 1970s, police/detective dramas became a staple, mirroring anxieties about the urban unrest of the time, precipitated by the decline of manufacturing and the loss of factory jobs. Americans' popular entertainment reflected the idea of heroic police and tenacious detectives protecting a nation from menacing forces that were undermining the economy and the cities. Such shows as *Hawaii Five-O* (1968–1980), *The Mod Squad* (1968–1973), and *The Rockford Files* (1974–1980) all ranked among the nation's top-rated programs during that time.

In contrast to chapter shows, **serial programs** are open-ended episodic shows; that is, most story lines continue from episode to episode. Cheaper to produce than chapter shows, employing just a few indoor sets, and running five days a week, daytime *soap operas* are among the longest-running serial programs in the history of television. Acquiring their name from soap product ads that sponsored these programs in the days of fifteen-minute radio dramas, soaps feature cliff-hanging story lines and intimate close-up shots that tend to create strong audience allegiance. Soaps also probably do the best job of any genre at imitating the actual open-ended rhythms of daily life. However, popular daytime network soaps have mostly disappeared in the digital age, with so many choices and small screens drawing away viewers, especially younger ones. But *General Hospital* (1963–), *The Young and the Restless* (1973–), and two other serials were still kicking in the 2013–14 TV season. Just ten years earlier, though, ten daytime soaps ran on the networks' daytime schedules.

Another type of drama is the *hybrid,* which developed in the early 1980s with the appearance of *Hill Street Blues* (1981–1987). Often mixing comic situations and grim plots, this multiple-cast show looked like an open-ended soap opera. On occasion, as in real life, crimes were not solved and recurring characters died. As a hybrid form, *Hill Street Blues* combined elements of both chapter and serial television by featuring some self-contained plots that were resolved in a single episode as well as other plotlines that continued from week to week.

LaunchPad ◉

macmillanhighered.com
/mediaculture10e

Television Drama: Then and Now
Head to LaunchPad to watch clips from two different drama series: one several decades old, and one recent.
Discussion: What evidence of storytelling changes can you see by comparing and contrasting the two clips?

This blend has been used by many successful dramatic hybrids, including *The X-Files* (1993–2002), *Buffy the Vampire Slayer* (1997–2003), *Lost* (2004–2010), TNT's *The Closer* (2005–2012), and AMC's *Breaking Bad* (2008–2013) and *The Walking Dead* (2010–).

TV Information: Our Daily News Culture

For about forty years (from the 1960s to the 2000s), broadcast news, especially on local TV stations, consistently topped print journalism in national research polls that asked which news medium was most trustworthy. Most studies at the time suggested that this has to do with TV's intimacy as a medium—its ability to create loyalty with viewers who connect personally with the news anchors we "invite" into our living rooms each evening. Print reporters and editors, by comparison, seemed anonymous and detached. But this distinction began breaking down as print reporters started discussing their work on cable TV news programs and became more accessible to their readers through e-mail, blogs, and newspaper Web sites. In this section, we focus on the traditional network evening news, its history, and the changes in TV news ushered in by twenty-four-hour cable news channels.

Network News

Originally featuring a panel of reporters interrogating political figures, NBC's weekly *Meet the Press* (1947–) is the oldest show on television. Daily evening newscasts, though, began on NBC in February 1948 with the *Camel Newsreel Theater*, sponsored by the cigarette company. Originally a ten-minute Fox Movietone newsreel that was also shown in theaters, it became a live, fifteen-minute broadcast in 1949. In 1956, the *Huntley Brinkley Report* debuted with Chet Huntley in New York and David Brinkley in Washington, D.C. This coanchored NBC program became the most popular TV evening news show at the time and served as the dual-anchor model for hundreds of local news broadcasts. After Huntley retired in 1970, the program was renamed *NBC Nightly News*. Tom Brokaw eventually settled in as sole anchor in September 1983 and passed the chair to Brian Williams in 2004.

Over at CBS, the network's flagship evening news program, *The CBS-TV News* with Douglas Edwards, premiered in May 1948. In 1956, the program became the first news show to be videotaped for rebroadcast on **affiliate stations** (stations that contract with a network to carry its programs) in Central and Western time zones. Walter Cronkite succeeded Edwards in 1962, starting a nineteen-year run as the influential anchor of the renamed *CBS Evening News*. Some critics believe Cronkite's eventual on-air opposition to the Vietnam War helped convince mainstream Americans to oppose it. Cronkite retired and gave way to Dan Rather in 1981. In 2006, CBS hired Katie Couric to serve as the first woman solo anchor on a network evening news program. But with stagnant ratings, she was replaced in 2011 by Scott Pelley.

After premiering an unsuccessful daily program in 1948, ABC launched a daily news show in 1953, anchored by John Daly—the head of ABC News and the host of CBS's evening game show *What's My Line?* After Daly left in 1960, John Cameron Swayze, Peter Jennings, Harry Reasoner, and Howard K. Smith all took a turn in the anchor's chair. In 1978, *ABC World News Tonight* premiered, featuring four anchors: Frank Reynolds in Washington, D.C.; Jennings in

Showtime Networks/Photofest

MASTERS OF SEX, an American period-drama series, has become a signature program for the premium cable channel Showtime. It tracks the real-life sexuality researchers William Masters and Virginia Johnson in the 1950s and early 1960s. Cable dramas typically use shorter seasons than their network counterparts; seasons of *Masters of Sex* run for twelve episodes instead of twenty or twenty-two. This shorter schedule enables cable shows to attract stars like Michael Sheen and Lizzy Caplan, who were previously best known for movie roles. The lack of broadcast limits on pay-cable stations also allows shows to tackle subjects like sexuality in a more frank and direct way than did many drama series of the past.

CBS Photo Archive/Getty Images

WALTER CRONKITE
In 1968, after popular CBS news anchor Walter Cronkite visited Vietnam, CBS produced the documentary *Report from Vietnam by Walter Cronkite*. At the end of the program, Cronkite offered this terse observation: "It is increasingly clear to this reporter that the only rational way out then will be to negotiate, not as victors but as an honorable people who lived up to their pledge to defend democracy, and did the best they could." Most political observers said that Cronkite's opposition to the war influenced President Johnson's decision not to seek reelection.

London; Barbara Walters in New York; and Max Robinson in Chicago. Robinson was the first black reporter to coanchor a network news program, while Walters was the first woman. In 1983, Jennings became the sole anchor of the broadcast. After Jennings's death in 2005, his spot was shared by coanchors Elizabeth Vargas and Bob Woodruff (who was severely injured covering the Iraq War in 2006) until Charles Gibson—from ABC's *Good Morning America*—took over in 2006. Gibson retired in 2009 and was replaced by Diane Sawyer, formerly of CBS's *60 Minutes* and ABC's *Good Morning America*.

Cable News Changes the Game

The first 24/7 cable TV news channel, Cable News Network (CNN), premiered in 1980 and was the brainchild of Ted Turner, who had already revolutionized cable with his Atlanta-based superstation WTBS (Turner Broadcast Service). When Turner turned a profit with CNN in 1985 (along with its sister Headline News channel), the traditional networks began to take notice of cable news. The success of CNN revealed a need and a lucrative market for twenty-four-hour news. Spawning a host of competitors in the United States and worldwide, CNN now battles for viewers with other twenty-four-hour news providers, including the Fox News Channel; MSNBC; CNBC; Euronews; British Sky Broadcasting; and thousands of Web and blog sites, like *Politico*, the *Huffington Post*, the *Drudge Report*, and *Salon*.

Cable news has significantly changed the TV news game by offering viewers information and stories in a 24/7 loop. Rather than waiting until 5:30 or 6:30 P.M. to watch the national network news, viewers can access news updates and breaking stories at any time. Cable news also challenges the network program formulas. Daily opinion programs, such as MSNBC's *Rachel Maddow Show* and Fox News' *Sean Hannity Show*, often celebrate argument, opinion, and speculation over traditional reporting based on verified facts. These programs emerged primarily because of their low cost compared with that of traditional network news. At the same time, satirical "fake news" programs like *The Daily Show with Jon Stewart* and *The Colbert Report* have challenged traditional news outlets by discussing the news in larger contexts, something the conventional thirty-minute daily broadcasts rarely do. (See Chapter 14 for more on fake news programs.)

Reality TV and Other Enduring Genres

Up to this point, we have focused on long-standing TV program trends, but many other genres have played major roles in TV's history, both inside and outside prime time. Talk shows like the *Tonight Show* (1954–) have fed our curiosity about celebrities and politicians and have offered satire on politics and business. Game shows like *Jeopardy!* (which has been around in some version since 1964) have provided families with easy-to-digest current events and historical trivia. Variety programs like the *Ed Sullivan Show* (1948–1971) took center stage in Americans' cultural lives by introducing new comics, opera divas, and popular musical phenomena like Elvis Presley and the Beatles. Newsmagazines like *60 Minutes* (1968–) shed light on major events, from the Watergate scandal in the 1970s to the reelection of President Obama in 2012. And all kinds of sporting events—from boxing and wrestling to the Olympics and the Super Bowl—have allowed us to follow our favorite teams and athletes.

Reality-based programs are the newest significant trend; they include everything from *The Voice* and *Deadliest Catch* to *Top Chef* and *Teen Mom*. One reason for their popularity is that these shows introduce us to characters and people who seem more "like us" and less like celebrities. Additionally, these programs have helped the networks and cable providers deal with the high cost of programming. Featuring nonactors, cheap sets, and no extensive scripts, reality shows are much less expensive to produce than sitcoms and dramas. While reality-based programs have played a major role in network prime time since the late 1990s, the genre was actually inspired by cable's *The Real World* (1992–), the longest-running program on MTV. Changing locations and casts from season to season, *The Real World* follows a group of strangers who live and work together for a few months and records their interpersonal entanglements and up-and-down relationships. *The Real World* has significantly influenced the structure of today's reality TV programs, including *Survivor*, *Project Runway*, *Teen Mom,* and *Dancing with the Stars*. (See "Media Literacy and the Critical Process: TV and the State of Storytelling" on page 210.)

Another growing trend is Spanish-language television, like Univision and Telemundo. For the 2013–14 TV season, the popular network Univision reached about 3 million viewers in prime time each day (compared with 1.9 million for the CW or 10.6 million for CBS, the top-rated network). That was down from 3.7 million in 2012–13. But in June 2014, Univision's ratings soared during soccer's World Cup. Sometimes beating ESPN throughout the World Cup, Univision had nearly 7 million viewers for the Brazil–Mexico match. The first foreign-language U.S. network began in 1961, when the owners of the nation's first Spanish-language TV station in San Antonio acquired a TV station in Los Angeles, setting up what was then called the Spanish International Network. It officially became Univision in 1986 and has built audiences in major urban areas with large Hispanic populations through its popular talk-variety programs and *telenovelas* (Spanish-language soap operas, mostly produced in Mexico), which air each weekday evening. Today, Univision Communications owns and operates more than sixty TV stations in the United States. Its Univision Network, carried by seventeen hundred cable affiliates, reaches almost all U.S. Hispanic households.

Discovery Channel/Photofest

DISCOVERY CHANNEL launched in 1985 and is one of the most widely distributed cable networks today. Its dedication to top-quality nonfictional and reality programming—typically on themes of popular science, nature, history, and geography—has won the channel several Emmy nominations and awards. One of its most popular programs, *Deadliest Catch* (2005–), focuses on several crab fishing crews. The drama comes from the nail-biting action on the fishing vessels, but the interpersonal relationships— and rivalries—among cast members provide juicy story lines.

Public Television Struggles to Find Its Place

Another key programmer in TV history has been public television. Under President Lyndon Johnson, and in response to a report from the Carnegie Commission on Educational Television, Congress passed the Public Broadcasting Act of 1967, establishing the Corporation for Public Broadcasting (CPB) and later, in 1969, the Public Broadcasting Service (PBS). In part, Congress intended public television to target viewers who were "less attractive" to commercial networks and advertisers. Besides providing programs for viewers over age fifty, public television has figured prominently in programming for audiences under age twelve, with children's series like *Mister Rogers' Neighborhood* (1968–2001), *Sesame Street* (1969–), and *Barney & Friends* (1991–). The major networks have largely abdicated the responsibility of developing educational series aimed at children under age twelve. When Congress passed a law in 1996 ordering the networks to offer three hours of children's educational programming per week, the networks sidestepped this mandate by taking advantage of the law's vagueness on what constituted

Media Literacy and the Critical Process

1 DESCRIPTION. Pick a current reality program and a current sitcom or drama. Choose programs that either started in the last year or two or have been on television for roughly the same period of time. Now develop a "viewing sheet" that allows you to take notes as you watch the two programs over a three- to four-week period. Keep track of main characters, plotlines, settings, conflicts, and resolutions. Also track the main problems that are posed in the programs and how they are portrayed or worked out in each episode. Find out and compare the basic production costs of each program.

2 ANALYSIS. Look for patterns and differences in the ways stories are told in the two programs. At a general level, what are the conflicts about? (For example, are they about men versus women, managers versus employees, tradition versus change, individuals versus institutions, honesty versus dishonesty, authenticity versus artificiality?) How complicated or simple are the tensions in the two programs, and how are problems resolved? Are there some conflicts that you feel should not be permitted—like pitting

TV and the State of Storytelling

The rise of the reality program over the past decade has more to do with the cheaper cost of this genre than with the wild popularity of these programs. In fact, in the history of television and viewer numbers, traditional sitcoms and dramas—and even prime-time news programs like *60 Minutes* and *20/20*—have been far more popular than successful reality programs like *American Idol*. But when national broadcast TV executives cut costs by reducing writing and production staffs and hiring "regular people" instead of trained actors, does the craft of storytelling suffer at the expense of commercial savings? Can good stories be told in a reality program? In this exercise, let's compare the storytelling competence of a reality program with that of a more traditional comedy or drama.

older contestants against younger or white against black? Are there noticeable differences between "the look" of each program?

3 INTERPRETATION. What do some of the patterns mean? What seems to be the point of each program? What do the programs say about relationships, values, masculinity or femininity, power, social class, and so on?

4 EVALUATION. What are the strengths and weaknesses of each program? Which program would you judge as better at telling a compelling story that you want to watch each week?

How could each program improve its storytelling?

5 ENGAGEMENT. Either through online forums or via personal contacts, find other viewers of these programs. Ask them follow-up questions about what they like or don't like about such shows, what they might change, and what the programs' creators might do differently. Then report your findings to the programs' producers through a letter, a phone call, or an e-mail. Try to elicit responses from the producers about the status of their programs. How did they respond to your findings?

"educational" to claim that many of their routine sitcoms, cartoons, and dramatic shows satisfied the legislation's requirements.

The original Carnegie Commission report also recommended that Congress create a financial plan to provide long-term support for public television, in part to protect it from political interference. However, Congress did not do this, nor did it require wealthy commercial broadcasters to subsidize public television (as many other countries do). As federal funding levels dropped in the 1980s, PBS depended more and more on corporate underwriting. By the early 2000s, corporate sponsors funded more than 25 percent of all public television, although corporate sponsorship declined in 2009 as the economy suffered. In 2010, Congress gave an extra $25 million to PBS to help during the economic downturn.[12] However, only about 15 percent of funding for public broadcasting (which includes both television and radio) has come from the federal government, with the bulk of support being provided by viewers, listeners, and corporations.

Despite support from the Obama administration, in 2011 the Republican-controlled House voted to ax all funding of the CPB in 2013. The Senate killed this effort, and the CPB did receive $430 million in federal funding for 2012. Anticipating decreased government support, public broadcasting began inserting promotional messages from sponsors every fifteen minutes in some programs beginning in fall 2011.[13] Some critics and public TV executives worried that such corporate messages would offend loyal viewers accustomed to uninterrupted programming and would compromise public television's mission to air programs that might be considered controversial or commercially less viable.

Also troubling to public television (in contrast to public radio, which increased its audience from two million listeners per week in 1980 to more than thirty million per week in 2010) is that the audience for PBS has declined. PBS content chief John Boland attributed the loss to the same market fragmentation and third-screen technology that has plagued the broadcast networks: "We are spread thin in trying to maintain our TV service and meet the needs of consumers on other platforms."[14] One viewer segment that PBS is watching closely is the children's audience—which declined 22 percent between 2010 and 2014. Initially PBS's toughest competitors were cable services like Nickelodeon, Nick Jr., Disney, Disney Junior, Sprout, and the Cartoon Network. But those channels saw similar ratings declines in that same time period. One report suggests that more and more parents are using on-demand services like Netflix to control what their children watch, while other reports indicate that educational video games and tablets are commanding more attention from younger viewers.[15]

Photofest

Regulatory Challenges to Television and Cable

Though cable cut into broadcast TV's viewership, both types of programming came under scrutiny from the U.S. government. Initially, thanks to extensive lobbying efforts, cable's growth was suppressed to ensure that no harm came to local broadcasters and traditional TV networks' ad revenue streams. Later, as cable developed, FCC officials worried that power and profits were growing increasingly concentrated in fewer and fewer industry players' hands. Thus the FCC set out to mitigate the situation through a variety of rules and regulations.

Government Regulations Temporarily Restrict Network Control

By the late 1960s, a progressive and active FCC, increasingly concerned about the monopoly-like impact of the Big Three networks, passed a series of regulations that began undercutting their power. The first, the **Prime Time Access Rule (PTAR)**, introduced in April 1970, reduced the networks' control of prime-time programming from four to three hours. This move was an effort to encourage more local news and public affairs programs, usually slated for the 6–7 P.M. time block. However, most stations simply ran thirty minutes of local news at 6 P.M. and then acquired syndicated quiz shows (*Wheel of Fortune*) or *infotainment* programs (*Entertainment Tonight*) to fill up the remaining half hour, during which they could sell lucrative regional ads.

In a second move, in 1970 the FCC created the Financial Interest and Syndication Rules—called **fin-syn**—which "constituted the most damaging attack against the network TV monopoly in FCC history," according to one historian.[16] Throughout the 1960s, the networks had run their own syndication companies. The networks sometimes demanded as much as 50 percent of the profits that TV producers earned from airing older shows as reruns in local TV markets. This was the case even though those shows were no longer on the networks and most of them had been developed not by the networks but by independent companies. The networks claimed that since popular TV series had gained a national audience because of the networks' reach, production companies owed them compensation even after shows completed their prime-time runs. The FCC banned the networks from reaping such profits from program syndication.

The Department of Justice instituted a third policy action in 1975. Reacting to a number of legal claims against monopolistic practices, the Justice Department limited the networks' production of non-news shows, requiring them to seek most of their programming from independent production companies and film studios. Initially, the limit was three hours of network-created prime-time entertainment programs per week, but this was raised to five hours by the late 1980s. In addition, the networks were limited to producing eight hours per week of in-house entertainment or non-news programs outside prime time, most of which were devoted to soap operas (which were inexpensive to produce and popular with advertisers). However, given that the networks could produce their own TV newsmagazines and select which programs to license, they retained a great deal of power over the content of prime-time television.

With the growth of cable and home video in the 1990s, the FCC gradually phased out the ban limiting network production because the TV market grew more competitive. Beginning in 1995, the networks were again allowed to syndicate and profit from rerun programs, but only from those they produced. The elimination of fin-syn and other rules opened the door for megadeals (such as Disney's acquisition of ABC in 1995) that have constrained independent producers from creating new shows and competing in prime time. Many independent companies and TV critics have complained that the corporations that now own the networks—Disney, CBS, 21st Century Fox, and Comcast—have exerted too much power and control over broadcast television content.

Balancing Cable's Growth against Broadcasters' Interests

By the early 1970s, cable's rapid growth, capacity for more channels, and better reception led the FCC to seriously examine industry issues. In 1972, the commission updated or enacted two regulations with long-term effects on cable's expansion: must-carry rules and access-channel mandates.

Must-Carry Rules

First established by the FCC in 1965 and reaffirmed in 1972, the **must-carry rules** required all cable operators to assign channels to and carry all local TV broadcasts on their systems. This rule ensured that local network affiliates, independent stations (those not carrying network programs), and public television channels would benefit from cable's clearer reception. However, to protect regional TV stations and their local advertising, the guidelines limited the number of distant commercial TV signals that a cable system could import to two or three independent stations per market. The guidelines also prohibited cable companies from bringing in network-affiliated stations from another city when a local station already carried that network's programming.

Access-Channel Mandates

In 1972, the FCC also mandated **access channels** in the nation's top one hundred TV markets, requiring cable systems to provide and fund a tier of nonbroadcast channels dedicated to local education, government, and the public. The FCC required large-market cable operators to

MEDIA & CULTURE

IS THE ERA OF A MASS AUDIENCE OVER?

p. 187

12M

the record-breaking first print run of
the last *Harry Potter* book

p. 349

$35.9B

total global movie box-office revenue in 2013

p. 255

CAN MOVIES CAUSE REAL-WORLD VIOLENCE?

p. 511

38%

THE AMOUNT OF HOUSEHOLDS WITH A
NETFLIX SUBSCRIPTION IN 2013

p. 261

▲
SEINFELD (1989–1998)
was not an immediate hit,
but it was in the ratings top
three for the final five of its
nine seasons. Now, over
twenty-five years after its first
episode, the show can still be
seen in heavy syndication on
TV. Produced by Sony Pictures
Television, *Seinfeld* is the type
of successful show the fin-syn
rules targeted to keep out of
the networks' hands.

© Castle Rock Entertainment/Everett Collection

assign separate channels for each access service, while cable operators in smaller markets (and with fewer channels) could require education, government, and the public to share one channel. In addition to free public-access channels, the FCC called for **leased channels**. Citizens could buy time on these channels and produce their own programs or present controversial views.

Cable's Role: Electronic Publisher or Common Carrier?

Because the Communications Act of 1934 had not anticipated cable, the industry's regulatory status was unclear at first. In the 1970s, cable operators argued that they should be considered **electronic publishers** and be able to choose which channels and content to carry. Cable companies wanted the same "publishing" freedoms and legal protections that broadcast and print media enjoyed in selecting content. Just as local broadcasters could choose to carry local news or *Jeopardy!* at 6 P.M., cable companies wanted to choose what channels to carry.

At the time, the FCC argued the opposite: Cable systems were **common carriers**, providing services that do not get involved in content. Like telephone operators, who do not question the topics of personal conversations ("Hi, I'm the phone company, and what are you going to be talking about today?"), cable companies, the FCC argued, should offer at least part of their services on a first-come, first-served basis to whoever could pay the rate.

In 1979, the debate over this issue ended in the landmark *Midwest Video* case, when the U.S. Supreme Court upheld the rights of cable companies to determine channel content and defined the industry as a form of "electronic publishing."[17] Although the FCC could no longer mandate channels' content, the Court said that communities could "request" access channels as part of contract negotiations in the franchising process. Access channels are no longer a requirement, but most cable companies continue to offer them in some form to remain on good terms with their communities.

Intriguingly, must-carry rules seem to contradict the *Midwest Video* ruling, since they require cable operators to carry certain local content. But this is a quirky exception to the *Midwest Video* ruling—mostly due to politics and economics. Must-carry rules have endured because of the lobbying power of the National Association of Broadcasters and the major TV networks. Over the years, these groups have successfully argued that cable companies should carry most local over-the-air broadcast stations on their systems so that local broadcasters can stay financially viable as cable systems expand their menus of channels and services.

Franchising Frenzy

After the *Midwest Video* decision, the future of cable programming was secure, and competition to obtain franchises to supply local cable service became intense. Essentially, a cable franchise is a mini-monopoly awarded by a local community to the most attractive bidder, usually for a fifteen-year period. Although a few large cities permitted two companies to build different parts of their cable systems, most communities granted franchises to only one company so that there wouldn't be more than one operator trampling over private property to string wire from utility poles or to bury cables underground. Most of the nation's cable systems were built between the late 1970s and the early 1990s.

During the franchising process, a city (or state) would outline its cable system needs and request bids from various cable companies. (Potential cable companies were prohibited from also owning broadcast stations or newspapers in the community.) In its bid, a company would make a list of promises to the city about construction schedules, system design, subscription rates, channel capacity, types of programming, financial backing, deadlines, and a *franchise fee*: the money the cable company would pay the city annually for the right to operate the local cable system. Lots of wheeling and dealing transpired in these negotiations, along with occasional corruption (e.g., paying off local city officials who voted on which company got the franchise), as few laws existed to regulate franchise negotiations. Often, battles over broken promises, unreasonable contracts, or escalating rates ended up in court.

Today, a federal cable policy act from 1984 dictates the franchise fees for most U.S. municipalities. This act helps cities and municipalities use such fees to establish and fund access channels for local government, educational, and community programming as part of their license agreement. For example, Groton, Massachusetts (population around ten thousand), has a cable contract with Charter Communications. According to the terms of the contract with Groton, Charter returned 4.25 percent of its revenue to the town (5 percent is the maximum a city can charge a cable operator). This money, which has amounted to about $100,000 a year, helped underwrite the city's cable-access programs and other community services.

The Telecommunications Act of 1996

Between 1984 and 1996, lawmakers went back and forth on cable rates and rules, creating a number of cable acts. One Congress would try to end *must-carry rules* or abandon rate regulation, and then a later one would restore the rules. Congress finally rewrote the nation's communications laws in the **Telecommunications Act of 1996**, bringing cable fully under the federal rules that had long governed the telephone, radio, and TV industries. In its most significant move, Congress used the Telecommunications Act to knock down regulatory barriers, allowing regional phone companies, long-distance carriers, and cable companies to enter one another's markets. The act allows cable companies to offer telephone services, and it permits phone companies to offer Internet services and buy or construct cable systems in communities with fewer than fifty thousand residents. For the first time, owners could operate TV or radio stations in the same market where they owned a cable system. Congress hoped that the new rules would spur competition and lower both phone and cable rates, but this has not usually happened. Instead, cable and phone companies have merged operations in many markets, keeping prices at a premium and competition to a minimum.

The 1996 act has had a mixed impact on cable customers. Cable companies argued that it would lead to more competition and innovations in programming, services, and technology. But in fact, there is not extensive competition in cable. About 90 percent of communities in the United States still have only one local cable company. In these areas, cable rates have risen faster; and in communities with multiple cable providers, the competition makes a difference—monthly rates are an average of 10 percent lower, according to one FCC study.[18] The rise of DBS companies like Dish in the last few years has also made cable prices more competitive.

Still, the cable industry has delivered on some of its technology promises, investing nearly $150 billion in technological infrastructure between 1996 and 2009, with most of the funds used for installing high-speed fiber-optic wires to carry TV and phone services. This has enabled cable companies to offer what they call the "triple play"—or the *bundling* of digital cable television, broadband Internet, and telephone service. By 2013, U.S. cable companies had signed more than forty-six million households to digital programming packages, while almost fifty million households had high-speed cable Internet service and twenty-six million households received their telephone service from cable companies.[19]

The Economics and Ownership of Television and Cable

It is not much of a stretch to define TV programming as a system that mostly delivers viewers to merchandise displayed in blocks of ads. And with more than $60 billion at stake in advertising revenues each year, networks and cable services work hard to attract the audiences and subscribers that bring in the advertising dollars. But although broadcast and cable advertising have declined in prominence, one recent study reported that more than 80 percent of consumers say that TV advertising—of all ad formats—has the most impact or influence on their buying decisions. A distant second, third, and fourth in the study were magazines (50 percent), online (47 percent), and newspapers (44 percent).[20] (See Figure 6.4 for costs for a thirty-second commercial during prime-time programs.) To understand the TV economy today, we need to examine the production, distribution, and syndication of programming;

FIGURE 6.4

PRIME-TIME NETWORK TV PRICING, 2013–14

The average costs are shown for a thirty-second commercial during prime-time programs on Monday and Thursday nights in 2013–14.

Data from: Jeanine Poggi, "TV Ad Prices: Football Is Still King," Advertising Age, October 20, 2013, adage.com/article/media/tv-ad-prices-football-king/244832/.

Note: * = Canceled shows

Monday

	8:00pm	8:30pm	9:00pm	9:30pm	10:00pm
ABC	Dancing with the Stars ($106,342)				Castle ($124,050)
CBS	How I Met Your Mother ($165,999)		2 Broke Girls ($175,508)	Mom ($139,070)	Hostages* ($133,185)
NBC	The Voice ($294,038)				The Blacklist ($201,650)
FOX	Bones ($159,932)		Sleepy Hollow ($137,610)		no network programming

Thursday

	8:00pm	8:30pm	9:00pm	9:30pm	10:00pm
ABC	Wonderland* ($97,138)		Grey's Anatomy ($204,658)		Scandal ($207,053)
CBS	The Big Bang Theory ($316,912)	The Millers* ($174,442)	The Crazy Ones* ($167,569)	Two and a Half Men ($183,904)	Elementary ($127,700)
NBC	Parks and Recreation ($78,146)	Welcome to the Family* ($62,368)	Sean Saves the World* ($80,939)	Michael J. Fox Show* ($95,663)	Parenthood ($89,278)
FOX	The X-Factor Results* ($169,255)		Glee ($171,757)		no network programming

the rating systems that set advertising rates; and the ownership structure that controls programming and delivers content to our homes.

Production

The key to the TV industry's success is offering programs that viewers will habitually watch each week—whether at scheduled times or via catch-up viewing. The networks, producers, and film studios spend fortunes creating programs that they hope will keep us coming back.

Production costs generally fall into two categories: below-the-line and above-the-line. *Below-the-line* costs, which account for roughly 40 percent of a new program's production budget, include the technical, or "hardware," side of production: equipment, special effects, cameras and crews, sets and designers, carpenters, electricians, art directors, wardrobe, lighting, and transportation. *Above-the-line*, or "software," costs include the creative talent: actors, writers, producers, editors, and directors. These costs account for about 60 percent of a program's budget, except in the case of successful long-running series (like *Friends* or *The Big Bang Theory*), in which salary demands by actors can drive up above-the-line costs to more than 90 percent.

Most prime-time programs today are developed by independent production companies that are owned or backed by a major film studio, such as Sony or Disney. In addition to providing and renting production facilities, these film studios serve as a bank, offering enough capital to carry producers through one or more seasons. In television, programs are funded through **deficit financing**. This means that the production company leases the show to a network or cable channel for a license fee that is actually lower than the cost of production. (The company hopes to recoup this loss later in lucrative rerun syndication.) Typically, a network leases an episode of a one-hour drama for about $1.5 million for two airings. Each episode, however, might cost the program's producers about $2.5 million to make, meaning they lose about $1 million per episode. After two years of production (usually forty-four to forty-six episodes), an average network show builds up a large deficit.

Because of smaller audiences and fewer episodes per season, costs for original programs on cable channels are lower than those for network broadcasts.[21] On average, in 2012–13 cable channels paid about $1 million per episode in licensing fees to production companies. Some cable shows, like AMC's *Breaking Bad*, cost about $3 million per episode, but since cable seasons are shorter (usually ten to thirteen episodes per season, compared to twenty-two to twenty-three for broadcast networks), cable channels build up smaller deficits. And unlike networks, cable channels have two revenue streams to pay for original programs—monthly subscription fees and advertising. (However, because network audiences are usually larger, ad revenue is higher for networks.) Cable channels also keep costs down by airing three to four new programs a year at most, compared to the ten to twenty that the broadcast networks air.

Still, both networks and cable channels build up deficits. This is where film studios like Disney, Sony, and Twentieth (now 21st) Century Fox have been playing a crucial role:

OFF-NETWORK SYNDICATION programs often include reruns of popular network sitcoms like *The Big Bang Theory*, which airs on local stations as well as cable channel TBS—where it sometimes beats network programming in the ratings.

CBS/Photofest

They finance the deficit and hope to profit on lucrative deals when the show—like *CSI*, *Friends*, *Bones*, or *The Office*—goes into domestic and international syndication.

To save money and control content, many networks and cable stations create programs that are less expensive than sitcoms and dramas. These include TV newsmagazines and reality programs. For example, NBC's *Dateline* requires only about half the outlay (between $700,000 and $900,000 per episode) demanded by a new hour-long drama. In addition, by producing projects in-house, networks and cable channels avoid paying license fees to independent producers and movie studio production companies.

Distribution

Programs are paid for in a variety of ways. Cable service providers (e.g., Time Warner Cable or Cablevision) rely mostly on customer subscriptions to pay for distributing their channels, but they also have to pay the broadcast networks **retransmission fees** to carry network channels and programming. While broadcast networks do earn carriage fees from cable and DBS providers, they pay *affiliate stations* license fees to carry their programs. In return, the networks sell the bulk of advertising time to recoup their fees and their investments in these programs. In this arrangement, local stations receive national programs that attract large local audiences and are allotted some local ad time to sell during the programs to generate their own revenue.

A common misconception is that TV networks own their affiliated stations. This is not usually true. Although traditional networks like NBC own stations in major markets like New York, Los Angeles, and Chicago, throughout most of the country networks sign short-term contracts to rent time on local stations. Years ago, the FCC placed restrictions on network-owned-and-operated stations (called **O & Os**). But the sweeping Telecommunications Act of 1996 abolished most ownership restrictions. Today, one owner is permitted to reach up to 39 percent of the nation's 120 million–plus TV households.

Although a local affiliate typically carries a network's entire lineup, a station may substitute a network's program. According to *clearance rules* established in the 1940s by the Justice Department and the FCC, all local affiliates are ultimately responsible for the content of their channels and must clear, or approve, all network programming. Over the years, some of the circumstances in which local affiliates have rejected a network's programming have been controversial. For example, in 1956 singer Nat King Cole was one of the first African American performers to host a network variety program. As a result of pressure applied by several white southern organizations, though, the program had trouble attracting a national sponsor. When some affiliates, both southern and northern, refused to carry the program, NBC canceled it in 1957. More recently, affiliates may occasionally substitute other programming for network programs they think may offend their local audiences, especially if the programs contain excessive violence or explicit sexual content.

Syndication Keeps Shows Going and Going . . .

Syndication—leasing TV stations or cable networks the exclusive right to air TV shows—is a critical component of the distribution process. Each year, executives from thousands of local TV stations and cable firms gather at the National Association of Television Program Executives (NATPE) convention to buy or barter for programs that are up for syndication. In so doing, they acquire the exclusive local market rights, usually for two- or three-year periods, to game shows, talk shows, and **evergreens**—popular old network reruns, such as *I Love Lucy*.

Syndication plays a large role in programming for both broadcast and cable networks. For local network-affiliated stations, syndicated programs are often used during **fringe time**—programming immediately before the evening's prime-time schedule (*early fringe*) and following the local evening news or a network late-night talk show (*late fringe*). Cable channels also syndicate network shows but are more flexible with time slots; for example, TNT may run older network syndicated episodes of *Law & Order* or *Bones* during its prime-time schedule, along with original cable programs like *Rizzoli & Isles* or *Major Crimes*.

Types of Syndication

In **off-network syndication** (commonly called "reruns"), older programs that no longer run during network prime time are made available for reruns to local stations, cable operators, online services, and foreign markets. This type of syndication occurs when a program builds up a supply of episodes (usually four seasons' worth) that are then leased to hundreds of TV stations and cable or DBS providers in the United States and overseas. A show can be put into rerun syndication even if new episodes are airing on network television. Rerun, or off-network, syndication is the key to erasing the losses generated by deficit financing. With a successful program, the profits can be enormous. For instance, the early rerun cycle of *Friends* earned nearly $4 million an episode from syndication in 250-plus markets, plus cable, totaling over $1 billion. Because the show's success meant the original production costs were already covered, the syndication market became almost pure profit for the producers and their backers. This is why deficit financing endures: Although investors rarely hit the jackpot, when they do, the revenues more than cover a lot of losses and failed programs.

First-run syndication is any program specifically produced for sale into syndication markets. Quiz programs such as *Wheel of Fortune* and daytime talk or advice shows like *The Ellen DeGeneres Show* or *Dr. Phil* are made for first-run syndication. The producers of these programs usually sell them directly to local markets around the country and the world.

Barter versus Cash Deals

Most financing of television syndication is either a cash deal or a barter deal. In a *cash deal*, the distributor offers a series for syndication to the highest bidder. Because of exclusive contractual arrangements, programs air on only one broadcast outlet per city in a major TV market or, in the case of cable, on one cable channel's service across the country. Whoever bids the most gets to syndicate the program (which can range from a few thousand dollars for a week's worth of episodes in a small market to $250,000 a week in a large market). In a variation of a cash deal called *cash-plus*, distributors retain some time to sell national commercial spots in successful syndicated shows (when the show is distributed, it already contains the national ads). While this means the local station has less ad time to sell, it also usually pays less for the syndicated show.

Although syndicators prefer cash deals, *barter deals* are usually arranged for new, untested, or older but less popular programs. In a straight barter deal, no money changes hands. Instead, a syndicator offers a program to a local TV station in exchange for a split of the advertising revenue. For example, in a 7/5 barter deal, during each airing the show's producers and syndicator retain seven minutes of ad time for national spots and leave stations with five minutes of ad time for local spots. As programs become more profitable, syndicators repackage and lease the shows as cash-plus deals.

FIRST-RUN SYNDICATION programs often include talk shows like *The Ellen DeGeneres Show*, which debuted in 2003 and is now one of the highest-rated daytime series.

Warner Bros. Television/Photofest

Measuring Television Viewing

Primarily, TV shows live or die based on how satisfied advertisers are with the quantity and quality of the viewing audience. Since 1950, the major organization that tracks and rates prime-time viewing has been the Nielsen Corporation, which estimates what viewers are watching in the nation's major markets. Ratings services like Nielsen provide advertisers, broadcast networks, local stations, and cable channels with considerable detail about viewers—from race and gender to age, occupation, and educational background.

The Impact of Ratings and Shares on Programming

In TV measurement, a **rating** is a statistical estimate expressed as the percentage of households that are tuned to a program in the market being sampled. Another audience measure is the **share**, a statistical estimate of the percentage of homes that are tuned to a specific program compared with those using their sets at the time of the sample. For instance, let's say on a typical night that 5,000 metered homes are sampled by Nielsen in 210 large U.S. cities, and 4,000 of those households have their TV sets turned on. Of those 4,000, about 1,000 are tuned to *The Voice* on NBC. The rating for that show is 20 percent—that is, 1,000 households watching *The Voice* out of 5,000 TV sets monitored. The share is 25 percent—1,000 homes watching *The Voice* out of a total of 4,000 sets turned on.

The importance of ratings and shares to the survival of TV programs cannot be overestimated. In practice, television is an industry in which networks, producers, and distributors target, guarantee, and "sell" viewers in blocks to advertisers. Audience measurement tells advertisers not only how many people are watching but, more important, what kinds of people are watching. Prime-time advertisers on the broadcast networks have mainly been interested in reaching relatively affluent eighteen- to forty-nine-year-old viewers, who account for most consumer spending. If a show is attracting those viewers, advertisers will compete to buy time during that program. Typically, as many as nine out of ten new shows introduced each fall on the networks either do not attain the required ratings or fail to reach the "right" viewers. The result is cancellation. Cable, in contrast, targets smaller audiences, so programs that do not attract a large audience might survive on cable because most of cable's revenues come from subscription fees rather than advertising. For example, on cable, AMC's award-winning *Breaking Bad* was considered successful. However, that show rarely attracted an audience of over 2 million in its first four seasons. But by the fifth and final season, its audience had grown to 6 million viewers, and the show's finale drew over 10 million viewers in 2013. (The show's creator, Vince Gilligan, has credited Netflix with *Breaking Bad*'s rating surge, because its streaming service allowed viewers to catch up with the series.) By comparison, CBS's *NCIS* drew an average audience of 21.6 million for each show in 2012–13.

Assessing Today's Converged and Multiscreen Markets

During the height of the network era, a prime-time series with a rating of 17 or 18 and a share of between 28 and 30 was generally a success. By the late 2000s, though, with increasing competition from cable, DVDs, and the Internet, the threshold for success had dropped to a rating of 3 or 4 and a share of under 10. In fact, with all the screen options and targeted audiences, it is

NICHE MARKETS
As TV's audience gets fragmented among broadcast, cable, DVRs, and the Internet, some shows have focused on targeting smaller niche audiences instead of the broad public. IFC's *Portlandia*, for example, has a relatively small but devoted fan base that supports the show's culturally specific satire.

Scott Green/© IFC/Everett Collection

Program	Network	Date	Rating
1 *M*A*S*H* (final episode)	CBS	2/28/83	60.2
2 *Dallas* ("Who Shot J.R.?" episode)	CBS	11/21/80	53.3
3 *The Fugitive* (final episode)	ABC	8/29/67	45.9
4 *Cheers* (final episode)	NBC	5/20/93	45.5
5 *Ed Sullivan Show* (Beatles' first U.S. TV appearance)	CBS	2/9/64	45.3
6 *Beverly Hillbillies*	CBS	1/8/64	44.0
7 *Ed Sullivan Show* (Beatles' second U.S. TV appearance)	CBS	2/16/64	43.8
8 *Beverly Hillbillies*	CBS	1/15/64	42.8
9 *Beverly Hillbillies*	CBS	2/26/64	42.4
10 *Beverly Hillbillies*	CBS	3/25/64	42.2

TABLE 6.1

THE TOP 10 HIGHEST-RATED TV SERIES; INDIVIDUAL PROGRAMS (SINCE 1960)

Note: The *Seinfeld* finale, which aired in May 1998, drew a rating of 41-plus and a total viewership of 76 million; in contrast, the final episode of *Friends* in May 2004 had a 25 rating and drew about 52 million viewers. (The *M*A*S*H* finale in 1983 had more than 100 million viewers.)

Data from: The World Almanac and Book of Facts, 1997 *(Mahwah, N.J.: World Almanac Books, 1996), 296;* Corbett Steinberg, TV Facts *(New York: Facts on File Publications, 1985);* A.C. Nielsen Media Research.

almost impossible for a TV program today to crack the highest-rated series list (see Table 6.1). Unfortunately, many popular programs have been canceled over the years because advertisers considered their audiences too young, too old, or too poor. To account for the rise of DVRs, Nielsen now offers three versions of its ratings: live; live plus twenty-four hours, counting how many DVR users played shows within a day of recording; and live plus seven days, adding in how many viewers played the shows within a week. During the 2011–12 TV season, many shows starting drawing much larger audiences when they added DVR playbacks to their original first-time scheduled showing on the networks.[22] This trend has continued, and those series that benefit from large boosts in live plus seven numbers include huge hits like *The Big Bang Theory*, moderate performers like *Agents of S.H.I.E.L.D.*, and more niche-specific shows like *New Girl*.[23]

In its efforts to keep up with TV's move to smaller screens, Nielsen is also using special software to track TV viewing on computers and mobile devices. Today, with the fragmentation of media audiences, the increase in third- and fourth-screen technologies, and the decline in traditional TV set viewing, targeting smaller niche markets and consumers has become advertisers' main game.

The biggest revenue game changer in the small-screen world will probably be Google's YouTube, which in 2011 and 2012 entered into a joint venture with nearly a hundred content producers to create niche online channels. YouTube advances up to $5 million to each content producer, and it keeps the ad money it collects until the advance is paid off; revenue after that is split between YouTube and the content producer. Some familiar names have signed on, including Madonna, Shaquille O'Neal, and Amy Poehler. Among the popular channels already launched are the music video site, Noisey, which had twenty-seven million visits in its first two months, and Drive, a channel for auto fans, which had seven million views in its first four months. (See "Tracking Technology: Changing Channels: Big Studios Diversify on YouTube" on page 222 for more on YouTube's foray into original programming.)

The way advertising works online differs substantially from the way it works on network TV, where advertisers pay as much as $400,000 to buy one thirty-second ad during NBC's *The Voice* or ABC's *Modern Family*. Online advertisers pay a rate called a CPM ("cost per mille"; *mille* is Latin for "one thousand"), meaning the rate per one thousand *impressions*—which is a single ad shown to a person visiting an online site. So if a product company or ad agency purchases one thousand online impressions at a $1 CPM rate, that means the company or agency would spend $10 to have its advertisement displayed ten thousand times. Popular online sites where advertisers are reaching targeted audiences could set a CPM rate between $10 and $100,

Changing Channels: Big Studios Diversify on YouTube

by Richard Verrier and Andrea Chang

The studio behind the *Shrek*, *How to Train Your Dragon*, and *Madagascar* movie franchises is targeting the Internet generation. The company is targeting the Internet generation with a family-oriented YouTube channel. The channel, DreamWorksTV, is part of an ongoing strategy to tap into the world's most popular online video platform. The channel includes a mix of original animated, live-action and reality shows, mostly two to five minutes long. It's also one of the most ambitious moves to date by a Hollywood studio to reach younger viewers, who watch more entertainment on multiple devices and in bite-size portions. "You could go out and buy a cable channel for $1 billion and spend $1 billion to program it, or you can go where the eyeballs are going fast and furious, which is mobile and online," says Brian Robbins, founder of the teen-targeting YouTube network AwesomenessTV, which was acquired by DreamWorks in 2013.

As more viewers and advertisers migrate online, studios have been scrambling to keep up with the shifting landscape: Disney has acquired Maker Studios Inc., the Culver City digital media company behind YouTube successes such as "Epic Rap Battles of History" and PewDiePie, while Fox has formed a multiyear partnership with Wigs, a new YouTube channel focusing on women. In some ways, the studios are following in the footsteps of TV personalities such as Ellen DeGeneres, Jimmy Fallon and Jimmy Kimmel, who host their own TV shows but turn to YouTube to build large fan communities.

DreamWorks has been building closer ties to YouTube, which attracts more than 1 billion unique visitors each month, as part of an ongoing effort to make DreamWorks Animation's operations less reliant on the volatile movie business by diversifying into television and other areas. The company last year signed a landmark deal to produce episodic TV shows for the global-streaming service Netflix.

Although DreamWorks will receive a share of advertising revenue from the YouTube channel, it's not counting on ventures like this to be its biggest moneymakers. Instead, the goal is to use the channel as a testing ground for potential new TV shows and movies. It can take at least four years and more than $100 million to produce a single animated movie. A typical show on DreamWorksTV would cost a few thousand dollars a minute. In a mass media landscape increasingly dominated by both gigantic brands and micro-targeted niches, DreamWorksTV approaches both trends, market-testing smaller ideas that could, in theory, be kicked up into movie-studio majors. ◢

Source: Richard Verrier and Andrea Chang, "DreamWorks Animation Launches Family-Oriented YouTube Channel," Los Angeles Times, June 17, 2014, www.latimes.com/entertainment/envelope /cotown/la-et-ct-dreamworks-animation-youtube -20140617-story.html.

while less popular sites might command only a $.10 to $.20 CPM rate from ad agencies and product companies. For some of its new YouTube TV channels, analysts are predicting that Google might be able to charge as much as $20 CPM for a relatively popular site.

The Major Programming Corporations

After deregulation began in the 1980s, many players in TV and cable consolidated to broaden their offerings, expand their market share, and lower expenses. For example, Disney now owns both ABC and ESPN and can spread the costs of sports programming over its networks and its various ESPN cable channels. This business strategy has produced an *oligopoly* in which just a handful of media corporations now controls programming.

The Major Broadcast Networks

Despite their declining reach and the rise of cable, the traditional networks have remained attractive business investments. In 1985, General Electric, which once helped start RCA-NBC, bought back NBC. In 1995, Disney bought ABC for $19 billion; in 1999, Viacom acquired CBS for $37 billion (Viacom and CBS split in 2005, but Viacom's CEO, Sumner Redstone, has remained CBS's main stockholder and executive chairman; in 2014, his holdings in both CBS and Viacom totaled $6 billion). And in January 2011, the FCC and the Department of Justice approved Comcast's purchase of NBC Universal from GE—a deal valued at $30 billion.

To combat audience erosion in the 1990s, the major networks began acquiring or developing cable channels to recapture viewers. Thus what appears to be competition between TV and cable is sometimes an illusion. NBC, for example, operates MSNBC, CNBC, and Bravo. ABC owns ESPN along with portions of Lifetime, A&E, and History. However, the networks continue to attract larger audiences than their cable or online competitors. For the 2013–14 season, CBS led the broadcast networks in ratings, followed by NBC, ABC, Fox, Univision, and the CW. CBS averaged over 11 million viewers per evening (while the CW drew about 1.5 million viewers each evening), although NBC reached more of the viewers most cherished by advertisers— eighteen- to forty-nine-year-olds.

Major Cable and DBS Companies

In the late 1990s, cable became a coveted investment, not so much for its ability to carry television programming as for its access to households connected with high-bandwidth wires. Today, there are about 5,200 U.S. cable systems, down from 11,200 in 1994. Since the 1990s, thousands of cable systems have been bought by large **multiple-system operators (MSOs)**, corporations like Comcast and Time Warner Cable (TWC) that own many cable systems. For years the industry called its major players **multichannel video programming distributors (MVPDs)**, a term that included DBS providers like DirecTV and Dish. By 2014, cable's main trade organization, the National Cable & Telecommunications Association (NCTA), had moved away from the MVPD classification and started using the term **video subscription services**, which now also includes Netflix and Hulu Plus (see Table 6.2 on page 224). Some critics suspect that the new classification term provides legal cover for the 2014 proposed merger between Comcast and TWC—for years the dominant two U.S. cable companies with by far the most cable subscribers. But if cable attorneys can argue that the on-demand service Netflix dwarfs Comcast and TWC—36.2 million subscribers compared to 22.6 and 11.4 respectively in 2014—then the FCC and Justice Department might permit the merger.

In cable, the industry behemoth today is Comcast, especially after its takeover of NBC and move into network broadcasting. Back in 2001, AT&T had merged its cable and broadband industry in a $72 billion deal with Comcast, then the third-largest MSO. The new Comcast instantly became the cable industry leader. In 2014, Comcast also owned E!, NBCSN, the Golf

TABLE 6.2
**TOP 10 VIDEO
SUBSCRIPTION SERVICES
IN 2014**

*Data from: National Cable &
Telecommunications Association,
"Industry Data," www.ncta.com
/industry-data.*

Rank	Video Subscription Service	Subscribers
1	Netflix	36.2 million
2	Comcast	22.6 million
3	DirecTV	20.3 million
4	Dish	4.1 million
5	Time Warner Cable	11.4 million
6	Hulu Plus	6.0 million
7	AT&T	5.7 million
8	Verizon FiOS	5.3 million
9	Charter Communications	4.4 million
10	Cox Communications	4.3 million

Channel, Universal Studios, Fandango (the online movie ticket site), and a 32 percent stake in Hulu (with Fox and Disney). In 2014, there were about 660 companies still operating cable systems. Along with Comcast, the other large MSOs included Time Warner Cable (formerly part of Time Warner, Inc.), Cox Communications, Charter Communications, and Cablevision Systems.

In the DBS market, DirecTV and Dish control virtually all the DBS service in the continental United States. In 2008, News Corp. sold DirecTV to cable service provider Liberty Media, which also owned the Encore and Starz movie channels. The independently owned Dish was founded as EchoStar Communications in 1980. In 2014, to counter the proposed merger talks between cable giants Comcast and TWC, DirecTV began investigating deals with both Dish and AT&T. Over the last few years, TV services (combined with existing voice and Internet services) offered by telephone giants AT&T (U-verse) and Verizon (FiOS) have developed into viable competitors for cable and DBS.

The Effects of Consolidation

There are some concerns that the trend toward cable, broadcasting, and telephone companies merging will limit expression of political viewpoints, programming options, and technical innovation, and lead to price-fixing. These concerns raise an important question: *In an economic climate in which fewer owners control the circulation of communication, what happens to new ideas or controversial views that may not always be profitable to circulate?*

The response from the industries is that, given the tremendous capital investment it takes to run television, cable, and other media enterprises, it is necessary to form business conglomerates in order to buy up struggling companies and keep them afloat. This argument suggests that without today's video subscription services, many smaller ventures in programming would not be possible. However, there is evidence that large MSOs and other big media companies can wield their monopoly power unfairly. Business disputes have caused disruptions as networks and cable providers have dropped one another from their services, leaving customers in the dark. For example, in October 2010, News Corp. pulled six channels—including the Fox network—from over three million Cablevision customers for two weeks. This standoff over retransmission fees meant Cablevision subscribers missed two World Series games, various professional football matches, and popular programs like *Glee* and *Family Guy*. Then, in August 2013, Time Warner Cable took CBS off its systems for a month in a bitter dispute over retransmission fee hikes the network sought. In addition to blacking out WCBS in New York, Los Angeles, Dallas, and five other markets, the cable company yanked Showtime from its systems. These examples illustrate what can happen when a few large corporations engage in relatively minor arguments over prices and programs: Consumers are often left with little recourse or choice in markets with minimal or no competition and programming from just a handful of large media companies.

Alternative Voices

After suffering through years of rising rates and limited expansion of services, some small U.S. cities have decided to challenge the private monopolies of cable giants by building competing, publicly owned cable systems. So far, the municipally owned cable systems number in the hundreds and can be found in places like Glasgow, Kentucky; Kutztown, Pennsylvania; Cedar Falls, Iowa; and Provo, Utah. In most cases, they're operated by the community-owned, non-profit electric utilities. There are more than two thousand such municipal utilities across the United States, serving about 14 percent of the population and creating the potential for more municipal utilities to expand into communications services. As nonprofit entities, the municipal operations are less expensive for cable subscribers, too.

The first town to take on a national commercial cable provider (Comcast now runs the cable service there) was Glasgow, Kentucky, which built a competing municipal cable system in 1989. The town of fourteen thousand had seven thousand municipal cable customers in 2014. William J. Ray, the town's Electric Plant Board superintendent and the visionary behind the municipal communications service, has argued that this is not a new idea:

Cities have long been turning a limited number of formerly private businesses into public-works projects. This happens only when the people making up a local government believe that the service has become so essential to the citizens that it is better if it is operated by the government. In colonial America, it was all about drinking water. . . . In the twentieth century, the issue was electric power and natural gas service. Now, we are facing the same transformation in broadband networks.[24]

More than a quarter of the country's two thousand municipal utilities offer broadband services, including cable, high-speed Internet, and telephone. How will commercial cable operators fend off this unprecedented competition? According to Ray, "If cable operators are afraid of cities competing with them, there is a defense that is impregnable—they can charge reasonable rates, offer consummate customer service, improve their product, and conduct their business as if they were a guest that owes their existence to the benevolence of the city that has invited them in."[25]

Television, Cable, and Democracy

In the 1950s, television's arrival significantly changed the media landscape—particularly the radio and magazine industries, both of which had to cultivate specialized audiences and markets to survive. In its heyday, television carried the egalitarian promise that it could bypass traditional print literacy and reach all segments of society. This promise was reenergized in the 1970s when cable-access channels gave local communities the chance to create their own TV programming. In such a heterogeneous and diverse nation, the concept of a visual, affordable mass medium, giving citizens entertainment and information that they could all talk about the next day, held great appeal. However, since its creation, commercial television has tended to serve the interests of profit more often than those of democracy. Despite this, television remains the main storytelling medium of our time.

The development of cable, VCRs and DVD players, DVRs, the Internet, and smartphone services has fragmented television's audience by appealing to viewers' individual and special needs. These changes and services, by providing more specialized and individual choices, also alter television's role as a national unifying cultural force, potentially de-emphasizing the idea that we are all citizens of a larger nation and world. Moreover, many cable channels have survived mostly by offering live sports or recycling old television shows and movies. Although cable and on-demand services like Netflix are creating more and more original high-quality programs, they rarely reach even the diminished audience numbers commanded by the traditional broadcast networks. In fact, given that the television networks and many leading cable channels are now owned by the same media conglomerates, cable has evolved into something of an extension of the networks. And even though cable audiences are growing and network viewership is contracting, the division between the two is blurring. New generations who have grown up on cable and the Internet rarely make a distinction between a broadcast network, a cable service, and an on-demand program. In addition, tablets, smartphones, and Internet services that now offer or create our favorite "TV" programs are breaking down the distinctions between mobile devices and TV screens. Cable, which once offered promise as a place for alternative programming and noncommercial voices, is now being usurped by the Internet, where all kinds of TV experiments are under way.

The bottom line is that television, despite the audience fragmentation, still provides a gathering place for friends and family at the same time that it provides anywhere access to a favorite show. Like all media forms before it, television is adapting to changing technology and shifting economics. As the technology becomes more portable and personal, TV-related industries continue to search for less expensive ways to produce stories and more channels

TV AND DEMOCRACY
The first televised presidential debates took place in 1960, pitting Massachusetts senator John F. Kennedy against Vice President Richard Nixon. Don Hewitt, who later created the long-running TV newsmagazine *60 Minutes*, directed the first debate and has argued that the TV makeup that Nixon turned down would have helped create a better appearance alongside that of his tanned opponent. In fact, one study at the time reported that a majority of radio listeners thought Nixon won the first debate while a majority of TV viewers believed Kennedy won.

▶

Paul Schutzer/Timepix-Getty Images

DIGITAL JOB OUTLOOK

Media Professionals Speak about Jobs in the Television Industry

Teresa Hein, Founder and CEO, My Media Jobs

The value of having an internship is key, not only for the experience but to help you know if you want to have a job in that field. Also, as you look for internships, don't just take any opportunity. Do as much as you can to get into a place that offers you the practical experience that is related to your desired field of interest. More and more students are doing two or more internships to expand their knowledge base. This gives visual experience to the paper résumé.

Darren Haynes, Studio Anchor, ESPN

As a college football player, I transferred from the University of Rhode Island to the University of New Haven. My former science education major at URI was not offered at UNH. So my mother said, "Darren, you have a passion for sports, you are not shy, you are well liked, and you have an outgoing personality. Why not look into majoring in sports broadcasting?" The rest is history. Now my mom wants 10 percent of my paycheck!

Anonymous Twentysomething on Becoming a Television Writer, as Described in *Forbes* Magazine

I turned the [online journalism] job down, bought a book on how to break into TV writing, and talked to anyone and everyone who would give me advice. I learned that (1) I needed to move to LA if I wanted to actually have a shot at this; (2) I needed to get an agent before I could get hired on any show; (3) I needed to write two spec scripts (original episodes of existing TV shows) before any agent would even look at me; and (4) I was going to spend every waking hour of the foreseeable future networking. And over the next few months, I wrote my spec scripts, talked to contacts, and planned my move. I knew it would be hard and risky, but that's the price, right?

Shonda Rhimes, Producer of *Grey's Anatomy* and *Scandal*, on How She Got Her Start in Writing

I was four and dictating stories into a tape recorder, and my mom typed them up.

---

on which to deliver them. But what will remain common ground on this shifting terrain is that television continues as our nation's chief storyteller, whether those stories come in the form of news bulletins, sporting events, cable dramas, network sitcoms, or YouTube vignettes.

TV's future will be about serving smaller rather than larger audiences. As sites like YouTube develop original programming and as niche cable services like the Weather Channel produce reality TV series about storms, no audience seems too small and no subject matter too narrow for today's TV world. For example, by 2013, *Duck Dynasty*—a program about an eccentric Louisiana family that got rich making products for duck hunters—had become a hit series on A&E. The program averaged a cable record 12.4 million viewers in 2012–13, but then lost half those numbers in 2013–14, as many viewers grew weary of the series. An overwhelming number of programming choices like this now exist for big and small TV screens alike. How might this converged TV landscape—with its volatile ups and downs in viewer numbers—change how audiences watch, and pay for, TV? With hundreds of shows available, will we adopt à la carte viewing habits, in which we download or stream only the shows that interest us, rather than pay for cable (or DBS) packages with hundreds of channels we don't watch? ▶

CHAPTER REVIEW

COMMON THREADS

One of the Common Threads discussed in Chapter 1 is mass media, cultural expression, and storytelling.
As television and cable change their shape and size, do they remain the dominant way our culture tells stories?

By the end of the 1950s, television had become an "electronic hearth," where families gathered in living rooms to share cultural experiences. By 2012, though, the television experience had splintered. Now we are watching programming on our laptops, smartphones, and tablets, making the experience increasingly individual rather than communal. Still, television remains the mass medium that can reach most of us at a single moment in time, whether it's during a popular sitcom or a presidential debate.

In this shift, what has been lost, and what has been gained? As an electronic hearth, television has offered coverage of special moments—inaugurations, assassinations, moonwalks, space disasters, Super Bowls, *Roots*, the Olympics, 9/11, hurricanes, presidential campaigns, Arab uprisings, World Cups—that brought large heterogeneous groups together for the common experience of sharing information, celebrating triumphs, mourning loss, and electing presidents.

Accessible now in multiple digitized versions, the TV image has become portable—just as radio became portable in the 1950s. Today, we can watch TV in cars, in the park, and in class (even when we're not supposed to).

The bottom line is that today television in all its configurations is both electronic hearth and digital encounter. It still provides a gathering place for friends and family, but now we can also watch a favorite show almost whenever or wherever we want. Like all media forms before it, television is adapting to changing technology and shifting economics. As technology becomes more portable and personal, the network TV, cable, and video subscription industries search for less expensive ways to produce and deliver television. Still, television remains the main place—whether it's the big LED screen or the handheld smartphone—where we go for stories. In what ways do you think this will change or remain the case in the future? Where do you prefer to get your stories?

KEY TERMS

The definitions for the terms listed below can be found in the glossary at the end of the book.
The page numbers listed with the terms indicate where the term is highlighted in the chapter.

analog, 191
digital, 192
prime time, 194
network era, 195
CATV, 195
narrowcasting, 196
basic cable, 197
superstations, 197
premium channels, 197
pay-per-view (PPV), 197
video-on-demand (VOD), 199
direct broadcast satellite (DBS), 199
time shifting, 200
third screens, 200
fourth screens, 202

kinescope, 203
sketch comedy, 204
situation comedy, 204
anthology dramas, 205
episodic series, 206
chapter shows, 206
serial programs, 206
affiliate stations, 207
Prime Time Access Rule (PTAR), 211
fin-syn, 212
must-carry rules, 212
access channels, 212
leased channels, 214
electronic publishers, 214
common carriers, 214

Telecommunications Act of 1996, 215
deficit financing, 217
retransmission fees, 218
O & Os, 218
syndication, 218
evergreens, 218
fringe time, 218
off-network syndication, 219
first-run syndication, 219
rating, 220
share, 220
multiple-system operators (MSOs), 223
multichannel video programming distributors (MVPDs), 223
video subscription services, 223

REVIEW QUESTIONS

The Origins and Development of Television

1. What were the major technical standards established for television in the 1940s? What happened to analog television?

2. Why did the FCC freeze the allocation of TV licenses between 1948 and 1952?

3. How did the sponsorship of network programs change during the 1950s?

The Development of Cable

4. What is CATV, and what were its advantages over broadcast television?

5. How did satellite distribution change the cable industry?

6. What is DBS? How well does it compete with the cable industry?

Technology and Convergence Change Viewing Habits

7. How have computers and mobile devices challenged the TV and cable industries?

8. What has happened to the audience in the digital era of third and fourth screens?

Major Programming Trends

9. What are the differences between sketch comedy and sitcoms on television?

10. Why did the anthology drama fade as a network programming staple?

11. How did news develop at the networks in the late 1940s and 1950s?

12. What are the challenges faced by public broadcasting today?

Regulatory Challenges to Television and Cable

13. What rules and regulations did the government impose to restrict the networks' power?

14. How did cable pose a challenge to broadcasting, and how did the FCC respond to cable's early development?

15. Why are cable companies treated more like electronic publishers than common carriers?

16. How did the Telecommunications Act of 1996 change the economic shape and future of the television and cable industries?

The Economics and Ownership of Television and Cable

17. Why has it become more difficult for independent producers to create programs for television?

18. What are the differences between off-network syndication and first-run syndication?

19. What are ratings and shares in TV audience measurement?

20. What are the main reasons some municipalities are building their own cable systems?

Television, Cable, and Democracy

21. Why has television's role as a national cultural center changed over the years? What are programmers doing to retain some of their influence?

QUESTIONING THE MEDIA

1. How much television do you watch today? How has technology influenced your current viewing habits?

2. If you were a television or cable executive, what changes would you try to make in today's programs? How would you try to adapt to third- and fourth-screen technologies?

3. Do you think the must-carry rules violate a cable company's First Amendment rights? Why or why not?

4. If you ran a public television station, what programming would you provide that isn't currently being supplied by commercial television? How would you finance such programming?

5. How do you think new technologies will further change TV viewing habits?

6. How could television be used to improve our social and political life?

LAUNCHPAD FOR *MEDIA & CULTURE*

Visit LaunchPad for *Media & Culture* at macmillanhighered.com/mediaculture10e for additional learning tools:

- REVIEW WITH LEARNINGCURVE
  LearningCurve, available on LaunchPad for *Media & Culture*, uses gamelike quizzing to help you master the concepts you need to learn from this chapter.

- VIDEO: WIRED OR WIRELESS: TELEVISION DELIVERY TODAY
  This video explores the switch to digital TV signals in 2009 and how it is changing television delivery.

7

Movies and the Impact of Images

233
Early Technology
and the Evolution
of Movies

238
The Rise of the
Hollywood Studio
System

241
The Studio System's
Golden Age

251
The Transformation
of the Studio System

255
The Economics of the
Movie Business

262
Popular Movies
and Democracy

In every generation, a film is made that changes the movie industry. In 1941, that film was Orson Welles's *Citizen Kane*. Welles produced, directed, wrote, and starred in the movie at age twenty-five, playing a newspaper magnate from a young man to old age. While the movie was not a commercial success initially (powerful newspaper publisher William Randolph Hearst, whose life was the inspiration for the movie, tried to suppress it), it was critically praised for its acting, story, and directing. *Citizen Kane*'s dramatic camera angles, striking *film noir*–style lighting, nonlinear storytelling, montages, and long deep-focus shots were considered technically innovative for the era. Over time, *Citizen Kane* became revered as a masterpiece, and in 1997, the American Film Institute named it the Greatest American Movie of All Time.

A generation later, the space epic *Star Wars* (1977) changed the culture of the movie industry. *Star Wars*—produced, written, and directed by George Lucas—departed from the personal filmmaking of the early 1970s and spawned a blockbuster mentality that formed a new primary audience for Hollywood—teenagers. It had all of the now-typical blockbuster characteristics, like massive promotion and lucrative merchandising tie-ins.

© Warner Bros. Pictures/
Everett Collection

Repeat attendance and positive buzz among young people made the first *Star Wars* the most successful movie of its generation.

Star Wars has influenced not only the cultural side of moviemaking but also the technical form. In the first *Star Wars* trilogy, produced in the 1970s and 1980s, Lucas developed technologies that are now commonplace in moviemaking—digital animation, special effects, and computer-based film editing. With the second trilogy, Lucas again broke new ground in the film industry. Several scenes of *Star Wars: Episode I—The Phantom Menace* (1999) were shot on digital video, easing integration with digital special effects. *The Phantom Menace* also used digital exhibition, becoming the first full-length motion picture from a major studio to use digital projectors, which have steadily been replacing standard film projectors. Another *Star Wars* trilogy will kick off in 2015.

For the current generation, no film has shaken up the film industry like *Avatar* (2009). Like *Star Wars* before it, *Avatar* was a groundbreaking blockbuster. Made for an estimated $250–$300 million, it became the all-time box-office champion, pulling in about $760 million domestic, and more than $2.7 billion worldwide. *Avatar* integrated 3-D movie technology seamlessly, allowing viewers to immerse themselves in the computer-generated world of the ethereal planet Pandora, home of the eleven-foot-tall blue beings called the Na'vi. Director James Cameron worked with Sony to develop new 3-D cameras (a major technical innovation), which were an essential element of the filmmaking process and story rather than a gimmicky add-on. The late film critic Roger Ebert likened the movie to a blockbuster he saw a generation earlier: "Watching *Avatar*, I felt sort of the same as when I saw *Star Wars* in 1977. That was another movie I walked into with uncertain expectations. . . . *Avatar* is not simply a sensational entertainment, although it is that. It's a technical breakthrough."[1]

Though *Avatar* was released in both conventional 2-D and 3-D versions, it was the 3-D version that not only most impressed viewers but also changed the business of Hollywood. Theaters discovered they could charge a premium for the 3-D screenings and still draw record crowds. The success of *Avatar* paved the way for plenty of 3-D imitators as well as new breakthroughs in how to use 3-D technology in movies like *The Hobbit: The Desolation of Smaug*; *Life of Pi*; and *Gravity*. *Gravity*'s director, Alfonso Cuarón, used special effects breakthroughs to tell a more intimate story with just a handful of characters and received an Academy Award for the film in 2014. But many effects-heavy movies will continue to chase spectacle: Cameron announced that production would soon begin on three sequels to *Avatar* that would tentatively be released three holiday seasons in a row, beginning December 2016.[2]

▲ **DATING BACK TO THE LATE 1800s,** films have had a substantial social and cultural impact on society. Blockbuster movies such as *Star Wars*, *E.T.*, *Titanic*, *Lord of the Rings*, *Shrek*, *Avatar*, and *The Avengers* represent what Hollywood has become—America's storyteller. Movies tell communal stories that evoke and symbolize our most enduring values and our secret desires (from *The Wizard of Oz* to *The Godfather* to the Batman series).

Visit **LaunchPad** for *Media & Culture* and use **LearningCurve** to review concepts from this chapter.

Films have also helped moviegoers sort through experiences that either affirmed or deviated from their own values. Some movies—for instance, *Last Tango in Paris* (1972), *Scarface* (1983), *Fahrenheit 9/11* (2004), *Brokeback Mountain* (2005), and *12 Years a Slave* (2013)—have allowed audiences to survey "the boundary between the permitted and the forbidden" and to experience, in a controlled way, "the possibility of stepping across this boundary."[3] Such films—criticized by some for appearing to glorify crime and violence, verge on pornography, trample on sacred beliefs, or promote unpatriotic viewpoints—have even, on occasion, been banned from public viewing.

Finally, movies have acted to bring people together. Movies distract us from our daily struggles: They evoke and symbolize universal themes of human experience (that of childhood, coming of age, family relations, growing older, and coping with death); they can help us understand and respond to major historical events and tragedies (for instance, the Holocaust and 9/11); and they encourage us to reexamine contemporary ideas as the world evolves, particularly in terms of how we think about race, class, spirituality, gender, and sexuality.

In this chapter, we examine the rich legacy and current standing of movies. We will:

- Consider film's early technology and the evolution of film as a mass medium
- Look at the arrival of silent feature films; the emergence of Hollywood; and the development of the studio system with regard to production, distribution, and exhibition
- Explore the coming of sound and the power of movie storytelling
- Analyze major film genres, directors, and alternatives to Hollywood's style, including independent films, foreign films, and documentaries
- Survey the movie business today—its major players, economic clout, technological advances, and implications for democracy
- Examine how convergence has changed the way the industry distributes movies and the way we experience them

As you consider these topics, think about your own relationship with movies. What is the first movie you remember watching? What are your movie-watching experiences like today? How have certain movies made you think differently about an issue, yourself, or others? For more questions to help you think through the role of movies in our lives, see "Questioning the Media" in the Chapter Review.

Early Technology and the Evolution of Movies

History often credits a handful of enterprising individuals with developing the new technologies that lead to new categories of mass media. Such innovations, however, are usually the result of simultaneous investigations by numerous people. In addition, the innovations of both known and unknown inventors are propelled by economic and social forces as well as by individual abilities.[4]

The Development of Film

The concept of film goes back as early as Leonardo da Vinci, who theorized in the late fifteenth century about creating a device that would reproduce reality. Other early precursors to film included the Magic Lantern developed in the seventeenth century, which projected images painted on glass plates using an oil lamp as a light source; the *thaumatrope* invented in 1824, a two-sided card with different images on each side that appeared to combine the images when twirled; and the *zoetrope* introduced in 1834, a cylindrical device that rapidly twirled images inside a cylinder, which appeared to make the images move.

Muybridge and Goodwin Make Pictures Move

The development stage of movies began when inventors started manipulating photographs to make them appear to move while simultaneously projecting them onto a screen. Eadweard Muybridge, an English photographer living in America, is credited with being the first to do both. He studied motion by using multiple cameras to take successive photographs of humans and animals in motion. One of Muybridge's first projects involved using photography to determine if a racehorse actually lifts all four feet from the ground at full gallop (it does). By 1880, Muybridge had developed a method for projecting the photographic images onto a wall for public viewing. These early image sequences were extremely brief, showing only a horse jumping over a fence or a man running a few feet, because only so many photographs could be mounted inside the spinning cylinder that projected the images.

Meanwhile, other inventors were also working on capturing moving images and projecting them. In 1884, George Eastman (founder of Eastman Kodak) developed the first roll film—a huge improvement over the heavy metal and glass plates used to make individual photos. The first roll film had a paper backing that had to be stripped off during the film developing stage. Louis Aimé Augustin Le Prince, a Frenchman living in England, invented the first motion picture camera using roll film. Le Prince, who disappeared mysteriously on a train ride to Paris in

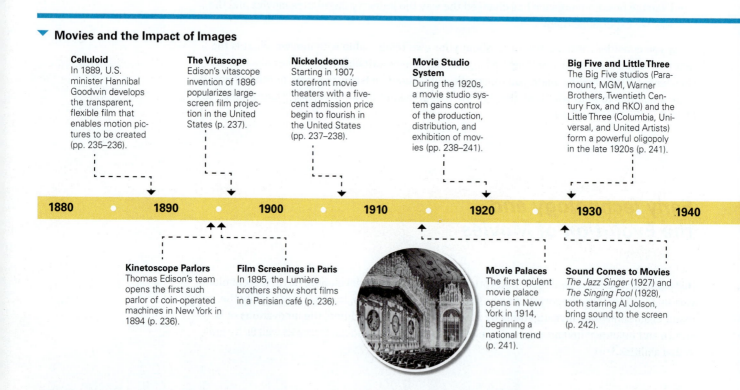

Movies and the Impact of Images

Celluloid
In 1889, U.S. minister Hannibal Goodwin develops the transparent, flexible film that enables motion pictures to be created (pp. 235–236).

The Vitascope
Edison's vitascope invention of 1896 popularizes large-screen film projection in the United States (p. 237).

Nickelodeons
Starting in 1907, storefront movie theaters with a five-cent admission price begin to flourish in the United States (pp. 237–238).

Movie Studio System
During the 1920s, a movie studio system gains control of the production, distribution, and exhibition of movies (pp. 238–241).

Big Five and Little Three
The Big Five studios (Paramount, MGM, Warner Brothers, Twentieth Century Fox, and RKO) and the Little Three (Columbia, Universal, and United Artists) form a powerful oligopoly in the late 1920s (p. 241).

1880 • 1890 • 1900 • 1910 • 1920 • 1930 • 1940

Kinetoscope Parlors
Thomas Edison's team opens the first such parlor of coin-operated machines in New York in 1894 (p. 236).

Film Screenings in Paris
In 1895, the Lumière brothers show short films in a Parisian café (p. 236).

Movie Palaces
The first opulent movie palace opens in New York in 1914, beginning a national trend (p. 241).

Sound Comes to Movies
The Jazz Singer (1927) and *The Singing Fool* (1928), both starring Al Jolson, bring sound to the screen (p. 242).

Eadweard Muybridge/Time Life Pictures/Getty Images

EADWEARD MUYBRIDGE'S study of horses in motion proved that a racehorse gets all four feet off the ground during a gallop. In his various studies of motion, Muybridge would use up to twelve cameras at a time.

1890, is credited with filming the first motion picture, *Roundhay Garden Scene*, in 1888. About two seconds' worth of the film survives today.

In 1889, a New Jersey minister, Hannibal Goodwin, improved Eastman's roll film by using thin strips of transparent, pliable material called **celluloid**, which could hold a coating of chemicals sensitive to light. Goodwin's breakthrough solved a major problem: It enabled a

The Hollywood Ten
The House Un-American Activities Committee investigates ten unwilling witnesses in 1947 on grounds of allegedly having communist sympathies (pp. 251–252).

Ratings System
In 1967, the MPAA introduces a system to rate movies for age appropriateness (p. 254).

The Rise of the Indies
Independent films, particularly those that screen at the Sundance Film Festival, become an important source for identifying new talent in the 1990s (p. 249).

DVDs
The new digital movie format is quickly adopted in 1997 as a format superior to the VHS cassette (p. 254).

Netflix
Netflix eliminates any waiting time with its streaming service in 2008, allowing customers instant access to thousands of films and television shows (p. 260).

Avatar
In 2009, the blockbuster becomes the all-time highest-earning film at the box office and propels 3-D into great popularity (p. 232).

| 1950 | 1960 | 1970 | 1980 | 1990 | 2000 | 2010 | 2020 |

Paramount Decision
In 1948, the Supreme Court forces studios to divest themselves of their theaters to end the vertical integration of the industry (p. 252).

Video Transforms the Industry
VHS-format videocassette recorders (VCRs) hit the consumer market in 1977, creating a movie rental and purchase industry (p. 254).

Megaplex Mania
A building wave of giant movie complexes begins in the mid-1990s (p. 258).

Digital Film Production
By 2000, the digital production and distribution format gains strength in Hollywood and with independents (pp. 261–262).

strip of film to move through a camera and be photographed in rapid succession, producing a series of pictures. Because celluloid was transparent (except for the images made on it during filming), it was ideal for projection, as light could easily shine through it. George Eastman, who also announced the development of celluloid film, legally battled Goodwin for years over the patent rights. The courts eventually awarded Goodwin the invention, but Eastman's company became the major manufacturer of film stock for motion pictures after buying Goodwin's patents.

Edison and the Lumières Create Motion Pictures

As with the development of sound recording, Thomas Edison takes center stage in most accounts of the invention of motion pictures. In the late 1800s, Edison initially planned to merge phonograph technology and moving images to create talking pictures (which would not happen in feature films until 1927). Because there was no breakthrough, however, Edison lost interest. He directed an assistant, William Kennedy Dickson, to combine Edison's incandescent lightbulb, Goodwin's celluloid, and Le Prince's camera to create another early movie camera, the **kinetograph**, and a single-person viewing system, the **kinetoscope**. This small projection system housed fifty feet of film that revolved on spools (similar to a library microfilm reader). Viewers looked through a hole and saw images moving on a tiny plate. In 1894, the first kinetoscope parlor, featuring two rows of coin-operated machines, opened on Broadway in New York.

Meanwhile, in France, brothers Louis and Auguste Lumière developed the *cinematograph*, a combined camera, film developer, and projection system. The projection system was particularly important, as it allowed more than one person at a time to see the moving images on a large screen. In a Paris café on December 28, 1895, the Lumières projected ten short movies for viewers who paid one franc each, on such subjects as a man falling off a horse and a child trying to grab a fish from a bowl. Within three weeks, twenty-five hundred people were coming each night to see how, according to one Paris paper, film "perpetuates the image of movement."

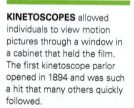

KINETOSCOPES allowed individuals to view motion pictures through a window in a cabinet that held the film. The first kinetoscope parlor opened in 1894 and was such a hit that many others quickly followed.

Everett Collection

With innovators around the world now dabbling in moving pictures, Edison's lab renewed its interest in film. Edison patented several inventions and manufactured a new large-screen system called the **vitascope**, which enabled filmstrips of longer lengths to be projected without interruption and hinted at the potential of movies as a future mass medium. Staged at a music hall in New York in April 1896, Edison's first public showing of the vitascope featured shots from a boxing match and waves rolling onto a beach. The *New York Times* described the exhibition as "wonderfully real and singularly exhilarating." Some members of the audience were so taken with the realism of the film images that they stepped back from the screen's crashing waves to avoid getting their feet wet.

Early movie demonstrations such as these marked the beginning of the film industry's entrepreneurial stage. At this point, movies consisted of movement recorded by a single continuous camera shot. Early filmmakers had not yet figured out how to move the camera around or how to edit film shots together. Nonetheless, various innovators were beginning to see the commercial possibilities of film. By 1900, short movies had become a part of the entertainment industry and were showing up in amusement arcades, traveling carnivals, wax museums, and vaudeville theater.

The Introduction of Narrative

The shift to the mass medium stage for movies occurred with the introduction of **narrative films**: movies that tell stories. Audiences quickly tired of static films of waves breaking on beaches or vaudeville acts recorded by immobile cameras. To become a mass medium, the early silent films had to offer what books achieved: the suspension of disbelief. They had to create narrative worlds that engaged an audience's imagination.

Some of the earliest narrative films were produced and directed by French magician and inventor Georges Méliès, who opened the first public movie theater in France in 1896. Méliès may have been the first director to realize that a movie was not simply a means of recording reality. He understood that a movie could be artificially planned and controlled like a staged play. Méliès began producing short fantasy and fairy-tale films—including *The Vanishing Lady* (1896), *Cinderella* (1899), and *A Trip to the Moon* (1902)—by increasingly using editing and existing camera tricks and techniques, such as slow motion and cartoon animation, which became key ingredients in future narrative filmmaking.

The first American filmmaker to adapt Méliès's innovations to narrative film was Edwin S. Porter. A cameraman who had studied Méliès's work in an Edison lab, Porter mastered the technique of editing diverse shots together to tell a coherent story. Porter shot narrative scenes out of order (for instance, some in a studio and some outdoors) and reassembled, or edited, them to make a story. In 1902, he made what is regarded as America's first narrative film, *The Life of an American Fireman*. It also contained the first close-up shot in U.S. narrative film history—a ringing fire alarm. Until then, moviemakers thought close-ups cheated the audience of the opportunity to see an entire scene. Porter's most important film, *The Great Train Robbery* (1903), introduced the western genre as well as chase scenes. In this popular eleven-minute movie, which inspired many copycats, Porter demonstrated the art of film suspense by alternating shots of the robbers with those of a posse in hot pursuit.

The Arrival of Nickelodeons

Another major development in the evolution of film as a mass medium was the arrival of **nickelodeons**—a form of movie

GEORGES MÉLIÈS trained as a stage magician before becoming interested in film—a talent he brought to his movies. Méliès is widely known as one of the first filmmakers to employ "tricks," or special effects, such as time-lapse photography, the stop trick, and multiple exposures. His impressive body of work includes the famous *A Trip to the Moon* (1902), *The Impossible Voyage* (1904), and *The Merry Frolics of Satan* (1906, pictured).

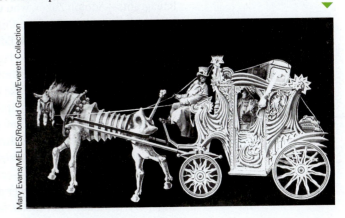

Mary Evans/MELIES/Ronald Grant/Everett Collection

theater whose name combines the admission price with the Greek word for "theater." According to media historian Douglas Gomery, these small and uncomfortable makeshift theaters were often converted storefronts redecorated to mimic vaudeville theaters: "In front, large, hand-painted posters announced the movies for the day. Inside, the screening of news, documentary, comedy, fantasy, and dramatic shorts lasted about one hour."[5] Usually a piano player added live music, and sometimes theater operators used sound effects to simulate gunshots or loud crashes. Because they showed silent films that transcended language barriers, nickelodeons flourished during the great European immigration at the turn of the twentieth century. These theaters filled a need for many newly arrived people struggling to learn English and seeking an inexpensive escape from the hard life of the city. Often managed by immigrants, nickelodeons required a minimal investment: just a secondhand projector and a large white sheet. Between 1907 and 1909, the number of nickelodeons grew from five thousand to ten thousand. The craze peaked by 1910, when entrepreneurs began to seek more affluent spectators, attracting them with larger and more lavish movie theaters.

The Rise of the Hollywood Studio System

By the 1910s, movies had become a major industry. Among the first to try his hand at dominating the movie business and reaping its profits, Thomas Edison formed the Motion Picture Patents Company, known as the *Trust*, in 1908. A cartel of major U.S. and French film producers, the company pooled patents in an effort to control film's major technology, acquired most major film distributorships, and signed an exclusive deal with George Eastman, who agreed to supply movie film only to Trust-approved companies.

However, some independent producers refused to bow to the Trust's terms. They saw too much demand for films, too much money to be made, and too many ways to avoid the Trust's scrutiny. Some producers began to relocate from the centers of film production in New York and New Jersey to Cuba and Florida. Ultimately, though, Hollywood became the film capital of the world. Southern California offered cheap labor, diverse scenery for outdoor shooting, and a mild climate suitable for year-round production. Geographically far from the Trust's headquarters in New Jersey, independent producers in Hollywood could also easily slip over the border into Mexico to escape legal prosecution brought by the Trust for patent violations.

Wanting to free their movie operations from the Trust's tyrannical grasp, two Hungarian immigrants—Adolph Zukor, who would eventually run Paramount Pictures, and William Fox, who would found the Fox Film Corporation (which later became Twentieth Century Fox)—played a role in the collapse of Edison's Trust. Zukor's early companies figured out ways to bypass the Trust, and a suit by Fox, a nickelodeon operator turned film distributor, resulted in the Trust's breakup due to restraint of trade violations in 1917.

Ironically, entrepreneurs like Zukor developed other tactics for controlling the industry. The strategies, many of which are still used today, were more ambitious than just monopolizing patents and technology. They aimed at dominating the movie business at all three essential levels—*production*, everything involved in making a movie, from securing a script and actors to raising money and filming; *distribution*, getting the films into theaters; and *exhibition*, playing films in theaters. This control—or **vertical integration**—of all levels of the movie business gave certain studios great power and eventually spawned a film industry that turned into an **oligopoly**, a situation in which a few firms control the bulk of the business.

Production

In the early days of film, producers and distributors had not yet recognized that fans would seek not only particular film stories—like dramas, westerns, and romances—but also particular film actors. Initially, film companies were reluctant to identify their anonymous actors for fear that their popularity would raise the typical $5 to $15 weekly salary. Eventually, though, the industry understood how important the actors' identities were to a film's success.

Responding to discerning audiences and competing against Edison's Trust, Adolph Zukor hired a number of popular actors and formed the Famous Players Company in 1912. His idea was to control movie production not through patents but through exclusive contracts with actors. One Famous Players performer was Mary Pickford. Known as "America's Sweetheart" for her portrayal of spunky and innocent heroines, Pickford was "unspoiled" by a theater background and better suited to the more subtle and intimate new medium. She became so popular that audiences waited in line to see her movies, and producers were forced to pay her increasingly higher salaries.

An astute businesswoman, Mary Pickford was the key figure in elevating the financial status and professional role of film actors. In 1910, Pickford made about $100 a week, but by 1914 she earned $1,000 a week, and by 1917 she received a weekly salary of $15,000. Having appeared in nearly two hundred films, Pickford was so influential that in 1919 she broke from Zukor to form her own company, United Artists. Joining her were actor Douglas Fairbanks (her future husband), comedian-director Charlie Chaplin, and director D. W. Griffith.

Although United Artists represented a brief triumph of autonomy for a few powerful actors, by the 1920s the **studio system** firmly controlled creative talent in the industry. Pioneered by director Thomas Ince and his company, Triangle, the studio system constituted a sort of assembly-line process for moviemaking: actors, directors, editors, writers, and others all worked under exclusive contracts for the major studios. Those who weren't under contract probably weren't working at all. Ince also developed the notion of the studio head; he appointed producers to handle hiring, logistics, and finances so that he could more easily supervise many pictures at one time. The system was so efficient that each major studio was producing a feature film every week. Pooling talent, rather than patents, was a more ingenious approach for movie studios aiming to dominate film production.

Distribution

An early effort to control movie distribution occurred around 1904, when movie companies provided vaudeville theaters with films and projectors on a *film exchange* system. In exchange for their short films, shown between live acts, movie producers received a small percentage of the vaudeville ticket-gate receipts. Gradually, as the number of production companies and the popularity of narrative films grew, demand for a distribution system serving national and international markets increased as well. One way Edison's Trust sought

Everett Collection

MARY PICKFORD
With legions of fans, Mary Pickford became the first woman ever to make a salary of $1 million in a year and gained the freedom to take artistic risks with her roles. (She would famously tell Adolph Zukor in 1915, "No, I really cannot afford to work for only $10,000 a week.") In 1919 she launched United Artists, a film distributing company, with Douglas Fairbanks, Charlie Chaplin, and D. W. Griffith. No woman since has been as powerful a player in the movie industry. Here she is seen with Buddy Rogers in *My Best Girl*.

to control distribution was by withholding equipment from companies not willing to pay the Trust's patent-use fees.

However, as with the production of film, independent film companies looked for distribution strategies outside of the Trust. Again, Adolph Zukor led the fight, developing **block booking** distribution. Under this system, to gain access to popular films with big stars like Mary Pickford, exhibitors had to agree to rent new or marginal films with no stars. Zukor would pressure theater operators into taking a hundred movies at a time to get the few Pickford titles they wanted. Such contracts enabled the new studios to test-market new stars without taking much financial risk. Although this practice was eventually outlawed as monopolistic, rising film studios used the tactic effectively to guarantee the success of their films in a competitive marketplace.

Another distribution strategy involved the marketing of American films in Europe. When World War I disrupted the once-powerful European film production industry, only U.S. studios were able to meet the demand for films in Europe. The war marked a turning point and made the United States the leader in the commercial movie business worldwide. After the war, no other nation's film industry could compete economically with Hollywood. By the mid-1920s, foreign revenue from U.S. films totaled $100 million. Today, Hollywood continues to dominate the world market.

Exhibition

Edison's Trust attempted to monopolize exhibition by controlling the flow of films to theater owners. If theaters wanted to ensure they had films to show their patrons, they had to purchase a license from the Trust and pay whatever price it asked. Otherwise, they were locked out of the Trust and had to try to find enough films from independent producers to show. Eventually, the flow of films from independents in Hollywood and foreign films enabled theater owners to resist the Trust's scheme.

After the collapse of the Trust, emerging studios in Hollywood had their own ideas on how to control exhibition. When industrious theater owners began forming film cooperatives to compete with block-booking tactics, producers like Zukor conspired to dominate exhibition by buying up theaters. By 1921, Zukor's Paramount owned three hundred theaters, solidifying its

MOVIE PALACES
Many movie palaces of the 1920s were elaborate, opulent buildings. The one pictured here includes space for a live band at the front of the theater, to provide music and sound effects for the movie.

Everett Collection

ability to show the movies it produced. In 1925, a business merger between Paramount and Publix (then the country's largest theater chain, with more than five hundred screens) gave Zukor enormous influence over movie exhibition.

Zukor and the heads of several major studios understood that they did not have to own all the theaters to ensure that their movies would be shown. Instead, the major studios (which would eventually include MGM, RKO, Warner Brothers, Twentieth Century Fox, and Paramount) only needed to own the first-run theaters (about 15 percent of the nation's theaters), which premiered new films in major downtown areas in front of the largest audiences, and which generated 85 to 95 percent of all film revenue.

The studios quickly realized that to earn revenue from these first-run theaters they would have to draw the middle and upper-middle classes to the movies. To do so, they built **movie palaces**, full-time single-screen movie theaters that provided a more hospitable moviegoing environment. In 1914, the three-thousand-seat Strand Theatre, the first movie palace, opened in New York. With elaborate architecture, movie palaces lured spectators with an elegant décor usually reserved for high-society opera, ballet, symphony, and live theater.

Another major innovation in exhibition was the development of *mid-city movie theaters*. These movie theaters were built in convenient locations near urban mass transit stations to attract the business of the urban and suburban middle class (the first wave of middle-class people moved from urban centers to city outskirts in the 1920s). This idea continues today, as **multiplexes** featuring multiple screens lure middle-class crowds to interstate highway crossroads.

By the late 1920s, the major studios had clearly established vertical integration in the industry. What had once been a fairly easy and cheap business to enter was now complex and expensive. What had been many small competitive firms in the early 1900s was now a few powerful studios, including the **Big Five**—Paramount, MGM, Warner Brothers, Twentieth Century Fox, and RKO—and the **Little Three** (which did not own theaters)—Columbia, Universal, and United Artists. Together, these eight companies formed a powerful oligopoly, which made it increasingly difficult for independent companies to make, distribute, and exhibit commercial films.

Everett Collection

BUSTER KEATON (1895–1966)
Born into a vaudeville family, Keaton honed his comic skills early on. He got his start acting in a few shorts in 1917 and went on to star in some of the most memorable silent films of the 1920s, including classics such as *Sherlock Jr.* (1924), *The General* (1927), and *Steamboat Bill Jr.* (1928). Because of Keaton's ability to match physical comedy with an unfailingly deadpan and stoic face, he gained the nickname the Great Stone Face.

The Studio System's Golden Age

Many consider Hollywood's Golden Age as beginning in 1915 with innovations in feature-length narrative film in the silent era, peaking with the introduction of sound and the development of the classic Hollywood style, and ending with the transformation of the Hollywood studio system post–World War II.

Hollywood Narrative and the Silent Era

D. W. Griffith, among the first "star" directors, was the single most important director in Hollywood's early days. Griffith paved the way for all future narrative filmmakers by refining many of the narrative techniques introduced by Méliès and Porter and using nearly all of them in one film for the first time, including varied camera distances, close-up shots, multiple story lines, fast-paced editing, and symbolic imagery. Despite the cringe-inducing racism of this pioneering and controversial film, *The Birth of a Nation* (1915) was the first *feature-length film* (more than an hour long) produced in America. The three-hour epic was also the first **blockbuster** and cost moviegoers a record $2 admission. Although considered a technical masterpiece, the film glorified the Ku Klux Klan and stereotyped southern blacks, leading to a campaign against the film by the NAACP and protests and riots at many screenings. Nevertheless, the movie triggered Hollywood's fascination with narrative films.

Feature films became the standard throughout the 1920s and introduced many of the film genres we continue to see produced today. The most popular films during the silent era were historical and religious epics, including *Napoleon* (1927), *Ben-Hur* (1925), and *The Ten Commandments* (1923), but the silent era also produced pioneering social dramas, mysteries, comedies, horror films, science-fiction films, war films, crime dramas, westerns, and even spy films. The silent era also introduced numerous technical innovations, established the Hollywood star system, and cemented the reputation of movies as a viable art form, when previously they had been seen as novelty entertainment.

The Introduction of Sound

With the studio system and Hollywood's worldwide dominance firmly in place, the next big challenge was to bring sound to moving pictures. Various attempts at **talkies** had failed since Edison first tried to link phonograph and moving picture technologies in the 1890s. During the 1910s, however, technical breakthroughs at AT&T's research arm, Bell Labs, produced prototypes of loudspeakers and sound amplifiers. Experiments with sound continued during the 1920s, particularly at Warner Brothers studios, which released numerous short sound films of vaudeville acts, featuring singers and comedians. The studio packaged them as a novelty along with silent feature films.

In 1927, Warner Brothers produced *The Jazz Singer*, a feature-length film starring Al Jolson, a charismatic and popular vaudeville singer who wore blackface makeup as part of his act. This further demonstrated, as did *The Birth of a Nation*, that racism in America carried into the film industry. An experiment, *The Jazz Singer* was basically a silent film interspersed with musical numbers and brief dialogue ("Wait a minute, wait a minute, you ain't heard nothin' yet"). At first there was only modest interest in the movie, which featured just 354 spoken words. But the film grew in popularity as it toured the Midwest, where audiences stood and cheered the short bursts of dialogue. The breakthrough film, however, was Warner Brothers' 1928 release *The Singing Fool*, which also starred Jolson. Costing $200,000 to make, the film took in $5 million and "proved to all doubters that talkies were here to stay."[6]

A SILENT COMEBACK
The Artist, a tribute to silent movies set around the dawn of the talkies, won the Academy Award for best picture of 2011. It was the first (mostly) silent movie to win since the first Academy Awards in 1927.

© The Weinstein Company/Everett Collection

Warner Brothers, however, was not the only studio exploring sound technology. Five months before *The Jazz Singer* opened, Fox studio premiered sound-film **newsreels**. Fox's newsreel company, Movietone, captured the first film footage with sound of the takeoff and return of Charles Lindbergh, who piloted the first solo, nonstop flight across the Atlantic Ocean in May 1927. Fox's Movietone system recorded sound directly onto the film, running it on a narrow filmstrip that ran alongside the larger image portion of the film. Superior to the sound-on-record system, the Movietone method eventually became film's standard sound system.

Boosted by the innovation of sound, annual movie attendance in the United States rose from sixty million a week in 1927 to ninety million a week in 1929. By 1931, nearly 85 percent of America's twenty thousand theaters accommodated sound pictures; and by 1935, the world had adopted talking films as the commercial standard.

The Development of the Hollywood Style

By the time sound came to movies, Hollywood dictated not only the business but also the style of most moviemaking worldwide. That style, or model, for storytelling developed with the rise of the studio system in the 1920s, solidified during the first two decades of the sound era, and continues to dominate American filmmaking today. The model serves up three ingredients that give Hollywood movies their distinctive flavor: the narrative, the genre, and the author (or director). The right blend of these ingredients—combined with timing, marketing, and luck—has led to many movie hits, from 1930s and 1940s classics like *It Happened One Night*, *Gone with the Wind*, *The Philadelphia Story*, and *Casablanca* to recent successes like *The Hunger Games* (2012) and *Gravity* (2013).

Hollywood Narratives

American filmmakers from D. W. Griffith to Steven Spielberg have understood the allure of *narrative*, which always includes two basic components: the story (what happens to whom) and the discourse (how the story is told). Further, Hollywood codified a familiar narrative structure across all genres. Most movies, like most TV shows and novels, feature recognizable character types (protagonist, antagonist, romantic interest, sidekick); a clear beginning, middle, and end (even with flashbacks and flash-forwards, the sequence of events is usually clear to the viewer); and a plot propelled by the main character experiencing and resolving a conflict by the end of the movie.

Within Hollywood's classic narratives, filmgoers find an amazing array of intriguing cultural variations. For example, familiar narrative conventions of heroes, villains, conflicts, and resolutions may be made more unique with inventions like computer-generated imagery (CGI) or digital remastering for an IMAX 3D Experience release. This combination of convention and invention—standardized Hollywood stories and differentiated special effects—provides a powerful economic package that satisfies most audiences' appetites for both the familiar and the distinctive.

Hollywood Genres

In general, Hollywood narratives fit a **genre**, or category, in which conventions regarding similar characters, scenes, structures, and themes recur in combination. (See Table 7.1 for a list of Hollywood's top movie genres.) Grouping films by category is another way for the industry to achieve the two related economic goals of *product standardization* and *product differentiation*. By making films that fall into popular genres, the movie industry provides familiar models that can be imitated. It is much easier for a studio to promote a film that already fits into a pre-existing category with which viewers are familiar. Among the most familiar genres are comedy,

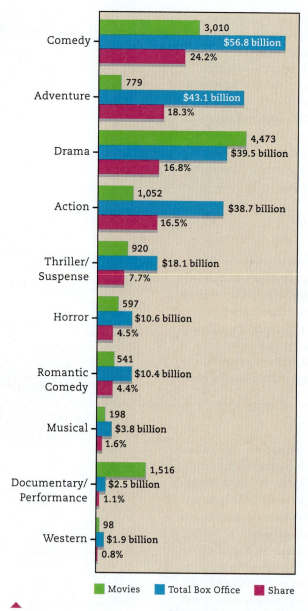

Comedy
3,010
$56.8 billion
24.2%

Adventure
779
$43.1 billion
18.3%

Drama
4,473
$39.5 billion
16.8%

Action
1,052
$38.7 billion
16.5%

Thriller/
Suspense
920
$18.1 billion
7.7%

Horror
597
$10.6 billion
4.5%

Romantic
Comedy
541
$10.4 billion
4.4%

Musical
198
$3.8 billion
1.6%

Documentary/
Performance
1,516
$2.5 billion
1.1%

Western
98
$1.9 billion
0.8%

■ Movies ■ Total Box Office ■ Share

TABLE 7.1

HOLLYWOOD'S TOP GENRES

Data from: "Market Share for Each Genre 1995–2014," The Numbers, June 28, 2014, www.the-numbers .com/market/genres.

adventure, drama, action, thriller/suspense, horror, romantic comedy, musical, documentary, western, gangster, fantasy–science fiction, and film noir.

Variations of dramas and comedies have long dominated film's narrative history. A western typically features "good" cowboys battling "evil" bad guys, as in *True Grit* (2010), or resolves tension between the natural forces of the wilderness and the civilizing influence of a town. Romances (such as *The Fault in Our Stars*, 2014) present conflicts that are mediated by the ideal of love. Another popular genre, thriller/suspense (such as *Prisoners*, 2013), usually casts "the city" as a corrupting place that needs to be overcome by the moral courage of a heroic detective.[7]

Because most Hollywood narratives try to create believable worlds, the artificial style of musicals is sometimes a disruption of what many viewers expect. Musicals' popularity peaked in the 1940s and 1950s, but they showed a small resurgence in the 2000s with *Moulin Rouge!* (2001), *Chicago* (2002), and *Les Misérables* (2012). Still, no live-action musicals rank among the top fifty highest-grossing films of all time.

Another fascinating genre is the horror film, which also claims none of the top fifty highest-grossing films of all time. In fact, from *Psycho* (1960) to *The Conjuring* (2013), this lightly regarded genre has earned only one Oscar for best picture: *Silence of the Lambs* (1991). Yet these movies are extremely popular with teenagers, among the largest theatergoing audience, who are in search of cultural choices distinct from those of their parents. Critics suggest that the teen appeal of horror movies is similar to the allure of gangster rap or heavy-metal music; they believe teens enjoy the horror genre because it is a cultural form that often carries anti-adult messages and does not appeal to most adults.

The *film noir* genre (French for "black film") developed in the United States in the late 1920s and hit its peak after World War II. Still, the genre continues to influence movies today. Using low-lighting techniques, few daytime scenes, and bleak urban settings, films in this genre (such as *The Big Sleep*, 1946, and *Sunset Boulevard*, 1950) explore unstable characters and the sinister side of human nature. Although the French critics who first identified noir as a genre place these films in the 1940s, their influence resonates in contemporary films—sometimes called *neo-noir*—including *Se7en* (1995), *L.A. Confidential* (1997), and *Sin City* (2005).

Hollywood "Authors"

In commercial filmmaking, the director serves as the main author of a film. Sometimes called "auteurs," successful directors develop a particular cinematic style or an interest in particular topics that differentiates their narratives from those of other directors. Alfred Hitchcock, for instance, redefined the suspense drama through editing techniques that heightened tension (*Rear Window*, 1954; *Vertigo*, 1958; *North by Northwest*, 1959; *Psycho*, 1960).

The contemporary status of directors stems from two breakthrough films: Dennis Hopper's *Easy Rider* (1969) and George Lucas's *American Graffiti* (1973), which became surprise box-office hits. Their inexpensive budgets, rock-and-roll soundtracks, and big payoffs created opportunities for a new generation of directors. The success of these films exposed cracks in the Hollywood system, which was losing money in the late 1960s and early 1970s. Studio executives seemed at a loss to explain and predict the tastes of a new generation of moviegoers. Yet Hopper and Lucas had tapped into the anxieties of the postwar baby-boom generation in its search for self-realization, its longing for an innocent past, and its efforts to cope with the turbulence of the 1960s.

This opened the door for a new wave of directors who were trained in California or New York film schools and were also products of the 1960s, such as Francis Ford Coppola (*The Godfather*, 1972), William Friedkin (*The Exorcist*, 1973), Steven Spielberg (*Jaws*, 1975), Martin Scorsese (*Taxi Driver*, 1976), Brian De Palma (*Carrie*, 1976), and George Lucas (*Star Wars*, 1977). Combining news or documentary techniques and Hollywood narratives, these films demonstrated how mass media borders had become blurred and how movies had become dependent on audiences who were used to television and rock and roll. These films signaled the start of a period that Scorsese has called "the deification of the director." A handful of successful directors gained the kind of economic clout and celebrity standing that had belonged almost exclusively to top movie stars.

Everett Collection

FILM GENRES

Psycho (1960), a classic horror film, tells the story of Marion Crane (played by Janet Leigh), who flees to a motel after embezzling $40,000 from her employer. There, she meets the motel owner, Norman Bates (played by Anthony Perkins), and her untimely death. The infamous shower scene, pictured above, is widely considered one of the most iconic horror film sequences.

Although the status of directors grew in the 1960s and 1970s, recognition for women directors of Hollywood features remained rare.[8] A breakthrough came with Kathryn Bigelow's best director Academy Award for *The Hurt Locker* (2009), which also won the best picture award. Prior to Bigelow's win, only three women had received an Academy Award nomination for directing a feature film: Lina Wertmüller in 1976 for *Seven Beauties*, Jane Campion in 1994 for *The Piano*, and Sofia Coppola in 2004 for *Lost in Translation*. Both Wertmüller and Campion are from outside the United States, where women directors frequently receive more opportunities for film development. Some women in the United States get an opportunity to direct because of their prominent standing as popular actors; Barbra Streisand, Jodie Foster, Penny Marshall, and Sally Field all fall into this category. Other women have come to direct films via their scriptwriting achievements. For example, Jennifer Lee, who wrote *Wreck-It Ralph* (2012), followed up by writing and directing *Frozen* (2013). Other women directors—like Bigelow, Catherine Hardwicke (*Twilight*, 2008), Lone Scherfig (*One Day*, 2011), Debra Granik (*Winter's Bone*, 2010), and Kimberly Peirce (*Carrie*, 2013)—have moved past debut films and proven themselves as experienced studio auteurs.

Members of minority groups, including African Americans, Asian Americans, and Native Americans, have also struggled for recognition in Hollywood. Still, some have succeeded as directors, crossing over from careers as actors or gaining notoriety through independent filmmaking. Among the most successful contemporary African American directors are Kasi Lemmons (*Black Nativity*, 2013), Lee Daniels (*The Butler*, 2013), John Singleton (*Abduction*, 2011), Tyler Perry (*A Madea Christmas*, 2013), and Spike Lee (*Oldboy*, 2013). (See "Case Study:

WOMEN DIRECTORS have long struggled in Hollywood. However, some, like Kathryn Bigelow, are making a name for themselves. Known for her rough-and-tumble style of filmmaking and her penchant for directing action and thriller movies, Bigelow became the first woman to win the Academy Award for best director for *The Hurt Locker* in 2010. Her *Zero Dark Thirty*, about the hunt for Osama bin Laden, followed in 2012.

LaunchPad ◉

macmillanhighered.com /mediaculture10e

Breaking Barriers with *12 Years a Slave*
Visit LaunchPad to view a short clip from the Oscar-winning movie from director Steve McQueen.
Discussion: How do you think *12 Years a Slave* differs from previous depictions of black history in America?

Breaking through Hollywood's Race Barrier" on page 247.) Asian Americans such as M. Night Shyamalan (*After Earth*, 2013), Ang Lee (*Life of Pi*, 2012), Wayne Wang (*Snow Flower and the Secret Fan*, 2011), and documentarian Arthur Dong (*Hollywood Chinese*, 2007) have built immensely accomplished directing careers. Chris Eyre (*Hide Away*, 2011) remains the most noted Native American director, working mainly as an independent filmmaker.

Outside the Hollywood System

Since the rise of the studio system, Hollywood has focused on feature-length movies that command popular attention and earn the most money. However, the movie industry has a long tradition of films made outside the Hollywood studio system. In the following sections, we look at three alternatives to Hollywood: international films, documentaries, and independent films.

Global Cinema

For generations, Hollywood has dominated the global movie scene. In many countries, American films capture up to 90 percent of the market. In striking contrast, foreign films constitute only a tiny fraction—less than 2 percent—of motion pictures seen in the United States today. Despite Hollywood's domination of global film distribution, other countries have a rich history of producing both successful and provocative short-subject and feature films. For example, cinematic movements of the twentieth century—such as German expressionism (capturing psychological moods), Soviet social realism (presenting a positive view of Soviet life), Italian neorealism (focusing on the everyday lives of Italians), and European new-wave cinema (experimenting with the language of film)—and post–World War II Japanese, Hong Kong, Korean, Australian, Indian, Canadian, and British cinema have all been extremely influential, demonstrating alternatives to the Hollywood approach.

Early on, Americans showed interest in British and French short films and in experimental films, such as Germany's *The Cabinet of Dr. Caligari* (1919). Foreign-language movies did reasonably well throughout the 1920s, especially in ethnic neighborhood theaters in large American cities. For a time, Hollywood studios even dubbed some popular American movies into Spanish, Italian, French, and German for these theaters. But the Depression brought cutbacks, and by the 1930s, the daughters and sons of turn-of-the-century immigrants—many of whom were trying to assimilate into mainstream American culture—preferred their Hollywood movies in English.[9]

Postwar prosperity, rising globalism, and the gradual decline of the studios' hold over theater exhibition in the 1950s and 1960s stimulated the rise of art-house theaters, and these decades saw a rebirth of interest in foreign-language films by such prominent directors as Sweden's Ingmar Bergman (*Wild Strawberries*, 1957), Italy's Federico Fellini (*La Dolce Vita*, 1960), France's François Truffaut (*Jules and Jim*, 1961), Japan's Akira Kurosawa (*Seven Samurai*, 1954), and India's Satyajit Ray (Apu Trilogy, 1955–1959). Catering to academic audiences, art houses made a statement against Hollywood commercialism as they sought to show alternative movies.

By the late 1970s, though, the home video market had emerged, and audiences began staying home to watch both foreign and domestic films. New multiplex theater owners rejected the smaller profit margins of most foreign titles, which lacked the promotional hype

© Summit Entertainment/Everett Collection

Breaking through Hollywood's Race Barrier

Despite inequities and discrimination, a thriving black cinema existed in New York's Harlem district during the 1930s and 1940s. Usually bankrolled by white business executives who were capitalizing on the black-only theaters fostered by segregation, independent films featuring black casts were supported by African American moviegoers, even during the Depression. But it was a popular Hollywood film, *Imitation of Life* (1934), that emerged as the highest-grossing film in black theaters during the mid-1930s. The film told the story of a friendship between a white woman and a black woman whose young daughter denied her heritage and passed for white, breaking her mother's heart. Despite African Americans' long support of the film industry, their moviegoing experience has not been the same as that of whites. From the late 1800s until the passage of Civil Rights legislation in the mid-1960s, many theater owners discriminated against black patrons. In large cities, blacks often had to attend separate theaters, where new movies might not appear until a year or two after white theaters had shown them. In smaller towns and in the South, blacks were often only allowed to patronize local theaters after midnight. In addition, some theater managers required black patrons to sit in less desirable areas of the theater.[1]

Changes took place during and after World War II, however. When the "white flight" from central cities began during the suburbanization of the 1950s, many downtown and neighborhood theaters began catering to black customers to keep from going out of business. By the late 1960s and early 1970s, these theaters had become major venues for popular commercial films, even featuring a few movies about African Americans, including *Guess Who's Coming to Dinner?* (1967), *In the Heat of*

the Night (1967), *The Learning Tree* (1969), and *Sounder* (1972).

Based on the popularity of these films, black photographer-turned-filmmaker Gordon Parks, who directed *The Learning Tree* (adapted from his own novel), went on to make commercial action/adventure films, including *Shaft* (1971, remade by John Singleton in 2000). Popular in urban theaters, especially among black teenagers, the movies produced by Parks and his son—Gordon Parks Jr. (*Super Fly*, 1972)—spawned a number of commercial imitators, labeled *blaxploitation* movies. These films were the subject of heated cultural debates in the 1970s; like some rap songs today, they were both praised for their realistic depictions of black urban life and criticized for glorifying violence. Nevertheless, these films reinvigorated urban movie attendance.

Opportunities for black film directors have expanded since the 1980s and 1990s, although even now there is still debate about what kinds of African American representation should be on the screen. Lee Daniels received only the second Academy Award nomination

for a black director for *Precious: Based on the Novel "Push" by Sapphire* in 2009 (the first was John Singleton for *Boyz N the Hood* in 1991). *Precious*, about an obese, illiterate black teenage girl subjected to severe sexual and emotional abuse, was praised by many critics but decried by others who interpreted it as more blaxploitation or "poverty porn."[2] Two more-recent films represented black characters based on real stories, and both found critical and commercial success. In 2013, Daniels returned as the director of *The Butler*, inspired by the real story of an African American man who experienced major events of the twentieth century from his position as a White House butler. In that same year, *12 Years a Slave*, by black British director Steve McQueen, told the story of a free African American man who was kidnapped and sold into slavery. The film adaptation of Solomon Northrup's 1853 memoir won three Academy Awards, including best picture, and a best director nomination for McQueen. McQueen became the first black director to win a best picture award. ◢

The Kobal Collection at Art Resource, NY

FOREIGN FILMS
China restricts the number of imported films shown and regulates the lengths of their runs in order to protect its own domestic film industry. Nonetheless, China has become a lucrative market—for both U.S. films and its own features, like *The Monkey King* (2014). This 3-D live-action film based on a classic Chinese folk story became one of China's biggest hits of 2014.

of U.S. films. As a result, between 1966 and 1990 the number of foreign films released annually in the United States dropped by two-thirds, from nearly three hundred to about one hundred titles per year.

With the growth of superstore video chains like Blockbuster in the 1990s, which were supplanted by online video services like Netflix in the 2000s, viewers gained access to a larger selection of foreign-language titles. The successes of *Amélie* (France, 2001), *The Girl with the Dragon Tattoo* (Sweden, 2009), and *Instructions Not Included* (Mexico, 2013) illustrate that U.S. audiences are willing to watch subtitled films with non-Hollywood perspectives. However, foreign films are losing ground as they compete with the expanding independent American film market for screen space.

Today, the largest film industry is in India, out of Bollywood (a play on words combining city names Bombay—now Mumbai—and Hollywood), where about a thousand films a year are produced—mostly romance or adventure musicals in a distinct style.[10] In comparison, Hollywood moviemakers release five hundred to six hundred films a year. (For a broader perspective, see "Global Village: Beyond Hollywood: Asian Cinema" on page 250.)

The Documentary Tradition

Both TV news and nonfiction films trace their roots to the movie industry's *interest films* and *newsreels* of the late 1890s. In Britain, interest films compiled footage of regional wars, political leaders, industrial workers, and agricultural scenes, and were screened with fiction shorts. Pioneered in France and England, newsreels consisted of weekly ten-minute magazine-style compilations of filmed news events from around the world. International news services began supplying theaters and movie studios with newsreels, and by 1911, they had become a regular part of the moviegoing menu.

Early filmmakers also produced *travelogues*, which recorded daily life in various communities around the world. Travel films reached a new status in Robert Flaherty's classic *Nanook of the North* (1922), which tracked an Inuit family in the harsh Hudson Bay region of Canada. Flaherty edited his fifty-five-minute film to both tell and interpret the story of his subject. Flaherty's second film, *Moana* (1925), a study of the lush South Pacific islands, inspired the term **documentary** in a 1926 film review by John Grierson, a Scottish film producer. Grierson defined Flaherty's work and the documentary form as "the creative treatment of actuality," or a genre that interprets reality by recording real people and settings.

Over time, the documentary developed an identity apart from its commercial presentation. As an educational, noncommercial form, the documentary usually required the backing of industry, government, or philanthropy to cover costs. In support of a clear alternative to Hollywood cinema, some nations began creating special units, such as Canada's National Film Board, to sponsor documentaries. In the United States, art and film received considerable support from the Roosevelt administration during the Depression.

By the late 1950s and early 1960s, the development of portable cameras had led to **cinema verité** (a French term for "truth film"). This documentary style allowed filmmakers to go where cameras could not go before and record fragments of everyday life more unobtrusively. Directly opposed to packaged, high-gloss Hollywood features, verité aimed to track reality, employing a rough, grainy look and shaky, handheld camera work. Among the key innovators in cinema verité was Drew Associates, led by Robert Drew, a former *Life* magazine photographer. Through his connection to Time Inc. (which owned *Life*) and its chain of TV stations, Drew shot the groundbreaking documentary *Primary*, which followed the 1960 Democratic presidential primary race between Hubert Humphrey and John F. Kennedy.

Perhaps the major contribution of documentaries has been their willingness to tackle controversial or unpopular subject matter. For example, American documentary filmmaker Michael Moore often addresses complex topics that target corporations or the government. His films include *Roger and Me* (1989), a comic and controversial look at the relationship between the city of Flint, Michigan, and General Motors; the Oscar-winning *Bowling for Columbine* (2002), an exploration of gun violence; *Fahrenheit 9/11* (2004), a critique of the Bush administration's Middle East policies; *Sicko* (2007), an investigation of the U.S. health-care system; and *Capitalism: A Love Story* (2009), a study of corporate culture in the United States. Moore's recent films were part of a resurgence in high-profile documentary filmmaking in the United States, which included *The Fog of War* (2003), *Super Size Me* (2004), *An Inconvenient Truth* (2006), *The Cove* (2009), and *Bully* (2012).

© Magnolia Pictures/Everett Collection

DOCUMENTARY FILMS
Blackfish, a documentary released in 2013, tracks the tragic life of Tilikum, a captive killer whale that attacked and killed his trainer. The documentary examines the controversial practice of training orca whales for entertainment venues like SeaWorld (the film's tagline is "Never capture what you can't control"). In fact, *Blackfish*, which first screened at the Sundance Film Festival, sparked anti-SeaWorld protests across the country.

The Rise of Independent Films

The success of documentary films like *Super Size Me* and *Fahrenheit 9/11* dovetails with the rise of **indies**, or independently produced films. As opposed to directors working in the Hollywood system, independent filmmakers typically operate on a shoestring budget and show their movies in thousands of campus auditoriums and at hundreds of small film festivals. The decreasing costs of portable technology, including smaller digital cameras and computer editing, have kept many documentary and independent filmmakers in business. They make movies inexpensively, relying on real-life situations, stage actors and nonactors, crews made up of friends and students, and local nonstudio settings. Successful independents like Sofia Coppola (*Lost in Translation*, 2003; *The Bling Ring*, 2013) and Jim Jarmusch (*Dead Man*, 1995; *Only Lovers Left Alive*, 2014) continue to find substantial audiences in college and art-house theaters and through online DVD and streaming services like Netflix, which promote work produced outside the studio system. Meanwhile, independent-minded filmmakers like Wes Anderson (*Rushmore*, 1998; *The Grand Budapest Hotel*, 2014), Darren Aronofsky (*Black Swan*, 2010; *Noah*, 2014), and David O. Russell (*The Fighter*, 2010; *American Hustle*, 2013) have established careers somewhere between fully independent and studio backed, often with smaller companies financing their films before they're picked up by bigger studios.

Distributing smaller films can be big business for the studios. The rise of independent film festivals in the 1990s—especially the Sundance Film Festival held every January in Park City, Utah—helped Hollywood rediscover low-cost independent films as an alternative to traditional movies with *Titanic*-size budgets. Films such as *Little Miss Sunshine* (2006), *500 Days of Summer* (2009), *The Way, Way Back* (2013), and *Whiplash* (2014) were able to generate industry buzz and garner major studio distribution deals through Sundance screenings, becoming star vehicles for several directors and actors. As with the recording industry, the

Beyond Hollywood: Asian Cinema

Asian nations easily outstrip Hollywood in quantity of films produced. India alone produces about a thousand movies a year. But from India to South Korea, Asian films are increasingly challenging Hollywood in terms of quality, and they have become more influential as Asian directors, actors, and film styles are exported to Hollywood and the world.

India

Part musical, part action, part romance, and part suspense, the epic films of Bollywood typically have fantastic sets, hordes of extras, plenty of wet saris, and symbolic fountain bursts (as a substitute for kissing and sex, which are prohibited from being shown). Indian movie fans pay from $.75 to $5 to see these films, and they feel shortchanged if the movies are shorter than three hours. With many films produced in less than a week, however, most of the Bollywood fare is cheaply produced and badly acted. But these production aesthetics are changing, as bigger-budget releases target middle and upper classes in India, the twenty-five million Indians living abroad, and Western audiences. *Jab Tak Hai Jaan* (2012), a romance starring Shahrukh Khan—India's most famous leading man—had the most successful U.S. box-office opening of any Bollywood film. The film was released just weeks after the death of Yash Chopra, its award-winning director.

China

Since the late 1980s, Chinese cinema has developed an international reputation. Leading this generation of directors are Yimou Zhang (*House of Flying Daggers*, 2004; *Coming Home*, 2014) and Kaige Chen (*Farewell My Concubine*, 1993; *Caught in the Web*, 2012), whose work has spanned such genres as historical epics, love stories, contemporary tales of city life, and action fantasy. These directors have also helped to make international stars out of Li Gong (*Memoirs of a Geisha*, 2005; *Coming Home*, 2014) and Ziyi Zhang (*Memoirs of a Geisha*, 2005; *Dangerous Liaisons*, 2012).

Hong Kong

Hong Kong films were the most talked about—and the most influential—film genre in cinema throughout the late 1980s and 1990s. The style of highly choreographed action with often breathtaking, balletlike violence became hugely popular around the world, reaching American audiences and in some cases even outselling Hollywood blockbusters. Hong Kong directors like John Woo, Ringo Lam, and Jackie Chan (who also acts in his movies) have directed Hollywood action films; and Hong Kong stars like Jet Li (*Lethal Weapon 4*, 1998; *The Expendables 3*, 2014), Yun-Fat Chow (*Pirates of the Caribbean: At World's End*, 2007; *The Monkey King*, 2014), and Malaysia's Michelle Yeoh (*Memoirs of a Geisha*, 2005; *The Lady*, 2011) are landing leading roles in American movies.

Japan

Americans may be most familiar with low-budget monster movies like *Godzilla*, but the widely heralded films of the late director Akira Kurosawa have had an even greater impact: His *Seven Samurai* (1954) was remade by Hollywood as *The Magnificent Seven* (1960), and *The Hidden Fortress* (1958) was George Lucas's inspiration for *Star Wars*. Hayao Miyazaki (*Ponyo*, 2009; *The Wind Rises*, 2013) is the country's top director of anime movies. Japanese thrillers like *Ringu* (1998), *Ringu 2* (1999), and *Ju-on: The Grudge* (2003) were remade into successful American horror films. Hirokazu Koreeda's drama *Like Father, Like Son* (2013) won the Jury Prize at the Cannes Film Festival and caught the attention of Steven Spielberg, who acquired the remake rights for his company DreamWorks.

BOLLYWOOD STAR Parineeti Chopra stars in *Hasee Toh Phasee* (2014; English: *She Smiles, She's Snared!*)

© Reliance Entertainment/Everett Collection

South Korea

The end of military regimes in the late 1980s and corporate investment in the film business in the 1990s created a new era in Korean moviemaking. Leading directors include Kim Jee-woon; Lee Chang-dong (nominated for the Palme d'Or award at Cannes for *Poetry*, 2010); and Chan-wook Park, whose Vengeance Trilogy films (*Sympathy for Mr. Vengeance*, 2002; *Oldboy*, 2003; and *Lady Vengeance*, 2005) have won international acclaim, including the Grand Prix at Cannes for *Oldboy*, which was remade in the United States in 2013 by director Spike Lee. Joon-ho Bong's science-fiction film *Snowpiercer* (2013), based on a French graphic novel, filmed in the Czech Republic, and starring a mostly English-speaking cast (including Chris Evans and Tilda Swinton) epitomizes the international outlook of Korean cinema.

major studios see these festivals—which also include New York's Tribeca Film Festival, the South by Southwest festival in Austin, and international film festivals in Toronto and Cannes—as important venues for discovering new talent. Some major studios even purchased successful independent film companies (Disney's purchase of Miramax) or have developed in-house indie divisions (Sony's Sony Pictures Classics) to specifically handle the development and distribution of indies.

But by 2010, the independent film business as a feeder system for major studios was declining due to the poor economy and studios' waning interest in smaller specialty films. Disney sold Miramax for $660 million to an investor group composed of Hollywood outsiders. Viacom folded its independent unit, Paramount Vantage, into its main studio, and Time Warner closed its Warner Independent and Picturehouse in-house indie divisions. Meanwhile, producers of low-budget independent films increasingly looked to alternative digital distribution models, such as Internet downloads, direct DVD sales, and on-demand screenings via cable and services like Netflix.

Daniel McFadden/© Relativity Media/Everett Collection

INDEPENDENT FILM FESTIVALS, like the Sundance Film Festival, are widely recognized in the film industry as a major place to discover new talent and acquire independently made films on topics that might otherwise be too controversial, too niche specific, or too original for a major studio-backed picture. One of the breakout hits of Sundance 2013, the comedy *Don Jon*, was directed by and starred Joseph Gordon-Levitt. Relativity Studios acquired distribution rights for $4 million, and the film (which had a $6 million production budget) earned $24.4 million in domestic box-office receipts.

The Transformation of the Studio System

After years of thriving, the Hollywood movie industry began to falter after 1946. Weekly movie attendance in the United States peaked at ninety million in 1946, then fell to under twenty-five million by 1963. Critics and observers began talking about the death of Hollywood, claiming that the Golden Age was over. However, the movie industry adapted and survived, just as it continues to do today. Among the changing conditions facing the film industry were the communist witch-hunts in Hollywood, the end of the industry's vertical integration, suburbanization, the arrival of television, and the appearance of home entertainment.

The Hollywood Ten

In 1947, in the wake of the unfolding Cold War with the Soviet Union, conservative members of Congress began investigating Hollywood for alleged subversive and communist ties. That year, aggressive witch-hunts for political radicals in the film industry by the House Un-American Activities Committee (HUAC) led to the famous **Hollywood Ten** hearings and subsequent trial. (HUAC included future president Richard M. Nixon, then a congressman from California.)

During the investigations, HUAC coerced prominent people from the film industry to declare their patriotism and to give up the names of colleagues suspected of having politically unfriendly tendencies. Upset over labor union strikes and outspoken writers, many film executives were eager to testify and provide names. For instance, Jack L. Warner of Warner Brothers suggested that whenever film writers made fun of the wealthy or America's political system in

▲

THE HOLLYWOOD TEN
While many studio heads, producers, and actors "named names" to HUAC, others, such as the group shown here, held protests to demand the release of the Hollywood Ten.

their work, or if their movies were sympathetic to "Indians and the colored folks,"[11] they were engaging in communist propaganda. Other "friendly" HUAC witnesses included actors Gary Cooper and Ronald Reagan, director Elia Kazan, and producer Walt Disney. Whether they believed it was their patriotic duty or they feared losing their jobs, many prominent actors, directors, and other film executives also "named names."

Eventually, HUAC subpoenaed ten unwilling witnesses who were questioned about their memberships in various organizations. The so-called Hollywood Ten—nine screenwriters and one director—refused to discuss their memberships or to identify communist sympathizers. Charged with contempt of Congress in November 1947, they were eventually sent to prison. Although jailing the Hollywood Ten clearly violated their free-speech rights, in the atmosphere of the Cold War many people worried that "the American way" could be sabotaged via unpatriotic messages planted in films. Upon release from jail, the Hollywood Ten found themselves blacklisted, or boycotted, by the major studios, and their careers in the film industry were all but ruined. The national fervor over communism continued to plague Hollywood well into the 1950s.

The Paramount Decision

Coinciding with the HUAC investigations, the government also increased its scrutiny of the movie industry's aggressive business practices. By the mid-1940s, the Justice Department demanded that the five major film companies—Paramount, Warner Brothers, Twentieth Century Fox, MGM, and RKO—end vertical integration, which involved the simultaneous control over production, distribution, and exhibition. In 1948, after a series of court appeals, the Supreme Court ruled against the film industry in what is commonly known as the **Paramount decision**, forcing the studios to gradually divest themselves of their theaters.

Although the government had hoped to increase competition, the Paramount case never really changed the oligopoly structure of the Hollywood film industry because it failed to challenge the industry's control over distribution. However, the 1948 decision did create opportunities in the exhibition part of the industry for those outside Hollywood. In addition to art houses showing documentaries or foreign films, thousands of drive-in theaters sprang up in farmers' fields, welcoming new suburbanites who embraced the automobile. Although drive-ins had been around since the 1930s, by the end of the 1950s, more than four thousand existed. The Paramount decision encouraged new indoor theater openings as well, but the major studios continued to dominate distribution.

Moving to the Suburbs

Common sense might suggest that television alone precipitated the decline in post–World War II movie attendance, but the most dramatic drop actually occurred in the late 1940s—before most Americans even owned TV sets.[12]

Everett Collection

MOVIES TAKE ON SOCIAL ISSUES
Rebel without a Cause (1955), starring James Dean and Natalie Wood, was marketed in movie posters as "Warner Bros. Challenging Drama of Today's Teenage Violence!" James Dean's memorable portrayal of a troubled youth forever fixed his place in movie history. He was killed in a car crash a month before the movie opened.

The transformation from a wartime economy and a surge in consumer production had a significant impact on moviegoing. With industries turning from armaments to appliances, Americans started cashing in their wartime savings bonds for household goods and new cars. Discretionary income that formerly went to buying movie tickets now went to acquiring consumer products, and the biggest product of all was a new house far from the downtown movie theaters—in the suburbs, where tax bases were lower. Home ownership in the United States doubled between 1945 and 1950, while the moviegoing public decreased just as quickly. Additionally, after the war, the average age for couples entering marriage dropped from twenty-four to nineteen. Unlike their parents, many postwar couples had their first child before they turned twenty-one. The combination of social and economic changes meant there were significantly fewer couples dating at the movies. Then, when television exploded in the late 1950s, there was even less discretionary income—and less reason to go to the movies.

Television Changes Hollywood

In the late 1940s, radio's popularity had a strong impact on film. Not only were 1948 and 1949 high points in radio listenership, but with the mass migration to the suburbs, radio offered Americans an inexpensive entertainment alternative to the movies (as it had during the Great Depression). As a result, many people stayed home and listened to radio programs until TV displaced both radio and movies as the medium of national entertainment in the mid-1950s. The movie industry responded in a variety of ways.

First, with growing legions of people gathering around their living room TV sets, movie content slowly shifted toward more serious subjects. At first, this shift was a response to the war and an acknowledgment of life's complexity, but later movies focused on subject matter that television did not encourage. This shift began with film noir in the 1940s but continued into the 1950s, as commercial movies, for the first time, explored larger social problems such as alcoholism (*The Lost Weekend*, 1945), anti-Semitism (*Gentleman's Agreement*, 1947), mental illness (*The Snake Pit*, 1948), racism (*Pinky*, 1949), adult–teen relationships (*Rebel without a Cause*, 1955), drug abuse (*The Man with the Golden Arm*, 1955), and—perhaps most controversial—sexuality (*Peyton Place*, 1957; *Butterfield 8*, 1960; *Lolita*, 1962).

These and other films challenged the authority of the industry's own prohibitive Motion Picture Production Code. Hollywood adopted the Code in the early 1930s to restrict film depictions of violence, crime, drug use, and sexual behavior and to quiet public and political concerns that the movie business was lowering the moral standards of America. (For more on the Code, see Chapter 16.) In 1967, after the Code had been ignored by producers for several years, the Motion Picture Association of America initiated the current ratings system, which rated films for age appropriateness rather than censoring all adult content.

Second, just as radio worked to improve sound to maintain an advantage over television in the 1950s, the film industry introduced a host of technological improvements to lure Americans away from their TV sets. Technicolor, invented by an MIT scientist in 1917, had improved and was being used in more movies to draw people away from their black-and-white TVs. In addition, Cinerama, CinemaScope, and VistaVision all arrived in movie theaters, featuring striking wide-screen images, multiple synchronized projectors, and stereophonic sound. Then 3-D (three-dimensional) movies appeared, although they wore off quickly as a novelty. Finally, Panavision, which used special Eastman color film and camera lenses that decreased the fuzziness of images, became the wide-screen standard throughout the industry. These developments, however, generally failed to address the movies' primary problem: the middle-class flight to the suburbs, away from downtown theaters.

Hollywood Adapts to Home Entertainment

Just as nickelodeons, movie palaces, and drive-ins transformed movie exhibition in earlier times, the introduction of cable television and the videocassette in the 1970s transformed contemporary movie exhibition. Although the video market became a financial bonanza for the movie industry, Hollywood ironically tried to stall the arrival of the VCR in the 1970s— even filing lawsuits to prohibit customers from copying movies from television. The 1997 introduction of the DVD helped reinvigorate the flat sales of the home video market as people began to acquire new movie collections on DVD. Today, home movie exhibition is again in transition, this time from DVD to Internet video. As DVD purchases began to decline, Hollywood endorsed the high-definition format Blu-ray in 2008 to revive sales, but the format didn't grow quickly enough to help the video store business. The biggest chain, Blockbuster, filed for bankruptcy in 2010, closed hundreds of stores, and was auctioned to the Dish Network in 2011, while the Movie Gallery–Hollywood Video chain shuttered all its stores. The only bright spot in DVD rentals has been at the low end of the market—automated kiosks like Redbox that rent movies for $1.50 to $2.00 a day—but even the kiosk rental business began to flatline by 2013.

The future of the video business is in Internet distribution. Movie fans can download or stream movies and television shows for rent or for purchase from services like Netflix, Amazon, Hulu, Google Play, and the iTunes store to their television sets through devices like Roku, Apple TV, TiVo Premiere, video game consoles, and Internet-ready TVs. As people invest in wide-screen TVs (including 3-D televisions) and sophisticated sound systems, home entertainment is getting bigger and keeping pace with the movie theater experience. Interestingly, home entertainment is also getting smaller—movies are increasingly available to stream and download on portable devices like tablets, laptop computers, and smartphones.

The Economics of the Movie Business

Despite the development of network and cable television, video-on-demand, DVDs, and Internet downloads and streaming, the movie business has continued to thrive. In fact, since 1963, Americans have purchased roughly 1 billion movie tickets each year; in 2013, 1.34 billion tickets were sold.[13] With first-run movie tickets in some areas rising to $15 (and 3-D movies costing even more), gross revenues from North American box-office sales have climbed to $10.9 billion, up from $8.8 billion annually in 2005 (see Figure 7.1). The bigger news for Hollywood studios is that global box-office revenues have grown at a much more rapid rate, especially in China (which adds an average of thirteen new movie screens every day), Russia, and Mexico.[14]

The growing global market for Hollywood films has helped cushion the industry as the home video market undergoes a significant transformation, with the demise of the video rental business and the rise of video streaming. In order to flourish, the movie industry has had to continually revamp its production, distribution, and exhibition system and consolidate its ownership.

Production, Distribution, and Exhibition Today

In the 1970s, attendance by young moviegoers at new suburban multiplex theaters made megahits of *The Godfather* (1972), *The Exorcist* (1973), *Jaws* (1975), *Rocky* (1976), and *Star Wars* (1977). During this period, *Jaws* and *Star Wars* became the first movies to gross more than $100 million at the U.S. box office in a single year. In trying to copy the success of these blockbuster hits, the major studios set in place economic strategies for future decades. (See "Media Literacy and the Critical Process: The Blockbuster Mentality" on page 259.)

Making Money on Movies Today

With 80 to 90 percent of newly released movies failing to make money at the domestic box office, studios need a couple of major hits each year to offset losses on other films. (See Table 7.2 on page 256 for a list of the highest-grossing films of all time.) The potential losses are great: Over

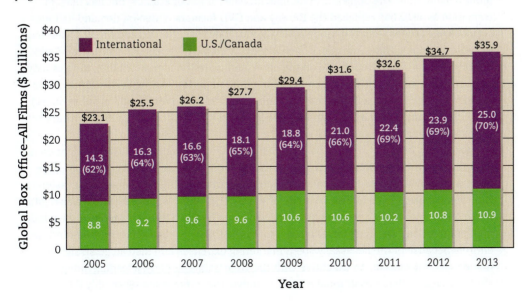

FIGURE 7.1

NORTH AMERICAN AND GLOBAL BOX-OFFICE REVENUE, 2005–2013 (IN $ BILLIONS)

Data from: Motion Picture Association of America, "Global Box Office—All Films (US$ Billions)," www.mpaa.org/wp-content /uploads/2014/03/MPAA-Theatrical -Market-Statistics-2013_032514 -v2.pdf.

TABLE 7.2

THE TOP 10 ALL-TIME BOX-OFFICE CHAMPIONS*

Data from: "All-Time Domestic Blockbusters," Box Office Guru, June 1, 2014, www.boxofficeguru .com/blockbusters.htm.

*Most rankings of the Top 10 most popular films are based on American box-office receipts. If these were adjusted for inflation, *Gone with the Wind* (1939) would become No. 1 in U.S. theater revenue. *Star Wars, Titanic,* and *E.T.* would all remain in the Top 10.

**Gross is shown in absolute dollars based on box-office sales in the United States and Canada.

Rank	Title/Date	Domestic Gross** ($ millions)
1	*Avatar* (2009)	760.5
2	*Titanic* (1997, 2012 3-D)	658.6
3	*The Avengers* (2012)	623.4
4	*The Dark Knight* (2008)	533
5	*Star Wars: Episode I—The Phantom Menace* (1999, 2012 3-D)	474.5
6	*Star Wars* (1977, 1997)	461
7	*The Dark Knight Rises* (2012)	447.8
8	*Shrek 2* (2004)	437.7
9	*E.T.: The Extra-Terrestrial* (1982, 2002)	435
10	*The Hunger Games: Catching Fire* (2013)	424.7

the past decade, a major studio film, on average, cost about $66 million to produce and about $37 million for domestic marketing, advertising, and print costs.[15]

With climbing film costs, creating revenue from a movie is a formidable task. Studios make money on movies from six major sources:

- First, the studios get a portion of the theater box-office revenue—about 40 percent of the box-office take (the theaters get the rest). More recently, studios have found that they can often reel in bigger box-office receipts for 3-D films and their higher ticket prices. For example, admission to the 2-D version of a film costs $15 at a New York City multiplex, while the 3-D version costs $19.50 at the same theater. In 2013, 3-D film screenings accounted for 16 percent of domestic box-office revenue. As Hollywood makes more 3-D films (the latest form of product differentiation), the challenge for major studios has been to increase the number of digital 3-D screens across the country. By 2013, about 37 percent of U.S. theater screens were capable of showing digital 3-D.

- Second, about three to four months after the theatrical release comes the home video market, which includes video-on-demand (VOD), subscription streaming, and the remaining Blu-ray and DVD sales and rental business. This release "window" generates more revenue than the domestic box-office income for major studios, but has been in transition as VOD has replaced the Blu-ray and DVD formats. Video-on-demand includes services like iTunes, Amazon, Google Play, Vudu, Hulu Plus, Netflix, and the VOD services of cable companies like Comcast, Time Warner Cable, Cox, Verizon, and satellite providers DirecTV and Dish. Depending on the agreement with the film distributer, movies may be purchased for instant viewing, rented for a limited period of time at a lower price, or (as in the case of Netflix, the largest streaming service with over 36 million subscribers) instantly streamed as part of a monthly fee for access to the company's entire library of licensed offerings.

Generally, discount rental kiosk companies like Redbox must wait twenty-eight days after films go on sale before they can rent them. Netflix has entered into a similar agreement with movie studios in exchange for more video streaming content—a concession to Hollywood's preference to first try to get the greater profits from selling movies as digital downloads or as DVDs before renting them or licensing them to a streaming service. Independent films and documentaries often bypass the theatrical box-office release window entirely because of the necessary steep marketing expenses and instead go straight to home video for release. An executive with the Weinstein Company, a leading independent studio, suggests that a traditional release to movie theaters makes sense only if the studio anticipates that the film will make gross revenues of more than $20 million.[16] There is pressure from services like Netflix for Hollywood to release films simultaneously to the home video market and to theaters, but the theater industry and their major studio allies have fiercely protected the three- to four-month exclusive window that theaters have for movie releases, arguing that to lose exclusivity would destroy the movie theater business.[17]

- Third are the next "windows" of release for a film: premium cable (such as HBO and Showtime), then network and basic cable showings, and finally the syndicated TV market. The price these cable and television outlets pay to the studios is negotiated on a film-by-film basis.
- Fourth, studios earn revenue from distributing films in foreign markets. In fact, at $25 billion in 2013, international box-office gross revenues are more than double the U.S. and Canadian box-office receipts, and they continue to climb annually, even as other countries produce more of their own films.
- Fifth, studios make money by distributing the work of independent producers and filmmakers, who hire the studios to gain wider circulation. Independents pay the studios between 30 and 50 percent of the box-office and home video money they make from movies.
- Sixth, revenue is earned from merchandise licensing and *product placements* in movies. In the early days of television and film, characters generally used generic products, or product labels weren't highlighted in shots. For example, Bette Davis's and Humphrey Bogart's cigarette packs were rarely seen in the actors' movies. But with soaring film production costs, product placements are adding extra revenue while lending an element of authenticity to the staging. Famous product placements in movies include Reese's Pieces in *E.T.* (1982), Pepsi-Cola in *Back to the Future II* (1989), and an entire line of toy products in *The Lego Movie* (2014).

Theater Chains Consolidate Exhibition

Film exhibition is controlled by a handful of theater chains; the leading five companies operate more than 50 percent of U.S. screens. Each of the major chains—Regal Cinemas, AMC

Zade Rosenthal/© Walt Disney Studios Motion Pictures/Everett Collection

BLOCKBUSTERS like *Captain America: The Winter Soldier* (2014), which draws on Disney's Marvel Comics property, are sought after despite their large budgets because they can potentially bring in twice their cost in box-office receipts, disc and video-on-demand sales, streaming, merchandising, and—studios hope—sequels that generate more of the same. *Captain America: The Winter Soldier*, sequel to *Captain America: The First Avenger* (2011), grossed $256.7 million in the United States and earned another $454.1 million worldwide (almost 64 percent of the film's earnings came from abroad). A third installment is set to be released in 2016.

Entertainment, Cinemark USA, Carmike Cinemas, and Cineplex Entertainment—owns thousands of screens in suburban malls and at highway crossroads, and most have expanded into international markets as well. Because distributors require access to movie screens, they do business with the chains that control the most screens. In a multiplex, an exhibitor can project a potential hit on two or three screens at the same time; films that do not debut well are relegated to the smallest theaters or bumped quickly for a new release.

The strategy of the leading theater chains during the mid-1990s was to build more **megaplexes** (facilities with fourteen or more screens), featuring upscale concession services and luxurious screening rooms with stadium-style seating and digital sound to make moviegoing a special event. By 2014, the movie exhibition business had grown to a record number (39,783) of indoor screens, most of them at megaplex locations. To further combat the home theater market, movie theater chains added IMAX screens and digital projectors in order to exhibit specially mastered 3-D blockbusters that carry higher ticket prices.[18]

Still, theater chains sought to be less reliant on Hollywood studios, and with new digital projectors they began to screen nonmovie events, including live sporting events, rock concerts, and classic TV show marathons. One of the most successful theater events is the live HD simulcast of the New York Metropolitan Opera's performances, which began in 2007 and during the 2014–15 season screened ten operas in more than 1,900 locations in sixty-four countries worldwide. The top two theater chains, Regal and AMC, also joined forces in 2011 to form their own film studio, Open Road Films, which became a successful production and distribution business for smaller movies, like the animated film *The Nut Job* (2014) and the indie comedy *Chef* (2014).

The Major Studio Players

The current Hollywood commercial film business is ruled primarily by six companies: Warner Brothers, Paramount, Twentieth Century Fox, Universal, Columbia Pictures, and Disney—the **Big Six**. Except for Disney, all these companies are owned by large parent conglomerates (see Figure 7.2). The six major studios account for about 77 percent of the revenue generated by commercial films. They also control more than half the movie market in Europe and Asia. In the United States, three independent studios—sometimes called mini-majors—have maintained modest market share for a number of years: Lionsgate (*The Hunger Games*, the *Twilight* series), which purchased indie Summit Entertainment in 2012; the Weinstein Company (*Django Unchained*, *Sin City: A Dame to Kill For*); and Relativity (*Oculus*, *Safe Haven*).

FIGURE 7.2

MARKET SHARE OF U.S. FILM STUDIOS AND DISTRIBUTORS, 2013 (IN $ MILLIONS)

Note: Based on gross box-office revenue, January 1, 2013–December 31, 2013. Overall gross for period: $10.927 billion.

Data from: Box Office Mojo, "Studio Market Share, 2013," www.boxofficemojo.com/studio/.

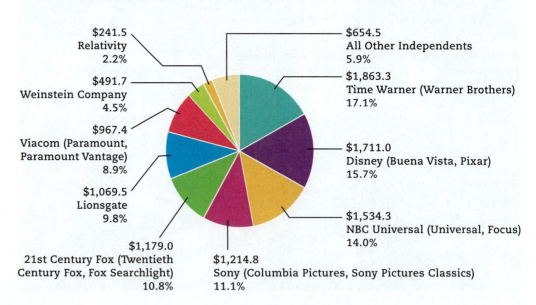

$241.5
Relativity
2.2%

$491.7
Weinstein Company
4.5%

$967.4
Viacom (Paramount, Paramount Vantage)
8.9%

$1,069.5
Lionsgate
9.8%

$1,179.0
21st Century Fox (Twentieth Century Fox, Fox Searchlight)
10.8%

$1,214.8
Sony (Columbia Pictures, Sony Pictures Classics)
11.1%

$654.5
All Other Independents
5.9%

$1,863.3
Time Warner (Warner Brothers)
17.1%

$1,711.0
Disney (Buena Vista, Pixar)
15.7%

$1,534.3
NBC Universal (Universal, Focus)
14.0%

Media Literacy and the Critical Process

1 **DESCRIPTION.** Consider a list of the all-time highest-grossing movies in the United States, such as the one on Box Office Mojo, http://boxofficemojo.com/alltime/domestic.htm.

2 **ANALYSIS.** Note patterns in the list. For example, of the thirty top-grossing films, twenty-four target young audiences (*The Passion of the Christ* is the only exception). Nearly all of these top-grossing films feature animated or digitally composited characters (*Frozen*, *Shrek*, *Jurassic Park*) or extensive special effects (*Transformers*, *The Avengers*). Nearly all of the films also either spawned or are a part of a series, like *The Lord of the Rings*, *Transformers*, *The Dark Knight*, and *Harry Potter*. More than half of the films fit into the action movie genre. Nearly all of the Top 30 had intense merchandising campaigns that featured action figures, fast-food tie-ins, and an incredible variety of products for sale; that is, hardly any were "surprise" hits.

The Blockbuster Mentality

In the beginning of this chapter, we noted Hollywood's shift toward a blockbuster mentality after the success of films like *Star Wars*. How pervasive is this blockbuster mentality, which targets an audience of young adults, releases action-packed big-budget films featuring heavy merchandising tie-ins, and produces sequels?

3 **INTERPRETATION.** What do the patterns mean? It's clear, economically, why Hollywood likes to have successful blockbuster movie franchises. But what kinds of films get left out of the mix? Hits like *Forrest Gump* (now bumped out of the Top 30), which may have had big-budget releases but lack some of the other attributes of blockbusters, are clearly anomalies of the blockbuster mentality, although they illustrate that strong characters and compelling stories can carry a film to great commercial success.

4 **EVALUATION.** It is likely that we will continue to see an increase in youth-oriented, animated/action movie franchises that are heavily merchandised and intended for wide international distribution. Indeed, Hollywood does not have a lot of motivation to put out the kinds of movies that don't fit these categories. Is this a good thing? Can you think of a film that you thought was excellent and that would have probably been a bigger hit with better promotion and wider distribution?

5 **ENGAGEMENT.** Watch independent and foreign films and see what you're missing. Visit foreignfilms.com or the Sundance Film Festival site and browse through the many films listed. Find these films on Netflix, Amazon, Google Play, or iTunes (and if the films are unavailable, let these services know). Write your cable company and request to have the Sundance Channel on your cable lineup. Organize an independent film night on your college campus and bring these films to a crowd.

In the 1980s, to offset losses resulting from box-office failures, the movie industry began to diversify, expanding into other product lines and other mass media. This expansion included television programming, print media, sound recordings, and home videos/DVDs, as well as cable and computers, electronic hardware and software, retail stores, and theme parks such as Universal Studios. To maintain the industry's economic stability, management strategies today rely on both heavy advance promotion (which can double the cost of a commercial film) and **synergy**—the promotion and sale of a product throughout the various subsidiaries of the media conglomerate. Companies promote not only the new movie itself but also its book form, soundtrack, calendars, T-shirts, Web site, and toy action figures, as well as "the-making-of" story on television, home video, and the Internet. The Disney studio, in particular, has been successful with its multiple repackaging of youth-targeted movies, including comic books, toys, television specials, fast-food tie-ins, and theme-park attractions. Since the 1950s, this synergy has been a key characteristic of the film industry and an important element in the flood of corporate mergers that have made today's Big Six even bigger.

The biggest corporate mergers have involved the internationalization of the American film business. Investment in American popular culture by the international electronics industry is particularly significant. This business strategy represents a new, high-tech kind of vertical integration—an attempt to control both the production of electronic equipment that

© Walt Disney Pictures/Everett Collection

SYNERGIES in feature films can be easy for Disney, which is a $45 billion multinational corporation. *Frozen* (2013) is one of Disney's biggest animated hits ever, and *Frozen* merchandise was in short supply in North America for fans wanting to celebrate the story of Anna and Elsa, two princess sisters who also became attractions at Disney resort parks. The movie's soundtrack hit No. 1 in sales, and Disney Cruise Line and the Adventures by Disney tour company experienced a huge increase in holiday business to Geirangerfjord, Norway, the fjord that inspired the film's fantasy kingdom of Arendelle.

consumers buy for their homes and the production and distribution of the content that runs on that equipment. This began in 1985 when Australia's News Corp. bought Twentieth Century Fox (News Corp. has since split into two separate companies; the film division is under the umbrella of 21st Century Fox). Sony bought Columbia in 1989 for $4 billion. Vivendi, a French utility, acquired Universal in 2000 but sold it to General Electric, the parent of NBC, in 2003. Comcast bought a controlling stake in NBC Universal in 2009, and government agencies approved the merger in 2011. In 2006, Disney bought its animation partner, Pixar. It also bought Marvel in 2009, which gave Disney the rights to a host of characters, including Spider-Man, Iron Man, the Hulk, the X-Men, and the Fantastic Four. In 2012, Disney bought Lucasfilm, gaining control of the *Indiana Jones* and *Star Wars* franchises, plus the innovative technologies of George Lucas's famed Industrial Light & Magic special effects company.

Convergence: Movies Adjust to the Digital Turn

The biggest challenge the movie industry faces today is the Internet. As broadband Internet service connects more households, movie fans are increasingly getting movies from the Web. After witnessing the difficulties that illegal file-sharing brought on the music labels (some of which share the same corporate parent as the Big Six), the movie industry has more quickly embraced the Internet for movie distribution. Apple's iTunes store began selling digital downloads of a limited selection of movies in 2006, and in 2008, iTunes began renting new movies from all the major studios for just $3.99. In the same year, online DVD rental service Netflix began streaming some movies and television shows to customers' computer screens and televisions.

The popularity of Netflix's streaming service opened the door to other similar services. Hulu, a joint venture by NBC Universal (Universal Studios), Twentieth Century Fox, and Disney, was created as the studios' attempt to divert attention from YouTube and get viewers to either watch free, ad-supported streaming movies and television shows online or subscribe to Hulu Plus, Hulu's premium service. Comcast operates a similar Web site, called Xfinity. Google's YouTube, the most popular online video service, moved to offer commercial films in 2010 by redesigning its interface to be more film-friendly and offering online rentals. Amazon, Vudu (owned by Walmart), and CinemaNow (owned by retailer Best Buy) also operate digital movie stores.

Movies are also increasingly available to stream or download on mobile phones and tablets. Several companies, including Netflix, Hulu, Amazon, Google, Apple, Redbox, and Blockbuster, have developed distribution to mobile devices. Small screens don't offer an optimal viewing experience, but if customers watch movies on their mobile devices, they will likely use the same company's service to continue viewing on the larger screens of computers and televisions.

The year 2012 marked a turning point: For the first time, movie fans accessed more movies through digital online media than physical copies, like DVD and Blu-ray.[19] For the movie industry, this shift to Internet distribution has mixed consequences. On one hand, the industry needs to offer movies where people want to access them, and digital distribution is a growing market. "We're agnostic about where the money comes from," says Eammon Bowles, president of the independent distributor Magnolia Pictures. "We don't care. Basically, our philosophy is we want to make the film available for however the customer wants to purchase it."[20] On the other hand, although streaming is less expensive than producing physical DVDs, the revenue is still much lower compared to DVD sales, which had a larger impact on the major studios that had grown reliant on healthy DVD revenue.

The digital turn creates two long-term paths for Hollywood. One path is that studios and theaters will lean even more heavily toward making and showing big-budget blockbuster film franchises with a lot of special effects, since people will want to watch those on the big screen (especially IMAX and 3-D) for the full effect—and they are easy to export for international audiences. The other path involves inexpensive digital distribution of lower-budget documentaries and independent films, which probably wouldn't get wide theatrical distribution anyway but could find an audience in those who watch from home.

The Internet has also become an essential tool for movie marketing, and one that studios are finding less expensive than traditional methods, like television ads or billboards. Films regularly have Web pages, but many studios now also use a full menu of social media to promote films in advance of their release. For example, the marketing plan for Lionsgate's 2012 movie *The Hunger Games*, which launched an enormously successful movie franchise, employed "near-constant use of Facebook and Twitter, a YouTube channel, a Tumblr blog, iPhone games and live Yahoo streaming from the premiere" to build interest that made it a hit film.[21]

Alternative Voices

With the major studios exerting such a profound influence on the worldwide production, distribution, and exhibition of movies, new alternatives have helped open and redefine the movie industry. The digital revolution in movie production is the most recent opportunity to wrest some power away from the Hollywood studios. Substantially cheaper and more accessible than standard film equipment, **digital video** is a shift from celluloid film; it allows filmmakers to replace expensive and bulky 16-mm and 35-mm film cameras with less expensive, lightweight digital video cameras. For moviemakers, digital video also means seeing camera work instantly instead of waiting for film to be developed, and being able to capture additional footage without concern for the high cost of film stock and processing.

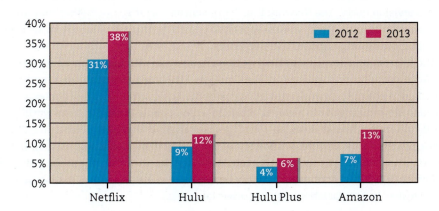

FIGURE 7.3

ONLINE VIDEO STREAMING MARKET SHARE RANKING IN 2013

Data from: Nielsen Newswire, "'Binging' Is the New Viewing for Over-the-Top Streamers," September 18, 2013, www.nielsen .com/us/en/newswire/2013/binging -is-the-new-viewing-for-over-the-top -streamers.html.

© Paramount Pictures/Photofest

PARANORMAL ACTIVITY
(2007), the horror film made by first-time director Oren Peli for a mere $15,000 with digital equipment, proves that you don't always need a big budget to make a successful film. Peli asked fans to "demand" the film be shown in their area via the Web site www.eventful.com, and Paramount agreed to a nationwide release if the film received one million "demands." *Paranormal Activity* was released nationwide on October 16, 2009, and went on to gross close to $200 million worldwide, spawning several sequels.

British director Mike Figgis achieved the milestone of producing the first fully digital release from a major studio with his film *Timecode* (2000). Though digital video has become commonplace on big studio productions, the greatest impact of digital technology has been on independent filmmakers. Low-cost digital video opened up the creative process to countless new artists. With digital video camera equipment and computer-based desktop editors, movies can be made for just a few thousand dollars, a fraction of what the cost would be on film. For example, *Paranormal Activity* (2007) was made for about $15,000 with digital equipment and went on to be a top box-office feature. Digital cameras are now the norm for independent filmmakers. Ironically, both independent and Hollywood filmmakers have to contend with issues of preserving digital content: Celluloid film stock can last a hundred years, whereas digital formats can be lost as storage formats fail and devices become obsolete.[22]

Because digital production puts movies in the same format as the Internet, independent filmmakers have new distribution venues beyond film festivals or the major studios. For example, Vimeo, YouTube, and Netflix have grown into leading Internet sites for the screening and distribution of short films and film festivals, providing filmmakers with their most valuable asset—an audience. Others have used the Web to sell DVDs directly, sell merchandise, or accept contributions for free movie downloads.

Popular Movies and Democracy

LaunchPad ◎
macmillanhighered.com
/mediaculture10e

More Than a Movie: Social Issues and Film
Independent filmmakers are using social media to get moviegoers involved.
Discussion: Do you think the convergence of digital media with social-issue movies helps such films make a larger impact? Why or why not?

At the cultural level, movies function as **consensus narratives**, a term that describes cultural products that become popular and provide shared cultural experiences. These consensus narratives operate across different times and cultures. In this sense, movies are part of a long narrative tradition, encompassing "the oral formulaic of Homer's day, the theater of Sophocles, the Elizabethan theater, the English novel from Defoe to Dickens, . . . the silent film, the sound film, and television during the Network Era."[23] Consensus narratives—whether they are dramas, romances, westerns, or mysteries—speak to central myths and values in an accessible language that often bridges global boundaries.

At the international level, countries continue to struggle with questions about the influence of American films on local customs and culture. Like other American mass media industries, the long reach of Hollywood movies is one of the key contradictions of contemporary life: Do such films contribute to a global village in which people throughout the world share a universal culture that breaks down barriers? Or does an American-based common culture stifle the development of local cultures worldwide and diversity in moviemaking? Clearly, the steady production of profitable action/adventure movies—whether they originate in the United States, Africa, France, or China—continues, not only because these movies appeal to mass audiences but also because they translate easily into other languages.

DIGITAL JOB OUTLOOK

Media Professionals Speak about Jobs in the Film Industry

Jeff White, Visual Effects Supervisor, Industrial Light & Magic

I was always interested in computer graphics and their application to visual effects. At the time I was going to college, there were very few formal programs in CG. I ended up studying cinema and photography with a minor in computer science. It actually turned out to be a nice combination of skills for a job in the field. I am terrible at drawing, so that route was not going to get me in, but studying film production, lighting, camera work, editing, was all very relevant to the job I do today.

Hossein Amini, Screenwriter (*Drive, The Wings of the Dove, Snow White and the Huntsman*)

I think you learn from doing lots and lots of stuff, but also you have to be quite tough about rejection and not getting breaks. I mean, I had tons of stuff. I kept on sending scripts out and getting rejection letters, often probably from people who sometimes hadn't even read them, I assume. I think that persistence and toughness are just so important. And I think everyone gets better; I don't think it's something you're born with. I do think it's something that hard work gets you further and further, and I think you improve.

Robert Rodriguez, Filmmaker (*Sin City, Spy Kids*), to the Graduating Class at the University of Texas

I didn't know that it was impossible to go make a movie for such a low budget with no film crew. . . . How did I figure it out? I'm from a big family. I can't waste money. It's against my genetic makeup. So I had to substitute money with creativity, and that's what made all the difference. So I had to make a movie in a way that broke the traditional mold and learn not to be a slave to tradition. Traditional thinking will hold you back.

Jennifer Lee, Filmmaker (*Frozen*), to the Graduating Class at the University of New Hampshire

When you are free from self-doubt, you fail better. You accept criticism and listen. . . . If I learned one thing, it is that self-doubt is one of the most destructive forces. It makes you defensive instead of open, reactive instead of active. . . . If you can learn to not take it personally, you'll be able to listen to constructive criticism and find it inspiring. It might motivate you and show you that you are capable of far more than you ever imagined.

With the rise of international media conglomerates, it has become more difficult to awaken public debate over issues of movie diversity and America's domination of the film business. Consequently, issues concerning increased competition and a greater variety of movies sometimes fall by the wayside. As critical consumers, those of us who enjoy movies and recognize their cultural significance must raise these broader issues in public forums as well as in our personal conversations. ▶

CHAPTER REVIEW

COMMON THREADS

One of the Common Threads discussed in Chapter 1 is mass media, cultural expression, and storytelling. The movie industry is a particularly potent example of this, as Hollywood movies dominate international screens. But Hollywood dominates our domestic screens as well. Does this limit our exposure to other kinds of stories?

In the 1920s, when the burgeoning film industries in Europe lay in ruins after World War I, Hollywood gained an international dominance it has never relinquished. Critics have long cited America's *cultural imperialism*, claiming America floods the world with its movies, music, television shows, fashion, and products. The strength of American cultural and economic power is evident when you witness a Thai man in a Tommy Hilfiger shirt watching *Transformers* at a Bangkok bar while eating a hamburger and drinking a Coke. Critics feel that American-produced culture overwhelms indigenous cultural industries, which will never be able to compete at the same level.

But other cultures are good at bending and blending our content. Hip-hop has been remade into regional music in places like Senegal, Portugal, Taiwan, and the Philippines. McDonald's is global, but in India you can get a McAloo Tikki sandwich—a spicy fried potato and pea vegetarian patty. In Turkey you can get a McTurco, a kebab with lamb or chicken. And in France you can order a beer with your meal.

While some may be proud of the success of America's cultural exports, we might also ask ourselves this: What is the impact of our cultural dominance on our own media environment? Foreign films, for example, account for less than 2 percent of all releases in the United States. Is this because we find subtitles or other languages too challenging? At points in the twentieth century, American moviegoers were much more likely to see foreign films. Did our taste in movies change on our own accord, or did we simply forget how to appreciate different narratives and styles?

Of course, international content does make it to our shores. We exported rock and roll, and the British sent it back to us, with long hair. They also gave us *The Office* and *House of Cards*. Japan gave us anime, Pokémon, *Iron Chef*, and Hello Kitty.

But in a world where globalization is a key phenomenon, Hollywood rarely shows us the world through another's eyes. The burden falls to us to search out and watch those movies until Hollywood finally gets the message.

KEY TERMS

The definitions for the terms listed below can be found in the glossary at the end of the book. The page numbers listed with the terms indicate where the term is highlighted in the chapter.

celluloid, 235
kinetograph, 236
kinetoscope, 236
vitascope, 237
narrative films, 237
nickelodeons, 237
vertical integration, 238
oligopoly, 238
studio system, 239
block booking, 240

movie palaces, 241
multiplexes, 241
Big Five, 241
Little Three, 241
blockbuster, 242
talkies, 242
newsreels, 243
genre, 243
documentary, 248
cinema verité, 248

indies, 249
Hollywood Ten, 251
Paramount decision, 252
megaplexes, 258
Big Six, 258
synergy, 259
digital video, 261
consensus narratives, 262

For review quizzes, chapter summaries, links to media-related Web sites, and more, go to macmillanhighered.com/mediaculture10e.

REVIEW QUESTIONS

Early Technology and the Evolution of Movies

1. How did film go from the novelty stage to the mass medium stage?

2. Why were early silent films popular?

3. What contribution did nickelodeons make to film history?

The Rise of the Hollywood Studio System

4. Why did Hollywood end up as the center of film production?

5. Why did Thomas Edison and the patents Trust fail to shape and control the film industry, and why did Adolph Zukor of Paramount succeed?

6. How does vertical integration work in the film business?

The Studio System's Golden Age

7. Why did a certain structure of film—called classic Hollywood narrative—become so dominant in moviemaking?

8. Why are genres and directors important to the film industry?

9. Why are documentaries an important alternative to traditional Hollywood filmmaking? What contributions have they made to the film industry?

The Transformation of the Studio System

10. What political and cultural forces changed the Hollywood system in the 1950s?

11. How did the movie industry respond to the advent of television?

12. How has the home entertainment industry developed and changed since the 1970s?

The Economics of the Movie Business

13. What are the various ways in which major movie studios make money from the film business?

14. How do a few large film studios manage to control most of the commercial industry?

15. How is the movie industry adapting to the Internet?

16. What is the impact of inexpensive digital technology on filmmaking?

Popular Movies and Democracy

17. Do films contribute to a global village in which people throughout the world share a universal culture? Or do U.S.-based films overwhelm the development of other cultures worldwide? Discuss.

QUESTIONING THE MEDIA

1. Do some research, and compare your earliest memory of going to a movie with a parent's or grandparent's earliest memory.

2. Do you remember seeing a movie you were not allowed to see? Discuss the experience.

3. Do you prefer viewing films at a movie theater or at home, either by playing a DVD or by streaming/downloading from the Internet? How might your viewing preferences connect to the way in which the film industry is evolving?

4. If you were a Hollywood film producer or executive, what kinds of films would you like to see made? What changes would you make in what we see at the movies?

5. Look at the international film box-office statistics in the latest issue of *Variety* magazine or online at www.boxofficemojo.com. Note which films are the most popular worldwide. What do you think about the significant role U.S. movies play in global culture? Should their role be less significant? Explain your answer.

LAUNCHPAD FOR *MEDIA & CULTURE*

Visit LaunchPad for *Media & Culture* *at* macmillanhighered.com/mediaculture10e *for additional learning tools:*

- REVIEW WITH LEARNINGCURVE
  LearningCurve, available on LaunchPad for *Media & Culture*, uses gamelike quizzing to help you master the concepts you need to learn from this chapter.

- VIDEO: *Gravity*
  Watch a brief clip from *Gravity*, and discuss how the movie uses the most advanced technical tools in service of classical storytelling.

PART 3
Words and Pictures

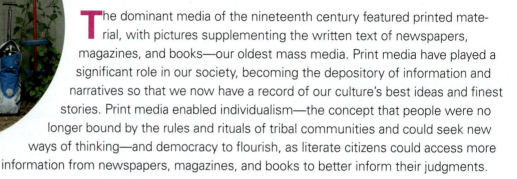

The dominant media of the nineteenth century featured printed material, with pictures supplementing the written text of newspapers, magazines, and books—our oldest mass media. Print media have played a significant role in our society, becoming the depository of information and narratives so that we now have a record of our culture's best ideas and finest stories. Print media enabled individualism—the concept that people were no longer bound by the rules and rituals of tribal communities and could seek new ways of thinking—and democracy to flourish, as literate citizens could access more information from newspapers, magazines, and books to better inform their judgments.

These media did not disappear when music, radio, and TV came along in the twentieth century. Rather, the newspaper, magazine, and book industries adapted. And in the twenty-first century, the story of our oldest media is still about adapting, but this time in the age of Apple and Amazon. As older media make the digital turn, daily papers, sports magazines, and romance novels are all transformed on digital tablets, like Apple's iPad and Amazon's Kindle. We are still reading newspapers, subscribing to magazines, and buying books; they now just come in multiple forms—from their old printed versions to their new digital incarnations.

Still, even with the rich older histories of our printed media, we wonder whether rising technological innovation and crumbling business models are obstacles too big to overcome. Indeed, online start-up companies like craigslist created havoc in the newspaper industry by demonstrating better and cheaper ways to display classified advertising. Great old newspapers like the *Chicago Tribune* and the *Los Angeles Times* still drift into bankruptcy as newspaper stock prices plunge and critics forecast their doom. In addition, we saw the venerable magazine *Newsweek*, around since 1933, sell for $1 in 2010 and then disappear in its print form in 2013 (although a new owner relaunched a print edition of *Newsweek* in March 2014). In 2011, we witnessed the demise of the megabookstore chain Borders, which failed to adapt fast enough to the digital turn and in the end could not compete with online behemoths like Amazon, only a few years ago a start-up company itself.

As we wrestle with the changes of the digital age, does it make any difference whether we get our news from a printed newspaper or an online Web site? Does it matter if we hold a physical magazine or even this textbook in our hands, or is an online version just as good? Digital versions of printed text can be updated, modified, and augmented far more easily, but they lack the traditional physical property of words and pictures printed on paper. What is clear is that newspapers, magazines, and books will continue in some form. Perhaps these forms will represent something entirely new, but the forms pioneered by earlier, physical versions of newspapers, magazines, and books will continue to shape that digital content, even as the ways they are read and interpreted change.

HOW WE READ NOW

NEWSPAPER PRINT ADVERTISING REVENUES FALL, ONLINE GROWS

*In millions of dollars.

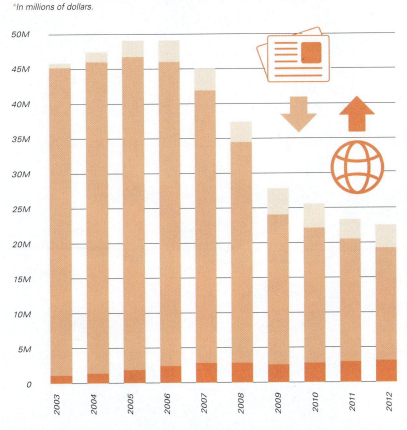

(Bar chart, y-axis from 0 to 50M in 5M increments, x-axis years 2003–2012)

TOP 10 iPAD NEWS APPS, 2013

1. NY TIMES
2. NEW YORK POST
3. **THE ECONOMIST**
4. **ZINIO**
5. **THE NEW YORKER**
6. THE WALL STREET JOURNAL
7. **NATIONAL GEOGRAPHIC**
8. **TIME**
9. **WIRED**
10. **POPULAR MECHANICS**

*Bold are magazine based; light are newspaper based.

IN THE PAST YEAR...

The typical adult read five books in the past year (five is the median, so half read more, half read fewer).

76% — 76% of adults (18 and over) report to have read at least one book.

69% — 69% of adults read a book in print in the past year.

28% — 28% of adults read an e-book.

14% — 14% of adults listened to an audiobook.

47% — 47% of adults 18–29 read an e-book in the past year.

AS TABLET OWNERSHIP GROWS, MORE USE THEM FOR E-BOOKS

*Among all e-book readers ages 18 and older, the % who read e-books on each device.

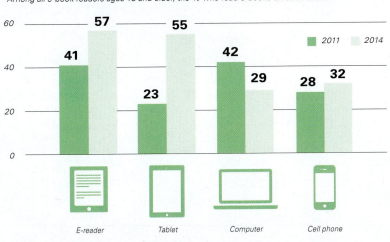

Legend: 2011 | 2014

E-reader: 41 / 57
Tablet: 23 / 55
Computer: 42 / 29
Cell phone: 28 / 32

metro

"THE GREATEST GLORY IN LIVING LIES NOT IN NEVER FALLING, BUT IN RISING EVERY TIME WE FALL."

1918-2013

NEW YORK CITY'S #1 FREE DAILY NEWSPAPER

8

Newspapers

The Rise and Decline of Modern Journalism

271
The Evolution of
American Newspapers

278
Competing Models
of Modern Print
Journalism

284
The Business
and Ownership
of Newspapers

296
Challenges Facing
Newspapers Today

303
Newspapers and
Democracy

Advertising Age reported back in 2013 that adult newspaper readership had fallen by 20 percent since 2001. Among major U.S. cities, Pittsburgh had the most adults—51 percent—claiming to still read a daily print newspaper; Atlanta ranked last with only 23 percent. In general, the South and Southwest had adult readership numbers around 25 percent, with the Northeast and Upper Midwest around 45 to 50 percent.[1]

Despite these numbers, investing guru Warren Buffett has been buying newspapers—more than sixty of them in 2012 and 2013—just as many traditional print companies, looking at the decline in readers, are trying to unload their papers. For example, in 2013, the Tribune Company—owner of the *Los Angeles Times* and the *Chicago Tribune*, two of the largest U.S. newspapers—considered selling the papers shortly after spending $2.7 billion to buy nineteen local TV stations (adding to the twenty-three it already owned), a purchase the *New York Times* described as "giving it one of the largest groups of local [TV] affiliates in the United States."[2] In 2014, Tribune did spin off its newspapers as a separate company called Tribune Publishing (with a $275 million debt load). In other words, Tribune executives today have bet that good old TV is the way to go—and they believe, as do other giant media companies like News Corp. and Time Warner, that splitting newspapers from TV interests may be the best move. Although TV viewing has declined dramatically in the smartphone and online era, broadcast programs still command the largest audiences. Buying TV stations gives the Tribune Company (now rid of its newspapers) access to retransmission fees (which cable companies now pay local broadcasters and national networks, mostly for traditional prime-time programs on ABC, CBS, Fox, and NBC), as well as a chunk of the lucrative political ad money that comes around to certain swing states every two years during election season.[3] Although digital advertising has overtaken newspapers in annual U.S. ad revenue, TV and cable still led all media in 2013, grabbing almost 39 percent of U.S. ad revenue. Digital advertising, including mobile phones, accounted for 25 percent of ad spending, while newspapers—for decades the U.S. ad leader—had just over a 10 percent share. Looking ahead, forecasters see newspaper advertising's share declining further, to just 7.5 percent by 2017.[4]

So against the backdrop of an uncertain digital future, what will happen to newspapers—and why is Warren Buffett buying them? While Buffett and his top executives have long held that "circulation, advertising and profits" in the newspaper business would decline in the digital age, they also think that news in general is still "good business." In 2013, Buffett argued, "I believe that papers delivering comprehensive and reliable information to tightly-bound communities . . . will remain viable for a long time."[5]

Just as the music and radio industries have adapted and survived over the years, newspapers will survive, too—probably at first by delivering a print version two or three days a week or moving to digital smartphone and tablet formats, where that advertising revenue is indeed growing. The *New Orleans Times-Picayune* and the *Cleveland Plain Dealer* in 2012 and 2013, respectively, reduced home delivery of their papers to just three days a week, while other newspapers, like the *Christian Science Monitor* and the *Seattle Post-Intelligencer*, have decided to go online only. Warren Buffett, a former newspaper boy, believes that in the age of the Internet, people want reliable information and good stories more than ever. In the end, his faith in the medium reminds us that media businesses are ultimately about telling and selling stories—regardless of format.

▲ **DESPITE THEIR CURRENT PREDICAMENTS,** newspapers and their online offspring play many roles in contemporary culture. As chroniclers of daily life, newspapers both inform and entertain. By reporting on scientific, technological, and medical issues, newspapers disseminate specialized knowledge to the public. In reviews of films, concerts, and plays, they shape cultural trends. Opinion pages trigger public debates and offer differing points of view. Columnists provide everything from advice on raising children to opinions on the U.S. role as an economic and military superpower. Newspapers help readers make choices about everything from what kind of food to eat to what kinds of leaders to elect.

Visit **LaunchPad** for *Media & Culture* and use **LearningCurve** to review concepts from this chapter.

Although newspapers have played a central role in daily life, in today's digital age the industry is losing both papers and readers. Newspapers have lost their near monopoly on classified advertising, much of which has shifted to free Web sites like craigslist and eBay. According to the Newspaper Association of America (NAA), in 2013 total newspaper ad revenues totaled more than $38 billion, a decline of 2.6 percent from 2012, when revenues fell 6 percent. Of that total, $24 billion came from ads across all platforms, $11 billion came from circulation, and $3.15 billion came from "other sources." In 2012, online ads accounted for about $3.4 billion in total revenue, while print advertising brought in more than $18.6 billion in ad revenue for the nation's papers—less than half of the ad money generated as recently as 2006. In 2013, online advertising rose just slightly—1.5 percent to $3.42 billion in total revenue. The NAA reported in 2013 that circulation revenue for U.S. newspapers recorded a second straight year of growth, rising 3.7 percent to $10.87 billion, according to NAA data (the first such growth since 2003). These two years of circulation growth provided a spark of hope in a time when the loss of papers, readers, advertising, and investor confidence raised concerns in a nation where daily news has historically functioned to "speak truth to power" by holding elected officials responsible and acting as a watchdog for democratic life.[6]

In this chapter, we examine the cultural, social, and economic impact of newspapers. We will:

- Trace the history of newspapers through a number of influential periods and styles
- Explore the early political-commercial press, the penny press, and yellow journalism
- Examine the modern era through the influence of the *New York Times* and journalism's embrace of objectivity
- Look at interpretive journalism in the 1920s and 1930s and the revival of literary journalism in the 1960s
- Review issues of newspaper ownership, new technologies, citizen journalism, declining revenue, and the crucial role of newspapers in our democracy

As you read this chapter, think about your own early experiences with newspapers and the impact they have had on you and your family. Did you read certain sections of the paper, like sports or comics? What do you remember from your childhood about your parents' reading habits? What are your own newspaper reading habits today? How often do you actually hold a newspaper? How often do you get your news online? For more questions to help you think through the role of newspapers in our lives, see "Questioning the Media" in the Chapter Review.

The Evolution of American Newspapers

The idea of news is as old as language itself. The earliest news was passed along orally from family to family, from tribe to tribe, by community leaders and oral historians. The earliest known written news account, or news sheet, *Acta Diurna* (Latin for "daily events"), was developed by Julius Caesar and posted in public spaces and on buildings in Rome in 59 BCE. Even in its oral and early written stages, news informed people on the state of their relations with neighboring tribes and towns. The development of the printing press in the fifteenth century greatly accelerated a society's ability to send and receive information. Throughout history, news has satisfied our need to know things we cannot experience personally. Newspapers today continue to document daily life and bear witness to both ordinary and extraordinary events.

Colonial Newspapers and the Partisan Press

The novelty and entrepreneurial stages of print media development first happened in Europe with the rise of the printing press. In North America, the first newspaper, *Publick Occurrences, Both Foreign and Domestick*, was published on September 25, 1690, by Boston printer Benjamin Harris. The colonial government objected to Harris's negative tone regarding British rule, and local ministers were offended by his published report that the king of France had an affair with his son's wife. The newspaper was banned after one issue.

In 1704, the first regularly published newspaper appeared in the American colonies—the *Boston News-Letter*, published by John Campbell. Because European news took weeks to travel by ship, these early colonial papers were not very timely. In their more spirited sections, however, the papers did report local illnesses, public floggings, and even suicides. In 1721, also in Boston, James Franklin, the older brother of Benjamin Franklin, started the *New England Courant*. The *Courant* established a tradition of running stories that interested ordinary readers rather than printing articles that appealed primarily to business and colonial leaders. In 1729, Benjamin Franklin, at age twenty-four, took over the *Pennsylvania Gazette* and created, according to historians, the best of the colonial papers. Although a number of colonial papers operated solely on subsidies from political parties, the *Gazette* also made money by advertising products.

▼ **Newspapers: The Rise and Decline of Modern Journalism**

First Colonial Newspaper
In 1690, Boston printer Benjamin Harris publishes the first North American newspaper—*Publick Occurrences, Both Foreign and Domestick* (p. 272).

First Precedent for Libel and Press Freedom
In 1734, printer John Peter Zenger is arrested for seditious libel; a jury rules in Zenger's favor in 1735, establishing freedom of the press and newspapers' right to criticize government (p. 273).

First Native American Newspaper
The *Cherokee Phoenix* appears in Georgia in 1828, giving a voice to tribal concerns as settlers encroach and move west (p. 290).

Yellow Journalism
Joseph Pulitzer buys the *New York World* in 1883; William Randolph Hearst buys the *New York Journal* in 1895 and battles Pulitzer during the heyday of the yellow journalism era (pp. 276–278).

| 1650 | 1800 | 1850 |

First U.S.-Based Spanish Paper
New Orleans' *El Misisipi* is founded in 1808 to serve Spanish-language readers (p. 289).

First African American Newspaper
Freedom's Journal begins its short-lived operation in 1827, establishing a tradition of newspapers speaking out against racism (p. 288).

Penny Press
Printer Benjamin Day founds the *New York Sun* in 1833 and sets the price at one cent, helping usher in the penny press era and news for the working and emerging middle classes (p. 274).

Another important colonial paper, the *New-York Weekly Journal*, appeared in 1733. John Peter Zenger had been installed as the printer of the *Journal* by the Popular Party, a political group that opposed British rule and ran articles that criticized the royal governor of New York. After a Popular Party judge was dismissed from office, the *Journal* escalated its attack on the governor. When Zenger shielded the writers of the critical articles, he was arrested in 1734 for *seditious libel*—defaming a public official's character in print. Championed by famed Philadelphia lawyer Andrew Hamilton, Zenger ultimately won his case in 1735. A sympathetic jury, in revolt against the colonial government, decided that newspapers had the right to criticize government leaders as long as the reports were true. After the Zenger case, the British never prosecuted another colonial printer. The Zenger decision would later provide a key foundation—the right of a democratic press to criticize public officials—for the First Amendment to the Constitution, adopted as part of the Bill of Rights in 1791. (See Chapter 16 for more on the First Amendment.)

By 1765, about thirty newspapers operated in the American colonies, with the first daily paper beginning in 1784. Newspapers were of two general types: political or commercial. Their development was shaped in large part by social, cultural, and political responses to British rule and by its eventual overthrow. The gradual rise of political parties and the spread of commerce also influenced the development of early papers. Although the political and commercial papers carried both party news and business news, they had different agendas. Political papers, known as the **partisan press**, generally pushed the plan of the particular political group that subsidized the paper. The *commercial press*, by contrast, served business leaders, who were interested in economic issues. Both types of journalism left a legacy. The partisan press gave us the editorial pages, while the early commercial press was the forerunner of the business section.

In the eighteenth and early nineteenth centuries, even the largest of these papers rarely reached a circulation of fifteen hundred. Readership was primarily confined to educated or

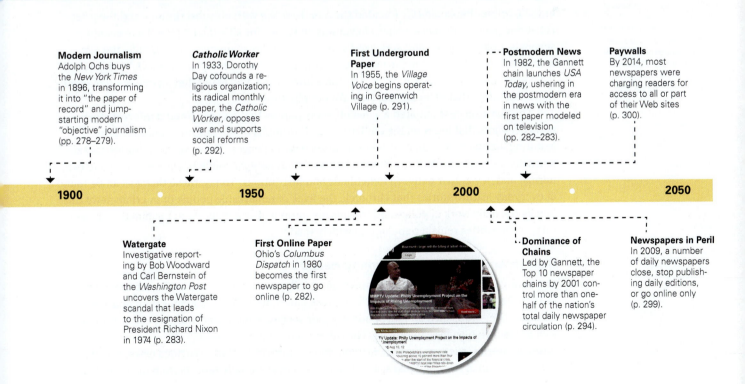

Modern Journalism
Adolph Ochs buys the *New York Times* in 1896, transforming it into "the paper of record" and jump-starting modern "objective" journalism (pp. 278–279).

Catholic Worker
In 1933, Dorothy Day cofounds a religious organization; its radical monthly paper, the *Catholic Worker*, opposes war and supports social reforms (p. 292).

First Underground Paper
In 1955, the *Village Voice* begins operating in Greenwich Village (p. 291).

Postmodern News
In 1982, the Gannett chain launches *USA Today*, ushering in the postmodern era in news with the first paper modeled on television (pp. 282–283).

Paywalls
By 2014, most newspapers were charging readers for access to all or part of their Web sites (p. 300).

1900   **1950**   **2000**   **2050**

Watergate
Investigative reporting by Bob Woodward and Carl Bernstein of the *Washington Post* uncovers the Watergate scandal that leads to the resignation of President Richard Nixon in 1974 (p. 283).

First Online Paper
Ohio's *Columbus Dispatch* in 1980 becomes the first newspaper to go online (p. 282).

Dominance of Chains
Led by Gannett, the Top 10 newspaper chains by 2001 control more than one-half of the nation's total daily newspaper circulation (p. 294).

Newspapers in Peril
In 2009, a number of daily newspapers close, stop publishing daily editions, or go online only (p. 299).

Num.b. LVI.

THE
New-York Weekly JOURNAL.

Containing the fresheft Advices, Foreign, and Domeftick.

MUNDAY December 2d, 1734.

© Bettmann/Corbis

COLONIAL NEWSPAPERS
During the colonial period, New York printer John Peter Zenger was arrested for seditious libel. He eventually won his case, which established the precedent that today allows U.S. journalists and citizens to criticize public officials. In this 1734 issue, Zenger's *New-York Weekly Journal* reported his own arrest and the burning of the paper by the city's "Common Hangman."

wealthy men who controlled local politics and commerce. During this time, though, a few pioneering women operated newspapers, including Elizabeth Timothy, the first American woman newspaper publisher (and mother of eight children). After her husband died of smallpox in 1738, Timothy took over the *South Carolina Gazette*, established in 1734 by Benjamin Franklin and the Timothy family. Also during this period, Anna Maul Zenger ran the *New-York Weekly Journal* throughout her husband's trial and after his death in 1746.[7]

The Penny Press Era: Newspapers Become Mass Media

By the late 1820s, the average newspaper cost six cents a copy and was sold through yearly subscriptions priced at ten to twelve dollars. Because that price was more than a week's salary for most skilled workers, newspaper readers were mostly affluent. By the 1830s, however, the Industrial Revolution made possible the replacement of expensive handmade paper with cheaper machine-made paper. During this time, the rise of the middle class spurred the growth of literacy, setting the stage for a more popular and inclusive press. In addition, breakthroughs in technology, particularly the replacement of mechanical presses by steam-powered presses, permitted publishers to produce as many as four thousand newspapers an hour, which lowered the cost of newspapers. **Penny papers** soon began competing with six-cent papers. Though subscriptions remained the preferred sales tool of many penny papers, they began relying increasingly on daily street sales of individual copies.

Day and the *New York Sun*

In 1833, printer Benjamin Day founded the *New York Sun* with no subscriptions and the price set at one penny. The *Sun*—whose slogan was "It shines for all"—highlighted local events, scandals, police reports, and serialized stories. Like today's supermarket tabloids, the *Sun* fabricated stories, including the infamous moon hoax, which reported "scientific" evidence of life on the moon. Within six months, the *Sun*'s lower price had generated a circulation of eight thousand, twice that of its nearest New York competitor.

The *Sun*'s success initiated a wave of penny papers that favored **human-interest stories**: news accounts that focus on the daily trials and triumphs of the human condition, often featuring ordinary individuals facing extraordinary challenges. These kinds of stories reveal journalism's ties to literary traditions, such as the archetypal conflicts between good and evil, normal and deviant, or between individuals and institutions. Today, these themes can be found in everyday feature stories that chronicle the lives of remarkable people or in crime news that details the daily work of police and the misadventures of criminals. As in the nineteenth century, crime stories remain popular and widely read.

Bennett and the *New York Morning Herald*

The penny press era also featured James Gordon Bennett's *New York Morning Herald*, founded in 1835. Bennett, considered the first U.S. press baron, freed his newspaper from political influence. He established an independent paper serving middle- and working-class readers as well as his own business ambitions. The *Herald* carried political essays, news about scandals, business stories, a letters section, fashion notes, moral reflections, religious news, society gossip, colloquial tales and jokes, sports stories, and eventually reports from the Civil War.

In addition, Bennett's paper sponsored balloon races, financed safaris, and overplayed crime stories. Charles Dickens, after returning to Britain from his first visit to America in the early 1840s, used the *Herald* as a model for the sleazy *Rowdy Journal*, the fictional newspaper in his novel *Martin Chuzzlewit*. By 1860, the *Herald* reached nearly eighty thousand readers, making it the world's largest daily paper at the time.

Changing Economics and the Founding of the Associated Press

The penny papers were innovative. For example, they were the first to assign reporters to cover crime, and readers enthusiastically embraced the reporting of local news and crime. By gradually separating daily front-page reporting from overt political viewpoints on an editorial page, penny papers shifted their economic base from political parties to the market—to advertising revenue, classified ads, and street sales. Although many partisan papers had taken a moral stand against advertising some controversial products and "services"—such as medical "miracle" cures, abortionists, and especially the slave trade—the penny press became more neutral toward advertisers and printed virtually any ad. In fact, many penny papers regarded advertising as consumer news. The rise in ad revenues and circulation accelerated the growth of the newspaper industry. In 1830, 650 weekly and 65 daily papers operated in the United States, reaching a circulation of 80,000. By 1840, a total of 1,140 weeklies and 140 dailies attracted more than 300,000 readers.

In 1848, six New York newspapers formed a cooperative arrangement and founded the Associated Press (AP), the first major news wire service. **Wire services** began as commercial organizations that relayed news stories and information around the country and the world using telegraph lines and, later, radio waves and digital transmissions. In the case of the AP, the New York papers provided access to both their own stories and those from other newspapers. In the 1850s, papers started sending reporters to cover Washington, D.C., and in the early 1860s, more than a hundred reporters from northern papers went south to cover the Civil War, relaying their reports back to their home papers via telegraph and wire services. The news wire companies enabled news to travel rapidly from coast to coast and set the stage for modern journalism.

Library of Congress

NEWSIES sold Hearst and Pulitzer papers on the streets of New York in the 1890s. With more than a dozen dailies competing, street tactics were ferocious, and publishers often made young "newsies"— news boys and girls—buy the papers they could not sell.

The marketing of news as a product and the use of modern technology to dramatically cut costs gradually elevated newspapers from an entrepreneurial stage to the status of a mass medium. By adapting news content, penny papers captured the middle- and working-class readers who could now afford the paper and also had more leisure time to read it. As newspapers sought to sustain their mass appeal, news and "factual" reports about crimes and other items of human interest eventually superseded the importance of partisan articles about politics and commerce.

The Age of Yellow Journalism: Sensationalism and Investigation

The rise of competitive dailies and the penny press triggered the next significant period in American journalism. In the late 1800s, **yellow journalism** emphasized profitable papers that carried exciting human-interest stories, crime news, large headlines, and more readable copy. Generally regarded as sensationalistic and the direct forerunner of today's tabloid papers, reality TV, and celebrity-centered shows like *Access Hollywood*, yellow journalism featured two major developments. First was the emphasis on overly dramatic—or sensational—stories about crimes, celebrities, disasters, scandals, and intrigue. Second, and sometimes forgotten, were early in-depth "detective" stories—the legacy for twentieth-century **investigative journalism**: news reports that hunt out and expose corruption, particularly in business and government. Reporting during this yellow journalism period increasingly became a crusading force for common people, with the press assuming a watchdog role on their behalf.

During this period, a newspaper circulation war pitted Joseph Pulitzer's *New York World* against William Randolph Hearst's *New York Journal*. A key player in the war was the first popular cartoon strip, *The Yellow Kid*, created in 1895 by artist R. F. Outcault, who once worked for Thomas Edison. The phrase *yellow journalism* has since become associated with the cartoon strip, which was shuttled back and forth between the Hearst and Pulitzer papers during their furious battle for readers in the mid to late 1890s.

Pulitzer and the *New York World*

Joseph Pulitzer, a Jewish-Hungarian immigrant, began his career in newspaper publishing in the early 1870s as part owner of the *St. Louis Post*. He then bought the bankrupt *St. Louis*

YELLOW JOURNALISM
Generally considered America's first comic-strip character, the Yellow Kid was created in the mid-1890s by cartoonist Richard (R. F.) Outcault. The cartoon was so popular that newspaper barons Joseph Pulitzer and William Randolph Hearst fought over Outcault's services, giving yellow journalism its name.

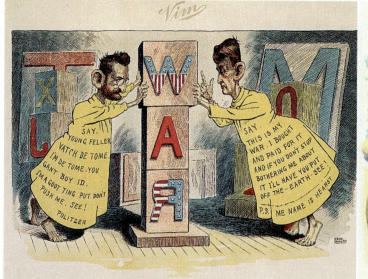

Library of Congress

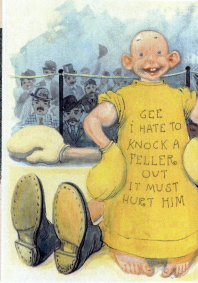

Dept. of Special Collections, Syracuse University Library

Dispatch for $2,500 at an auction in 1878 and merged it with the *Post*. The *Post-Dispatch* became known for stories that highlighted "sex and sin" ("A Denver Maiden Taken from Disreputable House") and satires of the upper class ("St. Louis Swells"). Pulitzer also viewed the *Post-Dispatch* as a "national conscience" that promoted the public good. He carried on the legacies of James Gordon Bennett: making money and developing a "free and impartial" paper that would "serve no party but the people." Within five years, the *Post-Dispatch* became one of the most influential newspapers in the Midwest.

In 1883, Pulitzer bought the *New York World* for $346,000. He encouraged plain writing and the inclusion of maps and illustrations to help immigrant and working-class readers understand the written text. In addition to running sensational stories on crime and sex, Pulitzer instituted advice columns and women's pages. Like Bennett, Pulitzer treated advertising as a kind of news that displayed consumer products for readers. In fact, department stores became major advertisers during this period. This development contributed directly to the expansion of consumer culture and indirectly to the acknowledgment of women as newspaper readers. Eventually (because of pioneers like Nellie Bly—see Chapter 14), newspapers began employing women as reporters.

The *World* reflected the contradictory spirit of the yellow press. It crusaded for improved urban housing, better conditions for women, and equitable labor laws. It campaigned against monopoly practices by AT&T, Standard Oil, and Equitable Insurance. Such popular crusades helped lay the groundwork for tightening federal antitrust laws in the early 1910s. At the same time, Pulitzer's paper manufactured news events and staged stunts, such as sending star reporter Nellie Bly around the world in seventy-two days to beat the fictional "record" in the popular 1873 Jules Verne novel *Around the World in Eighty Days*. By 1887, the *World*'s Sunday circulation had soared to more than 250,000, the largest anywhere.

Pulitzer created a lasting legacy by leaving $2 million to start the graduate school of journalism at Columbia University in 1912. In 1917, part of Pulitzer's Columbia endowment established the Pulitzer Prizes, the prestigious awards given each year for achievements in journalism, literature, drama, and music.

Hearst and the *New York Journal*

The *World* faced its fiercest competition when William Randolph Hearst bought the *New York Journal* (a penny paper founded by Pulitzer's brother Albert). Before moving to New York, the twenty-four-year-old Hearst took control of the *San Francisco Examiner* when his father, George Hearst, was elected to the U.S. Senate in 1887 (the younger Hearst had recently been expelled from Harvard for playing a practical joke on his professors). In 1895, with an inheritance from his father, Hearst bought the ailing *Journal* and then raided Joseph Pulitzer's paper for editors, writers, and cartoonists.

Taking his cue from Bennett and Pulitzer, Hearst focused on lurid, sensational stories and appealed to immigrant readers by using large headlines and bold layout designs. To boost circulation, the *Journal* invented interviews, faked pictures, and encouraged conflicts that might result in a story. One tabloid account describes "tales about two-headed virgins" and "prehistoric creatures roaming the plains of Wyoming."[8] In promoting journalism as mere dramatic storytelling, Hearst reportedly said, "The modern editor of the popular journal does not care for facts. The editor wants novelty. The editor has no objection to facts if they are also novel. But he would prefer a novelty that is not a fact to a fact that is not a novelty."[9]

Hearst is remembered as an unscrupulous publisher who once hired gangsters to distribute his newspapers. He was also, however, considered a champion of the underdog, and his paper's readership soared among the working and middle classes.

THE PENNY PRESS
The *World* (*top*) and the *New York Journal* (*bottom*) cover the same story in May 1898.

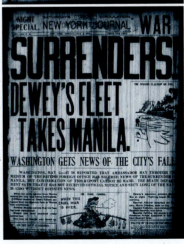

New York Public Library/Art Resource, NY (top and bottom)

In 1896, the *Journal*'s daily circulation reached 450,000, and by 1897, the Sunday edition of the paper rivaled the 600,000 circulation of the *World*. By the 1930s, Hearst's holdings included more than forty daily and Sunday papers, thirteen magazines (including *Good Housekeeping* and *Cosmopolitan*), eight radio stations, and two film companies. In addition, he controlled King Features Syndicate, which sold and distributed articles, comics, and features to many of the nation's dailies. Hearst, the model for Charles Foster Kane, the ruthless publisher in Orson Welles's classic 1940 film *Citizen Kane*, operated the largest media business in the world—the Disney or Google of its day.

Competing Models of Modern Print Journalism

The early commercial and partisan presses were, to some extent, covering important events impartially. These papers often carried verbatim reports of presidential addresses and murder trials, or the annual statements of the U.S. Treasury. In the late nineteenth century, as newspapers pushed for greater circulation, newspaper reporting changed. Two distinct types of journalism emerged: the *story-driven model*, dramatizing important events and used by the penny papers and the yellow press; and the *"just the facts" model*, an approach that appeared to package information more impartially and that the six-cent papers favored.[10] Implicit in these efforts was a question that is still debated today: Is there, in journalism, an ideal, attainable, objective model, or does the quest for objectivity actually conflict with journalists' traditional role of raising important issues about potential abuses of power in a democratic society?

"Objectivity" in Modern Journalism

As the consumer marketplace expanded during the Industrial Revolution, facts and news became marketable products. Throughout the mid-nineteenth century, the more a newspaper appeared not to take sides on its front pages, the more its readership base grew (although, as they are today, editorial pages were still often partisan). In addition, wire service organizations were serving a variety of newspaper clients in different regions of the country. To satisfy all clients, readers, and the wide range of political views, newspapers tried to appear more impartial.

Ochs and the *New York Times*

The ideal of an impartial, or purely informational, news model was championed by Adolph Ochs, who bought the *New York Times* in 1896. The son of immigrant German Jews, Ochs grew up in Ohio and Tennessee, where at age twenty-one he took over the *Chattanooga Times* in 1878. Known more for his business and organizational ability than for his writing and editing skills, he transformed the Tennessee paper. Seeking a national stage and business expansion, Ochs moved to New York and invested $75,000 in the struggling *Times*. Through strategic hiring, Ochs and his editors rebuilt the paper around substantial news coverage and provocative editorial pages. To distance his New York paper from the yellow press, the editors also downplayed sensational stories, favoring the documentation of major events or issues.

Partly as a marketing strategy, Ochs offered a distinct contrast to the more sensational Hearst and Pulitzer newspapers: an informational paper that provided stock and real estate reports to businesses, court reports to legal professionals, treaty summaries to political leaders, and theater and book reviews to educated general readers and intellectuals. Ochs's promotional gimmicks took direct aim at yellow journalism, advertising the *Times* under the motto "It does not soil the breakfast cloth." Ochs's strategy is similar to today's advertising tactic of targeting upscale viewers and readers who control a disproportionate share of consumer dollars.

With the Hearst and Pulitzer papers capturing the bulk of working- and middle-class readers, managers at the *Times* first tried to use their straightforward, "no frills" reporting to appeal to more affluent and educated readers. In 1898, however, Ochs lowered the paper's price to a penny. He believed that people bought the *World* and the *Journal* primarily because they were cheap, not because of their stories. The *Times* began attracting middle-class readers who gravitated to the now-affordable paper as a status marker for the educated and well informed. Between 1898 and 1899, its circulation rose from 25,000 to 75,000. By 1921, the *Times* had a daily circulation of 330,000, and 500,000 on Sunday. (For contemporary print and digital circulation figures, see Table 8.1 on page 280.)

"Just the Facts, Please"

Early in the twentieth century, with reporters adopting a more "scientific" attitude to news- and fact-gathering, the ideal of objectivity began to anchor journalism. In **objective journalism**, which distinguishes factual reports from opinion columns, modern reporters strive to maintain a neutral attitude toward the issue or event they cover; they also search out competing points of view among the sources for a story.

The story form for packaging and presenting this kind of reporting has been traditionally labeled the **inverted-pyramid style**. Civil War correspondents developed this style by imitating the terse, compact press releases (summarizing or imitating telegrams to generals) that came from President Abraham Lincoln and his secretary of war, Edwin M. Stanton.[11] Often stripped of adverbs and adjectives, inverted-pyramid reports began—as they do today—with the most dramatic or newsworthy information. They answered who, what, where, when (and, less frequently, why or how) questions at the top of the story and then narrowed down the story to presumably less significant details. If wars or natural disasters disrupted the telegraph transmission of these dispatches, the information the reporter led with had the best chance of getting through.

For much of the twentieth century, the inverted-pyramid style served as an efficient way to arrange a timely story. As one news critic pointed out, the wire services distributing stories to newspapers nationwide "had to deal with large numbers of newspapers with widely different political and regional interests. The news had to be 'objective' . . . to be accepted by such a heterogeneous group."[12] Among other things, the importance of objectivity and the reliance on the inverted pyramid signaled journalism's break from the partisan tradition. Although impossible to achieve (journalism is, after all, a literary practice, not a science), objectivity nonetheless became the guiding ideal of the modern press.

Despite the success of the *New York Times* and other modern papers, the more factual inverted-pyramid approach toward news has come under increasing scrutiny. As news critic and writing coach Roy Peter Clark has noted, "Some reporters let the pyramid control the content so that the news comes out homogenized. Traffic fatalities, three-alarm fires, and new city ordinances all begin to look alike. In extreme cases, reporters have been known to keep files of story forms. Fill in the blanks. Stick it in the paper."[13] Although the inverted-pyramid style has for years solved deadline problems for reporters and enabled editors to cut a story from the

AP Photo/Evan Agostini

THE *NEW YORK TIMES* had established itself as the official paper of record by the 1920s. The *Times* was the first modern newspaper, gathering information and presenting news in a straightforward way—without the opinion of the reporter. Today, the *Times* is known for its opinion columns and editorial pages as much as for its original reporting. In 2011, Jill Abramson (pictured) became its first woman executive editor. She was let go in 2014, setting off controversy and rumors over whether she was paid as much as her male predecessors.

TABLE 8.1

THE NATION'S TEN LARGEST DAILY NEWSPAPERS, 2014

Note: Count includes print and digital editions.

Data from: Cision, "Top 10 US Daily Newspapers," June 18, 2014, www.cision.com/us/2014/06 /top-10-us-daily-newspapers; and Alliance for Audited Media, www.auditedmedia.com /news/blog/top-25-us-newspapers -for-march-2013.aspx.

▶

Newspaper	2014 Weekday Circulation (print and digital)
1. *USA Today**	3,255,157
2. *Wall Street Journal*	2,294,093
3. *New York Times*	2,149,012
4. *Orange County Register*	681,512
5. *Los Angeles Times*	673,171
6. *San Jose Mercury News*	581,532
7. *New York Post*	477,314
8. (New York) *Daily News*	456,360
9. (Long Island, N.Y.) *Newsday*	443,362
10. *Washington Post*	436,601

*The Gannett-owned *USA Today* jumped from third in 2013 (1,674,306) to first in 2014 because since 2014, its circulation figures have included all the brief *USA Today* inserts found in Gannett's largest daily papers, such as the *Detroit Free Press*, the *Louisville Courier-Journal*, the *Nashville Tennessean*, and the *Cincinnati Enquirer*.

bottom to fit available space, it has also discouraged many readers from continuing beyond the key details in the opening paragraphs. Studies have demonstrated that the majority of readers do not follow a front-page story when it continues, or "jumps," inside the paper.

Interpretive Journalism

By the 1920s, there was a sense, especially after the trauma of World War I, that the impartial approach to reporting was insufficient for explaining complex national and global conditions. It was partly as a result of "drab, factual, objective reporting," one news scholar contended, that "the American people were utterly amazed when war broke out in August 1914, as they had no understanding of the foreign scene to prepare them for it."[14]

The Promise of Interpretive Journalism

Under the sway of objectivity, modern journalism had downplayed an early role of the partisan press: offering analysis and opinion. But with the world becoming more complex, some papers began to reexplore the analytical function of news. The result was the rise of **interpretive journalism**, which aims to explain key issues or events and place them in a broader historical or social context. According to one historian, this approach, especially in the 1930s and 1940s, was a viable way for journalism to address "the New Deal years, the rise of modern scientific technology, the increasing interdependence of economic groups at home, and the shrinking of the world into one vast arena for power politics."[15] In other words, journalism took an analytic turn in a world grown more interconnected and complicated.

Noting that objectivity and factuality should serve as the foundation for journalism, by the 1920s editor and columnist Walter Lippmann insisted that the press should do more. He ranked three press responsibilities: (1) "to make a current record"; (2) "to make a running analysis of it"; and (3) "on the basis of both, to suggest plans."[16] Indeed, reporters and readers alike have historically distinguished between informational reports and editorial (interpretive) pieces, which offer particular viewpoints or deeper analyses of the issues. Since the boundary between information and interpretation can be somewhat ambiguous, American papers have traditionally placed news analysis in separate, labeled columns and placed opinion articles on certain pages so that readers do not confuse them with "straight news." It was during this time that political columns developed to evaluate and provide context for news. Moving beyond the informational and storytelling functions of news, journalists and newspapers began to extend their role as analysts.

Broadcast News Embraces Interpretive Journalism

In a surprising twist, the rise of broadcast radio in the 1930s also forced newspapers to become more analytical in their approach to news. At the time, the newspaper industry was upset that broadcasters took their news directly from papers and wire services. As a result, a battle developed between radio journalism and print news. Although mainstream newspapers tried to copyright the facts they reported and sued radio stations for routinely using newspapers as their main news sources, the papers lost many of these court battles. Editors and newspaper lobbyists argued that radio should be permitted to do only commentary. By conceding this interpretive role to radio, the print press tried to protect its dominion over "the facts." It was in this environment that radio analysis began to flourish as a form of interpretive news. Lowell Thomas delivered the first daily network analysis for CBS on September 29, 1930, attacking Hitler's rise to power in Germany. By 1941, twenty regular commentators—the forerunners of today's radio talk-show hosts, "talking heads" on cable, and political bloggers—were explaining their version of the world to millions of listeners.

Some print journalists and editors came to believe, however, that interpretive stories, rather than objective reports, could better compete with radio. They realized that interpretation was a way to counter radio's (and later television's) superior ability to report breaking news quickly—even live. In 1933, the American Society of Newspaper Editors (ASNE) supported the idea of interpretive journalism. Most newspapers, however, still did not embrace probing analysis during the 1930s. So in most U.S. dailies, interpretation remained relegated to a few editorial and opinion pages. It wasn't until the 1950s—with the Korean War, the development of atomic power, tensions with the Soviet Union, and the anticommunist movement—that news analysis resurfaced on the newest medium: television. Interpretive journalism in newspapers grew at the same time, especially in such areas as the environment, science, agriculture, sports, health, politics, and business. Following the lead of the *New York Times*, many papers by the 1980s had developed an "op-ed" page—an opinion page opposite the traditional editorial page, which allowed a greater variety of columnists, news analyses, and letters to the editor.

Literary Forms of Journalism

By the late 1960s, many people were criticizing America's major social institutions. Political assassinations, Civil Rights protests, the Vietnam War, the drug culture, and the women's movement were not easily explained. Faced with so much change and turmoil, many individuals began to lose faith in the ability of institutions to oversee and ensure the social order. Members of protest movements as well as many middle- and working-class Americans began to suspect the privileges and power of traditional authority. As a result, key institutions—including journalism—lost some of their credibility.

Journalism as an Art Form

Throughout the first part of the twentieth century—journalism's modern era—journalistic storytelling was downplayed in favor of the inverted-pyramid style and the separation of fact from opinion. Dissatisfied with these limitations, some reporters began exploring a new model of reporting. **Literary journalism**, sometimes dubbed "new journalism," adapted fictional techniques, such as descriptive details and settings and extensive character dialogue, to nonfiction material and in-depth reporting. In the United States, literary journalism's roots are evident in the work of nineteenth-century novelists like Mark Twain, Stephen Crane, and Theodore Dreiser, all of whom started out as reporters. In the late 1930s and 1940s, literary journalism surfaced: Journalists, such as James Agee and John Hersey, began to demonstrate how writing about real events could achieve an artistry often associated only with fiction.

In the 1960s, Tom Wolfe, a leading practitioner of new journalism, argued for mixing the *content* of reporting with the *form* of fiction to create "both the kind of objective reality of

JOAN DIDION'S two essay collections—*Slouching Towards Bethlehem* (1968) and *The White Album* (1979)— are considered iconic pieces from the new journalism movement. Both books detail and analyze Didion's life in California, where she experienced everything from the counterculture movement in San Francisco to encounters with members of the Black Panther Party, the Doors, and even followers of Charles Manson.

journalism" and "the subjective reality" of the novel.[17] Writers such as Wolfe (*The Electric Kool-Aid Acid Test*), Truman Capote (*In Cold Blood*), Joan Didion (*The White Album*), Norman Mailer (*Armies of the Night*), and Hunter S. Thompson (*Hell's Angels*) turned to new journalism to overcome flaws they perceived in routine reporting. Their often self-conscious treatment of social problems gave their writing a perspective that conventional journalism did not offer. After the 1960s' tide of intense social upheaval ebbed, new journalism subsided as well. However, literary journalism not only influenced magazines like *Mother Jones* and *Rolling Stone* but also affected daily newspapers by emphasizing longer feature stories on cultural trends and social issues with detailed description or dialogue. Today, writers such as Adrian Nicole LeBlanc (*Random Family*), Dexter Filkins (*The Forever War*), and Åsne Seierstad (*The Bookseller of Kabul*) keep this tradition alive.

The Attack on Journalistic Objectivity

Former *New York Times* columnist Tom Wicker argued that in the early 1960s an objective approach to news remained the dominant model. According to Wicker, the "press had so wrapped itself in the paper chains of 'objective journalism' that it had little ability to report anything beyond the bare and undeniable facts."[18] Through the 1960s, attacks on the detachment of reporters escalated. News critic Jack Newfield rejected the possibility of genuine journalistic impartiality and argued that many reporters had become too trusting and uncritical of the powerful: "Objectivity is believing people with power and printing their press releases."[19] Eventually, the ideal of objectivity became suspect along with the authority of experts and professionals in various fields.

A number of reporters responded to the criticism by rethinking the framework of conventional journalism and adopting a variety of alternative techniques. One of these was *advocacy journalism*, in which the reporter actively promotes a particular cause or viewpoint. *Precision journalism*, another technique, attempts to make the news more scientifically accurate by using poll surveys and questionnaires. Throughout the 1990s, precision journalism became increasingly important. However, critics have charged that in every modern presidential campaign—including that of 2012—too many newspapers and TV stations became overly reliant on political polls, thus reducing campaign coverage to "racehorse" journalism, telling only "who's ahead" and "who's behind" stories rather than promoting substantial debates on serious issues. (See Table 8.2 for top works of American journalism.)

Contemporary Journalism in the TV and Internet Age

In the early 1980s, a postmodern brand of journalism arose from two important developments. In 1980, the *Columbus Dispatch* became the first paper to go online; today, nearly all U.S. papers offer some Web services. Then the colorful *USA Today*, started by Gannett, arrived in 1982, radically changing the look of most major U.S. dailies.

AP Images

	Journalist(s)	Title or Subject	Publisher	Year(s)
1	John Hersey	"Hiroshima"	*New Yorker*	1946
2	Rachel Carson	*Silent Spring*	Houghton Mifflin	1962
3	Bob Woodward/Carl Bernstein	Watergate investigation	*Washington Post*	1972–73
4	Edward R. Murrow	Battle of Britain	CBS Radio	1940
5	Ida Tarbell	"The History of the Standard Oil Company"	*McClure's Magazine*	1902–04
6	Lincoln Steffens	"The Shame of the Cities"	*McClure's Magazine*	1902–04
7	John Reed	*Ten Days That Shook the World*	Random House	1919
8	H. L. Mencken	Coverage of the Scopes "monkey" trial	*Baltimore Sun*	1925
9	Ernie Pyle	Reports from Europe and the Pacific during World War II	Scripps-Howard newspapers	1940–45
10	Edward R. Murrow/Fred Friendly	Investigation of Senator Joseph McCarthy	CBS Television	1954

TABLE 8.2

EXCEPTIONAL WORKS OF AMERICAN JOURNALISM

Working under the aegis of New York University's journalism department, thirty-six judges compiled a list of the Top 100 works of American journalism in the twentieth century. The list takes into account not just the newsworthiness of the event but the craft of the writing and reporting. What do you think of the Top 10 works listed here? What are some problems associated with a list like this? Do you think newswriting should be judged in the same way we judge novels or movies?

Data from: New York University, Department of Journalism, New York, N.Y., 1999.

USA Today Colors the Print Landscape

USA Today made its mark by incorporating features closely associated with postmodern forms, including an emphasis on visual style over substantive news or analysis and the use of brief news items that appealed to readers' busy schedules and shortened attention spans.

Now the second most widely circulated paper in the nation, *USA Today* represents the only successful launch of a new major U.S. daily newspaper in the last several decades. Showing its marketing savvy, *USA Today* was the first paper to openly acknowledge television's central role in mass culture: The paper used TV-inspired color and designed its first vending boxes to look like color TVs. Even the writing style of *USA Today* mimics TV news by casting many reports in present tense rather than the past tense (which was the print-news norm throughout the twentieth century).

Writing for *Rolling Stone* in March 1992, media critic Jon Katz argued that the authority of modern newspapers suffered in the wake of a variety of "new news" forms that combined immediacy, information, entertainment, persuasion, and analysis. Katz claimed that the news supremacy of most prominent daily papers, such as the *New York Times* and the *Washington Post*, was being challenged by "news" coming from talk shows, television sitcoms, popular films, and even rap music. In other words, we were changing from a society in which the transmission of knowledge depended mainly on books, newspapers, and magazines to a society dominated by a mix of print, visual, and digital information.

Online Journalism Redefines News

What started out in the 1980s as simple, text-only experiments for newspapers developed into more robust Web sites in the 1990s, allowing newspapers to develop an online presence. Today, online journalism is completely changing the industry. First, rather than subscribing to a traditional paper, many readers now begin their day on their iPads, smartphones, or computers scanning a wide variety of news Web sites, including those of print papers, cable news channels, newsmagazines, bloggers, and online-only news organizations. Such sources are increasingly taking over the roles of more traditional forms of news, helping set the nation's cultural, social, and political agendas. One of the biggest changes is that online news has sped up the news cycle to a constant stream of information and has challenged traditional news services to keep up. For instance, Matt Drudge, the conservative Internet gossip and news source behind the *Drudge Report*, hijacked the national agenda in January 1998 and launched a scandal when he posted a report that *Newsweek* had delayed the story about President Clinton's affair with White House intern Monica Lewinsky.

Another change is the way nontraditional sources and even newer digital technology help drive news stories. For example, the Occupy Wall Street (OWS) movement, inspired by the Arab Spring uprisings, began in September 2011 when a group of protesters gathered in Zuccotti Park in New York's financial district to express discontentment with overpaid CEOs, big banks, and Wall Street, all of which helped cause the 2008–09 financial collapse but still enjoyed a government bailout.

Mainstream media was slow to cover OWS, with early coverage simply pitting angry protesters against dismissive Wall Street executives and politicians, many of whom questioned the movement's longevity as well as its vague agenda. But as retirees, teachers, labor unions, off-duty police officers, firefighters, and other government workers joined the college students, the jobless, and the homeless in OWS protests across the country, the coverage and narratives in the media became more complicated and nuanced. As in the Arab uprisings, sites like Tumblr, Facebook, and Twitter became key organizational tools. But more than that, they became alternative media sources, documenting incidents of police brutality and arrests, and covering the issues protesters championed. In both the Arab Spring and the OWS stories, the Internet and social media gave ordinary people more agency than ever before. Still, it's important to remember that while successful movements need good communication and media coverage, they also require enough people willing to challenge power, just as they did in the days of the American Revolution and the Civil Rights movement.

In the digital age, newsrooms are integrating their digital and print operations and asking their journalists to tweet breaking news that links back to newspapers' Web sites. However, editors are still facing a challenge to get reporters and editors to fully embrace what news executives regard as a reporter's online responsibilities. In 2011, for example, then executive editor of the *New York Times* Jill Abramson noted that although the *Times* had fully integrated its online and print operations, some editors still tried to hold back on publishing a timely story online, hoping that it would make the front page of the print paper instead. "That's a culture I'd like to break down, without diminishing the [reporters'] thrill of having their story on the front page of the paper," said Abramson.[20] (For more about how online news ventures are changing the newspaper industry, see pages 298–300.)

LaunchPad ◉
macmillanhighered.com
/mediaculture10e

Newspapers and the Internet: Convergence
This video discusses the ways newspapers are adapting to online delivery of news.
Discussion: What different kinds of skills are needed to be effective in the new online world? What skills might remain the same?

The Business and Ownership of Newspapers

In the news industry today, there are several kinds of papers. *National newspapers* (such as the *Wall Street Journal*, the *New York Times*, and *USA Today*) serve a broad readership across the country. Other papers primarily serve specific geographic regions. Roughly 70 *metropolitan dailies* have a weekday paid circulation of approximately 100,000 (much more if we count digital hits on their Web sites). About 35 of these papers have a circulation of more than 200,000 during the workweek. In addition, about 100 daily newspapers are classified as medium dailies, with circulations between 50,000 and 100,000. By far the largest number of U.S. dailies—about 1,200 papers—fall into the small-daily category, with circulations under 50,000. While dailies serve urban and suburban centers, over 7,000 nondaily and *weekly newspapers* (down from 14,000 back in 1910) serve smaller communities and average over 8,000 copies per issue.[21]

No matter the size of the paper, each must determine its approach, target readers, and deal with ownership issues in a time of technological transition and declining revenue.

Consensus versus Conflict: Newspapers Play Different Roles

Smaller nondaily papers tend to promote social and economic harmony in their communities. Besides providing community calendars and meeting notices, nondaily papers focus on **consensus-oriented journalism**, carrying articles on local schools, social events, town government, property crimes, and zoning issues. Recalling the partisan spirit of an earlier era, small newspapers are often owned by business leaders who may also serve in local politics. Because consensus-oriented papers have a small advertising base, they are generally careful not to offend local advertisers, who provide the financial underpinnings for many of these papers. At their best, these small-town papers foster a sense of community; at their worst, they overlook or downplay discord and problems.

In contrast, national and metro dailies practice **conflict-oriented journalism**, in which front-page news is often defined primarily as events, issues, or experiences that deviate from social norms. Under this news orientation, journalists see their role not merely as neutral fact-gatherers but also as observers who monitor their city's institutions and problems. They often maintain an adversarial relationship with local politicians and public officials. These papers offer competing perspectives on such issues as education, government, poverty, crime, and the economy; and their publishers, editors, or reporters avoid playing major, overt roles in community politics. In theory, modern newspapers believe their role in large cities is to keep a wary eye fixed on recent local and state intrigue and events.

In telling stories about complex and controversial topics, conflict-oriented journalists often turn such topics into two-dimensional accounts, pitting one idea or person against another. This convention, or "telling both sides of a story," allows a reporter to take the position of a detached observer. Although this practice offers the appearance of balance, it usually functions to generate conflict and sustain a lively news story. Sometimes, though, good reporters ignore the notion that there are two sides to *every* story in order to tell the fullest and best story possible. However, often faced with deadline pressures, reporters do not always have the time—or the space—to develop a multifaceted and complex report or series of reports. But with the digital revolution releasing journalism from time and space constraints, news observers see the potential for more complex and longer stories developing online (see "Media Literacy and the Critical Process: Covering Business and Economic News" on page 286).

Newspapers Target Specific Readers

Historically, small-town weeklies and daily newspapers have served predominantly white, mainstream readers. However, ever since Benjamin Franklin launched the short-lived German-language *Philadelphische Zeitung* in 1732, newspapers aimed at ethnic groups have played a

Daniel Acker/Bloomberg via Getty Images

USA TODAY recently took the crown for largest circulation of any newspaper in the United States because inserts that the owner, Gannett, includes in its other high-circulation papers are now counted in *USA Today*'s figures.

Media Literacy and the Critical Process

1 DESCRIPTION. Check a week's worth of business news in your local paper. Examine both the business pages and the front and local sections for these stories. Devise a chart and create categories for sorting stories (e.g., promotion news, scandal stories, earnings reports, home foreclosures, auto news, unemployment, and media-related news), and gauge whether these stories are positive or negative. If possible, compare this coverage to a week's worth of news from the economic crisis in late 2008 or early 2009. Or compare your local paper's coverage of unemployment, home foreclosures, or company bankruptcies to the coverage in one of the nation's dailies, like the *New York Times*.

2 ANALYSIS. Look for patterns in the coverage. How many stories are positive? How many are negative? Do the stories show any kind of gender favoritism (such as men being covered or featured more than women) or class bias (such as management being favored over workers)? Compared to the coverage in the local paper, are there differences in the frequency and kinds of coverage offered in the national newspaper? Does your paper routinely cover the business of the parent company that owns the local paper? Does it cover national business stories? How many stories are there on the business of newspapers and media in general?

Covering Business and Economic News

The financial crisis and subsequent recession spotlighted newspapers' coverage of issues such as corporate corruption. For example, since 2008, articles have detailed the collapse of major investment firms like Lehman Brothers, the bailouts of GM and Chrysler, the fraud charges against Goldman Sachs, and of course the scandals surrounding the subprime mortgage–home foreclosure crisis. Over the years, critics have claimed that business news pages tend to favor issues related to management and downplay the role of everyday employees. Critics have also charged that business pages favor positive business stories—such as managers' promotions—and minimize negative news (unlike regional newspaper front pages, which often emphasize crime stories). In the aftermath of Wall Street scandals, major bankruptcies, and wild stock-market swings, check the business coverage in your local daily paper to see if these charges are accurate or if this pattern has changed since 2008.

3 INTERPRETATION. What do some of the patterns mean? Did you find examples in which the coverage of business seems comprehensive and fair? If business news gets more positive coverage than political news, what might this mean? If managers get more coverage than employees, what does this mean, given that there are many more regular employees than managers at most businesses? What might it mean if men are more prominently featured than women in business stories? What does it mean if certain businesses are not being covered adequately by local and national news operations? How do business stories cover the economy now in comparison to late 2008 or 2009?

4 EVALUATION. Determine which papers and stories you would judge as stronger models for how business should be covered, and which ones you would judge as weaker models. Are some elements that should be included missing from coverage? If so, make suggestions.

5 ENGAGEMENT. Either write or e-mail the editor to report your findings, or make an appointment with the editor to discuss what you discovered. Ask the editor if there may be issues or factors you've overlooked. Note what the newspaper is doing well, and make a recommendation on how to improve coverage.

major role in initiating immigrants into American society. During the nineteenth century, Swedish- and Norwegian-language papers informed various immigrant communities in the Midwest. The early twentieth century gave rise to papers written in German, Yiddish, Russian, and Polish, assisting the massive influx of European immigrants.

Throughout the 1990s and into the twenty-first century, several hundred foreign-language daily and nondaily presses published papers in at least forty different languages in the United States. Many are financially healthy today, supported by classified ads, local businesses, and

ELSEWHERE IN
MEDIA & CULTURE

$8.3B

THE PRICE OF THE BIGGEST NEWSPAPER MERGER EVER

p. 463

MARVEL COMICS ARE A BIG PART OF DISNEY'S CORPORATE STRATEGY

p. 460

1887

the year that Nellie Bly caused a sensation in the *New York World*

p. 477

$31.2B

the revenue that print advertising is expected to generate in 2017

p. 385

WHERE CAN YOU FIND JOURNALISTS' TWEETS COLLECTED IN ONE PLACE?

p. 499

increased ad revenue from long-distance phone companies and Internet services, which see the ethnic press as an ideal place to reach those customers most likely to need international communication services.[22] While the financial crisis took its toll and some ethnic newspapers failed, overall, loyal readers allowed such papers to fare better than the mainstream press.[23]

Most of these weekly and monthly newspapers serve some of the same functions for their constituencies—minorities and immigrants, as well as disabled veterans, retired workers, gay and lesbian communities, and the homeless—that the "majority" papers do. These papers, however, are often published outside the social mainstream. Consequently, they provide viewpoints that are different from the mostly middle- and upper-class establishment attitudes that have shaped the media throughout much of America's history. As noted by the Pew Research Center's Project for Excellence in Journalism, ethnic newspapers and media "cover stories about the activities of those ethnic groups in the United States that are largely ignored by the mainstream press, they provide ethnic angles to news that actually is covered more widely, and they report on events and issues taking place back in the home countries from which those populations or their family members emigrated. These outlets have also traditionally been leaders in their communities."[24]

FREDERICK DOUGLASS helped found the *North Star* in 1847. It was printed in the basement of the Memorial African Methodist Episcopal Zion Church, a gathering spot for abolitionists and "underground" activities in Rochester, New York. At the time, the white-owned *New York Herald* urged Rochester's citizens to throw the *North Star*'s printing press into Lake Ontario. Under Douglass's leadership, the paper came out weekly until 1860, addressing problems facing blacks around the country and offering a forum for Douglass to debate his fellow black activists.

Archive Photos/Getty Images

African American Newspapers

Between 1827 and the end of the Civil War in 1865, forty newspapers directed at black readers and opposed to slavery struggled for survival. These papers faced not only higher rates of illiteracy among potential readers but also hostility from white society and the majority press of the day. The first black newspaper, *Freedom's Journal*, operated from 1827 to 1829 and opposed the racism of many New York newspapers. In addition, it offered a public voice for antislavery societies. Other notable papers included the *Alienated American* (1852–1856) and the *New Orleans Daily Creole*, which began its short life in 1856 as the first black-owned daily in the South. The most influential oppositional newspaper was Frederick Douglass's *North Star*, a weekly antislavery newspaper in Rochester, New York, which was published from 1847 to 1860 and reached a circulation of three thousand. Douglass, a former slave, wrote essays on slavery and on a variety of national and international topics.

Since 1827, 5,500 newspapers have been edited or started by African Americans.[25] These papers, with an average life span of nine years, have taken stands against race baiting, lynching, and the Ku Klux Klan. They also promoted racial pride long before the Civil Rights movement. The most widely circulated black-owned paper was Robert C. Vann's weekly *Pittsburgh Courier*, founded in 1910. Its circulation peaked at 350,000 in 1947—the year professional baseball was integrated by Jackie Robinson, thanks in part to relentless editorials in the *Courier* that denounced the color barrier in pro sports. As they have throughout their history, these papers offer oppositional viewpoints to the mainstream press and record the daily activities of black communities by listing weddings, births, deaths, graduations, meetings, and church functions. Today, the National Association of Black Journalists (NABJ) reports that there are roughly two hundred African American newspapers, including Baltimore's *Afro-American*, New York's *Amsterdam News*, and the *Chicago Defender*, which celebrated its one hundredth anniversary in 2005.[26] None of these publish daily editions any longer, and most are weeklies.

The circulation rates of most black papers dropped sharply after the 1960s. The combined circulation of the local and national editions of the *Pittsburgh Courier*, for instance, dropped from 202,080 in 1944 to 20,000 in 1966, when it was reorganized as the *New Pittsburgh Courier*. Several factors contributed to these declines. First, television and black radio stations tapped into the limited pool of money that businesses allocated for advertising. Second, some advertisers, to avoid controversy, withdrew their support when the black press started giving favorable coverage to the Civil Rights movement in the 1960s. Third, the loss of industrial urban jobs in the 1970s and 1980s not only diminished readership but also hurt small neighborhood businesses, which could no longer afford to advertise in both the mainstream and the black press. Finally, after the enactment of Civil Rights and affirmative action laws, mainstream papers raided black papers, seeking to integrate their newsrooms with African American journalists. Black papers could seldom match the offers from large white-owned dailies.

While a more integrated mainstream press initially hurt black papers—an ironic effect of the Civil Rights laws—by 2011 that trend had reversed a bit, as some black reporters and editors returned to black press newsrooms.[27] Overall, however, the number of African Americans in newsrooms is declining—between 2006 and 2013, African American representation fell from 5.5 to 4.7 percent. The American Society of News Editors (ASNE) reported that in 1998, about 3,000 African Americans worked as journalists at daily newspaper, but that by 2013, that number had fallen to fewer than 1,800.

According to the ASNE's 2013 census, of the 38,000 reporters and editors at daily newspapers, "about 4,700 or 12.37 percent [were] racial minorities; the percentage of minority employees has consistently hovered between 12 and 13 percent for more than a decade." Among the ASNE's main goals, however, "is to have the percentage of minorities working in newsrooms nationwide reflect the percentage of the nation's population by 2025." In 2013, minorities made up about 37 percent of the U.S. population, and the U.S. Census Bureau has reported that the number will increase to more than 42 percent by 2025.[28]

© Lucien Aigner/Corbis

AFRICAN AMERICAN NEWSPAPERS
This 1936 scene reveals the newsroom of Harlem's *Amsterdam News*, one of the nation's leading African American newspapers. Ironically, the Civil Rights movement and affirmative action policies since the 1960s served to drain talented reporters from the black press by encouraging them to work for larger, mainstream newspapers.

Spanish-Language Newspapers

Bilingual and Spanish-language newspapers have served a variety of Mexican, Puerto Rican, Cuban, and other Hispanic readerships since 1808, when *El Misisipi* was founded in New Orleans. Throughout the 1800s, Texas had more than 150 Spanish-language papers.[29] Los Angeles' *La Opinión,* founded in 1926, is now the nation's largest Spanish-language daily. Other prominent publications are in Miami (*La Voz* and *Diario Las Americas*), Houston (*La Información*), Chicago (*El Mañana Daily News* and *La Raza*), and New York (*El Diario–La Prensa*). By 2011, about eight hundred Spanish-language papers operated in the United States, most of them weekly and nondaily papers, although since 2004, no new Hispanic papers have been founded.[30] Until the late 1960s, mainstream newspapers virtually ignored Hispanic issues and culture. But with the influx of Mexican, Puerto Rican, and Cuban immigrants throughout the 1980s and 1990s, many mainstream papers began to feature weekly Spanish-language supplements. The first was the *Miami Herald*'s "El Nuevo Herald," introduced in 1976. Other mainstream papers also joined in, but many had folded their Spanish-language supplements by the mid-1990s. In 1995, the *Los Angeles Times* discontinued its supplement, "Nuestro Tiempo," and the *Miami Herald* trimmed budgets and staff for "El Nuevo Herald." Spanish-language radio and television had beaten newspapers to these potential customers and advertisers. As the U.S. Hispanic population reached 17 percent in 2013, Hispanic journalists accounted for only about 4 percent of the newsroom workforce at U.S. daily newspapers.[31]

THE *WORLD JOURNAL* is a national daily paper that targets Chinese immigrants by focusing on news from China, Hong Kong, Taiwan, and other Southeast Asian communities.

Asian American Newspapers

In the 1980s, hundreds of small papers emerged to serve immigrants from Pakistan, Laos, Cambodia, and China. While people of Asian descent made up only about 5.3 percent of the U.S. population in 2013, this percentage is expected to rise to 9 percent by 2050.[32] Today, fifty small U.S. papers are printed in Vietnamese. Ethnic papers like these help readers both adjust to foreign surroundings and retain ties to their traditional heritage. In addition, these papers often cover major stories downplayed in the mainstream press. For example, in the aftermath of 9/11, airport security teams detained thousands of Middle Eastern–looking men. The *Weekly Bangla Patrika*—a Long Island, New York, paper—reported on the one hundred people the Bangladeshi community lost in the 9/11 attacks and on how it feels to be innocent yet targeted by ethnic profiling.[33]

A growth area in newspapers is Chinese publications. Even amid a poor economy, a new Chinese newspaper, *News for Chinese*, started in 2008. The Chinese-language paper began as a free monthly distributed in the San Francisco area. In early 2009, it began publishing twice a week. By 2014, the *World Journal*, the largest U.S.-based Chinese-language paper, was publishing editions in seven U.S. and Canadian cities: New York, Los Angeles, San Francisco, Chicago, Dallas, Vancouver, and Toronto.[34] In 2013, Asian American journalists accounted for 3 percent of newsroom jobs in the United States.[35]

Native American Newspapers

An activist Native American press has provided oppositional voices to mainstream American media since 1828, when the *Cherokee Phoenix* appeared in Georgia. Another prominent early paper was the *Cherokee Rose Bud*, founded in 1848 by tribal women in the Oklahoma territory. The Native American Press Association has documented more than 350 Native American papers, most of them printed in English but a few in tribal languages. Currently, two national papers are the *Native American Times*, which offers perspectives on "sovereign rights, civil rights, and government-to-government relationships with the federal government," and *Indian Country Today*, owned by the Oneida Nation in New York. In 2013, Native American journalists accounted for 0.37 percent of newsroom jobs in the United States—or about 140 reporters and editors.

To counter the neglect of Native American culture's viewpoints by the mainstream press, Native American newspapers have helped educate various tribes about their heritage and have helped build community solidarity. These papers have also reported on both the problems and the progress among tribes that have opened casinos and gambling resorts. Overall, these smaller papers provide a forum for debates on tribal conflicts and concerns, and they often signal the mainstream press on issues—such as gambling or hunting and fishing rights—that have particular significance for the larger culture.

The Underground Press

The mid to late 1960s saw an explosion of alternative newspapers. Labeled the **underground press** at the time, these papers questioned mainstream political policies and conventional values, often voicing radical opinions. Generally running on shoestring budgets, they were also erratic in meeting publication schedules. Springing up on college campuses and in major cities, underground papers were inspired by the writings of socialists and intellectuals from the 1930s and 1940s and by a new wave of thinkers and artists. Particularly inspirational were poets and writers (such as Allen Ginsberg, Jack Kerouac, LeRoi Jones, and Eldridge Cleaver) and "protest" musicians (including Bob Dylan, Pete Seeger, and Joan Baez). In criticizing social institutions, alternative papers questioned the official reports distributed by public relations agents, government spokespeople, and the conventional press (see "Case Study: Alternative Journalism: Dorothy Day and I. F. Stone" on page 292).

During the 1960s, underground papers played a unique role in documenting social tension by including the voices of students, women, African Americans, Native Americans, gay men and lesbians, and others whose opinions were often excluded from the mainstream press. The first and largest underground paper, the *Village Voice*, was founded in Greenwich Village in 1955. It is still distributed free, surviving through advertising, though its staff has been cut heavily in recent years. But circulation figures for free alternative weeklies are often difficult to pin down. While the Pew Research Center reported the *Village Voice* circulation at 144,000 in 2013, the Association of Alternative Newsweeklies (AAN) listed the paper's circulation at 80,000 in both 2013 and 2014.[36]

Among campus underground papers, the *Berkeley Barb* was the most influential, developing amid the free-speech movement in the mid-1960s. Despite their irreverent tone, many underground papers turned a spotlight on racial and gender inequities and occasionally goaded mainstream journalism to examine social issues. Like the black press, though, many early underground papers folded after the 1960s. Given their radical outlook, it was difficult for them to appeal to advertisers. In addition, as with the black press, mainstream papers raided alternatives and expanded their own coverage of culture by hiring the underground's best writers. Still, today more than 130 papers, reaching 25 million readers, are members of the AAN.

Newspaper Operations

Today, a weekly paper might employ only two or three people, while a major metro daily might have a staff of more than one thousand, including workers in the newsroom and online operations, and in departments for circulation (distributing the newspaper), advertising (selling ad space), and mechanical operations (assembling and printing the paper). In either situation, however, most newspapers distinguish business operations from editorial or news functions. Journalists' and readers' praise or criticism usually rests on the quality of a paper's news and editorial components, but business and advertising concerns today dictate whether papers will survive.

Most major daily papers would like to devote one-half to two-thirds of their pages to advertisements. Newspapers carry everything from full-page spreads for department stores to shrinking classified ads, which consumers can purchase for a few dollars to advertise used cars or old furniture (although many Web sites now do this for free). In most cases, ads are positioned in the paper first. The **newshole**—space not taken up by ads—accounts for the remaining 35 to 50 percent of the content of daily newspapers, including front-page news. The newshole and physical size of many newspapers had shrunk substantially by 2010.

News and Editorial Responsibilities

The chain of command at most larger papers starts with the publisher and owner at the top and then moves, on the news and editorial side, to the editor in chief and managing editor, who are in charge of the daily news-gathering and writing processes. Under the main editors, assistant editors have traditionally run different news divisions, including features, sports, photos, local news, state news, and wire service reports that contain major national and international news. Increasingly, many editorial positions are being eliminated or condensed to the job of

Alternative Journalism: Dorothy Day and I. F. Stone

Over the years, a number of unconventional reporters have struggled against the status quo to find a place for unheard voices and alternative ways to practice their craft. For example, Ida Wells fearlessly investigated violence against blacks for the *Memphis Free Speech* in the late nineteenth century. Newspaper lore offers a rich history of alternative journalists and their publications, such as Dorothy Day's *Catholic Worker* and *I. F. Stone's Weekly*.

In 1933, Dorothy Day (1897–1980) cofounded a radical religious organization with a monthly newspaper, the *Catholic Worker*, that opposed war and supported social reforms. Like many young intellectual writers during World War I, Day was a pacifist; she also joined the Socialist Party. Quitting college at age eighteen to work as an activist reporter for socialist newspapers, Day participated in the ongoing suffrage movement to give women the right to vote. Throughout the 1930s, her Catholic Worker organization invested in thirty hospices for the poor and homeless, providing food and shelter for five thousand people a day. This legacy endures today, with the organization continuing to fund soup kitchens and homeless shelters throughout the country.

For more than eighty years, the *Worker* has consistently advocated personal activism to further social justice, opposing anti-Semitism, Japanese American internment camps during World War II, nuclear weapons, the Korean War, military drafts, and the communist witch-hunts of the 1950s. The *Worker*'s circulation peaked in 1938 at 190,000, then fell dramatically during World War II, when Day's pacifism was at odds with much of America. Today, the *Catholic Worker* has a circulation of about 30,000.

I. F. Stone (1907–1989) shared Dorothy Day's passion for social activism. He also started early, publishing his own monthly paper at the age of fourteen and becoming a full-time reporter by age twenty. He worked as a Washington political writer for the *Nation* in the early 1940s and later for the *New York Daily Compass*. Throughout his career, Stone challenged the conventions and privileges of both politics and journalism. In 1941, for example, he resigned from the National Press Club when it refused to serve his guest, the nation's first African American federal judge. In the early 1950s, he actively opposed Joseph McCarthy's rabid campaign to rid government and the media of alleged communists.

When the *Daily Compass* failed in 1952, the radical Stone was unable to find a newspaper job and decided to create his own newsletter, *I. F. Stone's Weekly*, which he published for nineteen years. Practicing interpretive and investigative reporting, Stone became as adept as any major journalist at tracking down government records to discover contradictions, inaccuracies, and lies. Over the years, Stone questioned decisions by the Supreme Court, investigated the substandard living conditions of many African Americans, and criticized political corruption. He guided the *Weekly* to a circulation that reached seventy thousand during the 1960s, when he probed American investments of money and military might in Vietnam.

I. F. Stone and Dorothy Day embodied a spirit of independent reporting that has been threatened by first the rise of chain ownership, then the decline in readership. Stone, who believed that alternative ideas were crucial to maintaining a healthy democracy, once wrote that "there must be free play for so-called 'subversive' ideas—every idea 'subverts' the old to make way for the new. To shut off 'subversion' is to shut off peaceful progress and to invite revolution and war."[1]

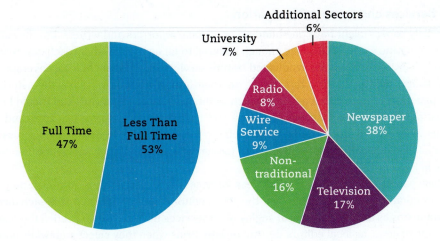

FIGURE 8.1

WHO REPORTS FROM U.S. STATEHOUSES? (PERCENTAGE OF ALL STATEHOUSE REPORTERS)

Note: The "less than full-time" category includes reporters who work during session only, as well as other staff, such as interns and videographers. "Additional sectors" represent the following: professional publications, multiplatform media companies, and "other," which includes freelancers, magazines, and alternative weeklies. Figures may not add up to 100 percent because of rounding.

Data from: Pew Research, "America's Shifting Statehouse Press Corp: Fewer Print Reporters Assigned to State Capitals," July 10, 2014, www.journalism.org/2014/07/10/americas-shifting-statehouse-press/.

a single editor, whose chief responsibility is often ensuring that stories are posted first online (to give them the immediacy that radio and TV news have always had), then updated, and then prepared for the print edition.

Reporters work for editors. *General assignment reporters* handle all sorts of stories that might emerge—or "break"—in a given day. *Specialty reporters* are assigned to particular beats (police, courts, schools, local and national government) or topics (education, religion, health, environment, technology). On large dailies, *bureau reporters* also file reports from other major cities. Large daily papers feature columnists and critics who cover various aspects of culture, such as politics, books, television, movies, and food. While papers used to employ a separate staff for their online operations, the current trend is to have traditional reporters file both online and print versions of their stories—accompanied by images or video they are responsible for gathering.

Recent consolidation and cutbacks have led to layoffs and the closing of bureaus outside a paper's city limits. For example, in 1985, more than 600 newspapers had reporters stationed in Washington, D.C.; in 2013, that number was under 250. The *Los Angeles Times*, the *Chicago Tribune*, and the *Baltimore Sun*—all owned now by Tribune Publishing—closed their independent bureaus in 2009, choosing instead to share reports.[37] In terms of state capital reporting, a 2014 Pew research study showed that the profession "lost a total of 164 full-time statehouse reporters—a decline of 35%—between 2003 and 2014."[38] That was slightly higher than the 30 percent decline of overall newspaper staffing during roughly the same period, according to ASNE census data.

The downside of these money-saving measures in our nation's capital and in various U.S. state capitals is that far fewer versions of stories are being produced, and readers must often rely on a single version of a news report. According to the ASNE, the workforce in daily U.S. newsrooms declined by 11,000 jobs in 2008 and 2009.[39] A small turnaround occurred in 2010 with 100 new jobs created overall, driven by the increase of 220 jobs in "freestanding digital news organizations."[40] But ASNE reported that from 2011 to 2012, the total number of newsroom jobs fell by 3,600, from 41,600 to 38,000.[41]

POLITICAL CARTOONS are often syndicated features in newspapers and reflect the issues of the day.

Wire Services and Feature Syndication

Major daily papers might have one hundred or so local reporters and writers, but they still cannot cover the world or produce enough material to fill up the newshole each day. Newspapers rely on wire services and syndicated feature services to supplement local coverage. A few major dailies, such as the *New York Times*, run their own wire services, selling their stories to other papers to reprint. Other agencies, such as the Associated Press (AP) and United Press International (UPI), have hundreds of staffers stationed throughout major U.S. cities and world capitals. They submit stories and photos each day for distribution to newspapers across the country. Some U.S. papers also subscribe to foreign wire services, such as Agence France-Presse in Paris or Reuters in London.

Daily papers generally pay monthly fees for access to all wire stories. Although they use only a fraction of what is available over the wires, editors monitor wire services each day for important stories and ideas for local angles. Wire services have greatly expanded the reach and scope of news, as local editors depend on wire firms when they select statewide, national, or international reports for reprinting.

In addition, traditional **feature syndicates**, such as United Features (now known as Universal Uclick) and Tribune Media Services (now known as Gracenote), operated historically as commercial outlets that contracted with newspapers to provide work from the nation's best political writers, editorial cartoonists, comic-strip artists, and self-help columnists. These companies served as brokers, distributing horoscopes and crossword puzzles as well as the political columns and comic strips that appealed to a wide audience. When a paper bid on and acquired the rights to a cartoonist or columnist, it signed exclusivity agreements with a syndicate to ensure that it was the only paper in the region to carry, say, Clarence Page, Maureen Dowd, Leonard Pitts, Connie Schultz, George Will, or cartoonist Mike Peters. Feature syndicates, like wire services, wielded great influence in determining which writers and cartoonists gained national prominence.

Newspaper Ownership: Chains Lose Their Grip

Edward Wyllis Scripps founded the first **newspaper chain**—a company that owns several papers throughout the country—in the 1890s. By the 1920s, there were about thirty chains in the United States, each owning an average of five papers. The emergence of chains paralleled the major business trend during the twentieth century: the movement toward oligopolies, in which a handful of corporations control each industry.

By the 1980s, more than 130 chains owned an average of nine papers each, with the 12 largest chains accounting for 40 percent of total circulation in the United States. By 2001, the top ten chains controlled more than one-half of the nation's total daily newspaper circulation. Gannett, for example, the nation's largest chain, owns over eighty daily papers (and hundreds of nondailies worldwide), ranging from small suburban papers to the *Cincinnati Enquirer*, the Nashville *Tennessean*, and *USA Today*.

Around 2005, consolidation in newspaper ownership leveled off because the decline in newspaper circulation and ad sales panicked investors, leading to drops in the stock value of newspapers. Many newspaper chains responded by significantly reducing their newsroom staffs and selling off individual papers.

For an example of this cost cutting, consider actions at the *Los Angeles Times* (then owned by the Chicago-based Tribune Company chain). Continuing demands from the corporate offices for cost reductions led to the resignations of editors and publishers. Cuts also caused the departures of some of the most talented staff members, including six Pulitzer Prize winners. In 2007, Chicago real estate developer Sam Zell bought the Tribune Company for $8 billion and made it private, insulating it for a time from market demands for high profit margins. However, by 2008, the company faced declining ad revenue and a tough economy and was forced to file for bankruptcy protection, which it received until the end of 2012, when it emerged from bankruptcy. While it continues to operate—as of 2014 as separate TV and newspaper companies—Tribune's history indicates the sorts of troubles once highly profitable major newspapers face.

About the same time, large chains started to break up, selling individual newspapers to private equity firms and big banks (like Bank of America and JPMorgan Chase) that deal in distressed and overleveraged companies with too much debt. For example, in 2006, Knight Ridder—then the nation's second-leading chain—was sold for $4.5 billion to the McClatchy Company. McClatchy then broke up the chain by selling off twelve of the thirty-two papers, including the *San Jose Mercury News* and Philadelphia Newspapers (which included the *Philadelphia Inquirer*). McClatchy also sold its leading newspaper, the *Minneapolis Star Tribune*, to a private equity company for $530 million, less than half of what it had paid to buy it eight years earlier.

On a more promising note, in 2012, billionaire philanthropist Warren Buffett, CEO of the investment firm Berkshire Hathaway, spent $344 million and bought more than sixty newspapers (the company planned to retain about thirty). A newspaper junkie and former paperboy, Buffett has owned the *Buffalo News* in New York since 1977 and has run it profitably. In 2011, he also bought his hometown paper, the *Omaha World-Herald*, for $200 million. Buffett has argued that many smaller and regional newspapers will thrive if they have a strong sense of their local communities and do a good job of mixing their print and digital products. The *New York Times* reported that Buffett planned to buy more papers—"three years after telling shareholders that he would not buy a newspaper at any price."[42] In 2013, Buffett's BH Media Group bought the *Tulsa World* in Oklahoma and the *Roanoke Times* in Virginia. By 2014, Buffett retained ownership of twenty-nine small and midsize daily newspapers.

While Warren Buffett concentrated on purchasing smaller regional papers, ownership of one of the nation's three national newspapers also changed hands. Back in 2007, the *Wall Street Journal*, held by the Bancroft family for more than one hundred years, accepted a bid of nearly $5.8 billion from News Corp. head Rupert Murdoch (News Corp. also owns the *New York Post* and many papers in the United Kingdom and Australia). At the time, critics raised serious concerns about takeovers of newspapers by large entertainment conglomerates (Murdoch's company at the time also owned TV stations, a network, cable channels, and a movie studio). As small subsidiaries in large media empires, newspapers are increasingly treated as just another product line that is expected to perform in the same way that a movie or TV program does. But in 2012, News Corp. decided to split its news and entertainment divisions, leading some critics to hope that Murdoch's news operations would no longer be subject to the same high-profit expectations of Hollywood movies and sitcoms.

As chains lose their grip, there are concerns about who will own papers in the future and the effect the papers' owners will have on content and press freedoms. Recent purchases by private equity groups are alarming, since these companies are usually more interested in turning a profit than supporting journalism. However, ideas exist for how to avoid this fate. For example, more support could be rallied for small independent owners, who could then make decisions based on what's best for the paper—not just what's best for the quarterly report. (For more on how newspapers and owners are trying new business models, see "New Models for Journalism" on pages 300–302.)

Joint Operating Agreements Combat Declining Competition

Although the amount of regulation preventing newspaper monopolies has decreased, the government continues to monitor the declining number of newspapers in various American cities as well as mergers in cities where competition among papers might be endangered. In the mid-1920s, about five hundred American cities had two or more newspapers with separate owners. However, by 2010, fewer than fifteen cities had independent, competing papers.

In 1970, Congress passed the Newspaper Preservation Act, which enabled failing papers to continue operating through a **joint operating agreement (JOA)**. Under a JOA, two competing papers keep separate news divisions while merging business and production operations for a period of years. Since the act's passage, twenty-eight cities have adopted JOAs. By 2003, sixteen of those JOAs had been terminated. By 2014, just six JOAs remained in place—in Charleston, West Virginia; Detroit; Fort Wayne, Indiana; Las Vegas; Salt Lake City; and York, Pennsylvania. Although JOAs and mergers have monopolistic tendencies, they have sometimes been the only way to maintain competition between newspapers.

For example, Detroit was one of the most competitive newspaper cities in the nation until 1989. The *Detroit News* and the *Detroit Free Press*, then owned by Gannett and Knight Ridder, respectively, both ranked among the ten most widely circulated papers in the country and sold their weekday editions for just fifteen cents a copy. Faced with declining revenue and increased costs, the papers' managers asked for and received a JOA in 1989. But problems continued. Then, in 1995, a prolonged and bitter strike by several unions sharply reduced circulation, as the strikers formed a union-backed paper to compete against the existing newspapers. Many readers dropped their subscriptions to the *News* and the *Free Press* to support the strikers. Before the strike (and the rise of the Internet), Gannett and Knight Ridder had both reported profit margins of well over 15 percent on all their newspaper holdings.[43] By 2010, Knight Ridder was out of the newspaper chain business, and neither Detroit paper ranked in the Top 20. In addition, the *News* and the *Free Press* became the first major papers to stop daily home delivery for part of the week, instead directing readers to the Web or to brief newsstand editions.

Challenges Facing Newspapers Today

Publishers and journalists today face worrisome issues, such as the decline in newspaper readership and the failure of many papers to attract younger readers. However, other problems persist as newspapers continue to converge with the Internet and grapple with the future of digital news.

Readership Declines in the United States

The decline in daily newspaper readership actually began during the Great Depression with the rise of radio. Between 1931 and 1939, six hundred newspapers ceased operation. Another circulation crisis occurred from the late 1960s through the 1970s with the rise in network television viewing and greater competition from suburban weeklies. In addition, with an increasing number of women working full-time outside the home, newspapers could no longer consistently count on one of their core readership groups.

Throughout the first decade of the twenty-first century, U.S. newspaper circulation dropped again, this time by more than 25 percent.[44] In the face of such steep circulation and readership declines, however, overall audiences did start growing again thanks to online readers, and Pew's *State of the News Media 2013* report saw reasons for optimism:

Companies have started to experiment in a big way with a variety of new revenue streams and major organizational changes. Some of the bright opportunities—such as offering social marketing services to local businesses—are ventures too new to be measured yet industry-wide. They show signs of stabilizing revenue.

Digital pay plans are being adopted at 450 of the country's 1,380 dailies and appear to be working not just at The New York Times *but also at small and mid-sized papers. Twinned with print subscription and single-copy price increases, the digital paywall movement has circulation revenues holding steady or rising. Together with the other new revenue streams, these added circulation revenues are rebalancing the industry's portfolio from its historic over-dependence on advertising.*[45]

Remarkably, while the United States continues to experience declines in newspaper readership and advertising dollars, many other nations—where Internet news is still emerging—have experienced increases. For example, the World Association of Newspapers (WAN) reported that between 2003 and 2009, there was an 8.8 percent growth in newspaper readership worldwide, mostly concentrated in Asia, Africa, and South America.[46] In 2013, WAN reported that between 2008 and 2013, "newspaper circulation dropped by 13 per cent in North America but rose 9.8 per cent in Asia," while ad revenue "declined by 42.1 per cent in North America but rose by 6.2 per cent in Asia."[47] In 2014, WAN reported that "around 2.5 billion people" worldwide read newspapers in print and about 800 million read them in digital forms. While digital ad sales continue to grow for newspapers worldwide, this still represents a small percentage of print news revenue. According to WAN, "Globally, 93 per cent of all newspaper revenues continue to come from print."[48]

Going Local: How Small and Campus Papers Retain Readers

Despite the doomsday headlines and predictions about the future of newspapers, it is important to note, as Pew's *State of the News Media 2010* report observed, that the problems of the newspaper business "are not uniform across the industry." In fact, according to the report, "Small dailies and community weeklies, with the exception of some that are badly positioned or badly managed," still do better than many "big-city papers."[49] That report back in 2010 also suggested that smaller papers in smaller communities remain "the dominant source for local information and the place for local merchants to advertise."[50]

Smaller newspapers continue to do better today for several reasons. First, small towns and cities often don't have local TV stations, big-city magazines, or numerous radio stations competing against newspapers for ad space. This means that smaller papers are more likely to retain their revenue from local advertisers. Second, whether they are tiny weekly papers serving small towns or campus newspapers serving university towns, such papers have a loyal and steady base of readers who cannot get information on their small communities from any other source. In fact, many college newspaper editors report that the most popular feature in their papers is the police report: It serves as a kind of local gossip, listing the names of students busted over the weekend for underage drinking or public intoxication.

Finally, because smaller newspapers tend to be more consensus-oriented than conflict-driven in their approach to news, these papers usually do not see the big dips in ad revenue that may occur when editors tackle complex or controversial topics that are divisive. For example, when a major regional newspaper does an investigative series on local auto dealers for poor service or shady business practices, those dealers—for a while—can cancel advertising that the paper sorely needs. While local papers fill in the gaps left by large mainstream papers and other news media sources, they still face some of the same challenges as large papers and must continue to adapt to retain readers and advertisers.

Blogs Challenge Newspapers' Authority Online

The rise of blogs in the late 1990s brought amateurs into the realm of professional journalism. It was an awkward meeting. As National Press Club president Doug Harbrecht said to conservative blogger Matt Drudge in 1998 while introducing him to the press club's members, "There aren't many in this hallowed room who consider you a journalist. Real journalists . . . pride themselves on getting it first and right; they get to the bottom of the story, they bend over backwards to get the other side. Journalism means being painstakingly thorough, even-handed, and fair."[51] Harbrecht's suggestion, of course, was that untrained bloggers weren't as scrupulous as professionally trained journalists. In the following decade, though, as blogs like *Daily Kos*, the *Huffington Post*, *The Dish: Biased and Balanced* (http://dish.andrewsullivan.com), and *Talking Points Memo* gained credibility and a large readership, traditional journalism slowly began to try blogging, allowing some reporters to write a blog in addition to their regular newspaper, television, or radio work. Some newspapers, such as the *Washington Post* and the *New York Times*, even hired journalists to blog exclusively for their Web sites.

By 2005, the wary relationship between journalism and blogging began to change. Blogging became less a journalistic sideline and more a viable main feature. Established journalists left major news organizations to begin new careers in the blogosphere. For example, in 2007, top journalists John Harris and Jim VandeHei left the *Washington Post* to launch *Politico*, a national blog (and, secondarily, a local newspaper) about Capitol Hill politics. Another breakthrough moment occurred when the *Talking Points Memo* blog, headed by Joshua Micah Marshall, won a George Polk Award for legal reporting in 2008. Explaining his view of blogging, Marshall has said, "I think of us as journalists; the medium we work in is blogging. We have kind of broken free of the model of discrete articles that have a beginning and end. Instead, there are an ongoing series of dispatches."[52] Increasingly, because of qualified journalists moving online, Pew reports that sites that started out as opinionated blogs have grown into legitimate news venues:

Digital players have exploded onto the news scene, bringing technological know-how and new money and luring top talent. BuzzFeed, once scoffed at for content viewed as "click bait," now has a news staff of 170, including top names like Pulitzer Prize–winner Mark Schoofs, and is the kind of place that ProPublica's Paul Steiger says he would want to work at if he were young again. Mashable now has a news staff of 70 and enticed former New York Times *assistant managing editor Jim Roberts to become its chief content officer. And in January of this year [2014], Ezra Klein left the* Washington Post *for Vox Media, which will become the new home for his explanatory journalism concept. Many of these companies are already successful digital brands—built around an innate understanding of technology—and are using revenues from other parts of the operation to get the news operations off the ground.*[53]

What distinguishes the best online news from so many opinion blogs still out there is the reliance on old-fashioned journalism—calling on reporters to interview people as sources, to look at documents, and to find evidence to support the story, whether it is in print or online.

Convergence: Newspapers Struggle in the Move to Digital

Because of their local monopoly status, many newspapers were slower than other media to confront the challenges of the Internet. But faced with competition from the 24/7 news cycle on cable,

Capecodonline.com

newspapers responded by developing online versions of their papers. While some observers think newspapers are on the verge of extinction as the digital age eclipses the print era, the industry is no dinosaur. In fact, the history of communication demonstrates that older mass media have always adapted; so far, books, newspapers, and magazines have adjusted to the radio, television, and movie industries. And with nearly fifteen hundred North American daily papers going online in 2010, newspapers are solving one of the industry's major economic headaches: the cost of newsprint. After salaries, paper is the industry's largest expense, typically accounting for more than 25 percent of a newspaper's total cost.

Online newspapers are truly taking advantage of the flexibility the Internet offers. Because space is not an issue online, newspapers can post stories and readers' letters that they aren't able to print in the paper edition. They can also run longer stories with more in-depth coverage, as well as offer immediate updates to breaking news. Also, most stories appear online before they appear in print; they can be posted at any time and updated several times a day.

Among the valuable resources that online newspapers offer are hyperlinks to Web sites that relate to stories and that link news reports to an archive of related articles. Free of charge or for a modest fee, a reader can search the newspaper's database from home and investigate the entire sequence and history of an ongoing story, such as a trial, over the course of several months. Taking advantage of the Internet's multimedia capabilities, online newspapers offer readers the ability to stream audio and video files—everything from presidential news conferences to local sports highlights to original video footage from a storm disaster. Today's online newspapers offer readers a dynamic, rather than a static, resource.

However, these advances have yet to pay off. Online ads in the United States accounted for about 13 percent of a newspaper's advertising in 2010—up about 3 percent from 2009. So

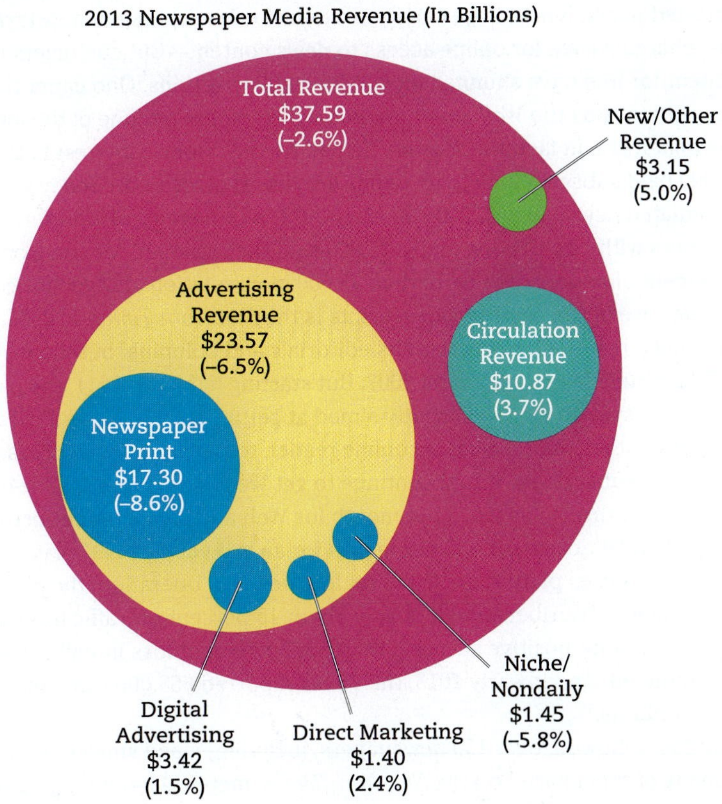

2013 Newspaper Media Revenue (In Billions)

Total Revenue
$37.59
(−2.6%)

New/Other
Revenue
$3.15
(5.0%)

Advertising
Revenue
$23.57
(−6.5%)

Circulation
Revenue
$10.87
(3.7%)

Newspaper
Print
$17.30
(−8.6%)

Digital
Advertising
$3.42
(1.5%)

Direct Marketing
$1.40
(2.4%)

Niche/
Nondaily
$1.45
(−5.8%)

FIGURE 8.2

NEWSPAPER MEDIA REVENUE, 2013

Data from: Newspaper Association of America, www.naa.org/Trends -and-Numbers/Newspaper-Revenue /Newspaper-Media-Industry -Revenue-Profile-2013.aspx.

Andrew Harrer/Bloomberg via Getty Images

PAYWALL
The *New York Times* began charging readers for access to all online content in early 2011, via either a print subscription or a stand-alone online subscription. Recognizing the fact that readers today are gravitating toward reading the news on their smartphones or tablets, all the plans offered by the *Times* include some form of mobile access. Still, in order to mitigate the decrease in online traffic and to alleviate resistance from those who feel as if they shouldn't have to pay for online content, the *Times* in 2014 allowed readers free access to ten articles a month, as well as free access to articles via a search link or a link posted on a social networking site.

newspapers, even in decline, are still heavily dependent on print ads. But this trend does not seem likely to sustain papers for long. Ad revenue for newspaper print ads in 2009 declined 25 to 35 percent at many newspapers.[54] To jump-start online revenue streams, more than four hundred daily newspapers collaborated with Yahoo! (the number-one portal to newspapers online) in 2006 to begin an advertising venture that aimed to increase papers' online revenue by 10 to 20 percent. By summer 2010, with the addition of the large Gannett chain, Yahoo! had nearly nine hundred papers in the ad partnership. During an eighteen-month period in 2009–10, the Yahoo! consortium sold over thirty thousand online ad campaigns in local markets, with most revenue shared 50/50 between Yahoo! and its partner papers.[55]

By 2014, online ad sales for newspapers accounted for about 17 percent of U.S. newspapers' advertising revenue, suggesting that online sales on average had risen just 1 percent a year since 2010. The Newspaper Association of America reported that print ad sales in 2013 had declined another 8.6 percent, which represented a loss of $1.6 billion. In terms of digital advertising—the revenue stream that could provide the foundation for a new business model for newspapers—sales were up just 1.5 percent in 2013. As the Nieman Journalism Lab noted: "In 2014, American newspapers still [got] 83 percent of their advertising revenue from print."[56]

One of the business mistakes that most newspaper executives made near the beginning of the Internet age was giving away online content for free. Whereas their print versions always had two revenue streams—ads and subscriptions—newspaper executives weren't convinced that online revenue would amount to much, so they used their online version as an advertisement for the printed paper. Since those early years, most newspapers are now trying to establish a **paywall**—charging a fee for online access to news content—but customers used to getting online content for free have shunned most online subscriptions. One paper that did charge early for online content was the *Wall Street Journal*, which pioneered one of the few successful paywalls in the digital era. In fact, the *Journal*, helped by the public's interest in the economic crisis and 400,000 paid subscriptions to its online service, replaced *USA Today* as the nation's most widely circulated newspaper in 2009. In early 2011, a University of Missouri study found 46 percent of papers with circulations under 25,000 said they charged for some online content, while only 24 percent of papers with more than 25,000 in circulation charged for content.[57]

An interesting case in the paywall experiments is the *New York Times*. In 2005, the paper began charging online readers for access to its editorials and columns, but the rest of the site was free. This system lasted only until 2007. But starting in March 2011, the paper added a paywall—a metered system that was mostly aimed at getting the *New York Times'* most loyal online readers, rather than the casual online reader, to pay for online access. Under this paywall system, print subscribers would continue to get Web access free. Online-only subscribers could opt for one of three plans: $15 per month for Web and smartphone access, $20 per month for Web and tablet access, or $35 per month for an "all-you-can-eat" plan that would allow access to all the *Times* platforms. In its first few weeks of operation, the paper gained more than 100,000 new subscribers and lost only about 15 percent of traffic from the days of free Web access—a more positive scenario than the 50 percent loss in online traffic some observers had predicted. And in early 2013, the *Times* reported 668,000 paid subscribers to all its various digital options.[58]

In the years that followed, over 150 newspapers, including many small ones, launched various paywalls, many of them based on the *New York Times'* metered model, trying to reverse years of giving away their print content online for free. Larger metro dailies, including the *Boston Globe*, *Dallas Morning News*, *Milwaukee Journal Sentinel*, and *Los Angeles Times*, have also started their own paywalls and metered models. But in 2014, the Nieman Journalism Lab reported on a number of studies and a report on Gannett's experiments with its various paywalls and concluded: "When you announce a paywall, you get a one-time boost from people who are willing to pay. But it plateaus. And maybe some of those subscribers eventually drop off. It's not a growth model that does anything like replace the ongoing decline in print advertising revenue—which continues to decline somewhere in the high single digits every year."[59]

New Models for Journalism

In response to the challenges newspapers face, a number of journalists, economists, and citizens are calling for new business models—with more potential than paywalls—for combating newspapers' decline. One avenue is developing new business ventures, such as the online-only papers begun by former print reporters. Started by former *Washington Post* reporters in 2007, *Politico* is a successful example. Another idea is for wealthy universities like Harvard and Yale to buy and support papers, thereby better insulating their public service and watchdog operations from the high profit expectations of the marketplace. Another possibility might be to get Internet companies involved. Amazon founder Jeff Bezos's purchase of the *Washington Post* in 2013 is one example. Earlier, Google—worried that a decline in the quality of journalism meant fewer sites on which to post ads and earn online revenue—pledged $5 million to news foundations and companies to encourage innovation in digital journalism. Wealthy Internet companies like Microsoft and Google could expand into the news business and start producing content for both online and print papers. In fact, in March 2010, Yahoo! began hiring reporters to increase the presence of its online news site. The company hired reporters from *Politico*, *BusinessWeek*, the *New York Observer*, the *Washington Post*, and *Talking Points Memo*, among others.

Reprinted with permission from *Politico*

POLITICO quickly became a reputable place for Washington insiders as well as the general population to go for political news and reporting, allowing the organization to thrive at a time when other papers were struggling. As editor in chief John Harris states on the site, *Politico* aims to be more than just a place for politics; it also "hope[s] to add to the conversation about what's next for journalism." What do you think its success means for the future of the news media?

Additional ideas are coming from universities (where journalism school enrollments are actually increasing). For example, the dean of Columbia University's Journalism School (started once upon a time with money bequeathed by nineteenth-century newspaper mogul Joseph Pulitzer) commissioned a study from Leonard Downie, former executive editor of the *Washington Post*, and Michael Schudson, Columbia journalism professor and media scholar. Their report, "The Reconstruction of American Journalism," focused on lost circulation, advertising revenue, and news jobs, and aimed to create a strategy for reporting that would hold public and government officials accountable.[60] After all, citizens in democracies require basic access to reports, data, and documentation in order to be well informed. Here is an overview of their recommendations, some of which have already been implemented:

- News organizations "substantially devoted to reporting on public affairs" should be allowed to operate as nonprofit entities in order to take in tax-deductible contributions while still collecting ad and subscription revenues. For example, the Poynter Institute owns and operates the *Tampa Bay Times* (formerly the *St. Petersburg Times*), Florida's largest newspaper. As a nonprofit, the *Times* is protected from the unrealistic 16 to 20 percent profit margins that publicly held newspapers had been expected to earn in the 1980s and 1990s.
- Public radio and TV, through federal reforms in the Corporation for Public Broadcasting, should reorient their focus to "significant local news reporting in every community served by public stations and their Web sites."
- Operating their own news services or supporting regional news organizations, public and private universities "should become ongoing sources of local, state, specialized subject and accountability news reporting as part of their educational mission."
- A national Fund for Local News should be created with money the Federal Communications Commission collects from "telecom users, television and radio broadcast licensees, or Internet service providers."
- News services, nonprofit organizations, and government agencies should use the Internet to "increase the accessibility and usefulness of public information collected by federal, state, and local governments."

As the journalism industry continues to reinvent itself and tries new avenues to ensure its future, not every "great" idea will work out. Some of the immediate backlash to Downie and Schudson's report raised questions about the government becoming involved with traditionally independent news media. What is important, however, is that newspapers continue to experiment with new ideas and business models so that they can adapt and even thrive in the Internet age. (For more on the challenges facing journalism, see Chapter 14.)

Alternative Voices

The combination of the online news surge and traditional newsroom cutbacks has led to a phenomenon known as **citizen journalism**, or *citizen media* (or *community journalism* for those projects in which the participants might not be citizens). As a grassroots movement, citizen journalism refers to people—activist amateurs and concerned citizens, not professional journalists—who use the Internet and blogs to disseminate news and information. In fact, with steep declines in newsroom staffs, many professional news media organizations—like CNN's iReport and many regional newspapers—are increasingly trying to corral citizen journalists as an inexpensive way to make up for the journalists lost to newsroom downsizing.

Back in 2008, one study reported that more than one thousand community-based Web sites were in operation, posting citizen stories about local government, police, and city development.[61] By 2013, as many as fifteen hundred such sites were running. Some sites simply aggregate video footage from YouTube, mostly from natural disasters and crises, such as the Boston Marathon terrorist bombing in 2013. These disaster and crisis videos represent by far the biggest contribution to news by amateurs. According to the Pew Research Center, more than 40 percent of the "most watched news videos" over a fifteen-month period in 2011 and 2012 "came directly from citizens."[62]

Beyond the citizen model, another Pew study in 2013 identified 170 specific nonprofit news organizations "with minimal staffs and modest budgets" that "range from the nationally known [like the investigative site ProPublica] to the hyperlocal" that are trying to compensate for the loss of close to 20,000 commercial newsroom jobs over the last decade.[63] In 2014, Pew studied 438 of these newer digital sites: "Of the 402 outlets that identified a business model, slightly more than half (204) are nonprofits compared with 196 that are commercial entities. In recent years, the nonprofit model has attracted a significant amount of foundation funding for news gathering." In its *State of the News Media 2014* report, Pew "estimated that roughly $150 million in philanthropy now goes to journalism annually. Some of that is used as seed money for digital nonprofit news organizations: 61% of the nonprofit news organizations surveyed by Pew Research began with a large start-up grant." Pew noted that the "goal for these organizations is ultimately finding a sustainable business model less reliant on big giving."[64]

Most journalists and many citizens want to see more professional models of journalism develop in the digital age so that people can decrease their reliance on unedited video footage and untrained amateurs as key sources for news. While many community-based sites and ordinary citizen reporters do not have the resources to provide the kind of regional news coverage that local newspapers once provided, there is still a lot of hope for community journalism moving forward. Some new digital sites have adopted what could be called a "pro-am" model for journalism, in which amateurs are trained by professionals. This practice is already followed at many universities, where students are trained by former and current journalists and then collaborate on print, broadcast, and online news projects with local news media.

Courtesy of Media Mobilizing

MEDIA MOBILIZING PROJECT (www.mediamobilizing.org) is a community-based organization in Philadelphia that helps nonprofit and grassroots organizations create and distribute news pieces about their causes and stories. Such organizations are key to getting out messages that matter deeply to communities but are often ignored by the mainstream media, such as documentation about the wealth disparity at the heart of the Occupy Wall Street movement in 2011 and 2012.

Newspapers and Democracy

Of all mass media, newspapers have played the leading role in sustaining democracy and championing freedom. Over the years, newspapers have fought heroic battles in places that had little tolerance for differing points of view. According to the Committee to Protect Journalists (CPJ), from 1992 through mid-2014, 1,062 reporters from around the world were killed while doing their jobs. In 2014, CPJ reported that since 1992, the five deadliest countries for journalists have been Iraq (164 killed), the Philippines (76 killed), Syria (64 killed), Algeria (60 killed), and Russia (56 killed). Of those killed, 13 percent died while "performing a dangerous assignment," 20 percent were killed in cross fire or combat, and 66 percent were murdered.[65] In the first half of 2014, 30 journalists and 5 media workers were killed, including 4 in Ukraine, 3 each in Syria and Iraq, and 2 each in Afghanistan and Brazil.

Many journalist deaths in the twenty-first century reported by CPJ came from the war in Iraq. From 2003 to 2011, 225 reporters, media workers, and support staff died in Iraq. For comparison, 63 reporters were killed while covering the Vietnam War, 17 died covering the Korean War, and 69 were killed during World War II.[66] Our nation and many others remain dependent on journalists who are willing to do this very dangerous reporting in order to keep us informed about what is going on around the world.

In addition to the physical danger, newsroom cutbacks, and the closing of foreign bureaus, a number of smaller concerns remain as we consider the future of newspapers. For instance, some charge that newspapers have become so formulaic in their design and reporting styles that they may actually discourage new approaches to telling stories and reporting news. Another criticism is that in many one-newspaper cities, only issues and events of interest to middle- and upper-middle-class readers are covered, resulting in the underreporting of the experiences and events that affect poorer and working-class citizens. In addition, given the rise of newspaper chains, the likelihood of including new opinions, ideas, and information in mainstream daily papers may be diminishing. Moreover, chain ownership tends to discourage watchdog journalism and the crusading traditions of newspapers. Like other business managers, many news executives have preferred not to offend investors or outrage potential advertisers by running too many investigative reports—especially business probes. This may be most evident in the fact that reporters have generally not reported adequately on the business and ownership arrangements in their own industry.

Finally, as print journalism shifts to digital culture, the greatest challenge is the upheaval of print journalism's business model. Most economists say that newspapers need new business models, but some observers think that local papers, ones that are not part of big overleveraged chains, will survive on the basis of local ads and coupons or "big sale" inserts. Increasingly, independent online firms will help bolster national reporting through special projects. In 2009, the Associated Press wire service initiated an experiment to distribute investigative reports from several nonprofit groups—including the Center for Public Integrity, the Center for Investigative Reporting, and ProPublica—to its fifteen hundred members as a news source for struggling papers that have cut back on staff. Also in 2009, the news aggregator *Huffington Post* hired a team of reporters to cover the economic crisis. Back in 2011, AOL (which purchased the *Huffington Post* for $315 million) had more than thirteen hundred reporters—most of them for Patch, a hyperlocal news initiative with over eight hundred separate editorial units serving small to midsize towns and cities across the United States. The Patch experiment hoped to restore local news coverage to areas that had been neglected due to newsroom cutbacks.[67] But by 2014, AOL had not made money, so it cut these local sites from nine hundred to six hundred and entered into a new joint venture controlled by Hale Global.[68]

Among the success stories in digital journalism, ProPublica has published more than a hundred investigative stories a year, often teaming up with traditional newspapers or public radio stations from around the country. It then offers these reports to traditional news outlets for free. In 2010, one story won a Pulitzer Prize for investigative reporting. Regional examples of this kind of public service news include the *Voice of San Diego* and *MinnPost*, both nonprofit online news ventures that feature news about the San Diego and the Twin Cities areas, respectively. Many of these news services have tried to provide reports for news outlets that have downsized and no longer have the reporting resources to do certain kinds of major investigations.

DIGITAL JOB OUTLOOK

Media Professionals Speak about Jobs in the Newspaper Industry

Mark Jurkowitz, Pew Research Journalism Project

At a time when print newsrooms continue to shed jobs, thousands of journalists are now working in the growing world of native digital news—at small nonprofits like *Charlottesville Tomorrow*, big commercial sites like the *Huffington Post*, and other content outlets, like BuzzFeed, that have moved into original news reporting. In a significant shift in the editorial ecosystem, most of these jobs have been created in the past half dozen years, and many have materialized within the last year alone [2014].

U.S. Bureau of Labor Statistics

Reporters, correspondents, and broadcast news analysts are expected to face strong competition for jobs [from 2012 to 2022], because of both the number of workers who are interested in entering the field and the projected employment declines of the occupations. Those with experience in the field—experience often gained through internships or by working for school newspapers, television stations, or radio stations—should have the best job prospects.

Multimedia journalism experience, including shooting and editing pieces, should also improve job prospects. Because stations are increasingly publishing content on multiple media platforms, particularly on the Web, employers may prefer applicants who have experience in Web site design and coding.

In addition, opportunities will likely be better in small local newspapers or television and radio stations.

Cubreporters.org

All of the gloomy reports about newspaper circulation rapidly dropping, network news ratings declining, and reporters being laid off might lead you to believe that journalism itself is dying. But journalism is alive and well. It is just that the way reporters do their job is changing.

As print journalism loses readers and advertisers to digital culture, what will become of newspapers, which do most of the nation's primary journalistic work? John Carroll presided over thirteen Pulitzer Prize–winning reports at the *Los Angeles Times* as editor from 2000 to 2005, but he left the paper to protest deep corporate cuts to the newsroom. He has lamented the future of newspapers and their unique role: "Newspapers are doing the reporting in this country. Google and Yahoo! and those people aren't putting reporters on the street in any numbers at all. Blogs can't afford it. Network television is taking reporters off the street. Commercial radio is almost nonexistent. And newspapers are the last ones standing, and newspapers are threatened. And reporting is absolutely an essential thing for democratic self-government. Who's going to do it? Who's going to pay for the news? If newspapers fall by the wayside, what will we know?"[69] In the end, there will be no return to any "golden age" of newspapers. The Internet is transforming journalism and relocating where we get our news; the print era is passing the news baton to the digital age. ▶

CHAPTER REVIEW

COMMON THREADS

One of the Common Threads discussed in Chapter 1 is the role that media play in a democracy. The newspaper industry has always played a strong role in our democracy by reporting news and investigating stories. Even in the Internet age, newspapers remain our primary source for content. How will the industry's current financial struggles affect our ability to demand and access reliable news?

With the coming of radio and television, newspapers in the twentieth century surrendered their title as the mass medium shared by the largest audience. However, to this day, newspapers remain the single most important source of news for the nation, even in the age of the Internet. Although today's readers may cite search engines like Google as the primary places they search for news, sites like Google are really directories and aggregators that guide readers to news stories—most often to online newspaper sites. This means that newspaper organizations are still the primary institutions doing the work of gathering and reporting the news. Even with all the newsroom cutbacks across the United States, newspapers remain the only journalistic organization in most towns and cities that still employs a significant staff to report news and tell the community's stories.

Newspapers link people to what matters in their communities, their nation, and their world. Few other journalistic institutions serve society as well. But with smaller news resources and the industry no longer able to sustain high profit margins, what will become of newspapers? Are digital news sites serving readers in their communities as well as newspapers once did? Who will gather the information needed to sustain a democracy, to serve as the watchdog over our key institutions, to document the comings and goings of everyday life? And perhaps more important, who will act on behalf of the people who don't have the news media's access to authorities or the ability to influence them?

KEY TERMS

The definitions for the terms listed below can be found in the glossary at the end of the book. The page numbers listed with the terms indicate where the term is highlighted in the chapter.

partisan press, 273
penny papers, 274
human-interest stories, 274
wire services, 275
yellow journalism, 276
investigative journalism, 276
objective journalism, 279

inverted-pyramid style, 279
interpretive journalism, 280
literary journalism, 281
consensus-oriented journalism, 285
conflict-oriented journalism, 285
underground press, 290
newshole, 291

feature syndicates, 294
newspaper chain, 294
joint operating agreement (JOA), 296
paywall, 300
citizen journalism, 302

For review quizzes, chapter summaries, links to media-related Web sites, and more, go to **macmillanhighered.com/mediaculture10e**.

REVIEW QUESTIONS

The Evolution of American Newspapers

1. What are the limitations of a press that serves only partisan interests? Why did the earliest papers appeal mainly to more privileged readers?

2. How did newspapers emerge as a mass medium during the penny press era? How did content changes make this happen?

3. What are the two main features of yellow journalism? How have Joseph Pulitzer and William Randolph Hearst contributed to newspaper history?

Competing Models of Modern Print Journalism

4. Why did objective journalism develop? What are its characteristics? What are its strengths and limitations?

5. Why did interpretive forms of journalism develop in the modern era? What are the limits of objectivity?

6. How would you define *literary journalism*? Why did it emerge in such an intense way in the 1960s? How did literary journalism provide a critique of so-called objective news?

The Business and Ownership of Newspapers

7. What is the difference between consensus- and conflict-oriented newspapers?

8. What role have ethnic, minority, and oppositional newspapers played in the United States?

9. Define *wire service* and *syndication*.

10. Why did newspaper chains become an economic trend in the twentieth century?

11. What is the impact of a joint operating agreement (JOA) on the business and editorial divisions of competing newspapers?

Challenges Facing Newspapers Today

12. What are the major reasons for the decline in U.S. newspaper circulation figures? How do these figures compare with circulations in other nations?

13. What major challenges does new technology pose to the newspaper industry?

14. With traditional ownership in jeopardy today, what are some other possible business models for running a newspaper?

15. What is the current state of citizen journalism?

16. What challenges do new online news sites face?

Newspapers and Democracy

17. What is a newspaper's role in a democracy?

18. What makes newspaper journalism different from the journalism of other mass media?

QUESTIONING THE MEDIA

1. What kinds of stories, topics, or issues are not being covered well by mainstream papers?

2. Why do you think people aren't reading U.S. daily newspapers as frequently as they once did? Why is newspaper readership going up in other countries?

3. Discuss whether newspaper chains are ultimately good or bad for the future of journalism.

4. Do newspapers today play a vigorous role as watchdogs of our powerful institutions? Why or why not? What impact will the downsizing and closing of newspapers have on this watchdog role?

5. Will tablets, or some other format, eventually replace the printed newspaper? Explain your response.

LAUNCHPAD FOR *MEDIA & CULTURE*

Visit **LaunchPad for *Media & Culture*** at **macmillanhighered.com/mediaculture10e** for additional learning tools:

- REVIEW WITH LEARNINGCURVE
  LearningCurve, available on LaunchPad for *Media & Culture*, uses gamelike quizzing to help you master the concepts you need to learn from this chapter.

- VIDEO: THE MEDIA AND DEMOCRACY
  This video traces the history of media's role in democracy from newspapers and television to the Internet.

9

Magazines in the Age of Specialization

311
The Early History
of Magazines

315
The Development
of Modern American
Magazines

325
The Domination
of Specialization

332
The Organization
and Economics
of Magazines

336
Magazines in a
Democratic Society

Cosmopolitan didn't always have cover photos of women with plunging necklines, or cover lines like "67 New Sex Tricks" and "The Sexiest Things to Do after Sex." As the magazine itself says, "The story of how a '60s babe named Helen Gurley Brown (you've probably heard of her) transformed an antiquated general-interest mag called *Cosmopolitan* into the must-read for young, sexy single chicks is pretty damn amazing."[1]

In fact, *Cosmopolitan* had at least four format changes before Helen Gurley Brown came along. The magazine was launched in 1886 as an illustrated monthly for the modern family (meaning it was targeted at married women) with articles on cooking, child care, household decoration, and occasionally fashion, featuring illustrated images of women in the hats and high collars of late-Victorian fashion.[2]

But the magazine was thin on content and almost folded. *Cosmopolitan* was saved in 1889, when journalist and entrepreneur John Brisben Walker gave it a second chance as an illustrated magazine of literature and insightful reporting.

JOANNA COLES, editor of *Cosmopolitan* magazine.
Robert Caplin/The New York Times/Redux

The magazine featured writers like Edith Wharton, Rudyard Kipling, and Theodore Dreiser and serialized entire books, including H. G. Wells's *The War of the Worlds*. And Walker, seeing the success of contemporary newspapers in New York, was not above stunt reporting. When Joseph Pulitzer's *New York World* sent reporter Nellie Bly to travel the world in less than eighty days in 1889 (challenging the premise of Jules Verne's 1873 novel, *Around the World in Eighty Days*), Walker sent reporter Elizabeth Bisland around the world in the opposite direction for a more literary travel account.[3] Walker's leadership turned *Cosmopolitan* into a respected magazine with increased circulation and a strong advertising base.

Walker sold *Cosmopolitan* at a profit to William Randolph Hearst (Pulitzer's main competitor) in 1905. Under Hearst, *Cosmopolitan* had its third rebirth—this

time as a muckraking magazine. As magazine historians explain, Hearst was a U.S. representative who "had his eye on the presidency and planned to use his newspapers and the recently bought *Cosmopolitan* to stir up further discontent over the trusts and big business."[4] *Cosmopolitan*'s first big muckraking series, David Graham Phillips's "The Treason of the Senate" in 1906, didn't help Hearst's political career, but it did boost the circulation of the

magazine by 50 percent and was reprinted in Hearst newspapers for even more exposure.

But by 1912, the progressive political movement that had given impetus to muckraking journalism was waning. *Cosmopolitan*, in its fourth incarnation, became a version of its former self—an illustrated literary monthly targeted to women, with short stories and serialized novels by such popular writers as Damon Runyon, Sinclair Lewis, and Faith Baldwin.

Cosmopolitan had great success as an upscale literary magazine, but by the early 1960s, the format had become outdated and readership and advertising had declined. At this point, the magazine had its most radical makeover. In 1962, Helen Gurley Brown, one of the country's top advertising copywriters, was recently married (at age forty) and wrote the best-selling book *Sex and the Single Girl*. When she proposed a magazine modeled on the book's vision of strong, sexually liberated women, the Hearst Corporation hired her in 1965 as editor in chief to reinvent *Cosmopolitan*. The new *Cosmopolitan* helped spark a sexual revolution and was marketed to the "Cosmo Girl": women aged eighteen to thirty-four with an interest in love, sex, fashion, and their careers.

Brown maintained a pink corner office in the Hearst Tower in New York until her death in 2012, but her vision of *Cosmo* continues today. It's the top women's fashion magazine—surpassing competitors like *Glamour*, *Marie Claire*, and *Vogue*—and has wide global influence, with sixty-one international editions. Although its present format is far from its origins, *Cosmopolitan* endures based on successful reinventions for over 129 years.

▲ *SINCE THE 1740s,* magazines have played a key role in our social and cultural lives, becoming America's earliest national mass medium. They created some of the first spaces for discussing the broad issues of the age, including public education, the abolition of slavery, women's suffrage, literacy, and the Civil War.

In the nineteenth century, magazines became an educational forum for women, who were barred from higher education and from the nation's political life. At the turn of the twentieth century, magazines' probing reports paved the way for investigative journalism, while their use of engraving and photography provided a hint of the visual culture to come. Economically, magazines brought advertised products into households, hastening the rise of a consumer society.

Today, more than twenty thousand commercial, alternative, and noncommercial magazines are published in the United States annually. Like newspapers, radio, movies, and television, magazines reflect and construct portraits of American life. They are catalogues for daily events and experiences, but they also show us the latest products, fostering our consumer culture. We read magazines to learn something about our community, our nation, our world, and ourselves.

In this chapter, we will:

- Investigate the history of the magazine industry, highlighting the colonial and early American eras, the arrival of national magazines, and the development of photojournalism
- Focus on the age of muckraking and the rise of general-interest and consumer magazines in the modern American era
- Look at the decline of mass market magazines, the impact of TV and the Internet, and how magazines have specialized in order to survive in a fragmented and converged market
- Investigate the organization and economics of magazines and their function in a democracy

As you think about the evolution of magazine culture, consider your own experiences. When did you first start reading magazines, and what magazines were they? What sort of magazines do you read today—popular mainstream magazines like *Cosmo* or *Sports Illustrated*, or niche publications that target very specific subcultures? How do you think printed magazines can best adapt to the age of the Internet? For more questions to help you think through the role of magazines in our lives, see "Questioning the Media" in the Chapter Review.

The Early History of Magazines

The first magazines appeared in seventeenth-century France in the form of bookseller catalogues and notices that book publishers inserted in newspapers. In fact, the word *magazine* derives from the French term *magasin*, meaning "storehouse." The earliest magazines were "storehouses" of writing and reports taken mostly from newspapers. Today, the word **magazine** broadly refers to collections of articles, stories, and advertisements appearing in nondaily (such as weekly or monthly) periodicals that are published in the smaller tabloid style rather than the larger broadsheet newspaper style.

The First Magazines

The first political magazine, called the *Review*, appeared in London in 1704. Edited by political activist and novelist Daniel Defoe (author of *Robinson Crusoe*), the *Review* was printed

COLONIAL MAGAZINES
The first issue of Benjamin Franklin's *General Magazine and Historical Chronicle* appeared in January 1741. Although it lasted only six months, Franklin found success in other publications, like his annual *Poor Richard's Almanac,* which started in 1732 and lasted twenty-five years.

Library of Congress

sporadically until 1713. Like the *Nation*, the *National Review*, and the *Progressive* in the United States today, early European magazines were channels for political commentary and argument. These periodicals looked like newspapers of the time, but they appeared less frequently and were oriented toward broad domestic and political commentary rather than recent news.

Regularly published magazines or pamphlets, such as the *Tatler* and the *Spectator*, also appeared in England around this time. They offered poetry, politics, and philosophy for London's elite, and they served readerships of a few thousand. The first publication to use the term *magazine* was *Gentleman's Magazine*, which appeared in London in 1731 and consisted of reprinted articles from newspapers, books, and political pamphlets. Later, the magazine began publishing original work by such writers as Defoe, Samuel Johnson, and Alexander Pope.

Magazines in Colonial America

Without a substantial middle class, widespread literacy, or advanced printing technology, magazines developed slowly in colonial America. Like the partisan newspapers of the time, these magazines served politicians, the educated, and the merchant classes. Paid circulations were low—between one hundred and fifteen hundred copies. However, early magazines did serve the more widespread purpose of documenting a new nation coming to terms with issues of taxation, state versus federal power, Indian treaties, public education, and the end of colonialism. George Washington, Alexander Hamilton, and John Hancock all wrote for early magazines, and Paul Revere worked as a magazine illustrator for a time.

The first colonial magazines appeared in Philadelphia in 1741, about fifty years after the first newspapers. Andrew Bradford started it all with *American Magazine, or A Monthly View of the Political State of the British Colonies*. Three days later, Benjamin Franklin's *General Magazine and Historical Chronicle* appeared. Bradford's magazine lasted only three monthly issues, due to circulation and postal obstacles that Franklin, who had replaced Bradford as Philadelphia's postmaster, put in its way. For instance, Franklin mailed his magazine without paying the high

▼ **Magazines in the Age of Specialization**

National Magazines
The *Saturday Evening Post* is launched in 1821, becoming the first major magazine to appeal directly to women. It becomes the longest-running magazine in U.S. history (p. 314).

Postal Act of 1879
Both postal rates and rail transportation costs plummet, allowing magazine distribution to thrive (p. 315).

| 1700 | 1750 | 1800 | 1850 |

Colonial Magazines
First appearing in Philadelphia in 1741, these generally unsuccessful magazines reprint material from local newspapers (pp. 312–313).

Engravings and Illustrations
By the mid-1850s, drawings, woodcuts, and other forms of illustration begin to fill the pages of magazines (pp. 314–315).

postal rates that he subsequently charged others. Franklin's magazine primarily duplicated what was already available in local papers. After six months it, too, stopped publication.

Nonetheless, following the Philadelphia experiments, magazines began to emerge in the other colonies, beginning in Boston in the 1740s. The most successful magazines simply reprinted articles from leading London periodicals, keeping readers abreast of European events. These magazines included New York's *Independent Reflector* and the *Pennsylvania Magazine*, edited by activist Thomas Paine, which helped rally the colonies against British rule. By 1776, about a hundred colonial magazines had appeared and disappeared. Although historians consider them dull and uninspired for the most part, these magazines helped launch a new medium that caught on after the American Revolution.

U.S. Magazines in the Nineteenth Century

After the revolution, the growth of the magazine industry in the newly independent United States remained slow. Delivery costs remained high, and some postal carriers refused to carry magazines because of their weight. Only twelve magazines operated in 1800. By 1825, about a hundred magazines existed, although about another five hundred had failed between 1800 and 1825. Nevertheless, during the first quarter of the nineteenth century, most communities had their own weekly magazines. These magazines featured essays on local issues, government activities, and political intrigue, as well as material reprinted from other sources. They sold some advertising but were usually in precarious financial straits because of their small circulations.

As the nineteenth century progressed, the idea of specialized magazines devoted to certain categories of readers developed. Many early magazines were overtly religious and boasted the largest readerships of the day. The Methodist *Christian Journal and Advocate*, for example, claimed twenty-five thousand subscribers by 1826. Literary magazines also emerged at this time. The *North American Review*, for instance, established the work of important writers

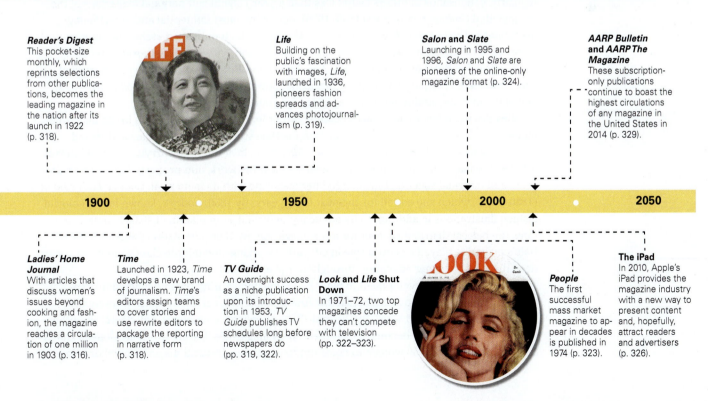

Reader's Digest
This pocket-size monthly, which reprints selections from other publications, becomes the leading magazine in the nation after its launch in 1922 (p. 318).

Life
Building on the public's fascination with images, *Life*, launched in 1936, pioneers fashion spreads and advances photojournalism (p. 319).

Salon and Slate
Launching in 1995 and 1996, *Salon* and *Slate* are pioneers of the online-only magazine format (p. 324).

AARP Bulletin and *AARP The Magazine*
These subscription-only publications continue to boast the highest circulations of any magazine in the United States in 2014 (p. 329).

1900   1950   2000   2050

Ladies' Home Journal
With articles that discuss women's issues beyond cooking and fashion, the magazine reaches a circulation of one million in 1903 (p. 316).

Time
Launched in 1923, *Time* develops a new brand of journalism. *Time's* editors assign teams to cover stories and use rewrite editors to package the reporting in narrative form (p. 318).

TV Guide
An overnight success as a niche publication upon its introduction in 1953, *TV Guide* publishes TV schedules long before newspapers do (pp. 319, 322).

Look and Life Shut Down
In 1971–72, two top magazines concede they can't compete with television (pp. 322–323).

People
The first successful mass market magazine to appear in decades is published in 1974 (p. 323).

The iPad
In 2010, Apple's iPad provides the magazine industry with a new way to present content and, hopefully, attract readers and advertisers (p. 326).

Northwind Picture Archives

COLOR ILLUSTRATIONS
first became popular in the
fashion sections of women's
magazines in the mid-
nineteenth century. The color
for this fashion image from
Godey's Lady's Book was
added to the illustration by
hand.

such as Ralph Waldo Emerson, Henry David Thoreau, and Mark Twain. In addition to religious and literary magazines, specialty magazines that addressed various professions, lifestyles, and topics also appeared, including the *American Farmer*, the *American Journal of Education*, the *American Law Journal*, *Medical Repository*, and the *American Journal of Science*. Such specialization spawned the modern trend of reaching readers who share a profession, a set of beliefs, cultural tastes, or a social identity.

The nineteenth century also saw the birth of the first general-interest magazine aimed at a national audience. In 1821, two young Philadelphia printers, Charles Alexander and Samuel Coate Atkinson, launched the *Saturday Evening Post*, which became the longest-running magazine in U.S. history. Like most magazines of the day, the early *Post* included a few original essays but "borrowed" many pieces from other sources. Eventually, however, the *Post* grew to incorporate news, poetry, essays, play reviews, and more. The *Post* published the writings of such prominent popular authors as Nathaniel Hawthorne and Harriet Beecher Stowe. Although the *Post* was a general-interest magazine, it also was the first major magazine to appeal directly to women, via its "Lady's Friend" column, which addressed women's issues.

National, Women's, and Illustrated Magazines

With increases in literacy and public education, the development of faster printing technologies, and improvements in mail delivery (due to rail transportation), a market was created for more national magazines like the *Saturday Evening Post*. Whereas in 1825 one hundred magazines struggled for survival, by 1850 nearly six hundred magazines were being published regularly. (Thousands of others lasted less than a year.) Significant national magazines of the era included *Graham's Magazine* (1840–1858), one of the most influential and entertaining magazines in the country; *Knickerbocker* (1833–1864), which published essays and literary works by Washington Irving, James Fenimore Cooper, and Nathaniel Hawthorne (preceding such national cultural magazines as the *New Yorker* and *Harper's*); the *Nation* (1865–present), which pioneered the national political magazine format; and *Youth's Companion* (1826–1929), one of the first successful national magazines for younger readers.

Besides the move to national circulation, other important developments in the magazine industry were under way. In 1828, Sarah Josepha Hale started the first magazine directed exclusively to a female audience: the *Ladies' Magazine*. In addition to carrying general-interest articles, the magazine advocated for women's education, work, and property rights. After nine years and marginal success, Hale merged her magazine with its main rival, *Godey's Lady's Book* (1830–1898), which she edited for the next forty years. By 1850, *Godey's*, known for its colorful fashion illustrations in addition to its advocacy, achieved a circulation of 40,000 copies—at the time, the biggest distribution ever for a U.S. magazine. By 1860, circulation swelled to 150,000. Hale's magazine played a central role in educating working- and middle-class women, who were denied access to higher education throughout the nineteenth century.

The other major development in magazine publishing during the mid-nineteenth century was the arrival of illustration. Like the first newspapers, early magazines were totally dependent on the printed word. By the mid-1850s, drawings, engravings, woodcuts, and other forms of illustration had become a major feature of magazines. During this time, *Godey's Lady's Book* employed up to 150 women to color-tint its magazine illustrations and stencil drawings by

© Bettmann/Corbis

hand. Meanwhile, *Harper's New Monthly Magazine*, founded in 1850, offered extensive woodcut illustrations with each issue. During the Civil War, many readers relied on *Harper's* for its elaborate battlefield sketches. Publications like *Harper's* married visual language to the printed word, helping transform magazines into a mass medium. Bringing photographs into magazines took a bit longer. Mathew Brady and his colleagues, whose thirty-five hundred photos documented the Civil War, helped to popularize photography by the 1860s. But it was not until the 1890s that magazines and newspapers possessed the technology to reproduce photos in print media.

The Development of Modern American Magazines

In 1870, about twelve hundred magazines were produced in the United States; by 1890, that number had reached forty-five hundred; and by 1905, more than six thousand magazines existed (see Figure 9.1 on page 316). Part of this surge in titles and readership was facilitated by the Postal Act of 1879, which assigned magazines lower postage rates and put them on an equal footing with newspapers delivered by mail, reducing distribution costs. Meanwhile, faster presses and advances in mass-production printing, conveyor systems, and assembly lines reduced production costs and made large-circulation national magazines possible.[5]

The combination of reduced distribution and production costs enabled publishers to slash magazine prices. As prices dropped from thirty-five cents to fifteen cents and then to ten cents, the working class was gradually able to purchase national publications. By 1905, there were about twenty-five national magazines, available from coast to coast and serving millions

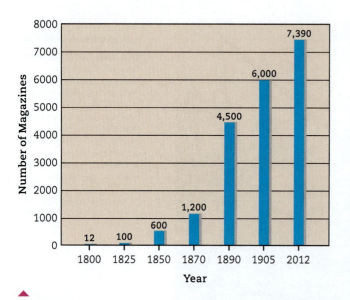

FIGURE 9.1

THE GROWTH OF MAGAZINES PUBLISHED IN THE UNITED STATES

Data from: Magazine Publishers of America, 2013/2014 Magazine Media Factbook, www.magazine .org/node/26924.

of readers.[6] As jobs and the population began shifting from farms and small towns to urban areas, magazines helped readers imagine themselves as part of a nation rather than as individuals with only local or regional identities. In addition, the dramatic growth of drugstores and dime stores, super-markets, and department stores offered new venues and shelf space for selling consumer goods, including magazines.

As magazine circulation began to skyrocket, advertising revenue soared. The economics behind the rise of advertising was simple: A magazine publisher could dramatically expand circulation by dropping the price of an issue below the actual production cost for a single copy. The publisher recouped the loss through ad revenue, guaranteeing large readerships to advertisers who were willing to pay to reach more readers. The number of ad pages in national magazines proliferated. *Harper's*, for instance, devoted only seven pages to ads in the mid-1880s, nearly fifty pages in 1890, and more than ninety pages in 1900.[7]

By the turn of the century, advertisers increasingly used national magazines to capture consumers' attention and build a national marketplace. One magazine that took advantage of these changes was *Ladies' Home Journal*, begun in 1883 by Cyrus Curtis. The women's magazine began publishing more than the usual homemaking tips, including also popular fiction, sheet music, and—most important, perhaps—the latest consumer ads. The magazine's broadened scope was a reflection of the editors' and advertisers' realization that women consumers constituted a growing and lucrative market. *Ladies' Home Journal* reached a circulation of over 500,000 by the early 1890s—the highest circulation of any magazine in the country. In 1903, it became the first magazine to reach a circulation of 1 million.

Social Reform and the Muckrakers

Better distribution and lower costs had attracted readers, but to maintain sales, magazines had to change content as well. Whereas printing the fiction and essays of the best writers of the day was one way to maintain circulation, many magazines also engaged in one aspect of *yellow journalism*—crusading for social reform on behalf of the public good. In the 1890s, for example, *Ladies' Home Journal* (*LHJ*) and its editor, Edward Bok, led the fight against unregulated patent medicines (which often contained nearly 50 percent alcohol), while other magazines joined the fight against phony medicines, poor living and working conditions, and unsanitary practices in various food industries.

The rise in magazine circulation coincided with rapid social change in America. While hundreds of thousands of Americans moved from the country to the city in search of industrial jobs, millions of new immigrants also poured in. Thus the nation that journalists had long written about had grown increasingly complex by the turn of the century. Many newspaper reporters became dissatisfied with the simplistic and conventional style of newspaper journalism and turned to magazines, where they were able to write at greater length and in greater depth about broader issues. They wrote about such topics as corruption in big business and government, urban problems faced by immigrants, labor conflicts, and race relations.

In 1902, *McClure's Magazine* (1893–1933) touched off an investigative era in magazine reporting with a series of probing stories, including Ida Tarbell's "The History of the Standard Oil Company," which took on John D. Rockefeller's oil monopoly, and Lincoln Steffens's "Shame of the Cities," which tackled urban problems. In 1906, *Cosmopolitan* magazine joined the fray with a series called "The Treason of the Senate," and *Collier's* magazine (1888–1957) developed "The Great American Fraud" series, focusing on patent medicines (whose ads accounted for 30 percent of the profits made by the American press by the 1890s). Much of this new reporting

A NAUSEATING JOB, BUT IT MUST BE DONE
(President Roosevelt takes hold of the investigating muck-rake himself in the packing-house scandal.)
From the *Saturday Globe* (Utica)

style was critical of American institutions. Angry with so much negative reporting, in 1906 President Theodore Roosevelt dubbed these investigative reporters **muckrakers**, because they were willing to crawl through society's muck to uncover a story. Muckraking was a label that Roosevelt used with disdain, but it was worn with pride by reporters such as Ray Stannard Baker, Frank Norris, and Lincoln Steffens.

Influenced by Upton Sinclair's novel *The Jungle*—a fictional account of Chicago's meatpacking industry—and by the muckraking reports of *Collier's* and *LHJ*, in 1906 Congress passed the Pure Food and Drug Act and the Meat Inspection Act. Other reforms stemming from muckraking journalism and the politics of the era include antitrust laws for increased government oversight of business, a fair and progressive income tax, and the direct election of U.S. senators.

The Rise of General-Interest Magazines

The heyday of the muckraking era lasted into the mid-1910s, when America was drawn into World War I. After the war and through the 1950s, **general-interest magazines** were the most prominent publications, offering occasional investigative articles but also covering a wide variety of topics aimed at a broad national audience. A key aspect of these magazines was **photojournalism**—the use of photos to document the rhythms of daily life (see "Case Study: The Evolution of Photojournalism" on pages 320–321).

IDA TARBELL (1857–1944) is best known for her work "The History of the Standard Oil Company," which appeared as a nineteen-part series in *McClure's Magazine* between November 1902 and October 1904. Tarbell once remarked on why she dedicated years of her life to investigating the company: "They had never played fair, and that ruined their greatness for me." For muckrakers and investigative journalists like Tarbell, exposing such corruption was a driving force behind their work.

(Left and right) The Granger Collection

High-quality photos gave general-interest magazines a visual advantage over radio, which was the most popular medium of the day. In 1920, about fifty-five magazines fit the general-interest category; by 1946, more than one hundred such magazines competed with radio networks for the national audience.

Saturday Evening Post

Although it had been around since 1821, the *Saturday Evening Post* concluded the nineteenth century as only a modest success, with a circulation of about ten thousand. In 1897, Cyrus Curtis, who had already made *Ladies' Home Journal* the nation's top magazine, bought the *Post* and remade it into the first widely popular general-interest magazine. Curtis's strategy for reinvigorating the magazine included printing popular fiction and romanticizing American virtues through words and pictures (a *Post* tradition best depicted in the three-hundred-plus cover illustrations by Norman Rockwell). Curtis also featured articles that celebrated the business boom of the 1920s. This reversed the journalistic direction of the muckraking era, in which business corruption was often the focus. By the 1920s, the *Post* had reached two million in circulation, the first magazine to hit that mark.

Reader's Digest

The most widely circulated general-interest magazine during this period was *Reader's Digest*. Started in a Greenwich Village basement in 1922 by Dewitt Wallace and Lila Acheson Wallace, *Reader's Digest* championed one of the earliest functions of magazines: printing condensed versions of selected articles from other magazines. In the magazine's early years, the Wallaces refused to accept ads and sold the *Digest* only through subscriptions. With its inexpensive production costs, low price, and popular pocket-size format, the magazine's circulation climbed to over 1 million during the Great Depression, and by 1946, it was the nation's most popular magazine. By the mid-1980s, it was the most popular magazine in the world, with a circulation of 20 million in America and 10 to 12 million abroad. However, by 2014 it was recovering from bankruptcy, and its circulation base had dropped to about 4.2 million, less than a quarter of its circulation thirty years earlier.

Time

During the general-interest era, national newsmagazines such as *Time* were also major commercial successes. Begun in 1923 by Henry Luce and Briton Hadden, *Time* developed a magazine brand of interpretive journalism, assigning reporter-researcher teams to cover stories, after which a rewrite editor would put the article in narrative form with an interpretive point of view. *Time* had a circulation of 200,000 by 1930, increasing to more than 3 million by the mid-1960s. *Time*'s success encouraged prominent imitators, including *Newsweek* (established in 1933); *U.S. News & World Report* (1948); and, more recently, *The Week* (2001). By 2014, economic decline, competition from the Web, and a shrinking number of readers and advertisers took their toll on the three top newsweeklies. *Time*'s circulation stagnated at 3.2 million, while *U.S. News* became a monthly magazine in 2008 and switched to an all-digital format in 2010 (and is now most famous for its "America's Best Colleges" reports). *Newsweek*'s circulation peaked in 1991 with 3.3 million readers. As its circulation and revenue sank, it was sold in 2010 for just $1

LIFE MAGAZINE published iconic photos during its original 1883–1972 run. Following nearly a century as a weekly, it has since been published as a monthly, an occasional commemorative publication, a newspaper supplement, and an online archive.

The LIFE Premium Collection/Getty Images

(Left and right) Margaret Bourke-White/Time Life Pictures/Getty Images

and the assumption of its debt. After an unsuccessful foray as a digital-only publication, *Newsweek* relaunched as a print publication in 2014 under new ownership and with an uncertain future.

Life

Despite the commercial success of *Reader's Digest* and *Time* in the twentieth century, the magazines that really symbolized the general-interest genre during this era were the oversized pictorial weeklies *Look* and *Life*. More than any other magazine of its day, *Life* developed an effective strategy for competing with popular radio by advancing photojournalism. Launched as a weekly by Henry Luce in 1936, *Life* appealed to the public's fascination with images (invigorated by the movie industry), radio journalism, and advertising and fashion photography. By the end of the 1930s, *Life* had a **pass-along readership**—the total number of people who come into contact with a single copy of a magazine—of more than seventeen million, rivaling the ratings of popular national radio programs.

Life's first editor, Wilson Hicks—formerly a picture editor for the Associated Press—built a staff of renowned photographer-reporters who chronicled the world's ordinary and extraordinary events from the late 1930s through the 1960s. Among *Life*'s most famous photojournalists were Margaret Bourke-White, the first female war correspondent to fly combat missions during World War II, and Gordon Parks, who later became Hollywood's first African American director of major feature films. Today, *Life*'s photographic archive is hosted online by Google (images.google.com/hosted/life).

The Fall of General-Interest Magazines

The decline of weekly general-interest magazines, which had dominated the industry for thirty years, began in the 1950s. By 1957, both *Collier's* (founded in 1888) and *Woman's Home Companion* (founded in 1873) had folded. Each magazine had a national circulation of more than four million the year it died. No magazine with this kind of circulation had ever shut down before. Together, the two publications brought in advertising revenues of more than $26 million in 1956. Although some critics blamed poor management, both magazines were victims of changing consumer tastes, rising postal costs, falling ad revenues, and, perhaps most important, television, which began usurping the role of magazines as the preferred family medium.

TV Guide Is Born

While other magazines were just beginning to make sense of the impact of television on their readers, *TV Guide* appeared in 1953. Taking its cue from the pocket-size format of *Reader's*

The Evolution of Photojournalism

by Christopher R. Harris

What we now recognize as photojournalism started with the assignment of photographer Roger Fenton, of the *Sunday Times of London*, to document the Crimean War in 1856. However, technical limitations did not allow direct reproduction of photodocumentary images in the publications of the day. Woodcut artists had to interpret the photographic images as black-and-white-toned woodblocks that could be reproduced by the presses of the period. Images interpreted by artists therefore lost the inherent qualities of photographic visual documentation: an on-site visual representation of facts for those who weren't present.

Woodcuts remained the basic method of press reproduction until 1880, when *New York Daily Graphic* photographer Stephen Horgan invented half-tone reproduction using a dot-pattern screen. This screen enabled metallic plates to directly represent photographic images in the printing process; now periodicals could bring exciting visual reportage to their pages.

In the mid-1890s, Jimmy Hare became the first photographer recognized as a photojournalist in the United States. Taken for *Collier's Weekly*, Hare's photo-reportage on the sinking of the battle-ship *Maine* in 1898 near Havana, Cuba, established his reputation as a newsman traveling the world to bring back images of news events. Hare's images fed into growing popular support for Cuban independence from Spain and eventual U.S. involvement in the Spanish-American War.

In 1888, George Eastman opened photography to the working and middle classes when he introduced the first flexible-film camera from Kodak, his company in Rochester, New York. Gone were the bulky equipment and fragile photographic plates of the past. Now families and journalists could more easily and affordably document gatherings and events.

JACOB RIIS
The Tramp, c. 1890. Riis, who emigrated from Denmark in 1870, lived in poverty in New York for several years before becoming a photojournalist. He spent much of his later life chronicling the lives of the poor in New York City. *The Museum of the City of New York/ Art Resource, NY.*

As photography became easier and more widespread, photojournalism began to take on an increasingly important social role. At the turn of the century, the documentary photography of Jacob Riis and Lewis Hine captured the harsh living and working conditions of the nation's many child laborers, including crowded ghettos and unsafe mills and factories. Reaction to these shockingly honest photographs resulted in public outcry and new laws against the exploitation of children. Photographs also brought the horrors of World War I to people far from the battlefields.

In 1923, visionaries Henry Luce and Briton Hadden published *Time*, the first modern photographic newsweekly; *Life* and *Fortune* soon followed. From coverage of the Roaring Twenties to the Great Depression, these magazines used images that changed the way people viewed the world.

Life, with its spacious 10-by-13-inch format and large photographs, became one of the most influential magazines in America, printing what are now classic images from World War II and the Korean War. Often, *Life* offered images that were unavailable anywhere else: Margaret Bourke-White's photographic proof of the unspeakably horrific concentration camps; W. Eugene Smith's gentle portraits of the humanitarian Albert Schweitzer in Africa; David Duncan's gritty images of the faces of U.S. troops fighting in Korea.

Television photojournalism made its quantum leap into the public mind as it documented the assassination of President Kennedy in 1963. In tele-vised images that were broadcast and rebroadcast, the public witnessed the actual assassination and the confusing aftermath, including live coverage of the murder of alleged assassin Lee Harvey Oswald and of President Kennedy's funeral procession. Photojournalism also provided visual documentation of the turbulent 1960s, including aggressive photographic coverage of the Vietnam War—its protesters and supporters. Pulitzer Prize–winning photographer Eddie Adams shook the emotions of the American public with his photographs of a South Vietnamese general's summary execution of a suspected Vietcong terrorist. Closer to home, shocking images of the Civil Rights movement culminated in pictures of Birmingham police and police dogs attacking Civil Rights protesters.

In the 1970s, new computer technologies emerged and were embraced by print and television media worldwide. By the late 1980s, computers could transform images into digital form and easily manipulate them with sophisticated software programs. Today, a reporter can take a picture and within minutes send it to news offices in Tokyo, Berlin, and New York; moments later, the image can be used in a late-breaking TV story or sent directly to that organization's Twitter followers. Such digital technology has revolutionized photojournalism, perhaps even more than the advent of roll film did in the late nineteenth century. Today's photojournalists post entire interactive photo slideshows alongside stories, sometimes adding audio explaining their artistic and journalistic process. Their photographs live on through online news archives and through photojournalism blogs, such as the Lens of the New York Times, where photojournalists are able to gain recognition for their work and find new audiences.

However, there is a dark side to all this digital technology. Because of the

Camille LePage/AFP/Getty Images

CAMILLE LEPAGE, a twenty-six-year-old French photojournalist, was killed in May 2014 while covering the chaotic civil war in the Central African Republic, which reignited in 2012. Her photos exposed the everyday life of civilians and soldiers in the Central African Republic and South Sudan, from refugees and the gravely injured in hospitals to African fashion-show models trying to maintain some sense of normalcy. Her work appeared in news media around the world, including in the New York Times, the Guardian, Le Monde, and Al Jazeera.

absence of physical film, there is a loss of proof, or veracity, of the authenticity of images. Original film has qualities that make it easy to determine whether it has been tampered with. Digital images, by contrast, can be easily altered, and such alteration can be very difficult to detect.

An egregious example of image-tampering involved the Ralph Lauren fashion model Filippa Hamilton. She appeared in a drastically Photoshopped advertisement that showed her hips as being thinner than her head—like a Bratz doll. The ad, published only in Japan, received intense criticism when the picture went viral. The 5'10", 120-pound model was subsequently dropped by the fashion label, because, as Hamilton explained, "they said I was overweight and I couldn't fit in their clothes anymore."[1] In today's age of Photoshop, it is common practice to make thin female models look even thinner and make

male models look unnaturally muscled. "Every picture has been worked on, some twenty, thirty rounds," Ken Harris, a fashion magazine photo-retoucher said; "going between the retoucher, the client, and the agency . . . [photos] are retouched to death."[2] And since there is no disclaimer saying these images have been retouched, it can be hard for viewers to know the truth.

Photojournalists and news sources are confronted today with unprecedented concerns over truth-telling. In the past, trust in documentary photojournalism rested solely on the verifiability of images ("what you see is what you get"). This is no longer the case. Just as we must evaluate the words we read, now we must also take a more critical eye to the images we view. ◢

Christopher R. Harris is a professor in the Department of Electronic Media Communication at Middle Tennessee State University.

1972		2014	
Rank/Publication	**Circulation**	**Rank/Publication**	**Circulation**
1 Reader's Digest	17,825,661	1 AARP The Magazine	22,274,096
2 TV Guide	16,410,858	2 AARP Bulletin	22,244,820
3 Woman's Day	8,191,731	3 Game Informer	7,629,995
4 Better Homes and Gardens	7,996,050	4 Better Homes and Gardens	7,615,641
5 Family Circle	7,889,587	5 Good Housekeeping	4,348,641
6 McCall's	7,516,960	6 Reader's Digest	4,288,529
7 National Geographic	7,260,179	7 Family Circle	4,092,525
8 Ladies' Home Journal	7,014,251	8 National Geographic	4,029,881
9 Playboy	6,400,573	9 People	3,527,541
10 Good Housekeeping	5,801,446	10 Woman's Day	3,311,803

Digest and the supermarket sales strategy used by women's magazines, *TV Guide*, started by Walter Annenberg's Triangle Publications, soon rivaled the success of *Reader's Digest* by addressing the nation's growing fascination with television by publishing TV listings. The first issue sold a record 1.5 million copies in ten urban markets. Because many newspapers were not yet listing TV programs, by 1962 the magazine became the first weekly to reach a circulation of 8 million, with its seventy regional editions tailoring its listings to TV channels in specific areas of the country. (See Table 9.1 for the circulation figures of the Top 10 U.S. magazines.)

TV Guide's story illustrates a number of key trends that affected magazines beginning in the 1950s. First, *TV Guide* highlighted America's new interest in specialized magazines. Second, it demonstrated the growing sales power of the nation's checkout lines, which also sustained the high circulation rates of women's magazines and supermarket tabloids. Third, *TV Guide* underscored the fact that magazines were facing the same challenge as other mass media in the 1950s: the growing power of television. *TV Guide* would rank among the nation's most popular magazines in the twentieth century.

In 1988, media baron Rupert Murdoch acquired Triangle Publications for $3 billion. Murdoch's News Corp. owned the new Fox network, and buying the then influential *TV Guide* ensured that the fledgling network would have its programs listed. In 2005, after years of declining circulation (TV schedules in local newspapers had increasingly undermined its regional editions), *TV Guide* became a full-size entertainment magazine, dropping its smaller digest format and its 140 regional editions. In 2008, *TV Guide*, once the most widely distributed magazine, was sold to a private venture capital firm for $1—less than the cost of a single issue. The TV Guide Network and TVGuide.com—both deemed more valuable assets—were sold to the film company Lionsgate Entertainment for $255 million in 2009. As *TV Guide* fell out of favor, *Game Informer*—a magazine about digital games—became a top title, as it chronicled the rise of another mass media industry.

Saturday Evening Post, Life, and Look Expire

Although *Reader's Digest* and women's supermarket magazines were not greatly affected by television, other general-interest magazines were. The *Saturday Evening Post* folded in 1969, *Look* in 1971, and *Life* in 1972. At the time, all three magazines were rated in the Top 10 in terms of paid circulation, and each had a readership that exceeded six million per issue. (A look at today's top-selling magazines—see Table 9.1—indicates just how large a readership this was.) Why did these magazines fold? First, to maintain these high circulation figures, their publishers were selling the magazines for far less than the cost of production. For example, a subscription to *Life* cost a consumer twelve cents an issue, yet it cost the publisher more than forty cents per copy to make and mail.

Second, the national advertising revenue pie that helped make up the cost differences for *Life* and *Look* now had to be shared with network television—and magazines' slices were getting smaller. *Life*'s high pass-along readership meant that it had a larger audience than many prime-time TV shows. But it cost more to have a single full-page ad in *Life* than it did to buy a minute of ad time during evening television. National advertisers were often forced to choose between the two, and in the late 1960s and early 1970s, television seemed a better buy to advertisers looking for the biggest audience.

Third, dramatic increases in postal rates had a particularly negative effect on oversized publications (those larger than the 8-by-10.5-inch standard). In the 1970s, postal rates increased by more than 400 percent for these magazines. The *Post* and *Life* cut their circulations drastically to save money. The *Post* went from producing 6.8 million to 3 million copies per issue; *Life*, which lost $30 million between 1968 and 1972, cut circulation from 8.5 million to 7 million. The economic rationale here was that limiting the number of copies would reduce production and postal costs, enabling the magazines to lower their ad rates to compete with network television. But in fact, with decreased circulation, these magazines became less attractive to advertisers trying to reach the largest general audience.

The general-interest magazines that survived the competition for national ad dollars tended to be women's magazines, such as *Good Housekeeping*, *Better Homes and Gardens*, *Family Circle*, *Ladies' Home Journal*, and *Woman's Day*. These publications had smaller formats and depended primarily on supermarket sales rather than on expensive mail-delivered subscriptions (like *Life* and *Look*). However, the most popular magazines, *TV Guide* and *Reader's Digest*, benefited not only from supermarket sales but also from their larger circulations (twice that of *Life*), their pocket size, and their small photo budgets. The failure of the *Saturday Evening Post*, *Look*, and *Life* as oversized general-audience weeklies ushered in a new era of specialization.

People Puts Life Back into Magazines

In March 1974, Time Inc. launched *People*, the first successful mass market magazine to appear in decades. With an abundance of celebrity profiles and human-interest stories, *People* showed a profit in two years and reached a circulation of more than two million within five years. *People* now ranks first in revenue from advertising and circulation sales—more than $1.5 billion a year—and ranks ninth in the United States in terms of circulation (see Table 9.1).

The success of *People* is instructive, particularly because only two years earlier television had helped kill *Life* by draining away national ad dollars. Instead of using a bulky oversized format and relying on subscriptions, *People* downsized and generated most of its circulation revenue from newsstand and supermarket sales. For content, it took its cue from our culture's fascination with celebrities. Supported by plenty of photos, its short articles are about one-third the length of the articles in a typical newsmagazine.

Although *People* has not achieved the broad popularity that *Life* once commanded, it does seem to defy the contemporary trend of specialized magazines aimed at narrow but well-defined audiences, such as *Tennis World*, *Game Informer*, and *Hispanic Business*. One argument suggests

LOOK
1/6 NOVEMBER 17, 1953

HOW TO FIGHT A BULL
A PICTURE STORY
By BARNABY CONRAD

DANNY THOMAS
Comic With a Heart

MARILYN MONROE

COMMUNIST INFILTRATION IN THE PROTESTANT CLERGY: TWO VIEWS

The Advertising Archives

THE RISE AND FALL OF *LOOK*
With large pages, beautiful photographs, and compelling stories on celebrities like Marilyn Monroe, *Look* entertained millions of readers from 1937 to 1971, emphasizing photojournalism to compete with radio. By the late 1960s, however, TV lured away national advertisers, postal rates increased, and production costs rose, forcing *Look* to fold despite a readership of more than eight million.

▲

REGIONAL MAGAZINES maintain a healthy readership in some areas, with sometimes award-winning coverage of local events, issues, and personalities. But even locally, there can be stiff competition: *Denver Magazine*, whose offices are pictured here, was closed and absorbed by rival *5280* in 2011.

Joe Amon/The Denver Post via Getty Images

that *People* is not, in fact, a mass market magazine but a specialized publication targeting people with particular cultural interests: a fascination with music, TV, and movie stars. If *People* is viewed as a specialty magazine, its financial success makes much more sense. It also helps explain the host of magazines that try to emulate it, including *Us Weekly*, *Entertainment Weekly*, *In Touch Weekly*, *Star*, and *OK! People* has even spawned its own spin-offs, including *People en Español* and *People StyleWatch*; the latter is a low-cost fashion magazine that began in 2007 and features celebrity styles at discount prices.

Convergence: Magazines Confront the Digital Age

Although the Internet was initially viewed as the death knell of print magazines, the industry now embraces it. The Internet has become the place where print magazines like *Time* and *Entertainment Weekly* can extend their reach, where some magazines like *FHM* and *PCWorld* can survive when their print version ends, or where online magazines like *Salon*, *Slate*, and *Wonderwall* can exist exclusively.

Magazines Move Online

Given the costs of paper, printing, and postage, creating magazine companion Web sites is a popular method for expanding the reach of consumer magazines. For example, *Wired* magazine has a print circulation of about 819,000. Online, Wired.com gets an average of 19 million unique visitors per month. Mobile magazine apps have become even more popular. Between 2010 and 2012, the number of U.S. consumer magazine iPad apps grew from 98 to 2,234.[8]

The Web and app formats give magazines unlimited space, which is at a premium in their printed versions, and the opportunity to do things that print can't do. Many online magazines now include blogs, original video and audio podcasts, social networks, games, virtual fitting rooms, and 3-D "augmented reality" (or AR) components that could never work in print. For example, PopularMechanics.com has added interactive 3-D models for do-it-yourself projects, so that a reader can go over plans to make an Adirondack chair, examining joints and parts from every angle. GQ.com has featured 3-D athletes in Calvin Klein underwear, and automotive magazines are using AR to bring car models to life. Additionally, many digital magazines (including *Lucky*, *Seventeen*, *GQ*, *Teen Vogue*, *Brides*, *Popular Science*, and *Maxim*) offer mobile-specific scanning apps that enable 3-D involvement on every page, not just those pages with a QR code (the square scannable bar codes that link to video and Web pages). Although QR codes are still a primary part of the mobile activation experience, they are more associated with promotions and coupons, whereas augmented reality is a vehicle for a stronger branding experience.

Paperless: Magazines Embrace Digital Content

Webzines such as *Salon* and *Slate*, which are magazines that appear exclusively online, were pioneers in making the Web a legitimate site for breaking news and discussing culture and politics. *Salon* was founded in 1995 by five former reporters from the *San Francisco Examiner* who wanted to break from the traditions of newspaper publishing and build "a different kind of newsroom" to create well-developed stories and commentary. *Salon* is a leading online magazine, claiming 15 million unique monthly visitors in 2014. Its main online competitor, *Slate*, founded in 1996 and now owned by the Washington Post Company, draws about 15.8 million unique monthly visitors.

Other online-only magazines have tried to reinvent the idea of a magazine, instead of just adapting the print product to the Web. For example, MSN's *Wonderwall* (www.wonderwall.com) uses a layout that is only possible in a digital magazine. Visitors are met by a vertical "wall" of more than sixty celebrity photographs, each linking to a story. *Lonny* (www.lonnymag.com), an interior design magazine, enables readers to flip through digital pages and then click through on items (such as pillows, chairs, fabrics) for purchase. As magazines create apps for smartphones and touchscreen tablets, editorial content is even more tightly woven with advertising. Readers can now, for example, read *Entertainment Weekly*'s top music recommendations on their iPhone or iPad and then click through to buy a song or album on iTunes. *Entertainment Weekly*, owned by Time Inc., then gets a cut of the sale it generated for iTunes, and the reader gets music almost instantly (see "Tracking Technology: The New 'Touch' of Magazines" on page 326).

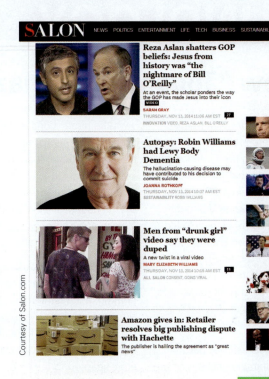

Courtesy of Salon.com

SALON, launched in 1995, is now a leading Internet entertainment magazine. Though it was created by former newspaper staffers, its mixture of topics and article lengths, as well as its national scope, makes it more akin to a general-interest magazine.

The Domination of Specialization

The general trend away from mass market publications and toward specialty magazines coincided with radio's move to specialized formats in the 1950s. With the rise of television, magazines ultimately reacted the same way radio and movies did: They adapted. Radio developed formats for older and younger audiences, for rock fans and classical music fans. At the movies, filmmakers focused on more adult subject matter that was off-limits to television's image as a family medium. And magazines traded their mass audience for smaller, discrete audiences that could be guaranteed to advertisers. This specialization continues today as the magazine industry adapts to the Internet. At least six of the nation's top twenty-five magazines in circulation are now linked to membership in a specialized organization: *AARP The Magazine* and *AARP Bulletin* (for members of the AARP), *Game Informer* (for a Pro membership card at GameStop stores), *AAA Living* (for members of the automobile organization, AAA), *American Rifleman* (one of four magazines for members of the National Rifle Association), and the *American Legion Magazine* (for members of the American Legion veterans organization). Linking the magazine subscription to organizational membership helps ensure audience loyalty to the magazine in the face of the Internet's many competing media options.

Magazines are now divided by advertiser type: *consumer magazines* (*O: The Oprah Magazine*, *Cosmopolitan*), which carry a host of general consumer product ads; *business* or *trade magazines* (*Advertising Age*, *Progressive Grocer*), which include ads for products and services for various occupational groups; and *farm magazines* (*Dairy Herd Management*, *Dakota Farmer*), which contain ads for agricultural products and farming lifestyles. Grouping by advertisers further distinguishes commercial magazines from noncommercial magazine-like periodicals. The noncommercial category includes everything from activist newsletters and scholarly journals

TRACKING TECHNOLOGY

The New "Touch" of Magazines

In the first decade of online magazines, there were relatively few great successes. Limited presentation and portability meant that readers did not clamor to sit down at a PC or with a laptop to read a magazine. Although many consumer magazines developed apps to put their titles on smartphones, these did not attract the attention of users. As one critic noted, "Whether squeezing facsimiles of print magazines onto a mobile phone is at all appealing to consumers is another issue."[1]

Now, though, magazines may have found their most suitable online medium in touchscreen tablets. Apple was the first to make a significant splash with the introduction of the iPad in 2010. The iPad is the closest a device has gotten to simulating the tactile experience of holding a magazine and flipping its pages,

with the dimensions and crisp color presentation similar to most consumer magazines. Since that time, the iPad has been released in even more sophisticated updates, and Amazon's Kindle Fire, the Samsung Galaxy Tab, the Google Nexus, and Microsoft's Surface have all emerged as worthy alternatives.

For the magazine industry, rocked by a recession and rising costs for paper, printing, and distribution, the iPad and other tablets offer the opportunity to reinvent magazines for a digital age. A number of popular magazines immediately adapted to the iPad, including *Vanity Fair, GQ, Glamour, Wired, Cosmopolitan, Time, National Geographic, Men's Health, Popular Science,* and *Entertainment Weekly.* And the publishing world seemed excited by the new opportunities tablets would provide for engaging readers and sharing content in new ways. As Chris Anderson, the editor in chief of *Wired,* said, "We finally have a digital platform that allows us to retain all the rich visual features of high-gloss print, from lavish design to glorious photography, while augmenting it with video, animations, additional content and full interactivity."[2] In fact, one of *Wired's* first issues on the iPad featured a cover article on *Toy Story 3,* that included videos and animations of the film that showed off the magazine's new capabilities.

The migration from print to digital editions of magazines is still a process that will take years, and maybe even one or two generations, says *Rolling Stone* publisher Jann Wenner. Wenner remains a strong advocate of the print magazine product. "To rush to throw away your magazine business and move it on the iPad is just sheer insanity and insecurity and fear," he says.[3] Ironically, Wenner Media's publications (*Rolling Stone, Us Weekly,* and *Men's Journal*) have some of the highest rates of digital readership compared to other major magazine publishers, with 45 percent of readers consuming digital-only or digital and print editions.[4] Still, the magazine industry is in the throes of a significant transition. Seventy-five percent of consumers responded that they feel digital magazine content complements print, and most of them still want a printed copy. But 25 percent of consumers feel digital *replaces* print, and those are readers the magazine industry won't want to lose.[5]

Perhaps the most encouraging news for the magazine industry is that digital magazines may provide unprecedented opportunities for advertisers. According to one study, about one-half of digital readers use the interactive features of the magazine.[6] If the digital magazine industry can structure more direct connections to its advertisers, the future of the magazine industry looks very promising. ◢

to business newsletters created by companies for distribution to employees. Magazines such as *Ms.*, *Consumer Reports*, and *Cook's Illustrated*, which rely solely on subscription and newsstand sales, also accept no advertising and fit into the noncommercial periodical category.

In addition to grouping magazines by advertising style, we can categorize popular consumer magazine styles by the demographic characteristics of their target audience—such as gender, age, or ethnic group—or by an audience interest area, such as entertainment, sports, literature, or tabloids.

Men's and Women's Magazines

One way the magazine industry competed with television was to reach niche audiences that were not being served by the new medium, creating magazines focused on more adult subject matter. *Playboy*, started in 1953 by Hugh Hefner, was the first magazine to do this by undermining the conventional values of pre–World War II America and emphasizing previously taboo subject matter. Scraping together $7,000, Hefner published his first issue, which contained a nude calendar reprint of the actress Marilyn Monroe, along with male-focused articles that criticized alimony payments and gold-digging women. With the financial success of that first issue, which sold more than fifty thousand copies, Hefner was in business.

Playboy's circulation peaked in the 1960s at more than seven million, but it fell gradually throughout the 1970s as the magazine faced competition from imitators and video, as well as criticism for "packaging" and objectifying women for the enjoyment of men. From the 1980s to today, *Playboy* and similar publications continue to publish, but newer men's magazines have shifted their focus to include health (*Men's Health*) and lifestyle (*Details* and *Maxim*).

Women's magazines had long demonstrated that gender-based publications were highly marketable, but during the era of specialization, the magazine industry sought the enormous market of magazine-reading women even more aggressively. *Better Homes and Gardens*, *Good Housekeeping*, *Ladies' Home Journal*, and *Woman's Day* focused on cultivating the image of women as homemakers and consumers. In the conservative 1950s and early 1960s, this formula proved to be enormously successful, but as the women's movement advanced in the late 1960s and into the 1970s, women's magazines grew more contemporary and sophisticated, incorporating content related to feminism (such as in Gloria Steinem's *Ms.* magazine, which first appeared in 1972), women's sexuality (such as in *Cosmopolitan* magazine, which became a young women's magazine under the editorship of Helen Gurley Brown in the 1960s), and career and politics—topics previously geared primarily toward men. Even so, *Better Homes and Gardens*, *Good Housekeeping*, *Ladies' Home Journal*, and *Woman's Day* are all still in the Top 20 list of U.S. highest-circulation magazines (see Table 9.1).

Sports, Entertainment, and Leisure Magazines

In the age of specialization, magazine executives have developed multiple magazines for fans of soap operas, running, tennis, golf, hunting, quilting, antiquing, surfing, and video games, to name only a few. Within categories, magazines specialize further, targeting older or younger runners, men or women golfers, duck hunters or bird-watchers, and midwestern or southern antique collectors.

The most popular sports and leisure magazine is *Sports Illustrated*, which took its name from a failed 1935 publication. Launched in 1954 by Henry Luce's Time Inc., *Sports Illustrated* was initially aimed at well-educated, middle-class men. It has become the most successful general sports magazine in history, covering everything from major-league sports and mountain climbing to foxhunting and snorkeling. Although frequently criticized for its immensely profitable but exploitative yearly swimsuit edition, *Sports Illustrated* has also done major investigative pieces—for example, on racketeering in boxing and on land conservation.

LaunchPad ⊙

macmillanhighered.com
/mediaculture10e

Magazine Specialization Today
Editors discuss motivations for magazine specialization and how the Internet is changing the industry.
Discussion: How have the types of magazines you read changed over the past ten years? Have their formats changed, too?

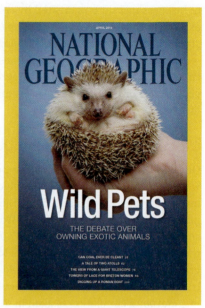

Courtesy of AARP. Photo © Kwaku Alston/Corbis Outline   Sports Illustrated/Getty Images   Vincent J. Musi/National Geographic Creative

SPECIALIZED MAGAZINES target a wide range of interests, from mainstream sports to hobbies like making model airplanes. Some of the more successful specialized magazines include *AARP The Magazine, Sports Illustrated,* and *National Geographic.*

Its circulation held steady at three million in 2014. *Sports Illustrated* competes directly with *ESPN The Magazine* and indirectly with dozens of leisure and niche sports magazine competitors, like *Golf Digest, Outside,* and *Pro Football Weekly.*

Another popular magazine type that fits loosely into the leisure category includes magazines devoted to music—everything from hip-hop's the *Source* to country's *Country Weekly.* The all-time circulation champ in this category is *Rolling Stone,* started in 1967 as an irreverent, left-wing political and cultural magazine by twenty-one-year-old Jann Wenner. Once considered an alternative magazine, *Rolling Stone* had paddled into the mainstream by 1982 with a circulation approaching 800,000; by 2014, it had a circulation of more than 1.4 million. Many fans of the early *Rolling Stone,* however, disappointed with its move to increase circulation and reflect mainstream consumer values, turned to less high-gloss alternatives, such as *Spin.*

Founded in 1888 by Boston lawyer Gardiner Green Hubbard and his famous son-in-law, Alexander Graham Bell, *National Geographic* promoted "humanized geography" and helped pioneer color photography in 1910. It was also the first publication to publish both undersea and aerial color photographs. In addition, many of *National Geographic*'s nature and culture specials on television, which began in 1965, rank among the most popular programs in the history of public television. *National Geographic*'s popularity grew slowly and steadily throughout the twentieth century, reaching 1 million in circulation in 1935 and 10 million in the 1970s. In the late 1990s, its circulation of paid subscriptions slipped to under 9 million. Other media ventures (for example, a cable channel and atlases) provided new revenue as circulation for the magazine continued to slide, falling to 4 million in 2014 (but with 3 million in international distribution). Despite its falling circulation, *National Geographic* is often recognized as one of the country's best magazines for its reporting and photojournalism. Today, *National Geographic* competes with other travel and geography magazines, such as *Discover, Smithsonian, Travel & Leisure, Condé Nast Traveler,* and its own *National Geographic Traveler.*

Magazines for the Ages

In the age of specialization, magazines have further delineated readers along ever-narrowing age lines, appealing more and more to very young readers and older readers, groups often ignored by mainstream television.

The first children's magazines appeared in New England in the late eighteenth century. Ever since, magazines such as *Youth's Companion*, *Boy's Life* (the Boy Scouts' national publication since 1912), *Highlights for Children*, and *Ranger Rick* have successfully targeted preschool and elementary-school children. The ad-free and subscription-only *Highlights for Children* topped the children's magazine category in 2014, with a circulation of more than two million.

In the popular arena, the leading female teen magazines have shown substantial growth; the top magazine for thirteen- to nineteen-year-olds is *Seventeen*, with a circulation of two million in 2014. Several established magazines responded to the growing popularity of the teen market by introducing specialized editions, such as *Teen Vogue* and *Girl's Life*. (For a critical take on women's fashion magazines, see "Media Literacy and the Critical Process: Uncovering American Beauty" on page 330.)

Targeting young men in their twenties, *Maxim*, launched in 1997, was one of the fastest-growing magazines of the late 1990s. *Maxim*'s covers boast the magazine's obsession with "sex, sports, beer, gadgets, clothes, fitness," a content mix that helped it eclipse rivals like *GQ* and *Esquire*. Today, *Maxim*'s circulation has leveled off at about two million.

In targeting audiences by age, the most dramatic success has come from magazines aimed at readers over age fifty, America's fastest-growing age segment. These publications have tried to meet the cultural interests of older Americans, who historically have not been prominently featured in mainstream consumer culture. The American Association of Retired Persons (AARP) and its magazine, *AARP The Magazine*, were founded in 1958 by retired California teacher Ethel Percy Andrus. Subscriptions to the bimonthly *AARP The Magazine* and the monthly *AARP Bulletin* come free when someone joins the AARP and pays the modest membership fee ($16 in 2014). By the early 1980s, *AARP The Magazine*'s circulation approached seven million. However, with the AARP signing up thirty thousand new members each week by the late 1980s, both *AARP The Magazine* and the newsletter overtook *TV Guide* and *Reader's Digest* as the top circulated magazines. By 2014, both had circulations of over twenty-two million, far surpassing the circulations of all other magazines (see Table 9.1). Article topics in the magazine cover a range of lifestyle, travel, money, health, and entertainment issues, such as sex at age fifty-plus, secrets for spectacular vacations, and how poker can create a sharper mind.

Elite Magazines

Although long in existence, *elite magazines* grew in popularity during the age of specialization. Elite magazines are characterized by their combination of literature, criticism, humor, and journalism and by their appeal to highly educated audiences, often living in urban areas. Among the numerous elite publications that grew in stature during the twentieth century were the *Atlantic Monthly* (now the *Atlantic*), *Vanity Fair*, and *Harper's*.

However, the most widely circulated elite magazine is the *New Yorker*. Launched in 1925 by Harold Ross, the *New Yorker* became the first city magazine aimed at a national upscale audience. Over the years, the *New Yorker* has featured many of the twentieth century's most prominent biographers, writers, reporters, and humorists, including A. J. Liebling, Dorothy Parker, Lillian Ross, John Updike, E. B. White, and Garrison Keillor, as well as James Thurber's cartoons and Ogden Nash's poetry. It introduced some of the finest literary journalism of the twentieth century, devoting an entire issue to John Hersey's *Hiroshima* and serializing Truman Capote's *In Cold Blood*. By the mid-1960s, the *New Yorker*'s circulation hovered around 500,000; by 2014, its print circulation stayed steady at over 1 million, and its digital circulation was healthy at more than 86,000 readers.

Minority-Targeted Magazines

Minority-targeted magazines, like newspapers, have existed since before the Civil War, including the African American antislavery magazines *Emancipator*, *Liberator*, and *Reformer*. One of

Media Literacy and the Critical Process

Uncovering American Beauty

How does the United States' leading fashion magazine define *beauty*? One way to explore this question is by critically analyzing the covers of *Cosmopolitan*.

1 DESCRIPTION. If you review a number of *Cosmopolitan* covers, you'll notice that they typically feature a body shot of a female model surrounded by blaring headlines often featuring the words *Hot* and *Sex* to usher a reader inside the magazine. The cover model is dressed provocatively and is positioned against a solid-color background. She looks confident. Everything about the cover is loud and brassy.

2 ANALYSIS. Looking at the covers over the last decade, and then the decade before it, what are some significant patterns? One thing you'll notice is that all of these models look incredibly alike, particularly when it comes to race: There is a disproportionate number of white cover models. But you'll notice that things are improving somewhat in this regard; *Cosmo* has used several Hispanic and African American cover models in recent years, but still they are few and far between. However, there is an even more consistent pattern regarding body type. Of cover model Hilary Duff, *Cosmo* said, "With long honey-colored locks, a smokin' bod, and killer confidence,

Hilary's looking every bit the hot Hollywood starlet." In *Cosmo*-speak, "smokin' bod" means ultrathin (sometimes made even more so with digital modifications).

3 INTERPRETATION. What does this mean? Although *Cosmo* doesn't provide height and weight figures for its models, the magazine is probably selling an unhealthy body weight (in fact, photos can be digitally altered to make the models look even thinner). In its guidelines for the fashion industry, the Academy for Eating Disorders suggests "for women and men over the age of 18, adoption of a minimum body mass index threshold of 18.5 kg/m^2 (e.g., a female model who is 5'9" [1.75 m] must weigh more than 126 pounds [57.3 kg]), which recognizes that weight below this is considered underweight by the World Health Organization."[1]

4 EVALUATION. *Cosmopolitan* uses thin cover models as aspirational objects for its readers—that is, as women its readers would like to look like. Thus these cover models become the image of what a "terrific" body is for its readers, who—by *Cosmopolitan*'s own account—are women age eighteen to twenty-four. *Cosmo* also notes that it's been the best-selling women's magazine in college bookstores for twenty-five years. But that target audience also happens to be the one most susceptible to body issues. As the Academy for Eating Disorders notes, "about one in 20 young women in the community has an eating disorder," which can include anorexia, bulimia, and binge eating.[2]

5 ENGAGEMENT. Contact *Cosmo*'s editor in chief, Joanna Coles, and request representation of healthy body types on the magazine's covers. You can contact her and the editorial department via e-mail (cosmo@hearst.com), telephone (212-649-3570), or U.S. mail: Joanna Coles, Editor, *Cosmopolitan*, 300 West 57th Street, New York, NY 10019. Your voice can be effective: In 2012, a thirteen-year-old girl started a petition on change.org and successfully got *Seventeen* to respond to the way it Photoshops images of models.

the most influential early African American magazines, the *Crisis*, was founded by W. E. B. Du Bois in 1910 and is the official magazine of the National Association for the Advancement of Colored People (NAACP).

In the modern age, the major magazine publisher for African Americans has been John H. Johnson, a former Chicago insurance salesman, who started *Negro Digest* in 1942 on $500 borrowed against his mother's furniture. By 1945, the *Digest* had a circulation of more than 100,000, and its profits enabled Johnson and a small group of editors to start *Ebony*, a picture-text magazine modeled on *Life* but serving black readers. The Johnson Publishing Company also successfully introduced *Jet*, a pocket-size supermarket magazine, in 1951. By 2014, *Ebony*'s circulation was rising to 1.3 million. *Essence*, the first major magazine geared toward African American women, debuted in 1969, and by 2014, it had a circulation of over 1 million. *Jet*, trailing the other two African American market magazines, announced in 2014 that it would begin publishing in a digital-only format.

Other minority groups also have magazines aimed at their own interests. The *Advocate*, founded in 1967 as a twelve-page newsletter, was the first major magazine to address issues of interest to gay men and lesbians, and it has in ensuing years published some of the best journalism about antigay violence, policy issues affecting the LGBT community, and AIDS—topics often not well covered by the mainstream press. *Out* is the top gay style magazine. Both are owned by Here Media, which also owns Here TV and several LGBT Web sites.

With increases in the Hispanic population and immigration, magazines appealing to Spanish-speaking readers have developed rapidly since the 1980s. In 1983, the De Armas Spanish Magazine Network began distributing Spanish-language versions of mainstream American magazines, including *Cosmopolitan en Español*; *Harper's Bazaar en Español*; and *Ring*, the prominent boxing magazine. *Latina* magazine was started in 1996, and is the most successful English-language publication for Hispanic women. The new magazines target the most upwardly mobile segments of the growing American Hispanic population, which numbered more than fifty-three million—about 17 percent of the U.S. population—by 2014. Today, *People en Español*, *Latina*, and *Vanidades* rank as the top three Hispanic magazines by ad revenue.

Although national magazines aimed at other minority groups were slow to arrive, there are magazines now that target virtually every race, culture, and ethnicity, including *Asian Week*, *Native Peoples*, and *Tikkun*.

Photograph by John Russo. Courtesy of Latina Media Ventures

LATINA, launched in 1996, has become the largest magazine targeted to Hispanic women in the United States. It counts a readership of three million bilingual, bicultural women and is also the top Hispanic magazine in advertising pages.

Supermarket Tabloids

With headlines like "Sex Secrets of a Russian Spy," "Extraterrestrials Follow the Teachings of Oprah Winfrey," and "Al-Qaeda Breeding Killer Mosquitoes," **supermarket tabloids** push the limits of both decency and credibility. Although they are published on newsprint, the Audit Bureau of Circulations, which checks newspaper and magazine circulation figures to determine advertising rates, counts weekly tabloids as magazines. Tabloid history can be traced to newspapers' use of graphics and pictorial layouts in the 1860s and 1870s, but the modern U.S. tabloid began with the founding of the *National Enquirer* by William Randolph Hearst in 1926. The *Enquirer* struggled until it was purchased in 1952 by Generoso Pope, who originally intended to use it to "fight for the rights of man" and "human decency and dignity."[9] In the interest of profit, though, Pope settled on the "gore formula" to transform the paper's anemic weekly circulation of seven thousand: "I noticed how auto accidents drew crowds and I decided that if it was blood that interested people, I'd give it to them."[10]

By the mid-1960s, the *Enquirer*'s circulation had jumped to over one million through the publication of bizarre human-interest stories, gruesome murder tales, violent accident accounts, unexplained-phenomena stories, and malicious celebrity gossip. By 1974, the magazine's weekly circulation had topped four million. Its popularity inspired the creation of other tabloids like *Globe* (founded in 1954) and *Star* (founded by News Corp. in 1974) and the adoption of a tabloid style by general-interest magazines such as *People* and *Us Weekly*. Today, tabloid magazine sales are down from their peak in the 1980s, but they continue to be popular. American Media in Boca Raton, Florida, owns several magazines, including two key supermarket tabloids: *Star* and *National Enquirer*.

The Organization and Economics of Magazines

Given the great diversity in magazine content and ownership, it is hard to offer a common profile of a successful magazine. However, large or small, online or in print, most magazines deal with the same basic functions: production, content, ads, and sales. In this section, we discuss how magazines operate, the ownership structure behind major magazines, and how smaller publications fulfill niche areas that even specialized magazines do not reach.

Magazine Departments and Duties

Unlike a broadcast station or a daily newspaper, a small newsletter or magazine can begin cheaply via computer-based **desktop publishing**, which enables an aspiring publisher-editor to write, design, lay out, and print or post online a modest publication. For larger operations, however, the work is divided into departments.

Editorial and Production

The lifeblood of a magazine is the *editorial department*, which produces its content, excluding advertisements. Like newspapers, most magazines have a chain of command that begins with a publisher and extends to the editor in chief, the managing editor, and a variety of subeditors. These subeditors oversee such editorial functions as photography, illustrations, reporting and writing, copyediting, layout, and print and multimedia design. Magazine writers generally include contributing staff writers, who are specialists in certain fields, and freelance writers: nonstaff professionals who are assigned to cover particular stories or a region of the country. Many magazines, especially those with small budgets, also rely on well-written unsolicited manuscripts to fill their pages. Most commercial magazines, however, reject more than 95 percent of unsolicited pieces.

Despite the rise of inexpensive desktop publishing, most large commercial magazines still operate several departments, which employ hundreds of people. The *production and technology department* maintains the computer and printing hardware necessary for mass market production. Because magazines are printed weekly, monthly, or bimonthly, it is not economically practical for most magazine publishers to maintain expensive print facilities. As with *USA Today*, many national magazines digitally transport magazine copy to various regional printing sites for the insertion of local ads and for faster distribution.

Advertising and Sales

The advertising and sales department of a magazine secures clients, arranges promotions, and places ads. Like radio stations, network television stations, and basic cable television stations, consumer magazines are heavily reliant on advertising revenue. The more successful the magazine, the more it can charge for advertisement space. Magazines provide their advertisers with rate cards, which indicate how much they charge for a certain amount of advertising space on a page. A top-rated consumer magazine like *People* might charge almost $340,000 for a full-page color ad and $108,700 for a third of a page black-and-white ad. However, in today's competitive world, most rate cards are not very meaningful: Almost all magazines offer 25 to 50 percent rate discounts to advertisers.[11] Although fashion and general-interest magazines carry a higher percentage of ads than do political or literary magazines, the average magazine contains about 45 percent ad copy and 55 percent editorial material, a figure that has remained fairly constant for the past decade.

The traditional display ad has been the staple of magazine advertising for more than a century. As magazines move to tablet editions, the options for ad formats have grown immensely. For example, Condé Nast magazines offer static display ads with a link for its editions on the iPad, Kindle Fire, Nexus 7, and Next Issue app. But they offer almost thirty other premium ad types, which can include audio, video, tap and reveal, and panoramic views. A single-issue Web-enabled ad in tablet editions of titles like *GQ*, *Wired*, *Vanity Fair*, the *New Yorker*, and *Vogue* would cost $5,000. A premium ad with effects such as animation or a slide show costs $25,000, while a premium plus ad with effects like a virtual tour or full interactivity costs $45,000. (The cost per ad is discounted with purchases of multiple issues.)

A few contemporary magazines, such as *Highlights for Children*, have decided not to carry ads and rely solely on subscriptions and newsstand sales instead. To protect the integrity of their various tests and product comparisons, *Consumer Reports* and *Cook's Illustrated* carry no advertising. To strengthen its editorial independence, *Ms.* magazine abandoned ads in 1990 after years of pressure from the food, cosmetics, and fashion industries to feature recipes and more complementary copy.

Some advertisers and companies have canceled ads when a magazine featured an unflattering or critical article about a company or an industry.[12] In some instances, this practice has put enormous pressure on editors not to offend advertisers. The cozy relationships between some advertisers and magazines have led to a dramatic decline in investigative reporting, once central to popular magazines during the muckraking era.

As television advertising siphoned off national ad revenues in the 1950s, publishers began introducing different editions of their magazines to attract advertisers. **Regional editions** are national magazines whose content is tailored to the interests of different geographic areas. For example, *Sports Illustrated* often prints five different regional versions of its College Football Preview and March Madness Preview editions, picturing regional stars on each of the five covers. In **split-run editions**, the editorial content remains the same, but the magazine includes a few pages of ads purchased by local or regional companies. Most editions of *Time* and *Sports Illustrated*, for example, contain a number of pages reserved for regional ads. **Demographic editions**, meanwhile, are editions of magazines targeted at particular groups of consumers. In this case, market researchers identify subscribers primarily by occupation, class, and zip code. *Time* magazine, for example, developed special editions of its magazine for top management, high-income zip-code areas, and ultrahigh-income professional/managerial households. Demographic editions guarantee advertisers a particular magazine audience, one that enables them to pay lower rates for their ads because the ads will be run in only a limited number of copies of the magazine. The magazine can then compete with advertising in regional television or cable markets and in newspaper supplements. Because of the flexibility of special editions, new sources of income opened up for national magazines. Ultimately, these marketing strategies permitted the massive growth of magazines in the face of predictions that television would cripple the magazine industry.

Circulation and Distribution

The circulation and distribution department of a magazine monitors single-copy and subscription sales. Toward the end of the general-interest magazine era in 1950, newsstand sales accounted for about 43 percent of magazine sales, and subscriptions constituted 57 percent. Since that time, subscriptions have risen to 91 percent of print magazine distribution and 75 percent of print magazine revenue. (Single copies are more expensive, so they generate more revenue.)[13] One tactic used by magazines' circulation departments to increase subscription sales is to encourage consumers to renew well in advance of their actual renewal dates. Magazines can thus invest and earn interest on early renewal money as a hedge against consumers who drop their subscriptions.

Other strategies include **evergreen subscriptions**—those that automatically renew on a credit card account unless subscribers request that the automatic renewal be stopped—and

TIME ON THE IPAD
Time, like many print publications, has an app with which users can purchase each weekly issue in digital form. The magazine also offers combination digital/print subscriptions.

controlled circulations, providing readers with a magazine at no charge by targeting captive audiences, such as airline passengers or association members. These magazines' financial support comes solely from advertising or corporate sponsorship.

The biggest strategy for reviving magazine sales is the migration to digital distribution (which also promises savings over the printing and physical distribution of glossy paper magazines). The number of magazines with iPad apps (which enable users to click on the app and launch the magazine) has grown rapidly. Although the iPad still reigns supreme in the world of tablets, other touchscreen color tablets, like the Amazon Kindle Fire, the Google Nexus 7, and the Samsung Galaxy Tab, have offered competition in the expanding market. Other models, such as the Next Issue app, offer unlimited access to 133 titles ($9.99 a month) or 143 titles ($14.99)—a Netflix-like plan for magazines.

Major Magazine Chains

In terms of ownership, the commercial magazine industry most closely resembles the cable television business, which patterned its specialized channels on the consumer magazine market (see Figure 9.2). Even though more than two hundred new commercial magazine titles appear each year—many of them independently owned—it is a struggle to survive in the competitive magazine marketplace.

Time Inc. is the largest U.S. magazine chain (by circulation) with twenty-three print titles in the United States—including *People*, *Time*, *Sports Illustrated*, and *InStyle*—and seventy international titles, plus forty-five Web sites.[14] In 2014, Time Inc. became an independent company, spun off from the media conglomerate Time Warner because of its weak financial performance. (It wasn't the first time Time Warner reduced its holdings; it spun off both Time Warner Cable and AOL in 2009.) Time Inc.'s fortunes reflect the difficult digital transition for the magazine industry: By 2014, its revenues had dropped to $370 million annually, compared to $1 billion in earnings less than ten years earlier.[15]

The Hearst Corporation, the leading magazine (and newspaper) chain early in the twentieth century, still remains a formidable publisher, with titles like *Cosmopolitan*, *Esquire*, *Elle*, and *O: The Oprah Magazine*. Long a force in upscale consumer magazines, Condé Nast is a division of Advance Publications, which operates the Newhouse newspaper chain. The Condé Nast group controls several key magazines, including *Vanity Fair*, *GQ*, and *Vogue*. The Meredith Corporation, based in Des Moines, Iowa, specializes in women's and home-related magazines (*Better Homes*

FIGURE 9.2

TOP U.S. CONSUMER MAGAZINE COMPANIES

Data from: Corporate reports of each publisher.

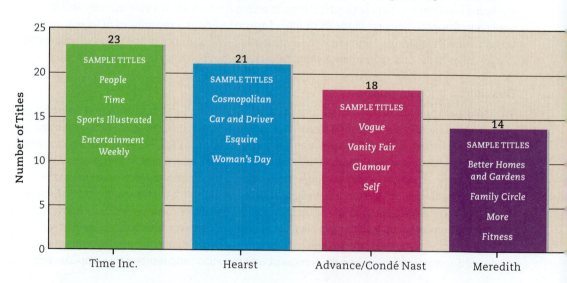

and Gardens, Family Circle). Other important commercial players include Rodale, a family-owned company that publishes health and wellness titles, such as *Prevention* and *Men's Health*.

In addition, a number of American magazines have carved out market niches worldwide. *Reader's Digest*, *Cosmopolitan*, *National Geographic*, and *Time*, for example, all produce international editions in several languages. In general, though, most American magazines are local, regional, or specialized and therefore less exportable than movies and television. Of the twenty thousand titles, only about two hundred magazines from the United States circulate routinely in the world market. Such magazines, however—like exported American TV shows and films—play a key role in determining the look of global culture.

Many major publishers, including Hearst, Meredith, Time Inc., and Rodale, generate additional revenue through custom publishing divisions, producing limited-distribution publications, sometimes called **magalogs**, which combine glossy magazine style with the sales pitch of retail catalogues. Magalogs are often used to market goods or services to customers or employees. For example, Rodale produces the biannual *Whole Foods Market Magazine* magalog, and Time produces the quarterly *My Ford*, distributed by the automobile company to buyers of its vehicles and also available digitally via the iTunes App Store.

Alternative Voices

Only eighty-five of the twenty thousand American magazines have circulations that top a million (see Figure 9.3), so most alternative magazines struggle to satisfy small but loyal groups of readers. At any given time, there are over two thousand alternative magazines in circulation, with many failing and others starting up every month.

Alternative magazines have historically defined themselves in terms of politics—published by either the Left (the *Progressive*, *In These Times*, the *Nation*) or the Right (the *National*

FIGURE 9.3

THE CIRCULATION REACH OF LEADING AMERICAN MAGAZINES

U.S. population data from U.S. Census Bureau, www.census.gov.

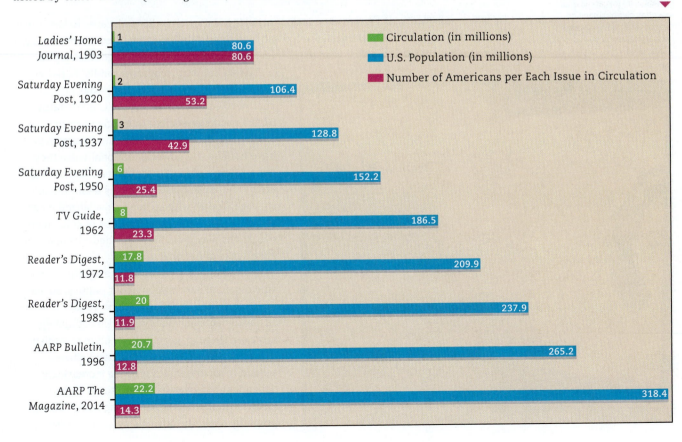

Review, *American Spectator*, *Insight*). However, what constitutes an alternative magazine has broadened over time to include just about any publication considered outside the mainstream, ranging from environmental magazines to alternative lifestyle magazines to punk-zines—the magazine world's answer to punk rock. (**Zines**, pronounced "zeens," is a term used to describe self-published magazines.) *Utne Reader*, widely regarded as "the *Reader's Digest* of alternative magazines," has defined *alternative* as any sort of "thinking that doesn't reinvent the status quo, that broadens issues you might see on TV or in the daily paper."

Occasionally, alternative magazines have become marginally mainstream. For example, during the conservative Reagan era in the 1980s, William F. Buckley's *National Review* saw its circulation swell to more than 100,000—enormous by alternative standards. By 2014, the magazine continued to be the leading conservative publication, with a circulation of about 150,000. On the Left, *Mother Jones* (named after labor organizer Mary Harris Jones), which champions muckraking and investigative journalism, had a circulation of 215,200 in 2014.

Most alternative magazines, however, are content to swim outside the mainstream. These are the small magazines that typically include diverse political, cultural, religious, international, and environmental subject matter, such as *Against the Current*, *Y'all*, *Buddhadharma*, *Home Education Magazine*, *Jewish Currents*, *Small Farmer's Journal*, and *Humor Times*.

Magazines in a Democratic Society

ZINES, mini-magazines that are often self-published or homemade, can give voices to marginalized populations or subcultures.

Like other mass media, magazines are a major part of the cluttered media landscape. To keep pace, the magazine industry has become fast-paced and high-risk. Of the seven hundred to one thousand new magazines that start up each year, fewer than two hundred will survive longer than a year.

Slim Lopez

As an industry, magazine publishing—like advertising and public relations—has played a central role in transforming the United States from a producer society to a consumer society. Since the 1950s, though, individual magazines have not had the powerful national voice they once possessed, uniting separate communities around important issues such as abolition and suffrage. Today, with so many specialized magazines appealing to distinct groups of consumers, magazines play a much-diminished role in creating a sense of national identity.

Contemporary commercial magazines provide essential information about politics, society, and culture, thus helping us think about ourselves as participants in a democracy. Unfortunately, however, these magazines have often identified their readers as consumers first and citizens second. With magazines growing increasingly dependent on advertising, and some of them (such as shopping magazines like *Lucky*) being primarily *about* the advertising, controversial

DIGITAL JOB OUTLOOK

Media Professionals Speak about Jobs in the Magazine Industry

Job Ad for *Slate* Magazine

We are looking for an energetic newshound with a passion for all things social to support us in growing our social media traffic. Do you have clear and snappy writing skills along with an innate understanding of how to get people to share things? Are you comfortable quickly whipping up sharable graphics in Photoshop? Have you ever made something go viral? Then you might be the right person for us. An active personal social media presence and one to two years' experience running institutional social media feeds are strong pluses.

Katherine Goldstein, Editor, *Vanity Fair*'s Web Site (Her Responsibilities Include Reading Magazine Job Applications)

Keep it short. I started putting word limits on cover letters because I couldn't stand, nor did I have the time to read, the epically long letters I'd receive. I'm going to give your letter maybe thirty seconds of my time. If you are interested in a job in journalism, you should be able to tell me about yourself and why I should hire you in less than two hundred words. I've never hired someone with a long-winded cover letter. Same goes for résumés. No one with fewer than four years of full-time work experience needs more than a page. Your summer lifeguarding job does not need five bullet points.

Gemma Askham, Deputy Feature Editor, *Glamour* Magazine U.K.

After a degree, a journalism postgrad, and three months' work experience, I ran out of money to work for free (and out of London-based relatives willing to let me squat in their spare room!). When my parents said, "When are you going to give up on being a writer and get a proper job?" I realised I had to get *any* magazine job. *Anywhere*. So I moved 150 miles to a tiny Midlands town to work—not on the dream women's glossy, but on two car magazines, *Planet 4x4* and *Total Off-Road*. And I'd urge anyone to start small.

Tehrene Firman, Web Editor, *J-14* Magazine

I make sure the Web site is updated with breaking celebrity news, conduct interviews with today's top stars, write up fun features, and update the magazine's social media accounts. . . . Get as much experience as you possibly can. Obviously your grades are important, but the people who will be hiring you are looking for writers who really know what they're doing. Write as much as you can, get editing experience, and if there aren't many options where you're from, don't let that stop you. I'm from an incredibly small town in Iowa and started my own online magazine to get experience. Your hard work won't go unnoticed. Trust me.

---

content sometimes has difficulty finding its way into print. More and more, magazines define their readers merely as viewers of displayed products and purchasers of material goods.

At the same time, magazines have arguably had more freedom than other media to encourage and participate in democratic debates. More magazine voices circulate in the marketplace than do broadcast or cable television channels. Moreover, many new magazines still play an important role in uniting dispersed groups of readers, often giving cultural minorities or newly arrived immigrants or alternative groups a sense of membership in a broader community. In addition, because magazines are distributed weekly, monthly, or bimonthly, they are less restricted by the deadline pressures experienced by newspaper publishers or radio and television broadcasters. Good magazines can usually offer more analysis of and insight into society than other media outlets can. In the midst of today's swirl of images, magazines and their advertisements certainly contribute to the commotion. But good magazines also maintain our connection to words, sustaining their vital role in an increasingly electronic and digital culture. ▶

CHAPTER REVIEW

COMMON THREADS

One of the Common Threads discussed in Chapter 1 is the commercial nature of mass media. The magazine industry is an unusual example of this. Big media corporations control some of the most popular magazines, and commercialism runs deep in many consumer magazines. At the same time, magazines are one of the most democratic mass media. How can that be?

There are more than twenty thousand magazine titles in the United States. But the largest and most profitable magazines are typically owned by some of the biggest media corporations. Advance Publications, for example, counts *GQ*, the *New Yorker*, *Vanity Fair*, and *Vogue* among its holdings. Even niche magazines that seem small are often controlled by chains. Supermarket tabloids like *Star* and the *National Enquirer* are owned by Florida-based American Media, which also publishes *Shape*, *Muscle & Fitness*, *Men's Fitness*, *Fit Pregnancy*, and *Flex*.

High-revenue magazines, especially those focusing on fashion, fitness, and lifestyle, can also shamelessly break down the firewall between the editorial and business departments. "Fluff" story copy serves as a promotional background for cosmetic, clothing, and gadget advertisements. Many titles in the new generation of online and tablet magazines further break down that firewall—with a single click on a story or image, readers are linked to an e-commerce site where they can purchase the item they clicked on. Digital retouching makes every model and celebrity thinner or more muscular, and always blemish-free. This altered view of their "perfection" becomes our ever-hopeful aspiration, spurring us to purchase the advertised products.

Yet the huge number of magazine titles—more than the number of radio stations, TV stations, cable networks, or yearly Hollywood releases—means that magazines span a huge range of activities and thought. Each magazine sustains a community—although some may think of readers more as consumers, others view them as citizens—and several hundred new launches each year bring new voices to the marketplace and search for their own community to serve.

So there is the glitzy, commercial world of the big magazine industry, with *Time*'s Person of the Year, the latest *Cosmo* girl, and the band on the cover of *Rolling Stone*. But many smaller magazines—like the *Georgia Review*, *Edutopia*, and *E–The Environmental Magazine*—account for the majority of magazine titles and the broad, democratic spectrum of communities that are their readers.

KEY TERMS

The definitions for the terms listed below can be found in the glossary at the end of the book. The page numbers listed with the terms indicate where the term is highlighted in the chapter.

magazine, 311
muckrakers, 317
general-interest magazines, 317
photojournalism, 317
pass-along readership, 319

Webzines, 324
supermarket tabloids, 331
desktop publishing, 332
regional editions, 333
split-run editions, 333

demographic editions, 333
evergreen subscriptions, 333
magalogs, 335
zines, 336

REVIEW QUESTIONS

The Early History of Magazines

1. Why did magazines develop later than newspapers in the American colonies?

2. Why did most of the earliest magazines have so much trouble staying financially solvent?

3. How did magazines become national in scope?

The Development of Modern American Magazines

4. How did magazines position women in the new consumer economy at the turn of the twentieth century?

5. What role did magazines play in social reform at the turn of the twentieth century?

6. When and why did general-interest magazines become so popular?

7. Why did some of the major general-interest magazines fail in the twentieth century?

8. What are the advantages of magazines' movement to digital formats?

The Domination of Specialization

9. What triggered the move toward magazine specialization?

10. What are the differences between regional and demographic editions?

11. What are the most useful ways to categorize the magazine industry? Why?

The Organization and Economics of Magazines

12. What are the four main departments at a typical consumer magazine?

13. How do digital editions of magazines change the format of magazine advertising?

14. What are some of the models for digital distribution of magazines?

15. What are the major magazine chains, and what is their impact on the mass media industry in general?

Magazines in a Democratic Society

16. How do magazines serve a democratic society?

17. How does advertising affect what gets published in the editorial side of magazines?

QUESTIONING THE MEDIA

1. What role did magazines play in America's political and social shift from being colonies of Great Britain to becoming an independent nation?

2. Why is the muckraking spirit—so important in popular magazines at the turn of the twentieth century—generally missing from magazines today?

3. If you were the marketing director of your favorite magazine, how would you increase circulation through the use of digital editions?

4. Think of stories, ideas, and images (illustrations and photos) that do not appear in mainstream magazines. Why do you think this is so? (Use the Internet, LexisNexis, or the library to compare your list with Project Censored, an annual list of the year's most underreported stories.)

5. Discuss whether your favorite magazines define you primarily as a consumer or as a citizen. Do you think magazines have a responsibility to educate their readers as both? What can they do to promote responsible citizenship?

6. Do you think touchscreen tablet editions will become the dominant format for magazines? Why or why not?

LAUNCHPAD FOR *MEDIA & CULTURE*

Visit LaunchPad for *Media & Culture* *at* macmillanhighered.com/mediaculture10e *for additional learning tools:*

- REVIEW WITH LEARNINGCURVE
LearningCurve, available on LaunchPad for *Media & Culture*, uses gamelike quizzing to help you master the concepts you need to learn from this chapter.

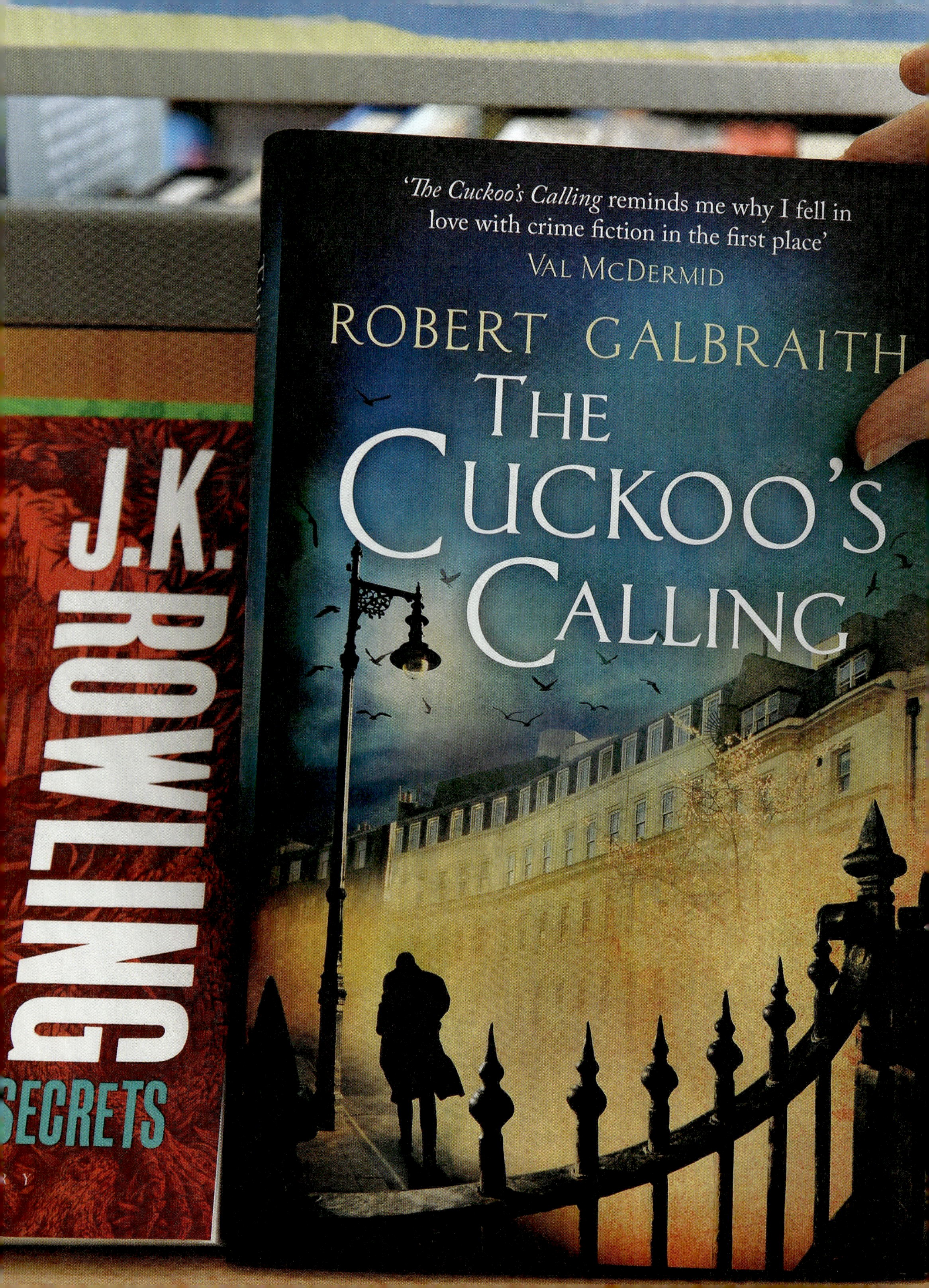

'*The Cuckoo's Calling* reminds me why I fell in love with crime fiction in the first place'
VAL McDERMID

ROBERT GALBRAITH

THE CUCKOO'S CALLING

J.K. ROWLING

SECRETS

Andy Rain/EPA/Newscom

10

Books and the Power of Print

344
The History of Books from Papyrus to Paperbacks

348
Modern Publishing and the Book Industry

355
Trends and Issues in Book Publishing

361
The Organization and Ownership of the Book Industry

367
Books and the Future of Democracy

Amazon is all about customer service. Its mission is plainly stated in its corporate documents: "We seek to be Earth's most customer-centric company.[1]

Yet in 2014, customers looking for books from a certain publisher on its Web site might not have found or purchased them so easily. For some books, Amazon's usual "one-click" buy buttons were missing or the period for shipping mysteriously expanded from just one to two days to one to four weeks. Prices also increased, while some book listings were missing entirely. Even blockbuster author J. K. Rowling's latest book (*The Silkworm*, written under her pseudonym, Robert Galbraith) wasn't immune from the problem. Amazon had removed the pre-order button from its listing for the book, which was expected to be a best-seller.[2]

The problem wasn't a few suddenly malfunctioning pages but Amazon's disagreement with Hachette, one of the world's largest publishers. In all, Hachette reported, "Amazon has limited its customers' ability to buy more than 5,000 Hachette titles."[3]

Amazon, which controls more than 40 percent of U.S. book sales, offered terms for new e-book contracts that were apparently unreasonable for Hachette. According to the *Atlantic*, Amazon wants control of e-book prices (rather than having the publishers set prices) and wants higher payments (often called co-op payments) from the publishers for the promotion of books on the Amazon Web site. Because Amazon now sells more e-books and printed books than any other entity, it has growing leverage to make these requests.[4]

The dispute took on David-versus-Goliath elements, with Amazon (annual revenues of $74.4 billion) taking on Hachette (annual revenues of $2.8 billion). Stephen Colbert, whose books are published by Hachette, said "this means war" and flipped off Amazon on his show. But award-winning author Sherman Alexie (whose books are also published by Hachette) argued to Colbert that it was "two giants fighting each other," and that people should "root for the authors," who were the real underdogs in the battle.[5]

Other retailers, including Walmart, Barnes & Noble, Powell's, and independent booksellers, took advantage of Amazon's snub to get a bigger piece of Hachette sales. Colbert even plugged one of the affected books, *California*—the first novel of Edan Lepucki—on his show to prove that he could "sell more books than Amazon."[6] The unexpected boost helped the novel make the *New York Times* best-seller fiction list.

For its defense, Amazon released a statement saying, "When we negotiate with suppliers, we are doing so on behalf of customers."[7] But Amazon's success in controlling prices, on behalf of its customers, would both enrich Amazon and change the entire nature of the publishing industry, the *Atlantic* argued: "More liberal discounting practices will give Amazon the power to continue to gain market share and it's easy to imagine a scenario where it controls three-quarters of all book sales in the U.S. At the same time, higher co-op payments would make book publishers less profitable and less likely to invest in riskier book projects."[8] Of course, many writers speak in favor of Amazon and its industry-changing store and Kindle readers.[9] Amazon offers independent authors a chance to sidestep publishing houses and earn a 70 percent royalty rate for books published with Amazon.

The dispute ended in November 2014, with Hachette retaining the power to set its own pricing on e-books. But Amazon continued other plans to remake the book industry with its new Netflix-style pricing scheme. Called Kindle Unlimited, Amazon's new service offers more than 600,000 book titles and audio books for reading and listening. Noticeably missing in the plan were the books of the five biggest trade book publishers: Penguin Random House, Macmillan, HarperCollins, Simon & Schuster, and Hachette. Advances in technology, distribution, and commerce continue—along with the battle over the future of the book industry.

Visit **LaunchPad** for *Media & Culture* and use **LearningCurve** to review concepts from this chapter.

◄ *IN THE 1950s AND 1960s,* cultural forecasters thought that the popularity of television might spell the demise of a healthy book industry, just as they thought television would replace the movie, sound recording, radio, newspaper, and magazine industries. Obviously, this did not happen. In 1950, more than 11,000 new book titles were introduced, and by 2011, publishers were producing over fifteen times that number—more than 177,000 titles per year (see Table 10.1). Despite the absorption of small publishing houses by big media corporations, thousands of different publishers—mostly small independents—issue at least one title a year in the United States alone.

Our oldest mass medium is also still our most influential and diverse one. The portability and compactness of books make them the preferred medium in many situations (e.g., relaxing at the beach, resting in bed, traveling on buses or commuter trains), and books are still the main repository of history and everyday experience, passing along stories, knowledge, and wisdom from generation to generation.

In this chapter, we consider the long and significant relationship between books and culture. We will:

- Trace the history of books, from Egyptian papyrus to downloadable e-books
- Examine the development of the printing press and investigate the rise of the book industry, from early publishers in Europe and colonial America to the development of publishing houses in the nineteenth and twentieth centuries
- Review the various types of books and explore recent trends in the industry—including audio books, the convergence of books onto online platforms, and book digitization

Year	Number of Titles
1778	461
1798	1,808
1880	2,076
1890	4,559
1900	6,356
1910	13,470 (peak until after World War II)
1919	5,714 (low point as a result of World War I)
1930	10,027
1935	8,766 (Great Depression)
1940	11,328
1945	6,548 (World War II)
1950	11,022
1960	15,012
1970	36,071
1980	42,377
1990	46,473
1996*	68,175
2001	114,487
2004*	164,020
2010	186,344
2013	192,633

TABLE 10.1

ANNUAL NUMBERS OF NEW BOOK TITLES PUBLISHED, SELECTED YEARS

Data from: Figures through 1945 from John Tebbel, A History of Book Publishing in the United States, *4 vols. (New York: R. R. Bowker, 1972–81); figures after 1945 from various editions of* The Bowker Annual Library and Book Trade Almanac *(Information Today, Inc.) and Bowker press releases.*

*Changes in the Almanac's methodology in 1997 and for years 2004–07 resulted in additional publications being assigned ISBNs and included in the counts.

- Consider the economic forces facing the book industry as a whole, from the growth of bookstore chains to pricing struggles in the digital age
- Explore how books play a pivotal role in our culture by influencing everything from educational curricula to popular movies

As you read through this chapter, think about the pivotal role books have played in your own life. What are your earliest recollections of reading? Is there a specific book that considerably influenced the way you think? How do you discover new books? Do you envision yourself reading more books on a phone or tablet in the future? Or do you prefer holding a paper copy and leafing through the pages? For more questions to help you understand the role of books in our lives, see "Questioning the Media" in the Chapter Review.

The History of Books, from Papyrus to Paperbacks

Before books, or writing in general, oral cultures passed on information and values through the wisdom and memories of a community's elders or tribal storytellers. Sometimes these rich traditions were lost. Print culture and the book, however, gave future generations different and often more enduring records of authors' words.

Ever since the ancient Babylonians and Egyptians began experimenting with alphabets some five thousand years ago, people have found ways to preserve their written symbols. These first alphabets mark the development stage for books. Initially, pictorial symbols and letters were drawn on wood strips or pressed with a stylus into clay tablets, and tied or stacked together

▼ Books and the Power of Print

Papyrus
Made from plant reeds found along the Nile, papyrus is first used as paper and rolled into scrolls around 2400 BCE (p. 345).

Codex
The first protomodern book is produced in the fourth century CE by the Romans, who cut and sew sheets of parchment together and then bind them with thin pieces of wood covered with leather (p. 345).

Movable Type
By assigning a separate piece of wood or metal to each Chinese character, the Chinese by 1000 CE can arrange a page quickly, significantly speeding up printing time (p. 346).

Printing Press
In Germany, Johannes Gutenberg turns a wine press into a printing press, forming the prototype for mass production in 1453. Among the first books mass-produced is the Bible (p. 346).

Encyclopedias
In 1751, French scholars begin compiling articles in alphabetical order. The first encyclopedias consist of radical and opinionated writings that spur debates across Europe (p. 354).

| 2400 BCE | 1000 BCE | 350 CE | 1000 | 1400 |

The Earliest Books
The Chinese make booklike objects from strips of wood and bamboo around 1000 BCE (p. 345).

Illuminated Manuscripts
Featuring decorative, colorful designs on each page, these books are created by priests and monks throughout Europe around 600 CE (p. 346).

The First Colonial Book
In Cambridge, Massachusetts, Stephen Daye prints a collection of biblical psalms in 1640 (p. 347).

to form the first "books." As early as 2400 BCE, the Egyptians wrote on **papyrus** (from which the word *paper* is derived), made from plant reeds found along the Nile River. They rolled these writings into scrolls, much as builders do today with blueprints. This method was adopted by the Greeks in 650 BCE and by the Romans (who imported papyrus from Egypt) in 300 BCE. Gradually, **parchment**—treated animal skin—replaced papyrus in Europe. Parchment was stronger, smoother, more durable, and less expensive because it did not have to be imported from Egypt.

At about the same time the Egyptians started using papyrus, the Babylonians recorded business transactions, government records, favorite stories, and local history on small tablets of clay. Around 1000 BCE, the Chinese also began creating booklike objects, using strips of wood and bamboo tied together in bundles. Although the Chinese began making paper from cotton and linen around 105 CE, paper did not replace parchment in Europe until the thirteenth century because of questionable durability.

The first protomodern book was probably produced in the fourth century by the Romans, who created the **codex**, a type of book made of sheets of parchment and sewn together along the edge, then bound with thin pieces of wood and covered with leather. Whereas scrolls had to be wound, unwound, and rewound, a codex could be opened to any page, and its configuration allowed writing on both sides of a page.

The Development of Manuscript Culture

During the Middle Ages (400–1500 CE), the Christian clergy strongly influenced what is known as **manuscript culture**, a period in which books were painstakingly lettered, decorated, and bound by hand. This period also marks the entrepreneurial stage in the evolution of books. During this time, priests and monks advanced the art of bookmaking; in many ways, they may be considered the earliest professional editors. Known as *scribes*, they transcribed most of the existing philosophical tracts and religious texts of the period, especially versions of the Bible. Through tedious and painstaking work, scribes became the chief caretakers of recorded

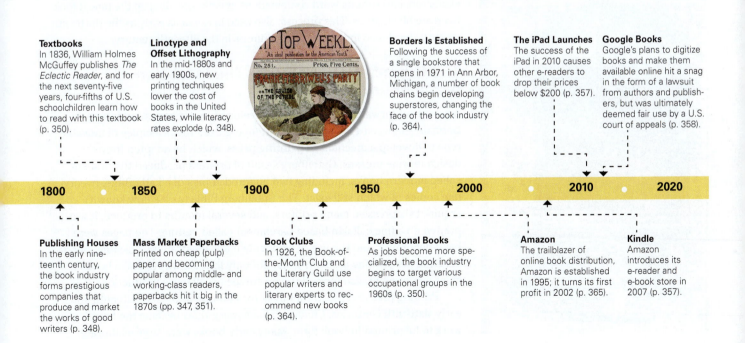

Textbooks
In 1836, William Holmes McGuffey publishes *The Eclectic Reader*, and for the next seventy-five years, four-fifths of U.S. schoolchildren learn how to read with this textbook (p. 350).

Linotype and Offset Lithography
In the mid-1880s and early 1900s, new printing techniques lower the cost of books in the United States, while literacy rates explode (p. 348).

Borders Is Established
Following the success of a single bookstore that opens in 1971 in Ann Arbor, Michigan, a number of book chains begin developing superstores, changing the face of the book industry (p. 364).

The iPad Launches
The success of the iPad in 2010 causes other e-readers to drop their prices below $200 (p. 357).

Google Books
Google's plans to digitize books and make them available online hit a snag in the form of a lawsuit from authors and publishers, but was ultimately deemed fair use by a U.S. court of appeals (p. 358).

1800 • 1850 • 1900 • 1950 • 2000 • 2010 • 2020

Publishing Houses
In the early nineteenth century, the book industry forms prestigious companies that produce and market the works of good writers (p. 348).

Mass Market Paperbacks
Printed on cheap (pulp) paper and becoming popular among middle- and working-class readers, paperbacks hit it big in the 1870s (pp. 347, 351).

Book Clubs
In 1926, the Book-of-the-Month Club and the Literary Guild use popular writers and literary experts to recommend new books (p. 364).

Professional Books
As jobs become more specialized, the book industry begins to target various occupational groups in the 1960s (p. 350).

Amazon
The trailblazer of online book distribution, Amazon is established in 1995; it turns its first profit in 2002 (p. 365).

Kindle
Amazon introduces its e-reader and e-book store in 2007 (p. 357).

history and culture, promoting ideas they favored and censoring ideas that were out of line with contemporary Christian thought.

Many books from the Middle Ages were **illuminated manuscripts**. Often made for churches or wealthy clients, these books featured decorative, colorful designs and illustrations on each page. Their covers were made from leather, and some were embedded with precious gems or trimmed with gold and silver. During this period, scribes developed rules of punctuation, making distinctions between small and capital letters and placing space between words to make reading easier. (Older Roman writing used all capital letters, and the words ran together on a page, making reading a torturous experience.) Hundreds of illuminated manuscripts still survive today in the rare book collections of museums and libraries.

The Innovations of Block Printing and Movable Type

While the work of the scribes in the Middle Ages led to advances in written language and the design of books, it did not lead to the mass proliferation of books, simply because each manuscript had to be painstakingly created one copy at a time. To make mechanically produced copies of pages, Chinese printers developed **block printing**—a technique in which sheets of paper were applied to blocks of inked wood with raised surfaces depicting hand-carved letters and illustrations—as early as the third century. This constituted the basic technique used in printing newspapers, magazines, and books throughout much of modern history. Although hand-carving each block, or "page," was time consuming, this printing breakthrough enabled multiple copies to be printed and then bound together. The oldest dated printed book still in existence is China's *Diamond Sutra* by Wang Chieh, from 868 CE. It consists of seven sheets pasted together and rolled up in a scroll. In 1295, explorer Marco Polo introduced these techniques to Europe after his excursion to China. The first block-printed books appeared in Europe during the fifteenth century, and demand for them began to grow among the literate middle-class populace emerging in large European cities.

The next step in printing was the radical development of movable type, first invented in China around the year 1000. Movable type featured individual characters made from reusable pieces of wood or metal, rather than entire hand-carved pages. Printers arranged the characters into various word combinations, greatly speeding up the time it took to create block pages. This process, also used in Korea as early as the thirteenth century, developed independently in Europe in the fifteenth century.

The Gutenberg Revolution: The Invention of the Printing Press

A great leap forward in printing was developed by Johannes Gutenberg. In Germany, between 1453 and 1456, Gutenberg used the principles of movable type to develop a mechanical **printing press**, which he adapted from the design of wine presses. Gutenberg's staff of printers produced the first so-called modern books, including two hundred copies of a Latin Bible, twenty-one copies of which still exist. The Gutenberg Bible (as it's now known) required six presses, many printers, and several months to produce. It was printed on a fine calfskin-based parchment called **vellum**. The pages were hand-decorated, and the use of woodcuts made illustrations possible. Gutenberg and his printing assistants had not only found a way to make books a mass medium but also formed the prototype for all mass production.

Printing presses spread rapidly across Europe in the late fifteenth and early sixteenth centuries. Chaucer's *Canterbury Tales* became the first English work to be printed in book form. Many early books were large, elaborate,

ILLUMINATED MANUSCRIPTS were handwritten by scribes and illustrated with colorful and decorative images and designs.

Erich Lessing/Art Resource, NY

and expensive, taking months to illustrate and publish. They were usually purchased by aristocrats, royal families, religious leaders, and ruling politicians. Printers, however, gradually reduced the size of books and developed less expensive grades of paper, making books cheaper so that more people could afford them.

The social and cultural transformations ushered in by the spread of printing presses and books cannot be overestimated. As historian Elizabeth Eisenstein has noted, when people could learn for themselves by using maps, dictionaries, Bibles, and the writings of others, they could differentiate themselves as individuals; their social identities were no longer solely dependent on what their leaders told them or on the habits of their families, communities, or social class. The technology of printing presses permitted information and knowledge to spread outside local jurisdictions. Gradually, individuals had access to ideas far beyond their isolated experiences, and this permitted them to challenge the traditional wisdom and customs of their tribes and leaders.[10]

The Birth of Publishing in the United States

In colonial America, English locksmith Stephen Daye set up a print shop in the late 1630s in Cambridge, Massachusetts. In 1640, Daye and his son Matthew printed the first colonial book, *The Whole Booke of Psalms* (known today as *The Bay Psalm Book*), marking the beginning of book publishing in the colonies. This collection of biblical psalms quickly sold out its first printing of 1,750 copies, even though fewer than 3,500 families lived in the colonies at the time. By the mid-1760s, all thirteen colonies had printing shops.

In 1744, Benjamin Franklin, who had worked in printing shops, imported Samuel Richardson's *Pamela; or, Virtue Rewarded* (1740) from Britain, the first novel reprinted and sold in colonial America. Both *Pamela* and Richardson's second novel, *Clarissa; or, The History of a Young Lady* (1747), connected with the newly emerging and literate middle classes—especially women, who were just starting to gain a social identity as individuals apart from their fathers, husbands, and employers. Richardson's novels portrayed women in subordinate roles; however, they also depicted women triumphing over tragedy, so he is credited as one of the first popular writers to take the domestic life of women seriously.

By the early nineteenth century, the demand for books was growing. To meet this demand, the cost of producing books needed to be reduced. By the 1830s, machine-made paper replaced more expensive handmade varieties, cloth covers supplanted more expensive leather ones, and **paperback books** with cheaper paper covers (introduced from Europe) helped make books more accessible to the masses. Further reducing the cost of books, Erastus and Irwin Beadle introduced paperback **dime novels** (so called because they sold for five or ten cents) in 1860. Ann Stephens authored the first dime novel, *Malaeska: The Indian Wife of the White Hunter*, a reprint of a serialized story Stephens wrote in 1839 for the *Ladies' Companion* magazine.[11] By 1870, dime novels had sold seven million copies. By 1885, one-third of all books published in the United States were popular paperbacks and dime novels, sometimes identified as **pulp fiction**, a reference to the cheap, machine-made pulp paper they were printed on.

The New York Public Library/Art Resource, NY

PULP FICTION
The weekly paperback series *Tip Top Weekly*, which was published between 1896 and 1912, featured stories of the most popular dime novel hero of the day, the fictional Yale football star and heroic adventurer Frank Merriwell. This issue, from 1901, follows Frank's exploits in the wilds of the Florida Everglades.

In addition, the printing process became quicker and more mechanized. In the 1880s, the introduction of **linotype** machines enabled printers to save time by setting type mechanically using a typewriter-style keyboard, while the introduction of steam-powered and high-speed rotary presses permitted the production of more books at lower costs. In the early 1900s, the development of **offset lithography** allowed books to be printed from photographic plates rather than from metal casts, greatly reducing the cost of color and illustrations and accelerating book production. With these developments, books disseminated further, preserving culture and knowledge and supporting a vibrant publishing industry.

Modern Publishing and the Book Industry

Throughout the nineteenth century, the rapid spread of knowledge and literacy as well as the Industrial Revolution spurred the emergence of the middle class. Its demand for books promoted the development of the publishing industry, which capitalized on increased literacy and widespread compulsory education. Many early publishers were mostly interested in finding quality authors and publishing books of importance. But with the growth of advertising and the rise of a market economy in the latter half of the nineteenth century, publishing gradually became more competitive and more concerned with sales.

The Formation of Publishing Houses

The modern book industry developed gradually in the nineteenth century with the formation of the early "prestigious" publishing houses: companies that tried to identify and produce the works of good writers.[12] Among the oldest American houses established at the time (all are now part of major media conglomerates) were J. B. Lippincott (1792); Harper & Bros. (1817), which became Harper & Row in 1962 and HarperCollins in 1990; Houghton Mifflin (1832); Little, Brown (1837); G. P. Putnam (1838); Scribner's (1842); E. P. Dutton (1852); Rand McNally (1856); and Macmillan (1869).

Between 1880 and 1920, as the center of social and economic life shifted from rural farm production to an industrialized urban culture, the demand for books grew. The book industry also helped assimilate European immigrants to the English language and American culture. In fact, 1910 marked a peak year in the number of new titles produced: 13,470, a record that would not be challenged until the 1950s. These changes marked the emergence of the next wave of publishing houses, as entrepreneurs began to better understand the marketing potential of books. These houses included Doubleday & McClure Company (1897), the McGraw-Hill Book Company (1909), Prentice-Hall (1913), Alfred A. Knopf (1915), Simon & Schuster (1924), and Random House (1925).

Despite the growth of the industry in the early twentieth century, book publishing sputtered from 1910 into the 1950s, as profits were adversely affected by the two world wars and the Great Depression. Radio and magazines fared better because they were generally less expensive and could more immediately cover topical issues during times of crisis. But after World War II, the book publishing industry bounced back.

Types of Books

The divisions of the modern book industry come from economic and structural categories developed both by publishers and by trade organizations, such as the Association of American

Publishers (AAP), the Book Industry Study Group (BISG), and the American Booksellers Association (ABA). The categories of book publishing that exist today include trade books (both adult and juvenile), professional books, elementary through high school (often called "el-hi") and college textbooks, mass market paperbacks, religious books, reference books, and university press books. (For sales figures for the book types, see Figure 10.1.)

Trade Books

One of the most lucrative parts of the industry, **trade books** include hardbound and paperback books aimed at general readers and sold at commercial retail outlets. The industry distinguishes among adult trade, juvenile trade, and comics and graphic novels. Adult trade books include hardbound and paperback fiction; current nonfiction and biographies; literary classics; books on hobbies, art, and travel; popular science, technology, and computer publications; self-help books; and cookbooks. (*Betty Crocker's Cookbook*, first published in 1950, has sold more than twenty-two million hardcover copies.)

Juvenile book categories range from preschool picture books to young-adult or young-reader books, such as Dr. Seuss books, the Lemony Snicket series, the *Fear Street* series, and the *Harry Potter* series. In fact, the *Harry Potter* series alone provided an enormous boost to the industry, helping create record-breaking first-press runs: 10.8 million for *Harry Potter and the Half-Blood Prince* (2005), and 12 million for the final book in the series, *Harry Potter and the Deathly Hallows* (2007).

Since 2003, the book industry has also been tracking sales of comics and *graphic novels* (long-form stories with frame-by-frame drawings and dialogue, bound like books). As with the similar Japanese *manga* books, graphic novels appeal to both youths and adults, as well as males and females. Will Eisner's *A Contract with God* (1978) is generally credited as the first graphic novel (and called itself so on its cover). Since that time, interest in graphic novels has grown, and in 2006, their sales surpassed comic books. Given their strong stories and visual nature, many comics and graphic novels, including *X-Men*, *The Dark Knight*, *Watchmen*, and

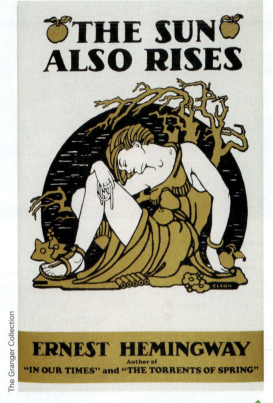

The Granger Collection

SCRIBNER'S—known more for its magazines in the late nineteenth century than for its books—became the most prestigious literary house of the 1920s and 1930s, publishing F. Scott Fitzgerald (*The Great Gatsby*, 1925) and Ernest Hemingway (*The Sun Also Rises*, 1926).

FIGURE 10.1

ESTIMATED U.S. BOOK REVENUE, 2013

Data from: Jim Milliot, "Book Sales Dipped in 2013," Publishers Weekly, June 27, 2014, www .publishersweekly.com/pw/by-topic /industry-news/publisher-news /article/63131-book-sales-dipped -in-2013.html.

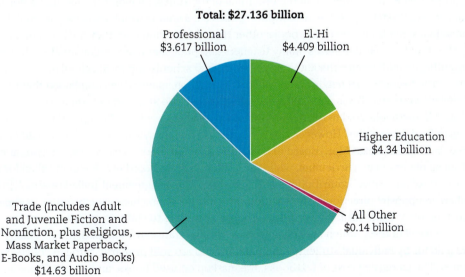

Total: $27.136 billion

Professional $3.617 billion

El-Hi $4.409 billion

Higher Education $4.34 billion

All Other $0.14 billion

Trade (Includes Adult and Juvenile Fiction and Nonfiction, plus Religious, Mass Market Paperback, E-Books, and Audio Books) $14.63 billion

© Superstock/age fotostock

WHEN THE TEXAS STATE BOARD OF EDUCATION voted to take its social studies curriculum in a more conservative direction in 2010, other states expressed concern that their textbooks would be affected by this controversial decision. However, publishers said they would not be creating a "one-size-fits-all" product, since customizing textbooks for different markets has become increasingly easier in recent years.

Captain America, have inspired movies. But graphic novels aren't only about warriors and superheroes. Maira Kalman's *Principles of Uncertainty* and Alison Bechdel's *Are You My Mother?* are both acclaimed graphic novels, but their characters are regular mortals in real settings (see "Case Study: Comic Books: Alternative Themes, but Superheroes Prevail" on pages 352–353).

Professional Books

The counterpart to professional trade magazines, **professional books** target various occupational groups and are not intended for the general consumer market. This area of publishing capitalizes on the growth of professional specialization that has characterized the job market, particularly since the 1960s. Traditionally, the industry has subdivided professional books into the areas of law, business, medicine, and technical-scientific works, with books in other professional areas accounting for a very small segment. These books are sold through mail order, the Internet, or sales representatives knowledgeable about the subject areas.

Textbooks

The most widely read secular book in U.S. history was *The Eclectic Reader*, an elementary-level reading textbook first written by William Holmes McGuffey, a Presbyterian minister and college professor. From 1836 to 1920, more than 100 million copies of this text were sold. Through stories, poems, and illustrations, *The Eclectic Reader* taught nineteenth-century schoolchildren to spell and read simultaneously—and to respect the nation's political and economic systems. Ever since the publication of the McGuffey reader (as it is often nicknamed), **textbooks** have served a nation intent on improving literacy rates and public education. Elementary school textbooks found a solid market niche in the nineteenth century, while college textbooks boomed in the 1950s, when the GI Bill enabled hundreds of thousands of working- and middle-class men returning from World War II to attend college. The demand for textbooks further accelerated in the 1960s as opportunities for women and minorities expanded. Textbooks are divided into elementary through high school (el-hi) texts, college texts, and vocational texts.

In about half of the states, local school districts determine which el-hi textbooks are appropriate for their students. In the other half of the states, including Texas and California—the two largest states—statewide adoption policies determine which texts can be used. If individual schools choose to use books other than those mandated, they are not reimbursed by the state for their purchases. Many teachers and publishers have argued that such sweeping authority undermines the autonomy of individual schools and local school districts, which have varied educational needs and problems. In addition, many have complained that the statewide system in Texas and California enables these two states to determine the content of all el-hi textbooks sold in the nation because publishers are forced to appeal to the content demands of these states. However, the two states do not always agree on what should be covered. In 2010, the Texas State Board of Education adopted more conservative interpretations of social history in its curriculum, while the California State Board of Education called for more coverage of minorities' contributions in U.S. history. The disagreement pulled textbook publishers in opposite directions. The solution, which is becoming increasingly easier to implement, involves customizing electronic textbooks according to state standards.

Unlike el-hi texts, which are subsidized by various states and school districts, college texts are paid for by individual students (and parents) and are sold primarily through college bookstores. The increasing cost of textbooks, the markup on used books, and the profit margins of

77.9¢

Textbook Wholesale Cost
Publisher's paper, printing, editorial, general and administrative costs; marketing costs and publisher's income. Also includes author income.

College Store Personnel
Store employee salaries and benefits to handle ordering, receiving, pricing, shelving, cashiers, customer service, refund desk, and sending extra textbooks back to the publisher.

11.0¢

2.7¢
Pre-Tax*

College Store Income
*Note: The amount of federal, state and/or local tax, and therefore the amount and use of any after-tax profit, is determined by the store's ownership, and usually depends on whether the college store is owned by an institution of higher education, a contract management company, a cooperative, a foundation, or by private individuals.

1.0¢

Freight Expense
The cost of getting books from the publisher's warehouse or bindery to the college store. *Part of cost of goods sold paid to freight company.*

7.4¢

College Store Operations
Insurance, utilities, building and equipment rent and maintenance, accounting and data processing charges, and other overhead paid by college stores.

FIGURE 10.2

WHERE THE NEW TEXTBOOK DOLLAR GOES*

Data from: © 2013 by the National Association of College Stores, www.nacs.org/research /industrystatistics.aspx.

*College store numbers are averages and reflect the most current data gathered by the National Association of College Stores.

local college bookstores (which in many cases face no on-campus competition) have caused disputes on most college campuses. A 2011–12 survey indicated that each college student spent an annual average of $420 on required course texts, including $296 on new textbooks and $124 on used ones.[13] (See Figure 10.2.)

As an alternative, some enterprising students have developed Web sites to trade, resell, and rent textbooks. Other students have turned to online purchasing, either through e-commerce sites like Amazon, Barnes & Noble, and eBay, or through college textbook sellers like eCampus .com and textbooks.com, or through book renters like Chegg.

Mass Market Paperbacks

Unlike the larger-size trade paperbacks, which are sold mostly in bookstores, **mass market paperbacks** are sold on racks in drugstores, supermarkets, and airports as well as in bookstores. Contemporary mass market paperbacks are often the work of blockbuster authors such as Stephen King, Nora Roberts, Patricia Cornwell, and John Grisham and are typically released in the low-cost (under $10) format months after publication of the hardcover version. But mass market paperbacks have experienced declining sales in recent years and now account for less than 6 percent of the book market, as e-books have become the preferred format for low-cost, portable reading.

Paperbacks became popular in the 1870s, mostly with middle- and working-class readers. This phenomenon sparked fear and outrage among those in the professional and educated classes, many of whom thought that reading cheap westerns and crime novels might ruin civilization. Some of the earliest paperbacks ripped off foreign writers, who were unprotected by copyright law and did not receive royalties for the books they sold in the United States. This changed with the International Copyright Law of 1891, which mandated that any work by any author could not be reproduced without the author's permission.

The popularity of paperbacks hit a major peak in 1939 with the establishment of Pocket Books by Robert de Graff. Revolutionizing the paperback industry, Pocket Books lowered the standard book price of fifty or seventy-five cents to twenty-five cents. To accomplish this, de Graff cut bookstore discounts from 30 to 20 percent, the book distributor's share fell from 46 to 36 percent of the cover price, and author royalty rates went from 10 to 4 percent. In its first three weeks, Pocket Books sold 100,000 books in New York City alone. Among its first titles was *Wake Up and Live* by Dorothea Brande, a 1936 best-seller on self-improvement that ignited an early wave of self-help books. Pocket Books also published *The Murder of Roger Ackroyd* by Agatha Christie; *Enough Rope*, a collection of poems by Dorothy Parker; and *Five Great*

Comic Books: Alternative Themes, but Superheroes Prevail

by Mark C. Rogers

At the precarious edge of the book industry are comic books, which are sometimes called *graphic novels* or simply *comix*. Comics have long integrated print and visual culture, and they are perhaps the medium most open to independent producers—anyone with a pencil and access to a photocopier can produce mini-comics. Nevertheless, two companies—Marvel and DC—have dominated the commercial industry for more than thirty years, publishing the routine superhero stories that have been so marketable.

Comics are relatively young, first appearing in their present format in the 1920s in Japan and in the 1930s in the United States. They began as simple reprints of newspaper comic strips, but by the mid-1930s, most comic books featured original material. Comics have always been published in a variety of genres, but their signature contribution to American culture has been the superhero. In 1938, Jerry Siegel and Joe Shuster created Superman for DC comics. Bob Kane's Batman character arrived the following year. In 1941, Marvel Comics introduced Captain America to fight Nazis, and except for a brief period in the 1950s, the superhero genre has dominated the history of comics.

After World War II, comic books moved away from superheroes and began experimenting with other genres, most notably crime and horror (e.g., *Tales from the Crypt*). With the end of the war, the reading public was ready for more moral ambiguity than was possible in the simple good-versus-evil world of the superhero. Comics became increasingly graphic and lurid as they tried to compete with other mass media, especially television and mass market paperbacks.

In the early 1950s, the popularity of crime and horror comics led to a moral panic about their effects on society. Fredric Wertham, a prominent psychiatrist, campaigned against them, claiming they led to juvenile delinquency. Wertham was joined by many religious and parent groups, and Senate hearings were held on the issue. In October 1954, the Comics Magazine Association of America adopted a code of acceptable conduct for publishers of comic books. One of the most restrictive examples of industry self-censorship in mass media history, the code kept the government from legislating its own code or restricting the sale of comic books to minors.

The code had both immediate and long-term effects on comics. In the short run, the number of comics sold in the United States declined sharply. Comic books lost many of their adult readers because the code confined comics' topics to those suitable for children. Consequently, comics have rarely been

taken seriously as a mass medium or as an art form; they remain stigmatized as the lowest of low culture—a sort of literature for the subliterate.

In the 1960s, Marvel and DC led the way as superhero comics regained their dominance. This period also gave rise to underground comics, which featured more explicit sexual, violent, and drug themes—for example, R. Crumb's *Mr. Natural* and Bill Griffith's *Zippy the Pinhead*. These alternative comics, like underground newspapers, originated in the 1960s counterculture and challenged the major institutions of the time. Instead of relying on newsstand sales, underground comics were sold through record stores, at alternative bookstores, and in a growing number of comic-book specialty shops.

In the 1970s, responding in part to the challenge of the underground form, "legitimate" comics began to increase the political content and relevance of their story lines. In 1974, a new method of distributing comics—direct sales—developed, catering to the increasing number of comic-book stores. This direct-sales method involved selling comics on a nonreturnable basis but with a higher discount than was available to newsstand distributors, who bought comics only on the condition that they could return unsold copies. The percentage of comics sold through specialty shops increased gradually, and by the early 1990s, more than 80 percent of all comics were sold through direct sales.

The shift from newsstand to direct sales enabled comics to once again approach adult themes and also created an explosion in the number of comics available and in the number of companies publishing comics. Comic books peaked in 1993, generating more than $850 million in sales. That year, the industry sold about 45 million comic books per month, but it then began a steady decline that led Marvel to declare bankruptcy in the late 1990s. After comic-book sales fell to $250 million in 2000 and Marvel reorganized, the industry rebounded. Today, the industry releases 70 to 80 million comics a year. Marvel and DC control more than 70 percent of comic-book sales, but challengers like Image, Dark Horse, and IDW plus another 150 small firms keep the industry vital by providing innovation and identifying new talent.

Meanwhile, the two largest firms focus on the commercial synergies of particular characters or superheroes. DC, for example, is owned by Time Warner, which has used the DC characters, especially Superman and Batman, to build successful film and television properties through its Warner Brothers division. Marvel, which was bought by Disney in 2009, also got into the act with film versions of *The Avengers* made by their in-house studios and series like *X-Men* licensed to outside studios.

Comics, however, are again about more than just superheroes. In 1992, comics' flexibility was demonstrated in *Maus: A Survivor's Tale* by Art Spiegelman, cofounder and editor of *Raw* (an alternative magazine for comics and graphic art). The first comic-style book to win a Pulitzer Prize, Spiegelman's two-book fable merged print and visual styles to recount his complex relationship with his father, a Holocaust survivor.

Today, there are few divisions among traditional books and graphic novels. In 2012–13, Seven Stories Press released a three-volume book, *The Graphic Canon: The World's Great Literature as Comics and Visuals*. The acclaimed collection uses 130 illustrators to reinterpret nearly 190 classic texts, from the ancient *Epic of Gilgamesh*, to Oscar Wilde's *The Picture of Dorian Gray*, to twentieth-century works like *Wild at Heart* by Barry Gifford.

As other writers and artists continue to adapt the form to both fictional and nonfictional stories, comics endure as part of popular and alternative culture. ◢

Mark C. Rogers teaches communication at Walsh University. He writes about television and the comic-book industry.

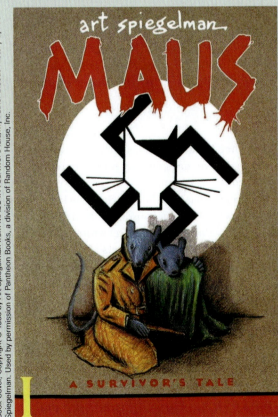

Tragedies by Shakespeare. Pocket Books' success spawned a series of imitators, including Dell, Fawcett, and Bantam Books.[14]

A major innovation of mass market paperback publishers was the **instant book**, a marketing strategy that involved publishing a topical book quickly after a major event occurred. Pocket Books produced the first instant book, *Franklin Delano Roosevelt: A Memorial*, six days after FDR's death in 1945. Similar to made-for-TV movies and television programs that capitalize on contemporary events, instant books enabled the industry to better compete with newspapers and magazines. Such books, however, like their TV counterparts, have been accused of circulating shoddy writing, exploiting tragedies, and avoiding in-depth analysis and historical perspective. Instant books have also made government reports into best-sellers. In 1964, Bantam published *The Report of the Warren Commission on the Assassination of President Kennedy*. After receiving the 385,000-word report on a Friday afternoon, Bantam staffers immediately began editing the Warren Report, and the book was produced within a week, ultimately selling over 1.6 million copies. Today, instant books continue to capitalize on contemporary events, including the inauguration of Barack Obama in 2009, the wedding of Prince William and Kate Middleton in 2011, and Superstorm Sandy in 2012.

Religious Books

The best-selling book of all time is the Bible, in all its diverse versions. Over the years, the success of Bible sales has created a large industry for religious books. After World War II, sales of religious books soared. Historians attribute the sales boom to economic growth and a nation seeking peace and security while facing the threat of "godless communism" and the Soviet Union.[15] By the 1960s, though, the scene had changed dramatically. The impact of the Civil Rights struggle, the Vietnam War, the sexual revolution, and the youth rebellion against authority led to declines in formal church membership. Not surprisingly, sales of some types of religious books dropped as well. To compete, many religious-book publishers extended their offerings to include serious secular titles on such topics as war and peace, race, poverty, gender, and civic responsibility.

Throughout this period of change, the publication of fundamentalist and evangelical literature remained steady. It then expanded rapidly during the 1980s, when the Republican Party began making political overtures to conservative groups and prominent TV evangelists. After a record year in 2004 (twenty-one thousand new titles), there has been a slight decline in the religious-book category. However, it continues to be an important part of the book industry, especially during turbulent social times.

Reference Books

Another major division of the book industry—**reference books**—includes dictionaries, encyclopedias, atlases, almanacs, and a number of substantial volumes directly related to particular professions or trades, such as legal casebooks and medical manuals.

The two most common reference books are encyclopedias and dictionaries. The idea of developing encyclopedic writings to document the extent of human knowledge is attributed to the Greek philosopher Aristotle. The Roman citizen Pliny the Elder (23–79 CE) wrote the oldest reference work still in existence, *Historia Naturalis*, detailing thousands of facts about animals, minerals, and plants. But it wasn't until the early eighteenth century that the compilers of encyclopedias began organizing articles in alphabetical order and relying on specialists to contribute essays in their areas of interest. Between 1751 and 1771, a group of French scholars produced the first multiple-volume set of encyclopedias.

The oldest English-language encyclopedia still in operation, *Encyclopaedia Britannica*, was first published in Scotland in 1768. U.S. encyclopedias followed, including *Encyclopedia Americana* (1829), *The World Book Encyclopedia* (1917), and *Compton's Pictured Encyclopedia* (1922). *Encyclopaedia*

Britannica produced its first U.S. edition in 1908. This best-selling encyclopedia's sales dwindled in the 1990s due to competition from electronic encyclopedias (like Microsoft's *Encarta*), and it went digital, too. *Encyclopaedia Britannica* and *The World Book Encyclopedia* (which still produces a printed set) are now the leading digital encyclopedias, although even they struggle today as young researchers increasingly rely on search engines such as Google or online resources like Wikipedia to find information (though many critics consider these sources inferior in quality).

Dictionaries have also accounted for a large portion of reference sales. The earliest dictionaries were produced by ancient scholars attempting to document specialized and rare words. During the manuscript period in the Middle Ages, however, European scribes and monks began creating glossaries and dictionaries to help people understand Latin. In 1604, a British schoolmaster prepared the first English dictionary. In 1755, Samuel Johnson produced the *Dictionary of the English Language*. Describing rather than prescribing word usage, Johnson was among the first to understand that language changes—that words and usage cannot be fixed for all time. In the United States in 1828, Noah Webster, using Johnson's work as a model, published the *American Dictionary of the English Language*, differentiating between British and American usages and simplifying spelling (for example, *colour* became *color* and *musick* became *music*). As with encyclopedias, dictionaries have moved mostly to online formats since the 1990s, and they struggle to compete with free online or built-in word-processing software dictionaries.

University Press Books

The smallest division in the book industry is the nonprofit **university press**, which publishes scholarly works for small groups of readers interested in intellectually specialized areas, such as literary theory and criticism, history of art movements, contemporary philosophy, and the like. Professors often try to secure book contracts from reputable university presses to increase their chances for *tenure*, a lifetime teaching contract. Some university presses are very small, producing as few as ten titles a year. The largest—Oxford University Press—publishes more than six thousand titles a year and has offices in fifty countries. One of the oldest and most prestigious presses in the United States is Harvard University Press, formally founded in 1913 but claiming roots that go back to 1640, when Stephen Daye published the first colonial book in a small shop located behind the house of Harvard's president.

University presses have not traditionally faced pressure to produce commercially viable books, preferring to encourage books about highly specialized topics by innovative thinkers. In fact, most university presses routinely lose money and are subsidized by their university. Even when they publish more commercially accessible titles, the lack of large marketing budgets prevents such books from reaching mass audiences. While large commercial trade houses are often criticized for publishing only blockbuster books, university presses often suffer the opposite criticism—that they produce mostly obscure books that only a handful of scholars read. To offset costs and increase revenue, some presses are trying to form alliances with commercial houses to help promote and produce academic books that have wider appeal.

Trends and Issues in Book Publishing

Ever since Harriet Beecher Stowe's abolitionist novel *Uncle Tom's Cabin* sold fifteen thousand copies in fifteen days back in 1852 (and three million total copies prior to the Civil War), many American publishers have stalked the *best-seller*, or blockbuster (just like in the movie business).

LaunchPad ◉

macmillanhighered.com
/mediaculture10e

**Based On: Making Books
into Movies**
Writers and producers discuss the process that brings
a book to the big screen.
Discussion: How is the
creative process of writing a
novel different from making
a movie? Which would you
rather do, and why?

THE FAULT IN OUR STARS,
a popular young adult–targeted
novel that crossed over to
a wider audience, became
a hit film in the summer of
2014. The film's star, Shailene
Woodley, has made her career
on book-to-film adaptations:
her starring roles in *Fault, The
Spectacular Now,* and the
Divergent series all originated
in books.

While most authors are professional writers, the book industry also reaches out to famous media figures, who may pen a best-selling book (Tina Fey, Jerry Seinfeld, Bill Clinton) or a commercial failure (Whoopi Goldberg, Jay Leno). Other ways publishers attempt to ensure popular success include acquiring the rights to license popular film and television programs or experimenting with formats like audio books and e-books. In addition to selling new books, other industry issues include the preservation of older books and the history of banned books and censorship.

Influences of Television and Film

There are two major facets in the relationship among books, television, and film: how TV can help sell books and how books serve as ideas for TV shows and movies. Through TV exposure, books by or about talk-show hosts, actors, and politicians such as Stephen Colbert, Julie Andrews, Barack Obama, and Hillary Clinton sell millions of copies—enormous sales in a business where 100,000 in sales constitutes remarkable success. In national polls conducted from the 1980s through today, nearly 30 percent of respondents said they had read a book after seeing the story or a promotion on television.

One of the most influential forces in promoting books on TV was Oprah Winfrey. Even before the development of Oprah's Book Club in 1996, Oprah's afternoon talk show had become a major power broker in selling books. In 1993, for example, Holocaust survivor and Nobel Prize recipient Elie Wiesel appeared on *Oprah*. Afterward, his 1960 memoir, *Night*, which had been issued as a Bantam paperback in 1982, returned to the best-seller lists. In 1996, novelist Toni Morrison's nineteen-year-old book *Song of Solomon* became a paperback best-seller after Morrison appeared on *Oprah*. In 1998, after Winfrey brought Morrison's *Beloved* to movie screens, the book version was back on the best-seller lists. Each Oprah's Book Club selection became an immediate best-seller, generating tremendous excitement within the book industry. *The Oprah Winfrey Show* ended in 2011.

The film industry gets many of its story ideas from books (more than 1,450 feature-length movie adaptations in the United States since 1980), which results in enormous movie-rights revenues for the book industry and its authors.[16] Robert M. Edsel's *The Monuments Men: Allied Heroes, Nazi Thieves, and the Greatest Treasure Hunt in History* (2009), Veronica Roth's *Divergent* (2011), and John Green's *The Fault in Our Stars* (2012), for instance, became Hollywood motion pictures in 2014. The most profitable movie successes for the book industry in recent years emerged from fantasy works. J. K. Rowling's best-selling *Harry Potter* books have become hugely popular movies, as has Peter Jackson's film trilogy of J. R. R. Tolkien's enduringly popular *The Lord of the Rings* (first published in the 1950s). The *Twilight* movie series has created a huge surge in sales of Stephenie Meyer's four-book saga, a success repeated by Suzanne Collins's *The Hunger Games* trilogy. Books have also inspired popular television programs, including *Game of Thrones* and *Boardwalk Empire* on HBO, *Dexter* on Showtime, and *Pretty Little Liars* on ABC Family. In each case, the television shows boosted the sales of the original books, too. Journalist H. G. Bissinger's *Friday Night Lights: A Town, a Team, and a Dream*

(1990), chronicling the story of a West Texas high school football team, inspired a 2004 film and then a 2006–2011 television series. The movie and television versions then spawned special editions of the book and frequent reprintings as the book became a classic sports account.

Audio Books

Another major development in publishing has been the merger of sound recording with publishing. *Audio books* generally feature actors or authors reading entire works or abridged versions of popular fiction and nonfiction trade books. Indispensable to many sightless readers and older readers whose vision is diminished, audio books are also popular among regular readers who do a lot of commuter driving or who want to listen to a book at home while doing something else—like exercising. The number of audio books borrowed from libraries soared in the 1990s and early 2000s, and small bookstore chains developed to cater to the audio book niche. Audio books are now readily available on the Internet for downloading to iPods and other portable devices. Amazon owns Audible, the largest provider of audio books.

Convergence: Books in the Digital Age

In 1971, Michael Hart, a student computer operator at the University of Illinois, typed up the text of the U.S. Declaration of Independence, and thus the idea of the **e-book**—a digital book read on a computer or a digital reading device—was born. Hart soon founded Project Gutenberg, which now offers more than forty thousand public domain books (older texts with expired copyrights) for free at www.gutenberg.org. Yet the idea of *commercial e-books*—putting copyrighted books like current best-sellers in digital form—took a lot longer to gain traction.

Print Books Move Online

Early portable reading devices from RCA and Sony in the 1990s were criticized for being too heavy, too expensive, or too difficult to read, while their e-book titles were scarce and had little cost advantage over full-price hardcover books. It is no surprise that these e-readers and e-books didn't catch on. Then, in 2007, Amazon, the largest online bookseller, developed an e-reader (the Kindle) and an e-book store that seemed inspired by Apple's music industry–changing iPod and iTunes. The first Kindle had an easy-on-the-eyes electronic paper display, held more than two hundred books, and did something no other device could do before: wirelessly download e-books from Amazon's online bookstore. Moreover, most Kindle e-books sold for $9.99, less than half the price of most new hardcovers. This time, e-books caught on quickly, and Amazon couldn't make Kindles fast enough to keep up with demand.

Amazon has continued to refine its e-reader, and in 2011 it introduced the Kindle Fire, a color touchscreen tablet with Web browsing, access to all the media on Amazon, and the Amazon Appstore. The Kindle devices are the best-selling products ever on Amazon. Of course, the Kindle is no longer the only portable reading device on the market. Apps have transformed the iPod Touch, the iPhone, and other smartphones into e-readers. In 2010, Apple introduced the iPad, a color touchscreen tablet that quickly outsold the Kindle. The immediate initial success of the iPad (introduced at a starting price of $499 and up), which sold three million units in less than three months, spurred other e-readers to drop their prices below $200. Like Amazon's Kindle Fire, other devices have mimicked the iPad by adding color, e-mail, and an app store.

By 2013, e-books accounted for 38 percent of adult fiction sales in the United States (in terms of revenue). Projections indicate that e-books will surpass the print book market by 2017.[17] As the market grows rapidly, several companies are vying to be the biggest seller of e-books. Apple's iBook Store serves the iPad, iPod, and iPhone exclusively. Amazon and Barnes & Noble sell e-books for their readers but also have apps for other devices so that, for example, an iPad user could buy e-books from their stores. Google started an e-book store

LaunchPad ⓞ

macmillanhighered.com
/mediaculture10e

Books in the New Millennium
Authors, editors, and bookstore owners discuss the future of book publishing. **Discussion:** Are you optimistic or pessimistic about the future of books in an age of computers and e-readers?

(now Google Play) that enables customers to access its cloud-based e-books anywhere via any device, a feature added by Amazon and Apple.

The Future of E-Books

E-books are demonstrating how digital technology can help the oldest mass medium adapt and survive. Distributors, publishers, and bookstores also use digital technology to print books on demand, reviving books that would otherwise go out of print and avoiding the inconveniences of carrying unsold books. But perhaps the most exciting part of e-books is their potential for reimagining what a book can be. Computers or tablet touchscreens such as an iPad can host e-books with embedded video, hyperlinks, and dynamic content, enabling, for example, a professor to reorganize, add, or delete content of an e-textbook to tailor it to the needs of a specific class. Children's books may also never be the same. An *Alice in Wonderland* e-book developed for the iPad uses the device's motion and touchscreen technologies to make "the pop-up book of the 21st-century." Such developments are changing the reading experience: "Users don't just flip the 'pages' of the e-book—they're meant to shake it, turn it, twist it, jiggle it, and watch the characters and settings in the book react."[18] E-books have also made the distribution of long-form journalism and novellas easier with products like the inexpensive Kindle Singles.

Preserving and Digitizing Books

Another recent trend in the book industry involves the preservation of older books, especially those from the nineteenth century printed on acid-based paper, which gradually deteriorates. At the turn of the twentieth century, research initiated by libraries concerned with losing valu-

E-BOOKS have opened up many new possibilities for children's books and are even going so far as to redefine how a book looks and acts. The classic *Alice in Wonderland* has been reimagined into a fully interactive experience. You can tilt your iPad to make Alice grow bigger or smaller, and shake your iPad to make the Mad Hatter even madder.

Sam Abell/National Geographic/Getty Images

able older collections provided evidence that acid-based paper would eventually turn brittle and self-destruct. The paper industry, however, did not respond, so in the 1970s, leading libraries began developing techniques to halt any further deterioration (although this process could not restore books to their original state). Finally, by the early 1990s, motivated almost entirely by economics rather than by the cultural value of books, the paper industry began producing acid-free paper. Libraries and book conservationists, however, still focused attention on older, at-risk books. Some institutions began photocopying original books onto acid-free paper and made the copies available to the public. Libraries then stored the originals, which were treated to halt further wear.

Another way to preserve books is through digital imaging. The most extensive digitization project, Google Books, which began in 2004, features partnerships with the New York Public Library and about twenty major university research libraries—including Harvard, Michigan, Oxford, and Stanford—to scan millions of books and make them available online. The Authors Guild and the Association of American Publishers initially sued Google for digitizing copyrighted books without permission. Google argued that displaying only a limited portion of the books was legal under fair-use rules. After years of legal battles, a U.S. Court of Appeals sided with Google's fair-use arguments in 2013 and dismissed the lawsuit. The Authors Guild vowed to appeal the decision. An alternative group, dissatisfied by Google Books' restriction of its scanned book content from use by other commercial search services, started a nonprofit service in 2007.

GLOBAL VILLAGE

France and the Anti-Amazon Law

by Pamela Druckerman

One of the maddening things about being a foreigner in France is that hardly anyone in the rest of the world knows what's really happening here. They think Paris is a Socialist museum where people are exceptionally good at eating small bits of chocolate and tying scarves. In fact, the French have all kinds of worthwhile ideas on larger matters. This occurred to me recently when I was strolling through my museum-like neighborhood in central Paris, and realized there were seven bookstores within a 10-minute walk of my apartment. Do the French know something about the book business that we Americans don't?

I was in a bookstore-counting mood because of the news that Amazon has delayed or stopped delivering some books, over its dispute with the publisher Hachette. This has prompted soul-searching over Amazon's 41 percent share of new book sales in America and its 65 percent share of new books sold online. For a few bucks off and the pleasure of shopping from bed, have we handed over a precious natural resource—our nation's books—to an ambitious billionaire with an engineering degree?

France, meanwhile, has just unanimously passed a so-called anti-Amazon law, which says online sellers can't offer free shipping on discounted books. ("It will be either cheese or dessert, not both at once," a French commentator explained.) The new measure is part of France's effort to promote "biblio-diversity" and help independent bookstores compete. Here, there's no big bookseller with the power to suddenly turn off the spigot. People in the industry estimate that Amazon has a 10 or 12 percent share

of new book sales in France. They handle around 70 percent of the country's online book sales—but just 18 percent of books are sold online.

The French secret is deeply un-American: fixed book prices. Its 1981 "Lang law," named after former Culture Minister Jack Lang, says that no seller can offer more than 5 percent off the cover price of new books. That means a book costs more or less the same wherever you buy it in France, even online. The Lang law was designed to make sure France continues to have lots of different books, publishers and booksellers. Fixing book prices may sound shocking to Americans, but it's common around the world, for the same reason. Six of the world's 10 biggest book-selling countries—Germany, Japan, France, Italy, Spain and South Korea—have versions of fixed book prices and there seems to be a link between those fixed prices and flourishing independent bookstores. In Britain, which abandoned its own fixed-price system in the 1990s, there are fewer than 1,000 independent bookstores left after a third of them closed in the past nine years, as supermarkets and Amazon discounted some books by more than 50 percent.

What underlies France's book laws isn't just an economic position—it's also a worldview. Quite simply, the French treat books as special. Some 70 percent of French people said they read at least one book last year; the average among French readers was 15 books. Readers say they trust books far more than any

URMAN LIONEL/SIPA/Newscom

other medium, including newspapers and TV. The French government classifies books as an "essential good," along with electricity, bread and water. People here have thought for centuries about what makes a book industry vibrant, and are watching developments in Britain and America as cautionary tales. "We don't sell potatoes," says Xavier Moni, co-owner of Comme Un Roman in Paris. "There are also ideas in books. That's what's dangerous. Because the day that you have a large seller that sells 80 percent of books, he's the one who will decide what's published, or what won't be published. That's what scares me." ◢

Source: Excerpted from Pamela Druckerman, "The French Do Buy Books. Real Books." New York Times, July 9, 2014, www.nytimes.com/2014/07/10/opinion/pamela-druckerman-the-french-do-buy-books-real-books.html.

Media Literacy and the Critical Process

1 DESCRIPTION. Identify two contemporary books that have been challenged or banned in two separate communities. (Check the American Library Association Web site [www.ala.org/advocacy/banned] for information on the most frequently challenged and banned books, or use the LexisNexis database.) Describe the communities involved and what sparked the challenges or bans. Describe the issues at stake and the positions students, teachers, parents, administrators, citizens, religious leaders, and politicians took with regard to the books. Discuss what happened and the final outcomes.

2 ANALYSIS. What patterns emerge? What are the main arguments given for censoring the books? What are the main arguments of those defending these particular books? Are there any middle-ground positions or unusual viewpoints raised in your book controversies? Did these communities take similar or different

Banned Books and "Family Values"

In *Free Speech for Me—but Not for Thee: How the American Left and Right Relentlessly Censor Each Other*, Nat Hentoff writes that "the lust to suppress can come from any direction." Indeed, *Ulysses* by James Joyce, *The Scarlet Letter* by Nathaniel Hawthorne, *Leaves of Grass* by Walt Whitman, *The Diary of a Young Girl* by Anne Frank, *Lolita* by Vladimir Nabokov, and *To Kill a Mockingbird* by Harper Lee have all been banned by some U.S. community, school, or library at one time or another. In fact, the most censored book in U.S. history is Mark Twain's *The Adventures of Huckleberry Finn*, the 1884 classic that still sells tens of thousands of copies each year. Often, the impulse behind calling for a book's banishment is to protect children in the name of a community's "family values."

approaches when dealing with these books?

3 INTERPRETATION. Why did these issues arise? What do you think are the actual reasons why people would challenge or ban a book? (For example, can you tell if people seem genuinely concerned about protecting young readers or are just personally offended by particular books?) How do people handle book banning and issues raised by First

Amendment protections of printed materials?

4 EVALUATION. Who do you think is right and wrong in these controversies? Why?

5 ENGAGEMENT. Read the two banned books. Then write a book review and publish it in a student or local paper, on a blog, or on Facebook. Through social media, link to the ALA's list of banned books and challenge other people to read and review them.

The Internet Archive's Open Library works with the Boston Public Library, several university libraries, Amazon, Microsoft, and Yahoo! to digitize millions of books with expired copyrights and make them freely available at openlibrary.org. In 2008, another group of universities formed the HathiTrust Digital Library to further archive and share digital collections. In 2010, these nonprofit archives joined other libraries to create the Digital Public Library of America.

Censorship and Banned Books

Over time, the wide circulation of books gave many ordinary people the same opportunities to learn that were once available to only a privileged few. However, as societies discovered the power associated with knowledge and the printed word, books were subjected to a variety of censors. Imposed by various rulers and groups intent on maintaining their authority, the censorship of books often prevented people from learning about the rituals and moral standards of other cultures. Political censors sought to banish "dangerous" books that promoted radical ideas or challenged conventional authority. In various parts of the world, some versions of the Bible, Karl Marx's *Das Kapital* (1867), *The Autobiography of Malcolm X* (1965), and Salman Rushdie's *The Satanic Verses* (1989) have all been banned at one time or another. In fact, one of

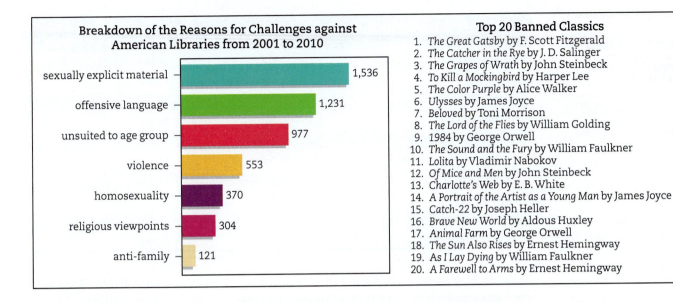

Breakdown of the Reasons for Challenges against American Libraries from 2001 to 2010

sexually explicit material	1,536
offensive language	1,231
unsuited to age group	977
violence	553
homosexuality	370
religious viewpoints	304
anti-family	121

Top 20 Banned Classics

1. *The Great Gatsby* by F. Scott Fitzgerald
2. *The Catcher in the Rye* by J. D. Salinger
3. *The Grapes of Wrath* by John Steinbeck
4. *To Kill a Mockingbird* by Harper Lee
5. *The Color Purple* by Alice Walker
6. *Ulysses* by James Joyce
7. *Beloved* by Toni Morrison
8. *The Lord of the Flies* by William Golding
9. *1984* by George Orwell
10. *The Sound and the Fury* by William Faulkner
11. *Lolita* by Vladimir Nabokov
12. *Of Mice and Men* by John Steinbeck
13. *Charlotte's Web* by E. B. White
14. *A Portrait of the Artist as a Young Man* by James Joyce
15. *Catch-22* by Joseph Heller
16. *Brave New World* by Aldous Huxley
17. *Animal Farm* by George Orwell
18. *The Sun Also Rises* by Ernest Hemingway
19. *As I Lay Dying* by William Faulkner
20. *A Farewell to Arms* by Ernest Hemingway

FIGURE 10.3

BANNED AND CHALLENGED BOOKS

Data from: American Library Association, www.ala.org/ala /issuesadvocacy/banned/index.cfm.

the triumphs of the Internet is that it allows the digital passage of banned books into nations where printed versions have been outlawed. (For more on banned books, see "Media Literacy and the Critical Process: Banned Books and 'Family Values'" on page 360.)

Each year, the American Library Association (ALA) compiles a list of the most challenged books in the United States. Unlike an enforced ban, a **book challenge** is a formal request to have a book removed from a public or school library's collection. Common reasons for challenges include sexually explicit passages, offensive language, occult themes, violence, homosexual themes, promotion of a religious viewpoint, nudity, and racism. (The ALA defends the right of libraries to offer material with a wide range of views and does not support removing material on the basis of partisan or doctrinal disapproval.) Some of the most challenged books of the past decade include *I Know Why the Caged Bird Sings* by Maya Angelou, *Forever* by Judy Blume, the *Harry Potter* series by J. K. Rowling, and the *Captain Underpants* series by Dav Pilkey (see Figure 10.3).

The Organization and Ownership of the Book Industry

Compared with the revenues earned by other mass media industries, the steady growth of book publishing has been relatively modest. From the mid-1980s to 2013, total revenues went from $9 billion to about $27.01 billion. Within the industry, the concept of who or what constitutes a publisher varies widely. A publisher may be a large company that is a subsidiary of a global media conglomerate and occupies an entire office building, or a one-person home office operation using a laptop computer.

Ownership Patterns

Like most mass media, commercial publishing is dominated by a handful of major corporations with ties to international media conglomerates. Mergers and consolidations have driven the book industry. For example, one of the largest publishing conglomerates is Germany's Bertelsmann. Beginning in the late 1970s with its purchase of Dell for $35 million and its 1980s purchase of

TABLE 10.2

WORLD'S TEN LARGEST BOOK PUBLISHERS (REVENUE IN MILLIONS OF DOLLARS), 2014

Data from: "The World's 56 Largest Book Publishers, 2014," Publishers Weekly, June 27, 2014, www.publishersweekly.com/pw/by-topic/industry-news/financial-reporting/article/63004-the-world-s-56-largest-book-publishers-2014.html.

Note: Cengage emerged from bankruptcy in 2014. It's ranking is based on 2012 revenue.

Rank/Publishing Company (Group or Division)	Home Country	Revenue in $ Millions
1 Pearson	U.K.	$9,330
2 Reed Elsevier	U.K./NL/U.S.	$7,288
3 Thomson Reuters	U.S.	$5,576
4 Wolters Kluwer	NL	$4,920
5 Penguin Random House (Bertelsmann & Pearson)	Germany/U.K.	$3,664
6 Hachette Livre (Lagardère)	France	$2,851
7 Holtzbrinck	Germany	$2,222
8 Grupo Planeta	Spain	$2,161
9 Cengage (Apax Partners)	U.S./Canada	$1,993
10 McGraw-Hill Education	U.S.	$1,992

BOOK MARKETING

In addition to traditional advertising and in-store placements, publishers take part in the annual BookExpo America convention to show off their books to buyers who decide what titles bookstores will purchase and sell.

Doubleday for $475 million, Bertelsmann has been building a publishing dynasty. In 1998, Bertelsmann shook up the book industry by adding Random House, the largest U.S. book publisher, to its fold for $1.4 billion. Bertelsmann's book company subsidiaries include Ballantine Bantam Dell, Doubleday Broadway, Alfred A. Knopf, and the Random House Publishing Group. In 2013, Random House merged with Penguin Books (owned by Pearson PLC, a British corporation), creating Penguin Random House and gaining control of about one-quarter of the book industry (see Table 10.2).

Penguin Random House (jointly owned since 2013 by Bertelsmann and Pearson), Simon & Schuster (owned by CBS), Hachette (owned by French-based Lagardère), HarperCollins (owned by News Corp.), and Macmillan (owned by German-based Holtzbrinck) are the five largest trade book publishers in the United States. From a corporate viewpoint, executives have argued that large companies can financially support a number of smaller firms or imprints while allowing their editorial ideas to remain independent from the parent corporation. With thousands of independent presses competing with bigger corporations, book publishing continues to produce volumes on an enormous range of topics. Still, the largest trade book publishers and independents alike find themselves struggling in the face of the industry's digital upheaval and the dominance of Amazon in the distribution of e-books.

AP Photo/Charles Sykes

The Structure of Book Publishing

A small publishing house may have a staff of a few to twenty people. Medium-size and large publishing houses employ hundreds of people. In the larger houses, divisions usually include acquisitions and development; copyediting, design, and production; marketing and sales; and administration and business. Unlike daily newspapers but similar to magazines, most publishing houses contract independent printers to produce their books.

Most publishers employ **acquisitions editors** to seek out and sign authors to contracts. For fiction, this might mean discovering talented writers through book agents or reading unsolicited manuscripts. For nonfiction, editors might examine manuscripts and letters of inquiry or match a known writer to a project (such as a celebrity

Hardcover Edition, $26 in Bookstore

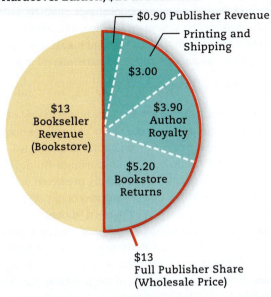

$0.90 Publisher Revenue

Printing and Shipping $3.00

$3.90 Author Royalty

$13 Bookseller Revenue (Bookstore)

$5.20 Bookstore Returns

$13 Full Publisher Share (Wholesale Price)

E-Book Edition, $12.99 Online

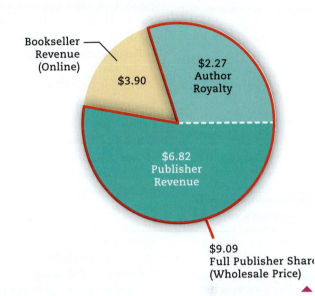

Bookseller Revenue (Online) $3.90

$2.27 Author Royalty

$6.82 Publisher Revenue

$9.09 Full Publisher Share (Wholesale Price)

biography). Acquisitions editors also handle **subsidiary rights** for an author—that is, selling the rights to a book for use in other media, such as a mass market paperback or as the basis for a screenplay.

As part of their contracts, writers sometimes receive *advance money*, an early payment that is subtracted from royalties earned from book sales (see Figure 10.4). Typically, an author's royalty is between 5 and 15 percent of the net price of the book. New authors may receive little or no advance from a publisher, but commercially successful authors can receive millions. For example, author J. K. Rowling hauled in an estimated $7 million advance from Little, Brown & Company/Hachette for *The Casual Vacancy* (2012), her first novel after the *Harry Potter* series. Nationally recognized authors, such as political leaders, sports figures, comedians, or movie stars, can also command large advances from publishers who are banking on the well-known person's commercial potential. For example, Sarah Palin received $1.25 million for her book *Going Rogue*, and George W. Bush got a $7 million advance for *Decision Points*, both released in 2010.

After a contract is signed, the acquisitions editor may turn the book over to a **developmental editor**, who provides the author with feedback, makes suggestions for improvements, and, in educational publishing, obtains advice from knowledgeable members of the academic community. If a book is illustrated, editors work with photo researchers to select photographs and pieces of art. Then the production staff enters the picture. While **copy editors** attend to specific problems in writing or length, production and **design managers** work on the look of the book, making decisions about type style, paper, cover design, and layout.

Simultaneously, plans are under way to market and sell the book. Decisions need to be made concerning the number of copies to print, ways to reach potential readers, and costs for promotion and advertising. For trade books and some scholarly books, publishing houses may send advance copies of a book to appropriate magazines and newspapers with the hope of receiving favorable reviews that can be used in promotional material. Prominent trade writers typically have book signings and travel the radio and TV talk-show circuit to promote their books. Unlike trade publishers, college textbook firms rarely sell directly to bookstores. Instead, they contact instructors through direct-mail brochures or sales representatives assigned to geographic regions.

To help create a best-seller, trade houses often distribute large illustrated cardboard bins, called *dumps*, to thousands of stores to display a book in bulk quantity. Like food merchants who

FIGURE 10.4

HOW A BOOK'S REVENUE IS DIVIDED

Booksellers are still dependent on printed books, but e-books are changing the nature of business expenses, profits, and costs to consumers. Here's where the money goes on a $26 trade book and the same title sold as a $12.99 e-book.

Data from: Ken Auletta, "Publish or Perish: Can the iPad Topple the Kindle, and Save the Book Business?" New Yorker, April 26, 2010, pp. 24–31.

Note: Publishers and booksellers must pay other expenses, such as employees and office/retail space, from their revenue share.

buy eye-level shelf placement for their products in supermarkets, large trade houses buy shelf space from major chains to ensure prominent locations in bookstores. Similarly, publishers are required to pay (co-op payments) for featured treatment on Amazon, as mentioned in the opening of this chapter. Publishers also buy ad space in newspapers and magazines and on buses, billboards, television, radio, and the Web—all in an effort to generate interest in a new book.

Selling Books: Brick-and-Mortar Stores, Clubs, and Mail Order

Traditionally, the final part of the publishing process involves the business and order fulfillment stages—shipping books to thousands of commercial outlets and college bookstores. Warehouse inventories are monitored to ensure that enough copies of a book will be available to meet demand. Anticipating such demand, though, is a tricky business. No publisher wants to be caught short if a book becomes more popular than originally predicted or get stuck with books it cannot sell, as publishers must absorb the cost of returned books. Independent bookstores, which tend to order more carefully, return about 20 percent of books ordered; in contrast, mass merchandisers such as Walmart, Sam's Club, Target, and Costco, which routinely overstock popular titles, often return up to 40 percent. Returns this high can have a serious impact on a publisher's bottom line. For years, publishers have talked about doing away with the practice of allowing bookstores to return unsold books to the publisher for credit.

Today, about 15,000 outlets sell books in the United States, including traditional bookstores, department stores, drugstores, used-book stores, and toy stores. Shopping-mall bookstores boosted book sales starting in the late 1960s. But it was the development of book superstores in the 1980s that really reinvigorated the business. Following the success of a single Borders store established in Ann Arbor, Michigan, in 1971, a number of book chains began developing book superstores that catered to suburban areas and to avid readers. A typical Barnes & Noble superstore stocks up to 200,000 titles. As superstores expanded, they began to sell recorded music and feature coffee shops and live performances. Borders grew from 14 superstores in 1991 to more than 508 superstores and 173 Waldenbooks in 2010, but the company declared bankruptcy and closed its last brick-and-mortar store in 2011. Since the shuttering of Borders, Barnes & Noble is the last national bookstore retail chain in the United States, operating 661 superstores and 700 college bookstores, but closing its smaller B. Dalton mall bookstores in 2010.

The rise of book superstores (and later, online bookstores) severely cut into independent bookstore business, which dropped from a 31 percent market share in 1991 to 4.3 percent by 2011.[19] The number of independent bookstores dropped from 5,100 in 1991 to about 1,900 today. Independent bookstores and superstore chains are being squeezed from multiple sides: online and e-book sales; discount retailers such as Walmart, Sam's Club, Target, and Costco; and specialty retailers like Anthropologie and Urban Outfitters that sell "lifestyle" books.[20]

Book clubs and mail-order services are two other traditional methods of selling books. Originally, these two tactics helped the industry when local bookstores were rarer and the Internet did not yet exist.

The Book-of-the-Month Club and the Literary Guild both started in 1926. Using popular writers and literary experts to recommend new books, the clubs were immediately successful. Book clubs have long served as editors for their customers, screening thousands of

INDEPENDENT BOOKSTORES
City Lights Books in San Francisco is both an independent bookstore and an independent publisher, publishing nearly two hundred titles since launching in 1955, including poet Allen Ginsberg's revolutionary work *Howl*. Customers from around the world now come to browse through the landmark store's three floors and to see the place where beatniks like Ginsberg got their start.

© James Kirkikis/age fotostock

titles and recommending key books in particular genres. During the 1980s, book clubs began a long decline in sales. Today, twenty remaining book clubs—including the Book-of-the-Month Club, the Literary Guild, and Doubleday—are consolidated by a single company, Pride Tree Holdings, which also owns DVD and music clubs.

Mail-order bookselling was pioneered in the 1950s by magazine publishers. They created special sets of books, including Time-Life Books, focusing on such areas as science, nature, household maintenance, and cooking. These series usually offered one book at a time and sustained sales through direct-mail flyers and other advertising. Although such sets are more costly due to advertising and postal charges, mail-order books still appeal to customers who prefer mail to the hassle of shopping or to those who prefer the privacy of mail order (particularly if they are ordering sexually explicit books or magazines). Today, mail-order bookselling is used primarily by trade, professional, and university press publishers.

Selling Books Online

Since the late 1990s, online booksellers have created an entirely new book distribution system on the Internet. The strength of online sellers lies in their convenience and low prices, and especially their ability to offer backlist titles and the works of less famous authors that retail stores aren't able to carry on their shelves. Online customers are also drawn to the interactive nature of these sites, which allow readers to post their own book reviews, read those of fellow customers, and receive book recommendations based on book searches and past purchases.

The trailblazer is Amazon, established in 1995 by then thirty-year-old Jeff Bezos, who left Wall Street to start a Web-based business. Bezos realized books were an untapped and ideal market for the Internet, with more than three million publications in print and plenty of distributors to fulfill orders. He moved to Seattle and started Amazon, so named because search engines like Yahoo! listed categories in alphabetical order, putting Amazon near the top of the list. In 1997, Barnes & Noble, the leading retail store bookseller, launched its own online book site, BN.com. The site's success, however, remains dwarfed by Amazon. By 2014, Amazon controlled 41 percent of book sales (print and e-books combined).[21]

But Amazon's bigger objective for the book industry was to transform the entire industry itself, from one based on bound paper volumes to one based on digital files. The introduction of the Kindle in 2007 made Amazon the fastest book delivery system in the world. Instead of going to a bookstore or ordering from Amazon and waiting for the book to be delivered in a box, one could buy a book in a few seconds from the Amazon store (see Figure 10.5). Amazon quickly grew to control 90 percent of the e-book market, which it used as leverage to

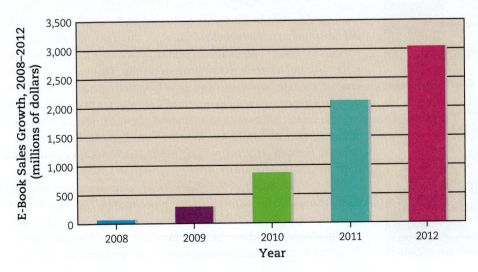

FIGURE 10.5

E-BOOK SALES GROWTH (IN MILLIONS OF DOLLARS), 2008–2012

Data from: Jim Miliot, "The E-Book Boom Years: The Format Moved from Sideline to Vital Category in Five Years," Book Expo America, 2013: The Digital Spotlight, Publishers Weekly, *May 2013, p. 1.*

force book publishers to comply with its low prices or risk getting dropped from Amazon's bookstore (something that has happened to several independent book publishers who complained).[22] Amazon has done the same in print book sales, where it is also a major player.

Amazon's price slashing caused most of the major trade book publishing corporations to endorse Apple's agency-model pricing, in which the publishers set the book prices and the digital bookseller gets a 30 percent commission. The new agency pricing system for e-books began in 2011; by 2013, Amazon's share of the e-book market had dropped from about 90 percent to about 60 percent, while Barnes & Noble and Apple each held about a 25 percent market share. When the U.S. Department of Justice ruled in 2013 that Apple and the major publishers had colluded to set book prices (thus denying consumers the lower prices that Amazon's deep discounts might offer), the booksellers responded that government investigators should be more concerned about Amazon, which has grown to be one of the most powerful players in the publishing industry. (See the opening of this chapter.) Of particular concern to publishers is that Amazon has been expanding into the field of traditional publishers with the establishment of Amazon Publishing, which has grown rapidly since 2009. With a publishing arm that can sign authors to book contracts, the Amazon store's distribution, and millions of Kindle devices in the hands of readers, Amazon is becoming a vertically integrated company and a too-powerful entity, traditional publishers fear.

Amazon's biggest rivals in the digital book business are those with their own tablet devices. Apple has its iBook Store, which is available for iPads and iPhones through an app in the iTunes store. Google Play, Google's digital media store, combines newly released and backlist books, along with the out-of-print titles that Google has been digitizing since 2004. Google also introduced its Nexus 7 tablet in 2012 to promote its store. Barnes & Noble has been less successful in shoring up its flagging brick-and-mortar bookstores with its Nook device and online store. (Barnes & Noble announced in 2014 that it would spin off its Nook Media division as a separate company.) The Kobo e-book device, introduced in 2010 by a Toronto-based company, has become the most popular e-book device in Canada and is making some inroads with independent booksellers in the United States.

Independent bookstores are an increasingly rare breed in the retail book industry. But to support independents, the American Booksellers Association created IndieCommerce, an e-commerce platform to give independent bookstores the ability to offer online service similar to Amazon's.

Alternative Voices

Even though the book industry is dominated by large book publishers and one big online retailer (Amazon), there are still alternative options for both publishing and selling books. One alternative idea is to make books freely available to everyone. This idea is not a new one—in the late nineteenth and early twentieth centuries, industrialist Andrew Carnegie used millions of dollars from his vast steel fortune to build more than twenty-five hundred public libraries in the United States, Britain, Australia, and New Zealand. Carnegie believed that libraries created great learning opportunities for citizens, especially for immigrants like himself.

One Internet source, NewPages, is working on another alternative to conglomerate publishing and chain bookselling by trying to bring together a vast array of alternative and university presses, independent bookstores, and guides to literary and alternative magazines. The site's listing of independent publishers, for example, includes

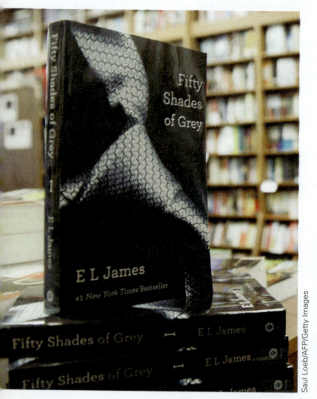

FIFTY SHADES OF GREY began its unlikely success story as *Twilight* fan fiction—an online phenomenon where fans of preexisting books, movies, or TV shows pen original stories about the characters from those works. These new stories can't be sold because they use copyrighted characters, but they're often shared for free online. Eventually, author E. L. James rewrote her fan fiction and self-published it as *Fifty Shades of Grey*; it was then picked up by a traditional publisher and became an even bigger hit, doubtless inspiring fan fiction of its own.

Saul Loeb/AFP/Getty Images

hundreds, mostly based in the United States and Canada, ranging from Academy Chicago Publishers (which publishes a range of fiction and nonfiction books) to Zephyr Press (which "publishes literary titles that foster a deeper understanding of cultures and languages").

Finally, because e-books make publishing and distribution costs low, **e-publishing** has enabled authors to sidestep traditional publishers. A new breed of large Internet-based publishing houses, such as Xlibris, iUniverse, Hillcrest Media, Amazon's CreateSpace, and Author Solutions, design and distribute books for a comparatively small price for aspiring authors who want to self-publish a title, which can even be formatted for the Kindle or iPad. Although sales are typically low for such books, the low overhead costs allow higher royalty rates for the authors and lower retail prices for readers.

Sometimes self-published books make it to the best-seller lists. British writer E. L. James's blockbuster erotic novel *Fifty Shades of Grey* was first written as fan fiction, posted to a busy *Twilight* fan forum beginning in 2009, where thousands read and commented on it. In 2012, Vintage bought the rights to *The Fifty Shades* trilogy for more than $1 million. Amanda Hocking, a writer in her mid-twenties from Minnesota, wrote several paranormal romance e-books that attracted attention from several publishers, and she signed a seven-figure advance contract with St. Martin's Press.[23] Some traditional publishers are considering the straight-to-e-book route themselves. Little, Brown & Company released Pete Hamill's *They Are Us* in digital format only.

Books and the Future of Democracy

As we enter the digital age, the book-reading habits of children and adults have become a social concern. After all, books have played an important role not only in spreading the idea of democracy but also in connecting us to new ideas beyond our local experience. The impact of our oldest mass medium—the book—remains immense. Without the development of printing presses and books, the idea of democracy would be hard to imagine. From the impact of Harriet Beecher Stowe's *Uncle Tom's Cabin*, which helped bring an end to slavery in the 1860s, to Rachel Carson's *Silent Spring*, which led to reforms in the pesticide industry in the 1960s, books have made a difference. They have told us things that we wanted—and needed—to know, and inspired us to action. And, quite suddenly, Americans are reading more again. In a sharp turnaround from a decade earlier, a 2009 National Endowment for the Arts (NEA) study, *Reading on the Rise*, reported that "for the first time in the history of the survey—conducted five times since 1982—the overall rate at which adults read literature (novels and short stories, plays, or poems) rose by seven percent." Interestingly, the most rapid increase in literary reading was in young adults ages eighteen to twenty-four, with significant increases among Hispanic and African American populations, and with fiction accounting for the new growth in all adult literary readers. The NEA surmised that millions of parents, teachers, librarians, and community leaders who endorsed reading and reading programs spurred the increase in reading. The survey found that America is basically divided in half: About 50 percent of Americans can be considered readers, and about 50 percent are nonreaders. Moreover, the NEA report noted that people who read regularly are more active in civic and cultural life and more likely to perform volunteer and charity work, crucial activities in a democratic society.[24]

AMAZON'S WAREHOUSES go far beyond the stockrooms of a typical brick-and-mortar store, housing more than one hundred employees in each location, of which there are dozens across the United States and around the world. Though Amazon still uses these warehouses to support its massive fulfillment needs, it owns a lot of virtual businesses, too, including cloud storage, e-publishing, e-commerce sites like Zappos, and social media like Goodreads, which Amazon bought in 2013.

Sean Gallup/Getty Images

CARNEGIE LIBRARIES
The Carnegie Library of Pittsburgh was first opened in 1895 with a $1 million donation from Andrew Carnegie (at the time, it was called Main Library). In total, eight branches were built in Pittsburgh as "Carnegie Libraries."

Although there is an increased interest in books, many people are concerned about the quality of books. Indeed, the economic clout of publishing houses run by large multinational corporations has made it more difficult for new authors and new ideas to gain a foothold. Often, editors and executives prefer to invest in commercially successful authors or those who have a built-in television, sports, or movie audience. In his book *The Death of Literature*, Alvin Kernan argues that serious literary work has been increasingly overwhelmed by the triumph of consumerism. People jump at craftily marketed celebrity biographies and popular fiction, he argues, but seldom read serious works. He contends that cultural standards have been undermined by marketing ploys that divert attention away from serious books and toward mass-produced works that are more easily consumed.[25]

DIGITAL JOB OUTLOOK

Media Professionals Speak about Jobs in the Publishing Industry

Joanna, Lead Technical Writer, Amazon's Consumer Web Site in Seattle

I have the unique opportunity to work directly with software developers to understand the needs of our customers and to write operations documentation to improve the overall customer experience. But, unlike at many other companies at which I have worked, here at Amazon, I am also encouraged to develop new, innovative ways of supporting our customer. My job is extremely fulfilling, as I know that my contributions, and opinions, have significant impact on the end user.

Jeremy Soldevilla, Publisher and Founder, Christopher Matthews Publishing

Build a platform for yourself.

- If you can, start before you graduate school. Are you a writer? Start a blog showcasing your writing. Post things regularly, no less than once a week. Include reviews of books. Join as many discussion groups on LinkedIn, Goodreads, Facebook, Twitter, and anywhere else that relates to writing and publishing.
- Join Guru.com as an editor.
- Create a Web site dedicated to book reviews—yours and/or other's reviews.
- Got Web design skills? Create a great Web site and focus the marketing of your design skills to self-publishers.
- Got art design skills? Create a Web site showcasing your portfolio and create some mock book covers.
- There is plenty of low-cost and free software available to format books and convert books to e-books. Get some, learn it, and offer your services online and through online author discussion groups.

Carolyn Zimatore, Talent Acquisition Manager, HarperCollins Publishers

Publishing internship experience is ideal, of course, but I do know that's not attainable for all. While in school, participate in extracurricular activities relating to publishing, like your school newspaper or literary magazine—that looks great on a résumé. If you are able to take courses on copyediting or anything digital—go for it! Also, one of the most valuable experiences you can have is to work at a bookstore.

Gina Gagliano, Marketing/Publicity Manager, First Second Books

You know when is a good time to be applying for an internship? . . . Applying at the beginning of the previous season is your best bet—which means September for winter/spring internships, January for summer internships, and May/June for fall internships. If you don't stick the timing on these things, you could be the best-ever intern possibility we've seen in our lives, but we're sorry—we've given the job to someone else already.

Yet books and reading have survived the challenge of visual and digital culture. Developments such as digital publishing, word processing, audio books, children's pictorial literature, and online services have integrated aspects of print and electronic culture into our daily lives. Most of these new forms carry on the legacy of books, transcending borders to provide personal stories, world history, and general knowledge to all who can read.

Since the early days of the printing press, books have helped us understand ideas and customs outside our own experiences. For democracy to work well, we must read. When we examine other cultures through books, we discover not only who we are and what we value but also who others are and what our common ties might be. ▶

CHAPTER REVIEW

COMMON THREADS

One of the Common Threads discussed in Chapter 1 is the commercial nature of mass media. Books have been products of a publishing industry in the United States since at least the early nineteenth century, but with the advent of digital technologies, the structure of the publishing industry is either evolving or dying. Is this a good or bad thing for the future of books?

Since the popularization of Gutenberg's printing press, there has always been some kind of gatekeeper in the publishing industry. Initially, it was religious institutions (which, for example, determined what would constitute the books of the Bible), then intellectuals, educators, and—with the development of publishing houses in the early nineteenth century—a fully formed commercial publishing industry.

Now, with the digital turn in publishing, anyone can be an author. Clay Shirky, a digital theorist at New York University, argues that this completely undercuts the work of publishers. "Publishing is going away," Shirky says. "Because the word 'publishing' means a cadre of professionals who are taking on the incredible difficulty and complexity and expense of making something public. That's not a job anymore. That's a button. There's a button that says 'publish,'

and when you press it, it's done."[26] Indeed, self-publishing is already a huge part of what the industry has become. As the *New York Times* noted, "Nearly 350,000 new print titles were published in 2011, and 150,000 to 200,000 of them were produced by self-publishing companies."[27] (Table 10.1 indicates that about 177,000 books were published in 2011, so nearly that many more books were self-published in the same year.)

An increase in the number of books in circulation is great for democracy, for the inclusion of more voices. But is there still value to the acquisition, editing, and marketing of books that publishers do? Are these traditional gatekeepers worth keeping around? Is it a legitimate concern that the quality of book content will suffer without publishers to find, develop, and promote the work of the best authors?

KEY TERMS

The definitions for the terms listed below can be found in the glossary at the end of the book.
The page numbers listed with the terms indicate where the term is highlighted in the chapter.

papyrus, 345
parchment, 345
codex, 345
manuscript culture, 345
illuminated manuscripts, 346
block printing, 346
printing press, 346
vellum, 346
paperback books, 347
dime novels, 347

pulp fiction, 347
linotype, 348
offset lithography, 348
trade books, 349
professional books, 350
textbooks, 350
mass market paperbacks, 351
instant book, 354
reference books, 354
university press, 355

e-book, 357
book challenge, 361
acquisitions editors, 362
subsidiary rights, 363
developmental editor, 363
copy editors, 363
design managers, 363
e-publishing, 367

REVIEW QUESTIONS

The History of Books, from Papyrus to Paperbacks

1. What distinguishes the manuscript culture of the Middle Ages from the oral and print eras in communication?

2. Why was the printing press such an important and revolutionary invention?

3. Why were books particularly important to women readers during the early periods of American history?

Modern Publishing and the Book Industry

4. Why did publishing houses develop?

5. Why is the trade book segment one of the most lucrative parts of the book industry?

6. What are the major issues that affect textbook publishing?

7. What has undermined the sales of printed encyclopedias?

8. What is the relationship between the book and movie industries?

9. Why did the Kindle succeed in the e-book market where other devices had failed?

Trends and Issues in Book Publishing

10. In what ways have e-books reimagined what a book can be?

11. What are the major issues in the debate over digitizing millions of books for Web search engines?

12. What is the difference between a book that is challenged and one that is banned?

The Organization and Ownership of the Book Industry

13. What are the current ownership patterns in the book industry? How do they affect the kinds of books that are published?

14. What are the general divisions within a typical publishing house?

15. What was the impact of the growth of book superstores on the rest of the bookstore industry?

16. How have online bookstores and e-books affected bookstores and the publishing industry?

17. What are the concerns over Amazon's powerful role in determining book pricing and having its own publishing divisions?

18. What is Andrew Carnegie's legacy in regard to libraries in the United States and elsewhere?

Books and the Future of Democracy

19. Why is an increasing interest in reading a signal for improved democratic life?

QUESTIONING THE MEDIA

1. As books shift to digital formats, what advantages of the bound-book format are we sacrificing?

2. Given the digital turn in the book industry, if you were to self-publish a book, what strategies would you use in marketing and distribution to help an audience find it?

3. Imagine that you are on a committee that oversees book choices for a high school library in your town. What policies do you think should guide the committee's selection of controversial books?

4. Why do you think the availability of television and cable hasn't substantially decreased the number of new book titles available each year? What do books offer that television doesn't?

5. What is the cultural significance of a bound volume, particularly a religious holy book, such as the Bible or Qur'an? If holy books are in digital form, does the format change their meaning?

LAUNCHPAD FOR *MEDIA & CULTURE*

Visit LaunchPad for *Media & Culture* *at* macmillanhighered.com/mediaculture10e *for additional learning tools:*

- REVIEW WITH LEARNINGCURVE
  LearningCurve, available on LaunchPad for *Media & Culture*, uses gamelike quizzing to help you master the concepts you need to learn from this chapter.

- VIDEO: TURNING THE PAGE: BOOKS GO DIGITAL
  Authors discuss how e-books are changing both how books are consumed and how they are written.

PART 4
The Business of Mass Media

The digital turn has brought about a shift in the locus of power in the mass media. For decades, the mass media have been dominated by giant corporations—such as Comcast (NBC Universal), Disney, Time Warner, News Corp., and CBS—which created the music, television, movies, and publications we consumed. Now a new digital market has grown up around them, displacing the way traditional mass media businesses operate, changing how advertising and public relations work, and breaking down the barriers of entry to start-up media companies:

- **Changes in the structure of media economics.** In just a few short years, legacy media companies, with their vast subsidiaries, have lost some of their power due to the rise of major digital companies, such as Apple, Amazon, Google, Microsoft, and Facebook. These digital corporations are the new media conglomerates, although they do not own many major content-creation companies. They control the devices and platforms that people use, thus controlling which media people consume. Traditional media companies now find themselves in a position in which they have to work with these companies (even if they balk at the 30 percent cut Apple takes, for example) or risk losing their audience.

- **The new digital ecosystem for advertising and public relations.** Professional media communicators are negotiating new terrain in the digital age, too. Not only are they figuring out what kinds of advertising or PR campaigns work best in the age of social media and mobile devices, but they also are dealing with an age in which it's much more difficult to control the flow of information and the framing of a story. This new environment can be good and bad. Everyone on the Internet is a potential customer but also a potential public critic.

- **Democracy and the redistribution of power.** The digital turn has allowed for more voices, more companies, and more creative start-ups, reversing many early concerns of mass media conglomerates. Now, content creators can enter the marketplace more easily: It's simple to get songs listed in the iTunes store, books placed in the Amazon catalog, and videos posted to YouTube.

THE BIG FIVE DIGITAL COMPANIES

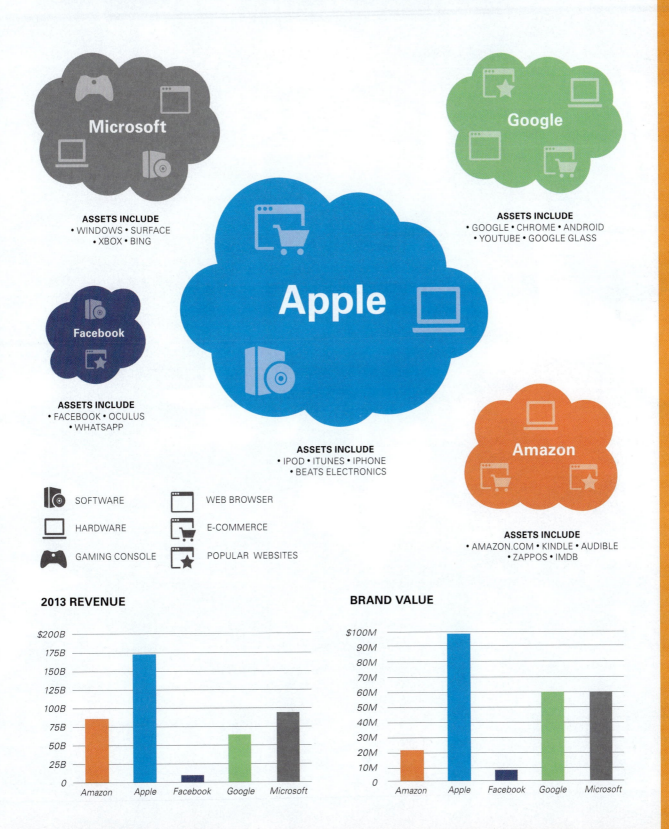

Microsoft

ASSETS INCLUDE
- WINDOWS • SURFACE
- XBOX • BING

Google

ASSETS INCLUDE
- GOOGLE • CHROME • ANDROID
- YOUTUBE • GOOGLE GLASS

Apple

ASSETS INCLUDE
- IPOD • ITUNES • IPHONE
- BEATS ELECTRONICS

Facebook

ASSETS INCLUDE
- FACEBOOK • OCULUS
- WHATSAPP

Amazon

ASSETS INCLUDE
- AMAZON.COM • KINDLE • AUDIBLE
- ZAPPOS • IMDB

SOFTWARE

HARDWARE

GAMING CONSOLE

WEB BROWSER

E-COMMERCE

POPULAR WEBSITES

2013 REVENUE

$200B	
175B	
150B	
125B	
100B	
75B	
50B	
25B	
0	

Amazon Apple Facebook Google Microsoft

BRAND VALUE

$100M	
90M	
80M	
70M	
60M	
50M	
40M	
30M	
20M	
10M	
0	

Amazon Apple Facebook Google Microsoft

11

Advertising and Commercial Culture

378
Early Developments in American Advertising

383
The Shape of U.S. Advertising Today

393
Persuasive Techniques in Contemporary Advertising

399
Commercial Speech and Regulating Advertising

408
Advertising, Politics, and Democracy

There's a saying in advertising: "Dollars always follow eyeballs."[1] That is, the advertising money flows to whichever medium is attracting people's attention. Over the past century, those eyeballs have shifted from newspapers and magazines to television to the Internet—and now the Internet as accessed via tablets and smartphones. With each new medium, advertisers get closer to us—in our workplaces, in our homes, and now in our hands with mobile devices. The next new medium could be even closer—right in front of our eyeballs.

Well, our right eyeball, for now. One of Google's most talked-about (and criticized) recent inventions, rolled out on a limited basis in 2014, is Google Glass, a mobile computer worn like eyeglasses, with a tiny camera and clear optical display over one's right eye. For $1,500, early adopters use voice commands to have "Glass" take a still photo, record video, send messages, search Google, and have a layer of *augmented reality* (for example, a map with directions) superimposed over one's view.

"In today's multi-screen world we face tremendous opportunities as a technology company focused on user benefit. It's an incredibly exciting time to be at Google," says Larry Page, CEO of Google.[2] But journalist Richard Tso reminds us that Google Glass might really be about more than just user benefit: "After the novelty of such a device begins to wear off, we can then examine how Google Glass may fit into the larger strategy down the road by Silicon Valley powerhouse Google. The company, after all, is an advertising company."[3]

With Glass, Google has invented a new screen for "today's multi-screen world" that can literally put ads right in front of our eyes. Imagine walking down a street, our view of shops and storefronts layered with translucent images of specials and sales. Would that be helpful or annoying? Google, which has always tried to be low key in its advertising style, will eventually find out. Richard Tso is even more concerned about information going in the other direction, from the Google Glass user back to the advertiser. Eye-tracking technology already exists and can determine where and for how long someone is looking. According to Tso, further advances in eye-tracking "will soon make it possible for ads to look right back at you, seeing where you look on a webpage and how long your gaze lingers on a banner or rich media advertisement for, say, Adidas or Starbucks."[4] Google Glass, if successful, could be a way for Google to further compete with its rival Apple. Google has been successful in making

advertising money from its popular search engine, but with Apple's self-enclosed app environments for its iPhone and iPod, Google sees the need for developing its own devices, to ensure more control over screens. Google, which is already the biggest advertising company in the world, bought AdMob, a company that serves ads to mobile screens, in 2010. With so many mobile phone and tablet devices (including Google's own Nexus 7 tablet) using the Android platform, Google has a ready network of devices for mobile advertising. Google hopes that Google Glass might become the next big device. Among the 2014 rollouts for "Glassware"—Google's nickname for its Glass apps—were Runtastic, a fitness app with a selection of workouts, and Duolingo, an app that promised game-based language learning.

Then again, Google Glass might not catch on. Beyond the hefty price tag, potential users may find it too intrusive to have ads delivered directly to their eyes and have their eyeballs tracked for data. Or perhaps people will look dorky in them. Google's key Glass partner, Leonardo Del Vecchio of Luxottica, the world's largest eyewear maker, said in September 2014, "I have not used Google Glass. It would embarrass me going around with that on my face. It would be OK in the disco, but I no longer go to the disco."[5]

If Google Glass does fail—or goes the way of disco—we can be certain of one thing: Advertisers will be looking for another way to follow our eyeballs.

▲ **TODAY, ADVERTISEMENTS ARE EVERYWHERE AND IN EVERY MEDIA FORM.** Ads take up more than half the space in most daily newspapers and consumer magazines. They are inserted into trade books and textbooks. They clutter Web sites on the Internet. They fill our mailboxes and wallpaper the buses we ride. Dotting the nation's highways, billboards promote fast-food and hotel chains, while neon signs announce the names of stores along major streets and strip malls. Ads are even found in the restrooms of malls, restaurants, and bars.

At local theaters and on DVDs, ads now precede the latest Hollywood movie trailers. Corporate sponsors spend millions for **product placement**: the purchase of spaces for particular goods to appear in a TV show, movie, or music video. Ads are part of a deejay's morning patter, and ads routinely interrupt our favorite TV and cable programs. By 2012, more than sixteen minutes of each hour of prime-time network television carried commercials, program promos, and public service announcements—an increase from thirteen minutes an hour in 1992. In addition, each hour of prime-time network TV carried about eleven minutes of product placements.[6] This means that about twenty-six minutes of each hour (or 43 percent) include some sort of paid sponsorship. According to the Food Marketing Institute, the typical supermarket's shelves are filled with thirty thousand to fifty thousand different brand-name packages, all functioning like miniature billboards. By some research estimates, the average American comes into contact with five thousand forms of advertising each day.[7]

Advertising comes in many forms, from classified ads to business-to-business ads, which provide detailed information on specific products. However, in this chapter, we will concentrate on the more conspicuous advertisements that shape product images and brand-name identities. Because so much consumer advertising intrudes into daily life, ads are often viewed in a negative light. Although business managers agree that advertising is the foundation of a healthy media economy—far preferable to government-controlled media—audiences routinely complain about how many ads they are forced to endure, and they increasingly find ways to avoid them, like zipping through television ads with TiVo and blocking pop-up ads with Web browsers. In response, market researchers routinely weigh consumers' tolerance—how long an ad or how many ads they are willing to tolerate to get "free" media content. Without consumer advertisements, however, mass communication industries would cease to function in their present forms. Advertising is the economic glue that holds most media industries together.

In this chapter, we will:

- Examine the historical development of advertising—an industry that helped transform numerous nations into consumer societies
- Look at the first U.S. ad agencies; early advertisements; and the emergence of packaging, trademarks, and brand-name recognition
- Consider the growth of advertising in the last century, such as the increasing influence of ad agencies and the shift to a more visually oriented culture
- Outline the key persuasive techniques used in consumer advertising
- Investigate ads as a form of commercial speech, and discuss the measures aimed at regulating advertising
- Look at political advertising and its impact on democracy

It's increasingly rare to find spaces in our society that don't contain advertising. As you read this chapter, think about your own exposure to advertising. What are some things you like or admire about advertising? For example, are there particular ad campaigns that give you enormous

THE "GOT MILK?" advertising campaign was originally designed by Goodby, Silverstein & Partners for the California Milk Processor Board in 1993. Since 1998, the National Milk Processor Board has licensed the "got milk?" slogan for its celebrity milk mustache ads, like this one.

Milk Processor Education Program

The game plan at breakfast.
got milk?
TheBreakfastProject.com

pleasure? How and when do ads annoy you? Can you think of any ways you intentionally avoid advertising? For more questions to help you understand the role of advertising in our lives, see "Questioning the Media" in the Chapter Review.

Early Developments in American Advertising

Advertising has existed since 3000 BCE, when shop owners in ancient Babylon hung outdoor signs carved in stone and wood so that customers could spot their stores. Merchants in early Egyptian society hired town criers to walk through the streets, announcing the arrival of ships and listing the goods on board. Archaeologists searching Pompeii, the ancient Italian city destroyed when Mount Vesuvius erupted in 79 CE, found advertising messages painted on walls. By 900 CE, many European cities featured town criers who not only called out the news of the day but also directed customers to various stores.

Other early media ads were on handbills, posters, and broadsides (long, newsprint-quality posters). English booksellers printed brochures and bills announcing new publications as early as the 1470s, when posters advertising religious books were tacked onto church doors. In 1622, print ads imitating the oral style of criers appeared in the first English newspapers. Announcing land deals and ship cargoes, the first newspaper ads in colonial America ran in the *Boston News-Letter* in 1704.

To distinguish their approach from the commercialism of newspapers, early magazines refused to carry advertisements. By the mid-nineteenth century, though, most magazines contained ads, and most publishers started magazines hoping to earn advertising dollars.

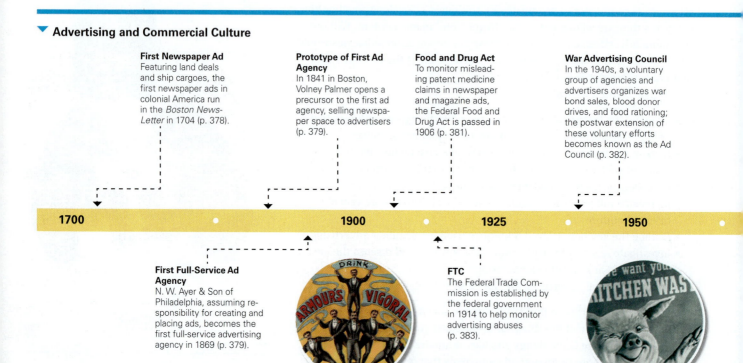

▼ **Advertising and Commercial Culture**

First Newspaper Ad
Featuring land deals and ship cargoes, the first newspaper ads in colonial America run in the *Boston News-Letter* in 1704 (p. 378).

Prototype of First Ad Agency
In 1841 in Boston, Volney Palmer opens a precursor to the first ad agency, selling newspaper space to advertisers (p. 379).

Food and Drug Act
To monitor misleading patent medicine claims in newspaper and magazine ads, the Federal Food and Drug Act is passed in 1906 (p. 381).

War Advertising Council
In the 1940s, a voluntary group of agencies and advertisers organizes war bond sales, blood donor drives, and food rationing; the postwar extension of these voluntary efforts becomes known as the Ad Council (p. 382).

| 1700 | | 1900 | | 1925 | | 1950 | |

First Full-Service Ad Agency
N. W. Ayer & Son of Philadelphia, assuming responsibility for creating and placing ads, becomes the first full-service advertising agency in 1869 (p. 379).

FTC
The Federal Trade Commission is established by the federal government in 1914 to help monitor advertising abuses (p. 383).

About 80 percent of these early advertisements covered three subjects: land sales, transportation announcements (stagecoach and ship schedules), and "runaways" (ads placed by farm and plantation owners whose slaves had fled).

The First Advertising Agencies

Until the 1830s, little need existed for elaborate advertising, as few goods and products were even available for sale. Before the Industrial Revolution, 90 percent of Americans lived in isolated areas and produced most of their own tools, clothes, and food. The minimal advertising that did exist usually featured local merchants selling goods and services in their own communities. In the United States, national advertising, which initially focused on patent medicines, didn't start in earnest until the 1850s, when railroads linking the East Coast to the Mississippi River valley began carrying newspapers, handbills, and broadsides—as well as national consumer goods—across the country.

The first American advertising agencies were newspaper **space brokers**, individuals who purchased space in newspapers and sold it to various merchants. Newspapers, accustomed to a 25 percent nonpayment rate from advertisers, welcomed the space brokers, who paid up front. Brokers usually received discounts of 15 to 30 percent but sold the space to advertisers at the going rate. In 1841, Volney Palmer opened a prototype of the first ad agency in Boston; for a 25 percent commission from newspaper publishers, he sold space to advertisers.

Advertising in the 1800s

The first full-service modern ad agency, N. W. Ayer & Son, worked primarily for advertisers and product companies rather than for newspapers. Opening in 1869 in Philadelphia, the agency helped create, write, produce, and place ads in selected newspapers and magazines. The traditional payment structure at this time had the agency collecting a fee from its advertising client for each ad placed; the fee covered the price that each media outlet charged for placement of

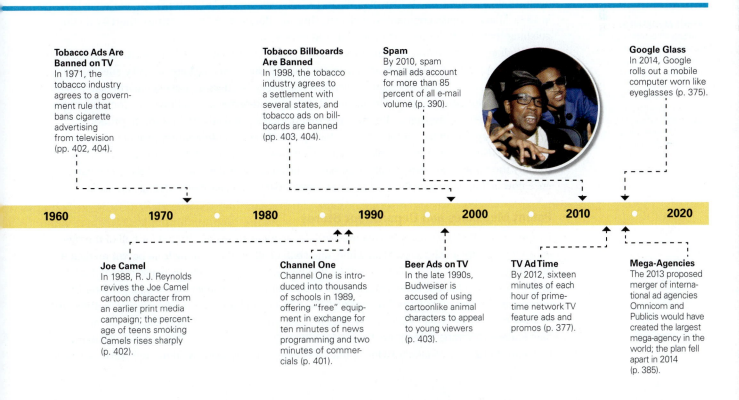

Tobacco Ads Are Banned on TV
In 1971, the tobacco industry agrees to a government rule that bans cigarette advertising from television (pp. 402, 404).

Tobacco Billboards Are Banned
In 1998, the tobacco industry agrees to a settlement with several states, and tobacco ads on billboards are banned (pp. 403, 404).

Spam
By 2010, spam e-mail ads account for more than 85 percent of all e-mail volume (p. 390).

Google Glass
In 2014, Google rolls out a mobile computer worn like eyeglasses (p. 375).

1960   1970   1980   1990   2000   2010   2020

Joe Camel
In 1988, R. J. Reynolds revives the Joe Camel cartoon character from an earlier print media campaign; the percentage of teens smoking Camels rises sharply (p. 402).

Channel One
Channel One is introduced into thousands of schools in 1989, offering "free" equipment in exchange for ten minutes of news programming and two minutes of commercials (p. 401).

Beer Ads on TV
In the late 1990s, Budweiser is accused of using cartoonlike animal characters to appeal to young viewers (p. 403).

TV Ad Time
By 2012, sixteen minutes of each hour of prime-time network TV feature ads and promos (p. 377).

Mega-Agencies
The 2013 proposed merger of international ad agencies Omnicom and Publicis would have created the largest mega-agency in the world; the plan fell apart in 2014 (p. 385).

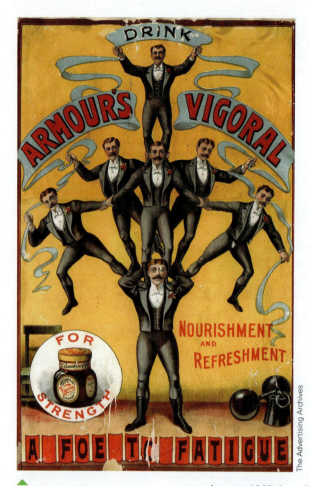

PATENT MEDICINES
Unregulated patent medicines, such as the one represented in this ad, created a bonanza for nineteenth-century print media in search of advertising revenue. After several muckraking magazine reports about deceptive patent medicine claims, Congress created the Food and Drug Administration in 1906.

the ad, plus a 15 percent commission for the agency. The more ads an agency placed, the larger the agency's revenue. Thus agencies had little incentive to buy fewer ads on behalf of their clients. Nowadays, however, many advertising agencies work for a flat fee, and some will agree to be paid on a performance basis.

Trademarks and Packaging

During the mid-1800s, most manufacturers served retail store owners, who usually set their own prices by purchasing goods in large quantities. Manufacturers, however, came to realize that if their products were distinctive and associated with quality, customers would ask for them by name. This would allow manufacturers to dictate prices without worrying about being undersold by stores' generic products or bulk items. Advertising let manufacturers establish a special identity for their products, separate from those of their competitors.

Like many ads today, nineteenth-century advertisements often created the impression of significant differences among products when in fact very few differences actually existed. But when consumers began demanding certain products—either because of quality or because of advertising—manufacturers were able to raise the prices of their goods. With ads creating and maintaining brand-name recognition, retail stores had to stock the desired brands.

One of the first brand names, Smith Brothers, has been advertising cough drops since the early 1850s. Quaker Oats, the first cereal company to register a trademark, has used the image of William Penn, the Quaker who founded Pennsylvania in 1681, to project a company image of honesty, decency, and hard work since 1877. Other early and enduring brands include Campbell Soup, which came along in 1869; Levi Strauss overalls in 1873; Ivory Soap in 1879; and Eastman Kodak film in 1888. Many of these companies packaged their products in small quantities, thereby distinguishing them from the generic products sold in large barrels and bins.

Product differentiation associated with brand-name packaged goods represents the single biggest triumph of advertising. Studies suggest that although most ads are not very effective in the short run, over time they create demand by leading consumers to associate particular brands with quality. Not surprisingly, building or sustaining brand-name recognition is the focus of many product-marketing campaigns. But the costs that packaging and advertising add to products generate many consumer complaints. The high price of many contemporary products results from advertising costs. For example, designer jeans that cost $150 (or more) today are made from roughly the same inexpensive denim that has outfitted farmworkers since the 1800s. The difference now is that more than 90 percent of the jeans' cost goes toward advertising and profit.

Patent Medicines and Department Stores

By the end of the 1800s, patent medicines and department stores accounted for half of the revenues taken in by ad agencies. Meanwhile, one-sixth of all print ads came from patent medicine and drug companies. Such ads ensured the financial survival of numerous magazines as "the role of the publisher changed from being a seller of a product to consumers to being a gatherer of consumers for the advertisers," according to Goodrum and Dalrymple in *Advertising in America.*[8] Bearing names like Lydia Pinkham's Vegetable Compound, Dr. Lin's Chinese Blood Pills, and William Radam's Microbe Killer, patent medicines were often made with water and 15 to 40 percent concentrations of ethyl alcohol. One patent medicine—Mrs. Winslow's Soothing Syrup—actually contained morphine. Powerful drugs in these medicines explain why people felt "better" after taking them; at the same time, they triggered lifelong addiction problems for many customers.

Many contemporary products, in fact, originated as medicines. Coca-Cola, for instance, was initially sold as a medicinal tonic and even contained traces of cocaine until 1903, when it was replaced by caffeine. Early Post and Kellogg's cereal ads promised to cure stomach and digestive problems. Many patent medicines made outrageous claims about what they could cure, leading to increased public cynicism. As a result, advertisers began to police their ranks and develop industry codes to restore customer confidence. Partly to monitor patent medicine claims, the Federal Food and Drug Act was passed in 1906.

Along with patent medicines, department store ads were also becoming prominent in newspapers and magazines. By the early 1890s, more than 20 percent of ad space was devoted to department stores. At the time, these stores were frequently criticized for undermining small shops and businesses, where shopkeepers personally served customers. The more impersonal department stores allowed shoppers to browse and find brand-name goods themselves. Because these stores purchased merchandise in large quantities, they could generally sell the same products for less. With increased volume and less money spent on individualized service, department store chains, like Target and Walmart today, undercut small local stores and put more of their profits into ads.

Advertising's Impact on Newspapers

With the advent of the Industrial Revolution, "continuous-process machinery" kept company factories operating at peak efficiency, helping produce an abundance of inexpensive packaged consumer goods.[9] The companies that produced those goods—Procter & Gamble, Colgate-Palmolive, Heinz, Borden, Pillsbury, Eastman Kodak, Carnation, and American Tobacco—were some of the first to advertise, and they remain major advertisers today (although many of these brand names have been absorbed by larger conglomerates).

The demand for newspaper advertising by product companies and retail stores significantly changed the ratio of copy at most newspapers. Whereas newspapers in the mid-1880s featured 70 to 75 percent news and editorial material and only 25 to 30 percent advertisements, by the early 1900s, more than half the space in daily papers was devoted to advertising. However, the recent recession hit newspapers hard: Their advertising revenue fell by half, from a peak of $49 billion in 2005 to $24 billion in 2013—as car, real estate, and help-wanted ads fell significantly.[10] For many papers, fewer ads meant smaller papers, not room for more articles. Some good news for newspapers in 2013, however, was that while ad dollars declined by 6.5 percent from 2012, circulation revenue—mostly from online growth and initiatives—grew almost 4 percent.

Promoting Social Change and Dictating Values

As U.S. advertising became more pervasive, it contributed to major social changes in the twentieth century. First, it significantly influenced the transition from a producer-directed to a consumer-driven society. By stimulating demand for new products, advertising helped manufacturers create new markets and recover product start-up costs quickly. From farms to cities, advertising spread the word—first in newspapers and magazines and later on radio and television.

© Bettmann/Corbis

WAR ADVERTISING COUNCIL
During World War II, the federal government engaged the advertising industry to create messages to support the U.S. war effort. Advertisers promoted the sale of war bonds; conservation of natural resources, such as tin and gasoline; and even saving kitchen waste so it could be fed to farm animals.

No one is jk or LOL now.

On the Road, Off the Phone.

National Safety Council

PUBLIC SERVICE ANNOUNCEMENTS
The Ad Council has been creating public service announcements (PSAs) since 1942. Supported by contributions from individuals, corporations, and foundations, the council's PSAs are produced pro bono by ad agencies. This PSA is the result of the Ad Council's long-standing relationship with the National Safety Council.

Second, advertising promoted technological advances by showing how new machines—such as vacuum cleaners, washing machines, and cars—could improve daily life. Third, advertising encouraged economic growth by increasing sales. To meet the demand generated by ads, manufacturers produced greater quantities, which reduced their costs per unit, although they did not always pass these savings along to consumers.

Appealing to Female Consumers

By the early 1900s, advertisers and ad agencies believed that women, who constituted 70 to 80 percent of newspaper and magazine readers, controlled most household purchasing decisions. (This is still a fundamental principle of advertising today.) Ironically, more than 99 percent of the copywriters and ad executives at that time were men, primarily based in Chicago and New York. They emphasized stereotyped appeals to women, believing that simple ads with emotional and even irrational content worked best. Thus early ad copy featured personal tales of "heroic" cleaning products and household appliances. The intention was to help female consumers feel good about defeating life's problems—an advertising strategy that endured throughout much of the twentieth century.

Dealing with Criticism

Although ad revenues fell during the Great Depression in the 1930s, World War II rejuvenated advertising. For the first time, the federal government bought large quantities of advertising space to promote U.S. involvement in a war. These purchases helped offset a decline in traditional advertising, as many industries had turned their attention and production facilities to the war effort.

Also during the 1940s, the industry began to actively deflect criticism that advertising created consumer needs that ordinary citizens never knew they had. Criticism of advertising grew as the industry appeared to be dictating values as well as driving the economy. To promote a more positive image, the industry developed the War Advertising Council—a voluntary group of agencies and advertisers that organized war bond sales, blood donor drives, and the rationing of scarce goods.

The postwar extension of advertising's voluntary efforts became known as the Ad Council. This organization has earned praise over the years for its Smokey the Bear campaign ("Only you can prevent forest fires"); its fund-raising campaign for the United Negro College Fund ("A mind is a terrible thing to waste"); and its "crash dummy" spots for the Department of Transportation, which substantially increased seat belt use. Choosing a dozen worthy causes annually, the Ad Council continues to produce pro bono *public service announcements* (PSAs) on a wide range of topics, including literacy, homelessness, drug addiction, smoking, and AIDS education.

Early Ad Regulation

The early 1900s saw the formation of several watchdog organizations. Partly to keep tabs on deceptive advertising, advocates in the business community in 1913 created the nonprofit Better Business Bureau, which now has more than one hundred branch offices in the United States. At the same time, advertisers wanted a formal service that tracked newspaper readership, guaranteed accurate audience measures, and ensured that papers would not overcharge ad agencies and their clients. As a result, publishers formed the Audit Bureau of Circulations (ABC) in 1914 (now known as the Alliance for Audited Media).

That same year, the government created the Federal Trade Commission (FTC), in part to help monitor advertising abuses. Thereafter, the industry urged self-regulatory measures in order to keep government interference at bay. For example, established in 1917, the American Association of Advertising Agencies (AAAA) tried to minimize government oversight by urging ad agencies to refrain from making misleading product claims.

Finally, the advent of television dramatically altered advertising. With this new visual medium, ads increasingly intruded on daily life. Critics also discovered that some agencies used **subliminal advertising**. This term, coined in the 1950s, refers to hidden or disguised print and visual messages that allegedly register in the subconscious and fool people into buying products. Noted examples of subliminal ads from that time include a "Drink Coca-Cola" ad embedded in a few frames of a movie and alleged hidden sexual activity drawn into liquor ads. Although research suggests that such ads are no more effective than regular ads, the National Association of Broadcasters banned the use of subliminal ads in 1958.

The Shape of U.S. Advertising Today

Until the 1960s, the shape and pitch of most U.S. ads were determined by a **slogan**, the phrase that attempts to sell a product by capturing its essence in words. With slogans such as "A Diamond Is Forever" (which De Beers first used in 1948), the visual dimension of ads was merely a complement. Eventually, however, through the influence of European design, television, and (now) multimedia devices, such as the iPad, images asserted themselves, and visual style became dominant in U.S. advertising and ad agencies.

The Influence of Visual Design

Just as a postmodern design phase developed in art and architecture during the 1960s and 1970s, a new design era began to affect advertising at the same time. Part of this visual revolution was imported from non-U.S. schools of design; indeed, ad-rich magazines such as *Vogue* and *Vanity Fair* increasingly hired European designers as art directors. These directors tended to be less tied to U.S. word-driven radio advertising because most European countries had government-sponsored radio systems with no ads.

By the early 1970s, agencies had developed teams of writers and artists, thus granting equal status to images and words in the creative process. By the mid-1980s, the visual techniques of MTV, which initially modeled its style on advertising, influenced many ads and most agencies. MTV promoted a particular visual aesthetic—rapid edits, creative camera angles, compressed narratives, and staged performances. Video-style ads soon saturated television and featured such prominent performers as Paula Abdul, Ray Charles, Michael Jackson, Elton John, and Madonna. The popularity of MTV's visual style also started a trend in the 1980s

MAD MEN
AMC's hit series *Mad Men* depicts the male-dominated world of Madison Avenue in the 1960s, as the U.S. consumer economy kicked into high gear and agencies developed ad campaigns for cigarettes, exercise belts, and presidential candidates. The show ended its run in 2015 after seven seasons and many awards.

Jaimie Trueblood/© AMC/Everett Collection

to license hit songs for commercial tie-ins. By the twenty-first century, a wide range of short, polished musical performances and familiar songs—including the work of Train (Samsung), the Shins (McDonald's), LMFAO (Kia Motors), and classic Louis Armstrong (Apple iPhone)—were routinely used in TV ads to encourage consumers not to click the remote control.

Most recently, the Internet and multimedia devices, such as computers, mobile phones, and portable media players, have had a significant impact on visual design in advertising. As the Web became a mass medium in the 1990s, TV and print designs often mimicked the drop-down menu of computer interfaces. In the twenty-first century, visual design has evolved in other ways, becoming more three-dimensional and interactive as full-motion, 3-D animation becomes a high-bandwidth multimedia standard. At the same time, design is also simpler, as ads and logos need to appear clearly on the small screens of smartphones and portable media players, and more international, as agencies need to appeal to the global audiences of many companies and therefore need to reflect styles from around the world.

Types of Advertising Agencies

About fourteen thousand ad agencies currently operate in the United States. In general, these agencies are classified as either **mega-agencies**—large ad firms that formed by merging several agencies and that maintain regional offices worldwide—or small **boutique agencies** that devote their talents to only a handful of select clients. With the economic crisis, both types of ad agencies suffered revenue declines in 2008 and 2009 but had slowly improved by 2013.

Mega-agencies

Mega-agencies provide a full range of services, from advertising and public relations to operating their own in-house radio and TV production studios. In 2014, the four global mega-agencies were WPP, Omnicom, Publicis, and Interpublic (see Figure 11.1).

FIGURE 11.1

GLOBAL REVENUE FOR THE WORLD'S LARGEST AGENCIES (IN BILLIONS OF DOLLARS)

Data from: Advertising Age Marketing Fact Pack 2014, *pp. 26–27.*

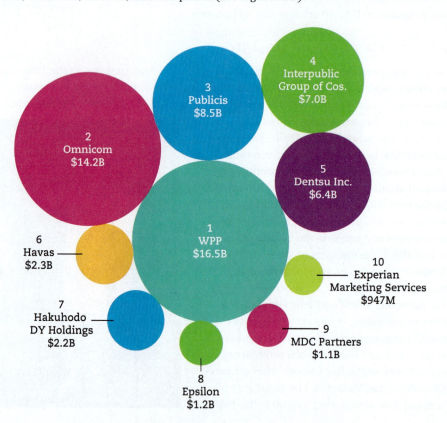

In 2013, Omnicom and Publicis announced a merger that would have created the world's largest mega-agency. But that plan fell apart in 2014, according to the *New York Times*, over a "mix of clashing personalities, disagreements about how the companies would be integrated and complications over legal and tax issues."[11] Based in New York, Omnicom in 2013 had more than 71,000 employees operating in more than 100 countries and currently owns the global advertising firms BBDO Worldwide, DDB Worldwide, and TBWA Worldwide. The company also owns three leading public relations agencies: Fleishman-Hillard, Ketchum, and Porter Novelli. The Paris-based Publicis Groupe has a global reach through agencies like Leo Burnett Worldwide, the British agency Saatchi & Saatchi, DigitasLBi, and the public relations firm MSL Group. Publicis employed more than 49,000 people worldwide in 2013.

The London-based WPP Group grew quickly in the 1980s with the purchases of J. Walter Thompson, the largest U.S. ad firm at the time; Hill & Knowlton, one of the largest U.S. public relations agencies; and Ogilvy & Mather Worldwide. In the 2000s, WPP Group continued its growth and acquired Young & Rubicam and Grey Global—both major U.S. ad firms. By 2013, WPP had 165,000 employees in 110 countries. The Interpublic Group, based in New York with 43,500 employees worldwide, holds global agencies like McCann Erickson (the top U.S. ad agency), FCB, and Lowe and Partners, and public relations firms Golin and Weber Shandwick.

This mega-agency trend has stirred debate among consumer and media watchdog groups. Some consider large agencies a threat to the independence of smaller firms, which are slowly being bought out. An additional concern is that these four firms now control more than half the distribution of advertising dollars globally. As a result, the cultural values represented by U.S. and European ads may undermine or overwhelm the values and products of developing countries. (See Figure 11.2 for a look at how advertising dollars are spent by medium.)

Boutique Agencies

The visual revolutions in advertising during the 1960s elevated the standing of designers and graphic artists, who became closely identified with the look of particular ads. Breaking

FIGURE 11.2

WHERE WILL THE ADVERTISING DOLLARS GO?*

*Years 2013–2017 are projections.

Data from: eMarketer, "US Total Media Ad Spend Inches Up, Pushed by Digital," August 22, 2013.

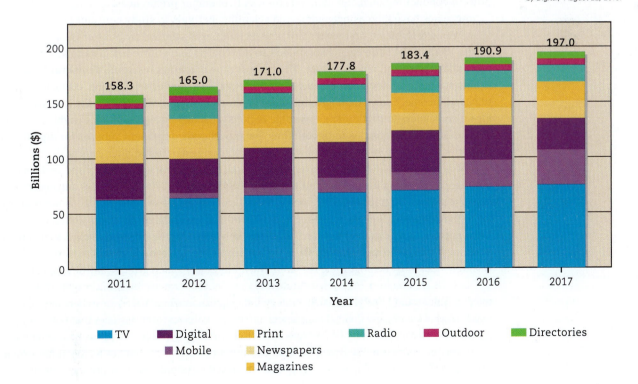

away from bigger agencies, many of these creative individuals formed small boutique agencies. Offering more personal services, the boutiques prospered, bolstered by innovative ad campaigns and increasing profits from TV accounts. By the 1980s, large agencies had bought up many of the boutiques. Nevertheless, these boutiques continue to operate as fairly autonomous subsidiaries within multinational corporate structures.

One independent boutique agency in Minneapolis, Peterson Milla Hooks (PMH), made its name with a boldly graphic national branding ad campaign for Target department stores. Target moved its business to another agency in 2011, but PMH—which employs only about sixty people—rebounded. By 2014, the agency's client list included Gap, Kohl's, Nine West, Mattel, Kmart, Sephora, Rooms To Go, Sleep Number, JCPenney, and Chico's.[12]

The Structure of Ad Agencies

Traditional ad agencies, regardless of their size, generally divide the labor of creating and maintaining advertising campaigns among four departments: account planning, creative development, media coordination, and account management. Expenses incurred for producing the ads are part of a separate negotiation between the agency and the advertiser. As a result of this commission arrangement, it generally costs most large-volume advertisers no more to use an agency than it does to use their own staff.

Account Planning, Market Research, and VALS

The account planner's role is to develop an effective advertising strategy by combining the views of the client, the creative team, and consumers. Consumers' views are the most difficult to understand, so account planners coordinate **market research** to assess the behaviors and attitudes of consumers toward particular products long before any ads are created. Researchers may study everything from possible names for a new product to the size of the copy for a print ad. Researchers also test new ideas and products with consumers to get feedback before developing final ad strategies. In addition, some researchers contract with outside polling firms to conduct regional and national studies of consumer preferences.

Agencies have increasingly employed scientific methods to study consumer behavior. In 1932, Young & Rubicam first used statistical techniques developed by pollster George Gallup. By the 1980s, most large agencies retained psychologists and anthropologists to advise them on human nature and buying habits. The earliest type of market research, **demographics**, mainly studied and documented audience members' age, gender, occupation, ethnicity, education, and income. Today, demographic data are much more specific. They make it possible to locate consumers in particular geographic regions—usually by zip code. This enables advertisers and product companies to target ethnic neighborhoods or affluent suburbs for direct mail, point-of-purchase store displays, or specialized magazine and newspaper inserts.

Demographic analyses provide advertisers with data on people's behavior and social status but reveal little about feelings and attitudes. By the 1960s and 1970s, advertisers and agencies began using **psychographics**, a research approach that attempts to categorize consumers according to their attitudes, beliefs, interests, and motivations. Psychographic analysis often relies on **focus groups**, a small-group interview technique in which a moderator leads a discussion about a product or an issue, usually with six to twelve people. Because focus groups are small and less scientific than most demographic research, the findings from such groups may be suspect.

In 1978, the Stanford Research Institute (SRI), now called Strategic Business Insights (SBI), instituted its **Values and Lifestyles (VALS)** strategy. Using questionnaires, VALS researchers measured psychological factors and divided consumers into types. VALS research assumes that not every product suits every consumer and encourages advertisers to vary their sales slants to find market niches.

Over the years, the VALS system has been updated to reflect changes in consumer orientations (see Figure 11.3). The most recent system classifies people by their primary consumer

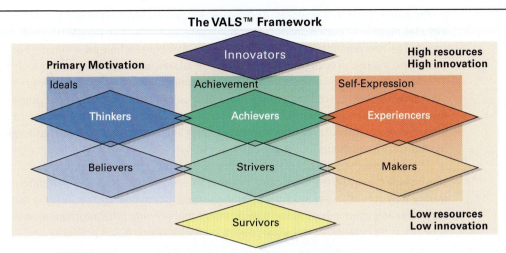

The VALS™ Framework

Innovators

Primary Motivation — High resources / High innovation

Ideals · Achievement · Self-Expression

Thinkers · Achievers · Experiencers

Believers · Strivers · Makers

Survivors — Low resources / Low innovation

VALS™ Types and Characteristics

Innovators Innovators are successful, sophisticated, take-charge people with high self-esteem and abundant resources. They exhibit all three primary motivations in varying degrees. They are change leaders and are the most receptive to new ideas and technologies. They are very active consumers, and their purchases reflect cultivated tastes for upscale, niche products and services.

Thinkers Thinkers are motivated by ideals. They are mature, satisfied, comfortable, and reflective people who value order, knowledge, and responsibility. They tend to be well educated and actively seek out information in the decision-making process. They are well informed about world and national events and are alert to opportunities to broaden their knowledge.

Achievers Motivated by the desire for achievement, Achievers have goal-oriented lifestyles and a deep commitment to career and family. Their social lives reflect this focus and are structured around family, their place of worship, and work. Achievers live conventional lives, are politically conservative, and respect authority and the status quo. They value consensus, predictability, and stability over risk, intimacy, and self-discovery.

Experiencers Experiencers are motivated by self-expression. As young, enthusiastic, and impulsive consumers, Experiencers quickly become enthusiastic about new possibilities but are equally quick to cool. They seek variety and excitement, savoring the new, the offbeat, and the risky. Their energy finds an outlet in exercise, sports, outdoor recreation, and social activities.

Believers Like Thinkers, Believers are motivated by ideals. They are conservative, conventional people with concrete beliefs based on traditional, established codes: family, religion, community, and the nation. Many Believers express moral codes that are deeply rooted and literally interpreted. They follow established routines, organized in large part around home, family, community, and social or religious organizations to which they belong.

Strivers Strivers are trendy and fun loving. Because they are motivated by achievement, Strivers are concerned about the opinions and approval of others. Money defines success for Strivers, who don't have enough of it to meet their desires. They favor stylish products that emulate the purchases of people with greater material wealth. Many see themselves as having a job rather than a career, and a lack of skills and focus often prevents them from moving ahead.

Makers Like Experiencers, Makers are motivated by self-expression. They express themselves and experience the world by working on it—building a house, raising children, fixing a car, or canning vegetables—and have enough skill and energy to carry out their projects successfully. Makers are practical people who have constructive skills and value self-sufficiency. They live within a traditional context of family, practical work, and physical recreation and have little interest in what lies outside that context.

Survivors Survivors live narrowly focused lives. With few resources with which to cope, they often believe that the world is changing too quickly. They are comfortable with the familiar and are primarily concerned with safety and security. Because they must focus on meeting needs rather than fulfilling desires, Survivors do not show a strong primary motivation.

FIGURE 11.3

VALS TYPES AND CHARACTERISTICS

Data from: Strategic Business Insights, 2010, http://strategicbusinessinsights.com/vals/ustypes.shtml.

motivations: ideals, achievement, or self-expression. The ideals-oriented group, for instance, includes *thinkers*—"mature, satisfied, comfortable, and reflective people who value order, knowledge, and responsibility." VALS and similar research techniques ultimately provide advertisers with microscopic details about which consumers are most likely to buy which products.

Agencies and clients—particularly auto manufacturers—have relied heavily on VALS to determine the best placement for ads. VALS data suggest, for example, that *achievers* and *experiencers* watch more sports and news programs; these groups prefer luxury cars or sport-utility vehicles. *Thinkers*, on the other hand, favor TV dramas and documentaries and like the functionality of minivans or the gas efficiency of hybrids.

VALS researchers do not claim that most people fit neatly into a category. But many agencies believe that VALS research can give them an edge in markets where few differences in quality may actually exist among top-selling brands. Consumer groups, wary of such research, argue that too many ads promote only an image and provide little information about a product's price, its content, or the work conditions under which it was produced.

Creative Development

Teams of writers and artists—many of whom regard ads as a commercial art form—make up the nerve center of the advertising business. The creative department outlines the rough sketches for print and online ads and then develops the words and graphics. For radio, the creative side prepares a working script, generating ideas for everything from choosing the narrator's voice to determining background sound effects. For television, the creative department develops a **storyboard**, a sort of blueprint or roughly drawn comic-strip version of the potential ad. For digital media, the creative team may develop Web sites, interactive tools, flash games, downloads, and **viral marketing**—short videos or other content that (marketers hope) quickly gains widespread attention as users share it with friends online or by word of mouth.

Often the creative side of the business finds itself in conflict with the research side. In the 1960s, for example, both Doyle Dane Bernbach (DDB) and Ogilvy & Mather downplayed research; they championed the art of persuasion and what "felt right." Yet DDB's simple ads for Volkswagen Beetles in the 1960s were based on weeks of intensive interviews with VW workers as well as on creative instincts. The campaign was remarkably successful in establishing the first niche for a foreign car manufacturer in the United States. Although sales of the VW Bug had been growing before the ad campaign started, the successful ads helped Volkswagen preempt the Detroit auto industry's entry into the small-car field.

Both the creative and the strategic sides of the business acknowledge that they cannot predict with any certainty which ads and which campaigns will succeed. Agencies say ads work best by slowly creating brand-name identities—by associating certain products over time with quality and reliability in the minds of consumers. Some economists, however, believe that much of the money spent on advertising is ultimately wasted because it simply encourages consumers to change from one brand name to another. Such switching may lead to increased profits for a particular manufacturer, but it has little positive impact on the overall economy.

Media Coordination: Planning and Placing Advertising

Ad agency media departments are staffed by media planners and **media buyers**: people who choose and purchase the types of media that are best suited to carry a client's ads, reach the targeted audience, and measure the effectiveness of those ad placements. For instance, a company like Procter & Gamble, currently the world's leading advertiser, displays its more than three hundred major brands—most of them household products like Crest toothpaste and Pampers diapers—on TV shows viewed primarily by women. To reach male viewers, however, media buyers encourage beer advertisers to spend their ad budgets on cable and network sports programming, evening talk radio, or sports magazines.

Along with commissions or fees, advertisers often add incentive clauses to their contracts with agencies, raising the fee if sales goals are met and lowering it if goals are missed. Incentive clauses can sometimes encourage agencies to conduct repetitive **saturation advertising**, in which a variety of media are inundated with ads aimed at target audiences. The initial Miller Lite beer campaign ("Tastes great, less filling"), which used humor and retired athletes to reach its male audience, became one of the most successful saturation campaigns in media history. It ran from 1973 to 1991 and included television and radio spots, magazine and newspaper ads, and billboards and point-of-purchase store displays. The excessive repetition of the campaign helped light beer overcome a potential image problem: being viewed as watered-down beer unworthy of "real" men.

The cost of advertising, especially on network television, increases each year. The Super Bowl remains the most expensive program for purchasing television advertising, with thirty seconds of time costing on average $4 million in 2014 on Fox—up from $3.8 million in 2013. (The network also reported that in 2014, the big game generated 25.3 million Tweets.) Running a thirty-second ad during a national prime-time TV show can cost from $50,000 to more than $500,000, depending on the popularity and ratings of the program. The prime-time average for a thirty-second TV spot was $112,100 in 2014, down from an all-time high of $129,600 in the prerecession year 2005.[13] (See "Case Study: Hey, Super Bowl Sponsors: Your Ads Are Already Forgotten," page 395.)

Account and Client Management

Client liaisons, or **account executives**, are responsible for bringing in new business and managing the accounts of established clients, including overseeing budgets and the research, creative, and media planning work done on their campaigns. This department also oversees new ad campaigns in which several agencies bid for a client's business, coordinating the presentation of a proposed campaign and various aspects of the bidding process, such as determining what a series of ads will cost a client. Account executives function as liaisons between the advertiser and the agency's creative team. Because most major companies maintain their

CREATIVE ADVERTISING
The New York ad agency Doyle Dane Bernbach created a famous series of print and television ads for Volkswagen beginning in 1959 (*below, left*) and helped usher in an era of creative advertising that combined a single-point sales emphasis with bold design, humor, and honesty. Arnold Worldwide, a Boston agency, continued the highly creative approach with its clever, award-winning "Drivers wanted" campaign for the New Beetle (*below*).

own ad departments to handle everyday details, account executives also coordinate activities between their agency and a client's in-house personnel.

The advertising business is volatile, and account departments are especially vulnerable to upheavals. One industry study conducted in the mid-1980s indicated that client accounts stayed with the same agency for about seven years on average, but since the late 1980s, clients have changed agencies much more often. Clients routinely conduct **account reviews**, the process of evaluating and reinvigorating a product's image by reviewing an ad agency's existing campaign or by inviting several new agencies to submit new campaign strategies, which may lead the product company to switch agencies. For example, when General Motors restructured its business in 2010, it put its advertising account for Chevrolet under review. Campbell Ewald (a subsidiary of Interpublic) had held the Chevy account since 1919, creating such campaigns as "The Heartbeat of America" and "Like a Rock," but after the review, it lost the $30 million account to Publicis.[14]

Trends in Online Advertising

The earliest form of Web advertising appeared in the mid-1990s and featured *banner ads*, the printlike display ads that load across the top or side of a Web page. Since that time, other formats have emerged, including video ads, sponsorships, and "rich media"—like pop-up ads, pop-under ads, flash multimedia ads, and **interstitials**, which pop up in new screen windows as a user clicks to a new Web page. Other forms of Internet advertising include classified ads and e-mail ads. Unsolicited commercial e-mail—known as **spam**—accounted for more than 85 percent of e-mail messages by 2010.

Paid search advertising has become the dominant format of Web advertising. Even though their original mission was to provide impartial search results, search sites such as Google, Yahoo!, and Bing have quietly morphed into advertising companies, selling sponsored links associated with search terms and distributing online ads to affiliated Web pages.[15]

Back in 2004, digital ads accounted for just over 4 percent of global ad spending. By 2012, the Internet had gained an 18 percent share of worldwide ad spending and was projected to become the second-largest global advertising medium in 2013, behind only television. In the United States, the Internet accounted for 19.1 percent of ad spending in 2012, making it the second-largest advertising medium, behind television.[16] According to an *Adweek* projection, spending on digital ads globally was excepted to grow to 17 percent in 2014, "marking the first

FIGURE 11.4

SHARE OF GLOBAL AD SPENDING BY MEDIUM

Data from: ZenithOptimedia, in Ricardo Bilton, "The Surprising State of Digital Ad Spending in 5 Charts," Digiday, June 17, 2014, http://digiday.com/brands/present-future-digital-ad-spending-5-charts/.

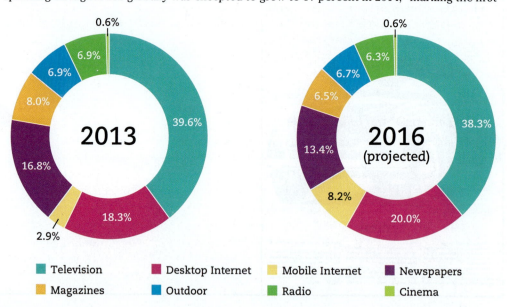

time digital will make up more than one-quarter of media spend."[17]

Online Advertising Challenges Traditional Media

Because Internet advertising is the leading growth area, advertising mega-agencies have added digital media agencies and departments to develop and sell ads online. For example, WPP has 24/7 Media and Xaxis, Omnicom owns Proximity Worldwide, Publicis has Digitas LBi and Razorfish, and Interpublic operates R/GA. Realizing the potential of their online ad businesses, major Web services have also aggressively expanded into the advertising market by acquiring smaller Internet advertising agencies. Google bought DoubleClick, the biggest online ad server; Yahoo! purchased Right Media, which auctions online ad space; and Microsoft acquired aQuantive, an online ad server and network that enables advertisers to place ads on multiple Web sites with a single buy. Google, as the top search engine, has surpassed the traditional mega-agencies in revenue, earning $59 billion in 2013, with almost all of that coming from advertising. Facebook, the top social networking site, is not yet in Google's league but remains poised to become a bigger advertising threat with an audience of over 1.3 billion users worldwide in 2014. Facebook earned $7.8 billion in 2013, most of that profit also coming from ads.[18]

Facebook has made its biggest strides in mobile advertising. While Google accounted for nearly 32 percent of all online global ad spending in 2013—over $120 billion—Facebook finished in second place, with roughly 6 percent of the total spent on online global advertising that year. In 2014, the *New York Times* reported that Facebook was closing the mobile gap, noting that the social media site accounted for nearly 16 percent of mobile advertising dollars in the previous year, while Google's share had dropped.[19]

As the Internet draws people's attention away from traditional mass media, leading advertisers are moving more of their ad campaigns and budget dollars to digital media. For example, the CEO of consumer product giant Unilever, a company with more than four hundred brands (including Dove, Hellmann's, and Lipton) and a multibillion-dollar advertising budget, doubled its spending on digital media back in 2010, since customers were spending much more time on the Internet and mobile phones. "I think you need to fish where the fish are," the Unilever CEO said. "So I've made it fairly clear that I'm driving Unilever to be at the leading edge of digital marketing."[20]

Online Marketers Target Individuals

Internet ads offer many advantages to advertisers, compared to ads in traditional media outlets like newspapers, magazines, radio, or television. Perhaps the biggest advantage—and potentially the most disturbing part for citizens—is that marketers can develop consumer profiles that direct targeted ads to specific Web site visitors. They do this by collecting information about each Internet user through cookies (see Chapter 2 for more on cookies) and online surveys. For example, when an ESPN.com contest requires you to fill out a survey to be eligible to win sports tickets, or when washingtonpost.com requires that you create an account for free access to the site, marketers use that information to build a profile about you. The cookies they attach to your profile allow them to track your activities on a certain site. They can also add to your profile by tracking what you search for and even by mining your profiles and data

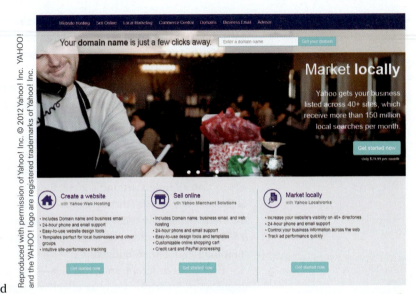

ONLINE ADS are mostly placed by large Internet companies like Google, Yahoo!, Microsoft, and AOL. Such services have allowed small businesses access to more customers than traditional advertising because the online ads are often cheaper to produce and are shown only to targeted users.

LaunchPad ⊙

macmillanhighered.com /mediaculture10e

Advertising in the Digital Age
This video discusses how ads evolve to overcome resistance to advertising. **Discussion:** Do you recall many ads from the last few times you used the Internet? What do you think this might mean for advertisers?

on social networking sites. Agencies can also add online and retail sales data (what you bought and where) to user profiles to create an unprecedented database, largely without your knowledge. Such data mining is a boon to marketers, but it is very troubling to consumer privacy advocates.

Internet advertising agencies can also track ad *impressions* (how often ads are seen) and *click-throughs* (how often ads are clicked on). This provides advertisers with much more specific data on the number of people who not only viewed the ad but also showed real interest by clicking on it. For advertisers, online ads are more beneficial because they are more precisely targeted and easily measured. For example, an advertiser can use Google AdWords to create small ads that are linked to selected key words and geographic targeting (from global coverage to a small radius around a given location). AdWords tracks and graphs the performance of the ad's key words (through click-through and sales rates) and lets the advertiser update the campaign at any time. This kind of targeted advertising enables smaller companies with a $500 budget, for example, to place their ads in the same location as larger companies with multimillion-dollar ad budgets.

Beyond computers, smartphones—the "third screen" for advertisers—are of increasing importance. Smartphones offer effective targeting to individuals, as does Internet advertising, but they also offer advertisers the bonus of tailoring ads according to either a specific geographic location (e.g., a restaurant ad goes to someone in close proximity) or the user demographic, since wireless providers already have that information. Google has also developed unique applications for mobile advertising and searching. For example, the Google Goggles smartphone app enables the user to take a photo of an object—such as a book cover, a landmark, a logo, or text—and then have Google return related search results. Google's Voice Search app lets users speak their search terms. Such apps are designed to maintain Google's dominant search engine position (which generates most of its profits) on the increasingly important mobile platform.

Advertising Invades Social Media

Social media, such as Facebook, Twitter, and Foursquare, provide a wealth of data for advertisers to mine. These sites and apps create an unprecedented public display of likes, dislikes, locations, and other personal information. And advertisers are using such information to further refine their ability to send targeted ads that might interest users. Facebook and other sites (like Hulu) go even further by asking users if they liked the ad or not. For example, clicking off a display ad in Facebook results in the question "Why didn't you like it?" followed by the choices "uninteresting," "misleading," "offensive," "repetitive," and "other." All that information goes straight back to advertisers so they can revise their advertising and try to engage you the next time. Beyond allowing advertisers to target and monitor their ad campaigns, most social media encourage advertisers to create their own online identity. For example, Ben & Jerry's Ice Cream's Facebook page has more than seven million "friends." Despite appearances, such profiles and identities still constitute a form of advertising and serve to promote products to a growing online audience for virtually no cost.

Companies and organizations also buy traditional paid advertisements on social media sites. A major objective of their *paid media* is to get *earned media*, or to convince online consumers to promote products on their own. Imagine that the environmental group the National Resources Defense Council buys an ad on Facebook that attracts your interest. That's a successful paid media ad for the council, but it's even more effective if it becomes earned media—that is, when you mark that you "Like" it, you essentially give the organization a personal endorsement. Knowing you like the ad, your friends view it; as they pass it along, it gets more earned media and eventually becomes viral—an even greater advertising achievement. As the Nielsen Media rating service says about online earned media, "Study after study has shown that consumers trust their friends and peers more than anyone else when it comes to making a purchase decision."[21] Social media are helping advertisers use such personal endorsements to further their own products and marketing messages—basically, letting consumers do the work for them.

A recent controversy in online advertising is whether people have to disclose if they are being paid to promote a product. For example, bloggers often review products or restaurants as part of their content. Some bloggers with large followings have been paid (either directly or by "gifts" of free products or trips) to give positive reviews or promote products on their site. When such instances, dubbed "blog-ola" by the press, came to light in 2008 and 2009, the bloggers argued that they did not have to reveal that they were being compensated for posting their opinions. At the time, they were right. However, in 2009, the Federal Trade Commission released new guidelines that require bloggers to disclose when an advertiser is compensating them to discuss a product. In 2010, a similar controversy erupted when it was revealed that many celebrities were being paid to tweet about their "favorite" products. One of Facebook's more recent ad ventures is called "sponsored stories." The way this works, according to the *New York Times*, is that companies, including Amazon, "pay Facebook to generate . . . automated ads" when a user clicks on the "Like" button for a Facebook participating brand partner or "references them in some other way." Sponsors and product companies like this service because they save money, since "no creative work is involved." However, in 2012, this practice resulted in Facebook's settling a state of California class action suit out of court. The lead plaintiff in the case, a costume designer from Seattle, innocently clicked the "Like" button for an online language course offered by Rosetta Stone. Then several months later, according to the *Times*, "she showed up in an ad for Rosetta Stone on her friends' Facebook pages."[22] Part of the case involved her resentment about not consenting to be used in an ad or receiving any compensation. As new ways to advertise or sponsor products through social media continue to develop, consumers need to keep a careful eye out for what is truly a friendly recommendation from a friend and what is advertising.

FOURSQUARE is using its recent popularity to increase revenues by partnering with businesses to provide "specials" to Foursquare users and "mayors." While it may seem like a great deal to offer free snacks or drinks to users, what Foursquare is really offering to businesses ("venues") is the chance to mine data and "be able to track how your venue is performing over time thanks to [Foursquare's] robust set of venue analytics."

© 2014, Foursquare Labs, Inc. All foursquare® logos and trademarks displayed are the property of Foursquare Labs, Inc.

Persuasive Techniques in Contemporary Advertising

Ad agencies and product companies often argue that the main purpose of advertising is to inform consumers about available products in a straightforward way. Most consumer ads, however, merely create a mood or tell stories about products without revealing much else. A one-page magazine ad, a giant billboard, or a thirty-second TV spot gives consumers little information about how a product was made, how much it costs, or how it compares with similar brands. In managing space and time constraints, advertising agencies engage in a variety of persuasive techniques.

Conventional Persuasive Strategies

One of the most frequently used advertising approaches is the **famous-person testimonial**, in which a product is endorsed by a well-known person. Famous endorsers include Justin Timberlake for Bud Light, Taylor Swift for Diet Coke, and Beyoncé for Pepsi. Athletes earn some of the biggest endorsement contracts. For example, Chicago Bulls player Derrick Rose has a

Denis Doyle/Getty Images for Kelloggs

▲
FAMOUS-PERSON TESTIMONIALS
Olympic glory comes not just with medals but with endorsement deals. Members of the USA's slopestyle skiing team, at the 2014 Winter Olympics in Sochi, appeared on a special-edition box of Kellogg's Corn Flakes.

$260 million, fourteen-year deal with Adidas, the same shoe company that has a $160 million deal with now-retired soccer star David Beckham. Tiger Woods remains one of the leading endorsers, despite his personal scandals in 2009. Although some sponsors—including Accenture, Gatorade, and Gillette—dropped him, companies such as Nike and Rolex either stayed with him or sought him out in deals that still totaled over $60 million a year in 2014—down from $80 million in 2012.

Another technique, the **plain-folks pitch**, associates a product with simplicity. Over the years, Volkswagen ("Drivers wanted"), General Electric ("We bring good things to life"), and Microsoft ("I'm a PC and Windows 7 was my idea") have each used slogans that stress how new technologies fit into the lives of ordinary people. In a way, the Facebook technique of sponsored stories fits this model, since it depends on friends' endorsements of products rather than the words or images of stars or athletes.

By contrast, the **snob-appeal approach** attempts to persuade consumers that using a product will maintain or elevate their social status. Advertisers selling jewelry, perfume, clothing, and luxury automobiles often use snob appeal. For example, the pricey bottled water brand Fiji ran ads in *Esquire* and other national magazines that said, "The label says Fiji because it's not bottled in Cleveland"—a jab intended to favorably compare the water bottled in the South Pacific to the drinking water of an industrial city in Ohio. (Fiji ended up withdrawing the ad after the Cleveland Water Department released test data showing that its water was more pure than Fiji water.)

Another approach, the **bandwagon effect**, points out in exaggerated claims that *everyone* is using a particular product. Brands that refer to themselves as "America's favorite" or "the best" imply that consumers will be left behind if they ignore these products. A different technique, the **hidden-fear appeal**, plays on consumers' sense of insecurity. Deodorant, mouthwash, and shampoo ads frequently invoke anxiety, pointing out that only a specific product could relieve embarrassing personal hygiene problems and restore a person to social acceptability.

A final ad strategy, used more in local TV and radio campaigns than in national ones, has been labeled **irritation advertising**: creating product-name recognition by being annoying or obnoxious. Although both research and common sense suggest that irritating ads do not work very well, there have been exceptions. In the 1950s and 1960s, for instance, an aspirin company ran a TV ad illustrating a hammer pounding inside a person's brain. Critics and the product's own agency suggested that people bought the product, which sold well, to get relief from the ad as well as from their headaches. On the regional level, irritation ads are often used by appliance discount stores or local car dealers, who dress in outrageous costumes and yell at the camera.

The Association Principle

Historically, American car advertisements have shown automobiles in natural settings—on winding roads that cut through rugged mountain passes or across shimmering wheat fields—but rarely on congested city streets or in other urban settings where most driving actually occurs. Instead, the car—an example of advanced technology—merges seamlessly into the natural world.

This type of advertising exemplifies the **association principle**, a widely used persuasive technique that associates a product with a positive cultural value or image even if it has little

Hey, Super Bowl Sponsors: Your Ads Are Already Forgotten

by Eric Chemi

With Super Bowl ad rates averaging $4 million per 30 seconds, total spending for commercials during this year's game approached $300 million. Here's the problem: Most of those commercials have already been forgotten. A survey of audience respondents conducted by marketing-research firm Db5 for *Bloomberg Businessweek* suggests they remembered less than 10 percent of Sunday's commercials. Despite what some so-called expert panels say about why certain ads are more successful than others, it's likely those results are too biased or subjective to tell us which ads were truly memorable. Db5 surveyed 504 people who watched the game in its entirety, and the results are surprising.

When asked to recall as many companies as possible that had ads during the big game, the average viewer in the survey could name only 5.4 brands. With more than 50 companies buying ads, that means less than 10 percent were recalled. The top winners were Budweiser, Doritos, Coca-Cola, PepsiCo, and GoDaddy—the only brands with viewer recall rates of more than 25 percent. Just 12 companies saw more than 10 percent recollection rates; the vast majority saw less than 10 percent recall. Even when viewers were given a sample list of advertisers and asked whether they remembered seeing an ad for each company, only 49 percent of those ads were recalled on average.

Daniel Goldstein, Db5's chief strategy officer, is a former ad executive who has worked on several major Super Bowl campaigns (Pepsi, Doritos, Visa). He says everybody is trying to copy the one-hit-wonder approach of Apple's famous "1984" ad. "Apple was the first to prove you could air a commercial only one time, during the Super Bowl, and have it bring you a ton of follow-up attention, praise, and sales," he says. Since then, that phenomenon has created a monster. Talking animals, talking babies, talking animal babies, big celebrities, bikinis, big-name Hollywood directors—the list of gimmicks is endless. Most of the audience can't keep up with all the tricks, and almost all the ads are quickly forgotten.

Some trends could have made a difference. Consistency may have been a factor; the most-remembered commercials came from companies who buy Super Bowl ads on an annual basis, such as Budweiser, Doritos, Coke, Pepsi, and GoDaddy. Another theory says that ads can be remembered better with advanced viewings, because they would give audiences more chances to see and process the spot. According to the data, however, that did not turn out to be the case. Ads that were seen for the first time did just as well as previously viewed ads.

The mathematical question for companies: Is 10 percent recall among 100 million people worth $4 million? With the increase of media fragmentation, there are so few opportunities to reach so many viewers at once. Goldstein says that this is not a knock against the Super Bowl as a platform for advertisers, but rather a signal that advertisers should not waste such a big opportunity for which they paid big bucks. The one trend that does seem to work is consistently showing up year after year, making the money a worthwhile investment in the long run. If companies want to go big, they should be going big every year. ◢

Source: Eric Chemi, "Hey, Super Bowl Sponsors: Your Ads Are Already Forgotten," Bloomberg Businessweek, *February 3, 2014, www .businessweek.com/articles/2014-02-03/hey-super -bowl-sponsors-your-ads-are-already-forgotten.*

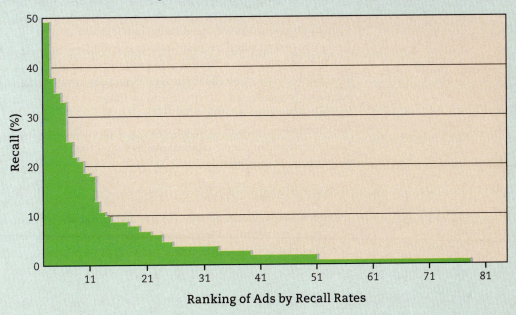

connection to the product. For example, many ads displayed visual symbols of American patriotism in the wake of the 9/11 terrorist attacks in an attempt to associate products and companies with national pride. Media critic Leslie Savan noted that in trying "to convince us that there's an innate relationship between a brand name and an attitude," advertising may associate products with nationalism, happy families, success at school or work, natural scenery, freedom, or humor.[23]

One of the more controversial uses of the association principle has been the linkage of products to stereotyped caricatures of women. In numerous instances, women have been portrayed either as sex objects or as clueless housewives who, during many a daytime TV commercial, need the powerful off-screen voice of a male narrator to instruct them in their own homes.

Another popular use of the association principle is to claim that products are "real" and "natural"—possibly the most familiar adjectives associated with advertising. For example, Coke sells itself as "the real thing," and the cosmetics industry offers synthetic products that promise to make women look "natural." The adjectives *real* and *natural* saturate American ads yet almost always describe processed or synthetic goods. Green marketing has a similar problem, as it is associated with goods and services that aren't always environmentally friendly.

Philip Morris's Marlboro brand has used the association principle to completely transform its product image. In the 1920s, Marlboro began as a fashionable women's cigarette. Back then, the company's ads equated smoking with a sense of freedom, attempting to appeal to women who had just won the right to vote. Marlboro, though, did poorly as a women's product, and new campaigns in the 1950s and 1960s transformed the brand into a man's cigarette. Powerful images of active, rugged men dominated the ads. Often, Marlboro associated its product with nature, displaying an image of a lone cowboy roping a calf, building a fence, or riding over a snow-covered landscape. In 2014, the branding consultancy BrandZ (a division of WPP) named Marlboro the world's ninth "most valuable global brand," having an estimated worth of $67 billion. (Google, Apple, IBM, Microsoft, McDonald's, Coca-Cola, Visa, and AT&T ranked ahead of Marlboro.)

Disassociation as an Advertising Strategy

As a response to corporate mergers and public skepticism toward impersonal and large companies, a *disassociation corollary* emerged in advertising. The nation's largest winery, Gallo, pioneered the idea in the 1980s by establishing a dummy corporation, Bartles & Jaymes, to sell jug wine and wine coolers, thereby avoiding the use of the Gallo corporate image in ads and on its bottles. The ads featured Frank and Ed, two low-key, grandfatherly types, as "co-owners" and ad spokesmen. On the one hand, as a *Business Week* article observed, the ad was "a way to connect with younger consumers who yearn for products that are handmade, quirky, and authentic."[24] On the other hand, this technique, by concealing the Gallo tie-in, allowed the wine giant to disassociate from the negative publicity of the 1970s—a period when labor leader Cesar Chavez organized migrant workers in a long boycott of Gallo.

In the 1990s, General Motors also used the disassociation strategy, according to the same *Business Week* report. Reeling from a declining corporate reputation, GM tried to package the Saturn as "a small-town enterprise, run by folks not terribly unlike Frank and Ed," who provide caring, personal service.[25] In 2009, however, GM shut down its struggling Saturn brand during the economic recession. As an ad strategy, disassociation often links new brands in a product line to eccentric or simple regional places rather than to images conjured up by big cities and multinational conglomerates.

Advertising as Myth and Story

Another way to understand ads is to use **myth analysis**, which provides insights into how ads work at a general cultural level. Here, the term *myth* does not refer simply to an untrue story or outright falsehood. Rather, myths help us define people, organizations, and social norms.

According to myth analysis, most ads are narratives with stories to tell and social conflicts to resolve. Three common mythical elements are found in many types of ads:

1. Ads incorporate myths in mini-story form, featuring characters, settings, and plots.
2. Most stories in ads involve conflicts, pitting one set of characters or social values against another.
3. Such conflicts are negotiated or resolved by the end of the ad, usually by applying or purchasing a product. In advertising, the product and those who use it often emerge as the heroes of the story.

Even though the stories that ads tell are usually compressed into thirty seconds or onto a single page, they still include the traditional elements of narrative. For instance, many SUV ads ask us to imagine ourselves driving out into the raw, untamed wilderness, to a quiet, natural place that only, say, a Jeep can reach. The audience implicitly understands that the SUV can somehow, almost magically, take us out of our fast-paced, freeway-wrapped urban world, plagued with long commutes, traffic jams, and automobile exhaust. This implied conflict between the natural world and the manufactured world is apparently resolved by the image of the SUV in a natural setting. Although SUVs typically clog our urban and suburban highways, get low gas mileage, and create tons of air pollution particulates, the ads ignore those facts. Instead, they offer an alternative story about the wonders of nature, and the SUV amazingly becomes the vehicle that negotiates the conflict between city/suburban blight and the unspoiled wilderness.

Most advertisers do not expect consumers to accept without question the stories or associations they make in ads. As media scholar Michael Schudson observed in his book *Advertising: The Uneasy Persuasion*, they do not "make the mistake of asking for belief."[26] Instead, ads are most effective when they create attitudes and reinforce values. Then they operate like popular fiction, encouraging us to suspend our disbelief. Although most of us realize that ads create a fictional world, we often get caught up in their stories and myths. Indeed, ads often work because the stories offer comfort about our deepest desires and conflicts—between men and women, nature and technology, tradition and change, the real and the artificial. Most contemporary consumer advertising does not provide much useful information about products. Instead, it tries to reassure us that through the use of familiar brand names, everyday tensions and problems can be managed (see "Media Literacy and the Critical Process: The Branded You" on page 399).

Product Placement

Product companies and ad agencies have become adept in recent years at *product placement*: strategically placing ads or buying space in movies, TV shows, comic books, video games, blogs, and music videos so that products appear as part of a story's set environment (see "Examining Ethics: Brand Integration, Everywhere" on page 398). For example, in 2009, Starbucks became a naming sponsor of MSNBC's show *Morning Joe*—which now includes "Brewed by Starbucks" in its logo. In 2013, the Superman movie *Man of Steel* had the most product placements ever for a film up to that time, with two-hundred-plus marketing partners in deals worth $160 million, including those with Hardee's, Gillette, Sears, Nikon, Nokia, 7-Eleven, IHOP, and the National Guard.

PRODUCT PLACEMENT in movies and television is more prevalent than ever. On television, placement is often most visible in reality shows, while scripted series and films tend to be more subtle—at least some of the time. Apple products are so ubiquitous in movies and television that many viewers have probably become accustomed to the prominent display of its logo on shows like *House of Cards*.

Nathaniel Bell/© Netflix/Everett Collection

Brand Integration, Everywhere

How clear should the line be between media content and media sponsors? Generations ago, this question was a concern mainly for newspapers, which worked to erect a "firewall" between the editorial and the business sides of their organizations, meant to prevent advertising concerns from creeping into articles and opinions. But early television and radio shows welcomed advertisers' sponsorship of programs—sometimes even including product names in show titles. After television's quiz-show scandal (see Chapter 6), networks relegated advertisers to buying spot ads during commercial breaks.

Today, however, advertisers have found new ways to cut through the clutter and put their messages right in the midst of media content.

In television, getting product placements (also known as "brand integration") during shows is much more desirable than running traditional ads. Reality TV programming, which can be structured around products and services, is especially saturated with brand integration. In fact, such episodes contain an average of 19 minutes

and 42 seconds of brand integration appearances per hour. This is more than the time allotted for network TV commercials per hour and nearly three times the amount of brand appearances in scripted programs (6 minutes and 59 seconds).[1] For example, *The Biggest Loser* chronicles the weight losses of its contestants, who work out at 24 Hour Fitness, one of the program's sponsors, and eat food from General Mills and Subway, two other advertisers.[2]

On the movie screen, a single product placement deal can translate into revenues ranging from several hundred thousand to millions of dollars. Sometimes the placements help fund production costs. Brandchannel, however, reported that placement in movies declined in 2013 to its lowest level since 2001, with an average of 9.1 products placed in all movies that ranked No. 1 at the box office. Brandchannel awarded Budweiser the 2013 Award for Overall Product Placement: "Budweiser appeared in nearly one-fifth of all of the films that reached No. 1 at the box office last year. Budweiser and Bud Light's appearance in 96 of the 502 top films (19.1 percent) during that period [including *Texas Chainsaw 3D*, *Bad Grandpa*, *Zero Dark Thirty*, *Man of Steel*, and *Iron Man 3*] make the beer giant the sixth most common brand, behind only Ford, Apple,

Coca-Cola, Chevrolet and Mercedes." Finally, Brandchannel reports, "Rounding out the year was Budweiser's over-the-top, galactically incongruous placement . . . in *Star Trek: Into Darkness*. (A Budweiser brewery was used as a stand-in for a spaceship in the film's climax.)"[3]

Now, digital technology makes it even easier to put product placements in visual media. Movies, TV shows, and video games can add or delete product placements; advertising can even be digitally integrated into older media that didn't originally include product placement. On the Internet, some bloggers and Twitter users write posts on topics or products because they've been paid or given gifts to do so.

The rules on disclosure for product placements are weak or nonexistent. Television credits usually include messages about "promotional consideration," which means there was some paid product integration, but otherwise, there are no warnings to the viewers. Movies have similar standards. The Writers Guild of America has criticized the practice, arguing that it "forces content creators to become ad writers."[4] In fact, some writers say that it is easier to get a studio to buy a script or finance a project if brand integrations are already secured.

In contrast, the Federal Trade Commission requires bloggers to disclose paid sponsorships or posts, but it's not yet clear how well product placements on the Internet are being monitored. In newspapers, where the "firewall" remains important, the Society of Professional Journalists Code of Ethics calls for journalism to "distinguish news from advertising and shun hybrids that blur the lines between the two." For the rest of the media, however, such hybrids are increasingly embraced as a common and effective form of advertising. ◢

UP IN THE AIR featured two major companies: Hilton Hotels and American Airlines (*shown*).

Paramount Pictures/Photofest

For many critics, product placement has gotten out of hand. What started out as subtle appearances in realistic settings—like Reese's Pieces in the 1982 movie *E.T.*—has turned into Coca-Cola's being almost an honorary cast member on Fox's *American Idol* set. The practice is now so pronounced that it was a subject of Hollywood parody in the 2006 film *Talladega Nights: The Ballad of Ricky Bobby*, starring Will Ferrell.

In 2005, watchdog organization Commercial Alert asked both the FTC and the FCC to mandate that consumers be warned about product placement on television. The FTC rejected the petition, whereas the FCC proposed product placement rules but had still not approved them by the fall of 2014. In contrast, the European Union recently approved product placement for television but requires programs to alert viewers of such paid placements. In Britain, for example, the letter *P* must appear in the corner of the screen at commercial breaks and at the beginning and end of a show to signal product placements.[27]

Commercial Speech and Regulating Advertising

In 1791, Congress passed and the states ratified the First Amendment to the U.S. Constitution, promising, among other guarantees, to "make no law . . . abridging the freedom of speech, or of the press." Over time, we have developed a shorthand label for the First Amendment, misnaming it the free-speech clause. The amendment ensures that citizens and journalists can generally say and write what they want, but it says nothing directly about **commercial speech**—any

Courtesy of adbusters.org

print or broadcast expression for which a fee is charged to organizations and individuals buying time or space in the mass media.

Whereas freedom of speech refers to the right to express thoughts, beliefs, and opinions in the abstract marketplace of ideas, commercial speech is about the right to circulate goods, services, and images in the concrete marketplace of products. For most of the history of mass media, only very wealthy citizens established political parties, and multinational companies could routinely afford to purchase speech that reached millions. The Internet, however, has helped to level that playing field. Political speech, like a cleverly edited mash-up video, or entertaining speech, like a music video by California teenager Rebecca Black singing about the weekend (the infamous "Friday" video on YouTube), can go viral and quickly reach millions, rivaling the most expensive commercial speech.

Although the mass media have not hesitated to carry product and service-selling advertisements and have embraced the concepts of infomercials and cable home-shopping channels, they have also refused certain issue-based advertising that might upset their traditional advertisers. For example, although corporations have easy access in placing paid ads, many labor unions have had their print and broadcast ads rejected as "controversial." The nonprofit Adbusters Media Foundation, based in Vancouver, British Columbia, has had difficulty getting networks to air its "uncommercials." One of its spots promotes the Friday after Thanksgiving (traditionally, the beginning of the holiday shopping season) as Buy Nothing Day.

Critical Issues in Advertising

In his 1957 book *The Hidden Persuaders*, Vance Packard expressed concern that advertising was manipulating helpless consumers, attacking our dignity, and invading "the privacy of our minds."[28] According to this view, the advertising industry was all-powerful. Although consumers have historically been regarded as dupes by many critics, research reveals that the consumer mind is not as easy to predict as some advertisers once thought. In the 1950s, for example, Ford could not successfully sell its midsize car, the oddly named Edsel, which was aimed at newly prosperous Ford customers looking to move up to the latest in push-button window wipers and antennas. After a splashy and expensive ad campaign, Ford sold only 63,000 Edsels in 1958 and just 2,000 in 1960, when the model was discontinued.

One of the most disastrous campaigns ever featured the now-famous "This is not your father's Oldsmobile" spots that began running in 1989 and starred celebrities like former Beatles drummer Ringo Starr and his daughter. Oldsmobile (which became part of General Motors in 1908) and its ad agency, Leo Burnett, decided to market to a younger generation after sales declined from a high of 1.1 million vehicles in 1985 to only 715,000 in 1988. But the campaign backfired, apparently alienating its older loyal customers (who may have felt abandoned by Olds and its catchy new slogan) and failing to lure younger buyers (who probably still had trouble getting past the name Olds). In 2000, Oldsmobile sold only 260,000 cars, and GM had phased out its Olds division by 2005.[29]

As these examples illustrate, most people are not easily persuaded by advertising. Over the years, studies have suggested that between 75 and 90 percent of new consumer products typically fail because they are not embraced by the buying public.[30] But despite public resistance to many new products, the ad industry has made contributions, including raising the American standard of living and financing most media industries. Yet serious concerns over the impact of advertising remain. Watchdog groups worry about the expansion of advertising's reach, and critics continue to condemn ads that stereotype or associate products with sex appeal, youth, and narrow definitions of beauty. Some of the most serious concerns involve children, teens, and health.

Children and Advertising

Children and teenagers, living in a culture dominated by TV ads, are often viewed as "consumer trainees." For years, groups such as Action for Children's Television (ACT) worked to limit advertising aimed at children. In the 1980s, ACT fought particularly hard to curb program-length commercials: thirty-minute cartoon programs (such as *G.I. Joe*, *My Little Pony and Friends*, *The Care Bear Family*, and *He-Man and the Masters of the Universe*) developed for television syndication primarily to promote a line of toys. This commercial tradition continued with programs such as *Pokémon* and *SpongeBob SquarePants*.

In addition, parent groups have worried about the heavy promotion of products like sugar-coated cereals during children's programs. Pointing to European countries, where children's advertising is banned, these groups have pushed to minimize advertising directed at children. Congress, hesitant to limit the protection that the First Amendment offers to commercial speech, and faced with lobbying by the advertising industry, has responded weakly. The Children's Television Act of 1990 mandated that networks provide some educational and informational children's programming, but the act has been difficult to enforce and has done little to restrict advertising aimed at kids.

Because children and teenagers influence nearly $500 billion a year in family spending—on everything from snacks to cars—they are increasingly targeted by advertisers.[31] A Stanford University study found that a single thirty-second TV ad can influence the brand choices of children as young as age two. Still, methods for marketing to children have become increasingly seductive as product placement and merchandising tie-ins become more prevalent. Most recently, companies have used seemingly innocuous online games to sell products like breakfast cereal to children.

Advertising in Schools

A controversial development in advertising was the introduction of Channel One into thousands of schools during the 1989–90 school year. The brainchild of Whittle Communications, Channel One offered "free" video and satellite equipment (tuned exclusively to Channel One) in exchange for a twelve-minute package of current events programming that included two minutes of commercials. Public pressure managed to get most junk-food ads removed from Channel One schools by 2006.

Over the years, the National Dairy Council and other organizations have also used schools to promote products, providing free filmstrips, posters, magazines, folders, and study guides adorned with corporate logos. Teachers, especially in underfunded districts, have usually been grateful for the support. Early on, however, Channel One was viewed as a more intrusive threat, violating the implicit cultural border between an entertainment situation (watching commercial television) and a learning situation (going to school). One study showed that schools with a high concentration of low-income students were more than twice as likely as affluent schools to receive Channel One.[32]

Texas and Ohio contain the highest concentrations of Channel One contracts, but many individual school districts and some state systems, including New York and California, have banned Channel One News. These school systems have argued that Channel One provides students with only slight additional knowledge about current affairs, and fear that students deem the products advertised—sneakers, clothing, cereal, and controversial sugar-flavored

LaunchPad ◉

macmillanhighered.com
/mediaculture10e

Images courtesy of

Advertising and Effects on Children
Scholars and advertisers analyze the effects of advertising on children.
Discussion: In the video, some argue that using cute, kid-friendly imagery in ads can lead children to begin drinking; others dispute this claim. What do you think, and why?

AS AMERICAN OBESITY CONTINUES TO RISE, ads touting fast food and soft drinks have been countered by health advocacy, as in this ad on the New York City subway warning riders about the sugar content of their morning coffee drinks.

© 2012 New York City Department of Health and Mental Hygiene/Elk Studios

juices like SunnyD, among others—more worthy of purchase because they are advertised in educational environments.[33] A 2006 study found that students remember "more of the advertising than they do the news stories shown on Channel One."[34] Though it has changed owners several times over the past ten years, Channel One is still in business.

Health and Advertising

Eating Disorders. Advertising has a powerful impact on the standards of beauty in our culture. A long-standing trend in advertising is the association of certain products with ultra-thin female models, promoting a style of "attractiveness" that girls and women are invited to emulate. Even today, despite the popularity of fitness programs, most fashion models are much thinner than the average woman. Some forms of fashion and cosmetics advertising actually pander to individuals' insecurities and low self-esteem by promising the ideal body. Such advertising suggests standards of style and behavior that may be not only unattainable but also harmful, leading to eating disorders such as anorexia and bulimia and an increase in cosmetic surgeries.

If advertising has been criticized for promoting skeleton-like beauty, it has also been blamed for the tripling of obesity rates in the United States since the 1980s, with more than two-thirds of adult Americans identified in 2014 as being overweight or obese. Corn syrup–laden soft drinks, fast food, and processed food are the staples of media ads and are major contributors to the nationwide weight problem. More troubling is that an obese nation is good for business (creating a multibillion-dollar market for diet products, exercise equipment, and self-help books), so media outlets see little reason to change current ad practices. The food and restaurant industry at first denied any connection between ads and the rise of U.S. obesity rates, instead blaming individuals who make bad choices. Increasingly, however, some fast-food chains offer healthier meals and calorie counts on various food items.

Tobacco. One of the most sustained criticisms of advertising is its promotion of tobacco consumption. Opponents of tobacco advertising have become more vocal in the face of grim statistics: Each year, an estimated 400,000 Americans die from diseases related to nicotine addiction and poisoning. Tobacco ads disappeared from television in 1971, under pressure from Congress and the FCC. However, over the years, numerous ad campaigns have targeted teenage consumers of cigarettes. In 1988, for example, R. J. Reynolds, a subdivision of RJR Nabisco, updated its Joe Camel cartoon character, outfitting him with hipper clothes and sunglasses. Spending $75 million annually, the company put Joe on billboards and store posters and in sports stadiums and magazines. One study revealed that before 1988, fewer than 1 percent of teens under age eighteen smoked Camels. After the ad blitz, however, 33 percent of this age group preferred Camels.

In addition to young smokers, the tobacco industry has targeted other groups. In the 1960s, for instance, the advertising campaigns for Eve and Virginia Slims cigarettes (reminiscent of ads during the suffrage movement in the early 1900s) associated their products with women's liberation, equality, and slim fashion models. And in 1989, Reynolds introduced a cigarette called Uptown, targeting African American consumers. The ad campaign fizzled due to public protests by black leaders and government officials. When these leaders pointed to the high concentration of cigarette billboards in poor urban areas and the high mortality rates among black male smokers, the tobacco company withdrew the brand.

The government's position regarding the tobacco industry began to change in the mid-1990s, when new reports revealed that tobacco companies had known that nicotine was addictive as early as the 1950s and had withheld that information from the public. In 1998, after four states won settlements against the tobacco industry and the remaining states threatened to bring more expensive lawsuits against the companies, the tobacco industry agreed to an unprecedented $206 billion settlement that carried significant limits on advertising and marketing tobacco products.

The agreement's provisions banned cartoon characters in advertising, thus ending the use of the Joe Camel character; prohibited the industry from targeting young people in ads and marketing and from giving away free samples, tobacco-brand clothing, and other merchandise; and ended outdoor billboard and transit advertising. The agreement also banned tobacco company sponsorship of concerts and athletic events, and it strictly limited other corporate sponsorships by tobacco companies. These agreements, however, do not apply to tobacco advertising abroad (see "Global Village: Smoking Up the Global Market" on page 404).

Alcohol. In 2013, 88,000 people died from alcohol-related diseases, and another 10,000 died in car crashes involving drunk drivers. As you can guess, many of the same complaints regarding tobacco advertising are also being directed at alcohol ads. (The hard liquor industry has voluntarily banned TV and radio ads for decades.) For example, one of the most popular beer ad campaigns of the late 1990s, featuring the Budweiser frogs (which croak "Budweis-errrr"), has been accused of using cartoonlike animal characters to appeal to young viewers. In fact, the Budweiser ads would be banned under the tough standards of the tobacco industry settlement, which prohibits the attribution of human characteristics to animals, plants, or other objects.

Alcohol ads have also targeted minority populations. Malt liquors, which contain higher concentrations of alcohol than beers do, have been touted in high-profile television ads for such labels as Colt 45 and Magnum. There is also a trend toward marketing high-end liquors to African American and Hispanic male populations. In a recent marketing campaign, Hennessy targeted young African American men with ads featuring hip-hop star Nas and sponsored events in Times Square and at the Governors Ball and Coachella music festivals. Hennessy also sponsored VIP parties with Latino deejays and hip-hop acts in Miami and Houston.

College students, too, have been heavily targeted by alcohol ads, particularly by the beer industry. Although colleges and universities have outlawed "beer bashes" hosted and supplied directly by major brewers, both Coors and Miller still employ student representatives to help "create brand awareness." These students notify brewers of special events that might be sponsored by and linked to a specific beer label. The images and slogans in alcohol ads often associate the products with power, romance, sexual prowess, or athletic skill. In reality, though, alcohol is a chemical depressant; it diminishes athletic ability and sexual performance, triggers addiction in roughly 10 percent of the U.S. population, and factors into many domestic abuse cases. A national study demonstrated "that young people who see more ads for alcoholic beverages tend to drink more."[35]

The Advertising Archives

ABSOLUT OBSESSION.

LIFESTYLE AD APPEALS
TBWA (now a unit of Omnicom) introduced Absolut Vodka's distinctive advertising campaign in 1980. The campaign marketed a little-known Swedish vodka as an exclusive lifestyle brand, an untraditional approach that parlayed it into one of the world's best-selling spirits. The long-running ad campaign ended in 2006, with more than 1,450 ads having maintained the brand's premium status by referencing fashion, artists, and contemporary music.

GLOBAL VILLAGE

Smoking Up the Global Market

By 2000, the status of tobacco companies and their advertising in the United States had hit a low point. A $206 billion settlement in 1998 between tobacco companies and state attorneys general ended tobacco advertising on billboards and severely limited the ways in which cigarette companies can promote their products in the United States. Advertising bans and antismoking public service announcements contributed to tobacco's growing disfavor in America, with smoking rates dropping from a high of 42.5 percent of the population in 1965 to just 18 percent fifty years later.

As Western cultural attitudes have turned against tobacco, the large tobacco multinationals have shifted their global marketing focus, targeting Asia in particular. Of the world's more than 1 billion smokers, 120 million adults smoke in India, 125 million adults smoke in Southeast Asia (Indonesia, Malaysia, the Philippines, Singapore, Thailand, Brunei, Burma, Cambodia, Laos, and Vietnam), and 350 million people smoke in China.[1] Underfunded government health programs and populations that generally admire American and European cultural products make Asian nations ill-equipped to resist cigarette marketing efforts. For example, in spite of China's efforts to control smoking (several Chinese cities have banned smoking in public places), recent studies have shown that nearly two-thirds of Chinese men and 10 percent of Chinese women are addicted to tobacco. Chinese women, who are now starting to smoke at increasing rates, are associating smoking with slimness, feminism, and independence.[2]

Advertising bans have actually forced tobacco companies to find alternative and, as it turns out, better ways to promote smoking. Philip Morris, the largest private tobacco company, and its global rival, British American Tobacco (BAT), practice "brand stretching"—linking their logos to race-car events, soccer leagues, youth festivals, concerts, TV shows, and popular cafés. The higher price for Western cigarettes in Asia has increased their prestige and has made packs of Marlboros symbols of middle-class aspiration.

The unmistakable silhouette of the Marlboro Man is ubiquitous throughout developing countries, particularly in Asia. In Hanoi, Vietnam, almost every corner boasts a street vendor with a trolley cart, the bottom half of which carries the Marlboro logo or one of the other premium foreign brands. Vietnam's Ho Chi Minh City has two thousand such trolleys. Children in Malaysia are especially keen on Marlboro clothing, which, along with watches, binoculars, radios, knives, and backpacks, they can win by collecting a certain number of empty Marlboro packages. (It is now illegal to sell tobacco-brand clothing and merchandise in the United States.)

Sporting events have proved to be an especially successful brand-stretching technique with men. In addition to Philip Morris's sponsorship of the Marlboro soccer league in China in the mid- to late 1990s, cigarette ads flourished on Chinese television (in the U.S., such ads have been banned by FCC rules since 1971). For the last twenty years, however, cigarette ads have been banned in China on TV and radio and in newspapers and magazines. But in 2014, the powerful government-controlled Chinese tobacco industry blocked a complete ban, according to Reuters, still permitting "cigarette product launches, and tobacco sponsorship for sporting events and schools."[3]

Critics suggest that the same marketing strategies will make their way into the United States and other Western countries, but that's unlikely. Tobacco companies are mainly interested in developing regions like Asia for two reasons. First, the potential market is staggering: Only one in twenty cigarettes now sold in China is a foreign brand, and women are just beginning to develop the habit. Second, many smokers in countries like China are unaware that smoking causes lung cancer. In fact, a million Chinese people die each year from tobacco-related health problems—around 50 percent of Chinese men will die before they are sixty-five years old, and lung cancer among Chinese women has increased by 30 percent in the past few years.[4] Smoking is projected to cause about eight million deaths a year by 2030.[5]

Prescription Drugs. Another area of concern is the recent surge in prescription drug advertising. Spending on direct-to-consumer advertising for prescription drugs increased from $266 million in 1994 to $5.3 billion in 2007—largely because of growth in television advertising, which today accounts for about two-thirds of such ads. The ads have made household names of prescription drugs such as Nexium, Claritin, Paxil, and Viagra. The ads are also very effective: Another survey found that nearly one in three adults has talked to a doctor and one in eight has received a prescription in response to seeing an ad for a prescription drug.[36] Between 2007 and 2011, direct-to-consumer TV advertising for prescription drugs dropped 23 percent—from $3.1 billion in 2007 to $2.3 billion in 2011—due to both doctors' concerns about being pressured by patients who see the TV ads for new drugs and to notable recalls of heavily advertised drugs like Vioxx, a pain reliever that was later found to have harsh side effects. Still, in 2011, Pfizer spent $156 million on TV ads for Lipitor (a cholesterol-lowering drug that reduces the risk of heart attack and stroke), the highest amount spent for any prescription drug that year. But then, in 2012, spending rose again to over $3 billion.[37]

The tremendous growth of prescription drug ads brings the potential for false and misleading claims, particularly because a brief TV advertisement can't possibly communicate all the relevant cautionary information. More recently, direct-to-consumer prescription drug advertising has appeared in text messages and on Facebook. Pharmaceutical companies have also engaged in "disease awareness" campaigns to build markets for their products. As of 2014, the United States and New Zealand were the only two nations to allow prescription drugs to be advertised directly to consumers.

Watching Over Advertising

A few nonprofit watchdog and advocacy organizations—Commercial Alert, as well as the Better Business Bureau and the National Consumers League—compensate in many ways for some of the shortcomings of the Federal Trade Commission and other government agencies in monitoring the excesses of commercialism and false and deceptive ads.

Excessive Commercialism

Since 1998, Commercial Alert, a nonprofit organization founded in part by longtime consumer advocate Ralph Nader and based in Portland, Oregon, has been working to "limit excessive commercialism in society" by informing the public about the ways that advertising has crept out of its "proper sphere." For example, Commercial Alert highlights the numerous deals for cross-promotion made between Hollywood studios and fast-food companies. These include Warner Brothers' partnership with Hardee's for *Man of Steel*, and DreamWorks Animation's partnership with McDonald's for family-friendly flicks like *The Croods* and *How to Train Your Dragon 2*.

These deals not only helped movie studios make money as DVD sales declined but also helped movies reach audiences that traditional advertising can't. As Jeffrey Godsick, Fox's executive VP of marketing, has said, "We want to hit all the lifestyle points for

CELEBRITY SPOKESPEOPLE Tennis champion Serena Williams recently endorsed the sleep supplement Sleep Sheets, an over-the-counter sleep aid that promises to combat insomnia and promote natural sleep. Although it is available without a prescription, Williams's vigorous ad campaign for the supplement, which she co-owns, attests to the persistence of prescription drug ads and the vulnerability of their audience.

Ben Gabbe/Getty Images

consumers. Partners get us into places that are nonpurchasable (as media buys). McDonald's has access to tens of millions of people on a daily basis—that helps us penetrate the culture."[38]

Commercial Alert is a lonely voice in checking the commercialization of U.S. culture. Its other activities have included challenges to specific marketing tactics, such as HarperCollins Children's Books' creation of the Mackenzie Blue series, which included "dynamic corporate partnerships," or product placements woven into the stories, written by the founder of a marketing group aimed at teens. In constantly questioning the role of advertising in democracy, the organization has aimed to strengthen noncommercial culture and limit the amount of corporate influence on publicly elected government bodies.

The FTC Takes on Puffery and Deception

Since the days when Lydia Pinkham's Vegetable Compound promised "a sure cure for all female weakness," false and misleading claims have haunted advertising. Over the years, the FTC, through its truth-in-advertising rules, has played an investigative role in substantiating the claims of various advertisers. A certain amount of *puffery*—ads featuring hyperbole and exaggeration—has usually been permitted, particularly when a product says it is "new and improved." However, ads become deceptive when they are likely to mislead reasonable consumers based on statements in the ad or because they omit information. Moreover, when a product claims to be "the best," "the greatest," or "preferred by four out of five doctors," FTC rules require scientific evidence to back up the claims.

A typical example of deceptive advertising is the Campbell Soup ad in which marbles in the bottom of a soup bowl forced more bulky ingredients—and less water—to the surface. In another instance, a 1990 Volvo commercial featured a monster truck driving over a line of cars and crushing all but the Volvo; the company later admitted that the Volvo had been specially reinforced and the other cars' support columns had been weakened. A more subtle form of deception featured the Klondike Lite ice cream bar—"the 93 percent fat-free dessert with chocolate-flavored coating." The bars were indeed 93 percent fat-free, but only after the chocolate coating was removed.[39]

In 2003, the FTC brought enforcement actions against companies marketing the herbal weight-loss supplement ephedra. Ephedra has a long-standing connection to elevated blood pressure, strokes, and heart attacks and has contributed to numerous deaths. Nevertheless, companies advertised ephedra as a safe and miraculous weight-loss supplement and, incredibly, as "a beneficial treatment for hypertension and coronary disease." According to the FTC, one misleading ad said: "Teacher loses 70 pounds in only eight weeks. . . . This is how over one million people have safely lost millions of pounds! No calorie counting! No hunger! Guaranteed to work for you too!" As the director of the FTC's Bureau of Consumer Protection summed up, "There is no such thing as weight loss in a bottle. Claims that you'll lose

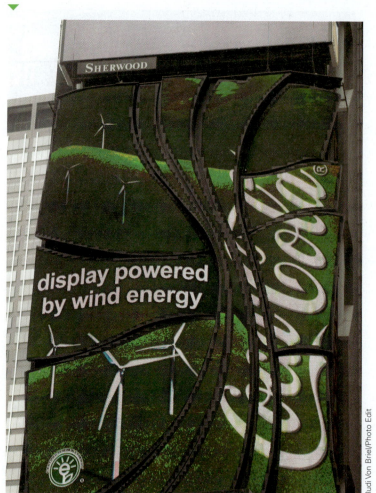

GREEN ADVERTISING
In response to increased consumer demand, companies have been developing and advertising green, or environmentally conscious, products to attract customers who want to lessen their environmental impact. How effective is this ad for you? What shared values do you look for or respond to in advertising?

display powered by wind energy

Rudi Von Briel/Photo Edit

substantial amounts of weight and still eat everything you want are simply false."[40] In 2004, the United States banned ephedra.

When the FTC discovers deceptive ads, it usually requires advertisers to change them or remove them from circulation. The FTC can also impose monetary civil penalties for companies, and it occasionally requires an advertiser to run spots to correct the deceptive ads.

Alternative Voices

One of the provisions of the government's multibillion-dollar settlement with the tobacco industry in 1998 established a nonprofit organization with the mission to counteract tobacco marketing and reduce youth tobacco use. That mission became a reality in 2000, when the American Legacy Foundation launched its antismoking/anti–tobacco industry ad campaign called "Truth."

Working with a coalition of ad agencies, a group of teenage consultants, and a $300 million budget, the foundation created a series of stylish, gritty print and television ads that deconstruct the images that have long been associated with cigarette ads—macho horse country, carefree beach life, sexy bar scenes, and daring skydives. These ads show teens dragging, piling, or heaving body bags across the beach or onto a horse, and holding up signs that say "What if cigarette ads told the Truth?" Other ads show individuals with lung cancer ("I worked where people smoked. I chose not to. But I got lung cancer anyway") or illustrate how many people are indirectly touched by tobacco deaths ("Yeah, my grandfather died April last year").

The TV and print ads prominently reference the foundation's Web site, www.thetruth.com, which offers statistics, discussion forums, and outlets for teen creativity. For example, the site provides facts about addiction (more than 80 percent of all adult smokers started smoking before they turned eighteen) and tobacco money (tobacco companies make $1.8 billion from underage sales) and urges site visitors to organize the facts in their own customized folders. By 2007, with its jarring messages and cross-media platform, the "Truth" anti-tobacco campaign was recognized by 80 percent of teens and was ranked in the Top 10 "most memorable teen brands."[41] The "Truth" campaign at least partly explains the reported decline in teen smoking. Back in 2000, according to University of Michigan studies, 23 percent of all teens said they smoked. In 2014, that figure was down to 9 percent.[42]

Courtesy TRUTH/American Legacy Foundation

ALTERNATIVE ADS
In 2005, "Truth," the national youth smoking prevention campaign, won an Emmy Award in the National Public Service Announcement category. "Truth" ads were created by the ad firms of Arnold Worldwide of Boston and Crispin Porter & Bogusky of Miami.

Advertising, Politics, and Democracy

Advertising as a profession came of age in the twentieth century, facilitating the shift of U.S. society from production-oriented small-town values to consumer-oriented urban lifestyles. With its ability to create consumers, advertising became the central economic support system for our mass media industries. Through its seemingly endless supply of pervasive and persuasive strategies, advertising today saturates the cultural landscape. Products now blend in as props or even as "characters" in TV shows and movies. In addition, almost every national consumer product now has its own Web site to market itself to a global audience 365 days a year. With today's digital technology, ad images can be made to appear in places where they don't really exist. For example, advertisements can be superimposed on the backstop wall behind the batter during a nationally televised baseball broadcast. Viewers at home see the ads, but fans at the game do not.

Advertising's ubiquity, especially in the age of social media, raises serious questions about our privacy and the ease with which companies can gather data on our consumer habits. But an even more serious issue is the influence of ads on our lives as democratic citizens. With fewer and fewer large media conglomerates controlling advertising and commercial speech, what is the effect on free speech and political debate? In the future, how easy will it be to get heard in a marketplace where only a few large companies control access to that space?

Advertising's Role in Politics

Since the 1950s, political consultants have been imitating market-research and advertising techniques to sell their candidates, giving rise to **political advertising**, the use of ad techniques to promote a candidate's image and persuade the public to adopt a particular viewpoint. In the early days of television, politicians running for major offices either bought or were offered half-hour blocks of time to discuss their views and the issues of the day. As advertising time became more valuable, however, local stations and the networks became reluctant to give away time in large chunks. Gradually, TV managers began selling thirty-second spots to political campaigns, just as they sold time to product advertisers.

During the 1992 and 1996 presidential campaigns, third-party candidate Ross Perot restored the use of the half-hour time block when he ran political infomercials on cable and the networks. Barack Obama also ran a half-hour infomercial in 2008, and in the 2012 presidential race, both major candidates and various political organizations supporting them ran many online infomercials that were much longer than the standard thirty- to sixty-second TV spot. However, only very wealthy or well-funded candidates can afford such promotional strategies, and television does not usually provide free airtime to politicians. Questions about political ads continue to be asked: Can serious information on political issues be conveyed in thirty-second spots? Do repeated attack ads, which assault another candidate's character, so undermine citizens' confidence in the electoral process that they stop voting?[43] And how does a democratic society ensure that alternative political voices, which are not well financed or commercially viable, still receive a hearing?

Although broadcasters use the public's airwaves, they have long opposed providing free time for political campaigns and issues, since political advertising is big business for television stations. TV broadcasters earned $400 million in political ad revenue in 1996 and took in more than $1.5 billion (of $4.14 billion total spending) from political ads during the presidential and congressional elections in 2004. In the historic 2008 election, more than $5.28 billion was spent on advertising by all presidential and congressional candidates and interest groups. In 2012 (with a total of $6.28 billion spent on all elections), more than $1.1 billion alone went to local broadcast TV stations in the twelve most highly contested states, with local cable raking in another $200 million in those states.[44]

DIGITAL JOB OUTLOOK

Media Professionals Speak about Jobs in the Advertising Industry

Paul Ten Haken, President and Chief Online Strategist, Click Rain, Inc.

If you want to work in the online space, you'll want to have an online footprint to match. Start a blog, polish up your social profiles, and make sure who Google says you are is who *you* say you are.

Winston Binch, Partner/Chief Digital Officer, Deutsch LA

Do your homework. Research the hell out of the place you want to work. Learn the history and facts about the people you're meeting with. Take it further. Come with questions. A lot of them. This is a great way to start a dialogue with someone you're interviewing with. And it proves you really want the job. If people don't know anything about my company, it's generally an immediate pass.

Nadja Bellan-White, Senior Partner and Managing Director, Ogilvy & Mather

I think for me, the best advice I've been given, and what I try to do, is really be good to the people around you—people you're competing against [and] your clients. Because the people that you see who you may think are your enemies could be your friends the next day. So be good to everybody. I try to tell that particularly to the younger folks coming in. They think you can be so competitive that you cut people off. You've got to be really, really good to the people around you.

Jonathan Goldhill, CEO and Head Marketing Coach, The Goldhill Group

The world will always need great storytellers (i.e., copy writers) and visual types (i.e., graphic designers). People who can turn abstract concepts and execute these complex programs will succeed because they can harness the creative ideas and concepts and see them through to execution. The industry will also always need good managers.

Debra Murphy, Marketing Coach and Founder, Masterful Marketing

Creativity is needed to develop the messages, and determine the right set of strategies to implement for achieving your goals. You also need to be flexible in order to take on whatever is needed to execute the strategy. And likeability is needed for the transparency that is critical in today's online marketing environment.

The Future of Advertising

Although commercialism—through packaging both products and politicians—has generated cultural feedback that is often critical of advertising's pervasiveness, the growth of the industry has not diminished. Ads continue to fascinate. Many consumers buy magazines or watch the Super Bowl just for the advertisements. Adolescents decorate their rooms with their favorite ads and identify with the images certain products convey. In 2013, the fourth straight year of increases, advertising spending in the United States totaled more than $140 billion.[45]

A number of factors have made possible advertising's largely unchecked growth. Many Americans tolerate advertising as a "necessary evil" for maintaining the economy, but many dismiss advertising as not believable and trivial. As a result, unwilling to downplay its centrality to global culture, many citizens do not think advertising is significant enough to monitor or reform. Such attitudes have ensured advertising's pervasiveness and suggest the need to escalate our critical vigilance.

As individuals and as a society, we have developed an uneasy relationship with advertising. Favorite ads and commercial jingles remain part of our cultural world for a lifetime, yet we detest irritating and repetitive commercials. We realize that without ads, many mass media would need to reinvent themselves. At the same time, we should remain critical of what advertising has come to represent: the overemphasis on commercial acquisitions and images of material success, and the disparity between those who can afford to live comfortably in a commercialized society and those who cannot. ▶

CHAPTER REVIEW

COMMON THREADS

One of the Common Threads discussed in Chapter 1 is the commercial nature of mass media. The U.S. media system, due to policy choices made in the early and mid-twentieth century, was built largely on a system of commercial sponsorship. Consumers' acceptance of this arrangement was based on a sense that media content and sponsors should remain independent of each other. In other words, sponsors and product companies should not control and create media content. Today, is that line between media content and advertising shifting—or even completely disappearing?

Although media consumers have not always been comfortable with advertising, they developed a resigned acceptance of it because it "pays the bills" of the media system. Yet media consumers have their limits. Moments in which sponsors stepped over the usual borders of advertising into the realm of media content—including the TV quiz-show and radio payola scandals, complimentary newspaper reports about advertisers' businesses, product placement in TV or movies, and now "sponsored stories" on Facebook—have generated the greatest legal and ethical debates about advertising.

Still, as advertising has become more pervasive and consumers have become more discriminating, ad practitioners have searched for ways to weave their work more seamlessly into the cultural fabric. Products now blend in as props or even as "characters" in TV shows and movies. Search engines deliver paid placements along with regular search results. Product placements are woven into video games. Advertising messages can also be the subject of viral videos—and consumers do the work of distributing the message.

Among the more intriguing efforts to become enmeshed in the culture are the ads that exploit, distort, or transform the political and cultural meanings of popular music. When Nike used the Beatles' song "Revolution" (1968) to promote Nike shoes in 1987 ("Nike Air is not a shoe . . . it's a revolution," the ad said), many music fans were outraged to hear the Beatles' music being used for the first time to sell products.

That was more than twenty-five years ago. These days, having a popular song used in a TV commercial is considered a good career move for musicians—even better than radio airplay. Similarly, while product placement in TV and movies was hotly debated in the 1980s and 1990s, the explosive growth of paid placements in video games hardly raises an eyebrow today. Even the lessons of the quiz-show scandals, which forced advertisers out of TV program production in the late 1950s, are forgotten or ignored today as advertisers have been warmly invited to help develop TV programs.

Are we as a society giving up on trying to set limits on the never-ending onslaught of advertising? Are we weary of trying to keep advertising out of media production? How do we feel about the growing encroachment of ads into social networks like Facebook and Twitter? Why do we now seem less concerned about the integration of advertising into the core of media culture?

KEY TERMS

The definitions for the terms listed below can be found in the glossary at the end of the book. The page numbers listed with the terms indicate where the term is highlighted in the chapter.

product placement, 377
space brokers, 379
subliminal advertising, 383
slogan, 383
mega-agencies, 384
boutique agencies, 384
market research, 386
demographics, 386
psychographics, 386
focus groups, 386

Values and Lifestyles (VALS), 386
storyboard, 388
viral marketing, 388
media buyers, 388
saturation advertising, 389
account executives, 389
account reviews, 390
interstitials, 390
spam, 390
famous-person testimonial, 393

plain-folks pitch, 394
snob-appeal approach, 394
bandwagon effect, 394
hidden-fear appeal, 394
irritation advertising, 394
association principle, 394
myth analysis, 396
commercial speech, 399
political advertising, 408

REVIEW QUESTIONS

Early Developments in American Advertising

1. Whom did the first ad agents serve?

2. How did packaging and trademarks influence advertising?

3. Explain why patent medicines and department stores figured so prominently in advertising in the late nineteenth century.

4. What role did advertising play in transforming America into a consumer society?

The Shape of U.S. Advertising Today

5. What influences did visual culture exert on advertising?

6. What are the differences between boutique agencies and mega-agencies?

7. What are the major divisions at most ad agencies? What is the function of each department?

8. What are the advantages of Internet and mobile advertising over traditional media like newspapers and television?

Persuasive Techniques in Contemporary Advertising

9. How do the common persuasive techniques used in advertising work?

10. How does the association principle work, and why is it an effective way to analyze advertising?

11. What is the disassociation corollary?

12. What is product placement? Cite examples.

Commercial Speech and Regulating Advertising

13. What is commercial speech?

14. What are four serious contemporary issues regarding health and advertising? Why is each issue controversial?

15. What is the difference between puffery and deception in advertising? How can the FTC regulate deceptive ads?

Advertising, Politics, and Democracy

16. What are some of the major issues involving political advertising?

17. What role does advertising play in a democratic society?

QUESTIONING THE MEDIA

1. What is your earliest recollection of watching a television commercial? Do you think the ad had a significant influence on you?

2. Why are so many people critical of advertising?

3. If you were (or are) a parent, what strategies would you use to explain an objectionable ad to your child or teenager? Use an example.

4. Should advertising aimed at children be regulated? Support your response.

5. Should tobacco or alcohol advertising be prohibited? Why or why not? How would you deal with First Amendment issues regarding controversial ads?

6. Would you be in favor of regular advertising on public television and radio as a means of financial support for these media? Explain your answer.

7. Is advertising at odds with the ideals of democracy? Why or why not?

LAUNCHPAD FOR *MEDIA & CULTURE*

Visit LaunchPad for *Media & Culture* at macmillanhighered.com/mediaculture10e
for additional learning tools:

- REVIEW WITH LEARNINGCURVE
LearningCurve, available on LaunchPad for *Media & Culture*, uses gamelike quizzing to help you master the concepts you need to learn from this chapter.

- VIDEO: BLURRING THE LINES: MARKETING PROGRAMS ACROSS PLATFORMS
An executive for MTV New Media explores how recent television programs blur the line between scripted and reality shows—and how MTV markets online to reach today's younger viewers.

12

Public Relations and Framing the Message

416
Early Developments in Public Relations

421
The Practice of Public Relations

433
Tensions between Public Relations and the Press

436
Public Relations and Democracy

Traditionally, public relations (PR) professionals try to influence audiences, often by attempting to gain positive coverage in the news media. Social media like Twitter, Facebook, YouTube, and Tumblr have shortened the path of communication; now PR pros can communicate directly with their audience—as can many of their famous clients. But entertainers, celebrities, and politicians who live by social media may also see their mistakes and foibles go viral on social media. Ashton Kutcher, Alec Baldwin, Amanda Bynes, Justin Bieber, and former congressman Anthony Weiner are among the celebrities who have damaged their images with ill-considered social media posts.

Beyoncé Knowles-Carter, best known by just her first name, is one of the world's most omnipresent media figures. She was the best-selling female artist of the first decade of the twenty-first century and, in 2013 and 2014, was among *Time* magazine's 100 most influential people in the world, listing her occupation as simply "Diva."[1] Since her marriage to Jay-Z, a rapper and one of music's wealthiest producers and entrepreneurs, the couple has achieved almost royalty status in American culture.

Kevin Mazur/WireImage for Parkwood Entertainment/ Getty Images

Beyoncé's successful career is a testament to her great talent and a public relations strategy that assiduously controls everything about her iconic image. Emblematic of this is the "temperature-controlled digital-storage facility that contains virtually every existing photograph of her" at her midtown Manhattan office suite. Since 2005, she has also employed a "visual director" who has recorded thousands of hours of footage of her private life. All the digital media are being archived in her own special catalog from which she can immediately retrieve any public or private record of herself.[2]

But Beyoncé's career over the past few years demonstrates the difficulty of completely controlling one's image in a world in which social media puts publicity power in so many other hands. For example, social media were abuzz in early 2013 with rumors that Beyoncé lip-synced her performance at President Obama's second inauguration. In response to the charges, she admitted she did lip-sync, but simply to control the quality of the performance (she said she was a "perfectionist"). In a masterful public relations move, she delivered a powerful a cappella version of "The Star-Spangled Banner" at a Super Bowl press conference a week later, which put any criticism of her singing abilities to rest.[3]

A few weeks later, Beyoncé's 2013 Super Bowl halftime show was a hit, but then Web sites like BuzzFeed and Gawker posted unflattering action photos of her performance—some of which her publicist asked BuzzFeed to remove (instead, the site printed the e-mail request and republished the photos).[4] For her 2013 Mrs. Carter tour, Beyoncé instituted tighter rules, prohibiting professional photographers from covering her concerts and issuing images taken only by her official photographer. The *Guardian* newspaper suggested that this policy was in response to the unflattering Super Bowl photos.[5]

Beyoncé continues to exert tight control over her media exposure; when HBO released the documentary *Beyoncé: Life Is But a Dream*, its subject also served as the writer, director, and executive producer of the autobiographical project. Then, in December 2013, Beyoncé released her fifth album with no promotion except for a message to her eight million Instagram followers that said "Surprise!" along with a fifteen-second video that introduced a "visual album" with seventeen videos and fourteen songs. Buzz about the surprise release immediately took over both traditional and social media, and the album became a million-seller on iTunes in less than a week. In a press release, Beyoncé said, "I didn't want to release my music the way I've done it. I'm bored with that. I feel like I am able to speak directly to my fans."[6]

▲ *THE BEYONCÉ STORY ILLUSTRATES A MAJOR DIFFERENCE* between advertising and public relations: Advertising is controlled publicity that a company or an individual buys; public relations attempts to secure favorable media publicity (which is more difficult to control) to promote a company or client.

Visit **LaunchPad** for *Media & Culture* and use **LearningCurve** to review concepts from this chapter.

Public relations covers a wide array of practices, such as shaping the public image of a politician or celebrity, establishing or repairing communication between consumers and companies, and promoting government agencies and actions, especially during wartime. Broadly defined, **public relations** refers to the total communication strategy conducted by a person, a government, or an organization attempting to reach and persuade an audience to adopt a point of view.[7] While public relations may sound very similar to advertising, which also seeks to persuade audiences, it is a different skill in a variety of ways. Advertising uses simple and fixed messages (e.g., "our appliance is the most efficient and affordable") that are transmitted directly to the public through the purchase of ads. Public relations involves more complex messages that may evolve over time (e.g., a political campaign or a long-term strategy to dispel unfavorable reports about "fatty processed foods") and that may be transmitted to the public indirectly, often through the news media.

The social and cultural impact of public relations has been immense. In its infancy, PR helped convince many American businesses of the value of nurturing the public, who became purchasers rather than producers of their own goods after the Industrial Revolution. PR set the tone for the corporate image-building that characterized the economic environment of the twentieth century and for the battles of organizations taking sides in today's environmental, energy, and labor issues. Perhaps PR's most significant effect, however, has been on the political process, in which individuals and organizations—on both the Right and the Left—hire spin doctors to shape their media images.

In this chapter, we will:

- Study the impact of public relations and the historical conditions that affected its development as a modern profession
- Look at nineteenth-century press agents and the role that railroad and utility companies played in developing corporate PR
- Consider the rise of modern PR, particularly the influences of former reporters Ivy Lee and Edward Bernays
- Explore the major practices and specialties of public relations
- Examine the reasons for the long-standing antagonism between journalists and members of the PR profession, and the social responsibilities of public relations in a democracy

As you read through this chapter, think about what knowledge you might already have about what public relations practitioners do, given that PR is an immensely powerful media industry and yet remains largely invisible. Can you think of a company or an organization, either national (like BP) or local (like your university or college), that might have engaged the help of a public relations team to handle a crisis? What did they do to make the public trust the organization more? When you see political campaign coverage, are you sometimes aware of the spin doctors who are responsible for making sure their candidate says or does the "right" thing at the "right" time in order to foster the most favorable public image that will gain the candidate the most votes? For more questions to help you understand the role of public relations in our lives, see "Questioning the Media" in the Chapter Review.

Early Developments in Public Relations

At the beginning of the twentieth century, the United States shifted to a consumer-oriented, industrial society, which fostered the development of new products and services as people moved to cities to find work. During this transformation from farm to factory, advertising and PR emerged as professions. While advertising drew attention and customers to new products, PR began in part to help businesses fend off increased scrutiny from the muckraking journalists and emerging labor unions of the time.[8]

The first PR practitioners were simply theatrical **press agents**: those who sought to advance a client's image through media exposure, primarily via stunts staged for newspapers. The advantages of these early PR techniques soon became obvious. For instance, press agents were used by people like Daniel Boone, who engineered various land-grab and real estate ventures, and Davy Crockett, who in addition to performing heroic exploits was also involved in the massacre of Native Americans. Such individuals often wanted press agents to repair and reshape their reputations as cherished frontier legends or as respectable candidates for public office.

P. T. Barnum and Buffalo Bill

The most notorious press agent of the nineteenth century was Phineas Taylor (P. T.) Barnum, who used gross exaggeration, fraudulent stories, and staged events to secure newspaper coverage for his clients, his American Museum, and later his circus. Barnum's circus, dubbed "The Greatest Show on Earth," included the "midget" General Tom Thumb, Swedish soprano Jenny Lind, Jumbo the Elephant, and Joice Heth (who Barnum claimed was the 161-year-old nurse of George Washington, but who was actually eighty when she died). These performers

---

▼ **Public Relations and Framing the Message**

Early Promotions through Media
In a career that spans the 1840s to the 1880s, theatrical agent P. T. Barnum employs early PR tactics to promote his many acts, including the Swedish soprano Jenny Lind and Jumbo, the twelve-foot-tall African elephant (pp. 416–417).

"Poison Ivy" Lee
After opening one of the first PR firms in New York in the first decade of the twentieth century, Lee, in 1914, works for the wealthy Rockefeller family, transforming the senior Rockefeller's reputation as a stingy curmudgeon into that of a child-loving philanthropist (pp. 419–420).

Walter Lippmann
In 1922, the newspaper columnist publishes the book *Public Opinion*, illustrating how slogans, stereotypes, and other media messages can shape public perception (p. 421).

| 1840 | 1860 | 1880 | 1900 | 1920 |

The Railroads
The PR practice of bribing reporters for positive news stories and deadheading (giving reporters free rail passes) reaches its height (p. 418).

Edward Bernays
In 1923, Bernays teaches the first public relations course at New York University and writes the first PR textbook (p. 420).

The Advertising Archives (left); © Bettmann/Corbis (right)

became some of the earliest nationally known celebrities because of Barnum's skill in using the media for promotion. Decrying outright fraud and cheating, Barnum understood that his audiences liked to be tricked. In newspapers and on handbills, he later often revealed the strategies behind his more elaborate hoaxes.

From 1883 to 1916, William F. Cody, who once killed buffalo for the railroads, promoted himself and his traveling show: "Buffalo Bill's Wild West and Congress of Rough Riders of the World." Cody's troupe—which featured bedouins, Cossacks, and gauchos, as well as "cowboys and Indians"—re-created dramatic gunfights, the Civil War, and battles of the Old West. The show employed sharpshooter Annie Oakley and Lakota medicine man Sitting Bull, whose legends were partially shaped by Cody's nine press agents. These agents were led by John Burke, who successfully promoted the show for its entire thirty-four-year run. Burke was one of the first press agents to use a wide variety of media channels to generate publicity: promotional newspaper stories, magazine articles and ads, dime novels, theater marquees, poster art, and early films. Burke and Buffalo Bill shaped many of the lasting myths

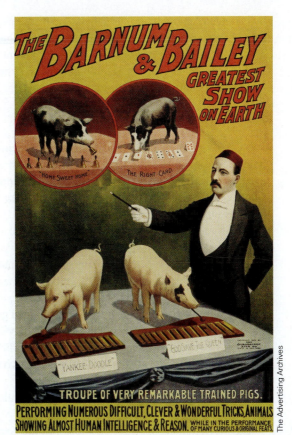

The Advertising Archives

EARLY PUBLIC RELATIONS
Originally called "P. T. Barnum's Great Traveling Museum, Menagerie, Caravan, and Hippodrome," Barnum's circus merged with Bailey's circus in 1881 and again with the Ringling Bros. in 1919. Even with the ups and downs of the Ringling Bros. and Barnum & Bailey Circus over the decades, Barnum's original catchphrase, "The Greatest Show on Earth," endures to this day.

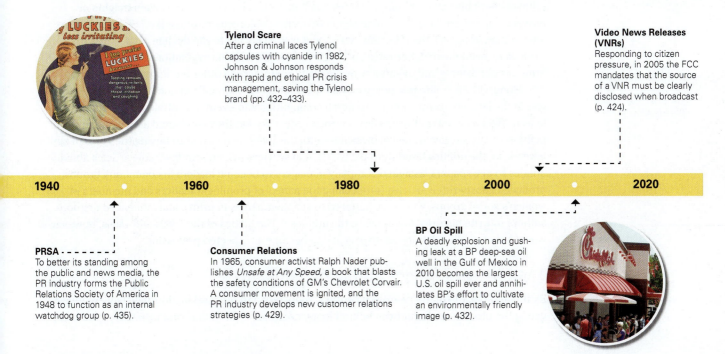

Tylenol Scare
After a criminal laces Tylenol capsules with cyanide in 1982, Johnson & Johnson responds with rapid and ethical PR crisis management, saving the Tylenol brand (pp. 432–433).

Video News Releases (VNRs)
Responding to citizen pressure, in 2005 the FCC mandates that the source of a VNR must be clearly disclosed when broadcast (p. 424).

1940		1960		1980		2000		2020

PRSA
To better its standing among the public and news media, the PR industry forms the Public Relations Society of America in 1948 to function as an internal watchdog group (p. 435).

Consumer Relations
In 1965, consumer activist Ralph Nader publishes *Unsafe at Any Speed*, a book that blasts the safety conditions of GM's Chevrolet Corvair. A consumer movement is ignited, and the PR industry develops new customer relations strategies (p. 429).

BP Oil Spill
A deadly explosion and gushing leak at a BP deep-sea oil well in the Gulf of Mexico in 2010 becomes the largest U.S. oil spill ever and annihilates BP's effort to cultivate an environmentally friendly image (p. 432).

about rugged American individualism and frontier expansion that were later adopted by books, radio programs, and Hollywood films about the American West. Along with Barnum, they were among the first to use **publicity**—a type of PR communication that uses various media messages to spread information about a person, a corporation, an issue, or a policy—to elevate entertainment culture to an international level.

Big Business and Press Agents

As P. T. Barnum, Buffalo Bill, and John Burke demonstrated, utilizing the press brought with it enormous power to sway the public and to generate business. So it is not surprising that during the nineteenth century, America's largest industrial companies—particularly the railroads—also employed press agents to win favor in the court of public opinion.

The railroads began to use press agents to help them obtain federal funds. Initially, local businesses raised funds to finance the spread of rail service. Around 1850, however, the railroads began pushing for federal subsidies, complaining that local fund-raising efforts took too long. For example, Illinois Central was one of the first companies to use government *lobbyists* (people who try to influence the voting of lawmakers) to argue that railroad service between the North and the South was in the public interest and would ease tensions, unite the two regions, and prevent a war.

The railroad press agents successfully gained government support by developing some of the earliest publicity tactics. Their first strategy was simply to buy favorable news stories about rail travel from newspapers through direct bribes. Another practice was to engage in *deadheading*—giving reporters free rail passes with the tacit understanding that they would write glowing reports about rail travel. Eventually, wealthy railroads received the federal subsidies they wanted and increased their profits, while the American public shouldered much of the financial burden of rail expansion.

Having obtained construction subsidies, the larger rail companies turned their attention to bigger game—persuading the government to control rates and reduce competition, especially from smaller, aggressive regional lines. Railroad lobbyists argued that federal support would lead to improved service and guaranteed quality because the government would be keeping a close watch. These lobbying efforts, accompanied by favorable publicity, led to passage of the Interstate Commerce Act in 1887, the first federal law to regulate private industry, which required railroads to publicize their shipping rates, banned special lower rates to certain freights or passengers, and established a commission to oversee enforcement of the law.[9] Historians have argued that, ironically, the PR campaign's success actually led to the decline of the railroads: Artificially maintained higher rates and burdensome government regulations forced smaller firms out of business and eventually drove many customers to other modes of transportation.

Along with the railroads, utility companies such as Chicago Edison and AT&T used PR strategies in the late nineteenth century to derail competition and eventually attain monopoly status. In fact, AT&T's PR and lobbying efforts were so effective that they eliminated all telephone competition—with the government's blessing—until the 1980s. In addition to buying the votes of key lawmakers, the utilities hired third-party editorial services, which sent favorable articles about utilities to newspapers, assigned company managers to become leaders in community groups, produced ghostwritten articles (often using the names of prominent leaders and members of women's social groups, who were flattered to see their names in print), and influenced textbook authors to write histories favorable to the utilities.[10] The tactics of the 1880s and 1890s, however, would haunt public relations as it struggled to become a respected profession.

The Birth of Modern Public Relations

By the first decade of the twentieth century, reporters and muckraking journalists were investigating the promotional practices behind many companies. As an informed citizenry paid more

© Bettmann/Corbis

Photo courtesy of Princeton University. Reprinted by permission.

attention, it became more difficult for large firms to fool the press and mislead the public. With the rise of the middle class, increasing literacy among the working classes, and the spread of information through print media, democratic ideals began to threaten the established order of business and politics—and the elite groups who managed them. Two pioneers of public relations—Ivy Lee and Edward Bernays—emerged in this atmosphere to popularize an approach that emphasized shaping the interpretation of facts and "engineering consent."

Ivy Ledbetter Lee

Most nineteenth-century corporations and manufacturers cared little about public sentiment. By the early 1900s, though, executives had realized that their companies could sell more products if they were associated with positive public images and values. Into this public space stepped Ivy Ledbetter Lee, considered one of the founders of modern public relations. Lee understood that the public's attitude toward big corporations had changed. He counseled his corporate clients that honesty and directness were better PR devices than the deceptive practices of the nineteenth century, which had fostered suspicion and an anti-big-business sentiment.

A minister's son, an economics student at Princeton University, and a former reporter, Lee opened one of the first PR firms in the early 1900s with George Park. Lee quit the firm in 1906 to work for the Pennsylvania Railroad, which, following a rail accident, hired him to help downplay unfavorable publicity. Lee's advice, however, was that Penn Railroad admit its mistake, vow to do better, and let newspapers in on the story. These suggestions ran counter to the then standard practice of hiring press agents to manipulate the media, yet Lee argued that an open relationship between business and the press would lead to a more favorable public image. In the end, Penn and subsequent clients, notably John D. Rockefeller, adopted Lee's successful strategies.

By the 1880s, Rockefeller controlled 90 percent of the nation's oil industry and suffered from periodic image problems, particularly after Ida Tarbell's powerful muckraking series about the ruthless business tactics practiced by Rockefeller and his Standard Oil Company appeared in *McClure's Magazine* in 1904. The Rockefeller and Standard Oil reputations reached a low point in April 1914, when tactics to stop union organizing erupted in tragedy at a coal

IVY LEE, a founding father of public relations (*above*), did more than just crisis work with large companies and business magnates. His PR work also included clients like transportation companies in New York City (*above right*) and aviator Charles Lindbergh.

company in Ludlow, Colorado. During a violent strike, fifty-three workers and their family members died, including thirteen women and children.

Lee was hired to contain the damaging publicity fallout. He immediately distributed a series of "fact" sheets to the press, telling the corporate side of the story and discrediting the tactics of the United Mine Workers, who had organized the strike. As he had done for Penn Railroad, Lee also brought in the press and staged photo opportunities. John D. Rockefeller Jr., who now ran the company, donned overalls and a miner's helmet and posed with the families of workers and union leaders. This was probably the first use of a PR campaign in a labor-versus-management dispute. Over the years, Lee completely transformed the wealthy family's image, urging the discreet Rockefellers to publicize their charitable work. To improve his image, the senior Rockefeller took to handing out dimes to children wherever he went—a strategic ritual that historians attribute to Lee.

Called "Poison Ivy" by corporate foes and critics within the press, Lee had a complex understanding of facts. For Lee, facts were elusive and malleable, begging to be forged and shaped. "Since crowds do not reason," he noted in 1917, "they can only be organized and stimulated through symbols and phrases."[11] In the Ludlow case, for instance, Lee noted that the women and children who died while retreating from the charging company-backed militia had overturned a stove, which caught fire and caused their deaths. One of his PR fact sheets implied that they had, in part, been victims of their own carelessness.

Edward Bernays

The nephew of Sigmund Freud, former reporter Edward Bernays inherited the public relations mantle from Ivy Lee. Beginning in 1919, when he opened his own office, Bernays was the first person to apply the findings of psychology and sociology to public relations, referring to himself as a "public relations counselor" rather than a "publicity agent." Over the years, Bernays's client list included General Electric, the American Tobacco Company, General Motors, *Good Housekeeping* and *Time* magazines, Procter & Gamble, RCA, the government of India, the city of Vienna, and President Coolidge.

Bernays also worked for the Committee on Public Information (CPI) during World War I, developing propaganda that supported America's entry into that conflict and promoting the image of President Woodrow Wilson as a peacemaker. Both efforts were among the first full-scale governmental attempts to mobilize public opinion. In addition, Bernays made key contributions to public relations education, teaching the first class called "public relations"—at New York University in 1923—and writing the field's first textbook, *Crystallizing Public Opinion*. For many years, his definition of PR was the standard: "Public relations is the attempt, by information, persuasion, and adjustment, to engineer public support for an activity, cause, movement, or institution."[12]

In the 1920s, Bernays was hired by the American Tobacco Company to develop a campaign to make smoking more publicly acceptable for women (similar campaigns are under way today in countries like China). Among other strategies, Bernays staged an event: placing women smokers in New York's 1929 Easter parade. He labeled cigarettes "torches of freedom" and encouraged women to smoke as a symbol of their newly acquired suffrage and independence from men. He also asked the women he placed in the parade to contact newspaper and newsreel companies in advance—to announce their symbolic protest. The campaign received plenty of free publicity from newspapers and magazines. Within weeks of the parade, men-only smoking rooms in New York theaters began opening up to women.

Through much of his writing, Bernays suggested that emerging freedoms threatened the established hierarchical order. He thought it was important for experts and leaders to control the direction of American society: "The duty of the higher strata of society—the cultivated, the learned, the expert, the intellectual—is therefore clear. They must inject moral and spiritual motives into public opinion."[13] For the cultural elite to maintain order and control, they would have to win the consent of the larger public. As a result, he described the shaping of public

© Bettmann/Corbis

20,679 Physicians say LUCKIES are *less irritating*

I too prefer LUCKIES *because ...*

Toasting removes dangerous irritants that cause throat irritation and coughing

LUCKY STRIKE "IT'S TOASTED" CIGARETTES

"It's toasted"

Your Throat Protection— against irritation—against cough.

The New York Public Library/Art Resource, NY

EDWARD BERNAYS with his business partner and wife, Doris Fleischman (*left*). Bernays worked on behalf of a client, the American Tobacco Company, to make smoking socially acceptable for women. For one of American Tobacco's brands, Lucky Strike, they were also asked to change public attitudes toward the color green. (Women weren't buying the brand because surveys indicated that the forest green package clashed with their wardrobes.) Bernays and Fleischman organized events such as green fashion shows and sold the idea of a new trend in green to the press. By 1934, green had become the fashion color of the season, making Lucky Strike cigarettes the perfect accessory for the female smoker. Interestingly, Bernays forbade his own wife to smoke, flushing her cigarettes down the toilet and calling smoking a nasty habit.

opinion through PR as the "engineering of consent." Like Ivy Lee, Bernays thought that public opinion was malleable and not always rational: In the hands of the right experts, leaders, and PR counselors, public opinion could be shaped into forms people could rally behind.[14] However, journalists like Walter Lippmann, who wrote the famous book *Public Opinion* in 1922, worried that PR professionals with hidden agendas, rather than journalists with professional detachment, held too much power over American public opinion.

Throughout Bernays's most active years, his business partner and later his wife, Doris Fleischman, worked with him on many of his campaigns as a researcher and coauthor. Beginning in the 1920s, she was one of the first women to work in public relations, and she introduced PR to America's most powerful leaders through a pamphlet she edited called *Contact*. Because she opened up the profession to women from its inception, PR emerged as one of the few professions—apart from teaching and nursing—accessible to women who chose to work outside the home at that time. Today, women outnumber men by more than three to one in the profession.

The Practice of Public Relations

Today, there are more than seven thousand PR firms in the United States, plus thousands of additional PR departments within corporate, government, and nonprofit organizations.[15] Since the 1980s, the formal study of public relations has grown significantly at colleges and universities. By 2014, the Public Relations Student Society of America (PRSSA) had more than eleven thousand members and over three hundred chapters in colleges and universities. As certified PR programs have expanded (often requiring courses or a minor in journalism), the profession has relied less and less on its traditional practice of recruiting journalists for its workforce. At the same time, new courses in professional ethics and issues management have expanded the responsibility of future practitioners. In this section, we discuss the differences between public relations agencies and in-house PR services and the various practices involved in performing PR.

Approaches to Organized Public Relations

The Public Relations Society of America (PRSA) offers this simple and useful definition of PR: "Public relations helps an organization and its publics adapt mutually to each other." To carry out this mutual communication process, the PR industry uses two approaches. First, there are independent PR agencies whose sole job is to provide clients with PR services. Second, most companies, which may or may not also hire independent PR firms, maintain their own in-house PR staffs to handle routine tasks, such as writing press releases, managing various media requests, staging special events, and dealing with internal and external publics.

Many large PR firms are owned by, or are affiliated with, multinational communications holding companies, such as Publicis, Omnicom, WPP, and Interpublic (see Table 12.1). Three of the largest PR agencies—Burson-Marsteller, Hill+Knowlton Strategies, and Ogilvy Public Relations—generated part of the $17.2 billion in revenue earned by their parent corporation, the WPP Group, in 2013. Founded in 1953, Burson-Marsteller has 158 offices and affiliate partners in 110 countries and lists Facebook, IKEA, Coca-Cola, Ford, Sony, and the United Arab Emirates among its clients. Hill+Knowlton, founded in 1927, has 90 offices in 52 countries and includes Johnson & Johnson, Nestlé, Proctor & Gamble, Canon, Splenda, and Latvia on its client list. Most independent PR firms are smaller and are operated locally or regionally. New York–based Edelman, the largest independent firm, is an exception, with global operations and clients like Starbucks, Microsoft, Hewlett-Packard, Samsung, and Unilever.

In contrast to these external agencies, most PR work is done in-house at companies and organizations. Although America's largest companies typically retain external PR firms, almost every company involved in the manufacturing and service industries has an in-house PR department. Such departments are also a vital part of many professional organizations, such as the American Medical Association, the AFL-CIO, and the National Association of Broadcasters, as well as large nonprofit organizations, such as the American Cancer Society, the Arthritis Foundation, and most universities and colleges.

TABLE 12.1

THE TOP 10 PUBLIC RELATIONS FIRMS, 2013 (BY WORLDWIDE REVENUE, IN MILLIONS OF U.S. DOLLARS)

Data from: "CRM/Direct and PR," Advertising Age, April 28, 2014, p. 31.

Rank	Agency	Parent Firm	Headquarters	Revenue
1	Edelman	Independent	New York/Chicago	$741
2	Weber Shandwick	Interpublic	New York	$567
3	Fleishman-Hillard	Omnicom	St. Louis	$551
4	MSL Group	Publicis	Paris	$501
5	Burson-Marsteller	WPP	New York	$466
6	Ketchum	Omnicom	New York	$464
7	Hill+Knowlton Strategies	WPP	New York	$390
8	Ogilvy Public Relations	WPP	New York	$296
9	BlueDigital	BlueFocus Communication Group	Beijing	$271
10	Brunswick Group	Independent	London	$231

Performing Public Relations

Public relations, like advertising, pays careful attention to the needs of its clients—politicians, small businesses, industries, and nonprofit organizations—and to the perspectives of its targeted audiences: consumers and the general public, company employees, shareholders, media organizations, government agencies, and community and industry leaders. To do so, PR involves providing a multitude of services, including publicity, communication, public affairs, issues management, government relations, financial PR, community relations, industry relations, minority relations, advertising, press agentry, promotion, media relations, social networking, and propaganda. This last service, **propaganda**, is communication strategically placed, either as advertising or as publicity, to gain public support for a special issue, program, or policy, such as a nation's war effort.

In addition, PR personnel (both PR technicians, who handle daily short-term activities, and PR managers, who counsel clients and manage activities over the long term) produce employee newsletters, manage client trade shows and conferences, conduct historical tours, appear on news programs, organize damage control after negative publicity, analyze complex issues and trends that may affect a client's future, manage Twitter and other social media accounts, and much more. Basic among these activities, however, are formulating a message through research, conveying the message through various channels, sustaining public support through community and consumer relations, and maintaining client interests through government relations.

© Corbis

WAR PRODUCTION CO-ORDINATING COMMITTEE

WORLD WAR II was a time when the U.S. government used propaganda and other PR strategies to drum up support for the war. One of the more iconic posters at the time asked women to join the workforce.

Research: Formulating the Message

Before anything else begins, one of the most essential practices in the PR profession is doing research. Just as advertising is driven today by demographic and psychographic research, PR uses similar strategies to project messages to appropriate audiences. Because it has historically been difficult to determine why particular PR campaigns succeed or fail, research has become the key ingredient in PR forecasting. Like advertising, PR makes use of mail, telephone, and Internet surveys and focus group interviews—as well as social media analytics tools such as Google Analytics, Twtrland, and Twitter Analytics—to get a fix on an audience's perceptions of an issue, policy, program, or client's image.

Research also helps PR firms focus the campaign message. For example, the Department of Defense hired the PR firm Fleishman-Hillard International Communications to help combat the rising rates of binge drinking among junior enlisted military personnel. The firm first verified its target audience by researching the problem, finding from the Department of Defense's triennial Health Related Behaviors Survey that eighteen- to twenty-four-year-old servicemen

MESSAGE FORMULATION
Appealing to the eighteen- to twenty-four-year-old target age group, the interactive Web site for the Department of Defense's "*That Guy!*" anti-binge-drinking campaign uses humorous terms like "Sloberus Sweatmuchus" and "Drunkus Obnoxious" to describe the stages of intoxication.

had the highest rates of binge drinking. It then conducted focus groups to refine the tone of its antidrinking message and developed and tested its Web site for usability. The finalized campaign concept and message—"Don't Be *That Guy!*"—has been successful: It has shifted binge drinkers' attitudes toward less harmful drinking behaviors through a Web site (www.thatguy .com) and multimedia campaign that combines humorous videos, mobile games, and cartoons with useful resources. By 2012, the campaign had been implemented in over eight hundred military locations across twenty-three countries, and the award-winning Web site had been viewed by approximately 1.3 million visitors.[16]

Conveying the Message

One of the chief day-to-day functions in public relations is creating and distributing PR messages for the news media or the public. There are several possible message forms, including press releases, VNRs, and various online options.

Press releases, or news releases, are announcements written in the style of news reports that give new information about an individual, a company, or an organization and pitch a story idea to the news media. In issuing press releases, PR agents hope that their client information will be picked up by the news media and transformed into news reports. Through press releases, PR firms manage the flow of information, controlling which media get what material in which order. (A PR agent may even reward a cooperative reporter by strategically releasing information.) News editors and broadcasters sort through hundreds of releases daily to determine which ones contain the most original ideas or are the most current. Most large media institutions rewrite and double-check the releases, but small media companies often use them verbatim because of limited editorial resources. Usually, the more closely a press release resembles actual news copy, the more likely it is to be used. Twitter has also become a popular format for releasing information—140 characters or less—to the news media.

Since the introduction of portable video equipment in the 1970s, PR agencies and departments have also been issuing **video news releases (VNRs)**—thirty- to ninety-second visual press releases designed to mimic the style of a broadcast news report. Although networks and large TV news stations do not usually broadcast VNRs, news stations in small TV markets regularly use material from VNRs. On occasion, news stations have been criticized for using video footage from a VNR without acknowledging the source. In 2005, the FCC mandated that broadcast stations and cable operators must disclose the source of the VNRs that they air. As with press releases, VNRs give PR firms some control over what constitutes "news" and a chance to influence what the general public thinks about an issue, a program, or a policy.

The equivalent of VNRs for nonprofits are **public service announcements (PSAs)**: fifteen- to sixty-second audio or video reports that promote government programs, educational projects, volunteer agencies, or social reform. As part of their requirement to serve the public interest, broadcasters have been encouraged to carry free PSAs. Since the deregulation of broadcasting began in the 1980s, however, there has been less pressure and no minimum obligation for TV and radio stations to air PSAs. When PSAs do run, they are frequently scheduled between midnight and 6:00 a.m., a less commercially valuable time slot.

Today, the Internet is an essential avenue for distributing PR messages. Companies upload or e-mail press releases, press kits, and VNRs for targeted groups. Social media has also transformed traditional PR communications. For example, a social media press release pulls together "remixable" multimedia elements, such as text, graphics, video, podcasts, and hyperlinks, giving journalists ample material to develop their own stories.

Media Relations

PR managers specializing in media relations promote a client or an organization by securing publicity or favorable coverage in the news media. This often requires an in-house PR person to speak on behalf of an organization or to direct reporters to experts who can provide information. Media-relations specialists also perform damage control or crisis management when negative publicity occurs. Occasionally, in times of crisis—such as a scandal at a university or a safety recall by a car manufacturer—a PR spokesperson might be designated as the only source of information available to news media. Although journalists often resent being cut off from higher administrative levels and leaders, the institution or company wants to ensure that rumors and inaccurate stories do not circulate in the media. In these situations, a game often develops between PR specialists and the media in which reporters attempt to circumvent the spokesperson and induce a knowledgeable insider to talk off the record, providing background details without being named directly as a source.

PR agents who specialize in media relations also recommend advertising to their clients when it seems appropriate. Unlike publicity, which is sometimes outside a PR agency's control, paid advertising may help focus a complex issue or a client's image. Publicity, however, carries the aura of legitimate news and thus has more credibility than advertising. In addition, media specialists cultivate associations with editors, reporters, freelance writers, and broadcast news

David Sherman/Getty Images

TWITTER MAKES A NEWS STORY
Less than 10 percent of U.S. adults get their news directly from Twitter, but more than half of journalists follow Twitter to get news tips. A tweet can be just as successful as a complete press release in gaining news media coverage. In this example, Priority Sports, a leading sports management firm based in Chicago and Los Angeles, tweeted that its client, NBA forward Robbie Hummel, had just re-signed with the Minnesota Timberwolves. This resulted in dozens of news stories, including one by *Sports Illustrated* online that incorporates an image of the tweet in its story, as well as Robbie Hummel's tweet that he's "excited to be back in Minneapolis for another season."

The NFL's Concussion Crisis

The stylized violence of hard-hitting is a favored American football tradition. Broadcasts of games repeat the most violent tackles with instant replay, often using slow motion to enhance the drama of the hit. Over the years, NFL Films has created several video collections featuring hours of player collisions, with titles like *Crunch Course*, *Moment of Impact*, and *NFL's Hardest Hits*.

But this celebration of big hits has begun to seem callous and cruel, as decades of professional football popularity have produced retired players in their thirties, forties, fifties, and older who are experiencing the trauma of brain damage. The diagnosis is CTE, chronic traumatic encephalopathy, which can leave its victims with problems like hearing loss, memory loss, aggression, depression, and overall dementia. The concussion problem for football players is caused not only by the big concussions that knock them unconscious but also by what researchers call smaller "subconcussions"—the hits to the head that happen many times during a game, and that can number in the hundreds and thousands over the course of a career.

CTE can best be confirmed upon death, when the interior of the brain can be examined to show the buildup of a protein that strangles neurons—not unlike what happens in much older patients with Alzheimer's disease. Several distraught players suffering the symptoms of CTE have committed suicide. Dave Duerson, who played in the NFL in the 1980s and 1990s,

killed himself in 2011 at age fifty, leaving a message to his family requesting that his brain be studied for CTE; researchers verified that he had the condition. In 2012, just two years after he retired from the field, NFL star Junior Seau committed suicide at age forty-three; as with Duerson, researchers checked his brain and confirmed that he had CTE.

In the 2013 book *League of Denial: The NFL, Concussions, and the Battle for Truth*, ESPN investigative reporters (and brothers) Mark Fainaru-Wada and Steve Fainaru explain that the NFL spent years responding to the crisis of concussions with dubious public relations tactics: first covering it up, then denying it, and then generating their own scientific studies to dispute the independent research. The NFL's response mirrors the same deceptive tactics used by big tobacco companies for decades to deny smoking's link to cancer.

The NFL has a lot to protect. Their business is a $10 billion industry, and the very nature of the game requires hulking players to knock their heads and bodies

into other very large players, often running at full speed.[1] As a result, more than four thousand retired players are suing the NFL to cover their head trauma expenses. These stories have begun to change the country's attitude toward the game. News stories about the effects of football concussions are increasingly common, and youth football league participation has dropped nearly 10 percent in the past two years, as parents have grown scared of the impact of the game on their children's health.

More recently, the NFL has responded by trying to change the conversation, acknowledging a concussion problem but emphasizing that the game has always evolved toward more safety in rules and technology (suggesting, perhaps, that it's just a matter of time before this forward march solves the concussion crisis). Indeed, the NFL hired a public relations counsel to help develop the NFLevolution .com site (motto: Forever Forward Forever Football). NFL's Corporate Communications Department also courted "mommy bloggers" to promote football as a healthy, safe activity for their children.

Chris Sweda/Chicago Tribune/MCT via Getty Images

Yet as players continue to come forward with fears or diagnoses of CTE, and as long as the game (and business) of football continues to be played this way, the NFL's public relations crisis will likely persist. As Fainaru-Wada and Fainaru write, "There has never been anything like this in the history of sports: a public health crisis that emerged from the playing fields of our twenty-first-century pastime."[2]

directors to ensure that press releases or VNRs are favorably received (see "Examining Ethics: What Does It Mean to Be Green?" on page 428).

Special Events and Pseudo-events

Another public relations practice involves coordinating *special events* to raise the profile of corporate, organizational, or government clients. Since 1967, for instance, the city of Milwaukee has run Summerfest, a ten-day music and food festival that attracts about a million people each year and now bills itself as "The World's Largest Music Festival." As the festival's popularity grew, various companies sought to become sponsors of the event. Today, Milwaukee's Miller Brewing Company sponsors one of the music festival's stages, which carries the Miller name and promotes Miller Lite as the "official beer" of the festival. Briggs & Stratton and Harley-Davidson are also among the local companies that sponsor stages at the event. In this way, all three companies receive favorable publicity by showing a commitment to the city in which their corporate headquarters are located.[17]

Noel Kessel/Newspix/Getty Images

LADY GAGA established the nonprofit Born This Way Foundation (BTWF) in 2011 to help address childhood bullying and to inspire young people to serve their communities. The organization has incorporated various media elements into its campaign, including a blog and online public service announcements.

More typical of special-events publicity is a corporate sponsor's aligning itself with a cause or an organization that has positive stature among the general public. For example, John Hancock Financial has been the primary sponsor of the Boston Marathon since 1986 and funds the race's prize money. The company's corporate communications department also serves as the PR office for the race, operating the pressroom and creating the marathon's media guide and other press materials. Eighteen other sponsors, including Adidas, Gatorade, PowerBar, and JetBlue Airways, also pay to affiliate themselves with the Boston Marathon. At the local level, companies often sponsor a community parade or a charitable fund-raising activity.

In contrast to a special event, a **pseudo-event** is any circumstance created for the sole purpose of gaining coverage in the media. Historian Daniel Boorstin coined the term in his influential book *The Image* when pointing out the key contributions of PR and advertising in the twentieth century. Typical pseudo-events are press conferences, TV and radio talk-show appearances, or any other staged activity aimed at drawing public attention and media coverage. The success of such events depends on the participation of clients, sometimes on paid performers, and especially on the media's attention to the event. In business, pseudo-events extend back at least as far as P. T. Barnum's publicity stunts, such as parading Jumbo the Elephant across the Brooklyn Bridge in the 1880s. In politics, Theodore Roosevelt's administration set up the first White House pressroom and held the first presidential press conferences in the early 1900s. By the twenty-first century, presidential pseudo-events involved a multimillion-dollar White House Communications Office. One of the most successful pseudo-events in recent years was a record-breaking space-diving project. On October 14, 2012, a helium balloon took Austrian skydiver Felix Baumgartner twenty-four miles into the stratosphere. He jumped from the capsule and went into a free dive for about four minutes, reaching a speed of 833.9 mph before deploying his parachute. Red Bull sponsored the project, which took more than five years of preparation.

As powerful companies, savvy politicians, and activist groups became aware of the media's susceptibility to pseudo-events, these activities proliferated. For example, to get free publicity, companies began staging press conferences to announce new product lines. During the 1960s, antiwar and Civil Rights protesters began their events only when the news media were assembled. One anecdote from that era aptly illustrates the principle of a pseudo-event:

What Does It Mean to Be Green?

Back in the 1930s, public relations pioneer Edward Bernays labored behind the scenes to make green a more fashionable color. Why? Bernays was working to change women's attitudes toward the forest green packaging of his client Lucky Strike's cigarettes so women would smoke them.

Today, public relations professionals are openly working on behalf of clients to promote a different kind of green—environmentally sustainable practices. The idea of green practices goes back at least as far as the very first Earth Day, April 22, 1970, which marked the beginnings of the modern environmental movement. The term *green* as a synonym for being environmentally conscious was inspired by Greenpeace, the international environmental conservation organization founded in 1971, and by a similar political ideology that gained roots in Europe and Australia in the 1970s that prized ecological practices, participatory democracy, nonviolence, and social justice.

TIMBERLAND'S green practices include a nutritional label to show customers the environmental impact of each pair of shoes.

Courtesy of Timberland

Corporations in the United States and elsewhere began adapting to the changing culture, integrating environmental claims into their marketing and public relations. But it wasn't always clear what constituted "green." In 1992, the Federal Trade Commission first issued its "Green Guides," guidelines to ensure that environmental marketing practices don't run afoul of its prohibition against unfair or deceptive acts or practices, sometimes called "greenwashing." As concern about global warming has grown in recent years, green marketing and public relations now extend into nearly every part of business and industry: product packaging (buzzwords include *recyclable*, *biodegradable*, *compostable*, *refillable*, *sustainable*, and *renewable*), buildings and textiles, renewable energy certificates and carbon offsets (funding projects to reduce greenhouse gas emissions in one place to offset carbon emissions produced elsewhere), labor conditions, and fair trade.

Although there have been plenty of companies that make claims of "green" products and services, only some have infused environmentally sustainable practices throughout their corporate culture. In the United States, the New Hampshire–based footwear and clothing company Timberland has been a model for green practices and PR. In 2008, Timberland released a short- and long-term plan for corporate social responsibility performance covering the areas of energy, product, workplace, and service, which represent the company's material impacts. Timberland's plan is particularly noteworthy in that it reports its key corporate social responsibility indicators quarterly (not just once a year) and encourages a two-way dialogue with its stakeholders using social media platforms.

Ultimately, green PR requires a global outlook, as sustainability responds to issues of an increasingly small planet. There are now more than 10,000 corporations in 145 nations belonging to the United Nations Global Compact, a strategic policy initiative launched in 2000 for businesses to align their operations and strategies with ten universally accepted principles in human rights, labor, environment, and anticorruption. Still, the move toward sustainable business practices has a long way to go, as there are more than six million business firms in the United States alone.

The good news for sustainability and green public relations is that executives around the world are embracing the concept. A study by the UN Global Compact in 2011 revealed that 93 percent of 766 CEOs surveyed believe that sustainability will be "important" or "very important" to the future success of their company.[1]

Yet putting sustainability ideas into practice is more difficult. *The 17th Annual Global CEO Survey* in 2014 found that only 46 percent of global CEOs agreed that resource scarcity and climate change would transform their business, and only 26 percent of them reported they would be addressing the risks of climate change and protecting diversity as a priority over the next three years.[2]

A reporter asked a student leader about the starting time for a particular protest; the student responded, "When can you get here?" Today, politicians running for office are particularly adept at scheduling press conferences and interviews to take advantage of TV's appetite for live remote feeds and breaking news.

Community and Consumer Relations

Another responsibility of PR is to sustain goodwill between an agency's clients and the public. The public is often seen as two distinct audiences: communities and consumers.

Companies have learned that sustaining close ties with their communities and neighbors not only enhances their image and attracts potential customers but also promotes the idea that the companies are good citizens. As a result, PR firms encourage companies to participate in community activities, such as hosting plant tours and open houses, making donations to national and local charities, and participating in town events like parades and festivals. In addition, more progressive companies may also get involved in unemployment and job-retraining programs, or donate equipment and workers to urban revitalization projects, such as Habitat for Humanity.

In terms of consumer relations, PR has become much more sophisticated since 1965, when *Unsafe at Any Speed*, Ralph Nader's groundbreaking book, revealed safety problems concerning the Chevrolet Corvair. Not only did Nader's book prompt the discontinuance of the Corvair line, but it also lit the fuse that ignited a vibrant consumer movement. After the success of Nader's book, along with a growing public concern over corporate mergers and corporations' lack of accountability to the public, consumers became less willing to readily accept the claims of corporations. As a result of the consumer movement, many newspapers and TV stations hired consumer reporters to track down the sources of customer complaints and embarrass companies by putting them in the media spotlight. Public relations specialists responded by encouraging companies to pay more attention to customers, establish product service and safety guarantees, and ensure that all calls and mail from customers were answered promptly. Today, PR professionals routinely advise clients that satisfied customers mean not only repeat business but also new business, based on a strong word-of-mouth reputation about a company's behavior and image.

Government Relations and Lobbying

While sustaining good relations with the public is a priority, so is maintaining connections with government agencies that have some say in how companies operate in a particular community, state, or nation. Both PR firms and the PR divisions within major corporations are especially interested in making sure that government regulation neither becomes burdensome nor reduces their control over their businesses.

Government PR specialists monitor new and existing legislation, create opportunities to ensure favorable publicity, and write press releases and direct-mail letters to persuade the public about the pros and cons of new regulations. In many industries, government relations has developed into **lobbying**: the process of attempting to influence lawmakers to support and vote for an organization's or industry's best interests. In seeking favorable legislation, some lobbyists contact government officials on a daily basis. In Washington, D.C., alone, there

EPA/Uwe Ansbach/Newscom

JP MORGAN organizes the JPMorgan Chase Corporate Challenge each year, a series of road races that raise money for several not-for-profit organizations around the world. Taking place in twelve major cities, including New York, Frankfurt, and Shanghai, these races, which are owned and operated by JPMorgan Chase, also allow the financial firm to gain valuable publicity.

FIGURE 12.1

TOTAL LOBBYING SPENDING AND NUMBER OF LOBBYISTS (2000–2013)

Data from: Figures are calculations by the Center for Responsive Politics based on data from the Senate Office of Public Records, accessed August 20, 2014, www.opensecrets.org/lobby.

*The number of unique, registered lobbyists who have actively lobbied.

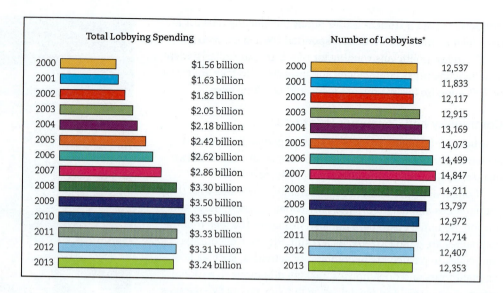

Total Lobbying Spending		Number of Lobbyists*	
2000	$1.56 billion	2000	12,537
2001	$1.63 billion	2001	11,833
2002	$1.82 billion	2002	12,117
2003	$2.05 billion	2003	12,915
2004	$2.18 billion	2004	13,169
2005	$2.42 billion	2005	14,073
2006	$2.62 billion	2006	14,499
2007	$2.86 billion	2007	14,847
2008	$3.30 billion	2008	14,211
2009	$3.50 billion	2009	13,797
2010	$3.55 billion	2010	12,972
2011	$3.33 billion	2011	12,714
2012	$3.31 billion	2012	12,407
2013	$3.24 billion	2013	12,353

are about thirteen thousand registered lobbyists—and thousands more government-relations workers who aren't required to register under federal disclosure rules. Lobbying expenditures targeting the federal government were at $3.24 billion in 2013, far above the $2.05 billion spent ten years earlier.[18] (See Figure 12.1.)

Lobbying can often lead to ethical problems, as in the case of earmarks and astroturf lobbying. *Earmarks* are specific spending directives that are slipped into bills to accommodate the interests of lobbyists and are often the result of political favors or outright bribes. In 2006, lobbyist Jack Abramoff (dubbed "the Man Who Bought Washington" in *Time*) and several of his associates were convicted of corruption related to earmarks, leading to the resignation of leading House members and a decline in the use of earmarks.

Astroturf lobbying is phony grassroots public affairs campaigns engineered by public relations firms. PR firms deploy massive phone banks and computerized mailing lists to drum up support and create the impression that millions of citizens back their client's side of an issue. For instance, the Center for Consumer Freedom (CCF), an organization that appears to serve the interests of consumers, is actually a creation of the Washington, D.C.–based PR firm Berman & Co. and is funded by the restaurant, food, alcohol, and tobacco industries. According to SourceWatch, which tracks astroturf lobbying, anyone who criticizes tobacco, alcohol, processed food, fatty food, soda pop, pharmaceuticals, animal testing, overfishing, or pesticides "is likely to come under attack from CCF."[19]

Public relations firms do not always work for the interests of corporations, however. They also work for other clients, including consumer groups, labor unions, professional groups, religious organizations, and even foreign governments. In 2005, for example, the California Center for Public Health Advocacy—a nonpartisan, nonprofit organization—hired Brown-Miller Communications, a small California PR firm, to rally support for landmark legislation that would ban junk food and soda sales in the state's public schools. Brown-Miller helped state legislators see obesity not as a personal choice issue but as a public policy issue, cultivated the editorial support of newspapers to compel legislators to sponsor the bills, and ultimately succeeded in getting a bill passed.

Presidential administrations also use public relations—with varying degrees of success—to support their policies. From 2002 to 2008, the Bush administration's Defense Department operated a "Pentagon Pundit" program, secretly cultivating more than seventy retired military officers to appear on radio and television talk shows and shape public opinion about the Bush agenda. In 2008, the *New York Times* exposed the unethical program, and its story earned a

Pulitzer Prize.[20] President Obama pledged to be more transparent on day one of his administration, but in 2014, an Associated Press analysis concluded that "the administration has made few meaningful improvements in the way it releases records."[21]

Public Relations Adapts to the Internet Age

Historically, public relations practitioners have tried to earn news media coverage (as opposed to buying advertising) to communicate their clients' messages to the public. While that is still true, the Internet, with its instant accessibility, offers public relations professionals a number of new routes for communicating with the public.

A company or an organization's Web site has become the home base of public relations efforts. Companies and organizations can upload and maintain their media kits (including press releases, VNRs, images, executive bios, and organizational profiles), giving the traditional news media access to the information at any time. And because everyone can access these corporate Web sites, the barriers between the organization and the groups that PR professionals ultimately want to reach are broken down.

The Web also enables PR professionals to have their clients interact with audiences on a more personal, direct basis through social media tools like Facebook, Twitter, YouTube, Wikipedia, and blogs. Now people can be "friends" and "followers" of companies and organizations. Corporate executives can share their professional and personal observations and seem downright chummy through a blog (e.g., Whole Foods Market's blog by CEO John Mackey). Executives, celebrities, and politicians can seem more accessible and personable through a Twitter feed. But social media's immediacy can also be a problem, especially for those who send messages into the public sphere without considering the ramifications.

Another concern about social media is that sometimes such communications appear without complete disclosure, which is an unethical practice. Some PR firms have edited Wikipedia entries for their clients' benefit, a practice Wikipedia founder Jimmy Wales has repudiated as a conflict of interest. A growing number of companies also compensate bloggers to subtly promote their products, unbeknownst to most readers. Public relations firms and marketers are particularly keen on working with "mom bloggers," who appear to be independent voices in discussions about consumer products but may receive gifts in exchange for their opinions. In 2009, the Federal Trade Commission instituted new rules requiring online product endorsers to disclose their connections to companies.

As noted earlier, Internet analytics tools enable organizations to monitor what is being said about them at any time. However, the immediacy of social media also means that public relations officials might be forced to quickly respond to a message or an image once it goes viral. For example, when two Domino's Pizza employees in North Carolina posted a YouTube video of themselves allegedly contaminating food in 2009, it spread like wildfire, much to the horror of the company. The traditional response of waiting for bad news to pass and quietly issuing a statement wasn't sufficient to defuse the situation. Ultimately, Domino's used the Internet to respond to the crisis; the company created a Twitter account to address customers' concerns, and the CEO posted his own apology video.

Public Relations during a Crisis

Since the Ludlow strike, one important duty of PR has been helping a corporation handle a public crisis or tragedy, especially if the

PR AND SOCIAL MEDIA
More companies are using social media tools like Twitter and Facebook to interact with their customers on a more personal level. Chick-fil-A used its Twitter feed in an attempt to counter bad press over the company president's antigay comments.

AP Photo/Longview News-Journal, Kevin Green

public assumes the company is at fault. Disaster management may reveal the best and the worst attributes of the company and its PR firm (see "Case Study: The NFL's Concussion Crisis" on page 426). Let's look at two contrasting examples of crisis management and the different ways they were handled.

One of the largest environmental disasters so far in the twenty-first century occurred in 2010. BP's Deepwater Horizon oil rig exploded on April 10 of that year, killing eleven workers. The oil gushed from the ocean floor for months, spreading into a vast area of the Gulf of Mexico, killing wildlife, and washing tar balls onto beaches. Although the company, formerly British Petroleum, officially changed its name to BP in 2001, adopting the motto Beyond Petroleum and a sunny new yellow and green logo in an effort to appear more "green-friendly," the disaster linked the company back to the hazards of its main business in oil. BP's many public relations missteps included its multiple underestimations of the amount of oil leaking, the chairman's reference to the "small people" of the Gulf region, the CEO's wish that he could "get his life back," and the CEO's attendance at an elite yacht race in England even as the oil leak persisted. In short, many people felt that BP failed to show enough remorse or compassion for the affected people and wildlife. BP tried to salvage its reputation by vowing to clean up the damaged areas, establishing a $20 billion fund to reimburse those economically affected by the spill, and creating a campaign of TV commercials to communicate its efforts. Nevertheless, harsh criticism persisted, and BP's ads were overwhelmed by online parodies and satires of its efforts. Years later, entire communities of fishermen and rig workers continue to be affected, and BP made its first $1 billion payment for Gulf restoration projects.

A decidedly different approach was taken in the 1982 tragedy involving Tylenol pain-relief capsules. Seven people died in the Chicago area after someone tampered with several bottles and laced them with poison. Discussions between the parent company, Johnson & Johnson, and its PR representatives focused on whether or not withdrawing all Tylenol capsules from store shelves might send a signal that corporations could be intimidated by a single deranged person. Nevertheless, Johnson & Johnson's chairman, James E. Burke, and the company's PR agency, Burson-Marsteller, opted for full disclosure to the media and the immediate recall of the capsules nationally, costing the company an estimated $100 million and cutting its market

RALPH LAUREN attracted media scrutiny when it was discovered that the 2012 U.S. Olympic Team uniforms the company designed were manufactured in China. After lawmakers publicly chastised the decision to outsource the uniforms, Lauren released a statement promising to produce the 2014 U.S. Olympic Team's uniforms in the United States.

Doug Mills/The New York Times/Redux Pictures

share in half. As part of its PR strategy to overcome the negative publicity and to restore Tylenol's market share, Burson-Marsteller tracked public opinion nightly through telephone surveys and organized satellite press conferences to debrief the news media. In addition, emergency phone lines were set up to take calls from consumers and health-care providers. When the company reintroduced Tylenol three months later, it did so with tamper-resistant bottles that were soon copied by almost every major drug manufacturer. Burson-Marsteller, which received PRSA awards for its handling of the crisis, found that the public thought Johnson & Johnson had responded admirably to the crisis and did not hold Tylenol responsible for the deaths. In fewer than three years, Tylenol recaptured its former (and dominant) share of the market.

Tensions between Public Relations and the Press

In 1932, Stanley Walker, an editor at the *New York Herald Tribune*, identified public relations agents as "mass-mind molders, fronts, mouthpieces, chiselers, moochers, and special assistants to the president."[22] Walker added that newspapers and PR firms would always remain enemies, even if PR professionals adopted a code of ethics (which they did in the 1950s) to "take them out of the red-light district of human relations."[23] Walker's tone captures the spirit of one of the most mutually dependent—and antagonistic—relationships in all of mass media.

Much of this antagonism, directed at public relations from the journalism profession, is historical. Journalists have long considered themselves part of a public service profession, but some regard PR as having emerged as a pseudo-profession created to distort the facts that reporters work hard to gather. Over time, reporters and editors developed the derogatory term **flack** to refer to a PR agent. The term, derived from the military word *flak*, meaning an antiaircraft artillery shell or a protective military jacket, symbolizes for journalists the protective barrier PR agents insert between their clients and the press. Today, the Associated Press manual for editors defines *flack* simply as "slang for press agent." Yet this antagonism belies journalism's dependence on public relations. Many editors, for instance, admit that more than half of their story ideas each day originate with PR people. In this section, we take a closer look at the relationship between journalism and public relations, which can be both adversarial and symbiotic.

Elements of Professional Friction

The relationship between journalism and PR is important and complex. Although journalism lays claim to independent traditions, the news media have become ever more reliant on public relations because of the increasing amount of information now available. Newspaper staff cutbacks, combined with television's need for local news events, have expanded the news media's need for PR story ideas.

Another cause of tension is that PR firms often raid the ranks of reporting for new talent. Because most press releases are written to imitate news reports, the PR profession has always sought good writers who are well connected to sources and savvy about the news business. For instance, the fashion industry likes to hire former style or fashion news writers for its PR staff, and university information offices seek reporters who once covered higher education. However, although reporters frequently move into PR, public relations practitioners seldom move into journalism; the news profession rarely accepts prodigal sons or daughters back into

the fold once they have left reporting for public relations. Nevertheless, the professions remain codependent: PR needs journalists for publicity, and journalism needs PR for story ideas and access.

Public relations, by making reporters' jobs easier, has often enabled reporters to become lazy. PR firms now supply what reporters used to gather for themselves. Instead of trying to get a scoop, many journalists are content to wait for a PR handout or a good tip before following up on a story. Some members of the news media, grateful for the reduced workload that occurs when they are provided with handouts, may be hesitant to criticize a particular PR firm's clients. Several issues shed light on this discord and on the ways in which different media professions interact.

Undermining Facts and Blocking Access

Journalism's most prevalent criticism of public relations is that it works to counter the truths reporters seek to bring to the public. Modern public relations redefined and complicated the notion of what "facts" are. PR professionals demonstrated that the facts can be spun in a variety of ways, depending on what information is emphasized and what is downplayed. As Ivy Lee noted in 1925: "The effort to state an absolute fact is simply an attempt to achieve what is humanly impossible; all I can do is to give you my interpretation of the facts."[24] With practitioners like Lee showing the emerging PR profession how the truth could be interpreted, the journalist's role as a custodian of accurate information became much more difficult.

Journalists have also objected that PR professionals block press access to key business leaders, political figures, and other newsworthy people. Before the prevalence of PR, reporters could talk to such leaders directly and obtain quotable information for their news stories. Now, however, journalists complain that PR agents insert themselves between the press and the newsworthy, thus disrupting the journalistic tradition in which reporters would vie for interviews with top government and business leaders. Journalists further argue that PR agents are now able to manipulate reporters by giving exclusives to journalists who are likely to cast a story in a favorable light or by cutting off a reporter's access to one of their newsworthy clients altogether if that reporter has written unfavorably about the client in the past.

Promoting Publicity and Business as News

Another explanation for the professional friction between the press and PR involves simple economics. As Michael Schudson noted in his book *Discovering the News: A Social History of American Newspapers*, PR agents help companies "promote as news what otherwise would have been purchased in advertising."[25] Accordingly, Ivy Lee wrote to John D. Rockefeller after he gave money to Johns Hopkins University: "In view of the fact that this was not really news, and that the newspapers gave so much attention to it, it would seem that this was wholly due to the manner in which the material was 'dressed up' for newspaper consumption. It seems to suggest very considerable possibilities along this line."[26] News critics worry that this type of PR is taking media space and time away from those who do not have the financial resources or the sophistication to become visible in the public eye. There is another issue: If public relations can secure news publicity for clients, the added credibility of a journalistic context gives clients a status that the purchase of advertising cannot offer.

Another criticism is that PR firms with abundant resources clearly get more client coverage from the news media than their lesser-known counterparts. For example, a business reporter at a large metro daily sometimes receives as many as a hundred press releases a day—far outnumbering the fraction of handouts generated by organized labor or grassroots organizations. Workers and union leaders have long argued that the money that corporations allocate to PR leads to more favorable coverage for management positions in labor disputes. Therefore, standard news reports may feature subtle language choices, with "rational, coolheaded management making offers" and "hotheaded workers making demands." Walter Lippmann saw such differences in 1922 when he wrote, "If you study the way many a strike is reported in the press, you will find very often that [labor] issues are rarely in the headlines, barely in the leading paragraph, and sometimes not even mentioned anywhere."[27] This imbalance is particularly significant in that the great majority of workers are neither managers nor CEOs, and yet these workers receive little if any media coverage on a regular basis. Most newspapers now have business sections that focus on the work of various managers, but few have a labor, worker, or employee section.[28]

Shaping the Image of Public Relations

Dealing with both a tainted past and journalism's hostility has often preoccupied the public relations profession, leading to the development of several image-enhancing strategies. In 1948, the PR industry formed its own professional organization, the PRSA (Public Relations Society of America). The PRSA functions as an internal watchdog group that accredits PR agents and firms, maintains a code of ethics, and probes its own practices, especially those pertaining to its influence on the news media. Most PRSA local chapters and national conventions also routinely invite reporters and editors to speak to PR practitioners about the news media's expectations of PR. In addition to the PRSA, independent agencies devoted to uncovering shady or unethical public relations activities publish their findings in publications like *Public Relations Tactics*, *PR Week*, and *PRWatch*. Ethical issues have become a major focus of the profession, with self-examination of these issues routinely appearing in public relations textbooks as well as in various professional newsletters (see Table 12.2).

Over the years, as PR has subdivided itself into specialized areas, it has used more positive phrases, such as *institutional relations*, *corporate communications*, and *news and information services* to describe what it does. Public relations' best press strategy, however, may be the limitations of the journalism profession itself. For most of the twentieth century, many reporters and editors clung to the ideal that journalism is, at its best, an objective institution that gathers information on behalf of the public. Reporters have only occasionally turned their pens, computers,

PRSA Member Statement of Professional Values

This statement presents the core values of PRSA members and, more broadly, of the public relations profession. These values provide the foundation for the Member Code of Ethics and set the industry standard for the professional practice of public relations. These values are the fundamental beliefs that guide our behaviors and decision-making process. We believe our professional values are vital to the integrity of the profession as a whole.

ADVOCACY
We serve the public interest by acting as responsible advocates for those we represent.
We provide a voice in the marketplace of ideas, facts, and viewpoints to aid informed public debate.

HONESTY
We adhere to the highest standards of accuracy and truth in advancing the interests of those we represent and in communicating with the public.

EXPERTISE
We acquire and responsibly use specialized knowledge and experience. We advance the profession through continued professional development, research, and education. We build mutual understanding, credibility, and relationships among a wide array of institutions and audiences.

INDEPENDENCE
We provide objective counsel to those we represent. We are accountable for our actions.

LOYALTY
We are faithful to those we represent, while honoring our obligation to serve the public interest.

FAIRNESS
We deal fairly with clients, employers, competitors, peers, vendors, the media, and the general public. We respect all opinions and support the right of free expression.

TABLE 12.2

PUBLIC RELATIONS SOCIETY OF AMERICA ETHICS CODE

In 2000, the PRSA approved a completely revised Code of Ethics, which included core principles, guidelines, and examples of improper conduct. Here is one section of the code.

Data from: The full text of the PRSA Code of Ethics is available at www.prsa.org.

Courtesy of Common Courage Press. Reprinted by permission.

TOXIC SLUDGE IS GOOD FOR YOU!

LIES, DAMN LIES AND THE PUBLIC RELATIONS INDUSTRY

JOHN STAUBER AND SHELDON RAMPTON

INTRODUCTION BY MARK DOWIE

"Terrific! Don't miss it."
—Molly Ivins

THE INVISIBILITY OF PUBLIC RELATIONS is addressed in a series of books by John Stauber and Sheldon Rampton.

and cameras on themselves to examine their own practices or their vulnerability to manipulation. Thus by not challenging PR's more subtle strategies, many journalists have allowed PR professionals to interpret "facts" to their clients' advantage.

Alternative Voices

Because public relations professionals work so closely with the press, their practices are not often the subject of media reports or investigations. Indeed, the multibillion-dollar industry remains virtually invisible to the public, most of whom have never heard of Burson-Marsteller, Hill+Knowlton, or Edelman. The Center for Media and Democracy (CMD) in Madison, Wisconsin, is concerned about the invisibility of PR practices and has sought to expose the hidden activities of large PR firms since 1993. Its *PRWatch* publication reports on the PR industry, with the goal of "investigating and countering PR campaigns and spin by corporations, industries and government agencies."[29] (See "Media Literacy and the Critical Process: The Invisible Hand of PR" on page 437.)

CMD staff members have also written books targeting public relations practices having to do with the Republican Party's lobbying establishment (*Banana Republicans*), U.S. propaganda on the Iraq War (*The Best War Ever*), industrial waste (*Toxic Sludge Is Good for You!*), mad cow disease (*Mad Cow USA*), and PR uses of scientific research (*Trust Us, We're Experts!*). Their work helps bring an alternative angle to the well-moneyed battles over public opinion. "You know, we feel that in a democracy, it's very, very critical that everyone knows who the players are, and what they're up to," said CMD founder and book author John Stauber.[30]

Public Relations and Democracy

From the days of PR's origins in the early twentieth century, many people—especially journalists—have been skeptical of communications originating from public relations professionals. The bulk of the criticism leveled at public relations argues that the crush of information produced by PR professionals overwhelms traditional journalism. However, PR's most significant impact may be on the political process, especially when organizations hire spin doctors to favorably shape or reshape a candidate's media image. In one example, former president Richard Nixon, who resigned from office in 1974 to avoid impeachment hearings regarding his role in the Watergate scandal, hired Hill & Knowlton to restore his postpresidency image. Through the firm's guidance, Nixon's writings, mostly on international politics, began appearing in Sunday op-ed pages. Nixon himself started showing up on television news programs like *Nightline* and spoke frequently before such groups as the American Newspaper Publishers Association and the Economic Club of New York. In 1984, after a media blitz by

Nixon's PR handlers, the *New York Times* announced, "After a decade, Nixon is gaining favor," and *USA Today* trumpeted, "Richard Nixon is back." Before his death in 1994, Nixon, who never publicly apologized for his role in Watergate, saw a large portion of his public image shift from that of an arrogant, disgraced politician to that of a revered elder statesman.[31] Many media critics have charged that the press did not counterbalance this PR campaign and treated Nixon too reverently. In 2014, on the fortieth anniversary of the Watergate scandal, former CBS news anchor Dan Rather remembered Nixon's administration as a "criminal presidency" but added, "There has been an effort to change history, and in some ways it has been successful the last 40 years, saying well, it wasn't all that bad."[32]

In terms of its immediate impact on democracy, the information crush delivered by public relations is at its height during national election campaigns. The 2012 presidential election was the most expensive in history, with President Barack Obama's and Republican candidate Mitt Romney's campaigns spending a combined $2.34 billion. Although much of that money was spent on television advertising, public relations helped hone each campaign's message. PR professionals assembled by *PR Week* magazine generally agreed that Obama's reelection campaign succeeded because it was able to change the focus of the campaign from a referendum on Obama's first term (the Romney campaign's goal) to a choice between candidates with two very different philosophies. They also acknowledged that there were unexpected events that aided Obama with his message. One was Romney's infamous comment at a private

$50,000-a-person fund-raiser. Romney told his supporters, "There are 47 percent of the people who will vote for the president no matter what" because they are "dependent on government," "believe that they are victims," and "believe that they are entitled to health care, to food, to housing. . . . My job is not to worry about those people." His comments were secretly video-taped by a bartender, and when they became a viral sensation, Romney had difficulty recovering from it. As public relations firm owner Carolyn Grisko noted, "The words that come out of a candidate's own mouth are ultimately the ones that resonate."[33] The other unexpected event was Superstorm Sandy, a hurricane that hit the Atlantic coast a week before the election. As president and commander in chief, Obama dominated news headlines in responding to the storm and received praise for his actions from Republican New Jersey governor Chris Christie. Christie later experienced his own public relations nightmare with the George Washington Bridge lane closure scandal. Several of his staff members and appointees ended up losing their jobs for conspiring to close lanes on a busy New Jersey toll plaza for several days in 2013, creating huge traffic jams. Christie denied any involvement in the bridge lane closings and hired a law firm that produced a report exonerating him, but the continuing cloud of scandal tarnished his future political prospects.

Though public relations often provides political information and story ideas, the PR profession bears only part of the responsibility for "spun" news; after all, it is the job of a PR agency to get favorable news coverage for the individual or group it represents. PR professionals police their own ranks for unethical or irresponsible practices, but the news media should also monitor the public relations industry, as they do other government and business activities. Journalism itself also needs to institute changes that will make it less dependent on PR and more conscious of how its own practices play into the hands of spin strategies. A positive example of change on this front is that many major newspapers and news networks now offer regular critiques of the facts and falsehoods contained in political advertising. This media vigilance should be on behalf of citizens, who are entitled to robust, well-rounded debates on important social and political issues.

Like advertising and other forms of commercial speech, PR campaigns that result in free media exposure raise a number of questions regarding democracy and the expression of ideas. Large companies and PR agencies, like well-financed politicians, have money to invest to figure out how to obtain favorable publicity. The question is not how to prevent that but how to ensure that other voices, less well financed and less commercial, also receive an adequate hearing. To that end, journalists need to become less willing conduits in the distribution of publicity. PR agencies, for their part, need to show clients that participating in the democratic process as responsible citizens can serve them well and enhance their image. ▶

DIGITAL JOB OUTLOOK

Media Professionals Speak about Jobs in the Public Relations Industry

Alex T. Williams, Pew Research Center

One factor behind the increase in public relations jobs has been digital technology. Agencies and companies are now able to reach out directly to the public in any number of ways and are hiring public relations specialists to help them do so.

Lindsay Groepper, Vice President, Blastmedia

When I first began my career in PR more than a decade ago, we would e-mail or fax (gasp!) the full press release text to the press. What we see now is new methods of distributing the info, driven by social media. Rather than e-mailing a press release, PR people are sending journalists to custom landing pages created just for that specific announcement, contacting them via Twitter with a BudURL link to the release, or even directing them to a YouTube video with a message from the CEO making the announcement.

Cara Stewart, Founder and Principal, Remarx Media

The most important platforms for PR pros in the future will be the ones most targeted for their clients. Twitter, LinkedIn and Facebook are "fun"; getting nitty-gritty into community sites that are industry-specific is less "fun," because PR pros have to really understand clients' technologies, business models, services, and more. Really, it's more about PR pros becoming better PR pros and understanding their clients' businesses, as well as what their clients do. . . . Social media is not a one-size-fits-all solution.

Erica Swallow, Owner, Southern Swallow Productions

There is also a growing demand for social platforms that make it easier for journalists and PR reps to contact one another. Help a Reporter Out (HARO), PRNewswire's ProfNet, NewsBasis, and Media Kitty are all enabling the communication lines to run in both directions. Rather than having PR reps make the first moves all the time, now members of the media can put out requests for pitches from particular types of experts.

CHAPTER REVIEW

COMMON THREADS

One of the Common Threads in Chapter 1 is the role that media play in a democracy. One key ethical contradiction that can emerge in PR is that (according to the PRSA Code of Ethics) PR should be honest and accurate in disclosing information while being loyal and faithful to clients and their requests for confidentiality and privacy. In this case, how does the general public know when public communications are the work of paid advocacy, particularly when public relations plays such a strong role in U.S. politics?

Public relations practitioners who are members of the Public Relations Society of America (PRSA) are obligated to follow the PRSA Code of Ethics. Members are asked to sign a pledge to conduct themselves "professionally, with truth, accuracy, fairness, and responsibility to the public."

Yet the code is not enforceable, and many public relations professionals simply ignore the PRSA. For example, only 14 of PR giant Burson-Marsteller's 2,200 worldwide employees are PRSA members.[34] Most lobbyists in Washington have to register with the House and Senate, so there is some public record of their activities to influence politics. Conversely, public relations professionals working to influence the political process don't have to register, so unless they act with the highest ethical standards and disclose what they are doing and who their clients are, they operate in relative secrecy.

According to National Public Radio (NPR), public relations professionals in Washington, D.C., work to engineer public opinion in advance of lobbying efforts to influence legislation.

As NPR reported, "For PR folks, conditioning the legislative landscape means trying to shape public perception. So their primary target is journalists like Lyndsey Layton, who writes for the *Washington Post*. She says she gets about a dozen emails or phone calls in a day."[35]

Less ethical work includes assembling phony "astroturf" front groups to engage in communication campaigns to influence legislators, spreading unfounded rumors about an opposing side, and entertaining government officials in violation of government reporting requirements—all things the PRSA code prohibits. Yet these are all-too-frequent practices in the realm of political public relations.

PRSA CEO Rosanna Fiske decries this kind of unethical behavior in her profession. "It's not that ethical public relations equals good public relations," Fiske says. "It is, however, that those who do not practice ethical public relations affect all of us, regardless of the environment in which we work, and the causes we represent."[36]

KEY TERMS

The definitions for the terms listed below can be found in the glossary at the end of the book. The page numbers listed with the terms indicate where the term is highlighted in the chapter.

public relations, 415
press agents, 416
publicity, 418
propaganda, 423

press releases, 424
video news releases (VNRs), 424
public service announcements
    (PSAs), 424

pseudo-event, 427
lobbying, 429
astroturf lobbying, 430
flack, 433

For review quizzes, chapter summaries, links to media-related Web sites, and more, go to **macmillanhighered.com/mediaculture10e**.

REVIEW QUESTIONS

Early Developments in Public Relations

1. What did people like P. T. Barnum and Buffalo Bill Cody contribute to the development of modern public relations in the twentieth century?

2. How did railroads and utility companies give the early forms of corporate public relations a bad name?

3. What contributions did Ivy Lee make toward the development of modern PR?

4. How did Edward Bernays affect public relations?

The Practice of Public Relations

5. What are two approaches to organizing a PR firm?

6. What are press releases, and why are they important to reporters?

7. What is the difference between a VNR and a PSA?

8. What is a pseudo-event? How does it relate to the manufacturing of news?

9. What special events might a PR firm sponsor to build stronger ties to its community?

10. Why have research and lobbying become increasingly important to the practice of PR?

11. How does the Internet change the way in which public relations communicates with an organization's many publics?

12. What are some socially responsible strategies that a PR specialist can use during a crisis to help a client manage unfavorable publicity?

Tensions between Public Relations and the Press

13. Explain the historical background of the antagonism between journalism and public relations.

14. How did PR change old relationships between journalists and their sources?

15. In what ways is conventional news like public relations?

16. How does journalism as a profession contribute to its own manipulation at the hands of competent PR practitioners?

Public Relations and Democracy

17. In what ways does the profession of public relations serve the process of election campaigns? In what ways can it impede election campaigns?

QUESTIONING THE MEDIA

1. What do you think of when you hear the term *public relations*? What images come to mind? Where did these impressions come from?

2. What might a college or university do to improve public relations with homeowners on the edge of a campus who have to deal with noisy student parties and a shortage of parking spaces?

3. What steps can reporters and editors take to monitor PR agents who manipulate the news media?

4. Overall, are social media platforms a good thing for practicing public relations, or do they present more problems than they are worth?

5. Considering the BP, Tylenol, and NFL concussion cases cited in this chapter, what are some key things an organization can do to respond effectively once a crisis hits?

LAUNCHPAD FOR *MEDIA & CULTURE*

Visit LaunchPad for *Media & Culture* *at* **macmillanhighered.com/mediaculture10e** *for additional learning tools:*

- REVIEW WITH LEARNINGCURVE
  LearningCurve, available on LaunchPad for *Media & Culture*, uses gamelike quizzing to help you master the concepts you need to learn from this chapter.

- VIDEO: GOING VIRAL: POLITICAL CAMPAIGNS AND VIDEO
  Online video has changed political campaigning forever. In this video, Peggy Miles of Intervox Communications discusses how politicians use the Internet to reach out to voters.

13

Media Economics and the Global Marketplace

445
Analyzing the Media Economy

448
The Transition to an Information Economy

455
Specialization, Global Markets, and Convergence

463
Social Issues in Media Economics

469
The Media Marketplace and Democracy

At some point in the book *The Circle*, the reader begins to realize that maybe it's not such a good thing that the world's biggest Internet company has gotten so big. The novel, a 2013 best-seller by Dave Eggers, tells the story of the Circle, the idealistic technology corporation headquartered in a vast, beautiful campus on the Pacific coast (not unlike the reality of so many other leading digital media companies). The corporation seems well intentioned: It wants to unify an individual's online identities into one account, with one identity (no anonymous or fake identities), one password, and one payment system—and all data, social media, and transactions simplified into a single account.

With all communication made public, good things start happening. Comment sites become more civil as the anonymous rants of trolls evaporate. People around the world are held accountable as tiny wireless cameras stream live video feeds from everywhere. Human rights violations such as those in Egypt's Tahrir Square? Everyone knows who the perpetrators are. Political dealings in smoke-filled rooms? Politicians are now more accountable, too, as they rise to the challenge to be fully "transparent" and wear a tiny camera that captures the work of all their waking hours. And, of course, advertisements become more focused because advertisers know more about each individual. People are encouraged to share comments, photos, and videos of everything they do, and to respond back with "smiles" or "frowns." Biometric bracelets linked to the Circle create a running log of people's exercise, diet, and health, helping catch any problems before they become serious. It is a technological utopia, whose existence is possible because of the dominance of the Circle in searching, e-mail, texting, and social media (subsuming Google, Facebook, and Twitter).

Yet a utopia in which everyone is encouraged to publicly share every bit of personal information is just a step away from a surveillance state where everyone is required to share, where the desire for privacy carries the social stigma of something to hide, where individuals become unable to control the information of their own lives, and where the lone dominant corporation becomes so big that it controls the flow of information—and perhaps everything else.

The fictional Circle sounds familiar. Google is an obvious comparison, but it also recalls the other major digital conglomerates—Apple, Microsoft, Amazon, Facebook, and others (perhaps Comcast and AT&T)—that would also like to become the dominant media corporation of our time. The question, How big should a media corporation be allowed to get? has long been a concern of media economics. Now, How deep into our lives should a media corporation be allowed to go? becomes an additional concern, as the digital mass media become so intimately enmeshed in our everyday lives.

▲ **THE MEDIA TAKEOVERS, MULTIPLE MERGERS, AND CORPORATE CONSOLIDATION**
over the last two decades have made our modern world very distinct from that of earlier generations—at least in economic terms. What's at the heart of this "brave new media world" is a media landscape that has been forever altered by the emergence of the Internet and a changing of the guard, from traditional media giants like Comcast and Time Warner to new digital giants like Amazon, Apple, Facebook, Google, and Microsoft. As the Yahoo! and Netflix ventures demonstrate, the Internet is marked by shifting and unpredictable terrain. In usurping the classified ads of newspapers and altering distribution for music, movies, and TV programs, the Internet has forced almost all media businesses to rethink not only the content they provide but the entire economic structure within which our capitalist media system operates.

Visit **LaunchPad for**
Media & Culture and
use **LearningCurve** to review
concepts from this chapter.

In this chapter, we examine the economic impact of business strategies on various media. We will:

- Explore the issues and tensions that are part of the current media economy
- Examine the rise of the Information Age, distinguished by flexible, specialized, and global markets
- Investigate the breakdown of economic borders, focusing on media consolidation, corporate mergers, synergy, deregulation, and the emergence of an economic global village
- Address ethical and social issues in media economics, investigating the limits of antitrust laws, the concept of consumer control, and the threat of cultural imperialism
- Examine the rise of new digital media conglomerates
- Consider the impact of media consolidation on democracy and on the diversity of the marketplace

As you read through this chapter, think about the different media you use on a daily basis. What media products or content did you consume over the past week? Do you know who owns them? How important is it to know this? Do you consume popular culture or read news from other countries? Why or why not? For more questions to help you understand the role of media economics in our lives, see "Questioning the Media" in the Chapter Review.

Analyzing the Media Economy

Given the sprawling scope of the mass media, the study of their economic conditions poses a number of complicated questions:

- What role does the government need to play in determining who owns the mass media and what kinds of media products are manufactured? Should it be a strong role, or should the government step back and let competition and market forces dictate what happens to mass media industries?
- Should citizen groups play a larger part in demanding that media organizations help maintain the quality of social and cultural life?
- Does the influence of American popular culture worldwide smother or encourage the growth of democracy and local cultures?
- Does the increasing concentration of economic power in the hands of several international corporations too severely restrict the number of players and voices in the media?

Answers to such questions span the economic and social spectrums. On the one hand, critics express concerns about the increasing power and reach of large media conglomerates. On the other hand, many free-market advocates maintain that as long as these structures ensure efficient operation and generous profits, they measure up as quality media organizations.

In order to probe these issues fully, we need to understand key economic concepts across two broad areas: media structure and media performance.[1]

The Structure of the Media Industry

Media industries are typically structured in one of three ways: as a **monopoly**, an **oligopoly** (the most common structure), or a **limited competition** (typical of the radio and newspaper industries).[2] For a detailed explanation of these structures, refer to Figure 13.1.

The Performance of Media Organizations

In analyzing the performance of media organizations, economists pay attention to a number of elements—from how media make money to how they set prices and live up to society's expectations.

Collecting Revenue

The media collect revenues in two ways: through direct and indirect payments. **Direct payment** involves media products supported primarily by consumers, who pay directly for a book, a movie, a music download, or an Internet or cable TV service. **Indirect payment** involves media products supported primarily by advertisers, who pay for the quantity or quality of audience members that a particular medium delivers. Over-the-air radio and TV broadcasting and most Web sites rely on indirect payments for the majority of their revenue.

Through direct payments, consumers communicate their preferences immediately. Through the indirect payments of advertising, "the client is the advertiser, not the viewer or listener or reader," according to media economist Douglas Gomery.[3] Advertisers, in turn, seek media channels that persuade customers to acquire new products or switch brand loyalties.

Many forms of mass media, of course, generate revenue both directly and indirectly, including newspapers, magazines, some video games, online services, and cable systems.

▼ **Media Economics and the Global Marketplace**

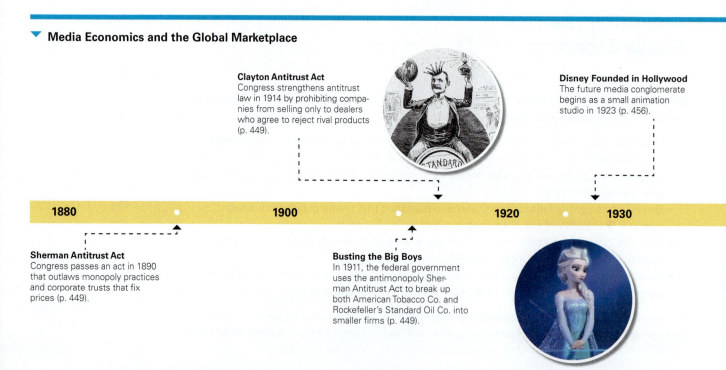

Clayton Antitrust Act
Congress strengthens antitrust law in 1914 by prohibiting companies from selling only to dealers who agree to reject rival products (p. 449).

Disney Founded in Hollywood
The future media conglomerate begins as a small animation studio in 1923 (p. 456).

1880   1900   1920   1930

Sherman Antitrust Act
Congress passes an act in 1890 that outlaws monopoly practices and corporate trusts that fix prices (p. 449).

Busting the Big Boys
In 1911, the federal government uses the antimonopoly Sherman Antitrust Act to break up both American Tobacco Co. and Rockefeller's Standard Oil Co. into smaller firms (p. 449).

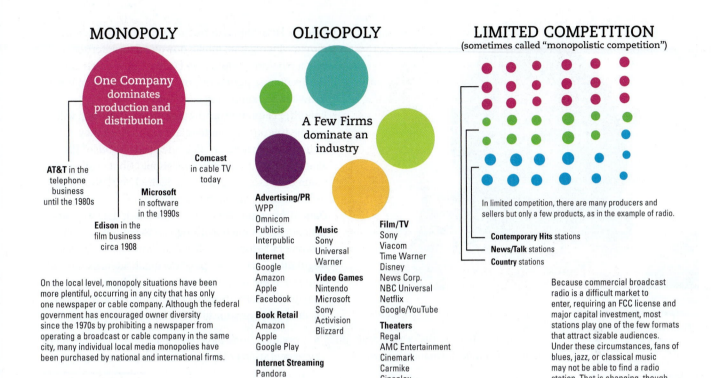

MONOPOLY

One Company dominates production and distribution

AT&T in the telephone business until the 1980s

Microsoft in software in the 1990s

Edison in the film business circa 1908

Comcast in cable TV today

On the local level, monopoly situations have been more plentiful, occurring in any city that has only one newspaper or cable company. Although the federal government has encouraged owner diversity since the 1970s by prohibiting a newspaper from operating a broadcast or cable company in the same city, many individual local media monopolies have been purchased by national and international firms.

OLIGOPOLY

A Few Firms dominate an industry

Advertising/PR
WPP
Omnicom
Publicis
Interpublic

Internet
Google
Amazon
Apple
Facebook

Book Retail
Amazon
Apple
Google Play

Internet Streaming
Pandora
Spotify
Deezer

Music
Sony
Universal
Warner

Video Games
Nintendo
Microsoft
Sony
Activision
Blizzard

Film/TV
Sony
Viacom
Time Warner
Disney
News Corp.
NBC Universal
Netflix
Google/YouTube

Theaters
Regal
AMC Entertainment
Cinemark
Carmike
Cineplex
Marcus

LIMITED COMPETITION
(sometimes called "monopolistic competition")

In limited competition, there are many producers and sellers but only a few products, as in the example of radio.

Contemporary Hits stations
News/Talk stations
Country stations

Because commercial broadcast radio is a difficult market to enter, requiring an FCC license and major capital investment, most stations play one of the few formats that attract sizable audiences. Under these circumstances, fans of blues, jazz, or classical music may not be able to find a radio station. That is changing, though, with the Internet.

FIGURE 13.1

MEDIA INDUSTRY STRUCTURES

Commercial Strategies

When selling media content (and selling their audience to their advertising clients), media industry executives look to the most advantageous balance in the commercial process, including program or product costs, price setting, marketing strategies, and regulatory practices. Following are some common questions for every media industry.

Celler-Kefauver Act
In 1950, corporate mergers and joint ventures that reduce competition are limited (p. 449).

Disney Buys ABC
The 1995 deal is approved despite concerns that ABC News will pull its punches in coverage of Disney's empire (pp. 451, 457).

EchoStar-DirecTV Merger Blocked
The FCC moves to block a deal in 2002 that would have created a direct broadcast satellite (DBS) monopoly (pp. 465, 467).

AOL buys the *Huffington Post*
Looking to reverse its decline, AOL acquires the *Huffington Post* for $315 million in 2011 (p. 451).

| 1950 | 1970 | 1990 | 2010 | 2020 |

GATT Established
The General Agreement on Tariffs and Trade is established in 1947, opening an era of increasing globalization. The signing of NAFTA in 1994 and formation of the WTO in 1995 further encourage trade and the export of certain jobs (p. 455).

GE Buys NBC
The 1985 merger sets off a wave of media consolidation (p. 450).

AOL Merges with Time Warner
Time Warner, already the largest media corporation, becomes even larger in 2001 with the addition of AOL, the largest Internet service provider (p. 451).

Yahoo! Buys Tumblr
In 2013, Yahoo! stakes its social media claim by buying the popular blogging site (p. 463).

AP Photo/The Canadian Press, Frank Gunn

OPRAH WINFREY has built a remarkable media empire over the course of her long career. From book publishing to filmmaking and television, where she got her start, Oprah has established an expansive sphere of influence. After ending her talk show, she launched the cable TV network *OWN* in 2011, which after a slow start moved toward stability on the strength of scripted television programs.

- **Price.** How high can the price be raised of a book, movie, video game, music download, or Internet service before people won't buy it? How much can Netflix charge per month before its subscribers begin to switch to competing services?
- **Length, Frequency, and Tolerance.** How long will people tolerate a commercial break before they switch the channel or click on something else? For example, how many seconds should Google allow a commercial to run prior to a desired YouTube video before a user can "skip the ad"?
- **Data Mining and Privacy.** How much data can media companies such as Google or Facebook collect on customers before they find it an invasion of privacy?
- **Regulation.** For example, how much advertising of alcohol to underage audiences can a media company get away with before drawing the attention of media critics, consumer organizations, and regulatory boards?

Economists, media critics, and consumer organizations have also asked the mass media to meet certain performance criteria. Some key expectations of media organizations include:

- Introducing new technologies to the marketplace (e.g., improving the speed of broadband connections)
- Making media products and services available to people of all economic classes
- Facilitating free expression and robust political discussion
- Monitoring society in times of crisis
- Playing a positive role in education
- Maintaining the quality of culture[4]

Although media industries live up to some of these expectations better than others, economic analyses permit consumers and citizens to examine the instances when the mass media fall short. For example, when corporate executives trim news budgets or fire news personnel, or use one reporter to do multiple versions of a story for TV, radio, newspaper, and the Internet, such decisions ultimately reduce the total number of distinct news stories that cover a crucial topic and may jeopardize the role of journalists as watchdogs of society. Media economic decisions thus affect the society in which we live.

The Transition to an Information Economy

The twentieth century can be divided in two. The first half of the century emphasized mass production, assembly lines, the rise of manufacturing plants, and the intense rivalry between U.S.-based businesses and businesses from other nations that produced competing products. By the 1950s, however, the U.S. economy was beginning a transition to a new cooperative global economy as the machines that drove the Industrial Age changed gears for the new Information Age. Offices slowly displaced factories as major work sites; centralized mass production declined and often gave way to internationalized, decentralized, and lower-paid service work; and the information-based economy became driven by computers and data.

As part of the shift to an information-based economy, various mass media industries began marketing music, movies, television programs, and computer software on a global level. The emphasis on mass production (e.g., television programs targeted to mass audiences, or magazines designed to appeal to a broad cross section of the U.S. population) slowly shifted to the cultivation of specialized niche media markets. The political and economic forces swung from regulating media industries (and industries in general) in the first half of the twentieth century to deregulating them in the second half. Decades of deregulation have led to media mergers and acquisitions, resulting in media powerhouses and more concentrated ownership in nearly every media sector.

Deregulation Trumps Regulation

During the rise of industry in the nineteenth century, entrepreneurs such as John D. Rockefeller in oil, Cornelius Vanderbilt in shipping and railroads, and Andrew Carnegie in steel created monopolies in their respective industries. There was so little regulation of these newly powerful industries that the companies became notorious for their exploitative labor practices (including child labor), corrupt corporate conduct, and manipulation of the competitive landscape. Corporations and their business partners were often organized as "trusts," but soon the word *trust* became equated with any large corporation—particularly large, unethical corporations that would try to drive out fair competition. Congress responded by enacting the first antitrust law in 1890, the Sherman Antitrust Act, which outlawed monopoly practices and corporate trusts that often fixed prices to force competitors out of business. Political progressives and muckraking journalists brought more anticompetitive trusts to light. In 1911, the government used the Sherman Antitrust Act to break up both the American Tobacco Company and Rockefeller's Standard Oil Company, which was divided into thirty smaller competing firms.

In 1914, Congress passed the Clayton Antitrust Act, prohibiting manufacturers from selling only to dealers and contractors who agree to reject the products of business rivals. The Celler-Kefauver Act of 1950 further strengthened antitrust rules by limiting any corporate mergers and joint ventures that reduced competition. Today, the Federal Trade Commission (established in 1914) and the antitrust division of the Department of Justice are responsible for enforcing these laws.

Deregulation Spurs Formation of Media Conglomerates

The corporate regulations introduced between 1890 and 1950 were meant to increase competition between companies and prevent any one company from having too much control over the market. However, corporations chafed under these economic rules, and with the rise of public relations tactics and aggressive lobbying campaigns from the 1920s onward, they worked to turn the anticorporate rhetoric so prominent throughout the first half of the twentieth century (particularly in light of the Great Depression) into a commonsense narrative that government

© Bettmann/Corbis

ANTITRUST REGULATION
During the late nineteenth century, John D. Rockefeller Sr., considered the richest businessman in the world, controlled more than 90 percent of the U.S. oil refining business. But antitrust regulations were used in 1911 to bust up Rockefeller's powerful Standard Oil into more than thirty separate companies. He later hired PR guru Ivy Lee to refashion his negative image as a greedy corporate mogul.

regulation was bad for business and bad for America.[5] Although the administration of President Jimmy Carter (1977–1981) actually initiated deregulation, under President Ronald Reagan (1981–1989) most controls on business were drastically weakened. Deregulation led to easier mergers, corporate diversifications, and increased tendencies in some sectors toward oligopolies (especially in air travel, energy, finance, and communications).[6]

The Telecommunications Act of 1996 (signed by President Bill Clinton) brought unprecedented deregulation to a broadcast industry that had been closely regulated for more than sixty years. The act transformed the industry:

- A single company could now own an almost unlimited number of radio and TV stations.
- Telephone companies could now own TV and radio stations.
- Cable companies could now compete in the local telephone business.
- Cable companies could freely raise rates.

Prior to this, a company could own no more than twenty AM, twenty FM, and twelve TV stations. After the act, several corporations quickly grew to owning hundreds of stations. As a result, radio and television ownership became increasingly consolidated. At the time, some economists thought the new competition would lower consumer prices. Others predicted more mergers and an oligopoly in which a few megacorporations would control most of the wires entering a home and thus dictate pricing.

As it turned out, the latter group was right. Ever-larger corporations control cable, telephone, and broadband service to households, and they have charged ever-increasing prices. For example, the average monthly price of basic cable service grew to $64.41 by 2013, a price increase almost triple the rate of inflation since 1995.[7] Of course, cable, telephone, and satellite companies are delivering even more channels to consumers. But because the industry "bundles" channels, most consumers pay for far more channels than they watch. The average U.S. home was receiving 189 TV channels by 2013, but watched only about 17 of them.[8]

Media Powerhouses: Consolidation, Partnerships, and Mergers

Despite their strength, the antitrust laws of the twentieth century have been unevenly applied, especially in terms of the media. When International Telephone & Telegraph (ITT) tried to acquire ABC in the 1960s, loud protests and government investigations sank the deal. But in the mid-1980s, just as the Justice Department was breaking up AT&T's century-old monopoly—creating telephone competition—the government was authorizing a number of mass media mergers that consolidated power in the hands of a few large companies. For example, when General Electric set out to purchase RCA/NBC in the 1980s, the FTC, the FCC, and the Justice Department had few objection. When NBC Universal changed hands again—in its 2011 purchase by cable giant Comcast that created the nation's largest traditional media conglomerate—the *New York Times* reported that "Comcast said it faced few onerous restrictions" from federal regulatory agencies and no requirements to sell any assets.[9]

MEDIA ACQUISITIONS like Comcast's purchase of NBC Universal enable a distribution company (Comcast) to also control the production (by NBC Universal) of much of its content. Comcast, the largest cable and broadband provider in the United States, now owns many of the channels that appear on its cable systems, including NBC, Telemundo, SyFy, E!, USA, Bravo, NBC Sports, the Golf Channel, MSNBC, CNBC, and the Weather Channel.

NBC/Photofest

In 1995, Disney acquired ABC for $19 billion. To ensure its rank as the world's largest media conglomerate, Time Warner countered and bought Turner Broadcasting in 1995 for $7.5 billion. In 2001, AOL acquired Time Warner for $164 billion—the largest media merger in history at the time. For a time, the company was called AOL–Time Warner. However, when the online giant saw its subscription service decline in the face of new high-speed broadband services from cable firms, the company went back to the Time Warner name and spun off AOL in 2009. Time Warner's failed venture in the volatile world of the Internet proved disastrous. The companies together were valued at $350 billion in 2000 but only at $50 billion in 2010. After suffering losses of over $700 million in 2010, AOL in 2011 bought the *Huffington Post*, a popular news and analysis Web site, for $315 million in an attempt to reverse its decline.

Also in 2001, the federal government approved a $72 billion deal uniting AT&T's cable division with Comcast, creating a cable company twice the size of its nearest competitor. (AT&T quickly left the merger, selling its cable holdings to Comcast for $47 billion late in 2001.) In 2009, Comcast struck a deal with GE to purchase a majority stake in NBC Universal, stirring up antitrust complaints from some consumer groups. In 2010, Congress began hearings on whether uniting a major cable company and a major broadcasting network under a single owner would decrease healthy competition between cable and broadcast TV and would hurt consumers. In 2011, the FCC approved the deal.

Until the 1980s, antitrust rules attempted to ensure diversity of ownership among competing businesses. Sometimes this happened, as in the breakup of AT&T, and sometimes it did not, as in the cases of cable monopolies and the mergers just discussed. What has occurred consistently, however, is media competition being usurped by media consolidation. Today, the same anticompetitive mind-set exists that allowed a few utility and railroad companies to control their industries in the days before antitrust laws.

Most media companies have skirted monopoly charges by purchasing diverse types of mass media rather than trying to control just one medium. For example, Disney, rather than trying to dominate one area, provides programming to TV, cable, and movie theaters. In 1995, then CEO Michael Eisner defended the company's practices, arguing that as long as large companies remain dedicated to quality—and as long as Disney did not try to buy the phone lines and TV cables running into homes—such mergers benefit America.

But Eisner's position raises questions: How is the quality of cultural products determined? If companies cannot make money on quality products, what happens? If ABC News cannot make a substantial profit, should Disney's managers cut back their national or international news staff? What are the potential effects of such layoffs on the public mission of news media and consequently on our political system? How should the government and citizens respond?

Business Tendencies in Media Industries

In addition to the consolidation trend, a number of other factors characterize the economics of mass media businesses. These are general trends or tendencies that cut across most business sectors and demonstrate how contemporary global economies operate.

Flexible Markets and the Decline of Labor Unions

Geographer David Harvey has observed that today's information culture is characterized by what business executives call flexibility—a tendency to emphasize "the new, the fleeting . . . and the contingent in modern life, rather than the more solid values implanted" during Henry Ford's day, when relatively stable mass production drove mass consumption.[10] The new elastic economy features the expansion of the service sector (most notably in health care, banking, real estate, fast food, Internet ventures, and computer software) and the need to serve individual consumer preferences. This type of economy has relied on cheap labor—sometimes exploiting poor workers in sweatshops—and on quick, high-volume sales to offset the costs of making so many niche products for specialized markets.

Given that 80 to 90 percent of new consumer and media products typically fail, a flexible economy has demanded rapid product development and efficient market research. Companies need to score a few hits to offset investments in failed products. For instance, during the peak summer movie season, studios premiere dozens of new feature films, such as *The Fault in Our Stars*, *Teenage Mutant Ninja Turtles*, and *Guardians of the Galaxy* in 2014. A few are hits but many more miss, and studios hope to recoup their losses via merchandising tie-ins and movie rentals and sales. Similarly, TV networks introduce scores of new programs each year but quickly replace those that fail to attract a large audience or the "right" kind of affluent viewers. Of course, this flexible media system heavily favors large companies with greater access to capital over small businesses that cannot easily absorb the losses incurred from failed products.

The era of flexible markets also coincided with the decline in the number of workers who belong to labor unions. Having made strong gains on behalf of workers after World War II, labor unions, at their peak in 1954, represented 34.8 percent of U.S. workers. Then manufacturers and other large industries began to look for ways to cut labor costs, which had increased as then-powerful labor unions successfully bargained for middle-class wages. With the shift to an information economy, many jobs—such as manufacturing computers, stereo systems, TV sets, and DVD players—were exported to avoid the high price of U.S. unionized labor. (See "Global Village: Designed in California, Assembled in China," in Chapter 2, which describes the conditions in which the Chinese company Foxconn currently makes electronic devices for Apple, Amazon, Microsoft, Sony, and a number of other electronics brands.) As large companies bought up small companies across national boundaries, commerce developed rapidly at the global level. According to the U.S. Department of Labor, union membership fell to 20.1 percent in 1983 and 11.3 percent three decades later, flattening out at the lowest rate in more than seventy years.[11]

Downsizing and the Wage Gap

With the apparent advantage to large companies in this flexible age, who is disadvantaged? From the beginning of the recession in December 2007 through 2009, the United States lost more than 8.4 million jobs (affecting 6.1 percent of all employers), creating the highest unemployment contraction since the Great Depression.[12] The unemployment rate started to recede in 2009, but from 2009 to 2012, as the economy slowly recovered, 95 percent of postrecession income growth was captured by the top 1 percent—those Americans with the greatest income.[13]

Inequality in the United States between the richest and everyone else has been growing since the 1970s. This is apparent in the skyrocketing rate of executive compensation and the growing ratio between executive pay and the typical pay of workers in corresponding industries. In 1965, the CEO-to-worker compensation ratio was 20:1 (i.e., the typical CEO earned 20 times the salary of the typical worker in that industry). By 2013, the ratio had climbed to 295.9:1 (see Figure 13.2).[14] Media corporations are among those with the highest wage gaps. In 2013, Robert Iger of Disney (No. 3 on the highest paid CEO list at $37.1 million), Philippe P. Dauman of Viacom (No. 5 at $33.3 million), and Rupert Murdoch of News Corp.

FIGURE 13.2

CEO-TO-WORKER WAGE GAP, 1965 AND 2013

Data from: Lawrence Mishel and Alyssa Davis, "CEO Pay Continues to Rise as Typical Workers Are Paid Less," Economic Policy Institute, June 12, 2014, www.epi.org/publication/ceo-pay-continues-to-rise/.

1965
CEO   Everyone Else

2013
CEO   Everyone Else

(No. 13 at $22.4 million) were among the highest paid CEOs of publicly traded companies in the United States.[15]

Corporate downsizing, which is supposed to make companies more flexible and more profitable, has served CEOs well but has not served workers well. This trend, spurred by government deregulation and a decline in worker protections, means that many employees today scramble for jobs, often working two or three part-time positions. Increasingly, the available positions have substandard pay. The National Employment Law Project reported that "more than one in four private sector jobs (26 percent) were low-wage positions paying less than $10 per hour."[16] This translates to a salary of about $20,000 a year or less. And the flexible economy keeps moving in that direction. The U.S. Bureau of Labor Statistics estimated in 2012 that 70 percent of the leading growth occupations for the next decade are low-wage ones.[17] Even as most big businesses had recovered from the recession and experienced record profits by 2011, their low-wage workers' wages still suffered. For example, at the top fifty low-wage employers, including Target, McDonald's, Panera, Macy's, and Abercrombie & Fitch, the highest-paid executives earned an average of $9.4 million a year. At that rate, they earned about $4,520 an hour, an amount it would take more than six hundred minimum-wage employees to earn in the same time period.[18] Based on Robert Iger's 2013 annual salary of $37.1 million, it would take 2,460 minimum-wage Disney employees to earn as much as he earns in a year.

Economics, Hegemony, and Storytelling

To understand why our society hasn't (until recently) participated in much public discussion about wealth disparity and salary gaps, it is helpful to understand the concept of hegemony. The word *hegemony* has roots in ancient Greek, but in the 1920s and 1930s, Italian philosopher and activist Antonio Gramsci worked out a modern understanding of hegemony: how a ruling class in a society maintains its power—not simply by military or police force but more commonly by citizens' consent and deference to power. He explained that people who are without power—the disenfranchised, the poor, the disaffected, the unemployed, exploited workers—do not routinely rise up against those in power because "the rule of one class over another does not depend on economic or physical power alone but rather on persuading the ruled to accept the system of beliefs of the ruling class and to share their social, cultural, and moral values."[19] **Hegemony**, then, is the acceptance of the dominant values in a culture by those who are subordinate to those who hold economic and political power.

How, then, does this process actually work in our society? How do lobbyists, the rich, and our powerful two-party political system convince regular citizens that they should go along with the status quo? Edward Bernays, one of the founders of modern public relations (see Chapter 12), wrote in his 1947 article "The Engineering of Consent" that companies and rulers couldn't lead people—or get them to do what the ruling class wanted—until the people consented to what those companies or rulers were trying to do, whether it was convincing the public to support women smoking cigarettes or to go to war. To pull this off, Bernays would convert a client's goals into "common sense"; that is, he tried to convince consumers and citizens that his clients' interests were the "natural" way things worked.

So if companies or politicians convinced consumers and voters that the interests of the powerful were common sense and therefore normal or natural, they also created an atmosphere and context in which there was less chance for challenge and criticism. Common sense, after all, repels self-scrutiny ("that's just plain common sense—end of discussion"). In this case, status quo values and conventional wisdom (e.g., hard work and religious belief are rewarded with economic success) and political arrangements (e.g., the traditional two-party system serves democracy best) become accepted as normal and natural ways to organize and see the world.

To argue that a particular view or value is common sense is often an effective strategy for stopping conversation and debate. Yet common sense is socially and symbolically constructed and shifts over time. For example, it was once common sense that the world was flat and that people who were not property-owning white males shouldn't be allowed to vote. Common sense is particularly powerful because it contains no analytical strategies for criticizing elite or dominant points of view and therefore certifies class, race, or sexual orientation divisions or mainstream political views as natural and given.

To buy uncritically into concepts presented as common sense inadvertently serves to maintain such concepts as natural, shutting down discussions about the ways in which economic divisions or political hierarchies are *not* natural and given. So when Democratic and Republican candidates run for office, the stories they tell about themselves espouse their connection to Middle American common sense and down-home virtues—for example, a photo of Mitt Romney eating a Subway sandwich or a video of Barack Obama playing basketball in a small Indiana high school gym. These ties to ordinary commonsense values and experience connect the powerful to the everyday, making their interests and ours appear to be seamless.

To understand how hegemony works as a process, let's examine how common sense is practically and symbolically transmitted. Here it is crucial to understand the central importance of storytelling to culture. The narrative—as the dominant symbolic way we make sense of experience and articulate our values—is often a vehicle for delivering common sense. Therefore, ideas, values, and beliefs can be carried in our mainstream stories—the stories we tell and find in daily conversations, in the local paper, in political ads, and on the evening news, or in books, magazines, movies, favorite TV shows, and online. The narrative, then, is the normal and familiar structure that aids in converting ideas, values, and beliefs to common sense—normalizing them into "just the way things are."

The reason that common narratives work is that they identify with a culture's dominant values; Middle American virtues include allegiances to family, honesty, hard work, religion, capitalism, health, democracy, moderation, loyalty, fairness, authenticity, modesty, and so forth. These kinds of Middle American virtues are the ones that our politicians most frequently align themselves with in the political ads that tell their stories. These virtues lie at the heart of powerful American Dream stories that for centuries have told us that if we work hard and practice such values, we will triumph and be successful. Hollywood, too, distributes these shared narratives, celebrating characters and heroes who are loyal, honest, and hardworking. Through this process, the media (and the powerful companies that control them) provide the commonsense narratives that keep the economic status quo relatively unchallenged and leave little room for alternatives.

In the end, hegemony helps explain why we occasionally support economic plans and structures that may not be in our best interest. We may do this out of altruism, as when wealthy people or companies favor higher taxes because of a sense of obligation to support those who are less fortunate. But more often, the American Dream story is so powerful in our media and popular culture that many of us believe that we have an equal chance of becoming rich and therefore successful and happy. So why do anything to disturb the economic structures that the dream is built on? In fact, in many versions of our American Dream story—from Hollywood films to political ads—the government often plays the role of villain, seeking to raise our taxes or undermine rugged individualism and hard

AMERICAN DREAM STORIES are distributed through our media. This is especially true of television shows in the 1950s and 1960s like *The Donna Reed Show,* which idealized the American nuclear family as central to the American Dream.

work. Pitted against the government in these stories, the protagonist is the little guy, at odds with burdensome regulation and bureaucratic oversight. However, many of these stories are produced and distributed by large media corporations and political leaders who rely on the rest of us to consent to the American Dream narrative in order to keep their privileged place in the status quo and reinforce this "commonsense" story as the way the world works.

Specialization, Global Markets, and Convergence

In today's complex and often turbulent economic environment, global firms have sought greater profits by moving labor to less economically developed countries that need jobs but have poor health and safety regulations for workers. The continuous outsourcing of many U.S. jobs and the breakdown of global economic borders accompanied this transformation. Bolstered by the passage of GATT (General Agreement on Tariffs and Trade) in 1947, the signing of NAFTA (North American Free Trade Agreement) in 1994, and the formation of the WTO (World Trade Organization, which succeeded GATT in 1995), global cooperation fostered transnational media corporations and business deals across international terrain.

But in many cases, this global expansion by U.S. companies ran counter to America's early-twentieth-century vision of itself. Henry Ford, for example, followed his wife's suggestion to lower prices so workers could afford Ford cars. In many countries today, however, most workers cannot even afford the computers and TV sets they are making primarily for U.S. and European markets.

The Rise of Specialization and Synergy

The new globalism coincided with the rise of specialization. The magazine, radio, and cable industries sought specialized markets both in the United States and overseas, in part to counter television's mass appeal. By the 1980s, however, even television—confronted with the growing popularity of home video and cable—began niche marketing, targeting affluent eighteen- to thirty-four-year-old viewers, whose buying habits are not as stable or predictable as those of older consumers. Younger and older audiences, abandoned by the networks, were sought by other media outlets and advertisers. Magazines such as *J-14* and *AARP The Magazine* now flourish. Cable channels such as Nickelodeon and the Cartoon Network serve the under-eighteen market, while the Hallmark Channel and Lifetime address female viewers over age fifty; in addition, cable channel BET targets young African Americans, helping define them as a consumer group (see "Case Study: Minority and Female Media Ownership: Why It Matters," on pages 458–459).

Beyond specialization, though, what really distinguishes current media economics is the extension of **synergy** to international levels. *Synergy* typically refers to the promotion and sale of different versions of a media product across the various subsidiaries of a media conglomerate (e.g., a Weather Channel segment on NBC's *Today Show*, or an NBC News reporter appearing on MSNBC for election coverage—all part of Comcast and its NBC Universal subsidiary). However, it also refers to global companies like Sony buying up popular culture—in this case, movie studios and record labels—to play on its various electronic products. Today, synergy is an important goal for large media corporations and is often the reason given for expensive mergers and acquisitions. But historically, half of all mergers and acquisitions are failures, and synergies are never realized.[20] (Consider, for example, the disastrous AOL–Time Warner merger of 2001 or the News Corp.'s expensive bad bet on the success of MySpace in 2005.)

Disney: A Postmodern Media Conglomerate

The Walt Disney Company is one of the most successful companies in leveraging its many properties to create synergies. For example, in 2014, ABC broadcast the prime-time special *The Story of* Frozen: *Making a Disney Animated Classic* to promote the Disney movie studio's enormous hit movie and soundtrack—and to hype ABC's *Once Upon a Time* series (which would soon feature a character from *Frozen*) along with Disney's next animated film, *Big Hero 6. Frozen* (as noted in Chapter 7) also taps into a huge array of licensed merchandise and even *Frozen*-themed vacation trips by Disney's tour company and cruise line. To fully understand the contemporary story of media economics and synergy, we need only examine the transformation of Disney from a struggling cartoon creator to one of the world's largest media conglomerates.

The Early Years

After Walt Disney's first cartoon company, Laugh-O-Gram, went bankrupt in 1922, Disney moved to Hollywood and found his niche. He created Mickey Mouse (originally named Mortimer) for the first sound cartoons in the late 1920s and developed the first feature-length cartoon, *Snow White and the Seven Dwarfs*, completed in 1937.

For much of the twentieth century, the Disney company set the standard for popular cartoons and children's culture. The *Silly Symphonies* series (1929–1939) established the studio's reputation for high-quality hand-drawn cartoons. Although Disney remained a minor studio, *Fantasia* and *Pinocchio*—the two top-grossing films of 1940—each made more than $40 million. Nonetheless, the studio barely broke even because cartoon projects took time—four years for *Snow White*—and commanded the company's entire attention.

Around the time of the demise of the cartoon film short in movie theaters, Disney expanded into other areas, with its first nature documentary short, *Seal Island* (1949); its first live-action feature, *Treasure Island* (1950); and its first feature documentary, *The Living Desert* (1953).

Disney was also among the first film studios to embrace television, launching a long-running prime-time show in 1954. Then, in 1955, Disneyland opened in Southern California. Eventually, Disney's theme parks would produce the bulk of the studio's revenues. (Walt Disney World in Orlando, Florida, began operation in 1971.)

In 1953, Disney started Buena Vista, a distribution company. This was the first step in making the studio into a major player. The company also began exploiting the power of its early cartoon features. *Snow White*, for example, was successfully rereleased in theaters to new generations of children before eventually going to videocassette and much later to DVD.

Global Expansion

The death of Walt Disney in 1966 triggered a period of decline for the studio. But in 1984, a new management team, led by Michael Eisner, initiated a turnaround. The newly created Touchstone movie division reinvented the live-action cartoon for adults as well as for children in *Who Framed Roger Rabbit* (1988). A string of hand-drawn animated hits followed, including *The Little Mermaid* (1989), *Beauty and the Beast* (1991), *The Lion King* (1994), *Mulan* (1998), and *Lilo & Stitch* (2002). Disney also distributed a string of computer-animated blockbusters from Pixar Animation Studios, including *Toy Story* (1995), *Monsters, Inc.* (2001), *Finding Nemo* (2003), and *The Incredibles* (2004); it later acquired Pixar outright and released movies including *Up* (2009), *Toy Story 3* (2010), and *Brave* (2012). Disney's in-house animation studio eventually got into the computer-animation business and had several major successes with *Wreck-It Ralph* (2012), *Frozen* (2013), and *Big Hero 6* (2014).

Disney also came to epitomize the synergistic possibilities of media consolidation. It can produce an animated feature for both theatrical release and DVD distribution. With its ABC

© Walt Disney Pictures/Everett Collection

network (purchased in 1995), it can promote Disney movies and television shows on programs like *Good Morning America*. A book version can be released through Disney's publishing arm, Disney Publishing Worldwide, and "the-making-of" versions can appear on cable's Disney Channel or ABC Family. Characters can become attractions at Disney's theme parks, which themselves have spawned Hollywood movies, such as the lucrative *Pirates of the Caribbean* franchise.

Throughout the 1990s, Disney continued to find new sources of revenue in both entertainment and distribution. Through its purchase of ABC, Disney also became the owner of the cable sports channels ESPN and ESPN2, and later expanded the brand with ESPNEWS, ESPN Classic, and ESPNU channels; *ESPN The Magazine*; ESPN Radio; and ESPN.go.com. In New York City, Disney renovated several theaters and launched versions of *Beauty and the Beast*, *The Lion King*, and *Spider-Man* as successful Broadway musicals.

Building on the international appeal of its cartoon features, Disney extended its global reach by opening Tokyo Disney Resort in 1983 and Disneyland Paris in 1991. On the home front, a proposed historical park in Virginia—Disney's America—suffered defeat at the hands of citizens who raised concerns about Disney misinterpreting or romanticizing American history. In 1995, shortly after the company purchased ABC, the news division was criticized for running a flattering profile about Disney on ABC's evening news program.

Despite criticism, little slowed Disney's global expansion. Orbit—a Saudi-owned satellite relay station based in Rome—introduced Disney's twenty-four-hour premium cable channel to twenty-three countries in the Middle East and North Africa in 1997. Disney opened more venues in Asia, with Hong Kong Disneyland Resort in 2005 and Shanghai Disney Resort, which broke ground in 2011. Disney exemplifies the formula for becoming a "great media conglomerate" as defined in the book *Global Dreams*: "Companies able to use visuals to sell sound, movies to sell books, or software to sell hardware would become the winners in the new global commercial order."[21]

Disney Today

Even as Disney grew into the world's No. 2 media conglomerate by the beginning of the twenty-first century, the cartoon pioneer experienced the multiple shocks of a recession, failed films and Internet ventures, and declining theme park attendance. By 2005, Disney had fallen to No. 5 among movie studios in U.S. box-office sales—down from No. 1 in 2003. In 2006, new CEO Robert Iger merged Disney and Pixar, and made Pixar and Apple Computer founder and CEO Steve Jobs a Disney board member. In 2009, Disney also signed a long-term deal to distribute movies from Steven Spielberg's DreamWorks Studios. But in 2010, Disney, still reeling from the economic recession, sold its independent film studio Miramax for $660 million to an investor group.

Minority and Female Media Ownership: Why It Matters

The giant merger in 2010 be-tween "Big Network" (NBC) and "Big Cable" (Comcast) signaled a key economic strategy for traditional media industries in the age of the Internet. By claiming that "Big Internet" companies like Google and Amazon (especially as they move into content development) pose enough of a threat to old media, traditional media companies pushed for the dissolution of remaining ownership restrictions. However, the big NBC-Comcast merger also brought to the forefront concerns about diminishing diversity in media ownership. Since the Telecommunica-tions Act of 1996, which made it easier for big media companies to consolidate, minority and female media owners have declined precipitously. For example, the nonpartisan media activist group

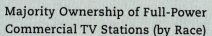

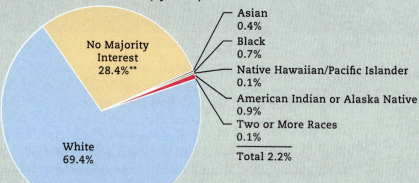

Free Press stated in 2012 that "racial or ethnic minorities currently own 43, or 3.2 percent of all the U.S. full-power commercial broadcast television sta-tions."[1] Critics fear that large media

conglomerations and more consolida-tion will mean even less diversity in media ownership.

Back in the 1970s, the FCC enacted rules that prohibited a single company from owning more than seven AM radio stations, seven FM radio stations, and seven TV stations (called "the 7-7-7 rule"). These restrictions were first put in place to encourage diverse and alterna-tive owners—and, therefore, diverse and alternative viewpoints. However, the rules were relaxed throughout the 1980s, and when almost all owner-ship restrictions were lifted in 1996, big media companies often bought up smaller radio and TV stations formerly controlled by minority and female owners. For example, by 2014, radio behemoth Clear Channel owned 840 radio stations, Cumulus owned 525, and Townsquare Media controlled 312.

In the United States, where women con-stitute slightly more than 50 percent of the population, blacks are about 13 per-cent of the population, and Hispanics are

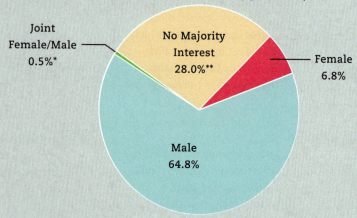

All chart data from: Federal Communications Commission, "Report on Ownership of Commercial Broadcast Stations," DA 12-1667, November 14, 2012.

*"Joint female/male" cases are those in which a female and a male each control a 50 percent interest in the station.

**"No majority interest" cases are those in which no party owns 50 percent (a majority) or more controlling interest in a station.

Majority Ownership of Commercial FM Radio Stations (by Gender)

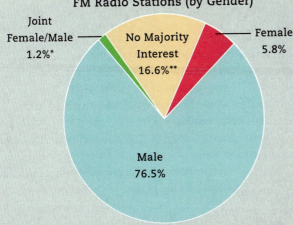

Joint Female/Male 1.2%*

No Majority Interest 16.6%**

Female 5.8%

Male 76.5%

destructive cycle disproportionately impacts women and minority owners, as they are far more likely to own just a single station in comparison to their white-male and corporate counterparts. Current female and minority owners are driven out of markets; and discrimination in access to deals, capital and equity, combined with the higher barriers to entry created by consolidation, shut out new female and minority owners.[4]

The only means at the FCC's disposal to prevent further erosion of diversity in media are limitations on station ownership, according to the United States Court of Appeals, which ruled in 2011 that the "Commission had failed to consider the effect on minority ownership of the repeal" of ownership restrictions.[5]

The point of diversity in ownership is to increase the variety of voices in the public sphere, which the FCC is required to do as part of its mission in the public interest. Yet there is continuing pressure applied to the FCC and Congress by large media conglomerates that want to grow even larger; thus, battle over ownership deregulation continues to be an issue worthy of close public attention. ◢

more than 16 percent of the population, television and radio broadcasting ownership diversity is poor by any measure.

The Free Press, in its formal response to the FCC's 2012 report on ownership, argued that "the level of female and minority ownership in the broadcast marketplace is disproportionately and embarrassingly low," with "a nearly 20 percent decline in the level of minority ownership since 2006."[2] (In 2014, FCC chairman Tom Wheeler acknowledged that African American ownership of television stations in the United States had dropped from nineteen in 2006 to just four in 2014. Moreover, in three of those four cases, the black station owners had a joint sales agreement with a larger media corporation, requiring them to turn over up to 90 percent of their profits to the corporate partner.)[3] The group criticized the FCC for not taking its obligations to serve the public interest seriously and for not fully studying the impact that relaxed ownership rules have on minority and female broadcast station ownership. (In its own calculations, the Free Press found even lower levels of diversity in station ownership than the FCC did.) It contended that large chains have enormous power in the

marketplace and ultimately harm minority and female ownership:

As markets become more concentrated, artificial economies of scale are created. This drives away potential new entrants in favor of existing large chains. Concentration also has the effect of diminishing the ability of existing smaller station groups and single-station owners to compete for both advertising and programming contracts. These effects combine to create immense pressure for smaller owners to sell their stations. And this

Majority Ownership of Commercial FM Radio Stations (by Race)

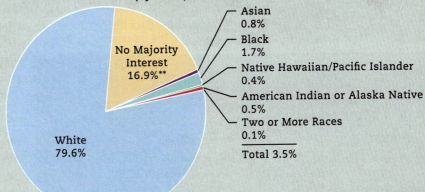

No Majority Interest 16.9%**

White 79.6%

Asian 0.8%

Black 1.7%

Native Hawaiian/Pacific Islander 0.4%

American Indian or Alaska Native 0.5%

Two or More Races 0.1%

Total 3.5%

The Pixar deal showed that Disney was ready to embrace the digital age. In an effort to focus on television, movies, and its online initiatives, Disney sold its twenty-two radio stations and the ABC Radio Network in 2007. Disney also made its movies and TV programs available at Apple's iTunes store and announced it would become a partner with NBC and Fox in the popular video site Hulu. In 2009, Disney purchased Marvel Entertainment for $4 billion, bringing Iron Man, Spider-Man, and X-Men into the Disney family; in 2012, it purchased Lucasfilm and with it the rights to the *Star Wars* and *Indiana Jones* movies and characters. This means that Disney now has access to whole casts of "new" characters—not just for TV programs, feature films, and animated movies but also for its multiple theme parks.

Global Audiences Expand Media Markets

As Disney's story shows, international expansion has allowed media conglomerates some advantages, including secondary markets in which to earn profits and advance technological innovations. First, as media technologies get cheaper and more portable (think Walkman to iPod), American media proliferate both inside and outside national boundaries. Today, greatly facilitated by the Internet, media products easily reach the eyes and ears of the world. Second, this globalism permits companies that lose money on products at home to profit abroad. Roughly 80 percent of U.S. movies, for instance, do not earn back their costs in U.S. theaters and depend on foreign circulation and video revenue to make up for losses.

In addition, satellite transmission has made North American and European TV available at the global level. Cable services such as CNN and MTV quickly took their national acts to the international stage, and by the twenty-first century, CNN and MTV were available in more than two hundred countries. Today, of course, the streaming of music, TV shows, and movies on the Internet through services like Spotify and Netflix (and through illegal file-sharing) has expanded the global flow of popular culture even further. (See "Media Literacy and the Critical Process: Cultural Imperialism and Movies" on page 461 for more on the dominance of the American movie industry.)

The Internet and Convergence Change the Game

For much of their history, media companies have been part of usually discrete or separate industries—that is, the newspaper business stood apart from book publishing, which was different from radio, which was different from the film industry. But the Internet and convergence have changed that—not only by offering a portal to view or read older media forms but also by requiring virtually all older media companies to establish an online presence. Today, newspapers, magazines, book publishers, music companies, radio and TV stations, and film studios all have Web sites that offer online versions of their product or Web services that enhance their original media form.

The Rise of the New Digital Media Conglomerates

The digital turn marks a shift in the media environment, from the legacy media powerhouses

HBO GO

Acclaimed HBO original programming, including *Last Week Tonight with John Oliver* and a variety of other TV series and movies, is available online through the company's HBO Go online service—but only to those who already subscribe to the premium channel through their cable company.

Eric Liebowitz/© HBO/Everett Collection

Media Literacy and the Critical Process

1 DESCRIPTION. Using international box-office revenue listings (www.boxofficemojo.com/intl is a good place to start), compare the recent weekly box-office rankings of the United States to those of five other countries. (Your sample could extend across several continents or focus on a specific region, like Southeast Asia.) Limit yourself to the top ten or fifteen films in box-office rank. Note where each film is produced (some films are joint productions of studios from two or more countries), and put your results in a table for comparison.

2 ANALYSIS. What patterns emerged in each country's box-office rankings? What percentage of films came from the United States? What percentage of films were domestic productions in each country? What percentage of films came from countries other than the United States? In the United States, what percentage of films originated with studios from other countries?

3 INTERPRETATION. So what do your discoveries mean? Can you

Cultural Imperialism and Movies

In the 1920s, the U.S. film industry became the leader in the worldwide film business. The images and stories of American films are well known in nearly every corner of the world. But with major film production centers in places like India, China, Hong Kong, Japan, South Korea, Mexico, the United Kingdom, Germany, France, Russia, and Nigeria, to what extent do U.S. films dominate international markets today? Conversely, how often do international films get much attention in the United States?

make an argument for or against the existence of cultural imperialism by the United States? Are there film industries in other countries that dominate movie theaters in their region of the world? How would you critique the reverse of cultural imperialism, wherein films from other countries rarely break into the Top 10 box-office list? Does this happen in any countries you sampled?

4 EVALUATION. Given your interpretation, is cultural dominance by one country a good thing or a bad thing? Consider the potential advantages of creating a global village of shared popular culture versus the potential disadvantages of cultural

imperialism. Also, is there any potential harm in a country's Top 10 box-office list being filled by domestic productions and rarely having international films featured?

5 ENGAGEMENT. Contact managers of your local movie theater (or executives at the headquarters of the chain that owns it). Ask them how they decide which films to screen. If they don't show many international films, ask them why not. Be ready to provide a list of three to five international films released in the United States (see the full list of current U.S. releases at www.boxofficemojo.com) that haven't yet been screened in the theater.

---

like Time Warner and Disney to the new digital media conglomerates. Five companies—Amazon, Apple, Facebook, Google, and Microsoft—reign in digital media, as detailed in Figure 13.3.

Each of the five leading companies has become powerful for different reasons. Amazon's entrée is that it has grown into the largest e-commerce site in the world. In recent years, Amazon has begun shifting from delivering physical products (e.g., bound books) to distributing digital products (e.g., e-books and downloadable music, movies, television shows, and more) on its digital devices (Kindle, Fire TV, and Fire Phone). Apple's strength has been creating the technology and the infrastructure to bring any media content to users' fingertips. When many traditional media companies didn't have the means to distribute online content easily, Apple developed the shiny devices (the iPod, iPhone, and iPad) and easy-to-use systems (the iTunes store) to do it, immediately transforming the media industries. Today, Apple has a hand in every media industry, as it offers the premiere platforms of the digital turn.

Facebook's strength has been its ability to become central to communication and social media. As Facebook's number of users surpassed one billion worldwide in 2012, the company still struggled to fully leverage those users (and the massive amounts of data they share about themselves) into advertising sales, particularly as its users moved to accessing Facebook via

AMAZON	APPLE	FACEBOOK	GOOGLE	MICROSOFT
est. 1995	est. 1976	est. 2004	est. 1998	est. 1975
Strength: **e-commerce**	Strengths: **technology infrastructure**	Strengths: **communication social media**	Strengths: **search advertising**	Strengths: **search game console**

FIGURE 13.3

RISE OF THE NEW DIGITAL MEDIA CONGLOMERATES

mobile phones. Unlike the other four digital companies, Facebook lacks hardware devices to access the Internet and digital media, although it began to remedy that problem with the purchase of the Oculus Rift virtual reality gaming headset for $2 billion in 2014. Google, which draws its huge numbers of users through its search function, has much more successfully translated those users (and the information provided by their search terms) into an advertising business worth more than $59 billion a year. Google is also moving into the same digital media distribution business that Apple and Amazon offer, via its Android phone operating system, Nexus 7 tablet, Chromebook, and Chromecast. Microsoft, one of the wealthiest digital companies in the world, is making the transition from being the top software company (a business that is slowly in decline) to competing in the digital media world with its Bing search engine and devices like its successful Xbox game console, Surface tablet, and Windows phone. Microsoft also owns Yammer, a business social network, and holds a small ownership share in Facebook.

Given how technologically adept these five digital corporations have proven to be, they still need to provide compelling narratives to attract people (to repeat a point from the beginning of the chapter). All five companies are weak in this regard, as they rely on other companies' media narratives (e.g., the sounds, images, words, and pictures) or the stories that their own users provide (as in Facebook posts or YouTube videos). Amazon is leading the other companies in content development, though, with its own publishing divisions (to compete with publishing companies) and its own original television series and online channels like Twitch (to compete with Netflix, Hulu, and YouTube. It's likely that the other digital companies will eventually do the same. The history of mass communication suggests that it is the content—the narratives—that endures, while the devices and distribution systems do not.

The Digital Age Favors Small, Flexible Start-Up Companies

All the leading digital companies of today were once small start-ups that emerged at important junctures of the digital age. The earliest, Microsoft and Apple, were established in the mid-1970s, with the rise of the personal computer. Amazon began in 1995, with the popularization of the Web and the beginnings of e-commerce. Google was established in 1998, as search engines became the best way of navigating the Web. And Facebook, beginning in 2004, proved to be the best social media site to emerge in the 2000s. For each success story, though, hundreds of other firms failed or flamed out quickly (e.g., MySpace).

Today, the juncture in the digital era is the growing importance of social media and mobile devices. Like in the earlier periods, the strategy for start-up companies is to find a niche market, connect with consumers, and get big fast, swallowing up or overwhelming competitors. Instagram, YouTube, Twitter, and Zynga are recent examples of this. The successful start-ups then take one of two paths—either be acquired by a larger company (e.g., Google buying YouTube, Facebook buying Instagram) or go it alone and try to get even bigger (e.g., Twitter). Either way, success might not last long, especially in an age when people's interests can move on very quickly. Witness Zynga, which had the top social media game when FarmVille debuted in 2009, but started to fizzle out a few years later without another hit game.

Social Issues in Media Economics

As the Disney-ABC merger demonstrates, recent years have brought a surplus of billion-dollar takeovers and mergers, including those between Time Inc. and Warner Communication, Time Warner and Turner, AOL and Time Warner, UPN and WB, Comcast and NBC Universal, Sirius and XM, Universal Music Group and EMI, Yahoo! and Tumblr, and proposed mergers between Comcast and Time Warner Cable and between AT&T and DirecTV (see Figure 13.4). This mergermania has accompanied stripped-down regulation, which has virtually suspended most ownership limits on media industries. As a result, a number of consumer advocates and citizen groups have raised questions about deregulation and ownership consolidation. Still, the 2008 financial crisis saw many of these megamedia firms overleveraged—that is, not making enough from stock investments to offset the debt they took on to add more companies to their empires. So in recent years we have seen Time Warner send AOL adrift, the New York Times

FIGURE 13.4

MAJOR MEDIA MERGERS AND ACQUISITIONS

MERGER AND ACQUISITION	PRICE	OUTCOME
New York Times + *Boston Globe* (1993)	$1.1 billion	The *Times* sells the *Globe* to the owner of the Boston Red Sox for $70 million in 2013.
Disney + ABC (1995)	$19 billion	The television network and ESPN become huge profit centers for Disney.
Time Warner + Turner Broadcasting (1995)	$7.5 billion	Time Warner grows even bigger than the combined Disney and ABC and adds CNN, TBS, and other cable channels.
Tribune Media Company + Times Mirror Company (2000)	$8.3 billion	Biggest newspaper merger ever combines the *Chicago Tribune*, the *Los Angeles Times*, and several others. The company files for bankruptcy in 2008 and spins off its newspaper division in 2014 (like several other newspaper conglomerates).
AOL + Time Warner (2001)	$164 billion	Biggest media merger failure ever. Time Warner spins off AOL in 2009.
Google + YouTube (2006)	$1.65 billion	One of Google's best acquisitions—YouTube makes several billion dollars each year.
Sirius + XM (2008)	$13 billion	A merger of equals makes a bigger company but reduces the number of satellite radio companies to one.
Google + Motorola (2011)	$12.5 billion	Google sold the Motorola mobile phone business to Lenovo in 2014 for $2.91 billion.
Comcast + NBC Universal (2011)	$28 billion	The biggest cable company becomes even bigger with a TV network, a movie studio, and more—though some of the media holdings aren't at peak performance.
Universal Music Group + EMI (2012)	$1.3 billion	Universal becomes the biggest music company in the world, leaving only three major sound recording corporations.
Comcast + Time Warner Cable (2014)	$45.2 billion	Under review. The merger would create the dominant wired broadband network in the United States.
AT&T + DirecTV (2014)	$48.5 billion	Under review. The merger of the largest mobile phone service and the largest satellite television provider would potentially create a giant telecommunication company.

ELSEWHERE IN
MEDIA & CULTURE

BIG STUDIOS PROGRAMMING FOR YOUTUBE

p. 222

24.9M

number of tweets by viewers of
Super Bowl XLVIII

p. 55

63.6%

amount of *Captain America* sequel grosses
that came from outside the United States

p. 257

$316,912

THE COST OF A THIRTY-SECOND ADVERTISEMENT
DURING *THE BIG BANG THEORY*

p. 216

HOW MUCH MONEY DO MUSICIANS MAKE FROM SPOTIFY?

p. 141

Company sell the *Boston Globe*, the Washington Post Company sell *Newsweek*, Disney unload Miramax, News Corp. spin off its newspaper and publishing divisions, and the Tribune Company and Gannett split off their newspapers divisions.

One longtime critic of media mergers, Ben Bagdikian, author of *The Media Monopoly*, has argued that although there are abundant products in the market—thousands of daily and weekly newspapers, radio and television stations, magazines, and book publishers—only a limited number of companies are in charge of those products.[22] Bagdikian and others fear that this represents a dangerous antidemocratic tendency, in which a handful of media moguls wield a disproportionate amount of economic control (see "Case Study: From Fifty to a Few: The Most Dominant Media Corporations" on page 466). The News Corp. phone hacking scandal that came to light in 2011 in the United Kingdom illustrates media power gone awry, with corruption involving top company executives, police, and government officials.[23]

The Limits of Antitrust Laws

Although meant to ensure multiple voices and owners, American antitrust laws have been easily subverted since the 1980s, as companies expanded by diversifying holdings and merging product lines with other big media firms. Large media firms have also become among the most active and powerful lobbyists in Washington, D.C., and other political capitals. The resulting consolidation of media owners has limited the number of independent voices in the market and reduced the number of owners who might be able to innovate and challenge established economic powers, leading to renewed interest in enforcing antitrust laws.

Diversification

Most media companies diversify among media products (such as television stations and film studios), never fully dominating a particular media industry. Time Warner, for example, spreads its holdings among its television programming, film, publishing, cable, and Internet divisions. However, the media giant actually competes with only a few other big companies, like Disney, Viacom, and 21st Century Fox (the cable, broadcast, and satellite company created in the 2013 split of the News Corp.).

Such diversification promotes oligopolies in which a few behemoth companies control most media production and distribution. This kind of economic arrangement makes it difficult for products offered outside an oligopoly to compete in the marketplace. For instance, in broadcast TV, the few networks that control prime time—all of them now owned by or in league with film studios—offer programs that are selected from known production companies that the networks either contract with regularly or own outright. Thus, even with a very good program or series idea, an independent production company—especially one that operates outside Los Angeles or New York—has a very difficult time entering the national TV market. The film giants even prefer buying from each other before dealing with independents. For example, in 2009 CBS sold syndication rights for its popular crime show *The Mentalist* to the TNT cable channel for over $2 million per episode. And for years, CBS's *Without a Trace* and NBC's *Law and Order* were both running in syndication on cable's TNT channel, owned by Time Warner, which also co-owns the CW network with CBS.

Applying Antitrust Laws Today

Occasionally, independent voices raise issues that aid the Justice Department and the FTC in their antitrust cases. For example, when EchoStar (now the Dish Network) proposed to purchase DirecTV in 2001, a number of rural, consumer, and Latino organizations spoke out against the merger for several reasons. Latino organizations opposed the merger because in many U.S. markets, direct broadcast satellite (DBS) service offers the only available Spanish-

LaunchPad ⓞ

macmillanhighered.com
/mediaculture10e

The Impact of Media Ownership
Media critics and professionals debate the pros and cons of media conglomerates. **Discussion:** This video argues that it is the drive for bottom-line profits that leads to conglomerates. What solution(s) might you suggest to make the media system work better?

From Fifty to a Few: The Most Dominant Media Corporations

In this graphic that lists the Top 10 media companies for 1980, 1997, and 2012, what patterns do you notice? How do these patterns reflect larger trends in the media? For example, seven of the major companies in 1980 were mostly print businesses, but what about in 2012? Should we trust how NBC News covers Comcast or how ABC News covers Disney? Should we be wary if *Time* magazine hypes a Warner Brothers film? More important, what actions can we take to ensure that the mass media function not just as successful businesses for stockholders but also as a necessary part of our democracy? Most of the large media companies have been profiled here and in Chapters 2 to 10 (illustrating their principal holdings). Although the subsidiaries of these companies often change, the graphic demonstrates the wide reach of today's large conglomerations. To get a better understanding of how the largest media corporations relate to one another and the larger world, see the folded insert at the beginning of the book.

Data from: Ad Age's 100 Leading Media Companies, *December 7, 1981;* "100 Companies by Media Revenue," Advertising Age, *August 18, 1997;* "Media 100," Advertising Age, *December 31, 2012.*

*The revenue in $billions is based on total net U.S. media revenue and does not include nonmedia and international revenue.

Top 10 U.S Media Companies

Revenue in $billions*

● 1980 ● 1997 ● 2012

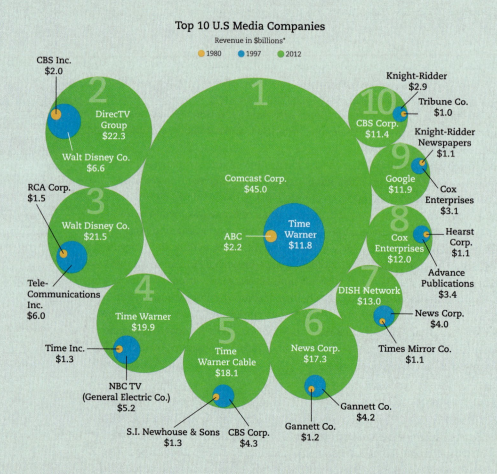

CBS Inc. $2.0

2 DirecTV Group $22.3

Walt Disney Co. $6.6

RCA Corp. $1.5

3 Walt Disney Co. $21.5

Tele-Communications Inc. $6.0

4 Time Warner $19.9

Time Inc. $1.3

NBC TV (General Electric Co.) $5.2

S.I. Newhouse & Sons $1.3

5 Time Warner Cable $18.1

CBS Corp. $4.3

Gannett Co. $1.2

6 News Corp. $17.3

Gannett Co. $4.2

1 Comcast Corp. $45.0

ABC $2.2

Time Warner $11.8

7 DISH Network $13.0

News Corp. $4.0

Times Mirror Co. $1.1

8 Cox Enterprises $12.0

Hearst Corp. $1.1

Advance Publications $3.4

9 Google $11.9

Cox Enterprises $3.1

10 CBS Corp. $11.4

Knight-Ridder $2.9

Tribune Co. $1.0

Knight-Ridder Newspapers $1.1

language television programming. The merger would have left the United States with just one major DBS company and created a virtual monopoly for EchoStar, which had fewer Spanish-language offerings than DirecTV. In 2002, the FCC declined to approve the merger, saying it would not serve the public interest, convenience, and necessity.

In 2011, AT&T moved to acquire T-Mobile, another wireless telecom giant (with more than thirty-three million customers), for $39 billion. The Justice Department opposed the merger on antitrust grounds (media watchdog groups said it would have left the country with just three major mobile phone companies, giving consumers far fewer options), leading AT&T to eventually scrap the deal. The proposed mergers between Comcast and Time Warner Cable and between AT&T and DirectTV will be even bigger tests of the U.S. government's enforcement of antitrust laws.

But antitrust laws have no teeth globally. Although international copyright laws offer some protection to musicians and writers, no international antitrust rules exist to prohibit trans-national companies from buying up as many media companies as they can afford. Still, as legal scholar Harry First points out, antitrust concerns are "alive and well and living in Europe."[24] For example, when Sony and Bertelsmann's BMG unit merged their music businesses, only the European Union (EU) raised questions about the merger on behalf of independent labels and musicians worried about the oligopoly structure of the music business. The EU frequently reviewed the merger, starting in 2004, but decided in late 2008 to withdraw its opposition.

The Fallout from a Free Market

Since the wave of media mergers began with gusto in the 1980s, a number of consumer critics have pointed to the lack of public debate surrounding the tightening oligopoly structure of international media. Economists and media critics have traced the causes and history of this void to two major issues: a reluctance to criticize capitalism and the debate over how much control consumers have in the marketplace.

Equating Free Markets with Democracy

In the 1920s and 1930s, commercial radio executives, many of whom befriended FCC members, succeeded in portraying themselves as operating in the public interest while labeling their noncommercial radio counterparts in education, labor, or religion as mere voices of propa-ganda. In these early debates, corporate interests succeeded in aligning the political ideas of democracy, misleadingly, with the economic structures of capitalism.

Throughout the Cold War period in the 1950s and 1960s, it became increasingly difficult to criticize capitalism, which had become a synonym for democracy in many circles. In this context, any criticism of capitalism became an attack on the free marketplace. This, in turn, appeared to be a criticism of free speech because the business community often sees its right to operate in a free marketplace as an extension of its right to buy commercial speech in the form of advertising. As longtime CBS chief William Paley told a group of educators in 1937, "He who attacks the funda-mentals of the American system" of commercial broadcasting "attacks democracy itself."[25]

Broadcast historian Robert McChesney, discussing the rise of commercial radio during the 1930s, has noted that leaders like Paley "equated capitalism with the free and equal market-place, the free and equal marketplace with democracy, and democracy with 'Americanism.'"[26] The collapse of the former Soviet Union's communist economy in the 1990s is often portrayed as a triumph for democracy. As we now realize, however, it was primarily a victory for capital-ism and free-market economies.

Consumer Choice versus Consumer Control

As many economists point out, capitalism is not structured democratically but arranged verti-cally, with powerful corporate leaders at the top and hourly wage workers at the bottom. But democracy, in principle, is built on a more horizontal model, in which each individual has an equal opportunity to have his or her voice heard and vote counted. In discussing free markets, economists distinguish between similar types of consumer power: *consumer control* over marketplace goods and freedom of *consumer choice*.[27] Most Americans and the citizens of other economically developed nations clearly have *consumer choice*: options among a range of media products. Yet consumers and even media employees have limited *consumer control*: power in deciding what kinds of media get created and circulated.

One recurring place for democratic production is the work of independent and alternative producers, artists, writers, and publishers. Despite the movement toward economic consolidation, the fringes of media industries still offer a diversity of opinions, ideas, and alternative products. In fact, when independent companies become even marginally popular, they are often pursued by large companies that seek to make them subsidiaries. For example, alternative music often taps into social concerns that are not normally discussed in the recording industry's corporate boardrooms. Moreover, business leaders "at the top" depend on independent ideas "from below" to generate new product lines. A number of transnational corporations encourage the development of local artists—talented individuals who might have the capacity to transcend the regional or national level and become the next global phenomenon.

Cultural Imperialism

The influence of American popular culture has created considerable debate in international circles. On the one hand, the notion of freedom that is associated with innovation and rebellion in American culture has been embraced internationally. The global spread of media and increased access to media have made it harder for political leaders to secretly repress dissident groups because police and state activity (such as the torture of illegally detained citizens) can now be documented digitally and easily dispatched by satellite, the Internet, and cell phones around the world.

On the other hand, American media are shaping the cultures and identities of other nations. American styles in fashion and food, as well as media fare, dominate the global market—a process known as **cultural imperialism**. Today, many international observers contend that the idea of consumer control or input is even more remote in countries inundated by American movies, music, television, and images of beauty. For example, consumer product giant Unilever sells Dove soap with its "Campaign for Real Beauty" in the United States, but markets Fair & Lovely products—a skin-lightening line—to poor women in India.

Although many indigenous forms of media culture—such as Brazil's telenovela (a TV soap opera), Jamaica's reggae, and Japan's anime—are extremely popular, U.S. dominance in producing and distributing mass media puts a severe burden on countries attempting to produce their own cultural products. For example, American TV producers have generally recouped their production costs by the time their TV shows are exported. This enables American distributors to offer these programs to other countries at bargain rates, undercutting local production companies that are trying to create original programs.

CULTURAL IMPERIALISM
Ever since Hollywood gained an edge in film production and distribution during World War I, U.S. movies have dominated the box office in Europe, in some years accounting for more than 80 percent of the revenues taken in by European theaters. Hollywood's reach has since extended throughout the world, including previously difficult markets such as China.

© Walt Disney Studios Motion Pictures/Everett Collection

Defenders of American popular culture argue that because some aspects of our culture challenge authority, national boundaries, and outmoded traditions, they create an arena in which citizens can raise questions. Supporters also argue that a universal popular culture creates a global village and fosters communication across national boundaries.

Critics, however, such as the authors of the book *Global Dreams*, believe that although American popular culture often contains protests against social wrongs, such protests "can be turned into consumer products and lose their bite. Protest itself becomes something to sell."[28] The harshest critics have also argued that American cultural imperialism both hampers the development of native cultures and negatively influences teenagers, who abandon their own rituals to adopt American tastes. The exportation of U.S. entertainment media is sometimes viewed as "cultural dumping" because it discourages the development of original local products and value systems.

Perhaps the greatest concern regarding a global village is the cultural disconnection for people whose standards of living are not routinely portrayed in contemporary media. About two-thirds of the world's population cannot afford most of the products advertised on American, Japanese, and European television. Yet more and more of the world's populations are able to glimpse consumer abundance and middle-class values through television, magazines, and the Internet.

As early as the 1950s, media managers feared political fallout—a backlash of rising expectations—in that ads and products would raise the hopes of poor people but not keep pace with their actual living conditions.[29] Furthermore, the conspicuousness of consumer culture makes it difficult for many of us to imagine other ways of living that are not heavily dependent on the mass media and brand-name products.

The Media Marketplace and Democracy

In the midst of today's major global transformations of economies, cultures, and societies, the best way to monitor the impact of transnational economies is through vigorous news attention and lively public discussion. Clearly, however, this process is being hampered. Starting in the 1990s, for example, news organizations, concerned about the bottom line, severely cut back the number of reporters assigned to cover international developments. This occurred—especially after 9/11—just as global news became more critical than ever to an informed citizenry.

We live in a society in which often-superficial or surface consumer concerns, stock market quotes, and profit aspirations, rather than broader social issues, increasingly dominate the media agenda. In response, critics have posed some key questions: As consumers, do we care who owns the media as long as most of us have a broad selection of products? Do we care who owns the media as long as multiple voices *seem* to exist in the market?

THE PRESIDENT AND COFOUNDER of Free Press, a national nonpartisan organization dedicated to media reform, Robert McChesney is one of the foremost scholars of media economics in the United States. For ten years, he hosted *Media Matters*, a radio call-in show in Central Illinois that discussed the relationship between politics and media. McChesney (*left*) most recently published *Dollarocracy: How the Money and Media Election Complex Is Destroying America* (2013) with journalist and Free Press cofounder John Nichols (*right*).

AP Photo/Jeff Chiu

The Effects of Media Consolidation on Democracy

Merged and multinational media corporations will continue to control more aspects of production and distribution. Of pressing concern is the impact of mergers on news operations, particularly the influence of large corporations on their news subsidiaries. These companies have the capacity to use major news resources to promote their products and determine national coverage.

Because of the growing consolidation of mass media, it has become increasingly difficult to sustain a public debate on economic issues. From a democratic perspective, the relationship of our mass media system to politics has been highly dysfunctional. Politicians in Washington, D.C., have regularly accepted millions of dollars in contributions from large media conglomerates and their lobbying groups to finance their campaigns. This changed in 2008 when the Obama campaign raised much of its financing from small donors. Still, corporations got a big boost from the Supreme Court in early 2010 in the *Citizens United* case. In a five-to-four vote, the court "ruled that the government may not ban political spending by corporations in candidate elections," the *New York Times* reported.[30] Justice Anthony Kennedy, writing for the majority, said, "If the First Amendment has any force, it prohibits Congress from fining or jailing citizens, or associations of citizens, for simply engaging in political speech." The ruling overturned two decades of precedents that had limited direct corporate spending on campaigns, including the Bipartisan Campaign Reform Act of 2002 (often called the McCain-Feingold Act, after the senators who sponsored the bill), which placed restrictions on buying TV and radio campaign ads.

As unfettered corporate political contributions count as "political speech," some corporations are experiencing backlash (or praise) once their customers discover their political positions. For example, in 2012 fast-food outlet Chick-fil-A's charitable foundation "was revealed to be funneling millions to groups that oppose gay marriage and, until recently, promoted gay 'cure' therapies," resulting in a firestorm of criticism but also a wave of support from others, the *Daily Beast* reported. In the same year, Amazon founder and CEO Jeff Bezos and his wife donated $2.5 million of their own money to support a same-sex marriage referendum in Washington State, gaining praise and criticism from some Amazon customers.[31]

Politicians have often turned to local television stations, spending record amounts during each election period to get their political ads on the air. In 2004, spending on the federal elections in the United States totaled $4.14 billion, with a large portion of that going to local broadcasters for commercials for congressional candidates and (in swing states like Ohio, Iowa, and Florida) for presidential candidates. In 2008, spending on federal elections topped $5.28 billion, and in 2012, it surpassed $6.28 billion.[32] But although local television stations have been happy to get part of the ever-increasing bounty of political ad money, the actual content of their news broadcasts has become less and less substantial, particularly when it comes to covering politics.

The Pew Research Center's Project for Excellence in Journalism reported that from 2005 to 2013, the amount of airtime given to weather, traffic, and sports on local news broadcasts expanded from 32 percent to 40 percent. Meanwhile, over that same period, the amount of time spent on politics and government stories slipped from 7 percent to 3 percent. The study's authors noted, "For some time, television consultants have been advising local television stations that viewers aren't interested in politics and government, and it appears that advice is being taken."[33]

Although television consultants might have concluded that local viewers aren't interested in politics and government, political consultants are only increasing the onslaught of political television ads every campaign season. Thus there is little news content to provide a counterpoint to all the allegations that might be hurled in the barrage of political ads.

The Media Reform Movement

Robert McChesney and John Nichols described the state of concern about the gathering consolidation of mainstream media power: "'Media Reform' has become a catch-all phrase to describe the broad goals of a movement that says consolidated ownership of broadcast and cable media, chain ownership of newspapers, and telephone and cable-company colonization of the Internet pose a threat not just to the culture of the Republic but to democracy itself."[34] While our current era has spawned numerous grassroots organizations that challenge media to do a better job for the sake of democracy, there has not been a large outcry from the general public for the kinds of concerns described by McChesney and Nichols. There is a reason for that. One key paradox of the Information Age is that for such economic discussions to be meaningful and democratic, they must be carried out in the popular media as well as in educational settings. Yet public debates and disclosures about the structure and ownership of the media are often not in the best economic interests of media owners.

Still, in some places, local groups and consumer movements are trying to address media issues that affect individual and community life. Such movements—like the National Conference for Media Reform—are usually united by geographic ties, common political backgrounds, or shared concerns about the state of the media. The Internet has also made it possible for media reform groups to form globally, uniting around such issues as contesting censorship or monitoring the activities of multinational corporations. The movement was also largely responsible for the success of preserving "net neutrality," which prevents Internet service providers from censoring or penalizing particular Web sites and online services (see Chapter 2).

With this reform victory and the 2008–09 economic crisis, perhaps we are more ready than ever to question some of the hierarchical and undemocratic arrangements of what McChesney, Nichols, and other reform critics call "Big Media." Even in the face of so many media mergers, the general public today seems open to such examinations, which might improve the global economy, improve worker conditions, and serve the public good. By better understanding media economics, we can play a more knowledgable role in critiquing media organizations and evaluating their impact on democracy. ▶

CHAPTER REVIEW

COMMON THREADS

One of the Common Threads discussed in Chapter 1 is the commercial nature of mass media. In thinking about media ownership regulations, it is important to consider how the media wield their influence.

During the 2000 presidential election, two marginal candidates—Pat Buchanan on the Right and Ralph Nader on the Left—shared a common view that both major-party candidates largely ignored. Buchanan and Nader warned of the increasing power of corporations to influence the economy and our democracy. In fact, between 2000 and 2012, total spending on lobbying in the nation's capital grew from $1.57 billion to more than $3 billion.[35] (See Chapter 12 for more on lobbyists.)

These warnings have generally gone unnoticed and unreported by mainstream media, whose reporters, editors, and pundits often work for the giant media corporations that not only are well represented by Washington lobbyists but also contribute generously to the campaigns of the major parties to influence legislation that governs media ownership and commercial speech.

Fast-forward to 2012. While politicians spoke of transparency and truth-telling, their campaign-funding process had few of those characteristics. In the aftermath of the U.S. Supreme Court's *Citizens United* (2010) decision, new Super PACs (political action committees) formed that can channel unlimited funds into political races as long as the Super PACs don't officially "coordinate" with the political campaigns. With his own Super PAC (named Americans for a Better Tomorrow, Tomorrow), comedian Stephen Colbert satirized the lax standards of Super PAC rules that enable hundreds of millions of dollars to be channeled into politics while obscuring disclosure of the contributors' identities. By December 2012, Super PACs had spent more than $644 million on the 2012 election cycle (mostly in negative attack ads), with the majority of contributions coming from a few dozen elite ultrawealthy donors. For example, Las Vegas casino magnate Sheldon Adelson and his wife donated in excess of $54 million to candidates and Super PACs in the 2012 election cycle.[36] In the 2014 midterm elections, billionaire Tom Steyer surpassed the Adelsons by donating at least $58 million, mostly through the NextGen Climate Action Super PAC. NPR noted that liberal climate activist Steyer was the "election's biggest donor—that we know of," a testament to the fact that most big donors like conservative billionaire brothers David and Charles Koch opt not to disclose most of their campaign expenditures because they aren't required to do so.[37] The huge influx of money was a boon for media advertising profits.

What both Buchanan and Nader argued in 2000 was that corporate influence is a bipartisan concern that we have in common and that all of us in a democracy need to be vigilant about how powerful and influential corporations become. This is especially true for the media companies that report the news and distribute many of our cultural stories. As media-literate consumers, we need to demand that the media serve as watchdogs over the economy and our democratic values. And when they fall down on the job, we need to demand accountability (through alternative media channels or the Internet), especially from those mainstream media—radio, television, and cable—that are licensed to operate in the public interest.

KEY TERMS

The definitions for the terms listed below can be found in the glossary at the end of the book. The page numbers listed with the terms indicate where the term is highlighted in the chapter.

monopoly, 446
oligopoly, 446
limited competition, 446

direct payment, 446
indirect payment, 446
hegemony, 453

synergy, 455
cultural imperialism, 468

For review quizzes, chapter summaries, links to media-related Web sites, and more, go to **macmillanhighered.com/mediaculture10e**.

REVIEW QUESTIONS

Analyzing the Media Economy

1. How are the three basic structures of mass media organizations—monopoly, oligopoly, and limited competition—different from one another?

2. What are the differences between direct and indirect payments for media products?

3. What are some of society's key expectations of its media organizations?

The Transition to an Information Economy

4. Why has the federal government emphasized deregulation at a time when so many media companies are growing so large?

5. How have media mergers changed the economics of mass media?

Specialization, Global Markets, and Convergence

6. How do global and specialized markets factor into the new media economy? How are regular workers affected?

7. Using Disney as an example, what is the role of synergy in the current climate of media mergers?

8. Why have Amazon, Apple, Facebook, Google, and Microsoft emerged as the leading corporations of the digital era?

Social Issues in Media Economics

9. What are the differences between consumer choice and consumer control?

10. What is cultural imperialism, and what does it have to do with the United States?

The Media Marketplace and Democracy

11. What do critics and activists fear most about the concentration of media ownership? How do media managers and executives respond to these fears?

12. What are some promising signs regarding the relationship between media economics and democracy?

QUESTIONING THE MEDIA

1. Why are consumers more likely to pay to download some digital content, like music and books, and less likely to pay for other content, like sports and news?

2. Why are narratives—media content—crucial to the success of a media corporation?

3. How does the concentration of media ownership limit the number of voices in the marketplace? Do we need rules limiting media ownership?

4. Is there such a thing as a global village? What does this concept mean to you?

LAUNCHPAD FOR *MEDIA & CULTURE*

Visit LaunchPad for *Media & Culture* *at* **macmillanhighered.com/mediaculture10e** *for additional learning tools:*

- REVIEW WITH LEARNINGCURVE
  LearningCurve, available on LaunchPad for *Media & Culture*, uses gamelike quizzing to help you master the concepts you need to learn from this chapter.

- VIDEO: THE MONEY BEHIND THE MEDIA
  Producers, advertisers, and advocates discuss how ownership systems and profits shape media production.

PART 5

Democratic Expression and the Mass Media

The freedom and openness of the Internet is a double-edged sword. In a digital world overloaded with data and news, it has become much easier to obtain information. With so many people paying attention to the details of everyday life, it is also easier to uncover wrongdoing by business and government, and even to hold these institutions to higher levels of transparency. The news media are helping to do this, but the digital turn and online outlets—particularly Facebook, Twitter, and YouTube—have provided new methods that allow ordinary citizens and nonprofit groups to do some of the work once performed by investigative journalists. The lack of centralized control over the Internet also means that people have been able to use digital technologies and our interconnectedness as a way to be heard and to effect change—especially in countries where press freedom has been limited or compromised. Both the Arab Spring uprisings in the Middle East and the Occupy Wall Street movement serve as examples.

At the same time, though, this ease of getting information has led to more situations involving ethically gray practices. For example, "hacktivists" like WikiLeaks and Anonymous and whistleblowers like Edward Snowden have raised issues regarding whether some government and business documents should remain secret—to protect national security, volatile economic markets, or vulnerable diplomats or other individuals at work in difficult areas of the world—or if all information should be made available to the public at all times. The fragmented and accessible nature of the Internet has led to concerns about how to best police the online world and control its overwhelming array of voices and traffic. There are also concerns that as traditional news media shrink, they might become subservient divisions of massive corporations that are able to dictate news content (the infographic on the right shows how overall news media revenue compares to some other well-known companies). We may be seeing similar conflicts, changes, and compromises in the years ahead as we continue to explore how powerful mass media fit into a democracy.

EXPRESSION AND THE MASS MEDIA

PRESS FREEDOM RANKINGS

*Ranking from 1 to 200

FREE

— The Netherlands (1)
— Norway (1)
— Belgium (4)
— Denmark (6)
— Monaco (12)
— Germany (18)
— Portugal (22)
— U.S.A. (30)
— France (33)
— U.K. (36)
— Japan (42)
— Poland (49)
— Spain (52)

PARTLY FREE

— Israel (62)
— Italy (64)
— South Korea (68)
— Serbia (74)
— India (78)
— Peru (87)
— Brazil (90)
— Greece (92)
— Indonesia (98)
— Argentina (106)
— Nicaragua (109)
— Colombia (115)
— Liberia (125)
— Kuwait (127)
— Mexico (132)

NOT FREE

— Ecuador (134)
— Ukraine (139)
— Pakistan (141)
— Afghanistan (147)
— Egypt (157)
— Iraq (171)
— Venezuela (171)
— Russia (176)
— Saudi Arabia (181)
— China (183)
— North Korea (197)

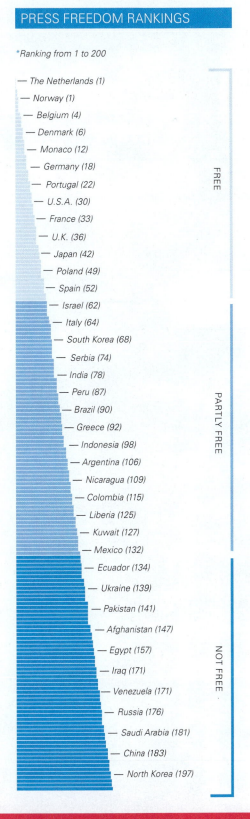

THE NEWS MEDIA

2013 Revenue

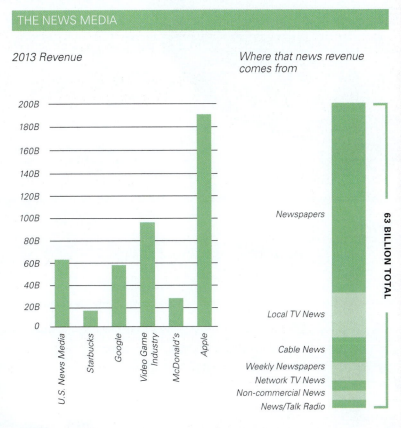

Where that news revenue comes from

Newspapers

Local TV News

Cable News
Weekly Newspapers
Network TV News
Non-commercial News
News/Talk Radio

63 BILLION TOTAL

MEDIA EFFECTS AND VIOLENCE

Rate of Firearm Homicide Deaths between 1981–2010
* Number of homicides per 100,000 people

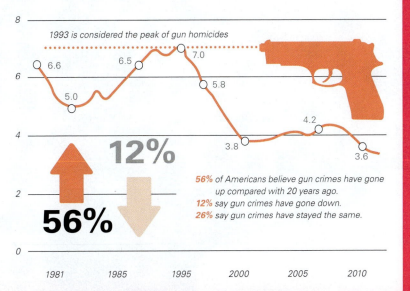

1993 is considered the peak of gun homicides

6.6   5.0   6.5   7.0   5.8   3.8   4.2   3.6

12%

56%

56% of Americans believe gun crimes have gone up compared with 20 years ago.
12% say gun crimes have gone down.
26% say gun crimes have stayed the same.

1981   1985   1995   2000   2005   2010

475

14

The Culture of Journalism

Values, Ethics, and Democracy

479
Modern Journalism in
the Information Age

485
Ethics and the News
Media

490
Reporting Rituals and
the Legacy of Print
Journalism

495
Journalism in the Age
of TV and the Internet

500
Alternative Models:
Public Journalism
and "Fake" News

505
Democracy and
Reimagining
Journalism's Role

In 1887, a young reporter left her job at the *Pittsburgh Dispatch* to seek her fortune in New York City. Only twenty-three years old, Elizabeth "Pink" Cochrane had grown tired of writing for the society pages and answering letters to the editor. She wanted to be on the front page. But at that time, it was considered "unladylike" for women journalists to use their real names, so the *Dispatch* editors, borrowing from a Stephen Foster song, had dubbed her "Nellie Bly."

After four months of persistent job-hunting and freelance writing, Nellie Bly earned a tryout at Joseph Pulitzer's *New York World*, the nation's biggest paper. Her assignment: to investigate the deplorable conditions at the Women's Lunatic Asylum on Blackwell's Island. Her method: to get herself declared mad and committed to the asylum. After practicing the look of a disheveled lunatic in front of mirrors, wandering city streets unwashed and seemingly dazed, and terrifying her fellow boarders in a New York rooming house by acting crazy, she succeeded in convincing doctors and officials to commit her. Other New York

The Granger Collection

newspapers reported her incarceration, speculating on the identity of this "mysterious waif," this "pretty crazy girl" with the "wild, hunted look in her eyes."[1]

Her two-part story appeared in October 1887 and caused a sensation. She was the first reporter to pull off such a stunt. In the days before so-called objective journalism, Nellie Bly's dramatic first-person accounts documented harsh cold baths ("three buckets of water over my head—ice cold water—into my eyes, my ears, my nose and my mouth"); attendants who abused and taunted patients; and newly arrived immigrant women, completely sane, who were committed to this "rat trap" simply because no one could understand them. After the exposé, Bly was famous. Pulitzer gave her a permanent job, and New York City committed $1 million toward improving its asylums.

Within a year, Nellie Bly had exposed a variety of shady scam artists, corrupt politicians and lobbyists, and unscrupulous business practices. Posing as an "unwed mother" with an unwanted child, she uncovered an outfit trafficking in newborn babies. And disguised as a sinner in need of reform, she revealed the appalling conditions at a home for "unfortunate women." A lifetime champion of women and the poor, Nellie Bly pioneered what was then called *detective* or *stunt* journalism. Her work inspired the twentieth-century practice of investigative journalism—from Ida Tarbell's exposés of oil corporations in 1902–1904 to the Pulitzer Prizes for investigative reporting, awarded in 2014 to Chris Hamby of the Center for Public Integrity in Washington, D.C., "for his reports on how some lawyers and

doctors rigged a system to deny benefits to coal miners stricken with black lung disease, resulting in remedial legislative efforts."[2]

One problem facing journalism today is that in the last few years, traditional print and broadcast newsrooms have dramatically cut back on news investigations, which are expensive and time consuming, even though readers and viewers want more of them, not fewer. Mary Walton, writing about the state of investigative reporting for *American Journalism Review*, made this point in 2010: "Kicked out, bought out or barely hanging on, investigative reporters are a vanishing species in the forests of dead tree media and missing in action on Action News. I-Teams are shrinking or, more often, disappearing altogether. Assigned to cover multiple beats, multitasking backpacking reporters no longer have time to sniff out hidden stories, much less write them." She reported that Investigative Reporters and Editors (IRE) membership "fell more than 30 percent, from 5,391 in 2003, to a 10-year low of 3,695 in 2009."[3] But encouragingly, the slack has been picked up, at least partially, by nontraditional and online media. In 2013, Jason Stverak, writing for Watchdog.org, noted, "Today, nonprofit news groups across the country are providing the 'unsexy and repetitive' coverage that the old-guard press began abandoning at the turn of the century. . . . Nonprofit news groups will lead the way in conducting investigative reports and keeping elected officials open and honest."[4] And in 2014, IRE reported that its membership had climbed again to more than five thousand.

▲ *JOURNALISM IS THE ONLY MEDIA ENTERPRISE* that democracy absolutely requires— and it is the only media practice and business that is specifically mentioned and protected by the U.S. Constitution. However, with the major decline in investigative reporting and traditional news audiences, the collapse of many newspapers, and the rise of twenty-four-hour cable news channels and Internet news blogs, mainstream journalism is searching for new business models and better ways to connect with the public.

In this chapter, we examine the changing news landscape and definitions of journalism. We will:

- Explore the values underlying news and ethical problems confronting journalists
- Investigate the shift from more neutral news models to partisan cable and online news
- Study the legacy of print-news conventions and rituals
- Investigate the impact of television and the Internet on news
- Consider contemporary controversial developments in journalism and democracy— specifically, the public journalism movement and satirical forms of news

As you read this chapter, think about how often you look at the news in a typical day. What are some of the recent events or issues you remember reading about in the news? Where is the first place you go to find information about a news event or issue? If you start with a search engine, what newspapers or news organizations do you usually end up looking at? Do you prefer opinion blogs over news organizations for your information? Why or why not? Do you pay for news—either by buying a newspaper or newsmagazine or by going online? For more questions to help you understand the role of journalism in our lives, see "Questioning the Media" in the Chapter Review.

Visit **LaunchPad** for
Media & Culture and
use **LearningCurve** to review
concepts from this chapter.

Modern Journalism in the Information Age

In modern America, serious journalism has sought to provide information that enables citizens to make intelligent decisions. Today, this guiding principle faces serious threats. Why? First, we may just be producing too much information. According to social critic Neil Postman, as a result of developments in media technology, society has developed an "information glut" that transforms news and information into "a form of garbage."[5] Postman believed that scientists, technicians, managers, and journalists merely pile up mountains of new data, which add to the problems and anxieties of everyday life. As a result, too much unchecked data—especially on the Internet—and too little thoughtful discussion emanate from too many channels of communication.

A second, related problem suggests that the amount of data the media now provide has questionable impact on improving public and political life. Many people feel cut off from our major institutions, including journalism. As a result, some citizens are looking to take part in public conversations and civic debates—to renew a democracy in which many voices participate. For example, one benefit of the controversial *Bush v. Gore* 2000 post–presidential election story was the way its legal and political complications engaged the citizenry at a much deeper level than the predictable, staged campaigns did.

What Is News?

In a 1963 staff memo, NBC news president Reuven Frank outlined the narrative strategies integral to all news: "Every news story should . . . display the attributes of fiction, of drama.

"DEEP THROAT"
The major symbol of twentieth-century investigative journalism, Carl Bernstein and Bob Woodward's (*above right*) coverage of the Watergate scandal for the *Washington Post* helped topple the Nixon White House. In *All the President's Men*, the newsmen's book about their investigation, a major character is Deep Throat, the key unidentified source for much of Woodward's reporting. Deep Throat's identity was protected by the two reporters for more than thirty years. Then, in summer 2005, he revealed himself as Mark Felt (*above*), the former No. 2 official in the FBI during the Nixon administration. (Felt died in 2008.)

It should have structure and conflict, problem and denouement, rising and falling action, a beginning, a middle, and an end."[6] Despite Frank's candid insights, many journalists today are uncomfortable thinking of themselves as storytellers. Instead, they tend to describe themselves mainly as information-gatherers.

News is defined here as the process of gathering information and making narrative reports—edited by individuals for news organizations—that offer selected frames of reference; within those frames, news helps the public make sense of important events, political issues, cultural trends, prominent people, and unusual happenings in everyday life.

Characteristics of News

Over time, a set of conventional criteria for determining **newsworthiness**—information most worthy of transformation into news stories—has evolved. Journalists are taught to select and develop news stories relying on one or more of these criteria: timeliness, proximity, conflict, prominence, human interest, consequence, usefulness, novelty, and deviance.

Most issues and events that journalists select as news are *timely*, or *new*. Reporters, for example, cover speeches, meetings, crimes, and court cases that have just happened. In addition, most of these events have to occur close by, or in *proximity* to, readers and viewers. Although local TV news and papers offer some national and international news, readers and viewers expect to find the bulk of news devoted to their own towns and communities.

Most news stories are narratives and thus contain a healthy dose of *conflict*—a key ingredient in narrative writing. In developing news narratives, reporters are encouraged to seek contentious quotes from those with opposing views. For example, stories on presidential elections almost always feature the most dramatic opposing Republican and Democratic positions. And many stories in the aftermath of the terrorist attacks of September 11, 2001, pitted the values of other cultures against those of Western culture—for example, Islam versus Christianity or premodern traditional values versus contemporary consumerism.

Reader and viewer surveys indicate that most people identify more closely with an individual than with an abstract issue. Therefore, the news media tend to report stories that feature *prominent*, powerful, or influential people. Because these individuals often play a role in shaping the rules and values of a community, journalists have traditionally been responsible for keeping a watchful eye on them and relying on them for quotes.

But reporters also look for *human-interest* stories: extraordinary incidents that happen to "ordinary" people. In fact, reporters often relate a story about a complicated issue (such as unemployment, war, tax rates, health care, or homelessness) by illustrating its impact on one "average" person, family, or town.

Two other criteria for newsworthiness are *consequence* and *usefulness*. Stories about isolated or bizarre crimes, even though they might be new, near, or notorious, often have little impact on our daily lives. To balance these kinds of stories, many editors and reporters believe that some news must also be of consequence to a majority of readers or viewers. For example, stories about issues or events that affect a family's income or change a community's laws have consequence. Likewise, many people look for stories with a practical use: hints on buying a used car or choosing a college, strategies for training a pet or removing a stain.

Finally, news is often about the *novel* and the *deviant*. When events happen that are outside the routine of daily life, such as a seven-year-old girl trying to pilot a plane across the country or an ex-celebrity involved in a drug deal, the news media are there. Reporters also cover events that appear to deviate from social norms, including murders, rapes, fatal car crashes, fires, political scandals, and gang activities. For example, as the war in Iraq escalated, any suicide bombing in the Middle East represented the kind of novel and deviant behavior that qualified as major news.

Values in American Journalism

Although newsworthiness criteria are a useful way to define news, they do not reveal much about the cultural aspects of news. News is both a product and a process. It is both the morning paper or evening newscast and a set of subtle values and shifting rituals that have been adapted to historical and social circumstances, such as the partisan press values of the eighteenth century or the informational standards of the twentieth century.

For example, in 1841, Horace Greeley described the newly founded *New York Tribune* as "a journal removed alike from servile partisanship on the one hand and from gagged, mincing neutrality on the other."[7] Greeley feared that too much neutrality would make reporters into wimps who stood for nothing. Yet the neutrality Greeley warned against is today a major value of conventional journalism, with mainstream reporters assuming they are acting as detached and all-seeing observers of social experience.

Neutrality Boosts Credibility—and Sales

As former journalism professor and reporter David Eason notes, "Reporters . . . have no special method for determining the truth of a situation nor a special language for reporting their findings. They make sense of events by telling stories about them."[8]

Even though journalists transform events into stories, they generally believe that they are—or should be—neutral observers who present facts without passing judgment on them. Conventions such as the inverted-pyramid news lead, the careful attribution of sources, the minimal use of adverbs and adjectives, and a detached third-person point of view all help reporters perform their work in an apparently neutral way.

Like lawyers, therapists, and other professionals, many modern journalists believe that their credibility derives from personal detachment. Yet the roots of this view reside in less noble territory. Jon Katz, media critic and former CBS News producer, discusses the history of the neutral pose:

The idea of respectable detachment wasn't conceived as a moral principle so much as a marketing device. Once newspapers began to mass market themselves in the mid-1880s, . . . publishers ceased being working, opinionated journalists. They mutated instead into businessmen eager to reach the broadest number of readers and antagonize the fewest. . . . Objectivity works well for publishers, protecting the status quo and keeping journalism's voice militantly moderate.[9]

To reach as many people as possible across a wide spectrum, publishers and editors realized as early as the 1840s that softening their partisanship might boost sales.

Partisanship Trumps Neutrality, Especially Online and on Cable

Since the rise of cable and the Internet, today's media marketplace has offered a fragmented world where appealing to the widest audience no longer makes the best economic sense. More options than ever exist, with newspaper readers and TV viewers embracing cable news, social networks, blogs, and Twitter. The old "mass" audience has morphed into smaller niche audiences who embrace particular hobbies, story genres, politics, and social networks. News media outlets that hope to survive appeal no longer to mass audiences but to interest groups—from sports fans and history buffs to conservatives or liberals. So, mimicking the news business of the eighteenth century, partisanship has become good business. For the news media today, muting political leanings to reach a mass audience makes no sense because such an audience no longer exists in the way it once did, especially in the days when only three major TV networks offered evening news for a half hour, once a day. Instead, news media now make money by targeting and catering to niche groups on a 24/7 news cycle.

In such a marketplace, we see the decline of a more neutral journalistic model that promoted fact-gathering, documents, and expertise and held up "objectivity" as the ideal for news practice. Rising in its place is a new era of partisan news—what Bill Kovach and Tom Rosenstiel call a "journalism of assertion"—marked partly by a return to journalism's colonial roots and partly by the downsizing of the "journalism of verification" that kept watch over our central institutions.[10] This transition is symbolized by the rise of the cable news pundit on Fox News or MSNBC as a kind of "expert" with more standing than verified facts, authentic documents, and actual experts. Today, the new partisan fervor found in news, both online and on cable, has been a major catalyst for the nation's intense political and ideological divide.

Other Cultural Values in Journalism

Even the neutral journalism model, which most reporters and editors still aspire to, remains a selective and uneven process. Reporters and editors turn some events into reports and discard many others. This process is governed by a deeper set of subjective beliefs that are not neutral. Sociologist Herbert Gans, who studied the newsroom cultures of CBS, NBC, *Newsweek*, and *Time* in the 1970s, generalized that several basic "enduring values" have been shared by most American reporters and editors. The most prominent of these values, which persist to this day, are ethnocentrism, responsible capitalism, small-town pastoralism, and individualism.[11]

By **ethnocentrism**, Gans meant that in most news reporting, especially foreign coverage, reporters judge other countries and cultures on the basis of how "they live up to or imitate American practices and values." Critics outside the United States, for instance, point out that CNN's international news channels portray world events and cultures primarily from an American point of view rather than through some neutral, global lens.

Gans also identified **responsible capitalism** as an underlying value, contending that journalists sometimes naïvely assume that

OCCUPY WALL STREET
On September 17, 2011, a group of protesters gathered in Zuccotti Park in New York's financial district and officially launched the Occupy Wall Street protest movement. Their slogan, "We are the 99 percent," addressed the growing income disparity in the United States, furthering the idea that the nation's wealth is unfairly concentrated among the top-earning 1 percent. Although forced out of Zuccotti Park on November 15, 2011, the movement resonated with people across the country and around the world. By the end of 2011, Occupy protests had spread to over 951 cities in eighty-two countries.

Lucas Jackson/Reuters/Landov

businesspeople compete with one another not primarily to maximize profits but "to create increased prosperity for all." Gans pointed out that although most reporters and editors condemn monopolies, "there is little implicit or explicit criticism of the oligopolistic nature of much of today's economy."[12] In fact, during the major economic recession of 2008–09, many journalists did not fully understand the debt incurred by media oligopolies and other financial conditions that led to the bankruptcies and shutdowns of numerous newspapers during this difficult time.

Another value that Gans found was the romanticization of **small-town pastoralism**: favoring the small over the large and the rural over the urban. Many journalists equate small-town life with innocence and harbor suspicions of cities, their governments, and urban experiences. Consequently, stories about rustic communities with crime or drug problems have often been framed as if the purity of country life had been contaminated by "mean" big-city values.

Finally, **individualism**, according to Gans, remains the most prominent value underpinning daily journalism. Many idealistic reporters are attracted to this profession because it rewards the rugged tenacity needed to confront and expose corruption. Beyond this, individuals who overcome personal adversity are the subjects of many enterprising news stories.

Often, however, journalism that focuses on personal triumphs neglects to explain how large organizations and institutions work or fail. Many conventional reporters and editors are unwilling or unsure of how to tackle the problems raised by institutional decay. In addition, because they value their own individualism and are accustomed to working alone, many journalists dislike cooperating on team projects or participating in forums in which community members discuss their own interests and alternative definitions of news.[13]

Facts, Values, and Bias

Traditionally, reporters have aligned facts with an objective position and values with subjective feelings.[14] Within this context, news reports offer readers and viewers details, data, and description. It then becomes the citizen's responsibility to judge and take a stand about the social problems represented by the news. Given these assumptions, reporters are responsible only for adhering to the tradition of the trade—"getting the facts." As a result, many reporters view themselves as neutral "channels" of information rather than selective storytellers or citizens actively involved in public life.

Still, most public surveys have shown that while journalists may work hard to stay neutral, the addition of partisan cable channels such as Fox News and MSNBC has undermined reporters who try to report fairly. So while conservatives tend to see the media as liberally biased, liberals tend to see the media as favoring conservative positions (see "Case Study: Bias in the News" on page 484). But political bias is complicated. During the early years of Barack Obama's presidency, many pundits on the political Right argued that Obama got much more favorable media coverage than did former president George W. Bush. But left-wing politicians and critics maintained that the right-wing media—especially news analysts associated with conservative talk radio and Fox's cable channel—rarely reported evenhandedly on Obama, painting him as a "socialist" or as "anti-American."

According to Evan Thomas of *Newsweek* magazine, "the suspicion of press bias" comes from two assumptions or beliefs that the public holds about news media: "The first is that reporters are out to get their subjects. The second is that the press is too close to its subjects."[15] Thomas argues that the "press's real bias is for conflict." He says that mainstream editors and reporters traditionally value scandals, "preferably sexual," and "have a weakness for war, the ultimate conflict." Thomas claims that in the end, journalists "are looking for narratives that reveal something of character. It is the human drama that most compels our attention."[16]

Bias in the News

All news is biased. News, after all, is primarily selective story-telling, not objective science. Editors choose certain events to cover and ignore others; reporters choose particular words or images to use and reject others. The news is also biased in favor of storytelling, drama, and conflict; in favor of telling "two sides of a story"; in favor of powerful and well-connected sources; and in favor of practices that serve journalists' space and time limits.

In terms of political bias, a 2012 Pew Research Center study reported that 37 percent of Americans see "a great deal of political bias" in the news—up from 31 percent in 2000 and 25 percent back in 1989 (see the figure below). In terms of political party affiliation, 49 percent of Republicans in this 2012 survey reported "a great deal" of bias, while only 32 percent of Democrats and 35 percent of Independents reported high levels of political bias. Since the late 1960s, the public perception has been that mainstream news media operate mostly with a liberal bias. This would seem to be supported by a 2004 Pew Research Center survey that found that 34 percent of national journalists

self-identify as liberal, 7 percent as conservative, and 54 percent as moderate.[1]

Given primary dictionary definitions of *liberal* (adj., "favorable to progress or reform, as in political or religious affairs") and *conservative* (adj., "disposed to preserve existing conditions, institutions, etc., or to restore traditional ones, and to limit change"), it is not surprising that a high percentage of liberals and moderates gravitate to mainstream journalism.[2] A profession that honors documenting change, checking power, and reporting wrongdoing would attract fewer conservatives, who are predisposed to "limit change." As sociologist Herbert Gans demonstrated in *Deciding What's News*, most reporters are socialized into a set of work rituals—especially getting the story first and telling it from "both sides" to achieve a kind of balance.[3] In fact, this commitment to political "balance" mandates that if journalists interview someone on the Left, they must also interview someone on the Right. Ultimately, such balancing acts require reporters to take middle-of-the-road or moderate positions.

Still, the "liberal bias" narrative persists. In 2001, Bernard Goldberg, a former producer at CBS News, wrote *Bias*. Using anecdotes

from his days at CBS, he maintained that national news slanted to the Left.[4] In 2003, Eric Alterman, a columnist for the *Nation*, countered with *What Liberal Media?* Alterman admitted that mainstream news media do reflect more liberal views on social issues but argued that they had become more conservative on politics and economics—as displayed in their support for deregulated media and concentrated ownership.[5] Alterman said that the liberal bias tale persists because conservatives keep repeating it in the major media. Conservative voices have been so successful that one study in *Communication Research* reported "a fourfold increase over the past dozen years in the number of Americans telling pollsters that they discerned a liberal bias in the news. But a review of the media's actual ideological content, collected and coded over a 12-year period, offered no corroboration whatever for this view."[6] However, a 2010 study in the *Harvard International Journal of Press/Politics* reported that both Democratic and Republican leaders are able "to influence perceptions of bias" by attacking the news media.[7]

Since journalists are primarily storytellers, and not scientists, searching for liberal or conservative bias should not be the main focus of our criticism. Under time and space constraints, most journalists serve the routine practices of their profession, which call on them to moderate their own political agendas. News reports, then, are always "biased," given human imperfection in storytelling and in communicating through the lens of language, images, and institutional values. Fully critiquing news stories must depend, then, on whether they are fair, represent an issue's complexity, provide verification and documentation, represent multiple views, and serve democracy.

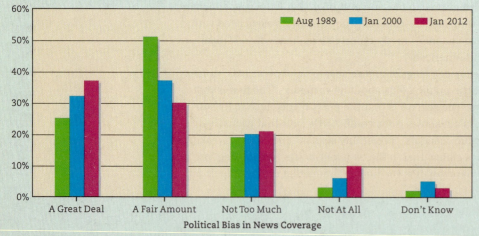

Data from: Pew Research Center Survey, January 5–8, 2012.
Note: Figures may not add up to 100 percent because of rounding.

Ethics and the News Media

National journalists occasionally face a profound ethical dilemma, especially in the aftermath of 9/11: When is it right to protect government secrets, and when should those secrets be revealed to the public? How must editors weigh such decisions when national security bumps up against citizens' need for information?

In 2006, Dean Baquet, then editor of the *Los Angeles Times* (in 2014, he became the executive editor of the *New York Times*), and Bill Keller, then executive editor of the *New York Times*, wrestled with these questions in a coauthored editorial:

Finally, we weigh the merits of publishing against the risks of publishing. There is no magic formula. . . . We make our best judgment.

When we come down on the side of publishing, of course, everyone hears about it. Few people are aware when we decide to hold an article. But each of us, in the past few years, has had the experience of withholding or delaying articles when the administration convinces us that the risk of publication outweighed the benefits. . . .

We understand that honorable people may disagree . . . to publish or not to publish. But making those decisions is a responsibility that falls to editors, a corollary to the great gift of our independence. It is not a responsibility we take lightly. And it is not one we can surrender to the government.[17]

What makes the predicament of these national editors so tricky is that in the war against terrorism, some politicians maintain that one value terrorists truly hate is "our freedom." At the same time, some of these same politicians criticized the *Times* for carefully editing and then publishing the WikiLeaks documents. There is irony here: What is more integral to liberty than the freedom of an independent press—so independent that for more than two hundred years U.S. courts have protected the news media's right to criticize our political leaders and, within boundaries, reveal government secrets?

Ethical Predicaments

What is the moral and social responsibility of journalists, not only for the stories they report but also for the actual events or issues they are shaping for millions of people? Wrestling with such media ethics involves determining the moral response to a situation through critical reasoning. Although national security issues raise problems for a few of our largest news organizations, the most frequent ethical dilemmas encountered in most newsrooms across the United States involve intentional deception, privacy invasions, and conflicts of interest.

Deploying Deception

Ever since Nellie Bly faked insanity to get inside an asylum in the 1880s, investigative journalists have used deception to get stories. Today, journalists continue to use disguises and assume false identities to gather information on social transgressions. Beyond legal considerations, though, a key ethical question comes into play: Does the end justify the means? For example, can a newspaper or TV newsmagazine use deceptive ploys to go undercover and expose a suspected fraudulent clinic that promises miracle cures at a high cost? Are news professionals justified in posing as clients desperate for a cure?

In terms of ethics, there are at least two major positions and multiple variations. At one end of the spectrum, *absolutist ethics* suggests that a moral society has laws and codes, including honesty, that everyone must live by. This means citizens, including members of the news media, should tell the truth at all times and in all cases. In other words, the ends (exposing a phony clinic) never justify the means (using deception to get the story). An editor who is an absolutist would cover this story by asking a reporter to find victims who have been ripped off by the clinic and then telling the story through their eyes. At the other end of the spectrum is *situational ethics*, which promotes ethical decisions on a case-by-case basis. If a greater public good could be served by using deceit, journalists and editors who believe in situational ethics would sanction deception as a practice.

Should a journalist withhold information about his or her professional identity to get a quote or a story from an interview subject? Many sources and witnesses are reluctant to talk with journalists, especially about a sensitive subject that might jeopardize a job or hurt another person's reputation. Journalists know they can sometimes obtain information by posing as someone other than a journalist, such as a curious student or a concerned citizen.

Most newsrooms frown on such deception. In particular situations, though, such a practice might be condoned if reporters and their editors believed that the public needed the information. The ethics code adopted by the Society of Professional Journalists (SPJ) is mostly silent on issues of deception. The code does say that "journalists should be honest, fair and courageous in gathering, reporting and interpreting information," and it also calls on journalists to "seek truth and report it" (see Figure 14.1 on page 487). So is it being "honest" for reporters to use deceptive tactics in the pursuit of truth?

Invading Privacy

To achieve "the truth" or to "get the facts," journalists routinely straddle a line between "the public's right to know" and a person's right to privacy. For example, journalists may be sent to hospitals to gather quotes from victims who have been injured. Often there is very little the public might gain from such information, but journalists worry that if they don't get the quote, a competitor might. In these instances, have the news media responsibly weighed the protection of individual privacy against the public's right to know? Although the latter is not constitutionally guaranteed, journalists invoke the public's right to know as justification for many types of stories.

One infamous example is the recent phone hacking scandal involving News Corp.'s now-shuttered U.K. newspaper, *News of the World*. In 2011, the *Guardian* reported that *News of the World* reporters had hired a private investigator to hack into the voice mail of thirteen-year-old murder victim Milly Dowler and had deleted some messages. Although there had been past allegations that reporters from *News of the World* had hacked into the private voice mails of the British royal family, government officials, and celebrities, this revelation on the extent of *News of the World*'s phone hacking activities caused a huge scandal and led to the arrests and resignations of several senior executives. Today, in the digital age, when reporters can gain access to private e-mail messages, Twitter accounts, and Facebook pages, as well as voice mail, such practices raise serious questions about how far a reporter should go to get information.

In the case of privacy issues, media companies and journalists should always ask these ethical questions: What public good is being served here? What significant public knowledge will be gained through the exploitation of a tragic private moment? Although journalism's code of ethics says, "The news media must guard against invading a person's right to privacy," this clashes with another part of the code: "The public's right to know of events of public importance and interest is the overriding mission of the mass media."[18] When these two ethical standards collide, should journalists err on the side of the public's right to know?

FIGURE 14.1

SOCIETY OF PROFESSIONAL JOURNALISTS' CODE OF ETHICS

Data from: Society of Professional Journalists (SPJ).

Code of Ethics

Preamble

Members of the Society of Professional Journalists believe that public enlightenment is the forerunner of justice and the foundation of democracy. The duty of the journalist is to further those ends by seeking truth and providing a fair and comprehensive account of events and issues. Conscientious journalists from all media and specialties strive to serve the public with thoroughness and honesty. Professional integrity is the cornerstone of a journalist's credibility.

Members of the Society share a dedication to ethical behavior and adopt this code to declare the Society's principles and standards of practice.

Seek Truth and Report It

Journalists should be honest, fair and courageous in gathering, reporting and interpreting information.

Journalists should:

- Test the accuracy of information from all sources and exercise care to avoid inadvertent error. Deliberate distortion is never permissible.
- Diligently seek out subjects of news stories to give them the opportunity to respond to allegations of wrongdoing.
- Identify sources whenever feasible. The public is entitled to as much information as possible on sources' reliability.
- Always question sources' motives before promising anonymity. Clarify conditions attached to any promise made in exchange for information. Keep promises.
- Make certain that headlines, news teases and promotional material, photos, video, audio, graphics, sound bites and quotations do not misrepresent. They should not oversimplify or highlight incidents out of context.
- Never distort the content of news photos or video. Image enhancement for technical clarity is always permissible. Label montages and photo illustrations.
- Avoid misleading re-enactments or staged news events. If re-enactment is necessary to tell a story, label it.
- Avoid undercover or other surreptitious methods of gathering information except when traditional open methods will not yield information vital to the public. Use of such methods should be explained as part of the story.
- Never plagiarize.
- Tell the story of the diversity and magnitude of the human experience boldly, even when it is unpopular to do so.
- Examine their own cultural values and avoid imposing those values on others.
- Avoid stereotyping by race, gender, age, religion, ethnicity, geography, sexual orientation, disability, physical appearance or social status.
- Support the open exchange of views, even views they find repugnant.
- Give voice to the voiceless; official and unofficial sources of information can be equally valid.
- Distinguish between advocacy and news reporting. Analysis and commentary should be labeled and not misrepresent fact or context.
- Distinguish news from advertising and shun hybrids that blur the lines between the two.
- Recognize a special obligation to ensure that the public's business is conducted in the open and that government records are open to inspection.

Minimize Harm

Ethical journalists treat sources, subjects and colleagues as human beings deserving of respect.

Journalists should:

- Show compassion for those who may be affected adversely by news coverage. Use special sensitivity when dealing with children and inexperienced sources or subjects.
- Be sensitive when seeking or using interviews or photographs of those affected by tragedy or grief.
- Recognize that gathering and reporting information may cause harm or discomfort. Pursuit of the news is not a license for arrogance.
- Recognize that private people have a greater right to control information about themselves than do public officials and others who seek power, influence or attention. Only an overriding public need can justify intrusion into anyone's privacy.
- Show good taste. Avoid pandering to lurid curiosity.
- Be cautious about identifying juvenile suspects or victims of sex crimes.
- Be judicious about naming criminal suspects before the formal filing of charges.
- Balance a criminal suspect's fair trial rights with the public's right to be informed.

Act Independently

Journalists should be free of obligation to any interest other than the public's right to know.

Journalists should:

- Avoid conflicts of interest, real or perceived.
- Remain free of associations and activities that may compromise integrity or damage credibility.
- Refuse gifts, favors, free travel and special treatment, and shun secondary employment, political involvement, public office and service in community organizations if they compromise journalistic integrity.
- Disclose unavoidable conflicts.
- Be vigilant and courageous about holding those with power accountable.
- Deny favored treatment to advertisers and special interests and resist their pressure to influence news coverage.
- Be wary of sources offering information for favors or money; avoid bidding for news.

Be Accountable

Journalists are accountable to their readers, listeners, viewers and each other.

Journalists should:

- Clarify and explain news coverage and invite dialogue with the public over journalistic conduct.
- Encourage the public to voice grievances against the news media.
- Admit mistakes and correct them promptly.
- Expose unethical practices of journalists and the news media.
- Abide by the same high standards to which they hold others.

Conflict of Interest

Journalism's code of ethics also warns reporters and editors not to place themselves in positions that produce a **conflict of interest**—that is, any situation in which journalists may stand to benefit personally from stories they produce. "Gifts, favors, free travel, special treatment or privileges," the code states, "can compromise the integrity of journalists and their employers. Nothing of value should be accepted."[19] Although small newspapers with limited resources and poorly paid reporters might accept such "freebies" as game tickets for their sportswriters and free meals for their restaurant critics, this practice does increase the likelihood of a conflict of interest that produces favorable or uncritical coverage.

On a broader level, ethical guidelines at many news outlets attempt to protect journalists from compromising positions. For instance, in most cities, U.S. journalists do not actively participate in politics or support social causes. Some journalists will not reveal their political affiliations, and some even decline to vote.

For these journalists, the rationale behind their decision is straightforward: Journalists should not place themselves in a situation in which they might have to report on the misdeeds of an organization or a political party to which they belong. If a journalist has a tie to any group, and that group is later suspected of involvement in shady or criminal activity, the reporter's ability to report on that group would be compromised—along with the credibility of the news outlet for which he or she works. Conversely, other journalists believe that not actively participating in politics or social causes means abandoning their civic obligations. They believe that fairness in their reporting, not total detachment from civic life, is their primary obligation.

In the digital age, conflict of interest cases surrounding opinion blogging have grown more complicated, especially when those opinion blogs run under the banner of traditional news media. For example, in 2010 David Weigel, whom the *Washington Post* hired to blog about the conservative movement, was forced to resign after private e-mails and Listserv messages were exposed in which he had used inflammatory rhetoric to vent about well-known conservatives like Matt Drudge, Ron Paul, and Rush Limbaugh. A *Post* editor commented at the time, "We can't have any tolerance for the perception that people are conflicted or bring a bias to their work. . . . There's abundant room on our Web site for a wide range of viewpoints, and we should be transparent about everybody's viewpoint."[20] Critics afterward noted that mainstream news media sites should make clear to their readers whether the bloggers are actually opinion writers or professional journalists trying to write fairly on subjects about which they may not agree. In this case, Weigel's credibility regarding his ability to blog fairly about right-wing politicians and pundits was compromised when his personal exchanges ridiculing conservatives came to light. This case illustrates the increasingly blurry line between the old journalism of verification and the new journalism of assertion.

Resolving Ethical Problems

When a journalist is criticized for ethical lapses or questionable reporting tactics, a typical response might be "I'm just doing my job" or "I was just getting the facts." Such explanations are troubling, though, because in responding this way, reporters are transferring personal responsibility for the story to a set of institutional rituals.

FAREED ZAKARIA, *Time* magazine editor-at-large and host of CNN's *GPS*, was briefly suspended from both *Time* and CNN in August 2012 when media blogs accused him of plagiarizing scholar Jill Lepore's essay on gun control in one of his columns. Reinstated after both *Time* and CNN found no evidence of deliberate plagiarism, Zakaria apologized for his "terrible mistake," which he explains came as a result of mixing up different notes from different sources. However, in 2014, the blog *Our Bad Media* was reporting several possible instances of additional plagiarism. These accusations underscore the potential consequences of an ethical lapse, even for journalists as high-profile as Zakaria.

Photoshot/Newscom

There are, of course, ethical alternatives to self-justifications such as "I'm just doing my job" that force journalists to think through complex issues. With the crush of deadlines and daily duties, most media professionals deal with ethical situations only on a case-by-case basis as issues arise. However, examining major ethical models and theories is a common strategy for addressing ethics on a general rather than a situational basis. The most well-known ethical standard, the Judeo-Christian command to "love your neighbor as yourself," provides one foundation for constructing ethical guidelines. Although we cannot address all major moral codes here, a few key precepts can guide us.

Aristotle, Kant, and Bentham and Mill

The Greek philosopher Aristotle offered an early ethical concept, the "golden mean"—a guideline for seeking balance between competing positions. For Aristotle, this was a desirable middle ground between extreme positions, usually with one regarded as deficient and the other as excessive. For example, Aristotle saw ambition as the balance between sloth and greed.

Another ethical principle entails the "categorical imperative" developed by German philosopher Immanuel Kant (1724–1804). This idea maintains that a society must adhere to moral codes that are universal and unconditional, applicable in all situations at all times. For example, the Golden Rule ("Do unto others as you would have them do unto you") is articulated in one form or another in most of the world's major religious and philosophical traditions and operates as an absolute moral principle. The First Amendment, which prevents Congress from abridging free speech and other rights, could be considered an example of an unconditional national law.

British philosophers Jeremy Bentham (1748–1832) and John Stuart Mill (1806–1873) promoted an ethical principle derived from "the greatest good for the greatest number," directing us "to distribute a good consequence to more people rather than to fewer, whenever we have a choice."[21]

Developing Ethical Policy

Arriving at ethical decisions involves several steps. These include laying out the case; pinpointing the key issues; identifying involved parties, their intents, and their competing values; studying ethical models; presenting strategies and options; and formulating a decision.

One area that requires ethics is covering the private lives of people who have unintentionally become prominent in the news. Consider Richard Jewell, the Atlanta security guard who, for eighty-eight days, was the FBI's prime suspect in the city park bombing at the 1996 Olympics. The FBI never charged Jewell with a crime, and he later successfully sued several news organizations for libel. The news outlets competed to be the first to report important developments in the case, and with the battle for newspaper circulation and broadcast ratings adding fuel to a complex situation, editors were reluctant to back away from the story once it began circulating.

At least two key ethical questions emerged: (1) Should the news media have named Jewell as a suspect even though he was never charged with a crime? (2) Should the media have camped out daily in front of his mother's house in an attempt to interview him and his mother? The Jewell case pitted the media's right to tell stories and earn profits against a person's right to be left alone.

Working through the various ethical stages, journalists formulate policies grounded in overarching moral principles.[22] Should reporters, for instance, follow the Golden Rule and be willing to treat themselves, their families, or their friends the way they treated the Jewells? Or should they invoke Aristotle's "golden mean" and seek moral virtue between extreme positions?

In Richard Jewell's situation, journalists could have developed guidelines to balance Jewell's interests and the news media's. For example, in addition to apologizing for using Jewell's name in early accounts, reporters might have called off their stakeout and allowed Jewell to set interview times at a neutral site, where he could talk with a small pool of journalists designated to relay information to other media outlets.

Reporting Rituals and the Legacy of Print Journalism

Unfamiliar with being questioned themselves, many reporters are uncomfortable discussing their personal values or their strategies for getting stories. Nevertheless, a stock of rituals, derived from basic American values, underlie the practice of reporting. These include focusing on the present, relying on experts, balancing story conflict, and acting as adversaries toward leaders and institutions.

Focusing on the Present

In the 1840s, when the telegraph first enabled news to crisscross America instantly, modern journalism was born. To complement the new technical advances, editors called for a focus on the immediacy of the present. Modern front-page print journalism began to de-emphasize political analysis and historical context, accenting instead the new and the now.

As a result, the profession began drawing criticism for failing to offer historical, political, and social analyses. This criticism continues today. For example, urban drug stories heavily dominated print and network news during the 1986 and 1988 election years. Such stories, however, virtually disappeared from the news by 1992, although the nation's serious drug and addiction problems had not diminished.[23] For many editors and reporters at the time, drug stories became "yesterday's news."

Modern journalism tends to reject "old news" for whatever new event or idea disrupts today's routines. During the 1996 elections, when statistics revealed that drug use among middle-class high school students was rising, reporters latched on to new versions of the drug story, but their reports made only limited references to the 1980s. And although drug problems and addiction rates did not diminish in subsequent years, these topics were virtually ignored by journalists during national elections from 2000 to 2012. Indeed, given the space and time constraints of current news practices, reporters seldom link stories to the past or to the ebb and flow of history. (To analyze current news stories, see "Media Literacy and the Critical Process: Telling Stories and Covering Disaster" on page 491.)

Getting a Good Story

Early in the 1980s, the Janet Cooke hoax demonstrated the difference between the mere telling of a good story and the social responsibility to tell the truth.[24] Cooke, a former *Washington Post* reporter, was fired for fabricating an investigative report for which she initially won a Pulitzer Prize. (It was later revoked.) She had created a cast of characters, featuring a mother who contributed to the heroin addiction of her eight-year-old son.

At the time the hoax was exposed, Chicago columnist Mike Royko criticized conventional journalism for allowing narrative conventions—getting a good story—to trump journalism's responsibility to the daily lives it documents: "There's something more important than a story here. This eight-year-old kid is being murdered. The editors should have said forget the story, find the kid. . . . People in any other profession would have gone right to the police."[25] Had editors at the *Post* done so, Cooke's hoax would not have gone as far as it did.

According to Don Hewitt, the creator and longtime executive producer of *60 Minutes*, "There's a very simple formula if you're in Hollywood, Broadway, opera, publishing, broadcasting, newspapering. It's four very simple words—tell me a story."[26] For most journalists, the bottom line is "Get the story"—an edict that overrides most other concerns. It is the standard against which many reporters measure themselves and their profession.

Media Literacy and the Critical Process

1 DESCRIPTION. Find print and broadcast news versions of the *same* disaster story (use LexisNexis if available). Make copies of each story, and note the pictures chosen to tell the story.

2 ANALYSIS. Find patterns in the coverage. How are the stories treated differently in print and on television? Are there similarities in the words chosen or images used? What kinds of experience are depicted? Who are the sources the reporters use to verify their information?

3 INTERPRETATION. What do these patterns suggest? Can you make any interpretations or arguments based on the kinds of disaster covered, sources used, areas covered, or words/images chosen? How are the stories told in relation to their importance to the entire community or nation? How complex are the stories?

Telling Stories and Covering Disaster

Covering difficult stories—such as natural disasters like Hurricane Sandy in 2012—may present challenges to journalists about how to frame their coverage. The opening sections, or leads, of news stories can vary depending on the source—whether it is print, broadcast, or online news—or even the editorial style of the news organization (e.g., some story leads are straightforward; some are very dramatic). And, although modern journalists claim objectivity as a goal, it is unlikely that a professional in the storytelling business can approximate any sort of scientific objectivity. The best journalists can do is be fair, reporting and telling stories to their communities and nation by explaining the complicated and tragic experiences they convert into words or pictures. To explore this type of coverage, try this exercise with examples from recent disaster coverage of a regional or national event.

4 EVALUATION. Which stories are the strongest? Why? Which are the weakest? Why? Make a judgment on how well these disaster stories serve your interests as a citizen and the interests of the larger community or nation.

5 ENGAGEMENT. In an e-mail or letter to the editor, share your findings with relevant editors and TV news directors. Make suggestions for improved coverage, and cite strong stories that you admired. Report to the class how the editors and news directors responded.

Getting a Story First

In a discussion on public television about the press coverage of a fatal airline crash in Milwaukee in the 1980s, a news photographer was asked to talk about his role in covering the tragedy. Rather than take up the poignant, heartbreaking aspects of witnessing the aftermath of such an event, the excited photographer launched into a dramatic recounting of how he had slipped behind police barricades to snap the first grim photos, which later appeared in the *Milwaukee Journal*. As part of their socialization into the profession, reporters often learn to evade authority figures to secure a story ahead of the competition.

The photographer's recollection points to the important role journalism plays in calling public attention to serious events and issues. Yet he also talked about the news-gathering process as a game that journalists play. It's now routine for local television stations, 24/7 cable news, and newspapers to run self-promotions about how they beat competitors to a story. In addition, during political elections, local television stations and networks project winners in particular races and often hype their projections when they are able to forecast results before the competition does. This practice led to the fiasco in November 2000 when the major networks and cable news services badly flubbed their predictions regarding the outcome of voting in Florida during the presidential election.

Journalistic *scoops* and exclusive stories attempt to portray reporters in a heroic light: They have won a race for facts, which they have gathered and presented ahead of their rivals.

It is not always clear, though, how the public is better served by a journalist's claim to have gotten a story first. In some ways, the 24/7 cable news, the Internet, and bloggers have intensified the race for getting a story first. With a fragmented audience and more media competing for news, the mainstream news often feels more pressure to lure an audience with exclusive, and sometimes sensational, stories. Although readers and viewers might value the aggressiveness of reporters, the earliest reports are not necessarily better, more accurate, or as complete as stories written later, with more context and perspective.

For example, in summer 2010, a firestorm erupted around the abrupt dismissal of Shirley Sherrod, a Georgia-based African American official with the U.S. Department of Agriculture, over a short clip of a speech posted by the late right-wing blogger Andrew Breitbart on his Web site BigGovernment.com. His clip implied that Sherrod had once discriminated against a white farm family who had sought her help when their farm was about to be foreclosed. FoxNews .com picked up the clip, and soon it was all over cable TV, where Sherrod and the Obama administration were denounced as "reverse racists." The secretary of agriculture, Tom Vilsack, demanded and got Sherrod's resignation. However, once reporters started digging deeper into the story and CNN ran an interview with the white farmers that Sherrod had actually helped, it was revealed that the 2½-minute clip had been re-edited and taken out of context from a 43-minute speech Sherrod had given at an NAACP event. In the speech, Sherrod talked about the discrimination that both poor white and black farmers had faced, and about rising above her own past. (Her father had been murdered forty-five years earlier, and an all-white Georgia grand jury did not indict the accused white farmer despite testimony from three witnesses.) Conservative pundits apologized, Glenn Beck demanded that Sherrod be rehired, and Tom Vilsack offered her a new job (which she ultimately declined).[27] In 2011, Sherrod sued Breitbart and his Web site for defamation of character. As described in a *Politico* blog, the case was still in the courts in 2014, complicated by Breitbart's unexpected death in 2012 and the Obama administration's resistance to requests for access to relevant government files and e-mails that could be used to prosecute or defend the case.[28]

This kind of scoop behavior, which has become rampant in the digital age, demonstrates pack or **herd journalism**, which occurs when reporters stake out a house; chase celebrities in packs; or follow a story in such herds that the entire profession comes under attack for invading people's privacy, exploiting their personal problems, or just plain getting the story wrong.

Relying on Experts

Another ritual of modern print journalism—relying on outside sources—has made reporters heavily dependent on experts. Reporters, though often experts themselves in certain areas by virtue of having covered them over time, are not typically allowed to display their expertise overtly. Instead, they must seek outside authorities to give credibility to seemingly neutral reports. *What* daily reporters know is generally subordinate to *who* they know.

During the early twentieth century, progressive politicians and leaders of opinion such as President Woodrow Wilson and columnist Walter Lippmann believed in the cultivation of strong ties among national reporters, government officials, scientists, business managers, and researchers. They wanted journalists supplied with expertise across a variety of areas. Today, the widening gap between those with expertise and those without it has created a need for public mediators. Reporters have assumed this role as surrogates who represent both leaders' and readers' interests. With their access to experts, reporters transform specialized and insider knowledge into the everyday commonsense language of news stories.

Reporters also frequently use experts to create narrative conflict by pitting a series of quotes against one another, or on occasion use experts to support a particular position. In addition, the use of experts enables journalists to distance themselves from daily experience;

they are able to attribute the responsibility for the events or issues reported in a story to those who are quoted.

To use experts, journalists must make direct contact with a source—by phone or e-mail or in person. Journalists do not, however, heavily cite the work of other writers; that would violate reporters' desire not only to get a story first but to get it on their own. Telephone calls and face-to-face interviews, rather than extensively researched interpretations, are the stuff of daily journalism.

Newsweek's Jonathan Alter once called expert sources the "usual suspects." Alter contended that "the impression conveyed is of a world that contains only a handful of knowledgeable people. . . . Their public exposure is a result not only of their own abilities, but of deadlines and a failure of imagination on the part of the press."[29]

In addition, expert sources have historically been predominantly white and male. Fairness and Accuracy in Reporting (FAIR) conducted a major study of the 14,632 sources used during 2001 on evening news programs on ABC, CBS, and NBC. FAIR found that only 15 percent of sources were women—and 52 percent of these women represented "average citizens" or "non-experts." By contrast, of the male sources, 86 percent were cast in "authoritative" or "expert" roles. Among U.S. sources for which race could be determined, the study found that white sources "made up 92 percent of the total, blacks 7 percent, Latinos and Arab Americans 0.6 percent each, and Asian Americans 0.2 percent."[30] (At that time, the 2000 census reported that the U.S. population stood at 69 percent white, 13 percent Hispanic, 12 percent black, and 4 percent Asian.) So as mainstream journalists increased their reliance on a small pool of experts, they probably alienated many viewers, who may have felt excluded from participation in day-to-day social and political life.

A 2005 study by the Pew Project for Excellence in Journalism found similar results. The study looked at forty-five news outlets over a twenty-day period, including newspapers, nightly network newscasts and morning shows, cable news programs, and Web news sites. Newspapers, the study found, "were the most likely of the media studied to cite at least one female source . . . (41% of stories)," while cable news "was the least likely medium to cite a female source (19% of stories)." The study also found that in "every [news] topic category, the majority of stories cited at least one male source," but "the only topic category where women crossed the 50% threshold was lifestyle stories." The study found that women were least likely to be cited in stories on foreign affairs, and sports sections of newspapers also "stood out in particular as a male bastion," with only 14 percent citing a female source.[31]

By 2012, the evidence again suggested little improvement. In fact, a study from the 4th Estate showed that over a six-month period during the 2012 election, men were "much more likely to be quoted on their subjective insight in newspapers and on television." This held true even on stories specifically dealing with women's issues. The 4th Estate study showed that "in front page articles about the 2012 election that mention[ed] abortion or birth control, men [were] 4 to 7 times more likely to be cited than women." The study concluded by noting that such a "gender gap undermines the media's credibility."[32]

By the late 1990s, many journalists were criticized for blurring the line between remaining neutral and being an expert. The boom in twenty-four-hour cable news programs at this time led to a news vacuum that was eventually filled with talk shows and interviews with journalists willing to give their views. During events with intense media coverage, such as the 2000 through 2012 presidential elections, 9/11, and the Iraq War, many print journalists appeared several times a day on cable programs acting as experts on the story, sometimes providing factual information but mostly offering opinion and speculation.

Some editors even encourage their reporters to go on these shows for marketing reasons. Today, many big-city newspapers have office space set aside for reporters to use for cable, TV, and Internet interviews. Critics contend that these practices erode the credibility of the profession by blending journalism with celebrity culture and commercialism. Daniel Schorr, who worked as a journalist for seventy years (he died in 2010), resigned from CNN when the cable network asked him to be a commentator during the 1984 Republican National Convention along with former Texas governor John Connally. Schorr believed that it was improper to mix a journalist and a politician in this way, but the idea seems innocent by today's blurred standards. As columnist David Carr pointed out in the *New York Times* in 2010, "Where there was once a pretty bright line between journalist and political operative, there is now a kind of continuum, with politicians becoming media providers in their own right, and pundits, entertainers and journalists often driving political discussions."[33]

Balancing Story Conflict

For most journalists, *balance* means presenting all sides of an issue without appearing to favor any one position. The quest for balance presents problems for journalists. On the one hand, time and space constraints do not always permit representing *all* sides; in practice, this value has often been reduced to "telling *both* sides of a story." In recounting news stories as two-sided dramas, reporters often misrepresent the complexity of social issues. The abortion controversy, for example, is often treated as a story that pits two extreme positions (staunchly pro-life versus resolutely pro-choice) against each other. Yet people whose views fall somewhere between these positions are seldom represented (studies show this group actually represents the majority of Americans). In this manner, "balance" becomes a narrative device to generate story conflict.

On the other hand, although many journalists claim to be detached, they often stake out a moderate or middle-of-the-road position between the two sides represented in a story. In claiming neutrality and inviting readers to share their detached point of view, journalists offer a distant, third-person, all-knowing point of view (a narrative device that many novelists use as well), enhancing the impression of neutrality by making the reporter appear value-free (or valueless).

The claim for balanced stories, like the claim for neutrality, disguises journalism's narrative functions. After all, when reporters choose quotes for a story, these are usually the most dramatic or conflict-oriented words that emerge from an interview, press conference, or public meeting. Choosing quotes sometimes has more to do with enhancing drama than with being fair, documenting an event, or establishing neutrality.

The balance claim has also served the financial interests of modern news organizations that stake out the middle ground. William Greider, a former *Washington Post* editor, makes the tie between good business and balanced news: "If you're going to be a mass circulation journal, that means you're going to be talking simultaneously to lots of groups that have opposing views. So you've got to modulate your voice and pretend to be talking to all of them."[34]

Acting as Adversaries

The value that many journalists take the most pride in is their adversarial relationship with the prominent leaders and major institutions they cover. The prime narrative frame for portraying this relationship is sometimes called a *gotcha story*, which refers to the moment when, through questioning, the reporter nabs "the bad guy," or wrongdoer.

This narrative strategy—part of the *tough questioning style* of some reporters—is frequently used in political reporting. Many journalists assume that leaders are hiding something and that the reporter's main job is to ferret out the truth through tenacious fact-gathering and "gotcha" questions. An extension of the search for balance, this stance locates the reporter in the middle, between "them" and "us," between political leaders and the people they represent.

Critics of the tough question style of reporting argue that while it can reveal significant information, when overused it fosters a cynicism among journalists that actually harms the democratic process. Although journalists need to guard against becoming too cozy with their political sources, they sometimes go to the other extreme. By constantly searching for what politicians may be hiding, some reporters may miss other issues or other key stories.

When journalists employ the gotcha model to cover news, being tough often becomes an end in itself. Thus reporters believe they have done their job just by roughing up an interview subject or by answering the limited "What is going on here?" question. Yet the Pulitzer Prize, the highest award honoring journalism, often goes to the reporter who asks ethically charged and open-ended questions, such as "Why is this going on?" and "What ought to be done about it?"

Journalism in the Age of TV and the Internet

The rules and rituals governing American journalism began shifting in the 1950s. At the time, former radio reporter John Daly hosted the CBS network game show *What's My Line?* When he began moonlighting as the evening TV news anchor on ABC, the network blurred the entertainment and information border, foreshadowing what was to come.

In the early days, the most influential and respected television news program was CBS's *See It Now.* Coproduced by Fred Friendly and Edward R. Murrow, *See It Now* practiced a kind of TV journalism lodged somewhere between the neutral and narrative traditions. Generally regarded as "the first and definitive" news documentary on American television, *See It Now* sought "to report in depth—to tell and show the American audience what was happening in the world using film as a narrative tool," according to A. William Bluem, author of *Documentary in American Television.*[35] Murrow worked as both the program's anchor and its main reporter, introducing the investigative model of journalism to television—a model that programs like *60 Minutes*, *20/20*, and *Dateline* would imitate. Later, of course, Internet news-gathering and reporting would further alter journalism.

Differences between Print, TV, and Internet News

Although TV news reporters share many values, beliefs, and conventions with their print counterparts, television transformed journalism in a number of ways. First, broadcast news is driven by its technology. If a camera crew and news van are dispatched to a remote location for a live broadcast, reporters are expected to justify the expense by developing a story, even if nothing significant is occurring. For instance, when a national political candidate does not arrive at the local airport in time for an interview on the evening news, the reporter may cover a flight delay instead. Print reporters, in contrast, slide their notebooks or laptops back into their bags and report on a story when it occurs. However, with print reporters now posting regular online updates to their stories, they offer the same immediacy that live television news reporting does. In fact, in most newsrooms today, the online version of a story is often posted before the newspaper or TV version appears.

Second, while print editors cut stories to fit the physical space around ads, TV news directors have to time stories to fit between commercials. Despite the fact that a much higher percentage of space is devoted to print ads (about 60 percent at most dailies), TV ads (which take up less than 25 percent of a typical thirty-minute news program) generally seem more intrusive to viewers, perhaps because TV ads take up time rather than space. The Internet has "solved" these old space and time problems by freeing stories from those constraints online.

Third, while modern print journalists are expected to be detached, TV news derives its credibility from live, on-the-spot reporting; believable imagery; and viewers' trust in the reporters and anchors. In fact, since the early 1970s, most annual polls have indicated that the majority of viewers find television news a more credible resource than print news. Viewers tend to feel a personal regard for the local and national anchors who appear each evening on TV sets in their living rooms. In fact, in the Pew Research Center's 2012 news credibility and believability study (which did not rate online news sources like *Politico* or the *Huffington Post*), the three top news outlets with the highest "positive" rating from those polled were "local TV news" (65 percent), *60 Minutes* (64 percent), and ABC News (59 percent). By comparison, Fox News, the *New York Times*, and *USA Today* were tied as the only organizations in the study to have higher negative than positive ratings—all at just 49 percent positive. The highest-rated newspaper in the study was the *Wall Street Journal*, with a 58 percent positive rating, while the "daily newspaper you know best"—that is, the paper from a respondent's local area or region—scored a 57 percent positive rating.[36]

By the mid-1970s, the public's fascination with the Watergate scandal, combined with the improved quality of TV journalism, helped local news departments realize profits. In an effort to retain high ratings, stations began hiring consultants, who advised news directors to invest in national prepackaged formats, such as Action News or Eyewitness News. Traveling the country, viewers noticed similar theme music and opening graphic visuals from market to market. Consultants also suggested that stations lead their newscasts with *crime blocks*: a group of TV stories that recount the worst local criminal transgressions of the day. A cynical slogan soon developed in the industry: "If it bleeds, it leads." This crime-block practice continues today at most local TV news stations.

Few stations around the country have responded to viewers and critics who complain about the overemphasis on crime. (In reality, FBI statistics reveal that crime and murder rates have fallen or leveled off in most major urban areas since the 1990s.) In 1996, the news director at KVUE-TV in Austin, Texas, created a new set of criteria that had to be met for news reports to qualify as responsible crime stories. She asked that her reporters answer the following questions: Do citizens or officials need to take action? Is there an immediate threat to safety? Is there a threat to children? Does the crime have significant community impact? Does the story lend itself to a crime prevention effort? With KVUE's new standards, the station eliminated many routine crime stories. Instead, the station provided a context for understanding crime rather than a mindless running tally of the crimes committed each day.[37]

Pretty-Face and Happy-Talk Culture

In the early 1970s at a Milwaukee TV station, consultants advised the station's news director that the evening anchor looked too old. The anchor, who showed a bit of gray, was replaced and went on to serve as the station's

MORNING NEWS SHOWS

are closely tended patches of the network news landscape. Competition between shows like *Today* and *Good Morning America* remains intense, and network executives sometimes intervene to make "fixes," like the controversial 2012 reassignment of former *Today* anchor Ann Curry. Gossip columnists buzzed that NBC didn't like the way she dressed or her refusal to cover her gray hair; others asserted that she was pushed out by coanchor Matt Lauer. Brian Stelter's 2013 book *Top of the Morning* covers the recent morning show saga in great detail.

NBC/Photofest

editorial director. He was thirty-two years old at the time. In the late 1970s, a reporter at the same station was fired because of a "weight problem," although that was not given as the official reason. Earlier that year, she had given birth to her first child. In 1983, Christine Craft, a former Kansas City television news anchor, was awarded $500,000 in damages in a sex discrimination suit against station KMBC (she eventually lost the monetary award when the station appealed). She had been fired because consultants believed she was too old, too unattractive, and not deferential enough to men.

Such stories are rampant in the annals of TV news. They have helped create a stereotype of the half-witted but physically attractive news anchor, reinforced by popular culture images (from Ted Baxter on TV's *Mary Tyler Moore Show* to Ron Burgundy in the *Anchorman* films). Although the situation has improved slightly, national news consultants set the agenda for what local reporters should cover (lots of crime) as well as how they should look and sound (young, attractive, pleasant, and with no regional accent). Essentially, news consultants—also known as *news doctors*—have advised stations to replicate the predominant male and female advertising images of the 1960s and 1970s in modern local TV news.

Another strategy favored by news consultants is *happy talk*: the ad-libbed or scripted banter that goes on among local news anchors, reporters, meteorologists, and sports reporters before and after news reports. During the 1970s, consultants often recommended such chatter to create a more relaxed feeling on the news set and to foster the illusion of conversational intimacy with viewers. Some also believed that happy talk would counter much of that era's "bad news," which included coverage of urban riots and the Vietnam War. A strategy still used today, happy talk often appears forced and may create awkward transitions, especially when anchors transition to reports on events that are sad or tragic.

Sound Bitten

Beginning in the 1980s, the term **sound bite** became part of the public lexicon. The TV equivalent of a quote in print news, a sound bite is the part of a broadcast news report in which an expert, a celebrity, a victim, or a person-in-the-street responds to some aspect of an event or issue. With increasing demands for more commercial time, there is less time for interview subjects to explain their views. As a result, sound bites have become the focus of intense criticism. Studies revealed that during political campaigns, the typical sound bite from candidates had shrunk from an average duration of forty to fifty seconds in the 1950s and 1960s to fewer than eight seconds by the late 1990s. With shorter comments from interview subjects, TV news sometimes seems like dueling sound bites, with reporters creating dramatic tension by editing competing viewpoints together, as if interviewees had actually been in the same location speaking to one another. Of course, print news also pits one quote against another in a story, even though the actual interview subjects may never have met. Once again, these reporting techniques, also at work in online journalism, are evidence of the profession's reliance on storytelling devices to replicate or create conflict.

Pundits, "Talking Heads," and Politics

The transformation of TV news by cable—with the arrival of CNN in 1980—led to dramatic changes in TV news delivery at the national level. Prior to cable news (and the Internet), most people tuned

ANDERSON COOPER has been the primary anchor of *Anderson Cooper 360°* since 2003. Although the program is mainly taped and broadcast from his New York City studio, and typically features reports of the day's main news stories with added analyses from experts, Cooper is one of the few "talking heads" who still reports live fairly often from the field for major news stories. Most recently and notably, he has done extensive coverage of the 2010 BP oil spill in the Gulf of Mexico (*below*), the February 2011 uprisings in Egypt, and the devastating earthquake in Japan in 2011.

ZUMA Press/Newscom

to their local and national news late in the afternoon or evening on a typical weekday, with each program lasting just thirty minutes. But today, the 24/7 news cycle means that we can get TV news anytime, day or night, and constant new content has led to major changes in what is considered news. Because it is expensive to dispatch reporters to document stories or maintain foreign news bureaus to cover international issues, the much less expensive "talking head" pundit has become a standard for cable news channels. Such a programming strategy requires few resources beyond the studio and a few guests.

Today's main cable channels have built their evening programs along partisan lines and follow the model of journalism as opinion and assertion: Fox News goes right with pundit stars like Bill O'Reilly (the ratings king of cable news) and Sean Hannity; MSNBC leans left with Rachel Maddow and Lawrence O'Donnell; and CNN stakes out the middle with hosts who try to strike a more neutral pose, like Anderson Cooper. CNN, the originator of cable news, does much more original reporting than Fox News and MSNBC and does better in nonpresidential election years, as well as during natural disasters and crime tragedies. After some up and down years, CNN dropped to a twenty-year audience low in 2014, with about 440,000 viewers per night in September 2014. MSNBC, which does better in national election years, dropped after 2012 (when it was averaging over 800,000 total viewers) but climbed back to 620,000 in September 2014. Fox News continued to lead cable prime-time news by a wide margin, averaging over 2.1 million in September 2014.[38]

Today's cable and Internet audiences seem to prefer partisan talking heads over traditional reporting. This suggests that in today's fragmented media marketplace, going after niche audiences along political lines is smart business—although not necessarily good journalism. What should concern us today is the jettisoning of good journalism—anchored in reporting and verification—that uses reporters to document stories and interview key sources. In its place, on cable and online, are highly partisan pundits who may have strong opinions and charisma but who may not have all their facts straight.

Convergence Enhances and Changes Journalism

For mainstream print and TV reporters and editors, online news has added new dimensions to journalism. Both print and TV news can continually update breaking stories online, and many reporters now post their online stories first and then work on traditional versions. This means that readers and viewers no longer have to wait until the next day for the morning paper or for the local evening newscast for important stories. To enhance the online reports, which do not have the time or space constraints of television or print, newspaper reporters are increasingly required to provide video or audio for their stories. This might allow readers and viewers to see full interviews rather than just selected print quotes in the paper or short sound bites on the TV report.

However, online news comes with a special set of problems. Print reporters, for example, can conduct e-mail interviews rather than leaving the office to question a subject in person. Many editors discourage this practice because they think relying on e-mail gives interviewees the chance to control and shape their answers. While some might argue that this provides more thoughtful answers, journalists say it takes the elements of surprise and spontaneity out of the traditional news interview, during which a subject might accidentally reveal information—something less likely to occur in an online setting.

Another problem for journalists, ironically, is the wide-ranging resources of the Internet. This includes access to versions of stories from other papers or broadcast stations. The mountain of information available on the Internet has made it all too easy for journalists to—unwittingly or intentionally—copy other journalists' work. In addition, access to databases and other informational sites can keep reporters at their computers rather than out cultivating sources, tracking down new kinds of information, and staying in touch with their communities.

LaunchPad ◉

macmillanhighered.com
/mediaculture10e

The Contemporary Journalist: Pundit or Reporter?
Journalists discuss whether the 24/7 news cycle encourages reporters to offer opinions more than facts.
Discussion: What might be the reasons why reporters should give opinions, and what might be the reasons why they shouldn't?

Most notable, however, for journalists in the digital age are the demands that convergence has made on their reporting and writing. Print journalists at newspapers (and magazines) are expected to carry digital cameras so they can post video along with the print versions of their stories. TV reporters are expected to write print-style news reports for their station's Web site to supplement the streaming video of their original TV stories. And both print and TV reporters are often expected to post the Internet versions of their stories first, before the versions they do for the morning paper or the six o'clock news. Increasingly, journalists today are also expected to tweet and blog.

Courtesy of muckrack.com

The Power of Visual Language

The shift from a print-dominated culture to an electronic-digital culture requires that we look carefully at differences among various approaches to journalism. For example, the visual language of TV news and the Internet often captures events more powerfully than do words. Over the past fifty years, television news has dramatized America's key events. Civil Rights activists, for instance, acknowledge that the movement benefited enormously from televised news that documented the plight of southern blacks in the 1960s. The news footage of southern police officers turning powerful water hoses on peaceful Civil Rights demonstrators and the news images of "white only" and "colored only" signs in hotels and restaurants created a context for understanding the disparity between black and white in the 1950s and 1960s.

Other enduring TV images are also embedded in the collective memory of many Americans: the Kennedy and King assassinations in the 1960s; the turmoil of Watergate in the 1970s; the first space shuttle disaster and the Chinese student uprisings in the 1980s; the Oklahoma City federal building bombing in the 1990s; the terrorist attacks on the Pentagon and World Trade Center in 2001; Hurricane Katrina in 2005; the historic election of President Obama in 2008; the Arab Spring uprisings in 2011; and the brutal murders of twenty schoolchildren and six adults in Newtown, Connecticut, in 2012. During these critical events, TV news has been a cultural reference point marking the strengths and weaknesses of our world.

Today, the Internet, for good or bad, functions as a repository for news images and video, alerting us to stories that the mainstream media missed or to videos captured by amateurs. Everyone remembers the video leaked to *Mother Jones* magazine in which candidate Mitt Romney proclaimed at a 2012 campaign fund-raiser: "There are 47 percent of the people who will vote for the president no matter what . . . who are dependent upon government, who believe that they are victims." That footage, played over and over on YouTube and cable news, hurt Romney's campaign. Then, in summer 2013, CIA employee Edward Snowden chose a civil liberties advocate and columnist for the London-based *Guardian* to receive leaked material on systematic surveillance of ordinary Americans by the National Security Agency. The video interview with the *Guardian* scored 1.5 million YouTube hits shortly after its release. As *New York Times* columnist David Carr noted at the time, "News no longer needs the permission of traditional gatekeepers to break through. Scoops can now come from all corners of the media map and find an audience just by virtue of what they reveal."[39]

NEWS IN THE DIGITAL AGE
Today, more and more journalists use Twitter in addition to performing their regular reporting duties. Muck Rack collects journalists' tweets in one place, making it easier than ever to access breaking news and real-time, one-line reporting.

LaunchPad ⓒ
macmillanhighered.com /mediaculture10e

Fake News/Real News: A Fine Line
The editor of the *Onion* describes how the publication critiques "real" news media. **Discussion:** How many of your news sources might be considered "fake" news as opposed to traditional news, and how do you decide which sources to consult?

Alternative Models: Public Journalism and "Fake" News

In 1990, Poland was experiencing growing pains as it shifted from a state-controlled economic system to a more open market economy. The country's leading newspaper, *Gazeta Wyborcza*, the first noncommunist newspaper to appear in Eastern Europe since the 1940s, was also undergoing challenges. Based in Warsaw with a circulation of about 350,000 at the time, *Gazeta Wyborcza* had to report on and explain the new economy and the new crime wave that accompanied it. Especially troubling to the news staff and Polish citizens were gangs that robbed American and Western European tourists at railway stations, sometimes assaulting them in the process. The stolen goods would then pass to an outer circle, whose members transferred the goods to still another exterior ring of thieves. Even if the police caught the inner circle members, the loot usually disappeared.

These developments triggered heated discussions in the newsroom. A small group of young reporters, some of whom had recently worked in the United States, argued that the best way to cover the story was to describe the new crime wave and relay the facts to readers in a neutral manner. Another group, many of whom were older and more experienced, felt that the paper should take an advocacy stance and condemn the criminals through interpretive columns on the front page. The older guard won this particular debate, and more interpretive pieces appeared.[40]

This story illustrates the two competing models that have influenced American and European journalism since the early twentieth century. The first—the *informational* or *modern model*—emphasizes describing events and issues from a seemingly neutral point of view. The second—a more *partisan* or *European model*—stresses analyzing occurrences and advocating remedies from an acknowledged point of view. For fictionalized representations of these differences, note the contrasts between the depiction of journalists on HBO's U.S. program *The Newsroom* (2012–2014) and on the Danish TV series *Borgen* (2010–). In *The Newsroom*, discussions of remedies and viewpoints take place off camera; in *Borgen*, journalists talk about these issues on and off camera.

In most American newspapers today, the informational model dominates the front page, while the partisan model remains confined to the editorial pages and an occasional front-page piece. However, alternative models of news—from the serious to the satirical—have emerged to challenge modern journalistic ideals.

CITIZEN JOURNALISM
One way technology has allowed citizens to become involved in the reporting of news is through cell phone photos and videos uploaded online. Witnesses can now pass on what they have captured to major mainstream news sources, like CNN's iReports, or post to their own blogs and Web sites.

Victoria Sinistra/AFP/Getty Images

The Public Journalism Movement

From the late 1980s through the 1990s, a number of papers experimented with ways to involve readers more actively in the news process. These experiments surfaced primarily at midsize daily papers, including the *Charlotte Observer*, the *Wichita Eagle*, the *Virginian-Pilot*, and the *Minneapolis Star Tribune*. Davis "Buzz" Merritt, editor of the *Wichita Eagle* at the time, defined key aspects of **public journalism**, including moving "beyond the limited mission

A Lost Generation of Journalists?

The economic crisis in 2008–09 added to the pile of problems facing traditional U.S. journalism, joining such obstacles as the Internet and loss of classified ad revenue. In 2014, a Pew Research Center study analyzing the U.S. Bureau of Labor Statistics specified one possible result of the economic downturn: "After years of grim news for the news industry marked by seemingly endless rounds of staff cutbacks, it's not unusual for those thinking about a career in journalism or veterans trying to find a new job to look at options in related fields. One field outpacing journalism both in sheer numbers and in salary growth is public relations."[1]

Back in the 1970s, the number of PR employees in the U.S. was roughly equal to the number of reporters working in print and broadcasting. That ratio became 2 to 1 by 2000, 3.2 to 1 by 2004, and was nearing 5 to 1 by 2013. Between 2004 and 2013, the number of reporters fell from 52,550 to 43,630, while the number of PR specialists "grew by 22 percent, from 166,210 to 202,530."[2]

The pay differences were also striking, according to the Pew study. Over the past decade, the salary gap between PR and news workers had, by 2013, grown to almost $20,000 per year; PR specialists earned an average of $54,940 annually, while reporters averaged $35,600. Nine years earlier, the disparity was not quite as large: $43,830 for PR and $31,320 for reporters.[3]

The decline in reporters and the rise of PR and political spin doctors raises significant concerns. During and following the digital turn, journalists have increasingly relied on press releases both for story ideas and for news copy. However, according to Robert McChesney and John Nichols in *The Death and Life of American Journalism*, "as editorial staffs shrink, there is less ability for news media to interrogate and counter the claims in press releases."[4] As an example, a 2012 Pew study reported that during the national election that year, journalists "often functioned as megaphones for political partisans, relaying assertions rather than contextualizing them."[5]

With the decrease in reporters and the increase in PR practitioners, far fewer journalists are available to vet information and fact-check the press releases that PR specialists pitch daily to multiple news organizations. For example, on the subject of health news, Pew researchers in 2014 reported on a *JAMA Internal Medicine* finding "that half of the stories examined relied on a single source or failed to disclose conflicts of interest from sources."[6]

Finally, the biggest concern may be the lost generation of journalists. More students coming from journalism schools are taking jobs as business writers and PR workers. The journalism profession, then, needs to not only figure out a new business model for the twenty-first century but also figure out how to recruit the best and brightest journalism students. Back in 1791, our founders offered special protection to journalists in the First Amendment—not to public relations specialists. Good journalism, after all, helps democracy work: It makes sense of key issues, documents events, keeps watch over our central institutions, and tells a community's significant stories. In the partisan era we now live in, overloaded with decontextualized information and undocumented punditry, these skills are more important than ever. Good journalism and compelling stories will eventually save and sustain the profession, no matter how the marketplace continues to fracture.

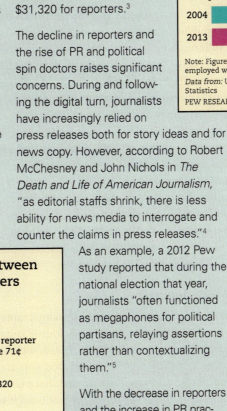

PR Specialists vs Reporters Over Time

Employee Ratio
Number of PR Specialists . . .   For Every

2004   3.2

2013   4.6

1 reporter

Total Employees
Reporters

2004   52,550

2013   43,630

PR Specialists

2004   166,210

2013   202,530

Note: Figures include full and part-time employees but not self-employed workers. Notebook icon by Garrett Knoll from The Noun Project.
Data from: U.S. Bureau of Labor Statistics Occupational Employment Statistics
PEW RESEARCH CENTER / Graphic by Jessica Schillinger

The Growing Income Gap Between PR Specialists and Reporters

In 2004

For every $1 a PR specialist made . . .   . . . a reporter made 71¢

$43,830 median annual income $31,320

By 2013

For every $1 a PR specialist made . . .   . . . a reporter made 65¢, a 6¢ loss

$54,940 $35,600

Note: Median annual income in current dollars, not adjusted for inflation. Dollar icon by Antonieta Gomez from The Noun Project.
Data from: U.S. Bureau of Labor Statistics Occupational Employment Statistics
PEW RESEARCH CENTER / Graphic by Jessica Schillinger

of 'telling the news' to a broader mission of helping public life go well," and moving "from see-ing people as consumers—as readers or nonreaders, as bystanders to be informed—to seeing them as a public, as potential actors in arriving at democratic solutions to public problems."[41]

Public journalism is best imagined as a conversational model for news practice. Modern journalism had drawn a distinct line between reporter detachment and community involve-ment; public journalism—driven by citizen forums, community conversations, and even talk shows—has obscured this line.

In the 1990s—before people felt the full impact of the Internet—public journalism served as a response to the many citizens who felt alienated from participating in public life. This alienation arose, in part, from viewers who watched passively as the political process seemed to play out in the news and on TV between party operatives and media pundits. Public journal-ism seemed to involve both the public and journalists more centrally in civic and political life. Editors and reporters interested in addressing citizen alienation—and reporter cynicism— began devising ways to engage people as conversational partners in determining the news. In an effort to draw the public into discussions about community priorities, these journalists began sponsoring citizen forums, where readers would have a voice in shaping aspects of the news that directly affected them.

An Early Public Journalism Project

Although isolated citizen projects and reader forums are sprinkled throughout the history of journalism, the public journalism movement began in earnest in 1987 in Columbus, Georgia. The city was suffering from a depressed economy, an alienated citizenry, and an entrenched leadership. In response, a team of reporters from the *Columbus Ledger-Enquirer* surveyed and talked with community leaders and other citizens about the future of the city. The paper then published an eight-part series based on the findings.

When the provocative series evoked little public response, the paper's leadership real-ized there was no mechanism or forum for continuing the public discussions about the issues raised in the series. Consequently, the paper created such a forum by organizing a town meeting and helped create a new civic organization to tackle issues such as racial tension and teenage antisocial behavior.

The Columbus project generated public discussion, involved more people in the news process, and eased race and class tensions by bringing various groups together in public con-versations. In the newsroom, the *Ledger-Enquirer* tried to reposition the place of journalists in politics: "Instead of standing outside the political community and reporting on its pathologies, they took up residence within its borders."[42]

Criticizing Public Journalism

By 2000, more than a hundred newspapers, many teamed with local television and public radio stations, had practiced some form of public journalism. Yet many critics remained skeptical of the experiment, raising a number of concerns, including the weakening of four journalistic hallmarks: editorial control, credibility, balance, and diverse views.[43]

First, some editors and reporters argued that public journalism had been co-opted by the marketing department and that those who practiced it were merely pandering to what read-ers wanted and taking editorial control away from newsrooms. They believed that focus group samples and consumer research—tools of marketing, not journalism—blurred the boundary between the editorial and the business functions of a paper. Some journalists also feared that by becoming more active in the community, they might be perceived as community boosters rather than as community watchdogs.

Second, critics worried that public journalism compromised the profession's credibility, which many believe derives from detachment. They argued that public journalism turned reporters into participants rather than observers. However, as the *Wichita Eagle*'s editor Davis Merritt pointed out, professionals who have credibility "share some basic values about life, some common ground about common good." Yet many journalists have insisted they "don't share values with anyone; that [they] are value-neutral."[44] Merritt argued that as a result, modern journalism actually has little credibility with the public, which the Pew Research Center's annual credibility surveys bear out.

Third, critics also contended that public journalism undermined balance and the both-sides-of-a-story convention by constantly seeking common ground and community consensus; therefore, it ran the risk of dulling the rough edges of democratic speech. Public journalists countered that they were trying to set aside more room for centrist positions. Such positions were often representative of many in the community but were missing in the mainstream news, which has always been more interested in the extremist views that make for a more dramatic story.

Fourth, many traditional reporters asserted that public journalism, which they considered merely a marketing tool, had not addressed the changing economic structure of the news business—especially the decline of reporting jobs and the boom in public relations work (see "Case Study: A Lost Generation of Journalists?," page 501). With more news outlets in the hands of fewer owners, both public journalists and traditional reporters needed to raise tough questions about the disappearance of competing daily papers and newsroom staff cutbacks at local monopoly newspapers. Facing little competition, in 2010 and 2011 newspapers continued to cut reporting staffs and expensive investigative projects, reduced the space for news, or converted to online-only operations. While such trends temporarily helped profits and satisfied stockholders, they limited the range of stories told and views represented in a community. In addition, the rise of PR made it much easier for companies to get stories about executive managers and corporate images into various news media, which needed new sources for story ideas with so many journalists out of work or switching careers.

"Fake" News and Satiric Journalism

For many young people, it is especially disturbing that two wealthy, established political parties—beholden to special interests and their lobbyists—control the nation's government. After all, 98 percent of congressional incumbents get reelected each year—not always because they've done a good job but often because they've made promises and done favors for the lobbyists and interests that helped get them elected in the first place.

Why shouldn't people, then, be cynical about politics? It is this cynicism that has drawn increasingly larger audiences to "fake" news shows like *The Daily Show*, *The Nightly Show*, and *Last Week Tonight*. Following in the tradition of *Saturday Night Live* (*SNL*), which began in 1975, news satires tell their audiences something that seems truthful about politicians and how they try to manipulate media and public opinion. But most important, these shows use humor to critique the news media and our political system. *SNL*'s sketches on GOP vice presidential candidate Sarah Palin in 2008 drew large audiences and shaped the way younger viewers thought about the election.

The Colbert Report satirized cable news hosts, particularly Fox's Bill O'Reilly and MSNBC's Chris Matthews, and the bombastic opinion-assertion culture promoted by their programs. In critiquing the limits of news stories and politics, *The Daily Show* parodies the narrative conventions of evening news programs: the clipped eight-second sound bite that limits meaning, and the formulaic shot of the TV news "stand up," which depicts reporters "on location," attempting to establish credibility by revealing that they were really there.

On *The Daily Show*, a cast of fake reporters are digitally superimposed in front of exotic foreign locales, Washington, D.C., or other U.S. locations. In a 2004 exchange with "political correspondent" Rob Corddry, host Jon Stewart asked him for his opinion about presidential

Jim Watson/AFP/Getty Images

Eric Liebowitz/© HBO/Everett Collection

NEWS AS SATIRE
Satirical news has become
something of a cottage
industry in recent years,
stemming from *Saturday Night
Live*'s "Weekend Update"
segment and dominated
by *The Daily Show*. Several
Daily Show correspondents
have gone on to their own
news-related shows and
have interviewed a variety of
political leaders and prominent
figures in the process.
Here Jon Stewart is shown
interviewing President Obama,
while upstart John Oliver,
whose *Last Week Tonight* now
airs on HBO, is pictured with
Fareed Zakaria.

campaign tactics. "My opinion? I don't have opinions," Corddry answered. "I'm a reporter, Jon. My job is to spend half the time repeating what one side says, and half the time repeating the other. Little thing called objectivity; might want to look it up."

During his reign as news court jester, Stewart, who stepped down from *The Daily Show* in 2015, has exposed the melodrama of TV news that nightly depicts the world in various stages of disorder while offering the stalwart, comforting presence of celebrity-anchors overseeing it all from their high-tech command centers. Even before CBS's usually neutral and aloof Walter Cronkite signed off the evening news with "And that's the way it is," network news anchors tried to offer a sense of order through the reassurance of their individual personalities.

Yet even as fake anchors, satirists like Stewart and Oliver display much greater range of emotion—a range that may match our own—than we get from our detached "hard news" anchors: more amazement, irony, outrage, laughter, and skepticism. For example, during Stewart's coverage of the 2012 presidential election, he often showed genuine irritation or even outrage—coupled with irony and humor—whenever a politician or political ad presented information that was untrue or misleading.

While fake news programs often mock the formulas that real TV news programs have long used, they also present an informative and insightful look at current events and the way "traditional" media cover them. For example, he exposes hypocrisy by juxtaposing what a politician said recently in the news with the opposite position articulated by the same politician months or years earlier. Indeed, many Americans have admitted that they watch satires such as *The Daily Show* not only to be entertained but also to stay current with what's going on in the world. In fact, a prominent Pew Research Center study back in 2007 found that people who watched these satiric shows were more often "better informed" than most other news consumers, usually because these viewers tended to get their news from multiple sources and a cross section of news media.[45]

Although the world has changed, local TV news story formulas (except for splashy opening graphics and Doppler weather radar) have gone virtually unaltered since the 1970s, when *SNL*'s "Weekend Update" first started making fun of TV news. Newscasts still limit reporters' stories to two minutes or less and promote stylish anchors, a "sports guy," and a certified meteorologist as familiar personalities whom we invite into our homes each evening. Now that a generation of viewers has been raised on the TV satire and political cynicism of "Weekend Update," David Letterman, Jimmy Fallon, Conan O'Brien, *The Daily Show*, and *The Colbert Report*, the slick, formulaic packaging of political ads and the canned, cautious sound bites offered in news packages are simply not as persuasive as they once were.

Journalism should break free from tired formulas—especially in TV news—and reimagine better ways to tell stories. In fictional television, storytelling has evolved over time, becoming increasingly complex. Although the Internet and 24/7 cable news have introduced new models of journalism and commentary, why has TV news remained virtually unchanged over the past forty years? Are there no new ways to report the news? Maybe audiences would value news that matches the complicated storytelling that surrounds them in everything from TV dramas to interactive video games to their own conversations. We should demand news story forms that better represent the complexity of our world.

Democracy and Reimagining Journalism's Role

Journalism is central to democracy: Both citizens and the media must have access to the information that we need to make important decisions. As this chapter illustrates, however, this is a complicated idea. For example, in the aftermath of 9/11, some government officials claimed that reporters or columnists who raised questions about fighting terrorism, invading Iraq, or developing secret government programs were being unpatriotic. Yet the basic principles of democracy require citizens and the media to question our leaders and government. Isn't this, after all, what the American Revolution was all about? (See "Examining Ethics: WikiLeaks, Secret Documents, and Good Journalism" on page 506.)

Conventional journalists will fight ferociously for the principles that underpin journalism's basic tenets—freedom of the press, the obligation to question government, the public's right to know, and the belief that there are two sides to every story. These are mostly worthy ideals, but they do have limitations. These tenets, for example, generally do not acknowledge any moral or ethical duty for journalists to improve the quality of daily life. Rather, conventional journalism values its news-gathering capabilities and the well-constructed news narrative, leaving the improvement of civic life to political groups, nonprofit organizations, business philanthropists, individual citizens, and practitioners of Internet activism.

Social Responsibility

Although reporters have traditionally thought of themselves first and foremost as observers and recorders, some journalists have acknowledged a social responsibility. Among them was James Agee in the 1930s. In his book *Let Us Now Praise Famous Men*, which was accompanied by the Depression-era photography of Walker Evans, Agee said that he regarded conventional journalism as dishonest, partly because the act of observing intruded on people and turned them into story characters that newspapers and magazines then exploited for profit.

Agee also worried that readers would retreat into the comfort of his writing—his narrative—instead of confronting what for many families was the horror of the Great Depression. For Agee, the question of responsibility extended not only to journalism and to himself but to the readers of his stories as well: "The reader is no less centrally involved than the authors and those of whom they tell."[46] Agee's self-conscious analysis provides insights into journalism's hidden agendas and the responsibility of all citizens to make public life better.

Deliberative Democracy

According to advocates of public journalism, when reporters are chiefly concerned with maintaining their antagonistic relationship to politics and are less willing to improve political

EXAMINING ETHICS

WikiLeaks, Secret Documents, and Good Journalism

Since its inception in 2006, the controversial Web site WikiLeaks has released millions of documents—from revelations of toxic dumps in Africa to the 2013 release of 1.5 million U.S. diplomatic records, many involving President Nixon's secretary of state, Henry Kissinger. WikiLeaks' main spokesperson and self-identified "editor in chief," Julian Assange, an Australian online activist, has been called everything from a staunch free-speech advocate to a "hi-tech terrorist" (by U.S. vice president Joe Biden). Certainly, government leaders around the world have faced embarrassment from the site's many document dumps and secrecy breaches.

In its most controversial move, in 2010 WikiLeaks offered 500,000-plus documents, called the "War Logs," to three mainstream print outlets—the *Guardian* in the United Kingdom, the German magazine *Der Spiegel*, and the *New York Times*. These documents were mainly U.S. military and state department dispatches and internal memos related to the Afghan and Iraq wars—what Bill Keller, then executive editor of the *New York Times*, called a "huge breach of secrecy" for those running the wars. Keller described working with WikiLeaks as an adventure that "combined the cloak-and-dagger intrigue of handling a vast secret archive with the more mundane feat of sorting, searching and understanding a mountain of data."[1] Indeed, one of the first major stories the *Times*

wrote, based on the "War Logs" project, reported on "Pakistan's ambiguous role as an American ally."[2] Then, just a few months later, Osama bin Laden was found hiding in the middle of a Pakistani suburb.

WikiLeaks presents a number of ethical dilemmas and concerns for both journalists and citizens. News critic and journalism professor Jay Rosen has called WikiLeaks "the world's first stateless news organization."[3] But is WikiLeaks actually engaging in journalism—and therefore entitled to First Amendment protections? Or is it merely an important "news source, news provider, content host, [or] whistleblower," exposing things that governments would rather keep secret, as one critic from the Nieman Journalism Lab suggests?[4] And should *any* document or material obtained by WikiLeaks be released for public scrutiny, or should some kinds of documents and materials be withheld?

Examining Ethics Activity

As a class or in smaller groups, consider the ethical concerns laid out above. Following the ethical template outlined on page 19 in Chapter 1, begin by researching the topic, finding as much information and analysis as possible. Read Bill Keller's *New York Times Magazine* piece, "The Boy Who Kicked the Hornet's Nest" (January 30, 2011), or his longer 2011 *Times* report, "Open Secrets: WikiLeaks, War and American Diplomacy" (www.nytimes.com/opensecrets). See also Nikki Usher's work for Harvard's Nieman Journalism Lab and Jay Rosen's blog, *PressThink*. Consider also journalism criticism and news study sites, such as the *Columbia Journalism Review*, the Pew Research Center, and the First Amendment Center. Watch Julian Assange's interview on CBS's *60 Minutes* from January 2011.

Next, based on your research and informed analysis, decide whether WikiLeaks is a legitimate form of journalism and whether there should be newsroom policies that restrict the release of some kinds of documents when in partnership with a resource like WikiLeaks (such as the "War Logs" project described here). Create an outline for such policies. ▲

Carl Court/AFP/Getty Images

discourse, news and democracy suffer. The late *Washington Post* columnist David Broder thought that national journalists like him—through rising salaries, prestige, and formal education—have distanced themselves "from the people that [they] are writing for and have become much, much closer to people [they] are writing about."[47] Broder believed that journalists need to become activists, not for a particular party but for the political process and in the interest of reenergizing public life. For those who advocate for public journalism, this might also involve mainstream media spearheading voter registration drives or setting up pressrooms or news bureaus in public libraries or shopping malls, where people converge in large numbers.

Public journalism offers people models for how to deliberate in forums, and then it covers those deliberations. This kind of community journalism aims to reinvigorate a *deliberative democracy* in which citizen groups, local government, and the news media work together more actively to shape social, economic, and political agendas. In a more deliberative democracy, a large segment of the community discusses public life and social policy before advising or electing officials who represent the community's interests.

In 1989, historian Christopher Lasch argued that "the job of the press is to encourage debate, not to supply the public with information."[48] Although he overstated his case—journalism does both and more—Lasch made a cogent point about how conventional journalism had lost its bearings. In the so-called objective era of modern journalism, mainstream news media had lost touch with its partisan roots. The early mission of journalism—to advocate opinions and encourage public debate—had been relegated to alternative magazines, the editorial pages, news blogs, and cable news channels starring allegedly elite reporters. Tellingly, Lasch connected the gradual decline in voter participation, which began in the 1920s, to more professionalized conduct on the part of journalists. With a modern "objective" press, he contended, the public increasingly began to defer to the "more professional" news media to watch over civic life on its behalf.

As the advocates of public journalism acknowledged, people had grown used to letting their representatives think and act for them. Today, more community-oriented journalism and other civic projects offer citizens an opportunity to deliberate and to influence their leaders. This may include broadening the story models and frames they use to recount experiences, paying more attention to the historical and economic contexts of these stories, doing more investigative reports that analyze both news conventions and social issues, taking more responsibility for their news narratives, participating more fully in the public life of their communities, admitting to their cultural biases and occasional mistakes, and ensuring that the verification model of reporting is not overwhelmed by the new journalism of assertion.

Arguing that for too long journalism has defined its role only in negative terms, news scholar Jay Rosen notes: "To be adversarial, critical, to ask tough questions, to expose scandal and wrongdoing . . . these are necessary tasks, even noble tasks, but they are negative tasks." In addition, he suggests that journalism should assert itself as a positive force, not merely as a watchdog or as a neutral information conduit to readers but as "a support system for public life."[49] ▶

CHAPTER REVIEW

COMMON THREADS

One of the Common Threads discussed in Chapter 1 is the role that media play in a democracy. Today, one of the major concerns is the proliferation of news sources. How well is our society being served by this trend—especially on cable and the Internet—compared with the time when just a few major news media sources dominated journalism?

Historians, media critics, citizens, and even many politicians argue that a strong democracy is only possible with a strong, healthy, skeptical press. In the old days, a few legacy or traditional media—key national newspapers, three major networks, and three newsmagazines—provided most of the journalistic common ground for discussing major issues confronting U.S. society.

In today's online and 24/7 cable world, though, the legacy media have ceded some of their power and many of their fact-checking duties to new media forms, especially in the blogosphere. As discussed in this chapter and in Chapter 8, this power shortage is partly because substantial losses in advertising (which has gone to the Internet) have led to severe cutbacks in newsroom staffs, and partly because bloggers, 24/7 cable news media, and news satire shows like *The Daily Show* and *The Colbert Report* (prior to Stephen Colbert's leaving to host CBS's *Late Night* program in 2015) are fact-checking the

media as well as reporting stories that used to be the domain of professional news organizations.

The case before us then goes something like this: In the old days, the major news media provided us with reports and narratives to share, discuss, and argue about. But in today's explosion of news and information, that common ground has eroded or is shifting. Instead, today we often rely only on those media sources that match our comfort level, cultural values, or political affiliations; increasingly these are blog sites, radio talk shows, or cable channels. Sometimes these opinion sites and channels are not supported with the careful fact-gathering and verification that has long been a pillar of the best kinds of journalism.

So in today's media environment, how severely have technological and cultural transformations undermined the common-ground function of mainstream media? And are these changes ultimately good or bad for democracy?

KEY TERMS

The definitions for the terms listed below can be found in the glossary at the end of the book. The page numbers listed with the terms indicate where the term is highlighted in the chapter.

news, 480
newsworthiness, 480
ethnocentrism, 482
responsible capitalism, 482

small-town pastoralism, 483
individualism, 483
conflict of interest, 488
herd journalism, 492

sound bite, 497
public journalism, 500

REVIEW QUESTIONS

Modern Journalism in the Information Age

1. What are the drawbacks of the informational model of journalism?

2. What is news?

3. Explain the values shift in journalism today from a more detached or neutral model to a more partisan or assertion model.

Ethics and the News Media

4. How do issues such as deception and privacy present ethical problems for journalists?

5. Why is getting a story first important to reporters?

6. What are the connections between so-called neutral journalism and economics?

Reporting Rituals and the Legacy of Print Journalism

7. Why have reporters become so dependent on experts?

8. Why do many conventional journalists (and citizens) believe firmly in the idea that there are two sides to every story?

Journalism in the Age of TV and the Internet

9. How is credibility established in TV news as compared with print journalism?

10. With regard to TV news, what are sound bites and happy talk?

11. What roles are pundits now playing in 24/7 cable news?

12. In what ways has the Internet influenced traditional forms of journalism?

Alternative Models: Public Journalism and "Fake" News

13. What is public journalism? In what ways is it believed to make journalism better?

14. What are the major criticisms of the public journalism movement, and why do the main-stream national media have concerns about public journalism?

15. What role do satirical news programs like *SNL*'s "Week-end Update," *The Daily Show*, and *The Colbert Report* play in the world of journalism?

Democracy and Reimagining Journalism's Role

16. What is deliberative democracy, and what does it have to do with journalism?

QUESTIONING THE MEDIA

1. What are your main criticisms of the state of news today? In your opinion, what are the news media doing well?

2. If you were a reporter or an editor, would you quit voting in order to demonstrate your ability to be neutral? Why or why not?

3. Is the trend toward opinion-based partisan news programs on cable and the Internet a good thing or a bad thing for democracy?

4. Is there political bias in front-page news stories? If so, cite some current examples.

5. How would you go about formulating an ethical policy with regard to using deceptive means to get a story?

6. For a reporter, what are the dangers of both detachment from and involvement in public life?

7. Do satirical news programs make us more cynical about politics and less inclined to vote? Why or why not?

8. What steps would you take to make journalism work better in a democracy?

LAUNCHPAD FOR *MEDIA & CULTURE*

Visit **LaunchPad for** *Media & Culture* *at* **macmillanhighered.com/mediaculture10e** *for additional learning tools:*

- REVIEW WITH LEARNINGCURVE
  LearningCurve, available on LaunchPad for *Media & Culture*, uses gamelike quizzing to help you master the concepts you need to learn from this chapter.

- VIDEO: THE OBJECTIVITY MYTH
  Pulitzer Prize–winning journalist Clarence Page and *Onion* editor Joe Randazzo explore how objectivity began in journalism and how reporter biases may nonetheless influence news stories.

15

Media Effects and Cultural Approaches to Research

513
Early Media Research
Methods

518
Research on Media
Effects

526
Cultural Approaches
to Media Research

532
Media Research
and Democracy

In 1966, NBC showed the Rod Serling made-for-television thriller *The Doomsday Flight*, the first movie to depict an airplane hijacking. In the story, a man plants a bomb and tries to extract ransom money from an airline. In the days following the telecast, the nation's major airlines reported a dramatic rise in anonymous bomb threats, some of them classified as teenage pranks. The network agreed not to run the film again.

In 1985, the popular heavy-metal band Judas Priest made headlines when two Nevada teenagers shot themselves after listening to the group's allegedly subliminal suicidal message on their 1978 *Stained Class* album. One teen died instantly; the other lived for three more years, in constant pain from severe facial injuries. The teenagers' parents lost a civil product liability suit against the British metal band and CBS Records.

In 1995, an eighteen-year-old woman and her boyfriend went on a killing spree in Louisiana after reportedly watching Oliver Stone's 1994 film

Natural Born Killers more than twenty times. The family of one of the victims filed a lawsuit against Stone and Time Warner, charging that the film—starring Juliette Lewis and Woody Harrelson as a demented, celebrity-craving young couple on a murderous rampage—irresponsibly incited real-life violence. Stone and Time Warner argued that the lawsuit should be dismissed on the grounds of free speech, and the case was finally thrown out in 2001. There was no evidence, according to the judge, that Stone had intended to incite violence.

In 1999, two heavily armed students wearing trench coats attacked Columbine High School in Littleton, Colorado. They planted as many as fifty bombs and murdered twelve fellow students and a teacher before killing themselves. In the wake of this tragedy, many people blamed the mass media, speculating that the killers had immersed themselves in the dark lyrics of shock rocker Marilyn Manson and were desensitized to violence by "first-person-shooter" video games such as *Doom*.

In April 2007, a student massacred thirty-two people on the Virginia Tech campus before killing himself. Gunman Seung-Hui Cho was mentally disturbed and praised "martyrs like Eric and Dylan," the infamous Columbine killers. But Cho's rampage included a twist: During the

attack, he sent a package of letters, videos, and photos of himself to NBC News. The images and ramblings of his "multimedia manifesto" became a major part of the news story (as did ethical questions about the news media broadcasting clips of his videos) while the country tried to make sense of the tragedy.

Yet another tragic shooting occurred in 2012 in Aurora, Colorado, at a midnight screening of *The Dark Knight Rises*. A shooter opened fire in the darkened theater, killing twelve people and injuring fifty-eight. The gunman was identified as James Holmes, a twenty-four-year-old wearing a gas mask and trench coat and carrying several semiautomatic firearms. Holmes repeatedly identified himself as "the Joker" to police.

Each of these events and recent political battles over the need for gun control laws have renewed long-standing cultural debates over the suggestive power of music, visual imagery, and screen violence. Since the emergence of popular music, movies, television, and video games as influential mass media, the relationship between make-believe stories and real-life imitation has drawn a great deal of attention. Concerns have been raised not only by parents, teachers, and politicians but also by several generations of mass communication researchers.

▲ **AS THESE TRAGIC TALES OF VIOLENCE ILLUSTRATE,** many believe that media have a powerful effect on individuals and society. This belief has led media researchers to focus most of their efforts on two types of research: media effects research and cultural studies research.

Media effects research attempts to understand, explain, and predict the effects of mass media on individuals and society. The main goal of this type of research is to uncover whether there is a connection between aggressive behavior and violence in the media, particularly in children and teens. In the late 1960s, government leaders—reacting to the social upheavals of that decade—first set aside $1 million to examine this potential connection. Since that time, thousands of studies have told us what most teachers and parents believe instinctively: Violent scenes on television and in movies stimulate aggressive behavior in children and teens—especially young boys.

The other major area of mass media research is **cultural studies**. This research approach focuses on how people make meaning, apprehend reality, articulate values, and order experience through their use of cultural symbols. Cultural studies scholars also examine the way status quo groups in society, particularly corporate and political elites, use media to circulate their messages and sustain their interests. This research has attempted to make daily cultural experience the focus of media studies, keying on the subtle intersections among mass communication, history, politics, and economics.

In this chapter, we will:

- Examine the evolution of media research over time
- Focus on the two major strains of media research, investigating the strengths and limitations of each
- Conclude with a discussion of how media research interacts with democratic ideals

As you get a sense of media effects and cultural studies research, think of some research questions of your own. Consider your own Internet habits. How do the number of hours you spend online every day, the types of online content you view, and your motivations for where you spend your time online shape your everyday behavior? Also, think about the ways your gender, race, sexuality, or class play into other media you consume—like the movies and television you watch and the music you like. For more questions to help you understand the effects of media in our lives, see "Questioning the Media" in the Chapter Review.

Visit **LaunchPad** for *Media & Culture* and use **LearningCurve** to review concepts from this chapter.

Early Media Research Methods

In the early days of the United States, philosophical and historical writings tried to explain the nature of news and print media. For instance, the French political philosopher Alexis de Tocqueville, author of *Democracy in America*, noted differences between French and American newspapers in the early 1830s:

In France the space allotted to commercial advertisements is very limited, and . . . the essential part of the journal is the discussion of the politics of the day. In America three quarters of the enormous sheet are filled with advertisements and the remainder is frequently occupied by political intelligence or trivial anecdotes; it is only from time to time that one finds a corner devoted to the passionate discussions like those which the journalists of France every day give to their readers.[1]

Scott Olson/Getty Images

PUBLIC OPINION RESEARCH
Public opinion polls suggest that the American public's attitude toward same-sex marriage has evolved. Just weeks before the Supreme Court ruled to strike down the Defense of Marriage Act (DOMA), a 2013 *Washington Post*–ABC News poll found that 63 percent of Americans were already in favor of extending federal benefits to legally married same-sex couples.

During most of the nineteenth century, media analysis was based on moral and political arguments, as demonstrated by the de Tocqueville quote.[2]

More scientific approaches to mass media research did not begin to develop until the late 1920s and 1930s. In 1920, Walter Lippmann's *Liberty and the News* called on journalists to operate more like scientific researchers in gathering and analyzing factual material. Lippmann's next book, *Public Opinion* (1922), was the first to apply the principles of psychology to journalism. Described by media historian James Carey as "the founding book in American media studies,"[3] it led to an expanded understanding of the effects of the media, emphasizing data collection and numerical measurement. According to media historian Daniel Czitrom, by the 1930s "an aggressively empirical spirit, stressing new and increasingly sophisticated research techniques, characterized the study of modern communication in America."[4] Czitrom traces four trends between 1930 and 1960 that contributed to the rise of modern media research: propaganda analysis, public opinion research, social psychology studies, and marketing research.

Propaganda Analysis

After World War I, some media researchers began studying how governments used propaganda to advance the war effort. They found that during the war, governments routinely relied on propaganda divisions to spread "information" to the public. According to Czitrom, though propaganda was considered a positive force for mobilizing public opinion during the war, researchers after the war labeled propaganda negatively, calling it "partisan appeal based on half-truths and devious manipulation of communication channels."[5] Harold Lasswell's important 1927 study *Propaganda Technique in the World War* focused on propaganda in the media, defining it as "the control of opinion by significant symbols, . . . by stories, rumors, reports, pictures and other forms of social communication."[6] **Propaganda analysis** thus became a major early focus of mass media research.

Public Opinion Research

Researchers soon went beyond the study of war propaganda and began to focus on more general concerns about how the mass media filtered information and shaped public attitudes. In the face of growing media influence, Walter Lippmann distrusted the public's ability to function as knowledgeable citizens as well as journalism's ability to help the public separate truth from lies. In promoting the place of the expert in modern life, Lippmann celebrated the social scientist as part of a new expert class that could best make "unseen facts intelligible to those who have to make decisions."[7]

Today, social scientists conduct *public opinion research*, or citizen surveys; these have become especially influential during political elections. On the upside, public opinion research on diverse populations has provided insights into citizen behavior and social differences, especially during election periods or following major national events. For example, a 2013 *Washington Post*–ABC News poll confirmed what several other reputable polls reported: A majority of Americans support same-sex marriage. Since 1988, when more than 70 percent of Americans opposed same-sex marriage, the balance has been shifting toward support—gradually at first and more rapidly since 2009.[8]

On the downside, journalism has become increasingly dependent on polls, particularly for political insight. Some critics argue that this heavy reliance on measured public opinion has begun to adversely affect the active political involvement of American citizens. Many people do not vote because they have seen or read poll projections and have decided that their votes will not make a difference. Furthermore, some critics of incessant polling argue that the public is just passively responding to surveys that mainly measure opinions on topics of interest to business, government, academics, and the mainstream news media. A final problem is the pervasive use of unreliable **pseudo-polls**, typically call-in, online, or person-in-the-street polls that the news media use to address a "question of the day." The National Council of Public Opinion Polls notes that "unscientific pseudo-polls are widespread and sometimes entertaining, but they never provide the kind of information that belongs in a serious report," and discourages news media from conducting them.[9]

Social Psychology Studies

While opinion polls measure public attitudes, *social psychology studies* measure the behavior and cognition of individuals. The most influential early social psychology study, the Payne Fund Studies, encompassed a series of thirteen research projects conducted by social psychologists between 1929 and 1932. Named after the private philanthropic organization that funded the research, the Payne Fund Studies were a response to a growing national concern about the effects of motion pictures, which had become a particularly popular pastime for young people in the 1920s. These studies, which were later used by some politicians to attack the movie industry, linked frequent movie attendance to juvenile delinquency, promiscuity, and other antisocial behaviors, arguing that movies took "emotional possession" of young filmgoers.[10]

Photofest

SOCIAL AND PSYCHOLOGICAL EFFECTS OF MEDIA Concerns about film violence are not new. The 1930 movie *Little Caesar* follows the career of gangster Rico Bandello (played by Edward G. Robinson, shown), who kills his way to the top of the crime establishment and gets the girl as well. The Motion Picture Production Code, which was established a few years after this movie's release, reined in sexual themes and profane language, set restrictions on film violence, and attempted to prevent audiences from sympathizing with bad guys like Rico.

FIGURE 15.1

TV PARENTAL GUIDELINES

The TV industry continues to study its self-imposed rating categories, promising to fine-tune them to ensure that the government keeps its distance. These standards are one example of a policy that was shaped in part by media research. Since the 1960s, research has attempted to demonstrate links between violent TV images and increased levels of aggression among children and adolescents.

Data from: TV Parental Guidelines Monitoring Board, accessed November 24, 2014, www.tvguidelines.org.

The following categories apply to programs designed solely for children:

TVY All Children
This program is designed to be appropriate for all children. Whether animated or live-action, the themes and elements in this program are specifically designed for a very young audience, including children from ages 2–6. This program is not expected to frighten young children.

TVY7FV Directed to Older Children— Fantasy Violence
For those programs where fantasy violence may be more intense or more combative than other programs in this category, such programs will be designated **TV-Y7-FV**.

TVY7 Directed to Older Children
This program is designed for children age 7 and above. It may be more appropriate for children who have acquired the developmental skills needed to distinguish between make-believe and reality. Themes and elements in this program may include mild fantasy violence or comedic violence, or may frighten children under the age of 7. Therefore, parents may wish to consider the suitability of this program for their very young children.

The following categories apply to programs designed for the entire audience:

TVG General Audience
Most parents would find this program suitable for all ages. Although this rating does not signify a program designed specifically for children, most parents may let younger children watch this program unattended. It contains little or no violence, no strong language and little or no sexual dialogue or situations.

TVPG Parental Guidance Suggested
This program contains material that parents may find unsuitable for younger children. Many parents may want to watch it with their younger children. The theme itself may call for parental guidance and/or the program may contain one or more of the following: some suggestive dialogue (D), infrequent coarse language (L), some sexual situations (S), or moderate violence (V).

TV14 Parents Strongly Cautioned
This program contains some material that many parents would find unsuitable for children under 14 years of age. Parents are strongly urged to exercise greater care in monitoring this program and are cautioned against letting children under the age of 14 watch unattended. This program may contain one or more of the following: intensely suggestive dialogue (D), strong coarse language (L), intense sexual situations (S), or intense violence (V).

TVMA Mature Audiences Only
This program is specifically designed to be viewed by adults and therefore may be unsuitable for children under 17. This program may contain one or more of the following: crude indecent language (L), explicit sexual activity (S), or graphic violence (V).

In one of the Payne studies, for example, children and teenagers were wired with electrodes and galvanometers, mechanisms that detected any heightened response via the subject's skin. The researchers interpreted changes in the skin as evidence of emotional arousal. In retrospect, the findings hardly seem surprising: The youngest subjects in the group had the strongest reaction to violent or tragic movie scenes, while the teenage subjects reacted most strongly to scenes with romantic and sexual content. The researchers concluded that films could be dangerous for young children and might foster sexual promiscuity among teenagers. The conclusions of this and other Payne Fund Studies contributed to the establishment of the Motion Picture Production Code, which tamed movie content from the 1930s through the 1950s (see Chapter 16). As forerunners of today's TV violence and aggression research, the Payne Fund Studies became the model for media research. (See Figure 15.1 for one example of a contemporary policy that has developed from media research. Also see "Case Study: The Effects of TV in a Post-TV World" on page 517.)

Marketing Research

A fourth influential area of early media research, *marketing research,* developed when advertisers and product companies began conducting surveys on consumer buying habits in the 1920s. The emergence of commercial radio led to the first ratings systems that measured how many people were listening on a given night. By the 1930s, radio networks, advertisers, large stations, and advertising agencies all subscribed to ratings services. However, compared with print media, whose circulation departments kept careful track of customers' names and

The Effects of TV in a Post-TV World

Since TV's emergence as a mass medium, there has been persistent concern about the effects of violence, sex, and indecent language seen in television programs. The U.S. Congress had its first hearings on the matter of television content in 1952 and has held hearings in every subsequent decade.

In its coverage of congressional hearings on TV violence in 1983, the *New York Times* accurately captured the nature of these recurring public hearings: "Over the years, the principals change but the roles remain the same: social scientists ready to prove that television does indeed improperly influence its viewers, and network representatives, some of them also social scientists, who insist that there is absolutely nothing to worry about."[1]

One of the central focuses of the TV debate has been television's effect on

Jason LaVeris/FilmMagic/Getty Images

children. In 1975, the major broadcast networks (then ABC, CBS, and NBC) bowed to congressional and FCC pressure and agreed to a "family hour" of programming in the first hour of prime-time television (8–9 P.M. eastern or 7–8 P.M. central). Shows such as *Happy Days*, the *Cosby Show*, and *Little House on the Prairie* flourished in that time slot. By 1989, Fox had arrived as a fourth major network and successfully counterprogrammed in the family hour with dysfunctional family shows like *Married . . . with Children*.

The most prominent watchdog monitoring prime-time network television's violence, sex, and indecent language has been the Parents Television Council (PTC), formed in 1995. The lobbying group's primary mission is to "promote and restore responsibility and decency to the entertainment industry in answer to America's demand for positive, family-oriented television programming. The PTC does this by fostering changes in TV programming to make the early hours of prime time family-friendly and suitable for viewers of all ages."[2] The PTC (through its Web campaign) played a leading role in inundating the FCC with complaints and getting the FCC to approve a steep increase in its fines for broadcast indecency.

Yet to address the ongoing concerns of parent groups and Congress, it's worth asking: What are the effects of TV in what researchers now call a "post-TV" world? In just the past few years, digital video recorders have become common, and services like Hulu, YouTube, Netflix, iTunes, and

on-demand cable viewing mean that viewers can access TV programming of all types at any time of the day. Although Americans are watching more television than ever before, it's increasingly time-shifted programming. How should we consider the possible harmful effects of prime-time network television given that most American families are no longer watching during the appointed broadcast network prime-time hours? Does the American public care about such media effects in this post-TV world?

These days, the Parents Television Council still releases its weekly "Family Guide to Prime Time Television" on its Web site. A sample of its guide from summer 2014, for example, listed no shows as "family-friendly," while shows as diverse as *The Big Bang Theory*, *Person of Interest*, *America's Got Talent*, and *Arrow* received a red-light designation for sexual content, language, and violence.

Of course, as television viewers move away from broadcast networks and increasingly watch programming from multiple sources on a range of devices, the PTC's traditional concern about prime-time network viewing can seem outdated. In recent years, the PTC announced it was giving its seal of approval to the Inspiration Network cable channel "for programming that embraces time-honored values."[3] The channel's lineup featured shows like *The Waltons*; *Dr. Quinn, Medicine Woman*; *Little House on the Prairie*; and *Happy Days*—all shows from an era decades before our post-TV world. ◢

addresses, radio listeners were more difficult to trace. This problem precipitated the development of increasingly sophisticated marketing research methods to determine consumer preferences and media use, such as direct-mail diaries, television meters, phone surveys, telemarketing, and Internet tracking. In many instances, product companies paid consumers nominal amounts of money to take part in these studies.

Research on Media Effects

As concern about public opinion, propaganda, and the impact of the media merged with the growth of journalism and mass communication departments in colleges and universities, media researchers looked more and more to behavioral science as the basis of their research. Between 1930 and 1970, as media historian Daniel Czitrom has noted, "Who says what to whom with what effect?" became the key question "defining the scope and problems of American communications research."[11] In addressing this question specifically, media effects researchers asked follow-up questions such as this: If children watch a lot of TV cartoons (stimulus or cause), will this repeated act influence their behavior toward their peers (response or effect)? For most of the twentieth century, media researchers and news reporters used different methods to answer similar sets of questions—who, what, when, and where—about our daily experiences (see "Media Literacy and the Critical Process: Wedding Media and the Meaning of the Perfect Wedding Day" on page 523).

Early Theories of Media Effects

A major goal of scientific research is to develop theories or laws that can consistently explain or predict human behavior. The varied impacts of the mass media and the diverse ways in which people make popular culture, however, tend to defy predictable rules. Historical, economic, and political factors influence media industries, making it difficult to develop systematic theories that explain communication. Researchers developed a number of small theories, or models, that help explain individual behavior rather than the impact of the media on large populations. But before these small theories began to emerge in the 1970s, mass media research followed several other models. Developing between the 1930s and the 1970s, these major approaches included the hypodermic-needle, minimal-effects, and uses and gratifications models.

The Hypodermic-Needle Model

One of the earliest media theories attributed powerful effects to the mass media. A number of intellectuals and academics were fearful of the influence and popularity of film and radio in the 1920s and 1930s. Some social psychologists and sociologists who arrived in the United States after fleeing Germany and Nazism in the 1930s had watched Hitler use radio, film, and print media as propaganda tools. They worried that the popular media in America also had a strong hold over vulnerable audiences. The concept that powerful media affect weak audiences has been labeled the **hypodermic-needle model**, sometimes also called the *magic bullet theory* or the *direct-effects model*. It suggests that the media shoot their potent effects directly into unsuspecting victims.

One of the earliest challenges to this theory involved a study of Orson Welles's legendary October 30, 1938, radio broadcast of *War of the Worlds*, which presented H. G. Wells's Martian invasion novel in the form of a news report and frightened millions of listeners who didn't realize it was fictional (see Chapter 5). In a 1940 book-length study of the broadcast, *The Invasion from Mars: A Study in the Psychology of Panic*, radio researcher Hadley Cantril argued that

LaunchPad ◉
macmillanhighered.com
/mediaculture10e

Media Effects Research
Experts discuss how media effects research informs media development.
Discussion: Why do you think the question of media's effects on children has continued to be such a big concern among researchers?

contrary to expectations based on to the hypodermic-needle model, not all listeners thought the radio program was a real news report. Instead, Cantril, after conducting personal interviews and a nation-wide survey of listeners and analyzing newspaper reports and listener mail to CBS Radio and the FCC, noted that although some did believe it to be real (mostly those who missed the disclaimer at the beginning of the broadcast), the majority reacted out of collective panic, not out of a gullible belief in anything transmitted through the media. Although the hypodermic-needle model over the years has been disproved by social scientists, many people still attribute direct effects to the mass media, particularly in the case of children.

The Minimal-Effects Model

Cantril's research helped lay the groundwork for the **minimal-effects model**, or *limited model*. With the rise of empirical research techniques, social scientists began discovering and demonstrating that media alone cannot cause people to change their attitudes and behaviors. Based on tightly controlled experiments and surveys, researchers argued that people generally engage in **selective exposure** and **selective retention** with regard to the media. That is, people expose themselves to the media messages that are most familiar to them, and they retain the messages that confirm the values and attitudes they already hold. Minimal-effects researchers have argued that in most cases, mass media reinforce existing behaviors and attitudes rather than change them. The findings from the first comprehensive study of children and television—by Wilbur Schramm, Jack Lyle, and Edwin Parker in the late 1950s—best capture the minimal-effects theory:

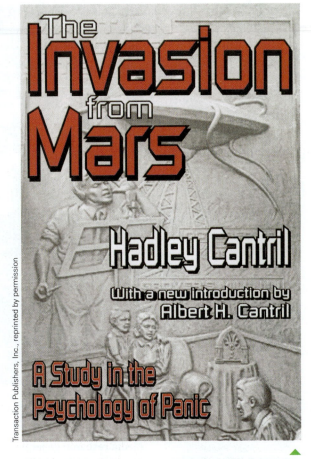

Transaction Publishers, Inc., reprinted by permission

For some children, under some conditions, some television is harmful. For other children under the same conditions, or for the same children under other conditions, it may be beneficial. For most children, under most conditions, most television is probably neither particularly harmful nor particularly beneficial.[12]

In addition, Joseph Klapper's important 1960 research study, *The Effects of Mass Communication*, found that the mass media only influenced individuals who did not already hold strong views on an issue and that the media had a greater impact on poor and uneducated audiences. Solidifying the minimal-effects argument, Klapper concluded that strong media effects occur largely at an individual level and do not appear to have large-scale, measurable, and direct effects on society as a whole.[13]

The minimal-effects theory furthered the study of the relationship between the media and human behavior, but it still assumed that audiences were passive and were acted upon by the media. Schramm, Lyle, and Parker suggested that there were problems with the position they had taken on effects:

In a sense the term "effect" is misleading because it suggests that television "does something" to children. The connotation is that television is the actor, the children are acted upon. Children are thus made to seem relatively inert; television, relatively active. Children are sitting victims; television bites them. Nothing can be further from the fact. It is the children who are most active in this relationship. It is they who use television, rather than television that uses them.[14]

Indeed, as the authors observed, numerous studies have concluded that viewers—especially young children—are often *actively* engaged in using media.

MEDIA EFFECTS?
In *The Invasion from Mars: A Study in the Psychology of Panic*, Hadley Cantril (1906–1969) argued against the hypodermic-needle model as an explanation for the panic that broke out after the *War of the Worlds* radio broadcast. A lifelong social researcher, Cantril also did a lot of work in public opinion research, even working with the government during World War II.

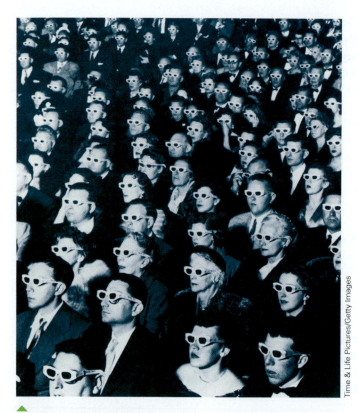

USES AND GRATIFICATIONS In 1952, audience members at the Paramount Theater in Hollywood donned 3-D glasses for the opening-night screening of *Bwana Devil*, the first full-length color 3-D film. The uses and gratifications model of research investigates the appeal of mass media, such as going out to the movies.

The Uses and Gratifications Model

A response to the minimal-effects theory, the **uses and gratifications model** was proposed to contest the notion of a passive media audience. Under this model, researchers— usually using in-depth interviews to supplement survey questionnaires—studied the ways in which people used the media to satisfy various emotional or intellectual needs. Instead of asking, "What effects do the media have on us?" researchers asked, "Why do we use the media?" Asking the *why* question enabled media researchers to develop inventories cataloguing how people employed the media to fulfill their needs. For example, researchers noted that some individuals used the media to see authority figures elevated or toppled, to seek a sense of community and connectedness, to fulfill a need for drama and stories, and to confirm moral or spiritual values.[15]

Although the uses and gratifications model addressed the *functions* of the mass media for individuals, it did not address important questions related to the impact of the media on society. Once researchers had accumulated substantial inventories of the uses and functions of media, they often did not move in new directions. Consequently, uses and gratifications never became a dominant or an enduring theory in media research.

Conducting Media Effects Research

Media research generally comes from the private or public sector, and each type has distinguishing features. *Private research*, sometimes called *proprietary research*, is generally conducted for a business, a corporation, or even a political campaign. It is usually applied research in the sense that the information it uncovers typically addresses some real-life problem or need. *Public research*, in contrast, usually takes place in academic and government settings. It involves information that is often more *theoretical* than applied; it tries to clarify, explain, or predict the effects of mass media rather than to address a consumer problem.

Most media research today focuses on the effects of the media in such areas as learning, attitudes, aggression, and voting habits. This research employs the **scientific method**, a blueprint long used by scientists and scholars to study phenomena in systematic stages. The steps in the scientific method include the following:

1. Identifying the research problem
2. Reviewing existing research and theories related to the problem
3. Developing working hypotheses or predictions about what the study might find
4. Determining an appropriate method or research design
5. Collecting information or relevant data
6. Analyzing results to see if the hypotheses have been verified
7. Interpreting the implications of the study to determine whether they explain or predict the problem

The scientific method relies on *objectivity* (eliminating bias and judgments on the part of researchers); *reliability* (getting the same answers or outcomes from a study or measure during repeated testing); and *validity* (demonstrating that a study actually measures what it claims to measure).

In scientific studies, researchers pose one or more **hypotheses**: tentative general statements that predict the influence of an *independent variable* on a *dependent variable*. For example, a researcher might hypothesize that frequent TV viewing among adolescents (independent variable) causes poor academic performance (dependent variable). Or another researcher might hypothesize that playing first-person-shooter video games (independent variable) is associated with aggression in children (dependent variable).

Broadly speaking, the methods for studying media effects on audiences have taken two forms—experiments and survey research. To supplement these approaches, researchers also use content analysis to count and document specific messages that circulate in mass media.

Experiments

Like all studies that use the scientific method, **experiments** in media research isolate some aspect of content; suggest a hypothesis; and manipulate variables to discover a particular medium's impact on attitude, emotion, or behavior. To test whether a hypothesis is true, researchers expose an *experimental group*—the group under study—to a selected media program or text. To ensure valid results, researchers also use a *control group*, which serves as a basis for comparison; this group is not exposed to the selected media content. Subjects are picked for each group through **random assignment**, which simply means that each subject has an equal chance of being placed in either group. Random assignment ensures that the independent variables researchers want to control are distributed to both groups in the same way.

For instance, to test the effects of violent films on preadolescent boys, a research study might take a group of ten-year-olds and randomly assign them to two groups. Researchers expose the experimental group to a violent action movie that the control group does not see. Later, both groups are exposed to a staged fight between two other boys so that the researchers can observe how each group responds to an actual physical confrontation. Researchers then determine whether or not there is a statistically measurable difference between the two groups' responses to the fight. For example, perhaps the control subjects tried to break up the fight but the experimental subjects did not. Because the groups were randomly selected and the only measurable difference between them was the viewing of the movie, researchers may conclude that under these conditions, the violent film caused a different behavior. (See the "Bobo doll" experiment photos on page 524.)

When experiments carefully account for independent variables through random assignment, they generally work well to substantiate direct cause-effect hypotheses. Such research takes place both in laboratory settings and in field settings, where people can be observed using the media in their everyday environments. In field experiments, however, it is more difficult for researchers to control variables. In lab settings, researchers have more control, but other problems may occur. For example, when subjects are removed from the environments in which they regularly use the media, they may act differently—often with fewer inhibitions—than they would in their everyday surroundings.

Experiments have other limitations as well. First, they are not generalizable to a larger population; they cannot tell us whether cause-effect results can be duplicated outside of the laboratory. Second, most academic experiments today are performed on college students, who are convenient subjects for research but are not representative of the general public. Third, while most experiments are fairly good at predicting short-term media effects under controlled conditions, they do not predict how subjects will behave months or years later in the real world.

Survey Research

In the simplest terms, **survey research** is the collecting and measuring of data taken from a group of respondents. Using random sampling techniques that give each potential subject an equal chance to be included in the survey, this research method draws on much larger populations than those used in experimental studies. Surveys may be conducted through direct mail, personal interviews, telephone calls, e-mail, and Web sites, enabling survey researchers to accumulate large amounts of information by surveying diverse cross sections of people. These data help researchers examine demographic factors such as educational background, income level, race, ethnicity, gender, age, sexual orientation, and political affiliations, along with questions directly related to the survey topic.

Two other benefits of surveys are that they are usually generalizable to the larger society and that they enable researchers to investigate populations in long-term studies. For example, survey research can measure subjects when they are ten, twenty, and thirty years old to track changes in how frequently they watch television and what kinds of programs they prefer at different ages. In addition, large government and academic survey databases are now widely available and contribute to the development of more long-range or **longitudinal studies**, which make it possible for social scientists to compare new studies with those conducted years earlier.

Like experiments, surveys have several drawbacks. First, survey investigators cannot account for all the variables that might affect media use; therefore, they cannot show cause-effect relationships. Survey research can, however, reveal **correlations**—or associations—between two variables. For example, a random questionnaire survey of ten-year-old boys might demonstrate that a correlation exists between aggressive behavior and watching violent TV programs. Such a correlation, however, does not explain what is the cause and what is the effect—that is, do violent TV programs cause aggression, or are more aggressive ten-year-old boys simply drawn to violent television? Second, the validity of survey questions is a chronic problem for survey practitioners. Surveys are only as good as the wording of their questions and the answer choices they present. For example, as NPR reported, "If you ask people whether they support or oppose the death penalty for murderers, about two-thirds of Americans say they support it. If you ask whether people prefer that murderers get the death penalty or life in prison without parole, then you get a 50-50 split."[16]

Content Analysis

Over the years, researchers recognized that experiments and surveys focused on general topics (violence) while ignoring the effects of specific media messages (gun violence, fistfights). As a corrective, researchers developed a method known as **content analysis** to study these messages. Such analysis is a systematic method of coding and measuring media content.

Although content analysis was first used during World War II for radio, more recent studies have focused on television, film, and the Internet. Probably the most influential content analysis studies were conducted by George Gerbner and his colleagues at the University of Pennsylvania. Beginning in the late 1960s, they coded and counted acts of violence on network television. Combined with surveys, their annual "violence profiles" showed that heavy watchers of television, ranging from children to retired Americans, tend to overestimate the amount of violence that exists in the actual world.[17]

The limits of content analysis, however, have been well documented. First, this technique does not measure the effects of the messages on audiences, nor does it explain how those messages are presented. For example, a content analysis sponsored by the Kaiser Family Foundation that examined more than eleven hundred television shows found that 70 percent featured sexual content.[18] But the study didn't explain how viewers interpreted the content or the context of the messages.

Second, problems of definition occur in content analysis. For instance, in the case of coding and counting acts of violence, how do researchers distinguish slapstick cartoon aggression from the violent murders or rapes in an evening police drama? Critics point out that such varied depictions may have diverse and subtle effects on viewers that are not differentiated by content analysis. Third, critics point out that as content analysis grew to be a primary tool in media

Media Literacy and the Critical Process

1 DESCRIPTION. Select three or four bridal media and compare them. Possible choices include magazines such as *Brides*, *Bridal Guide*, and *Martha Stewart Weddings*; reality TV shows like *My Fair Wedding*, *Bridezillas*, *Say Yes to the Dress*, *My Big Fat American Gypsy Wedding*, and *Four Weddings*; Web sites like The Knot, Southern Bride, and Project Wedding; and games like *My Fantasy Wedding*, *Wedding Dash*, and *Imagine Wedding Designer*.

2 ANALYSIS. What patterns do you find in the wedding media? (Consider what isn't depicted as well.) Are there limited ways in which femininity is defined? Do men have an equal role in the planning of wedding events? Are weddings depicted as something just for heterosexuals? Do the wedding media presume that weddings are first-time experiences for the couple getting married? What seem to be the standards in terms of consumption—the expense, size, and number of things to buy and rent to make a "perfect" day?

3 INTERPRETATION. What do the wedding media seem to say

Wedding Media and the Meaning of the Perfect Wedding Day

According to media researcher Erika Engstrom, the bridal industry in the United States generates $50 to $70 billion annually, with more than two million marriages a year.[1] Supporting that massive industry are books, magazines, Web sites, reality TV shows, and digital games (in addition to fictional accounts in movies and music) that promote the idea of what a "perfect" wedding should be. What values are wrapped up in these wedding narratives?

about what it is to be a woman or a man on her or his wedding day? What do these gender roles for the wedding suggest about the appropriate gender roles for married life after the wedding? What do the wedding media infer about the appropriate level of consumption? In other words, consider the role of wedding media in constructing *hegemony*: In their depiction of what makes a perfect wedding, do the media stories attempt to get us to accept the dominant cultural values relating to things like gender relations and consumerism?

4 EVALUATION. Come to a judgment about the wedding media analyzed. Are they good or bad on

certain dimensions? Do they promote gender equality? Do they promote marriage equality (that is, gay marriage)? Do they offer alternatives to having a "perfect" day without buying all the trappings of so many weddings?

5 ENGAGEMENT. Talk to friends about what weddings are supposed to celebrate, and whether an alternative conception of a wedding would be a better way of celebrating a union of two people. (In real life, if there is discomfort in talking about alternative ways to celebrate a wedding, that's probably the pressure of hegemony. Why is that pressure so strong?) Share your criticisms and ideas on wedding Web sites as well.

---

research, it sometimes pushed to the sidelines other ways of thinking about television and media content. Broad questions concerning the media as a popular art form, as a measure of culture, as a democratic influence, or as a force for social control are difficult to address through strict measurement techniques. Critics of content analysis, in fact, have objected to the kind of social science that reduces culture to acts of counting. Such criticism has addressed the tendency by some researchers to favor measurement accuracy over intellectual discipline and inquiry.[19]

Contemporary Media Effects Theories

By the 1960s, the first departments of mass communication began graduating Ph.D.-level researchers schooled in experiment and survey research techniques, as well as content analysis. These researchers began documenting consistent patterns in mass communication and developing new theories. Five of the most influential contemporary theories that help explain media effects are social learning theory, agenda-setting, the cultivation effect, the spiral of silence, and the third-person effect.

SOCIAL LEARNING THEORIES

These photos document the "Bobo doll" experiments conducted by Albert Bandura and his colleagues at Stanford University in the early 1960s. Seventy-two children from the Stanford University Nursery School were divided into experimental and control groups. The "aggressive condition" experimental group subjects watched an adult in the room sit on, kick, and hit the Bobo doll with hands and a wooden mallet while saying such things as "Sock him in the nose," "Throw him in the air," and "Pow." (In later versions of the experiment, children watched filmed versions of the adult with the Bobo doll.) Afterward, in a separate room filled with toys, the children in the "aggressive condition" group were more likely than the other children to imitate the adult model's behavior toward the Bobo doll.

Courtesy of Albert Bandura

Social Learning Theory

Some of the most well-known studies that suggest a link between the mass media and behavior are the "Bobo doll" experiments, conducted on children by psychologist Albert Bandura and his colleagues at Stanford University in the 1960s. Bandura concluded that the experiments demonstrated a link between violent media programs, such as those on television, and aggressive behavior. Bandura developed **social learning theory** as a four-step process: *attention* (the subject must attend to the media and witness the aggressive behavior), *retention* (the subject must retain the memory for later retrieval), *motor reproduction* (the subject must be able to physically imitate the behavior), and *motivation* (there must be a social reward or reinforcement to encourage modeling of the behavior).

Supporters of social learning theory often cite real-life imitations of media aggression (see the beginning of the chapter) as evidence of social learning theory at work. Yet critics note that many studies conclude just the opposite—that there is no link between media content and aggression. For example, millions of people have watched episodes of *CSI* and *The Sopranos* without subsequently exhibiting aggressive behavior. As critics point out, social learning theory simply makes television, film, and other media scapegoats for larger social problems relating to violence. Others suggest that experiencing media depictions of aggression can actually help viewers let off steam peacefully through a catharsis effect.

Agenda-Setting

A key phenomenon posited by contemporary media effects researchers is **agenda-setting**: the idea that when the mass media focus their attention on particular events or issues, they determine—that is, set the agenda for—the major topics of discussion for individuals and society. Essentially, agenda-setting researchers have argued that the mass media do not so much tell us what to think as *what to think about*. Traceable to Walter Lippmann's notion in the early 1920s that the media "create pictures in our heads," the first investigations into agenda-setting began in the 1970s.[20]

Over the years, agenda-setting research has demonstrated that the more stories the news media do on a particular subject, the more importance audiences attach to that subject. For instance, when the media seriously began to cover ecology issues after the first Earth Day in 1970, a much higher percentage of the population began listing the environment as a primary social concern in surveys. When *Jaws* became a blockbuster in 1975, the news media started featuring more shark attack stories; even landlocked people in the Midwest began ranking sharks as a major problem, despite the rarity of such incidents worldwide. More recently, extensive news coverage about the documentary *An Inconvenient Truth* and its companion best-selling book in 2006 sparked the highest-ever public concern about global warming, according to national surveys. But in the following years, the public's sense of urgency faltered somewhat as stories about the economy and other topics dominated the news agenda.

AP Photo/Baba Ahmed

MALI
The West African nation of Mali has been in the midst of a political crisis since its northern region was seized by rebel forces in 2012. One of the most devastating outcomes of the country's political strife is the recruitment of child soldiers, as desperate, poor families often give up their children to rebels in exchange for food and money. Despite the devastation in Mali, many feel the international response to Mali's crisis has been woefully inadequate and the mass media's coverage equally insufficient.

The Cultivation Effect

Another mass media phenomenon—the **cultivation effect**—suggests that heavy viewing of television leads individuals to perceive the world in ways that are consistent with television portrayals. This area of media effects research has pushed researchers past a focus on how the media affects individual behavior and toward a focus on larger ideas about the impact on perception.

The major research in this area grew from the attempts of George Gerbner and his colleagues to make generalizations about the impact of televised violence. The cultivation effect suggests that the more time individuals spend viewing television and absorbing its viewpoints, the more likely their views of social reality will be "cultivated" by the images and portrayals they see on television.[21] For example, Gerbner's studies concluded that although fewer than 1 percent of Americans are victims of violent crime in any single year, people who watch a lot of television tend to overestimate this percentage. Such exaggerated perceptions, Gerbner and his colleagues argued, are part of a "mean world" syndrome, in which viewers with heavy, long-term exposure to television violence are more likely to believe that the external world is a mean and dangerous place.

According to the cultivation effect, media messages interact in complicated ways with personal, social, political, and cultural factors; they are one of a number of important factors in determining individual behavior and defining social values. Some critics have charged that cultivation research has provided limited evidence to support its findings. In addition, some have argued that the cultivation effects recorded by Gerbner's studies have been so minimal as to be benign and that when compared side by side, the perceptions of heavy television viewers and nonviewers in terms of the "mean world" syndrome are virtually identical.

The Spiral of Silence

Developed by German communication theorist Elisabeth Noelle-Neumann in the 1970s and 1980s, the **spiral of silence** theory links the mass media, social psychology, and the formation of public opinion. The theory proposes that those who believe that their views on controversial issues are in the minority will keep their views to themselves—that is, become silent—for fear of social isolation, which diminishes or even silences alternative perspectives. The theory is based on social psychology studies, such as the classic conformity research studies of Solomon Asch in 1951. In Asch's study on the effects of group pressure, he demonstrated that a test subject is more likely to give clearly wrong answers to questions about line lengths if all other people in the room unanimously state an incorrect answer. Noelle-Neumann argued that mass media, particularly television, can exacerbate this effect by communicating real or presumed majority opinions widely and quickly.

According to the theory, the mass media can help create a false, overrated majority; that is, a true majority of people holding a certain position can grow silent when they sense an opposing majority in the media. One criticism of the theory is that some people may fail to fall into a spiral of silence either because they don't monitor the media or because they mistakenly perceive that more people hold their position than really do. Noelle-Neumann acknowledges that in many cases, "hard-core" nonconformists exist and remain vocal even in the face of social isolation and can ultimately prevail in changing public opinion.[22]

The Third-Person Effect

Identified in a 1983 study by W. Phillips Davison, the **third-person effect** theory suggests that people believe others are more affected by media messages than they are themselves.[23] In other words, it proposes the idea that "we" can escape the worst effects of media while still worrying about people who are younger, less educated, more impressionable, or otherwise less capable of guarding against media influence.

Under this theory, we might fear that other people will, for example, take tabloid newspapers seriously, imitate violent movies, or get addicted to the Internet, while dismissing the idea that any of those things could happen to us. It has been argued that the third-person effect is instrumental in censorship, as it would allow censors to assume immunity to the negative effects of any supposedly dangerous media they must examine.

Evaluating Research on Media Effects

The mainstream models of media research have made valuable contributions to our understanding of the mass media, submitting content and audiences to rigorous testing. This wealth of research exists partly because funding for studies on the effects of the media on young people remains popular among politicians and has drawn ready government support since the 1960s. Media critic Richard Rhodes argues that media effects research is inconsistent and often flawed but continues to resonate with politicians and parents because it offers an easy-to-blame social cause for real-world violence.[24] (For more on real-world gun violence in the United States, see "Case Study: Our Masculinity Problem" on page 529.)

Funding restricts the scope of some media effects and survey research, particularly if government, business, or other administrative agendas do not align with researchers' interests. Other limits also exist, including the inability to address how media affect communities and social institutions. Because most media research operates best when examining media and individual behavior, fewer research studies explore media's impact on community and social life. Some research has begun to address these deficits and also to turn more attention to the increasing impact of media technology on international communication.

Cultural Approaches to Media Research

During the rise of modern media research, approaches with a stronger historical and interpretive edge developed as well, often in direct opposition to the scientific models. In the late 1930s, some social scientists began to warn about the limits of "gathering data" and "charting trends," particularly when these kinds of research projects served only advertisers and media organizations and tended to be narrowly focused on individual behavior, ignoring questions like "Where are institutions taking us?" and "Where do we want them to take us?"[25]

In the United States in the 1960s, an important body of research—loosely labeled *cultural studies*—arose to challenge mainstream media effects theories. Since that time, cultural studies research has focused on how people make meaning, understand reality, and order experience by using cultural symbols that appear in the media. This research has attempted to make everyday culture the centerpiece of media studies, focusing on how subtly mass communication shapes and is shaped by history, politics, and economics. Other cultural studies work examines the relationships between elite individuals and groups in government and politics and how media play a role in sustaining the authority of elites and, occasionally, in challenging their power.

Early Developments in Cultural Studies Research

In Europe, media studies have always favored interpretive rather than scientific approaches; in other words, researchers there have approached the media as if they were literary or cultural critics rather than experimental or survey researchers. These approaches were built on the writings of political philosophers such as Karl Marx and Antonio Gramsci, who investigated how mass media support existing hierarchies in society. They examined how popular culture and sports distract people from redressing social injustices, and they addressed the subordinate status of particular social groups, something emerging media effects researchers were seldom doing.

In the United States, early criticism of media effects research came from the Frankfurt School, a group of European researchers who emigrated from Germany to America to escape Nazi persecution in the 1930s. Under the leadership of Max Horkheimer, T. W. Adorno, and Leo Lowenthal, this group pointed to at least three inadequacies of traditional scientific approaches to media research, arguing that they (1) reduced large "cultural questions" to measurable and "verifiable categories"; (2) depended on "an atmosphere of rigidly enforced neutrality"; and (3) refused to place "the phenomena of modern life" in a "historical and moral context."[26] The researchers of the Frankfurt School did not completely reject the usefulness of measuring and counting data. They contended, however, that historical and cultural approaches were also necessary to focus critical attention on the long-range effects of the mass media on audiences.

Since the time of the Frankfurt School, criticisms of the media effects tradition and its methods have continued, with calls for more interpretive studies of the rituals of mass communication. Academics who have embraced a cultural approach to media research try to understand how media and culture are tied to the actual patterns of communication in daily life. For example, in the 1970s, Stuart Hall and his colleagues studied the British print media and the police, who were dealing with an apparent rise in crime and mugging incidents. Arguing that the close relationship between the news and the police created a form of urban surveillance, the authors of *Policing the Crisis* demonstrated that the mugging phenomenon was exacerbated, and in part created, by the key institutions assigned the social tasks of controlling crime and reporting on it.[27]

Conducting Cultural Studies Research

Cultural studies research focuses on the investigation of daily experience, especially on issues of race, gender, class, and sexuality, and on the unequal arrangements of power and status in contemporary society. Such research emphasizes how some social and cultural groups have been marginalized and ignored throughout history. Consequently, cultural studies have attempted to recover lost or silenced voices, particularly among African American; Native American; Asian and Asian American; Arab; Latino; Appalachian; lesbian, gay, bisexual, and transgender (LGBT); immigrant; and women's cultures. The major analytical approaches in cultural studies research today are textual analysis, audience studies, and political economy studies.

Textual Analysis

In cultural studies research, **textual analysis** highlights the close reading and interpretation of cultural messages, including those found in books, movies, and TV programs. It is the equivalent of measurement methods like experiments and surveys and content analysis. While media effects research approaches media messages with the tools of modern science—replicability, objectivity, and data—textual analysis looks at rituals, narratives, and meaning. One type of textual analysis is *framing research*, which looks at recurring media story structures, particularly in news stories. Media sociologist Todd Gitlin defines media frames as "persistent patterns of cognition, interpretation, and presentation, of selection, emphasis, and exclusion, by which symbol-handlers routinely organize discourse, whether verbal or visual."[28]

Although textual analysis has a long and rich history in film and literary studies, it became significant to media in 1974, when Horace Newcomb's *TV: The Most Popular Art* became the first serious academic book to analyze television shows. Newcomb studied why certain TV programs and formats became popular, especially comedies, westerns, mysteries, soap operas, news reports, and sports programs. Newcomb took television programs seriously, examining patterns in the most popular programs at the time, such as the *Beverly Hillbillies*, *Bewitched*, and *Dragnet*, which traditional researchers had usually snubbed or ignored. Trained as a literary scholar, Newcomb argued that content analysis and other social science approaches to popular media often ignored artistic traditions and social context. For Newcomb, "the task for the student of the popular arts is to find a technique through which many different qualities of the work—aesthetic, social, psychological—may be explored" and to discover "why certain formulas . . . are popular in American television."[29]

Before Newcomb's work, textual analysis generally focused only on "important" or highly regarded works of art—debates, films, poems, and books. But by the end of the 1970s, a new generation of media studies scholars, who had grown up on television and rock and roll, began to study less elite forms of culture. They extended the concept of what a "text" is to include architecture, fashion, tabloid magazines, pop icons like Madonna, rock music, hip-hop, soap operas and telenovelas, movies, cockfights, shopping malls, reality TV, Martha Stewart, and professional wrestling—trying to make sense of the most taken-for-granted aspects of everyday media culture. Often the study of these seemingly minor elements of popular culture provides insight into broader meanings within our society. By shifting the focus to daily popular culture artifacts, cultural studies succeeded in focusing scholarly attention not just on significant presidents, important religious leaders, prominent political speeches, or military battles but on the more ordinary ways that "normal" people organize experience and understand their daily lives.

Audience Studies

Cultural studies research that focuses on how people use and interpret cultural content is called **audience studies**, or *reader-response research*. Audience studies differs from textual analysis because the subject being researched is the audience for the text, not the text itself. For example, in *Reading the Romance: Women, Patriarchy, and Popular Literature*, Janice Radway studied a group of midwestern women who were fans of romance novels. Using her training in literary criticism and employing interviews and questionnaires, Radway investigated the meaning of romance novels to the women. She argued that reading romance novels functions as personal time for some women, whose complex family and work lives leave them very little time for themselves. The study also suggested that these particular romance-novel fans identified with the active, independent qualities of the romantic heroines they most admired. As a cultural study, Radway's work did not claim to be scientific, and her findings are not generalizable to all women. Rather, Radway was interested in investigating and interpreting the relationship between reading popular fiction and ordinary life.[30]

Our Masculinity Problem

There have been at least seventy mass shootings in the United States since 1982, and nearly half of them have happened since 2006.[1] Just some of those that made headlines include the Washington Navy Yard in 2013 (13 dead, 8 injured); Sandy Hook Elementary in Newtown, Connecticut, in 2012 (28 dead, 2 injured); the movie theater in Aurora, Colorado, in 2012 (12 dead, 58 injured); and Virginia Tech in 2007 (33 dead, 23 injured).

What are the reasons? Our news media respond with a number of usual suspects: the easy availability of guns in the United States; influential movies, television shows, and video games; mental illness; bad parenting. But Jackson Katz, educator, author, and filmmaker (of *Tough Guise* and *Tough Guise 2*), sees another major factor. The least-talked-about commonality in all the shootings is the one so obvious most of us miss it: Nearly all the mass murderers are male (and usually white).

What would psychologists, pundits, and other talking heads be saying if women were responsible for nearly every mass shooting for more than three decades? "If a woman were the shooter," Katz says, "you can bet there would be all sorts of commentary about shifting cultural notions of femininity and how they might have contributed to her act, such as discussions in recent years about girl gang violence."[2]

But a woman was responsible for only one of the seventy mass shootings; all the others had a man (or men) behind the trigger. "Because men represent the dominant gender, their gender is rendered invisible in the discourse about violence," Katz says.[3] In fact, the dominance of masculinity is the norm in our mainstream mass media. Dramatic content is often about the performance of heroic, powerful masculinity (e.g., many action films, digital games, and sports). Similarly, humorous content often derives from calling into question the standards of masculinity (e.g., a man trying to cook, clean, or take care of a child). The same principles apply for the advertising that supports the content. How many automobile, beer, shaving cream, and food commercials peddle products that offer men a chance to maintain or regain their rightful masculinity?

Rachel Kalish and Michael Kimmel, sociologists at SUNY Stonybrook, analyzed the problem of mass shootings that usually end in suicide. They found that males and females have similar rates of suicide attempts. "Feeling aggrieved, wronged by the world—these are typical adolescent feelings, common to many boys and girls," they report.

The result of these attempts, though, differ by gender. Female suicide behaviors are more likely to be a cry for help. Male suicide behaviors, informed by social norms of masculinity, often result in a different outcome: "aggrieved entitlement." Kalish and Kimmel define this as "a gendered emotion, a fusion of that humiliating loss of manhood and the moral obligation and entitlement to get it back. And its gender is masculine."[4] Retaliation, which is considered acceptable in lesser forms (think of all the cultural narratives in which the weak or aggrieved character finally gets his revenge), becomes horrifying when combined with the immediacy and lethal force of assault firearms.

Elliot Rodger, the Isla Vista shooter in 2014, posted similar thoughts on a YouTube video titled "Retribution" before

Archive Photos/Getty Images

gunning down students at the University of California in Santa Barbara:

> *Tomorrow is the day of retribution, the day in which I will have my revenge. You girls have never been attracted to me. I don't know why you girls aren't attracted to me, but I will punish you all for it.*[5]

There is some evidence that the gun industry understands the sense of masculine entitlement but uses that knowledge to sell guns, not to consider how they might be misused. A marketing campaign begun in 2010 for the Bushmaster .223-caliber semiautomatic rifle showed an image of the rifle with the large tagline "Consider Your Man Card Reissued." The Bushmaster was the same civilian assault rifle used by the shooter who massacred twenty-eight people at the Newtown elementary school in 2012.

How do we find a way out of this cultural cycle? "Make gender—specifically the idea that men are gendered beings—a central part of the national conversation about rampage killings," Katz says. "It means looking carefully at how our culture defines manhood, how boys are socialized, and how pressure to stay in the 'man box' not only constrains boys' and men's emotional and relational development, but also their range of choices when faced with life crises."[6]

The Granger Collection

▲

PUBLIC SPHERE
Conversations in eighteenth-century English coffeehouses (like the one shown) inspired Jürgen Habermas's public-sphere theory. However, Habermas expressed concerns that the mass media could weaken the public sphere by allowing people to become passive consumers of the information distributed by the media instead of entering into debates with one another about what is best for society. What do you think of such concerns? Has the proliferation of political cable shows, Internet bloggers, and other mediated forums decreased serious public debate, or has it just shifted the conversation to places besides coffeehouses?

Radway's influential cultural research used a variety of interpretive methods, including literary analysis, interviews, and questionnaires. Most important, these studies helped define culture in broad terms—as being made up of both the *products* a society fashions and the *processes* that forge those products.

Political Economy Studies

A focus on the production of popular culture and the forces behind it is the topic of **political economy studies**, which specifically examine interconnections among economic interests, political power, and how that power is used. Among the major concerns of political economy studies is the increasing conglomeration of media ownership. The increasing concentration of ownership means that the production of media content is being controlled by fewer and fewer organizations, investing those companies with more and more power. In addition, the domination of public discourse by for-profit corporations may mean that the bottom line for all public communication and popular culture is money, not democratic expression.

Political economy studies work best when combined with textual analysis and audience studies, which provide context for understanding the cultural content of a media product, its production process, and how the audience responds. For example, a major media corporation may, for commercial reasons, create a film and market it through a number of venues (political economy), but the film's meaning or popularity makes sense only within the historical and narrative contexts of the culture (textual analysis), and it may be interpreted by various audiences in ways both anticipated and unexpected (audience studies).

Cultural Studies' Theoretical Perspectives

Developed as an alternative to the predictive theories of social science research (e.g., if X happens, the result will be Y), cultural studies research on media is informed by more general perspectives about how the mass media interact with the world. Two foundational concepts in cultural studies research are (1) the public sphere, and (2) the idea of communication as culture.

The Public Sphere

The idea of the **public sphere**, defined as a space for critical public debate, was first advanced by German philosopher Jürgen Habermas in 1962.[31] Habermas, a professor of philosophy, studied late-seventeenth-century and eighteenth-century England and France, and he found those societies to be increasingly influenced by free trade and the rise of the printing press. At that historical moment, an emerging middle class began to gather to discuss public life in coffeehouses, meeting halls, and pubs and to debate the ideas of novels and other publications in literary salons and clubs. In doing so, this group (which did not yet include women, peasants, the working classes, and other minority groups) began to build a society beyond the control of aristocrats, royalty, and religious elites. The outcome of such critical public debate led to support for the right to assembly, free speech, and a free press.

Habermas's research is useful to cultural studies researchers when they consider how democratic societies and the mass media operate today. For Habermas, a democratic society should always work to create the most favorable communication situation possible—a public sphere. Basically, without an open communication system, there can be no democratically functioning society. This fundamental notion is the basis for some arguments on why an open, accessible mass media system is essential. However, Habermas warned that the mass media could also be an enemy of democracy; he cautioned modern societies to beware of "the manipulative deployment of media power to procure mass loyalty, consumer demand, and 'compliance' with systematic imperatives" of those in power.[32]

Communication as Culture

As Habermas considered the relationship between communication and democracy, media historian James Carey considered the relationship between communication and culture. Carey rejected the "transmission" view of communication—that is, that a message goes simply from sender to receiver. Carey argued that communication is more of a cultural ritual; he famously defined communication as "a symbolic process whereby reality is produced, maintained, repaired, and transformed."[33] Thus communication creates our reality and maintains that reality in the stories we tell ourselves. For example, think about novels; movies; and other stories, representations, and symbols that explicitly or tacitly supported discrimination against African Americans in the United States prior to the Civil Rights movement. When events occur that question reality (like protests and sit-ins in the 1950s and 1960s), communication may repair the culture with adjusted narratives or symbols, or it may completely transform the culture with new dominant symbols. Indeed, analysis of media culture in the 1960s and afterward (including books, movies, TV, and music) suggests a U.S. culture undergoing repair and transformation.

Carey's ritual view of communication leads cultural studies researchers to consider communication's symbolic process as culture itself. Everything that defines our culture—our language, food, clothing, architecture, mass media content, and the like—is a form of symbolic communication that signifies shared (but often still-contested) beliefs about culture at a point in historical time. From this viewpoint, then, cultural studies is tightly linked with communication studies.

CULTURAL STUDIES researchers are interested in the production and meaning of a wide range of elements within communication culture, as well as audiences' responses to these. Some researchers have focused on the meaning of the recent trend of dark subject matter in young-adult novels like the *Twilight* series by Stephenie Meyer, the *Hunger Games* trilogy by Suzanne Collins, and *Wintergirls* by Laurie Halse Anderson. As such books are made into movies, researchers may also study the cultural fascination with actors who appear in them (like Jennifer Lawrence, the star of the *Hunger Games* films, shown here).

Evaluating Cultural Studies Research

In opposition to media effects research, cultural studies research involves interpreting written and visual "texts" or artifacts as symbolic representations that contain cultural, historical, and political meaning. For example, the wave of police and crime TV shows that appeared in the mid-1960s can be interpreted as a cultural response to concerns and fears people had about urban unrest and income disparity. Audiences were drawn to the heroes of these dramas, who often exerted control over forces that, among society in general, seemed out of control. Similarly, people today who participate in radio talk shows, Internet forums, and TV reality shows can be viewed, in part, as responding to their feelings of disconnection from economic success or political power. Taking part in these

Murray Close/© Lionsgate/Everett Collection

forums represents a popular culture avenue for engaging with media in ways that are usually reserved for professional actors or for the rich, famous, and powerful. As James Carey put it, the cultural approach, unlike media effects research, which is grounded in the social sciences, "does not seek to explain human behavior, but to understand it. . . . It does not attempt to predict human behavior, but to diagnose human meanings."[34] In other words, a cultural approach does not provide explanations for laws that govern how mass media behave. Rather, it offers interpretations of the stories, messages, and meanings that circulate throughout our culture.

One of the main strengths of cultural studies is the freedom it affords researchers to broadly interpret the impact of the mass media. Because cultural work is not bound by the precise control of variables, researchers can more easily examine the ties between media messages and the broader social, economic, and political world. For example, media effects research on politics has generally concentrated on election polls and voting patterns, while cultural research has broadened the discussion to examine class, gender, and cultural differences among voters and the various uses of power by individuals and institutions in authority. Following Horace Newcomb's work, cultural investigators have expanded the study of media content beyond "serious" works. They have studied many popular forms, including music, movies, and prime-time television.

Just as media effects research has its limits, so does cultural studies research. Sometimes cultural studies have focused exclusively on the meanings of media programs or texts, ignoring their effect on audiences. Some cultural studies, however, have tried to address this deficiency by incorporating audience studies. Both media effects and cultural studies researchers today have begun to look at the limitations of their work more closely, borrowing ideas from one another to better assess the complexity of the media's meaning and impact.

Media Research and Democracy

One charge frequently leveled at academic studies is that they fail to address the everyday problems of life, often seeming to have little practical application. The growth of mass media departments in colleges and universities has led to an increase in specialized jargon, which tends to alienate and exclude nonacademics. Although media research has built a growing knowledge base and dramatically advanced what we know about the effect of mass media on individuals and societies, the academic world has paid a price. That is, the larger public has often been excluded from access to the research process even though cultural research tends to identify with marginalized groups. The scholarship is self-defeating if its complexity removes it from the daily experience of the groups it addresses. Researchers themselves have even found it difficult to speak to one another across disciplines because of discipline-specific language used to analyze and report findings. For example, understanding the elaborate statistical analyses used to document media effects requires special training.

In some cultural research, the language used is often incomprehensible to students and to other audiences who use the mass media. A famous hoax in 1996 pointed out just how inaccessible some academic jargon can be. Alan Sokal, a New York University physics professor, submitted an impenetrable article, "Transgressing the Boundaries: Toward a Transformative Hermeneutics of Quantum Gravity," to a special issue of the academic journal *Social Text* devoted to science and postmodernism. As he had expected, the article—a hoax designed to point out how dense academic jargon can sometimes mask sloppy thinking—was published.

According to the journal's editor, about six reviewers had read the article but didn't suspect that it was phony. A public debate ensued after Sokal revealed his hoax. Sokal said he worries that jargon and intellectual fads cause academics to lose contact with the real world and "undermine the prospect for progressive social critique."[35]

In addition, increasing specialization in the 1970s began isolating many researchers from life outside of the university. Academics were locked away in their ivory towers, concerned with seemingly obscure matters to which the general public couldn't relate. Academics across many fields, however, began responding to this isolation and became increasingly active in political and cultural life in the 1980s and 1990s. For example, literary scholar Henry Louis Gates Jr. began writing essays for *Time* and the *New Yorker* magazines. Linguist Noam Chomsky has written for decades about excessive government and media power; he was also the subject of an award-winning documentary, *Manufacturing Consent: Noam Chomsky and the Media*. Essayist and cultural critic Barbara Ehrenreich has written often about labor and economic issues in magazines such as *Time* and the *Nation*. In her 2008 book, *This Land Is Their Land: Reports from a Divided Nation*, she investigates incidents of poverty among recent college graduates, undocumented workers, and Iraq War military families, documenting the wide divide between rich and poor. Georgetown University sociology professor Michael Eric Dyson, author of the book *April 4, 1968: Martin Luther King, Jr.'s Death and How It Changed America*, made frequent appearances on network and cable news channels during the 2008 presidential campaign to speak on the issues of race and the meaning of Barack Obama's historic candidacy. Melissa Harris-Perry, a political science professor at Tulane, writes about race, class, and politics for the *Nation* and also hosts a news and opinion show for MSNBC.

In recent years, public intellectuals have also encouraged discussion about media production in a digital world. Harvard law professor Lawrence Lessig has been a leading advocate of efforts to rewrite the nation's copyright laws to enable noncommercial "amateur culture" to flourish on the Internet. American University's Pat Aufderheide, longtime media critic for the alternative magazine *In These Times*, worked with independent filmmakers to develop the *Documentary Filmmakers' Statement of Best Practices in Fair Use*, which calls for documentary filmmakers to have reasonable access to copyrighted material for their work.

Like public journalists, public intellectuals based on campuses help carry on the conversations of society and culture, actively circulating the most important new ideas of the day and serving as models for how to participate in public life. ▶

Charles Sykes/NBC/NBCU Photo Bank via Getty Images

PUBLIC INTELLECTUALS
Melissa Harris-Perry writes about race, class, and politics for the *Nation* and also hosts a weekend news and opinion show for MSNBC. Her most recent book is *Sister Citizen: Shame, Stereotypes, and Black Women in America.*

CHAPTER REVIEW

COMMON THREADS

One of the Common Threads discussed in Chapter 1 is the commercial nature of mass media. In controversies about media content, how much of what society finds troubling in the mass media is due more to the commercial nature of the media than to any intrinsic quality of the media themselves?

For some media critics, such as former advertising executive Jerry Mander in his popular book *Four Arguments for the Elimination of Television* (1978), the problems of the mass media are inherent in the technology of the medium (e.g., the hypnotic lure of a light-emitting screen) and can't be fixed or reformed. Other researchers focus primarily on the effects of media on individual behavior.

But how much of what critics dislike about television and other mass media—including violence, indecency, immorality, inadequate journalism, and unfair representations of people and issues—derives from the way in which the mass media are organized in our culture rather than from anything about the technologies themselves or their effects on behavior? In other words, are many of the criticisms of television and other mass media merely masking what should be broader criticisms of capitalism?

One of the keys to accurately analyzing television and the other mass media is to tease apart the effects of a capitalist economy (which organizes media industries and relies on advertising, corporate underwriting, and other forms of sponsorship to profit from them) from the effects of the actual medium (television, movies, the Internet, radio, newspapers,

etc.). If our media system wasn't commercial in nature—if it wasn't controlled by large corporations—would the same "effects" exist? Would the content change? Would different kinds of movies fill theaters? Would radio play the same music? What would the news be about? Would search engines generate other results?

Basically, would society be learning other things if the mass media were organized in a noncommercial way? Would noncommercial mass media set the same kind of political agenda, or would they cultivate a different kind of reality? What would the spiral of silence theory look like in a noncommercial media system?

Perhaps noncommercial mass media would have their own problems. Indeed, there may be effects that can't be unhitched from the technology of a mass medium no matter what the economy is. But it's worth considering whether any effects are due to the economic system that brings the content to us. If we determine that the commercial nature of the media is a source of negative effects, then we should also reconsider our policy solutions for trying to deal with those effects.

KEY TERMS

The definitions for the terms listed below can be found in the glossary at the end of the book. The page numbers listed with the terms indicate where the term is highlighted in the chapter.

media effects research, 513
cultural studies, 513
propaganda analysis, 514
pseudo-polls, 515
hypodermic-needle model, 518
minimal-effects model, 519
selective exposure, 519
selective retention, 519
uses and gratifications model, 520

scientific method, 520
hypotheses, 521
experiments, 521
random assignment, 521
survey research, 521
longitudinal studies, 522
correlations, 522
content analysis, 522
social learning theory, 524

agenda-setting, 524
cultivation effect, 525
spiral of silence, 525
third-person effect, 526
textual analysis, 528
audience studies, 528
political economy studies, 530
public sphere, 530

REVIEW QUESTIONS

Early Media Research Methods

1. What were the earliest types of media studies, and why weren't they more scientific?

2. What were the major influences that led to scientific media research?

Research on Media Effects

3. What are the differences between experiments and surveys as media research strategies?

4. What is content analysis, and why is it significant?

5. What are the differences between the hypodermic-needle model and the minimal-effects model in the history of media research?

6. What are the main ideas behind social learning theory, agenda-setting, the cultivation effect, the spiral of silence, and the third-person effect?

7. What are some strengths and limitations of modern media research?

Cultural Approaches to Media Research

8. Why did cultural studies develop in opposition to media effects research?

9. What are the features of cultural studies?

10. How is textual analysis different from content analysis?

11. What are some of the strengths and limitations of cultural research?

Media Research and Democracy

12. What is a major criticism about specialization in academic research at universities?

13. How have public intellectuals contributed to society's debates about the mass media? Give examples.

QUESTIONING THE MEDIA

1. Think about instances in which the mass media have been blamed for a social problem. Could there be another, more accurate cause (an underlying variable) of that problem?

2. One charge leveled against a lot of media research—both the effects and the cultural models—is that it has very little impact on our media institutions. Do you agree or disagree, and why?

3. Do you have a major concern about media in society that hasn't been, but should be, addressed by research? Explain your answer.

4. Can you think of a media issue on which researchers from different fields at a university could team up to study together? Explain.

LAUNCHPAD FOR *MEDIA & CULTURE*

Visit LaunchPad for *Media & Culture* at macmillanhighered.com/mediaculture10e for additional learning tools:

- REVIEW WITH LEARNINGCURVE
  LearningCurve, available on LaunchPad for *Media & Culture*, uses gamelike quizzing to help you master the concepts you need to learn from this chapter.

- VIDEO: VIOLENCE IN MOVIES
  Watch a clip from a film and analyze how it treats violent subject matter.

16

Legal Controls and Freedom of Expression

539
**The Origins of Free
Expression
and a Free Press**

553
**Film and the First
Amendment**

557
**Expression in the
Media: Print,
Broadcast, and Online**

565
**The First Amendment
and Democracy**

Politicians and their constituents can talk, but money as speech speaks much louder. Aspects of our present political system amount to a legal pay-to-play system, in which the wealthiest can leverage indirect influence over elections (manipulating issues by buying lots of advertising) and more direct influence over legislation (manipulating politicians who desperately want money to pay for campaign advertising).[1] There is plenty of evidence that a majority of Americans dislike this system. For example, a national poll in 2014 found that 75 percent of Americans think "wealthy Americans have a better chance than others of influencing the election process." Another 71 percent responded that campaign contributions by individuals should be limited, and 76 percent said spending on ads by unaffiliated groups should be limited.[2] This influence has been defended on First Amendment grounds. Here is what the First Amendment (adopted in 1791) says about money as speech in political campaigns:

> Congress shall make no law respecting an establishment of religion, or prohibiting the free exercise thereof; or abridging the freedom of speech, or of the press; or the right

© Shawn Thew/epa/Corbis

of the people peaceably to assemble, and to petition the Government for a redress of grievances.

In other words, it says nothing explicitly about money. Yet money now counts as speech, protected by the First Amendment. So how did we end up here?

Ironically, it started with Congress's intention to control the amount of money in elections. In 1974, emerging from the Watergate scandal (President Nixon's illegal tactics in the 1972 election), Congress amended federal election law to further limit campaign contributions. Two years later, in *Buckley v. Valeo* (1976), the U.S. Supreme Court suggested for the first time that political contributions count as speech. The court argued that restrictions on campaign money "necessarily reduce[d] the quantity of expression by restricting the number of issues discussed, the depth of the exploration, and the size of the audience reached. This is because virtually every means of communicating ideas in today's mass society requires the expenditure of money."

Over the ensuing years, Congress has tried to again rein in campaign finance with new laws, but federal courts, beholden to the idea that money equals speech, have always struck them down. This brings us to the current state of our national elections. The two main political parties and their supporters spent an estimated $6 billion on campaign advertising for the 2012 election, more than doubling the previous record. The main reason for the new record was the unlimited amount that corporations and rich individuals could now spend, thanks to another decision by the Supreme Court, *Citizens United v. Federal Election Commission* (2010). The five-to-four decision said that it was a violation of First Amendment free-speech rights for the federal government to limit corporate or union spending for TV and radio advertising, usually done through organized Super PACs (political action committees), which are

most often sponsored by corporate interests or super-rich donors.

While the Supreme Court decision ran counter to public opinion, many advocates on the political Right and some on the Left offered that the First Amendment means what it says: "Congress shall make no law." Traditional First Amendment supporters like Gene Policinski of the First Amendment Center argue that the "good intentions" behind the idea of limiting campaign spending "don't justify ignoring a basic concept that the Supreme Court majority pointed out in its ruling: Nothing in the First Amendment provides for 'more or less' free-speech protection depending on who is speaking."[3]

An advantage in advertising spending is only one of many variables; Obama still won reelection in 2012 despite more national party, Super PAC, and campaign spending.[4] Nevertheless, those with limited means are at a clear disadvantage compared to those who have money when it comes to buying expensive commercial speech and shaping the direction of a presidential campaign. Harvard Law School professor Lawrence Lessig argues that money corrupted American politics long before the *Citizens United* ruling. "Politicians are dependent upon 'the funders'—spending anywhere from 30 percent to 70 percent of their time raising money from these funders," he wrote. "But 'the funders' are not 'the People': .26 percent of Americans give more than $200 in a congressional campaign; .05 percent give the max to any congressional candidate; .01 percent—the 1 percent of the 1 percent—give more than $10,000 in an election cycle; and .0000063 percent have given close to 80 percent of the super PAC money spent in this election so far. That's 196 Americans."[5] Given the *Citizens United* ruling, what can be done to give all citizens a voice in the campaign finance system and make them "patrons" of the political process?

Visit **LaunchPad** for *Media & Culture* and use **LearningCurve** to review concepts from this chapter.

▲ **THE CULTURAL AND POLITICAL STRUGGLES OVER WHAT CONSTITUTES FREE SPEECH** or free expression have defined American democracy. In 1989, when Supreme Court Justice William Brennan Jr. was asked to comment on his favorite part of the Constitution, he replied, "The First Amendment, I expect. Its enforcement gives us this society. The other provisions of the Constitution really only embellish it." Of all the issues that involve the mass media and popular culture, none is more central—or explosive—than freedom of expression and the First Amendment. Our nation's historical development can often be traced to how much or how little we tolerated speech during particular periods.

The current era is as volatile a time as ever for free-speech issues. Contemporary free-speech debates include copyright issues, hate-speech codes on college and university campuses, explicit lyrics in music, violent images in film and television, the swapping of media files on the Internet, and the right of the press to publish government secrets.

In this chapter, we will:

- Examine free-expression issues, focusing on the implications of the First Amendment for a variety of mass media
- Investigate the models of expression, the origins of free expression, and the First Amendment
- Examine the prohibition of censorship and how the First Amendment has been challenged and limited throughout U.S. history
- Focus on the impact of gag orders, shield laws, the use of cameras in the courtroom, and some of the clashes between the First Amendment and the Sixth Amendment
- Review the social and political pressures that gave rise to early censorship boards and the current film ratings system
- Discuss First Amendment issues in broadcasting, considering why broadcasting has been treated differently from print media
- Explore the newest frontier in free expression—the Internet

One of the most important laws relating to the media is the First Amendment (see pages 537–538 for its full text). While you've surely heard about its protections, do you know how or why it was put in place? Have you ever known someone who had to fight to express an idea— for example, was anyone in your high school ever sent home for wearing a certain T-shirt or hat that school officials deemed "offensive"? Have you ever felt that your access to some media content was restricted or censored? What were the circumstances, and how did you respond? For more questions to help you understand the role of freedom of expression in our lives, see "Questioning the Media" in the Chapter Review.

The Origins of Free Expression and a Free Press

When students from other cultures attend school in the United States, many are astounded by the number of books, news articles, editorials, cartoons, films, TV shows, and Web sites that make fun of U.S. presidents, the military, and the police. Many countries' governments throughout history have jailed, or even killed, their citizens for such speech "violations." For instance, between 1992 and September 2014, more than one thousand international journalists were killed in the line of duty, often because someone disagreed with what they wrote or reported.[6] In the United States, however, we have generally taken for granted our right to criticize and

AP Photo/John Moore

JOURNALISTS IN IRAQ
During the Iraq War, journalists
were embedded with
troops to provide "frontline"
coverage. The freedom the
U.S. press had to report on the
war came at a cost. According
to the Committee to Protect
Journalists, 249 journalists and
media workers were killed in
Iraq between 2003 and 2014
as a result of hostile actions.

poke fun at the government and other authority figures.
Moreover, many of us are unaware of the ideas that underpin our freedoms and don't realize the extent to which those
freedoms surpass those in most other countries.

In fact, a 2014 survey related that sixty-six nations allow
virtually no freedom of the press, with those governments
exercising tight control over the news media and even
intimidating, jailing, and executing journalists. Only one
in seven people on the planet live in a country with a free
media system.[7]

Models of Expression

Since the mid-1950s, four conventional models for speech
and journalism have been used to categorize the widely
differing ideas underlying free expression.[8] These models
include the authoritarian, communist, social responsibility,
and libertarian concepts. They are distinguished by the levels of freedom permitted and by the
attitudes of the ruling and political classes toward the freedoms granted to the average citizen.
Today, given the diversity among nations, the experimentation of journalists, and the collapse
of many communist press systems, these categories are no longer as relevant. Nevertheless,
they offer a good point of departure for discussing the press and democracy.

The **authoritarian model** developed at about the time the printing press first arrived in
sixteenth-century England. Its advocates held that the general public, largely illiterate in those
days, needed guidance from an elite, educated ruling class. Government criticism and public
dissent were not tolerated, especially if such speech undermined "the common good"—an
ideal that elites and rulers defined and controlled. Censorship was also frequent, and the government issued printing licenses primarily to publishers who were sympathetic to government
and ruling-class agendas.

Today, many authoritarian systems operate in developing countries throughout Asia, Latin
America, and Africa, where journalism often joins with government and business to foster economic growth, minimize political dissent, and promote social stability, because state leaders
believe that too much speech freedom would undermine the delicate stability of their nations'
social infrastructures. In these societies, criticizing government programs may be viewed as an
obstacle to keeping the peace, and both reporters and citizens may be punished if they question leaders and the status quo too fiercely.

In the authoritarian model, the news is controlled by private enterprise. But under the
communist or state model, the press is controlled by the government because state leaders
believe the press should serve the goals of the state. Although some government criticism is
tolerated under this model, ideas that challenge the basic premises of state authority are not.
Although state media systems were in decline throughout the 1990s, there are still a few countries using this model, including Myanmar (Burma), China, Cuba, and North Korea.

The **social responsibility model** characterizes the ideals of mainstream journalism in the
United States. The concepts and assumptions behind this model were outlined in 1947 by the
Hutchins Commission, which was formed to examine the increasing influence of the press.
The commission's report called for the development of press watchdog groups because the
mass media had grown too powerful and needed to become more socially responsible. Key
recommendations encouraged comprehensive news reports that put issues and events in
context; more news forums for the exchange of ideas; better coverage of society's range of
economic classes and social groups; and stronger overviews of our nation's social values,
ideals, and goals.

A socially responsible press is usually privately owned (although the government technically operates the broadcast media in most European democracies). In this model, the press functions as a **Fourth Estate**—that is, as an unofficial branch of government that monitors the legislative, judicial, and executive branches for abuses of power. In theory, private ownership keeps the news media independent of government. Thus they are better able to watch over the system on behalf of citizens. Under this model, the press supplies information to citizens so that they can make informed decisions regarding political and social issues.

Courtesy of Freedom House

The flip side of the state and authoritarian models and a more radical extension of the social responsibility model, the **libertarian model** encourages vigorous government criticism and supports the highest degree of individual and press freedoms. Under a libertarian model, no restrictions would be placed on the mass media or on individual speech. Libertarians tolerate the expression of everything, from publishing pornography to advocating anarchy. In North America and Europe, many alternative newspapers and magazines operate on such a model. Placing a great deal of trust in citizens' ability to distinguish truth from fabrication, libertarians maintain that speaking out with absolute freedom is the best way to fight injustice and arrive at the truth.

The First Amendment of the U.S. Constitution

To understand the development of free expression in the United States, we must first understand how the idea for a free press came about. In various European countries throughout the seventeenth century, in order to monitor—and punish, if necessary—the speech of editors and writers, governments controlled the circulation of ideas through the press by requiring printers to obtain licenses from them. However, in 1644, English poet John Milton, author of *Paradise Lost*, published his essay *Areopagitica*, which opposed government licenses for printers and defended a free press. Milton argued that all sorts of ideas, even false ones, should be allowed to circulate freely in a democratic society because eventually the truth would emerge. In 1695, England stopped licensing newspapers, and most of Europe followed. In many democracies today, publishing a newspaper, magazine, or newsletter remains one of the few public or service enterprises that requires no license.

Less than a hundred years later, the writers of the U.S. Constitution were ambivalent about the freedom of the press. In fact, the Constitution as originally ratified in 1788 didn't include a guarantee of freedom of the press. Constitutional framer Alexander Hamilton thought it impractical to attempt to define "liberty of the press" and believed that whatever declarations might be added to the Constitution, its security would ultimately depend on public opinion. At that time, though, nine of the original thirteen states had charters defending the freedom of the press, and the states pushed to have federal guarantees of free speech and press approved at the first session of the new Congress. The Bill of Rights, which contained the first ten amendments to the Constitution, was adopted in 1791.

The commitment to freedom of the press, however, was not resolute. In 1798, the Federalist Party, which controlled the presidency and Congress, passed the Sedition Act to silence opposition to an anticipated war against France. Led by President John Adams, the Federalists believed that defamatory articles by the opposition Democratic-Republican Party might stir up discontent against the government and undermine its authority. Over the next three years, twenty-five individuals were arrested and ten were convicted under the act, which was also used to prosecute anti-Federalist newspapers. After failing to curb opposition, the Sedition Act expired in 1801 during Thomas Jefferson's presidency. Jefferson, a Democratic-Republican who had challenged the act's constitutionality, pardoned all defendants convicted under it.[9] Ironically, the Sedition Act, the first major attempt to constrain the First Amendment, became the defining act in solidifying American support behind the notion of a free press. As journalism historian Michael Schudson explained, "Only in the wake of the Sedition Act did Americans boldly embrace a free press as a necessary bulwark of a liberal civil order."[10]

Censorship as Prior Restraint

In the United States, the First Amendment has theoretically prohibited censorship. Over time, Supreme Court decisions have defined censorship as **prior restraint**. This means that courts and governments cannot block any publication or speech before it actually occurs, on the principle that a law has not been broken until an illegal act has been committed. In 1931, for example, the Supreme Court determined in *Near v. Minnesota* that a Minneapolis newspaper could not be stopped from publishing "scandalous and defamatory" material about police and law officials whom they felt were negligent in arresting and punishing local gangsters.[11] However, the Court left open the idea that the news media could be ordered to halt publication in exceptional cases. During a declared war, for instance, if a U.S. court judged that the publication of an article would threaten national security, such expression could be restrained prior to its printing. In fact, during World War I, the U.S. Navy seized all wireless radio transmitters. This was done to ensure control over critical information about weather conditions and troop movements that might inadvertently aid the enemy. In the 1970s, though, the Pentagon Papers decision and the *Progressive* magazine case tested important concepts underlying prior restraint.

The Pentagon Papers Case

In 1971, with the Vietnam War still in progress, Daniel Ellsberg, a former Defense Department employee, stole a copy of the forty-seven-volume report *History of U.S. Decision-Making Process on Vietnam Policy*. A thorough study of U.S. involvement in Vietnam since World War II, the report was classified by the government as top secret. Ellsberg and a friend leaked the study— nicknamed the Pentagon Papers—to the *New York Times* and the *Washington Post*. In June 1971, the *Times* began publishing articles based on the study. To block any further publications, the Nixon administration applied for and received a federal court injunction against the *Times*, arguing that the publication of these documents posed "a clear and present danger" to national security.

A lower U.S. district court supported the newspaper's right to publish, but the government's appeal put the case before the Supreme Court less than three weeks after the first article was published. In a six-to-three vote, the Court sided with the newspaper. Justice Hugo Black, in his majority opinion, attacked the government's attempt to suppress publication: "Both the history and language of the First Amendment support the view that the press must

be left free to publish news, whatever the source, without censorship, injunctions, or prior restraints."[12] (See "Media Literacy and the Critical Process: Who Knows the First Amendment?" on page 544.)

The *Progressive* Magazine Case

The issue of prior restraint for national security surfaced again in 1979, when an injunction was issued to block publication of the *Progressive*, a national left-wing magazine, in which the editors planned to publish an article titled "The H-Bomb Secret: How We Got It, Why We're Telling It." The dispute began when the editor of the magazine sent a draft to the Department of Energy to verify technical portions of the article. Believing that the article contained sensitive data that might damage U.S. efforts to halt the proliferation of nuclear weapons, the Energy Department asked the magazine not to publish it. When the magazine said it would proceed anyway, the government sued the *Progressive* and asked a federal district court to block publication.

Judge Robert Warren sought to balance the *Progressive*'s First Amendment rights against the government's claim that the article would spread dangerous information and undermine national security. In an unprecedented action, Warren sided with the government, deciding that "a mistake in ruling against the United States could pave the way for thermonuclear annihilation for us all. In that event, our right to life is extinguished and the right to publish becomes moot."[13] During appeals and further litigation, several other publications, including the *Milwaukee Sentinel* and *Scientific American*, published their own articles related to the H-bomb, getting much of their information from publications already in circulation. None of these articles, including the one eventually published in the *Progressive*—after the government dropped the case during an appeal—contained the precise technical details needed to actually design a nuclear weapon, nor did they provide information on where to obtain the sensitive ingredients.

Even though the article was eventually published, Warren's decision stands as the first time in American history that a prior-restraint order imposed in the name of national security actually stopped the initial publication of a controversial news report.

Unprotected Forms of Expression

Despite the First Amendment's provision that "Congress shall make no law" restricting speech, the federal government has made a number of laws that do just that, especially concerning false or misleading advertising, expressions that intentionally threaten public safety, and certain speech that compromises war strategy and other issues of national security.

PRIOR RESTRAINT
In 1971, Daniel Ellsberg surrendered to government prosecutors in Boston. Ellsberg was a former Pentagon researcher who turned against America's military policy in Vietnam and leaked information to the press. He was charged with unauthorized possession of top-secret federal documents. Later called the Pentagon Papers, the documents contained evidence on the military's bungled handling of the Vietnam War. In 1973, an exasperated federal judge dismissed the case when illegal government-sponsored wiretaps of Ellsberg's psychoanalyst came to light during the Watergate scandal.

Media Literacy and the Critical Process

1 DESCRIPTION. Working alone or in small groups, find eight to ten people you know from two different age groups: (1) from your peers and friends or younger siblings, and (2) from your parents' or grandparents' generations. (Do not choose students from your class.) Interview your subjects individually, in person, by phone, or by e-mail, and ask them this question: If Congress were considering the following law—then offer the First Amendment (see pages 537–538), but don't tell them what it is—would they approve? Then ask them to respond to the following series of questions, adding any other questions that you think would be appropriate:

1. Do you agree or disagree with the freedoms? Explain.
2. Which do you support, and which do you think are excessive or provide too much freedom?
3. Ask them if they recognize the law. Note how many identify it as the First Amendment to the U.S. Constitution and how many do not. Note the percentage from each age group.

Who Knows the First Amendment?

Enacted in 1791, the First Amendment supports not just press and speech freedoms but also religious freedom and the right of people to protest and to "petition the government for a redress of grievances." It also says that "Congress shall make no law" abridging or prohibiting these five freedoms. To investigate some critics' charge that many citizens don't exactly know the protections offered in the First Amendment, conduct your own survey. Discuss with friends, family, or colleagues what they know or think about the First Amendment.

4. Optional: Ask if your respondents are willing to share their political leanings—Republican, Democrat, Independent, not sure, disaffected, apathetic, or other. Record their answers.

2 ANALYSIS. What patterns emerge in the answers from the two groups? Are their answers similar or different? How? Note any differences in the answers based on gender, level of education, or occupation.

3 INTERPRETATION. What do these patterns mean? Are your interview subjects supportive or unsupportive of the First Amendment? What are their reasons?

4 EVALUATION. How do your interviewees judge the freedoms? In general, what did your interview subjects know about the First Amendment? What impresses you about your subjects' answers? Do you find anything alarming or troubling in their answers?

5 ENGAGEMENT. Research free expression and locate any national studies that are similar to this assignment. Then, check the recent national surveys on attitudes toward the First Amendment at www.newseuminstitute.org/first-amendment-center. Based on your research, educate others. Do a presentation in class or at your college or university about the First Amendment.

Beyond the federal government, state laws and local ordinances have on occasion curbed expression, and over the years the court system has determined that some kinds of expression do not merit protection under the Constitution, including seditious expression, copyright infringement, libel, obscenity, the right to privacy, and expression that interferes with the Sixth Amendment.

Seditious Expression

For more than a century after the Sedition Act of 1798, Congress passed no laws prohibiting dissenting opinion. But by the twentieth century, the sentiments of the Sedition Act reappeared in times of war. For instance, the Espionage Acts of 1917 and 1918, which were enforced during World Wars I and II, made it a federal crime to disrupt the nation's war effort, authorizing severe punishment for seditious statements.

In the landmark *Schenck v. United States* (1919) appeal case during World War I, the Supreme Court upheld the conviction of a Socialist Party leader, Charles T. Schenck, for distributing leaflets urging American men to protest the draft, in violation of the recently passed Espionage Act. In upholding the conviction, Justice Oliver Wendell Holmes wrote two of the more famous interpretations and phrases in the First Amendment's legal history:

But the character of every act depends upon the circumstances in which it is done. The most stringent protection of free speech would not protect a man in falsely shouting fire in a theater and causing a panic.

The question in every case is whether the words used are used in such circumstances and are of such a nature as to create a clear and present danger that they will bring about the substantive evils that Congress has a right to prevent.

In supporting Schenck's sentence—a ten-year prison term—Holmes noted that the Socialist leaflets were entitled to First Amendment protection, but only during times of peace. In establishing the "clear and present danger" criterion for expression, the Supreme Court demonstrated the limits of the First Amendment.

And in 2010, after WikiLeaks released thousands of confidential U.S. embassy cables into the public domain, the U.S. Justice Department contemplated charging the Web site's founder, Julian Assange, with violating the 1917 Espionage Act. In June 2012, Assange took refuge inside the Ecuadorian embassy in London, where he was granted diplomatic asylum. The U.S. government instead pursued Espionage Act charges against Private First Class Bradley (now Chelsea) Manning, an intelligence analyst in Iraq, who admitted to releasing the information to WikiLeaks to show the flaws of U.S. strategies in Iraq and Afghanistan. Manning was convicted and sentenced to thirty-five years in prison in August 2013.

Copyright Infringement

Appropriating a writer's or an artist's words or music without consent or payment is also a form of expression that is not protected as speech. A **copyright** legally protects the rights of authors and producers to their published or unpublished writing, music, lyrics, TV programs, movies, or graphic art designs. When Congress passed the first Copyright Act in 1790, it gave authors the right to control their published works for fourteen years, with the opportunity for a renewal for another fourteen years. After the end of the copyright period, the work enters the **public domain**, which gives the public free access to the work. The idea was that a period of copyright control would give authors financial incentive to create original works, and that the public domain gives others incentive to create derivative works.

Over the years, as artists lived longer and, more important, as corporate copyright owners became more common, copyright periods were extended by Congress. In 1976, Congress extended the copyright period to the life of the author plus fifty years, or seventy-five years for a corporate copyright owner. In 1998 (as copyrights on works such as Disney's Mickey Mouse were set to expire), Congress again extended the copyright period for twenty additional years—the eleventh time in forty years that the terms for copyright had been extended.[14] As Timothy B. Lee of the *Washington Post* points out, "The big question now is whether incumbent copyright holders will try to get yet another extension of copyright terms before works begin falling into the public domain again on January 1, 2019."[15] (See "Examining Ethics: A Generation of Copyright Criminals?" on page 564.)

Corporate owners have millions of dollars to gain by keeping their properties

Camera Press/Richard Stonehouse/Redux Pictures

THE LIMITS OF COPYRIGHT
The iconic album art for the Velvet Underground's 1967 debut, a banana print designed by artist Andy Warhol, has been a subject of controversy in recent years, as a copyright dispute between the Andy Warhol Foundation for the Visual Arts and the rock band has continued to flourish. The most recent disagreement occurred when the Warhol Foundation, which had previously accused the Velvet Underground of violating its claim to the print, announced plans to license the banana design for iPhone cases. Accusing the foundation of copyright violation, the band filed a copyright claim to the design, which a federal judge later dismissed.

out of the public domain. Disney, a major lobbyist for the 1998 extension, would have lost its copyright to Mickey Mouse in 2004 but now continues to earn millions on its movies, T-shirts, and Mickey Mouse watches through 2024. Warner/Chappell Music, which owns the copyright to the popular "Happy Birthday to You" song, will keep generating money on the song at least through 2030, and even longer if corporations successfully pressure Congress for another extension.

Today, nearly every innovation in digital culture creates new questions about copyright law. For example, is a video mash-up that samples copyrighted sounds and images a copyright violation or a creative accomplishment protected under the concept of *fair use* (the same standard that enables students to legally quote attributed text from other works in their research papers)? Is it fair use for a blog to quote an entire newspaper article as long as it has a link and an attribution? Should news aggregators like Google News and Yahoo! News pay something to financially strapped newspapers when they link to their articles? One of the laws that tips the debates toward stricter enforcement of copyright is the Digital Millennium Copyright Act of 1998, which outlaws any action or technology that circumvents copyright protection systems. In other words, it may be illegal to merely create or distribute technology that enables someone to make illegal copies of digital content, such as a music file or a DVD.

Libel

The biggest legal worry that haunts editors and publishers is the issue of libel, a form of expression that, unlike political expression, is not protected as free speech under the First Amendment. **Libel** refers to defamation of character in written or broadcast form; libel is different from **slander**, which is spoken language that defames a person's character. Inherited from British common law, libel is generally defined as a false statement that holds a person up to public ridicule, contempt, or hatred or injures a person's business or occupation. Examples of libelous statements include falsely accusing someone of professional dishonesty or incompetence (such as medical malpractice), falsely accusing a person of a crime (such as drug dealing), falsely stating that someone is mentally ill or engages in unacceptable behavior (such as public drunkenness), or falsely accusing a person of associating with a disreputable organization or cause (such as the Mafia or a neo-Nazi military group).

Since 1964, the *New York Times v. Sullivan* case has served as the standard for libel law. The case stems from a 1960 full-page advertisement placed in the *New York Times* by the Committee to Defend Martin Luther King and the Struggle for Freedom in the South.

LIBEL AND THE MEDIA
The 1960 *New York Times* advertisement that triggered one of the most influential and important libel cases in U.S. history criticized law-enforcement tactics used against Martin Luther King and the Civil Rights movement. The behind-the-scenes machinations of King's later Alabama demonstrations are the subject of the recent film *Selma*.

Howard Sochurek/The LIFE Picture Collection/Getty Images

Without naming names, the ad criticized the law-enforcement tactics used in southern cities—including Montgomery, Alabama—to break up Civil Rights demonstrations. The ad condemned "southern violators of the Constitution" bent on destroying King and the movement. Taking exception, the city commissioner of Montgomery, L. B. Sullivan, sued the *Times* for libel, claiming the ad defamed him indirectly. Although Alabama civil courts awarded Sullivan $500,000, the newspaper's lawyers appealed to the Supreme Court, which unanimously reversed the ruling, holding that Alabama libel law violated the *Times*' First Amendment rights.[16]

As part of the *Sullivan* decision, the Supreme Court asked future civil courts to distinguish whether plaintiffs in libel cases are public officials or private individuals. Citizens with more "ordinary" jobs, such as city sanitation employees, undercover police informants, nurses, or unknown actors, are normally classified as private individuals. Private individuals have to prove (1) that the public statement about them was false, (2) that damages or actual injury occurred (such as the loss of a job, harm to reputation, public humiliation, or mental anguish), and (3) that the publisher or broadcaster was negligent in failing to determine the truthfulness of the statement.

There are two categories of public figures: (1) public celebrities (movie or sports stars) or people who "occupy positions of such pervasive power and influence that they are deemed public figures for all purposes" (presidents, senators, mayors), and (2) individuals who have thrown themselves—usually voluntarily but sometimes involuntarily—into the middle of "a significant public controversy," such as a lawyer defending a prominent client, an advocate for an antismoking ordinance, or a labor union activist.

Public officials also have to prove falsehood, damages, negligence, and **actual malice** on the part of the news medium; actual malice means that the reporter or editor knew the statement was false and printed or broadcast it anyway, or acted with a reckless disregard for the truth. Because actual malice against a public official is hard to prove, it is difficult for public figures to win libel suits. The *Sullivan* decision allowed news operations to aggressively pursue legitimate news stories without fear of continuous litigation. However, the mere threat of a libel suit still scares off many in the news media. Plaintiffs may also belong to one of many vague classification categories, such as public high school teachers, police officers, and court-appointed attorneys. Individuals from these professions end up as public or private citizens depending on a particular court's ruling.

Defenses against Libel Charges

Since the 1730s, the best defense against libel in American courts has been the truth. In most cases, if libel defendants can demonstrate that they printed or broadcast statements that were essentially true, such evidence usually bars plaintiffs from recovering any damages—even if their reputations were harmed.

In addition, there are other defenses against libel. Prosecutors, for example, who would otherwise be vulnerable to being accused of libel are granted *absolute privilege* in a court of law so that they are not prevented from making accusatory statements toward defendants. The reporters who print or broadcast statements made in court are also protected against libel; they are granted conditional or **qualified privilege**, allowing them to report judicial or legislative proceedings even though the public statements being reported may be libelous.

Another defense against libel is the rule of **opinion and fair comment**. Generally, libel applies only to intentional misstatements of factual information rather than opinion, and therefore opinions are protected from libel. However, because the line between fact and opinion is often hazy, lawyers advise journalists first to set forth the facts on which a viewpoint is based and then to state their opinion based on those facts. In other words, journalists should make it clear that a statement of opinion is a criticism and not an allegation of fact.

AP Photo/BH

LIBEL AND OBSCENITY
Prior to his 1984 libel trial, *Hustler* magazine publisher Larry Flynt was also convicted of pandering obscenity. Here, Flynt answers questions from newsmen on February 9, 1977, as he is led to jail.

One of the most famous tests of opinion and fair comment occurred in 1983, when Larry Flynt, publisher of *Hustler* magazine, published a spoof of a Campari advertisement depicting conservative minister and political activist Jerry Falwell as a drunk and as having had sexual relations with his mother. In fine print at the bottom of the page, a disclaimer read: "Ad parody—not to be taken seriously." Often a target of Flynt's irreverence and questionable taste, Falwell sued for libel, asking for $45 million in damages. In the verdict, the jury rejected the libel suit but found that Flynt had intentionally caused Falwell emotional distress, awarding Falwell $200,000. The case drew enormous media attention and raised concerns about the erosion of the media's right to free speech. However, Flynt's lawyers appealed, and in 1988 the Supreme Court unanimously overturned the verdict. Although the Court did not condone the *Hustler* spoof, the justices did say that the magazine was entitled to constitutional protection. In affirming *Hustler*'s speech rights, the Court suggested that even though parodies and insults of public figures might indeed cause emotional pain, denying the right to publish them and awarding damages for emotional reasons would violate the spirit of the First Amendment.[17]

Libel laws also protect satire, comedy, and opinions expressed in reviews of books, plays, movies, and restaurants. Such laws may not, however, protect malicious statements in which plaintiffs can prove that defendants used their free-speech rights to mount a damaging personal attack.

Obscenity

For most of this nation's history, legislators have argued that **obscenity** does not constitute a legitimate form of expression protected by the First Amendment. The problem, however, is that little agreement has existed on how to define an obscene work. In the 1860s, a court could judge an entire book obscene if it contained a single passage believed capable of "corrupting" a person. In fact, throughout the nineteenth century, certain government authorities outside the courts—especially U.S. post office and customs officials—held the power to censor or destroy material they deemed obscene.

This began to change in the 1930s, during the trial involving the celebrated novel *Ulysses* by Irish writer James Joyce. Portions of *Ulysses* had been serialized in the early 1920s in an

American magazine, *Little Review*, copies of which were later seized and burned by postal officials. The publishers of the magazine were fined $50 and nearly sent to prison. Because of the four-letter words contained in the novel and the book-burning and fining incidents, British and American publishing houses backed away from the book, and in 1928, the U.S. Customs Office officially banned *Ulysses* as an obscene work. Ultimately, however, Random House agreed to publish the work in the United States if it was declared "legal." Finally, in 1933, a U.S. judge ruled that an important literary work such as *Ulysses* was a legitimate, protected form of expression, even if portions of the book were deemed objectionable by segments of the population.

In a landmark 1957 case, *Roth v. United States*, the Supreme Court offered this test of obscenity: whether to an "average person," applying "contemporary standards," the major thrust or theme of the material "taken as a whole" appealed to "prurient interest" (in other words, was intended to "incite lust"). By the 1960s, based on *Roth*, expression was not obscene if only a small part of the work lacked "redeeming social value."

The current legal definition of obscenity derives from the 1973 *Miller v. California* case, which stated that to qualify as obscenity, the material must meet three criteria: (1) the average person, applying contemporary community standards, would find that the material as a whole appeals to prurient interest; (2) the material depicts or describes sexual conduct in a patently offensive way; and (3) the material, as a whole, lacks serious literary, artistic, political, or scientific value. The *Miller* decision contained two important ideas not present in *Roth*. First, it acknowledged that different communities and regions of the country have different values and standards with which to judge obscenity. Second, it required that a work be judged *as a whole*, so that publishers could not use the loophole of inserting a political essay or literary poem into pornographic materials to demonstrate in court that their publications contained redeeming features.

Since the *Miller* decision, courts have granted great latitude to printed and visual obscenity. By the 1990s, major prosecutions had become rare—aimed mostly at child pornography—as the legal system accepted the concept that a free and democratic society must tolerate even repulsive kinds of speech. Most battles over obscenity are now online, where the global reach of the Internet has eclipsed the concept of community standards. A new complication in defining pornography has emerged with cases of "sexting," in which minors produce and send sexually graphic images of themselves via cell phones or the Internet (see "Case Study: Is 'Sexting' Pornography?" on page 550).

The Right to Privacy

Whereas libel laws safeguard a person's character and reputation, the right to privacy protects an individual's peace of mind and personal feelings. In the simplest terms, the **right to privacy** addresses a person's right to be left alone, without his or her name, image, or daily activities becoming public property. Invasions of privacy occur in different situations, the most common of which are intrusion into someone's personal space via unauthorized tape recording, photographing, wiretapping, and the like; making available to the public personal records, such as health and phone records; disclosing personal information, such as religion, sexual activities, or personal

PAPARAZZI
Prince William and Catherine, Duchess of Cambridge, have been an object of ongoing fascination since marrying in 2011. The media frenzy surrounding the royal couple came to a head when the French tabloid *Closer* published images of what appears to be the Duchess sunbathing topless while on vacation, prompting the royal family to press criminal charges against the publication. A greater frenzy accompanied the birth of the couple's first child in 2013. The British royal family is sadly all too familiar with the paparazzi; Prince William's mother, Diana, Princess of Wales, died in a car accident after being chased by paparazzi in 1997.

Vincent Thian/AFP/Getty Images

Is "Sexting" Pornography?

According to U.S. federal and state laws, when someone produces, transmits, or possesses images with graphic sexual depictions of minors, it is considered child pornography. Digital media have made the circulation of child pornography even more pervasive, according to a 2006 study on child pornography on the Internet. About one thousand people are arrested each year in the United States for child pornography, and according to a U.S. Department of Justice guide for police, they have few distinguishing characteristics other than being "likely to be white, male, and between the ages of 26 and 40."[1]

Now, a social practice has challenged the common wisdom of what is obscenity and who are child pornographers: What happens when the people who produce, transmit, and possess images with graphic sexual depictions of minors are minors themselves?

The practice in question is "sexting," the sending or receiving of sexual images via mobile phone text messages or via the Internet. Sexting occupies a gray area of obscenity law—yes, these are images of minors; but no, they don't fit the intent of child pornography laws, which are designed to stop the exploitation of children by adults.

While such messages are usually meant to be completely personal, technology makes it otherwise. "All control over the image is lost—it can be forwarded repeatedly all over the school, town, state, country and world," says Steven M. Dettelbach, U.S. attorney for the Northern District of Ohio.[2] And given the endless archives of the Internet, such images never really go away but can be accessed by anyone with enough skills to find them.

A recent national survey found that 15 percent of teens ages twelve to seventeen say they have received sexually suggestive nude or nearly nude images of someone they know via text messaging. Another 4 percent of teens ages twelve to seventeen say they have sent sexually suggestive nude or nearly nude images of themselves via text messaging. The rates are even higher for teens at age seventeen—8 percent have sent such images, and 30 percent have received them.[3]

Some recent cases illustrate how young people engaging in sexting have gotten caught up in a legal system designed to punish pedophiles. In 2008, Florida resident Phillip Alpert, then eighteen, sent nude images of his sixteen-year-old girlfriend to friends after they got in an argument. He was convicted of child pornography and is required to be registered as a sex offender for the next twenty-five years. In Iowa, eighteen-year-old Jorge Canal Jr. was also convicted as a sex offender after sending a photo of his genitals to a fourteen-year-old girl—a friend who asked him to send the photo as a joke. Her parents found the photo and pressed charges. In 2009, three Pennsylvania girls took seminude pictures of themselves and sent the photos to three boys. All six minors were charged with child pornography. A judge later halted the charges in the interest of freedom of speech and parental rights. In all these cases, and others like them, technology and social trends challenged the status quo beliefs on obscenity laws and the media. The problem of texting potentially embarrassing photos can be solved technologically with Snapchat, an app introduced in 2011 that enables users to send photos that self-destruct in a few seconds. (More recently, however, a forensics company figured out how to resurrect Snapchat photos.) In the legal realm, by 2014 at least twenty states enacted legislation on sexting, often amending laws so that teens involved in sexting are treated with misdemeanor charges rather than being subject to harsher felony laws against child pornography. How do you think sexting should be handled by the law?

Rana Faure/Aurora Photos

activities; and unauthorized appropriation of someone's image or name for advertising or other commercial purposes. In general, the news media have been granted wide protections under the First Amendment to do their work. For instance, the names and pictures of both private individuals and public figures can usually be used without their consent in most news stories. Additionally, if private citizens become part of public controversies and subsequent news stories, the courts have usually allowed the news media to treat them like public figures (that is, to record their quotes and use their images without the individuals' permission). The courts have even ruled that accurate reports of criminal and court records, including the identification of rape victims, do not normally constitute privacy invasions. Nevertheless, most newspapers and broadcast outlets use their own internal guidelines and ethical codes to protect the privacy of victims and defendants, especially in cases involving rape and child abuse.

Public figures, however, have received some legal relief, as many local municipalities and states have passed "anti-paparazzi" laws that protect individuals from unwarranted scrutiny and surveillance of personal activities on private property or outside public forums. Some courts have ruled that photographers must keep a certain distance from celebrities, although powerful zoom lens technology usually overcomes this obstacle. However, every year brings a few stories of a Hollywood actor or sports figure punching a tabloid photographer or TV cameraman who got too close. And in 2004, the Supreme Court ruled—as an exception to the Freedom of Information Act—that families of prominent figures who have died have the right to object to the release of autopsy photos, so that the images are not exploited.

A number of laws also protect the privacy of regular citizens. For example, the Privacy Act of 1974 protects individuals' records from public disclosure unless individuals give written consent. The Electronic Communications Privacy Act of 1986 extended the law to computer-stored data and the Internet, although subsequent court decisions ruled that employees have no privacy rights in electronic communications conducted on their employer's equipment. The USA PATRIOT Act of 2001, however, weakened the earlier laws and gave the federal government more latitude in searching private citizens' records and intercepting electronic communications without a court order.

First Amendment versus Sixth Amendment

Over the years, First Amendment protections of speech and the press have often clashed with the Sixth Amendment, which guarantees an accused individual in "all criminal prosecutions . . . the right to a speedy and public trial, by an impartial jury." In 1954, for example, the Sam Sheppard case garnered enormous nationwide publicity and became the inspiration for the TV show and film *The Fugitive*. Featuring lurid details about the murder of Sheppard's wife, the press editorialized in favor of Sheppard's quick arrest; some papers even pronounced him guilty. A prominent and wealthy osteopath, Sheppard was convicted of the murder, but twelve years later Sheppard's new lawyer, F. Lee Bailey, argued before the Supreme Court that his client had not received a fair trial because of prejudicial publicity in the press. The Court overturned the conviction and freed Sheppard.

Gag Orders and Shield Laws

A major criticism of recent criminal cases concerns the ways in which lawyers use the news media to comment publicly on cases that are pending or are in trial. After the Sheppard reversal in the 1960s, the Supreme Court introduced safeguards that judges could employ to ensure fair trials in heavily publicized cases. These included sequestering juries (Sheppard's jury was not sequestered); moving cases to other jurisdictions; limiting the number of reporters; and placing restrictions, or **gag orders**, on lawyers and witnesses. In some countries, courts have issued gag orders to prohibit the press from releasing information or giving commentary that might prejudice jury selection or cause an unfair trial. In the United States, however, especially since a Supreme Court review in 1976, gag orders have been struck down as a prior-restraint violation of the First Amendment.

In opposition to gag orders, **shield laws** have favored the First Amendment rights of reporters, protecting them from having to reveal their sources for controversial information used in news stories. The news media have argued that protecting the confidentiality of key sources maintains a reporter's credibility, protects a source from possible retaliation, and serves the public interest by providing information that citizens might not otherwise receive. In the 1960s, when the First Amendment rights of reporters clashed with Sixth Amendment fair-trial concerns, judges usually favored the Sixth Amendment arguments. In 1972, a New Jersey journalist became the first reporter jailed for contempt of court for refusing to identify sources in a probe of the Newark housing authority. Since that case, forty states and the District of Columbia have adopted some type of shield law, and other states (except Wyoming) have established some shield law protection through legal precedent. There is no federal shield law in the United States, leaving journalists exposed to subpoenas from federal prosecutors and courts. Revelations that the U.S. Department of Justice had obtained phone records of the Associated Press renewed calls for a federal shield law in 2013.

Cameras in the Courtroom

The debates over limiting intrusive electronic broadcast equipment and photographers in the courtroom actually date to the sensationalized coverage of the Bruno Hauptmann trial in the mid-1930s. Hauptmann was convicted and executed for the kidnap-murder of the nineteen-month-old son of Anne and Charles Lindbergh (the aviation hero who made the first solo flight across the Atlantic Ocean in 1927). During the trial, Hauptmann and his attorney complained that the circus atmosphere fueled by the presence of radio and flash cameras prejudiced the jury and turned the public against him.

After the trial, the American Bar Association amended its professional ethics code, Canon 35, stating that electronic equipment in the courtroom detracted "from the essential dignity of the proceedings." Calling for a ban on photographers and radio equipment, the association believed that if such elements were not banned, lawyers would begin playing to audiences and negatively alter the judicial process. For years after the Hauptmann trial, almost every state banned photographic, radio, and TV equipment from courtrooms.

As broadcast equipment became more portable and less obtrusive, however, and as television became the major news source for most Americans, courts gradually reevaluated their bans on broadcast equipment. In fact, in the early 1980s, the Supreme Court ruled that the presence of TV equipment did not make it impossible for a fair trial to occur, leaving it up to each state to implement its own system. The ruling opened the door for the debut of Court TV (now truTV) in 1991 and the televised O.J. Simpson trial of 1994 (the most publicized case in history). All states today allow television coverage of cases, although most states place certain restrictions on coverage of courtrooms, often leaving it up to the discretion of the presiding judge. While U.S. federal courts now allow limited TV coverage of their trials, the Supreme Court continues to ban TV from its proceedings, but in 2000 the Court broke its anti-radio rule by permitting delayed radio broadcasts of the hearings on the Florida vote recount case that determined the winner of the 2000 presidential election.

As libel law and the growing acceptance of courtroom cameras indicate, the legal process has generally, though not always, tried to ensure that print and other news media are able to cover public issues broadly, without fear of reprisals.

AP Images

Film and the First Amendment

When the First Amendment was ratified in 1791, even the most enlightened leaders of our nation could not have predicted the coming of visual media such as film and television. Consequently, new communication technologies have not always received the same kinds of protection under the First Amendment as those granted to speech or print media, including newspapers, magazines, and books. Movies, in existence since the late 1890s, only earned legal speech protection after a 1952 Supreme Court decision. Prior to that, social and political pressures led to both censorship and self-censorship in the movie industry.

Social and Political Pressures on the Movies

During the early part of the twentieth century, movies rose in popularity among European immigrants and others from modest socioeconomic groups. This, in turn, spurred the formation of censorship groups, which believed that the movies would undermine morality. During this time, according to media historian Douglas Gomery, criticism of movies converged on four areas: "the effects on children, the potential health problems, the negative influences on morals and manners, and the lack of a proper role for educational and religious institutions in the development of movies."[18]

Public pressure on movies came both from conservatives, who saw them as a potential threat to the authority of traditional institutions, and from progressives, who worried that children and adults were more attracted to movie houses than to social organizations and urban education centers. As a result, civic leaders publicly escalated their pressure, organizing local *review boards* that screened movies for their communities. In 1907, the Chicago City Council created an ordinance that gave the police authority to issue permits for the exhibition of movies. By 1920, more than ninety cities in the United States had some type of movie censorship board made up of vice squad officers, politicians, and citizens. By 1923, twenty-two states had established such boards.

Meanwhile, social pressure began to translate into law as politicians, wanting to please their constituencies, began to legislate against films. Support mounted for a federal censorship bill. When Jack Johnson won the heavyweight championship in 1908, boxing films became the target of the first federal censorship law aimed at the motion-picture industry. In 1912, the government outlawed the transportation of boxing movies across state lines. The laws against boxing films, however, had more to do with Johnson's race than with concern over violence in movies. The first black heavyweight champion, he was perceived as a threat to some in the white community.

The first Supreme Court decision regarding film's protection under the First Amendment was handed down in 1915 and went against the movie industry. In *Mutual v. Ohio*, the Mutual Film Company of Detroit sued the state of Ohio, whose review board had censored a number of the distributor's films. On appeal, the case arrived at the Supreme Court, which unanimously ruled that motion pictures were not a form of speech but "a business pure and simple" and, like a circus, merely a "spectacle" for entertainment with "a special capacity for evil." This ruling would stand as a precedent for thirty-seven years, although a movement to create a national censorship board failed.

Self-Regulation in the Movie Industry

As the film industry expanded after World War I, the impact of public pressure and review boards began to affect movie studios and executives who wanted to ensure control over their economic well-being. In the early 1920s, a series of scandals rocked Hollywood: actress Mary

CENSORSHIP
A native of Galveston, Texas, Jack Johnson (1878–1946) was the first black heavyweight boxing champion, from 1908 to 1914. His stunning victory over white champion Jim Jeffries (who had earlier refused to fight black boxers) in 1910 resulted in race riots across the country and led to a ban on the interstate transportation of boxing films. A 2005 Ken Burns documentary, *Unforgivable Blackness*, chronicles Johnson's life.

© Bettmann/Corbis

Pickford's divorce and quick marriage to actor Douglas Fairbanks; director William Desmond Taylor's unsolved murder; and actor Wallace Reid's death from a drug overdose. But the most sensational scandal involved aspiring actress Virginia Rappe, who died a few days after a wild party in a San Francisco hotel hosted by popular silent-film comedian Fatty Arbuckle. After Rappe's death, the comedian was indicted for rape and manslaughter, in a case that was sensationalized in the press. Although two hung juries could not reach a verdict, Arbuckle's career was ruined. Censorship boards across the country banned his films. Even though he was acquitted at his third trial in 1922, the movie industry tried to send a signal about the kinds of values and lifestyles it would tolerate: Arbuckle was banned from acting in Hollywood. He later resurfaced to direct several films under the name Will B. Goode.

In response to the scandals, particularly the first Arbuckle trial, the movie industry formed the Motion Picture Producers and Distributors of America (MPPDA) and hired as its president Will Hays, a former Republican National Committee chair. Also known as the Hays Office, the MPPDA attempted to smooth out problems between the public and the industry. Hays blacklisted promising actors or movie extras with even minor police records. He also developed an MPPDA public relations division, which stopped a national movement for a federal law censoring movies.

The Motion Picture Production Code

During the 1930s, the movie business faced a new round of challenges. First, various conservative and religious groups—including the influential Catholic Legion of Decency—increased their scrutiny of the industry. Second, deteriorating economic conditions during the Great Depression forced the industry to tighten self-regulation in order to maintain profits and keep harmful public pressure at bay. In 1927, the Hays Office had developed a list of "Don'ts and Be Carefuls" to steer producers and directors away from questionable sexual, moral, and social themes. Nevertheless, pressure for a more formal and sweeping code mounted. As a result, in the early 1930s the Hays Office established the Motion Picture Production Code, whose overseers were charged with officially stamping Hollywood films with a moral seal of approval.

The Code laid out its mission in its first general principle: "No picture shall be produced which will lower the moral standards of those who see it. Hence the sympathy of the audience shall never be thrown to the side of crime, wrong-doing, evil or sin." The Code dictated how producers and directors should handle "methods of crime," "repellent subjects," and "sex hygiene." A section on profanity outlawed a long list of phrases and topics, including "toilet gags" and "traveling salesmen and farmer's daughter jokes." Under "scenes of passion," the Code dictated that "excessive and lustful kissing, lustful embraces, suggestive postures and gestures are not to be shown," and it required that "passion should be treated in such a manner as not to stimulate the lower and baser emotions." The section on religion revealed the influences of a Jesuit priest and a Catholic publisher, who helped write the Code: "No film or episode may throw ridicule on any religious faith," and "ministers of religion . . . should not be used as comic characters or as villains."

Adopted by 95 percent of the industry, the Code influenced nearly every commercial movie made between the mid-1930s and the early 1950s. It also gave the industry a relative degree of freedom, enabling the major studios to remain independent of outside regulation. When television arrived, however, competition from the new family medium forced movie producers to explore more adult subjects.

The *Miracle* Case

In 1952, the Supreme Court heard the *Miracle* case—officially *Burstyn v. Wilson*—named after Roberto Rossellini's film *Il Miracolo* (*The Miracle*). The movie's distributor sued the head of the

New York Film Licensing Board for banning the film. A few New York City religious and political leaders considered the 1948 Italian film sacrilegious and pressured the film board for the ban. In the film, an unmarried peasant girl is impregnated by a scheming vagrant who tells her that he is St. Joseph and she has conceived the baby Jesus. The importers of the film argued that censoring it constituted illegal prior restraint under the First Amendment. Because such an action could not be imposed on a print version of the same story, the film's distributor argued that the same freedom should apply to the film. The Supreme Court agreed, declaring movies "a significant medium for the communication of ideas." The decision granted films the same constitutional protections as those enjoyed by the print media and other forms of speech. Even more important, the decision rendered most activities of film review boards unconstitutional because these boards had been engaged in prior restraint. Although a few local boards survived into the 1990s to handle complaints about obscenity, most of them had disbanded by the early 1970s.

The MPAA Ratings System

The current voluntary movie rating system—the model for the advisory labels for music, television, and video games—developed in the late 1960s after discontent again mounted over movie content, spurred on by such films as 1965's *The Pawnbroker*, which contained brief female nudity, and 1966's *Who's Afraid of Virginia Woolf?*, which featured a level of profanity and sexual frankness that had not been seen before in a major studio film. In 1966, the movie industry hired Jack Valenti to run the MPAA (the Motion Picture Association of America, formerly the MPPDA), and in 1968 he established an industry board to rate movies. Eventually, G, PG, R, and X ratings emerged as guideposts for the suitability of films for various age groups. In 1984, prompted by the releases of *Gremlins* and *Indiana Jones and the Temple of Doom*, the MPAA added the PG–13 rating and sandwiched it between PG and R to distinguish slightly higher levels of violence or adult themes in movies that might otherwise qualify as PG-rated films (see Table 16.1).

The MPAA copyrighted all ratings designations as trademarks except for the X rating, which was gradually appropriated as a promotional tool by the pornographic film industry. In fact, between 1972 and 1989, the MPAA stopped issuing the X rating. In 1990, however, based on protests from filmmakers over movies with adult sexual themes that they did not consider pornographic, the industry copyrighted the NC–17 rating—no children age seventeen or under. In 1995, *Showgirls* became the first movie to intentionally seek an NC–17 to demonstrate that the rating was commercially viable. However, many theater chains refused to carry NC–17 movies, fearing economic sanctions and boycotts by their customers or religious groups. Many newspapers also refused to carry ads for NC–17 films. Panned by the critics, *Showgirls* flopped at the box office. Since then, the NC–17 rating has not proved commercially viable, and distributors avoid releasing films with the rating, preferring to label such films "unrated" or to

TABLE 16.1

THE VOLUNTARY MOVIE RATING SYSTEM

Data from: Motion Picture Association of America, "Understanding the Film Ratings," accessed November 24, 2014, www.mpaa .org/film-ratings.

▶

Rating	Description
G	**General Audiences:** Nothing that would offend parents for viewing by their children.
PG	**Parental Guidance Suggested:** Parents urged to give "parental guidance." May contain some material parents might not like for their young children.
PG–13	**Parents Strongly Cautioned:** Parents are urged to be cautious. Some material may be inappropriate for pre-teenagers.
R	**Restricted:** Contains some adult material. Parents are urged to learn more about the film before taking their young children with them.
NC–17	**No one 17 and under admitted:** Clearly adult. Children are not admitted.

cut the film to earn an R rating, as happened with *Clerks* (1994), *Eyes Wide Shut* (1999), *Brüno* (2009), and *The Wolf of Wall Street* (2013). Today, there is mounting protest against the MPAA, which many argue is essentially a censorship board that limits the First Amendment rights of filmmakers.

Expression in the Media: Print, Broadcast, and Online

During the Cold War, a vigorous campaign led by Joseph McCarthy, an ultraconservative senator from Wisconsin, tried to rid both government and the media of so-called communist subversives who were allegedly challenging the American way of life. In 1950, a publication called *Red Channels: The Report of Communist Influence in Radio and Television* aimed "to show how the Communists have been able to carry out their plan of infiltration of the radio and television industry." *Red Channels*, inspired by McCarthy and produced by a group of former FBI agents, named 151 performers, writers, and musicians who were "sympathetic" to communist or left-wing causes. Among those named were Leonard Bernstein, Will Geer, Dashiell Hammett, Lillian Hellman, Lena Horne, Burgess Meredith, Arthur Miller, Dorothy Parker, Pete Seeger, Irwin Shaw, and Orson Welles. For a time, all were banned from working in television and radio even though no one on the list was ever charged with a crime.[19]

Although the First Amendment protects an individual's right to hold controversial political views, network executives either sympathized with the anticommunist movement or feared losing ad revenue. At any rate, the networks did not stand up to the communist witch-hunters. In order to work, a blacklisted or "suspected" performer required the support of the program's sponsor. Though *I Love Lucy*'s Lucille Ball, who in sympathy with her father once registered to vote as a communist in the 1930s, retained Philip Morris's sponsorship of her popular program, other performers were not as fortunate.

Although no evidence was ever introduced to show how entertainment programs circulated communist propaganda, by the early 1950s the TV networks were asking actors and other workers to sign loyalty oaths denouncing communism—a low point for the First Amendment.

The communist witch-hunts demonstrated key differences between print and broadcast protection under the First Amendment. On the one hand, licenses for printers and publishers have been outlawed since the eighteenth century. On the other hand, in the late 1920s commercial broadcasters themselves asked the federal government to step in and regulate the airwaves. At that time, they wanted the government to clear up technical problems, channel noise, noncommercial competition, and amateur interference. Ever since, most broadcasters have been trying to free themselves from the government intrusion they once demanded.

THE HOUSE UN-AMERICAN ACTIVITIES COMMITTEE attempted to expose performers, writers, and musicians as "communist subversives," blacklisting them from working in Hollywood without any evidence of criminal wrongdoing. In 1947, movie stars like Humphrey Bogart, Evelyn Keyes, and Lauren Bacall, pictured here, visited Washington to protest the committee's methods.

© Bettmann/Corbis

ELSEWHERE IN
MEDIA & CULTURE

ARE VIDEO GAMES MISOGYNISTIC?

pp. 94–95

THE ADVENTURES OF HUCKLEBERRY FINN IS STILL THE MOST-BANNED BOOK IN U.S. HISTORY

p. 360

HOW IS ADVERTISING SPENDING CHANGING?

39%

Share of U.S. advertising
dollars that go to television

25%

Share of U.S. advertising
dollars that go to digital/mobile

10%

Share of U.S. advertising
dollars that go to newspapers

p. 385

HOW PIRACY CHANGED THE MUSIC INDUSTRY

p. 140

The FCC Regulates Broadcasting

Drawing on the argument that limited broadcast signals constitute a scarce national resource, the Communications Act of 1934 mandated that radio broadcasters operate in "the public interest, convenience, and necessity." Since the 1980s, however, with cable and, later, DBS increasing channel capacity, station managers have lobbied to own their airwave assignments. Although the 1996 Telecommunications Act did not grant such ownership, stations continue to challenge the "public interest" statute. They argue that because the government is not allowed to dictate content in newspapers, it should not be allowed to control broadcasting via licenses or mandate any broadcast programming.

Two cases—*Red Lion Broadcasting Co. v. FCC* (1969) and *Miami Herald Publishing Co. v. Tornillo* (1974)—demonstrate the historic legal differences between broadcast and print. The *Red Lion* case began when WGCB, a small-town radio station in Red Lion, Pennsylvania, refused to give airtime to Fred Cook, author of a book that criticized Barry Goldwater, the Republican Party's presidential candidate in 1964. A conservative radio preacher and Goldwater fan, the Reverend Billy James Hargis, verbally attacked Cook on the air. Cook asked for response time from the two hundred stations that carried the Hargis attack. Most stations complied, granting Cook free reply time. But WGCB offered only to sell Cook time. He appealed to the FCC, which ordered the station to give Cook free time. The station refused, claiming that its First Amendment rights granted it control over its program content. On appeal, the Supreme Court sided with the FCC, deciding that whenever a broadcaster's rights conflict with the public interest, the public interest must prevail. In interpreting broadcasting as different from print, the Supreme Court upheld the 1934 Communications Act by reaffirming that broadcasters' responsibilities to program in the public interest may outweigh their right to program whatever they want.

In contrast, five years later, in *Miami Herald Publishing Co. v. Tornillo*, the Supreme Court sided with the newspaper. A political candidate, Pat Tornillo Jr., requested space to reply to an editorial opposing his candidacy. Previously, Florida had a right-to-reply law, which permitted a candidate to respond, in print, to editorial criticisms from newspapers. Counter to the *Red Lion* decision, the Court in this case struck down the Florida state law as unconstitutional. The Court argued that mandating that a newspaper give a candidate space to reply violated the paper's First Amendment rights to control what it chose to publish. The two decisions demonstrate that the unlicensed print media receive protections under the First Amendment that have not always been available to licensed broadcast media.

Dirty Words, Indecent Speech, and Hefty Fines

In theory, communication law prevents the government from censoring broadcast content. Accordingly, the government may not interfere with programs or engage in prior restraint, although it may punish broadcasters for **indecency** or profanity after the fact. Over the years, a handful of radio stations have had their licenses suspended or denied after an unfavorable FCC review of past programming records. Concerns over indecent broadcast programming began in 1937 when NBC was scolded by the FCC for running a sketch featuring comic actress Mae West on ventriloquist Edgar Bergen's network program. West had the following conversation with Bergen's famous wooden dummy, Charlie McCarthy:

WEST: That's all right. I like a man that takes his time. Why don't you come home with me? I'll let you play in my woodpile . . . you're all wood and a yard long. . . .
CHARLIE: Oh, Mae, don't, don't . . . don't be so rough. To me love is peace and quiet.
WEST: That ain't love—that's sleep.[20]

INDECENT SPEECH
The sexual innuendo of an "Adam and Eve" radio sketch between sultry film star Mae West and dummy Charlie McCarthy (voiced by ventriloquist Edgar Bergen) on a Sunday evening in December 1937 enraged many listeners of Bergen's program. The networks banned West from further radio appearances for what was considered indecent speech.

© Bettmann/Corbis

After the sketch, West did not perform on radio for years. Ever since, the FCC has periodically fined or reprimanded stations for indecent programming, especially during times when children might be listening.

In the 1960s, *topless radio* featured deejays and callers discussing intimate sexual subjects in the middle of the afternoon. The government curbed the practice in 1973, when the chairman of the FCC denounced topless radio as "a new breed of air pollution . . . with the suggestive, coaxing, pear-shaped tones of the smut-hustling host."[21] After an FCC investigation, a couple of stations lost their licenses, some were fined, and topless radio was temporarily over. It reemerged in the 1980s, this time with doctors and therapists—instead of deejays—offering intimate counsel over the airwaves.

The current precedent for regulating broadcast indecency stems from a complaint to the FCC in 1973. In the middle of the afternoon, WBAI, a nonprofit Pacifica network station in New

York, aired George Carlin's famous comedy sketch about the seven dirty words that could not be uttered by broadcasters. A father, riding in a car with his fifteen-year-old son, heard the program and complained to the FCC, which sent WBAI a letter of reprimand. Although no fine was issued, the station appealed on principle and won its case in court. The FCC, however, appealed to the Supreme Court. Although no court had legally defined indecency (and still hasn't), the Supreme Court's unexpected ruling in the 1978 *FCC v. Pacifica Foundation* case sided with the FCC and upheld the agency's authority to require broadcasters to air adult programming at times when children are not likely to be listen-

CBS/Photofest

2 BROKE GIRLS has become a favorite target of the Parents Television Council (PTC) since its debut in 2011. The PTC, which collects indecency complaints via its Web site and directs them to the Federal Communications Commission (FCC), evaluates shows based on occurrences of gratuitous sex, explicit dialogue, violent content, or obscene language. *2 Broke Girls* attracts the PTC's ire for its frequent references to sex.

ing. The Court ruled that so-called indecent programming, though not in violation of federal obscenity laws, was a nuisance and could be restricted to late-evening hours. As a result, the FCC banned indecent programs from most stations between 6:00 A.M. and 10:00 P.M. In 1990, the FCC tried to ban such programs entirely. Although a federal court ruled this move unconstitutional, it still upheld the time restrictions intended to protect children.

This ruling provides the rationale for the indecency fines that the FCC has frequently leveled against programs and stations that have carried indecent programming during daytime and evening hours. While Howard Stern and his various bosses held the early record for racking up millions in FCC indecency fines in the 1990s—before Stern moved to unregulated satellite radio—the largest-ever fine was for $3.6 million, leveled in 2006 against 111 TV stations that broadcast a 2004 episode of the popular CBS program *Without a Trace* that depicted teenage characters taking part in a sexual orgy.

After the FCC later fined broadcasters for several instances of "fleeting expletives" during live TV shows, the four major networks sued the FCC on grounds that their First Amendment rights had been violated. In its fining flurry, the FCC was partly responding to organized campaigns aimed at Howard Stern's vulgarity and at the Janet Jackson exposed-breast incident during the 2004 Super Bowl halftime show. In 2006, Congress substantially increased the FCC's maximum allowable fine to $325,000 per incident of indecency—meaning that one fleeting expletive in a live entertainment, news, or sports program could cost millions of dollars in fines, as it is repeated on affiliate stations across the country. But in 2010, a federal appeals court rejected the FCC's policy against fleeting expletives, arguing that it was constitutionally vague and had a chilling effect on free speech "because broadcasters have no way of knowing what the FCC will find offensive."[22]

Political Broadcasts and Equal Opportunity

In addition to indecency rules, another law that the print media do not encounter is **Section 315** of the 1934 Communications Act, which mandates that during elections, broadcast stations must provide equal opportunities and response time for qualified political candidates. In other words, if broadcasters give or sell time to one candidate, they must give or sell the same opportunity to others. Local broadcasters and networks have fought this law for years, complaining that it has required them to give marginal third-party candidates with little hope for success equal airtime in political discussions. Broadcasters claim that because no similar rule applies to newspapers or magazines, the law violates their First Amendment right to control content. In fact, because of this rule, many stations avoid all political programming, ironically reversing the rule's original intention. The TV networks managed to get the law amended in 1959 to exempt newscasts, press conferences, and other events—such as political debates—that qualify as news. For instance, if a senator running for office appears in a news story, opposing candidates cannot invoke Section 315 and demand free time. The FCC has subsequently ruled that interview portions of programs like the *700 Club* and *TMZ* also count as news.

Due to Section 315, many stations from the late 1960s through the 1980s refused to air movies starring Ronald Reagan. Because his film appearances did not count as bona fide news stories, politicians opposing Reagan as a presidential candidate could demand free time in markets that ran old Reagan movies. For the same reason, in 2003, TV stations in California banned the broadcast of Arnold Schwarzenegger movies when he became a candidate for governor, and dozens of stations nationwide preempted an episode of *Saturday Night Live* that was hosted by Al Sharpton, a Democratic presidential candidate.

However, supporters of the equal opportunity law argue that it has provided forums for lesser-known candidates representing views counter to those of the Democratic and Republican parties, further noting that the other main way for alternative candidates to circulate their messages widely is to buy political ads, thus limiting serious outside contenders to wealthy candidates, such as Ross Perot, Steve Forbes, or members of the Bush or Clinton families.

The Demise of the Fairness Doctrine

Considered an important corollary to Section 315, the **Fairness Doctrine** was to controversial issues what Section 315 is to political speech. Initiated in 1949, this FCC rule required stations (1) to air and engage in controversial-issue programs that affected their communities, and (2) to provide competing points of view when offering such programming. Antismoking activist John Banzhaf ingeniously invoked the Fairness Doctrine to force cigarette advertising off television in 1971. When the FCC mandated antismoking public service announcements to counter "controversial" smoking commercials, tobacco companies decided not to challenge an outright ban rather than tolerate a flood of antismoking spots authorized by the Fairness Doctrine.

Over the years, broadcasters argued that mandating opposing views every time a program covered a controversial issue was a burden not required of the print media, and that it forced many of them to refrain from airing controversial issues. As a result, the Fairness Doctrine ended with little public debate in 1987 after a federal court ruled that it was merely a regulation rather than an extension of Section 315 law.

Since 1987, however, periodic support for reviving the Fairness Doctrine has surfaced. Its supporters argue that broadcasting is fundamentally different from—and more pervasive than—print media, requiring greater accountability to the public. Although many broadcasters disagree, supporters of fairness rules insist that as long as broadcasters are licensed as public trustees of the airwaves—unlike newspaper or magazine publishers—legal precedent permits the courts and the FCC to demand responsible content and behavior from radio and TV stations.

Communication Policy and the Internet

Many have looked to the Internet as the one true venue for unlimited free speech under the First Amendment because it is not regulated by the government, it is not subject to the

LaunchPad ⊚
macmillanhighered.com /mediaculture10e

Bloggers and Legal Rights
Legal and journalism scholars discuss the legal rights and responsibilities of bloggers.
Discussion: What are some of the advantages and disadvantages of the audience's turning to blogs, rather than traditional sources, for news?

Communications Act of 1934, and little has been done in regard to self-regulation. Its current global expansion is comparable to that of the early days of broadcasting, when economic and technological growth outstripped law and regulation. At that time, noncommercial experiments by amateurs and engineering students provided a testing ground that commercial interests later exploited for profit. In much the same way, amateurs, students, and various interest groups have explored and extended the communication possibilities of the Internet. In fact, they have experimented so successfully that commercial vendors have raced to buy up pieces of the Internet since the 1990s.

Nate Beeler/Cagle Cartoons

Public conversations about the Internet have not typically revolved around ownership. Instead, the debates have focused on First Amendment issues, such as civility and pornography. Not unlike the public's concern over television's sexual and violent images, the scrutiny of the Internet is mainly about harmful images and information online, not about who controls it and for what purposes. However, as we watch the rapid expansion of the Internet, an important question confronts us: Will the Internet continue to develop as a democratic medium? By 2014, the answer to that question was still unclear. In late 2010, the FCC created net neutrality rules for wired (cable and DSL) broadband providers, requiring that they provide the same access to all Internet services and content. But the FCC's net neutrality rules have been rejected by federal courts twice, most recently in 2014. The courts argued that because the FCC had not defined the Internet as a utility, it couldn't regulate it in this manner. Telecommunication companies were pleased with the decision, as they don't want any rules governing how they distribute access to the Internet. However, citizens and entrepreneurs have opposed an unregulated system that would allow telecommunication companies to create fast lanes (for those who pay more) and slow lanes on the Internet. The debate generated a record number of comments to the FCC—more than 3 million by mid-September 2014—the vast majority in favor of net neutrality.[23]

The eventual outcome will determine whether broadband Internet connections will be defined as an *essential utility* to which everyone has access and for which rates are controlled (like electricity or phone service) or as an *information service* for which Internet service providers can charge as much as they wish (as with cable TV).

Critics and observers hope that a vigorous debate about ownership will develop—a debate that will go beyond First Amendment issues. The promise of the Internet as a democratic forum encourages the formation of all sorts of regional, national, and global interest groups. In fact, many global movements use the Internet to fight political forms of censorship. Human Rights Watch, for example, encourages free-expression advocates to use blogs "for disseminating information about, and ending, human rights abuses around the world."[24] Where oppressive regimes have tried to monitor and control Internet communication, Human Rights Watch suggests bloggers post anonymously to safeguard their identity. Just as fax machines, satellites, and home videos helped expedite and document the fall of totalitarian regimes in Eastern Europe in the late 1980s, the Internet helps spread the word and activate social change today.

EXAMINING ETHICS

A Generation of Copyright Criminals?

As a student reading this book, you have probably already composed plenty of research papers and quoted, with attribution, from various printed sources. This is a routine practice, and you are within the legal bounds of fair use of the sources you sampled. The concept of *fair use* has existed in U.S. case law for more than 150 years.

But what if you are composing a song or creating a video, and you decide to sample bits of music or a clip of film? Under current law, you have little protection and may be subject to a lawsuit from the recording or motion-picture industry alleging copyright infringement.

As inexpensive digital technology became available, artists began sampling sounds and images, much like scholars and writers might sample texts. University of Iowa communication studies professor Kembrew McLeod explains that in the late 1980s, sampling "was a creative window that had been forced open by hip-hop artists," but "by the early 1990s, the free experimentation was over. . . . Everyone had to pay for the sounds that they sampled or risk getting sued."[1] The cost for most acts was far too prohibitive. Fees to use snippets of copyrighted sounds in the Beastie Boys' 1989 sample-rich *Paul's Boutique* recording cost $250,000.[2] Today, a recording based on creative mash-ups of samples probably couldn't even be made, as some copyright owners demand up to $50,000 for sampling just a few seconds of a song.

Nevertheless, some artists are still trying. Pittsburgh-based mash-up

deejay Girl Talk (Gregg Gillis) has no problem performing his sample-heavy music, in which he remixes a dozen or more samples on his laptop with some of his own beats to create a new song. Copyright royalties are covered for his live public performances, since many venues already have public performance agreements with copyright management agencies BMI, ASCAP, and SESAC. (These are the same agencies that collect fees from restaurants and radio stations for publicly performed music.) But—and this is one of the many inconsistencies in copyright law—if Gillis wants to make a recording of his music, the cost of the copyright royalty payments (should they even be granted by the copyright holder) would exceed the revenue generated by selling the recording. On the other hand, if he doesn't get copyright permission for the samples used, he risks hundreds of thousands of dollars in penalties.

Despite the threat of lawsuits, Gillis and an independent label—appropriately named Illegal Art—released the acclaimed *Night Ripper* album in 2006 and Feed the Animals (which uses 322 samples) in 2008. His 2010 album *All Day* was released as a free download with 372 samples. In defending the recording against potential lawsuits, Gillis and his label argue that they are protected from copyright infringement by the fair-use exemption, which allows

DJ GIRL TALK mixes his beats with samples from other artists to create new music.

for *transformative use*—creating new work from bits of copyrighted work.[3]

The uneven and unclear rules for the use of sound, images, video, and text have become one of the most contentious issues of today's digital culture. As digital media make it easier than ever to create and re-create cultural content, copyright law has yet to catch up with these new forms of expression.

"There's no way to kill this technology. You can only criminalize its use," Harvard Law professor and Internet activist Lawrence Lessig notes. "If this is a crime, we have a whole generation of criminals."[4]

The First Amendment and Democracy

For most of our nation's history, citizens have counted on journalism to monitor abuses in government and business. During the muckraking period, writers like Upton Sinclair, Ida Tarbell, and Sinclair Lewis made strong contributions in reporting corporate expansion and social change. Unfortunately, however, news stories about business issues today are usually reduced to consumer affairs reporting. In other words, when a labor strike, factory recall, or business shutdown is covered, the reporter mainly tries to answer the question, "How do these events affect consumers?" Although this is an important news angle, discussions about media ownership or labor management ethics are not part of the news that journalists typically report. Similarly, when companies announce mergers, reporters do not routinely question the economic wisdom or social impact of such changes but instead focus on how consumers will be affected.

Courtesy of kickstarter.com

At one level, journalists have been compromised by the ongoing upheavals of their own media businesses. As newspapers, magazines, and broadcast stations consolidate, downsize, outsource, or close down completely, and digital outlets spring up without a history or mission of news reporting, there are fewer journalists available to adequately cover and lead discussions on issues of politics, the economy, and media ownership. In fact, the very companies they work for are the prime buyers and sellers of major news-media outlets and are often participants in a political system rife with advertising money in campaign season.

As a result, it is becoming increasingly important that the civic role of watchdog be shared by both citizens and journalists. Citizen action groups like Free Press, the Media Access Project, and the Center for Digital Democracy have worked to bring media ownership issues into the mainstream. However, it is important to remember that the First Amendment protects not only the news media's free-speech rights but also the rights of all of us to speak out. Mounting concerns over who can afford access to the media go to the heart of free expression. As we struggle to determine the future of converging print, electronic, and digital media and to strengthen the democratic spirit underlying media technology, we need to stay engaged in spirited public debates about media ownership and control, and about the differences between commercial speech and free expression. As citizens, we need to pay attention to who is included and excluded from opportunities not only to buy products but also to speak out and shape the cultural landscape. To accomplish this, we need to challenge our journalists and our leaders. More important, we need to challenge ourselves to become watchdogs—critical consumers and engaged citizens—who learn from the past, care about the present, and map mass media's future. ▶

NET NEUTRALITY DAY OF ACTION
On September 10, 2014, several popular Internet sites—including Netflix, Kickstarter, Reddit, Tumblr, Foursquare, Etsy, and Vimeo—held a Day of Action to support net neutrality and oppose the FCC's proposal to have fast and slow lanes. The companies featured messages on their pages to contact the FCC and Congress along with images of spinning wheels to signify what the slow lane of an Internet without net neutrality might look like.

CHAPTER REVIEW

COMMON THREADS

One of the Common Threads discussed in Chapter 1 is the role that media play in a democracy. Is a free media system necessary for democracy to exist, or must democracy first be established to enable a media system to operate freely? What do the mass media do to enhance or secure democracy?

In 1787, as the Constitution was being formed, Thomas Jefferson famously said, "Were it left to me to decide whether we should have a government without newspapers, or newspapers without a government, I should not hesitate a moment to prefer the latter." Jefferson supported the notion of a free press and free speech. He stood against the Sedition Act, which penalized free speech, and did not support its renewal when he became president in 1801.

Nevertheless, as president, Jefferson had to withstand the vitriol and allegations of a partisan press. In 1807, near the end of his second term, Jefferson's idealism about the press had cooled, as he remarked, "The man who never looks into a newspaper is better informed than he who reads them, inasmuch as he who knows nothing is nearer the truth than he whose mind is filled with falsehoods and errors."

Today, we contend with mass media that extend far beyond newspapers—a media system that is among the biggest and most powerful institutions in the country. Unfortunately, it is also a media system that too often envisions us as consumers of capitalism, not citizens of a democracy. Media sociologist Herbert Gans argues that the media alone can't guarantee a democracy.[25] "Despite much disingenuous talk about citizen empowerment by politicians and merchandisers, citizens have never had much clout. Countries as big as America operate largely through organizations," Gans explains.

But in a country as big as America, the media constitute one of those critical organizations that can help or hurt us in creating a more economically and politically democratic society. At their worst, the media can distract or misinform us with falsehoods and errors. But at their Jeffersonian best, the media can shed light on the issues, tell meaningful stories, and foster the discussions that can help a citizens' democracy flourish.

KEY TERMS

The definitions for the terms listed below can be found in the glossary at the end of the book. The page numbers listed with the terms indicate where the term is highlighted in the chapter.

authoritarian model, 540
communist or state model, 540
social responsibility model, 540
Fourth Estate, 541
libertarian model, 541
prior restraint, 542
copyright, 545

public domain, 545
libel, 546
slander, 546
actual malice, 547
qualified privilege, 547
opinion and fair comment, 547
obscenity, 548

right to privacy, 549
gag orders, 551
shield laws, 552
indecency, 559
Section 315, 561
Fairness Doctrine, 562

REVIEW QUESTIONS

The Origins of Free Expression and a Free Press

1. Explain the various models of the news media that exist under different political systems.

2. What is the basic philosophical concept that underlies America's notion of free expression?

3. What happened with the passage of the Sedition Act of 1798, and what was its relevance to the United States' new First Amendment?

4. How has censorship been defined historically?

5. What is the public domain, and why is it an important element in American culture?

6. Why is the case of *New York Times v. Sullivan* so significant in First Amendment history?

7. What does a public figure have to do to win a libel case? What are the main defenses that a newspaper can use to thwart a charge of libel?

8. What is the legal significance of the *Falwell v. Flynt* case?

9. How has the Internet changed battles over what constitutes obscenity?

10. What issues are at stake when First Amendment and Sixth Amendment concerns clash?

Film and the First Amendment

11. Why were films not constitutionally protected as a form of speech until 1952?

12. Why did film review boards develop, and why did they eventually disband?

13. How did both the Motion Picture Production Code and the current movie rating system come into being?

Expression in the Media: Print, Broadcast, and Online

14. The government and the courts view print and broadcasting as different forms of expression. What are the major differences?

15. What's the difference between obscenity and indecency?

16. What is the significance of Section 315 of the Communications Act of 1934?

17. Why didn't broadcasters like the Fairness Doctrine?

The First Amendment and Democracy

18. What are the similarities and differences between the debates over broadcast ownership in the 1920s and those over Internet ownership today?

19. Why is the future of watchdog journalism in jeopardy?

QUESTIONING THE MEDIA

1. Have you ever had an experience in which you thought personal or public expression went too far and should be curbed? Explain. How might you remedy this situation?

2. If you owned a community newspaper and had to formulate a policy for your editors about which letters from readers could appear in a limited space on your editorial page, what kinds of letters would you eliminate, and why? Would you be acting as a censor in this situation? Why or why not?

3. The writer A. J. Liebling once said that freedom of the press belonged only to those who owned one. Explain why you agree or disagree.

4. Should the United States have a federal shield law to protect reporters?

5. What do you think of the current movie rating system? Should it be changed? Why or why not?

6. Should the Fairness Doctrine be revived? Why or why not?

7. Should corporations, unions, and rich individuals be able to contribute any amount of money they want to support particular candidates and pay for TV ads? Why or why not?

LAUNCHPAD FOR *MEDIA & CULTURE*

Visit LaunchPad for *Media & Culture* at macmillanhighered.com/mediaculture10e for additional learning tools:

- REVIEW WITH LEARNINGCURVE
  LearningCurve, available on LaunchPad for *Media & Culture*, uses gamelike quizzing to help you master the concepts you need to learn from this chapter.

- VIDEO: THE FIRST AMENDMENT AND STUDENT SPEECH
  Legal and newspaper professionals explain how student newspapers are protected by the First Amendment.

Extended Case Study

Social Media and Finding Real Happiness

Social media connect us in so many different ways, expanding our human interactions beyond the limits of meeting in person. As noted in Chapter 2, social media include any blogs, collaborative projects, content communities, social networking sites, virtual game worlds, and virtual social worlds that expand our social horizons. But while social media connect us, they disconnect us in other ways, taking up time in which we might experience real physical connection and replacing it with short, highly mediated messages. With social media, we are both the media and the subject, and we create the online version of ourselves.

For at least some of us, the social mediated version of ourselves becomes the predominant way we experience the world. As *Time* magazine noted in 2014, "Experiences don't feel fully real" until you have "tweeted them or tumbled them or YouTubed them—and the world has congratulated you for doing so."[1] The flip side of promoting our own experiences on social media as the most awesome happenings ever (with the added subtext of "too bad you aren't here") is the social anxiety associated with reading about other people's experiences—and the accompanying realization that you are not actually there.

The problem is called Fear of Missing Out (FOMO), and one report defines it as "the uneasy and sometimes all-consuming feeling that you're missing out—that your peers are doing, in the know about, or in possession of more or something better than you."[2] This fear has been around long before social media was invented. Photos, postcards, holiday family letters, and plain old bragging have usually put the most positive spin on people's lives. But social media and mobile technology make being exposed to the interactions you missed a 24/7 phenomenon. Exposure to a hypothetical better experience or better life is potentially constant.

According to a report in *Computers in Human Behavior*, with FOMO there is a "desire to stay continually connected with what others are doing," so the person suffering from the anxiety continues to be tethered to social media, tracking "friends" and sacrificing time that might be spent having in-person, unmediated experiences.[3] Some related social media problems can get even more serious. A study by University of Michigan researchers found that the use of Facebook (the most popular social media site) makes people feel worse about themselves. The study of college students over two weeks found that the more they used Facebook, the more two components of well-being declined: how people feel moment-to-moment and how satisfied they are with their lives. These declines occurred regardless of how many Facebook "friends" they had in their network.[4]

▲ THE IDEA THAT SOCIAL MEDIA COULD BE CREATING NEW FORMS OF ANXIETY AND UNDERMINING OUR HAPPINESS PRESENTS AN IMPORTANT QUESTION ABOUT OUR CULTURE TO INVESTIGATE. For this case study, we will look at social media in our lives and whether they help expand our friendships, undermine our social well-being, or offer a mixed result of good and bad outcomes.

As detailed in Chapter 1 and throughout the book, a media-literate perspective involves mastering five overlapping critical stages that build on each other: (1) *description*: paying close attention, taking notes, and researching the subject under study; (2) *analysis*: discovering and focusing on significant patterns that emerge from the description stage; (3) *interpretation*: asking and answering the "What does that mean?" and "So what?" questions about our findings; (4) *evaluation*: arriving at a judgment about whether something is good, bad, poor, or mediocre, which involves subordinating our personal views to the critical assessment resulting from the first three stages; and (5) *engagement*: taking some action that connects our critical interpretations and evaluations with our responsibility as citizens.

Step 1: Description

In the description phase, you will need to not only draw on your own experiences with social media but also research others' experiences systematically. For example, you might do qualitative research in the form of interviews with five or ten people to learn more about how social media makes them feel.

One tool to analyze social media use and the Fear of Missing Out was developed by a team of researchers in the United Kingdom and the United States.[5] They created a ten-item questionnaire to measure levels of FOMO. Respondents answer each question on a five-point scale. A reproduction of that scale and questionnaire follows.

Respondents answer each question on a five-point scale, as follows: (1) not at all true of me; (2) slightly true of me; (3) moderately true of me; (4) very true of me; or (5) extremely true of me.

1. I fear others have more rewarding experiences than me.
2. I fear my friends have more rewarding experiences than me.
3. I get worried when I find out my friends are having fun without me.
4. I get anxious when I don't know what my friends are up to.
5. It is important that I understand my friends' "in jokes."
6. Sometimes, I wonder if I spend too much time keeping up with what is going on.
7. It bothers me when I miss an opportunity to meet up with friends.
8. When I have a good time, it is important for me to share the details online (e.g., updating status).
9. When I miss out on a planned get-together, it bothers me.
10. When I go on vacation, I continue to keep tabs on what my friends are doing.

Other information to gather for your subjects could include the number of social media platforms they use (Facebook, Twitter, Tumblr, LinkedIn, Pinterest, Google+, Instagram, Vine, and so on) and how frequently they use them. It would also be interesting to know if the subjects ever took a break from social media, and if so, why and for how long. For example, one sixteen-year-old female high school student reported, "I have disabled my Facebook a couple of times and it's been nice, but I felt like I missed out on too much, so I went back to it." To completely give up Facebook would be harder, she said. "I would just have to learn how to not know what people are doing all the time, and more importantly, not to care."

Step 2: Analysis

In the second stage of the critical process, you will isolate patterns that emerged from the interviews that call for closer attention. The following questions can help you identify patterns in your results:

- How did the total score on the ten-item FOMO questionnaire correspond to the number and frequency of use of social media platforms for each person?
- Are your interview subjects aware of the Fear of Missing Out in their lives? Do they see social media as a good thing overall in their lives or as something in which they would like to be less involved if they could? Do they feel forced to participate in social media because so many other people they know (or want to know) are on it?
- What kinds of things do subjects spend less time doing because of time spent on social media?
- Do your subjects who spend less time with social media report a higher level of satisfaction?

INSTAGRAM is intended to be used on a mobile device as an app; the browser-based version of the service actually makes it difficult to upload photos not taken with a phone or other devices with wireless-enabled cameras. This means that Instagram users are encouraged to check their feeds on their phones. How might this affect how posts are perceived?

▶

Thomas Coex/AFP/Getty Images

- Are there aspects of the particular social media sites that your subjects find most valuable or least valuable? That is, do some social media make them feel better than others?

Our sample sixteen-year-old student noted that she uses Instagram and Tumblr just for finding cool images, but that texting has the potential to induce anxiety and unhappiness: "You feel bad when someone doesn't text you back. I know someone who is notoriously bad at responding, and honestly it makes me feel really bad when they don't respond. So you start second guessing yourself. It's really stressful." Your subjects might have experienced other events with social media—from finding good friends or someone they love, to being bullied or humiliated. Are there any patterns here?

Step 3: Interpretation

In the interpretation stage, you will determine the larger meanings of the patterns you have analyzed. The most difficult stage in criticism, interpretation demands an answer to the questions "So what?" and "What does all this mean?"

For example, is there social pressure to present ourselves in the best way possible in social media photos, videos, and texts, thus creating an inaccurate public presentation of our lives? (Or think about it this way: Are we presenting ourselves in the same way that a business might present itself on social media? Should we treat our own lives like a business communication?)

Do we overshare in social media, revealing too much of ourselves to people who really aren't close friends, in the traditional sense? Are we being pathetic in constantly seeking approval by collecting "Likes" for our pictures and posts? Is social media use leaving us feeling more alienated, alone, and depressed?

Ellen DeGeneres/Twitter via Getty Images

SELFIE CULTURE got a national showcase at the 2014 Academy Awards ceremony, where host Ellen DeGeneres quickly convinced a gaggle of huge stars, including Jennifer Lawrence, Brad Pitt, Meryl Streep, and Bradley Cooper, to pose for a selfie to be posted on her Twitter account. It quickly became one of the most retweeted images in the history of Twitter.

Step 4:
Evaluation

The evaluation stage of the critical process is about making informed judgments. Building on description, analysis, and interpretation, you can better evaluate the impact of social media on its users.

Based on your critical research, consider what happens to people who use social media—do they find positive social connections, do they feel like they are missing out, do they feel bullied, or does their constant use of social media leave them feeling less satisfied with their life? Thus, on balance, are social media sites and tools that people use for interpersonal interaction a good thing or a bad thing for society?

Merrick Morton/© Columbia Pictures/Everett Collection

THE FICTIONALIZED VERSION OF MARK ZUCKERBERG in David Fincher's 2010 film *The Social Network* portrayed the Facebook founder as wildly successful, but still on some level, desperately lonely.

Step 5:
Engagement

The fifth state of the critical process—engagement—encourages you to take action, adding your own voice to the process of shaping our culture and environment.

Studies about happiness routinely conclude that the best path to subjective well-being (i.e., happiness) and life satisfaction is to have a community of close personal relationships. Social psychologists Ed Diener and Robert Biswas-Diener acknowledge that the high use of mobile phones, text messaging, and social media is evidence that people want to connect. But they also explain that "we don't just need relationships: we need close ones."[6] Frequent contact isn't enough to create the kinds of relationships that produce the most happiness.

According to Diener and Biswas-Diener, "The close relationships that produce the most happiness are those characterized by mutual understanding, caring, and validation of the other person as worthwhile. People feel secure in these types of relationships, and are often able to share intimate aspects of themselves with the other. Importantly, they can count on the other person for help if they need it. Although acquaintances and casual friends can be fun, it is the supportive close relationships that are essential to happiness."[7]

One way to take action might be to think about how to use social media without creating FOMO in others. Is there a way communications can be structured so that they don't seem exclusionary?

Eileen Bach/Getty Images

Another way might be to decrease use of social media whenever possible and to make a concerted effort to put the time you would have devoted to social media into having in-person human interactions and developing close personal relationships.

Also, experiment with a "vacation" from social media—go do something fun or enriching by yourself or with friends, and don't make a social media record of it. Or take a several-day break from social media (and encourage other friends to do so, and perhaps your whole class or your entire college or university), and discover the possibilities of life without social media.

Notes

1 Mass Communication: A Critical Approach

1. See The Editorial Board, "The Worst Voter Turnout in 72 Years," *New York Times*, November 11, 2104, http://www.nytimes.com/2014/11/12/opinion/the-worst-voter-turnout-in-72-years.html.
2. See American Presidents Project, http://www.presidency.ucsb.edu/data/turnout.php, accessed November 10, 2014.
3. See Chris Cillizza, "The 2014 Election Cost $3.7 Billion. We Spend Twice That Much on Halloween," Washingtonpost.com, November 6, 2014, http://www.washingtonpost.com/blogs/the-fix/wp/2014/11/06/the-2014-election-cost-3-7-billion-we-spend-twice-that-much-on-halloween.
4. Brian Stelter, "You Won't Miss Those Annoying Political Ads. Stations Will Miss the Money," CNNMoney, November 4, 2014, http://money.cnn.com/2014/11/04/media/political-ads-midterms.
5. Cass Sunstein, "'Partyism' Now Trumps Racism," Bloomberg View, September 22, 2014, http://www.bloombergview.com/articles/2014-09-22/partyism-now-trumps-racism.
6. Neil Postman, *Amusing Ourselves to Death: Public Discourse in the Age of Show Business* (New York: Penguin Books, 1985), 19.
7. James W. Carey, *Communication as Culture: Essays on Media and Society* (Boston: Unwin Hyman, 1989), 203.
8. Postman, *Amusing Ourselves to Death,* 65. See also Elizabeth Eisenstein, *The Printing Press as an Agent of Change,* 2 vols. (Cambridge: Cambridge University Press, 1979).
9. James Fallows, "How to Save the News," *Atlantic*, June 2010, http://www.theatlantic.com/magazine/archive/2010/06/how-to-save-the-news/8095/.
10. "Generation M2: Media in the Lives of 8- to 18-Year-Olds," A Kaiser Family Foundation Study, p. 2, accessed May 24, 2010, http://www.kff.org/entmedia/upload/8010.pdf.
11. Jefferson Graham, "For TV Networks, Social Is Hugely Important," *USA Today*, May 3, 2012, http://www.usatoday.com/tech/columnist/talkingtech/story/2012-05-02/social-media-tv/54705524/1.
12. Jerome Bruner, *Making Stories: Law, Literature, Life* (New York: Farrar, Straus & Giroux, 2002), 8.
13. Roger Rosenblatt, "I Am Writing Blindly," *Time,* November 6, 2000, p. 142.
14. See Plato, *The Republic*, Book II, 377B.
15. For a historical discussion of culture, see Lawrence Levine, *Highbrow/Lowbrow: The Emergence of Cultural Hierarchy in America* (Cambridge, Mass.: Harvard University Press, 1988).
16. For an example of this critical position, see Allan Bloom, *The Closing of the American Mind: How Higher Education Has Failed Democracy and Impoverished the Souls of Today's Students* (New York: Simon & Schuster, 1987).
17. For overviews of this position, see Postman, *Amusing Ourselves to Death*; and Stuart Ewen, *Captains of Consciousness: Advertising and the Social Roots of the Consumer Culture* (New York: McGraw-Hill, 1976).
18. See James W. Carey, *Communication as Culture: Essays on Media and Society* (Boston: Unwin Hyman, 1989).
19. Walter Lippmann, *Public Opinion* (New York: Free Press, 1922), 11, 19, 246–247.
20. See William Romanowski, *Pop Culture Wars: Religion & the Role of Entertainment in American Life* (Downers Grove, Ill.: InterVarsity Press, 1996).
21. For more on this idea, see Cecelia Tichi, *Electronic Hearth: Creating an American Television Culture* (New York: Oxford University Press, 1991), 187–188.
22. See Jon Katz, "Rock, Rap and Movies Bring You the News," *Rolling Stone*, March 5, 1992, p. 33.

◢ EXAMINING ETHICS   Covering War, p. 18

1. Bill Carter, "Some Stations to Block 'Nightline' War Tribute," *New York Times*, April 30, 2004, p. A13.
2. For reference and guidance on media ethics, see Clifford Christians, Mark Fackler, and Kim Rotzoll, *Media Ethics: Cases and Moral Reasoning,* 4th ed. (White Plains, N.Y.: Longman, 1995); and Thomas H. Bivins, "A Worksheet for Ethics Instruction and Exercises in Reason," *Journalism Educator* (Summer 1993): 4–16.

◢ CASE STUDY   Is *Anchorman* a Comedy or a Documentary?, p. 22

1. John Cawelti, *Adventure, Mystery, and Romance: Formula Stories as Art and Popular Culture* (Chicago: University of Chicago Press, 1976), 39.
2. Bill Kovach and Tom Rosenstiel, *The Elements of Journalism: What People Should Know and the Public Should Expect* (New York: Three Rivers Press, 2007), 187.
3. Steven Johnson, *Everything Bad Is Good for You: How Today's Popular Culture Is Actually Making Us Smarter* (New York: Riverhead Books, 2005), 115.
4. Steven Johnson, "Watching TV Makes You Smarter," *New York Times Magazine*, April 24, 2005, http://www.nytimes.com/2005/04/24/magazine/24TV.html.

◢ GLOBAL VILLAGE   Bedouins, Camels, Transistors, and Coke, p. 31

1. Václav Havel, "A Time for Transcendence," *Utne Reader*, January/February 1995, p. 53.
2. Dan Rather, "The Threat to Foreign News," *Newsweek*, July 17, 1989, p. 9.

Part 1 Opener

http://www.digitalbuzzblog.com/infographic-2013-mobile-growth-statistics/comment-page-3/

2 The Internet, Digital Media, and Media Convergence

1. "Market Shares of Purchase Transactions Worldwide 2013," The Nilson Report, March 2014, http://www.nilsonreport.com/publication_chart_and_graphs_archive.php.
2. Adam Satariano, "Would You Give This Guy $25 Million?" *Bloomberg Businessweek*, March 17, 2014, pp. 29–30.
3. Michelle Goodman, "How Dwolla Disrupted the Digital Payment Industry," *Entrepreneur*, October 2, 2013, http://www.entrepreneur.com/article/227960.
4. Susannah Fox and Lee Rainie, "The Web at 25 in the U.S.," Pew Research Internet Project, February 27, 2014, http://www.pewinternet.org/2014/02/27/the-web-at-25-in-the-u-s/.
5. David Landis, "World Wide Web Helps Untangle Internet's Labyrinth," *USA Today*, August 3, 1994, p. D10.

6. "Broadband vs. Dial-Up Adoption over Time," Pew Research Internet Project, September 2013, http://www.pewinternet.org/data-trend/internet-use/connection-type/.

7. Hibah Hussain, Danielle Kehl, Patrick Lucey, and Nick Russo, "The Cost of Connectivity 2013," New America Foundation, October 28, 2013, http://oti.newamerica.net/publications/policy/the_cost_of_connectivity_2013.

8. Peter H. Lewis, "The Computer Always Beeps Twice," *New York Times*, April 28, 1994, p. 1.

9. "Desktop Search Engine Market Share," NetMarketShare, March 2014, http://www.netmarketshare.com/search-engine-market-share.aspx?qprid=4&qpcustomd=0&qptimeframe=M.

10. Lawrence Lessig, *Remix: Making Art and Commerce Thrive in the Hybrid Economy* (New York: Penguin, 2009).

11. Andreas M. Kaplan and Michael Haenlein, "Users of the World, Unite! The Challenges and Opportunities of Social Media," *Business Horizons* 53, no. 1 (2010): 59–68.

12. United States Securities and Exchange Commission, Form S-1 Registration Statement, Twitter, Inc., October 3, 2013, http://www.sec.gov/Archives/edgar/data/1418091/000119312513390321/d564001ds1.htm; and "Twitter Reports Fourth Quarter and Fiscal Year 2013 Results," Twitter, February 5, 2014, https://investor.twitterinc.com/releasedetail.cfm?ReleaseID=823321.

13. Lucien Tessier, "Boy Scouts: Vote to End Your Anti-gay Policy So My Brother Can Earn His Eagle Award," Change.org, May 2013, http://www.change.org/petitions/boy-scouts-vote-to-end-your-anti-gay-policy-so-my-brother-can-earn-his-eagle-award.

14. Renee Guarriello Heath, Courtney Vail Fletcher, and Ricardo Munoz, eds., *Understanding Occupy from Wall Street to Portland: Applied Studies in Communication Theory* (Lanham, Md.: Lexington Books, 2013).

15. "Protest Shows Xi Jinping Giving the Finger in Paris," Reporters without Borders, March 27, 2014, https://en.rsf.org/chine-protest-shows-xi-jinping-giving-27-03-2014,46048.html.

16. Peter J. Schuyten, "The Computer Entering Home," *New York Times*, December 6, 1978, p. D4.

17. Adam Lella, "comScore Reports February 2014 U.S. Smartphone Subscriber Market Share," comScore, April 4, 2014, https://www.comscore.com/Insights/Press_Releases/2014/4/comScore_Reports_February_2014_US_Smartphone_Subscriber_Market_Share.

18. Chris Anderson and Michael Wolff, "The Web Is Dead. Long Live the Internet," *Wired*, August 17, 2010, http://www.wired.com/magazine/2010/08/ff_webrip. See also Charles Arthur, "Walled Gardens Look Rosy for Facebook, Apple—and Would-Be Censors," *Guardian*, April 17, 2012, http://www.guardian.co.uk/technology/2012/apr/17/walled-gardens-facebook-apple-censors.

19. Arthur, "Walled Gardens."

20. Tim Berners-Lee, James Hendler, and Ora Lassila, "The Semantic Web," *Scientific American*, May 17, 2001.

21. Ibid.

22. Liam F. McCabe, "Europe's Appliances Are Cooler, Prettier, and More Popular," Reviewed.com, September 5, 2013, http://refrigerators.reviewed.com/features/ifa-2013-highlights-culture-gap-between-american-and-european-appliances.

23. Farhad Manjoo, "The Great Tech War of 2012: Apple, Facebook, Google, and Amazon Battle for the Future of the Innovation Economy," *Fast Company*, October 19, 2011, http://www.fastcompany.com/magazine/160/tech-wars-2012-amazon-apple-google-facebook.

24. Seth Fiegerman, "Google Tops Exxon Mobil to Become World's 2nd Most Valuable Company," *Mashable*, February 7, 2014, http://mashable.com/2014/02/07/google-second-most-valuable-company/.

25. Vindu Goel, "Facebook Profit Tripled in First Quarter," *New York Times*, April 23, 2014, http://www.nytimes.com/2014/04/24/technology/facebook-profit-tripled-in-first-quarter.html.

26. Internet Advertising Bureau, "2013 Internet Ad Revenues Soar to $42.8 Billion," April 10, 2014, http://www.iab.net/about_the_iab/recent_press_releases/press_release_archive/press_release/pr-041014.

27. Mark Zuckerberg, "Our Commitment to the Facebook Community," *The Facebook Blog*, November 29, 2011, http://blog.facebook.com/blog.php?post=10150378701937131.

28. "Cookies: Leaving a Trail on the Web," Federal Trade Commission, November 2011, http://www.consumer.ftc.gov/articles/0042-cookies-leaving-trail-web.

29. See Federal Trade Commission, *Privacy Online: Fair Information Practices in the Electronic Marketplace*, May 2000, http://www.ftc.gov/sites/default/files/documents/reports/privacy-online-fair-information-practices-electronic-marketplace-federal-trade-commission-report/privacy2000.pdf.

30. Bureau of Justice Statistics, "16.6 Million People Experienced Identity Theft in 2012," December 12, 2013, http://www.bjs.gov/content/pub/press/vit12pr.cfm.

31. American Library Association, "CIPA Questions and Answers," July 16, 2003, http://www.ala.org/advocacy/sites/ala.org.advocacy/files/content/advleg/federallegislation/cipa/cipaqa-1.pdf.

32. "Internet User Demographics," Pew Research Internet Project, January 2014, http://www.pewinternet.org/data-trend/internet-use/latest-stats/. See also Kathryn Zickuhr and Aaron Smith, "Home Broadband 2013," Pew Research Internet Project, August 26, 2013, http://www.pewinternet.org/2013/08/26/home-broadband-2013/.

33. Ibid.

34. ClickZ, "Stats-Web Worldwide," http://www.clickz.com/showPage.html?page=stats/web_worldwide.

35. Timothy B. Lee, "Comcast's Deal with Netflix Makes Network Neutrality Obsolete," *Washington Post*, February 23, 2014, http://www.washingtonpost.com/blogs/the-switch/wp/2014/02/23/comcasts-deal-with-netflix-makes-network-neutrality-obsolete/.

36. Federal Communications Commission, *In the Matter of Preserving the Open Internet Broadband Industry Practices*, Report and Order FCC 10-201, December 23, 2010, http://madison.techcrunch.com/assets/pdfs/FCC-10-201A1.pdf.

37. Editorial Board, "Creating a Two-Speed Internet," *New York Times*, April 24, 2014, http://www.nytimes.com/2014/04/25/opinion/creating-a-two-speed-internet.html.

38. David Bollier, "Saving the Information Commons," Remarks to American Library Association Convention, Atlanta, June 15, 2002, http://www.ala.org/acrl/aboutacrl/directoryofleadership/committees/copyright/piratesbollier.

39. Douglas Gomery, "In Search of the Cybermarket," *Wilson Quarterly* (Summer 1994): 10.

◢ EXAMINING ETHICS The "Anonymous" Hackers of the Internet, p. 50

1. Matt Liebowitz, "Anonymous Targets Monsanto Again in Latest Data Dump," MSNBC, March 2, 2012, http://www.msnbc.msn.com

/id/46606307/ns/technology_and_science-security/t/anonymous
-targets-monsanto-again-latest-data-dump/#.UBFr216chs8.

2. Chris Landers, "Serious Business: Anonymous Takes On Scientology (and Doesn't Afraid of Anything)," *Baltimore City Paper*, April 2, 2008, http://www2.citypaper.com/columns/story .asp?id=15543.

3. David Kushner, "Anonymous vs. Steubenville," *Rolling Stone*, November 27, 2013, http://www.rollingstone.com/culture/news /anonymous-vs-steubenville-20131127.

4. David E. Sanger, "Obama Order Sped Up Wave of Cyberattacks against Iran," *New York Times,* June 1, 2012, http://www.nytimes .com/2012/06/01/world/middleeast/obama-ordered-wave-of -cyberattacks-against-iran.html.

▲ **GLOBAL VILLAGE   Designed in California, Assembled in China, p. 61**

1. Charles Duhigg and Keith Bradsher, "How the U.S. Lost Out on iPhone Work," *New York Times*, January 21, 2012, http://www .nytimes.com/2012/01/22/business/apple-america-and-a-squeezed -middle-class.html.

2. Ibid. See also Charles Duhigg and David Barboza, "In China, Human Costs Are Built into an iPad," *New York Times,* January 25, 2012, http://www.nytimes.com/2012/01/26/business/ieconomy- apples-ipad-and-the-human-costs-for-workers-in-china.html.

3. Bill Weir, "A Trip to the iFactory: 'Nightline' Gets an Unprecedent- ed Glimpse inside Apple's Chinese Core," *ABC News*, February 20, 2012, http://abcnews.go.com/International/trip-ifactory-nightline -unprecedented-glimpse-inside-apples-chinese/story?id=15748745# .T9AQTu2PfpA.

4. Barbara Demick and David Sarno, "Firm Shaken by Suicides," *Los Angeles Times*, May 26, 2010, http://articles.latimes.com/2010/may /26/world/la-fg-china-suicides-20100526.

5. Fair Labor Association, "Fair Labor Association Secures Commitment to Limit Workers' Hours, Protect Pay at Apple's Largest Supplier," March 29, 2012, http://www.fairlabor.org/blog /entry/fair-labor-association-secures-commitment-limit-workers -hours-protect-pay-apples-largest.

▲ **Media Literacy and the Critical Process   Tracking and Recording Your Every Move, p. 63**

1. Robert Epstein, "Google's Gotcha: 15 Ways Google Monitors You," *U.S. News & World Report*, May 10, 2013, http://www.usnews.com /opinion/articles/2013/05/10/15-ways-google-monitors-you.

3 Digital Gaming and the Media Playground

1. Chris Gaither, "Technology & Media; Video Game Field Becomes Crowded and Highly Profitable," *New York Times*, December 17, 2001, http://www.nytimes.com/2001/12/17/business/technology -media-video-game-field-becomes-crowded-and-highly-profitable .html.

2. Roger Kay, "Facebook's $2 Billion Purchase of Oculus Is Just Crazy," *Forbes*, March 26, 2014, http://www.forbes.com/sites /rogerkay/2014/03/26/facebooks-2-billion-purchase-of-oculus-is -just-crazy/. See also Jeff Reeves, "Why Facebook Was Smart to Buy Oculus," *MarketWatch*, March 31, 2014, http://www.marketwatch .com/story/why-facebook-was-smart-to-buy-oculus-2014-03-31.

3. Mark Zuckerberg, Facebook, March 25, 2014, https://www .facebook.com/zuck/posts/10101319050523971.

4. Gartner, "Gartner Says Worldwide Video Game Market to Total $93 Billion in 2013," October 29, 2013, http://www.gartner.com /newsroom/id/2614915.

5. Erkki Huhtamo, "Slots of Fun, Slots of Trouble: An Archaeology of Arcade Gaming," in Joost Raessens and Jeffrey Goldstein, eds., *Handbook of Computer Game Studies* (Cambridge, Mass.: MIT, 2005), 10.

6. Ibid., 9–10.

7. Seth Porges, "11 Things You Didn't Know about Pinball History," *Popular Mechanics*, accessed August 7, 2014, http://www.popular mechanics.com/technology/gadgets/toys/4328211-new#fbIndex.

8. David Winter, "Magnavox Odyssey," accessed June 20, 2012, http://www.pong-story.com/odyssey.htm.

9. "Industry Demographics," Fantasy Sports Trade Association, accessed May 19, 2014, http://www.fsta.org/?page=Demographics.

10. Chris Taylor, "Facebook: 375 Million Users Play Games Each Month," *Mashable*, March 19, 2014, http://mashable.com/2014/03/19 /facebook-games-stats/.

11. Keith Stuart, "Nintendo Game Boy—25 Facts for Its 25th Anniversary," *Guardian*, April 21, 2014, http://www.theguardian .com/technology/2014/apr/21/nintendo-game-boy-25-facts-for-its -25th-anniversary.

12. See Mark Rogowsky, "Without Much Fanfare, Apple Has Sold Its 500 Millionth iPhone," *Forbes*, March 25, 2014, http://www.forbes .com/sites/markrogowsky/2014/03/25/without-much-fanfare-apple -has-sold-its-500-millionth-iphone/. See also Shara Tibken, "Six Takeaways from Apple CEO Cook's Earnings Call," CNET, April 24, 2014, http://www.cnet.com/news/six-takeaways-from-apple-ceo -cooks-earnings-call/.

13. See Richard Verrier, "CinemaCon 2014: Global Box Office Hits Record $35 Billion in 2013," *Los Angeles Times*, March 25, 2014, http://www.latimes.com/entertainment/envelope/cotown/la-et-ct -cinemacon-global-box-office-2013-record-20140325-story .html#axzz2ynuWdlt4. See also Gartner, "Gartner Says Worldwide Video Game Market to Total $93 Billion in 2013."

14. Sam Anderson, "Just One More Game . . . Angry Birds, Farmville and Other Hyperaddictive 'Stupid Games,'" *New York Times*, April 4, 2012, http://www.nytimes.com/2012/04/08/magazine/angry-birds -farmville-and-other-hyperaddictive-stupid-games.html.

15. Entertainment Software Association, *2014 Essential Facts about the Computer and Video Game Industry*, 2014, p. 12, http://www .theesa.com/wp-content/uploads/2014/10/ESA_EF_2014.pdf.

16. Ian Sherr, "Player Tally for 'League of Legends' Surges," *Wall Street Journal*, January 27, 2014, http://blogs.wsj.com/digits/2014 /01/27/player-tally-for-league-of-legends-surges/.

17. Editorial: "Final Eclipse of Conversation?" *Milwaukee Journal*, December 19, 1981, p. 12.

18. Pierre Lévy, *Collective Intelligence: Mankind's Emerging World in Cyberspace* (New York: Basic Books, 1997), xxviii.

19. *World of Warcraft*, "Beginner's Guide, Chapter III: Playing Together," accessed May 20, 2014, http://us.battle.net/wow/en/game /guide/playing-together.

20. Entertainment Software Association, *In-Game Advertising*, 2012, http://www.theesa.com/games-improving-what-matters /advertising.asp.

21. Ibid.

22. D. A. Gentile, H. Choo, A. Liau, T. Sim, D. Li, D. Fung, and A. Khoo, "Pathological Video Game Use among Youths: A Two-Year Longitudinal Study," *Pediatrics* 127, no. 2 (2011), doi:10.1542/peds .2010-1353.

23. Florian Rehbein and Dirk Baier, "Family-, Media-, and School-Related Factors of Video Game Addiction: A 5-Year Longitudinal Study," *Journal of Media Psychology: Theories, Methods, and Application* 25, no. 3 (2013): 118–128.

24. Andrew Salmon, "Couple: Internet Gaming Addiction Led to Baby's Death," CNN, April 1, 2010, http://articles.cnn.com/2010-04 -01/world/korea.parents.starved.baby_1_gaming-addiction -internet-gaming-gaming-industry?_s=PM:WORLD.

25. Jason Epstein, "10 of the Most Delightfully Violent Video Games of All Time," Guyism, February 13, 2012, http://guyism.com/tech /gadgets/10-of-the-most-violent-video-games-of-all-time.html.

26. Patrick Markey and Charlotte N. Markey, "Vulnerability to Violent Video Games: A Review and Integration of Personality Research," *Review of General Psychology* 14, no. 2 (2010): 82–91.

27. National Center for Women & Information Technology, "NCWIT Factsheet," accessed June 26, 2012, http://www.ncwit.org/sites /default/files/resources/ncwitfactsheet.pdf. See also Claire Cain Miller, "Technology's Man Problem," *New York Times*, April 5, 2014, http://www.nytimes.com/2014/04/06/technology/technologys-man -problem.html.

28. Daniel Engber, "How Do Video Games Get Rated?" *Slate*, July 15, 2005, http://www.slate.com/articles/news_and_politics/explainer /2005/07/how_do_video_games_get_rated.html.

29. Janna Anderson and Lee Rainie, "The Future of Gamification," Pew Internet & American Life Project, May 18, 2012, http://pewinternet.org /Reports/2012/Future-of-Gamification/Overview.aspx.

30. Entertainment Software Association, *2013 Essential Facts about the Computer and Video Game Industry.*

31. John Markoff, "Company News; Sony Starts a Division to Sell Game Machines," *New York Times*, May 19, 1994, http://www .nytimes.com/1994/05/19/business/company-news-sony-starts-a -division-to-sell-game-machines.html.

32. Business Wire, "Nintendo 64 Sold Out; Company Pushes for More Product; Frenzied Consumers Demand to Buy Before Product Officially Launches," October 2, 1996, http://www.thefreelibrary. com/Nintendo+64+Sold+Out%3B+Company+Pushes+for+More+ Product%3B+Frenzied...-a018745127

33. "Tired of Waiting for Prices to Fall, Consumers Are Returning to Video Games," *New York Times*, January 26, 1998, http://www .nytimes.com/1998/01/26/business/tired-of-waiting-for-prices-to -fall-consumers-are-returning-to-video-games.html.

34. John Markoff, "Microsoft's Game Plan; Xbox to Go Head to Head with Sony," *New York Times*, September 4, 2000, http://www.nytimes .com/2000/09/04/business/microsoft-s-game-plan-xbox-to-go-head -to-head-with-sony.html.

35. Craig Glenday, ed., "Hardware History II," in *Guinness World Records Gamer's Edition 2008* (London: Guinness World Records, 2008), 27.

36. "Mission Statement," Blizzard Entertainment, accessed May 20, 2014, http://us.blizzard.com/en-us/company/about/mission.html.

37. Alex Pham, "Star Wars: The Old Republic—the Costliest Game of All Time?" *Los Angeles Times,* January 20, 2012, http://latimesblogs .latimes.com/entertainmentnewsbuzz/2012/01/star-wars-old -republic-cost.html.

38. Matt Brian, "Rovio's Angry Birds Titles Hit 1 Billion Cumulative Downloads," *TNW Blog*, May 9, 2012, http://thenextweb.com/mobile /2012/05/09/rovios-angry-birds-titles-hit-1-billion-cumulative- downloads/.

39. Rob Waugh, "Star Wars Epic Uses the Force—and $100M—to Take on World of Warcraft," *Mail Online*, December 20, 2011, http:// www.dailymail.co.uk/sciencetech/article-2076105/Star-Wars-epic -takes-4-billion-titan-online-gaming-World-Warcraft.html.

40. "John Madden Net Worth," Celebrity Networth, accessed July 5, 2012, http://www.celebritynetworth.com/richest-athletes/nfl/ john-madden-net-worth/.

41. Joshua Brustein, "Grand Theft Auto V Is the Most Expensive Game Ever—and It's Almost Obsolete," *Bloomberg Businessweek*, September 18, 2013, http://www.businessweek.com/articles /2013-09-18/grand-theft-auto-v-is-the-most-expensive-game-ever -and-it-s-almost-obsolete. See also Superannuation, "How Much Does It Cost to Make a Big Video Game?" *Kotaku*, January 15, 2014, http://kotaku.com/how-much-does-it-cost-to-make-a-big-video -game-1501413649.

42. Erik Kain, "'Grand Theft Auto V' Crosses $1B in Sales, Biggest Entertainment Launch in History," *Forbes*, September 20, 2013, www.forbes.com/sites/erikkain/2013/09/20/grand-theft-auto-v -crosses-1b-in-sales-biggest-entertainment-launch-in-history/.

43. Ian Hamilton, "Blizzard's World of Warcraft Revenue Down," *Orange County Register*, November 8, 2010, http://ocunwired.ocregister .com/2010/11/08/blizzards-world-of-warcraft-revenue-down/.

44. GameStop Corp., *10K Annual Report*, April 2, 2014, http://www .sec.gov/Archives/edgar/data/1326380/000119312512134615 /d283661d10k.htm.

45. "Steam: Valve's Ingenious Digital Store," Daily Infographic, February 24, 2012, http://dailyinfographic.com/steam-valves -ingenious-digital-store-infographic.

46. Matthew Sabatini, "Google Play (Android Market) vs Apple App Store—2012," *Android Authority*, April 24, 2012, http://www .androidauthority.com/google-play-vs-apple-app-store-2012-76566/.

47. Jeff Beer, "Rise of Mobile Gaming Surprises Big Video-Game Developers," *Canadian Business*, April 2, 2012, p. 30.

48. Aaron Leitko, "Kickstarter.com Helps Video Game Developers Reboot Old Titles," *Washington Post*, May 25, 2012, http://www .washingtonpost.com/lifestyle/style/kickstartercom-helps-video-game -developers-reboot-old-titles/2012/05/25/gJQAMeFipU_story.html.

49. Evan Narcisse, "Supreme Court: 'Video Games Qualify for First Amendment Protection,'" *Time*, June 27, 2011, http://techland.time .com/2011/06/27/supreme-court-video-games-qualify-for-first -amendment-protection/.

50. Entertainment Software Association, *2014 Essential Facts about the Computer and Video Game Industry,* April 2014, http://www .theesa.com/wp-content/uploads/2014/10/ESA_EF_2014.pdf.

51. Charlie Jane Anders, "*Prometheus* Writer Jon Spaihts on How to Create a Great Space Movie," io9, May 10, 2012, http://io9 .com/5909279/prometheus-writer-jon-spaihts-on-how-to-create-a -great-space-movie.

52. Ray Muzyka, "To Mass Effect 3 Players, from Dr. Ray Muzyka, Co-founder of BioWare," *BioWare*, March 21, 2012, http://blog .bioware.com/2012/03/21/4108/.

▲ **CASE STUDY** *Watch Dogs* **Hacks Our Surveillance Society, p. 85**
1. Chris Suellentrop, "New Consoles' Special Game: Waiting," *New York Times*, September 6, 2013, http://www.nytimes.com/2013/09/08/arts/video-games/for-playstation-4-and-xbox-one-best-games-may-have-to-wait.html.
2. Charlie Hall, "Watch Dogs: Invasion_," Polygon, October 16, 2013, http://www.polygon.com/features/2013/10/16/4817988/watch-dogs-invasion.
3. *Watch Dogs*, "Ultimate Preview Trailer," Ubisoft Entertainment, 2013, http://watchdogs.ubi.com/watchdogs/en-us/home/index.aspx.
4. Sean Hollister, "'Watch Dogs' Adds Real Guilt to Fake Killing," The Verge, April 23, 2014, http://www.theverge.com/2014/4/23/5640896/watch-dogs-preview.

▲ **GLOBAL VILLAGE** **South Korea's Gaming Obsession, p. 96**
1. Chico Harlan, "S. Korean Gamers Now Have Plenty to Cheer About," *Washington Post*, August 17, 2010, p. A8.
2. Seth Schiesel, "Land of the Video Geek," *New York Times*, October 8, 2006, www.nytimes.com/2006/10/08/arts/08schi.html.
3. Brett Staebell, "BoxeR in Brief," *Escapist*, April 6, 2010, http://www.escapistmagazine.com/articles/view/issues/issue_248/7378-BoxeR-in-Brief.
4. "Tournaments, Live Broadcasts Herald Rise of E-sports," *Korea Times*, February 8, 2012, http://www.koreatimes.co.kr/www/news/art/2012/05/201_104371.html.
5. Schiesel, "Land of the Video Geek."
6. Ibid.
7. Harlan, "S. Korean Gamers."
8. Carolyn Sun, "South Korea Is the Most-Wired Country in the World—and Online Games Are the New Drug of Choice for Its Youth," *Newsweek*, International Edition, October 24, 2011.

▲ **Media Literacy and the Critical Process** **First-Person Shooter Games: Misogyny as Entertainment?, p. 98**
1. Seth Schiesel, "Way Down Deep in the Wild, Wild West," *New York Times*, May 16, 2010, http://www.nytimes.com/2010/05/17/arts/television/17dead.html.
2. Ibid.
3. The Red Dragon, "Red Dead Redemption Coolest Achievement Ever—Dastardly Tutorial," YouTube video, posted May 19, 2010, http://www.youtube.com/watch?v=Vmtdvpp9dMc&feature=related.
4. Tracy Clark-Flory, "Grand Theft Misogyny," *Salon*, May 3, 2008, http://www.salon.com/life/broadsheet/2008/05/03/gta.
5. Matt Cabral, "A History of GTA and How It Helped Shape Red Dead Redemption," *PCWorld Australia*, July 13, 2010, http://www.pcworld.idg.com.au/article/352981/history_gta_how_it_helped_shape_red_dead_redemption/.

Part 2 Opener
http://www.asymco.com/2010/09/08/itunes-app-total-downloads-to-overtake-songs-this-year/
http://appleinsider.com/articles/14/02/11/app-store-growth-makes-apples-itunes-business-alone-more-valuable-than-xerox-cbs
http://seekingalpha.com/article/462301-apple-and-pandora-are-working-in-tandem
http://digitalquarters.net/

http://www.movingpicture.com/email/201308cheatsheet/Producers-Cheatsheet_201308.html
http://www.ongamers.com/articles/wall-street-journal-chart-lists-twitch-tv-fourth-in-u-s-peak-traffic/1100-824/
http://drupal.kurthanson.com/category/tags/triton-digital

4 **Sound Recording and Popular Music**
1. Nolan Feeney, "Macklemore's 'Thrift Shop' Is First Indie Hit to Top Charts in Nearly Two Decades," *Time*, January 25, 2013, http://newsfeed.time.com/2013/01/25/macklemores-thrift-shop-is-first-indie-hit-to-top-charts-in-nearly-two-decades/.
2. James C. Mckinley Jr., "Stars Align for a Gay Marriage Anthem," *New York Times*, June 30, 2013, http://www.nytimes.com/2013/07/01/arts/music/stars-align-for-a-gay-marriage-anthem.html.
3. "Édouard-Léon Scott de Martinville's Phonautograms," First Sounds, accessed August 21, 2014, http://www.firstsounds.org/sounds/scott.php.
4. Thomas Edison, quoted in Marshall McLuhan, *Understanding Media* (New York: McGraw-Hill, 1964), 276.
5. Mark Coleman, *Playback: From the Victrola to MP3* (Cambridge, Mass.: Da Capo Press, 2003).
6. Shawn Fanning, quoted in Steven Levy, "The Noisy War over Napster," *Newsweek*, June 5, 2000, p. 46.
7. Ethan Smith, "LimeWire Found to Infringe Copyrights," *Wall Street Journal*, May 12, 2010, http://online.wsj.com/article/SB10001424052748704247904575240572654422514.html.
8. Ben Sisario, "Spotify Hits 10 Million Subscribers, a Milestone," *New York Times*, May 21, 2014, http://www.nytimes.com/2014/05/22/business/media/spotify-hits-milestone-with-10-million-paid-subscribers.html.
9. IFPI, "IFPI Digital Music Report 2014," 2014, http://www.ifpi.org/downloads/Digital-Music-Report-2014.pdf.
10. Brian X. Chen, "Apple to Pay $3 Billion to Buy Beats," *New York Times*, May 28, 2014, http://www.nytimes.com/2014/05/29/technology/apple-confirms-its-3-billion-deal-for-beats-electronics.html.
11. See Bruce Tucker, "'Tell Tchaikovsky the News': Postmodernism, Popular Culture and the Emergence of Rock 'n' Roll," *Black Music Research Journal* 9, no. 2 (Fall 1989): 280.
12. Robert Palmer, *Deep Blues: A Musical and Cultural History of the Mississippi Delta* (New York: Penguin, 1982), 15.
13. LeRoi Jones, *Blues People* (New York: Morrow Quill, 1963), 168.
14. Mick Jagger, quoted in Jann S. Wenner, "Jagger Remembers," *Rolling Stone,* December 14, 1995, p. 66.
15. Little Richard, quoted in Charles White, *The Life and Times of Little Richard: The Quasar of Rock* (New York: Harmony Books, 1984), 65–66.
16. Quoted in Dave Marsh and James Bernard, *The New Book of Rock Lists* (New York: Fireside, 1994), 15.
17. Tucker, "'Tell Tchaikovsky the News,'" 287.
18. See Gerri Hershey, *Nowhere to Run: The Story of Soul Music* (New York: Penguin Books, 1984).
19. Ken Tucker, quoted in Ed Ward, Geoffrey Stokes, and Ken Tucker, *Rock of Ages: The Rolling Stone History of Rock and Roll* (New York: Simon & Schuster, 1986), 521.
20. Stephen Thomas Erlewine, "Nirvana," in Michael Erlewine, ed., *All Music Guide: The Best CDs, Albums, & Tapes,* 2nd ed. (San Francisco: Miller Freeman Books, 1994), 233.

21. Joshua P. Friedlander, "News and Notes on 2013 RIAA Music Industry Shipment and Revenue Statistics," accessed August 21, 2014, http://76.74.24.142/2463566A-FF96-E0CA-2766-72779A364D01.pdf; and IFPI, "Digital Music Report 2014."

22. IFPI, "Digital Music Report 2014."

23. Spotify, "Some Fast Figures," accessed June 7, 2014, http://press.spotify.com/us/information/.

24. Spotify, "Spotify Explained," accessed June 7, 2014, http://www.spotifyartists.com/spotify-explained/.

25. Stuart Dredge, "Streaming Music Payments: How Much Do Artists Really Receive?" *Guardian*, August 19, 2013, http://www.theguardian.com/technology/2013/aug/19/zoe-keating-spotify-streaming-royalties.

26. Jeff Leeds, "The Net Is a Boon for Indie Labels," *New York Times*, December 27, 2005, p. E1.

27. Nat Hentoff, "Many Dreams Fueled Long Development of U.S. Music," *Milwaukee Journal*/United Press International, February 26, 1978, p. 2.

◢ CASE STUDY Psy and the Meaning of "Gangnam Style," p. 142

1. Jeff Yang, "Gangnam Style's U.S. Popularity Has Koreans Puzzled, Gratified," *Wall Street Journal*, August 28, 2012, http://blogs.wsj.com/speakeasy/2012/08/28/gangnam-style-viral-popularity-in-u-s-has-koreans-puzzled-gratified/.

5 Popular Radio and the Origins of Broadcasting

1. Tom Lewis, *Empire of the Air: The Men Who Made Radio* (New York: HarperCollins, 1991), 181.

2. Captain Linwood S. Howeth, USN (Retired), *History of Communications-Electronics in the United States Navy* (Washington, D.C.: Government Printing Office, 1963), http://earlyradiohistory.us/1963hw.htm.

3. Margaret Cheney, *Tesla: Man out of Time* (New York: Touchstone, 2001).

4. William J. Broad, "Tesla, a Bizarre Genius, Regains Aura of Greatness," *New York Times*, August 28, 1984, http://query.nytimes.com/gst/fullpage.html?res=9400E4DD1038F93BA1575BC0A9629482
60&sec=health&spon=&partner=permalink&exprod=permalink.

5. Michael Pupin, "Objections Entered to Court's Decision," *New York Times*, June 10, 1934, p. E5.

6. Lewis, *Empire of the Air*, 73.

7. For a full discussion of early broadcast history and the formation of RCA, see Eric Barnouw, *Tube of Plenty* (New York: Oxford University Press, 1982); Susan Douglas, *Inventing American Broadcasting, 1899–1922* (Baltimore: Johns Hopkins University Press, 1987); and Christopher Sterling and John Kitross, *Stay Tuned: A Concise History of American Broadcasting* (Belmont, Calif.: Wadsworth, 1990).

8. See Jefferson Cowie, *Capital Moves: RCA's Seventy-Year Quest for Cheap Labor* (New York: New Press, 2001).

9. Robert W. McChesney, *Telecommunications, Mass Media & Democracy: The Battle for Control of U.S. Broadcasting, 1928–1935* (New York: Oxford University Press, 1994).

10. Michele Hilmes, *Radio Voices: American Broadcasting, 1922–1952* (Minneapolis: University of Minnesota Press, 1997).

11. "Amos 'n' Andy Show," Museum of Broadcast Communications, http://www.museum.tv/archives/etv/A/htmlA/amosnandy/amosnandy.htm.

12. StreamingRadioGuide, "Radio Stations Streaming on the Internet," accessed October 5, 2014, http://streamingradioguide.com/.

13. Arbitron, "The Infinite Dial 2013: Navigating Digital Platforms," 2013, http://www.edisonresearch.com/wp-content/uploads/2013/04/Edison_Research_Arbitron_Infinite_Dial_2013.pdf.

14. Ed Christman, "RIAA, Pandora, NARAS, NAB Square Off on Capitol Hill," Billboard.biz, June 7, 2012, http://www.billboard.biz/bbbiz/industry/legal-and-management/riaa-pandora-naras-nab-square-off-on-capitol-1007257152.story.

15. National Association of Broadcasters, "Equipping Mobile Phones with Broadcast Radio Capability for Emergency Preparedness Additional Resources," accessed June 13, 2014, http://www.nab.org/advocacy/issueResources.asp?id=2354&issueID=1082.

16. Nielsen, "State of the Media: Audio Today 2014, How America Listens," February 6, 2014, http://www.nielsen.com/us/en/reports/2014/state-of-the-media-audio-today-2014.html.

17. Radio Advertising Bureau, "Network, Digital, Off-Air Shine as Radio Ends 2013 in the Black," March 14, 2014, http://www.rab.com/public/pr/revenue_detail.cfm?id=132.

18. Federal Communications Commission, "Broadcast Station Totals as of March 31, 2014," April 9, 2014, http://www.fcc.gov/document/broadcast-station-totals-march-31-2014.

19. Peter DiCola, "False Premises, False Promises: A Quantitative History of Ownership Consolidation in the Radio Industry," Future of Music Coalition, December 13, 2006, http://futureofmusic.org/article/research/false-premises-false-promises.

20. "Statement of FCC Chairman William E. Kennard on Low Power FM Radio Initiative," March 27, 2000, http://www.fcc.gov/Speeches/Kennard/Statements/2000/stwek024.html.

◢ GLOBAL VILLAGE Radio Mogadishu, p. 176

1. Committee to Protect Journalists, "53 Journalists Killed in Somalia since 1992 / Motive Confirmed," accessed June 15, 2014, http://www.cpj.org/killed/africa/somalia/.

2. Mohammed Ibrahim, "Somali Radio Stations Halt Music," *New York Times*, April 13, 2010, http://www.nytimes.com/2010/04/14/world/africa/14somalia.html.

3. Jeffrey Gettleman, "A Guiding Voice amid the Ruins of a Capital City," *New York Times*, March 29, 2010, http://www.nytimes.com/2010/03/30/world/africa/30mogadishu.html.

4. CISA News Africa, "Somali: Another Journalist Killed," July 9, 2013, http://cisanewsafrica.com/somali-another-journalist-killed/.

5. Patrick Jackson, "Somali Anger at Threat to Music," BBC, April 7, 2010, http://news.bbc.co.uk/2/hi/africa/8604830.stm.

6 Television and Cable: The Power of Visual Culture

1. Amanda Kondolojy, "'ABC World News with Diane Sawyer' Closes Total Viewing Gap with 'NBC Nightly News' by 3%," TV by the Numbers, June 5, 2012, http://tvbythenumbers.zap2it.com/2012/06/05/abc-world-news-with-diane-sawyer-closes-total-viewing-gap-with-nbc-nightly-news-by-3/136864/.

2. See Greg Jarboe, "YouTube Now Gets More Than 1 Billion Unique Visitors Every Month," Search Engine Watch, March 22, 2013, www

.searchenginewatch.com/article/2256759 and also https://www
.youtube.com/yt/press/statistics.html, accessed October 3, 2014.
3. See Nielsen, "The Digital Consumer," February 2014, http://www
.nielsen.com/content/dam/corporate/us/en/reports-downloads
/2014%20Reports/the-digital-consumer-report-feb-2014.pdf.
4. See National Cable & Telecommunication Association, "Industry
Data," accessed August 18, 2014, https://www.ncta.com/industry-data.
5. See Edmund Lee, "Netflix CEO Reed Hastings: We Won't Compete
with Cable TV," *Advertising Age*, May 4, 2011, http://adage.com
/article/mediaworks/netflix-ceo-reed-hastings-compete-cable
-tv/227364/.
6. See Sam Schechner, "Comcast Takes Aim at Netflix," *Wall Street
Journal*, February 22, 2012, http://online.wsj.com/article/SB10001424
052970204909104577237321153043092.html.
7. See Nielsen, "The Digital Consumer."
8. J. Fred MacDonald, *One Nation under Television: The Rise and
Decline of Network TV* (Chicago: Nelson-Hall Publishers, 1994), 70.
9. Edgar Bergen, quoted in MacDonald, *One Nation under Television*,
78.
10. See Horace Newcomb, *TV: The Most Popular Art* (Garden City,
N.Y.: Anchor Books, 1974), 31, 39.
11. Ibid., 35.
12. Association of Public Television Stations (APTS), "Congress
Provides Critical Funding Increases to Public Broadcasting for
FY2010," December 15, 2009, http://archive.today/Ue9iE.
13. See Elizabeth Jensen, "PBS Plans Promotional Breaks within
Programs," *New York Times*, May 31, 2011, http://www.nytimes
.com/2011/05/31/business/media/31adco.html.
14. John Boland, quoted in Katy June-Friesen, "Surge of Channels . .
. Depress PBS Ratings," *Current.org*, December 8, 2008, http://www
.current.org/2008/12/surge-of-channels-people-meter-chaos
-depress-pbs-ratings/.
15. See Dru Sefton, "PBS Mulls Strategy to Boost Kids' Ratings,"
Current.org, March 11, 2014, www.current.org/2014/03/pbs
-mulls-strategy-to-boost-kids-ratings.
16. MacDonald, *One Nation under Television,* 181.
17. *United States v. Midwest Video Corp.*, 440 U.S. 689 (1979).
18. Federal Communications Commission, "Report on Cable
Industry Prices," January 16, 2009, http://hraunfoss.fcc.gov/edocs
_public/attachmatch/DA-09-53A1.pdf.
19. National Cable & Telecommunication Association, "Operating
Metrics," accessed July 12, 2012, http://www.ncta.com/StatsGroup
/OperatingMetric.aspx.
20. See Jack Loechner, "TV Advertising Most Influential,"
MediaPost, March 23, 2011, http://www.mediapost
.com/publications/article/147033.
21. Bill Carter, "Cable TV, the Home of High Drama," *New York
Times*, April 5, 2010, pp. B1, B3.
22. See Josef Adalian, "The 2011–12 TV Season: What We Watched
and What We Skipped," Vulture, June 21, 2012, www.vulture.com
/2012/06/201112-tv-season-by-the-numbers.html.
23. See Sara Bibel, "Live+7 DVR Ratings: Complete 2013–2014
Season," TV by the Numbers, June 9, 2014, http://tvbythenumbers
.zap2it.com/2014/06/09/live7-dvr-ratings-complete-2013-14-season
-the-big-bang-theory-leads-adults-18-49-ratings-increase-raising
-hope-earns-biggest-percentage-increase-the-blacklist-tope
-viewership-gains/271900/.

24. William J. Ray, "Private Enterprise, Privileged Enterprise, or
Free Enterprise," accessed February 21, 2012, http://www.glasgow
-Ky.com/papers/#PrivateEnterprise.
25. Ibid.

⬛ CASE STUDY   ESPN: Sports and Stories, p. 198
1. See Linda Haugsted, "ESPN's First-Place Finish," *Multichannel
News*, March 3, 2008, p. 21.

7 Movies and the Impact of Images
1. Roger Ebert, "Avatar," December 11, 2009, http://rogerebert
.suntimes.com/apps/pbcs.dll/article?AID=/20091211/REVIEWS
/912119998.
2. Michael Cieply, "For Fox, Much Is Riding on 3 Sequels to 'Avatar,'"
New York Times, June 15, 2014, http://www.nytimes.com/2014/06/16
/business/media/fox-expects-3-avatar-sequels-to-be-worth-the
-wait.html.
3. John Cawelti, *Adventure, Mystery, and Romance: Formula Stories
as Art and Popular Culture* (Chicago: University of Chicago Press,
1976), 35.
4. See Charles Musser, *The Emergence of Cinema: The American
Screen to 1907* (New York: Scribner's, 1991).
5. Douglas Gomery, *Shared Pleasures: A History of Movie Presentation in the United States* (Madison: University of Wisconsin Press,
1992), 18.
6. Douglas Gomery, *Movie History: A Survey* (Belmont, Calif.:
Wadsworth, 1991), 167.
7. See Cawelti, *Adventure, Mystery, and Romance*, 80–98.
8. See Barbara Koenig Quart, *Women Directors: The Emergence of a
New Cinema* (New York: Praeger, 1988).
9. See Gomery, *Shared Pleasures*, 171–180.
10. Ismail Merchant, "Kitschy as Ever, Hollywood Is Branching Out,"
New York Times, November 22, 1998, sec. 2, pp. 15, 30.
11. See Eric Barnouw, *Tube of Plenty: The Evolution of American Television,* rev. ed. (New York: Oxford University Press, 1982), 108–109.
12. See Douglas Gomery, "Who Killed Hollywood?" *Wilson Quarterly*
(Summer 1991): 106–112.
13. Motion Picture Association of America, "Theatrical Market
Statistics," 2013, http://www.mpaa.org/wp-content/uploads/2014/03
/MPAA-Theatrical-Market-Statistics-2013-032514-v2.pdf.
14. Chris Dodd, "CinemaCon 2014—Remarks as Prepared for
Delivery," March 25, 2014, http://www.mpaa.org/wp-content
/uploads/2014/03/MPAA-DODD-CinemaCon-2014-As-Prepared-For
-Delivery-MG.pdf.
15. Based on authors' calculations and Motion Picture Association
of America, "Theatrical Market Statistics," 2011.
16. Tambay A. Obenson, "Is a Theatrical Release Still Essential in
2014, or Will VOD, Digital Distribution Suffice?" Indiewire, January
28, 2014, http://blogs.indiewire.com/shadowandact/is-a-theatrical
-release-still-essential-in-2014-or-will-vod-digital-distribution-suffice.
17. Andrew Wallenstein and Ramin Setoodeh, "The Movie Deal
Netflix Wants to Make—and It's Not Day-and-Date," *Variety*,
November 5, 2013, http://variety.com/2013/biz/news/netflix-to
-preem-movies-the-same-day-they-bow-in-theaters-1200796130/.
18. Jeff Gammage, "Digital or Die: Theaters Scramble for Pricey New
Projectors," *Philadelphia Inquirer*, January 13, 2013, p. A01.

19. Julianne Pepitone, "Americans Now Watch More Online Movies Than DVDs," CNN/Money, March 22, 2012, http://money.cnn.com/2012/03/22/technology/streaming-movie-sales/index.htm.

20. Jake Coyle, "Clicking through the Wild West of Video-on-Demand," *Bloomberg Businessweek*, March 29, 2012, http://www.businessweek.com/ap/2012-03/D9TQAOI00.htm.

21. Brooks Barnes, "How 'Hunger Games' Built Up Must-See Fever," *New York Times*, March 18, 2012, http://www.nytimes.com/2012/03/19/business/media/how-hunger-games-built-up-must-see-fever.html.

22. David S. Cohen, "Academy to Preserve Digital Content," *Variety*, August 3, 2007, http://www.variety.com/article/VR1117969687.html.

23. David Thorburn, "Television as an Aesthetic Medium," *Critical Studies in Mass Communication* (June 1987): 168.

▲ **CASE STUDY** **Breaking through Hollywood's Race Barrier, p. 247**

1. Douglas Gomery, *Shared Pleasures: A History of Movie Presentation in the United States* (Madison: University of Wisconsin Press, 1992), 155–170.

2. Felicia R. Lee, "To Blacks, *Precious* Is 'Demeaned' or 'Angelic,'" *New York Times*, November 20, 2009, http://www.nytimes.com/2009/11/21/movies/21precious.html. See also Mary Mitchell, "Precious Little Patience for Blaxploitation; Degradation of Black Folks Not My Idea of Entertainment," *Chicago Sun-Times*, December 17, 2009, p. 12.

Part 3 Opener

http://www.pewinternet.org/2014/01/16/a-snapshot-of-reading-in-america-in-2013/

http://www.journalism.org/2014/03/26/the-revenue-picture-for-american-journalism-and-how-it-is-changing/news_revenue8

http://stateofthemedia.org/2013/newspapers-stabilizing-but-still-threatened/newspapers-by-the-numbers/

http://www.magazine.org/node/26924

8 **Newspapers: The Rise and Decline of Modern Journalism**

1. "The Best (and Worst) Cities for Newspapers," *Advertising Age*, June 10, 2013, p. 3.

2. Brian Stelter and Christine Haughney, "Tribune in $2.7 Billion Deal for 19 Local TV Stations," *New York Times*, July 2, 2013, pp. B1, 4.

3. Ibid.

4. "US Total Media Ad Spending Share, by Media, 2012–2018," eMarketer, June 2014, http://www.emarketer.com/Article/Total-US-Ad-Spending-See-Largest-Increase-Since-2004/1010982.

5. See David Ress, "Warren Buffett Is Confident in the Future of Newspapers," roanoke.com, May 30, 2013, http://www.roanoke.com/news/local/roanoke/warren-buffett-is-confident-in-the-future-of-newspapers/article_3847f2e4-4796-552f-9fbb-a054913b9ef6.html.

6. See Newspaper Association of America, "The American Newspaper Media Industry Revenue Profile 2012," April 8, 2013, http://www.naa.org/trends-and-numbers/newspaper-revenue/newspaper-media-industry-revenue-profile-2012.aspx. For 2013 data, see Newspaper Association of America, "Newspaper Revenue 2013," April 8, 2014, http://www.naa.org/Trends-and-Numbers/Newspaper-Revenue/Newspaper-Media-Industry-Revenue-Profile-2013.aspx.

7. See Kay Mills, *A Place in the News: From the Women's Pages to the Front Page* (New York: Dodd, Mead, 1988).

8. Piers Brendon, *The Life and Death of the Press Barons* (New York: Atheneum, 1983), 136.

9. William Randolph Hearst, quoted in Brendon, *The Life and Death of the Press Barons*, 134.

10. Michael Schudson, *Discovering the News: A Social History of American Newspapers* (New York: Basic Books, 1978), 23.

11. See David T. Z. Mindich, "Edwin M. Stanton, the Inverted Pyramid, and Information Control," *Journalism Monographs* 140 (August 1993).

12. John C. Merrill, "Objectivity: An Attitude," in Merrill and Ralph L. Lowenstein, eds., *Media, Messages and Men* (New York: David McKay, 1971), 240.

13. Roy Peter Clark, "A New Shape for the News," *Washington Journalism Review*, March 1984, 47.

14. Curtis D. MacDougall, *The Press and Its Problems* (Dubuque: William C. Brown, 1964), 143, 189.

15. See Edwin Emery, *The Press and America: An Interpretative History of the Mass Media*, 3rd ed. (Englewood Cliffs, N.J.: Prentice-Hall, 1972), 562.

16. Walter Lippmann, *Liberty and the News* (New York: Harcourt, Brace and Howe, 1920), 92.

17. Tom Wolfe, quoted in Leonard W. Robinson, "The New Journalism: A Panel Discussion," in Ronald Weber, ed., *The Reporter as Artist: A Look at the New Journalism Controversy* (New York: Hastings House, 1974), 67. See also Tom Wolfe and E. E. Johnson, eds., *The New Journalism* (New York: Harper & Row, 1973).

18. Tom Wicker, *On Press* (New York: Viking, 1978), 3–5.

19. Jack Newfield, "The 'Truth' about Objectivity and the New Journalism," in Charles C. Flippen, ed., *Liberating the Media* (Washington, D.C.: Acropolis Books, 1973), 63–64.

20. Jill Abramson, quoted in Nat Ives, "Abramson and Keller, NYT's Incoming and Outgoing Top Editors, Talk Challenges and Changes," *Advertising Age*, June 2, 2011, http://adage.com/article/mediaworks/q-a-york-times-jill-abramson-bill-keller/227928/.

21. See Newspaper Association of America, "Trends and Numbers," accessed July 5, 2013, http://www.naa.org/Trends-and-Numbers.aspx; and National Newspaper Association, "Community Newspaper Facts and Figures," accessed July 5, 2013, http://nnaweb.org/about-nna?articleCategory=community-facts-figures.

22. See Sreenath Sreenivasan, "As Mainstream Papers Struggle, the Ethnic Press Is Thriving," *New York Times*, July 22, 1996, p. C7.

23. Pew Research Center's Project for Excellence in Journalism, "Ethnic: Summary Essay," *State of the News Media 2010*, http://stateofthemedia.org/2010/ethnic-summary-essay/.

24. Ibid.

25. See Barbara K. Henritze, *Bibliographic Checklist of American Newspapers* (Baltimore: Clearfield, 2009).

26. April Turner, "Black Journalists Ranks Cut by Nearly 1,000 in Past Decade," National Association of Black Journalists newsletter, April 4, 2012, http://www.nabj.org/news/88558.

27. Pamela Newkirk, "The Not-So-Great Migration," *Columbia Journalism Review*, May 25, 2011, http://www.cjr.org/feature/the_not-so-great_migration.php.

28. See American Society of News Editors (ASNE), "Table A—Minority Employment in Daily Newspapers," accessed July 5, 2013, http://asne.org/content.asp?pl=140&sl=129&contentid=129, and "Table B—Minority Employment by Race and Job Category," accessed July 5, 2013, http://asne.org/content.asp?pl=140&sl=130&contentid=130.

29. Special thanks to Mary Lamonica and her students at New Mexico State University.

30. Pew Research Center's Project for Excellence in Journalism, *State of the News Media 2010*, http://www.stateofthenewsmedia.org/2010/. See also Emily Guskin and Monica Anderson, "Developments in the Hispanic Market," Pew Research Journalism Project, March 26, 2014, http://www.journalism.org/2014/03/26/developments-in-the-hispanic-media-market.

31. ASNE, "Table A" and "Table B."

32. See United States Census Bureau, "State & County Quick Facts," July 8, 2014, http://quickfacts.census.gov/qfd/states/00000.html. See also Pew Research Center's Project for Excellence in Journalism, *State of the News Media 2010*.

33. Wil Cruz, "The New *New Yorker*: Ethnic Media Fill the Void," *Newsday*, June 26, 2002, p. A25.

34. See Chinese Advertising Agencies, "About *Chinese Daily News*," accessed September 3, 2014, http://www.chineseadvertisingagencies.com/mediaguide/Chinese-Daily-News.html.

35. ASNE, "Table A" and "Table B."

36. See Monica Anderson, "5 Facts about Alternative Weeklies," Pew Research Center, July 11, 2014, http://www.pewresearch.org/fact-tank/2014/07/11/5-facts-about-alternative-weeklies; and Association of Alternative Newsweeklies, "AAN Publications," accessed September 3, 2014, http://www.altweeklies.com/aan/Directories/Newsweeklies.

37. Pew Research Center Publications, "The New Face of Washington's Press Corps," February 11, 2009, http://pewresearch.org/pubs/1115/washington-press-corps-study.

38. Jodi Enda, Katerina Eva Matsa, and Jan Lauren Boyles, "America's Shifting Statehouse Press: Can New Players Compensate for Lost Legacy Reporters?" July 10, 2014, http://www.journalism.org/2014/07/10/americas-shifting-statehouse-press/.

39. American Society of News Editors, "Decline in Newsroom Jobs Slows," accessed June 8, 2010, http://asne.org/content.asp?pl=121&sl=150&contentid=150.

40. Rick Edmonds, "ASNE Newsroom Census Total Reflects Decline in Traditional Journalism Jobs," Poynter, May 6, 2011, http://www.poynter.org/latest-news/business-news/the-biz-blog/130184.

41. See Rick Edmonds, "ASNE Census Finds 2,600 Newsroom Jobs Were Lost in 2012," Poynter, June 26, 2013, www.poynter.org/latest-news/the-biz-blog/216617.

42. See Mac Ryan, "Amid Industry Cuts, Warren Buffett Says He Is Looking to Buy More Newspapers," *Forbes*, May 24, 2012, http://www.forbes.com/sites/ryanmac/2012/05/24/warren-buffett-says-he-is-looking-to-buy-more-newspapers/; and Christine Haughney, "Newspaper Work, with Warren Buffett as Boss," *New York Times*, June 17, 2012, http://www.nytimes.com/2012/06/18/business/media/newspaper-work-with-warren-buffett-as-the-boss.html?_r=0.

43. See Philip Meyer, "Learning to Love Lower Profits," *American Journalism Review*, December 1995, 40–44.

44. Pew Research Center's Project for Excellence in Journalism, "Newspapers: Summary Essay," *State of the News Media 2010*, http://stateofthemedia.org/2010/newspapers-summary-essay/.

45. Pew Research Center's Project for Excellence in Journalism, *State of the News Media 2013*, http://www.stateofthenewsmedia.org/2013.

46. World Association of Newspapers (WAN), "Newspaper Circulation Grows Despite Economic Downturn," May 27, 2009, http://www.wan-press.org/article18148.html.

47. Achara Deboonme, "Floppy Discs, Walkmans and Now Newspapers?" *Nation* (Thailand), June 4, 2013, www.nationmultimedia.com/opinion/Floppy-discs-Walkmans-and-now-newspapers-30207480.html.

48. World Association of Newspapers (WAN), "World Press Trends: Print and Digital Together Increasing Newspaper Audiences," June 9, 2014, http://www.wan-ifra.org/press-releases/2014/06/09/world-press-trends-print-and-digital-together-increasing-newspaper-audience.

49. Pew Research Center's Project for Excellence in Journalism, "Newspapers: Summary Essay," *State of the News Media 2010*.

50. Ibid.

51. "Anyone with a Modem Can Report on the World," Liberty Round Table Library Essays, address before the National Press Club, June 2, 1998, http://bhs.cc/journalism/pdf/future/Liberty%20Round%20Table_%20Essays_%20Matt%20Drudge%20Speech.pdf.

52. Joshua Micah Marshall, quoted in Noam Cohen, "Blogger, Sans Pajamas, Rakes Muck and a Prize," *New York Times*, February 25, 2008, http://www.nytimes.com/2008/02/25/business/media/25marshall.html?pagewanted=all.

53. See Amy Mitchell, "State of the News Media 2014: Overview," Pew Research Journalism Project, March 26, 2014, http://www.journalism.org/2014/03/26/state-of-the-news-media-2014-overview.

54. Richard Pérez-Peña, "Newspaper Ad Revenue Could Fall as Much as 30%," *New York Times*, April 15, 2009, p. B3.

55. See "Gannett Newspapers and Yahoo Create Local Advertising Partnership," Chicago Press Release Services, July 19, 2010, http://chicagopressrelease.com/technology/gannett-newspapers-and-yahoo; Evan Hessel, "Yahoo!'s Dangerous Newspaper Deal?" *Forbes*, June 22, 2009, http://www.forbes.com/2009/06/22/advertising-newspapers-internet-business-media-yahoo.html; and Kate Kaye, "Media General Expands Yahoo Partnership to TV-Only Markets," Clickz Marketing News, June 11, 2010, http://www.clickz.com/clickz/news/1721928/media-general-xpands-yahoo-partnership.

56. Rick Edmonds, "Newspaper Industry Narrowed Revenue Loss in 2013 as Paywall Plans Increased," Poynter, April 18, 2014, http://www.poynter.org/latest-news/top-stories/247555/newspaper-industry-narrowed-revenue-loss-in-2013-as-paywall-plans-increased.

57. D. M. Levine, "Small Papers Lead the Way on Paywalls," *Adweek*, June 3, 2011, http://www.adweek.com/news/press/small-papers-lead-way-paywalls-132203.

58. Seth Fiegerman, "*New York Times* Digital Subscription Growth Slows Ad Revenue Decline," Mashable, accessed February 7, 2013, http://mashable.com/2013/02/07/new-york-times-digital-subscribers-2/.

59. Neiman Journalism Lab, "Paywalls Are Not a Cure-All: Evidence from Gannett," February 4, 2014, http://www.niemanlab.org/2014/02/paywalls-are-not-a-cure-all-evidence-from-gannett.

60. Leonard Downie and Michael Schudson, "The Reconstruction of American Journalism," Columbia Journalism Report, October 19, 2009, pp. 77–91. See www.cjr.org for the full report. All quoted material below is from the report. See also Leonard Downie Jr. and Michael Schudson, "Finding a New Model for News Reporting," *Washington Post*, October 19, 2009, http://www.washingtonpost.com.

61. Brian Deagon, "You, Reporting Live: Citizen Journalism Relies on Audience; Now, Everyone's a Stringer . . . ," *Investor's Business Daily*, March 31, 2008, p. A4.

62. Mark Jurkowitz and Paul Hitlin, "Citizen Eyewitnesses Provide Majority of Top Online News Videos," Pew Research Center, May 20, 2013, www.pewresearch.org/fact-tank/2013/05/22/citizen -eyewitnesses-provide-majority-of-top-online-news-videos.

63. Amy Mitchell, Mark Jurkowitz, Jesse Holcomb, Jodi Enda, and Monica Anderson, "Nonprofit Journalism—A Growing but Fragile Part of the U.S. News System," Pew Research Journalism Project, June 10, 2013, http://www.journalism.org/2013/06/10/nonprofit-journalism/.

64. Jesse Holcomb and Amy Mitchell for Pew Research Journalism Project, "Personal Wealth, Capital Investments, and Philanthropy," March 26, 2014, http://www.journalism.org/2014/03/26/personal -wealth-capital-investments-and-philanthropy/.

65. Committee to Protect Journalists, accessed August 2014, http:// www.cpj.org/killed/2014/.

66. Marc Santora and Bill Carter, "War in Iraq Becomes the Deadliest Assignment for Journalists in Modern Times," *New York Times*, May 30, 2006, p. A10.

67. See Matthew Ingram, "Which Will Save AOL: *Huffington Post* or Patch?" *Gigaom*, June 9, 2011, http://www.gigaom.com/2011/06/09 /which-will-save-aol-huffington-post-or-patch.

68. Jondi Gumz, "Patch.com Shuts News Websites, Lays Off Hundreds," *Santa Cruz Sentinel*, January 29, 2014, Business and Financial section.

69. John Carroll, "News War, Part 3," *Frontline*, PBS, February 27, 2007, http://www.pbs.org/wgbh/pages/frontline/newswar/etc/script3.html.

◢ **CASE STUDY** Alternative Journalism: Dorothy Day and I. F. Stone, p. 292

1. I. F. Stone, quoted in Jack Lule, "I. F. Stone: Professional Excellence in Raising Hell," *QS News* (Summer 1989): 3.

9 Magazines in the Age of Specialization

1. Jennifer Benjamin, "How Cosmo Changed the World," accessed August 13, 2012, http://www.cosmopolitan.com/about/a1746/about -us_how-cosmo-changed-the-world/.

2. Sammye Johnson, "Promoting Easy Sex without the Intimacy: *Maxim* and *Cosmopolitan* Cover Lines and Cover Images," in Mary-Lou Galician and Debra L. Merskin, eds., *Critical Thinking about Sex, Love, and Romance in the Mass Media* (Mahwah, N.J.: Erlbaum, 2007), 55–74.

3. Karen S. H. Roggenkamp, "'Dignified Sensationalism': Elizabeth Bisland, *Cosmopolitan*, and Trips around the World," *American Periodicals: A Journal of History, Criticism, and Bibliography* 17, no. 1 (2007) 26–40.

4. John Tebbel and Mary Ellen Zuckerman, *The Magazine in America, 1741–1990* (New York: Oxford University Press, 1991), 116.

5. See Theodore Peterson, *Magazines in the Twentieth Century* (Urbana: University of Illinois Press, 1964), 5.

6. See Richard Ohmann, *Selling Culture: Magazines, Markets, and Class at the Turn of the Century* (New York: Verso, 1996).

7. See Peterson, *Magazines*, 5.

8. Magazine Publishers of America, *2012/2013 Magazine Media Factbook*, http://www.magazine.org/sites/default/files/factbook -2012.pdf; and Magazine Publishers of America, *2013/2014 Magazine Media Factbook*, http://www.magazine.org/node/26924.

9. Generoso Pope, quoted in William H. Taft, *American Magazines for the 1980s* (New York: Hastings House, 1982), 226–227.

10. See S. Elizabeth Bird, *For Enquiring Minds: A Cultural Study of Supermarket Tabloids* (Knoxville: University of Tennessee Press, 1992), 24.

11. See Robin Pogrebin, "The Number of Ad Pages Does Not Make the Magazine," *New York Times*, August 26, 1996, p. C1.

12. See Gloria Steinem, "Sex, Lies and Advertising," *Ms.*, July/August 1990, pp. 18–28.

13. Magazine Publishers of America, *2013/2014 Magazine Media Factbook*, p. 87.

14. Time Inc., Form 10-Q, May 14, 2014, https://invest.timeinc.com /invest/financials/sec-filings/default.aspx.

15. David Carr and Ravi Somaiya, "Time Inc. to Set a Lonely Course after a Spinoff," *New York Times*, June 8, 2014, http://www.nytimes .com/2014/06/09/business/media/time-inc-to-set-a-lonely-course -after-a-spinoff.html.

◢ **CASE STUDY** The Evolution of Photojournalism, p. 320

1. Carrie Melago, "Ralph Lauren Model Filippa Hamilton: I Was Fired Because I Was Too Fat!" *New York Daily News*, October 14, 2009, http://www.nydailynews.com/lifestyle/fashion/2009/10 /14/2009-10-14_model_fired_for_being_too_fat.html #ixzz0riJa9skc.

2. Ken Harris, quoted in Jesse Epstein, "Sex, Lies, and Photoshop," *New York Times*, March 8, 2009, http://video.nytimes.com/video /2009/03/09/opinion/1194838469575/sex-lies-and-photoshop.html.

◢ **TRACKING TECHNOLOGY** The New "Touch" of Magazines, p. 326

1. Steve Smith, "Zinio Brings Digital Newsstand to iPhone," *MinOnline*, January 12, 2010, http://www.minonline.com/news /Zinio-Brings-Digital-Newsstand-to-iPhone_13188.html.

2. Chris Anderson, "The Wired Tablet App: A Video Demonstration," *Wired*, February 16, 2010, http://www.wired.com/epicenter/2010/02 /the-wired-ipad-app-a-video-demonstration/.

3. Steve Meyers, "Wenner: Publishers' Rush to iPad Is 'Sheer Insanity and Insecurity and Fear,'" Poynter, May 30, 2011, http:// www.poynter.org/latest-news/romenesko/134162/wenner-publishers -rush-to-ipad-is-sheer-insanity-and-insecurity-and-fear/.

4. Katerina-Eva Matsa, Jane Sasseen, and Amy Mitchell, "Magazines: Are Hopes for Tablets Overdone?" *State of the News Media 2012*, Pew Research Center's Project for Excellence in Journalism, http:// stateofthemedia.org/2012/magazines-are-hopes-for-tablets-overdone/.

5. Jared Keller, "Will Digital Reading Entirely Replace Print?" *Atlantic*, June 24, 2011, http://www.theatlantic.com/technology /archive/2011/06/will-digital-reading-entirely-replace-print/240967.

6. Magazine Publishers of America, *2013/2014 Magazine Media Factbook*, http://www.magazine.org/node/26924, p. 73.

◢ **Media Literacy and the Critical Process** Uncovering American Beauty, p. 330

1. Academy for Eating Disorders, "Guidelines for the Fashion Industry," accessed November 18, 2014, http://www.aedweb.org /web/index.php/23-get-involved/position-statements/95-aed -statement-on-body-shaming-and-weight-prejudice-in-public -endeavors-to-reduce-obesity-9.

2. Academy for Eating Disorders, "Fast Facts on Eating Disorders," accessed November 18, 2014, http://aedweb.org/web/index.php /education/eating-disorder-information/eating-disorder -information-14#8.

🔟 Books and the Power of Print

1. Amazon.com, *2013 Annual Report*, Form 10-K, p. 3, http://phx .corporate-ir.net/phoenix.zhtml?c=97664&p=irol-reportsannual.
2. Leslie Kaufman and Elizabeth A. Harris, "J. K. Rowling's 'The Silkworm' a Boon for Other Booksellers as Hachette and Amazon Brawl," *New York Times*, June 18, 2014, http://www.nytimes .com/2014/06/19/business/media/jk-rowlings-the-silkworm-a-boon -for-other-booksellers-as-hachette-and-amazon-brawl.html.
3. "Hachette Puts Out Response to Amazon Statement, Rejects Author Pool before Agreement Is Reached," *Digital Book World*, May 28, 2014, http://www.digitalbookworld.com/2014/hachette-puts-out-response-to -amazon-statement-rejects-author-pool-before-agreement-is-reached/.
4. Jeremy Greenfield, "How the Amazon-Hachette Fight Could Shape the Future of Ideas," *Atlantic*, May 28, 2014, http://www .theatlantic.com/business/archive/2014/05/how-the-amazon -hachette-fight-could-shape-the-future-of-ideas/371756/.
5. Stephen Colbert, *The Colbert Report*, June 4, 2014, http:// thecolbertreport.cc.com/videos/t1nxwu/amazon-vs–hachette— sherman-alexie.
6. Ibid.
7. Amazon, "Announcement: Hachette/Amazon Business Interrup- tion," May 27, 2014, http://www.amazon.com/forum/kindle?_encoding =UTF8&cdForum=Fx1D7SY3BVSESG&cdThread=Tx1UO5T446WM5YY.
8. Greenfield, "How the Amazon-Hachette Fight Could Shape the Future of Ideas," 2014.
9. Blair Hanley Frank, "Surprise: These Authors Are Sticking Up for Amazon in Its Hachette Battle," *GeekWire*, July 3, 2014, http://www .geekwire.com/2014/surprise-authors-sticking-amazon-hachette-battle/.
10. See Elizabeth Eisenstein, *The Printing Press as an Agent of Change* (Cambridge: Cambridge University Press, 1980).
11. See Quentin Reynolds, *The Fiction Factory: From Pulp Row to Quality Street* (New York: Street & Smith/Random House, 1955), 72–74.
12. For a comprehensive historical overview of the publishing industry and the rise of publishing houses, see John A. Tebbel, *A History of Book Publishing in the United States*, 4 vols. (New York: R. R. Bowker, 1972–1981).
13. National Association of College Stores, "Higher Education Retail Market Facts & Figures, 2013," http://www.nacs.org/research /industrystatistics/higheredfactsfigures.aspx.
14. For a historical overview of paperbacks, see Kenneth Davis, *Two-Bit Culture: The Paperbacking of America* (Boston: Houghton Mifflin, 1984).
15. See John P. Dessauer, *Book Publishing: What It Is, What It Does* (New York: R. R. Bowker, 1974), 48.
16. Mid-Continent Public Library, "Based on the Book," accessed July 23, 2014, http://www.mymcpl.org/books-movies-music/based -book.
17. Jim Milliot, "Book Sales Dipped in 2013," *Publishers Weekly*, June 27, 2014, http://www.publishersweekly.com/pw/by-topic/industry -news/publisher-news/article/63131-book-sales-dipped-in-2013.html. See also Laura Hazard Owen, "PwC: The U.S. Consumer Ebook

Market Will Be Bigger Than the Print Book Market by 2017," *Gigaom*, June 4, 2013, https://gigaom.com/2013/06/04/pwc-the-u-s-consumer -ebook-market-will-be-bigger-than-the-print-book-market-by-2017/.
18. "Alice in Wonderland iPad App Reinvents Reading (Video)," *Huffington Post*, April 14, 2010, http://www.huffingtonpost.com /2010/04/14/alice-in-wonderland-ipad_n_537122.html.
19. Jim Milliot, "Tracking the Transition: Bookstats," *Publishers Weekly*, August 12, 2011, http://www.publishersweekly.com/pw /by-topic/industry-news/financial-reporting/article/48348-tracking -the-transition-bookstats.html.
20. Stephanie Clifford and Julie Bosman, "Publishers Look beyond Bookstores," *New York Times,* February 27, 2011, http://www .nytimes.com/2011/02/28/business/media/28bookstores.html.
21. Jim Milliot, "BEA 2014: Can Anyone Compete with Amazon?" *Publishers Weekly*, May 28, 2014, http://www.publishersweekly .com/pw/by-topic/industry-news/bea/article/62520-bea-2014-can -anyone-compete-with-amazon.html.
22. Steve Wasserman, "The Amazon Effect," *Nation,* May 29, 2012, http://www.thenation.com/article/168125/amazon-effect#.
23. Neal Pollack, "The Case for Self-Publishing," *New York Times*, May 20, 2011, http://www.nytimes.com/2011/05/22/books/review/the -case-for-self-publishing.html. See also Amanda Hocking, "An Epic Tale of How It All Happened," *Amanda Hocking's Blog*, August 27, 2010, http://amandahocking.blogspot.com/2010/08/epic-tale-of-how -it-all-happened.html.
24. National Endowment for the Arts, *Reading on the Rise*, January 12, 2009, http://www.arts.gov/research/ReadingonRise.pdf.
25. Alvin Kernan, *The Death of Literature* (New Haven: Yale University Press, 1990).
26. "How We Will Read: Clay Shirky," interview by Sonia Saraiya, *Findings*, April 5, 2012, http://blog.findings.com/post/20527246081 /how-we-will-read-clay-shirky.
27. Alan Finder, "The Joys and Hazards of Self-Publishing on the Web," *New York Times*, August 15, 2012, http://www.nytimes.com /2012/08/16/technology/personaltech/ins-and-outs-of-publishing -your-book-via-the-web.html.

Part 4 Opener

Infographic sources:
http://www.interbrand.com/en/best-global-brands/2013/Best -Global-Brands-2013.aspx
http://google.client.shareholder.com/investorkit.cfm
http://investor.apple.com/sef.cfm#filings
http://investor.fb.com
http://www.microsoft.com/investor/SEC/default.aspx
http://phx.corporte-ir.net/phoenix.zhtml?c=97664&p=irol -reportsanual

🔟 Advertising and Commercial Culture

1. Nat Worden, "Web Advertising Eclipsed Newspapers in 2010," *Wall Street Journal*, April 14, 2011, http://online.wsj.com/article/SB10 001424052748703551304576261092386405686.html#ixzzlOv1Xih57.
2. Google, "Google Inc. Announces Fourth Quarter and Fiscal Year 2012 Results," January 22, 2013, http://investor.google.com/earnings /2012/Q4_google_earnings.html.

3. Richard Tso, "How Eye-Tracking Technologies Will Change the Advertising Game," *Huffington Post*, June 19, 2013, http://www.huffingtonpost.com/richard-tso/eye-tracking-technologies_b_3457397.html.

4. Ibid.

5. Leonardo Del Vecchio, quoted in Rolfe Winkler and Manuela Mesco, "Founder of Luxottica, Key Google Partner, Says Embarrassed by Glass," *Digits*, *Wall Street Journal*, September 3, 2014, http://blogs.wsj.com/digits/2014/09/03/founder-of-luxottica-key-google-partner-says-embarrassed-by-glass/.

6. Teresa F. Lindeman, "Product Placement Nation: Advertisers Pushing the Boundaries to Bring in More Bucks," *Pittsburgh Post-Gazette*, May 13, 2011, http://www.post-gazette.com/pg/11133/1146175-28-0.stm.

7. Caitlin A. Johnson, "Cutting through Advertising Clutter," *CBS Sunday Morning*, September 16, 2006, http://www.cbsnews.com/stories/2006/09/17/sunday/main2015684.shtml.

8. For a written and pictorial history of early advertising, see Charles Goodrum and Helen Dalrymple, *Advertising in America: The First 200 Years* (New York: Harry N. Abrams, 1990), 31.

9. Michael Schudson, *Advertising: The Uneasy Persuasion* (New York: Basic Books, 1984), 164.

10. Newspaper Association of America, "Business Model Evolving, Circulation Revenue Rising," April 14, 2014, http://www.naa.org/Trends-and-Numbers/Newspaper-Revenue/Newspaper-Media-Industry-Revenue-Profile-2013.aspx.

11. David Gelles, "At Odds, Omnicom and Publicis End Merger, *New York Times*, May 8, 2014, chttp://dealbook.nytimes.com/2014/05/08/ad-agency–giants-said-to-call-off-35-billion-merger/.

12. Natalie Zmuda, "Peterson Milla Hooks Is Ad Age's Comeback Agency of the Year," January 28, 2013, *Advertising Age*, http://adage.com/article/special-report-agency-alist-2013/comeback-agency-year-peterson-milla-hooks/239306/. See also PMH Web site at http://www.pmhadv.com/about/.

13. See TVB, "TV Cost & CPM Trends—Network TV Primetime (M–Su), accessed September 19, 2014, http://www.tvb.org/trends/4718/4709.

14. Andrew McMains and Noreen O'Leary, "GM Shifts Chevy Biz to Publicis from C-E," *Adweek*, April 23, 2010, http://www.adweek.com/aw/content_display/news/account-activity/e3i091074075f7ed276cf510b1df8dddbcd.

15. Bettina Fabos, "The Commercialized Web: Challenges for Libraries and Democracy," *Library Trends* 53, no. 4 (Spring 2005): 519–523.

16. "Share of Ad Spending by Medium: U.S.," *Advertising Age*, December 31, 2012, p. 16.

17. Lauren Johnson, "Digital to Pass 25% of Global Media Spend for First Time," *Adweek*, July 9, 2014, http://www.adweek.com/news/technology/digital-pass-25-global-media-spend-first-time-158815.

18. Google, "Form 10-K for the Fiscal Year Ended December 31, 2012," http://www.sec.gov/Archives/edgar/data/1288776/000119312513028362/d452134d10k.htm; eMarketer, "Google Takes Home Half of Worldwide Mobile Internet Ad Revenues," June 13, 2013, http://www.emarketer.com/Article/Google-Takes-Home-Half-of-Worldwide-Mobile-Internet-Ad-Revenues/1009966; Facebook, "Form 10-K for the Fiscal Year Ended December 31, 2012," http://investor.fb.com/secfiling.cfm?filingID=1326801-13-3.

19. See Mike Isaac, "Google's Quarterly Results Show Its Continuing Struggle with Mobile Advertising," *New York Times*, July 17, 2014, http://www.nytimes.com/2014/07/18/technology/googles-earnings-show-its-struggle-with-mobile-ads.html.

20. Jack Neff, "Unilever to Double Digital Spending This Year," *Advertising Age*, June 25, 2010, http://adage.com/cannes2010/article?article_id=144672.

21. Jon Gibs and Sean Bruich, "Advertising Effectiveness: Understanding the Value of a Social Media Impression," Nielsen, April 2010, http://www.iab.net/media/file/NielsenFacebookValueofSocialMediaImpressions.pdf.

22. See Somini Sengupta, "Like It or Not, His Face Is on Ad," *New York Times*, June 1, 2012, p. A1.

23. Leslie Savan, "Op Ad: Sneakers and Nothingness," *Village Voice*, April 2, 1991, p. 43.

24. See Mary Kuntz and Joseph Weber, "The New Hucksterism," *BusinessWeek*, July 1, 1999, 79.

25. Ibid.

26. Schudson, *Advertising*, 210.

27. Eric Pfanner, "Your Brand on TV for a Fee, in Britain," *New York Times*, March 6, 2011, http://www.nytimes.com/2011/03/07/business/media/07iht-adco.html.

28. Vance Packard, *The Hidden Persuaders* (New York: Basic Books, 1957, 1978), 229.

29. See Eileen Dempsey, "Auld Lang Syne," *Columbus Dispatch*, December 28, 2000, p. 1G; John Reinan, "The End of the Good Old Days," *Minneapolis Star Tribune*, August 31, 2004, p. 1D.

30. See Schudson, *Advertising*, 36–43; Andrew Robertson, *The Lessons of Failure* (London: MacDonald, 1974).

31. Kim Campbell and Kent Davis-Packard, "How Ads Get Kids to Say, I Want It!" *Christian Science Monitor*, September 18, 2000, p. 1.

32. See Jay Mathews, "Channel One: Classroom Coup or a 'Sham'?" *Washington Post*, December 26, 1994, p. A1ff.

33. See Michael F. Jacobson and Laurie Ann Mazur, *Marketing Madness: A Survival Guide for a Consumer Society* (Boulder, Colo.: Westview Press, 1995), 29–31.

34. "Ads Beat News on School TVs," *Pittsburgh Post-Gazette,* March 6, 2006, p. A7.

35. Hilary Waldman, "Study Links Advertising, Youth Drinking," *Hartford Courant*, January 3, 2006, p. A1.

36. Alix Spigel, "Selling Sickness: How Drug Ads Changed Healthcare," National Public Radio, October 13, 2009, http://www.npr.org/templates/story/story.php?storyid=113675737.

37. PorCon.org, "Should Prescription Drugs Be Advertised Directly to Consumers?" updated March 2014, http://prescriptiondrugs.procon.org/view.answers.php?questionID=001603.

38. Jeffrey Godsick, quoted in T. L. Stanley, "Hollywood Continues Its Fast-Food Binge," *Adweek*, June 6, 2009, http://www.adweek.com/news/advertising-branding/hollywood-continues-its-fast-food-binge-105907.

39. Douglas J. Wood, "Ad Issues to Watch for in '06," *Advertising Age*, December 19, 2005, p. 10.

40. Associated Press, "Two Ephedra Sellers Fined for False Ads," *Washington Post*, July 2, 2003, p. A7.

41. Beth Harskovits, "Corporate Profile: Legacy's Truth Finds Receptive Audience," *PR Week*, June 12, 2006, p. 9.

42. See Truth, "We Are Here to Empower, Not Judge," accessed September 19, 2014, http://www.thetruth.com/about.

43. See Stephen Ansolabehere and Shanto Iyengar, *Going Negative: How Attack Ads Shrink and Polarize the Electorate* (New York: Free Press, 1996).

44. Center for Responsive Politics, "The Money behind the Elections," accessed June 14, 2013, http://www.opensecrets.org/bigpicture/.

45. Kantar Media, "KM Reports U.S. Advertising Expenditures Increased 0.9 Percent in 2013, Fueled by Larger Advertisers," March 25, 2014, http://kantarmedia.us/press/kantar-media-reports-us-advertising-expenditures-increased-09-percent-2013.

▲ **EXAMINING ETHICS   Brand Integration, Everywhere, p. 398**

1. Kantar Media, "Kantar Media Reports U.S. Advertising Expenditures Increased 5.1% in the First Quarter of 2010," May 26, 2010, http://www.businesswire.com/news/home/20100526005260/en/Kantar-Media-Reports-U.S.-Advertising-Expenditures-Increased#.VFo-q1eLMo4.

2. "A Place for Everything: Product Placements These Days Go beyond Putting a Coke Can in the Background," *Media Week*, March 1, 2010, p. 12.

3. See Abe Sauer, "The Envelope, Please: The 2014 Brandcameo Product Placement Awards," Brandchannel, February 27, 2014, http://www.brandchannel.com/home/post/2014/02/27/140227-2014-Brandcameo-Product-Placement-Awards.aspx.

4. Writers Guild of America, West, "Product Integration," accessed September 8, 2010, http://www.wga.org/content/default.aspx?id=1405.

▲ **GLOBAL VILLAGE   Smoking Up the Global Market, p. 404**

1. Peh Shing Huei, "7 Chinese Cities All Fired Up to Curb Smoking," *Straits Times*, January 23, 2010, p. 4.

2. Cheng Yingqi, "Women Now Main Target of Tobacco Firms," *China Daily*, May 19, 2010, http://www.chinadaily.com.cn/china/2010-05/19/content_9865347.htm.

3. See Li Hui and Ben Blanchard, "China Tobacco Monopoly Blocks Full Ban on Tobacco," Reuters, September 4, 2014, http://www.reuters.com/article/2014/09/05/us-china-smoking-idUSKBN0H001N20140905.

4. Cheng Yingqi, "Women Now Main Target of Tobacco Firms," *China Daily*, May 19, 2010, http://www.chinadaily.com.cn/china/2010-05/19/content_9865347.htm.

5. National Institutes of Health, "Fact Sheet: Global Tobacco Research," October 2010, http://report.nih.gov/nihfactsheets/Pdfs/GlobalTobaccoResearch%28FIC%29.pdf.

12   Public Relations and Framing the Message

1. Baz Luhrmann, "The 2013 Time 100: Beyoncé," April 18, 2013, *Time*, http://time100.time.com/2013/04/18/time-100/slide/beyonce/.

2. Amy Wallace, "Miss Millennium: Beyoncé," *GQ*, February 2013, http://www.gq.com/women/photos/201301/beyonce-cover-story-interview-gq-february-2013.

3. CBS News, "Beyoncé Admits Inauguration Day Lip Sync, Says She'll 'Absolutely Be Singing Live' at Super Bowl," January 31, 2013, http://www.cbsnews.com/8301-207_162-57566981/beyonce-admits-inauguration-day-lip-sync-says-shell-absolutely-be-singing-live-at-super-bowl/.

4. BuzzFeed, "The 'Unflattering' Photos Beyoncé's Publicist Doesn't Want You to See," February 5, 2013, http://www.buzzfeed.com/buzzfeedceleb/the-unflattering-photos-beyonces-publicist-doesnt-want-you-t.

5. Sean Michaels, "Beyoncé Bans Press Photographers from Mrs Carter World Tour," *Guardian*, April 24, 2013, http://www.guardian.co.uk/music/2013/apr/24/beyonce-bans-photographers-mrs-carter.

6. Eric R. Danton, "Beyonce Surprises with New Album Release," *Rolling Stone*, December 13, 2013, http://www.rollingstone.com/music/news/beyonce-surprises-with-new-album-release-20131213.

7. Matthew J. Culligan and Dolph Greene, *Getting Back to the Basics of Public Relations and Publicity* (New York: Crown Publishers, 1982), 100.

8. See Stuart Ewen, *PR! A Social History of Spin* (New York: Basic Books, 1996).

9. Marvin N. Olasky, "The Development of Corporate Public Relations, 1850–1930," *Journalism Monographs* 102 (April 1987): 14.

10. Ibid., 15.

11. Ivy Lee, quoted in Anthony Fellow, *American Media History* (Boston: Cengage Learning, 2012), 202.

12. Edward Bernays, "The Theory and Practice of Public Relations: A Résumé," in E. L. Bernays, ed., *The Engineering of Consent* (Norman: University of Oklahoma Press, 1955), 3–25.

13. Edward Bernays, *Crystallizing Public Opinion* (New York: Horace Liveright, 1923), 217.

14. Michael Schudson, *Discovering the News: A Social History of American Newspapers* (New York: Basic Books, 1978), 136.

15. PRSA, "PR by the Numbers," accessed June 12, 2013, http://media.prsa.org/pr-by-the-number/.

16. Fleishman Hillard, "Department of Defense/TRICARE: That Guy," accessed June 12, 2013, http://fleishmanhillard.com/work/department-of-defensetricare-management-activity-that-guy/.

17. The lead author of this book, Richard Campbell, worked briefly as the assistant PR director for Milwaukee's Summerfest in the early 1980s.

18. Center for Responsive Politics, "Lobbying Database," accessed August 26, 2012, http://opensecrets.org/lobby.

19. SourceWatch, "Center for Consumer Freedom," accessed August 20, 2014, http://www.sourcewatch.org/index.php?title=Center_for_Consumer_Freedom.

20. David Barstow, "Message Machine: Behind TV Analysis, Pentagon's Hidden Hand," *New York Times*, April 20, 2008, http://www.nytimes.com/2008/04/20/us/20generals.html.

21. Associated Press, "Open Government Study: Secrecy Up," *Politico*, March 16, 2014, http://www.politico.com/story/2014/03/open-government-study-secrecy-up-104715.html.

22. Stanley Walker, "Playing the Deep Bassoons," *Harper's*, February 1932, p. 365.

23. Ibid., p. 370.

24. Ivy Lee, *Publicity* (New York: Industries Publishing, 1925), 21.

25. Schudson, *Discovering the News*, 136.

26. Ivy Lee, quoted in Ray Eldon Hiebert, *Courtier to the Crowd: The Story of Ivy Lee and the Development of Public Relations* (Ames: Iowa State University Press, 1966), 114.

27. See Walter Lippmann, *Public Opinion* (New York: Free Press, 1922, 1949), 221.

28. Christopher R. Martin, *Framed! Labor and the Corporate Media* (Ithaca, N.Y.: Cornell University Press, 2003).

29. *PRWatch*, "About Us," accessed August 26, 2012, http://www.prwatch.org/cmd.

30. John Stauber, "Corporate PR: A Threat to Journalism?" *Background Briefing: Radio National*, March 30, 1997, http://www.abc.net.au/radionational/programs/backgroundbriefing/corporate-pr-a-threat-to-journalism/3563876.

31. See Alicia Mundy, "Is the Press Any Match for Powerhouse PR?" in Ray Eldon Hiebert, ed., *Impact of Mass Media* (White Plains, N.Y.: Longman, 1995), 179–188.

32. Dan Rather, interviewed in "Forty Years after Watergate: Carl Bernstein & Dan Rather with CNN's Candy Crowley," *State of the Union with Candy Crowley,* CNN, August 3, 2014, http://cnnpressroom.blogs.cnn.com/2014/08/03/forty-years-after-watergate-carl-bernstein-dan-rather-with-cnns-candy-crowley/.

33. "PR Pros Call the 2012 Election in Advance for Obama," *PR Week*, November 6, 2012, http://www.prweek.com/article/1277656/pr-pros-call-2012-election-advance-obama.

34. Rosanna Fiske, "PR Pros: Haven't We Learned Anything about Disclosure?" PRSay, May 11, 2011, http://prsay.prsa.org/index.php/2011/05/11/pr-and-communications-pros-havent-we-learned-anything-about-disclosure/.

35. Elizabeth Blair, "Under the Radar, PR's Political Savvy," National Public Radio, May 19, 2011, http://www.npr.org/2011/05/19/136436263/under-the-radar-pr-s-political-savvy.

36. Fiske, "PR Pros."

◢ CASE STUDY   The NFL's Concussion Crisis, p. 426

1. Brent Schrotenboer, "NFL Takes Aim at $25 Billion, but at What Price?" *USA Today*, February 5, 2014, http://www.usatoday.com/story/sports/nfl/super/2014/01/30/super-bowl-nfl-revenue-denver-broncos-seattle-seahawks/5061197/.

2. Mark Fainaru-Wada and Steve Fainaru, *League of Denial: The NFL, Concussions, and the Battle for Truth* (New York: Crown, 2013), 6.

◣ EXAMINING ETHICS   What Does It Mean to Be Green?, p. 428

1. United Nations Global Compact, "A New Era of Sustainability," May 25, 2011, http://www.unglobalcompact.org/news/126-05-25-2011.

2. PwC, "Business Success beyond the Short Term: CEO Perspectives on Sustainability," *The 17th Annual Global CEO Survey*, 2014, http://www.pwc.com/gx/en/ceo-survey/2014/sustainability-perspective.jhtml.

◢ Media Literacy and the Critical Process   The Invisible Hand of PR, p. 437

1. John Stauber, "Corporate PR: A Threat to Journalism?" *Background Briefing: Radio National*, March 30, 1997, http://www.abc.net.au/radionational/programs/backgroundbriefing/corporate-pr-a-threat-to-journalism/3563876.

13 Media Economics and the Global Marketplace

1. For this section, the authors are indebted to the ideas and scholarship of Douglas Gomery, a media economist and historian, formerly from the University of Maryland.

2. Douglas Gomery, "The Centrality of Media Economics," in Mark R. Levy and Michael Gurevitch, eds., *Defining Media Studies* (New York: Oxford University Press, 1994), 202.

3. Ibid., 200.

4. Ibid., 203–204.

5. Elizabeth Fones-Wolf, *Selling Free Enterprise: The Business Assault on Labor and Liberalism, 1945–60* (Urbana: University of Illinois Press, 1994).

6. David Harvey, *The Condition of Postmodernity: An Enquiry into the Origins of Cultural Change* (Oxford: Basil Blackwell, 1989), 171.

7. Federal Communications Commission, "Report on Cable Industry Prices," DA 14-672A1, May 16, 2014, http://transition.fcc.gov/Daily_Releases/Daily_Business/2014/db0516/DA-14-672A1.pdf.

8. Nielsen, "Changing Channels: Americans View Just 17 Channels Despite Record Number to Choose From," May 6, 2014, http://www.nielsen.com/us/en/insights/news/2014/changing-channels-americans-view-just-17-channels-despite-record-number-to-choose-from.html.

9. Tim Arango and Brian Stelter, "Comcast Receives Approval for NBC Universal Merger," *New York Times*, January 11, 2011, http://www.nytimes.com/2011/01/19/business/media/19comcast.html.

10. Harvey, *The Condition of Postmodernity*, 158.

11. Bureau of Labor Statistics, "Union Members Summary," January 24, 2014, http://www.bls.gov/news.release/union2.nr0.htm.

12. Economic Policy Institute, "The State of Working America: The Great Recession," August 17, 2012, http://stateofworkingamerica.org/great-recession/.

13. Dave Gilson, "Survival of the Richest," *Mother Jones*, September/October 2014, pp. 32–35.

14. Lawrence Mishel and Alyssa Davis, "CEO Pay Continues to Rise as Typical Workers Are Paid Less," Economic Policy Institute, June 12, 2014, http://www.epi.org/publication/ceo-pay-continues-to-rise/.

15. Equilar, "The New York Times 100 Highest-Paid CEOs," 2013, http://www.equilar.com/corporate-governance/2013-reports/the-new-york-times-100-highest-paid-ceos.

16. National Employment Law Project, "Big Business, Corporate Profits, and the Minimum Wage," July 2012, http://www.nelp.org/page/-/rtmw/NELP-Big-Business-Corporate-Profits-Minimum-Wage.pdf.

17. Ibid.

18. Ibid.

19. Antonio Gramsci, *Selections from the Prison Notebooks* (New York: International Publishers, 1971), 12–13.

20. Robert Sher, "Why Half of All M&A Deals Fail, and What You Can Do about It," *Forbes*, March 19, 2012, http://www.forbes.com/sites/forbesleadershipforum/2012/03/19/why-half-of-all-ma-deals-fail-and-what-you-can-do-about-it/.

21. Richard J. Barnet and John Cavanagh, *Global Dreams: Imperial Corporations and the New World Order* (New York: Simon & Schuster, 1994), 131.

22. Ben Bagdikian, *The Media Monopoly*, 6th ed. (Boston: Beacon Press, 2000), 222.

23. Nick Davies, *Hack Attack: The Inside Story of How the Truth Caught Up with Rupert Murdoch* (New York: Faber and Faber, 2014).

24. Harry First, "Bring Back Antitrust!" *Nation*, June 2, 2008, pp. 7–8.

25. William Paley, quoted in Robert W. McChesney, *Telecommunications, Mass Media and Democracy: The Battle for Control of U.S. Broadcasting, 1928–1935* (New York: Oxford University Press, 1993), 251.

26. McChesney, *Telecommunications, Mass Media and Democracy*, 264.

27. Edward Herman, "Democratic Media," *Z Papers* (January–March 1992): 23.

28. Barnet and Cavanagh, *Global Dreams*, 38.

29. Richard J. Barnet and Ronald E. Muller, *Global Reach: The Power of Multinational Corporations* (New York: Simon & Schuster, 1974), 175.

30. See Adam Liptak, "Justices, 5–4, Reject Corporate Spending Limits," *New York Times*, January 22, 2010, http://www.nytimes.com/2010/01/22/us/politics/22scotus.html.

31. David Sessions, "Chick-fil-A's Place in the Church of Fast Food," *Daily Beast*, July 29, 2012, http://www.thedailybeast.com/articles /2012/07/29/chick-fil-a-s-place-in-the-church-of-fast-food.html; and Michael D. Shear, "Amazon's Founder Pledges $2.5 Million in Support of Same-Sex Marriage," *New York Times*, July 27, 2012, http://thecaucus.blogs.nytimes.com/2012/07/27/amazons-founder -pledges-2-5-million-in-support-of-same-sex-marriage.

32. Center for Responsive Politics, "The Money behind the Elections," accessed June 14, 2013, http://www.opensecrets.org /bigpicture/.

33. Pew Research Center Project for Excellence in Journalism, *State of the News Media 2013*, accessed June 14, 2013, http://stateofthemedia .org/2013/special-reports-landing-page/the-changing-tv-news -landscape/.

34. Robert McChesney and John Nichols, "Who'll Unplug Big Media? Stay Tuned," *Nation*, May 29, 2008, http://www.thenation.com /article/wholl-unplug-big-media-stay-tuned.

35. Center for Responsive Politics, "Lobbying Database," October 15, 2012, http://www.opensecrets.org/lobby/index.php.

36. Center for Responsive Politics, "2012 Top Donors to Outside Spending Groups," September 1, 2012, http://www.opensecrets.org /outsidespending/summ.php?cycle=2012&disp=D&type=V.

37. Peter Overby, "Democratic Climate Activist Is Election's Biggest Donor—That We Know Of," NPR, October 23, 2014, http://www.npr .org/2014/10/23/358238870/big-spending-democrat-faces-off-with -koch-brothers-in-campaign-ads.

◢ CASE STUDY Minority and Female Media Ownership: Why It Matters, p. 458

1. "Comments of Free Press before the Federal Communications Commission, in the Matter of MB Docket No. 09-182 and MB Docket No. 07-294," December 21, 2012, p. 15.

2. Ibid., p. 3.

3. Lauren Wilson, "FCC Chairman Wheeler and Commissioner Pai Duke It Out over Broadcast Diversity," Free Press, March 26, 2014, http://www.freepress.net/blog/2014/03/26/fcc-chairman-wheeler -and-commissioner-pai-duke-it-out-over-broadcast-diversity.

4. "Comments of Free Press," p. 21.

5. *Prometheus Radio Project v. FCC*, 652 F.3d 431,471 (3d Cir. 2011).

Part 5 Opener

Infographic sources:
http://www.journalism.org/2014/03/26/the-revenue-picture-for -american-journalism-and-how-it-is-changing/news_revenue8/
http://freedomhouse.org/report/freedom-press-2014/press-freedom -rankings#.U_5Ht0iVyF8

14 **The Culture of Journalism: Values, Ethics, and Democracy**

1. See Brooke Kroeger, *Nellie Bly: Daredevil, Reporter, Feminist* (New York: Times Books/Random House, 1994).

2. The Pulitzer Prizes, "The 2014 Pulitzer Prize Winners: Investigative Reporting," accessed October 3, 2014, http://www.pulitzer.org /citation/2014-Investigative-Reporting.

3. Mary Walton, "Investigative Shortfall," *American Journalism Review*, September 2010, www.ajr.org/Article.asp?id=4904.

4. Jason Stverak, "Investigative Journalism Is Alive and Well Outside Mainstream Media," Watchdog.org, January 18, 2013, www .watchdog.org/66865/investigative-journalism-is-alive-and-well -outside-mainstream-media/.

5. Neil Postman, "Currents," *Utne Reader*, July/August 1995, p. 35.

6. Reuven Frank, "Memorandum from a Television Newsman," reprinted as Appendix 2 in A. William Bluem, *Documentary in American Television* (New York: Hastings House, 1965), 276.

7. Horace Greeley, quoted in Christopher Lasch, "Journalism, Publicity and the Lost Art of Argument," *Gannett Center Journal* 4, no. 2 (Spring 1990): 2.

8. David Eason, "Telling Stories and Making Sense," *Journal of Popular Culture* 15, no. 2 (Fall 1981): 125.

9. Jon Katz, "AIDS and the Media: Shifting out of Neutral," *Rolling Stone*, May 27, 1993, p. 32.

10. Bill Kovach and Tom Rosenstiel, *The Elements of Journalism* (New York: Three Rivers Press, 2007), 78–112.

11. Herbert Gans, *Deciding What's News* (New York: Pantheon, 1979), 42–48.

12. Ibid.

13. Ibid., 48–51.

14. See Michael Schudson, *Discovering the News: A Social History of American Newspapers* (New York: Basic Books, 1978), 3–11.

15. Evan Thomas (with Suzanne Smalley), "The Myth of Objectivity: Is the Mainstream Press Unbiased?" *Newsweek*, March 10, 2008, p. 36.

16. Ibid.

17. Dean Baquet and Bill Keller, "When Do We Publish a Secret?" *New York Times*, July 1, 2006, p. A27.

18. Code of Ethics, reprinted in Melvin Mencher, *News Reporting and Writing*, 3rd ed. (Dubuque, Iowa: William C. Brown, 1984), 443–444.

19. Ibid.

20. See Howard Kurtz, "*Post* Blogger Resigns after Messages Leaked," *Washington Post*, June 26, 2010, p. C1.

21. For reference and guidance on media ethics, see Clifford Christians, Mark Fackler, and Kim Rotzoll, *Media Ethics: Cases and Moral Reasoning*, 4th ed. (White Plains, N.Y.: Longman, 1995); and Thomas H. Bivins, "A Worksheet for Ethics Instruction and Exercises in Reason," *Journalism Educator* (Summer 1993): 4–16.

22. Christians, Fackler, and Rotzoll, *Media Ethics*, 15.

23. See Jimmie Reeves and Richard Campbell, *Cracked Coverage: Television News, the Anti-Cocaine Crusade, and the Reagan Legacy* (Durham, N.C.: Duke University Press, 1994).

24. See David Eason, "On Journalistic Authority: The Janet Cooke Scandal," *Critical Studies in Mass Communication* 3, no. 4 (December 1986): 429–447.

25. Mike Royko, quoted in "News Media: A Searching of Conscience," *Newsweek*, May 4, 1981, p. 53.

26. Don Hewitt, interview conducted by Richard Campbell on *60 Minutes*, CBS News, New York, February 21, 1989.

27. See Frank Rich, "There's a Battle Outside and It's Still Ragin'," *New York Times*, July 25, 2010, Week in Review, p. 8; James Rainey, "On the Media: Short Clip, Untold Harm," *Los Angeles Times*, July 24, 2010, p. D1; John Loring, "Shirley Sherrod at the Centre of a Racially Tinged Firestorm over a Mischief-Making Viral Video," *Globe and Mail* (Canada), July 24, 2010, p. F2; and Sheryl Gay Stolberg, Shaila Dewan, and Brian Stelter, "For Fired Agriculture Official, Flurry of Apologies and Job Offer," *New York Times*, July 22, 2010, p. A15.

28. Josh Gerstein, "Judge Rips Feds in Sherrod-Breitbart Lawsuit," *Politico*, February 20, 2014, http://www.politico.com/blogs/under-the-radar/2014/02/judge-rips-feds-in-sherrodbreitbart-lawsuit-183689.html.

29. Jonathan Alter, "News Media: Round Up the Usual Suspects," *Newsweek*, March 25, 1985, p. 69.

30. Ina Howard, "Power Sources: On Party, Gender, Race, and Class, TV News Looks to the Most Powerful Groups," *Extra!*, Fairness and Accuracy in Reporting, May 1, 2002, http://www.fair.org/extra-online/articles/power-sources.

31. Pew Research Center's Project for Excellence in Journalism, "The Gender Gap," May 23, 2005, http://www.journalism.org/node/141.

32. The 4th Estate, "Silenced: Gender Gap in Election Coverage," accessed September 3, 2012, http://www.4thestate.net/female-voices-in-media-infographic/.

33. David Carr, "Journalist, Provocateur, Maybe Both," *New York Times*, July 26, 2010, p. B2.

34. William Greider, quoted in Mark Hertsgaard, *On Bended Knee: The Press and the Reagan Presidency* (New York: Farrar, Straus & Giroux, 1988), 78.

35. Bluem, *Documentary in American Television*, 94.

36. Pew Research Center, "Further Decline in Credibility Ratings for Most News Organizations," August 16, 2012, www.people-press.org/2012/08/16/further-decline-in-credibility-ratings.

37. See Joe Holley, "Should the Coverage Fit the Crime?" *Columbia Journalism Review* 35, no. 1 (May/June 1996): 27.

38. See Amanda Kondolojy, "Cable News Ratings for Thursday, September 11, 1014," September 12, 2014, zap2it, http://tvbythenumbers.zap2it.com/2014/09/12/cable-news-ratings-for-thursday-september-11-2014/302051.

39. See David Carr, "Big News Forges Its Own Path," *New York Times*, June 16, 2013, http://www.nytimes.com/2013/06/17/business/media/big-news-forges-its-own-path.html.

40. Based on notes made by the lead author's wife, Dianna Campbell, after a visit to Warsaw and discussions with a number of journalists working for *Gazeta Wyborcza* in 1990.

41. Davis "Buzz" Merritt, *Public Journalism and Public Life: Why Telling the News Is Not Enough* (Hillsdale, N.J.: Lawrence Erlbaum, 1995), 113–114.

42. Jay Rosen, "Politics, Vision, and the Press: Toward a Public Agenda for Journalism," in Jay Rosen and Paul Taylor, *The New News v. the Old News: The Press and Politics in the 1990s* (New York: Twentieth Century Fund, 1992), 14.

43. See Jonathan Cohn, "Should Journalists Do Community Service?" *American Prospect* (Summer 1995): 15.

44. Davis Merritt and Jay Rosen, "Imagining Public Journalism: An Editor and a Scholar Reflect on the Birth of an Idea," *Roy W. Howard Public Lecture*, no. 5 (Bloomington: Indiana University, 1995), 12.

45. Katharine Q. Seelye, "Best-Informed Also View Fake News, Study Finds," *New York Times*, April 16, 2007, http://www.nytimes.com/2007/04/16/business/media/16pew.html.

46. James Agee and Walker Evans, *Let Us Now Praise Famous Men* (Boston: Houghton Mifflin, 1960), xiv.

47. David Broder, quoted in "Squaring with the Reader: A Seminar on Journalism," *Kettering Review* (Winter 1992): 48.

48. Lasch, "Journalism, Publicity and the Lost Art of Argument," 1.

49. Jay Rosen, "Forming and Informing the Public," *Kettering Review*, Winter 1992, 69–70.

◢ **CASE STUDY** Bias in the News, p. 484

1. Pew Research Center for the People and the Press, "Bottom-Line Pressures Now Hurting Coverage, Say Journalists," May 23, 2004, http://www.people-press.org/reports/display.php3?PageID=829.

2. *Random House Webster's Unabridged Dictionary*, 2nd ed., s.vv. "conservative," "liberal."

3. Herbert Gans, *Deciding What's News* (New York: Vintage, 1980).

4. See Bernard Goldberg, *Bias: A CBS Insider Exposes How the Media Distort the News* (New York: Perennial, 2003).

5. See Eric Alterman, *What Liberal Media? The Truth about Bias and the News* (New York: Basic Books, 2003).

6. M. D. Watts et al., "Elite Cues and Media Bias in Presidential Campaigns: Explaining Public Perceptions of a Liberal Press," *Communication Research* 26 (1999): 144–175.

7. See Glen R. Smith, "Politicians and the News Media: How Elite Attacks Influence Perceptions of Media Bias," *International Journal of Press/Politics* 15, no. 3 (2010), 319–343.

◢ **CASE STUDY** A Lost Generation of Journalists?, p. 501

1. Alex T. Williams, "The Growing Pay Gap between Journalism and PR," Pew Research Center, August 11, 2014, http://www.pewresearch.org/fact-tank/2014/08/11/the-growing-pay-gap-between-journalism-and-public-relations.

2. See Robert McChesney and John Nichols, *The Death and Life of American Journalism* (New York: Nation Books, 2010), 46–50; and Williams, Pew Research Center.

3. See Williams, Pew Research Center.

4. McChesney and Nichols, 48.

5. See Pew Research Center, "The Master Character Narratives in Campaign 2012," August 23, 2012, http://www.journalism.org/2012/08/23/2012-campaign-character-narratives.

6. See Williams, Pew Research Center.

◢ **EXAMINING ETHICS** WikiLeaks, Secret Documents, and Good Journalism, p. 506

1. Bill Keller, "The Boy Who Kicked the Hornet's Nest," *New York Times Magazine*, January 30, 2011, pp. 33–34.

2. Ibid., p. 37.

3. Jay Rosen, "The Afghanistan War Logs Released by Wikileaks, the World's First Stateless News Organization," *PressThink*, July 26, 2010, http://www.pressthink.org/2010/07/the-afghanistan-war-logs-released-by-wikileaks-the-worlds-first-stateless-news-organization.

4. Nikki Usher, "Why WikiLeaks' Latest Document Dump Makes Everyone in Journalism—and the Public—a Winner," Nieman Journalism Lab, December 3, 2010, http://www.niemanlab.org/2010/12/why-wikileaks-latest-document-dump-makes-everyone-in-journalism-and-the-public-a-winner/.

15 Media Effects and Cultural Approaches to Research

1. Alexis de Tocqueville, *Democracy in America* (New York: Modern Library, 1835, 1840, 1945, 1981), 96–97.

2. Steve Fore, "Lost in Translation: The Social Uses of Mass Communications Research," *Afterimage*, no. 20 (April 1993): 10.

3. James Carey, *Communication as Culture: Essays on Media and Society* (Boston: Unwin Hyman, 1989), 75.

4. Daniel Czitrom, *Media and the American Mind: From Morse to McLuhan* (Chapel Hill: University of North Carolina Press, 1982), 122–125.

5. Ibid., 123.

6. Harold Lasswell, *Propaganda Technique in the World War* (New York: Alfred A. Knopf, 1927), 9.

7. Walter Lippmann, *Public Opinion* (New York: Macmillan, 1922), 18.

8. Jon Cohen, "Gay Marriage Support Hits New High in *Post*–ABC Poll," *Washington Post*, March 18, 2013, http://www.washingtonpost.com/blogs/the-fix/wp/2013/03/18/gay-marriage-support-hits-new-high-in-post-abc-poll/.

9. Sheldon R. Gawiser and G. Evans Witt, "20 Questions a Journalist Should Ask about Poll Results," 2nd ed., http://www.ncpp.org/qajsa.htm.

10. See W. W. Charters, *Motion Pictures and Youth: A Summary* (New York: Macmillan, 1934); and Garth Jowett, *Film: The Democratic Art* (Boston: Little, Brown, 1976), 220–229.

11. Czitrom, *Media and the American Mind*, 132. See also Harold Lasswell, "The Structure and Function of Communication in Society," in Lyman Bryson, ed., *The Communication of Ideas* (New York: Harper and Brothers, 1948), 37–51.

12. Wilbur Schramm, Jack Lyle, and Edwin Parker, *Television in the Lives of Our Children* (Stanford, Calif.: Stanford University Press, 1961), 1.

13. See Joseph Klapper, *The Effects of Mass Communication* (New York: Free Press, 1960).

14. Schramm, Lyle, and Parker, *Television,* 1.

15. For an early overview of uses and gratifications, see Jay Blumler and Elihu Katz, *The Uses of Mass Communication* (Beverly Hills, Calif.: Sage, 1974).

16. National Public Radio, "Death-Penalty Option Varies Depending on Question," *Weekend Edition,* July 2, 2006.

17. See George Gerbner et al., "The Demonstration of Power: Violence Profile No. 10," *Journal of Communication* 29, no. 3 (1979): 177–196.

18. Kaiser Family Foundation, *Sex on TV 4* (Menlo Park, Calif.: Henry C. Kaiser Family Foundation, 2005).

19. Robert P. Snow, *Creating Media Culture* (Beverly Hills, Calif.: Sage, 1983), 47.

20. See Maxwell McCombs and Donald Shaw, "The Agenda-Setting Function of Mass Media," *Public Opinion Quarterly* 36, no. 2 (1972): 176–187.

21. See Nancy Signorielli and Michael Morgan, *Cultivation Analysis: New Directions in Media Effects Research* (Newbury Park, Calif.: Sage, 1990).

22. John Gastil, *Political Communication and Deliberation* (Beverly Hills, Calif.: Sage, 2008), 60.

23. W. Phillips Davison, "The Third-Person Effect in Communication," *Public Opinion Quarterly* 47, no. 1 (1983): 1–15, doi:10.1086/268763.

24. Richard Rhodes, *The Media Violence Myth*, 2000, http://www.abffe.com/myth1.htm.

25. Robert Lynd, *Knowledge for What? The Place of Social Science in American Culture* (Princeton, N.J.: Princeton University Press, 1939), 120.

26. Czitrom, *Media and the American Mind*, 143; and Leo Lowenthal, "Historical Perspectives of Popular Culture," in Bernard Rosenberg and David White, eds., *Mass Culture: The Popular Arts in America* (Glencoe, Ill.: Free Press, 1957), 52.

27. See Stuart Hall et al., *Policing the Crisis: Mugging, the State, and Law and Order* (London: Macmillan, 1978).

28. Todd Gitlin, *The Whole World Is Watching* (Berkeley: University of California Press, 1980), 7.

29. Horace Newcomb, *TV: The Most Popular Art* (Garden City, N.Y.: Anchor Books, 1974), 19, 23.

30. See Janice Radway, *Reading the Romance: Women, Patriarchy, and Popular Literature* (Chapel Hill: University of North Carolina Press, 1984).

31. Jürgen Habermas, *The Structural Transformation of the Public Sphere* (Cambridge, Mass.: MIT Press, 1962/1994).

32. Craig Calhoun, ed., *Habermas and the Public Sphere* (Cambridge, Mass.: MIT Press, 1994), 452.

33. James W. Carey, *Communication as Culture* (New York: Routledge, 1989), 23.

34. James Carey, "Mass Communication Research and Cultural Studies: An American View," in James Curran, Michael Gurevitch, and Janet Woollacott, eds., *Mass Communication and Society* (London: Edward Arnold, 1977), 418, 421.

35. Alan Sokal, quoted in Scott Janny, "Postmodern Gravity Deconstructed, Slyly," *New York Times*, May 18, 1996, p. 1. See also The Editors of Lingua Franca, eds., *The Sokal Hoax: The Sham That Shook the Academy* (Lincoln, Neb.: Bison Press, 2000).

◢ **CASE STUDY The Effects of TV in a Post-TV World, p. 517**

1. Frank J. Prial, "Congressmen Hear Renewal of Debate over TV Violence," *New York Times*, April 16, 1983, http://www.nytimes.com/1983/04/16/arts/congressmen-hear-renewal-of-debate-over-tv-violence.html.

2. Parents Television Council, "What Is the PTC's Mission?" accessed May 15, 2011, http://www.parentstv.org/PTC/faqs/main.asp#What%20is%20the%20PTCs%20mission.

3. Parents Television Council, "INSP Network Earns PTC Seal of Approval," May 23, 2012, http://www.parentstv.org/PTC/news/release/2012/0523.asp.

◢ **Media Literacy and the Critical Process Wedding Media and the Meaning of the Perfect Wedding Day, p. 523**

1. Erika Engstrom, *The Bride Factory: Mass Media Portrayals of Women and Weddings* (New York: Peter Lang, 2012).

◢ **CASE STUDY Our Masculinity Problem, p. 529**

1. Mark Follman, Gavin Aronsen, and Deanna Pan, "A Guide to Mass Shootings in America," *Mother Jones*, May 24, 2014, http://www.motherjones.com/politics/2012/07/mass-shootings-map. See also John Wihbey, "Mass Murder, Shooting Sprees and Rampage Violence: Research Roundup," Journalist's Resource, April 3, 2014, http://journalistsresource.org/studies/government/criminal-justice/mass-murder-shooting-sprees-and-rampage-violence-research-roundup.

2. Jackson Katz, "Memo to Media: Manhood, Not Guns or Mental Illness, Should Be Central in Newtown Shooting," *Huffington Post*, updated February 17, 2013, http://www.huffingtonpost.com/jackson-katz/men-gender-gun-violence_b_2308522.html.

3. Ibid.

4. Rachel Kalish and Michael Kimmel, "Suicide by Mass Murder: Masculinity, Aggrieved Entitlement, and Rampage School Shootings," *Health Sociology Review* 19, no. 4 (2010): 451–464.

5. Elliot Rodger, quoted in ibid.

6. See Ralph Ellis and Sara Sidner, "Deadly California Rampage: Chilling Video, but No Match for Reality," CNN, May 27, 2014, http://www.cnn.com/2014/05/24/justice/california-shooting-deaths/.

16 Legal Controls and Freedom of Expression

1. Allan J. Lichtman, "Who Rules America?" *The Hill*, August 12, 2014, http://thehill.com/blogs/pundits-blog/civil-rights/214857-who-rules-america.

2. Sarah Dutton, Jennifer De Pinto, Anthony Salvanto, and Fred Backus, "Americans' View of Congress: Throw 'Em Out," CBS News, May 21, 2014, http://www.cbsnews.com/news/americans-view-of-congress-throw-em-out/.

3. Gene Policinski, "Amendment to Undo *Citizens United* Won't Do," First Amendment Center, September 21, 2011, http://www.firstamendmentcenter.org/amendment-to-undo-citizens-united-wont-do.

4. "2012 Presidential Race," OpenSecrets.org, accessed October 3, 2014, http://www.opensecrets.org/pres12/#out.

5. Lawrence Lessig, "An Open Letter to the Citizens against Citizens United," *Atlantic*, March 23, 2012, http://www.theatlantic.com/politics/archive/2013/03/an-open-letter-to-the-citizens-against-citizens-united/254902/.

6. Committee to Protect Journalists, "1076 Journalists Killed since 1992," accessed September 10, 2014, http://www.cpj.org/killed/.

7. Freedom House, "Freedom of the Press 2014," accessed September 10, 2014, http://www.freedomhouse.org/report/freedom-press/freedom-press-2014.

8. Fred Siebert, Theodore Peterson, and Wilbur Schramm, *Four Theories of the Press* (Urbana: University of Illinois Press, 1956).

9. See Douglas M. Fraleigh and Joseph S. Tuman, *Freedom of Speech in the Marketplace of Ideas* (New York: St. Martin's Press, 1997), 71–73.

10. Michael Schudson, *The Good Citizen: A History of American Civic Life* (Cambridge, Mass.: Harvard University Press, 1998), 77.

11. See Fraleigh and Tuman, *Freedom of Speech*, 125.

12. Hugo Black, quoted in "*New York Times Company v. U.S.*: 1971," in Edward W. Knappman, ed., *Great American Trials: From Salem Witchcraft to Rodney King* (Detroit: Visible Ink Press, 1994), 609.

13. Robert Warren, quoted in "*U.S. v. The Progressive*: 1979," in Knappman, ed., *Great American Trials*, 684.

14. Lawrence Lessig, "Opening Plenary—Media at a Critical Juncture: Politics, Technology and Culture," National Conference on Media Reform, Minneapolis, Minnesota, June 7, 2008.

15. Timothy B. Lee, "15 Years Ago, Congress Kept Mickey Mouse out of the Public Domain. Will They Do It Again?" *Washington Post*, October 25, 2013, http://www.washingtonpost.com/blogs/the-switch/wp/2013/10/25/15-years-ago-congress-kept-mickey-mouse-out-of-the-public-domain-will-they-do-it-again.

16. See Knappman, ed., *Great American Trials*, 517–519.

17. Ibid., 741–743.

18. Douglas Gomery, *Movie History: A Survey* (Belmont, Calif.: Wadsworth, 1991), 57.

19. See Eric Barnouw, *Tube of Plenty: The Evolution of American Television,* rev. ed. (New York: Oxford University Press, 1982), 118–130.

20. See "Dummy and Dame Arouse the Nation," *Broadcasting-Telecasting*, October 15, 1956, p. 258; and Lawrence Lichty and Malachi Topping, *American Broadcasting: A Source Book on the History of Radio and Television* (New York: Hastings House, 1975), 530.

21. Dean Burch, quoted in Peter Fornatale and Joshua Mills, *Radio in the Television Age* (Woodstock, N.Y.: Overlook Press, 1980), 85.

22. *Fox Television Stations, Inc. v. FCC*, No. 06-1760 (2nd Cir. 2010).

23. Brooks Boliek, "Sorry, Ms. Jackson: FCC Hits New Record," *Politico*, September 10, 2014, http://www.politico.com/story/2014/09/fcc-net-neutrality-record-110818.html.

24. Human Rights Watch, "Become a Blogger for Human Rights," http://hrw.org/blogs.htm.

25. Herbert J. Gans, *Democracy and the News* (Oxford: Oxford University Press, 2003), ix.

▲ CASE STUDY Is "Sexting" Pornography?, p. 550

1. Richard Wortley and Stephen Smallbone, "Child Pornography on the Internet," U.S. Department of Justice, updated May 2012, http://www.cops.usdoj.gov/files/ric/Publications/e04062000.pdf.

2. Steven Dettelbach, quoted in Tracy Russo, "'Sexting' Town Hall Meeting Held in Cleveland," *Criminal Justice News*, March 19, 2010, http://criminal-justice-online.blogspot.com/2010/03/sexting.html.

3. Amanda Lenhart, "Teens and Sexting," Pew Internet & American Life Project, December 15, 2009, http://pewresearch.org/pubs/1440/teens-sexting-text-messages.

▲ EXAMINING ETHICS A Generation of Copyright Criminals?, p. 564

1. Kembrew McLeod, *Freedom of Expression®: Overzealous Copyright Bozos and Other Enemies of Creativity* (New York: Doubleday, 2005), 67–68.

2. Ibid.

3. Michael D. Ayers, "White Noise: Girl Talk," *Billboard*, June 14, 2008.

4. Lawrence Lessig, quoted in *Rip: A Remix Manifesto*, dir. Brett Gaylor, 2008.

Extended Case Study: Social Media and Finding Real Happiness, p. 568

1. Lev Grossman and Matt Vella, "iNeed?" *Time*, September 22, 2014, p. 44.

2. JWT, "Fear of Missing Out," May 2011, http://www.jwtintelligence.com/production/FOMO_JWT_TrendReport_May2011.pdf.

3. Andrew K. Przybylski et al., "Motivational, Emotional, and Behavioral Correlates of Fear of Missing Out," *Computers in Human Behavior* 29 (2013): 1841–1848.

4. Ethan Kross et al., "Facebook Use Predicts Declines in Subjective Well-Being in Young Adults," *PLOS ONE* 8, no. 8 (2013), doi:10.1371/journal.pone.0069841.

5. Przybylski et al.

6. Ed Diener and Robert Biswas-Diener, *Happiness: Unlocking the Mysteries of Psychological Wealth* (Malden, Mass: Wiley-Blackwell, 2008), Chapter 4.

7. Ibid., 51.

Glossary

A&R (artist & repertoire) agents talent scouts of the music business who discover, develop, and sometimes manage performers.

access channels in cable television, a tier of nonbroadcast channels dedicated to local education, government, and the public.

account executives in advertising, client liaisons responsible for bringing in new business and managing the accounts of established clients.

account reviews in advertising, the process of evaluating or reinvigorating an ad campaign, which results in either renewing the contract with the original ad agency or hiring a new agency.

acquisitions editors in the book industry, editors who seek out and sign authors to contracts.

action games games emphasizing combat-type situations that ask players to test their reflexes and to punch, slash, shoot, or throw as accurately as possible so as to strategically make their way through a series of levels.

actual malice in libel law, a reckless disregard for the truth, such as when a reporter or an editor knows that a statement is false and prints or airs it anyway.

adult contemporary (AC) one of the oldest and most popular radio music formats, typically featuring a mix of news, talk, oldies, and soft rock.

adventure games games requiring players to interact with individual characters and a sometimes hostile environment in order to solve puzzles.

advergames video games created for purely promotional purposes.

affiliate station a radio or TV station that, though independently owned, signs a contract to be part of a network and receives money to carry the network's programs; in exchange, the network reserves time slots, which it sells to national advertisers.

agenda-setting a media-research argument that says that when the mass media pay attention to particular events or issues, they determine—that is, set the agenda for—the major topics of discussion for individuals and society.

album-oriented rock (AOR) the radio music format that features album cuts from mainstream rock bands.

alternative rock nonmainstream rock music, which includes many types of experimental music and some forms of punk and grunge.

AM amplitude modulation; a type of radio and sound transmission that stresses the volume or height of radio waves.

analog in television, standard broadcast signals made of radio waves (replaced by digital standards in 2009).

analog recording a recording that is made by capturing the fluctuations of the original sound waves and storing those signals on records or cassettes as a continuous stream of magnetism—analogous to the actual sound.

analysis the second step in the critical process, it involves discovering significant patterns that emerge from the description stage.

anthology dramas a popular form of early TV programming that brought live dramatic theater to television; influenced by stage plays, anthologies offered new teleplays, casts, directors, writers, and sets from week to week.

arcade an establishment that gathers multiple coin-operated games together and can be considered a newer version of the penny arcade.

ARPAnet the original Internet, designed by the U.S. Defense Department's Advanced Research Projects Agency (ARPA).

association principle in advertising, a persuasive technique that associates a product with some cultural value or image that has a positive connotation but may have little connection to the actual product.

astroturf lobbying phony grassroots public affairs campaigns engineered by public relations firms; coined by U.S. Senator Lloyd Bentsen of Texas (it was named after AstroTurf, the artificial-grass athletic field surface).

audience studies cultural studies research that focuses on how people use and interpret cultural content. Also known as reader-response research.

audiotape lightweight magnetized strands of ribbon that make possible sound editing and multiple-track mixing; instrumentals or vocals can be recorded at one location and later mixed onto a master recording in another studio.

authoritarian model a model for journalism and speech that tolerates little public dissent or criticism of government; it holds that the general public needs guidance from an elite and educated ruling class.

avatar a graphic interactive "character" situated within the world of a game, such as *World of Warcraft* or *Second Life*.

bandwagon effect an advertising strategy that incorporates exaggerated claims that everyone is using a particular product, so you should, too.

basic cable in cable programming, a tier of channels composed of local broadcast signals, nonbroadcast access channels (for local government, education, and general public use), a few regional PBS stations, and a variety of cable channels downlinked from communication satellites.

Big Five/Little Three from the late 1920s through the late 1940s, the major movie studios that were vertically integrated and that dominated the industry. The Big Five were Paramount, MGM, Warner Brothers, Twentieth Century Fox, and RKO. The Little Three were those studios that did not own theaters: Columbia, Universal, and United Artists.

Big Six the six major Hollywood studios that currently rule the commercial film business: Warner Brothers, Paramount, Twentieth Century Fox, Universal, Columbia Pictures, and Disney.

block booking an early tactic of movie studios to control exhibition, involving pressuring theater operators to accept marginal films with no stars in order to get access to films with the most popular stars.

blockbuster the type of big-budget special effects film that typically has a summer or holiday release date, heavy promotion, and lucrative merchandising tie-ins.

block printing a printing technique developed by early Chinese printers, who hand-carved characters and illustrations into a block of wood, applied ink to the block, and then printed copies on multiple sheets of paper.

blogs sites that contain articles in reverse chronological journal-like form, often with reader comments and links to other articles on the Web (from the term *Weblog*).

blues originally a kind of black folk music, this music emerged as a distinct category in the early 1900s; it was influenced by African American spirituals, ballads, and work songs in the rural South, and by urban guitar and vocal solos from the 1930s and 1940s.

book challenge a formal complaint to have a book removed from a public or school library's collection.

boutique agencies in advertising, small regional ad agencies that offer personalized services.

broadband data transmission over a fiber-optic cable—a signaling method that handles a wide range of frequencies.

broadcasting the transmission of radio waves or TV signals to a broad public audience.

browsers information-search services, such as Microsoft's Internet Explorer, Firefox, and Google Chrome, that offer detailed organizational maps to the Internet.

cartridge early physical form of video games that were played on consoles manufactured by companies like Nintendo, Sega, and Atari.

casual games games that have very simple rules and are usually quick to play, such as *Tetris* or *Angry Birds*.

CATV (community antenna television) an early cable system that originated where mountains or tall buildings blocked TV signals; because of early technical and regulatory limits, CATV contained only twelve channels.

celluloid a transparent and pliable film that can hold a coating of chemicals sensitive to light.

chapter show in television production, any situation comedy or dramatic program whose narrative structure includes self-contained stories that feature a problem, a series of conflicts, and a resolution from week to week (for contrast, see **serial program** and **episodic series**).

cinema verité French term for *truth film*, a documentary style that records fragments of everyday life unobtrusively; it often features a rough, grainy look and shaky, handheld camera work.

citizen journalism a grassroots movement wherein activist amateurs and concerned citizens, not professional journalists, use the Internet and blogs to disseminate news and information.

codex an early type of book in which paperlike sheets were cut and sewed together along an edge, then bound with thin pieces of wood and covered with leather.

collective intelligence the sharing of knowledge and ideas, particularly in the world of gaming.

commercial speech any print or broadcast expression for which a fee is charged to the organization or individual buying time or space in the mass media.

common carrier a communication or transportation business, such as a phone company or a taxi service, that is required by law to offer service on a first-come, first-served basis to whoever can pay the rate; such companies do not get involved in content.

communication the process of creating symbol systems that convey information and meaning (for example, language, Morse code, film, and computer codes).

Communications Act of 1934 the far-reaching act that established the Federal Communications Commission (FCC) and the federal regulatory structure for U.S. broadcasting.

communist or state model a model for journalism and speech that places control in the hands of an enlightened government, which speaks for ordinary citizens and workers in order to serve the common goals of the state.

compact discs (CDs) playback-only storage discs for music that incorporate pure and very precise digital techniques, thus eliminating noise during recording and editing sessions.

conflict of interest considered unethical, a compromising situation in which a journalist stands to benefit personally from the news report he or she produces.

conflict-oriented journalism found in metropolitan areas, newspapers that define news primarily as events, issues, or experiences that deviate from social norms; journalists see their role as observers who monitor their city's institutions and problems.

consensus narratives cultural products that become popular and command wide attention, providing shared cultural experiences.

consensus-oriented journalism found in small communities, newspapers that promote social and economic harmony by providing community calendars and meeting notices and carrying articles on local schools, social events, town government, property crimes, and zoning issues.

consoles devices people use specifically to play video games.

contemporary hit radio (CHR) originally called *Top 40 radio*, this radio format encompasses everything from hip-hop to children's songs; it appeals to many teens and young adults.

content analysis in social science research, a method for studying and coding media texts and programs.

content communities online communities that exist for the sharing of all types of content, from text to photos and videos.

convergence the first definition involves the technological merging of media content across various platforms (see also **cross platform**). The second definition describes a business model that consolidates various media holdings under one corporate umbrella.

cookies information profiles about a user that are usually automatically accepted by a Web browser and stored on the user's own computer hard drive.

copy editors the people in magazine, newspaper, and book publishing who attend to specific problems in writing, such as style, content, and length.

copyright the legal right of authors and producers to own and control the use of their published or unpublished writing, music, and lyrics; TV programs and movies; or graphic art designs.

Corporation for Public Broadcasting (CPB) a private, nonprofit corporation created by Congress in 1967 to funnel federal funds to nonprofit radio and public television.

correlations observed associations between two variables.

country claiming the largest number of radio stations in the United States, this radio format includes such subdivisions as old-time, progressive, country-rock, western swing, and country-gospel.

cover music songs recorded or performed by musicians who did not originally write or perform the music; in the 1950s, some white producers and artists capitalized on popular songs by black artists by "covering" them.

critical process the process whereby a media-literate person or student studying mass communication forms and practices employs the techniques of description, analysis, interpretation, evaluation, and engagement.

cross platform a particular business model that involves a consolidation of various media holdings—such as cable

connection, phone service, television transmission, and Internet access—under one corporate umbrella (also known as **convergence**).

cultivation effect in media research, the idea that heavy television viewing leads individuals to perceive reality in ways that are consistent with the portrayals they see on television.

cultural imperialism the phenomenon of American media, fashion, and food dominating the global market and shaping the cultures and identities of other nations.

cultural studies in media research, the approaches that try to understand how the media and culture are tied to the actual patterns of communication used in daily life; these studies focus on how people make meanings, apprehend reality, and order experience through the use of stories and symbols.

culture the symbols of expression that individuals, groups, and societies use to make sense of daily life and to articulate their values; a process that delivers the values of a society through products or other meaning-making forms.

data mining the unethical gathering of data by online purveyors of content and merchandise.

deficit financing in television, the process whereby a TV production company leases its programs to a network for a license fee that is actually less than the cost of production; the company hopes to recoup this loss later in rerun syndication.

demographic editions national magazines whose advertising is tailored to subscribers and readers according to occupation, class, and zip code.

demographics in market research, the study of audiences or consumers by age, gender, occupation, ethnicity, education, and income.

description the first step in the critical process, it involves paying close attention, taking notes, and researching the cultural product to be studied.

design managers publishing industry personnel who work on the look of a book, making decisions about type style, paper, cover design, and layout.

desktop publishing a computer technology that enables an aspiring publisher/editor to inexpensively write, design, lay out, and even print a small newsletter or magazine.

development the process of designing, coding, scoring, and testing a game.

developmental editor in book publishing, the editor who provides authors with feedback, makes suggestions for improvements, and obtains advice from knowledgeable members of the academic community.

digital in television, the type of signals that are transmitted as binary code.

digital communication images, texts, and sounds that use pulses of electric current or flashes of laser light and are converted (or encoded) into electronic signals represented as varied combinations of binary numbers (ones and zeros); these signals are then reassembled (decoded) as a precise reproduction of a TV picture, a magazine article, or a telephone voice.

digital divide the socioeconomic disparity between those who do and those who do not have access to digital technology and media, such as the Internet.

digital recording music recorded and played back by laser beam rather than by needle or magnetic tape.

digital video the production format that is replacing celluloid film and revolutionizing filmmaking because the cameras are more portable and production costs are much less expensive.

dime novels sometimes identified as pulp fiction, these cheaply produced and low-priced novels were popular in the United States beginning in the 1860s.

direct broadcast satellite (DBS) a satellite-based service that for a monthly fee downlinks hundreds of satellite channels and services; DBS began distributing video programming directly to households in 1994.

direct payment in media economics, the payment of money, primarily by consumers, for a book, a music CD, a movie, an online computer service, or a cable TV subscription.

documentary a movie or TV news genre that documents reality by recording actual characters and settings.

domestic comedy a TV hybrid of the sitcom in which characters and settings are usually more important than complicated situations; it generally features a domestic problem or work issue that characters have to solve.

drive time in radio programming, the periods between 6 and 10 A.M. and 4 and 7 P.M., when people are commuting to and from work or school; these periods constitute the largest listening audiences of the day.

e-book a digital book read on a computer or electronic reading device.

e-commerce electronic commerce, or commercial activity, on the Web.

electromagnetic waves invisible electronic impulses similar to visible light; electricity, magnetism, light, broadcast signals, and heat are part of such waves, which radiate in space at the speed of light, about 186,000 miles per second.

electronic publishers communication businesses, such as broadcasters or cable TV companies, that are entitled to choose what channels or content to carry.

e-mail electronic mail messages sent over the Internet; developed by computer engineer Ray Tomlinson in 1971.

engagement the fifth step in the critical process, it involves actively working to create a media world that best serves democracy.

Entertainment Software Rating Board (ESRB) a self-regulating organization that assigns ratings to games based on six categories: EC (Early Childhood), E (Everyone), E 10+, T (Teens), M 17+, and AO (Adults Only 18+).

episodic series a narrative form well suited to television because the main characters appear every week, sets and locales remain the same, and technical crews stay with the program; episodic series feature new adventures each week, but a handful of characters emerge with whom viewers can regularly identify (for contrast, see **chapter show**).

e-publishing Internet-based publishing houses that design and distribute books for comparatively low prices for authors who want to self-publish a title.

ethnocentrism an underlying value held by many U.S. journalists and citizens, it involves judging other countries and cultures according to how they live up to or imitate American practices and ideals.

evaluation the fourth step in the critical process, it involves arriving at a judgment about whether a cultural product is good, bad, or mediocre; this requires subordinating one's personal taste to the critical assessment resulting from the first three stages (description, analysis, and interpretation).

evergreens in TV syndication, popular, lucrative, and enduring network reruns, such as the *Andy Griffith Show* or *I Love Lucy*.

evergreen subscriptions magazine subscriptions that automatically renew on the subscriber's credit card.

experiments in regard to the mass media, research that isolates some aspect of content, suggests a hypothesis, and manipulates variables to discover a particular medium's impact on attitudes, emotions, or behavior.

Fairness Doctrine repealed in 1987, this FCC rule required broadcast stations to both air and engage in controversial-issue programs that affected their communities and, when offering such programming, to provide competing points of view.

famous-person testimonial an advertising strategy that associates a product with the endorsement of a well-known person.

feature syndicates commercial outlets or brokers, such as United Features and King Features, that contract with newspapers to provide work from well-known political writers, editorial cartoonists, comic-strip artists, and self-help columnists.

Federal Communications Commission (FCC) an independent U.S. government agency charged with regulating interstate and international communications by radio, television, wire, satellite, cable, and the Internet.

Federal Radio Commission (FRC) a body established in 1927 to oversee radio licenses and negotiate channel problems.

feedback responses from receivers to the senders of messages.

fiber-optic cable thin glass bundles of fiber capable of transmitting along cable wires thousands of messages converted to shooting pulses of light; these bundles of fiber can carry broadcast channels, telephone signals, and all sorts of digital codes.

fin-syn (Financial Interest and Syndication Rules) FCC rules that prohibited the major networks from running their own syndication companies or from charging production companies additional fees after shows had completed their prime-time runs; most fin-syn rules were rescinded in the mid-1990s.

first-person shooter (FPS) games that allow players to feel as if they are actually holding a weapon and to feel physically immersed in the drama.

first-run syndication in television, the process whereby new programs are specifically produced for sale in syndication markets rather than for network television.

flack a derogatory term that, in journalism, is sometimes applied to a public relations agent.

FM frequency modulation; a type of radio and sound transmission that offers static-less reception and greater fidelity and clarity than AM radio by accentuating the pitch or distance between radio waves.

focus groups a common research method in psychographic analysis in which moderators lead small-group discussions about a product or an issue, usually with six to twelve people.

folk music music performed by untrained musicians and passed down through oral traditions; it encompasses a wide range of music, from Appalachian fiddle tunes to the accordion-led zydeco of Louisiana.

folk-rock amplified folk music, often featuring politically overt lyrics; influenced by rock and roll.

format radio the concept of radio stations developing and playing specific styles (or formats) geared to listeners' age, race, or gender; in format radio, management, rather than deejays, controls programming choices.

Fourth Estate the notion that the press operates as an unofficial branch of government, monitoring the legislative, judicial, and executive branches for abuses of power.

fourth screens technologies like smartphones, iPods, iPads, and mobile TV devices that are forcing major changes in consumer viewing habits and media content creation.

fringe time in television, the time slot either immediately before the evening's prime-time schedule (called *early fringe*) or immediately following the local evening news or the network's late-night talk shows (called *late fringe*).

gag orders legal restrictions prohibiting the press from releasing preliminary information that might prejudice jury selection.

gameplay the way in which a game's rules, rather than the graphics, sound, and narrative style, structure how players interact with a game.

gangster rap a style of rap music that depicts the hardships of urban life and sometimes glorifies the violent style of street gangs.

gatekeepers editors, producers, and other media managers who function as message filters, making decisions about what types of messages actually get produced for particular audiences.

general-interest magazines types of magazines that address a wide variety of topics and are aimed at a broad national audience.

genre a narrative category in which conventions regarding similar characters, scenes, structures, and themes recur in combination.

grunge rock music that takes the spirit of punk and infuses it with more attention to melody.

guilds or clans in gaming, coordinated, organized teamlike groups that can be either small and easygoing or large and demanding.

HD radio a digital technology that enables AM and FM radio broadcasters to multicast two to three additional compressed digital signals within their traditional analog frequency.

hegemony the acceptance of the dominant values in a culture by those who are subordinate to those who hold economic and political power.

herd journalism a situation in which reporters stake out a house or follow a story in such large groups that the entire profession comes under attack for invading people's privacy or exploiting their personal tragedies.

hidden-fear appeal an advertising strategy that plays on a sense of insecurity, trying to persuade consumers that only a specific product can offer relief.

high culture a symbolic expression that has come to mean "good taste"; often supported by wealthy patrons and corporate donors, it is associated with fine art (such as ballet, the symphony, painting, and classical literature), which is available primarily in theaters or museums.

hip-hop music that combines spoken street dialect with cuts (or samples) from older records and bears the influences of social politics, male boasting, and comic lyrics carried forward from blues, R&B, soul, and rock and roll.

Hollywood Ten the nine screenwriters and one film director subpoenaed by the House Un-American Activities Committee (HUAC) who were sent to prison in the late 1940s for refusing to disclose their memberships or to identify communist sympathizers.

HTML (hypertext markup language) the written code that creates Web pages and links; a language all computers can read.

human-interest stories news accounts that focus on the trials and tribulations of the human condition, often featuring ordinary individuals facing extraordinary challenges.

hypodermic-needle model an early model in mass communication research that attempted to explain media effects by arguing that the media figuratively shoot their powerful effects into unsuspecting or weak audiences; sometimes called the *bullet theory* or *direct effects model*.

hypotheses in social science research, tentative general statements that predict a relationship between a dependent variable and an independent variable.

illuminated manuscripts books from the Middle Ages that featured decorative, colorful designs and illustrations on each page.

indecency an issue related to appropriate broadcast content; the government may punish broadcasters for indecency or profanity after the fact, and over the years a handful of radio stations have had their licenses suspended or denied over indecent programming.

indies independent music and film production houses that work outside industry oligopolies; they often produce less mainstream music and film.

indirect payment in media economics, the financial support of media products by advertisers, who pay for the quantity or quality of audience members that a particular medium attracts.

individualism an underlying value held by most U.S. journalists and citizens, it favors individual rights and responsibilities above group needs or institutional mandates.

in-game advertisements integrated, often subtle advertisements, such as billboards, logos, or storefronts in a game, that can be either static or dynamic.

instant book in the book industry, a marketing strategy that involves publishing a topical book quickly following a major event.

instant messaging a Web feature that enables users to chat with buddies in real time via pop-up windows assigned to each conversation.

intellectual properties in gaming, the stories, characters, personalities, and music that require licensing agreements.

Internet the vast network of telephone and cable lines, wireless connections, and satellite systems designed to link and carry computer information worldwide.

Internet radio online radio stations that either "stream" simulcast versions of on-air radio broadcasts over the Web or are created exclusively for the Internet.

Internet service provider (ISP) a company that provides Internet access to homes and businesses for a fee.

interpretation the third step in the critical process, it asks and answers the "What does that mean?" and "So what?" questions about one's findings.

interpretive journalism a type of journalism that involves analyzing and explaining key issues or events and placing them in a broader historical or social context.

interstitials advertisements that pop up in a screen window as a user attempts to access a new Web page.

inverted-pyramid style a style of journalism in which news reports begin with the most dramatic or newsworthy information—answering *who*, *what*, *where*, and *when* (and less frequently *why* or *how*) questions at the top of the story—and then trail off with less significant details.

investigative journalism news reports that hunt out and expose corruption, particularly in business and government.

irritation advertising an advertising strategy that tries to create product-name recognition by being annoying or obnoxious.

jazz an improvisational and mostly instrumental musical form that absorbs and integrates a diverse body of musical styles, including African rhythms, blues, big band, and gospel.

joint operating agreement (JOA) in the newspaper industry, an economic arrangement, sanctioned by the government, that permits competing newspapers to operate separate editorial divisions while merging business and production operations.

kinescope before the days of videotape, a 1950s technique for preserving television broadcasts by using a film camera to record a live TV show off a studio monitor.

kinetograph an early movie camera developed by Thomas Edison's assistant in the 1890s.

kinetoscope an early film projection system that served as a kind of peep show in which viewers looked through a hole and saw images moving on a tiny plate.

leased channels in cable television, channels that allow citizens to buy time for producing programs or presenting their own viewpoints.

libel in media law, the defamation of character in written expression.

libertarian model a model for journalism and speech that encourages vigorous government criticism and supports the highest degree of freedom for individual speech and news operations.

limited competition in media economics, a market with many producers and sellers but only a few differentiable products within a particular category; sometimes called *monopolistic competition*.

linotype a technology introduced in the nineteenth century that enabled printers to set type mechanically using a typewriter-style keyboard.

literary journalism news reports that adapt fictional story-telling techniques to nonfictional material; sometimes called *new journalism*.

Little Three See **Big Five/Little Three**.

lobbying in governmental public relations, the process of attempting to influence the voting of lawmakers to support a client's or an organization's best interests.

longitudinal studies a term used for research studies that are conducted over long periods of time and often rely on large government and academic survey databases.

low culture a symbolic expression supposedly aligned with the questionable tastes of the "masses," who enjoy the commercial "junk" circulated by the mass media, such as soap operas, rock music, talk radio, comic books, and monster truck pulls.

low-power FM (LPFM) a new class of noncommercial radio stations approved by the FCC in 2000 to give voice to local groups lacking access to the public airwaves; the 10-watt and 100-watt stations broadcast to a small, community-based area.

magalog a combination of a glossy magazine and retail catalogue that is often used to market goods or services to customers or employees.

magazine a nondaily periodical that comprises a collection of articles, stories, and ads.

manuscript culture a period during the Middle Ages when priests and monks advanced the art of bookmaking.

market research in advertising and public relations agencies, the department that uses social science techniques to assess the behaviors and attitudes of consumers toward particular products before any ads are created.

mass communication the process of designing and delivering cultural messages and stories to diverse audiences through media channels as old as the book and as new as the Internet.

massively multiplayer online role-playing games (MMORPGs) role-playing games set in virtual fantasy worlds that require users to play through an avatar.

mass market paperbacks low-priced paperback books sold mostly on racks in drugstores, supermarkets, and airports, as well as in bookstores.

mass media the cultural industries—the channels of communication—that produce and distribute songs, novels, news, movies, online computer services, and other cultural products to a large number of people.

mass media channel newspapers, books, magazines, radio, movies, television, or the Internet.

media buyers in advertising, the individuals who choose and purchase the types of media that are best suited to carry a client's ads and reach the targeted audience.

media effects research the mainstream tradition in mass communication research, it attempts to understand, explain, and predict the impact—or effects—of the mass media on individuals and society.

media literacy an understanding of the mass communication process through the development of critical-thinking tools—description, analysis, interpretation, evaluation, engagement—that enable a person to become more engaged as a citizen and more discerning as a consumer of mass media products.

mega-agencies in advertising, large firms or holding companies that are formed by merging several individual agencies and that maintain worldwide regional offices; they provide both advertising and public relations services and operate in-house radio and TV production studios.

megaplexes movie theater facilities with fourteen or more screens.

messages the texts, images, and sounds transmitted from senders to receivers.

microprocessors miniature circuits that process and store electronic signals, integrating thousands of electronic components into thin strands of silicon along which binary codes travel.

minimal-effects model a mass communication research model based on tightly controlled experiments and survey findings; it argues that the mass media have limited effects on audiences, reinforcing existing behaviors and attitudes rather than changing them.

modding the most advanced form of **collective intelligence**; slang for modifying game software or hardware.

modern the term describing a historical era spanning the time from the rise of the Industrial Revolution in the eighteenth and nineteenth centuries to the present; its social values include celebrating the individual, believing in rational order, working efficiently, and rejecting tradition.

monopoly in media economics, an organizational structure that occurs when a single firm dominates production and distribution in a particular industry, either nationally or locally.

Morse code a system of sending electrical impulses from a transmitter through a cable to a reception point; developed by the American inventor Samuel Morse.

movie palaces ornate, lavish single-screen movie theaters that emerged in the 1910s in the United States.

MP3 short for MPEG-1 Layer 3, an advanced type of audio compression that reduces file size, enabling audio to be easily distributed over the Internet and to be digitally transmitted in real time.

muckrakers reporters who used a style of early-twentieth-century investigative journalism that emphasized a willingness to crawl around in society's muck to uncover a story.

multichannel video programming distributors (MVPDs) the cable industry's name for its largest revenue generators, including cable companies and DBS providers.

multiple-system operators (MSOs) large corporations that own numerous cable television systems.

multiplexes contemporary movie theaters that exhibit many movies at the same time on multiple screens.

must-carry rules rules established by the FCC requiring all cable operators to assign channels to and carry all local TV broadcasts on their systems, thereby ensuring that local network affiliates, independent stations (those not carrying network programs), and public television channels would benefit from cable's clearer reception.

myth analysis a strategy for critiquing advertising that provides insights into how ads work on a cultural level; according to this strategy, ads are narratives with stories to tell and social conflicts to resolve.

narrative the structure underlying most media products, it includes two components: the story (what happens to whom) and the discourse (how the story is told).

narrative films movies that tell a story, with dramatic action and conflict emerging mainly from individual characters.

narrowcasting any specialized electronic programming or media channel aimed at a target audience.

National Public Radio (NPR) noncommercial radio established in 1967 by the U.S. Congress to provide an alternative to commercial radio.

net neutrality the principle that every Web site and every user—whether a multinational corporation or you—has the right to the same Internet network speed and access.

network a broadcast process that links, through special phone lines or satellite transmissions, groups of radio or TV stations that share programming produced at a central location.

network era the period in television history, roughly from the mid-1950s to the late 1970s, that refers to the dominance of the Big Three networks—ABC, CBS, and NBC—over programming and prime-time viewing habits; the era began eroding with a decline in viewing and with the development of VCRs, cable, and new TV networks.

news the process of gathering information and making narrative reports—edited by individuals in a news organization—that create selected frames of reference and help the public make sense of prominent people, important events, and unusual happenings in everyday life.

newshole the space left over in a newspaper for news content after all the ads are placed.

newspaper chain a large company that owns several papers throughout the country.

newsreels weekly ten-minute magazine-style compilations of filmed news events from around the world organized in a sequence of short reports; prominent in movie theaters between the 1920s and the 1950s.

news/talk/information the fastest-growing radio format in the 1990s, dominated by news programs or talk shows.

newsworthiness the often unstated criteria that journalists use to determine which events and issues should become news reports, including timeliness, proximity, conflict, prominence, human interest, consequence, usefulness, novelty, and deviance.

nickelodeons the first small makeshift movie theaters, which were often converted cigar stores, pawnshops, or restaurants redecorated to mimic vaudeville theaters.

ninjas game players who snatch loot out of turn and then leave a group, or **PUG**.

noobs game players who are clueless beginners.

O & Os TV stations "owned and operated" by networks.

objective journalism a modern style of journalism that distinguishes factual reports from opinion columns; reporters strive to remain neutral toward the issue or event they cover, searching out competing points of view among the sources for a story.

obscenity expression that is not protected as speech if these three legal tests are all met: (1) the average person, applying contemporary community standards, would find that the material as a whole appeals to prurient interest; (2) the material depicts or describes sexual conduct in a patently offensive way; (3) the material, as a whole, lacks serious literary, artistic, political, or scientific value.

off-network syndication in television, the process whereby older programs that no longer run during prime time are made available for reruns to local stations, cable operators, online services, and foreign markets.

offset lithography a technology that enabled books to be printed from photographic plates rather than metal casts, reducing the cost of color and illustrations and eventually permitting computers to perform typesetting.

oligopoly in media economics, an organizational structure in which a few firms control most of an industry's production and distribution resources.

online fantasy sports games in which players assemble teams and use actual sports results to determine scores in their online games. These games reach a mass audience, have a major social component, and take a managerial perspective on the game.

online piracy the illegal uploading, downloading, or streaming of copyrighted material, such as music or movies.

open-source software noncommercial software shared freely and developed collectively on the Internet.

opinion and fair comment a defense against libel that states that libel applies only to intentional misstatements of factual information rather than to statements of opinion.

opt-in or **opt-out policies** controversial Web site policies over personal data gathering: *opt-in* means Web sites must gain explicit permission from online consumers before the site can collect their personal data; *opt-out* means that Web sites can automatically collect personal data unless the consumer goes to the trouble of filling out a specific form to restrict the practice.

option time a business tactic, now illegal, whereby a radio network in the 1920s and 1930s paid an affiliate station a set fee per hour for an option to control programming and advertising on that station.

Pacifica Foundation a radio broadcasting foundation established in Berkeley, California, by journalist and World War II pacifist Lewis Hill; he established KPFA, the first nonprofit community radio station, in 1949.

paperback books books made with less expensive paper covers, introduced in the United States in the mid-1800s.

papyrus one of the first substances to hold written language and symbols; produced from plant reeds found along the Nile River.

Paramount decision the 1948 U.S. Supreme Court decision that ended vertical integration in the film industry by forcing the studios to divest themselves of their theaters.

parchment treated animal skin that replaced papyrus as an early pre-paper substance on which to document written language.

partisan press an early dominant style of American journalism distinguished by opinion newspapers, which generally argued one political point of view or pushed the plan of the particular party that subsidized the paper.

pass-along readership the total number of people who come into contact with a single copy of a magazine.

payola the unethical (but not always illegal) practice of record promoters paying deejays or radio programmers to favor particular songs over others.

pay-per-view (PPV) a cable-television service that allows customers to select a particular movie for a fee, or to pay $25 to $40 for a special one-time event.

paywall an online portal that charges consumers a fee for access to news content.

penny arcade the first thoroughly modern indoor playground, filled with coin-operated games.

penny papers (also *penny press*) refers to newspapers that, because of technological innovations in printing, were able to drop their price to one cent beginning in the 1830s, thereby making papers affordable to the working and emerging middle classes and enabling newspapers to become a genuine mass medium.

phishing an Internet scam that begins with phony e-mail messages that appear to be from an official site and request that customers send their credit card numbers and other personal information to update their account.

photojournalism the use of photos to document events and people's lives.

pinball machine the most prominent mechanical game, in which players score points by manipulating the path of a metal ball on a playfield in a glass-covered case.

plain-folks pitch an advertising strategy that associates a product with simplicity and the common person.

podcasting a distribution method (coined from "iPod" and "broadcasting") that enables listeners to download audio program files from the Internet for playback on computers or digital music players.

political advertising the use of ad techniques to promote a candidate's image and persuade the public to adopt a particular viewpoint.

political economy studies an area of academic study that specifically examines interconnections among economic interests, political power, and how that power is used.

pop music popular music that appeals either to a wide cross section of the public or to sizable subdivisions within the larger public based on age, region, or ethnic background; the word *pop* has also been used as a label to distinguish popular music from classical music.

portal an entry point to the Internet, such as a search engine.

postmodern the term describing a contemporary historical era spanning the 1960s to the present; its social values include opposing hierarchy, diversifying and recycling culture, questioning scientific reasoning, and embracing paradox.

premium channels in cable programming, a tier of channels that subscribers can order at an additional monthly fee over their basic cable service; these may include movie channels and interactive services.

press agent the earliest type of public relations practitioner, who seeks to advance a client's image through media exposure.

press releases in public relations, announcements—written in the style of news reports—that give new information about an individual, a company, or an organization, and pitch a story idea to the news media.

prime time in television programming, the hours between 8 and 11 P.M. (or 7 and 10 P.M. in the Midwest), when networks have traditionally drawn their largest audiences and charged their highest advertising rates.

Prime Time Access Rule (PTAR) an FCC regulation that reduced networks' control of prime-time programming to encourage more local news and public-affairs programs, often between 6 and 7 P.M.

printing press a fifteenth-century invention whose movable metallic type technology spawned modern mass communication by creating the first method for mass production. It reduced the size and cost of books; made them the first mass medium affordable to less affluent people; and provided the impetus for the Industrial Revolution, assembly-line production, modern capitalism, and the rise of consumer culture.

prior restraint the legal definition of censorship in the United States; it prohibits courts and governments from blocking any publication or speech before it actually occurs.

product placement the advertising practice of strategically placing products in movies, TV shows, comic books, and video games so that the products appear as part of a story's set environment.

professional books technical books that target various occupational groups and are not intended for the general consumer market.

Progressive Era a period of political and social reform that lasted from the 1890s to the 1920s.

progressive rock an alternative music format that developed as a backlash to the popularity of Top 40.

propaganda in advertising and public relations, a communication strategy that tries to manipulate public opinion to gain support for a special issue, program, or policy, such as a nation's war effort.

propaganda analysis the study of propaganda's effectiveness in influencing and mobilizing public opinion.

pseudo-events in public relations, circumstances or events created solely for the purpose of obtaining coverage in the media.

pseudo-polls typically call-in, online, or person-in-the-street nonscientific polls that the news media use to address a "question of the day."

psychographics in market research, the study of audience or consumer attitudes, beliefs, interests, and motivations.

Public Broadcasting Act of 1967 the act by the U.S. Congress that established the Corporation for Public Broadcasting, which oversees the Public Broadcasting Service (PBS) and National Public Radio (NPR).

Public Broadcasting Service (PBS) noncommercial television established in 1967 by the U.S. Congress to provide an alternative to commercial television.

public domain the end of the copyright period for a work, at which point the public may begin to access it for free.

publicity in public relations, the positive and negative messages that spread controlled and uncontrolled information about a person, a corporation, an issue, or a policy in various media.

public journalism a type of journalism, driven by citizen forums, that goes beyond telling the news to embrace a broader mission of improving the quality of public life; also called *civic journalism.*

public relations the total communication strategy conducted by a person, a government, or an organization attempting to reach and persuade its audiences to adopt a point of view.

public service announcements (PSAs) reports or announcements, carried free by radio and TV stations, that promote government programs, educational projects, voluntary agencies, or social reform.

public sphere those areas or arenas in social life—like the town square or coffeehouse—where people come together regularly to discuss social and cultural problems and try to influence politics; the public sphere is distinguished from governmental spheres, where elected officials and other representatives conduct affairs of state.

PUGs in gaming, temporary teams usually assembled by match-making programs integrated into a game (short for Pick-Up Groups).

pulp fiction a term used to describe many late-nineteenth-century popular paperbacks and dime novels, which were constructed of cheap machine-made pulp material.

punk rock rock music that challenges the orthodoxy and commercialism of the recording business; it is characterized by loud, unpolished qualities, a jackhammer beat, primal vocal screams, crude aggression, and defiant or comic lyrics.

qualified privilege a legal right allowing journalists to report judicial or legislative proceedings even though the public statements being reported may be libelous.

Radio Act of 1912 the first radio legislation passed by Congress, it addressed the problem of amateur radio operators cramming the airwaves.

Radio Act of 1927 the second radio legislation passed by Congress; in an attempt to restore order to the airwaves, the act stated that licensees did not own their channels but could license them if they operated to serve the "public interest, convenience, or necessity."

Radio Corporation of America (RCA) a company developed during World War I that was designed, with government approval, to pool radio patents; the formation of RCA gave the United States almost total control over the emerging mass medium of broadcasting.

radio waves a portion of the electromagnetic wave spectrum that was harnessed so that signals could be sent from a transmission point and obtained at a reception point.

random assignment a social science research method for assigning research subjects; it ensures that every subject has an equal chance of being placed in either the experimental group or the control group.

rating in TV audience measurement, a statistical estimate expressed as a percentage of households tuned to a program in the local or national market being sampled.

receivers the targets of messages crafted by senders.

reference books dictionaries, encyclopedias, atlases, and other reference manuals related to particular professions or trades.

regional editions national magazines whose content is tailored to the interests of different geographic areas.

responsible capitalism an underlying value held by many U.S. journalists and citizens, it assumes that businesspeople should compete with one another not primarily to maximize profits but to increase prosperity for all.

retransmission fee the fee that cable providers pay to broadcast networks for the right to carry their channels.

rhythm and blues (or **R&B**) music that merges urban blues with big-band sounds.

right to privacy addresses a person's right to be left alone, without his or her name, image, or daily activities becoming public property.

rockabilly music that mixes bluegrass and country influences with those of black folk music and early amplified blues.

rock and roll music that merges the African American influences of urban blues, gospel, and R&B with the white influences of country, folk, and pop vocals.

role-playing games (RPGs) games that are typically set in a fantasy or sci-fi world in which each player (there can be multiple players in a game) chooses to play as a character that specializes in a particular skill set.

rotation in format radio programming, the practice of playing the most popular or best-selling songs many times throughout the day.

satellite radio pay radio services that deliver various radio formats nationally via satellite.

saturation advertising the strategy of inundating a variety of print and visual media with ads aimed at target audiences.

scientific method a widely used research method that studies phenomena in systematic stages; it includes identifying a research problem, reviewing existing research, developing working hypotheses, determining appropriate research design, collecting information, analyzing results to see if the hypotheses have been verified, and interpreting the implications of the study.

search engines sites or applications that offer a more automated route to finding content by allowing users to enter key words or queries to locate related Web pages.

Section 315 part of the 1934 Communications Act; it mandates that during elections, broadcast stations must provide equal opportunities and response time for qualified political candidates.

selective exposure the phenomenon whereby audiences seek messages and meanings that correspond to their preexisting beliefs and values.

selective retention the phenomenon whereby audiences remember or retain messages and meanings that correspond to their preexisting beliefs and values.

senders the authors, producers, agencies, and organizations that transmit messages to receivers.

serial program a radio or TV program, such as a soap opera, that features continuing story lines from day to day or week to week (for contrast, see **chapter show**).

share in TV audience measurement, a statistical estimate of the percentage of homes tuned to a certain program, compared with those simply using their sets at the time of a sample.

shield laws laws protecting the confidentiality of key interview subjects and reporters' rights not to reveal the sources of controversial information used in news stories.

simulation games games that involve managing resources and planning worlds that are typically based in reality.

situation comedy a type of comedy series that features a recurring cast and set as well as several narrative scenes; each episode establishes a situation, complicates it, develops increasing confusion among its characters, and then resolves the complications.

sketch comedy short television comedy skits that are usually segments of TV variety shows; sometimes known as *vaudeo*, the marriage of vaudeville and video.

slander in law, spoken language that defames a person's character.

slogan in advertising, a catchy phrase that attempts to promote or sell a product by capturing its essence in words.

small-town pastoralism an underlying value held by many U.S. journalists and citizens, it favors the small over the large and the rural over the urban.

snob-appeal approach an advertising strategy that attempts to convince consumers that using a product will enable them to maintain or elevate their social station.

social learning theory a theory within media effects research that suggests a link between the mass media and behavior.

social media digital applications that allow people worldwide to have conversations, share common interests, and generate their own media content online.

social networking sites sites on which users can create content, share ideas, and interact with friends.

social responsibility model a model for journalism and speech, influenced by the libertarian model, that encourages the free flow of information to citizens, so they can make wise decisions about political and often more social issues.

soul music that mixes gospel, blues, and urban and southern black styles with slower, more emotional, and melancholic lyrics.

sound bite in TV journalism, the equivalent of a quote in print; the part of a news report in which an expert, a celebrity, a victim, or a person on the street is interviewed about some aspect of an event or issue.

space brokers in the days before modern advertising, individuals who purchased space in newspapers and sold it to various merchants.

spam a computer term referring to unsolicited e-mail.

spiral of silence a theory that links the mass media, social psychology, and the formation of public opinion; the theory says that people who hold minority views on controversial issues tend to keep their views silent.

split-run editions editions of national magazines that tailor ads to different geographic areas.

spyware software with secretive codes that enable commercial firms to "spy" on users and gain access to their computers.

stereo the recording of two separate channels or tracks of sound.

storyboard in advertising, a blueprint or roughly drawn comic-strip version of a proposed advertisement.

strategy games games in which perspective is omniscient and the player must survey the entire "world" or playing field and make strategic decisions.

studio system an early film production system that constituted a sort of assembly-line process for moviemaking; major film studios controlled not only actors but also directors, editors, writers, and other employees, all of whom worked under exclusive contracts.

subliminal advertising a 1950s term that refers to hidden or disguised print and visual messages that allegedly register on the subconscious, creating false needs and seducing people into buying products.

subsidiary rights in the book industry, selling the rights to a book for use in other media forms, such as a mass market paperback, a CD-ROM, or the basis for a movie screenplay.

supermarket tabloids newspapers that feature bizarre human-interest stories, gruesome murder tales, violent accident accounts, unexplained phenomena stories, and malicious celebrity gossip.

superstations local independent TV stations, such as WTBS in Atlanta or WGN in Chicago, that have uplinked their signals onto a communication satellite to make themselves available nationwide.

survey research in social science research, a method of collecting and measuring data taken from a group of respondents.

syndication leasing TV stations or cable networks the exclusive right to air TV shows.

synergy in media economics, the promotion and sale of a product (and all its versions) throughout the various subsidiaries of a media conglomerate.

talkies movies with sound, beginning in 1927.

Telecommunications Act of 1996 the sweeping update of telecommunications law that led to a wave of media consolidation.

telegraph invented in the 1840s, it sent electrical impulses through a cable from a transmitter to a reception point, transmitting Morse code.

textbooks books made for the el-hi (elementary and high school) and college markets.

textual analysis in media research, a method for closely and critically examining and interpreting the meanings of culture, including architecture, fashion, books, movies, and TV programs.

third-person effect the theory that people believe others are more affected by media messages than they are themselves.

third screens the computer-type screens on which consumers can view television, movies, music, newspapers, and books.

time shifting the process whereby television viewers record shows and watch them later, when it is convenient for them.

Top 40 format the first radio format, in which stations played the forty most popular hits in a given week, as measured by record sales.

trade books the most visible book industry segment, featuring hardbound and paperback books aimed at general readers and sold at bookstores and other retail outlets.

transistors invented by Bell Laboratories in 1947, these tiny pieces of technology, which receive and amplify radio signals, make portable radios possible.

trolls players who take pleasure in intentionally spoiling a gaming experience for others.

underground press radical newspapers, run on shoestring budgets, that question mainstream political policies and conventional values; the term usually refers to a journalism movement of the 1960s.

university press the segment of the book industry that publishes scholarly books in specialized areas.

urban contemporary one of radio's more popular formats, primarily targeting African American listeners in urban areas with dance, R&B, and hip-hop music.

uses and gratifications model a mass communication research model, usually employing in-depth interviews and survey questionnaires, that argues that people use the media to satisfy various emotional desires or intellectual needs.

Values and Lifestyles (VALS) a market-research strategy that divides consumers into types and measures psychological factors, including how consumers think and feel about products and how they achieve (or do not achieve) the lifestyles to which they aspire.

vellum a handmade paper made from treated animal skin, used in the Gutenberg Bibles.

vertical integration in media economics, the phenomenon of controlling a mass media industry at its three essential levels: production, distribution, and exhibition; the term is most frequently used in reference to the film industry.

video news releases (VNRs) in public relations, the visual counterparts to press releases; they pitch story ideas to the TV news media by mimicking the style of a broadcast news report.

video-on-demand (VOD) cable television technology that enables viewers to instantly order programming, such as movies, to be digitally delivered to their sets.

video subscription services a new term for cable and video-on-demand providers introduced to include streaming-only companies, like Hulu Plus and Netflix.

viral marketing short videos or other content that marketers hope will quickly gain widespread attention as users share it with friends online or by word of mouth.

vitascope a large-screen movie projection system developed by Thomas Edison.

Webzine a magazine that publishes on the Internet.

wiki Web sites Web sites that are capable of being edited by any user; the most famous is Wikipedia.

wireless telegraphy the forerunner of radio, a form of voiceless point-to-point communication; it preceded the voice and sound transmissions of one-to-many mass communication that became known as broadcasting.

wireless telephony early experiments in wireless voice and music transmissions, which later developed into modern radio.

wire services commercial organizations, such as the Associated Press, that share news stories and information by relaying them around the country and the world, originally via telegraph and now via satellite transmission.

World Wide Web (WWW) a data-linking system for organizing and standardizing information on the Internet; the WWW enables computer-accessed information to associate with—or link to—other information, no matter where it is on the Internet.

yellow journalism a newspaper style or era that peaked in the 1890s, it emphasized high-interest stories, sensational crime news, large headlines, and serious reports that exposed corruption, particularly in business and government.

zines self-published magazines produced on personal computer programs or on the Internet.

Credits

Page 42, Figure 2.1: Katie Hafner and Matthew Lyon, "Distributed Networks," from *Where Wizards Stay Up Late*. Copyright © 1996 by Katie Hafner and Matthew Lyon. Reprinted with permission of Simon & Schuster, Inc. **85, Case Study:** Olivia Hottle, "*Watch Dogs* Hacks Our Surveillance Society." Used by courtesy of Olivia Hottle Mossman. **138, Tracking Technology:** John Seabrook, "The Song Machine: The Hitmakers Behind Rihanna," from the *New Yorker,* March 26, 2012. Copyright © 2012 by John Seabrook. Used by permission of the author. **142, Case Study:** Michael K. Park, "Psy-zing Up to Mainstream of 'Gangnam Style.'" Used by permission of the author. **171, Case Study:** David Foster Wallace, excerpt from "Host: The Origin of Talk Show Radio." Originally published in the *Atlantic*, April 2005, pp. 66–68. Reprinted by permission of The David Foster Wallace Literary Trust. **222, Tracking Technology:** Richard Verrier and Andrea Chang, "Changing Channels: Big Studios Diversify on YouTube." Copyright © *Los Angeles Times*. Reprinted with permission. **352, Case Study:** Mark C. Rogers, "Comic Books: Alternative Themes, but Superheroes Prevail." Used by permission of the author. **359, Global Village:** Pamela Druckerman, "France and the Anti-Amazon Law," from the *New York Times*, July 9, 2014. Used by permission and protected by the Copyright Laws of the United States. The printing, copying, redistribution, or retransmission of the Material without express written permission is prohibited. **435, Table 12.2:** Public Relations Society of America, Ethics Code. Used by permission of the Public Relations Society of America. **487, Figure 14.1:** Society of Professional Journalists' Code of Ethics. Copyright © Society of Professional Journalists. Reprinted with permission.

Index

AAA Living magazine, 325
A&E, 223, 227
A&R (artist & repertoire) agents, 139
AARP (American Association of Retired Persons), 329
AARP Bulletin, 313, 325, 329
  circulation of, 336
AARP The Magazine, 313, 325, 329
  circulation of, 336
ABC (American Broadcasting Company), 162, 187, 270
  Disney's purchase of, 198, 212, 447, 451, 463
  loss of audience by, 9
  ratings of, 223
  trends in programming and, 195
"ABC" (Jackson 5), 130
ABC/Disney, 200
ABC Family, 457
ABC News, 207, 496
  as media corporation, 468
  profits of, 451
ABC Radio Network, 460
ABC World News Tonight, 207
Abdi Shire Jama (Jooqle), 176
Abduction, 245
Abdul, Paula, 383
Abercrombie & Fitch, wage gap and, 453
el-Abidine Ben ali, Zine, 50
above-the-line costs, 217
Abramson, Jill, 284
absolute ethics, 486
Absolut Vodka, advertising of, 403
Academy Chicago Publishers, 367
Accenture, 394
access-channel mandates, 212, 214
Access Hollywood, 28, 276
account executives, 389–390
accounts, 67
  advertising and planning of, 386–393
  reviews of, 390
acquisitions editors, 362–363
Acta Diurna, 271–272
action digital games, 75, 86, 88
Action for Children's Television (ACT), 401
Action News, 496
Activision Blizzard, 101–102, 103
actual malice, 547
Adams, Eddie, 321
Adams, John, 542
Adams, Ryan, 125
Adbusters Media Foundation, 400
Ad Council, 382
addiction, electronic gaming and, 94
Adele, 114, 137, 139

Adidas, 394, 427
  advertising of, 376
AdMob, 59, 376
Adorno, T. W., 527
Advanced Research Projects Agency (ARPA), 42
advance money, 363
Advance Publications, 334–335
advancing graphics, 79–80
adventure games, 75, 88
Adventure, Mystery, and Romance (Cawelti), 22
Adventures of Huckleberry Finn (Twain), 360
advergames, 93
adversaries, journalists as, 494–495
advertising
  account, 386–393
  alcohol and, 403
  appeal of, to consumers, 382
  association principle in, 394, 396
  bandwagon effect in, 394
  beer, 379, 395, 398, 403
  brand integration in, 398
  business-to-business, 377
  children and, 401
  classified, 377
  commercial speech and regulating, 399–403, 405–407
  cost of, 389
  critical issues in, 400–403
  deceptive, 406–407
  digital, 270, 372
  early American, 378–383
  in the 1800s, 379–381
  electronic gaming and, 93
  flow of money in, 375
  future of, 409
  in global market, 404
  green, 406
  grouping magazines by style of, 326–327
  health and, 402–403, 405
  impressions of, 392
  indirect payments of, 446
  in-game, 93
  irritation, 394
  jobs in, 409
  as myth and story, 396–397
  newspaper, 378, 381
  online trends in, 390–393
  persuasive techniques in, 393–394, 396–397, 399–401
  plain-folks pitch in, 394
  political, 4
  politics of, 408
  pop-up, 377
  of prescription drugs, 405
  product placement and, 397, 399

  in promoting social change and dictating values, 381–382
  on radio, 178–179
  saturation, 389
  in schools, 401–402
  seductive, 21
  shape of United States, 383–393
  in social media, 392–393
  subliminal, 383
  for Super Bowl, 395
  targeted, 60, 62
  television, 333
  tobacco, 379, 402–403, 407
  watching over, 405–407
Advertising Age, 269, 325
advertising agencies
  first, 378, 379
  mega, 379
  structure of, 386–393
  types of, 384–386
Advertising in America (Goodrum and Dalrymple), 380–381
advertising magazines, 332–333
Advertising: The Uneasy Persuasion (Schudson), 397
advocacy journalism, 282
Advocate, The, 331
Aerosmith, 135
affiliate stations, 207, 218
Affleck, Ben, 28
AFL-CIO, 422
African Americans
  breaking through Hollywood's race barrier and, 247
  media ownership, 458–459
  newspapers of, 272, 288–289
Afro-American, 288
After Earth, 246
Against the Current magazine, 336
Agee, James, 281, 505
Agence France-Presse, 294
agenda-setting, 524–525
Agents of S.H.I.E.L.D., 221
Age of Conan, 91
ages, magazines for all, 328–329
"Aiden Pearce," 85
"Ain't That a Shame," 127
Air1, 181
Akira, 93
Akuma, 93
album-oriented rock (AOR), 169, 172
alcohol, advertising and, 403
Alexander, Charles, 314
Alexie, Sherman, 342
Alfred Hitchcock Presents, 203, 205
Alice in Chains, 135
Alienated American, 288
Alkaline Trio, 143
"All along the Watchtower," 127
Allen, Gracie, 161

Allen, Woody, 204
Alliance for Audited Media, 382
Allied Heroes (Edsel), 356
All the President's Men, 480
All Things Considered, 173
Ally McBeal, 205
Alpert, Phillip, 550
Al-Qaeda, 176
Al-Shabaab, 176
Altamont racetrack, 132
Alter, Jonathan, 493
Alterman, Eric, 484
alternative journalism, 292
alternative magazines, 335–336
alternative rock music, 134
AM (amplitude modulation), 166, 167, 180
amateur radio, 152
Amazing Spider-Man, The, 92
Amazon, 393, 462
  apps on, 357
  Appstore on, 105, 357
  Barnes & Noble and, 365–366
  book digitizing and, 360
  book distribution and, 345
  business strategy of, 12
  Cloud Player and, 60
  comparison to *The Circle* and, 444
  CreateSpace and, 367
  customer service of, 341
  digital gaming industry and, 73, 74
  digital media and, 57, 139, 461
  disagreement with Hachette, 341–342
  dot-com companies and, 68
  e-reader and e-book store and, 345
  Foxconn's electronic devices for, 452
  Internet and, 67
  as media giant, 373, 445
  mobile device distribution and, 260
  mobile payment system of, 40
  movie downloads on, 254, 260
  net neutrality and, 67
  new story "content" of, 23
  "one-click" buy buttons of, 341
  online purchasing of college textbooks, 351
  original programming of, 188
  print media and, 266
  sounds and image distribution on, 110
  start of, 43, 56, 60
  streaming music and, 121
  as video game store, 105
  video-on-demand service of, 256
  warehouses of, 367

Amazon Fire Phone, bringing media content to users, 461
Amazon Fire TV, 53
  bringing media content to users, 461
Amazon Kindle, 54, 60, 61
  Amazon's development of, 357
  introduction of, 345, 365
  media content of, 461
  print media and, 266
Amazon Kindle Fire, 54, 60, 326, 333, 357
  competition and, 334
Amazon Kindle Unlimited, 342
AMC Entertainment, 23, 188, 207, 257, 258
Amélie, 248
American Association of Advertising Agencies (AAAA), 383
American Bandstand, 128
American Booksellers Association (ABA), 349
American Broadcasting Company (ABC). See ABC (American Broadcasting Company)
American Cancer Society, 422
American Dictionary of the English Language, 355
American dream stories, 454–455
American Family Association, 181
American Farmer, 314
American Graffiti, 245
American Horror Story, 206
American Hustle, 249
American Idol, 399
American Journalism Review, 478
American Journal of Education, 314
American Journal of Science, 314
American Law Journal, 314
American Legion Magazine, 325
American Library Association, 361
American Magazine, 312
American Marconi, 153
  RCA and, 156
  Sarnoff, David, and, 159
  as subsidiary of British Marconi, 156
  Wireless Telephone Company competition with, 154
American Media, 331
American Medical Association, 422
American Morning, 193
American Newspaper Publishers Association, 436

American Revolution, 284
American Rifleman Magazine, 325
American Society of Composers, Authors, and Publishers (ASCAP), 121
American Society of Newspaper Editors (ASNE), 281, 289
  workforce decline and, 293
American Spectator, 336
American Tobacco Company, 381, 446
  Bernays, Edward's, hiring by, 420
  Sherman Antitrust Act and, 449
America's Got Talent, 517
AM/FM radio, 177, 180
Amini, Hossein, 263
Amos 'n' Andy, 163
  all black cast of, 189
  broadcasting of in restaurants and movie theaters, 164
Amsterdam News, 288
analog recording, 118
analog standard, 191, 192
Anchorman, 22–23, 497
Anderson, Chris, 326
Anderson, Wes, 22, 249
Anderson Cooper 360°, 497
Andreessen, Marc, 45
Andrews, Julie, 356
Andrews Sisters, 123
Android Market, 83–84
android phones, 54
Android Wear, 59
Andrzejewski, Alexa, 69
Andy Griffith, 24
Angel, 28
Angelou, Maya, 361
Angels, 129
Angry Birds, 84, 89, 101, 102, 104, 106
Anik, 196
Animals on American Top 40 charts, 129
Annenberg, Walter, 322
"Annie Had a Baby," 124
Anonymous, 474
anthology dramas, 205–206
anti-Amazon law, France and, 359
anti-paparazzi laws, 551
antislavery magazines, 329–330
antitrust laws, 449
  charging of RCA with violations of, 160–161
  Clayton Antitrust Act as, 446, 449
  limits of, 465, 467
  Sherman Antitrust Act, 446, 449
AOL, 43, 45, 304, 334

as leading force on Internet, 57
merger and acquisitions of, 447, 451, 455, 463
AOL Instant Messenger (AIM), 46
Apple. See also iPad; iPhone; iPod
advertising branding of, 398
agency-model pricing and, 366
Apps store of, 54, 106
comparison to The Circle and, 444
competition with Google, 376
computers made by, 61
devices of, 55
as digital company, 40, 57, 373
digital gaming industry and, 73, 74
dot-com companies and, 68
e-book percentage of sales of, 366
establishment of, 59, 462
Foxconn's electronic devices for, 452
Game Center of, 83
global marketing brand of, 396
iChat of, 46
iCloud of, 59
introduction of social gaming and, 77
Jobs, Steve, and, 457
as media giant, 12, 445
Napster and, 56
print media and, 266
purchase of Beats music by, 121
selling of music, 36
The Simpsons allusions to, 25
Siri, 36, 56–57
Apple TV, 53, 254
appropriateness, 64–65
apps, 55
April 4, 1968: Martin Luther King, Jr.'s Death and How It Changed America (Dyson), 533
Apu Trilogy, 246
Arab Spring uprisings (2011 and 2012), 50, 499
beginning of, 49, 52
Occupy Wall Street movement inspired by, 284
press freedom and, 474
use of smartphones and laptops during, 31
Arbuckle, Fatty, 555
Arcade Fire, 143
arcades, 78–79
Archon, 102
Arctic Monkeys, 134
Areopagitica (Milton), 541
Are You My Mother? (Bechdel), 350
Aristotle, 15, 489
Armies of the Night (Mailer), 282

Armstrong, Edwin, 154
  predicting of radio's demise, 166–167
Armstrong, Louis, 123, 384
Arnaz, Desi, 203
Arnold Worldwide, 389
Aronofsky, Darren, 249
Around the World in Eighty Days (Verne), 277, 310
ARPAnet, 42
Arrested Development, 55
Arrow, 517
art form, journalism as an, 281–282
art-house theaters, 246
Arthritis Foundaton, 422
Artist, The, 242
Asian American newspapers, 290
Asian cinema, 250
Asian Week, 331
Assange, Julian, 506, 545
Assassin's Creed, 80, 91, 102
Associated Press (AP), 303
  founding of, 275–276
  manual for editors, 433
  wire services and feature syndication and, 294
Association of Alternative Newsweeklies (AAN), 291
Association of American Publishers (AAP), 348–349, 358
association principle in advertising, 394, 396
Asteroids, 78
Astro Boy, 93
astroturf lobbying, 430–431
Atari, 78, 79, 104
  consoles of, 79, 101
A-Team, The, 28
Atkinson, Samuel Coate, 314
Atlantic Monthly, 329
Atlantic's Cat label, 127
AT&T, 40, 120
  affiliates of, 159
  broadband access and, 66
  Comcast merger and, 451
  comparison to The Circle and, 444
  development into competitor for cable and DBS, 224
  DirecTV and, 467
  global marketing brand of, 396
  launch of Telstar, 196
  making and selling of radio receivers by, 158
  merger and acquisitions of, 223, 463
  monopoly practices by, 277
  public relations and, 418
  radio stations owned by, 158

RCA and, 156, 159
WEAF on, 163
attention, 524
audience
    global, 460
    studies of, 528, 530
audio books, 357
Audion, 154
audiotapes, 116, 118
Audit Bureau of Circulations, 331, 382
augmented reality, 324, 375
Aulderheide, Pat, 533
auteurs, 244
authoritarian model, 540
Authors Guild, 358
Author Solutions, 367
Autobiography of Malcolm X, The (Marx), 360
Avalon, Frankie, 129
Avatar, 232, 233, 235, 256
avatars, 79, 87
Avengers, The, 233, 256, 353
Avett Brothers, 125
Awesomeness TV, 222

Babbage's, 105
"Baby Love," 131
Bach, 17
Back to the Future II, 257
Bad Boy Entertainment, 135
Bad Grandpa, 398
Bad Religion, 143
Baer, Ralph, 78
Baez, Joan, 131, 291
bagatelles, 76
Bagdikian, Ben, 465
Bailey, F. Lee, 551
Baker, Belle, 123
Baker, Ray Stannard, 317
Baldwin, Alec, 413
Baldwin, Faith, 310
Ball, Lucille, 203, 557
Ballantine Bantam Dell, 362
Baltimore Sun, 293
Bancroft, Anne, 205
Bandello, Roco, 515
Band Perry, The, 122
Bandura, Albert, 524
bandwagon effect in advertising, 394
Bank of America, 295
banned books, 360–361
Banshees, 133
Bantam Books, 354
Baquet, Dean, 485
Bard's Tale, The, 102
Barnes & Noble
    apps on, 357
    brick-and-mortar bookstores of, 366

e-book sales of, 366
Hachette sales and, 342
online purchasing of college textbooks, 351
store closings by, 364
Barney & Friends, 209
Barnum, Phineas Taylor (P.T.), 416–417, 427
barter deals, 219
Bartles & Jaymes, 396
Basecamp, 48
basic cable services, 197
Basie, Count, 123
Batman: Arkham Asylum, 93
Batman for DC comics, 93, 352, 353
Battlefield, 102
Baumgartner, Felix, 427
Baxter, Ted, 497
Bay Psalm Book, The (Daye), 347
BBDO Worldwide, 385
Beach Boys, 129
Beastie Boys, 135
Beatles, 17, 25
    drug arrests of, 132
    imitation of Chuck Berry and Little Richard by, 129–130
    as musical phenomena, 208
Beats by Dr. Dre headphones, 120, 121
Beats Music, 120, 121
    as streaming service, 141
Beat the Clock, 163
Beauty and the Beast, 456, 457
Bechdel, Allison, 350
Beck, Glenn, 169, 171, 492
Beckham, David, 394
Bee Gees, 134
beer advertising, 379, 395, 398, 403
Bejeweled, 84, 102
Bell, Alexander Graham, 116–117, 328
Bell, Chichester, 116–117
Bellan-White, Nadja, 409
Bell Labs, 242
Beloved (Morrison), 356
below-the-line costs, 217
Ben-Hur, 242
Ben & Jerry's Ice Cream's Facebook page, 392
Bennett, James Gordon, 274–275, 277
Benny, Jack, 161
Bentham, Jeremy, 489
Bergen, Candice, 204
Bergen, Edgar, 204, 559–560
Bergman, Ingmar, 246
Berkeley Barb, 291
Berle, Milton, 204

Berlin, Irving, 122, 123
Berliner, Emile, 115, 117
Berman & Co., 430
Bernays, Edward, 161, 416, 420–421, 428, 453
Berners-Lee, Tim, 45, 56
Bernstein, Carl, 283, 480
Bernstein, Leonard, 557
Berry, Chuck, 28, 124–125, 134
    arrest of, 128
    Beatles imitation of, 129
    British invasion and, 129
    "duck walk" of, 125
    influence of, on rock and roll music, 125
Bertelsmann and Pearson, 361–362
Best Buy, 105, 139
    DVD sales at, 200
    luring customers with wholesale prices, 140
best-sellers, 355–356
BET, 197
Betamax (Beta), 200
Better Business Bureau, 382
    nonprofit advertising and, 405
Better Homes and Gardens, 322, 323, 327, 334
Betty Crocker's Cookbook, 349
Beverly Hillbillies, 221, 528
Bewitched, 528
Beyoncé, 114, 136, 138, 141, 393, 412, 413–414
Beyoncé: Life Is But a Dream, 414
Bezos, Jeff, 56
    establishment of Amazon by, 365
    purchase of *Washington Post* by, 301
    same-sex marriage referendum and, 470
BH Media Group, 295
Bianchini, Gina, 69
bias
    in the news, 484
    political, 483
Bias (Goldberg), 484
Biden, Joe, 506
Bieber, Justin, 30, 143, 413
Big Bang, 142
Big Bang Theory, 203, 206, 517
    as huge hit, 221
    salary demands by actors of, 217
    as situation comedy, 204
big business, press agents and, 418
Big C, The, 205
Big Cable, 458
Bigelow, Kathryn, 245, 246
Big Five studios, 234, 241

Biggest Loser, The, 398
Big Hero 6, 456
Big Juice, 138
Big Machine Label Group, 122, 177
Big Machine Records, 137
"Big Mac" theory, 21
Big Media, 471
Big Network, 458
Big Sleep, The, 244
Big Three networks, 203, 211
Bill of Rights, 273, 542
Binch, Winston, 409
Bing, 59
    advertising and, 390
    search on, 462
    travel pages on, 93
biometric bracelets, 444
BioShock, 28
BioWare, 102
Bipartisan Campaign Reform Act (2002), 470
Birth of a Nation, The, 242
Bisland, Elizabeth, 310
Bissinger, H. G., 356
Biswas-Diener, Robert, 574
bits, 46, 79
BitTorrent, 120
Black, Hugo, 542–543
Black, Rebecca, 400
Blackberry, 53
Blacklist, The, 22, 203
Black Nativity, 245
Black Panther Party, 282
blacks. *See* African Americans
Black Swan, 249
Blackwell, Otis, 126
Blade Runner (Scott), 29
Blade Runner in Pop Culture Wars (Romanowski), 29
blaxploitation, 247
Blek, 83
Bling Ring, The, 249
Blizzard Entertainment, 88, 92
BlizzCon, 92
block booking, 240
Blockbuster
    distribution to mobile devices by, 260
    filing of bankruptcy by, 254
blockbuster mentality, 259
block printing, 7, 346
block Web sites, 50
Blogger (blogging platform), 48, 52, 59
blogs/blogging, 12, 33, 43, 47–48, 297–298, 304
    public relations and, 431
Blondie, 133
"Blueberry Hill," 125
Blue Bloods, 203

BlueDigital, 422
Bluem, A. William, 495
Blues Brothers, The, 204
blues music, 123–124
Blume, Judy, 361
Blumlein, Alan, 118
Blu-ray, 83, 200, 254, 256
Bly, Nellie, 277, 310
BMG, 137
  merger of Sony and, 137
Boardwalk Empire, 356
Bob & Tom Show, The, 179
Bogart, Humphrey, 257
"Bohemian Rhapsody" (song), 28
Bok, Edward, 316
Boland, John, 211
Bollier, David, 68
Bollywood, 248, 250
Bonanza, 187
Bones, 218, 219
Bon Iver, 143
Bonzer, Eric, 69
book(s), 341–389
  audio, 357
  college text, 349, 350–351
  comic, 352–353
  early, 7, 344
  future of democracy and,
    367–368
  Google, 345
  history of, 344–348
  influences of television and
    film on, 356–357
  instant, 354
  manga, 349
  modern publishing and book
    industry, 348–351, 354–355
  online, 365–366
  paperback, 345, 347
  preserving and digitizing, 357,
    358, 360
  professional, 345, 350
  reference, 354–355
  religious, 349, 354
  selling, 364–366
  trade, 349, 362, 363
  trends and issues in publish-
    ing, 355–358, 360–361
  types of, 348–349
  university press, 355
book challenge, 361
book clubs, 345, 364–365
Book-of-the-Month Club, 345,
  364–365
book publishing
  organization and ownership of,
    361–367
  structure of, 362–364
Bookseller of Kabul, The
  (Seierstad), 282
Boone, Daniel, 416

Boone, Pat, 127–128
Boorstin, Daniel, 427
Borden, 381
Borders, 266
  as book superstore, 364
  establishment of, 345
Borgen, 500
"Born This Way," 114
bosses, 87
Boston, 133
Boston Globe, 300, 465
  merger and acquisitions of, 463
Boston Marathon terrorist bomb-
  ing (2013), 302
Boston News-Letter, 272
Boston Public Library, 360
Bouazizi, Mohamed, 49, 52
Bourke-White, Margaret, 319, 320
boutique agencies, 384, 385–386
Bowie, David, 125, 133, 134
Bowles, Eammon, 261
Bowling for Columbine, 249
BoxeR, 96
Boy George, 125
Boy's Life, 329
Boyz N the Hood, 247
Bradford, Andrew, 312
Brady, Matthew, photographs of,
  315
Braintree, 40
Brande, Dorothea, 351
brand integration, 398
brands, influence of, on
  consumer, 399
BrandZ, 396
Brant Rock, Massachusetts, 155
Brave, 92, 456
Brave New World (Huxley), 26
Bravo, 188, 197, 200, 223
Breaking Bad, 22, 23, 188, 207,
  217, 220
Breeders, 134
Breitbart, Andrew, 492
Brennan, William, Jr., 539
brick-and-mortar stores, 364, 366
Brides, 324
British American Tobacco (BAT),
  advertising bans and, 404
British Marconi, 156
British Petroleum oil spill, 417,
  432
broadband, 45
broadcasting, 155
  cable threats to, 196–197
  FCC regulation of, 559
  toll, 158
Broadcasting Corporation of
  America (BCA), 159, 160
broadcast news, interpretive
  journalism and, 281
Broder, David, 507

Brokaw, Tom, 207
Brokeback Mountain, 233
Brookings Institution, 27
Brooklyn Eagle, 163
Brooks, Mel, 17, 204
Brown, Chris, 138, 143
Brown, Helen Gurley, 309, 310,
  327
Brown, James, audiences of, 130
Brown, Jay, 138
Brown, Margaret Wise, 24
Brown-Miller Communications,
  430
Brown v. Board of Education, 124
browsers, 45
Bruner, Jerome, 14
Brüno, 557
Brunswick Group, 422
Bryan, Luke, 136
Bubble Island, 102
Bubble Witch Saga, 102
Buckley, William F., 336
Buckley v. Valeo, 538
Buddhadharma, 336
Bud Light, 393
Budweiser, advertising of, 395,
  398, 403
Buena Vista, 456
Buffalo News, 295
Buffett, Warren, 270, 295
Buffy the Vampire Slayer, 28, 207
Buick Circus Hour, 193
Bully, 249
bundling of digital cable
  television, 215
bureau reporters, 293
Burger King, 93
Burgundy, Ron, 497
Burke, James E., 432
Burke, John, 417
Burnett, Leo, 400
Burns, George, 161
Burson-Marsteller, 422, 436
  Tylenol tragedy and, 432–433
Burstyn v. Wilson, 555–556
Bush, George W., 363
  criticism of news media by, 19
  media coverage of, 483
Bushido Blade, 86
Bush v. Gore, 479
business magazines, 325
business news, 434–435
  covering, 286
business tendencies in media
  industries, 451–454
business-to-business ads, 377
BusinessWeek, 301
Butler, The, 245, 247
Butterfield 8, 254
Buzzcocks, 133
BuzzFeed, 305, 414

Bynes, Amanda, 413
Byrds, 131

Cabinet of Dr. Caligari, The, 246
cable, 9, 187–188, 191, 197, 460
  balancing growth against
    broadcasters' interests,
    212, 214
  basic services, 197
  democracy and, 225–227
  development of, 195–197, 199
  digital, 197
  economics and ownership of,
    216–221, 223–225
  premium services, 197, 199
  regulatory challenges to,
    211–215
  threats to broadcasting,
    196–197
  wires and satellites behind,
    195–196
Cablevision, 120, 202, 218, 224
Caesar, Julius, 272
Caesar, Sid, 204
Cage the Elephant, 172
Cairo, Egypt, pro-democracy
  gatherings in, 52
Cajun music, 16
California (Lepucki), 342
California, Channel one
  contracts in, 401
California Center for Public
  Health Advocacy, 430
California State Board of
  Education, 350
"Call Me Maybe," 136
Call of Duty, 94, 98, 101, 102
Camel News Caravan, 193
Camel Newsreel Theater, 207
cameras in courtroom, 552
Cameron, James, 232
Campbell, Clive, 135
Campbell, John, 272
Campbell Ewald, 390
Campbell Soup, 380, 406
Campion, Jane, 245
Canada's National Film Board,
  248
Canal, Jorge, Jr., 550
Candy Crush Saga, 81, 82, 89, 101,
  102
Cannes Film Festival, 250, 251
Canon, 422
Canterbury Tales (Chaucer),
  346–347
"Can't Hold Us," 113
Cantor, Eddie, 123
Cantril, Hadley, 518–519
Capcom, Marvel vs., 86, 93
capitalism, responsible, 482–483
Capitalism: A Love Story, 249

Capote, Truman, 282, 329
Captain America, 93, 257, 350, 352
Captain Underpants (Pilkey), 361
card games, computerized
    versions of, 75
Care Bear Family, The, 401
Carey, James, 514, 531
Carlin, George, 561
Carmike Cinemas, 258
Carnation, 381
Carnegie, Andrew, 366, 449
Carnegie Commission on
    Educational Television,
    209–210
Carnegie libraries, 368
Carolina Hurricanes, 198
Carr, David, 494, 499
Carrie, 245
Carroll, John, 304
Carson, Rachel, 283, 367
Carter, Chris, 60
Carter, Jimmy, 450
Cartoon Network, 211, 455
cartridge, 100–101
Casablanca, 243
cash, 40
cash deal, 219
Cash Money Records, 139
cash-plus, 219
cassette players, 118
cassettes, 117, 118
Castle, 203
casual games, 89
Casual Vacancy, The (Rowling),
    363
catch-up services, 201–202
categorical imperative, 489
cathode ray tubes (CRTs), 76, 78,
    190
Catholic Worker, 292
CATV (community antenna
    television), 190, 195
Caught in the Web, 250
Cawelti, John, 22
CBGB, 133
CBS (Columbia Broadcasting
    System), 9, 187, 195, 270, 465
    creation of name of, 161
    forming of oligopoly by, 241
    mass media and, 372
    newsroom cultures of, 482–483
    radio programming and, 163,
        179
    television news on, 207
    Time Warner and, 188
    Viacom's split with, 223
CBS News, 54
CBS Records, 118
CD Baby, 141
CDs, 117, 119
celebrity spokespeople, 405

Celler-Kefauver Act (1950), 447,
    449
celluloid, 234, 235–236
censorship, 360–361, 554
    fears of corruption and,
        128–129
    as prior restraint, 542–543
Center for Consumer Freedom
    (CCF), 430–431
Center for Digital Democracy,
    565
Center for Investigative
    Reporting, 304
Center for Public Integrity, 303,
    478
Centipede, 80
CEO-to-worker compensation
    ratio, 452
Chan, Jackie, 250
Chancellor Media Corporation,
    180
Chang-dong, Lee, 250
Change.org, 48
Channel One, 379, 401–402
"Chantilly Lace," 128–129
Chaplin, Charlie, 26, 29, 102, 239
chapter shows, 206–207
Charles, Ray, 126, 128, 383
Charleston, 115
Charlie's Angels, 28
Charlotte Observer, 500
Charmed, 28
Charter Communications, 215,
    224
Charter Internet service
    provider (ISP), 45
Chase, Melissa, 183
Chattanooga Times, 278
Chaucer, 346
Chavez, Cesar, 396
Cheers, 13, 221
Chef, 258
Chegg, 351
Chelsea Lately, 142
Chen, Kaige, 250
Cherokee Phoenix, 272, 290
Cherokee Rose Bud, 290
Chess, 80, 137
Chester Cheetah, 93
Chevrolet, advertising branding
    of, 398
Chic, 135
Chicago, 244
Chicago Defender, 288
Chicago Edison, public relations
    and, 418
Chicago Tribune, 266, 269, 293
Chick-fil-A, 470
Chico, advertising of, 386
Chieh, Wang, 346
child labor, 449

Child of Light, 80
Child Online Protection Act
    (1998), 65
children
    advertising and, 401
    Internet and, 65
    magazines for, 329, 333
    television for, 209, 401
Children's Internet Protection
    Act (2000), 65
Children's Television Act (1990),
    401
Child's Play, 91
China
    community control of mass
        communication in, 52
    student uprisings in, 499
Cho, Seung-Hui, 512
Chomsky, Noam, 533
Chopra, Parineeti, 250
Chopra, Yash, 250
Chords, 127
Chow, Yun-Fat, 250
Christian Science Monitor, 270
Christie, Agatha, 351
Christie, Chris, 438
Chrome (Web browser), 45, 59
Chromebook, 462
Chromecast, 59, 462
Chuck E. Cheese pizza-arcade
    restaurant chain, 78
Chun-Li, 93
Cincinnati Enquirer, 294
Cinderella, 237
CinemaNow, 260
Cinemark USA, 258
CinemaScope, 254
cinematograph, 236
cinema verité, 248
Cineplex Entertainment, 258
Cinerama, 254
Circle, The (Eggers), 443–444
circulation and distribution
    magazines, 333–334
Citadel, settlement of FCC payola
    investigation and, 179
citizen journalism, 302–303, 500
Citizen Kane, 25, 231, 278
*Citizens United v. Federal Election
    Commission,* 4, 470, 538
civil rights, 190
Civil Rights movement, 13, 284,
    289, 321
Civil War
    magazines in, 315
    photography in, 315
clans, 90
Clara, 163
Clarissa (Richardson), 347
Claritin, advertising for, 405
Clark, Dick, 126, 128

Clark, Roy Peter, 279
Clarke, Arthur C., 195
Clarkson, Kelly, 138
Clash, 133
Clash of Clans, 104
classical music, 16
classic games, arcades and,
    78–79
classic rock music, 134, 172
classified ads, 377
Clayton Antitrust Act, 446, 449
clearance rules, 218
Clear Channel, 122, 150, 177, 180,
    458
    settlement of FCC payola
        investigation and, 179
Cleaver, Eldridge, 291
Clerks, 557
Cleveland Plain Dealer, 270
click-throughs, 392
Clinton, Hillary, 356
Clinton, William (Bill), 356, 450
    affair with Lewinsky, 13, 284
Closer, The, 207
Club Penguin, 82
CNBC, 208, 223
CNN
    arrival of, 497
    availability of, in other
        countries, 198
    cable services of, 196, 197
    drop in audience of, 498
    as first 24/7 cable TV news
        channel, 208
    global audiences and, 460
    network shows lose to, 9
Cobain, Kurt, 134, 135
Coca-Cola, 381, 422
    advertising of, 395, 398
    global marketing brand of, 396
    product placement and, 399
Cochrane, Elizabeth "Pink"
    (Nellie Bly), 477
codex, 344, 345
Cody, William F., 417
Colbert, Stephen, 33, 342, 356
Colbert Report, 23, 28, 208, 503, 504
Cold War, 467
Cole, Nat King, music-variety
    shows hosted by, 193, 218
Coles, Joanna, 330
Colgate Comedy Hour, 193
Colgate-Palmolive, 163, 381
collaborative projects, 48
collective intelligence, 90–91
college textbooks, 349, 350–351
Collier's, 316, 317, 319, 320
Collins, Suzanne, 356
colonial America
    magazines in, 312–313
    newspapers in, 272–273, 274

color TV standard, 190
Colt 45, advertising and, 403
Columbia Broadcasting System (CBS). *See* CBS (Columbia Broadcasting System)
Columbia Dispatch, 282
Columbia Phonograph Broadcasting System (CPBS), 161
Columbia Pictures
  current film business ruled by, 258
  Sony's ownership of, 260
Columbus Ledger-Enquirer, 502
Combs, Sean "Diddy," 135
Comcast, 120, 188, 224
  comparison to *The Circle* and, 444
  control of broadband access, 66
  future of television and, 188
  mass media and, 372
  as media giant, 223, 445, 468
  merger and acquisitions of, 223, 463, 467
  NBCUniversal and, 260
  Netflix and, 67, 201
  on-demand service of, 223
comedies
  domestic, 204
  situation, 204
  sketch, 204
Comedy Central, 9, 197, 503
  The Daily Show on, 23, 28, 208, 503, 504
Comedy poetry, 22
"Come See about Me," 131
comic books, 352–353
Comics Magazine Association of America, 352
Coming Home, 250
comment sites, 443
Commerce, U.S. Department of, 158
Commercial Alert, 399
  in checking commercialization of United States culture, 406
  as nonprofit advertising watchdog, 405
commercial e-books, 357
commercialization of the Internet, 44–47
commercial radio, 152
commercial speech, regulating advertising and, 399–403, 405–407
commercial strategies in media industry, 446–448
Comme Un Roman, 359
Committee on Public Information, 420

Committee to Defend Martin Luther King and the Struggle for Freedom in the South, 546
Committee to Protect Journalists, 303, 540
common carriers, 214
communication
  channels of, 6
  as culture, 5–10, 531
  defined, 6
  digital, 8–9
  Internet and, 562–563
  oral, 6–7, 12
  print, 12
  written, 6–7
Communications Act (1934), 153, 162, 214, 559
  Internet and, 562–563
  Section 315 of, 561
  Wagner-Hatfield Amendment to, 173
Communications Decency Act (1996), 65
communist model, 540
Community, 201
community, public relations and, 429
compact discs (CDs), 117, 119
Compton's Pictured Encyclopedia, 354
computer-generated imagery (CGI), 243
computer technology, photojournalism and, 321
concussion, 426
Condé Nast magazines, 328, 333, 334–335
conflict of interest, 488
conflict-oriented journalism, 285
Conjuring, The, 244
Connally, John, 494
Conrad, Frank, 157, 158
consensus narratives, 262
consensus-oriented journalism, 285
conservatives, 32
consumer magazines, 325
consumer relations, public relations and, 429
Consumer Reports, 333
consumers
  appeal of advertising and, 382
  choices of, 467–468
Contact, 421
contemporary hit radio (CHR), 172, 176
contemporary media effects theories, 523–526
content analysis, 522

content communities, 48–49
Contract with God, A (Eisner), 349
control group, 521
controlled circulation, 334
conventions, 91–92
convergence. *See* media convergence
Cook, Fred, 559
cookies, 62, 391–392
Cook's Illustrated, 327, 333
Coolidge, Calvin, 158–159, 420
Cooper, Anderson, 497, 498
Cooper, Gary, 252
Cooper, James Fenimore, 314
Coors, advertising by, 403
Coppola, Francis Ford, 245
Coppola, Sofia, 245, 249
copy editors, 363
copyright, 545
Copyright Act (1790), 545
Copyright Royalty Board, 177
Corddry, Rob, 503–504
Cornwell, Patricia, 351
corporate communications, 435
corporate downsizing, 453
Corporation for Public Broadcasting (CPB), 173, 174, 209, 211, 301
correlations, 522
Correll, Charles, 163, 164
Cosby Show, 13, 187, 517
Cosmo, 311
Cosmo Girl, 310
Cosmopolitan, 278, 309, 325, 326, 335
  covers of, 330
  as part of Hearst Corporation, 310, 334
  "Treason of the Senate, The" of, 316
  Walker, John Brisben and, 309–310
  women's sexuality and, 327
  writers for, 310
Cosmopolitan en Español, 331
Costco
  independent bookstores and, 364
  returned books and, 364
counter machines, 76
Counter-Strike, 81, 91, 105
country music, 172, 176
Country Weekly, 328
Couric, Katie, 207
courtrooms, cameras in, 552
Cove, The, 249
cover music, 123
Cox Communications, 45, 66, 224
CPM (cost per mile), 221
Crackberry, 53
Craft, Christine, 497

Crane, Stephen, 281
creative development, advertising in, 388
credibility, neutrality in boosting, 481–482
crime blocks, 496
Criminal Minds, 203
Crisis, 330
crisis, public relations during a, 431–433
critical perspective, benefits of, 30–33
critical process
  defined, 30
  media literacy and, 32–33, 63, 330, 360, 399, 437, 461, 491, 523, 544
criticism, dealing with, 382
Crockett, Davy, 416
Cronkite, Walter, 207, 208, 504
Croods, The, 405
Crosby, Bing, 13, 123
cross platform, 12
Cruise, Tom, 50
Crumb, R., 353
Crysis, 102
Crystallizing Public Opinion, 420
CSI: Crime Scene Investigation, 203, 206, 218, 524
C-SPAN, 197
Cuarón, Alfonso, 232
Cubreporters.org, 305
cultivation effect, 525
cultural approaches to media research, 526–528, 530
cultural change, media convergence and, 13
cultural imperialism, 461, 468–469
cultural landscape, surveying, 16–17, 20–21
cultural studies research, 513, 527
  conducting, 527–528, 530
  early developments in, 527
  evaluating, 531–532
  theoretical perspectives, 530–531
cultural values and ideals, 6
culture
  communication as, 531
  critiquing, 29–30, 32–33
  defined, 6
  evolution of mass communication, 5–10
  high, 17
  low, 17
  map as, 21, 24–26
  oral, 9
  skyscraper as, 16, 17, 20, 21
Cumulus Media, 149–150, 181
Curb Your Enthusiasm, 204

Curry, Ann, 496
Curtis, Cyrus, 316, 318
Czitrom, Daniel, 514, 518

Daily Compass, 292
Daily Herd Management, 325
Daily Kos, 298
daily media consumption by
   platform, 16
Daily Show with Jon Stewart, 23,
   28, 208, 503, 504
Dakota Farmer, 325
Dallas, 23, 221
Dallas Morning News, 300
Daly, John, 207, 495
Dance Dance Revolution, 90, 93
dance games, 90
Dancing with the Stars, 14, 203, 209
Dangerous, 135
Dangerous Liaisons, 250
Daniels, Lee, 245, 247
Dark Knight, The, 256, 349, 512
Dark Souls, 102
Das Kapital (Marx), 360
data mining, 62
   privacy and, 448
   targeted advertising and, 60, 62
Dateline, 218, 495
DatPiff, 136, 144
Dauman, Philippe P., 452
Davis, Bette, 257
Davis, Ossie, 205
Davis, Ziff, 91
Davison, W. Phillips, 526
Day, Benjamin, 272, 274
Day, Dorothy, 291, 292
Daye, Matthew, 347
Daye, Stephen, 344, 347
Db5, 395
DC Comics, 352–353
DC Universe Online, 104
DDB Worldwide, 385
DDoS (Distributed Denial of
   Service), 50
dead air, 168
Deadbeat, 188
deadheading, 418
Deadliest Catch, 14, 209
Dead Man, 249
Dead Weather, 172
Deafheaven, 134
Dean, Ester, 138
Dean, James, 205, 253
De Armas Spanish Magazine
   Network, 331
*Death and Life of American
   Journalism, The*
   (McChesney), 501
Death of Literature, The (Kernan),
   368
Death Race, 98

De Beers, 383
deception, deploying, 485–486
deceptive advertising, 406–407
Deciding What's News (Gans), 484
Decision Points (Bush), 363
deep throat, 480
Deezer, 121, 136
Defense, U.S. Department of,
   Pentagon Pundit program,
   430–431
Defense of Marriage Act
   (DOMA), 114, 514
deficit financing, 217
Def Jam, 138
Defoe, Daniel, 311–312
De Forest, Lee, 152, 154, 159, 167
DeGeneres, Ellen, 222
de Graff, Robert, 351
Deitz, Corey, 183
Delaine, Aubry, 138
deliberative democracy, 505, 507
Delilah, 180
Dell, 61
   Bertelsmann's purchase of, 361
   Linux and, 67
Del Rey, Lana, 136
Del Vecchio, Leonardo
   (Luxottica), 376
democracy
   books and future of, 367–368
   cable and, 225–227
   deliberative, 505, 507
   effects of media consolidation
      on, 470
   equating free markets with, 467
   First Amendment and, 565
   Internet and, 68–69
   magazines in, 336–337
   media marketplace and,
      469–471
   media research and, 532–533
   movies and, 262–263
   newspapers and, 303–304
   public relations and, 436–438
   radio and, 182–183
   redistribution of power and, 372
   reimagining journalism's role
      and, 505, 507
   social media and, 49, 52
   sound recordings and, 144–145
   television and, 225–227
Democracy in America
   (Tocqueville), 513–514
Democratic-Republican Party, 542
demographic editions, 333
demographics, 386
demos, 139
De Palma, Brian, 245
department stores, advertising
   in, 380–381
dependent variables, 521

deregulation, 449
Der Spiegel, 506
Derulo, Jason, 136
design managers, 363
desktop publishing, 332
"Desolation Row," 168
Destiny, 80
Details, 327
detective journalism, 478
Detroit, soul music in, 130
Dettelbach, Steven M., 550
Deus Ex, 102
developmental editors, 363
development budget, 103
Dexter, 30, 356
Diablo, 81, 92, 102
Diamond Dash, 102
Diamond Sutra (Chieh), 346
Diario Las Americas, 289
Diary of a Young Girl, The
   (Frank), 360
Dickens, Charles, 275
Dickinson, Emily, 24
Dickson, William Kennedy, 236
dictionaries, 355
*Dictionary of the English
   Language,* 355
Diddley, Bo, 125
Didion, Joan, 282
Diener, Ed, 574
Diet Coke, 393
digital age, 8–9
   advertising in, 270
   books in, 357
   magazines and, 324–325
   start-up companies in, 462
digital archiving, 68
digital cable, 197
digital communication, 8–9, 45–46
digital distribution, 105
digital divide, preventing, 65–66
digital film production, 235
digital gaming
   business of, 99–106
   development of, 75–81
   First Amendment freedom of
      speech rights and, 75
   free speech, democracy and,
      106–107
   licensing of, 103–104
   marketing of, 104
   Microsoft's use of, 74
   ownership and organization of,
      100–102
   selling, 104–105
   structure of, 103–104
   trends and issues in, 92–95,
      98–99
digital imaging, 358
digital media, convergence and,
   36–37

Digital Millennium Copyright Act
   (1988), 546
digital music, 137, 139
Digital Public Library of
   America, 360
digital recording, 118–119
digital signals, 192
digital sound recording,
   evolution of, 119
digital technology, 42
digital theft, crackdown on, 120
digital transactions, cost to, 40
digital turn, 36
digital TV standard, 191
digital versions of printed text, 266
digital video, 261
Digitas LBi, 385, 391
dime novels, 347
Direct Broadcast Satellite (DBS),
   191, 199, 447, 465, 467
direct effects model, 518
directors, women, 246
direct payment, 446
direct sales, 353
DirecTV, 199, 224, 463, 465, 467
disassociation as advertising
   strategy, 396
disaster management, 432
"Disco Sucks," 133
Discover, 328
*Discovering the News: A Social
   History of American
   Newspapers* (Schudson), 434
Discovery, 202
disease awareness campaigns, 405
Dish, The: Biased and Balanced,
   298
Dish Network, 199, 202, 254, 465
Disney, 197, 198, 211, 456–457,
   465, 546
   ABC and, 212, 447, 451
   CEO's annual salary and, 453
   current film business ruled by,
      258
   diversification and, 451, 465
   ESPN and, 198
   failed suit against Sony, 200
   founding of, 446
   future of television and, 188
   Iger, Robert of, 452
   Marvel and, 260, 353, 460
   mass media and, 372
   as media corporations, 468
   merger and acquisitions of, 463
   Miramax and, 251
   partnership of, 201
   Pixar and, 260
   syndication and, 217
   YouTube and, 260
Disney, Walt, 252
Disney Channel, 457

Disney Junior, 211
Disneyland, 456
Disneyland Paris, 457
Disney Publishing, 457
Disney studio, 259
Distributed Denial of Service
        (DDoS), 50
distributed networks, 42
dithyrambic poetry, 22
Divergent (Roth), 356
diversification, 465
Django Unchained, 258
DJ Kool Here, 135
Doc Martin, 206
Dr. Lin's Chinese Blood Pills, 380
Dr. Seuss books, 349
Documentary Filmmakers'
        Statement of Best Practices
        in Fair Use, 533
documentary films, 248–249
Documentary in American
        Television, 495
Dollarocracy: How the Money and
        Media Election Complex Is
        Destroying America
        (McChesney), 469
domestic comedies, 204
Domino, Fats, 125, 127
Domino's Pizza, 431
Dong, Arthur, 246
Don Jon, 251
Donkey Kong, 78, 100
"Do Not Track" options, 64
Don't Look Back, 133
Don't Touch the White Tile 4, 83
Doom, 81, 86
Doomsday Fight, The, 511
Doors, The, 132, 133, 169, 282
Doritos, advertising at Super
        Bowl, 395
Dorsey, Jack, 40
Dorsey, Tommy, 123
DoubleClick, 391
Doubleday, 365
    Bertelsmann's purchase of,
        361–362
Doubleday & McClure Company,
        348
Doubleday Broadway, 362
Douglass, Frederick, 288
Dove, 391
Dowd, Maureen, 294
Downey, Morton, Jr., 171
"Down Hearted Blues," 124
Downie, Leonard, 301, 302
downloading, 202
downsizing, 452–453
Downton Abbey, 203, 206
Doyle Dane Bernbach (DDB), 388,
        389
Dr. Dre, 121

Dr. Phil, 219
Dr. Quinn, Medicine Woman, 517
Dragnet, 528
Dragon Age: Origins, 102
Drake, 139
dramas, anthology, 205–206
Draw Something, 102
DreamWorks, 222, 250
    partnership with McDonald's,
        405
Dreiser, Theodore, 281, 310
Drew, Robert, 249
Drive, 263
drive time, 169
drop lines, 196
Drudge, Matt, 283–284, 298, 488
Drudge Report, 208, 284
Dualtone Records, 137
Du Bois, W. E. B., 30, 330
Duck Dynasty, 14, 227
"duck walk," 125
Duerson, Dave, 426
Duff, Hilary, 330
Dugdale, Scott, 120
Duke Ellington, 123
dumps, 363
Duncan, David, 320
Dungeons & Dragons, 88
duolingo, 376
Dutton, E. P., 348
DVDs, 235, 254
    high-definition, 200
DVRs (digital video recorders),
        13, 199, 200
Dwolla, 40
Dylan, Bob, 127, 131, 133, 168, 291
Dynasty, 23, 32
Dyson, Michael Eric, 533

E!, 188, 223
Eagles, 125
Earle, Steve, 125
early fringe, 218
Early Show, The, 193
earmarks, 430
earned media, 392
Eason, David, 481
Eastman, George, 234, 236, 320
Eastman Kodak, 234, 380, 381
Easy Rider, 245
eating disorders, advertising and,
        402
eBay, 64
    net neutrality and, 67
    online purchasing of college
        textbooks, 351
Ebert, Roger, 232
Ebony, 330
e-books, 357. *See also* Amazon
        Kindle
    future of, 358

eCampus, 351
EchoStar Communications, 224,
        465, 467
    DirecTV merger and, 447
Eclectic Reader, The (McGuffey),
        350
e-commerce, 62
Economic Club of New York, 436
economic divide, 65
economics
    coverage of news on, 286
    issues of the Internet and, 57–60
    of magazines, 332–336
economy
    analyzing the media, 445–448
    transition to information,
        448–455
Edelman, 422
Edison, Thomas, 115, 155, 234,
        242
    development of sound
        recording and, 236–237
    diligence of, 10–13
    forming of Motion Picture
        Patents Company, 238
Edison's Trust, 239–240
editorial magazines, 332
editor in chief, 291
editors
    acquisitions, 362–363
    copy, 363
    managing, 291
eDonkey, 120
Edsel, Robert M., 356
Ed Sullivan Show, 15, 163, 208,
        221
Educational Media Foundation,
        181
Edwards, Douglas, 207
Effects of Mass Communication,
        The (Klapper), 519
EFM Media, 171
Eggers, Dave, 443
Ehrenreich, Barbara, 533
8 tracks, 177
Eisenstein, Elizabeth, 347
Eisner, Michael, 451, 456
Eisner, Will, 349
Elder Scrolls, The, 91
El Diario-La Prensa, 289
elections, and advertising, 3–4
electric guitars, 124
Electric Kool-Aid Acid Test, The
        (Wolfe), 282
electromagnetic waves, 152, 154
Electronic Arts, 101, 102, 105
Electronic Communications
        Privacy Act (1986), 551
Electronic Entertainment Expo
        (E3), 92
electronic era, 8

electronic gaming
    advertising and, 93
    media culture and, 92–93
electronic publishing, 214
electronic technology, 190–193
Elementary, 203
Elements of Journalism, The
        (Kovach and Rosenstiel), 23
el-hi texts, 349, 350–351
elite magazines, 329
Elle, 334
Ellen DeGeneres Show, 142, 219
Ellsberg, Daniel, 542, 543
El Mañana Daily News, 289
El Misisipi, 272, 289
Em, 163
e-mail, 9, 42, 46. *See also* Internet
    defined, 43
Emancipator, 329–330
Emerson, Ralph Waldo, 314
EMI, 137
    merger and acquisitions of, 463
Eminem, 135
eMule, 120
Encyclopaedia Britannica, 354–355
Encyclopedia Americana, 354
encyclopedias, 344
"The End," 169
engineering consent, 419, 421
engraving and illustrations, 312
Engstrom, Erika, 523
Entercom, settlement of FCC
        payola investigation and,
        179
entertainment magazines,
        327–328
Entertainment Software
        Association (ESA), 84,
        94–95, 100
Entertainment Software Rating
        Board (ESRB), 99
Entertainment Tonight, 28, 211
Entertainment Weekly, 324, 325,
        326
entrepreneurial stage, 11
Environs, 25
Ephedra, 406
Epic of Gilgamesh, 353
Epic poetry and tragedy, 22
episodic series, 206–207
Epitaph, 143
e-publishing, 367
equal opportunity, political
        broadcasts and, 561–562
Equitable Insurance, monopoly
        practices by, 277
Eriksen, Mikkel, 138
Espionage Act (1917), 544, 545
ESPN (Entertainment Sports
        Programming Network),
        196, 197, 198, 457

ESPN Classic, 198, 457
ESPN Deportes, 198
ESPNEWS, 198, 457
ESPN.go.com, 457
ESPN-HD, 198
ESPN Radio, 198, 457
ESPN The Magazine, 198, 328, 457
ESPNU channels, 457
Esquire, 334
E.T.: The Extra-Terrestrial, 233,
    256, 257, 399
ethics
    absolute, 486
    codes of, 398, 486, 487
    news media and, 485–489
    policy development and, 489
    predicaments in, 485–486, 488
    problem resolutions and,
        488–489
    situational, 486
ethnocentrism, 482
Euripides, 14
Euronews, 208
European model, 500
European Union, 467
Eve cigarettes, advertising for, 402
Eveready Hour, 163
evergreens, 218
evergreen subscriptions, 333–334
EverQuest, 104
Everquest II, 99
everyday life, power of media
    stories in, 14–16
Everything Bad Is Good for You, 23
Exorcist, The, 245, 255
Expendables 3, The, 250
experimental group, 521
experiments, 521
experts, relying on, 492–494
exposure, selective, 10
expression
    in media, 557–563
    unprotected forms of, 543–544
Eyes Wide Shut, 557
eye-tracking technology, 376
Eyewitness News, 496
Eyre, Chris, 246

Fabian, 129
Facebook, 422
    as advertising threat, 391
    audience of, 60
    birth of, 36
    business strategy of, 12
    Cairo protesters connection to,
        52
    Candy Crush Saga on, 81, 82, 89,
        101, 102
    closed Internet and, 55
    comparison to *The Circle* and,
        444

competing for young music
    fans, 177
digital gaming and, 73, 74
digital world of, 31, 57, 461
dot-com companies and, 68
friends on, 69
as key player in news and
    politics, 9
launching of, 43
live blogs on, 55
mass media and, 474
as media giant, 373, 445
near-constant use of, 261
net neutrality and, 67
as organizational tool, 284
pages on, 392
Pandora and, 177
public debate and news and, 33
public relations and, 431
as social media site, 49, 83
strength of, 461–462
venue of, 29
video-sharing service of, 48
Words with Friends on, 74, 89
Facebook Chat, 46
facts, 483
Fahrenheit 9/11, 233, 249
Fainaru, Steve, 426
Fainaru-Wada, Mark, 426
Fairbanks, Douglas, 102, 239, 555
Fair Labor Association (FLA), 61
Fairness and Accuracy in
    Reporting (FAIR), 493
Fairness Doctrine, 171, 562
fair use, 546, 564
    rules for, 358
"fake" news, 500, 502–505
Fallon, Jimmy, 222, 504
Fallows, James, 12
Falwell, Jerry, 548
Family Circle, 322, 323, 334
family entertainment games, 75
Family Guy, 23, 224
family hour, 517
family values, banned books and,
    360
famous-person testimonial,
    393–394
Famous Players Company, 239
Fandango, 224
FanFiction.net, 48
Fanning, Shawn, 119
Fantasia, 456
Fantastic Four characters, 260
Fantasy Focus, 92
fantasy sports leagues, 75
Fantasy Sports Trade Associa-
    tion, 82
Farber, Erica, 183
Farewell My Concubine, 250
Fargo, 22, 23

Farm Heroes Saga, 82–83
farm magazines, 325
FarmVille, 74, 93, 102, 462
Farnsworth, Philo, 190–191, 192
Fat Boys, 135
Fault in Our Stars, The (Green),
    244, 356, 452
FCB, 385
FCC v. Pacifica Foundation, 561
Fear Factor, 163
Fear of Missing Out, 571
Fear Street series, 349
feature-length film, 242
feature syndicates, 294
Federal Communications Act,
    128
Federal Communications
    Commission (FCC)
    access-channel mandates, 212,
        214
    adoption of analog standard,
        191
    in assigning frequency and
        freezing of licenses, 192
    call for stricter warnings on
        radio news, 165
    collection from telecom users
        by, 301
    EchoStar-DirecTV merger and,
        447, 467
    Fairness Doctrine and, 171,
        562–563
    introduction of color television,
        192–193
    must-carry rules, 212
    net neutrality rules of, 66
    regulation of broadcasting, 559
Federal Food and Drug Act
    (1906), 381
Federalist Party, 542
Federal Radio Commission (FRC),
    162
Federal Trade Commission (FTC),
    449
    advertising regulation and,
        406–407
    on bloggers, 398
    Bureau of Consumer Protection
        of, 406–407
    charging of RCA with violations
        of antitrust laws and,
        160–161
    creation of, 383
    information-gathering software
        of, 62–63
    monitoring advertising abuses
        and, 378
    shortcomings of, 405
feedback, 9
feeder cables, 196
Fellini, Federico, 246

female media ownership, 458–459
feminism, women's magazines
    and, 327
Fenton, Roger, 320
Ferrell, Will, 22, 399
Fessenden, Reginald, 154, 155
Fey, Tina, 356
FHM, 324
Fiasco, Lupe, 135
Fibber McGee and Molly, 163
fiber-optic cable, 43, 44
fictional storytelling, evolution
    of, 23
Field, Sally, 245
FIFA (soccer), 102
Fifty Shades of Grey (James), 366,
    367
Fighter, The, 249
fighting games, 75
Fiji, 394
Filkins, Dexter, 282
film(s). *See also* movies
    development of, 234–237
    documentary, 248–249
    First Amendment and, 553–557
    foreign, 248
    independent, 249, 251
    influences on books, 356–357
    jobs in, 263
    narrative, 237
    screenings of, in Paris, 234
film exchange system, 239
film noir genre, 244
Filo, David, 46
Final Fantasy, 84, 88, 101, 102
Financial Interest and Syndica-
    tion Rules, 212
Finding Nemo, 456
fine art, 17
"finger pointin'" music, 131
Finnegans Wake (Joyce), 25
fin-syn, 212
Firefox (Web browser), 45
fireside chats, 163, 164
Firman, Tehrene, 337
First, Harry, 467
First Amendment, 273, 470, 489
    Brennan, William, Jr. and, 539
    defending of, 537
    democracy and, 565
    development of free expression
        and, 541–542
    enacting of, 544
    film and, 553–557
    Sixth Amendment versus,
        551–552
first-person perspective, 87
first-person shooter games, 86,
    98
first-run syndication, 219
Fitzgerald, F. Scott, 349

Five Great Tragedies (Shakespeare), 351, 354
500 Days of Summer, 249
flack, 433
Flaggis, Mike, 262
Flaherty, Robert, 248
flat disk, 116
Flatts, Rascal, 137
Fleischman, Doris, 421
Fleishman-Hillard advertising agency, 385, 422
Flickr, 47
  blocking of, 52
  as content community, 48
Flynt, Larry, 548
FM (frequency modulation), 153, 166, 167, 180
focus groups, 386
Fog of War, The, 249
folk music, 131
folk-rock music, 129, 131
Food Marketing Institute, 377
Foodspotting, 69
Ford, Henry, 455
Ford Company, 422
  advertising branding of, 398
foreign-language movies, 246, 248
"Forever," 143
Forever (Blume), 361
Forever War, The (Filkins), 282
Forgotify, 140
format radio, 167–168
format specialization, 169–170
45-rpm record, 118
Foster, Jodie, 245
Foster, Stephen, 477
4AD (independent record label), 143
Foursquare, 62
Fourth Estate, 541
fourth-screen technologies, 202
Four Tops, 130
Fox, William, 238
Foxconn, 61
Fox & Friends, 193
Fox Film Corporation, 238
Fox Movietone, 207, 243
Fox News, 9, 200, 208, 270, 482
  as partisan cable channel, 483
  partnership of, 201
  programs on, 22, 498
  pundit stars on, 498
  ratings of, 496
framing research, 528
France, anti-Amazon law and, 359
franchise fee, 215
Francis, Connie, 129
Frank, Ann, 360
Frank, Reuven, 479–480

Franken, Al, 204
Franken Berry cereal, 17
Frankenstein (Shelley), 17
Franklin, Aretha, audiences of, 130
Franklin, Benjamin, 272, 312
  launching of *Philadelphische Zeitung* by, 285
  sale of colonial novels and, 347
  South Carolina Gazette established by, 274
Franklin, James, 272
Franklin Delano Roosevelt: A Memorial, 354
fraud, online, 64
Freed, Alan, 124, 126, 128
Freedom of Information Act, 551
Freedom's Journal, 272, 288
free expression, origins of, and free press, 539–549, 551–552
Freegate, 52
free market, fallout from, 467–468
freemium, 104
Free Press, 458, 459, 469, 565
Free Speech for Me (Hentoff), 360
free-to-play games, 104
Freud, Sigmund, 25, 420
Friday Night Lights: A Town, a Team, and a Dream (Bissinger), 356
Friedkin, William, 245
Friendly, Fred, 283, 495
Friends, 217, 218, 219
Fringe, 28
fringe time, 218
Frogger, 80, 93
Frozen, 245, 456
Fruit Ninja, 84
Fugitive, The, 221, 551
full-body interactivity, 77
funk, 130
FX, 188, 200

G. I. Joe, 401
Gagliano, Gina, 369
gag orders, 551–552
Galavision, 181
Galbraith, Robert, 341
Gallo, marketing of, 396
Game Boy, 73, 89
game consoles, 79–80, 83, 89, 100–101, 202
GameFly, 105
Game Informer, 105, 322, 323, 325
Game of Thrones, 197
  audiences of, 55
  multifunctionality and portability of devices showing, 202

  storytelling of, 23
  as TV narrative, 22, 356
GamePad, 80
gameplay, 84, 86, 89–90
game publishers, 101–102
games
  action digital, 75, 86, 88
  adventure, 75, 88
  card, 7
  casual, 89
  classic, 78–79
  dance, 90
  family entertainment, 75
  fighting, 75
  first-person shooter, 86, 98
  free-to-play, 104
  future of, 99
  on home computers, 80–81
  Internet in transforming, 81–82
  licensing of digital, 103–104
  maze, 86, 88
  MMORPGs, 77, 81–82, 88, 97, 103, 104
  music, 89
  platform, 86, 88
  racing, 75
  regulating, 98–99
  role-playing, 75, 88
  shooter, 75, 86, 88
  simulation, 75 88–89
  in social media, 74
  sports, 75, 89, 198
  strategy, 75, 88
  survival horror, 88
  video, 76, 78, 86–88, 105, 107
game sites, 91
gamespeak, 90
GameStop, 91, 99–100, 105, 325
GameTrailers, 91
"Gangnam Style," 142
gangster rap music, 135
Gannett Company, 299, 465
  as largest newspaper chain, 294
  starting of *USA Today* by, 282
Gans, Herbert, 482–483, 484
Ganz, 82
Gap stores, 28
  advertising of, 386
Garland, Judy, music-variety shows hosted by, 193
gatekeepers, 9
Gates, Henry Louis, Jr., 533
Gatorade, 394, 427
Gauging Your Distraction, 99
Gawker, 48, 50
Gawker Media, 91, 414
Gaye, Marvin, 130
Gazeta Wyborcza, 500
Geer, Will, 557
Gelbart, Larry, 204

gender, as factor in game addiction, 94
General, The, 241
General Agreement on Tariffs and Trade (1994), 455
  establishment of, 447
general assignment reporters, 293
General Electric (GE), 155, 156, 160, 188
  advertising for, 394
  Bernays, Edward, and, 420
  helping start up RCA/NBC, 223
  NBC and, 447, 450
  radio group and, 159
  radio stations owned by, 158
  RCA and, 156, 161
  Universal and, 260
General Hospital, 206
general-interest magazines, 309
  fall of, 319, 322–324
  rise of, 317–319
General Magazine and Historical Chronicle (Franklin), 312
General Motors, 60, 160, 249
  advertising for, 390, 400
  Bernays, Edward, and, 420
General Motors Family Party, 163
generations, music preferences across, 132
genres, Hollywood, 243–244
Gentleman's Agreement, 254
Gentleman's Magazine, 312
geosynchronous orbit, 196
Gerbner, George, 522, 525
Geritol, 194
Gershwin, George, 122
Gibson, Charles, 208
Gibson, Don, 128
Gifford, Barry, 353
Gillette, advertising of, 397
Gilligan, Vince, 220
Gillis, Gregg, 564
Ginsberg, Allen, 291
Gio magazine as online spin-off, 325
Girls, 23, 197
Girl's Life, 329
Girl Talk, 564
Girl with the Dragon Tattoo, The, 50, 248
Gitlin, Todd, 528
Glamour, 310, 326
Glee, 55, 205, 224
Glenn Beck Program, 180
global audiences, 460
global cinema, 246, 248
Global Dreams, 457, 469
global market, advertising in, 404
global village, 469

Globe, 331
Gmail, 46, 59
GoDaddy, advertising at Super
    Bowl, 395
Godey's Lady's Book, 314–315
Godfather, The, 233, 245, 255
Godsick, Jeffrey, 405–406
Godzilla, 93, 250
Goffin, Gerry, 122
Going Rogue (Palin), 363
Goldberg, Bernard, 484
Goldberg, Whoopi, 356
golden age of radio, 153
golden mean, 489
Golden Rule, 489
Goldhill, Jonathan, 409
Goldsmith, Thomas T., 78
Goldstein, Daniel, 395
Goldwater, Barry, 559
Golf Channel, 224
Golf Digest, 328
Golin, 385
Gomery, Douglas, 68, 238, 446, 554
Gone with the Wind, 243
Goode, Will B., 555
Good Housekeeping, 278, 322,
    323, 327
   Bernays, Edward, and, 420
Goodman, Benny, 123
Good Morning America, 193, 208,
    457, 496
Goodnight Moon (Brown), 24
"Good Times," 135
Good Wife, The, 22, 23
Goodwin, Hannibal, 234, 235–237
Google, 12, 40, 43, 304, 458
   advertising and, 376, 390
   Ad Words, 392
   Apple and, 376
   comparison to *The Circle* and,
    444
   digital gaming industry and,
    73, 74
   digital media and, 461
   distribution to mobile devices
    by, 260
   dot-com companies and, 68
   establishment of, 59
   fair use arguments in, 358
   global marketing brand of, 396
   as leading force on Internet, 57
   Life's photographic archive on,
    319
   as media giant, 373, 445
   merger and acquisitions of, 463
   net neutrality and, 67
   Nexus and, 54, 326, 334, 376
   number of users of, 462
   open Internet and, 56
   Play, 59
   purchase of DoubleClick, 391

   two-speed Internet and, 67
   Voice Search app, 392
Google+
   circles of, 69
   as social networking site, 49
Google Analytics, 423
Google Books, 345, 358
Google Chat, 46
Google Chromecast, 53
Google Glass, 59, 375–376, 379
Google Goggles, 47, 392
Google Maps, 48, 58
Google News, 546
Google Now, 56
Google Play, 54, 83–84, 105, 106
   combination of new released
    and backlist books, 366
   movie downloads on, 254
   start up of, 357–358
   video-on-demand service of,
    256
Google Play Music, 121
Google Voice Search, 47
Gordon-Levitt, Joseph, 251
Gordy, Berry, 130
Gore, Lesley, 129
Gosden, Freeman, 163, 164
government relations, public
    relations and, 429–431
government surveillance, 64
GQ, 324, 326, 329
   as part of Condé Nast division,
    334–335
   Web-enabled ads on, 333
GQ.com, 324
Gracenote, 294
Graham's Magazine, 314
gramophone, 117
Gramsci, Antonio, 453, 527
Grand Budapest Hotel, The, 249
Grandmaster Flash and the
    Furious Five, 135
Grand Ole Opry, 128, 172
Grand Theft Auto, 85, 88, 91, 95,
    98, 104
Granik, Debra, 245
*Graphic Canon, The: World's
    Great Literature as Comics
    and Visuals,* 353
graphic novels, 349–350, 352
graphophone, 116–117
Grateful Dead, 68, 132
Gravity, 232, 243
"Great American Fraud" series,
    in *Collier's,* 316
"Great Balls of Fire," 126
Greatest Treasure Hunt in History
    (Edsel), 356
Great Gatsby, The (Fitzgerald),
    349
Great Train Robbery, The, 237

Greeley, Horace, 481
Green, John, 356
green advertising, 406
Green Day, 134
Green Hornet, The, 163
green marketing, 396
Greenpeace, 428
greenwashing, public relations
    and, 428
Greenwich Village, 131
Gremlins, 556
Grey Global, 385
Grierson, John, 248
Griffith, Bill, 353
Griffith, D. W., 22, 102, 239, 242,
    243
Grisham, John, 351
Grisko, Carolyn, 438
Groepper, Lindsay, 439
Grokster, 120
Grooveshark, 144
grunge music, 134
Guardian, 506
Guardians of the Galaxy, 452
Guess Who's Coming to Dinner?,
    247
guilds, 90
guitar, electric, 124
Guitar Hero, 90, 102
"Gulf Coast Blues," 124
Gunsmoke, 206
Guns N' Roses, 24
Gutenberg, Johannes, 7, 344, 346
Gutenberg Bible, 346
Guthrie, Arlo, 131
Guthrie, Woody, 131
Guy, Buddy, 124

Habermas, Jürgen, 530–531
Hachette, 342, 362
   disagreement with Amazon,
    341–342
hackers, 50–51
Hadden, Briton, 318
Haken, Paul Ten, 409
Hale, Sarah Josepha, 314
Haley, Alex, 206
Haley, Bill, 124
Half-Life, 81, 91
Hallmark Channel, 455
Halo, 80, 91, 94, 101
Hamby, Chris, 478
Hamill, Pete, 367
Hamilton, Alexander, 312, 541
Hamilton, Filippa, 321
Hammett, Dashiell, 557
Hancock, John, 312
handheld gaming, 84
Hannity, Sean, 498
happiness, social media and
    finding, 569–575

Happy Days, 517
happy talk, 497
Harbrecht, Doug, 297–298
Hardee's
   advertising of, 397
   Warner Brothers and, 405
Hardwicke, Catherine, 245
Hare, Jimmy, 320
Harmonix Systems, 89
Harper & Bros., 348
Harper & Row, 348
HarperCollins, 342, 348, 362, 369
Harper's, 314, 329
Harper's Bazaar en Español, 331
Harper's New Monthly Magazine,
    315
Harrelson, Woody, 512
Harris, Benjamin, 272
Harris, Jim, 298
Harris, Ken, 321
Harris-Perry, Melissa, 533
Harry, Debbie, 133
Harry Potter series (Rowling),
    349, 356, 361, 363
Hart, Michael, 357
Harvey, David, 451
Hasee Toh Phasee, 250
Hatfields and McCoys, 206
HathiTrust Digital Library, 360
Hauptmann, Bruno, 552
Havel, Václav, 31
Hawaii Five-O, 206
Hawthorne, Nathaniel, 314, 360
Haynes, Darren, 227
Hays, William, 555
Hays Office, 555
HBO (Home Box Office), 23, 188,
    196, 197, 201
   audiences of, 199
   release of films and, 257
HBO GO, 460
HD radio, 175
HDTV (high-definition
    television), 192
headend, 196
Headline News channel, 208
health, advertising and, 402–403,
    405
Hearst, George, 277
Hearst, William Randolph, 231, 331
   media ownership of, 276,
    277–278, 310
Hearst Corporation, 310, 334, 335
Hearts, 80
"Heat Wave," 130
Hefner, Hugh, 327
hegemony, 453
Hein, Teresa, 227
Heinz, 381
Hellman, Lillian, 557
Hellmann, 391

Hell's Angels, 132–133

Hell's Angels (Thompson), 282

He-Man and the Masters of the Universe, 401

Hemingway, Ernest, 349

Hendrix, Jimi, 127, 132, 134
  death of, 133

Hentoff, Nat, 360

herd journalism, 492

Here Media, 331

Here TV, 331

Heritage Foundation, 27

Hermansen, Tor, 138

Herman's Hermits, 129

Herrold, Charles "Doc," 158

Hersey, John, 281, 283, 329

Heth, Joice, 416

Hewitt, Don, 490

Hewlett-Packard, 61, 422

Hicks, Wilson, 319

Hidden Blade, 86

Hidden Chronicles, 102

hidden-fear appeal, 394

Hidden Fortress, The, 250

Hidden Persuaders, The (Packard), 400

Hide Away, 246

high culture, 17
  diminished audience for, 21
  tendency to exploit, 17

high-definition DVDs, 200

Highlights for Children, 329, 333

Hill, Lewis Kimball, 173

Hillcrest Media, 367

Hill-Knowlton, 385, 422, 436

Hill Street Blues, 206–207

Hine, Lewis, 320

hip-hop music, 115, 117, 124, 134–135

Hiroshima (Hersey), 329

Hispanic Broadcasting, 181

Hispanic Business, 323–324

Historia Naturalis, 354

History, 223

History of a Young Lady, The (Richardson), 347

"History of the Standard Oil Company" (Tarbell), 316

Hitchcock, Alfred, 244

Hits Now!, 179

The Hobbit: The Desolation of Smaug, 232

Hocking, Amanda, 367

Hole, 134

Holkins, Jerry, 91

Holly, Buddy, 125, 126
  death of, 128

Hollywood
  adaptation to, 254
  breaking through race barrier in, 247

Golden Age of, 14

impact of television on, 253–254

studio system in, 238–241

Hollywood Chinese, 246

Hollywood genres, 243–244

Hollywood narratives, 243

Hollywood style, development of, 243–246

Hollywood Ten, 235, 251–252

Holmes, James, 512

Holmes, Oliver Wendell, 544–545

Holtzbrinck, 362

home computers, gaming on, 80–81

home dubbing, 118

Home Education, 336

home entertainment, 254

Homeland, 23, 188, 197, 201

home video, 200

Hong Kong Disneyland Resort, 457

Hon Hai Precision Industry Co., Ltd., 61

Hoover, Herbert, 162

Hope, Bob, 192

Hopper, Dennis, 245

Horgan, Stephen, 320

Horkheimer, Max, 527

Horne, Lena, 557

horror film, 244

HotAir, 48

hot clock, 168

Hot Country, 179

Hotmail, 46

Hottle, Olivia, 85n

Houghton Mifflin, 348

"Hound Dog," 125

House of Cards, 22

House of Flying Daggers, 250

House Un-American Activities Committee (HUAC), 235, 251, 557

Howlin' Wolf, 123, 124

Howth Castle, 25

How to Train Your Dragon, 222, 405

HTC, 54

Hubbard, Gardiner Green, 328

Huffington Post, 48, 208, 298, 496
  AOL purchase of, 447, 451
  coverage of economic crisis and, 304
  credibility of, 298

Hulk, 93

Hulu, 13, 36, 55, 110, 460
  as attempt to divert attention from YouTube, 260
  competition with, 462
  as data-heavy service, 67
  distribution to mobile devices by, 260

future of television and, 188

movie downloads on, 254

parents groups and, 517

streaming programming from, 83

watching of videos online and, 200

Hulu Plus, 191
  starting of, by Hulu, 201
  video-on-demand service of, 256
  as video subscription service, 223

human-interest stories, 274

Human Rights Watch, 563

Humor Times, 336

Humphrey, Hubert, 249

Hunger Games, The, 24, 104, 243, 256, 258, 261, 356

Huntley Brinkley Report, 207

Hurricane Katrina (2005), 499

Hurricane Sandy, 491

Hurt Locker, The, 245, 246

Hushmail, 52

Hüsker Dü, 134

Hutchins Commission, 540

Huxley, Aldous, 26

hybrid, 206–207

Hyman, Mark, 19

Hynde, Chrissie, 133

Hype Machine, 144

hypertext, 43, 45

hypodermic-needle model, 518–519

hypotheses, 521

IBM, 61
  global marketing brand of, 396
  operating of Linux and, 67

"I Can't Help Myself," 130

"I Can't Stop Loving You," 128

Ice-T, 135

iconscope, 191

"Ida Red," 125

identity theft, 64

Iger, Robert, 452, 453

Iggy Pop, 133

IGN, 91, 99–100

"I Got a Woman," 126

"I Hear a Symphony," 131

"I Heard It through the Grapevine," 130

iHeartMedia, 122, 150, 180, 181

iHeartRadio, 110, 122, 140, 141, 177

IHOP, advertising of, 397

Ikea, 422

I Know Why the Caged Bird Sings (Angelou), 361

Illinois Central, 418

illuminated manuscripts, 344, 346

illustrations in magazines, 314–315

Il Miracolo (The Miracle), 555–556

I Love Lucy, 203, 204, 557
  network reruns of, 218
  as situation comedy, 204

IMAX, 243, 258, 261

Imitation of Life, 247

Impossible Voyage, The, 237

Imus, Don, 171

Ince, Thomas, 239

In Cold Blood (Capote), 282, 329

Inconvenient Truth, An, 249, 525

Incredibles, The, 456

indecency, 559–560

independent bookstores, 366

independent films
  festivals for, 251
  rise of, 249, 251

independent labels, 143

Independent Reflector, 313

independent studios, 258

independent variables, 521

Indiana Jones, 260, 460, 556

Indian Country Today, 290

IndieCommerce, 366

indies, 137, 139, 249
  rise of, 235

indirect payments, 446

individualism, 483
  print media and, 266

Industrial Light & Magic special effects company, 260, 263

Industrial Revolution, 7, 26, 75

inFAMOUS Second Son, 80

information age, journalism in, 479–483

informational model, 500

information economy, transition to, 448–455

information glut, 479

Information Please, 163

information superhighway, 41

infotainment programs, 211

in-game advertisements, 93

in-game chat, 90

Insight, 336

Instagram, start-up of, 462

instant books, 354

instant messaging (IM), 46

institutional relations, 435

Instructions Not Included, 248

InStyle, 334

intellectual properties, 103–104

interactive environments, future of, 99

interest films, 248

International Copyright Law (1891), 351

International Telephone & Telegraph (ITT), 450
Internet, 9, 29
 advertising for, 62
 birth of, 41–43
 changing relationship with, 55–56
 commercialization of, 44–47
 communication policy and, 562–563
 controlling, 57–60
 democracy and, 68–69
 economics and issues of, 57–60
 freedom and openness of, 474
 hackers of, 50–51
 jobs in, 69
 magazines on, 324–325, 326
 maintaining open, 66–67
 public relations and, 431
 rise of, 10
 in transforming gaming, 81–82
 TV convergence with, 200–202
 widening of, 43–44
Internet Archive's Open Library, 360
Internet Explorer, 45
Internet radio, 175, 177
Internet service provider (ISP), 45
interpretive journalism, 280–281
Interpublic Group, 384, 385
Interscope Geffen A&M, 114
Interstate Commerce Act (1887), 418
interstitials, 390
In the Heat of the Night, 247
In These Times, 335, 533
In Touch Weekly, 324
Invasion from Mars, The: A Study in the Psychology of Panic (Cantril), 518–519
inverted-pyramid style, 279
investigative journalism, 276, 485–486
Investigative Reporters and Editors (IRE), 478
Iovine, Jimmy, 121
iPad, 61, 202, 266, 326
 Apple's release of, 43
 attracting readers and advertisers, 313
 iBook store services for, 357
 introduction of, 36, 345
 iPhone and, 54
 magazines on, 326, 333, 334
 reading on, 325
 in transforming media industry, 461
iPhone, 43, 53–54, 61, 325
 applications for, 54, 376
 as e-readers, 357

iBook store services for, 357
introduction of, 53–54
in transforming media industry, 461
iPod, 61, 202
 app environments for, 376
 iBook store services for, 357
 in transforming media industry, 461
iPod Touch, 54
 devices for, 83
 as e-readers, 357
Iraq, journalists in, 540
Iron Man, 260, 398, 460
irritation advertising, 394
Irving, Washington, 314
Island Records, 143
isometric perspective, 87
It Happened One Night, 243
It's Always Sunny in Philadelphia, 204
iTunes, 55, 59, 67, 120, 260, 325
 Apple's launch of, 36, 120
 competing for music fans on, 177
 digital downloads of, 139
 distributor of sounds and images, 110
 Fox and, 460
 listing songs on, 372
 movie downloads on, 254
 parents groups and, 517
 partnering with NBC, 460
 producing of massive hit on, 136
 profits of, 140
 reemergence of pop music and, 135
 selling of twenty-fifth billion song download, 117
 video-on-demand service of, 256
 video rental and, 200
iUniverse, 367

Jab Tak Hai Jaan, 250
Jack FM, 179
Jackson, Janet, 561
Jackson, Michael, 14, 135, 383
Jackson, Peter, 356
Jackson 5, 130
Jacor Communications, 180
Jae-Sang, Park, 142
Jagger, Mick, 125, 130
James, E. L., 366, 367
Jan & Dean, 129
Jarmusch, Jim, 249
Jaws, 245, 255, 525
Jay-Z, 140, 413
jazz music, 16, 115, 123
Jazz Singer, 234, 242, 243

JCPenney, advertising of, 386
Jee-woon, Kim, 250
Jefferson, Thomas, 542
Jefferson Airplane, 132
Jenckes, Marcien, 201
Jennings, Peter, 207–208
Jeopardy!, 208, 214
Jepsen, Carly Rae, 136
Jersey Shore, 14
Jet, 330
JetBlue Airways, 427
Jet Li, 250
Jetpack Joyride, 106
Jett, Joan, 133
Jewish Currents, 336
"Jimmy Iovine," 114
jitterbug, 115
"JK Wedding Entrance Dance," 143
jobs
 in advertising industry, 409
 in film industry, 263
 in Internet industry, 69
 in magazine industry, 337
 media, 227
 in music industry, 145
 in newspaper industry, 305
 in public relations industry, 439
 in publishing industry, 369
 in radio industry, 183
 in television industry, 227
 in video game industry, 107
Jobs, Steve, 59, 61, 457
Joe Camel, 379
John, Elton, 125, 133, 383
John Madden Football, 102
"Johnny B. Goode," 125
Johnson, Jack, 68
Johnson, John H., 330
Johnson, Lyndon B., 209
Johnson, Robert, 123, 124
Johnson, Samuel, 312, 355
Johnson & Johnson, 417, 422, 432
joint operating agreements, 295–296
Jolie, Angelina, 28
Jolson, Al, 123, 242
Jones, Grace, 125
Jones, LeRoi, 291
Jones, Mary Harris, 336
Joplin, Janis, 132, 133
Joplin, Scott, 122
journalism
 advocacy, 282
 alternative, 292
 as art form, 281–282
 of assertion, 482
 attack on objectivity in, 282
 citizen, 302–303, 500

conflict-oriented, 285
consensus-oriented, 285
contemporary, in television and Internet age, 282–284
cultural values of, 482–483
culture of, 477–507
democracy and reimagining role of, 505, 507
detective or stunt, 478
herd, 492
impact of convergence, 498–499
in information age, 479–483
interpretive, 280–281
investigative, 276, 485–486
in Iraq, 540
literary forms of, 281–282
modern print, 278–284
new, 281
new models for, 300–302
objectivity in modern, 278–280
online, 283–284
precision, 282
pro-am model for, 303
public, 500, 502–505
satiric, 503–505
scoops in, 491–492
values in American, 481–482
yellow, 272, 276–278, 316
Joyce, James, 25, 360, 548–549
Joyner, Tom, 169
JPMorgan Chase, 295
 Corporate Challenge of, 429
Jules and Jim, 246
Jumbo the Elephant, 416, 427
Jungle, The (Sinclair), 317
Ju-on: The Grudge, 250
Jurkowitz, Mark, 305
Just Dance, 90
Justified, 22, 188
"just the facts" model, 278
JVC, 200

Kafka, 25
Kalish, Rachel, 529
Kalman, Maira, 350
Kaltenborn, H. V., 163
Kane, Bob, 352
Kane, Charles Foster, 278
Kansas, 133
Kant, Immanuel, 489
Karloff, Boris, 17
Katz, Jackson, 529
Katz, Jon, 283, 481–482
Kazaa, 120
Kazan, Ella, 252
KCBS, 158
KCOR, 172
KDJE-FM, 183
KDKA, 157, 158
Keating, Zoë, 141

Keaton, Buster, 241
Keller, Bill, 485, 506
Kellor, Garrison, 329
Kelly, Grace, 205
Kennard, William E., 181
Kennedy, Anthony, 470
Kennedy, John F., 249
   assassination of, 189, 320–321,
      499
Kernan, Alvin, 368
Kerouac, Jack, 291
Ke$ha, 138
Ketchum advertising agency,
   385, 422
Keys, Alicia, 172
KGO, 171
Khan, Shahrukh, 250
Kia Motors, advertising of, 384
Kickstarter, 48, 74, 106
Kidman, Nicole, 250
Kid Rock, 135
Killing, The, 55
Kimmel, Jimmy, 222
Kimmel, Michael, 529
Kindle entries. *See* Amazon
      Kindle
Kinect, 77
kinescope, 203
kinetograph, 236
kinetoscope, 76, 236
kinetoscope parlors, 234
King (game developer), 82–83,
   102
King, B. B., 124
King, Carole, 122
King, Martin Luther, Jr.,
   assassination of, 189, 499
King, Stephen, 351
King Features Syndicate, 278
Kings of Leon, 125
Kinks on American Top 40
   charts, 129
Kipling, Rudyard, 310
Kiss, 134
Kissinger, Henry, 506
Klapper, Joseph, 519
Klein, Calvin, 324
Klein, Ezra, 298
Klondike Lite ice cream bar, 406
K-Love, 181
Kmart, advertising of, 386
KMBC, 497
K'naan, 176
Knickerbocker, 314
Knight Ridder, 295
Knopf, Alfred A., 348, 362
KNOW, 175
Knowles-Carter, Beyoncé, 114,
   136, 138, 141, 393, 412,
   413–414
Kobo e-book device, 366

Kodak camera, 320
Kohl's, advertising of, 386
Koppel, Ted, 19
Korean War, photography of,
   320
Koreeda, Hirokazu, 250
Kotaku, 91
Kovach, Bill, 23, 482
"K-pop," 142
Kraft's Cheez Whiz, 205
Kraft Television Theater, 205
Krahulik, Mike, 91
Kravitz, Lenny, 134
Ku Klux Klan (KKK), 242, 288
Kurosawa, Akira, 246, 250
Kutcher, Ashton, 413
KVUE-TV, 496
Kweli, Talib, 135

L.A. Confidential, 244
"La Bamba," 128
Labor Statistics, U.S. Bureau of,
   305
labor unions, decline of,
   451–452
Laden, Osama bin, 18, 506
Ladies' Companion, 347
Ladies Home Journal
   advertising in, 316
   circulation of, 313, 327, 336
   Curtis, Cyrus, and, 318
   muckraking reports and, 317
   national ad dollars and, 323
   ranking of, 322
Ladies' Magazine, 314
La Dolce Vita, 246
Lady, The, 250
Lady Gaga, 9–10, 114, 125, 138
   establishment of nonprofit
      organization, 427
Lady Vengeance, 250
Lagardère, 362
La Información, 289
Lam, Ringo, 250
Lamar, Kendrick, 136
Lambert, Adam, 125
Lambert, Mary, 114
lamp black, 116
*Land Is Their Land, The: Reports
      from a Divided Nation*
      (Ehrenreich), 533
Lang, Jack, 359
Lang law, 359
language
   foreign, movies, 246, 248
   power of visual, 499
   Spanish, 172, 209, 289
La Opinión, 289
Lara Croft: Tomb Raider series,
   92
La Raza, 289

Lasch, Christopher, 507
Lassie, 24
Lasswell, Harold, 514
Last.fm, 177
Last Stand, The, 250
Last Tango in Paris, 233
late fringe, 218
Latino
   launching of, 331
   as online spin-off, 325
Latvia, 422
Lauer, Matt, 496
Laugh-O-Gram, 456
Lauren, Ralph, 321, 432
La Voz, 289
Law & Order, 219, 465
LBET, 455
Lead Belly (Huddie Ledbetter),
   131
"Leader of the Pack," 129
League, The, 92
*League of Denial: The NFL,
   Concussions, and the Battle
   for Truth* (ESPN), 426
League of Legends, 81, 88
Learning Tree, 247
leased channels, 214
least objectionable programming
   (LOP) strategy, 17, 21
Leaves of Grass (Whitman), 360
LeBlanc, Adrian Nicole, 282
Lee, Ang, 246
Lee, Harper, 360
Lee, Ivy Ledbetter, 419–420,
   434
Lee, Jennifer, 245
Lee, "Poison Ivy," 416
Lee, Spike, 245, 250
Lee, Timothy B., 545
Legend of Zelda, 101
Lego Movie, The, 257
Lehman Brothers, 286
Leiber, Jerry, 122
Leigh, Janet, 245
leisure magazines, 327–328
leisure time, emergence of, 75
Lemony Snicket series, 349
Lennox, Annie, 125
Leno, Jay, 356
Lens, 321
Leo Burnett Worldwide, 385
LePage, Camille, 321
Lepore, Jill, 488
Le Prince, Louis Aimé Augustin,
   234–235
Lepucki, Edan, 342
Les Misérables, 244
Lessig, Lawrence, 533, 564
Lethal Weapon 4, 250
"Let's Spend Some Time
   Together," 130

"Let's Spend the Night Together,"
   130
Letterman, David, 504
Let Us Now Praise Famous Men
   (Agee), 505
Levi Strauss, 380
Lévy, Pierre, 91
Lewinsky, Monica, 13, 284
Lewis, Jerry Lee, 126, 128
Lewis, Juliette, 512
Lewis, Macklemore & Ryan, 136
Lewis, Ryan, 113–114
Lewis, Sinclair, 310, 565
LG, 54
LGBT community, 331
libel, 272, 546–547
   defenses against, 547–548
   obscenity and, 548
   seditious, 273
liberal, 32
   bias of, 484
libertarian model, 541
Liberty and the News (Lippmann),
   514
Liberty Media, 224
Library of Congress, 68
licensing of digital games,
   103–104
Lieberman, Joe, 99
Liebling, A. J., 329
Life, 193, 249, 322, 323, 330
   close of, 313
   as general-interest genre, 319
Life of an American Fireman, The,
   237
Life of Pi, 232, 246
lifestyle ad appeals, 403
Lifetime, 223, 455
Li Gong, 250
Like, 323
Like Father, Like Son, 250
Lilo & Stitch, 456
Limbaugh, Rush, 30, 169, 488
LimeWire, 120
limited competition, 446
limited model, 519
Limp Bizkit, 135
Lincoln, Abraham, 279
Lind, Jenny, 416
Lind, Phil, 128
Lindbergh, Anne, 552
Lindbergh, Charles, 160, 243, 552
Lineage, 96
linear model of mass communi-
   cation, 9
LinkedIn, 49
linotype, 345, 348
Linux, 67–68
Lion King, The, 456, 457
Lionsgate Entertainment, 258,
   261, 322

Lipitor, advertising for, 405
Lippmann, Walter
  agenda-setting and, 524
  as author of *Public Opinion*, 421
  influence of, 27
  informed radical society and, 27
  journalism, psychology, and, 514
  promoting publicity and, 434–435
  public perception and, 416
  responsibilities of journalists and, 280
  ties among national reporters and, 492
Lipton, 391
literary forms of journalism, 281–282
Literary Guild, 345, 364–365
Little, Brown & Company, 348, 367
Little Caesar, 515
Little House on the Prairie, 517
Little Mermaid, The, 456
Little Miss Sunshine, 249
Little Review, 549
Little Richard (Penniman), 125, 126
  Beatles imitation of, 129
  British invasion and, 129
  image of, 128
  "Long Tall Sally" and, 127
Little Three, 241
LiveJournal, 49
live-tweeting, 13
LL Cool J, 135
lobbying, 418, 429–430
  astroturf, 430–431
Local Community Radio Act (2011), 182
Lolita (Nabokov), 254, 360
Lone Ranger, The, 163, 189
Long Island Newsday, 280
longitudinal studies, 522
long lines, 159
long-playing record (LP), 118
"Long Tall Sally," 127–128
Lonny, 325
Look, 322
  close of, 313, 323
Lord of the Rings, The (Tolkien), 233, 356
Los Angeles Times
  bankruptcy at, 266
  consolidation and cutbacks at, 293
  as daily newspaper, 280
  ethics and, 485
  launching of paywalls, 300
  Pulitzer Prize–winning reports at, 304

Spanish-language supplement of, 289
Tribune Company ownership of, 269, 294
Lost, 28, 207
Lost in Translation, 245, 249
Lostutter, Deric, 51
Lost Weekend, The, 254
low culture, 17
Lowe and Partners, 385
Lowenthal, Leo, 527
low-power FM (LPFM), 181–182
LSD, 132
Lu, 163
Lucas, George/Lucasfilm, 231–232
  American Graffiti and, 245
  Indiana Jones and, 260, 460, 556
  Industrial Light & Magic special effects company of, 260
  Star Wars and, 231–232, 233, 245, 255, 256, 259, 260, 460
Luce, Henry, 318, 319, 327
Luckey, Palmer, 74
Lucky, 324, 336–337
Lucky Strike Orchestra, 163
Ludlow, Colorado, coal strike in, 419–420
Lumière, Auguste, 236
Lumière, Louis, 236
Lumineers, The, 137
Lyle, Jack, 519

MacFarlane, Seth, 142
MacGruber, 204
Mackey, John, 431
Macklemore, 113–114, 136
Macmillan, 342, 348, 362
Macy's, wage gap at, 453
Madagascar, 222
Mad Catz, 89
Madden, John, 89, 102
Madden NFL, 81, 82, 89
Maddow, Rachel, 498
Madea Christmas, A, 245
Mad Men, 23, 55, 188, 201
Madonna, 10, 221, 383
magalogs, 335
magazines. *See also specific by name*
  advertising in, 332–333
  age and, 328–329
  alternative, 335–336
  business, 325
  children's, 329
  circulation and distribution of, 333–334
  in colonial America, 312–313
  consumer, 325
  defined, 311

in democratic society, 336–337
  departments and duties, 332–334
  development of modern American, 313–319, 322–325
  devoted to music, 328
  digital age and, 324–325
  domination of specialization, 325, 327–331
  early history of, 311–315
  editorial, 332
  elite, 329
  farm, 325
  general interest, 317–319, 322–324
  growth of published, 316
  illustrations in, 314–315
  jobs in, 337
  major chains, 334–335
  minority-targeted, 329–331
  narrowcasting in, 332
  national, 314, 315–316
  organization and economics of, 332–336
  production, 332
  sales, 332–333
  sports, entertainment, and leisure, 327–328
  trade, 325
  for women, 311, 314
magic bullet theory, 518
Magic Lantern, 234
Magna Carta Holy Grail, 140–141
Magnavox, 78
  release of *Odyssey*, 78
Magnificent Seven, The, 250
Magnolia Pictures, 261
Magnum, advertising and, 403
"Magnum Pleasure Hunt," 93
Mailer, Norman, 282
mail-order services, 364–365
Maine, sinking of, in Spanish-American War, 320
Mainstream Media's Liberal Bias (MMLB), 171
Major Crimes, 219
Maker Studios Inc., 222
Making Stories (Bruner), 14
Malaeska: The Indian Wife of the White Hunter (Stephens), 347
Maleficent, 92
Mali, 525
malice, actual, 547
managing editors, 291
manga books, 349
Mann, Estle Ray, 78
Manning, Bradley (now Chelsea), 545
Man of Steel, 397, 398, 405

Manson, Charles, 133, 282
Manson, Marilyn, 125, 512
Manufacturing Consent: Noam Chomsky and the Media, 533
manuscript culture, development of, 345–346
manuscripts, illuminated, 344, 346
Man with the Golden Arm, The, 254
"Maple Leaf Rag," 122
map model, 16, 21, 24–26
Marconi, Guglielmo, 152–154
Marconi Wireless Telegraph Company, 153
Marie Claire, 310
Mario, 91
Mario Bros., 79, 80
Mario Kart 8, 80
marketing
  of digital games, 104
  green, 396
  viral, 388
marketing research, 386, 516, 518
Mark Levin Show, The, 179
Markoff, John, 101
Married with Children, 517
Mars, Bruno, 127
Marshall, Penny, 245
Martha and the Vandellas, 130
Martin Chuzzlewit (Dickens), 275
Marvel Entertainment, 257, 352–353
  Captain America and, 352
  Disney's ownership of, 260, 353, 460
Marvel vs Capcom, 86, 93
Marx, Groucho, 161
Marx, Karl, 360, 527
Mary Tyler Moore Show, 497
masculinity problem, 529
*M*A*S*H*, 204, 221
Mashable, 48
"mash-up," 26
mass communication
  cultural model for understanding, 9–10
  defined, 6
  linear model of, 9
Mass Effect, 102
massively multiplayer online role-playing games (MMORPGs), 77, 81–82, 88, 103, 104
  banning of teenagers under sixteen, 97
mass market paperbacks, 345, 351
mass media, 6
  business of, 372
mass media channel, 9

mass medium stage, 11
Masterpiece Classic, 206
Masterpiece Mystery!, 206
Masterpiece Theatre, 206
Masters of Sex, 197
Matador, 143
Mattel, advertising of, 386
Matthews, Christopher, 369, 503
Matthews, Christopher,
   Publishing, 369
Maus: A Survivor's Tale (Spiegel-
   man), 353
Maxim, 324, 327, 329
Maxwell, James, 152, 172
"Maybellene," 125
maze games, 86, 88
MC5, 133
MCA, failed suit against Sony, 200
McCain-Feingold Act, 470
McCall's, 322
McCann Erickson, 385
McCarthy, Charlie, 559–560
McCarthy, Joseph, 205, 557
McChesney, Robert, 467, 469,
   471, 501
McClatchy Company, 295
McClure Magazine, 316, 419
McDonald's
   advertising of, 384
   DreamWorks partnership with,
      405
   global marketing brand of, 396
   wage gap and, 453
McGraw, Tim, 122
McGraw-Hill Book Company, 348
McGuffey, William Holmes, 345,
   350
McKay, Adam, 22
McLaughlin, Ed, 171
McLean, Don, 129
McLeod, Kembrew, 564
McNally, Rand, 348
McQueen, Steve, 247
Meat Inspection Act (1906), 317
mechanical gaming, 76–77
media
   critiquing, 29–30, 32–33
   early promotions through, 416
   evolution of, 10–13
   expression in, 557–563
   and politics, 3–4
   stories as foundation of, 13–14
Media Access Project, 565
media buyers, 388
media companies
   in converged world, 12
   top United States, 468
media conglomerates
   deregulation in spurring
      formation of, 449–450
   rise of new digital, 460–462

media consolidation, 456–457
   effects of, on democracy, 470
media convergence, 6, 11–13
   cultural change and, 13
   digital media and, 36–37, 54–56
   dual roles of, 11–12
   media businesses and, 12
   mobile media and, 53–57
   on PCs and TVs, 53
   radio and, 175, 177–178
media coordination, advertising
   in, 388–389
media culture, electronic gaming
   and, 92–93
media economics
   analyzing, 445–448
   changes in structure of, 372
   social issues in, 463–465, 467
media effects
   early theories of, 518–520
   evaluating research on, 526
   research on, 518–526
media effects research, 513
   conducting, 520–523
media industries
   business tendencies in,
      451–454
   structure of, 446–448
media jobs, 227
media literacy, 4
   critical process and, 32–33, 63,
      286, 330, 360, 399, 437, 461,
      491, 523, 544
   defined, 30
media marketplace, democracy
   and, 469–471
Media Matters, 469
Media Monopoly, The (Bagdikian),
   465
media multitasking, 13
media powerhouses, 450–451
media production company, 325
media reform movement, 471
media relations, public relations
   and, 425, 427
media research
   cultural approaches to,
      526–528, 530
   democracy and, 532–533
   early methods of, 513–516, 518
media stories, power of, in
   everyday life, 14–16
media takeovers, 445
Medical Repository, 314
Meet the Press, 207
mega-agencies, 384–385
megaplexes, 235, 258
Méliès, Georges, 237
Memoirs of a Geisha, 250
Memorial African Methodist
   Episcopal Zion Church, 288

Memphis Free Speech, 292
Mencken, H. L., 283
Men's Health, 326, 327, 335
Men's Journal, 326
Mentalist, The, 465
Mercedes, advertising branding
   of, 398
Mercury label, 127
Mercury Theater of the Air, 164
Meredith, Burgess, 557
Meredith Corporation, 335
Merge Records, 143
Merritt, Davis "Buzz," 500
Merriwell, Frank, 347
Merry Frolics of Satan, The, 237
"The Message," 135
messages
   in public relations, 423–425
   wide range of, 25
Metal Gear, 91
*Methodist Christian Journal and
   Advocate,* 313
Metroid, 83, 88
metropolitan dailies, 284
Meyer, Stephenie, 356
MGM, 234, 241
   Supreme Court's ruling against,
      252
M.I.A., 135
Miami Herald, 289
*Miami Herald Publishing Co. v.
   Tornillo,* 559
Michelson, Ingrid, 48
Mickey Mouse, 456, 546
Microbe Killer, 380
microprocessors, 42, 43
Microsoft, 103, 422. *See also*
   Xbox
   advertising for, 394
   comparison to *The Circle* and,
      444
   competition between console
      makers and, 79–80
   competition in digital media
      world, 462
   digital gaming industry and,
      73, 74
   digitizing of books with
      expired copyrights, 360
   domination of, 100
   Encarta, 355
   Foxconn's electronic devices
      for, 452
   Games Marketplace of, 105
   global marketing brand of, 396
   HD DVD format and, 200
   maintaining of controlling hand
      with dot-com companies,
      68
   as media giant, 57, 59, 373, 445,
      461

   net neutrality and, 67
   video game business of, 78
Microsoft (Surface), 54, 326
Microsoft Cortana, 56
Microsoft Skype, 46
Microsystems, operating of
   Linux and, 67
mid-city movie theaters, 241
Middle American virtues, 454
Middleton, Kate, 354
midterm election, 2008, 3–4
midterm election, 2014, 3–4
Midwest Video, ruling in case of,
   191, 214
Mightybell, 69
Mill, John Stuart, 489
Miller, Arthur, 557
Miller, Glenn, 123
Miller Brewing, 427
   advertising and, 403
Miller v. California, 549
Milne, Ben, 40
Milton, John, 541
Milwaukee Journal Sentinel, 300,
   543
Minaj, Nicki, 138, 139
Minecraft, 88
Minecraft-Pocket Edition, 83
mini-majors, 258
minimal-effects model, 519
miniseries, 206
Minneapolis Star Tribune, 295,
   500
MinnPost, 304
minority media ownership,
   458–459
minority-targeted magazines,
   329–331
Minow, Newton, 171
Minutemen, 134
Miracle case, 555–556
Miracles, 130
Miramax, 465
   Disney's selling of, 457, 460
   purchase of, by Disney, 251
misogyny, electronic gaming
   and, 94–95
Mission Impossible, 28
Mister Rogers' Neighborhood, 209
Miyamoto, Shigeru, 79
Miyazaki, Hayao, 250
MNF, 198
Moana, 248
mobile gaming, 83–84
mobile media
   convergence and, 53–57
   impact of media convergence
      on, 54–56
mobile video, 202
modding, 91

models of expression, 540–541
Modern Family, 203, 204, 221
modern model, 500
modern period, cultural values of, 26–27
modern print journalism, competing models of, 278–284
Modern Times (Chaplin), 26, 29
Mod Squad, The, 206
Monday Night Football, 198, 203
money exchange devices, 40
Moni, Xavier, 359
Monkey King, The, 248
monopoly, 156, 446
Monroe, Marilyn, 327
Monsanto, 50
Monsters, Inc., 456
Monthly View of the Political State of the British Colonies, A, 312
Monuments Men, The, 356
Moore, Michael, 249
Morning Edition, 173
Morning Joe, 397
morning news shows, 496
Morpheus, 120
Morris, Philip, 557
Morrison, Jim, death of, 133
Morrison, Toni, 356
Morse, Samuel, 151, 152
Morse code, 151
Morsi, Mohamed, 52
Mortal Kombat, 99
Mother Jones, 282, 336, 499
Motion Picture Association of America, 254
Motion Picture Production Code, 254, 515, 555
  establishment of, 516
motion pictures, 115
motivation, 524
Motorola, 54, 61
  merger and acquisitions of, 463
motor reproduction, 524
Motown, 129, 130, 137
Moulin Rouge!, 244
Mountain Goats, The, 143
movable type, 344, 346
Movie Gallery, 254
movie palaces, 234, 240, 241
movies, 231–263. *See also* film(s)
  adjustment to digital turn, 260–261
  arrival of nickelodeons, 237–238
  Asian cinema, 250
  democracy and, 262–263
  documentary, 248–249
  economics of business of, 255–262

evolution of, 233–238
golden age of, 241–246, 248–249, 251
Hollywood style of, 238–241, 243–246
independent films and, 249, 251
narratives in, 237
outside the Hollywood system, 246, 248–249, 251
race barrier and, 247
self-regulation and, 554–556
social and political pressures on, 554
sound in, 234, 242–243
studio system and, 251–254
Movietone, 243
movie trailers, advertising and, 377
Mozart in the Jungle, 188
MP3 file format, 117, 120
MPAA ratings system, 556–557
Mr. Natural (Crumb), 353
Mrs. Winslow's Soothing Syrup, 380–381
"Mr. Tambourine Man," 131
Ms., 327, 333
Ms. Consumer Reports, 327
MSL Group, 385, 422
MSNBC, 9, 208, 223, 482, 498
  election coverage on, 455
  as partisan cable channel, 483
MTV, 9, 197, 198
  global audiences and, 460
  visual techniques of, 383–384
muckrakers, 310, 316–317
Mulan, 456
M.U.L.E., 102
multichannel video programming distributors (MVPDs), 223
multimedia manifesto, 512
multiplexes, 241
Munsters, The, 17
Murder of Roger Ackroyd, The (Christie), 351
Murdoch, Rupert, 156, 295, 322, 453
Murphy, Debra, 409
Murrow, Edward R., 161, 283, 495
music
  alternative rock, 134
  blues, 123–124
  Cajun, 16
  classical, 16
  classical rock, 172
  country, 172, 176
  cover, 123
  digital, 137, 139
  folk, 131
  folk-rock, 129, 131
  gangster, 135

grunge, 134
hip-hop, 115, 117, 124, 134–135
jazz, 16, 115, 123
magazines devoted to, 328
pop, 115, 122–139
preferences across generations, 132
progressive rock, 168
psychedelic, 129, 132–133
rhythm and blues, 124
rock, 122, 168
rock and roll, 16, 115, 117, 123–129
salsa, 16
soul, 130
streaming, 121
white cover, 127–128
musicals, 244
music formats, 172–173
music games, 89
music labels, influence of, 137, 139
music streaming, 117
must-carry rules, 212, 215
Mutual v. Ohio, 554
Muybridge, Eadweard, 234, 235
My Best Girl, 239
"My Boyfriend's Back," 129
My Ford, 335
"My Girl," 130
"My Guy," 130
My Little Pony and Friends, 401
My Morning Jacket's songs, 143
MySpace, 114, 144, 455, 462
  Facebook eclipsing of, 49
Myst, 81, 88
myths
  advertising as, 396–397
  analysis of, 396–397

Nabokov, Vladimir, 360
Nader, Ralph, 417, 429
Namco Bandal, 102
Nanook of the North, 248
Napoleon, 242
Napster, 110
  Apple's response to, 56
  Fanning, Shawn's development of, 119
  file-sharing of, 114
  free file-sharing service of, 120
narrative films, 237
narratives, 14, 454
  consensus, 262
  creating conflict in, 492–493
  introduction of, 237
narrowcasting, 155, 196
  in magazines, 332
Naruto, 93
Nas, 403
NASCAR (racing), 102

Nation, 312, 314, 335
National, The, 143
National Association for the Advancement of Colored People (NAACP), 330
National Association of Black Journalists (NABJ), 288
National Association of Broadcasters (NAB), 178, 180, 214, 383, 422
National Association of Television Program Executives (NATPE) convention, 218
National Broadcasting Company (NBC). *See* NBC (National Broadcasting Company)
National Cable & Telecommunications Association (NCTA), 223
National Center for Supercomputing Applications (NCSA), 45
National Conference for Media Reform, 471
National Consumer League, 405
National Council of Public Opinion Polls, 515
National Dairy Council, 401
National Employment Law Project, 453
National Endowment for the Arts, 367
National Enquirer, 331
National Federation for Decency, 181
National Football League (NFL), concussion crisis in, 426
National Geographic, 322, 326, 328, 335
National Geographic Traveler, 328
National Guard, advertising of, 397
nationalism, printing press in fostering, 8
national magazines, 314, 315–316
National Music Publishers Association, 143
national newspapers, 284
National Press Club, 292
National Public Radio (NPR), 158, 173, 174, 175
National Resources Defense Council, 392
National Review, 312, 335–336
National Rifle Association, 325
National Security Agency (NSA), 64, 85
National Television Systems Committee (NTSC), 191
National Union of Somali Journalists, 176

Native American newspapers, 290
Native American Times, 290
Native Peoples, 331
Natural Born Killers, 512
Nazi Thieves (Edsel), 356
NBC (National Broadcasting Company), 9, 160, 187, 188, 195, 223, 270, 465
  challenging, 161
  General Electric purchase of, 447
  newsroom cultures of, 482–483
  partnership of, 201
  rights to special programming and, 193
NBC-Blue network, 160, 163
NBC.com, 110
NBC-Comcast merger, 458
NBC News, 468
NBC Nightly News, 33, 207
NBC-Red network, 160, 163
NBCSN, 223
NBC Universal, 200, 223, 450, 455
  Comcast's stake in, 260, 451
  mass media and, 372
  merger and acquisitions of, 463
NCIS, 22, 203
Near v. Minnesota, 542
Need for Speed, 92
Negro Digest, 330
Negroponte, Nicholas, 66
Nelson, Ricky, 129
neo-noir, 244
Nestlé, 422
Netflix, 13, 23, 36, 110, 188
  comparison to Comcast, 201
  competition with, 462
  as data-heavy service, 67
  as digital distribution model, 251
  distribution to mobile devices by, 260
  expanding global flow and, 460
  foreign-language films and, 248
  movie downloads on, 254
  parents groups and, 517
  production of "Amazon Originals," 60
  revival of canceled series on, 55
  screening of short films and film festivals on, 262
  streaming service of, 83, 201, 235
  two-speed Internet and, 67
  video-on-demand service of, 256–257
  video rental and, 200
  as video subscription service, 223

net neutrality, 43, 66–67, 471
  Day of Action, 565
network era, 195
network news, 207–208
networks
  building first, 158–159
  distributed, 42
neutrality
  in boosting credibility, 481–482
  partisanship and, 482
Nevermind, 134, 135
Neverwinter Nights, 88
Newcomb, Horace, 528
New England Courant, 272
New England Whalers, 198
Newfield, Jack, 282
New Girl, 201
  as niche-specific show, 221
  as situation comedy, 204
new journalism, 281
Newman, Paul, 205
New Orleans Daily Creole, 288
New Orleans Times-Picayune, 270
NewPages, 366–367
New Pittsburgh Courier, 288–289
news
  bias in, 484
  characteristics of, 480–481
  defined, 479–481
  differences between print, TV, and Internet, 495–498
  "fake," 500, 502–505
  information services and, 435
  network, 207–208
  promoting publicity and business as, 434–435
  as satire, 504
News Corp., 270, 362
  CEO of, among highest paid, 453
  diversification and, 465
  founding of *Star* by, 331
  mass media and, 372
  Murdoch, Rupert as head of, 157
  News of the World of, 486
  ownership of Twentieth Century Fox, 260
  owning of Fox network, 322
  selling of DirecTV, 224
  split if, 465
  success of MySpace and, 455
news doctors, 497
News for Chinese, 290
newshole, 291
newsies, 275
news media, ethics and, 485–489
News of the World, 486
newspaper(s), 12, 269–305. *See also* journalism
  advertising impact on, 381
  African American, 288–289

  Asian American, 290
  business and ownership of, 284–291
  chains in, 294
  challenges facing, today, 296–303
  college, 297
  colonial, 272–273, 274
  compiling models of modern print journalism and, 278–284
  decline in readership, 296–297
  democracy and, 303–304
  evolution of American, 271–278
  fall in readership, 269
  founding of Associated Press (AP), 275–276
  jobs in, 305
  joint operating agreements, 295–296
  move to digital, 298–300
  national, 284
  Native American, 290
  operations of, 291, 293–294
  ownership of, 294–295
  partisan press and, 273–274
  penny press era, 274–276
  readers targeted by, 285–291
  roles of, 285
  Spanish-language, 289
  underground press, 290–291
  weekly, 284
  wire services and feature syndication, 294
  yellow journalism and, 276–278
Newspaper Association of America (NAA), 271
  print ad sales and, 299–300
newsreels, 243, 248
Newsroom, The, 500
news/talk/information format, 170
New Super Mario Bros., 79–80
Newsweek, 266, 284, 318–319, 465
  newsroom cultures of, 482–483
newsworthiness, 480
New York, Channel one contracts in, 401
New York Daily Graphic, 320
New York Daily News, 280
New York Dolls, 133
New Yorker, 314, 329
  Web-enabled ads on, 333
New York Herald, 288
New York Journal, 276
  Hearst's purchase of, 277–278
New York Metropolitan Opera, 258
New York Morning Herald, 274–275

New York Observer, 301
New York Post, 280
New York Public Library, 358
New York Sun, 274
New York Times, 269, 295, 450
  availability of, in print, 11
  bestseller fiction list in, 342
  charging readers for access to online content, 300
  Citizens United case and, 470
  democracy and, 32
  ethics and, 485
  evaluating fairness of reports in, 33
  hiring of journalists to blog, 298
  "huge breach of secrecy" for those running the wars and, 506
  integration of online and print operations of, 284
  lens of, 321
  merger and acquisitions of, 463
  as national newspaper, 284
  Ochs, Adolph's purchase of, 278–279
  as official paper of record, 279
  paywall experiments and, 300
  ratings of, 496
  success of, 279
  supremacy of, 283
  weekday circulation of, 280
  wire services and feature syndication and, 294
New York Times v. Sullivan, 546–547
New York Tribune, 481
New York Weekly Journal, 273, 274
New York World, 276, 277, 310, 477
Nexium, advertising for, 405
Next Issue app, 333
Nexus 7, 333, 462
NFLevolution, 426
niche markets, 220
Nichols, John, 469, 471, 501
nickelodeons, 197, 211, 234, 237–238, 455
Nick Jr., 211
Nielsen Corporation, 220
  rating systems of, 221
Nielsen Media rating service, 392–393
Night (Wiesel), 356
Nightline, 19, 436
Night Ripper, 564
Night Trap, 99
Nike, 394

Nikon, advertising of, 397
Nine Inch Nails, 134, 144
Nine West, advertising of, 386
ninjas, 90
Nintendo 3DS, 83
Nintendo Entertainment, 76, 103, 104
    competition between console makers and, 79–80
    domination of, 100
    Koreans shunning of, 96
    motion-controlled games and, 99
    popularization of handheld digital games by, 83
    release of first, 79
    release of Nintendo 64, 100–101
    rivalry between Sony and, 101
    Super Mario Bros. of, 73
    video game business of, 78
Nipkow, Paul, 190, 191
Nirvana, 134, 135
Nixon, Richard M., 251
    Watergate scandal and, 538
Noah, 249
Noelle-Neumann, Elisabeth, 525–526
Nokia, advertising of, 397
noncommercial networks, creation of first, 173
nonprofit radio, 173–174
noobs, 90
Norris, Frank, 317
North Alabama White Citizens Council, 125
North American Free Trade Agreement (NAFTA), 455
North American Review, 313–314
North by Northwest, 244
Northrup, Solomon, 247
North Star, 288
nostalgia, 25–26, 28
Notorious B.I.G., 135
NSFNET, 44
NSF Network, 42
Nut Job, The, 258

O: The Oprah Magazine, 325, 334
Oakley, Annie, 417
Obama, Barack, 3–4, 354, 408
    election of 2008, 3, 499
    election of 2012, 3
    historic candidacy of, 533
    public relations and, 437
    transparency of, 430–431
    video of, playing basketball, 454
objective journalism, 279, 478
objectivity
    in modern journalism, 278–280
    scientific method and, 520

O'Brien, Conan, 504
obscenity, 548–549
Occupy Wall Street movement, 284, 474, 482
Ochs, Adolph, 278–279
Ochs, Phil, 131
Oculus, 77, 258
Oculus Rift, 74, 462
Oculus VR, 60, 74
O'Donnell, Lawrence, 498
Odyssey, 78, 100
    release of, 78
Odyssey 100, 78
Office, The, 143, 218
off-network syndication, 217, 219
offset lithography, 345, 348
Ogilvy & Mather Worldwide, 385, 388
Ogilvy Public Relations, 422
Ohio, Channel one contracts in, 401
OK!, 324
Oldboy, 245, 250
Old Time Spelling Bee, 163
oligopoly, 137, 223, 238, 446
Olympics, 208
Omaha World-Herald, 295
Omnicom, 384, 391, 422
    merger of Publicis and, 385
On Air with Ryan Seacrest, 180
Once Upon a Time series, 456
On-Demand, 13
O'Neal, Shaquille, 221
One Day, 245
OneDrive, 59
100 Balls, 104
Oneida Nation, 290
online advertising, trends in, 390–393
online fantasy sports, 82
online fraud, 64
online journalism, 283–284
online music stores, 117
online piracy, 140
Only Lovers Left Alive, 249
O & Os, 218
Open Road Films, 258
open-source software, 67–68
Opera (Web browser), 45
opinion and fair comment, 547
"Oppa Gangnam Style," 142
Oprah's Book Club, 356
Oprah Winfrey Show, 356
opt-in policies, 63
option time, 161
opt-out policies, 63
Ora, Rita, 92
oral communication, 12
oral culture, 9
oral era in communication, 6–7
Orange County Register, 280

Orange Is the New Black, 188
Orbit, 457
Oregon Trail, The, 89
O'Reilly, Bill, 498, 503
Origin, 105
Orkut as social networking site, 49
Oswald, Lee Harvey, 321
Our Idiot Brother, 249
Out, 331
Outcault, R. F., 276
Outside, 328

Pacifica Foundation, 173
packaging, trademarks and, 380
Packard, Vance, 400
packet switching, 42
Pac-Man, 78, 79, 80, 86
Page, Clarence, 294
Page, Larry, 376
paid media, 392
Paine, Thomas, 313
Paley, William, 153, 161, 193, 467
Palin, Sarah, 363, 503
Palmer, Amanda, 144
Palmolive Hour, 163
Pamela (Richardson), 347
Pandora
    competition for young music fans, 177
    creation of individual stations, 177
    as distributor of sounds and images, 110
    launching of, 153
    planet of, in *Avatar,* 232
    radio industry and, 183
    royalties on, 141
    as streaming radio service, 140
Panera, wage gap and, 453
paperbacks, 345, 347
papyrus, 344, 345
Paradise Lost (Milton), 541
paradox, willingness to accept, 28
Paramount Pictures, 234, 235, 238, 241
    current business of, 258
    merger between Publix and, 241
    Supreme Court's ruling against, 252
    theaters owned by, 240–241
Paramount Vantage, 251
Paranormal Activity, 262
parchment, 345
Parents Television Council (PTC), 517
Paris, film screenings in, 234
Park, George, 419
Parker, Dorothy, 329, 351, 557
Parker, Edwin, 519

Parks, Gordon, 247, 319
Parks and Recreation, 204
Parquet Courts, 133
partisan model, 500
partisan press, 273–274
partisanship, 4
    neutrality and, 482
    partyism and, 4
pass-along readership, 319
Patch, 304
patent medicines, advertising of, 380–381
Patton, Charley, 124
Paul, Ron, 488
Pavement, 143
Pawnbroker, The, 556
Pawn Stars, 14
Paxil, advertising for, 405
pay models, 104
Payne Fund Studies, 515–516
payola
    manipulating playlists with, 179
    as scandal in rock and roll music, 128
PayPal, 40, 64
pay-per-view (PPV) programs, 197
paywall, 300
PC bangs, 96
PCWorld, 324
Pearl Jam, 134, 135
Pearson PLC, 362
peer-to-peer (P2P) systems, 120
"Peggy Sue," 128
Peirce, Kimberly, 245
Peli, Oren, 262
Penguin Books, 362
Penguin Random House, 342, 362
Penn, William, 380
Pennsylvania Gazette, 272
Pennsylvania Magazine, 313
Pennsylvania Railroad, 419, 420
penny arcade, 76, 91
Penny Arcade Expo (PAX), 91, 92
Penny Dreadful, 22, 197
penny press, 272, 274
Pentagon Papers case, 542–543
People, 313, 323–324, 331, 332, 334
People en Español, 324, 331
People StyleWatch, 324
Pepsi-Cola, 257
    advertising at Super Bowl, 395
Percy, Ethel, 329
Perkins, Anthony, 245
Perkins, Carl, 125, 126
Perot, Ross, 408
Perry, Katy, 126, 136, 138
Perry, Tyler, 245
personal computers (PCs), 43–44
    media convergence on, 53

Person of Interest, 203, 517
Peter, Paul, and Mary, 131
Peter Pan, 193
Peters, Mike, 294
Peterson Milla Hooks (PMH), 386
Pet Rescue Saga, 83
Pew Internet & American Life Project, 65
Pew Project for Excellence in Journalism, 288, 470, 493
Peyton Place, 254
Philadelphia Inquirer, 295
Philadelphia Story, 243
Philadelphische Zeitung, 285
Philip Morris, advertising bans and, 404
Philip Morris Marlboro, 396
Philips, designing of digitally recorded disc and player, 119
Phillips, David Graham, 310
Phillips, Sam, 126
phishing, 64
phonograph, 116, 121
Photobucket, 47
  as content community, 48
photography, civil war, 315
photojournalism, 313, 317
  evolution of, 320–321
  National Geographic and, 328
  television, 320–321
Photoshop, 321
Piano, The, 245
Pickett, Wilson, 130
Pickford, Mary, 102, 239, 240, 554–555
Picture of Dorian Gray (Wilde), 353
picture radio, 115
Pilkey, Dav, 361
Pillsbury, 381
Pinball Construction Set, 102
pinball machine, 76
Pink, 138
Pinkham, Lydia, 380, 406
Pink Lloyd, 169
Pinky, 254
Pinocchio, 456
Pinterest, 49
Pirate Bay, The, 50
Pirates of the Caribbean, 250, 457
Pitchfork, 134
Pitts, Leonard, 294
Pittsburgh Courier, 288
Pittsburgh Dispatch, 477
Pixar, 456, 457
  digital age and, 460
  Disney ownership of, 260
plain-folks pitch in advertising, 394
Plants vs. Zombies, 102

platform games, 86, 88
Plato, 7, 15
Playboy, 322, 327
playlists, manipulating, with payola, 179
PlayStation, 77, 89, 101, 105–106, 200
  capabilities for music playing CDs, 100
  establishment of online community by, 80
  Koreans shunning of, 96
PlayStation Move, 80
PlayStation Network, 80
PlayStation Portable (PSP), 83
PlayStation Vita, 83
Pliny the Elder, 354
Pocket Books, 351, 354
podcasting, 153, 177–178
Podio, 48
Poehler, Amy, 221
Poitier, Sidney, 205
Pokémon, 91, 401
Pokémon Red/Blue, 83
political advertising, 4, 408
political bias, 483
political broadcasts, equal opportunity and, 561–562
political cartoons, 293
political economy studies, 530
political pressures, on movies, 554
political speech, 400, 470
Politico, 208, 298, 301, 496
politics, and the media, 3–4
Polo, Marco, 346
Polygon, 85
Polygram, 137
Pong, 75, 76, 78, 79
Poor Richard's Almanac, 312
PopCap Games, 102
Pope, Alexander, 312
Pope, Generoso, 331
Popmoney, 40
pop music, 122
  formation of rock and, 122–129
  impact of, 115
  reemergence of, 135–136
  reformations in, 129–136
  rise of, 122–123
Popov, Alexander, 153, 154
PopularMechanics.com, 324
Popular Party, 273
Popular Science, 324, 326
populism, 28
pop-up ads, 377
pornography, sexting as, 550
portable players, 83–84
portal, 57
Porter, Cole, 122, 242
Porter, Edwin S., 237

Porter Novelli advertising agency, 385
Postal Act (1879), 312
Postman, Neil, 479
postmodern culture, 27–29
postmodern period, 27
Powell's, Hachette sales and, 342
PowerBar, 427
Poynter Institute, 301
Precious, 247
precision journalism, 282
premium cable services, 197, 199
Prentice-Hall, 348
prescription drugs, advertising of, 405
Presley, Elvis, 126
  censorship of, on television, 128
  class bias and racism as basis of objections to, 15
  legacy of, 127
  pegged pants and gyrating hips of, 125
  popularity of, 15, 208
  record sales of, 127
press
  origins of a free, 539–549, 551–552
  tension between public relations and, 433–436
press agents, 416, 418
press releases, 424
PressThink, 506
pretty face and happy-talk culture, 496–497
Prevention, 335
Priest, Judas, 511
Primary, 249
prime time, 169, 194
Prime Time Access Rule (PTAR), 211
Primettes, 131
Prince, 125, 134
Princess Bride, The, 24
Princess Peach, 88
Princess Toadstool, 88
Principles of Uncertainty (Kalman), 350
print communication, 12
printed text, digital versions of, 266
printing presses, 26, 344
  in fostering nationalism, 8
  invention and development of, 7, 272, 346–347
print journalism, reporting rituals and legacy of, 490–495
print media, 266
print revolution, 7–8

prior restraint, censorship as, 542–543
PRISM program, 85
Prisoners, 244
privacy
  data mining and, 448
  invading, 486
  right to, 549, 551
Privacy Act (1974), 551
private research, 520
private sector monopoly, 156
pro-am model for journalism, 303
Procter & Gamble, 381, 388, 420, 422
product differentiation, 243, 380
production, 332
product placement, 257, 377
  advertising in, 397, 399
product standardization, 243
professional books, 345, 350
professional friction, elements of, 433–435
Professor Quiz, 163
Pro Football Weekly, 328
program log, 168
programming, impact of ratings and shares on, 220
Progressive, 312, 335, 543
Progressive Era, 27, 310
Progressive Grocer, 325
progressive rock music, 168
Project Gutenberg, 357
Project Runway, 209
Prometheus Radio Project, 182
propaganda, 423
  analysis of, 514
Propaganda Technique in the World War (Lasswell), 514
proprietary research, 520
ProPublica, 304
Proximity Worldwide, 391
PRWatch, 435, 437
PR Week, 435
PS4, 53
  functioning also as DVD players, 83
pseudo-events, 427, 429
pseudo-polls, 515
Psy, 142
psychedelic music, 129, 132–133
Psycho, 25, 244, 245
psychographics, 386
Public Broadcasting Act (1967), 173, 209
Public Broadcasting Service (PBS), 173, 191, 197, 200
public domain, 545
Public Enemy, 135
Publicis Groupe, 384, 385, 422
  Omnicom merger with, 385
publicity, 418, 434–435

public journalism, 500, 502–505
Publick Occurrences, Both Foreign and Domestick, 272
Public Opinion (Lippmann), 27, 416, 421, 514
public opinion research, 514–515
public relations, 413–439
  adaption to the Internet age, 431
  approaches to organized, 422
  big business and press agents, 418
  birth of modern, 418–421
  community and consumer relations, 429
  during crisis, 431–433
  defined, 415
  democracy and, 436–438
  digital ecosystem for, 372
  early developments in, 416–421
  government relations and lobbying, 429–431
  greenwashing and, 428
  industry of, 437
  invisible hand of, 437
  media relations and, 425, 427
  message in, 423–425
  NFL's concussion crisis in, 426
  performing, 423–425, 427
  practice of, 421–425, 427, 429–433
  shaping of image, 435–436
  social and cultural impact of, 415
  special events and pseudo-events in, 427, 429
  tensions between press and, 433–436
Public Relations Society of America (PRSA), 417, 435
  Member Statement of Professional Values, 435
Public Relations Student Society of America (PRSSA), 422
Public Relations Tactics, 435
public research, 520
public service announcements (PSAs), 382, 424
public sphere, 530–531
public TV, 190, 209
publishing houses, 345
  formation, 348
  origin of, in United States, 347–348
Publix, merger between Paramount and, 241
puffery, 406
PUGs, 90
Pulitzer, Albert, 277
Pulitzer, Joseph, 272, 301, 310, 477
  New York World and, 276–277
pulp fiction, 347

punk rock, 133
Pure Food and Drug Act (1906), 317
Push (Sapphire), 247
Putnam, G. P., 348
Pyle, Ernie, 283

QR code, 324
quadraphonic or four-track sound, 118
Quake, 81
Quaker Oats, 380
qualified privilege, 547
Queen (musical group), 28, 169
Queen Latifah, 135
Quiz Kids, 163
quiz shows
  rise and fall of, on television, 194
  scandals involving, 190, 194–195

Rachel Maddow Show, 208
racing games, 75
Radam, William, 380
radio, 8, 11–12, 116, 149–183
  advertising on, 178–179
  AM/FM, 177
  authority of, 164–165
  building first networks, 158–159
  commercial, 152
  comparing commercial and noncommercial, 174
  convergence and, 175, 177–178
  democracy and, 182–183
  early technology and development of, 151–157
  economics of broadcast, 178–182
  evolution of, 157–165
  golden age of, 153, 163–165
  HD, 175
  Internet, 175, 177
  music formats of, 172–173
  news, 170
  news, talk, and information, 170
  nonprofit, 173–174
  portable, 166
  reinvention of, 165–169
  relationship between records and, 121–122
  rise of format and Top 40, 167–168
  satellite, 175
  sounds of commercial, 169–170, 172–175, 177–178
  talk, 9, 153, 170, 171
Radio Act (1912), 156, 162
Radio Act (1927), 153, 161–162

Radio Advertising Bureau, 183
Radio Corporation of America (RCA), 12, 156
  formation of, 156
  General Electric's purchase of, 161
  radio group and, 159
radio group, 159
radio industry, jobs in, 183
Radio Mogadishu, 176
radio ownership, 179–181
radio programming, 163–164
radio suffers, 153
radio waves, 152, 166
  discovery of, 152
  as natural resource, 156
Radway, Janice, 528, 530
railroads, public relations for, 416, 418
Rain, 142
Rainey, Ma, 124
Raising Hell, 135
Raitt, Bonnie, 123
Ramones, 133
random assignment, 521
Random Family (LeBlanc), 282
Random House, 348, 362, 549
Ranger Rick, 329
Rappe, Virginia, 555
"Rapper's Delight," 135
Rasmussen, Bill, 198
Rather, Dan, 31, 207
  Watergate scandal and, 437
rating, 220
Ray, Johnnie, 124
Ray, Satyajit, 246
Ray, William J., 225
Rayman, 102
Razorfish, 391
RCA, 160
  Bernays, Edward, and, 420
  charges with violations of antitrust laws and, 160–161
  manufacturing of equipment of, 156
  monopoly power of, 158
  portable reading devices from, 357
  Zworykin's innovations for, 191
RCA/NBC
  General Electric's purchase of, 450
  government scrutiny in ending, 160–161
RCA Records, 118
RCA Victor, 160
Rdio, 121, 136
  ad-support of, 140
  as streaming service, 141
reader-response research, 528

Reader's Digest, 318
  circulation of, 335, 336
  commercial success of, 319
  competition to, 329
  launch of, 313
  rivalry of, 322
  supermarket sales and, 323
Reading on the Rise, 367
Reading the Romance: Women, Patriarchy, and Popular Literature (Radway), 528, 530
Reagan, Ronald, 171, 252, 450, 562
Real Housewives, 14
reality, augmented, 375
reality TV, 208–209
real-time strategy game (RTS), 88
Real World, The, 28, 209
Rear Window, 244
Reasoner, Harry, 207
Rebel without a Cause, 253
receivers, 9
records, relationship between radio and, 121–122
Redbox
  as discount rental kiosk, 256
  distribution to mobile devices by, 260
Red Channels: The Report of Communist Influence in Radio and Television, 557
Red Dead Redemption, 98
Redding, Otis, 127, 130
Redford, Robert, 205
Red Lion Broadcasting Co. v. FCC, 559
Reed, John, 283
Reed, Lou, 133
Reese's Pieces, 257
  product placement and, 399
reference books, 354–355
reformations in popular music, 129–136
Reformer, 329–330
Regal Cinemas, 257, 258
regional editions, 333
regulation, 449
Reid, Wallace, 555
Reiner, Carl, 204
Relativity Studios, 251, 258
reliability, scientific method and, 520
religious books, 349, 354
R.E.M., 134
REO Speedwagon, 133
Report of the Warren Commission on the Assassination of President Kennedy, The, 354

Republic, The (Plato), 15
Republican Party, 3
reruns, 219
Resident Evil, 28, 88, 92, 93
responsible capitalism, 482–483
Resurrection, 203
retention, 524
retransmission fees, 218
Reuters wire services and
    feature syndication and,
    294
revenue, collecting, in media
    industry, 446
Revere, Paul, 312
Review, 311–312
review boards, 554
Review of General Psychology, 95
Revlon, 194
Reynolds, Frank, 207
Reynolds, R. J., 402
R/GA, 391
Rhapsody, 121, 139, 144
rhythm and blues (R&B) music,
    124
Richardson, Samuel, 347
Right Media, Yahoo! purchase of,
    391
right to privacy, 549, 551
Rihanna, 136, 138
Riis, Jacob, 320
Ring, 331
Ringling Bros. and Barnum &
    Bailey Circus, 417
ringtones, 140
Ringu, 250
Ringu 2, 250
rituals, reporting, and legacy of
    print journalism, 490–495
Rizzoli & Isles, 219
RKO, 234, 241
    Supreme Court's ruling against,
    252
Roanoke Times, 295
Robbins, Brian, 222
Roberts, Jim, 298
Roberts, Nora, 351
Robinson, Edward G., 515
Robinson, Jackie, 288
Robinson, Max, 208
Robinson Crusoe (Defoe), 311–312
rockabilly, 125
rock and roll music, 16, 115, 117,
    123–129
    battles in, 126–129
    payola scandals in, 128
Rock Band, 81, 89, 90, 102
Rockefeller, John D., 316, 419,
    420, 449
Rockford Files, The, 206
rock music, 122
    progressive, 168

Rockstar Games, 98, 104
Rockwell, Norman, 318
Rocky, 255
Roc Nation, 138
Roc the Mic Studios, 138
Rodale, 335
Rodger, Elliot, 529
Rodriguez, Robert, 263
Roger and Me, 249
Rogers, Buddy, 239
Roku, 53, 202
    television device for download-
    ing, 254
role-playing games (RPGs), 75,
    88
Rolex, 394
roll film, 234
Rolling Stone, 282, 283, 326, 328
Rolling Stones, 89, 125, 127
    as "bad boys" of rock and roll,
    130
    drug arrests of, 132
    on top charts, 129
"Roll Over Beethoven" (song),
    28, 124, 125
Romanowski, William, 29
Rome, Jim, 169
Romney, Mitt, 454, 499
    public relations and, 437
Rooms To Go, advertising of, 386
Roosevelt, Franklin D., 156
    fireside chats of, 163, 164
Roosevelt, Theodore, 427
    muckrakers and, 317
Roots, 206
Rose, Derrick, 393–394
Roseanne, 13
Rosen, Jay, 507
Rosenblatt, Roger, 14
Rosenstiel, Tom, 23, 482
Rosing, Boris, 190–191
Ross, Diana, 130, 131
Ross, Harold, 329
Ross, Lillian, 329
Rossellini, Roberto, 555–556
rotation, 167
Roth, Veronica, 356
Roth v. United States, 549
Roundhay Garden Scene, 235
Rovio, 102, 106
Rowdy Journal, 275
Rowling, J. K., 341, 356, 361, 363
Royal Pains, 188
royalty rate, 140
Royko, Mike, 490
rugged individualism as
    American ideal, 6
Run-DMC, 135
Runtastic, 376
Runyon, Damon, 310
Rushdie, Salman, 360

Rush Limbaugh Show, 171, 180
Rushmore, 249
Russell, David O., 249

Saatchi & Saatchi, 385
Safari (Web browser), 45
Safe Haven, 258
St. Louis Blues, 124
St. Louis Dispatch, 276–277
St. Louis Post, 276–277
St. Martin's Press, 367
St. Petersburg Times, 301
Saints Row: Red Faction, 102
Salander, Lisbeth, 50–51
sales magazines, 332–333
Salon, 208, 313, 324
salsa music, 16
Salt-N-Pepa, 135
"Same Love," 113–114
Samoff, David, 153
Sam's Club, bookstore business
    of, 364
Samsung, 54, 326, 422
    advertising of, 384
    App for, 141
    competition in expanding
    markets and, 334
Sandbox (or open-world)
    role-playing games (RPGs),
    88
San Francisco Examiner, 277, 324
San Jose Mercury News, 280, 295
Santa Barbara, 32
Sapkowski's saga, 93
Sapphire, 247
Sarnoff, David, 159–160
    as head of RCA/NBC, 193
    negotiation in using Farns-
    worth's patents, 191
    predicting of radio's demise,
    166–167
    proposal of company to buy
    shares of RCA, 160–161
Satanic Verses, The (Rushdie), 360
satellite radio, 175
satire, news as, 504
satiric journalism, 503–505
"Satisfaction," 127
saturation advertising, 389
Saturday Evening Post, 318
    circulation of, 323, 336
    failure of, 322, 323
    launching of, 312
    as longest-running magazine,
    314
Saturday Night Live, 22–23, 142,
    503
    preempting of Sharpton, Al, on,
    562
    sketch comedy of, 204
    "Weekend Update," 23

Saturn, 396
Savages, 134
Savan, Leslie, 396
Sawyer, Diane, 208
Scalia, Antonin, 106–107
Scandal, 203
scanning disk, 190
Scarface, 233
Scarlet Letter, The (Hawthorne),
    360
Schenck, Charles T., 544–545
Schenck v. United States,
    544–545
Scherfig, Lone, 245
Schoofs, Mark, 298
"School Day," 125
schools, advertising in, 401–402
Schorr, Daniel, 494
Schramm, Wilbur, 519
Schudson, Michael, 301, 302, 397,
    434, 542
Schultz, Connie, 294
Schwarzenegger, Arnold, 250,
    562
Schweitzer, Albert, 320
Scientific American, 543
scientific method, 520–521
Scorsese, Martin, 245
Scott, Ridley, 29
Scott de Martinville, Édouard-
    Léon, 116
Scribner's, 348
Scripps, Edward Wyllis, 294
Seacrest, Ryan, 169
Seal Island, 456
Sean Hannity Show, 208
search engines, 46–47
Sears, 78
    advertising of, 397
Seattle Post-Intelligencer, 270
Second Life, 82
Sedition Act (1798), 542, 544
seditious expression, 544–545
seditious libel, 273
seductive advertising, 21
Seeger, Pete, 131, 291, 557
See It Now, 495
Sega, 102, 104
    as console maker, 101
    Koreans shunning of, 96
Sega Dreamcast, 79, 81
Sega Genesis, 79
Sega Saturn, 89
Seierstad, Asne, 282
Seinfeld, 24
    as situation comedy, 204
Seinfeld, Jerry, 356
selective exposure, 10, 519
selective retention, 519
self-regulation, 76
    in movie industry, 554–556

semantic Web, 56–57
Sendak, Maurice, 24
senders, 9
"separate but equal" laws, 124
Sephora, advertising of, 386
September 11 terrorist attacks (2001), 64, 189
  Internet censorship after, 65
serialized TV shows, 206
serial programs, 163–164, 206
Serling, Rod, 511
Sesame Street, 209
Se7en, 142, 244
Seven Beauties, 245
Seven Cities of Gold, 102
7-Eleven, advertising of, 397
700 Club, 562
Seven Samurai, 246, 250
7-7-7 rule, 458
Seven Stories Press, 353
Seventeen, 324, 329, 330
78-rpm records, 118
Sex and the City, 205
Sex and the Single Girl (Brown), 310
Sex Pistols, 133
sexting as pornography, 550
sexuality, women's magazines and, 327
"Sexy Ways," 124
Shadow, The, 163, 165
Shaft, 247
"Shake, Rattle, and Roll," 125
Shakespeare, William, 17
Shakur, Tupac, 135
"Shame of the Cities" (Steffens), 316
Shanghai Disney Resort, 457
Shangri-Las, 129
share, 220
Sharpton, Al, 562
Shaw, Irwin, 557
"Sh-Boom," 127
She & Him, 143
shellac discs, 117
Shelley, Mary Wollstonecraft, 17
Sheppard, Sam, 551
Sherlock, 206
Sherlock Jr., 241
Sherman Antitrust Act (1890), 446, 449
Sherrod, Shirley, 492
She Smiles, She's Snared!, 250
shield laws, 552
shooter games, 75, 86, 88
  first-person, 98
"Shop Around," 130
Showtime, 188, 197, 356
  release of films and, 257
Shrek, 222, 233
Shrek 2, 256

Shuster, Joe, 352
Shyamalan, M. Night, 246
Siegel, Jerry, 352
signal scrambling, 199
Silence of the Lambs, 244
Silent Spring (Carson), 367
Silkworm, The, 341
Silly Symphonies series, 456
simCity, 88–89, 94
Simon, Neil, 204
Simon & Schuster, 342, 348, 362
Simpson, O. J., 552
Simpsons, The, 17, 23, 25
Sims Social, The, 93
simulation games, 75, 88–89
Sinatra, Frank, 161
  music-variety shows hosted by, 193
  parlaying of music and radio into movie stardom, 123
Sin City, 244, 258, 263
Sinclair, Upton, 317, 565
Sinclair Broadcast Group, 19
Singing Fool, The, 234, 242
Singleton, John, 245, 247
Siouxsie, 133
Siri, 56–57
Sirius, 175
  merger and acquisitions of, 463
Sirius XM, 175, 177
sitcoms, 204, 206
Sitting Bull, 417
situational ethics, 486
situation comedy, 204
16 and Pregnant, 28
Sixth Amendment, First Amendment versus, 551–552
60 Minutes
  evaluating fairness of reports of, 33
  investigative model of journalism and, 495
  media literacy and, 32
  melodrama and, 22
  news credibility ratings and, 496
  shedding of light on major events, 208
$64,000 Challenge, 194
$64,000 Question, 194
sketch comedy, 204
Sky Broadcasting, 208
Skype, net neutrality and, 67
skyscraper model, 16, 17, 20, 21
Slacker, 177
  determining royalties on, 141
slander, 546
Slate, 313, 324
Sleep Number, advertising of, 386
slogans, 383

Slouching Towards Bethlehem (Didion), 282
Small Farmer's Journal, 336
small-town pastoralism, 483
smartphones, 39, 202
  use of, 65
smartwatches, 54
Smashing Pumpkins, 68
"Smells Like Teen Spirit," 134
Smiley, Tavis, 169
Smith, Bessie, 124
Smith, Patti, 133
Smith, W. Eugene, 320
Smith Brothers, 380
Smithsonian, 68, 328
Smokey Robinson, 130
Smokey the Bear campaign, 382
snail mail, 9
Snake Pit, The, 254
Sneak King, 93
SNK as console maker, 101
snob-appeal approach in advertising, 394
Snowden, Edward, 64, 85, 474, 499
Snow Flower and the Secret Fan, 246
Snow White, 24
Snow White and the Huntsman, 263
Snow White and the Seven Dwarfs, 456
soap operas, 163–164, 206
  Spanish-language, 209
social change, role of advertising in, 381–382
social issues in media economics, 463–465, 467
social learning theory, 524
socially responsible press, 541
social media, 9
  advertising in, 392–393
  defined, 47
  democracy and, 49, 52
  emergence of, 9
  finding real happiness and, 569–575
  games in, 74
  rise of, 10
  types of, 47–49
social networking, 47, 49
social pressures on movies, 554
social psychology studies, 515–516
social reform, muckrakers and, 316–317
social responsibility, 505, 540
social viewing, 55
society, role of media in, 10–16
Society of Professional Journalists Code of Ethics, 398, 486, 487

Socrates, 7, 14
software
  costs of, 217
  open-source, 67–68
Sokal, Alan, 532–533
Soldevilla, Jeremy, 369
Solitaire, 80
"Someday We'll Be Together," 131
Song of Solomon (Morrison), 356
Son House, 124
Sonic the Hedgehog, 91, 102
Sonic Youth, 134, 143
Sony, 137, 422. *See also* PlayStation
  competition between console makers and, 79–80
  court ruling in favor of, 200
  designing of digitally recorded disc and player, 119
  domination of, 100
  Foxconn's electronic devices for, 452
  introduction of pocket radio, 166
  merger of BMG and, 137
  ownership of Columbia, 260
  portable reading devices from, 357
  rivalry between Nintendo and, 101
  syndication and, 217
  3-D cameras of, 232
  video game business of, 78
Sony and Bertelsmann, 467
Sony Music Entertainment, 137
Sony Pictures Classics, 251
Sony Walkman, 118
Sopranos, The, 188, 524
soul music, 130
sound
  addition to movies, 242–243
  in movies, 234
sound bite, 497
SoundCloud, 144
Sounder, 247
SoundExchange, 141
Soundgarden, 134, 135
sound recordings, 113–145
  business of, 136–141, 143–144
  development of, 115–122
  free expression and democracy, 144–145
  in Internet age, 119–121
  reformations in popular music, 129–136
  U.S. popular music and formation of rock, 122–129
Source, The, 328
Sousa, John Philip, 122
South by Southwest festival, 251
South Carolina Gazette, 274

South Korea, gaming obsession in, 96–97

South Park, 23, 94

space brokers, advertising agencies as, 379

Space Invaders, 79, 80

space shuttle disaster, 499

Spades, 80

spam, 379, 390

Spanish-American War, sinking of *Maine* in, 320

Spanish International Network, 209

Spanish-language newspapers, 289

Spanish-language radio, 172

Spanish-language soap operas, 209

Spanish-language television, 209

Spears, Britney, 142

special events, 427, 429

specialization
 in magazines, 325, 327–331
 rise of, 455

specialty reporters, 293

Spectator, 312

Spector, Phil, 138

speech
 commercial, in regulating advertising, 399–403, 405–407
 political, 400

Speedy Ortiz, 133

Spider-Man, 93, 104, 260, 457, 460

Spiegelman, Art, 353

Spielberg, Steven, 22, 243, 245, 250

Spike TV, 92

Spin, 328

Spinutech, 69

spiral of silence theory, 525–526

Splenda, 422

Splinter Cell: Chaos Theory, 93

split-run editions, 333

SpongeBob SquarePants, 401

sponsored stories, 393

Spore, 91

sports games, 75, 89
 ESPN and, 198

Sports Illustrated, 311, 327–328, 333, 334

sports magazines, 327–328

Spotify, 136, 139
 ad-support of, 140
 competing for young music fans, 177
 expanding global flow and, 460
 as streaming service, 141

Springsteen, Bruce, 133, 175

Sprout, 211

Spy Kids, 263

spyware, 62

Square, 40

Square Cash, 40

Square Enix, 102

Square Wallet, 40

Staehle, Albert, 318

Stained Class album, 511

Standard Oil, 446
 breaking up of, with Sherman Antitrust Act, 449
 monopoly practices by, 277

Stanton, Edwin M., 279

Star, 324, 331

Starbucks, 40, 422
 advertising of, 376
 as naming sponsor, 397

StarCraft, 88, 92, 96, 102

Starflight, 102

Stargate, 138

Starr, Ringo, 400

Star Trek, 25, 206

start-up companies in digital age, 462

Star Wars, 102, 103, 104, 231–232, 233, 245, 255, 256, 460
 Lucasfilm's control of, 260
 success of, 259

state model, 540

State of the News Media, 296
 2010 report of, 297

Stauber, John, 437

Stax, 137

Steam, 105

Steamboat Bill Jr., 241

Steffens, Lincoln, 283, 316, 317

Steiger, Paul, 298

Steinem, Gloria, 327

Stelter, Brian, 496

Stephens, Ann, 347

stereo, 118

Stern, Howard, 175
 indecency fines and, 561

Stewart, Cara, 439

Stewart, Jon, 33, 503–504

Stewart, Martha, 175

Stockham, Thomas, 118

Stoker, 250

Stoller, Mike, 122

Stone, I. F., 291, 292

Stone, Oliver, 511–513

Stone Temple Pilots, 135

Stooges, 133

"Stop! In the Name of Love," 130, 131

stories
 balancing conflict, 494
 comfort of familiar, 24
 covering difficult, 491
 getting first, 491–492
 getting good, 490
 TV and state of, 210

storyboard, 388

story-driven model, 278

Story of Frozen, The: Making a Disney Animated Classic, 456

Storz, Todd, 167

Stowe, Harriet Beecher, 314, 355–356, 367

Strand Theatre, 241

strategy games, 75, 88

streaming, 121, 141, 144, 175, 202

Street Fighter, 86, 93

Streisand, Barbra, 245

Stripe, 40

Stuart Saves His Family, 204

StubHub, 57

studio system, 239

stunt journalism, 478

Stverak, Jason, 478

Styx, 133

subconcussion, 426

subliminal advertising, 383

subscription streaming, 256

subsidiary rights, 363

suburbs, moving to, 252–253

Sugarhill Gang, 135

Sullivan, Ed, 130

Sullivan, L. B., 547

Summer, Donna, 134

Summit Entertainment, 258

Sun, 137

Sun Also Rises, The (Hemingway), 349

Sundance Channel, 25

Sundance Film Festival, 249

Sunday Night Football, 203

Sunday Times of London, 320

Sun Records, 126

Sunset Boulevard, 244

Super Bowl, 187, 208
 advertising in, 395

Super Fly, 247

Superman for DC comics, 352, 353

Super Mario Bros., 73, 79
 bundling of NES console with, 100
 as platform game, 86, 88

supermarket tabloids, 331

Super Monkey Ball, 102

super-PACs, 538

Super Size Me, 249

superstations, 197

Supremes, 130, 131

Surface tablet, 59, 462

survey research, 521–522

survival horror games, 88

Survivor, 209

Swallow, Erica, 439

Swayze, John Cameron, 207

"Sweet Little Sixteen," 125

Swift, Taylor, 114, 122, 137, 177, 393

Syfy, 188

Sympathy for Mr. Vengeance, 250

synchronization fees, 140

syndication, 218–219

synergy, 259, 260, 455

"synths," 138

tablets, 99

Tahrir Square (Egypt), 443

Tainter, Charles Sumner, 116–117

Tales from the Crypt, 352

talkies, 242

talking heads, 133, 498

Talking Points Memo, 298, 301

talk radio, 9, 153, 171

Talladega Nights: The Ballad of Ricky Bobby, 399

Tamla label, 131

Tampa Bay Times, 301

Tangled, 456

tap lines, 196

Tarbell, Ida, 283, 419, 565
 exposés of oil corporations, 478
 "History of the Standard Oil Company" of, 316–317
 investigative journalism and, 317

Target, 105, 139
 graphic branding ad campaign for, 386
 percentage of returned books by, 364
 squeezing out of independent bookstore businesses, 364
 undercutting of small local stores by, 381
 wage gap and, 453

targeted advertising, data mining and, 60, 62

Tattler, 312

Taxi Driver, 245

Taylor, William Desmond, 555

TBWA Worldwide, 385

TechCrunch, 48

Technicolor, 254

technology, electronic, 190–193

Teenage Mutant Ninja Turtles, 452

Teen Mom, 209

Teen Vogue, 324, 329

Tejano music, 16

Tekken, 102

Telecommunications Act (1996), 450, 458, 559
 consequences of, 180
 consolidation in radio ownership and, 153
 defined, 215
 elimination of most radio and television ownership rules, 162

overhaul of nation's communications regulations and, 57
passage of, 68–69
paving way for television
consolidation and, 191
radio ownership and, 179–180
telegraph, 8, 115, 151–152
Telemundo, 197, 209
telenovelas, 209, 468
"Telephone" (2010 song), 9–10
telephone group, 159
telephones, 115
teleplays, 205
Teletubbies, 25
television (TV)
advertising on, 333
anthology dramas on, 205–206
assigning frequencies and
freezing licenses to, 192
cable, 187–188
changes in viewing habits,
199–202
children's, 209, 401
color, 192–193
controlling content on, 193–195
democracy and, 225–227
economics and ownership of,
216–221, 223–225
effects of, in post-TV world, 517
electronic technology and,
190–191
episodic series, 206–207
ESPN on, 198
as final link to true mass
communication, 187
first transmissions on, 190
future of, 227
influence on books, 356–357
jobs in, 227
measuring viewing, 220–221
media convergence on, 53
miniseries in, 206
origins and development of,
189–195
photojournalism and, 320–321
programming trends in, 203–211
public, 209
quiz shows on, 194–195
reality, 208–209
regulatory challenges to,
211–215
setting technical standards,
191–192
specials on, 193
storytelling and, 210
technology in, 190
Telstar, 190, 196
Temple Run, 104, 106
Temptations, 130
Ten Commandments, The, 242
Tennessean, 294

Tennis World, 323
tenure, 355
Tesla, Nikola, 152, 154, 155
Tessler, Lucien, 48
Tetris, 78–79, 83, 84, 89
Texaco Star Theater, 204
Texas, Channel one contracts in,
401
Texas Chainsaw 3D, 398
Texas Instruments, 166
Texas State Board of Education,
350
text, 90
textbooks, 345, 350–351
textual analysis, 528
thaumatrope, 234
theater chains, 257–258
Them on American Top 40
charts, 129
They Are Us (Hamill), 367
Thicke, Robin, 172
ThinkProgress, 48
third-person effect, 526
third-person perspective, 87
third screen, 200–202
This American Life, 54
"This Land Is Your Land," 131
Thomas, Dylan, 133
Thomas, Evan, 483
Thompson, Hunter S., 282
Thoreau, Henry David, 314
Thornton, Willie Mae "Big
Mama," 125
THQ, 102
3-D cameras, 232
3-D graphics, 81, 89
3-D movies, 254
3-D sports games, 89
"Thrift Shop," 113
"Thriller" video (Jackson,
Michael), 14
Thug Life, 135
Thurber, James, 329
Tikkun, 331
Timberlake, Justin, 393–394
Timberland, 428
Time, 33, 193, 313, 318–319, 326,
333, 335
Bernays, Edward, and, 420
extending reach of, 324
on iPad, 334
as media corporations, 334, 468
newsroom cultures of, 482–483
Time, Inc., 249, 327, 334, 335
Timecode, 262
Time-Life Books, 365
time shifting, 200
Times Mirror Cable (TWC)
on demand service of, 233
mergers and acquisitions of,
463

Time Warner Cable, 45, 120, 218,
224, 334
closing of Warner Independent
by, 251
Comcast merger with, 467
control of broadband access,
66
dispute over retransmission
fees, 224
diversification and, 465
as HBO's parent company, 188
Internet service provider and,
45
making programs available for
downloading, 201
mass media and, 372
as media giant, 445
merger and acquisitions of,
447, 451, 463
as owner of many cable
systems, 223
reducing of holdings, 334
releasing of iPad apps by, 202
splitting of newspapers from
TV interests, 270
Warner Brothers division of,
353
Timothy, Elizabeth, 274
Tin Pan Alley, 122, 123, 129
Tiny Wings, 106
Tip Top Weekly, 347
Titanfall, 80
Titanic, 156, 233, 256
TiVo, 377
TiVo Premiere, television device
for downloading, 254
TMZ, 562
TNT, 188, 465
tobacco, advertising of, 379,
402–403, 407
Tocqueville, Alexis de, 513–514
Today Show, 142, 193, 194, 455,
496
To Kill a Mockingbird (Lee), 360
Tokyo Disney Resort, 457
Tokyo Game Show, 92
Tolkien, J. R. R., 356
toll broadcasting, 158
Tomb Raider, 28
Tomlinson, Ray, 43
Tom Thumb, 416
Tonight Show, 193, 208
Top 40 format, 138, 168–169
Top 40 radio, 135
Top Chef, 14, 55, 209
Top of the Morning (Stelter), 496
Tornillo, Pat, Jr., 559
Torvalds, Linus, 67
Toshiba, 61, 200
Total Request Live, 135
Tough Guise, 529

Townsquare Media, 181, 458
Toy Story, 456
TPM Muckraker, 48
trade books, 349, 362, 363
trade magazines, 325
trademarks, packaging and, 380
Tramp, The (Riis), 320
Transformers: Dark of the Moon,
92
transistors, 166
Travel & Leisure, 328
travelogues, 248
Treasure Island, 456
Triangle, 239
Triangle Publications, 322
Tribeca Film Festival, 251
Tribune Company, 269–270, 293,
294, 465
Chicago Tribune and, 266, 269,
293
Los Angeles Times and, 294
merger and acquisitions of, 463
triode, 154
triple play, 215
Trip to the Moon, A, 237
Troggs, 129
trolls, 90
Tron, 92
True Detective, 188, 197, 206
True Grit, 244
Truffaut, François, 246
Truman, Harry S., 124
trunk cables, 196
Trust, 238
trusts, 449
Truth or Consequences, 163
Tso, Richard, 376
Tucker, Ken, 133
Tucker, Sophie, 123
Tulsa World, 295
Tumblr, 47, 48
as organizational tool, 284
Yahoo!'s purchase of, 447
Turner, Big Joe, 125
Turner, Frank, 143
Turner, Ike and Tina, audiences
of, 130
Turner, Ted, 196
CNN as brainchild of, 208
Turner Broadcasting, 208
merger and acquisitions of, 463
Time Warner's purchase of, 451
"Tutti-Frutti," 127
TV. *See* Television
TV: The Most Popular Art
(Newcomb), 528
TV ad time, 379
TV Guide, 313, 319, 322, 323
circulation and population of,
336
competition to, 329

TV Guide Network and TVGuide. com, 322
TV information, 207–208
TV on the Go, 191
TV parental guidelines, 516
Twain, Mark, 281, 314, 360
12 Years a Slave, 233, 246, 247, 248–249
Twentieth Century Fox, 234, 238, 241
    current film business ruled by, 258
    News Corp. ownership of, 260
    Supreme Court's ruling against, 252
    syndication and, 217
    YouTube and, 260
24/7 news cycle, 498
24/7 Media, 391
Twenty-First Century Fox
    diversification and, 465
    future of television and, 188
Twenty-One, 194
20/20, 495
Twilight, 245, 258, 356
Twilight Zone, 205
Twitch, 92
Twitter, 7, 9, 29, 31, 33
    blocking of, 52
    Cairo protesters connection to, 52
    introduction of Vine App by, 48
    as key organizational tool, 284
    late-breaking TV stories and, 321
    live blogs on, 55
    mass media and, 474
    near-constant use of, 261
    news story of, 425
    public relations and, 431
    start-up of, 462
Twitter Analytics, 423
2001: A Space Odyssey, 195
Tylenol, 1982 tragedy involving, 432–433
Tyler the Creator, 172

U2, 134
Ubisoft, 80, 85, 102
Ultrasurf, 52
Ulysses (Joyce), 360, 548–549
Uncle Tom's Cabin (Stowe), 355–356, 367
underground press, 290–291
Unilever, 391, 422
UniMás, 181
United Arab Emirates, 422
United Artists, 234, 239, 241
United Features, 294
United Independent Broadcasters (UIB), 161

United Mine Workers, 420
United Nations Global Compact, 428
United Negro College Fund, 382
United Press International (UPI), wire services and feature syndication and, 294
Universal Music Group, 114, 137, 143
    merger and acquisitions of, 463
Universal Studios, 137, 188, 224, 234
    as attempt to divert attention from YouTube, 260
    current film business ruled by, 258
    forming of oligopoly by, 241
    General Electric's ownership of, 260
    Theme Park of, 259
    Vivendi's ownership of, 260
Universal Uclick, 294
University Press Books, 355
Univision, 209
Univision Online, 181
Univision Radio
    settlement of payola and end of FCC investigation and, 179
    takeover of Hispanic Broadcasting by, 181
Unsafe at Any Speed (Nader), 417, 429
Up, 456
Updike, John, 329
urban contemporary, 172
USA Network, 188, 197, 200
USA Patriot Act (2001), 64, 551
USA Today, 54, 280
    Gannett's ownership of, 294
    as national newspaper, 284
    online service of, 300
    print landscape and, 283
    ratings of, 496
    representing first successful U.S. daily newspaper, 283
    starting of, by Gannett Company, 282
uses and gratifications model, 520
U.S. News & World Report, 318–319
US Weekly, 324, 331
Utne Reader, 336

vacuum, 154
Valens, Ritchie, airplane death of, 128
validity, scientific method and, 520
Vallée, Rudy, 123
values

cultural, of modern period, 26–27
    in postmodern culture, 27–29
    role of advertising in, 381–382
Values and Lifestyles (VAL) strategy, 386–388
Valve Corporation, 91, 105
Vampire Weekend, 134, 139
VandeHei, Jim, 298
Vanderbilt, Cornelius, 449
Van Doren, Charles, 194, 195
Vanidades, 331
Vanishing Lady, The, 237
Vanity Fair, 326, 329
    advertising in, 383
    as part of Condé Nast division, 334–335
    Web-enabled ads on, 333
Vann, Robert C., 288
Vargas, Elizabeth, 208
variables
    dependent, 521
    independent, 521
vaudeville, 163
Vaughan, Stevie Ray, 123
Vazquez, Betzy, 172
VCRs, 254
vellum, 346
Velvet Underground, 133
Verizon, 120
    control of broadband access, 66
    development into competitor for cable and DBS, 224
    as Internet service provider, 45
Verizon Wireless, 40
Verne, Jules, 277, 310
vertical and side scrolling, 87
vertical integration, 238, 252, 259–260
Vertigo, 244
Vevo, 110
    ad-support of, 140
    music videos licensed for use on, 143
    popularity of, 144
    video service of, 141
VHS (Video Home System), 200
Viacom, 202, 452
    diversification and, 465
Viagra, advertising for, 405
Victor Talking Machine Company, 11–12, 117, 160, 161
Victrolas, 116, 117
videocassette recorders (VCRs), 200
video games
    conventions for, 87
    first, 78
    genres of, 84, 86–88
    jobs in, 107

stores for, 105
    violence in, 76
video news releases (VNRs), 417, 424
video-on-demand (VOD), 199, 256
video services, 141–142
video-style ads, 383
video subscription services, 223
Vietnam War, photographic coverage of, 321
Village People, 134
Village Voice, 291
Vilsack, Tom, 492
Vimeo, 48, 50
    screening of short films and film festivals on, 262
Vine, 48
violence
    electronic gaming and, 94–95
    video game, 76
Vioxx, advertising for, 405
viral marketing, 388
Virginian-Pilot, 500
Virginia Slims cigarettes, advertising campaign for, 402
virtual communities, 90
virtual game worlds, 49
virtual reality, 75
virtual social worlds, 49, 75
Virtue Rewarded (Richardson), 347
Visa, 60
    global marketing brand of, 396
VistaVision, 254
visual design, influence on advertising, 383–384
visual director, 414
visual language, power of, 499
vitascope, 234, 237
Vivendi, ownership of Universal Studios by, 260
Vogue, 310
    advertising in, 383
    as part of Condé Nast division, 334–335
    Web-enabled ads on, 333
voice, 90
Voice, The, 55, 202, 203, 220
    as reality-based program, 209
Voice of San Diego, 304
voice-track, 150
Volkswagen, 388
    advertising for, 394
Volvo, 406
voter turnout, 3
Vox media, 298
Vudu
    as digital movie stores, 260
    video-on-demand service of, 256

wage gap, 452–453
Wagner-Hatfield Amendment to Communications Act (1934), 173
Wake Up and Live (Brande), 351
Waldenbooks, 364
Wales, Jimmy, 431
Walker, John Brisben, 309–310
Walker, Stanley, 433
Walking Dead, The, 22, 188, 203, 207
"Walk This Way," 135
Wallace, Christopher (a.k.a. Biggie Smalls), 135
Wallace, Dewitt, 318
Wallace, Lila Acheson, 318
wallet, 39
Wall Street Journal, 33, 280
    as national newspaper, 284
    online content of, 300
    ratings of, 496
Walmart, 105, 120, 139
    Hachette sales and, 342
    leading sellers of DVDs, 200
    percentage of returned books by, 364
    selling at wholesale prices to lure customers, 140
    squeezing out of independent bookstore businesses, 364
    undercutting of small local stores by, 381
Walt Disney World, 456
Walters, Barbara, 208
Walton, Mary, 478
Waltons, The, 517
Wang, Wayne, 246
war, media coverage of, 18–19
War Advertising Council, 382
Warhol, Andy, 28, 545
Warhol, Andy, Foundation for the Visual Arts, 545
"War Logs," 506
Warner, Jack L., 251
Warner Brothers, 137, 234, 241–243, 251
    current film business ruled by, 258
    as one of most dominate media corporations, 468
    partnership with Hardee's, 405
    Supreme Court's ruling against, 252
Warner/Chappell Music, 546
Warner Music Group, 137
War of the Worlds (Wells), 164, 165, 310, 518
Warren, Robert, 543
Warren Report, 354
Washington, George, 312

Washington Post, 280, 283, 324, 465, 514
    Bezos's purchase of, 56
    hiring of journalists to blog, 298
    Politico started by reporters from, 301
    purchased by Bezos, Jeff, 301
Wasikowska, Mia, 250
Wasteland, 102
Watch Dogs, 85
Watchmen, 349
Watergate scandal, 499
Waters, Muddy, 123, 124
wax records, 117
Way, Way Back, The, 249
Wayne's World, 204
WBAI, 560–561
WEAF, 158
Weather Channel, 188, 197
Weaver, Sigourney, 193
Weaver, Sylvester "Pat," 193
Weavers, 131
web browsers, 43
Webcaster Settlement Act (2009), 153, 177
Weber Shandwick, 385, 422
Webkinz game, 82
Webkinz Jr., 82
webzines, 324–325
wedding day, meaning of perfect, 523
Weebly (blogging platform), 48
Weekly, 292
Weekly Bangla Patrika, 290
weekly newspapers, 284
Weigel, David, 488
Weiner, Anthony, 413
Weinstein Company, 256–257, 258
Welles, Orson, 22, 164, 557
    in *Citizen Kane,* 231
    as radio voice of *The Shadow,* 165
Wells, H. G., 164
    War of the Worlds and, 310
Wells, Ida, 292
Wells, Mary, 130
Wenner, Jann, 326, 328
Wertham, Fredric, 352
Wertmüller, Lina, 245
Wesker, Albert, 93
West, Mae, 560
Westar, 196
Westergren, Tim, 177, 183
Western Union, 8
Westinghouse, 156, 157, 158, 160
    radio stations owned by, 158
    RCA's competition with, 161
    Zworykin's innovations for, 191

Westwood One, 179, 180
WGCB, 559
WGN, 163, 197
WGY, 159
Wharton, Edith, 310
What Liberal Media?, 484
WhatsApp, 60, 62
What's My Line?, 207, 495
Wheeler, Tom, 67, 459
Wheel of Fortune, 211, 219
"Where Did Our Love Go," 130, 131
Where the Wild Things Are (Sendak), 24
whistleblowers, 474
White, E. B., 329
White, Jeff, 263
White Album, The (Didion), 282
white cover music, 127–128
Whitman, Walt, 360
Whittle Communications, 401–402
Who Framed Roger Rabbit, 456
Whole Booke of Psalms, The (Daye), 347
Whole Foods Market, 431
Whole Foods Market Magazine, 335
Who on American Top 40 charts, 129
Who's Afraid of Virginia Woolf?, 556
Who Wants to Be a Millionaire, 195
Wichita Eagle, 500
Wickham, Rich, 97
Wiesel, Elie, 356
Wii, 53
    Nintendo's release of new kind of console, 79–80
Wii Fit, 80, 94
Wii Sports, 79, 80
Wii U, 80
wiki, 48
WikiLeaks, 48, 85, 474, 485, 506, 545
Wikimapia, 48
Wikipedia, 355, 431
Wikitravel, 48
Wiki Web sites, 48
Wild at Heart (Gifford), 353
Wilde, Oscar, 353
Wildmon, Donald, 181
Wild Strawberries, 246
"Wild Wild Young Men," 124
Will, George, 294
William (Prince), 354
will.i.am, 135
Williams, Alex T., 439
Williams, Brian, 207

Williams, Serena, 405
Williams, Tennessee, 25
Williams, Wendy, 172
Williamson, Sonny Boy, 124
Wilson, Woodrow, 156, 420, 492
Windows 7, advertising for, 394
Wind Rises, The, 250
Winfrey, Oprah, 175, 356, 448
Wings of the Dove, The, 263
Winter's Bone, 245
Wired, 324, 326
    Web-enabled ads on, 333
Wired.com, 324
wireless cable, 199
Wireless Ship Act (1910), 152, 156, 162
wireless technology, use for, 152
wireless telegraphy, 8, 115, 152–154
Wireless Telephone Company, 154
wire services, 275, 294
Witcher, The, 93
Without a Trace, 465, 561
Wix (blogging platform), 48
Wizard of Oz, The, 233
Wiz Khalifa, 172
WJZ, 159
WNBC, 158
Wolfe, Tom, 281–282
Wolf of Wall Street, The, 557
Wolfram Alpha, 57
Wolverine, 93
Woman's Day, 322, 323, 327
Woman's Home Companion, 319
women
    as directors, 246
    magazines for, 311, 314
Women's Lunatic Asylum, 477
Wonderwall, 324, 325
Wonder Years, The, 205
Woo, John, 250
Wood, Natalie, 253
woodcuts, 320
Woodruff, Bob, 208
Woods, Tiger, 394
Woodstock (1969), 132
Woodward, Bob, 283, 480
Woodward, Joanne, 205
Wooga, 102
Woozworld, 82
WordPress (blogging platform), 48
    blocking of, 52
Words with Friends, 74, 89
workouts, 376
World Association of Newspapers (WAN), 297
World Book Encyclopedia, The, 354
World Journal, 290

World of Warcraft, 94, 104
  collective intelligence and, 91
  competition of, 102
  as multiplayer online game, 94
  as popular massively multi-
    player online role-playing
    games, 82
  in stage of script and film
    development, 28
  as subscription game, 81
  as top franchise, 92
World Trade Organization
    (WTO), 455
World War I
  impact of, 156
  photography of, 320
World War II
  photography of, 320
  propaganda in, 423
World Wide Web (www), 44–45
  search engines in organization
    of, 46–47
  semantic, 56–57
Wozniak, Steve, 59
WPP Group, 384, 385, 391, 422
Wreck-It Ralph, 245, 456
Writers Guild of America, 398
written era in communication,
    6–7
WTBS, 196, 208
WURV-FM, 183

Xaxis, 391
Xbox, 53, 59, 61, 73–74, 101
  Electronic Entertainment Expo
    (E3) streamed to, 92
  establishment of online
    community by, 80

functioning also as DVD
    players, 83
representing commitment from
    Microsoft, 101
streaming programming from,
    83
success of, 462
Xbox 360, 105–106
Xbox Kinect, 89, 93, 99
Xbox LIVE, 77, 80
  connection to online service of,
    101
  revival of generation with, 92
Xbox One, 73–74, 80
X-Files, 25, 28, 207
Xfinity, 201, 260
Xlibris, 367
XL Recordings, 137, 139
XM, 175
  merger and acquisitions of, 463
X-Men, 102, 260, 349, 353, 460

Yahoo!, 46, 304
  advertising and, 390
  digitizing of books with
    expired copyrights, 360
  as leading force on Internet, 57
  purchase of Right Media by,
    391
  purchase of Tumblr by, 447
  putting Amazon near the top in
    its searches, 365
  supporting of net neutrality by,
    67
Yahoo! Messenger, 46
Yahoo! News, 546
Y'all, 336
Yammer, 462

Yang, Jerry, 46
Yardbirds, 129
Yeah Yeah Yeahs, 133
Yeats, William Butler, 24
yellow journalism, 272, 276–278,
    316
Yellow Kid, The, 276
Yelp, 57, 62
Yeoh, Michelle, 250
Yo-hwan, Lim, 96
Yo La Tengo, 143
"You Can't Hurry Love," 131
Young and the Restless, The, 206
Young & Rubicam, 385, 386
Young Frankenstein (Brooks), 17
Your Show of Shows, 204
Youth's Companion, 314, 329
YouTube
  ad-support of, 140
  aggregation of video footage
    from, 302
  as biggest revenue game
    changer, 221
  Black, Rebecca, on, 400
  blocking of, 52
  Cairo protesters connection to,
    52
  competition with, 110, 177, 462
  as content community, 48
  as data-heavy service, 67
  diversification of, 222
  exposure level of, 114
  "Gangnam Style" on, 142
  instant success of, 59
  mass media and, 474
  merger and acquisitions of, 463
  music videos licensed for use
    on, 143

near-constant use of, 261
parents groups and, 517
popularity of, 41, 144, 201, 260
public relations and, 431
screening of short films and
    film festivals on, 262
Sony's licensing of video on, 143
successful start-up of, 462
trend of, 31
TV channels of, 223
uploading of video mash-up to,
    10
videos on, 47, 93, 141, 200, 372,
    462

Zakaria, Fareed, 488
Zappos, 60
Zelda, 88
Zell, Sam, 294
Zenger, Anna Maul, 274
Zenger, John Peter, 272, 273, 274
Zephyr Press, 367
Zero Dark Thirty, 246, 398
Zhang, Yimou, 250
Zhang, Ziyi, 250
Zimatore, Carolyn, 369
Zimmerman, Robert Allen, 133
zines, 336
Zippy the Pinhead (Griffith), 353
zoeltrope, 234
Zombies, 129
Zqorykin, Vladimir, 190–191
Zuckerberg, Mark, 55, 74
  settlement with FTC by, 62
Zukor, Adolph, 238, 239, 240–241
Zworykin, Vladimir, 191
Zynga, 102, 462
Zynga Poker, 102

Experience Media with LaunchPad.

Throughout the new integrated media edition of *Media & Culture*, the book directs you to LaunchPad for *Media & Culture*, where you can watch video clips from popular media and interviews with media industry insiders, complementing and enhancing the material in the text. The book lists additional related videos under the "LaunchPad for *Media & Culture*" heading in the Chapter Review section at the end of each chapter. Here is a list, by chapter, of all the videos featured in the book. For directions on how to access these videos online, please see instructions to the right.

Chapter 1: Mass Media and the Cultural Landscape
Agenda Setting and Gatekeeping (see p. 15)
The Media and Democracy

Chapter 2: The Internet, Digital Media, and Media Convergence
The Internet in 1995: *The Net* (see p. 47)
Net Neutrality (see p. 66)
User-Generated Content
The Rise of Social Media

Chapter 3: Digital Gaming and the Media Playground
Video Games at the Movies: *Resident Evil* (see p. 92)
Tablets, Technology, and the Classroom

Chapter 4: Sound Recording and Popular Music
Recording Music Today (see p. 120)
Alternative Strategies for Music Marketing (see p. 141)
Streaming Music Videos (see p. 144)

Chapter 5: Popular Radio and the Origins of Broadcasting
Going Visual: Video, Radio, and the Web (see p. 175)
Radio: Yesterday, Today, and Tomorrow (see p. 178)

Chapter 6: Television and Cable: The Power of Visual Culture
Television Networks Evolve (see p. 199)
Television Drama: Then and Now (see p. 206)
What Makes Public Television Public? (see p. 211)
Reality on *Project Runway*
Changes in Prime-Time
Wired or Wireless: Television Delivery Today

Chapter 7: Movies and the Impact of Images
Breaking Barriers with *12 Years a Slave* (see p. 246)
More than a Movie: Social Issues and Film (see p. 262)
Technology in *Gravity*

Chapter 8: Newspapers: The Rise and Decline of Modern Journalism
Newspapers and the Internet: Convergence (see p. 284)
Community Voices: Weekly Newspapers (see p. 298)
Newspapers Now: Balancing Citizen Journalism and Investigative Reporting

Chapter 9: Magazines in the Age of Specialization
Magazine Specialization Today (see p. 327)
Narrowcasting in Magazines (see p. 332)

Chapter 10: Books and the Power of Print
Based On: Making Books into Movies with Tom Perrotta and Anne Rice (see p. 356)
Books in the New Millennium: Anne Rice and Others Discuss the Future of the Publishing Industry (see p. 357)
Turning the Page: Books Go Digital

Chapter 11: Advertising and Commercial Culture
Advertising in the Digital Age (see p. 391)
Advertising and Effects on Children (see p. 401)
Product Placement in the Movies: *E.T.*
Blurring the Lines: Marketing Programs Across Platforms

Chapter 12: Public Relations and Framing the Message
Give and Take: Public Relations and Journalism (see p. 434)
Filling the Holes: Video News Releases
Going Viral: Political Campaigns and Video

Chapter 13: Media Economics and the Global Marketplace
Disney's Global Brand: *Frozen* (see p. 456)
The Impact of Media Ownership (see p. 465)
The Money behind the Media

Chapter 14: The Culture of Journalism: Values, Ethics, and Democracy
The Contemporary Journalist: Pundit or Reporter? (see p. 498)
Fake News/Real News with Joe Randazzo of *The Onion* (see p. 499)
Journalism Ethics: What News Is Fit to Print?
The Objectivity Myth
Shield Laws and Non-Traditional Journalists

Chapter 15: Media Effects and Cultural Approaches to Research
Media Effects Research (see p. 518)

Chapter 16: Legal Controls and Freedom of Expression
Bloggers and Legal Rights (see p. 562)
The First Amendment and Student Speech
Freedom of Information